Lecture Notes in Artificial Intelligence 2689

Edited by J. G. Carbonell and J. Siekmann

Subseries of Lecture Notes in Computer Science

Springer
Berlin
Heidelberg
New York
Hong Kong
London
Milan
Paris
Tokyo

Kevin D. Ashley   Derek G. Bridge (Eds.)

Case-Based Reasoning Research and Development

5th International Conference
on Case-Based Reasoning, ICCBR 2003
Trondheim, Norway, June 23-26, 2003
Proceedings

Springer

Series Editors

Jaime G. Carbonell, Carnegie Mellon University, Pittsburgh, PA, USA
Jörg Siekmann, University of Saarland, Saarbrücken, Germany

Volume Editors

Kevin D. Ashley
University of Pittsburgh, Learning Research and Development Center
3939 O'Hara Street, Pittsburgh PA 15260, USA
E-mail: ashley@pitt.edu

Derek G. Bridge
University College Cork, Department of Computer Science
The Kane Building, College Road, Cork, Ireland
E-mail: d.bridge@cs.ucc.ie

Cataloging-in-Publication Data applied for

A catalog record for this book is available from the Library of Congress.

Bibliographic information published by Die Deutsche Bibliothek.
Die Deutsche Bibliothek lists this publication in the Deutsche Nationalbibliografie;
detailed bibliographic data is available in the Internet at <http://dnb.ddb.de>.

CR Subject Classification (1998): I.2, J.4, J.1, F.4.1

ISSN 0302-9743
ISBN 3-540-40433-3 Springer-Verlag Berlin Heidelberg New York

This work is subject to copyright. All rights are reserved, whether the whole or part of the material is
concerned, specifically the rights of translation, reprinting, re-use of illustrations, recitation, broadcasting,
reproduction on microfilms or in any other way, and storage in data banks. Duplication of this publication
or parts thereof is permitted only under the provisions of the German Copyright Law of September 9, 1965,
in its current version, and permission for use must always be obtained from Springer-Verlag. Violations are
liable for prosecution under the German Copyright Law.

Springer-Verlag Berlin Heidelberg New York
a member of BertelsmannSpringer Science+Business Media GmbH

http://www.springer.de

© Springer-Verlag Berlin Heidelberg 2003
Printed in Germany

Typesetting: Camera-ready by author, data conversion by PTP-Berlin GmbH
Printed on acid-free paper   SPIN: 10927854   06/3142   5 4 3 2 1 0

Preface

The International Conference on Case-Based Reasoning (ICCBR) is the preeminent international meeting on case-based reasoning (CBR). ICCBR 2003 (http://www.iccbr.org/iccbr03/) is the fifth in this series of biennial international conferences highlighting the most significant contributions to the field of CBR. The conference took place from June 23 through June 26, 2003 at the Norwegian University of Science and Technology in Trondheim, Norway. Previous ICCBR conferences have been held in Vancouver, Canada (2001), Seeon, Germany (1999), Providence, Rhode Island, USA (1997), and Sesimbra, Portugal (1995).

Day 1 of ICCBR 2003, Industry Day, provided hands-on experiences utilizing CBR in cutting-edge knowledge-management applications (e.g., help-desks, e-business, and diagnostics). Day 2 featured topical workshops on CBR in the health sciences, the impact of life-cycle models on CBR systems, mixed-initiative CBR, predicting time series with cases, and providing assistance with structured vs. unstructured cases. Days 3 and 4 comprised presentations and posters on theoretical and applied CBR research and deployed CBR applications, as well as invited talks from three distinguished scholars: David Leake, Indiana University, Héctor Muñoz-Avila, Lehigh University, and Ellen Riloff, University of Utah.

The presentations and posters covered a wide range of CBR topics of interest both to practitioners and researchers, including case representation, similarity, retrieval, adaptation, case library maintenance, multi-agent collaborative systems, data mining, soft computing, recommender systems, knowledge management, legal reasoning, software reuse and music.

This volume comprises papers for all of the presentations and posters. These 51 papers have survived a highly selective process. Of a total of 92 submissions, the Program Committee selected 19 papers for oral presentation and 32 papers for poster presentation. Each submission was identified as being in one of three categories and judged using the following criteria: 1. Theoretical research paper (scientific significance, originality, technical quality, and clarity); 2. Applied research paper (significance for scientific research or innovative commercial deployment, originality, technical quality, and clarity); 3. Deployed application paper (demonstrated practical, social, environmental or economic significance; originality; treatment of issues of engineering, management and user acceptance; and clarity).

Many people participated in making ICCBR 2003 a success. Agnar Aamodt, Norwegian University of Science and Technology, served as Conference Chair, with Derek Bridge, University College Cork, and Kevin Ashley, University of Pittsburgh, as Program Co-chairs. We would especially like to thank Lorraine McGinty, University College Dublin, for serving as Workshop Coordinator and Mehmet H. Göker, Kaidara Software, for chairing Industry Day. We thank the Program Committee and the additional reviewers for their thoughtful and timely participation in the paper selection process. The members of the Local Organizing Committee at the Norwegian University of Science and Technology worked long and hard: Jörg Cassens (Webmaster, Technical Support), Anders Kofod-Petersen (Social Events Program), Pinar Özturk (Conference Site Management), and Frode Sørmo (Public Relations). Finally, we gratefully acknowledge the generous support of the sponsors of ICCBR 2003 and of Springer-Verlag for its continuing support in publishing the proceedings of ICCBR.

April 2003   *Kevin Ashley*
                                                        Derek Bridge

Program Chairs

Kevin Ashley, University of Pittsburgh, USA
Derek Bridge, University College Cork, Ireland

Conference Chair

Agnar Aamodt, Norwegian University of Science and Technology, Norway

Industry Day Coordinator

Mehmet H. Göker, Kaidara Software, Los Altos, USA

Workshop Coordinator

Lorraine McGinty, University College Dublin, Ireland

Program Committee

Agnar Aamodt	Norwegian University of Science and Technology
David W. Aha	Naval Research Laboratory, USA
Vincent Aleven	Carnegie Mellon University, USA
Klaus-Dieter Althoff	Fraunhofer IESE, Germany
Kevin Ashley	University of Pittsburgh, USA
Paolo Avesani	IRST Povo, Italy
Brigitte Bartsch-Spörl	BSR Consulting, Germany
Carlos Bento	University of Coimbra, Portugal
Ralph Bergmann	University of Hildesheim, Germany
Enrico Blanzieri	University of Trento, Italy
L. Karl Branting	LiveWire Logic, Inc., USA
Derek Bridge	University College Cork, Ireland
Robin Burke	DePaul University, Chicago, USA
Hans-Dieter Burkhard	Humboldt University Berlin, Germany
Bill Cheetham	General Electric Co., USA
Michael T. Cox	Wright State University, Dayton, USA
Susan Craw	Robert Gordon University, Scotland, UK
Pádraig Cunningham	Trinity College Dublin, Ireland
Boi Faltings	EPFL Lausanne, Switzerland
Peter Funk	Mälardalen University, Sweden
Ashok Goel	Georgia Institute of Technology, USA
Mehmet H. Göker	Kaidara Software, Los Altos, USA
Andrew Golding	Lycos, Inc., USA
Pedro A. González-Calero	Univ. Complutense de Madrid, Spain
Igor Jurisica	Ontario Cancer Institute, Canada
Mark Keane	University College Dublin, Ireland
David Leake	Indiana University, USA

Brian Lees	University of Paisley, Scotland, UK
Ramon López de Mántaras	IIIA-CSIC, Spain
Michel Manago	Kaidara Software, Paris, France
Cindy Marling	Ohio University, USA
Bruce McLaren	Carnegie Mellon University, USA
David McSherry	University of Ulster, Northern Ireland, UK
Erica Melis	DFKI, Saarbrücken, Germany
Alain Mille	Université Claude Bernard, France
Héctor Muñoz-Avila	Lehigh University, USA
Bart Netten	TNO TPD, The Netherlands
Petra Perner	IBaI Leipzig, Germany
Enric Plaza	IIIA-CSIC, Spain
Luigi Portinale	University of Eastern Piedmont, Italy
Lisa S. Purvis	Xerox Corporation, NY, USA
Francesco Ricci	IRST Povo, Italy
Michael M. Richter	University of Kaiserslautern, Germany
Edwina Rissland	University of Massachusetts, USA
Rainer Schmidt	Universität Rostock, Germany
Barry Smyth	University College Dublin, Ireland
Katia Sycara	Carnegie Mellon University, USA
Manuela Veloso	Carnegie Mellon University, USA
C. Gresse von Wangenheim	Univ. do Vale do Itajai, Brazil
Ian Watson	AI-CBR, University of Auckland, New Zealand
Rosina Weber	Drexel University, USA
David C. Wilson	University College Dublin, Ireland
Qiang Yang	Hong Kong University of Science & Technology

Additional Reviewers

Josep Lluis Arcos	Rafał Latkowski	Martin Schaaf
Liliana Ardissono	John Loughrey	Sascha Schmitt
Marco Botta	Diego Magro	Kay Schröter
Stefanie Brüninghaus	Paolo Massa	Mikael Sollenborn
Lorcan Coyle	Kerstin Maximini	Frode Sørmo
Björn Decker	Rainer Maximini	Marco Spinelli
Johan Erikson	Mirjam Minor	Armin Stahl
Jason Ernst	Markus Nilsson	Alexander Tartakovski
Andrea Freßmann	Francisco C. Pereira	Carsten Ullrich
Joseph Giampapa	Jörg Rech	Torsten Willrich
Paulo Gomes	Thomas Reichherzer	Nirmalie Wiratunga
Roger Jonsson	Thomas Roth-Berghofer	Ke Xu

Sponsoring Institutions

ICCBR 2003 was supported by Kaidara Software, empolis and the Norwegian University of Science and Technology, Department of Computer and Information Science.

Table of Contents

Invited Talks

Human-Centered CBR: Integrating Case-Based Reasoning with
Knowledge Construction and Extension 1
  David B. Leake

On the Role of the Cases in Case-Based Planning 2
  Héctor Muñoz-Avila

From Manual Knowledge Engineering to Bootstrapping:
Progress in Information Extraction and NLP 4
  Ellen Riloff

Scientific Papers

SOFT-CBR: A Self-Optimizing Fuzzy Tool for Case-Based Reasoning ... 5
  *Kareem S. Aggour, Marc Pavese, Piero P. Bonissone,
  William E. Cheetham*

Extracting Performers' Behaviors to Annotate Cases in a
CBR System for Musical Tempo Transformations 20
  Josep Lluís Arcos, Maarten Grachten, Ramon López de Mántaras

Case-Based Ranking for Decision Support Systems 35
  Paolo Avesani, Sara Ferrari, Angelo Susi

Analogical Reasoning for Reuse of Object-Oriented Specifications 50
  Solveig Bjørnestad

Combining Case-Based and Model-Based Reasoning for Predicting the
Outcome of Legal Cases 65
  Stefanie Brüninghaus, Kevin D. Ashley

Measuring the Similarity of Labeled Graphs 80
  Pierre-Antoine Champin, Christine Solnon

Global Grade Selector: A Recommender System for Supporting the
Sale of Plastic Resin... 96
  William E. Cheetham

Maximum Likelihood Hebbian Learning Based Retrieval Method for
CBR Systems 107
    Juan M. Corchado, Emilio S. Corchado, Jim Aiken, Colin Fyfe,
    Florentino Fernandez, Manuel Gonzalez

An Evaluation of the Usefulness of Case-Based Explanation 122
    Pádraig Cunningham, Dónal Doyle, John Loughrey

Adaptation Guided Retrieval Based on Formal Concept Analysis 131
    Belén Díaz-Agudo, Pablo Gervás, Pedro A. González-Calero

Club ♣ (Trèfle): A Use Trace Model 146
    Elöd Egyed-Zsigmond, Alain Mille, Yannick Prié

Case-Based Plan Recognition in Computer Games 161
    Michael Fagan, Pádraig Cunningham

Solution Verification in Software Design: A CBR Approach 171
    Paulo Gomes, Francisco C. Pereira, Paulo Carreiro, Paulo Paiva,
    Nuno Seco, José Luís Ferreira, Carlos Bento

Evaluation of Case-Based Maintenance Strategies in Software Design 186
    Paulo Gomes, Francisco C. Pereira, Paulo Paiva, Nuno Seco,
    Paulo Carreiro, José Luís Ferreira, Carlos Bento

Optimal Case-Based Refinement of Adaptation Rule Bases for
Engineering Design 201
    Hans-Werner Kelbassa

Detecting Outliers Using Rule-Based Modeling for Improving
CBR-Based Software Quality Classification Models 216
    Taghi M. Khoshgoftaar, Lofton A. Bullard, Kehan Gao

An Empirical Analysis of Linear Adaptation Techniques for
Case-Based Prediction 231
    Colin Kirsopp, Emilia Mendes, Rahul Premraj, Martin Shepperd

A Framework for Historical Case-Based Reasoning 246
    Jixin Ma, Brian Knight

An Investigation of Generalized Cases 261
    Kerstin Maximini, Rainer Maximini, Ralph Bergmann

On the Role of Diversity in Conversational Recommender Systems 276
    Lorraine McGinty, Barry Smyth

Similarity and Compromise 291
  David McSherry

The General Motors Variation-Reduction Adviser: Evolution of a
CBR System 306
  Alexander P. Morgan, John A. Cafeo, Diane I. Gibbons,
  Ronald M. Lesperance, Gulcin H. Sengir, Andrea M. Simon

Diversity-Conscious Retrieval from Generalized Cases: A Branch
and Bound Algorithm 319
  Babak Mougouie, Michael M. Richter, Ralph Bergmann

Assessing Elaborated Hypotheses: An Interpretive Case-Based
Reasoning Approach 332
  J. William Murdock, David W. Aha, Leonard A. Breslow

Soft Interchangeability for Case Adaptation 347
  Nicoleta Neagu, Boi Faltings

Supporting the IT Security of eServices with CBR-Based
Experience Management 362
  Markus Nick, Björn Snoek, Torsten Willrich

Improving Similarity Assessment with Entropy-Based Local Weighting ... 377
  Héctor Núñez, Miquel Sànchez-Marrè, Ulises Cortés

Collaborative Case Retention Strategies for CBR Agents 392
  Santiago Ontañón, Enric Plaza

Efficient Real Time Maintenance of Retrieval Knowledge in
Case-Based Reasoning 407
  David W. Patterson, Mykola Galushka, Niall Rooney

Incremental Learning of Retrieval Knowledge in a Case-Based
Reasoning System... 422
  Petra Perner

Case Base Management for Analog Circuits Diagnosis Improvement 437
  Carles Pous, Joan Colomer, Joaquim Melendez, Josep Lluís de la Rosa

Empirical Analysis of Case-Based Reasoning and Other Prediction
Methods in a Social Science Domain: Repeat Criminal Victimization 452
  Michael A. Redmond, Cynthia Blackburn Line

A Hybrid System with Multivariate Data Validation and Case Base
Reasoning for an Efficient and Realistic Product Formulation 465
   Sina Rezvani, Girijesh Prasad

Product Recommendation with Interactive Query Management and
Twofold Similarity 479
   Francesco Ricci, Adriano Venturini, Dario Cavada, Nader Mirzadeh,
   Dennis Blaas, Marisa Nones

Unifying Weighting and Case Reduction Methods Based on Rough Sets
to Improve Retrieval 494
   Maria Salamó, Elisabet Golobardes

A Knowledge Representation Format for Virtual IP Marketplaces 509
   Martin Schaaf, Andrea Freßmann, Marco Spinelli, Rainer Maximini,
   Ralph Bergmann

Managing Experience for Process Improvement in Manufacturing 522
   Radhika B. Selvamani, Deepak Khemani

Using Evolution Programs to Learn Local Similarity Measures 537
   Armin Stahl, Thomas Gabel

Playing Mozart Phrase by Phrase 552
   Asmir Tobudic, Gerhard Widmer

Using Genetic Algorithms to Discover Selection Criteria for
Contradictory Solutions Retrieved by CBR 567
   Costas Tsatsoulis, Brent Stephens

Using Case-Based Reasoning to Overcome High Computing Cost
Interactive Simulations 581
   Javier Vázquez-Salceda, Miquel Sànchez-Marrè, Ulises Cortés

Predicting Software Development Project Outcomes 595
   Rosina Weber, Michael Waller, June Verner, William Evanco

An SQL-Based Approach to Similarity Assessment within a
Relational Database 610
   Graeme M. West, James R. McDonald

Knowledge Capture and Reuse for Geo-spatial Imagery Tasks........... 622
   David C. Wilson, Michela Bertolotto, Eoin McLoughlin,
   Dympna O'Sullivan

Index Driven Selective Sampling for CBR 637
  Nirmalie Wiratunga, Susan Craw, Stewart Massie

Case Base Reduction Using Solution-Space Metrics.................... 652
  Fei Ling Woon, Brian Knight, Miltos Petridis

CBM-Gen+: An Algorithm for Reducing Case Base Inconsistencies in
Hierarchical and Incomplete Domains................................ 665
  Ke Xu, Héctor Muñoz-Avila

Maintaining Consistency in Project Planning Reuse 679
  Ke Xu, Héctor Muñoz-Avila

Case Mining from Large Databases.................................. 691
  Qiang Yang, Hong Cheng

Case Base Maintenance for Improving Prediction Quality 703
  Farida Zehraoui, Rushed Kanawati, Sylvie Salotti

Context-Awareness in User Modelling: Requirements Analysis for a
Case-Based Reasoning Application 718
  Andreas Zimmermann

Author Index 733

Human-Centered CBR: Integrating Case-Based Reasoning with Knowledge Construction and Extension*

David B. Leake

Computer Science Department
Indiana University
Lindley Hall 215
150 S. Woodlawn Avenue
Bloomington, IN 47405, U.S.A.
leake@cs.indiana.edu

Human-centered computing studies methods to improve the interactions and performance of combined human/machine systems. Case-based reasoning provides a natural method for supporting knowledge capture and access in such systems. However, the human-centered approach raises numerous questions about how best to address variations in individual human needs. These questions include how to reflect individual perspectives, how to adjust to changing task contexts, and how each part of the combined system can help to extend the capabilities of the other. This talk describes ongoing research addressing these questions in the context of case-based support for human knowledge modeling and construction.

This project focuses on developing and implementing integrated intelligent methods to support large-scale distributed knowledge capture, refinement, reuse and sharing. It aims to empower domain experts to directly construct, navigate, share, and criticize knowledge models, and to facilitate their use in support of user tasks. Its primary approach is to augment interactive computer tools for concept mapping with knowledge access methods inspired by CBR, to index knowledge models and perform context-sensitive retrieval as they are needed. A range of methods enable the system to suggest knowledge models that have proven useful in similar prior knowledge modeling episodes, as well as to formulate queries to retrieve supplementary types of information such as task-relevant documents and images. The retrievals provide real-time support to the knowledge modeler; the resulting knowledge models enrich the case library. In addition, the system extends its initial knowledge not only by case capture, but also by mining the web to identify new but related areas for the user to consider adding to system knowledge.

The talk closes by discussing the relationship of this work to fundamental CBR issues, considering lessons, questions, and potential opportunities that the work suggests for case representation, case adaptation, and case-base maintenance, and illustrating potential benefits of a human-centered computing approach to CBR as a whole.

---

* This research is supported in part by NASA under award No NCC 2-1216. It is done in collaboration with Ana Maguitman and Thomas Reichherzer of Indiana University and with Alberto Cañas and the concept mapping group of The Institute for Human and Machine Cognition, at the University of West Florida.

K.D. Ashley and D.G. Bridge (Eds.): ICCBR 2003, LNAI 2689, p. 1, 2003.
© Springer-Verlag Berlin Heidelberg 2003

On the Role of the Cases in Case-Based Planning

Héctor Muñoz-Avila

Department of Computer Science and Engineering
19 Memorial Drive West
Lehigh University
Bethlehem, PA 18015, USA
hem4@lehigh.edu

Abstract. One of the first CBR systems was CHEF, a case-based planner that reuses cooking recipes for creating new ones. Since then, a wide variety of applications of case-based planning (CBP) have been proposed including manufacturing, military planning and emergency prediction. In this talk, the speaker will discuss the evolution of the role of the cases in CBP. In early CBP systems like CHEF, cases provide domain knowledge. Later, cases provided control knowledge to guide first-principles planners. More recently, the speaker has developed a theory explaining how cases can play both roles. This theory facilitates the use of CBP for a number of new applications including project planning and plan discovery.

1 Introduction

Planning, generating a sequence of actions meeting pre-defined specifications, was one of the earliest problems targeted by case-based reasoning (CBR) (Hammond, 1989). Since then, case-based planning (CBP) has been a recurrent research topic covering a wide range of application areas including manufacturing (Kambhampati, 1994; Bergmann & Wilke, 1995; Muñoz-Avila & Weberskirch, 1996), military planning (Mitchell, 1997; Muñoz-Avila et. al. 1999), route planning (Haig & Veloso, 1995; Branting & Aha; 1995) and emergency prediction (Avesani et. al., 1993).

Cases in early CBP systems such as CHEF contain domain knowledge; in such systems, cases provide instances of successful problem-solving episodes that can be used to cope with the absence of a domain theory. Later, research on CBP has concentrated on guiding first-principles planners. Cases in these systems provide meta-knowledge on how to use the domain theory to solve new problems efficiently (e.g., (Veloso, 1995)). More recently, we developed a theory that explains how cases can play both roles (Muñoz-Avila et. al., 2001). This theory facilitates the use of CBP for a number of new applications including project planning ((Muñoz-Avila et. al., 2002) and Plan Discovery.

K.D. Ashley and D.G. Bridge (Eds.): ICCBR 2003, LNAI 2689, pp. 2–3, 2003.
© Springer-Verlag Berlin Heidelberg 2003

References

Avesani, P., Perini, A. & Ricci, F. (1993) Combining CBR and Constraint Reasoning in Planning Forest Fire Fighting. *Proceedings of First European Workshop on Case-based Reasoning (EWCBR-93)*. Kaiserslautern: Technical Report. AG Richter. University of Kaiserslautern.

Bergmann R., & Wilke W. (1995). Building and refining abstract planning cases by change of representation language. *Journal of Artificial Intelligence Research*. 3, 53–118.

Branting, L.K., & Aha, D. W.(1995). tratified case-based reasoning: Reusing hierarchical problem solving episodes. *Proceedings of the Fourteenth International Joint Conference on Artificial Intelligence*. ontreal, Canada: Morgan Kaufmann.

Costas, T, & Kashyan, P. (1993) Case-based reasoning and learning in manufacturing with TOTLEC planner. *IEEE Transactions on Systems, Man, and Cybernetics*. 23(iv) July/August

Haigh, K.Z., & Veloso, M. (1995). Route Planning by Analogy. *Proceedings of the First International Conference on Case-based Reasoning (ICCBR-95)*. Sesimbra: Springer.

Hammond, K. (1989). *Case-based planning: Viewing planning as a memory task*. Boston, MA: Academic Press.

Kambhampati, S. (1994). Expoiting causal structure to control retrieval and refitting during plan reuse. *Computational Intelligence*, 10(2).

Mitchell, S.W. (1997). A hybrid architecture for real-time mixed-initiative planning and control. In: *Proceedings of the Ninth Conference on Innovative Applications of AI*. Providence, RI: AAAI Press

Muñoz-Avila, H. & Weberskirch F.: *Planning for Manufacturing Workpieces by Storing, Indexing and Replaying Planning Decisions*. In: Proceedings of the 3rd International Conference on AI Planning Systems (AIPS-96), AAAI-Press, 1996.

Muñoz-Avila, H., Aha, D.W., Nau D. S., Breslow, L.A., Weber, R., & Yamal, F. SiN: Integrating Case-based Reasoning with Task Decomposition. In: *Proceedings of the Seventeenth International Joint Conference on Artificial Intelligence (IJCAI-2001)*. Seattle, WA: AAAI Press, 2001.

Muñoz-Avila, H., Gupta, K., Aha, D.W., Nau, D.S. Knowledge Based Project Planning. in *Knowledge Management and Organizational Memories*. 2002.

Veloso, M.M. (1994). *Planning and learning by analogical reasoning*. Berlin: Springer.

From Manual Knowledge Engineering to Bootstrapping: Progress in Information Extraction and NLP

Ellen Riloff

School of Computing
University of Utah
Salt Lake City, UT 84112-9205, U.S.A.
riloff@cs.utah.edu

The last decade has seen dramatic changes in the landscape of natural language processing in general and *information extraction* in particular. *Information extraction* (IE) systems are designed to extract factual information about a specific domain from text sources. For example, IE systems have been built to extract facts from news reports of terrorist incidents (e.g., extracting the names of the perpetrators, victims, and targets) and business articles about corporate acquisitions (e.g., extracting the acquired company, the buyer, and the amount paid).

The early information extraction systems required large amounts of manual knowledge engineering, including syntactic and semantic dictionaries, domain-specific extraction patterns, and discourse knowledge. Over the past decade, many techniques have been developed to automate the construction of this knowledge. Long gone are the days when researchers spent weeks and months painstakingly building domain-specific dictionaries and knowledge bases by hand. Researchers now focus their efforts on developing and applying machine learning techniques to automatically acquire syntactic and semantic knowledge from annotated training texts. NLP researchers are beginning to push the envelope even further by developing bootstrapping methods that can learn from raw texts and a few seed examples, requiring virtually no special training data at all.

In many ways, the evolution of IE research mirrors the evolution of natural language processing as a whole. We will overview the general trend in NLP research toward supervised and weakly supervised learning methods and describe the major advances in information extraction research over the past decade.

K.D. Ashley and D.G. Bridge (Eds.): ICCBR 2003, LNAI 2689, p. 4, 2003.
© Springer-Verlag Berlin Heidelberg 2003

SOFT-CBR: A Self-Optimizing Fuzzy Tool for Case-Based Reasoning

Kareem S. Aggour, Marc Pavese, Piero P. Bonissone, and William E. Cheetham

GE Global Research
One Research Circle
Niskayuna, NY 12309
{aggour, pavese, bonissone, cheetham}@research.ge.com

Abstract. A generic Case-Based Reasoning tool has been designed, implemented, and successfully used in two distinct applications. SOFT-CBR can be applied to a wide range of decision problems, independent of the underlying input case data and output decision space. The tool supplements the traditional case base paradigm by incorporating Fuzzy Logic concepts in a flexible, extensible component-based architecture. An Evolutionary Algorithm has also been incorporated into SOFT-CBR to facilitate the optimization and maintenance of the system. SOFT-CBR relies on simple XML files for configuration, enabling its widespread use beyond the software development community. SOFT-CBR has been used in an automated insurance underwriting system and a gas turbine diagnosis system.

1 Introduction

Case-Based Reasoning (CBR) is a popular technique that relies on past cases with known solutions to make decisions on new cases (Aamodt & Plaza 1994). Fuzzy Logic (FL), a superset of Boolean logic that supports the concept of partial truth, is an approximate reasoning technique used in situations where information is imprecise or incomplete (Zadeh 1965). Evolutionary Algorithms (EAs) are stochastic search techniques that can perform optimization without relying on gradient information or becoming trapped in local minima (Goldberg 1989). The trade-off in using EAs for optimization is that their robust global search, which can also be applied to discrete landscapes, cannot guarantee an optimal solution, but only regions of good solutions. Soft Computing (SC) is an approach to computing which parallels the ability of the human mind to reason and learn in an environment of uncertainty and imprecision. SC combines knowledge, techniques, and methodologies from Fuzzy Logic, Neural Networks, Probabilistic Reasoning, and Evolutionary Algorithms to create intelligent systems (Bonissone et al 1999). Our goal was to combine CBR and SC techniques into a generic, Self-Optimizing Fuzzy Tool for Case-Based Reasoning (SOFT-CBR) capable of handling a wide variety of problems in which an existing case base would be used to build solutions to new cases.

General Electric (GE) requires automated decision tools such as SOFT-CBR to bring consistency, accuracy, and speed to decision-making processes throughout the company. This fits with GE's 6σ Quality initiative, since we often observe that

K.D. Ashley and D.G. Bridge (Eds.): ICCBR 2003, LNAI 2689, pp. 5–19, 2003.
© Springer-Verlag Berlin Heidelberg 2003

variability and inconsistency in decision-making is the root cause of many process defects. GE has applied both CBR and SC in various applications (Cheetham 1997, Bonissone & Cheetham 1998, and Bonissone et al 2002), and opportunities for further use are growing throughout the company. As we move forward, it is critical that researchers be able to invest their time researching these opportunities rather than rewriting code. It was therefore our intention to combine the technologies described above in a flexible tool capable of being applied to a wide range of problem domains. SOFT-CBR is designed to be extensible so that if new functionality is required it can be easily incorporated into the system without having to rewrite or recompile existing components. In addition, EA technology is incorporated to facilitate system maintenance by searching for a set of parameters to make the CBR output as accurate as possible. The EA optimization is configurable like the rest of the tool to handle domain-specific problems.

Section 2 provides background information, including a review of some past CBR work relevant to this paper. Major design choices and system architecture are described in Section 3. Section 4 provides a more detailed view of the design, including a discussion of major SOFT-CBR components such as the EA. The successful use of SOFT-CBR in two applications, an Automated Insurance Underwriting system and a Gas Turbine Diagnosis system, is described in Section 5.

2   Background & Prior Art

2.1 Brief Summary of Fuzzy Case-Based Reasoning Systems

The use of Fuzzy Logic in CBR systems goes back to the early 90's, when researchers began to use attributes with fuzzy values and a fuzzy pattern matcher for case retrieval (Plaza & Lopez de Mantaras 1990, Dubois & Prade 1992). In fact, FL techniques have proven to be very useful in addressing many other problems typical of CBR systems. For example, FL can be used in case representation to provide a characterization of imprecise and uncertain information. It can also be used for case adaptation through the concept of gradual rules (Dubois & Prade 1992). FL is enabled within SOFT-CBR through:

- Case Representation: Approximate or incomplete knowledge of case attributes can be represented by fuzzy intervals or sets, which in turn can be associated with linguistic terms stored as text.
- Case Retrieval: A concept of "neighborhood" or partial match has been implemented for numeric attributes. Non-numeric attributes (such as fuzzy linguistic terms) can either be handled by adjusting the distance calculation or by extending the current components.
- Case Similarity: Distance calculation is highly customizable. A fuzzy similarity based on the Generalized Bell function exists. Alternative fuzzy similarity measures can also be coded and used.

A brief description of some existing Fuzzy CBR systems follows. The list is by no means complete. For a more detailed review, see (Bonissone & Lopez de Mantaras 1998).

The memory organization of the ARC system (Plaza & Lopez de Mantaras 1990) is a hierarchy of classes and cases. Each class is represented by a fuzzy prototype describing the features common to most of the cases belonging to the class. The retrieval step consists of selecting the most promising classes by means of a fuzzy pattern-matching algorithm. Next, cases are selected based on the similarities and differences between the classes and the cases. Finally, near misses are used to avoid repeating past failures.

The CAREFUL system (Jaczynski & Trousse 1994) focuses on the first two steps of a case-based reasoner: case and problem representation and case retrieval. The representation is based on a hierarchy of fuzzy classes. Fuzzy sets represent imprecise values of the attributes of the cases. The retrieval process proceeds in two steps. First, the problem specification and case filtering, which guides the operator in specifying the problem and identifies potentially interesting cases, and second, the selection that chooses the nearest cases. In the second step, each value of a problem attribute represents a fuzzy constraint and the process selects those cases that better satisfy the constraints according to a weighted fuzzy pattern matching technique.

In PROFIT (Bonissone & Cheetham 1998), a fuzzy CBR system was developed to estimate residential property values for real estate transactions. The system enhances CBR techniques with fuzzy predicates expressing preferences in determining similarities between subject and comparable properties. These similarities guide the selection and aggregation process, leading to the final property value estimate. PROFIT has been successfully tested on thousands of real estate transactions.

2.2 Brief Summary of Evolutionary Algorithms to Tune CBR Systems

The proper integration of SC technologies such as fuzzy logic and EAs has resulted in the improvement of many reasoning systems (Bonissone et al 1999). There is a small body of literature dealing with the tuning of CBR parameters using EAs, however. While some authors have combined or integrated EA and CBR systems (Inazumi et al 1999, Kuriyama et al 1998, Job et al 1999), few researchers have used EAs as design tools for developing and maintaining a CBR system. Ishii et al (1998) proposed an EA-based method for learning feature weights in a similarity function. Jarmulak et al (2000) proposed the use of evolutionary algorithms to determine the relevance of case features and to find optimal retrieval parameters. They consider this approach to be a self-optimizing CBR retrieval because the optimization is performed using the data in the case base.

Bonissone et al (2002) described the use of evolutionary algorithms for automating the tuning and maintenance of two fuzzy decision systems: a rule-based and a case-based classifier for insurance underwriting. A configurable multi-stage mutation-based EA tunes the decision thresholds and internal parameters of fuzzy rule-based and case-based systems that decide the risk categories of insurance applications. The encouraging results of that work motivated the implementation of SOFT-CBR.

2.3 Other CBR Tools

In the following, we cite some of the interesting CBR tools known to us. Citations with URLs are provided in the references section. CBR*Tools from INRIA is a generic software library that requires some programming to produce a CBR system. The CBR Shell from AIAI is developed in Java and uses an EA for weight learning. CASPIAN, from the University of Wales, Aberystwyth, relies on a custom case language configuration file and is developed in C. Finally, orenge from empolis GmbH is a comprehensive and extensible CBR tool. Its architecture seems very close in spirit to SOFT-CBR. We believe SOFT-CBR has useful features that together are not covered in any one tool above. First, it incorporates an EA for parameter optimization. Second, it performs dynamic component invocation through XML configuration files without requiring code rewrites. Third, it has a simple, open architecture that allows integration of new functionality with zero impact to the other components.

3   System Architecture

SOFT-CBR is written in Java, is platform independent, and has been executed on UNIX and Windows operating systems. A simple, flexible component-based architecture has been adopted using Object-Oriented design paradigms. The components are logically and functionally distinct and each implement a major step in the CBR process:

1 **Neighbor Retrieval** ("**Retrieve**" component): Compares a probe case against the case base of past cases and retrieves any cases that are similar to the probe case.
2 **Distance Calculation** ("**Distance**" component): Calculates a distance between each retrieved case and the probe to quantify the similarity between the two cases.
3 **Decision Making** ("**Decide**" component): Determines a solution for the probe case using the known solutions for the retrieved cases and their distances to the probe case.

A fourth major component, "**CaseBase**", is used within the Retrieve component to perform case base access. An abstract interface for each component has been defined, and a library of components is provided in the "core" SOFT-CBR, providing a significant amount of well-tested, generally applicable functionality. These components are likely to be useful for many applications, but SOFT-CBR is intended to be useful even in situations that are not covered by pre-existing components. New functionality can be added (and existing components can be extended) to cover more complex situations. If and when additional functionality is required, a software developer can easily program new components that obey the appropriate Java interface definitions.

The traditional CBR cycle as described in (Aamodt & Plaza 1994) has four processes: retrieve, reuse, revise, and retain. A new case is solved by retrieving one or more previously experienced cases, reusing those cases to produce a solution, revising that solution through simulation or test execution, and retaining the new experience by incorporating it into the existing case base.   The SOFT-CBR components "Retrieve", "Distance", and "Case Base" together implement the retrieve process from the traditional CBR cycle.   In our case, the flexible case base access requirement introduces additional complexity to the retrieve process.   Neighbor retrieval is performed based on range queries defined around features in the probe case.   Then, distance is refined using partial ordering induced from fuzzy membership functions.   The SOFT-CBR component "Decide" implements the reuse process from the traditional CBR cycle.   The core Decide components do not feature any adaptations, but they can be included in future Decide modules as required.   The revise and retain processes are handled outside of SOFT-CBR.

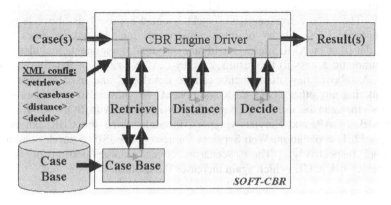

Fig. 1. Decision Process Modules

SOFT-CBR is configured using a file written in eXtensible Mark-up Language (XML). In this file one can specify what components to use for each of the functional steps. All of the parameters required to configure each component are also exposed to the user in appropriate sections of this file. Hayes and Cunningham (1999) use XML for CBR case representation, which incorporates similar technologies but with different objectives. Performing tasks such as changing the attributes used to define cases, changing the method by which distance calculations are performed, and determining what types of outputs are valid can all be done by modifying this file. Typically, no code writing or compilation is required—one does not need to be a software developer to use SOFT-CBR.   A main "engine driver" in the tool is responsible for parsing the configuration file and determining what components to load dynamically at run time. Therefore, any component can be extended or replaced by another that implements the same interface. The driver passes data from one component to the next, acting as the glue between the components and allowing them to work together to make decisions, as illustrated in Figure 1.

   When a probe case is sent to the engine, the engine first passes the case to the retrieve class. Retrieve invokes a case base class that connects to a data store and obtains neighbors to the probe based on range queries around features in the probe case. The case base class obtains a set of neighbors and feeds them back through the retrieve class to the engine driver. The allowable variation of retrieved cases from the probe case is specified in the XML configuration file. The engine driver then passes the probe case and its neighbors to the distance class, which calculates the distance between the probe and each neighbor using fuzzy membership functions. The XML file specifies the relative weights of each parameter in the case base, as well as other configurable parameters used to calculate the distance. These distances are then returned to the engine. Finally, the driver passes the neighbor cases and their distances to the decide class, which reuses the solutions of the retrieved cases to generate a solution for the probe case. This solution adaptation procedure is configured in the XML file.

To build a CBR decision model with SOFT-CBR, we need a framework for connecting to different data sources (read new cases for evaluation), run the engine, and generate output (allow access to CBR results on those cases) in whatever format is desired. The same componentized, object-oriented approach as above is adopted for this purpose. Our library of input components includes taking cases from a database, flat files, or XML files. Our library of output components includes an API for programmatic access to the results, or they can be written in flat file and XML formats. As above, new components can be developed and used as needs arise, without altering any other SOFT-CBR component. We have also developed a set of "wrappers" that can be used interchangeably to integrate with SOFT-CBR. These include EJB, SOAP, and Servlet wrappers, through which the CBR can be used within any J2EE application, Web Services framework, or JSP or Servlet-based Web application, respectively. These scenarios cover a large portion of the new development work at GE, which again increases the usefulness of the tool.

4   System Features & Design

4.1 Engine Initialization and Operation

Upon initialization, an XML file laid out as shown in Figure 2 is passed to the engine. This file contains three top-level elements: *<retrieve>*, *<distance>*, and *<decide>*, that configure the major components of SOFT-CBR.

In Figure 2, the "..." within the various elements indicate that content has been left out for simplicity. Within each of these three XML elements, a *<class>* element is required to specify the Java class to use for that step. The engine driver reads each of the *<class>* elements and uses Java's reflection API (run-time class loading) to instantiate those classes. This is how the engine can operate without knowing exactly what type of distance calculation it is performing, for example—all the engine has to know is what class to invoke. After the *<class>* element, all additional information within the XML block is used to initialize that component. For example, any additional information in *<retrieve>* is passed to the Retrieve component that was loaded by the engine driver. No constraints are placed on the information a given component can require. This affords users of SOFT-CBR a great deal of flexibility in the implementation of new components.

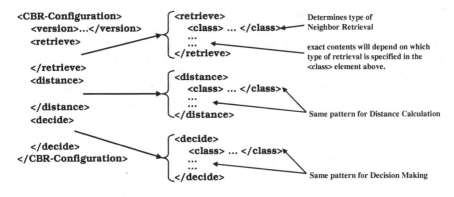

Fig. 2. Example Initialization File

4.2 Core Components

The "core" SOFT-CBR provides a library of generally useful components.

4.2.1 Neighbor Retrieval

One neighbor retrieval component exists, referred to as "Basic Retrieve." The Basic Retrieve component does not access the case base directly, but uses a case base component to perform the data source access. The reason for using a separate component to do the case base access is flexibility. The user may wish to connect to different case base types while still using the same neighbor retrieval component. The case base component is responsible for connecting to a data source (a database or flat file, for example) and then providing neighbor cases back to the retrieve component.

4.2.2 Case Base Access

Currently, two simple but quite general case base components have been developed that allow cases to be accessed from a table in any JDBC compliant database. Individual cases must exist in the table as single rows. The table containing the case base data may also contain other fields which SOFT-CBR does not use. The case base components are responsible for constructing the query that retrieves neighbors of the probe case, and then returning those cases to the retrieve component. In the present implementation, the query is described by ranges of values around each attribute used for retrieval. Other retrieval algorithms may also be incorporated into SOFT-CBR, as necessary. By way of the case base class, the retrieve component returns all cases that appear similar to the probe, and then the engine uses a distance calculation component to rank them. The existing components assume cases have the same representation, but sparse representation can be handled in future implementations.

4.2.3   Distance Calculation

Two distance calculation components have been implemented.   They are: "Manhattan" and "Generalized Bell Function" distance.

For two points in an N-dimensional space, the Manhattan Distance is defined as the weighted sum of the absolute values of the differences between each of the dimensions.   In this application, each case is a point and each attribute can be considered a dimension.   Therefore, we can define the Manhattan Distance between cases $c1$ and $c2$ to be

$$dist(c1, c2) = \sum_{k=1}^{n} w(k) * |c1(k) - c2(k)| \tag{1}$$

The notation $c1(k)$ represents the value of attribute k for case $c1$, $c2(k)$ represents the value of attribute k for case $c2$, $w(k)$ represents the weight for attribute k, and n is the total number of attributes.

The Generalized Bell Function (GBF) Distance is used to favor values that are close together and penalize those that are far apart.   Different Bell function shapes are defined around each attribute in the input case, and the distance that the neighbor case's value falls on the Bell curve is used as the distance between those two attributes.   The absolute values of the distances are then summed for all of the attributes to create the overall distance between two cases.   We can define the GBF Distance to be

$$dist(c1, c2) = \sum_{k=1}^{n} w(k) * (1 - \frac{1}{1 + \left(\frac{|c1(k) - c2(k)|}{a} \right)^{2b}}) \tag{2}$$

Here $c1(k)$, $c2(k)$, and $w(k)$ have the same meaning as in Equation 1.   The parameters a and b control the shape of the Bell function.

These distance calculation components each assume the attributes are numeric. For non-numeric attributes, these components both assign a distance of 0 to exact matches and a distance of 1 to mismatches.   One can easily extend these classes to implement fuzzy similarity relations over non-numeric attributes.   Both of these components also allow us to assign weights to the attributes. These weights take into account any potential unit conversion issues, as well as the fact that one attribute may be more significant than another in terms of case similarity.   The distance calculation components determine how similar the neighbors are to the probe case, and the CBR engine driver then passes this data to the decision making step to make a final decision for the probe case.

4.2.4   Decision Making

Two decision-making components have been implemented.   They are: "Single Nearest Neighbor" (SNN) and "Weighted Mode" decide.   Both of these components are for discrete decision problems.   The SNN Decide component takes the solution from the single closest neighbor and uses it as the decision.   The Weighted Mode Decide component builds a weighted histogram of possible solutions based on the known solutions from the nearest neighbors and their distances to the input case. The weighting of the neighbor case solutions is based on the distance of the neighbor to the probe—the closer the neighbor, the larger the weight its solution is assigned. Once the histogram is complete, this component assigns the decision that has the most weight. If no neighbors are retrieved, a default value specified in the configuration file is used. This default value represents "no decision" from the engine.

4.3 Maintenance & Optimization with Evolutionary Algorithms

Maintenance of a CBR system is critical to its long-term usefulness since, over time, the configuration of the system may become sub-optimal. It is therefore critical to have the ability to optimize the configuration in a convenient manner. The implementation of an Evolutionary Algorithm directly into SOFT-CBR greatly simplifies this task.

EAs (Goldberg 1989, Holland 1994) define an optimization paradigm based on the theory of evolution and natural selection. Figure 3 visualizes how the EA and CBR interact in SOFT-CBR. Our EA is composed of a population of individuals ("chromosomes"), each of which contains a vector of elements that represent distinct tunable parameters within the CBR configuration. Any numerical value in the SOFT-CBR configuration (in any of the four major components) can be tuned, so the size of the chromosome depends on the number of parameters being tuned. Example tunable parameters include the range of each parameter used to retrieve neighbor cases and the relative weights associated with each parameter used for distance calculation. One of the most important aspects of the SOFT-CBR EA is its ability to dynamically determine the structure of the chromosomes. One can specify directly in the configuration file what attributes should be tuned and within what range for each attribute. This enables one to dynamically define the search space over which the EA will optimize. Any combination of SOFT-CBR parameters may be tuned while others remain static.

Since a chromosome defines a complete configuration of the CBR, an instance of the CBR can be initialized for each chromosome, as shown in Figure 3. On the left-hand side there is a population $P(t)$ of chromosomes c_i, each of which go through a decoding process to allow them to initialize a CBR on the right. The CBR then goes through a round of leave-one-out testing. We can determine the quality of that CBR instance (the "fitness" of the chromosome) by analyzing the results.

A fitness function f is used to give a quantitative representation of the quality of the output. We define a generic fitness function for discrete classification problems using two matrices. The first matrix M_{TxT} is a confusion matrix that contains frequencies of correct and incorrect classifications for all possible combinations of the benchmark and model decisions (see Figure 4 for an example). For instance, cell (i,j) contains the frequency of class i being misclassified as class j. Clearly, all the cells on the main diagonal represent correct classifications. This matrix is often used in character recognition problems, and is a valuable tool for visualizing the accuracy and coverage of the CBR. The second matrix P_{TxT} is a reward/penalty matrix and is of equal dimension as M_{TxT}. Here, cell (i,j) represents the penalty for misclassifying a class i as a class j. Rewards are assigned to elements on the main diagonal.

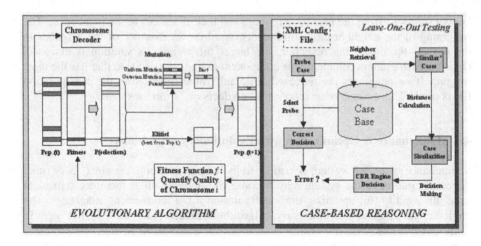

Fig. 3. EA and CBR Interaction

The fitness function f takes the confusion matrix M_{TxT} (produced from a run of leave-one-out testing of the CBR configured with chromosome c_i) and combines it with the matrix P_{TxT} using the formula in Equation 3 to produce a single value.

$$f(c_i) = \sum_{j=1}^{T} \sum_{k=1}^{T} M(j,k) * P(j,k) \qquad (3)$$

When tuning is invoked in SOFT-CBR, a second configuration file is specified. This file includes the entire set of configuration information required to initialize the tuning process, including the number of generations to run for the EA and how many chromosomes to include in the population. The fitness/penalty matrix is also specified directly and flexibly in this configuration file. Finally, through this file one can also optimize the engine on only a portion of the case base. This is valuable when running a complete iteration of leave-one-out testing is time consuming.

As shown in Figure 3, our EA uses mutation (randomly permuting parameters of a single chromosome) to produce new individuals in the population. The more fit chromosomes in generation t will be more likely to be selected for this and pass their genetic material to the next generation $t+1$. Similarly, the less fit solutions will be culled from the population. At the conclusion of the EA's execution, the single best chromosome is written to the SOFT-CBR configuration file so that it can be used as the CBR's new configuration.

5   Applications

SOFT-CBR has been successfully used in two distinct applications: Automated Insurance Underwriting for GE Financial Assurance (GEFA), and Gas Turbine Diagnosis for GE Power Systems (GEPS). These two applications are vastly different in the data they use and the decisions they make, but were both implemented by writing XML configuration files for the same underlying software—SOFT-CBR. The rapid and successful development of these two applications is a direct testimony to the flexibility and extensibility of SOFT-CBR.

5.1 Automated Insurance Underwriting

Insurance underwriting is a complex decision-making task traditionally performed by trained individuals. An underwriter must evaluate each insurance application in terms of its risk of generating a claim. A given insurance application is compared against standards adopted by the insurance company, which are based on actuarial principles relating to the insured risk (e.g., mortality in the case of life insurance). The application is then classified into one of the risk categories available for the type of insurance requested. These risk categories are discrete "bins" into which the underwriter places applicants with similar risk profiles. The assigned risk category, in conjunction with other factors such as gender and age, will then determine the appropriate premium that the applicant must pay for an insurance policy. Therefore, we may consider the underwriting process as a discrete classification problem that maps an input vector of applicant data into the decision space of rate categories. Our goal was to automate as high a fraction of these underwriting decisions as possible using AI and Soft Computing techniques. A major constraint faced was the need for interpretability of decisions—no black box models could be used due to consumer communication considerations.

Specializing to life insurance, there is a natural dichotomy in applicants—those who have medical impairments (such as hypertension or diabetes) and those who do not (who are "clean"). Clean case underwriting is relatively simple and we have been able to represent it by a compact set of fuzzy logic rules (Bonissone et al 2002). Impaired underwriting is more difficult, as the applicant's medical data is more complex. Underwriters thus use more judgment and experience in these cases. Therefore, rather than create an enormous and un-maintainable fuzzy rule base, we turned to CBR to handle the impaired cases. However, to validate the use of CBR for insurance underwriting, we first applied both FL and CBR systems to the same clean case data set. This has an added benefit as the CBR model can be used to guide auditing and quality assurance of the FL model. For example, cases for which the two models give different results might be suspect and therefore subject to more frequent audits. In addition, this provided an opportunity to compare a CBR model with other modeling techniques on the same data.

To develop the underwriting models, we created a "standard reference" dataset of approximately 3000 cases taken from a stratified random sample of the historical clean case population. Each of these cases received a rate category decision when it was originally underwritten. However, to reduce variability in these decisions, a team of experienced underwriters reviewed the cases blind to the original underwriter's decisions and determined the "standard reference" decisions. These cases were then used to create and optimize both the FL and CBR models.

In Figure 4 we present the results of comparing the standard reference decisions to (A) the CBR model, and (B) the Fuzzy Logic model. As indicated in (C), the models are of similar coverage and accuracy. This performance reflects a significant reduction in variability in comparison to the original underwriter decisions. The details of the FL model have been described in (Bonissone et al 2002). The CBR model was implemented with SOFT-CBR using the GBF distance calculation and the Weighted Mode decide method. For the CBR, automating the optimization with an EA had a significant effect on the overall accuracy. A manually-tuned prototype CBR system (created before SOFT-CBR existed) displayed only 34% global accuracy and 36% coverage, which is easily surpassed by the 90%+ accuracy and coverage shown in Figure 4.

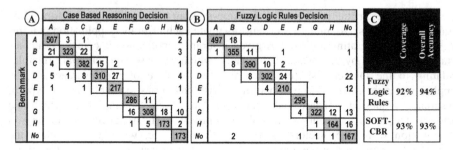

Fig. 4. Confusion Matrices for Clean Case Insurance Underwriting

5.2 Gas Turbine Diagnosis

GE gas turbines are used to generate electrical power for everything from cruise ships to large cities. A typical turbine costs between 20 and 40 million US dollars and provides enough electricity for a moderately sized town. It is important to keep the turbines in proper working condition and repair them quickly when a problem occurs. Every minute that a turbine is not working is lost revenue for the power generator and a potential shortage of electricity for their customers. GE Energy Services helps its customers monitor turbines and diagnose failures. This condition monitoring is a complex decision-making task traditionally performed by trained field service technicians. In order to assist the technicians, GE is creating a set of intelligent decision aids using rule-based and case-based reasoning. SOFT-CBR has been used to create the Case-Based Reasoning tool.

		Case Based Reasoning Decision			Coverage	Overall Accuracy
		Other	High Ex	Unknown		
Benchmark	Other	220	13	4	98%	91%
	High Ex	8	68	3		
	Unknown	0	0	0		

Fig. 5. Confusion Matrix for Gas Turbine Diagnosis

GE gas turbines are operated using an embedded control system that is equipped with an On-Site-Monitor (OSM), which records the values of over 100 sensors on the turbine. Automatic condition monitoring and anomaly detection is currently done in the areas of vibration, thermal performance, and combustion. The control system is also equipped with a remote notification module, which provides immediate notification to GE technicians at a central site when anomalies are detected. The central site technicians perform initial processing, logging, and viewing of alarm data. SOFT-CBR will assist the central site technicians in diagnosing the root cause of failures.

SOFT-CBR is currently able to diagnose a subset of the possible causes for gas turbine failures, called "High Exhaust" (High Ex) failures. High Ex failures are the most common type of failure, representing about 25% of all failures. They include a set of root causes, all of which produce an unsafe temperature variation in the turbine. A case consists of a summary of the relevant sensor readings immediately preceding the failure and the verified cause of the failure. A case base that includes every turbine failure for the past year on a fleet of 500 turbines has been created. The performance of the current system is shown in Figure 5. The second row of the figure shows that 68 of the 79 "High Ex" failures in our test set were classified correctly, 8 were classified incorrectly ("Other"), and 3 were too close to call ("Unknown"). Of the 237 "Other" failures (not "High Ex") 220 were classified correctly, 13 were incorrect, and 4 were too close to call.

6   Conclusions & Future Work

A Self-Optimizing Fuzzy Tool for Case Based Reasoning (SOFT-CBR) has been developed. It has been used successfully in two distinct applications. A key aspect of the tool is its flexible and extensible design. A library of components is available for users to quickly configure new CBR systems. When necessary, new components can be easily integrated into SOFT-CBR and used in combination with the pre-existing ones. A second key aspect of SOFT-CBR is the incorporation of an EA optimizer. Any and all numeric parameters in any component of SOFT-CBR can be tuned to refine the accuracy and coverage of the CBR results. We hope that SOFT-CBR will gain wide acceptance in facilitating the implementation of CBR systems, allowing other developers to add new functionality to the core system. As this occurs, the class of problems treatable with pre-existing SOFT-CBR components will grow.

Future work includes automating the design of the case base and developing a module that calculates the confidence in a SOFT-CBR result. Insurance underwriting exemplifies an application in which legal and compliance constraints require the system to exhibit reasoning transparency while using a specific set of input variables. These regulations constrain the design of the CBR system and limit the number and type of features that can be used to index a case. Therefore, any improvement in the CBR performance (measured in term of coverage and accuracy) can only be obtained by parametric tuning. However, there are other applications in which these regulations are not present. In such cases, EAs can be used for structural selection and tuning, such as feature determination and variable transformations, in addition to parametric tuning. We intend to explore this approach in the use of EAs to improve upon the design of CBR's for other GE applications. Since the simultaneous optimization of CBR structures and parameters might affect the EAs search convergence, we plan to use domain knowledge to create an initial library of features, a subset of which will then be selected by the EA. When using other reasoning techniques whose structures are defined by network topologies, we will use efficient representation of those structures, such as grammatical encoding, to further address the EA convergence problem. A confidence module will be used to calculate a predicted error in the result of SOFT-CBR. If the predicted error is low, the result does not need to be checked by a human and can be automated (e.g., automatically approving a life insurance policy or notifying a turbine operator of the root cause of a failure). For low confidence decisions, a human could review the result before taking any action.

References

Aamodt, A. and Plaza, E. 1994. Case-Based Reasoning: Foundational Issues, Methodological Variations, and System Approaches, *Artificial Intelligence Communications*, vol. 7, no. 1, pp 39–59

Bonissone, P. and Cheetham, W. 1998. Fuzzy Case-Based Reasoning for Residential Property Valuation, *Handbook on Fuzzy Computing* (G 15.1), Oxford University Press

Bonissone, P., Chen, Y.-T., Goebel, K. and Khedkar, P. S. 1999. Hybrid Soft Computing Systems: Industrial and Commercial Applications, *Proceedings of the IEEE*, vol. 87, no. 9, pp 1641–1667

Bonissone, P. and Lopez de Mantaras, R. 1998. Fuzzy Case-based Reasoning Systems, *Handbook on Fuzzy Computing* (F 4.3), Oxford University Press

Bonissone, P., Subbu, R. and Aggour, K.S. 2002. Evolutionary Optimization of Fuzzy Decision Systems for Automated Insurance Underwriting, *Proceedings of the 2002 IEEE International Conference on Fuzzy Systems*, Honolulu, Hawaii, USA, vol. 2, pp 1003–1008

CASPIAN, University of Wales, Aberystwyth, Wales, http://www.aber.ac.uk/compsci/Research/mbsg/cbrprojects/getting_caspian.shtml

CBR Shell, Artificial Intelligence Applications Institute (AIAI), University of Edinburgh, Scotland, http://www.aiai.ed.ac.uk/project/cbr/

CBR*Tools, Institut National de Recherche en Informatique et en Automatique (INRIA), France, http://www-sop.inria.fr/aid/cbrtools/manual-eng/doc_web/Abstract98.html

Cheetham, W. 1997. Case-Based Reasoning for Color Matching, *Lecture Notes in Artificial Intelligence*, Springer Verlag, vol. 1266

Dubois, D. and Prade, H. 1992. Gradual Inference Rules in Approximate Reasoning, *Information Science*, vol. 61, pp 103–122

Goldberg, D.E. 1989. *Genetic Algorithms in Search, Optimization, and Machine Learning.* Addison-Wesley, Massachusetts

Hayes, C. and Cunningham, P., 1999. Shaping a CBR View with XML, *Proceedings of the 3rd International Conference on Case-Based Reasoning, Lecture Notes in Artificial Intelligence*, Springer Verlag, vol. 1650, pp 468–481

Holland, J.H. 1994. *Adaptation in Natural and Artificial Systems: an Introductory Analysis with Applications to Biology, Control, and Artificial Intelligence, 3rd edition,* The MIT Press, Cambridge, Massachusetts

Inazumi, H., Suzuki, K. and Kusumoto, K. 1999. A New Scheme of Case-Based Decision Support Systems by Using DEA and GA Techniques, *Proceedings, IEEE International Conference on Systems, Man, and Cybernetics*, Tokyo, Japan, vol. 3, pp 1036–1041

Ishii, N. and Yong Wang 1998. Learning Feature Weights for Similarity Using Genetic Algorithms, *Proceedings, IEEE International Joint Symposia on Intelligence and Systems*, Rockville, MD, USA, pp 27–33

Jaczynski, M. and Trousse, B. 1994. Fuzzy Logic for the Retrieval Step of a Case-Based Reasoner, *Proceedings Second European Workshop on Case-Based Reasoning*, pp 313–322

Jarmulak, J., Craw, S. and Rowe, R. 2000. Self-Optimising CBR Retrieval, *Proceedings, 12th IEEE International Conference on Tools with Artificial Intelligence*, Vancouver, BC, Canada, pp 376–383

Job, D., Shankararaman, V. and Miller, J. 1999. Combining CBR and GA for Designing FPGAs, *Proceedings, Third International Conference on Computational Intelligence and Multimedia Applications*, New Delhi, India, pp 133–137

Kuriyama, K., Terano, T. and Numao, M. 1998. Authoring Support by Interactive Genetic Algorithm and Case Based Retrieval, *Proceedings, Second International Conference on Knowledge-Based Intelligent Electronic Systems*, Adelaide, SA, Australia, vol. 1, pp 390–395

Orenge, Empolis GmbH, http://www.empolis.com/

Plaza, E. and Lopez de Mantaras, R. 1990. A Case-Based Apprentice that Learns from Fuzzy Examples, *Methodologies for Intelligent Systems, 5th edition*, Ras, Zemankova and Emrich, Elsevier, pp 420–427

Zadeh, L. 1965. Fuzzy Sets, *Information and Control*, vol. 8, pp 338–353

Extracting Performers' Behaviors to Annotate Cases in a CBR System for Musical Tempo Transformations

Josep Lluís Arcos, Maarten Grachten, and Ramon López de Mántaras

IIIA, Artificial Intelligence Research Institute
CSIC, Spanish Council for Scientific Research
Campus UAB, 08193 Bellaterra, Catalonia, Spain.
{arcos,maarten,mantaras}@iiia.csic.es, http://www.iiia.csic.es

Abstract. In this paper we describe a method, based on the edit distance, to construct cases of musical performances by annotating them with the musical behavior of the performer. The cases constructed with this knowledge are used in *Tempo-Express*, a CBR system for applying tempo transformations to musical performances, preserving musical expressiveness.

1   Introduction

In the design of a case-based reasoning system, one of the key issues is the case base acquisition. One possible option for acquiring cases is the development of tools for manually incorporating cases into the case base. Another alternative is the development of tools for automatically—or semi-automatically—importing cases from a pre-existing source—either from publicly available archives [4] or problem specific data bases.

For classification or identification tasks, a case can be easily represented by the input data (the case problem) and the class or the enumerated collection of classes the case belongs (the case solution). In other tasks such as planning or design problems, a solution can be a composite structure. Moreover, the solution structure can contain the solution itself and additionally knowledge about the decisions taken when constructing the solution. For instance, *derivational analogy* [5] is based on augmenting the case solution by means of detailed knowledge of the decisions taken while solving the problem, and this recorded information (e.g. decisions, options, justifications) is used to "replay" the solution in the context of the new problem. As originally defined in derivational analogy for planning systems the cases contain *traces* from planning processes performed to solve them; also it is stated that in Prodigy/Analogy stored plans are annotated with plan *rationale* and reuse involves adaptation driven by this rationale [18].

Another task example, where case representation has to be augmented with detailed knowledge of the decisions taken while solving the problem, is the generation of expressive music. As our previous experience in the SaxEx system has demonstrated [1], the problem of the automatic generation of expressive musical performances is that human performers use musical knowledge that is not explicitly noted in musical scores. This knowledge is difficult to verbalize and therefore AI approaches based on declarative knowledge representations have serious limitations. An alternative approach is that of directly using the knowledge implicit in examples from recordings of human performances. Then, when we import recordings to be incorporated as cases in our case base, besides representing the musician performance as the case solution, we also need to *extract* the decisions performed by the musician when playing a melody (in other words, the performers' behavior). These decisions—such as playing additional notes, leaving out some notes, changing note durations, etc—are what we call annotations in this paper.

In this paper we focus our attention on the automatic annotation process developed for *Tempo-Express*, a case-based reasoning system for tempo transformation of musical performances, that preserves expressivity in the context of standard jazz themes. Expressive tempo transformations are a common manual operation in audio post-processing tasks. A CBR system can be a useful tool for automating this task. As we will explain in the next section, the annotation process is used when incorporating cases into the system and when the system must solve a new problem (that is, a new performance must be generated).

Case annotation is based on a dynamic programming algorithm based on the concept of *edit distance*. Edit distance is a technique for assessing the distance between two sequences and calculates this distance as the minimum total cost of transforming one sequence (the source sequence) into the other (the target sequence), given a set of allowed edit operations and a cost function that defines the cost of each edit operation. The output of the algorithm is a quantity that is proportional to the *distance*, or *dis*similarity between the sequences. Moreover, the edit distance provides the sequence of edit operations that yielded this value. Edit distance was first adapted to musical applications by Mongeau and Sankoff in [14].

The paper is organized as follows: In section 2 we briefly introduce the *Tempo-Express* application and their main inference modules. In section 3 we describe the edit distance mechanism. In section 4 we describe the the use of edit distance in the case annotation process. In section 5 we report the experiments performed in annotating cases. The paper ends with a discussion of the results, and the planned future work.

2   Tempo-Express

Tempo-Express is a case-based reasoning system for generating expressive tempo transformations in the context of standard jazz themes. Changing the tempo of a given melody is a problem that cannot be reduced to just applying a uniform transformation to all the notes of a musical piece. When a human performer plays a given melody at different tempos, she does not perform uniform transformations. On the contrary, the relative importance of the notes will determine, for each tempo, the performer's decisions. For instance, if the tempo is very fast, the performer will, among other things, tend to emphasize the most important notes by not playing the less important ones. Alternatively, in the case of slow tempos, the performer tends to delay some notes and anticipate others.

In the development of *Tempo-Express* we are using the experience acquired in developing the SaxEx system [1]. The goal of SaxEx was also to generate expressive music performances but the task was centered on transforming a non expressive input performance into an expressive new sound file taking into account the user preferences regarding the desired expressive output characterized along three affective dimensions (tender-aggressive, sad-joyful, calm-restless). The task of *Tempo-Express* is to perform tempo transformations with 'musical meaning' to an already expressive input performance. That is, a recording has to be replayed at a user required tempo that can be very different from the input tempo.

Below, we briefly present the main *Tempo-Express* modules and the inference flow (see Figure 1). The input of *Tempo-Express* is a recording of a jazz performance at a given tempo T_i (a sound file), its corresponding score (a MIDI file) and the desired output tempo. The score contains the melodic and the harmonic information of the musical piece and is analyzed automatically in terms of the Implication/Realization Model [15] (this analysis is used in the retrieval step and is not further discussed in this paper). The recording is parsed by the performance analysis module that produces a XML file containing the performance melody segmentation (onset points and duration of notes). Then, the melody segmentation is compared to its corresponding score by the Annotation process (see the detailed description in section 4). The annotated performance and the desired output tempo T_o are the input for the case-based reasoning. The task of the case-based reasoning modules is to determine a sequence of operations that achieves the desired tempo transformation while maintaining a form of musical expressivity that is appropriate for that tempo. Finally, the output of the system is a new version of the original melody, at the desired tempo, generated by the synthesis process.

Tempo-Express is implemented in *Noos* [3,2], an object-centered representation language designed to support the development of knowledge intensive case based reasoning systems. The melodic (performance) Analysis and synthesis processes have been implemented by the Music Technology Group (MTG) of the Pompeu Fabra University using signal spectral modeling techniques (see [17,8] for a detailed description). Below, we briefly describe the case-based reasoning components.

The Case Base. A case is represented as a complex structure embodying three different kinds of knowledge: (1) the representation of the musical score (notes and chords), (2) the musical model of the score (automatically inferred from the score using Narmour's Implication/Realization model and Lerdahl and Jackendoff's Generative Theory of Tonal Music as background musical knowledge [15, 12]), and (3) a collection of annotated performances. For the case acquisition, several saxophone performances were recorded from 5 jazz standards, each one

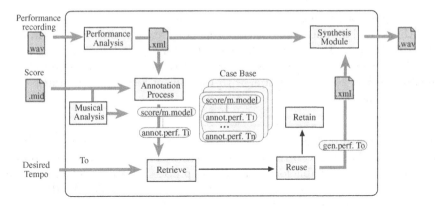

Fig. 1. General view of *Tempo-Express* modules.

consisting of 4–5 distinct phrases. The performances were played by a professional performer, at 9–14 different tempos per phrase. From this, the initial case base was constructed, containing 20 scores of musical phrases, each with about 11 annotated performances (in total more than 5.000 performed notes). See section 5 for more details of the data set.

The Retrieval Step. The retrieval mechanism is organized in three phases. In a first phase the input melody is compared with the melodies of the case base using melodic similarity measures (see [9] for a detailed description) for retrieving only those case melodies really similar—For instance, given a slow ballad as input, we are not interested in comparing it with be-bop themes.

In a second phase, we focus on the similarity of the musical models. This phase uses similarity criteria such as: Narmour's musical grouping structures (e.g melodic progressions, repetitions, changes in registral directions); the harmonic stability of the note according to jazz harmony; the metrical strengths of the notes; or the hierarchical relations of the notes in the phrase melodies according to the Generative Theory of Tonal Music (GTTM) model.

Finally, in a third phase the similarities among performances are assessed. For example, in figure 1 the annotated input performance (T_i) is compared to the annotated performances ($T_1 \ldots T_n$) of the case base whose tempos are the closest to the tempo of T_i. This set of annotated performances is ranked according to the degrees of similarity between their annotations and the annotation of T_i. The output of the retrieval step is a collection of candidate annotations for each note in the input melody.

The Adaptation Step. The adaptation mechanism has been implemented using *constructive adaptation* [16], a generative technique for reuse in CBR systems. The adaptation mechanism deals with two kinds of criteria: local criteria and coherence criteria. Local criteria deal with the transformations to be performed to each note—i.e. how retrieved candidate annotations can be reused in each input note. Coherence criteria try to balance smoothness and hardness. Smoothness and hardness are basically contradictory: the first tends to iron out strong deviations with respect to the score, while the second tends to favor strong deviations. The resulting expressive performance is a compromise between the smoothness and hardness criteria, with the aim of keeping an overall balance pleasant to the ear.

The Retain Step. The user decides whether or not each new tempo performance should be added to the memory of cases. The newly added tempo performances will be available for the reasoning process in future problems. At this moment *Tempo-Express* has no specific criteria to automatically decide whether to store a newly solved problem.

3   The Edit Distance Approach

In general, the edit distance (also known as Levenshtein distance [13]) between two sequences can be defined as the minimum total cost of transforming one sequence (the source sequence) into the other (the target sequence), given a set of allowed edit operations and a cost function that defines the cost of each edit operation. The sequences under comparison are not restricted to consist of quantitative data, and they do not even have to be of the same nature, since the edit operations and their costs can be designed to handle any kind of data.

The set of edit operations used for most purposes contains insertion, deletion, and replacement. Insertion is the operation of adding an element at some point in the target sequence; deletion refers to the removal of an element from the source sequence; replacement is the substitution of an element from the target sequence for an element of the source sequence. Although the effect of a replacement could be established by removing the source sequence element and inserting the target sequence element, the replacement operation expresses the idea that the source and target elements somehow correspond to each other. Ideally, if a source element and a target element are thought to correspond, this is reflected by the fact that the cost of replacing the source element by the target element is lower than the sum of the costs of deleting the source element and inserting the target element. Many other operations can be added, depending on the nature of the sequences, like one-to-many and many-to-one replacements, or transpositions (reversing the order of elements).

The edit distance approach has been applied in a variety of domains, such as text search, molecular biology and genetics. Mongeau and Sankoff [14] have described a way of applying this measure of distance to monophonic melodies (represented as sequences of notes). They extended basic set of edit operations (insertion, deletion and replacement) with *fragmentation* and *consolidation*, i.e. one-to-many and many-to-one replacements respectively. These operations cater for the phenomenon where a sequence of two or more notes (usually with the same pitch) are replaced by one long note of the same pitch, or vice versa.

Phrases that are considered to be melodic variations of each other often contain such kind of variations.

The weights for the edit operations defined by Mongeau and Sankoff take into account the pitch and duration information of the notes. The costs of deletion and insertion are directly related to the duration of the deleted/inserted notes. Replacements are charged by calculating the differences in pitch and duration between the notes to be replaced. The costs of fragmentation and consolidation are similar, where the duration of one note is compared to the summed duration of the set of notes in the other sequence.

3.1   Computing the Distances

Computing the edit distance is done by calculating the minimum cost of transforming a source sequence into a target sequence. This can be done relatively fast, using the following recurrence equation for the distance $d_{m,n}$ between two sequences $\langle a_1, a_2, ..., a_m \rangle$ and $\langle b_1, b_2, ..., b_n \rangle$:

$$d_{i,j} = min \begin{cases} d_{i-1,j} + w(a_i, \emptyset) & \text{(deletion)} \\ d_{i,j-1} + w(\emptyset, b_j) & \text{(insertion)} \\ d_{i-1,j-1} + w(a_i, b_j) & \text{(replacement)} \\ d_{i-1,j-k} + w(a_i, b_{j-k+1}, ..., b_j), 2 \le k \le j & \text{(fragmentation)} \\ d_{i-k,j-1} + w(a_{i-k+1}, ..., a_i, b_j), 2 \le k \le i & \text{(consolidation)} \end{cases}$$

for all $0 \le i \le m$ and $0 \le j \le n$, where m is the length of the source sequence and n is the length of the target sequence. Additionally, the initial conditions for the recurrence equation are:

$$d_{i,0} = d_{i-1,j} + w(a_i, \emptyset) \qquad \text{(deletion)}$$
$$d_{0,j} = d_{i,j-1} + w(\emptyset, b_j) \qquad \text{(insertion)}$$
$$d_{0,0} = 0$$

The weight function w, defines the cost of operations, such that e.g. $w(a_4, \emptyset)$ returns the cost of deleting element a_4 from the source sequence, and $w(a_3, b_5, b_6, b_7)$ returns the cost of fragmenting element a_3 from the source sequence into the subsequence $\langle b_5, b_6, b_7 \rangle$ of the target sequence.

For two sequences a and b, consisting of m and n elements respectively, the values $d_{i,j}$ (with $0 \le i \le m$ and $0 \le j \le n$) are stored in an $n + 1$ by $m + 1$ matrix. The value in the cell at the lower-right corner, $d_{m,n}$ is taken as the distance between a and b, that is, the minimal cost of transforming the sequence $\langle a_0, ..., a_m \rangle$ into $\langle b_0, ..., b_n \rangle$.

3.2   Optimal Alignments

After the distance value between two sequences has been calculated, it can be easily found out what was the sequence of transformations that yielded this value. To do this, it is necessary to store for each value $d_{i,j}$ ($0 \le i \le m$ and

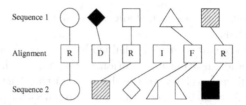

Fig. 2. A possible alignment between two sequences of geometric symbols.

$0 \leq i \leq m$, where m and n are the lengths of the source and target sequence respectively) which was the last operation that was performed to arrive at $d_{i,j}$. From this operation it can be inferred how much each of the indices for the source and the target sequence should be decreased (for example in the case of deletion i is decreased by 1 and j is not decreased). By traversing the matrix in this way from $d_{m,n}$ to $d_{0,0}$, the sequence of operations that yielded the value $d_{m,n}$, can be found.

The sequence of operations that transform the source sequence into the target sequence can be regarded as an alignment between the two sequences, i.e. a correspondence is established between elements in the source sequence and elements in the target sequence, respectively. In the next section we will see that this alignment is the key aspect of the automatic annotation process.

An alignment example is shown in figure 2. For simplicity, the two aligned sequences consist of geometric figures, instead of musical elements. The alignment is shown in between the sequences, as a sequence of operations. The letters in operations stand for replacement (R), deletion (D), insertion (I) and fragmentation (F), respectively. The example shows how matches are made between identical or near identical elements from sequence 1 and sequence 2. When for a particular element in one sequence there is no matchable element at hand in the other sequence, a deletion or insertion operation is performed. A fragmentation occurs between the triangle in sequence 1 and the two half triangles in sequence 2, since the two half triangles taken together, match with the whole triangle. Which of all possible alignments is *optimal* (i.e. has the lowest total cost) obviously depends on the costs assigned to the operations that occur in the alignments.

4   The Annotation Process

To analyze a performance of a melody, a crucial problem is to identify which element in the performance corresponds to each note of the score of the melody. Especially in jazz performances, which is the area on which we will focus, this problem is not trivial, since jazz performers often favor a 'liberal' interpretation of the score. This does not only involve changes in expressive features of the score elements as they are performed, but also omitting or adding notes. Thus, one can normally not assume that the performance contains a corresponding element for every note of the score, neither that every element in the performance corresponds to a note of the score. Taking these performance liberties into account, a description of a musical performance could take the form of a sequence of operations that are applied to the score elements.

From this perspective the edit distance, as described in the previous section, will be very useful. The edit distance has been used before in the performance-to-score mapping problem by Dannenberg [6] and Large [11], among others. The application area has been score-tracking for automatic accompaniment as well as performance timing research. Other approaches to performance-to-score matching have also been proposed. See [7] and [10] for an overview and comparison of several approaches.

The application of the edit distance in the context of comparing performances to scores is somewhat different from the case where scores are comparing to other scores. In the first case, we deal with sequences of different nature. The performance itself is not necessarily a discrete sequence but could be for example a continuous (audio) stream. Although matching score elements to fragments of audio data is not inconceivable, it is probably more convenient to make a transcription of the performance into a sequence of note elements before matching. The resulting sequence of note elements is more appropriate for comparing with scores, but it must be kept in mind that transcription of audio to note sequences is a reductive procedure. For example, pitch and dynamics envelopes are usually reduced to single values.

Another difference between score-performance matching and score-score matching is more conceptual. In score-performance matching, the performance is thought to be *derived* from the score, that is, the elements of the score sequence are *transformed* into performance elements, rather than *replaced* by them. For this reason, in the context of score-performance matching it is more appropriate to talk of *transformation* operations instead of *replace* operations.

4.1   The Edit Operations

The various edit operations can be classified (see figure 3) to make explicit the characteristics of their behavior. Firstly, all the operations refer to one or more elements in the sequences that are aligned. We can distinguish, within this general class of *Reference* operations, those that refer to notes in the score sequence and those that refer to elements in the performance sequence. Deletion operations refer to notes of the score sequence that are not present in the performance sequence (i.e. the notes that are not played), therefore they can be be classified as *Score-Reference* operations. Conversely, insertion operations refer only to elements in the performance sequence (i.e. the notes that were added), so they form a subclass of *Performance-Reference* operations. Transformation, consolidation and fragmentation operations refer to elements from both the score and the performance and thus form a shared subclass of Score-Reference and Performance-Reference operations. We call this class *Correspondence* operations. Figure 3 summarizes the relations between the classes of edit operations.

In our particular case, we are not primarily interested in comparing performance elements to score elements itself, but rather in the changes that are

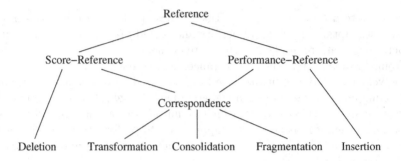

Fig. 3. A hierarchical representation of edit operations for performance annotation.

made to values of score notes when they are transformed into performance elements. Therefore, we view transformation operations as compositions of several transformations, e.g. *pitch transformations*, *duration transformations* and *onset transformations*. Following the same idea, fragmentation and consolidation operations (as described in section 3), can be elaborated by such transformation operations. For example, a consolidation operation could be composed of a duration transformation that specifies how the total duration of the consolidated score notes deviates from the duration of the corresponding performance element.

Based on the fact that the phrases in our data set were played by a professional musician and they were performed quite closely to the score, it may be thought that the performances could be described by only correspondence operations, that map a score element to a performance element, perhaps with minor adjustments of duration and onset. However, as mentioned before, most actual performances, and indeed the performances at our disposal, contain extra notes, or lack some notes from the score. Listening to the performances revealed that these were not unintentional performance errors, since they were often found on the same places in various performances of the same phrase and the effect sounded natural. This implies that in addition to correspondence operations, insertion and deletion operations are also required. Furthermore, we also observed that *consolidation* (as described in the previous section) occurred in some performances. Occasionally, we found cases of *fragmentation*. Other transformations, such as transposition (reversal of the temporal order of notes) were not encountered. Thus, the set of operations shown in figure 3 are basically sufficient for mapping the performances to their scores in our application.

4.2   The Cost Values

Once the set of edit-operations is determined, we need to decide good cost values for each of them. Ideally, the cost values will be such that the resulting optimal alignment corresponds to an intuitive judgment of how the performance aligns to the score (in practice, the subjectivity that is involved in establishing this mapping by ear, tuns out to be largely unproblematic). The main factors that determine which of all the possible alignments between score and performance is optimal, will be on the one hand the features of the note elements that are involved in calculating the cost of applying an operation, and on the other hand the relative costs of the operations with respect to each other.

In establishing which features of the compared note elements are considered in the comparison, we adopted much of the choices made by Mongeau and Sankoff [14]. Primarily, pitch and duration information were taken into to account in order to assign the cost of a transformation operation. For insertions and deletions, only the duration of the inserted/deleted notes is considered. Fragmentation and consolidation both use pitch and duration information. The cost functions w for each operations are given below. P and D are functions such that $P(x)$ returns the pitch (as a MIDI number) of a score or performance element x, and $D(x)$ returns its duration. Equations 1, 2, 3, 4, 5 define the costs of deletion, insertion, transformation, consolidation and fragmentation, respectively.

$$w(s_i, \emptyset) = D(s_i) \tag{1}$$

$$w(\emptyset, p_j) = D(p_j) \tag{2}$$

$$w(s_i, p_j) = |P(s_i) - P(p_j)| + |D(s_i) - D(p_j)| \tag{3}$$

$$w(s_i, ..., s_{j+K}, p_j) = \sum_{k=0}^{K} |P(s_{i+k}) - P(p_j)| + |D(p_j) - \sum_{k=0}^{K} D(s_{i+k})| \tag{4}$$

$$w(s_i, p_j, ..., p_{j+L}) = \sum_{l=0}^{L} |P(s_i) - P(p_{j+l})| + |D(s_i) - \sum_{l=0}^{L} D(p_{j+l})| \tag{5}$$

From the equations it can be seen that the cost of transformation will be zero if the score and performance elements have the same pitch and duration, and the fragmentation cost will be zero if a score note is fragmented into a sequence of performance notes whose durations add up to the duration of the score note and whose pitches are all equal to the pitch of the score element.

From a musical perspective, it can be argued that a the cost mapping two elements with different pitches should not depend on the difference of the absolute pitches, but rather on the different roles the pitches play with respect to the underlying harmonies, or their scale degree, as these features have more perceptual relevance than absolute pitch difference. This would certainly be essential in order to make good alignments between scores and performances that very liberally paraphrase the score (e.g. improvisations on a melody) and also in the case where alignment is constructed for assessing the similarity between different scores. In our case however, we currently deal with performances that are relatively 'clean' interpretations of the score. As such, changes of pitch are very uncommon in our data. Still, it is desirable to have a more sophisticated pitch comparison approach, to accommodate more liberal performances in the future.

We have also considered incorporating the difference in position in the costs of the correspondence operations (transformation, consolidation and fragmentation). This turned out to improve the alignment in some cases. One such case occurs when one note in a row of notes with the same pitch and duration is omitted in the performance. Without taking into account positions, the optimal alignment will delete an arbitrary note of the sequence, since the deletions of each of these notes are equivalent based on pitch and duration information only. When position *is* taken into account, the remaining notes of the performance will all be mapped to the closest notes in the score, so the deletion operation will be performed on the score note that remains unmapped, which is often the desired result.

The other factor of importance for determining the optimal alignment between score and performance is the relative costs of the operations are with respect to each other. The relative costs of each kind of operation can be controlled simply by adding a constant scaling factor to each of the cost equations above. Experimentation with several settings showed that the score-performance alignments were stable within certain ranges of relative costs. Only when certain values were exceeded the alignments would change. For example, gradually decreasing the cost of deletions and insertions did initially not affect the alignments. Only after reaching a certain threshold, more and more correspondence operations were left out of the alignment and replaced by the deletion and insertion of the involved sequence elements. The stability of the alignments under changing cost functions is probably due to the fact that the performances are generally quite close to the score, i.e. it is mostly unambiguous which notes the performer played at each moment. If the performances had been less faithful representations of the score, it would be less clear whether notes would have just been changed in time and pitch, or rather that some notes have been deleted and others are played instead. This would probably result on a lack of stable alignments. In general, the desired alignments of the different phrases performed at different tempos could be obtained using the same values cost function parameters.

In the calculation of the alignment it is not necessary to take into account low-level operations like onset transformation or duration transformation, because they can be inferred, from the note attributes, once a correspondence between notes in the score and notes in the performance has been established. Also the order in which e.g. a transformation operation is split into pitch transformation, duration transformation and onset transformation, is irrelevant, since all these operations act on the same performance element.

5   Experimentation and Results

Our set of audio data currently consists of alto saxophone recordings of five jazz standards ('Once I Loved' (A.C. Jobim), 'Up Jumped Spring' (F. Hubbard), 'Donna Lee' (C. Parker), 'Like Someone in Love' (Van Heusen/Burke) and 'Body and Soul' (J. Green)), played at various tempos. Each song is played at about 12 different tempos, spread around the original tempo at intervals of approximately 10 beats per minute. These tempos are assumed to cover most of the musically

Fig. 4. Graphical representation of the annotations extracted for the first phrase of 'Body and Soul' at 100 beats per minute.

acceptable range of tempos at which the melodies can be performed. The songs were performed by a professional jazz musician, playing along with a metronome. The performer was instructed to stick to the score as much as possible, and play in a consistent expressive way, that is, without intentionally changing the mood. After recording, the performances were segmented into phrases manually, which resulted in a data set consisting of 219 recorded musical phrases. These phrases were transcribed using a melody extraction tool that is being developed by the Music Technology Group (MTG) of the Pompeu Fabra University of Barcelona [8]. The transcriptions are in XML format and comply to the MPEG7 standard for melody description. The note entries in the melody description contain attributes such as the MIDI number of the pitch, onset (in seconds), duration (in seconds) and dynamics. Since the tempo of the performance and the position of the metronome ticks is known, duration and onset values can be easily converted from seconds to metrical beats.

A general analysis of the annotation results, perhaps unsurprisingly, show the extracted annotations showed that more insertions were found in phrases that were performed at slower tempos, and deletions and consolidations more often occurred in faster performances. Closer inspection showed that the inserted notes were mainly ornamental 'leading' notes: notes with a very short duration played 'as an introduction' to the following note. The pitch was often just one semitone above or below the pitch of the note that it embellished. Deletions of notes often occurred in sequences of notes with the same pitch. In some of these cases, the duration of the previous or next note was increased slightly, so it was hard to tell if the note was really deleted, or rather that it had been consolidated together with its predecessor or successor into one large note. Both possibilities could be obtained, respectively by increasing and decreasing the cost of consolidation.

More concretely, table 1 shows the annotations extracted comparing the score and one performance of the first phrase of 'Body and Soul' at tempo 100. The numbers in the table are the deviations with respect to the score. Negative (resp. positive) values for onset transformations mean that the note has been anticipated (resp. delayed). Negative (resp. positive) values for duration transformations mean that the note has been shortened (resp. prolonged). C5 in the table is a note added by the performer between notes 16-17. A♭4 consolidates

Table 1. Quantified annotations extracted for the first phrase of 'Body and Soul' at tempo 100. Duration and onset transformations are shown in metrical beat units.

Note	Dur. Tr.	Onset Tr.	Pitch Tr.	Ins.	Del.	Cons.	Frag.
1	0.024	0.105					
2	-0.058	0.129					
3	-0.126	0.071					
4	-0.021	-0.054					
5	0.068	-0.075					
6	0.054	-0.007					
7	0.490	0.048					
8	0.051	0.037					
9	-0.031	0.088					
10	0.024	0.058					
11	-0.024	0.082					
12	0.017	0.058					
13	0.061	0.075					
14	-0.030	0.136					
15	0.016	0.106					
16	0.837	0.122					
			C5				
17	-0.110	0.183					
18	0.034	0.088					
19	0.068	0.122					
20	-0.136	0.191					
21	-0.034	0.055					
22	0.535	0.020					
23	-0.078	0.126					
24	-0.085	0.048					
25	0.031	-0.037					
26/27						A♭4	
28	0.000	0.068					
29	-0.030	0.068					
30	-0.150	0.038					

notes 26-27. Empty entries mean that the corresponding transformation was not applied.

Figure 4 shows a summary of the same annotations in a graphical form. The alignment between the score and the performance is represented by the letters T (Transformation), I (Insertion), and C (Consolidation). For the Transformation operations, the duration and onset deviations of performance are shown in bars. The size of the bars show the amount of deviation. Bars above the line indicate a longer duration or later onset, respectively. Bars below the line indicate a shorter duration or earlier onset.

6   Conclusions and Future Work

We have presented a system to annotate cases of musical performances. The annotations are automatically extracted from human performances. This is done by finding the optimal alignment between the score and a transcription of the performance, using the edit distance algorithm.

It should be noticed that even in performances that were intended to be relatively literal interpretations of the score, deletions and insertions of note elements occur. This implies that an annotation scheme that labels performance elements as the one presented in this paper is very useful in music performance processing systems.

This paper has focused on extracting performers' behaviors to annotate cases within the *Tempo-Express* CBR system. The whole system has been only briefly described. Such a system is useful to automatically achieve musically sensible tempo transformations that presently are manually done in audio-processing studios.

At some stages of the annotation process, improvements and elaborations are possible: the hierarchy of edit operations could be specified in further detail, for example by distinguishing between the insertions/deletions of ornamental notes (that often have an intricate relationship to their neighboring notes) versus non-grace notes. Other improvements could be made in the cost calculation of the edit operations. For example, the costs of transformation operations could involve a comparison of the harmonic role of the pitches, rather than the absolute pitch difference. This would be especially valuable in cases where the performance is a liberal paraphrase, or an improvisation on the score.

Acknowledgments. The authors acknowledge the Music Technology Group of the Pompeu Fabra University for providing the XML transcriptions of the performances. This research has been partially supported by the Spanish Ministry of Science and Technology under the project TIC 2000-1094-C02 "Tabasco: Content-based Audio Transformation using CBR".

References

1. Josep Lluís Arcos and Ramon López de Mántaras. An interactive case-based reasoning approach for generating expressive music. *Applied Intelligence*, 14(1):115–129, 2001.
2. Josep Lluís Arcos and Enric Plaza. Inference and reflection in the object-centered representation language Noos. *Journal of Future Generation Computer Systems*, 12:173–188, 1996.
3. Josep Lluís Arcos and Enric Plaza. Noos: An integrated framework for problem solving and learning. In *Knowledge Engineering: Methods and Languages*, 1997.
4. C. Blake, E. Keogh, and C. Merz. *UCI Repository of Machine Learning Algorithms Databases.* University of California. Department of Information and Computer Science, Irvine, CA, 1998.

5. Jaime Carbonell. Derivational analogy: A theory of reconstructive problem solving and expertise acquisition. In R. S. Michalski, J. G. Carbonell, and T. M. Mitchell, editors, *Machine Learning*, volume 2, pages 371–392. Morgan Kaufmann, 1986.
6. R. Dannenberg. An on-line algorithm for real-time accompaniment. In *Proceedings of the 1984 International Computer Music Conference*. International Computer Music Association, 1984.
7. P. Desain, H Honing, and H. Heijink. Robust score-performance matching: Taking advantage of structural information. In *Proceedings of the 1997 International Computer Music Conference*, pages 337–340, San Francisco, 1997. International Computer Music Association.
8. E. Gómez, , A. Klapuri, and B. Meudic. Melody description and extraction in the context of music content processing. *Journal of New Music Research*, 32(1), 2003. (In Press).
9. Maarten Grachten, Josep Lluís Arcos, and Ramon López de Mántaras. A comparison of different approaches to melodic similarity. In *IInd International Conference on Music and Artificial Intelligen ce*, 2002.
10. H. Heijink, P. Desain, H. Honing, and L. Windsor. Make me a match: An evaluation of different approaches to score-performance matching. *Computer Music Journal*, 24(1):43–56, 2000.
11. E. W. Large. Dynamic programming for the analysis of serial behaviors. *Behavior Research Methods, Instruments & Computers*, 25(2):238–241, 1993.
12. Fred Lerdahl and Ray Jackendoff. An overview of hierarchical structure in music. In Stephan M. Schwanaver and David A. Levitt, editors, *Machine Models of Music*, pages 289–312. The MIT Press, 1993. Reproduced from Music Perception.
13. V. I. Levenshtein. Binary codes capable of correcting del etions, insertions and reversals. *Soviet Physics Doklady*, 10:707–710, 1966.
14. Marcel Mongeau and David Sankoff. Comparison of musical sequences. *Computers and the Humanities*, 24:161–175, 1990.
15. Eugene Narmour. *The Analysis and cognition of basic melodic structures : the implication-realization model*. University of Chicago Press, 1990.
16. Enric Plaza and Josep Ll. Arcos. Constructive adaptation. In Susan Craw and Alun Preece, editors, *Advances in Case-Based Reasoning*, number 2416 in Lecture Notes in Artificial Intelligence, pages 306–320. Springer-Verlag, 2002.
17. Xavier Serra, Jordi Bonada, Perfecto Herrera, and Ramon Loureiro. Integrating complementary spectral methods in the design of a musical synthesizer. In *Proceedings of the ICMC'97*, pages 152–159. San Francisco: International Computer Music Association., 1997.
18. Manuela M. Veloso, Alice M. Mulvehill, and Michael T. Cox. Rationale-supported mixed-initiative case-based planning. In *AAAI/IAAI*, pages 1072–1077, 1997.

Case-Based Ranking for Decision Support Systems

Paolo Avesani, Sara Ferrari, and Angelo Susi

ITC-IRST,
Via Sommarive 18 - Loc. Pantè, I-38050 Povo, Trento, Italy
{avesani,susi,sferrari}@itc.it

Abstract. Very often a planning problem can be formulated as a ranking problem: i.e. to find an order relation over a set of alternatives. The ranking of a finite set of alternatives can be designed as a preference elicitation problem. While the case-based preference elicitation approach is more effective with respect to the first principle methods, still the scaling problem remains an open issue because the elicitation effort has a quadratic relation with the number of alternative cases. In this paper we propose a solution based on the machine learning techniques. We illustrate how a boosting algorithm can effectively estimate pairwise preferences and reduce the effort of the elicitation process. Experimental results, both on artificial data and a real world problem in the domain of civil defence, showed that a good trade-off can be achieved between the accuracy of the estimated preferences, and the elicitation effort of the end user.

1 Introduction

Very often a planning problem can be formulated as a ranking problem: i.e. to find an order relation over a set of alternatives. This order relation is usually interpreted as a sort of priority index that supports a selection policy.

Although the problem of finding an order over a set of items is ubiquitous, we have conducted our research in the domain of environmental decision support systems. A typical problem in civil defence is arranging emergency plans for a set of areas with high environmental hazard. Since preparing a single emergency plan requires a great deal of effort, a new issue arises: to establish an order over the candidate areas that indicates how to proceed. A similar problem arises when the training of civile population has to be planned: the simulation of a single emergency plan is expensive and has a great impact on everyday life.

Both scheduling the preparation of the emergency plans and scheduling the simulation of these plans require to take into account many factors, because the final order of a set of alternatives has to combine multiple criterias. For example, the relevance of an emergency plan requires combining the assessment of elements such as the environmenatal hazard and the systemic hazard. Usually it is hard to understand in advance the mutual dependecies of these criterias; in many cases the solution is proceeding with an elicitation process of all the relevant factors. The ranking problem can be designed as a preference elicitation problem.

The preference elicitation can be designed as an ex-ante process or as an ex-post process. In the former case, the preferences are formulated before we know the alternatives, while in the latter case, the preferences are formulated after establishing a finite

K.D. Ashley and D.G. Bridge (Eds.): ICCBR 2003, LNAI 2689, pp. 35–49, 2003.
© Springer-Verlag Berlin Heidelberg 2003

set of alternatives. It is worthwhile to note that, in this context, the goal is not to find the top rank but to produce the total order.

The focus of this work is on the ex-post approach, where the real cases (i.e. the alternatives) play a key role in the preference elicitation process. In particular we are interested in developing a methodology where such a process is guided by the cases, not by general principles. We believe that by reasoning on cases, we may support the emergence of relevance factors in determining a rank over a finite set.

The main contribution of this paper is the design of a case-based elicitation process to support the planning problem in terms of rank assessment. More specifically, we adopt a pairwise approach in which the preference elicitation strategy is based on the comparison of two alternatives. In this paper, we propose a simple iterative model based on two automated steps: the development of a case selection policy, and the approximation of case preferences. The former aims at supporting a strategy for pairwise comparison, and the latter aims at reducing the elicitation effort.

A well known drawback of the case-based elicitation approach is the restriction on the case base size: this constraint results from the interactive process of acquiring preferences from the end users. As the size of the case base increases, the number of preferences that must be elicited grows quadratically. Usually the threshold is around ten cases [17].

The objective of this work is to illustrate how the use of machine learning techniques, like boosting [11], enables us to increase the threshold on the size of the case base while reducing the cognitive load of the end user. The preliminary results, both on artificial data and data obtained from real world experiments, showed that our solution is effective in finding a good balance between the size of the case base and the end users effort.

The structure of the paper is as follows. In the next section, we describe our motivation for this work. In the third section we discuss related work. In the fourth section we introduce the case-based model for the pairwise elicitation process. The fifth section explains how the machine learning techniques have been exploited in the case-based model, and the sixth and the seventh sections will present and discuss the experimental results on artificial and real world data respectively.

2   Motivation

The preference elicitation problem is well known in many scientific communities and it has been extensively investigated [3,12,14,18]. The ex-ante approach is based on the notion of utility functions, which are designed to combine the various factors involved. This way of proceeding doesn't take into account the real set of cases where the utility function has to be applied. The basic assumption is that it is always possible to encode the first principle rationality in terms of an utility function.

A typical example is represented by the overlay model [2], widely used in the environmental sciences. In this domain, the following equation can be used to estimate the natural risk: $R = HVv$ (risk, hazard, vulnerability and value respectively). The values of these three features are acquired separately for each case and the risk value for each of them is derived by the equation. The total rank of the cases follows from the order relation of numbers.

Although the development of Geographical Information Systems (GIS) has made this approach very popular, there are many drawbacks [6]. First of all the unrealistic assumption that the acquisition of the feature values is context independent; a further related assumption that simplifies the complexity of the problem is concerned with the homogeneity of the case description. Moreover this method sometime produces only partial orders. When the main purpose of an order relation is supporting a decision-making step a partial rank could be not satisfactory.. In general, with the ex-ante approaches it is not possible to know in advance whether a predefined criteria will produce a total or a partial order because the final outcome is strongly related to the given set of cases.

To overcome this drawback an alternative approach has been proposed by Saaty [17] where the order relation is derived from the analysis of the cases. The pairwise comparison allows the simplification of the elicitation process that iteratively acquires the preference relation with respect to two alternative cases. Through this method the rationality of ranking can emerge from the comparison of the real cases and not from a generalized first principle. The elicitation process requires filling an half matrix where both rows and columns represent the same set of cases, and each entry a pair of cases (we assume that the preference structure is invariant with respect to the order of pair presentation).

The average effort to accomplish this task is related to the size of the case base: $|C|(|C|-1)/2$. It can become very hard for the end user to afford this approach when the number of cases increases. For this reason the literature has identified a threshold of 9 cases [17]. Given this constraint only an approach based on preference approximation will be sustainable once the size of the case base exceed the threshold above. A new challenge arises to design innovative strategies that do not require an exhaustive acquisition of all the pairwise preferences. Our objective is to find a trade-off between the elicitation effort and the accuracy of the estimated preferences.

In the fourth section we will introduce a model for a case-based preference elicitation process that supports a mixed-initiative strategy to achieve a total order of a finite set of cases. A step of pairwise analysis is in charge of the end user, and a step of preference approximation is in charge of the computer. The role of the machine learning techniques is twofold: estimating the rank, and shortening the iterative process of preference elicitation.

These two roles are closely related and together aim at making the case-based approach of preference elicitation competitive against the first principle one.

3   Related Work

The preference elicitation problem has received a growing attention in recent years with the advance of the Internet. The growing importance of e-commerce has promoted the development of personalization services that automatically elicit preferences from users.

However, preference elicitation in the domain of e-commerce is slightly different than in the domain of environmental resource management. Although existing work attempts to exploit the notion of case-based comparison [13] or to support the retrieval through an order relation [4], their foci are the selection of the top of a set of alternatives. In the domain of e-commerce, the objective is similar to that of information filtering, while in environmental planning the ultimate goal is a total ranking because it is more suitable to support a policy of case selection. Let us remind that in a decision support system the interest is on the rank of the whole set of items, while in a recommendation system the interest is on a single item, i.e. the top rank.

In this perspective, the work most similar to ours is the Analytical Hierarchy Process (AHP) and its variations [17,15]. This method has been developed in the last decade in the domain of environmental resource management. The basic idea is to exploit a case-based pairwise comparison to elicit the preference structure and consequently to derive a rank according to a predefined goal. For all possible pairs from a finite set of cases, each expert is asked which of the two cases he prefers. Once the matrix of the pairwise preferences is filled, the corresponding rank is synthesized for the set of cases. It is not worthwhile to go in detail to explain the role of the hierarchy in AHP since it is not meaningful for the purpose of this paper, nevertheless it has to be stressed that this method is a successful alternative to the first principle approaches and has been applied in many domains [16].

Although it has been widely used, AHP suffers of two main drawbacks that prevents the method from scaling up on the number of cases, as we have already mentioned before. First, the cardinality of the set of cases has to be less than ten; second, the constraint on the preference range has to be elicited from a scale of nine values (to state how much a case has to be preferred with respect to the other). A non trivial boolean preference increases the cognitive overload of the user, making the method prone to the error because it assumes the capability to vote independently from the context. In a real world application, if the user is not familiar with the scale of values or the related semantic is not well defined in advance, the acquired information will be noisy. An additional objective of our work is to relax this constraint and to enable a boolean pairwise preference.

A recent work in the area of preference elicitation has developed a system that acquires the preference structure of the end user interactively: VEIL [3]. This system supports an incremental utility elicitation process on large datasets, to allow the building of a model of the user's preferences. In particular the system addresses the problem of visualizing many alternatives emphasizing some of their features considered of interest for the users. When the users are interacting with the system the whole set of cases are simultaneously presented to them. The user's operations are interpreted to implicitly derive from them the preference structure. This approach doesn't allow a rich visualization of the case descriptions. Moreover, the users are not supported in browsing the space of alternatives, and they are in charge of focusing their attention on relevant cases. In the next section we will show how our model takes this issue into account, and how the machine learning techniques can be effective in supporting the pair selection.

The works mentioned above do not fit the typical case-based reasoning loop [1], although we have stressed the role of cases in the elicitation process. The classical perspective of case-based reasoning has been adopted by work developed in the decision theory community. In [12] it is assumed that a set of preference structures, complete or incomplete, has been elicited from a set of users; the goal is the elicitation of the preferences of a new user incrementally, using the closest existing preference structures as potential defaults. This work explore the use of three different distance measures to compute the similarity between the preference structures. These similarity metrics among order relations are crucial to support the retrieval step of a CBR loop. In the case-based approach to decision support systems, we don't have an explicit step of retrieval; rather, an approximation step. The similarity metrics on preference structures are of potential use to design nearest neighbour classifiers supporting the preference approximation. In the following section, we explain the use of a classifier to approximate a partial unknown preference structure.

Our approach to the approximation of the preference elicitation is based on the work described in [10] where the RankBoost methodology is described and used in the context of information retrieval. In particular, the goal of this work is discovering a total order relation for a given set of instances described with some features, given a set of ordering functions for this features and a target user ordering function represented as a binary preference relation between couples of instances. Although these techniques have not been developed to support the approximation of preference structures, we will show in the section 5 how we have applied them to support the problem of preference elicitation.

To summarize, we are interested in exploiting the machine learning techniques mentioned above to combine a solution for the twofold problem: supporting the pairwise elicitation selection and the pairwise preferences approximation. In the next section, we explain the process that integrates the two steps in such a way that each one can benefit from the other.

4   A Model for Case-Based Preference Elicitation

The objectives of this work can be summarized as follows:

– **Elicitation advisory process.**
  Designing a case-based decision support system to support the interactive elicitation of a preference structure over a finite set of cases.
– **Pairwise preference elicitation.**
  Supporting the elicitation of a boolean preference structure through a pairwise comparison of cases.
– **Preference acquisition policy.**
  Developing an acquisition policy to support the expert in the process of preference elicitation: i.e. recommendation of the pairs of cases tha have to be analyzed first.
– **Preference learning step.**
  Exploiting learning techniques to approximate the unknown pair preferences taking advantage of the previously elicited preferences.
– **Error and effort minimization.**
  Achieving a good trade-off between the accuracy of approximated rank and the effort required to collect the explicit definition of the preference structure.
– **Mutual recursive benefit.**
  Improving the accuracy of rank approximation taking advantage of an effective acquisition policy, and at the same time improving the acquisition policy taking advantage of the by product result of the learning step (i.e. the pairs where the learner fails).

Before introducing the interactive case-based preference elicitation model we briefly sketch the general architecture that underlies the generic process. Figure 1 illustrates the schema of the process; the abstract view highlights the interactive and the static components.

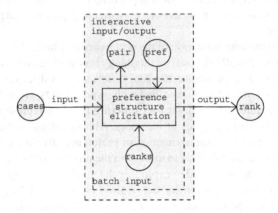

Fig. 1. Generic architecture for the preference elicitation process.

The types of data involved in the elicitation process can be detailed as follows:

- data - The input data represent the finite collection of cases that has to be ranked. The data are the initial input of a case-based preference elicitation process.
- pair - A pair is a couple of alternative cases where the end user preference is unknown. Given a pair the end user is interactively asked for preference elicitation. The pairs are generated run time by an automated process.
- pref - The pref is the order relation between two alternative cases elicited by the end user. The preference is formulated as a boolean choice from a pair, i.e. two alternative cases.
- ranks - The ranks are a collection of order relations defined on the finite collection of cases. When the ranks are derived by the feature-based description of the cases they are referred as *r*anking features.
- rank - The rank represents the target preference structure and it is the main output of the whole process. The rank produced in output could be an approximation of the exact rank.

Starting from this generic architecture, we can design at least four different models of the iterative process that enable the ranking of a set of cases through the interactive acquisition of pairwise preference: the basic single-user loop model, the iterated single-user loop model, the basic multi-user loop model and the self multi-user loop model.

The basic single-user loop model is depicted in Figure 2 and it is based on an iteration of three steps in the following sequence:

1. Pair sampling
   An automated procedure selects from the case base a pair of cases whose relative preference is unknown according to a predefined acquisition policy.

2. Preference acquisition

Given a pair of alternative cases the end user chooses which one is to be preferred with respect to the ultimate goal.

3. Rank learning

Given a partial elicitation of the user preferences a learning algorithm produces an approximation of the unknown preferences and then a correspondent ranking of the whole set of cases is derived.

If the result of the learning step is considered enough accurate or the end user has been overloaded the iteration halts and the latest approximated rank is given as output; otherwise an other cycle of the loop is carried on. It is to be noticed that the first and the third steps are automated while the second step is in charge to the end user.

The basic single-user loop model is characterized by two elements: first only one user takes part to the elicitation process, second it is assumed that the preference elicitation is monotonic (i.e. the user doesn't see a pair twice).

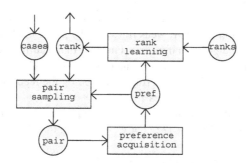

Fig. 2. Basic single-user loop: monotonic elicitation process.

In the iterated single-user loop model there is the assumption that the preference acquisition is context sensitive or better is history dependent. The choice between two alternative cases depends on what has been previously elicited. Because the opinion of the users may change and they should have the opportunity to revise their preferences presenting to them the same pair of alternative cases.

The basic multi-user loop and the self multi-user loop models refer the scenario where many users take part to the elicitation process in order to take into account multiple points of view. More specifically the fourth model introduces a further restrictive condition: the learning step can't take advantage of the predefined order relations over the set of cases.

In the following we will restrict our attention to the basic single-user loop model.

5   The Learning Step

In this section we will focus our attention on the approximation of a preference structure. To explain how a boosting approach can be exploited for this purpose we arrange an abstraction of the problem definition.

The basic elements we have seen until now are the case base, the ranking features, the target rank and the elicited pairwise preferences. The case base is defined as a finite set C of cases. The ranking features $F = (f_1, \ldots, f_N)$ are defined as a finite set of N features that describe the case, where $f_i : C \to \bar{\mathbb{R}}$ ($\bar{\mathbb{R}} = \mathbb{R} \cup \{\bot\}$) and the interpretation of the inequality $f_i(c_0) > f_i(c_1)$ means that c_0 is ranked above c_1 by f_i and $f_i(c) = \bot$ if c is unranked by f_i. The target rank is defined as a feedback function $\Phi : C \times C \to \mathbb{R}$ whose interpretation is that $\Phi(c_0, c_1)$ represents how important it is that c_1 be ranked above c_0; positive values means that c_1 should be ranked above c_0; $\Phi(c_0, c_1) = 0$ indicates that there is no preference between c_0 and c_1 (we assume $\Phi(c, c) = 0$ and $\Phi(c_0, c_1) = -\Phi(c_1, c_0)$ for all $c_0, c_1 \in C$). Finally the set of pairwise elicited preferences is defined as $C_\Phi = \{c \in C | \exists c' \in C : \Phi(c, c') \neq 0\}$ that represents the feedback of the user or the finite support of Φ.

The goal of the learning step is to produce a ranking of all cases in C, including those not ranked by the f_i, represented in the form of a function $H : C \to \mathbb{R}$ with a similar interpretation to that of the ranking features (c_1 is ranked higher than c_0 by H if $H(c_1) > H(c_0)$).

The methodology we have choosen is boosting, a method to produce highly accurate prediction rules by combining many weak rules which may be moderately accurate; here we refer to the boosting algorithm introduced in [10]. In the current setting the objective is a learning algorithm that will produce a function $H : C \to \mathbb{R}$ whose induced ordering of C will approximate the relative orderings encoded by the feedback function Φ using the information from the set of features F.

Before introducing the boosting algorithm we require to define an additional notion of *crucial pair*, a density function $D : C \times C \to \mathbb{R}$ such that

$$D(c_0, c_1) = max(\{0, \Phi(c_0, c_1)\})\gamma$$

setting to 0 all negative entries of Φ; γ is a positive constant chosen so that

$$\sum_{c_0, c_1} D(c_0, c_1) = 1$$

A pair c_0, c_1 is said to be *crucial* if $\Phi(c_0, c_1) > 0$, so that the pair receives non-zero weight under D. The algorithm we used is designed to find an order function H with a small weighted number of crucial-pair misorderings, in other words with a small ranking loss $rloss_D(H)$ defined as:

$$rloss_D(H) = \sum_{c_0, c_1} D(c_0, c_1)[\![H(c_1) \leq H(c_0)]\!] = Pr_{(c_0, c_1) \sim D}[H(c_1) \leq H(c_0)]$$

where $[\![H(c_1) \leq H(c_0)]\!] = 1$ if $H(c_1) \leq H(c_0)$ is true, 0 otherwise.

The algorithm *RankBoost* in Figure 3 operates in rounds. The basic round is based on two procedures called *WeakLearner* and *ChooseAlpha* that are invoked to produce respectively a *weak hypothesis* h and the value for the parameter α. *RankBoost* maintains a distribution D_t over $C \times C$ that is passed on round t to the weak learner. The algorithm chooses D_t to emphasize different parts of the training data. A high weight assigned to

Algorithm **RankBoost**
Input: initial distribution D over $C \times C$
Output: the final Hypothesis $H(c)$

begin
    Initialize $D_1 = D$;
    For $t = 1, \ldots, T$:
        $h_t = WeakLearner(.)$, where $h_t : C \rightarrow \mathbb{R}$;
        $\alpha_t = ChooseAlpha(.)$, where $\alpha_t \in \mathbb{R}$;
        $D_{t+1}(c_0, c_1) = \frac{D_t(c_0, c_1)}{Z_t} e^{\alpha_t(h_t(c_0) - h_t(c_1))}$;
    return $H(c) = \sum_{t=1}^{T} \alpha_t h_t(c)$;
end.

Fig. 3. RankBoost algorithm.

a pair of cases indicates a great importance and the weak learner has to order that pair correctly.

Weak hypotheses have the form $h_t : C \rightarrow \mathbb{R}$. The boosting algorithm uses the weak hypothesis h to update the distribution as shown in the algorithm. Suppose that c_0, c_1 is a crucial pair so that we want c_1 to be ranked higher than c_0 (in all other cases D_t is 0). Assuming that the parameter $\alpha_t > 0$ this rule decreases the weight $D_t(c_0, c_1)$ if h_t gives a correct ranking ($h_t(c_1) > h_t(c_0)$) and increases the weight otherwise. Thus, D_t tends to concentrate on the pairs whose relative ranking is hardest to determine. The final hypothesis H is the α_t weighted sum of the weak hypothesis h_t.

During the development of the system we have implemented the weak learner proposed in [10] that takes as input the ranking features $f_1, \ldots, f_N$ and the distribution D, and as output the learner h. Other possible weak learner schemas can be designed, for example the nearest neighbour learners based on the similarity metrics proposed in [12]; nevertheless combining nearest neighbour learners with a boosting schema produces classifiers more sensitive to the variance of the data.

6 The Pair Sampling Step

If the learning step illustrated in the previous section plays a key role in producing an accurate approximation of the target rank, an other task remains to be tackled: to reduce the elicitation effort of the end users. The purpose of the acquisition policy is to sample the pairs whose relative preferences is unknown. Of course if the number of elicited preferences increases, the approximation error tends to decrease. When the acquisition process is exhaustive the approximation error is zero because all the information is elicited. The challenge is to find a kind of minimum set that maximize the accuracy of the estimated rank. Although the model enables a one-shot pairs sample, the basic intuition is that an incremental strategy could be much more effective because after each learning step a new awareness on what is difficult to approximate is acquired. Therefore an acquisition policy can take advantage focusing the sampling on the pairs where the estimated preferences are not enough accurate [5].

As we have seen in the previous section the boosting technique produces, as a by-product of the learning algorithm, a distribution of weights that emphasizes the pair of cases for which it was harder to approximate the right preference. The rationality of acquisition policy combines this information with an other source of knowledge: the notion of problem complexity [9]. The complexity of the approximation problem can be characterized by the relationship between the target rank and the order relation used as the base of the inductive process. Four types of categories can be defined with increasing degree of complexity: *isotonic, antitonic, non-monotonic* and *non-projective*.

Although many acquisition policies can be designed all of them share the same structure based on two components: a bootstrap component and a feedback component. The former samples a set of pairs without any hints because at the beginning no information are avaliable (remind that the sampling step is the first of the process), the latter implements the rationality that we sketched above.

In the experiments illustrated in the following section we have adopted a "bipartite" strategy for bootstrapping the pair sampling. The hypothesis is to maximize the minimum coverage of the all cases: the pairs are generated without selecting the same case twice.

The next two sections are devoted to the experimentations of the model looking first at the evaluation setup and then at the empirical results.

7 Evaluation Setup

The evaluation of the case-based preference elicitation model presented until now has been organized distinguishing between on-line and off-line experiments. The off-line experiments have been designed to assess the properties of the process and of the proposed solutions. The on-line experiments have been performed as a case study on a real world problem and with real users in the domain of the civil defence (see Section 9 for the details). As depicted in the Figure 4 all the experiments have tested the same three steps loop using the same acquisition policy and the same learning algorithm. Only the preference acquisition was different: in the on-line experiments the real users have been directly involved while in the off-line experiments they have been simulated.

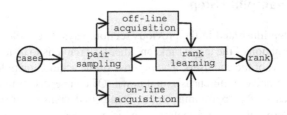

Fig. 4. Experimental Loops: the on-line and off-line elicitation.

For the off-line experiments many artificial datasets have been synthesized producing case bases with a number of instances ranging from ten to hundred. For each case base an arbitrary preference function Φ has been associated as the target rank and in a similar way the ranking features f_i have been derived from the case description. The Φ function has been used both to simulate the real user in the preference acquisition step and to assess the accuracy of the approximated rank function H.

The assessment of the accuracy has been performed using the notion of disagreement [7] between the two preference functions Φ and H: i.e. the percentage of approximated pair relations not aligned with the correspondent pair relations defined by the target rank. Of course such a measure depends on the total amount of elicited pairwise preferences. It is formulated as percentage of the total amount of pairs without taking into account the symmetrical pair relations.

To simulate more difficult problems different target functions Φ have been configured on the same case base changing their relationships with the ranking features f_i, whose definition is strongly related to the specific case base. Problems with different complexity degree have been generated using the four categories mentioned above.

8   Experimental Results

We performed many trials to assess the properties of the proposed model and overall to provide empirical evidence that it could be effective.

The aim of the first set of experiments was to assess the claim that a target order relation can approximated taking advantage of a set of orders defined on the same collection of cases, e.g. the ranking features. The results are illustrated on the left side of the Figure 5 where on the y axis is illustrated the disagreement measure and on the x axis the elicitation effort. The elicitation effort is formulated as the percentage of the $|C|(|C| - 1)/2$ total amount of relations; the figure doesn't provide the detail of the incremental dynamics of the acquisition policy. The plots refer to the behaviour of the model on a case base of 50 instances and a case description of 20 features. The different curves correspond to different types of problem complexity without changing the case base size. The values represent the average performance over 50 trials. It is worthwhile to notice that, although it is not reported on the plots, the performance of the model is invariant respects with the dimension of the case base and the number of ranking features.

There is a lower bound for the elicitation effort because the end users are constrained to see all the cases at least once, i.e. $|C|/2$ pairs of cases. Such a threshold is around the 2%: the leftmost point of the plots. Even though the performance is already good with the 5% of pairs, the performance of the method becomes stable around 10%, i.e. $2|C|$ pairs of cases. We can conclude that elicitating a number of preferences double respects with the number of cases it possible to lower the approximation error less than 5%. We claim that improving the acquisition policy could lower the elicitation effort achieving a number of pairs equal to the size of the case base.

The second plot of Figure 5 illustrates the results of the experiments related to the comparison between the boolean and the rated pairwise preferences. In these experiments we modified the configuration of the preference function Φ extending the values range from $\{-1, 1\}$ to $[-9, 9]$. The two curves show how the two different ways to elicit preferences don't differ with respect to the disagreement measure; this similarity increases with the cardinality of the case base, so we can conclude that the cognitive overload required by a user to provide a rated preference relation doesn't reduce the approximation error.

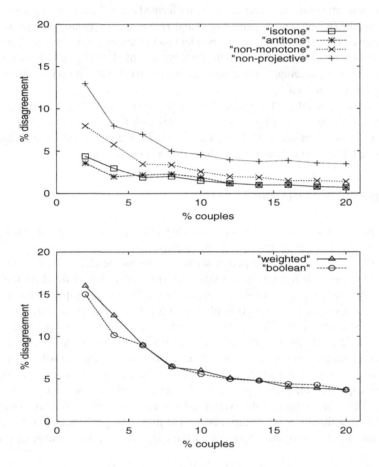

Fig. 5. Evaluation tests: on the y axis is shown the percentage of the wrong pairwise order relations with respect to the target ones: i.e. the disagreement between the approximated ranks and the exact rank; on the x axis is shown the amount of relations given to the learning algorithm: i.e. the percentage of pairs presented to the users. The first plot shows the performance of the method on few case bases of 50 instances with incresing difficulties; the second plot shows the comparison between a boolean choice of alternatives and a fined grained elicitation of preferences.

9   The Case Study of Civile Defence

After the good results achieved in the laboratory, there was the challenge of confirming this success also with a test on the field. We chose to arrange a real world experimentation in collaboration with the Geological Department of Trentino, an Italian northern region.

The expert selected the following problem: ranking a set of areas that a preliminary and rough analysis has recognized as risky from the hydrogeological point of view. The ultimate goal was to implicitly elicit a rationality for planning further studies of deeper analysis and the related emergency plans. In particular this process of assessment was required to take into account the systemic vulnerability, i.e. the capability of the social organizations to deal with unexpected events.

The starting point was a collection of 30 areas, mainly landslides, divided into two categories of risk (the source database is "Aree Vulnerable Italiane" developed by a project led by the National Research Council of Italy). From this perspective the goal was to confirm this partition of the areas and at the same time to achieve a total order of the areas of the two sets. An area was represented by a detailed map and by a record with a quite rich description including the geographical positioning, the administrative information, the risk analysis (with data like the landslide volume, land chemical composition, the site slope, the involved infrastructures, the threatened people, ...). Part of these features have been used to induce the order relation functions.

Experimental sessions have been performed with three experts of the Geological Department acting as a single decision maker. The typical session was characterized by the direct interaction of the users (not mediated by a technician) with the web-based interface developed to deploy the implementation of the model. Although the experimentation has not been modified with respects to the definition given in the Section 4, the two steps of sampling and approximation were transparent to the users.

At the beginning of the experimental session a set of pairs of alternative cases was presented to the users that were free to choose which couple of cases to inspect. At this stage the team of expert negotiated the order relation between the two alternative cases, eventually annotating the single case: sometimes extending the case description with new features, sometimes modifying the original values of the case description.

Once the user has elicited the preferences for all the proposed pairs of cases there are two choices: to ask for a new set of pairs or to ask for a synthesis of the approximated rank. Our experts carried on three cycles of the loop with a set of 15 pairs for each step.

At the end of the elicitation phase the final rank was synthesized and the coverage [8] of the induced order relation has been tested with the team of expert. The disagreement on the coverage of the order relation was 4%, a result obtained presenting only the 10% of pairs to the experts. These achievements, accomplished on the field in a real world setting, agree with the promising results of the previous off-line experiments.

10   Conclusions and Future Work

In this paper we presented a case-based model for the mixed initiative elicitation process that combines a step of a pairwise case selection and a step of a pairwise preference approximation. We illustrated how a case-based approach can be sustainable also with a large number of cases whether learning phase is combined with the end user elicitation. Moreover we have provided the experimental evidence that a rankboost algorithm is effective to achieve a good trade-off between the accuracy of the final rank and the elicitation effort. A meaningful result is concerned with the boolean preference: we have showed that when the number of cases increases the rated preference and the related cognitive overload become useless.

For lack of the space, we have not included a further interesting result on the characterization of the problem complexity. Four categories of increasing complexity have been introduced discriminating with respect to the relationship between the target rank and the order relations derived from the supporting funtions. A paper devoted to this aspect is in preparation.

The paper omitted illustrating the design detail of the acquisition policy. Up to now we refer to a baseline that has allowed achieving the results above. We are currently working on the enhancement of this baseline to obtain a much more effective acquisition policy that would enable a better exploitation of the available information: the by product of the boosting step and the understanding of the problem complexity.

Last but not least, after these preliminary promising results, a new challenge is open: to extend this approach dealing with the multiple viewpoints or the multiagents architecture, according to a decision theory or an artificial intellingence perspective respectively.

Acknowledgments. We would like to thank the Geological Department of Provincia Autonoma di Trento and in particular Silvana Arnoldi and Roberto Cavazzana for their invaluable support to accomplish the case study.

References

1. A. Aamodt and E. Plaza. Case-based reasoning: Foundational issues, methodological variations, adn system approaches. *AI Communications*, 7(1):39–59, 1994.
2. E. Beinat and P. Nijkamp. *Multicriteria Evaluation in Land-Use Management: Methodologies and Case Studies*. Kluwer, 1998.
3. Jim Blythe. Visual Exploration and Incremental Utitlity Elicitation. In *Proceedings of AAAI/IAAI 2002*, pages 526–532, Edmonton, Alberta, CA, July 2002.
4. K. Bradley and B. Smyth. Personalized information ordering: A case study in online recruitment. In *Proceedings of the Twenty-second SGAI International Conference on Knowledge Based Systems and Applied Artificial Intelligence*, Cambridge, UK, 2002.
5. B. Caprile, C. Furlanello, and S. Merler. Highlighting hard patterns via Adaboost weights evolution. In J. Kittler and F. Roli, editors, *Multiple Classifier Systems, Lecture Notes in Computer Science 2364*, pages 72–80. Springer, 2002.
6. A. Carrara. Potentials and pitfalls of gis technology in assessing natural hazards. *Earth Surface Processes and Landforms*, 16:427–445, 1991.
7. William W. Cohen, Robert E. Schapire, and Yoram Singer. Learning to Order Things. In Michael I. Jordan, Michael J. Kearns, and Sara A. Solla, editors, *Advances in Neural Information Processing Systems*, volume 10. The MIT Press, 1998.
8. B.A. Davey and H.A.Priestley. *Introduction to lattices and order*. Cambridge University Press, 1990.
9. G. Devetag and M. Warglien. Representing others' preferences in mixed motive games: Was schelling right? *to appear*, 2002.
10. Y. Freund, R. Iyer, R. Schapire, and Y. Singer. An Efficient Boosting Algorithm for Combining Preferences. In *Proceedings 15th International Conference on Machine Learning*, 1998.
11. Y. Freund and R. Schapire. A Short Introduction to Boosting, 1999.

12. Vu Ha and Peter Haddawy. Toward case-based preference elicitation: Similarity measures on preference structures. In Gregory F. Cooper and Serafín Moral, editors, *Proceedings of the 14th Conference on Uncertainty in Artificial Intelligence (UAI-98)*, pages 193–201, San Francisco, July 24–26 1998. Morgan Kaufmann.

13. McGinty L. and Smyth B. Comparison-based recommendation. In Springer, editor, *Proceedings of the European Conference on Case-Based Reasoning*, Aberdeen, Scotland, 2002.

14. G. Linden, S. Hanks, and N. Lesh. Interactive assessment of user preference models. In *User Modeling*, 1994.

15. Thomas L. Saaty. Fundamentals of the analytic network process. In *Proceedings of International Symposium on Analytical Hierarchy Process*, 1999.

16. Thomas L. Saaty and Luis G. Vargas. *Decision Making in Economic, Political, Social and Technological Environments With the Analytic Hierarchy Process*. RWS Publications, 1994.

17. Thomas L. Saaty and Luis G. Vargas. *Models, Methods, Concepts & Applications of the Analytic Hierarchy Process*. Kluwer Academic, 2000.

18. J. von Neumann and O. Morgestern. *Theory of Games and Economic Behaviour*. Princeton University Press, 1994.

Analogical Reasoning for Reuse of Object-Oriented Specifications

Solveig Bjørnestad

Department of Information Science, University of Bergen, N-5020 Bergen, Norway
solveig@ifi.uib.no
http://www.ifi.uib.no

Abstract. Software reuse means to use again software components built successfully for previous projects. To be successful, techniques for reuse should be incorporated into the development environment. This paper presents an approach where analogical reasoning is used to identify potentially reusable analysis models. A prototype implementation with focus on the repository and analogical reasoning mechanism is presented. All models in the repository are described in terms of their structure. Semantic similarity among models is found by identifying distance in a semantic net built on WordNet, an electronic, lexical database. During retrieval of potential analogies, information about structure and semantics of models is used. During mapping, genetic algorithms are used to optimize the mapping between two models based on their structure and semantics.

Experiments are described in which analogies are identified from the models in the repository. The results reported show that this approach is viable.

1 Introduction

The problem of software reuse has received much attention during the last few decades. Main incentives for this effort have been increasing software development expenses and problems related to software quality. While previously claiming that artificial intelligence (AI) had not contributed to software reuse, in 1994 Tracz states that he believes that "software reuse is the common ground where AI and software engineering will meet" [1]. This is due to the strength of AI within knowledge acquisition and representation experience. AI would be particularly important when trying to reuse artifacts from early stages of the software development process.

The goal of this project [2] is to study how analogical reasoning (AR) can be used to reuse object-oriented specifications. Reuse candidates should be identified early during a software project, as this may reduce the project's use of resources, and result in a product of higher quality.

It has long been realized that software reuse must be planned, and that it must be integrated in the software development process itself. This field has received increased interest during recent years [3,4]. Schmidt [5], in 1999, says that although *opportunistic* reuse has taken place when software developers have

K.D. Ashley and D.G. Bridge (Eds.): ICCBR 2003, LNAI 2689, pp. 50–64, 2003.
© Springer-Verlag Berlin Heidelberg 2003

Fig. 1. An OOram role model with a stimulus role called *borrower*

been cutting and pasting code previously developed by themselves or others within a small group, such reuse does not scale. The goal is to achieve *systematic* software reuse, and this requires both organizational and technical changes.

In recent years, focus has shifted more and more towards component-based development. One effect is that the developer has less control over the architecture and design of a new system because so many design decisions are already made by the component developers. The design decisions are now, according to Wallnau et al. [6], shifted more towards selecting components, rather than towards designing your own components.

According to Maiden [7], evidence has been established that experienced software developers use analogies when they solve new problems, while novices are more concerned with the constructs of the programming language itself. I suggest the incorporation of AR techniques into a computer-aided software engineering (CASE) tool to help the systems developer reuse components from previous systems. The developer should be aided through the process of creating software artifacts by getting suggestions of potentially reusable artifacts found in a repository. For reuse to be successful, reusable artifacts should be identified during the analysis phase. This would prevent too much time being wasted on designing components that could otherwise be reused.

The reusable artifacts used in this work, are OOram (Object-oriented role analysis modelling) role models [8]. They are examples of high level object-oriented analysis models that emphasize the roles objects play using application domain terms. At this early stage in the development process no decisions are made as to what objects will play the different roles and what classes are needed to implement them. An example OOram role model is given in figure 1. Ovals represent roles, small circles represent ports, and lines represent paths between the roles. The stimulus role, *borrower*, is initiating the activity in the role model. If there is a port next to a role, it means that this role knows about the role at the other end of the path. A double, or MANY, port indicates that the role knows about multiple occurrences of the role at the other end.

Theory from AR advocates that structural similarities be used to identify analogies. AR is used as the foundation for the current approach. The methodology must be fine-tuned, however, with respect to what information is actually present in a repository of reusable components. I suggest a hybrid approach where the similarity measure is based on both structural and semantic information. How these similarity measures are to be balanced will thus be a question of analysis.

I show through a set of experiments that it is in fact possible to use AR within a realistic framework to identify analogous, and reusable, analysis models.

2   Approach

2.1   Analogical Reasoning

Analogical problem solving is important for how humans solve problems. Transfer of concepts and relations from one domain to another lies in the bottom of common sense reasoning, learning, and complex problem solving. Research within AR states that the underlying structure of the problem is important for identifying analogies [9]. Analogical problem solving can briefly be described as an attempt to reuse and adapt a problem solution in a new situation, maybe within a completely different domain.

According to Kedar-Cabelli, computational models for analogical problem solving can be described in 4 steps [10]:

1. *Retrieval*—from a target case, search the knowledge base for a *base* case that resembles the target and has a reusable solution.
2. *Elaboration*—derive attributes, relations and causal chains that involve the base case.
3. *Mapping*—match attributes, relations, causal chains from the base case to the target case.
4. *Justification*—ensure that the derived properties, obtained from matching, are in fact valid. If not, correct or modify.

Kedar-Cabelli adds a fifth step, *learning*, that involves accepting the computed properties of the target and adding those to the knowledge base [11], and derivation of general knowledge from the base and target solution [12,13].

The most difficult of the four (or five) steps seems to be *retrieval* of base cases. The process should ensure that the retrieved cases are relevant and can be mapped to the target case after the elaboration process. The most promising methods seem to involve indexing by common generalizations, negative associations (reasons for wrong classification), prototypes and important differences between cases. Such techniques are described by Kolodner, Simpson et al. [14], and further improved by Bareiss, Porter et al. [15].

Thagard [16] presents two criteria for evaluating computational approaches to analogy. First, how well does a computational account of analogy correspond to the experimental facts of human thinking? Second, how powerful is the computational approach: What tasks does it perform, and how efficiently does it perform them? In this work the emphasis is on the second of these criteria.

According to Thagard, computational approaches to analogy are often organized along four general dimensions: representation, retrieval, exploitation, and learning. Along each dimension we can distinguish between syntactic, semantic and pragmatic approaches. Syntax deals with the properties that symbols have due to their form. Semantics is concerned with the relations of symbols to the world, and finally *pragmatics* deals with the use of symbols.

2.2 Our Support for Analogical Reasoning

When a software developer performs analysis for a new project, he should have the option to use AR at any point in the process to identify components from previous projects that are similar enough to be reused, in part or in whole. The system should give an estimate of the closeness of the match, to indicate the amount of work needed for modifications.

The current project supports the retrieval and mapping phases of AR. Although structural similarity is said to be the basis for analogies, I propose a similarity model based on a combined measure of structural and semantic belief values both during the retrieval and mapping phases. Models created from within the same application domain are thought to be more reusable, since less replacement or rewriting of components is thought to be required. Semantic similarity is thus also taken into consideration.

To handle structure information during retrieval, information about a role model's most important sub-structures is computed automatically and stored in the repository when the model is stored [17]. The purpose of structure descriptions is to have a rapid way to extract the models that are similar to the *target model*. A sub-structure can be a *ring*, *tree*, *star*, or *chain*. Information about the size of the structure is also stored. At most 3 sub-structures are described.

The process of finding analogies can be described in the following points.

- When a search for analogous role models is activated by the software developer, the structural descriptions of the role models are first searched to find the role models that resemble the *target model*.
- The next step is to find the best possible candidates for semantic similarity.
- The results from the structural and semantic search are combined. An interesting problem is what weight to give to the semantic similarity compared to the structural similarity during retrieval.
- When retrieval is completed, and all *base models* are ranked based on a combination of structural and semantic similarity, a number of models are selected for mapping. The software developer should be able to select models based on a lower threshold for the computed probability of a base model being analogous and an upper limit of models to perform the mapping on.
- The elaboration phase is supported in the sense that the role models themselves, rather than their structure descriptions, are utilized in the mapping.
- A genetic algorithm based on GAlib [18] is used during mapping.
- When the selected models are mapped, the user is presented with the resulting models, ranked according to their analogy values, to let him decide whether any of the suggestions are acceptable.
- If the analogy is accepted, this information is stored in the repository for future use.

2.3 Prototype

To be able to test the suggested approach, a prototype for the CASE tool environment is developed. The OOram models are stored in a repository. Information about the models' structure is used during retrieval, as mentioned above,

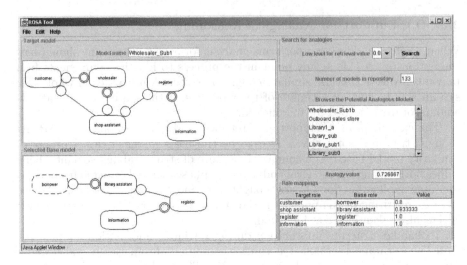

Fig. 2. The CASE Tool after search and selection of a potential analogy

together with information about the names that are used to describe role names. A role is named by creating a link to a *word meaning* in a *term space*. A further description of the term space is given in section 2.4.

The user starts the search for analogies by selecting a *target model* as shown in the upper left pane of figure 2. He then chooses to see all models with an analogy value above a certain leverl, here 0.0, i.e., all models (upper right side of the window), and starts the search by pressing the Search button. When the search is completed, a list of *base models* are shown in a pane on the right side of the window ranked according to their analogy value. Above the list, the number of role models in the repository is shown.

When selecting a model in the list, it is displayed in the lower left pane. The roles that are mapped between target and base models are shown in the lower right pane, together with the semantic similarity value between the pairs of mapped roles. For each role in the target model there may be a mapping to a role in the base. Figure 2 shows the system after a user has performed a search for a target model.

2.4   Semantic Description

Available knowledge from work within lexical and semantic research is used as a basis to measure semantic similarity between any two components in the repository. WordNet [19], a lexical database that supports conceptual, rather than merely alphabetical, search, is an interesting system in this respect. It combines features from both a dictionary and thesaurus, and it contains the full range of common English vocabulary.

The basic relationship used in WordNet is the *synonym*, and words are organized in synonym sets, or *synsets*, consisting of all words that express a common concept, and with relationships between these synsets. Each *word form*, i.e., written word, can have several *word meanings*. A word form belongs to one of the word categories nouns, verbs, adjectives, or adverbs. This implies that the words in a synset are interchangeable in some, although not in all, contexts. Between the synsets there can be several types of relationships, e.g., specialization, generalization, and containment. Some short phrases, or collocations, that would normally not be included in a dictionary, are also included in WordNet.

The most important relationship *between* noun synsets is specialization which organizes synsets into a lexical hierarchy, or rather in a set of hierarchies, each with a *unique beginner* at its root. There are 25 such unique beginners. A unique beginner is a primitive semantic component representing all words in its hierarchically structured semantic field. Examples of unique beginners are {*artifact*} and {*act, activity*}. The unique beginners are organized into 11 hierarchies, and by doing this, a few more general synsets are introduced, e.g., {*entity*} and {*object*}. The hierarchies tend to be fairly shallow, and lexical inheritance systems are never more than 14 levels (applies to version 1.6).

2.5 Semantic Requirements of the Analogy Machine

Research in AR emphasizes deeper, structural similarities. However, surface similarities, like the names used, may play an important role for improving the analogies. An analogy machine should quickly be able to identify the models that most closely resemble the structure of the *target* model.

Tests performed on graphs illudating OOram models using genetic algorithms [20] indicate that when using additional linguistic knowledge, the search for good analogies is improved. These experiments used names chosen from a restricted set, and the graphs were not conversions of role models. Also, the names were not related through a semantic net. It was therefore only possible to say whether the names were the same or not. The addition of a semantic net could enhance the importance of using semantics as an aid to identify analogies. Therefore, the results after searching for structural similarities should be combined with a search for semantic similarity.

We want to identify properties of WordNet useful for finding similarities among OOram components. OOram components can be named as follows: *Roles* and *attributes* are named using nouns, *messages* using verbs, and *message arguments* using nouns. If one term is not enough to name a component, a combination of terms might be necessary. The term *library assistant* does not exist in WordNet, so to use it in a model, it could be added to the term space. Alternatively, a *modifier*, i.e., an extra name part that is used in addition to the main name, could be introduced. For role names, a modifier can be an additional noun, e.g., the main name is *assistant*, with the modifier *library*, in the example above. Modifiers removes the need for adding new synsets to the repository.

2.6 Semantic and Structural Similarity

Semantic information in the CASE repository is organized in a *term space* filled with the noun part of the WordNet database. The terms, or *word forms*, are stored in a hash table with pointers from each word form to each of its meanings. The meanings are organized into synsets. The synsets are organized hierarchically through specialization and generalization relationships. Thus there is a many-to-many relationship between word forms and synsets. In the CASE tool, OOram roles are named by creating a pointer to a particular *word meaning*.

The semantic similarity between two OOram roles is found by calculating the distance between the synsets that represent them in the term space. The further apart they are in the term space, the lower the similarity value. Since the term space is organized as a set of hierarchies, there are two base situations. If the two role names are found in the same hierarchy, they get a similarity value, sim > 0. If they belong to different hierarchies, sim = 0.

Several semantic similarity models are tried out. The model selected takes into account that when two nodes in a hierarchy are compared, one should not only take into account the distance between them, but also their difference in abstraction level. The greater the difference in abstraction level, the greater the semantic difference. This reduction should be dependent on the level at which the two roles are found.

We use a notation where w_t and w_b represent the word meanings of target and base roles respectively, w_a is their nearest common ancestor, $\text{sim}(w_t, w_b)$, is the semantic similarity value between w_t and w_b, and $\text{lev}(w_x)$ is the level of a word meaning, w_x, in a WordNet hierarchy, such that $0 \leq \text{sim}(w_t, w_b) \leq 1$. The similarity model used is shown in equation 1.

$$
\begin{aligned}
&\text{sim}(w_t, w_b) \\
&= 1 - \frac{(\text{lev}(w_t) - \text{lev}(w_a)) + (\text{lev}(w_b) - \text{lev}(w_a))}{\text{lev}(w_t) + \text{lev}(w_b)} - k\frac{|\text{lev}(w_t) - \text{lev}(w_b)|}{\text{lev}(w_t) + \text{lev}(w_b)} \\
&= \frac{2 * \text{lev}(w_a) - k * |\text{lev}(w_t) - \text{lev}(w_b)|}{\text{lev}(w_t) + \text{lev}(w_b)}.
\end{aligned}
\tag{1}
$$

The effect of the difference in abstraction level is controlled by a constant k, whose value is decided through testing.

During *retrieval*, the mapping of roles is not known, so the algorithm finds the best semantic match for each role name in the *target* model, and the mean similarity value for roles in the target model is calculated according to equation 2.

$$
\text{sim}(t, b) = \frac{\sum_{j=1}^{m} max_{i=1}^{n} \text{sim}(w_i^b, w_j^t)}{m}.
\tag{2}
$$

where $sim(w_i^b, w_j^t)$ is the similarity between a role in the target model and one of the roles in a base model in equation 1, and m and n are the number of roles in target and base models, respectively. The function max_j calculates the maximum similarity between role j in the target model and each of the roles, i, in the base model. $\text{sim}(t, b)$ thus represents an upper bound on the average semantic similarity between the target model and a base model.

Based on Dempster-Shafer theory of evidence [21], this value is converted into a belief function, Bel_{sem}^b. Based on the belief function, a probability value for semantic similarity, p_{sem}^b, is calculated, i.e., an *optimistic* approach is used. During *mapping*, however, when roles are mapped structurally, only the names of roles that are structurally mapped are compared.

2.7 Retrieval

Structural similarity is based on a search through a collection of structure descriptions. An example of a structure description is: T 3 4, meaning a tree with trunk length 3 and 2 branches. The structure descriptions of two role models are compared, and a belief function for structural similarity, Bel_{str}^b, is calculated. The more roles included in a structure description, the higher value the description gets during comparison.

When semantic and structural similarity are found, the two belief functions are combined, and a combined probability, p_c^b, that base model b is analogous to the target, is calculated. This probability is used to rank the models after retrieval. The probability is given by

$$p_c^b(a) = m(\{a\}) + k \cdot m(\{a, \neg a\}).$$
(3)

where m is the mass assignment, a represents the proposition that the two models are analogous, and the value of k decides whether the function is optimistic (1), pessimistic (0) or neutral (1/2). We use a neutral approach. The semantic and structural belief functions are given equal weight.

2.8 Mapping

The best candidates for analogy identified during retrieval are selected for the mapping phase. During mapping, specific roles from target and base models are mapped according to their structural *positions*. The genetic algorithm has a fitness function that gives score for isomorphic graphs, while using the value of the semantic similarity between mapped roles to strenghen or weakening the mapping. The best mapping is taken to be the one that gives the highest total value, i.e., it maps as many roles in the target as possible. The analogy value is taken to be the average value of the $\text{sim}(b, t)/n$, where n is the number of roles in the target model.

3 Experimental Design

The suggested approach is tested and improved through a set of experiments. The term space is filled with all nouns from a Prolog version of WordNet. The repository is filled with a set of 133 role models. The models differ in size, application area, and complexity. 24 models are chosen as target models for each experiment. For some of these cases, there are other models known to be similar to the target, while other target models do not have any close analogies. Most models are simple—the smallest is a chain containing 2 roles—but typically they contain 3–5 roles with differing structure. On the other end of the scale there are more complex models that typically represents a higher level of synthesis. The most complex model contains 16 roles and 36 ports.

The simplest role model is a chain with one structure description. The most complex role models is described by many structure descriptions. Since only the three most important structure descriptions are stored, not all roles will be part of one of the descriptions that are stored and later used during retrieval. The intention of our approach to reuse is to find analogies among sub-models, but it is also interesting to see how the system degrades as the models grow larger and more complex.

The same set of base models are used for each experiment. A main goal is to find if the best analogies are identified during retrieval, so that we can safely limit the number of models sent to the mapping phase. The models are kept in an XML format and are therefore easy to add to the database. When roles are named using word forms with more than one meaning in WordNet, a particular meaning is chosen by identifying a **synsetID** in the XML file. The synsetIDs are found using the WordNet graphical user interface. In a future system, this functionality will be supported by giving the user an option to choose from a set of meanings displayed with synonyms, descriptions, and examples.

After each experiment, we select the following information for each case: For each base model, its name, rank after retrieval and computed probability that the model is analogous after retrieval, and its analogy value and rank after the mapping phase is completed.

3.1   Establish Base Situation

The approach described so far is tested with the 24 cases. Later, small variations are tried out, and the results are compared to this base. There are two main goals for the experiments; 1) get as good mappings, i.e., as high analogy values, as possible, and 2) improve the retrieveal by moving the best analogies as high as possible in the ranked list after retrieval.

Figure 3 shows the base situation as curve A. The x-axis represents the number of base models chosen for mapping after retrieval. The y-axis shows in how many of the 24 experiment cases the highest ranked analogy after mapping in fact would have been chosen for mapping. To be certain that the best analogy is included in all cases we would have to choose 67 candidates for mapping. If we accept that the best analogy is found in only a fraction of 0.75 of the cases, we only have to map the two highest ranked models after retrieval.

3.2   Add Information about Multiplicity on Ports

In the base situation, A, OOram MANY ports are not distinguished from ONE ports during mapping. I want to test if the distinction between these two types of ports will improve the mappings. By this I mean that the analogies get higher values. Such information is added in situation B in this experiment. Information about how many base models from retrieval must be passed on to the mapping phase, is collected as above. Figure 3 compares situation B with situation A.

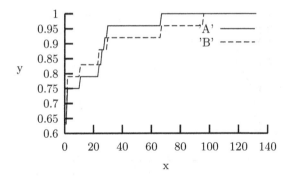

Fig. 3. Fraction of best analogies found at position x after retrieval

The left part of the curve shows an improved situation in B. A possible explanation of this fact may be that in situation A the genetic algorithm fixes the structure too early due to greater semantic similarity. At about position 30, the number of analogies found in situation B is lower than in situation A. This poorer performance of B at higher positions is explained by the fact that some mappings in A between ONE and MANY ports, that were considered good, are lost, since they get a lower score than a mapping between two ports of the same kind. In situation B, the best analogy is found among the two highest ranked models after retrieval in a fracton of 0.79 of the cases, compared to 0.75 in situation A.

It is not only interesting to see how the best analogy is performing, so I also look at the 5 best analogies in each experimental case. The use of such information may in some situations result in mappings with lower values, but if these do not show up among the 5 best analogies, it is of no importance. I compare the two situations to see whether better analogy values are identified when multiplicity information is considered. A change in analogy value is measured as $\delta_{ij} = a_{ij}^B - a_{ij}^A$, where a_{ij}^x is the analogy value for the ith ranked base model in experimental case j, and x is the situation A or B. There is one test case for each target model j.

The *Wilcoxon sign test* is used to analyze the results [22]. When considering the 5 highest ranked models in either A or B, B gives significantly higher analogy values than A. I will therefore include the multiplicity information in the AR approach.

3.3 Weight of Structural and Semantic Similarity during Retrieval

The best analogies should be ranked as high as possible after retrieval to avoid the mapping of too many models. In my approach, structural and semantic similarity are given equal weight during retrieval. As theory within AR states that deeper, structural similarities are important for finding analogies [9], an experiment is performed to see whether more weight on structure will give good analogies a higher rank after retrieval. This situation is termed C.

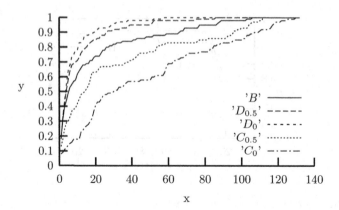

Fig. 4. Comparison of effect of increase of structural and semantic weight for 5 best analogies

The weight given to the semantic belief function is *reduced* to 0.9, 0.8, 0.7, 0.5, and 0.0 of its original weight in a set of tests. The same set of target models were used in each situation. For each situation, the weight of Bel_{sem} is reduced before being combined with Bel_{str}. The 5 best analogies for each of the 24 experimental cases in the two situations are compared using

$$x_{ij}^y = \pi_y(a_{ij}). \qquad (4)$$

where $\pi_y(a_{ij})$ calculates the position after retrieval of the ith analogy in case j using method y. A change in x_{ij}^y is measured as $\delta_{ij} = x_{ij}^B - x_{ij}^A$. If the 5 best analogies are ranked in C, the median of δ will be less than zero. The *sign test for median* is used to analyze the data.

This experiment showed no improvement in the ranks of the best analogies after retrieval. On the contrary, it seemed that the 5 best analogies were moved down the list after retrieval, contrary to the theory. Due to this, a new experiment was performed to see if an *increase* in weight on semantic similarity would improve the ranks of the best analogies after retrieval. This new situation is termed D. Except for this change, the experiment was similar to the one above. The result shows that when reducing the weight on structure during retrieval, the best analogies are in fact moved to better positions during retrieval.

I am still not willing to conclude that structure is less important. The results *may* be caused by properties among the models used in the experiments, e.g., they may be more similar semantically than structurally, or it may be that the structure description algorithm used is not able to capture the true structure of the models. The last point would probably play a greater role for the biggest models in the repository.

These two experiments try to show opposite effect, and it is therefore natural to show the results combined. Figure 4 compares the relative number of 5 best analogies that will be found at each position in the list after retrieval for both the emphasis on structural and semantic belief. For both the situations C and

D we show the results when the weight for Bel_{str} or Bel_{sem} has been reduced to 0.5 and to 0, respectively. The situation with no weight on Bel_{str}, gives the best result, while the situation with no weight on Bel_{sem} gives the poorest result.

3.4 Use of Fitness Function from the GA to Rank Analogies

Previous results indicate that structure is less important than semantics during retrieval, thus contradicting current theory regarding AR. One explanation is that the values of the analogies are given too much emphasis on semantics.

Alternatively, the fitness function used by the genetic algorithm during mapping can be used to calculate the value of the analogy. The fitness function takes into account information on both structure and semantics. The base case for this experiment is situation B from the experiment in section 3.2. Here the value of the analogy calculated as the mean semantic similarity of the roles from the target model that is mapped. In the alternative case, E, the analogy gets the value of the best genome returned from the fitness function. It is not possible to compare the analogy values in B and E because they are incomparable. I want to see whether this approach to ranking the analogies will result in an order that is more in line with the rank of the role models after retrieval.

Experiments show that the original approach is significantly better than the fitness function, for all weightings of structure and semantics in the retrieval ranking. The weight on Bel_{sem} and Bel_{str} were varied as in section 3.3, and for all situations the fitness function gave a poorer result.

3.5 Results

The results show that if the 10 top ranked models after retrieval are passed on to mapping, I identify a fraction of 0.6 of the 5 best analogies in these 24 cases in situation B. In situation D_0 with $\mathrm{Bel}_{sem} = 0$, a fraction of 0.8 of the 5 best analogies are found. In situation $C_{0.5}$, with a weight on $\mathrm{Bel}_{str} = 0.5$, only a fraction of 0.2 of these models are found.

Multiplicity information on roles gives better results, although, in a few cases, the best analogy is ranked lower. A firm conclusion cannot be made unless it has been tested with a wider set of models. When it comes to weight of semantics and structural information during retrieval, I think it would be right to let the user decide the lower limit of the number of models that should be used during mapping. The user may have some knowledge about the content of the repository that can make him want to spend more time waiting for a positive result.

I am more certain when it comes to how the analogy values are calculated. Use of the fitness function does not give better results than does the function where the mean value of the semantic similarity value between the roles that are mapped by the genetic algorithm.

4   Related Work

During the 90s, there was increased interest in the use of AR for reusing software artifacts, and particularly within reuse of specifications. Maiden and Sutcliffe [23] use AR in a *domain matcher*, a hybrid computational mechanism for AR between a requirement specification and one or more domain abstractions. They use techniques similar to SME [24] by Falkenhainer and ACME [25] by Holyoak and Thagard.

Lung and Urban [26] integrate domain analysis in an analogical approach to software reuse. They stress that reuse cannot occur without domain analysis, and that the requirements of AR should be part of the *standard* products of the domain analysis process. When the domain at hand is poorly understood, an analogy could be compared to a well defined domain [27]. For this to be a viable approach, domain models must be classified, and they present a hybrid classification scheme based on hierarchical and faceted classification, i.e., it consists of a hierarchy of facets, where each facet describes a key aspect of the software.

Spanoudakis and Constantopoulos define a quantitative similarity relation between descriptions of software artifacts to promote analogical reuse [28]. A generic method for computing similarity between object-oriented qualitative descriptions is presented. Analogies are elaborated by functions measuring conceptual distances between objects with respect to semantic modelling abstractions.

There are other examples where attempts have been made to reuse code through the use of AR, e.g., Jeng and Cheng [29]. This is not considered relevant to our work, though, as we are interested in the reuse of artifacts from the early phases of software development.

5   Conclusion and Further Work

The suggested approach to integrate AR in a CASE tool, seems promising. Both the retrieval and mapping phases of AR are supported. Retrieval is based on both structure, using structure descriptions, and semantics, using a term space modelled after WordNet. The two are combined in a belief of whether a base model is analogous to a target or not. The ranking of base models after retrieval decides what models are passed to the mapping phase. The models that are eventually mapped, should, after retrieval, be ranked similar to the rank they get after mapping. This goal should be reached with as little effort as possible. Mapping of models is based on a genetic algorithm combining knowledge about their structure and semantics. The use of WordNet ensures that there is a large vocabulary that is modelled by expert lexicographers, and this strenghtens our belief in the results.

The experiments performed show that it is possible to use analogical reasoning to identify OOram role models that are similar to a target model. The potentially best analogies, where similarity is based on both model structure and semantics, are, for the experiments performed, found among the 10 highest ranked models after retrieval in a fraction of 0.6 cases when weigth is equally balanced between semantics and structure information.

The base models with highest analogy values are identified, but no work has been done as to decide how good these analogies really are. This will to a great extent dependent on the user's judgment during justification. Also, no experiments are performed as to find out whether the implementations of the analogous models are reusable. This should be the ultimate goal of a project such as this. To be able to answer this question, a repository should contain models of systems that are implemented, and selected analogies should be tried adapted to fit the new needs.

A final question is whether the results, related to OOram role models, would also be valid for other methodologies, e.g., UML analysis models. Since the OOram models are transformed into directed graphs before the mapping phase, it is reasonable to believe that a repository of models that can be converted into directed graphs, can profit from a solution as the one suggested here.

References

1. Will Tracz. Software reuse myths revisited. In *Proc. of the 16th International Conference on Software Engineering*, pp. 271–272, 1994.
2. Bjørnar Tessem and Solveig Bjørnestad. Analogy and complex software modeling. *Computers in Human Behavior*, 13(4):465–486, 1997.
3. Reidar Conradi. Process support for reuse. In *Proc. of the 10th International Software Process Workshop (1996): Process Support of Software Product Lines*, pp. 43–47, 1998.
4. W. Lam, S. Jones, and C. Britton. Technology transfer for reuse: a management model and process improvement framework. In *Proc. of the 3rd International Conference on Requirements Engineering*, pp. 233–240, 1998.
5. Douglas C. Schmidt. Why software reuse has failed and how to make it work for you. *C++ Report*, January 1999.
6. Kurt Wallnau, Scott Hissam, and Robert Seacord. *Building Systems from Commercial Components*. Addison Wesley, 2002.
7. Neil A. Maiden. *Analogical Specification Reuse During Requirements Analysis*. PhD thesis, School of Informatics, City University, London, 1992.
8. Trygve Reenskaug, Per Wold, and Odd A. Lehne. *Working With Objects. The OOram Software Engineering Method*. Manning Publications Co, 1996.
9. Dedre Gentner. Structure mapping: A theoretical framework for analogy. *Cognitive Science*, 7(2):155–170, 1983.
10. Smadar Kedar-Cabelli. Analogy—from a unified perspective. In D.H. Helman, editor, *Analogical Reasoning*, pp. 65–103. Kluwer Academic Publishers, 1988.
11. T. G. Evans. A program for the solution of geometric analogy intelligence test questions. In M. Minsky, editor, *Semantic Information Processing*. MIT Press, Cambridge, 1968.
12. J.G. Carbonell. Learning by analogy: Formulating and generalizing plans from past experience. In R.S. Michalski, J.G. Carbonell, and T.M. Mitchell, editors, *Machine Learning: An Artificial Intelligence Approach*, pp. 137–161. Palo Alto, CA, 1983.
13. Patrick Henry Winston. Learning new principles from precedents and exercises. *Artificial Intelligence*, 19(3):321–350, 1982.
14. J.L. Kolodner, R.L. Simpson, and K. Sycara-Cyranski. A process model of case-based reasoning in problem solving. In *Proc. IJCAI-9*, pp. 284–290, Los Angeles, CA, 1985.
15. Bruce W. Porter, Ray Bareiss, and Robert C. Holte. Concept learning and heuristic classification in weak-theory domains. *Artificial Intelligence*, 45:229–263, 1990.
16. Paul Thagard. Dimensions of analogy. In D.H. Helman, editor, *Analogical Reasoning*, pp. 105–124. Kluwer Academic Publishers, 1988.

17. Bjørnar Tessem. Structure abstractions in retrieval of analogical software models. *Expert Systems with Applications*, 15:341–348, 1998.
18. Matthew Wall. Galib documentation. http://lancet.mit.edu/galib-2.4/, 1996. Version 2.4.2.
19. Christiane Fellbaum, editor. *WordNet, an Electronic Lexical Database*. The MIT Press, Cambridge, USA, 1998.
20. Bjørnar Tessem. Genetic algorithms for analogical mapping. In D. Aha and D. Wettschereck, editors, *Workshop Notes on Case-Based Learning: Beyond Classification of Feature Vectors*, 9th European Conf. on Machine Learning, pp. 61–67, Prague, April 1997.
21. Glenn Shafer. *A Mathematical Theory of Evidence*. Princteon University Press, Princeton, NJ, 1976.
22. Claes Wohlin, Per Runeson, Martin Höst, Magnus C. Ohlsson, Björn Regnell, and Anders Wesslén. *Experimentation in Software Engineering. An Introduction*. Kluwer Academic Publishers, 2000.
23. N.A.M. Maiden and A.G. Sutcliffe. Computational mechanisms for reuse of domain knowledge during requirements engineering. Technical Report NATURE-94-08, Centre for Human-Computer Interface Design, City University, London, UK, 1994.
24. Brian Falkenhainer, Kenneth D. Forbus, and Dedre Gentner. The structure-mapping engine: Algorithm and examples. *Artificial Intelligence*, 41:1–63, 1989.
25. Keith J. Holyoak and Paul Thagard. Analogical mapping by constraint satisfaction. *Cognitive Science*, 13:295–355, 1989.
26. Chung-Horng Lung and Joseph E. Urban. Integration of domain analysis and analogical approach for software reuse. In *ACM SAC'93*, pp. 48–53, 1993.
27. Chung-Horng Lung and Joseph E. Urban. An approach to the classification of domain models in support of analogical reuse. In M. Samadzadeh and M. Zand, editors, *Proc. ACM SRR'95*, pp. 169–178, Seattle, WA, April 1995. ACM Press.
28. George E. Spanoudakis and Panos Constantopoulos. Integrating specifications: A similarity reasoning approach. *Automated Software Engineering Journal*, 2(4):311–342, December 1995.
29. Jun-Jang Jeng and Betty H. C. Cheng. Using analogy and formal methods for software reuse. In *Proc. of IEEE 5th International Conference on Tools with AI*, pages 113–116, 1993.

Combining Case-Based and Model-Based Reasoning for Predicting the Outcome of Legal Cases

Stefanie Brüninghaus and Kevin D. Ashley

Learning Research and Development Center,
Intelligent Systems Program, and School of Law
University of Pittsburgh
3939 O'Hara Street; Pittsburgh, PA 15260 (USA)
{steffi,ashley}@pitt.edu

Abstract. This paper presents an algorithm called IBP that combines case-based and model-based reasoning for an interpretive CBR application, predicting the outcome of legal cases. IBP uses a weak model of the domain to identify the issues raised in a case, and to combine the analyses for these issues; it reasons with cases to resolve conflicting evidence related to each issue. IBP reasons symbolically about the relevance of cases and uses evidential inferences. Experiments with a collection of historic cases show that IBP's predictions are better than those made with its weak model or with cases alone. IBP also has higher accuracy compared to standard inductive and instance-based learning algorithms.

1 Reasoning with Cases for Prediction

1.1 Predicting the Outcome of Legal Cases

In determining the outcome of a new case, courts in common-law jurisdictions like the US are bound by past decisions. Given that courts are supposed to follow the relevant precedents, it is reasonable to expect that to some extent, one might predict the outcomes of new cases based on past precedents. There is, moreover, a large, and growing, body of data. Legal cases are published on the WWW; tens of thousands of full-text opinions are available in commercial databases like Westlaw and Lexis; and many law firms maintain their own case management systems, where case documents are indexed and stored for future reference.

It may appear, then, that the law is a prime candidate for applying machine learning (ML) or data mining techniques to predict the outcomes of new cases or induce rules about the domain. However, purely statistical methods are of limited use in the law, because they generate numerical scores, rather than a human-interpretable explanation. Likewise, rule-learning algorithms have serious limitations, even though their output is easier to understand for a human. These algorithms tend to focus on a subset of features to find a small set of rules to capture regularities in the data. We found that these induced regularities

K.D. Ashley and D.G. Bridge (Eds.): ICCBR 2003, LNAI 2689, pp. 65–79, 2003.
© Springer-Verlag Berlin Heidelberg 2003

may lead to correct predictions, but they do not correspond to legal reasoning, and the output of such systems is not an acceptable explanation for human experts. Instead, case-based methods are most appropriate. The evidence in legal disputes often favors both sides, but there usually are no rules how to weigh the conflicting features. Advocates and courts make arguments how to resolve these conflicts by analogizing the new case to similar precedents, thereby considering the features of a case in context. In addition, the features and arguments are described textually in long complex texts, and it is very difficult automatically to extract predictive features. Doing so manually, on the other hand, requires knowledge and becomes prohibitively expensive for very large collections.

We have developed a hybrid algorithm for predicting the outcomes of legal cases that avoids some of these pitfalls and problems. The algorithm, called IBP for issue-based prediction, integrates CBR techniques and a weak domain model to predict outcomes with a comparatively small case database and provides meaningful explanations. More specifically, IBP (1) uses its model of the domain to identify which issues were raised, (2) applies CBR techniques to evaluate evidence which side is favored for each issue, and (3) derives a prediction from this issue-analysis following its model of the domain. An evaluation shows that IBP achieves more accurate predictions using this combination of actual cases and a weak predictive theory compared to predictions made with either knowledge source alone. IBP's performance is also better than standard ML algorithms.

1.2   Case-Based Reasoning in the Law

IBP is based on the approach developed in the interpretive CBR programs HYPO and CATO (Ashley 1990; Aleven 1997), which are designed to make arguments with cases and implemented for trade secret law. The cases are represented in terms of Factors, stereotypical patterns of fact that strengthen or weaken a plaintiff's claim. The outcome of a case may either be for the plaintiff, the party that brings the lawsuit, or for the defendant, the party that is being sued. (In the remainder of the paper, we refer to Factors as Fi, and use subscript π and δ to indicate which side they favor.) HYPO's argumentation model introduced Factors to reason symbolically about cases, and defined similarity by the inclusiveness of the set of Factors a case shares with another problem. HYPO does not employ schemes for assigning quantitative feature weights, which are problematic. They are not sensitive to a problem's particular context or do not support reasonable legal explanations. CATO extended HYPO's model by introducing the Factor Hierarchy, a representation that links the Factors to intermediate legal conclusions and higher-level legal issues and that provides a specially designed inference mechanism. With the Factor Hierarchy, CATO can make arguments about the relevance of distinctions between cases.

Recently, methods from CATO and HYPO have been applied to predict the outcome of cases (Aleven 2003). In this approach, prediction was based on a simple criterion: If all cases that satisfy a relevance criterion R were won by the same side, then predict that side, else abstain. The relevance criteria used in the experiment are based on HYPO's definitions of most-on-point and best-untrumped cases (HYPO-BUC), and on CATO's reasoning about the relevance of distinctions between cases (NoSignDist/BUC). Both methods made few mistakes, at cost of abstaining frequently; see Table 1, Nrs. 3 and 8.

1.3 Combining Model-Based and Case-Based Reasoning

The integration of CBR with other techniques has long been a focus of CBR research; see (Marling *et al.* 2002) for a comprehensive overview.

Probably most similar to IBP is CARMA (Branting, Hastings, & Lockwood 2001), which also integrated a weakly predictive model and historical cases for prediction. In CARMA's domain, expert models were too weak for accurate prediction from scratch but they could be used successfully to adapt predictions based on prototypical cases. The program broke down a new case into subcases based on its model, used CBR to retrieve an approximate solution, and applied the model to refine and adapt that solution. Evaluation demonstrated that CARMA's hybrid of model and cases did better than either method alone.

Anapron, another hybrid program, improved the accuracy of its predictions of how names are pronounced by combining independent case-based and rule-based evidential sources (Golding & Rosenbloom 1996). Before applying a rule whose antecedents were satisfied, the program checked for any case exceptions to the rule. If the program found a "compelling analogy" between the problem and a case exception, it applied the exception rather than rule in making a prediction. Experiments showed that the combination improved accuracy over a purely rule-based or case-based version of the program. Anapron differs from IBP in that both reasoners can generate competing solutions.

CASEY (Koton 1989) combined case-based reasoning and a strong causal model of heart disease, not to fill gaps in the causal model, but to make it more efficient to reason with the computationally expensive model. Evidence principles and a justified match procedure determined under what circumstances a past case's explanation could be adapted to diagnose a new problem.

Interestingly, two other hybrid approaches, GREBE (Branting 1999) and CABARET (Rissland & Skalak 1989) were developed for the legal domain. Both programs use a combination of rule-based and case-based reasoning for generating arguments. IBP is similar to these programs in that its model summarizes requirements for a claim in its domain. However, CABARET's domain, home office deduction, is statutory, which means that its model of domain is stronger than in IBP. Like Anapron, it has a more complete set of rules which can be applied at the same time as CBR, and in each reasoning step, meta-knowledge is used to pick the best reasoner. Likewise, GREBE was developed for a domain with a stronger set of rules, compared to IBP's weak model. Moreover, GREBE's representation is more structured than CATO's and includes intermediate conclusions, which are similar to issues in IBP. Most importantly, CABARET and GREBE generate arguments, not predictions.

SHYSTER (Popple 1993) was an early attempt to use a nearest-neighbor approach in the law. It used the outcome of the most similar case as prediction for a problem, and generated a quasi-argument by listing shared and unshared features, which is overly simplistic compared to IBP's output; see Fig. 3.

The rest of this paper is organized as follows. In Sec. 2, we describe the knowledge represented in IBP. In Sec. 3, we discuss how IBP works and illustrate it with an example. In Sec. 4, we focus on further details of the algorithm. In Sec. 5, we present the results of our experiments. In Sec. 6, we conclude by summarizing the most interesting observations from a CBR point-of-view.

2   Knowledge Sources for IBP

2.1   Cases and Factors

The most important knowledge source in common-law domains, such as trade secret law, are cases. The outcome of a new problem is influenced by the existing body of case law. Courts are bound by their decisions, and may only be overruled by higher courts. Judges and attorneys reason with cases, trying to find the most relevant and favorable precedents.

We are using CATO's case database, which comprises 148 trade secret law cases. These cases come from a wide range of jurisdictions and procedural settings. Most were selected for their pedagogical utility, and the collection was compiled long before the work on IBP was envisioned. The case database is not truly representative for the domain in that only litigated cases frequently involving hard choices among evenly balanced conflicting strengths and weaknesses may be reported; the rest get settled outside of court and are not available for inclusion in the sample. The cases are represented in terms of CATO's 26 Factors (Aleven 1997; Ashley 1990). These Factors were derived from treatises, e.g., the Restatement of Torts, 2nd, as well as from studying the courts' decisions.

2.2   Weak Model

While we do not know of any rules that can be used to determine the outcome of a case in trade secret law, the domain has some higher-level structure. The Uniform Trade Secrets Act, and the Restatement of Torts, 2nd, give the following high-level definitions for the concepts trade secret, and misappropriation, respectively:

"Trade secret" means information, [...] that:
    (i) derives independent economic value, [...] from not being generally known [...], and not being readily ascertainable by proper means [...] and
    (ii) is the subject of efforts that are reasonable under the circumstances to maintain its secrecy.
One [...] is liable [for trade secret misappropriation if]
    (a) he discovered the secret by improper means, or
    (b) his disclosure or use constitutes a breach of confidence [...]

These definitions are represented in Fig. 1, which captures the relations between the five major issues below the definition of the concept trade secret misappropriation. These issues are Information-Unique, Maintain-Secrecy,

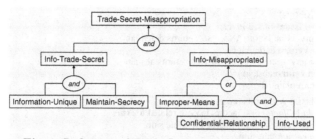

Fig. 1. Definition of Trade Secret Misappropriation

Improper-Means, Information-Used, and Confidential Relationship. For each issue, we worked out a list of related Factors.

3   How IBP Works

The process of IBP's reasoning when making a prediction can be broken down into three steps. (1) Given a new fact situation, the program identifies the issues raised and the related facts, using its weak model of the domain and knowledge about the Factors. (2) For each issue raised in the fact situation, IBP determines which side is favored, reasoning with cases and its knowledge about the Factors. (3) It combines the analysis from the issues following the domain model to make its prediction. From an implementation point of view, the first and third step are comparatively simple. Most work happens in the second step.

3.1   *K&G* Example

We will illustrate the algorithm with a real case, *K & G Oil Tool & Service Co. v. G & G Fishing Tool Service, 314 S.W.2d 782 (K&G)*. In this case, the plaintiff K & G developed a tool to remove metal debris from oil and gas wells. The internal construction of the device was not generally known in the business. There was testimony that the design could be determined by thoroughly examining the tool, even without disassembling it. K & G had entered into a licensing agreement with defendant G & G by which the defendant would sublease the K & G device to other companies. According to the agreement, the defendant was prohibited from disassembling plaintiff's device. It was mutually understood that the purpose of this agreement was to guard against anyone determining the internal construction of the tool. However, G & G did take apart the device in order to examine its internal construction and used the information that it gained from the examination to construct its own device, which was substantially the same as plaintiff's. The plaintiff had not disclosed information about the internal construction of its device to others outside its business.

This case has strengths for both sides. The plaintiff is favored by the following Factors: The information was unique ($F15_\pi$); the plaintiff took security measures ($F6_\pi$); the defendant was on notice that the information was confidential ($F21_\pi$); defendant's product was identical to plaintiff's ($F18_\pi$); and the

function IBP (*cfs*)
    issues ← issues raised in *cfs*
    if for any issue ISSUE-ANALYSIS returns defendant
        then return defendant
    elsif for any issue ISSUE-ANALYSIS returns abstain
        then return abstain
    else return plaintiff

function ISSUE-ANALYSIS (*case, issue*)
    issue-related-factors ← factors in *case* related to *issue*
    if all *issue-related-factors* favor the same side
        then return that side
    elsif there are cases where the *issue-related-factors* apply
        then return the result of THEORY-TESTING (*issue-related-factors*)
    else return the result of BROADEN-QUERY (*issue-related-factors*)

function THEORY-TESTING (*factors*)
    if all cases retrieved by query with *factors* favor the same side
        then return that side
    else return the outcome of EXPLAIN-AWAY (*retrieved-cases, cfs, factors*)

function EXPLAIN-AWAY (*retrieved-cases, cfs, factors*)
    hypothesis ← outcome of majority of *retrieved-cases*
    exceptions ← *retrieved-cases* with outcome opposite to *hypothesis*
    if all *exceptions* are DISTINGUISHABLE from *cfs* and *retrieved-cases* that follow *hypothesis*
        then return *hypothesis*, else return abstain

function DISTINGUISHABLE (*exception, cases, hypothesis*)
    if *exception* has KO-Factors that do not apply in *cases*
        and that can cause an outcome *opposite* to *hypothesis*
        then return true, **else return** false

function BROADEN-QUERY (*factors*)
    side ← side favored by at least 2 *factors*
    pro-side-factors ← *factors* favoring *side*
    if there is a *pro-side-factor* for which DROP-FACTOR still favors *side*
        and there is no *pro-side-factor* for which DROP-FACTOR favors opposite of *side*
        then return side, else return abstain

function DROP-FACTOR (*factor, factors*)
    remaining-factors ← REMOVE (*factor, factors*)
    return the result of THEORY-TESTING (*remaining-factors*)

Fig. 2. Outline of IBP Algorithm (top) with Subfunctions

defendant used materials clearly identified as confidential ($F14_\pi$). On the other hand, the evidence for the defendant includes that the information could be duplicated ($F16_\delta$), and that the defendant reverse-engineered the device ($F25_\delta$).

When IBP is asked to make a prediction for a case, it first determines which issues from Fig. 1 were raised in that case. The Factors in *K&G* indicate that the issues Maintain-Secrecy ($F6_\pi$), Confidential-Relationship ($F21_\pi$), Unique-Product ($F15_\pi$, $F16_\pi$), and Information-Used ($F25_\delta$, $F18_\pi$, $F14_\pi$) were relevant.

3.2   Weak-Model-Prediction

The first two issues in *K&G* are Maintain-Secrecy and Confidential-Relationship (Fig. 3). For Maintain-Secrecy, there is one Factor, $F6_\pi$, Security-Measures, which favors plaintiff. There is also just one Factor related to Confidential-Relationship, $F21_\pi$, Knew-Info-Confidential, which also favors plaintiff. For both

```
Prediction for KG, which was won by PLAINTIFF
   Factors favoring plaintiff: (F21 F18 F15 F14 F6)
   Factors favoring defendant: (F25 F16]

Issue raised in this case is MAINTAIN-SECRECY                Weak-Model-
   Relevant factors in case: F6(P)
The issue-related factors all favor the outcome PLAINTIFF.    Prediction

Issue raised in this case is CONFIDENTIAL-RELATIONSHIP
   Relevant factors in case: F21(P)
The issue-related factors all favor the outcome PLAINTIFF.

Issue raised in this case is INFO-VALUABLE                 Theory-Testing
   Relevant factors in case: F16(D) F15(P)
Theory testing has no clear outcome, try to explain away exceptions.
Cases won by plaintiff:
   AMERICAN-CAN (F4 F6 F15 F16 F18)
   HENRY-HOPE (F4 F6 F15 F16)
   ILG-INDUSTRIES (F7 F10 F12 F15 F16 F21)
   KAMIN (F1 F10 F16 F18 F15)
   KUBIK (F7 F15 F16 F18 F21)
   MASON (F15 F16 F6 F21 F1)
   TELEVATION (F6 F10 F12 F15 F16 F18 F21)
Cases won by defendant:
   NATIONAL-REJECTORS (F7 F10 F15 F16 F18 F19 F27)
Trying to explain away the exceptions favoring DEFENDANT
NATIONAL-REJECTORS can be explained away with unshared ko-factor(s) (F27 F19)
Therefore, PLAINTIFF is favored.

Issue raised in this case is INFO-USED                      Broaden-Query
   Relevant factors in case: F25(D) F18(P) F14(P)
Theory testing did not retrieve any cases, broadening the query.
For INFO-USED, the query can be broadened for PLAINTIFF.
Each of the pro-P Factors (F14 F18) is dropped for new theory testing.
Theory testing with Factors (F14 F25) gets the following cases:
   (TECHNICON PLAINTIFF F6 F10 F12 F14 F16 F21 F25)
   In this broadened query, PLAINTIFF is favored.
Theory testing with Factors (F18 F25) gets the following cases:
   (MINERAL-DEPOSITS PLAINTIFF F1 F16 F18 F25)
   In this broadened query, PLAINTIFF is favored.
By a-forteriori argument, the PLAINTIFF is favored for INFO-USED.

Outcome of the issue-based analysis:
   For issue CONFIDENTIAL-RELATIONSHIP, PLAINTIFF is favored.
   For issue INFO-VALUABLE, PLAINTIFF is favored.
   For issue INFO-USED, PLAINTIFF is favored.
   For issue MAINTAIN-SECRECY, PLAINTIFF is favored.
=> Predicted outcome for KG is PLAINTIFF, which is correct.
```

Fig. 3. IBP's annotated output for the *K&G* example

issues, the relevant evidence is unequivocal, and IBP records that plaintiff is favored. This part of the prediction is part of IBP's top-level function; see Fig. 2.

3.3   Theory-Testing and Explaining-Away

The third issue in *K&G* is Information-Unique; Factors related to this issue favor both sides (Fig. 3). In order to resolve this conflict, IBP carries out a form of reasoning called THEORY-TESTING. This technique was inspired by and named after a pedagogical strategy pioneered in CATO (Aleven 1997) and based on scientific hypothesis testing. In the CATO instruction, a general question about the domain was presented to the students. They were asked to pose a theory or hypothesis based on factors, use it to make a prediction, test it by submitting a query to the case database, and examine any counterexamples to the theory. For IBP, we implemented a procedure that can be carried out automatically, and that does not require a human to formulate the theory or hypothesis. Moreover, we developed a method that can attempt to salvage a theory even when there are counterexamples.

The motivation behind THEORY-TESTING is as follows. If there are Factors favoring both sides related to an issue, there are two possible hypotheses. The first possible hypothesis is that, where the issue-related Factors apply, plaintiff is favored for the issue. The alternative hypothesis is that defendant is favored. IBP reasons with its cases to determine which hypothesis to pick. If all past cases in which the conflicting Factors apply were won by the same side, there is reason to believe that the conflict between the opposing Factors should be resolved for that side. However, quite often, there will be cases won by both sides. In this situation, IBP pursues the more probable hypothesis, based on the side favored by the majority of cases, and tries to salvage it by explaining away the opposite outcome of the counterexamples or exceptions.

More concretely, $K\&G$ has two Factors, $F15_\pi$ and $F16_\delta$, related to the issue Info-Unique. There are two possible hypotheses how the issue, and the conflict between $F15_\pi$ and $F16_\delta$, should be resolved. The first hypotheses is that plaintiff is favored for this issue, the alternative hypothesis is that defendant is favored for the issue. IBP uses its cases to find which hypothesis is supported. Thus, IBP submits a query for Factors $F15_\pi$ and $F16_\delta$. If the retrieved cases favor either plaintiff or defendant, there is reason to select the respective hypothesis and assume that this side is also favored in $K\&G$. However, the query for $F15_\pi$ and $F16_\delta$ does not permit that inference. It retrieves seven cases where the plaintiff won, and one case, *National-Rejectors*, where the defendant won. In this situation, which is fairly typical, the more probable hypothesis, which is adopted by IBP, would be that plaintiff is favored, and that *National-Rejectors* is an exception. Here, IBP calls EXPLAIN-AWAY; see Fig. 2. With this function, IBP tries to save the hypothesis even though there are exceptions. It looks for a way to distinguish the exceptions and thus explain their outcome consistently with the hypothesis. In the $K\&G$ example, IBP checks whether *National-Rejectors* has some Factors not present in $K\&G$ that may be reasons that defendant won, and that can be used to distinguish *National-Rejectors* from $K\&G$ and the other seven cases retrieved. *National-Rejectors* has Factors $F7_\pi$, $F10_\delta$, $F15_\pi$, $F16_\delta$, $F18_\pi$, $F19_\delta$, and $F27_\delta$. Here, the program notices that the plaintiff did not take necessary security measures ($F19_\delta$) and even disclosed the alleged trade secret in a public forum ($F27_\delta$). Both Factors are almost always fatal to plaintiff's claim. These two *KO-Factors*, as they are called in IBP, can be used to distinguish and explain away *National-Rejectors*. Therefore, the result of the THEORY-TESTING for $F15_\pi$ and $F16_\delta$ is for plaintiff.

3.4   Broadening a Query

The fourth issue in $K\&G$ is Information-Used. Again, the Factors related to the issue favor both sides, and IBP calls THEORY-TESTING with Factors $F18_\pi$, $F14_\pi$, $F25_\delta$. However, there are no precedents in the case database with the Factors;

the query is too specific. Accordingly, IBP calls BROADEN-QUERY in an attempt to find more general hypotheses that can be tested.

BROADEN-QUERY is a technique that leverages our knowledge about which side a Factor favors. Here is the basic idea behind the technique.[1] In a situation like the issue Information-Used in *K&G*, which has two Factors for plaintiff and only one Factor for defendant, we can not infer from the fact that "plaintiff has more Factors" that plaintiff is favored for the issue. Factors have different predictive strengths, which often depend on the context; see Sec. 4.2 and 4.3. However, we can safely assume that this situation is stronger for the plaintiff compared to a hypothetical situation where only one of the Factors favoring plaintiff and the Factor favoring defendant apply. So, if we "drop" a constraint, by removing one of the Factors favoring plaintiff, and if *Theory-Testing* with the remaining Factors favors plaintiff, we can make an *a-fortiori* argument that with the initial set of Factors, plaintiff's position is even stronger. (If theory testing with the remaining Factors favors the defendant, we can only conclude that the initial conflict can not be resolved, and abstain.)

The implemented BROADEN-QUERY drops both Factors favoring plaintiff in turn, and carries out THEORY-TESTING with the remaining Factors; see Fig. 2. If both variations allow for an *a-fortiori* argument (for plaintiff), IBP records that the plaintiff is favored for the issue. If dropping the pro-p Factors for one query favors plaintiff, and for the other query does not retrieve any cases, we can still conclude that plaintiff is favored for the issue. However, in any other case (in particular if the THEORY-TESTING retrieves only cases won by defendant), IBP will explicitly abstain on the issue.

Returning to the *K&G* example, IBP drops the two Factors $F14_\pi$ and $F18_\pi$ in turn. THEORY-TESTING retrieves one case favoring plaintiff, respectively. Thus, after running BROADEN-QUERY, the plaintiff is favored in IBP for the issue Information-Used.

One may wonder why IBP does not drop Factor $F25_\delta$, too. This Factor favors the defendant, and is the reason that there is conflicting evidence related to the issue. Dropping this Factor would leave two Factors, $F14_\pi$ and $F18_\pi$, favoring the plaintiff. All one could conclude is that if there was no Factor favoring the defendant, the plaintiff would be favored for the issue, but it does not allow any inferences about how the conflicting evidence should be resolved.

Finally, IBP combines the results from analyzing the issues in its top-level function; see Fig. 2. For each of the four issues raised in the *K&G* case, the plaintiff is favored. Hence, IBP's prediction is that the plaintiff should win, which was indeed the outcome of that case.

---

[1] For easier understanding, we limit this discussion to the case with two pro-p and one pro-d Factor. IBP is of course more general; apart from the symmetric situation favoring defendant, the implementation also covers a 3-1 and a 2-2 balance of Factors favoring each side. Space limitations do not allow us to discuss this in more depth.

4   Details of the Algorithm

4.1   Missing Issues and Abstentions in the Weak Model

While the logical structure in Fig. 1 is fairly simple, reasoning in cases tends to be less straight forward. Not every issue is raised in every case. Sometimes, the facts are so clear that a court completely skips the issue, because the parties choose not to litigate it. In other cases, the fact situation may simply not be related to an issue. If an issue is not present in a case, we assume that neither side was favored and ignore the issue and its logical implications.

Even when an issue is raised, IBP may not be able to resolve the conflicting evidence, for instance when it can not EXPLAIN-AWAY. In those situations, it abstains on the issue. The implications of an abstention depend on the context. If defendant is favored for another issue, then the abstention does not really matter. If for the other issues plaintiff is favored, then an abstention takes precedence. For the purpose of this paper, we simplify the reasoning, and only use the following rule (see function IBP in Fig. 2): If there is an issue where defendant is favored, then predict that defendant will win. Otherwise, if there is an abstention for an issue, then abstain for the case. In all other cases, predict that plaintiff will win.

4.2   Knockout-Factors

When IBP tries to explain away counterexamples to a theory, like *National-Rejectors*, it looks for evidence that could have caused the outcome. In the *National-Rejectors* case, the plaintiff had publicly disclosed the information, which corresponds to Factor $F27_\delta$, and had not taken any measures to keep the information a secret, which corresponds to Factor $F19_\delta$. Intuitively, the presence of those Factors implies that the information did not meet the requirements of a trade secret in Fig. 1; there was no Unique-Product or Maintain-Secrecy. Thus, defendant should win. If we look at all cases in the case database, we find that both $F27_\delta$ and $F19_\delta$ are highly predictive for the outcome of a case: Of the 22 cases with $F19_\delta$, 20 were won by the defendant, and of the 14 cases with $F27_\delta$, 12 were won by defendant. We call Factors like F19 and F27 KO-Factors.

More formally, we require that these Factors are suitable for explaining exceptions, in terms of their predictive strength and meaning. In finding KO-Facors, we first selected those Factors with a probability that the favored side wins of more than 80%. Among those, we focussed on the Factors that correspond to a clear violation of the requirements for a trade secret in Fig. 1. We call these Factors contra-definition. We also included Factors that capture particularly outrageous behavior by the defendant, like Factor $F26_\pi$, Deception, or that can be used as an affirmative defense for defendant, like Factor $F14_\delta$, Independent-Development. Such Factors can be characterized as "good actor/bad actor."

4.3   Insufficient Evidence from Weak Factors

IBP's KO-Factors are very decisive. On the other hand, there are also very weak Factors, which are not very predictive for the outcome of a case. While these

Factors are important, in particular in the context of other Factors, in isolation they should not be used to draw conclusions about issues.

Consider Factor $F10_\delta$, Information-Disclosed-Outsiders, favoring the defendant. This Factor is related to the issue Maintain-Secrecy. However, the fact that the information was known to persons outside of plaintiff's business does not necessarily imply that plaintiff failed to take reasonable measures to keep the information secret. It may, for instance, be that confidential disclosures were customary in the business and that the disclosees were well aware of the secret nature of the information. Factor $F10_\delta$ is also not very predictive. It applies in 30 cases, only 12 of which (less than half) were won by defendant. The probability that defendant wins a case is about the same, whether we know nothing about the case ($p(_\delta) = 0.39$), or whether we know that $F10_\delta$ applies ($p(\delta|F10)$ = 0.40). In a case where we only have Factor $F10_\delta$ as issue-related evidence, we therefore do not consider this sufficient evidence to draw conclusions that the issue was raised and that the defendant was favored. In general, we require for a Factor that the odds of the favored side winning should increase by at least 20% compared to the baseline (Table 1, Nr. 11). Otherwise, we do not take this Factor alone as sufficient evidence that the related issue was raised.

Weak Factors should not be confused with noise, though. Factors, by definition, always have a side they favor, sometimes to a stronger degree, sometimes to a lesser degree. There are several reasons for this. Not all Factors are equally predictive, a Factor's influence may depend on the other Factors in a case, and some Factors have a degree or magnitude, which was represented in HYPO's dimensions, but is not captured in Factors. We found that for all Factors the probability of the favored side winning given that a Factor was present was larger than probability of that side winning, thus, none of the Factors can be considered noisy.

5   Experiments

5.1   Experiment Setup

For evaluating IBP, we used our existing collection of 148 trade secret law cases, the case database, which had been compiled for the evaluation of the CATO instructional environment. We also included 38 new cases, which we had analyzed and marked up before the work on IBP began, and which we added to the collection after the implementation was complete. Of the overall 186 cases, 108 (58.1%) were won by the plaintiff, 78 (41.9%) were won by the defendant.

For the combined collection of 186 cases, IBP correctly predicts the outcome of 170 cases, makes a mistake for 15 cases, and abstains on 1 case. This corresponds to an accuracy of 91.4% (Table 1, Nr. 1). Accuracy was better for the 38 new cases, which suggests that we did not optimize the algorithm for the collection we had used in the program's development.

In our first set of experiments, we tested whether combining a weak model with cases in IBP would lead to better performance, compared to either component alone. In an ablation study, we modified IBP such that it would not

Table 1. Experimental results

	Algorithm	correct	errors	abstain	accuracy	p
1	IBP	170	15	1	0.914	n/a
2	Naive Bayes	161	25	0	0.865	0.03
3	NoSignDist/BUC	152	19	22	0.778	0.00
4	C4.5-pruned	158	28	0	0.849	0.01
5	C4.5-rules	155	31	0	0.833	0.01
6	Ripper	154	32	0	0.828	0.00
7	IB1	153	33	0	0.823	0.00
8	HYPO-BUC	127	9	50	0.683	0.00
9	IBP-model	99	15	38	0.726	0.00
10	IB3	96	52	0	0.649	0.00
11	Baseline	108	78	0	0.581	0.00

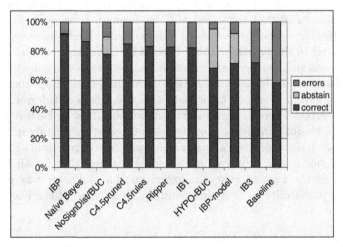

Fig. 4. Overview of experimental results

use cases and disabled THEORY-TESTING and BROADEN-QUERY. This version, called IBP-model, got 72.6% accuracy, and 20.4% abstentions (Table 1, Nr. 9).

We also wanted to know how well one could predict outcomes using only cases. We selected David Aha's IBL package[2] as a purely case-based reasoning method (Aha 1991). On our collection, IB1 had the best performance, with 82.3% accuracy (Table 1, Nr. 7). IB3, which is designed to deal with noisy data, had the worst performance of the IBL algorithms (Table 1, Nr. 10). This is not surprising, since in the law, cases are hardly ever considered noisy. Every case is decided based on the particular facts it presents. As discussed is Sec. 4.3, the whole set of Factors is relevant. There is also no basis for determining whether the outcome of a case is noise. The court decides and records whether plaintiff or defendant prevails; there are no measurement errors or missing data as in technical domains.

---

[2] http://www.aic.nrl.navy.mil/~aha/software/

Summarizing, IBP, which uses the weak model and cases, clearly outperforms the comparison methods IBP-model and IBL, which only rely on the weak model and on the cases, respectively.

In a second set of experiments, our goal was to see how IBP's performance compares to ML algorithms. While IBP's argument-like explanation of its reasoning is already a significant advantage over the output of a learning algorithm, IBP should also lead to better performance. We selected Naive Bayes (Mitchell 1997),[3] C4.5 (Quinlan 1993), Ripper (Cohen 1996), and IBL (Aha 1991).

As in the previous experiment, IBP outperformed its competitors, although by smaller margins. The best competitor was Naive Bayes, with 86.6% accuracy. We used McNemar's test (Ditterich 1996) to determine whether the observed differences were statistically significant, or merely caused by random variation in the data. When we compared IBP's results to each of the other algorithms, we found that all p-values, which capture the probability that the observed differences are due to chance, were below 0.05. Thus, the differences are statistically significant.

The output of the ML algorithms, in particular Ripper, was also interesting. Ripper learned the following rules when trained on the full collection:

1. If there are No-Security-Measures ($F19_\delta$), but no Competitive-Advantage ($F8_\pi$), then defendant wins.
2. If there is Information-Known-to-Outsiders ($F20_\delta$), then defendant wins.
3. In all other cases, plaintiff wins.

One interpretation is that Ripper did not learn "Trade Secret Misappropriation", it learned the opposite of the concept, an observation sometimes expressed by researchers after applying ML algorithms. Ripper relies on Factors that are KO-Factors in IBP. And, by default, it predicts the majority class (plaintiff). We also saw a similar behavior in C4.5, even though it was less pronounced. While the output of these algorithms can be instructive for humans, it is far less useful than the kind of analysis generated for each case by IBP; see Fig. 3.

5.2   Error Analysis

As part of our experiments, we also analyzed IBP's mistakes. We found that the distribution of incorrectly predicted cases won by plaintiff and defendant was very similar to the original distribution. 64% of the errors were cases won by the defendant; overall, 58% of the cases were won by the plaintiff. Thus, there is no evidence that IBP's predictions are skewed for either side.

We then explored whether some cases are hard to predict for different algorithms and counted for each case how many of the algorithms made an error in predicting its outcome. Intuitively, those cases where more algorithms make mistakes must be harder to predict. First, we observed that there was a set of cases for which more than half of the algorithms made errors, which suggests that these cases are hard to predict. Second, we saw that all of these cases are

---

[3] We used Ray Mooney's publicly available implementation.

among IBP's errors. Thus, we conclude that when IBP makes a mistake, it is likely that the case is hard to predict.

We then examined in depth the cases for which IBP made a mistake. In one case, *Franke*, the court decided for the plaintiff, even though the information did not strictly qualify as a trade secret. The judge argued that the defendant's behavior was so outrageous, that this outweighed the plaintiff's otherwise fatal weaknesses. Here, IBP lacks the judge's moral values. In another case, *Goldberg*, the court reasoned in a similar way, that the plaintiff should win, even though he had not taken reasonable measures to keep the information secret. Like IBP, which did not agree with the court, a judge in a later decision argued that the decision in *Goldberg* was a mistake.

For several other cases, our interpretation of the facts differed from their Factor representation in the case database. In some cases, there was an issue whether the security measures taken by the plaintiff were sufficient and reasonable under the circumstances. For instance, the court may have argued that minimal measures were sufficient. In *Junkunc*, all Factors in its representation favored plaintiff. The defendant won, however, because the court reasoned that plaintiff's security measures were insufficient; there were too many security holes.

This suggests that no matter how careful and knowledgeable a human may be in translating legal cases from the text to the corresponding Factor representation, there is still room for individual interpretation of cases. Our research in Textual CBR (Brüninghaus & Ashley 2001) is related to this problem; we are working on automatically identifying sentences related to Factors. If a system can present to a human indexer those sentences that it found as evidence for a Factor, together with links into previously indexed cases, this could lead to a better, more consistent case representation, and ultimately, to better prediction.

6 Conclusions

In this paper, we presented a new algorithm called IBP that integrates case-based and model-based reasoning for the prediction of legal case outcomes. IBP uses its weak model of the domain to break a case into issues, and to combine the analysis of each issue to make its prediction. It uses CBR to resolve conflicting evidence related to issues. Interestingly, IBP uses a kind of scientific evidential reasoning to reason about whether positive or negative case instances of each issue should prevail. Experiments with a collection of historic cases show that IBP's predictions are better than those made with its weak model or with cases alone. IBP also had higher accuracy compared to standard inductive and instance-based learning algorithms.

The experiments provided some interesting insights into the task, and the potential benefits of CBR. First, our experiments suggest that ML algorithms may not be the best choice for a complex domain. These algorithms have a tendency to learn just a few, overly simplistic rules that cover exceptions. CBR is a much better choice for applications like the law, where the target concepts are complex and cannot simply be captured in a set of rules.

Second, thinking of cases as noisy is not always useful in a CBR domain. If there are regularities in the training data that allow for the identification of noisy cases, then one does not need CBR; rule-induction is the better choice. On the other hand, in a CBR domain like the law, the full set of cases with all features is needed for best performance.

References

Aha, D. 1991. Case-based learning algorithms. In *Proce. DARPA Case-Based Reasoning Workshop*, 147–158.

Aleven, V. 1997. *Teaching Case-Based Argumentation through a Model and Examples.* Ph.D. Dissertation, University of Pittsburgh.

Aleven, V. 2003. Using Background Knowledge in Case-Based Legal Reasoning: A Computational Model and an Intelligent Learning Environment. *Artificial Intelligence.* Special Issue on Artificial Intelligence and Law. In Press.

Ashley, K. 1990. *Modeling Legal Argument, Reasoning with Cases and Hypotheticals.* MIT-Press.

Branting, K.; Hastings, J.; and Lockwood, J. 2001. CARMA: A Case-Based Range Management Advisor. In *Proc. IAAI-2001*, 3–10.

Branting, L. 1999. *Reasoning with Rules and Precedents - A Computational Model of Legal Analysis.* Kluwer Academic Publishers.

Brüninghaus, S., and Ashley, K. 2001. The Role of Information Extraction for Textual CBR. In *Proce. ICCBR-01*, 74–89.

Cohen, W. 1996. Learning Trees and Rules with Set-valued Features. In *Proc. AAAI-96*, 709–716.

Ditterich, T. 1996. Statistical Tests for Comparing Supervised Classification Learning Algorithms. Oregon State University Technical Report.

Golding, A., and Rosenbloom, P. 1996. Improving Accuracy by Combining Rule-Based and Case-Based Reasoning. *Artificial Intelligence* 87(1-2):215–254.

Koton, P. 1989. *Using experience in learning and problem solving.* Ph.D. Dissertation, Massachusetts Institute of Technology, Laboratory of Computer Science.

Marling, C.; Sqalli, M.; Rissland, E.; Munoz-Avila, H.; and Aha, D. 2002. Case-Based Reasoning Integrations. *AI Magazine* 23(1):69–86.

Mitchell, T. 1997. *Machine Learning.* Mc Graw Hill.

Popple, J. 1993. *SHYSTER: A Pragmatic Legal Expert System.* Ph.D. Dissertation, Australian National University, Canberra, Australia.

Quinlan, R. 1993. *C4.5: Programs for Machine Learning.* Morgan Kaufman.

Rissland, E., and Skalak, D. 1989. Combining Case-Based and Rule-Based Reasoning: A Heuristic Approach. In *Proc. IJCAI-89*, 534–529.

Measuring the Similarity of Labeled Graphs

Pierre-Antoine Champin and Christine Solnon

LIRIS, bât. Nautibus, University of Lyon I
43 Bd du 11 novembre, 69622 Villeurbanne cedex, France
{champin,csolnon}@bat710.univ-lyon1.fr

Abstract. This paper proposes a similarity measure to compare cases represented by labeled graphs. We first define an expressive model of directed labeled graph, allowing multiple labels on vertices and edges. Then we define the similarity problem as the search of a best mapping, where a mapping is a correspondence between vertices of the graphs. A key point of our approach is that this mapping does not have to be univalent, so that a vertex in a graph may be associated with several vertices of the other graph. Another key point is that the quality of the mapping is determined by generic functions, which can be tuned in order to implement domain-dependant knowledge. We discuss some computational issues related to this problem, and we describe a greedy algorithm for it. Finally, we show that our approach provides not only a quantitative measure of the similarity, but also qualitative information which can prove valuable in the adaptation phase of CBR.

1   Introduction

Case based reasoning (CBR) relies on the hypothesis that similar problems have similar solutions. Hence, a CBR system solves a new problem by retrieving a similar one, for which a solution is known, then reusing that solution in the current context [1]. The retrieving phase requires an accurate similarity measure, so that cases are actually reusable whenever they are considered similar to the problem at hand.

In many situations, cases can be represented as a set of attribute-value pairs (usually called "vector cases"). Similarity between such cases can be defined in a rather straightforward way, as a weighted combination of each attribute-value pair similarity, and it can be efficiently computed [5]. However, more structured representations can be necessary for solving more complex problems, *e.g.*, feature terms [14], hierarchical decompositions [15], directed or non-directed labeled graphs [7,13].

In this paper, we focus on directed labeled graphs, *i.e.*, directed graphs whose vertices and edges are associated with one or more labels, and consider the problem of characterizing and computing their similarity. Such labeled graphs provide a rich mean for modeling structured objects. In particular in the ARDECO project [4], from which this work is originated, we use them to represent design objects in a computer aided design (CAD) application. Figure 1 displays two

K.D. Ashley and D.G. Bridge (Eds.): ICCBR 2003, LNAI 2689, pp. 80–95, 2003.
© Springer-Verlag Berlin Heidelberg 2003

design objects, borrowed from this application, and allows us to introduce some key points that should be addressed when measuring their similarity. Roughly speaking, one would say these two design objects are similar since the four beams a, b, c, d respectively correspond to the beams 1, 2, 3, 4, and the walls e and f correspond to 5. However, they are not absolutely similar: first, the beams have different shapes (I on the left and U on the right); besides, the number of walls is different from one case to the other (the wall 5 plays alone the role of the two walls e and f).

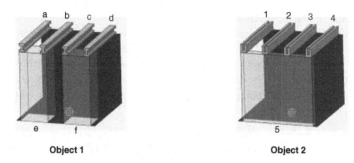

Fig. 1. Two similar design objects

This example first shows that, in order to measure the similarity between two objects, we must find a mapping which pairs their different components. Furthermore, this mapping should be the "best" one, i.e., the one that maps "similar" components as much as possible, where their similarity depends on the features they share, as well as the relations they have with other components. This example also shows that this mapping is not necessarily one-to-one: the role of wall 5 in object 2 is held by both walls e and f in object 1. To provide accurate comparison of complex structured objects, it is essential to allow such multiple mappings and to take them into account when defining a similarity measure. Finally, a similarity measure should not only be *quantitative*, indicating how much two objects are similar, but also *qualitative*, giving information about commonalities and differences between the two objects.

In the next section (2), we formally define labeled graphs, and illustrate their expressive power on the design example of figure 1. In section 3, we propose our general similarity measure based on the notion of mapping between graph vertices, and we show how application-dependant similarity knowledge can be implemented in our framework. Section 4 discusses some computational issues related to our similarity problem: we first study the tractability of a complete approach, and then describe an efficient greedy algorithm. In section 5, we discuss the benefits of our similarity measure in the reuse phase of CBR. Finally, we conclude by showing the genericity of this work with respect to other proposals for graph comparison, and we give further research directions.

2   Labeled Graphs

2.1   Definitions and Notations

A *labeled graph* is a directed graph such that vertices and edges are associated with labels. Without loss of generality, we shall assume that every vertex and edge is associated with at least one label: if some vertices (resp. edges) have no label, one can add an extra anonymous label that is associated with every vertex (resp. edge). More formally, given a finite set of vertex labels L_V, and a finite set of edge labels L_E, a labeled graph will be defined by a triple $G = \langle V, r_V, r_E \rangle$ such that:

- V is a finite set of vertices,
- $r_V \subseteq V \times L_V$ is the relation that associates vertices with labels, *i.e.*, r_V is the set of couples (v_i, l) such that vertex v_i has label l,
- $r_E \subseteq V \times V \times L_E$ is the relation that associates edges with labels, *i.e.*, r_E is the set of triples (v_i, v_j, l) such that edge (v_i, v_j) has label l. Note that from this edge relation r_E, one can define the set E of edges as $E = \{(v_i, v_j) | \exists l, (v_i, v_j, l) \in r_E\}$.

We respectively call the tuples from r_V and r_E, the *vertex features* and *edge features* of G. We then define the *descriptor* of a graph $G = \langle V, r_V, r_E \rangle$ as the set of all its features: $descr(G) = r_V \cup r_E$. This descriptor completely describes the graph and will be used to measure the similarity between two graphs. Finally, a *similarity problem* is defined by two graphs $G_1 = \langle V_1, r_{V_1}, r_{E_1} \rangle$ and $G_2 = \langle V_2, r_{V_2}, r_{E_2} \rangle$ that have disjoint sets of vertices, *i.e.*, $V_1 \cap V_2 = \emptyset$.

2.2   Example

Let us consider again the two design objects displayed in figure 1. To represent these two objects with labeled graphs, we first define the sets of vertex and edge labels that respectively characterize their components and relationships between components:

$$L_V = \{\, beam, I, U, wall \,\}$$
$$L_E = \{\, on, next\_to \,\}$$

Given these sets of labels, the two design objects of figure 1 may be represented by the two labeled graphs of figure 2 (the left part of the figure displays their graphical representations; the right part gives their associated formal definitions by means of vertex and edge features).

Note that vertices a, b, c and d have the two labels *beam* and I, whereas vertices $1, 2, 3$ and 4 have the two labels *beam* and U. This allows us to express that the corresponding objects share the feature "being a beam", even though their shapes are different.

More generally, the fact that edges and vertices may have more than one label is used to express inheritance (specialization) relationships by inclusion of sets of labels. With such an inclusive expression of inheritance, the similarity of two vertices, or edges, can be defined by means of their common labels, corresponding to their common ancestors in the inheritance hierarchy.

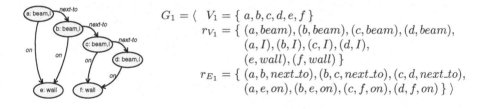

$$G_1 = \langle \ V_1 = \{\, a, b, c, d, e, f \,\}$$
$$r_{V_1} = \{\ (a, beam), (b, beam), (c, beam), (d, beam),$$
$$(a, I), (b, I), (c, I), (d, I),$$
$$(e, wall), (f, wall) \,\}$$
$$r_{E_1} = \{\ (a, b, next\_to), (b, c, next\_to), (c, d, next\_to),$$
$$(a, e, on), (b, e, on), (c, f, on), (d, f, on) \,\} \ \rangle$$

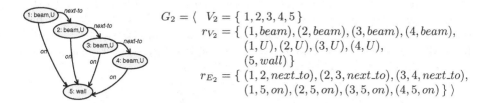

$$G_2 = \langle \ V_2 = \{\, 1, 2, 3, 4, 5 \,\}$$
$$r_{V_2} = \{\ (1, beam), (2, beam), (3, beam), (4, beam),$$
$$(1, U), (2, U), (3, U), (4, U),$$
$$(5, wall) \,\}$$
$$r_{E_2} = \{\ (1, 2, next\_to), (2, 3, next\_to), (3, 4, next\_to),$$
$$(1, 5, on), (2, 5, on), (3, 5, on), (4, 5, on) \,\} \ \rangle$$

Fig. 2. Labeled graphs $G1$ and $G2$ describing objects 1 and 2 of figure 1

3   A Measure of Similarity for Labeled Graphs

3.1   Mapping of Labeled Graphs

To measure the similarity of two labeled graphs, one first has to find a mapping that matches their vertices in order to identify their common features. More precisely, a mapping between two labeled graphs $G_1 = \langle V_1, r_{V_1}, r_{E_1}\rangle$ and $G_2 = \langle V_2, r_{V_2}, r_{E_2}\rangle$, such that $V_1 \cap V_2 = \emptyset$, is a relation $m \subseteq V_1 \times V_2$. Note that such a mapping can associate to each vertex of one graph, zero, one, or more vertices of the other graph. By extension, we shall use the functional notation $m(v)$ to denote the set of vertices that are associated with a vertex v by the relation m, i.e.,

$$\forall v_1 \in V_1, \quad m(v_1) \doteq \{v_2 \in V_2 |\ (v_1, v_2) \in m\}$$
$$\forall v_2 \in V_2, \quad m(v_2) \doteq \{v_1 \in V_1 |\ (v_1, v_2) \in m\}$$

Even though we may use a functional notation, one should keep in mind that a mapping is a relation, i.e., a set of couples of vertices, so that we can apply set operators on mappings.

Example: For the labeled graphs of figure 2, one can define, e.g., the two following mappings

$$m_A = \{(a, 1), (b, 2), (c, 3), (d, 4), (e, 5), (f, 5)\}$$
$$m_B = \{(a, 1), (b, 2), (a, 3), (b, 4)), (e, 5)\}$$

The first mapping m_A respectively matches a, b, c and d to 1, 2, 3 and 4, and both e and f to 5; in this mapping, the set of vertices associated with, e.g., 5 will be noted $m_A(5) = \{e, f\}$. The second mapping m_B matches both 1 and 3 to a, both 2 and 4 to b, and e to 5; in this mapping, the set of vertices associated with f will be noted $m_B(f) = \emptyset$.

3.2   Similarity with Respect to a Mapping

In order to measure the similarity between two objects, it is intuitive and usual to compare the amount of features which are common to both objects, to the total amount of their features [9]. In the field of psychology, Tversky [17] has demonstrated the cognitive plausibility of this intuition, giving the following mathematical model of a similarity measure between two objects a and b described respectively by two sets of features A and B:

$$sim_{\mathrm{Tversky}}(a,b) = \frac{f(A \cap B)}{f(A \cup B) - \alpha f(A - B) - \beta f(B - A)}$$

where f is a non-decreasing positive function, monotonic with respect to inclusion, and α and β are positive values, allowing to define *asymmetrical* similarity measures. We shall set them to zero from now on, since in our case, their role can be held by function f; this will be discussed in section 3.5.

A labeled graph G, as we defined it in section 2, is described by the set $descr(G)$ of all its vertex and edge features. Hence, the similarity of two different graphs $G_1 = \langle V_1, r_{V_1}, r_{E_1} \rangle$ and $G_2 = \langle V_2, r_{V_2}, r_{E_2} \rangle$ depends on both the common features of $descr(G_1)$ and $descr(G_2)$, and the set of all their features. However, since $V_1 \cap V_2 = \emptyset$, the intersection of the two graphs descriptors will always be empty. We must instead compute this intersection *with respect* to a given mapping m, which pairs vertices from G_1 with vertices from G_2:

$$
\begin{aligned}
descr(G_1) \sqcap_m descr(G_2) \doteq\ & \{(v,l) \in r_{V_1} | \ \exists v' \in m(v), (v',l) \in r_{V_2}\} \\
\cup\ & \{(v,l) \in r_{V_2} | \ \exists v' \in m(v), (v',l) \in r_{V_1}\} \\
\cup\ & \{(v_i, v_j, l) \in r_{E_1} | \\
& \ \exists v_i' \in m(v_i), \exists v_j' \in m(v_j)\, (v_i', v_j', l) \in r_{E_2}\} \\
\cup\ & \{(v_i, v_j, l) \in r_{E_2} | \\
& \ \exists v_i' \in m(v_i), \exists v_j' \in m(v_j)\, (v_i', v_j', l) \in r_{E_1}\}
\end{aligned}
$$

This set contains all the features from both G_1 and G_2 whose vertices or edges are matched, according to m, to at least one vertex or edge with the same feature.

Given this definition of commonalities between G_1 and G_2, we can apply Tversky's formula to define the similarity between G_1 and G_2 with respect to a mapping m:

$$sim1_m(G_1, G_2) = \frac{f(descr(G_1) \sqcap_m descr(G_2))}{f(descr(G_1) \cup descr(G_2))} \qquad (1)$$

Example: Let us consider the two labeled graphs, and their associated descriptors, of figure 2. The intersections of these descriptors, with respect to the mappings m_A and m_B proposed in section 3.1, are:

$$
\begin{aligned}
descr(G_1) \sqcap_{m_A} descr(G_2) = \quad & descr(G_1) \cup descr(G_2) \\
& -\{\, (a,I),(b,I),(c,I),(d,I), \\
& \qquad (1,U),(2,U),(3,U),(4,U) \,\} \\
descr(G_1) \sqcap_{m_B} descr(G_2) = \{\, & (a,beam),(b,beam),(e,wall), \\
& (1,beam),(2,beam),(3,beam),(4,beam),(5,wall), \\
& (a,b,next\_to), \\
& (1,2,next\_to),(3,4,next\_to), \\
& (a,e,on),(b,e,on), \\
& (1,5,on),(2,5,on),(3,5,on),(4,5,on) \,\}
\end{aligned}
$$

3.3   Evaluation of Splits

The definition of $sim1_m$ in equation 1 is not entirely satisfying. For example, let us consider the two labeled graphs of figure 2 and suppose the beams of both objects have the same shape. In this case, the mapping $m_A = \{(a,1),(b,2),(c,3),(d,4),(e,5),(f,5)\}$ would match every feature of each graph to a perfectly similar one from the other graph, so that $descr(G_1) \sqcap_{m_A} descr(G_2) = descr(G_1) \cup descr(G_2)$ and $sim1_{m_A}(G_1,G_2) = 1$. This would mean that the two graphs are perfectly similar, whatever the chosen function f. Nevertheless, one might be annoyed that vertex 5 is paired with two vertices (e and f), and prefer another mapping such as, *e.g.*, $m_3 = \{(a,1),(b,2),(c,3),(d,4),(e,5)\}$, even though some features were not matched. We do not intend to mean that one mapping is strictly better than the other one, nor that only isomorphic graphs or subgraphs should be matched. Indeed, this obviously depends on the application domain. On the contrary, we want the model to be tunable in order to allow for either interpretation.

Therefore, to enhance the model, we introduce the function *splits* which returns the set of split vertices (*i.e.*, vertices paired with more than one vertex) together with the set s_v of vertices they are paired with. We also define an extended inclusion operator $\sqsubseteq$ on those sets, by considering inclusion on sets of paired vertices s_v.

$$
splits(m) \doteq \{(v, s_v)\mid v \in V_1 \cup V_2,\ s_v = m(v),\ |m(v)| \geq 2\}
$$

$$
splits(m_1) \sqsubseteq splits(m_2) \Leftrightarrow \forall (v, s_v) \in splits(m_1),\ \exists (v, s_v') \in splits(m_2),\ s_v \subseteq s_v'
$$

For example, the mappings proposed in section 3.1 have the following splits: $splits(m_A) = \{\, (5, \{e,f\}) \,\}$ and $splits(m_B) = \{\, (a, \{1,3\}),\ (b, \{2,4\}) \,\}$.

We can now modify equation 1 so as to take the value of splits into account:

$$
sim_m(G_1, G_2) = \frac{f(descr(G_1) \sqcap_m descr(G_2)) - g(splits(m))}{f(descr(G_1) \cup descr(G_2))} \tag{2}
$$

where function g is defined with the same properties as f: it is positive, monotonic and non-decreasing with respect to extended inclusion $\sqsubseteq$. Hence the similarity will be decreasing as the number of splits is increasing.

3.4   Maximum Similarity of Labeled Graphs

We have defined the similarity of two graphs with respect to a given mapping between the graphs vertices. Now, we can define the *maximum similarity* of two graphs G_1 and G_2 as the similarity induced by the best mapping:

$$sim(G_1, G_2) = \max_{m \subseteq V_1 \times V_2} \frac{f(descr(G_1) \sqcap_m descr(G_2)) - g(splits(m))}{f(descr(G_1) \cup descr(G_2))} \qquad (3)$$

Note that, if the similarity value induced by a given mapping m (sim_m) is always between 0 and 1 when m does not contain any split (*i.e.*, when every vertex is associated with at most one vertex), it may become negative when some vertices are associated with more than one vertex: this occurs if the weight of splits, defined by g, is higher than the weight of common features, defined by f. However, in any cases, the maximum similarity sim will always be between 0 and 1 since the similarity induced by the empty mapping $m = \emptyset$ is null.

Note also that determining which of the mappings between G_1 and G_2 is the "best", actually completely depends on functions f and g that respectively quantify vertex and edge features and splits. As a consequence, those functions must be carefully chosen depending on the application domain. This will be discussed in section 3.5.

3.5   Similarity Knowledge

The notions presented so far about similarity measures are quite generic. However, in order to be accurate, an actual similarity measure has to take into account similarity knowledge which is of course application dependant. The functions f and g used in the above definitions are the place where such application dependant knowledge can be implemented. An easy way of defining them while ensuring their being monotonic, is to define them as a sum of positive (or null) weights assigned to each element of the measured sets (namely, features and splits), i.e., given a set of vertex and edge features F and a set of splits S,

$$f(F) = \sum_{(v,l) \in F} weight_{fV}(v, l) + \sum_{(v_1, v_2, l) \in F} weight_{fE}(v_1, v_2, l)$$

$$g(S) = \sum_{(v, s_v) \in S} weight_g(v, s_v)$$

Without much domain knowledge, one could assign the same weight to every feature (that is, f is the cardinality function). Every split (v, s_v) could receive the same weight or a weight proportional to the cardinality of s_v.

If *generic* knowledge is available, the weight of a feature could be defined on the basis of its label only: one could thus represent the facts that being a beam is more significant than being U-shaped, or that a composition relation is more significant than a "next-to" relation, for example.

Finally, if specific or *contextual* knowledge is available, one could assign a specific weight to each feature or split. For example, one could express the facts that it is more significant for a to be I-shaped than it is for b, that it is more significant for a and b to be in relation than it is for b and c, or that it is less annoying for a to be split into 1 and 2 than it is for c.

One may be concerned that we constrained parameters α and β in Tversky's formula to be zero. Those parameters make it possible to define asymmetrical similarity measures, which is often considered a desirable property in CBR. However, the definition of *sim* enables such asymmetrical similarity measures: features and splits can be weighted differently depending on which graph they belong to. For example, assigning a null weight to any feature of G_2 allows to measure how much G_1 "matches" (or "fits into") G_2.

4 Computing the Maximum Similarity of Labeled Graphs

Given two labeled graphs G_1 and G_2, we now consider the problem of computing their maximum similarity, *i.e.*, finding a mapping m that maximizes formula 2. One should note that the denominator $f(descr(G_1) \cup descr(G_2))$ of this formula does not depend on the mapping. Indeed, this denominator is introduced to normalize the similarity value between zero and one. Hence, to compute the maximum similarity between two graphs G_1 and G_2, one has to find the mapping m that maximizes the score function

$$score(m) = f(descr(G_1) \sqcap_m descr(G_2)) - g(splits(m))$$

This problem is highly combinatorial. Indeed, it is more general than, *e.g.*, the subgraph isomorphism problem[1] which is known to be NP-complete [12]. In this section, we first study the tractability of a complete search, and then propose a greedy incomplete algorithm for it.

4.1 Tractability of a Complete Search

The search space of the maximum similarity problem is composed of all different mappings —all subsets of $V_1 \times V_2$— and it contains $2^{|V_1| * |V_2|}$ states. This search space can be structured in a lattice by the set inclusion relation, and it can be explored in an exhaustive way with a "branch and bound" approach. Such a complete approach is actually tractable if there exists a "good" bounding function that can detect as soon as possible when a node can be pruned, *i.e.*,

---

[1] We do not present the proof here, since it involves some technical tricks which would require more space than available.

when the score of all the nodes that can be constructed from the current node is worse than the best score found so far. In our case, the potential successors of the node associated with a partial mapping $m \subset V_1 \times V_2$ are all the mappings that are supersets of m. However, the score function is not monotonic with respect to set inclusion, *i.e.*, the score of a mapping may either increase or decrease when one adds a new couple to it. Indeed, this score is defined as a difference between a function of the common features and a function of the splits, and both sides of this difference may increase when adding a couple to a mapping. More precisely, one can show that for all mappings m and m' such that $m \subseteq m'$,

$$descr(G_1) \sqcap_m descr(G_2) \subseteq descr(G_1) \sqcap_{m'} descr(G_2)$$
$$\text{and} \qquad splits(m) \sqsubseteq splits(m')$$

and therefore, since the f and g functions are monotonic,

$$f(descr(G_1) \sqcap_m descr(G_2)) \leq f(descr(G_1) \sqcap_{m'} descr(G_2))$$
$$\text{and} \qquad g(splits(m)) \leq g(splits(m'))$$

However, we can use the fact that the intersection of graph features is bounded by the set of all graph features to define a bounding function. Indeed, for every mapping m, one can trivially show that

$$descr(G_1) \sqcap_m descr(G_2) \subseteq descr(G_1) \cup descr(G_2)$$

and, as f and g are monotonic, for every mapping m' such that $m' \supseteq m$,

$$score_{m'}(G_1, G_2) = f(descr(G_1) \sqcap_{m'} descr(G_2)) - g(splits(m'))$$
$$\leq f(descr(G_1) \cup descr(G_2)) - g(splits(m))$$

As a consequence, one can prune the node associated with a matching m if $f(descr(G_1) \cup descr(G_2)) - g(splits(m))$ is smaller or equal to the score of the best mapping found so far. In this case, all the nodes corresponding to mappings that are supersets of m will not be explored as their score cannot be higher than the best score found so far.

A first remark about this bounding function is that its effectiveness in reducing the search tree highly depends on the relative "weights" of functions f and g: the higher the weight of splits, the more nodes can be pruned. Actually, this bounding function is generic, and it can be applied to any kind of labeled graphs, with any f and g functions (provided that they are monotonic). More accurate bounding functions could be defined when considering more specific cases.

Also, one may introduce *ad-hoc* rules to reduce the search space. In particular, one can remove from the search space every mapping that contains a couple (v_i, v_j) such that v_i and v_j do not have any common features (vertex features, but also features of edges starting from or ending to v_i and v_j). Further more, during the exploration, one can remove from the partial search tree the root of which is a mapping m, every mapping $m' \supseteq m$ containing a couple (v_i, v_j) such that all the common features of v_i and v_j already belong to $descr(G_1) \sqcap_m descr(G_2)$.

Finally, the tractability of any complete branch and bound approach strongly depends on ordering heuristics, which determine an order for developing the nodes of the search tree: a good ordering heuristic allows the search to quickly find a good mapping, the score of which is high, so that more nodes can be cut. We describe in the next subsection a greedy algorithm that uses such ordering heuristics to quickly build a "good" mapping.

4.2   Greedy Algorithm

Figure 3 describes a greedy algorithm that introduces ordering heuristics to build a mapping m: the algorithm starts from the empty mapping, and iteratively adds to this mapping a couple of vertices that most increases the score function. At each step, this set of candidate couples that most increase the score function — called *cand*— often contains more than one couple. To break ties between them, we look ahead the potentiality of each candidate $(u_1, u_2) \in cand$ by taking into account the features that are shared by edges starting from (resp. ending to) both u_1 and u_2 and that are not already in $descr(G_1) \sqcap_{m \cup \{(u_1, u_2)\}} descr(G_2)$. Hence, we select the next couple to enter the mapping within the set *cand'* of couples whose looked-ahead common edge features maximize f.

function Greedy$(G_1=\langle V_1, r_{V_1}, r_{E_1}\rangle, G_2=\langle V_2, r_{V_2}, r_{E_2}\rangle)$ **returns** a mapping $m \subseteq V_1 \times V_2$
    $m \leftarrow \emptyset$
    $best_m \leftarrow \emptyset$
    loop
        $cand \leftarrow \{(u_1, u_2) \in V_1 \times V_2 - m \mid score(m \cup \{(u_1, u_2)\})$ is maximal$\}$
        $cand' \leftarrow \{(u_1, u_2) \in cand \mid f(look\_ahead(u_1, u_2))$ is maximal$\}$
            where $look\_ahead(u_1, u_2) = \{(u_1, v_1, l) \in r_{E_1} \mid \exists v_2 \in V_2, (u_2, v_2, l) \in r_{E_2}\}$
                              $\cup \{(u_2, v_2, l) \in r_{E_2} \mid \exists v_1 \in V_1, (u_1, v_1, l) \in r_{E_1}\}$
                              $\cup \{(v_1, u_1, l) \in r_{E_1} \mid \exists v_2 \in V_2, (v_2, u_2, l) \in r_{E_2}\}$
                              $\cup \{(v_2, u_2, l) \in r_{E_2} \mid \exists v_1 \in V_1, (v_1, u_1, l) \in r_{E_1}\}$
                              $- descr(G_1) \sqcap_{m \cup \{(u_1, u_2)\}} descr(G_2)$
      exit loop when $\forall (u_1, u_2) \in cand', score(m \cup \{(u_1, u_2)\}) \leq score(m)$ and
                              $look\_ahead(u_1, u_2) = \emptyset$
        choose randomly one couple (u_1, u_2) in $cand'$
        $m \leftarrow m \cup \{(u_1, u_2)\}$
        if $score(m) > score(best_m)$ **then** $best_m \leftarrow m$
    end loop
    return $best_m$

Fig. 3. Greedy search of a mapping

Let us consider for example the two graphs of figure 2, and let us suppose that the f and g functions are both defined as the set cardinality function. At the first iteration, when the current mapping m is empty, the set of couples that most increase the score function contains every couple that matches two vertices sharing one vertex label, i.e., $cand = \{a, b, c, d\} \times \{1, 2, 3, 4\} \cup \{e, f\} \times \{5\}$. Within this set of candidates, $(b, 2)$ (resp. $(c, 3)$)) has $3+3$ potential common edge features, so that $f(look\_ahead(b, 2)) = f(look\_ahead(c, 3)) = 6$; also $(e, 5)$ and $(f, 5)$ have 6 potential common edge features (the 4 edges ending to 5 plus the 2 edges ending to e or f); other candidates all have a smaller number of potential common edge features. Hence, the greedy algorithm will randomly select one couple within the set $cand' = \{(b, 2), (c, 3), (e, 5), (f, 5)\}$. Let us suppose now that the selected couple is, e.g., $(e, 5)$. Then, at the second iteration, $cand$ will contain $(a, 1)$ and $(b, 2)$, which both increase the score function of $2 + 2$, whereas $cand'$ will only contain $(b, 2)$ as it has more potential common edge features than $(a, 1)$. Hence, the next couple to enter the mapping will be $(b, 2)$. At the third iteration, $cand$ will only contain $(a, 1)$, which increases the score function of $3 + 3$, so that $(a, 1)$ will enter the mapping... and so on.

This greedy algorithm stops iterating when every couple neither directly increases the score function nor has looked-ahead common edge features. Note that the score of the mapping m under construction may decrease from one step to another: this occurs when the couple that enters the mapping introduces more new splits than new common features, but it has looked-ahead common edge features, so that the score function is expected to increase at the next iteration. Hence, the algorithm returns the best computed mapping —$best_m$— since the beginning of the run.

This greedy algorithm has a polynomial time complexity of $\mathcal{O}((|V_1| \times |V_2|)^2)$, provided that the computation of the f and g functions have linear time complexities with respect to the size of the mapping (note that the "look_ahead" sets can be computed in an incremental way). As a counterpart of this rather low complexity, this algorithm never backtracks and is not complete. Hence, it may not find the best mapping, the score of which is maximal; moreover, even if it actually finds the best mapping, it cannot be used to prove its optimality. Note however that, since this algorithm is not deterministic, we may run it several times for each case, and keep the best found mapping.

4.3   Discussion

Both algorithms have been implemented in C++. Generally speaking, first experiments have shown us that the complete branch and bound approach can be applied on small graphs only (up to 10 vertices in the general case), even though it performs better when increasing the relative weight of splits with respect to the weights of the common features. Experiments have also confirmed that the greedy algorithm is actually efficient, computing mappings for graphs with 50 nodes and 150 edges in a few seconds of CPU time.

Actually, tractability is all the more critical in CBR that the target case must be compared to numerous cases from the case base. Usually, a first pass filters out a majority of cases, then the most promising candidates are precisely compared. The filtering pass can use a less accurate but efficient algorithm [15], like the greedy algorithm presented here. It can also limit the comparison to representative sub-graphs [10], or even to a vector of characteristics [6]. In the ARDECO implementation, we plan to use a one-pass of our greedy algorithm to select from the case base the most promising candidates. Then, for these most promising candidates, we plan to run several more times the greedy algorithm, trying to find better mappings. As discussed in section 6, we shall further enhance our greedy algorithm by integrating some local search mechanisms.

5   Similarity and Adaptation

5.1   Reusing Qualitative Similarity Information

One of the goals pursued in this work was to provide not only a quantitative similarity measure, but also the *qualitative* information used to compute this measure. Indeed, from the best mapping m —the one that maximizes the two graphs similarity— one can define the set of *differences* between these two graphs as the set of both split vertices and features which are not shared by the graphs:

$$diff(G1, G2) = splits(m) \cup (descr(G1) \cup descr(G2)) - (descr(G1) \sqcap_m descr(G2))$$

We believe that this set of differences can be valuable when reusing a case. For example, the ARDECO assistant aims at helping designers (using a CAD application) to reuse their experience, represented as *design episodes* [4]. Episodes are composed of an initial state and a final state, both represented by labeled graphs. Reusability of an episode is estimated according to the similarity between its initial state and the current state of the designer's work. Adaptation is performed by transforming the current state into a new state which has the same differences with the final state than the current state has with the initial state (cf. figure 4).

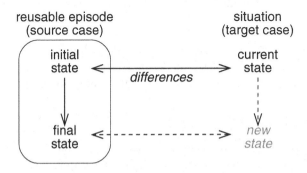

Fig. 4. Adapting a design episode in ARDECO

This approach can be compared to *similarity paths* proposed by [8]: the similarity between two cases is estimated by finding a path between them in the problem space, and this path is translated in the solution space in order to follow it "backward" during adaptation. This is another example of eliciting and reusing qualitative similarity information.

In our approach, the computed set of differences $diff(G1, G2)$ can be seen as a set of elementary operations (feature addition/deletion and vertex splitting/merging) which are reversible. Our model relies however on the assumption that such elementary operations are independent and unordered, while steps in similarity paths are strictly ordered and global (each of them can affect the whole graph).

5.2 Adaptation Guided Similarity

In the introduction, we underlined the fact that remembering and reusing are tightly related. Therefore from the point of view of CBR, a similarity measure is accurate if the cases considered similar are actually reusable. This has been pointed out by several authors [15,8], the latter even prove that their retrieval mechanism (the similarity paths mentioned above) is correct and complete with respect to adaptation (meaning that all and only adaptable cases are retrieved).

It seems therefore important to emphasize again on the design of functions f and g. It has been discussed in section 3.5 how similarity knowledge can be implemented in these functions, but such knowledge must be consistent with adaptation knowledge: a feature must be all the more weighted that its addition (resp. deletion) is expensive or difficult in the adaptation process. Hence general purpose similarities as proposed by [9] are not necessarily adequate to CBR.

6 Conclusion

We have proposed a representation model for cases as labeled directed graphs, where vertices and edges may have more than one label. We have defined a similarity measure on such graphs, and discussed two approaches for computing that measure: the complete branch and bound algorithm appears to be intractable in the very general case, but an efficient greedy algorithm is proposed. This model is suited to CBR for it enables flexible modelling of similarity knowledge, and provides qualitative similarity information which can prove useful for adaptation.

6.1 A Generic Model

Graphs are versatile representation tools, that have been used and studied in a wide range of application domains. Comparing two graphs is an important problem which has been tackled under various modalities: are two graphs identical (problem of graph isomorphism), is one of them more general than the other (problem of subsumption), to what extent (quantitatively or qualitatively) are they different ?

Most of these graph comparison problems can be addressed by our similarity measure in a very straightforward way. For instance, isomorphism is trivially the search for a perfect mapping (with a similarity of 1) where f and g assign any non-null value to every feature and split. Subgraph isomorphism has already been discussed in section 4, and can easily be modelled, as well as partial graph or subgraph isomorphism. It has also been discussed in section 2 how multiple labels can be used to represent hierarchically structured types of vertex or edge. Determining if a graph G_1 subsumes a graph G_2, as does the projection algorithm [16], can be achieved by ignoring (i.e., assigning a null weight to) every feature and every split from G_2, and looking for a similarity of 1. On the other hand, using a symmetrical similarity measure and considering similarity values lower than 1 corresponds to looking for the most specific subsumer of G_1 and G_2, as does the anti-unification algorithm [14].

In the field of knowledge representation, exact subsumption is sometimes too constraining —for ill-designed knowledge basis, or during incremental design. Approximative subsumption measures have been proposed [2,18] to address this kind of problem. In the field of image recognition, [11] proposed an algorithm of fuzzy-projection, by extending the conceptual graphs formalism. Other theoretical work cope with error-tolerant isomorphism [3], computing similarity on the basis of how many elementary transformations are necessary to make the graphs isomorphic. However, all the above propositions miss some interesting features of our model, e.g., approximate edge matching (most focus on vertices), handling splits, flexible tuning.

It is also worth mentioning the recent work of Petrovic et al. [13] about graph retrieval in the field of CBR. Their approach is quite similar to ours —it expresses similarity of a mapping between vertices, and looks for the maximizing mapping— but it is lacking some flexibility with regard to our requirements: splits are not allowed (mappings are univalent functions), graph elements have exactly one label each, and furthermore, function f is pre-defined and corresponds to the cardinality function. However, they went further in addressing tractability issues, by implementing an efficient Tabu search.

6.2   Further Work

The genericity of our model explains to a large extent its complexity and the induced tractability issue. We plan to focus in three research directions to address that issue.

First, we shall further explore heuristic approaches. More work can be done on the *look_ahead* function in the greedy algorithm, in order to find a good trade-off between accurate predictions and efficiency. Other incomplete approaches, such as Tabu search, can also be used in order to refine results of the greedy algorithm by locally exploring the search space around the constructed mapping.

Second, in situations where graphs have remarkable properties, tractability issues are usually addressed by using *ad hoc* heuristics. We plan to study such heuristics from less generic approaches, in order to be able to integrate them, either by tuning f and g functions or by other means when necessary.

Finally, we are particularly interested in systems that aim at assisting the user (rather than standalone systems). In such situations, the retrieving and reusing phase of CBR should be performed interactively. This is possible thanks to the qualitative information elicited by our approach (mapping, commonalities and differences). Not only can interaction allow users to guide the system, thus reducing combinatorial complexity; but user guidance can also provide contextual knowledge about specific cases, which will make the system more knowledgeable and accurate for future uses.

Acknowledgment. We would like to thank Sébastien Sorlin for enriching discussions on this work, and the implementation of the two presented algorithms.

References

1. Agnar Aamodt and Enric Plaza. Case-Based Reasoning: Foundational Issues, Methodological Variations, and System Approaches. *AI Communications*, 7(1):39–59, 1994.
2. Gilles Bisson. *Why and How to Define a Similarity Measure for Object Based Representation Systems*, pages 236–246. IOS Press, Amsterdam (NL), 1995.
3. Horst Bunke. Error Correcting Graph Matching: On the Influence of the Underlying Cost Function. *IEEE Transaction on Pattern Analysis and Machine Intelligence*, 21(9):917–922, 1999.
4. Pierre-Antoine Champin. *Modéliser l'expérience pour en assister la réutilisation : de la Conception Assistée par Ordinateur au Web Sémantique.* Thèse de doctorat en informatique, Université Claude Bernard, Lyon (FR), 2002.
5. Edwin Diday. *Éléments d'analyse de données.* Dunod, Paris (FR), 1982.
6. Christophe Irniger and Horst Bunke. Graph Matching: Filtering Large Databases of Graphs Using Decision Trees. In *IAPR-TC15 Workshop on Graph-based Representation in Pattern Recognition*, pages 239–249, 2001.
7. Jean Lieber and Amedeo Napoli. Using Classification in Case-Based Planning. In *proceedings of ECAI 96*, pages 132–136, 1996.
8. Jean Lieber and Amedeo Napoli. Correct and Complete Retrieval for Case-Based Problem-Solving. In *proceedings of ECAI 98*, pages 68–72, 1998.
9. Dekang Lin. An Information-Theoretic Definition of Similarity. In *proceedings of ICML 1998, Fifteenth International Conference on Machine Learning*, pages 296–304. Morgan Kaufmann, 1998.
10. Bruno T. Messmer and Horst Bunke. A New Algorithm for Error-Tolerant Subgraph Isomorphism Detection. *IEEE Transaction on Pattern Analysis and Machine Intelligence*, 20(5):493–504, 1998.
11. Philippe Mulhem, Wee Kheng Leow, and Yoong Keok Lee. Fuzzy Conceptual Graphs for Matching Images of Natural Scenes. In *proceedings of IJCAI 01*, pages 1397–1404, 2001.
12. Christos H. Papadimitriou. *Computational complexity.* Addison-Wesley, Boston, MA (US), 1994.
13. Sanja Petrovic, Graham Kendall, and Yong Yang. A Tabu Search Approach for Graph-Structured Case Retrieval. In *proceedings of STAIRS 02*, volume 78 of *Frontiers in Artificial Intelligence and Applications*, pages 55–64. IOS Press, 2002.
14. Enric Plaza. Cases as terms: A feature term approach to the structured representation of cases. In *proceedings of ICCBR 95*, number 1010 in LNCS, pages 265–276. Springer Verlag, 1995.

15. Barry Smyth and Matk T. Keane. Retrieval and Adaptation in Déjà Vu, a Case-Based Reasoning System for Software Design. In *AAAI Fall Symposium on Adaptation of Knowledge for Reuse*. AAAI, 1995.
16. John Sowa. *Knowledge Representation: Logical, Philosophical, and Computational Foundations*. PWS Publishing Co., 1999.
17. Amos Tversky. Features of Similarity. *Psychological Review*, 84(4):327–352, 1977.
18. Petko Valtchev. *Construction automatique de taxonomies pour l'aide à la représentation de connaissances par objets*. Thèse de doctorat en informatique, Université Joseph Fourier, Grenoble (FR), 1999.

Global Grade Selector: A Recommender System for Supporting the Sale of Plastic Resin

William Cheetham

General Electric, 1 Research Circle, Niskayuna, NY 12309
cheetham@research.ge.com

Abstract. Selecting the appropriate grade of plastic for a customer from the 3000 grades available is an important knowledge intensive job for the General Electric sales force. A case-based reasoning recommender system, called Global Grade Selector, was created to capture, maintain, and constantly learn information about grades and the knowledge that is needed to correctly select them. Global Grade Selector was fielded to the 800 people in the GE Plastics worldwide sales force in July 2002. During the second half of 2002 it was used for 4700 sales opportunities.

1 Introduction

In the 1967 movie "The Graduate" Dustin Hoffman's character was advised, "The future is Plastics." Since that time plastics have grown to be used for applications as diverse as water bottles, computer casings, coatings for compact disks, and car bumpers. General Electric's (GE) Plastics division sells over 3,000 different grades of plastic resin, which are pea-sized pellets that are later molded into their desired form. Each grade has different properties, which makes different grades appropriate for different applications. The selection of the appropriate grade for a customers' application is a knowledge intensive task that, in GE, is done by a sales force of 800 people worldwide. In order to support this sales force, a Case-Based Reasoning (CBR) [1, 5] tool was created and deployed to the global sales force in 2002. This paper describes that tool, which is called Global Grade Selector (GGS).

1.1 Plastic Sales Process

The plastics sales process starts with the customer describing what their requirements are for their application. Different customers, with different technical understanding of plastic, will describe their requirements in different ways. One customer might just say what their application is, for example a car bumper, and have the sales person determine the appropriate properties of the plastic. Another customer may specify the set of properties that they want the plastic to meet. The properties could be strength, flexibility, flame resistance, cost, and many other mechanical, thermal, electrical, and

K.D. Ashley and D.G. Bridge (Eds.): ICCBR 2003, LNAI 2689, pp. 96–106, 2003.
© Springer-Verlag Berlin Heidelberg 2003

chemical properties. Yet another customer might say they want a grade similar to another grade with one or more different properties (e.g., like grade ABC but stronger). Customers will usually not specify values for all possible properties, just the ones that are the most important for their application.

After the major desired properties are identified a salesperson and possibly an engineer at GE Plastics will determine if any of the existing grades of plastic meet the properties specified by the customer. This is a multi-criteria decision making problem [4], since we need to find a single grade that correctly satisfies all the properties specified by the customer. Before GGS was created the determination of the best grade was done by using descriptions of the properties for each grade, database queries, personal experience, or asking other experts. Once the grade is selected a description of the grade, and possibly a sample, would be sent to the customer. The customer can accept the grade, specify some new properties, or ask GE to develop a new grade specifically for them. Determining the grade that best matches the desired properties is important because if the best matching grade is not suggested we would not be satisfying the customer to the maximum degree possible and may loose the sale to a competitor that suggests a more appropriate grade. Furthermore, if no grade is found to match when one does exist we might spend time trying to create a new grade where none is needed.

1.2 Recommender Systems

Recommender systems are one of the application areas where the CBR methodology has been frequently used. The FAQ Finder and Entrée systems [2] use CBR to find information from Usenet FAQ's and recommend restaurants respectively. PTV [3] is a commercially fielded recommender that uses the television viewing habits of people to construct personalized TV listings that recommend shows the viewers should find of interest. GGS is a recommender that stores and learns knowledge about plastic grades in order to recommend ones appropriate for a customer.

2 Global Grade Selector Description

The creation of GGS began in 2001. A database of properties for all grades already existed and there was a simple material selector that a salesperson could use to query the database. However, there were problems with these. The database had many missing values and different properties for plastics developed in different countries. For example, the strength of the plastic could be measured with one test in the United States a different test in Europe. The simple material selector only returned grades when they matched or exceeded all properties used in the query. It did not retrieve close matches that did not meet all properties or rank the grades that were selected from best to worst. The GGS was to be a better version of the material selector.

2.1 Demonstration

The first step in using GGS is to enter as much information as possible about the desired grade, the user interface for this is shown in Figure 1. There are a few types of information that can be entered. A user can

- Select he name of a known grade, called a Benchmark Material, and find grades similar to it,
- Enter an Application and find grades used for that application,
- Enter specific Critical Properties of the desired grade and find grades with similar properties, or
- Enter any combination of the information above and find grades that are similar.

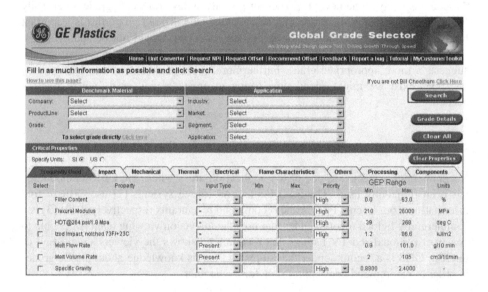

Fig. 1. Input Screen

The known grade is entered by selecting the Company that makes the grade, either GE or any other plastic manufacturer, from the select box under the heading "Benchmark Material." After the Company is selected, the ProductLine select box is updated to have just the families of plastics made by the selected company. When a family is chosen, the Grade select box is updated to just have the grades in the family of that company. After the grade is selected the user can click on Search to find GE grades that have been previously identified as similar to the selected grade, see Figure 2. An alternative way to select a grade is to click on the words "To select a grade directly Click Here," this displays a pop-up window that shows all grades from all companies. Selecting a grade from this pop-up window fills in the Company, ProductLine, and Grade select boxes. A known grade search is useful when our salesperson is trying to sell to a customer who has been using a competitors grade, when a customers requirements change slightly and the current grade is not sufficient, or when we stop producing a grade that a customer has used.

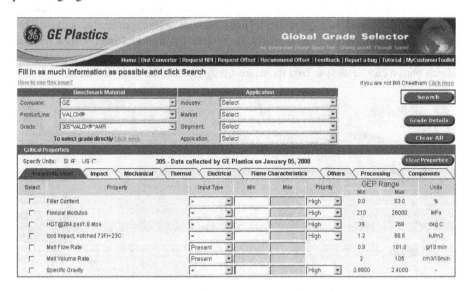

Fig. 2. Input Screen – Benchmark Material

An application is entered using the select boxes for Industry, Market, Segment, and Application. An application is an end use of a grade where the grade has been successfully sold to a customer. Example applications are water bottles or car bumpers. The four selection boxes list the levels of a taxonomy of all applications where each Industry has many Markets, each Market has multiple Segments, and each Segment has Applications. Grades can be associated with any level of the taxonomy. Once any of these select boxes is entered the user can click on Search, which brings back all grades that are appropriate for the specified level of the taxonomy and below. An example is given in Figure 3. The application search is useful when we are trying to sell to a customer for an application where we are already selling a grade to another customer. Using a grade that has already been used for an application simplifies the selection process because some tests are not required for every grade, but are needed for some applications. For instance, a grade used for a water bottle can't change the taste of the water, a grade for a car bumper can't fade in the sun, and an office chair wheel can't squeak. There are many properties like these where we do not have complete information about all grades because the tests are expensive and only done when needed. Using an existing grade eliminates the need for these tests and reduces unexpected application related issues.

Entering critical properties is done by first selecting the check box next to the property that is desired. There are nine tabs with properties that can be selected (i.e., Frequently Use, Impact, Mechanical, ...), the user can select any properties from any tabs, see

Figure 4. Next, the user selects the desired values for that property. Numeric properties can have their InputType be equal to, greater than, or less than a value or between two values. Boolean properties can have their InputType be Present or Missing. Next, the user selects the priority of the property (Low, Medium, or High). Some information about the properties is provided to help the user select appropriate values. This information is the units of the property along with the min and max values for that property in the case base. Once the values are selected for all checked properties the Search button can be used to find the nearest neighbors to the desired values.

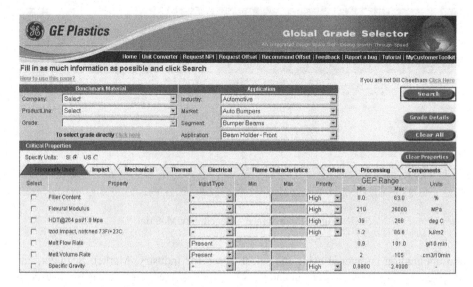

Fig. 3. Input Screen – Benchmark Material

Specifying critical properties is the most frequent way that a grade is selected. Most of our customers identify the critical properties that are needed for their application before they request a grade from us. In this case we can just enter the properties and perform a search. If the customers have not identified the properties we can use GGS to go through the list of possible properties and check off the ones they are interested in. This keeps us from realizing a property is important only after a grade is selected and sent to the customer, a problem we have had in the past.

An example of the output produced is given in Figure 5. This output includes the number of properties that were met by the grade, "CTQ's Met", the similarity score for the grade, Score, the name of the grade, Grade Name, the GE product line the grade is in, Product, the area of the world where the grade is currently produced, mfg Region, the current availability of the grade, Status, and the actual values in the case base for every property that was selected.

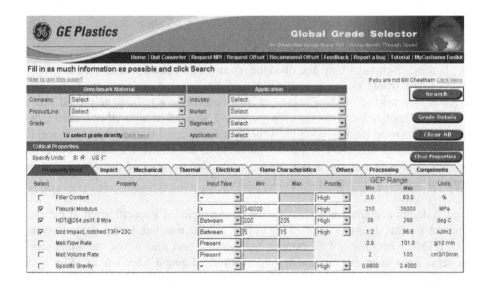

Fig. 4. Input Screen – Critical Properties

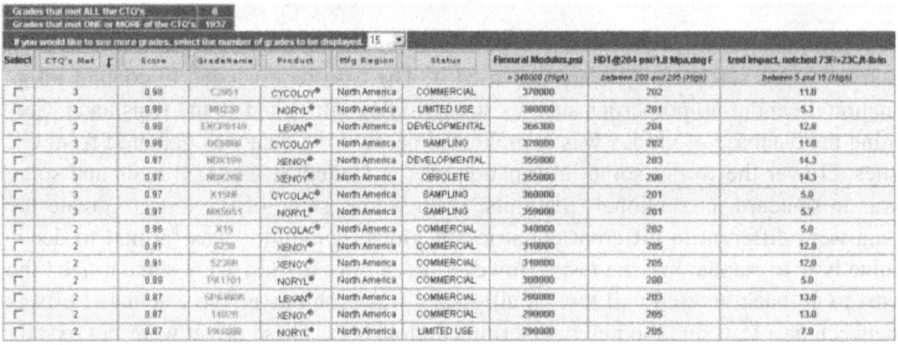

Fig. 5. Output Screen – Critical Properties

If the benchmark material and/or application is entered along with critical properties then the benchmark and application are considered another property when the search is done and results are displayed. The user can select any of the returned grades for a more detailed comparison by clicking on the appropriate select check box.

2.2 Design

Before we began the design of GGS we gathered requirements from a dozen salespeople. In these discussions they described the resources they used, process they followed, features they would like to have in GGS, and detailed use cases of actual customer requests they worked on. One source of information that was frequently used was a database of application areas for each grade. We also talked with other software developers who were creating other tools for the sales force. One ongoing project was to create a database that had GE grades that could be substituted for each of our competitors' grades. During the design phase, we decided to integrate the information on application areas and competitors grades into GGS.

Next, a design document was created. The design included a specification of the system architecture, descriptions of all algorithms needed, user interface paper prototypes (i.e., HTML where none of the buttons do anything), and a set of use cases that show the input (user interface) processing (algorithms) and output (user interface) for each use case. This document was shown to the dozen salespeople and modified based on their comments. When the document was completed the development was ready to begin.

2.3 Development

The two major tasks in development were creating the case base of grade information and the grade selection software that used it. The case base needed to contain information on about 50 properties such as strength, flexibility, and flame resistance. Creating the database of grades was complicated because the data was gathered from GE sites all over the world, some information was in United States (US) units and some was in standard international (SI) units. Even worse, some of the tests to create the data were different in different countries. A global committee was formed to determine how to standardize the tests. However, even after the test were standardized the cost to go back and redo all test on all grades was prohibitive. We calculated offsets between past tests and the newly determined global set. These offset were not exactly correct, but they allowed us to create a starting case base that included all grades. The cases with calculated offsets would be updated when those tests were needed in the future.

The software created for the property search retrieves potentially matching cases from an Oracle database, calculates the similarity of each retrieved case to the desired properties, and displays the results to a user. The similarity calculation for a retrieved grade is a weighted sum of the similarities for each selected property where the weight is 5 for high priority, 3 for low priority, and 1 for low priority. The similarity of a single property is between 0 and 1, with 1 being most similar, and depends on the InputType (equal to, greater than, less than, or between). A property that has Input-Type "equal to" is given a similarity of 1 if the value in the case exactly matches the

desired value. The similarity linearly decreases to zero when the value in the case is
10% different than the desired value, as shown in figure 6.

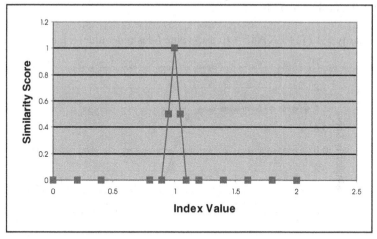

Fig. 6. Equal-to Membership Function

A property that has InputType "greater than" is given a similarity value that is close to
zero when the retrieved case's value is less than the desired value, increase exponentially to 0.9 when the values are equal and continues to increase towards 1.0 when the
retrieved value is greater than the desired value. The formula for this is given in
Equation 1 and shown in Figure 7.

$$\text{Similarity} = 1 / (1 + \text{EXP}(-15 * ((case\_value / desired\_value) - 0.85))) \tag{1}$$

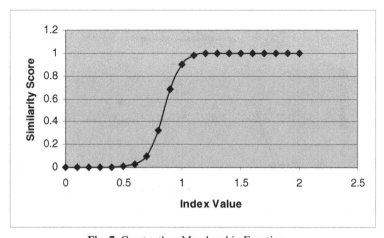

Fig. 7. Greater than Membership Function

A property that has InputType "less than" is given a similarity value that is close to
zero when the retrieved case's value is greater than the desired value, increase expo-

nentially to 0.9 when the values are equal and continues to increase towards 1.0 when the retrieved value is less than the desired value. The formula for this is given in Equation 2 and shown in Figure 8.

$$\text{Similarity} = 1 / (1+ \text{EXP}(15 * ((\text{case\_value} / \text{desired\_value}) - 1.15))) \tag{2}$$

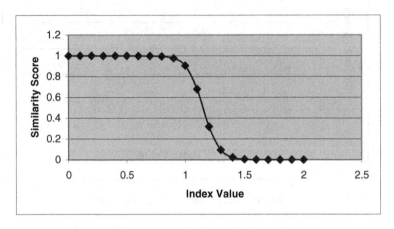

Fig. 8. Less than Membership Function

A property that has InputType "between" is given a similarity value 1.0 when the retrieved case's value within the min and max desired values. The similarity linearly decreases to zero when the retrieved values is outside the desired region by ½ the size of the desired region, as is shown in Figure 9.

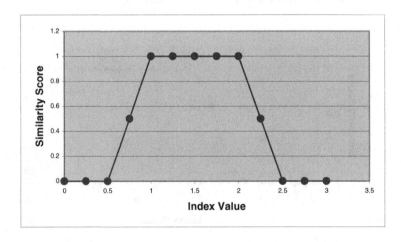

Fig. 9. Between Membership Function

2.4 Knowledge Maintenance

When a grade is selected for an application the sales person who makes that selection has to report what application the grade is being used for and if it is replacing a different grade that has been used. If the application is a new one for the grade then the grade may be added to the application taxonomy. If the grade is replacing another grade then it may be added to the benchmark material offsets.

New grades are being researched constantly at many GE sites throughout the world. Whenever one of these new product introduction (NPI) projects is successful (i.e., a new grade is found to fill some purpose that was not previously satisfied) then the new grade is added to the case base.

3 Formulation Predictor

Any fielded CBR recommender system should have a plan for what to do when no case is similar to the desired values. The simple thing to do when there is no grade that satisfies a customers needs is to start a NPI to create a grade that does. The NPI process involves

1. Searching through any past experiments that were done for previous grades, which did or did not turn into production grades.
2. Determining the most promising set of past experiments.
3. Constructing a new set of experiments based on the past ones.
4. Then determining if the new experiments produced a grade that meets the customers needs.

We are in the process of creating a CBR tool, called formulation predictor, that has a case base of every experiment that is run by GE throughout the world. Formulation predictor selects the most promising experiments and has adaptation algorithms that construct suggested experiments. Combining GGS with FP is planned for 2003.

4 Usages and Payoff

A pilot version of GGS was initially written for just one type of product line. This simplified the creation and validation of the case base, allowed us to focus on feedback from just a portion of the sales force, and gave us time to improve the user interface before showing it to a wider audience. The pilot version was completed in December of 2001. Feedback was collected from the pilot users and the full system released to the GE Plastics sales force throughout the world in July 2002. The sales force consists of 800 people working at multiple sites including North and South America, Europe, Asia, Africa, and Australia, see Figure 10. From July to December of 2002 GGS was used 4700 times. Details of each usage of GGS are stored in a reporting database. The following pieces of information are a subset of the items stored in the database for each usage of GGS: users name, date and time of usage, location of user, properties selected, grades suggested, and text field containing user feedback if any was entered. Reports that describe the tools usage are periodically generated from this database.

Fig. 10. Countries with GGS in use (Gray)

When GGS was introduced in July 2002 there were about 150 NPI research projects in place. GGS was used to find existing grades that could be used to satisfy the requirements of the NPIs. If GGS could find a grade the customer could be satisfied without having to wait for the NPI, usually 3 to 6 months, and the NPI could be cancelled, saving time for the researchers. GGS was able to find grades satisfying 11 of the NPI efforts. These 11 grades resulted in $9.5 million USD in sales. A patent for GGS has been filed with the United States patent office.

References

1. Aamodt, A., Case-Based Reasoning: Foundational Issues, Methodological Variations, and System Approaches, AICOM, Vol. 7, No. 1, (March 1994)
2. Hammond, K., Burke, R., Schmidt, K. A Case-Based Approach to Knowledge Navigation, In Case-Based Reasoning: Experiences, Lessons, & Future Directions Ed. Leake, AAAI Press/MIT Press, Menlo Park, CA (1996)
3. Smyth, B., Cotter P. A Personalized TV Listening Service for the Digital TV Age. Journal of Knowledge-Based Systems. 13(2-3), pp. 53–59 (2000)
4. Triantaphyllou, E., Multi-Criteria Decision Making Methods: A Comparative Study, Kluwer Academic Publishers, Dordrecht/Boston/London (2000)
5. Watson, I., Applying Case-Based Reasoning: Techniques for Enterprise Systems. San Francisco, Cal. Morgan Kaufmann Publishers (1997)

Maximum Likelihood Hebbian Learning Based Retrieval Method for CBR Systems

Juan M. Corchado[1], Emilio S. Corchado[3], Jim Aiken[2], Colin Fyfe[3],
Florentino Fernandez[4], and Manuel Gonzalez[1]

[1] Dept. de Informática y Automática, University of Salamanca, Plaza de la Merced s/n,
37008, Salamanca, Spain
corchado@usal.es

[2] Dept. de Ingeniería Civil, University of Burgos, Esc. Politécnica Superior, Edificio C, C/
Francisco de Vitoria, Burgos, Spain

[3] Plymouth Marine Laboratory, Prospect Place, West Hoe, Plymouth, PL1 - 3DH, UK

[4] Computing and Information System Dept. University of Paisley, PA1-2BE, Paisley, UK

[5] Dept. Informática. University of Vigo, Campus As Lagoas, Ourense, Spain

Abstract. CBR systems are normally used to assist experts in the resolution of problems. During the last few years researchers have been working in the development of techniques to automate the reasoning stages identified in this methodology. This paper presents a Maximum Likelihood Hebbian Learning-based method that automates the organisation of cases and the retrieval stage of case-based reasoning systems. The proposed methodology has been derived as an extension of the Principal Component Analysis, and groups similar cases, identifying clusters automatically in a data set in an unsupervised mode. The method has been successfully used to completely automate the reasoning process of an oceanographic forecasting system and to improve its performance.

1 Introduction

Case based reasoning (CBR) systems have been successfully used in several domains such as diagnosis, prediction, control and planning [1], [10], [23], [26]. However, a major problem with these systems is the difficulty in case retrieval and case matching when the number of cases increases; large case bases are difficult to handle and require efficient indexing mechanisms and optimised retrieval algorithms, as explained later. Also there are very few standard techniques to automate their construction, since each problem may be represented by a different data set and requires a customised solution. This paper presents a method that can be used to alleviate these problems.

In the CBR cycle there is normally some human interaction. Whilst case retrieval and reuse may be automated, case revision and retention are often undertaken by human experts. This is a current weakness of CBR systems and one of their major chal-

K.D. Ashley and D.G. Bridge (Eds.): ICCBR 2003, LNAI 2689, pp. 107–121, 2003.
© Springer-Verlag Berlin Heidelberg 2003

lenges. For several years we have been working in the identification of techniques to automate the reasoning cycle of CBR systems [4], [8], [10], [19]. This paper presents a Maximum Likelihood Hebbian Learning (MLHL) based model to automate the process of case indexing and retrieval, that may be used in problems in which the cases are characterised predominantly by numerical information.

Maximum Likelihood Hebbian Learning (MLHL) based models were first developed as an extension of Principal Component Analysis [21], [22]. Maximum Likelihood Hebbian Learning Based Method attempts to identify a small number of data points, which are necessary to solve a particular problem to the required accuracy. These methods have been successfully used in the unsupervised investigation of structure in data sets [2], [3]. We have previously investigated the use of Artificial Neural Networks [8] and Kernel Principal Component Analysis (KPCA) [11], [12] to identify cases, which will be used in a case based reasoning system. In this paper, we present a novel hybrid technique.

Maximum Likelihood Hebbian Learning Based models can be used in case based reasoning systems when cases can be represented in the form of numerical feature vectors, examples of which would be temperature (°C), distance (m), time (hh,mm,ss), dates (dd,mm,yy) etc. This is normally the case in most instance based reasoning systems (IBR) [19]. Large case/instance bases may have negative consequences for the performance of the CBR/IBR systems. This has been shown in several projects such as INRECA [27] and ORKA [5], [6]. When a CBR system is used in a real time problem, such as the oceanographic one presented latter in this paper, it may not be possible to manage a large case base and the necessary pre-processing algorithms with reasonable computational power. As has been shown in the ORKA project, new and updated cases should be included and maintained in the case base, and obsolete and redundant cases should be eliminated or transformed to maintain a case base with a stable size, in order to control the response time of the system and maintain its efficiency. The transformation of a number of cases into one representative case may help to reduce the volume of information stored in the case base without losing accuracy. The ability of the Maximum Likelihood Hebbian Learning-based methods presented in this paper to cluster cases/instances and to associate cases to clusters can be used to successfully prune the case-base without losing valuable information.

An instance based reasoning system developed for predicting oceanographic time series and to identify oceanographic fronts ahead of an ongoing vessel [4], [5], in real time, will be used to illustrate the efficiency of the solution here discussed. The identification of oceanographic fronts (areas in which two or more water masses converge) is very important for nuclear submarines [6]. This paper first presents the Maximum Likelihood Hebbian Learning Based Method and its theoretical background. The oceanographic problem in which this technique has been used is presented, and finally we show how this approach has been implemented to forecast oceanographic thermal time series in real time.

2 Maximum Likelihood Hebbian Learning Based Method

The use of Maximum Likelihood Hebbian Learning Based Method has been derived from the work of [3], [11], [12], [13], etc. in the field of pattern recognition as an extension of Principal Component Analysis (PCA) [21], [22]. We first review Principal Component Analysis (PCA) which has been the most frequently reported linear operation involving unsupervised learning for data compression, which aims to find that orthogonal basis which maximises the data's variance for a given dimensionality of basis. Then the Exploratory Projection Pursuit (EPP) theory is outlined. It is shown how Maximum Likelihood Hebbian Learning Based Method may be derived from PCA and it could be viewed as a method of performing EPP. Finally we show why Maximum Likelihood Hebbian Learning Based Method is appropriated for this type of problems.

2.1 Principal Component Analysis (PCA)

Principal Component Analysis (PCA) is a standard statistical technique for compressing data; it can be shown to give the best linear compression of the data in terms of least mean square error. There are several artificial neural networks which have been shown to perform PCA e.g. [21], [22]. We will apply a negative feedback implementation [9].

The basic PCA network is described by equations (1)-(3). Let us have an N-dimensional input vector at time t, $x(t)$, and an M-dimensional output vector, y, with W_{ij} being the weight linking input j to output i. η is a learning rate. Then the activation passing and learning is described by

Feedforward:

$$y_i = \sum_{j=1}^{N} W_{ij} x_j \, , \forall i \tag{1}$$

Feedback:

$$e_j = x_j - \sum_{i=1}^{M} W_{ij} y_i \tag{2}$$

Change weights:

$$\Delta W_{ij} = \eta e_j y_i \tag{3}$$

We can readily show that this algorithm is equivalent to Oja's Subspace Algorithm [21]:

$$\Delta W_{ij} = \eta e_j y_i = \eta (x_j - \sum_k W_{kj} y_k) y_i \tag{4}$$

and so this network not only causes convergence of the weights but causes the weights to converge to span the subspace of the Principal Components of the input data. We might ask then why we should be interested in the negative feedback formulation rather than the formulation (4) in which the weight change directly uses negative feedback. The answer is that the explicit formation of residuals (2) allows us to consider probability density functions of the residuals in a way which would not be brought to mind if we use (4).

Exploratory Projection Pursuit (EPP) is a more recent statistical method aimed at solving the difficult problem of identifying structure in high dimensional data. It does this by projecting the data onto a low dimensional subspace in which we search for its structure by eye. However not all projections will reveal the data's structure equally well. We therefore define an index that measures how "interesting" a given projection is, and then represent the data in terms of projections that maximise that index.

The first step in our exploratory projection pursuit is to define which indices represent interesting directions. Now "interesting" structure is usually defined with respect to the fact that most projections of high-dimensional data onto arbitrary lines through most multi-dimensional data give almost Gaussian distributions [7]. Therefore if we wish to identify "interesting" features in data, we should look for those directions onto which the data-projections are as far from the Gaussian as possible.

It was shown in [16] that the use of a (non-linear) function creates an algorithm to find those values of W which maximise that function whose derivative is f() under the constraint that W is an orthonormal matrix. This was applied in [9] to the above network in the context of the network performing an Exploratory Projection Pursuit. Thus if we wish to find a direction which maximises the kurtosis of the distribution which is measured by s4, we will use a function f(s) $\approx$ s3 in the algorithm. If we wish to find that direction with maximum skewness, we use a function f(s) $\approx$ s2 in the algorithm.

2.2 ε-Insensitive Hebbian Learning

It has been shown [28] that the nonlinear PCA rule

$$\Delta W_{ij} = \eta \left(x_j f(y_i) - f(y_i) \sum_k W_{kj} f(y_k) \right) \qquad (5)$$

can be derived as an approximation to the best non-linear compression of the data. Thus we may start with a cost function

$$J(W) = 1^T E\left\{ \left(x - Wf(W^T x) \right)^2 \right\} \qquad (6)$$

which we minimise to get the rule (5). [18] used the residual in the linear version of (6) to define a cost function of the residual

$$J = f_1(\mathbf{e}) = f_1(\mathbf{x} - W\mathbf{y}) \qquad (7)$$

where $f_1 = \|.\|^2$ is the (squared) Euclidean norm in the standard linear or nonlinear PCA rule. With this choice of $f_1(\ )$, the cost function is minimised with respect to any set of samples from the data set on the assumption that the residuals are chosen independently and identically distributed from a standard Gaussian distribution. We may show that the minimisation of J is equivalent to minimising the negative log probability of the residual, **e**. , if **e** is Gaussian.

$$\text{Let } p(\mathbf{e}) = \frac{1}{Z}\exp(-\mathbf{e}^2) \tag{8}$$

Then we can denote a general cost function associated with this network as

$$J = -\log p(\mathbf{e}) = (\mathbf{e})^2 + K \tag{9}$$

where K is a constant. Therefore performing gradient descent on J we have

$$\Delta W \propto -\frac{\partial J}{\partial W} = -\frac{\partial J}{\partial \mathbf{e}}\frac{\partial \mathbf{e}}{\partial W} \approx \mathbf{y}(2\mathbf{e})^T \tag{10}$$

where we have discarded a less important term. See [16] for details.

In general [25], the minimisation of such a cost function may be thought to make the probability of the residuals greater dependent on the probability density function (pdf) of the residuals. Thus if the probability density function of the residuals is known, this knowledge could be used to determine the optimal cost function. [11] investigated this with the (one dimensional) function:

$$p(\mathbf{e}) = \frac{1}{2+\varepsilon}\exp\left(-|\mathbf{e}|_\varepsilon\right) \tag{11}$$

where

$$|e|_\varepsilon = \begin{cases} o & \forall |e| < \varepsilon \\ |e| - \varepsilon & otherwise \end{cases} \tag{12}$$

with ε being a small scalar ≥ 0.

[11] described this in terms of noise in the data set. However we feel that it is more appropriate to state that, with this model of the pdf of the residual, the optimal $f_1(\ )$ function is the ε-insensitive cost function:

$$f_1(\mathbf{e}) = |\mathbf{e}|_\varepsilon \tag{13}$$

In the case of the negative feedback network, the learning rule is

$$\Delta W \propto -\frac{\partial J}{\partial W} = -\frac{\partial f_1(\mathbf{e})}{\partial \mathbf{e}}\frac{\partial \mathbf{e}}{\partial W} \qquad (14)$$

which gives:

$$\Delta W_{ij} = \begin{cases} o & if |e_j| < \varepsilon \\ otherwise & \eta y(sign(e)) \end{cases} \qquad (15)$$

The difference with the common Hebb learning rule is that the sign of the residual is used instead the value of the residual. Because this learning rule is insensitive to the magnitude of the input vectors x, the rule is less sensitive to outliers than the usual rule based on mean squared error. This change from viewing the difference after feedback as simply a residual rather than an error permits us to consider a family of cost functions each member of which is optimal for a particular probability density function associated with the residual.

2.3 Applying Maximum Likelihood Hebbian Learning

The Maximum Likelihood Hebbian Learning algorithm is constructed now on the bases of the previously presented concepts as outlined here. Now the ε-insensitive learning rule is clearly only one of a possible family of learning rules which are suggested by the family of exponential distributions. This family was called an exponential family in [15] though statisticians use this term for a somewhat different family. Let the residual after feedback have probability density function

$$p(\mathbf{e}) = \frac{1}{Z}\exp(-|\mathbf{e}|^p) \qquad (16)$$

Then we can denote a general cost function associated with this network as

$$J = E(-\log p(\mathbf{e})) = E(|\mathbf{e}|^p + K) \qquad (17)$$

where K is a constant independent of W and the expectation is taken over the input data set. Therefore performing gradient descent on J we have

$$\Delta W \propto -\frac{\partial J}{\partial W}\Big|_{W(t-1)} = -\frac{\partial J}{\partial \mathbf{e}}\frac{\partial \mathbf{e}}{\partial W}\Big|_{W(t-1)} \approx E\{\mathbf{y}(p|\mathbf{e}|^{p-1} sign(\mathbf{e}))^T|_{W(t-1)}\} \qquad (18)$$

where T denotes the transpose of a vector and the operation of taking powers of the norm of e is on an elementwise basis as it is derived from a derivative of a scalar with respect to a vector.

Computing the mean of a function of a data set (or even the sample averages) can be tedious, and we also wish to cater for the situation in which samples keep arriving as we investigate the data set and so we derive an online learning algorithm. If the conditions of stochastic approximation [17] are satisfied, we may approximate this with a difference equation. The function to be approximated is clearly sufficiently smooth and the learning rate can be made to satisfy $\eta_k \geq 0, \sum_k \eta_k = \infty, \sum_k \eta_k^2 < \infty$ and so we have the rule:

$$\Delta W_{ij} = \eta.y_i.sign(e_j)|e_j|^{p-1} \tag{19}$$

We would expect that for leptokurtotic residuals (more kurtotic than a Gaussian distribution), values of p<2 would be appropriate, while for platykurtotic residuals (less kurtotic than a Gaussian), values of p>2 would be appropriate. Researchers from the community investigating Independent Component Analysis [14], [15] have shown that it is less important to get exactly the correct distribution when searching for a specific source than it is to get an approximately correct distribution i.e. all supergaussian signals can be retrieved using a generic leptokurtotic distribution and all subgaussian signals can be retrieved using a generic platykutotic distribution. Our experiments will tend to support this to some extent but we often find accuracy and speed of convergence are improved when we are accurate in our choice of p. Therefore the network operation is:

Feedforward:

$$y_i = \sum_{j=1}^{N} W_{ij} x_j, \ \forall_i \tag{20}$$

Feedback:

$$e_j = x_j - \sum_{i=1}^{M} W_{ij} y_i \tag{21}$$

Weights change:

$$\Delta W_{ij} = \eta.y_i.sign(e_j)|e_j|^{p-1} \tag{22}$$

[11] described their rule as performing a type of PCA, but this is not strictly true since only the original (Oja) ordinary Hebbian rule actually performs PCA. It might be more appropriate to link this family of learning rules to Principal Factor Analysis since PFA makes an assumption about the noise in a data set and then removes the assumed noise from the covariance structure of the data before performing a PCA. We are doing something similar here in that we are basing our PCA-type rule on the assumed distribution of the residual. By maximising the likelihood of the residual with respect to the actual distribution, we are matching the learning rule to the probability density function of the residual.

More importantly, we may also link the method to the standard statistical method of Exploratory Projection Pursuit: now the nature and quantification of the interesting-ness is in terms of how likely the residuals are under a particular model of the prob-ability density function of the residuals. In the results reported later, we also sphere the data before applying the learning method to the sphered data and show that with this method we may also find interesting structure in the data.

2.4 Sphering of the Data g

Because a Gaussian distribution with mean a and variance x is no more or less inter-esting than a Gaussian distribution with mean b and variance y - indeed this second order structure can obscure higher order and more interesting structure - we remove such information from the data. This is known as "sphering". That is, the raw data is translated till its mean is zero, projected onto the principal component directions and multiplied by the inverse of the square root of its eigenvalue to give data which has mean zero and is of unit variance in all directions. So for input data X we find the covariance matrix.

$$\Sigma = \left\langle \left(X - \langle X \rangle\right)\left(X - \langle X \rangle\right)^T \right\rangle = UDU^T \tag{23}$$

Where U is the eigenvector matrix, D the diagonal matrix of eigenvalues, T de-notes the transpose of the matrix and the angled brackets indicate the ensemble aver-age. New samples, drawn from the distribution are transformed to the principal com-ponent axes to give y where

$$y_i = \frac{1}{\sqrt{D_i}} \sum_{j=1}^{n} U_{ij}\left(X_i - \langle X_i \rangle\right), \, for 1 \le i \le m \tag{24}$$

Where n is the dimensionality of the input space and m is the dimensionality of the sphered data.

3   IBR for Oceanographic Real-Time Forecasting

A forecasting system capable of predicting the temperature of the water ahead of an ongoing vessel in real time has been developed using a IBR system [4], [6]. An IBR system was selected for its capacity of handling huge amounts of data, of adapting to the changes in the environment and to provide real time forecast.

In Figure 1, shadowed words represent the four steps of a typical IBR life cycle [1], the arrows represent data coming in or out of the instance-base (situated in the centre of the diagram) and the text boxes represent the result obtained by each of the four stages of the IBR life-cycle. Data are recorded in real time by sensors in the vessels and satellite pictures are received weekly. A *Knowledge Acquisition module* is in charge of collecting, handling and *indexing* the data in the instance-base. Once the real-time system is activated on an ongoing vessel, a *new instance* is generated every 2 km using the temperatures recorded by the vessel during the last 40km. This new instance is used to retrieve *m cases* from a collection of previous cases using Kernel methods [10]. The *m-retrieved instances* are adapted by an Unsupervised Kernel method during the reuse phase to obtain an initial *(proposed) forecast* [10]. Though the revision process, the proposed solution is adjusted to generate the *final forecast* using the confidence limits from the knowledge base [5]. *Learning* (retaining) is achieved by updating the Kernels. A complete description of this system can be obtained in [10]. This IBR system has been successfully tested and it is presently operative in several oceanographic vessels. Improving this system has been our challenge and this section will outline the modifications that has been done to it with the intention of demonstrating that the Maximum Likelihood Hebbian Learning algorithm can provide successful results and automate the instances indexing and the instance retrieval process. The following tables shows the changes that have been done in the IBR system for real time oceanographic forecasting.

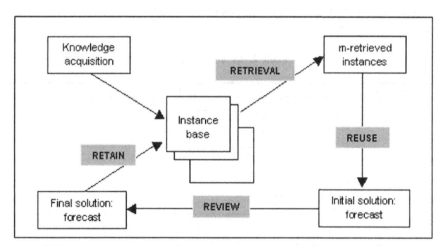

Fig. 1. IBR system architecture.

Table 1. Changes in the IBR system for real time oceanographic forecasting

STEP	Operating IBR system	Modifications and improvements
Indexing	Rule based system	Maximum Likelihood Hebbian Learning algorithm
Retrieval	Kernel methods	Maximum Likelihood Hebbian Learning algorithm
Reuse	Unsupervised Kernel methods	Unsupervised Kernel methods
Retrain	Kernel methods	Kernel methods / Maximum Likelihood Hebbian Learning algorithm

Table 1 outlines the changes made to the original system. The first column of the table indicates in which parts of the IBR system the changes have been made, the second column indicates the method originally used (and now eliminated) and column three indicates which methods have been included in the system. The changes indicated in table 1 have been introduced with the intention of developing a robust model, based on a technology easy to implement and that can automate the process of defining the retrieval step of the IBR system, facilitating the indexing of cases and helping in the learning and adaptation stage. The Maximum Likelihood Hebbian Learning algorithm automates these processes, clustering the instances and facilitating the retrieval of the most similar cases to a problem case. In this particular application the adaptation stage is carried out by an unsupervised kernel network, which structure need to be identified in advance, and tuned manually. We now present the structure of a case and indicate how the Maximum Likelihood Hebbian Learning algorithm has been used in the mentioned IBR parts.

3.1   The Instance

Each stored instance contains information relating to a specific situation and consists of an *input profile* (i.e. a vector of temperature values) together with the various fields shown in Table 2. A 40 km data profile has been found to give sufficient resolution to characterise the problem instance [6].

Table 2. Instance structure.

Instance Field	Explanation
Identification	unique identification: a positive integer in the range 0 to 64000
Input Profile, I	A 40 km temperature input vector of values Ij, (where j = 1, 2, ... 40) Representing the structure of the water between the present position of the vessel and its position 40 km back.
Output Value, F	A temperature value representing the water temperature 5 km ahead of the present location
Time	Time when recorded (although redundant, this information helps to ensure fast retrieval)
Date	Date when the data were recorded (included for the same reasons as for the previous field).
Location	Geographical co-ordinates of the location where the value I_{40} (of the input profile) was recorded.
Orientation	Approximate direction of the data track, represented by an integer x, $(1 \leq x \leq 12)$.
Retrieval Time	Time when the instance was last retrieved.
Retrieval Date	Date when the instance was last retrieved.
Retrieval Location	Geographical co-ordinates of the location at which the instance was last retrieved.
Average Error	Average error over all forecasts for which the instance has been used during the adaptation step.

The parametric features of the different water masses that comprise the various oceans vary substantially, not only geographically, but also seasonally. Because of these variations it is therefore inappropriate to attempt to maintain an instance base representing patterns of ocean characteristics on a global scale; such patterns, to a large extent, are dependent on the particular water mass in which the vessel may currently be located. Furthermore, there is no necessity to refer to instances representative of all the possible orientations that a vessel can take in a given water mass. Vessels normally proceed in a given predefined direction. So, only instances corresponding to the current orientation of the vessel are normally required at any one time.

3.2 Indexing and Retrieving Instances the Maximum Likelihood Hebbian Learning Algorithm

To explore the structure of a data set we are using Maximum Likelihood Hebbian Learning. Applying equations 20 to 22 to the Case-base, the MLHL algorithm groups the cases in clusters automatically. The proposed indexing mechanism classifies the cases/instances automatically, clustering together those of similar structure. This technique attempts to find interesting low dimensional projections of the data so that humans can investigate the structure of the data even by eye. One of the great advantages of this technique is that it is an unsupervised method so we do not need to have any information about of the data before hand. When a new case is presented to the IBR system, it is identified as belonging to a particular type by applying also equations 20 to 22 to it. This mechanism may be used as an universal retrieval and indexing mechanism to be applied to any problem similar to the presented here.

3.3 Forecasting with the Instance-Base Reasoning System

Several experiments have been carried out to illustrate the effectiveness of the IBR system, which incorporates the MLHL algorithm. Experiments have been carried out using data from the Atlantic Meridian Transept (AMT) Cruise 4 [6]. We show in Figure 2 the errors on a data set of 500 instances randomly taken from the AMT 2000 data set (composed of more than 150.000 instances) using the Kernel based CBR system. Figure 3 shows the results obtained with the new MLHL proposed modification. The mean absolute error, when forecasting the temperature of the water 5 Km ahead of an ongoing vessel, along 10.000 km (form the UK to the Falkland Island) was 0.0205 °C [10]. With the new proposal, the average error have been reduced to 0.0167 °C, for the whole data set, which compares very favourably with the initial Instance based reasoning system and other previous methods [6]. Using the MLHL algorithm the number of predictions with an error higher than 0,1 has been reduced in more than 30%. The reason may be that the data selection carried out with the MLHL algorithm facilitate the creation of more consistent models during the adaptation stage than with the Unsupervised Kernel algorithm. We have compared the proposal presented in this paper with several classification algorithms that may be used for the indexing and retrieval of cases: Principal Components Analysis (PCA), Kernel Methods and Growing Cells Structures (GCS) [20]. The Maximum Likelihood Hebbian Learning method outperforms the others techniques improving the final results clustering the instances adequately for a future adaptation using and Unsupervised Kernel algorithm. The average forecasting error obtained with the PCA method was of 0.0310 °C, with the Kernel Method was of 0.0205 °C and with the GCS was of 0.0231°C.

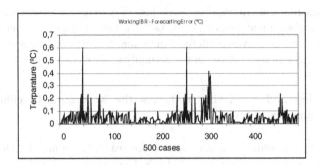

Fig. 2. Average error of the working IBR system in 500 forecasts carried out during the AMT 2000 cruise from the UK to the Falkland Island.

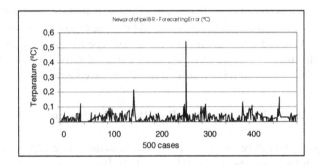

Fig. 3. Average error with IBR system using MLHL algorithms in the same 500 predictions as the ones showed in Figure 2.

For pedagogical purposes, we illustrate the method on a small sample of cases. 150 instances which characterise the oceanographic problem has been selected from five different areas of the Atlantic ocean (five water masses with different properties). This has been done because it is useless to represent the 150000 instances in one Figure. Figure 4 shows the classification ability of the MLHM proposed, which gives a rather better separation of the individual five oceanographic areas found in the data set. We are using an unsupervised learning technique in the field of artificial neural networks so generally we do not need any information about the data. Of course, the data must have some kind of structure (correlation, redundancy, etc). The only condition that we need is to set the dimension of the output vector (M), i.e. the number of output neurons, to be greater than the number of patterns or factors (number of water masses, in this case), otherwise some outputs will have found two or more patters simultaneously. We have used 10 output neurons in this experiment.

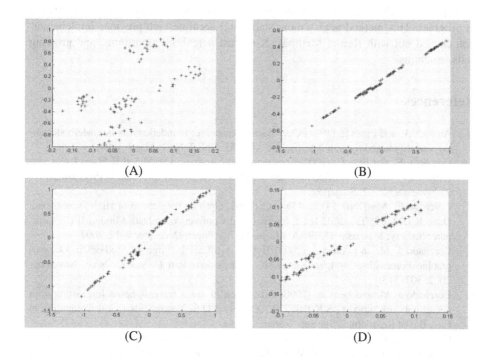

Fig. 4. Figure A shows the results of the Maximum Likelihood Hebbian learning network using $p=0$. The Maximum Likelihood Method identifies a projection, which spread the data out identifying the five different clusters. Figure B presents the result obtained with the PCA method, Figure C shows the clusters obtained with the Kernel Method and Figure D presents the results obtained with the GCS methods.

4   Conclusion

We have demonstrated a new technique for case/instance indexing and retrieval, which could be used to construct instance based reasoning systems. The basis of the method is a Maximum Likelihood Hebbian Learning algorithm. This method provides us with a very robust model for indexing the data and retrieving instances without any need of information about the structure of the data set in advance. It has been shown to give extremely accurate results on an exemplar-forecasting task: our results of 0.0167 °C error are among the best we have ever achieved on this data set. This is very important in the identification of fronts in these large bodies of water particularly since such fronts have an extremely adverse effect on underwater communications. The retrieval of the best matching instance is a very simple operation using the proposed method and presents no major computational obstacles. The whole system may be used with any number-based data set; an area of ongoing research is the application of algorithms that combine MLHL and kernel methods. We believe that this method may be improved with Competence-coverage techniques [24], and several experiments are in progress. This method is also more stable and accurate than previous implementation carried out with Kernel Methods, K-nearest neighbour algorithms, and growing cells structures.

References

1. Aamodt A. and Plaza E. (1994) Case-Based Reasoning: foundational Issues, Methodological Variations, and System Approaches. AICOM. Vol. 7. No 1. March 1994.
2. Corchado E. and Fyfe C. (2002) Maximum and Minimum Likelihood Hebbian Rules as a Exploratory Method. 9th International Conference on Neural Information Processing. 18–22 November 2002. Singapore.
3. Corchado E., MacDonald D. and Fyfe C. (2002) Optimal Projections of High Dimensional Data. ICDM '02. The 2002 IEEE International Conference on Data Mining, IEEE Computer Society; Maebashi TERRSA, Maebashi City, Japan December 9–12, 2002
4. Corchado J. M. and Aiken J. (2003) Hybrid Artificial Intelligence Methods in Oceanographic Forecasting Models. IEEE SMC Transactions Part C. Vol.32, No.4, November 2002: 307–313.
5. Corchado J. M. and Lees B. (2000) Adaptation of cases for case-based forecasting with neural network support., S.K Pal, T.S. Dillon and D.S. Yeung (Eds.), Soft Computing in Case Based Reasoning", Springer Verlag, London.
6. Corchado J. M., Aiken J. and Rees N. (2001) Artificial Intelligence Models for Oceanographic Forecasting. Plymouth Marine Laboratory, U.K, 2001. ISBN: 0-9519618-4-5.
7. Diaconis P. and Freedman D. (1984) Asymptotics of Graphical Projections. The Annals of Statistics. 12(3): 793–815.
8. Fdez-Riverola F. and Corchado J. M. (2003) FSfRT: Forecasting System for Red Tides. Applied Intelligence. Soft Computing in Case-Based Reasoning. In press. ISSN: 0924-669X.
9. Fyfe C. and Baddeley R. (1995) Non-linear data structure extraction using simple Hebbian networks, Biological Cybernetics 72(6), p533–541.
10. Fyfe C. and Corchado J. M. (2001) Automating the construction of CBR Systems using Kernel Methods. International Journal of Intelligent Systems. Vol 16, No. 4, April 2001. ISSN 0884–8173.
11. Fyfe C. and MacDonald D. (2001) ε– Insensitive Hebbian learning, Neuro Computing.
12. Fyfe C. and Corchado E. (2002a). Maximum Likelihood Hebbian Rules. 10th European Symposium on Artificial Neural Networks, ESANN"2002, Bruges, April 24-25-26, 2002.
13. Fyfe C. and Corchado E., (2002b) A New Neural Implementation of Exploratory Projection Pursuit. IDEAL2002 Third International Conference on Intelligent Data Engineering and Automated Learning. Manchester, UK . 12–14 August, 2002.
14. Hyvärinen A. (2001) Complexity Pursuit: Separating interesting components from time series. Neural Computation, 13: 883–898.
15. Hyvärinen A. Karhunen J. and Oja E. (2002) Independent Component Analysis, Wiley, ISBN 0-471-40540-X.
16. Karhunen J. and Joutsensalo J. (1994.) Representation and Separation of Signals Using Non-linear PCA Type Learning, Neural Networks, 7:113–127.
17. Kashyap R. L., Blaydon C. C., and Fu K. S. (1994.) Stochastic Approximation. in A Prelude to Neural Networks: Adaptive and Learning Systems, Ed Jerry M. Mendel, Prentice Hall, ISBN 0-13-147448-0.

18. Lai P. L., Charles D., and Fyfe C., (2000.) Seeking Independence using Biologically In-spired Artificial Neural Networks, in Developments in Artificial Neural Network Theory : Independent Component Analysis and Blind Source Separation, Editor M. A. Girolami, Springer Verlag.
19. Lees B. and Corchado J. M. (1999) Integrated case-based approach to problem solving. In: Lecture Notes in Artificial Intelligence 1570, XPS-99: Knowledge-Based Systems – Sur-vey and Future Directions, edited by Frank Puppe, Springer, Berlin, pp. 157–166.
20. MacDonald D. and Fyfe C. (2000) The Kernel self-organising map. In R.J Howlett and L.C. Jain, editors, Fourth International Conference on Knowledge-based Intelligent Engi-neering Sustems and Allied Technologies, KES 20000.
21. Oja E. (1989) Neural Networks, Principal Components and Subspaces, International Journal of Neural Systems, 1:61–68.

An Evaluation of the Usefulness of Case-Based Explanation

Pádraig Cunningham, Dónal Doyle, and John Loughrey

Department of Computer Science
Trinity College Dublin
Padraig.Cunningham@cs.tcd.ie

Abstract. One of the perceived benefits of Case-Based Reasoning (CBR) is the potential to use retrieved cases to explain predictions. Surprisingly, this aspect of CBR has not been much researched. There has been some early work on knowledge-intensive approaches to CBR where the cases contain explanation patterns (e.g. SWALE). However, a more knowledge-light approach where the case similarity is the basis for explanation has received little attention. To explore this, we have developed a CBR system for predicting blood-alcohol level. We compare explanations of predictions produced by this system with alternative rule-based explanations. The case-based explanations fare very well in this evaluation and score significantly better than the rule-based alternative.

1 Introduction

Most tutorials on Case-Based Reasoning (CBR) would point to the advantages arising from the transparency and interpretability of the CBR approach. This transparency has particular advantages for explanation as pointed out by Leake (1996):

> *"...neural network systems cannot provide explanations of their decisions and rule-based systems must explain their decisions by reference to their rules, which the user may not fully understand or accept. On the other hand, the results of CBR systems are based on actual prior cases that can be presented to the user to provide compelling support for the system's conclusions."*

Given this potential for explanation it is perhaps surprising that explanation is not more prominent in CBR applications and is not a bigger issue in CBR research and development. Indeed, a study of physicians' expectations and demands on computer based consultation systems found that the ability to explain reasoning was the single most important requirement for an advice giving system in medicine (Ramberg 1996).

In this paper we question the usefulness of case-based explanation (CBE) to users of decision support systems. Are explanations based on specific examples as useful as those based on general principles? Although we are interested in this question from the perspective of medical decision support systems we have used a different domain for the evaluation. We have developed a case-based Breathalyser system to predict whether a subject is over the drink-driving limit based on a case-like description of

K.D. Ashley and D.G. Bridge (Eds.): ICCBR 2003, LNAI 2689, pp. 122–130, 2003.
© Springer-Verlag Berlin Heidelberg 2003

the subject (see Fig. 2). We have developed this application because of the ready availability of subjects with some knowledge of the domain who can provide feedback on the explanations. It would be very difficult to get the same volume of feedback from medical practitioners in a specialised domain.

Before describing the evaluation we have performed, we review existing research on explanation in CBR in section 2. In this evaluation we compare two distinct approaches, the knowledge-light approach and the more knowledge-intensive approach. In section 3 the experimental set-up for the evaluation is described. The details of the two alternative approaches to explanation (i.e. rule-based and case-based) that have been evaluated are described in section 4. The results of the evaluation are presented in section 5. The paper finishes with some conclusions and recommendations for future work in section 6.

2   Case-Based Explanation

As stated in the Introduction, our review of the literature suggests that work on CBE can be divided into knowledge-light and knowledge-intensive approaches. However, all approaches to explanation in CBR will share an important characteristic. On the spectrum of possibilities between 'specific' and 'general', the case-based explanation will be at the specific end of the spectrum. When discussing explanation patterns (see (Kass & Leake, 1988) for instance) Kolodner (1996) argues that what differentiates CBR from similar ideas in model-based reasoning is the concreteness of the cases. So, whether knowledge-light or knowledge intensive, case-based explanation is *case-based*.

There is still disagreement among CBR researchers on the implications CBR has for knowledge engineering effort. Some, such as Mark et al. (1996) argue that CBR still entails a "full knowledge acquisition effort". Others would argue that knowledge-intensive CBR is missing the point of CBR, which is the potential CBR has to *finesse* knowledge engineering effort by manipulating cases that are compiled chunks of knowledge. These alternative views of CBR are reflected in the different approaches to CBE.

2.1   Knowledge-Intensive CBE

A knowledge-intensive approach to CBE will incorporate mechanisms such as rule-based or model-based inference that can be used to generate explanations. Developing knowledge-intensive case-based applications will, in the words of Mark et al (1996), involve a "full scale knowledge acquisition effort". Amongst the earliest examples of this approach is the work on SWALE and its descendants (the CBR systems not the horses). These systems incorporate explanation patterns (XPs) that can be used for explanation. Typically, these XPs are pretty specific, e.g. the JANIS-JOPLIN-XP. Even the more abstract XPs are pretty specific; the MAFIA-REVENGE-XP can be instantiated directly. The key point is that the system designers have incorporated model-based representations that can be used for explanation.

XPs are made up of facts and belief-support nodes that link the facts together. The facts include the premise, intermediate facts and conclusions. The intermediate facts are inferred from the facts. The JANIS JOPLIN XP is shown in Fig. 1. Janis Joplin was a young rock star who died as a result of a drugs overdose. The fact that she is a "Rock Star", leads to intermediate facts that she has "Wealth", "Drug Using Friends" and "Stress". In turn "Wealth and "Drug-Using Friends", leads to another intermediate fact that she has "Access to Drugs" and so forth. Finally this explanation pattern concludes with "Death" due to a "Drug Overdose". The idea with SWALE is that this explanation can be invoked to explain target cases that map appropriately to this explanation pattern.

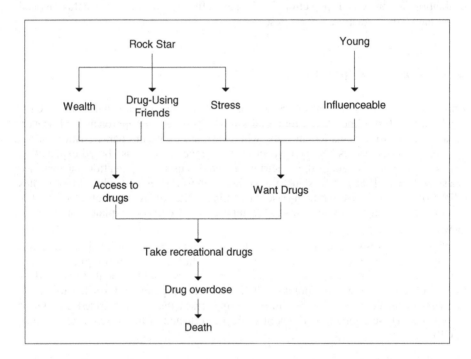

Fig. 1. An illustration of the JANIS JOPLIN XP from (Kass 1988).

Another more recent example of a knowledge-intensive approach to CBE is the DIRAS system for assessing long-term risks in diabetes (Armengol et al., 2001). The approach in DIRAS is more dynamic than that in the SWALE systems in that the explanation is built at run-time using a process called *Lazy Induction of Descriptions.*

2.2 Knowledge-Light CBE

The majority of commercially successful CBR applications have been knowledge-light systems; usually retrieval-only systems or mixed initiative systems involving interactive adaptation. In CBR systems that use a feature-value based representation, the retrieved cases can be used in explanation as follows:

"The system predicts that the outcome will be X *because that was the outcome in case* C1 *that differed from the current case only in the value of feature* F *which was* f2 *instead of* f1.
In addition the outcome in C2 was also X *..."*

Explanation in these terms (i.e. expressed in the vocabulary of the case features) will not always be adequate but in some situations, such as in medical decision support, it can be quite useful. The main difference between this and the more knowledge-intensive approach described in section 2.1 is that the explanation is expressed in terms of similarity only. The more knowledge-intensive system still produce explanations that reference the retrieved case but the explanation is expressed in terms of causal interactions rather than simple similarity.

A good example of knowledge-light explanation in CBR is the Strategist system developed by McSherry (2001) for fault diagnosis in a toy domain. Strategist organizes its cases into a decision tree using decision tree induction and it can use that tree to explain its reasoning. Explanation in Strategist is focused on explanation of reasoning (for example the relevance of a question) rather than explanation of diagnoses/predictions. Another example of the knowledge-light approach to CBE is the CARES system for predicting recurrence of colorectal cancer developed by Ong, et al. (1997). The approach to explanation in the CARES system is to present the feature-value representations of the retrieved cases and the target case to the user for examination. The commercial CBR tool Orenge from Empolis* also relies on comparison to retrieved cases as a mechanism for explanation.

3   The Experiment

Eight unique problem cases were used in the experiment. 37subjects were presented with each of these problem cases three times, once with predictions and case-based explanations, once with predictions and rule-based explanations (RBE) and once with predictions only without explanation. The rule-based and case-based explanations were presented together but the order was varied to avoid any bias due to familiarity. The format in which the cases and explanations were presented to the user is shown in Fig. 2 and Fig. 3. Fig. 2 shows the case-based explanation while Fig. 3 shows the rule-based explanation.

The subjects were asked to score how convinced they were by the explanations on a 5-point scale (No, Maybe No, Maybe, Maybe Yes, Yes). In the evaluation of the results these scores were interpreted as numeric values from 1-5. The target cases were presented in turn to the subjects and the subjects were able to backtrack to change their scores.

The subjects were all staff and postgraduate students in the TCD Computer Science Department and it was explained to them that the objective of the experiment was to compare the usefulness of case-based and rule-based explanation.

---

* See the White Paper on Orenge available at www.empolis.com.

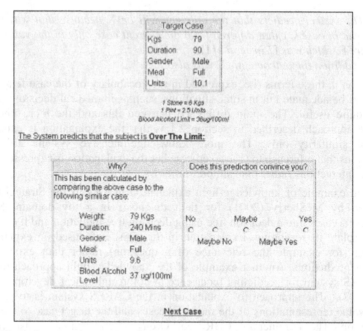

Fig. 2. An example case-based prediction and explanation frrm the experiment.

Target Case

Kgs	79
Duration	90
Gender	Male
Meal	Full
Units	10.1

1 Stone = 6 Kgs
1 Pint = 2.5 Units
Blood Alcohol Limit = 36ug/100ml

The System predicts that the subject is **Over the Limit**

Why?	Does this prediction convince you?
Satisfies the following rules: Rule: Units > 9.1 AND Kgs > 7.1 AND Meal = Full	No ○ ○ ○ Maybe ○ ○ Yes Maybe No Maybe Yes

Next Case

Fig. 3. An example rule-based prediction and explanation from the experiment.

4 The Prediction and Explanation Systems

89 cases were collected in pubs in the centre of Dublin. The alcohol measurements were taken with an Alcho Sensor IV* breath testing system which is an 'evidence

---

* see www.intox.com

grade' system. In addition to the alcohol measurements, the attributes shown in Table 1 were recorded for each case.

Table 1. The features gathered for the experiment.

Age	Weight
Gender	Height
Elapsed Time (time since last drink)	Meal (None, Snack, Lunch, Full)
Duration (time spent drinking)	Amount (in Units)
	Blood Alcohol Content

Using a Wrapper-based feature selection technique, we found that using only the features; Weight, Gender, Meal, Duration and Amount produced the best results. Thus the case-based and rule-based prediction and explanation systems were built using 89 cases described by five features. The systems were implemented using the nearest neighbour and decision tree classification code available in the Weka toolkit.[**]

4.1 Rule-Based Explanation

Weka provides the J48 algorithm, a decision tree-learning algorithm, which is an extension of the C4.5 algorithm (Quinlan, 1993). This code was used to produce the decision tree from which the rules were extracted (see Figure 3). Weka provides code for automatically extracting rules from a decision tree. This code was not used as the rules it produces are designed to be applied in order. Because of this, rules late in the order are incomplete if used as explanations. Instead we extracted complete rules with a comprehensive rule describing each of the possible paths from the root to the leaves of the tree shown in Figure 3. When a new case is passed to the resulting rule-based system for classification, the prediction is produced from the rule that covers it and the rule is also returned as explanation (see Fig. 3). A 10-fold cross validation assessment of the accuracy of the prediction system produced a figure of 80%.

4.2 Case-Based Explanation

The Case-Based Explanation system was also developed on top of Weka. Given the feature values for a query case, the system looks at all the existing cases and retrieves the most similar cases from the Case-Base. In the similarity metric used, nominal values such as Gender and Meal simply contribute binary similarity scores.

The accuracy of the Case-Based Prediction system was assessed using 10 fold cross-validation. Using a single nearest neighbour for prediction yielded an accuracy of 81%. In the evaluation, the nearest neighbour was returned as an explanation of the prediction.

[**] www.cs.waikato.ac.nz/ml/weka

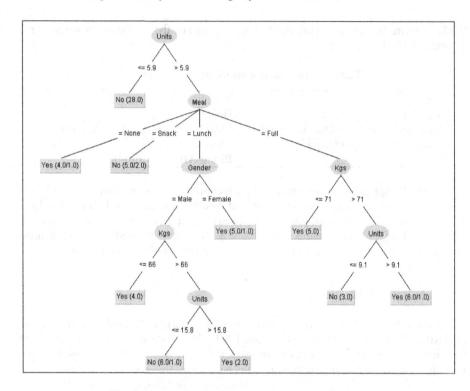

Fig. 4. The decision tree on which the RBE system is built.

5 Evaluation

In all 37 subjects evaluated 24 predictions, eight in each category. An incorrect prediction coupled with a poor explanation was included in each category to help assess the attention paid by the subjects to the evaluation. The average rating for these poor predictions was 1.5 while the average for the other predictions was 3.9 (on a scale of 1-5). The ratings for these poor predictions were not considered further in the evaluation. The averages of the remaining ratings are shown in Fig. 5.

Two things to note are the strong performance of the Case-Based explanation and the fact that the predictions without explanation were still found to be quite convincing. Statistical tests were run on the data and a paired t-test showed that the CBE was better than the RBE (P value = 0.0005) and better than No Explanation (P value = 0.005). If we count the Wins and Draws between the rule-based and case-based alternatives we find that CBE wins 105 times, RBE wins 48 times and there are 106 draws.

This disappointing performance of RBE is not surprising if we remember the work of Clancey on explanation in Mycin/Guidon. Clancey (1983) found that simple rule structures linking symptoms to diagnoses were not very useful as explanations – well, not in a tutoring context anyway. Despite this negative assessment of RBE from

Clancey, rules are the dominant mechanism for explanation in data-mining research (Han & Kamber, 2001). So the preliminary results reported here suggest that the explanation potential of CBR could have significant impact if explored further.

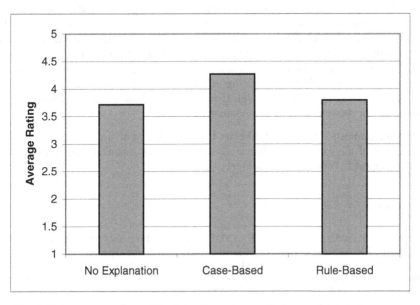

Fig. 5. The average ratings of the three alternative prediction and explanation systems.

6 Conclusions and Future Work

This evaluation provides some support for the use of CBR in applications where explanation of predictions is important. It shows that, in this application area, CBE is considered more convincing than the rule-based alternative. Because of the nature of this type of evaluation it is difficult to perform evaluations across a range of data-sets or domains. So what are the caveats associated with drawing conclusions from this single evaluation?

- Because of the inherent instability of decision tree building algorithms there are alternative decision trees that would have produced different rules that might have scored better.
- CBE may inherently suit this task because it considers all features in the decision making process. The RBE only considers a subset of features and this may be more acceptable in other domains.
- The comparatively simple case representation may favour CBE. It might fare less well with more complex cases (i.e. more features).
- Results may be different in domains where the subjects have more insight or less insight into the underlying mechanisms.

6.1   Future Work

We plan to perform similar evaluations in other domains to explore this question further.

This detailed exploration of the usefulness of knowledge-light CBE suggests ways in which the process might be improved. Comments from evaluators suggest that cases that are perceived to be between the target case and the decision surface are more convincing. For instance, if the target has consumed 10 units and is predicted to be over the limit then a case of 8 units in support of that prediction is more convincing than one of 12 units (other things being equal). It is difficult to select for this using conventional similarity based retrieval. However, order-based retrieval (Bridge 2002) might allow for the selection of more convincing cases.

Acknowledgements. We would like to thank Ruth Byrne for her advice on the organization of the experiment. We would like to thank Science Foundation Ireland for their support in funding this research.

References

Armengol, E., Palaudàries, A., Plaza, E., (2001) Individual Prognosis of Diabetes Long-term Risks: A CBR Approach. Methods of Information in Medicine. Special issue on prognostic models in Medicine. vol. 40, pp. 46–51

Bridge, D., Ferguson, A., (2002) An Expressive Query Language for Product Recommender Systems, *Artificial Intelligence Review*, vol.18, pp.269–307

Clancey, W. J. (1983) The epistemology of a rule-based expert system: A framework for explanation, *Artificial Intelligence*, 20, 3, 215–251.

Kass, A.M., Leake, D.B., (1988) Case-Based Reasoning Applied to Constructing Explanations, in Proceedings of 1988 Workshop on Case-Based Reasoning, ed. J. Kolodner, pp190–208, Morgan Kaufmann. San Mateo, Ca

Kohavi, R., John, G., (1998) The Wrapper Approach, in *Feature Selection for Knowledge Discovery and Data Mining*, H. Liu and H. Motoda (eds.), Kluwer Academic Publishers, pp33–50.

Kolodner, J., (1996) Making the Implicit Explicit: Clarifying the Principles of Case-Based Reasoning, in Leake, D.B. (ed) Case-Based Reasoning: Experiences, Lessons and Future Directions, pp349–370, MIT Press

Leake, D., B., (1996) CBR in Context: The Present and Future, in Leake, D.B. (ed) Case-Based Reasoning: Experiences, Lessons and Future Directions, pp3–30, MIT Press

Mark, W., Simoudis, E., Hinkle, D., (1996) Case-Based Reasoning: Expectations and Results, in Leake, D.B. (ed) Case-Based Reasoning: Experiences, Lessons and Future Directions, pp269–294, MIT Press

McSherry, D. (2001) Interactive Case-Based Reasoning in Sequential Diagnosis. *Applied Intelligence* 14 , 65–76

Ong, L.S., Sheperd, B., Tong, L.C., Seow-Choen, F., Ho, Y.H., Tong, L.C., Ho Y.S, Tan, K. (1997) The Colorectal Cancer Recurrence Support (CARES) System. Artificial Intelligence in Medicine 11(3): 175–188.

Quinlan, J.R., (1993) C4.5: Programs for Machine Learning, Morgan Kaufmann, San Mateo, Ca, USA.

Ramberg, R., (1996) Constructing and Testing Explanations in a Complex Domain, in *Computers in Human Behaviour*, Vol 12, No 1, pp. 29–48.

Riesbeck, C.K., (1988) An Interface for Case-Based Knowledge Acquisition, in *Proceedings of 1988 Workshop on Case-Based Reasoning*, ed. J. Kolodner, pp312–326, Morgan Kaufmann. San Mateo, Ca.

Adaptation Guided Retrieval Based on Formal Concept Analysis*

Belén Díaz-Agudo, Pablo Gervás, and Pedro A. González-Calero

Dep. Sistemas Informáticos y Programación
Universidad Complutense de Madrid, Spain
{belend, pgervas, pedro}@sip.ucm.es

Abstract. In previous papers [5,4] we have proved the usefulness of Formal Concept Analysis (FCA) as an inductive technique that elicits knowledge embedded in a case library. The dependency knowledge implicitly contained in the case base is captured during the FCA process in the form of dependence rules among the attributes describing the cases. A substitution-based adaptation process is proposed that profits from these dependence rules since substituting an attribute may require to substitute dependant attributes. Dependence rules will guide an interactive query formulation process which favors retrieving cases where successful adaptations can be accomplished. In this paper we exemplify the use of FCA to help query formulation in an application to generate Spanish poetry versions of texts provided by the user.

1 Introduction

Structured domains are characterized by the fact that there is an intrinsic dependency between certain elements in the domain. Considering these dependencies leads to better performance of CBR systems and it is an important factor for determining the relevance of the cases stored in a case base [10,5]. Although dependency knowledge could be manually identified from a domain expert, we consider that the case library itself can be used as the dependency knowledge source as it contains useful knowledge beyond the individual specific pieces of problem solving experiences to be reused.

We use Formal Concept Analysis (FCA) [13,7] as an inductive technique that elicits knowledge embedded in a concrete case library. In previous papers [5,4] we have described the use of FCA to support CBR application designers in the task of discovering knowledge embedded in a case base. The application of FCA provides an internal view of the conceptual structure of the case base and it uncovers patterns of regularity among the cases. In [5] we showed how the dependency knowledge implicitly contained in the case base is captured during the FCA process in the form of dependence rules among the attributes describing the cases. These dependence rules are used to guide the process of formulating a CBR query. Moreover, the concept lattice that results from the FCA application can be used as a case organization structure: the formal concepts represent maximal groupings of cases with shared properties. Within this structure we

---

* Supported by the Spanish Committee of Science & Technology (TIC2002-01961)

K.D. Ashley and D.G. Bridge (Eds.): ICCBR 2003, LNAI 2689, pp. 131–145, 2003.
© Springer-Verlag Berlin Heidelberg 2003

can access together all the cases sharing a set of properties with the given query, because they are grouped under the same concept. The extracted knowledge is dependent on the case library and it will be used to complete the knowledge already acquired by other techniques of domain modelling. In [4] we focused in classification based retrieval and the utility of Galois lattices as structures to classify and retrieve planning cases that are described by the goals satisfied by the solution and the precondition properties needed to apply the case solution. In this paper we review the use of FCA to extract dependency knowledge from a case base an exemplify it using an specific application to generate Spanish poetry versions of texts provided by the user [2]. In this application we define processes for adaptation guided retrieval [12] and substitution-based adaptation that can be enhanced by applying dependency knowledge to take into account correlated substitutions.

The poetry generation application is introduced in Section 2. Section 3 describes the basics of the Formal Concept Analysis technique and how we are applying it for knowledge elicitation on case bases. Section 4 describes how this knowledge can be used during the query formulation and retrieval tasks. Section 5 briefly describes how the rest of the CBR cycle works within this application. Finally the conclusions and limitations of our approach are discussed.

2   Poetry Generation with CBR

In [2] we chose poetry generation as an example of the use of the COLIBRI (Cases and Ontology Libraries Integration for Building Reasoning Infrastructures) system. COLIBRI assists during the design of knowledge intensive CBR (KI-CBR) systems that combine cases with various knowledge types and reasoning methods. It is based on CBROnto [3,6], an ontology that incorporates reusable CBR knowledge and serves as a domain-independent framework to develop CBR systems based on generic components like domain ontologies and Problem Solving Methods (PSMs).

Our approach to poetry generation with CBR uses an specific process that is conceptually based on a procedure universally employed when not-specially-talented individuals need to personalise a song, for instance, for a birthday, a wedding, or a particular event: pick a song that everybody knows and rewrite the lyrics to suit the situation under consideration. This particular approach to the problem of generating customised lyrics or poetry has the advantage of being easily adapted to a formal CBR architecture. No claims whatsoever regarding the general suitability of this approach for poetry composition in a broad sense should be read into this particular choice.

This paper does not aim to describe all the details application but to exemplify one of the CBROnto PSMs. Interested readers will find the details of the application in [2]. The following sections introduce the basic rules of Spanish poetry and how the required knowledge and the cases are represented in this application.

2.1 Basic Rules of Spanish Poetry

Formal poetry in Spanish is governed by a set of rules that determine a valid verse form and a valid strophic form. A given poem can be analysed by means of these rules in order to establish what strophic form is being used. Another set of rules is applied to analyse (or *scan*) a given verse to count its metrical syllables.

Given that words are divided into syllables and each word has a unique syllable that carries the prosodic stress, the constraints that the rules have to account for are the following:

Metric Syllable Count. Specific strophic forms require different number of syllables to a line. Metric syllables may be run together thereby shortening the syllable count of the line involved. When a word ends in a vowel and the following word starts with a vowel, the last syllable of the first word and the first syllable of the following word constitute a single syllable (*synaloepha*).

Word Rhyme. Each strophic form requires a different rhyming pattern.

Stanza or Strophic Form. For the purpose of this application only poems of the following regular strophic forms are considered: *cuarteto*, a stanza of four lines of 11 syllables where the two outer lines rhyme together and the two inner lines rhyme together; and *terceto*, a stanza of three lines of 11 syllables where the either the two outer lines rhyme together or the three lines have independent rhymes.

2.2 Poetry Domain Knowledge Ontology and Poem Case Base

The COLIBRI approach to building KI-CBR systems takes advantage of the explicit representation of domain knowledge. An initial sketch of an ontology about the domain of application has been developed for purposes of illustration, resulting in a knowledge base containing 86 concepts, 22 relations and 606 individuals [2].

Cases describe a solved problem of poem composition. We describe cases using the CBROnto case description language and domain knowledge terminology. We choose a case representation structure where both description and solution are linked to a correct poem.

Within our representation, a poem is a text made up of words, and built up as a series of stanzas, which are groups of a definite number of lines of a specific length in syllables, satisfying a certain rhyme pattern. Each word is represented as an individual which is an instance of the domain concept *Word* and is described in terms of the following attributes: the number of syllables that the word has, the position of the stressed syllable of the word counted from the beginning of the word, the rhyme of the word, whether the word begins or ends with a vowel, and the part-of-speech tags associated with that word. There are currently 4872 words in the vocabulary, of which 313 appear in the cases and the rest is additional vocabulary available for adaptation during the generation of new poems.

Part-of-speech Tags. In our representation each word of the available vocabulary has one Part Of Speech (POS) tag representing the syntactical category of this word. To this purpose we use the tags used in the CRATER project and its POS tagger [8] that extracts automatically the syntactical category associated to a given word. These tags are common and easy to understand so that not specific linguistic knowledge is required to use the system. What follows is an example of a poem of the case base and the POS tags associated to its words.

marchitara la rosa el viento helado
todo lo mudara la edad ligera
por no hacer mudanza en su costumbre[1]
VLFI3S ARTDFS NCFS ARTDMS NCMS ADJGMS
QUXMS ARTDNS VLFI3S ARTDFS NCFS ADJGFS
PREP NEG VLINF NCFS PREP PPOSPS NCFS

The poem uses a subset of the more than 300 POS tags identified in this project. In particular it uses the following POS tags:

- VLFI3S Lexical verb. Indicative future tense third person singular
- VLINF Lexical verb. Infinitive
- ARTDFS Feminine singular definite article
- ARTDMS Masculine singular definite article
- ADJGFS Feminine singular general positive adjective
- ADJGMS Masculine singular general positive adjective
- NCFS Feminine singular common noun
- NCMS Masculine singular common noun
- ARTDNS Neuter singular definite article
- PREP Preposition

For the sake of a comprehensive exposition we can not use the whole set of tags but we present a reduced example using the subset of tags appearing in the poem example.

3   Formal Concept Analysis

FCA [13,7] is a mathematical approach to data analysis based on the lattice theory of Garret Birkhoff [1]. It provides a way to identify groupings of objects with shared properties. FCA is especially well suited when we have to deal with a collection of items described by properties. This is a clear characteristic of the case libraries where there are cases described by features. A *formal context* is defined as a triple $\langle G, M, I \rangle$ where there are two sets G (of objects) and M (of attributes), and a binary (incidence) relation $I \subseteq G{\times}M$, expressing which attributes describe each object (or which objects are described using an attribute), i.e., $(g, m) \in I$ if the object g carries the attribute m, or m is a descriptor of the object g. With a general perspective, a concept represents a group of objects and is described by using *attributes* (its intent) and *objects* (its extent). The extent covers all objects belonging to the concept while the intent comprises all attributes (properties) shared by all those objects. With $A \subseteq G$ and $B \subseteq M$ the following operator (*prime*) is defined as:

---

[1] The icy wind will cause the rose to wilt,// and all things will be changed by fickle time,// so as to never change its own routine.

$$A\prime = \{m \in M \mid (\forall g \in A)(g, m) \in I\}$$
$$B\prime = \{g \in G \mid (\forall m \in B)(g, m) \in I\}$$

A pair (A,B) where $A \subseteq G$ and $B \subseteq M$, is said to be a *formal concept* of the context $\langle G, M, I \rangle$ if $A' = B$ and $B' = A$. A and B are called the *extent* and the *intent* of the concept, respectively.

It can also be observed that, for a concept (A, B), $A'' = A$ and $B'' = B$, which means that all objects of the extent of a formal concept, have all the attributes of the intent of the concept, and that there is no other object in the set G having all the attributes of (the intent of) the concept.

The set of all the formal concepts of a context $\langle G, M, I \rangle$ is denoted by $\beta(G, M, I)$. The most important structure on $\beta(G, M, I)$ is given by the subconcept-superconcept order relation denoted by $\leq$ and defined as follows: $(A1, B1) \leq (A2, B2)$ if $A1 \subseteq A2$ (which is equivalent to $B2 \subseteq B1$ see [7]).

Basic Theorem for Concept Lattices. [13]
Let $\langle G, M, I \rangle$ be a context. Then $\langle \beta(G, M, I), \leq \rangle$ is a complete lattice, called the concept lattice of the context $\langle G, M, I \rangle$, for which infimum and supremum can be described as follows:

$$Inf\beta(G, M, I) = \left[\bigwedge_\alpha (A_\alpha, B_\alpha) = \bigcap_\alpha A_\alpha, \left(\bigcup_\alpha B_\alpha \right)'' \right]$$

$$Sup\beta(G, M, I) = \left[\bigvee_\alpha (A_\alpha, B_\alpha) = \left(\bigcup_\alpha A_\alpha \right)'', \bigcap_\alpha B_\alpha \right]$$

Graphically, contexts are usually described by cross-tables while concept lattices are visualized by Hasse diagrams. The following sections illustrate how FCA is applied to our simple example, and how the dependency knowledge is extracted from the concept lattice interpretation.

3.1   FCA Application Example

We propose the application of FCA as an automatic technique to elicit the knowledge about attribute co-appearance implicit in a case library.

In the example presented in this paper we apply FCA to compute the concept lattice taking the POS tags of the words as the features under consideration. In the formal context (G, M, I), the set of objects (G) consists of all the cases in the case base[2], the set of attributes (M) consists of all the POS tags appearing in these cases[3], and the incidence relation (I) between G and M indicates that a poem has a word with a certain POS tag.

That way, the lattice captures formal concepts representing the co-appearance of POS tags that appear in the poems of the case base. We are using POS tags and not other characteristics of the words (or poems) because

---

[2] Case7 corresponds to the example case presented in Section 2.2
[3] In the example we are using the reduced set presented in Section 2.2

	ARTDFS	ARTDMS	ARTDNS	ADJGFS	ADJGMS	VLFI3S	VLINF	NCFS	NCMS	PREP
Caso1	☑	☑		☑		.		☑	☑	☑
Caso2	☑	☑		☑		☑	☑	☑		☑
Caso3			☑		☑		☑	☑	☑	☑
Caso4		☑			☑				☑	
Caso5	☑	☑			☑			☑	☑	☑
Caso6	☑	☑		☑	☑			☑	☑	
Caso7	☑	☑	☑	☑	☑	☑	☑	☑	☑	☑
Caso8		☑		☑	☑		☑	☑	☑	☑
Caso9					☑				☑	☑
Caso10								☑	☑	☑

Fig. 1. Case base formal context

of the kind of adaptation that we propose. The high level idea of the adaptation process is to substitute as many words from the poem with words from the query, without loosing the syntactic structure of the poem lines. We assume that the query is a meaningful sentence and, therefore, if we can accommodate those words into the poem in a similar order it is plausible to think that the new poem will reflect, to a certain extent, the original message in the query. In order to maintain the syntactic correctness of the poem, and taking into account that the system has no additional syntactic knowledge, we constrain substitutions to words with exactly the same POS tag.

So, POS tags of the words in the cases are interpreted as formal contexts, and represented by using the incidence tables in Fig. 1.

Besides the cross table representation, there is a graphical representation of formal contexts using Hasse diagrams. Fig. 2 shows Hasse diagrams of the concept lattice associated to the context in Fig. 1. Each node in the diagram represents a formal concept of the context, and the ascending paths of line segments represent the subconcept-superconcept relation. The lattice (Fig. 2) contains exactly the same information that the cross table (Fig. 1), so that the incidence relation I can always be reconstructed from the lattice.

In the Hasse Diagram, labels meaning attributes from the intent are marked by [ ] and labels meaning object from the extent are marked by {}. A lattice node is labelled with the attribute m∈M if it is the upper node having m in its intent; and a lattice node is labelled with the object g∈G if it is the lower node having g in its extent. Using this labelling, each label (attribute or object name) is used exactly once in the diagram. If a node C is labelled by the attribute [m] and the object {g} then all the concepts greater than C (above C in the graph) have the object g in their extents, and all the concepts smaller than C (below C in the graph) have the attribute m in their intents. In a Hasse diagram, the intent of a concept can be obtained as the union of the attributes in its label [ ] and attributes in the labels [ ] of the concepts above it in the lattice. Conversely, the extent of a concept, is obtained as the union of the objects in its label {} and objects in the labels {} of the concepts below it in the lattice.

To reconstruct a row of the original incidence relations in Fig. 1, look for the unique concept C whose label {} contains the object name heading the row and mark with a cross (in the row we are reconstructing) the column of each one of the attributes of the intent of C.

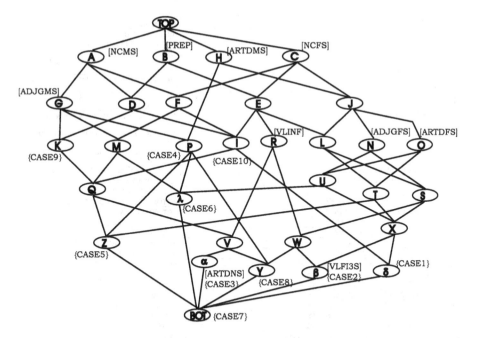

Fig. 2. FCA applied to the poem case base

For example, to reconstruct the cross table row of Case4, mark with a cross the columns corresponding to the intent of concept P in the lattice: [ADJGMS, ARTDMS, NCMS]. Dually, to reconstruct a table column, look for the concept C which label [ ] contains the attribute name heading the column, and mark with a cross the row of each one of the objects of the extent of C. For example, to reconstruct the column named VLINF in the cross table, mark the rows corresponding to the concept R extent: {CASE2, CASE3, CASE7, CASE8}. Figure 3 shows the complete extent and intent of the formal concepts in the diagram of Figure 2.

Besides the hierarchical conceptual clustering of the cases, the concept lattice provides a set of implications between attributes: *dependence rules* [5]. A dependence rule between two attribute sets (written $M1 \rightarrow M2$, where $M1, M2 \subseteq M$) means that any object having all attributes in $M1$ has also all attributes in $M2$. We can read the dependence rules in the graph as follows:

- Each line between nodes labelled with attributes means a dependence rule between the attributes from the lower node to the upper one.
- When there are several attributes in the same label it means that there is a co-appearance of all these attributes for all the cases in the sample.

We can read the following set of dependence rules in Fig. 2. Besides other rules can be obtained by transitivity:
{ADJGMS → NCMS ; VLINF → NCFS ; VLINF → PREP; ADJGFS → NCFS ; ARTDFS → NCFS ; ADJGFS → ARTDMS; ARTDFS → ARTDMS ; VLFI3S → VLINF ; VLFI3S → ADJGFS; VLFI3S → ARTDFS ; ARTDNS → VLINF ; ARTDNS → ADJGMS; ARTDNS → NCMS ; ARTDNS → NCFS ; ARTDNS → PREP }

	EXTENT	INTENT
BOT	CASE7	ARTDFS ARTDMS ARTDNS ADJGFS ADJGMS VLFI3S VLINF NCFS NCMS PREP.
χ	CASE6,CASE7	ARTDFS ARTDMS ADJGFS ADJGMS NCFS NCMS
δ	CASE1,CASE7	ARTDFS ARTDMS ADJGFS NCFS NCMS PREP.
β	CASE2,CASE7	ARTDFS ARTDMS ADJGFS VLFI3S VLINF NCFS PREP
α	CASE3,CASE7	ARTDNS ADJGMS VLINF NCFS NCMS PREP.
Z	CASE5,CASE7	ARTDFS ARTDMS ADJGMS NCFS NCMS PREP.
Y	CASE7,CASE8	ARTDMS ADJGFS ADJGMS VLINF NCFS NCMS PREP
X	CASE1,CASE2,CASE7	ARTDFS ARTDMS ADJGFS NCFS PREP
W	CASE2,CASE7,CASE8	ARTDMS ADJGFS VLINF NCFS PREP
V	CASE3,CASE7,CASE8	ADJGMS VLINF NCFS NCMS PREP.
U	CASE6,CASE1,CASE2,CASE7	ARTDFS ARTDMS ADJGFS NCFS
T	CASE1,CASE2,CASE5,CASE7	ARTDFS ARTDMS NCFS PREP
S	CASE1,CASE2,CASE7,CASE8	ARTDMS ADJGFS NCFS
R	CASE2,CASE3,CASE7,CASE8	VLINF NCFS PREP
Q	CASE3,CASE5,CASE7,CASE8	ADJGMS NCFS NCMS PREP
P	CASE4,CASE6,CASE5,CASE7,CASE8	ARTDMS ADJGMS NCMS
O	CASE6,CASE1,CASE2,CASE5,CASE7	ARTDFS ARTDMS NCFS
N	CASE6,CASE1,CASE2,CASE7,CASE8	ARTDMS ADJGFS NCFS
M	CASE6,CASE3,CASE5,CASE7,CASE8	ADJGMS NCFS NCMS
L	CASE1,CASE2,CASE5,CASE7,CASE8	ARTDMS NCFS PREP
K	CASE3,CASE5,CASE7,CASE8,CASE9	ADJGMS NCMS PREP
J	CASE6,CASE1,CASE2,CASE5,CASE7,CASE8	ARTDMS NCFS
I	CASE1,CASE3,CASE5,CASE7,CASE8,CASE10	NCFS NCMS PREP
H	CASE4,CASE6,CASE1,CASE2,CASE5,CASE7,CASE8	ARTDMS
G	CASE4,CASE6,CASE3,CASE5,CASE7,CASE8,CASE9	ADJGMS NCMS
F	CASE6,CASE1,CASE3,CASE5,CASE7,CASE8,CASE10	NCFS NCMS
E	CASE1,CASE2,CASE3,CASE5,CASE7,CASE8,CASE10	NCFS PREP
D	CASE1,CASE3,CASE5,CASE7,CASE8,CASE9,CASE10	NCMS PREP
C	CASE6,CASE1,CASE2,CASE3,CASE5,CASE7,CASE8,CASE10	NCFS
B	CASE1,CASE2,CASE3,CASE5,CASE7,CASE8,CASE9,CASE10	PREP.
A	CASE4,CASE6,CASE1,CASE3,CASE5,CASE7,CASE8,CASE9,CASE10	NCMS
TOP	CASE1, CASE2, CASE3, CASE4, CASE5, CASE6, CASE7, CASE8, CASE9, CASE10, CASE11, CASE12	∅

Fig. 3. Formal Concepts in the Poetry Domain

We apply FCA as a complementary way of knowledge acquisition and although it is not general knowledge about the domain, but knowledge associated to this concrete case base, it suggests concepts and rules to be added to the general domain model.

4   Retrieval over the Formal Concept Lattice

We propose an organization structure using an inductive technique over the case base, that is guided by the domain knowledge. FCA application to a case library provides a conceptual hierarchy, because it extracts the formal concepts and the hierarchical relations among them, where related cases are clustered according to their shared properties. Concepts in the lattice represent maximal groupings of cases with shared properties, and for a given query, we can access all the cases that share properties with the query at the same time so that they are grouped under the same concept [5]. The order between concepts allows us to structure the library according to the attributes describing the cases. The lower in the graph, the more characteristics can be attributed to the cases; i.e. the more general concepts are higher up than the more specific ones.

Classification based retrieval [11,4] over a concept taxonomy is typically implemented as a three step process: first, a query is represented as an individual and it is classified or recognized in its corresponding place in a certain hierarchy; second, a number of individuals are retrieved from the most specific concepts of which this individual is an instance, and, third, one (or more) of them is chosen by applying a selection function or by the user.

Classification based retrieval on the formal concept lattice makes use of the case library to guide the search. The properties of the lattice justify how this approach always finds the *best* case without travelling through all cases, but taking advantage of the formal concepts clustering the cases.

The query is given as a sequence of words that we want to inspire our poem. In the example, the cases with the largest number of POS tag in common with the query should be retrieved. This way, during adaptation it will be easy to substitute words in the retrieved poem with words from the query without loosing syntactic correctness. Furthermore, dependence rules are used to suggest additional words to be included in the query, not only for retrieval purpose, but also to improve the quality of the resulting poem by imposing correlated substitutions.

Query formulation guided by dependencies

As we have described, FCA applied on a case library allows us to capture its specific dependencies, i.e. it detects regularities satisfied by all the cases in the library. We propose an interactive query definition process where the user is guided towards the definition of "good" queries for this case base. During the query description process, the user provides certain descriptors (POS tags) while the system proposes others using the dependence rules captured during the FCA. This begins an interaction cycle where the system requests the assistance of the user using the knowledge extracted from the case library, so the cases themselves are guiding the query formulation process. That allows an exact matching process where the retrieved cases fulfills all the query POS tags when it is possible (but not its words).

The query completion mechanism applies the dependence rules extracted from the lattice to help the user to make a good query (according to this case base). For instance, rule {ADJGMS → NCMS} indicates that every case having a general adjective that is masculine and singular goes together with a common name that is also masculine and singular. Similarly, rule {ARTDFS → NCFS } indicates that feminine singular definite articles appear together with feminine singular common nouns.

This method uses the rules to complete the user's queries and carry out a process of exact retrieval, in the sense that the retrieved cases satisfy exactly the requirements of the query employed (considering as a requisite that the syntactical categories of the words in the query must be maintained). The lattice in the figure has been constructed using as attributes of the formal context (some of) the syntactic categories of the words that make up the poems in the cases. This process implies that the query is interpreted as the succession of the syntactic categories of the given words.

Dependence rules provide patterns to complete the query with words that are similar to the ones in the cases (which may be used to substitute them during adaptation, given that they have the same syntactic categories). The correction characteristics are determined with respect to the dependence rules that are extracted from the casebase. When completing the query by using the dependence rules, intuitively, what we are doing is to guide the user towards more specific and defined concepts in the lattice. Note, this kind of retrieval over the lattice finds all the cases where all the query descriptors appear, i.e. the cases retrieved as similar are those with the greater number of properties (POS tags) shared with the query. From the adaptation point of view, dependence rules can be seen as imposing additional adaptations induced by the words already in the query. Whenever a word in the query leads to the substitution of a poem word, the system suggests that candidates substitutes should also be provided for words linked to the substituted one by dependence rules.

After that, the system explicitly constructs an individual with the query case description, classifies it in the lattice, and retrieves individuals placed near it. We use a Description Logic (DL) system, LOOM [9], whose recognition module automatically classifies the new individual in its corresponding place in the lattice (belonging to the extent of certain formal concept). All instances classified under the most specific concept the query instance belongs to, are retrieved as similar. Moreover, as this concept will be typically specialized by other most specific concepts, the goal of the query definition module is to guide the user from general concepts towards their subconcepts. The DLs reasoning mechanisms are useful to automatically organize the concept lattice and to keep the cases automatically organized under them. Besides, the instance recognition mechanism is used for the direct retrieval of the siblings of the query individual.

Example 1:
Let us assume that the user chooses "*descansara(VLFI3S)*" (will rest) as a reference word to inspire our poem. The system (using the dependence rules VLFI3S → ADJGFS; VLFI3S → ARTDFS; VLFI3S → VLINF) will suggest to the user that she complete her query with other words having the obtained POS tags: ARTDFS, VLINF, ADJGFS. The system could also offer a list of vocabulary words with a certain POS tag so that the user chooses between them. In particular, there is only one word "la" (the, feminine and singular) with the POS tag ARTDFS[4]. That way the system can directly include this word in the query, and suggest that the user include of other words using the dependence rules: {ARTDFS → ARTDMS ; ARTDFS → NCFS }. The process continues until the user decides to stop the query formulation process and begin the classification based retrieval of cases over the lattice.

Word: descansara(VLFI3S)
Rules: VLFI3S → ARTDFS; VLFI3S → ADJGFS; VLFI3S → VLINF
 − VLFI3S → ARTDFS
   Word: la(ARTDFS) (unique choice)

---

[4] as with ARTDMS and ARTDNS

Rules: ARTDFS → ARTDMS ; ARTDFS → NCFS
- ARTDFS → ARTDMS
  Word: el(ARTDMS) (unique choice)
  Rules: ∅
- ARTDFS → NCFS
  Word: flor(NCFS) (multiple choices)
  Rules: ∅
− VLFI3S → ADJGFS
  Word: helada(ADJGFS)(multiple choices)
  Rules: ADJGFS → NCFS
  - ADJGFS → NCFS
    Word: noche(NCFS)[5]
    Rules: ∅
− VLFI3S → VLINF
  Word: cambiar(VLINF)
  Rules: VLINF → PREP ; VLINF → NCFS
  - VLINF → PREP
    Word: por(PREP). Do not change the original preposition.
    Rules: ∅
  - VLINF → NCFS
    Word: mirada(NCFS)

The resultant query is: *"descansara(VLFI3S) la(ARTDFS) flor(NCFS) la(ARTDFS) noche(NCFS) helada(ADJGFS) mirada(NCFS) por(PREP) el (ARTDMS) cambiar(VLINF)"* (The flower will rest the frozen night glance for a change). This query is represented as an individual that is classified below concept β in the lattice, and CASE7 AND CASE2 are retrieved as they share all the query POS tags (consult β intent in Figure 3).

Example 2:
The user begins a query with the word "maravilloso(ADJGMS)" (marvellous). The system then detects a dependency among the POS tags ADJGMS and NCMS, meaning that in this case library there are no poems that have an ADJGMS and not a NCMS. So, the query formulation process will guide the user towards these concrete cases (instances of the concept G in the lattice). To get the query individual classified below concept G, the system requires a NCMS to participate in the query. The user can provide one word with this POS tag (for example, "dia" –day–). If she does not provide a word the system will use the word that belong to the original poem. As there are no more applicable rules the user could choose between beginning with the retrieval process or giving additional words. At this point the retrieval process would create an instance that would be automatically classified under the concept G. The cases resulting from the current retrieval query are those from the G extent, i.e CASE4,CASE6,CASE3,CASE5,CASE7,CASE8,CASE9 (see Figure 3). If the user wants to choose another query descriptor, she will be guided towards more specific concepts in the lattice[6], i.e. those classified below G. If the user decides finishing

---

[5] As word flor has already this POS tag it is not necessary to include a different word, but it will provide more vocabulary to make substitutions.

[6] Reducing the descriptor set when needed as it was described in [5]

the query, a selection method based on similarity computation (Section 7) is applied to filter one between the seven retrieved cases. Similarity computation will take into account the rest of the word features (as the number of syllables, rhyme, accent, and so on).

Suppose now that the user gives another word: "despertar(VLINF)". The system applies the rules VLINF → NCFS; VLINF → PREP and lets the user include two additional words: "flor(NCFS)" (flower) and "de(PREP)" (of).

The resulting query *"despertar flor de dia maravilloso"* is classified below the concept V in the lattice, and cases CASE3, CASE7, CASE8 are retrieved because they all have as common features the POS tags: ADJGMS, VLINF, NCFS, NCMS, PREP (see V intent in Figure 3).

A dependence rule detects a regularity satisfied by all the cases in the library, but we cannot assure its applicability for every possible case in the domain. In this example, there are some rules representing how to build correct phrases in Spanish, for example, that an adjective always accompanies a noun ADJGMS → NCMS ; ADJGFS → NCFS. These are general rules that will be useful in this domain for every case base. But in the general case, the rules[7] mean a co- apparition of a set of attributes for all the cases in this particular case base but not representing general domain rules, i.e., they are not general rules to build correct phrases in Spanish. For example, the rule ARTDFS → ARTDMS. In any case, the rules are useful to retrieve cases over this particular case base because they represent properties that are satisfied by all the cases in this case base.

The system proposes (and not imposes) certain POS tags using the dependence rules to maintain the semantic sense of certain groups of words. For example, the rule ADJGMS → NCMS suggests changing the noun that accompanies an adjective if the latter changes. If the user does not follow the system suggestion the system will use the original word in the query (or even could randomly select a word from the vocabulary).

Complementary methods of retrieval. As we have explained in previous papers, the advantage of COLIBRI is that it allows us to experiment with different methods that solve the CBR tasks. In the method presented in this paper a retrieval process is carried out guided by the adaptation, since we guide the user to build well-structured query, which will insure retrieval of a case that guarantees a possible substitution for all the given words during adaptation. This takes place under the assumption that only the syntactic categories, and not the rest of the properties of the words (number of syllables, begins or ends with a vowel, rhyme). As a result, the metric of the poem will be disrupted, and a stronger process of revision is required at a later stage. In last year's paper [2] a different method was presented, that retrieved the cases with highest number of syntactic categories in common with the query. This was guided by the same idea of guaranteeing the required possibilities for substitution during adaptation. After the initial filtering, a measure of the similarity value that took into account the rest of the attributes of the words (such as number of syllables, begins or ends with a vowel) was applied. In this way, subsequent revision was minimized.

---

[7] specially in a reduced example as the one used in the paper

5 Illustration of the Rest of the CBR Cycle

To give an idea about how the whole system works, in this section we briefly introduce the adaptation and revision processes.

Lets suppose we are using the query of Example 1 from Section 4: *"descansara(VLFI3S) la(ARTDFS) flor(NCFS) la(ARTDFS) noche(NCFS) helada(ADJGFS) mirada(NCFS) por(PREP) el (ARTDMS) cambiar(VLINF)"*. And the selected case to be adapted is CASE7 that is the one we used to get the example POS tag subset in Section 2.2:

marchitara la rosa el viento helado
todo lo mudara la edad ligera
por no hacer mudanza en su costumbre

The adaptation process consists of substitution certain words in the retrieved poem using the words given by the query (in italic):

descansara la noche el viento helado
todo lo pintara *la flor* helada
por no *cambiar mirada* en *su* primavera

During the proposed adaptation process, we only have considered the POS tags of the substituted words and not the rest of the word properties, like the number of syllables, if a word begins or ends with a vowel (to check the *synaloephas* in the lines), or the rhyme. That is why, even though the substitutions maintain the syntactical correctness of the sentences, the metric of the poem can be damaged and the revision process is in charged of fixing the metric of the poem. In particular the revision process fixes the number of syllables of the verses and their rhyme. The original poem in the example was (before adaptation) a *Terceto* with a stanza of three lines of 11 syllables where the three lines have independent rhymes.

After adaptation, the revision process is in charge of evaluating and, if needed, repairing the proposed poem. It consists of identifying one by one the problems we have to fix and repair them. As we have described in [2] we propose a classification based evaluation method that compares the classification between the adapted case and the retrieved case. The concepts under which the retrieved case is classified in the domain model are used as declarative descriptions of the properties that should be maintained by the adapted case after transformations. In the example the retrieved case is recognized as *Poem*, the stanza is recognized as a *Terceto* and each one of its poem lines are recognized as *Endecasilabos*.

Before substitutions, the copy of the retrieved case that will be adapted has the same classification. If substitutions provokes a change in the concepts the system recognizes for a certain individual, the evaluation task classifies this individual below a concept representing a type of problem. The revision is implemented as the process of substituting words in the adapted poem so that the detected problems can be repaired. In the example we have reused a poem without rhyme, so revision is restricted to the number of syllables of the lines.

In the example, we have substituted a word by other of the same POS tag but possibly different number of syllables. The problem type called *Syllables-count-failure* involves the domain concept *Endecasilabo*. When an individual leaves this concept it is recognized as an instance of *Syllables-count-failure*. The problem type has associated a repair strategy that tries to put the individual representing each line, back as an instance of the goal concept *Endecasilabo*.

The first and third lines have 12 syllables instead of 11. In the first line the words *helado* and *viento* are candidates to be substituted as they do not belong to the query. In order to find a replacement for this word, we search for a word with the same POS tag and one less syllable than the candidate one. For example, the word *triste (ADJGMS)* meets those requirements when substituting *helado*. The next loop tries to repair the number of syllables of the third poem line. The candidate to be substituted is the word *primavera (NCFS)* that is substituted by a word with the same POS tag and three syllables. For example, the word *juventud*. After these substitutions, the number of syllables are automatically recomputed and the individuals representing the lines are re-classified as instances of the concept *Endecasilabo*. The resulting poem is:

descansara la noche el viento triste
todo lo pintara *la flor helada*
por no *cambiar mirada* en *su* juventud[8]

6   Conclusions

FCA has been successfully used in many data analysis applications. We use it as a complementary technique to enrich the domain taxonomy, providing an alternative organization of the case library that facilitates a direct and guided access to the cases. FCA application provides an internal sight of the case base conceptual structure and allows finding patterns and regularities among the cases.

We have described the application of FCA to a CBR system to generate well-formed Spanish poetry versions of texts provided by the user. The knowledge acquired through FCA is used during the query formulation and retrieval tasks. Dependence rules provide patterns to complete the query with words that are similar to the ones in the cases (which may be used to substitute them during adaptation, given that they have the same syntactic categories). Furthermore, dependence rules require new words that impose further adaptations.

Although our approach have clear advantages we have illustrated in this paper, we have identified certain limitations of our proposal. For example, FCA does not allow to extract disjunctive rules like ARTDMS → NCMS OR VLINF, meaning that ARTDMS words always appear together with a NCMS or a VLINF. We think that kind of rules would be also very useful but FCA detects POS tags co-occurrences for *all* the cases in the casebase. That is also the main reason for other limitation: the strong noise sensibility of this technique. Besides, our proposal only consider if a POS tag appears or does not appear in a case, but it does not take into account the situations where several words with the same POS tag belong to the same poem. They are all considered as one POS tag occurrence.

---

[8] The night will ease the sorrowful wind,//and all things will be tinted by the frozen bloom// so as not to exchange a glance in its prime

Even considering these limitations we have illustrated the usefulness of the lattice structure obtained by FCA application, to organize the case base and support an adaptation guided retrieval process that takes into account the semantic meaning of the parts that compose the poems.

References

1. G. Birkhoff. Lattice theory, third editon. In *American Math. Society Coll. Publ. 25, Providence, R.I.* 1973.
2. B. Díaz-Agudo, P. Gervás, and P. A. González-Calero. Poetry generation in COLIBRI. In *Procs 6th European Conference on Case Based Reasoning(ECCBR'02). Springer LNAI 2416, pp. 73-87.* 2002.
3. B. Díaz-Agudo and P. A. González-Calero. An architecture for knowledge intensive CBR systems. In E. Blanzieri and L. Portinale, editors, *Advances in Case-Based Reasoning - (EWCBR'00).* Springer-Verlag, Berlin Heidelberg New York, 2000.
4. B. Díaz-Agudo and P. A. González-Calero. Classification based retrieval using formal concept analysis. In *Procs. of the (ICCBR 2001).* Springer-Verlag, 2001.
5. B. Díaz-Agudo and P. A. González-Calero. Formal concept analysis as a support technique for CBR. In *Knowledge-Based Systems, 14 (3-4), June,.* Elsevier. (ISSN:0950-7051), pp. 163-172., 2001.
6. B. Díaz-Agudo and P. A. González-Calero. CBROnto: a task/method ontology for CBR. In S. Haller and G. Simmons, editors, *Procs. of the 15th International FLAIRS'02 Conference (Special Track on CBR,* pages 101-106. AAAI Press, 2002.
7. B. Ganter and R. Wille. Formal concept analysis. mathematical foundations. 1997.
8. F. S. León. Corpus resources and terminology extraction project (mlap-93/20), 1993.
9. R. Mac Gregor and R. Bates. The loom knowledge representation language. ISI Reprint Series ISI/RS-87-188, University of Southern California, 1987.
10. H. Muñoz-Avila and J. Hullen. Retrieving cases in structured domains by using goal dependencies. In *CBR Research and development(ICCBR'95).* Springer-Verlag, 1995.
11. A. Napoli, J. Lieber, and R. Courien. Classification-based problem solving in cbr. In I. Smith and B. Faltings, editors, *Advances in Case-Based Reasoning - (EWCBR'96).* Springer-Verlag, Berlin Heidelberg New York, 1996.
12. B. Smyth and M. T. Keane. Adaptation-guided retrieval: Questioning the similarity assumption in reasoning. *Artificial Intelligence,* 102(2):249-293, 1998.
13. R. Wille. Conceptual lattices and conceptual knowledge systems. In *Computers and Mathematics with Apps, 23 (6-9),* pages 493-515. 1992.

Club ♣ (Trèfle): A Use Trace Model

Elöd Egyed-Zsigmond, Alain Mille, and Yannick Prié

LIRIS – Université Lyon 1
Bâtiment Nautibus,
69622 Villeurbanne CEDEX, France
Firstname.Surname@lisi.univ-lyon1.fr

Abstract. In this paper we present a use trace model which allows the collection and reuse of user experience, based on a homogeneous and interconnected representation of users, procedures and objects. All these notions form a connected labeled directed graph containing highly connected and explained use traces. This model enables assistance in non trivial, creativity requiring situations. Our model uses the Case Based Reasoning (CBR) paradigm in order to reuse experience. After a formal description of the model we discuss how it can serve to capitalize and re-use experience.

1 Introduction

A constantly growing large public is using computers and networked electronic devices for a large variety of tasks. "Generic" computer applications like text processors, development environments, etc. became a support for these tasks by providing the required resources. We mean by resource a service delivering data, knowledge, processing... The large variety of uses of these applications and the diverse backgrounds of their users make illusory the development of software assistants capable to help *a priori* the user in fulfilling his task.

Indeed, generic applications allow carrying out complex tasks, providing a high degree of freedom to users. By definition, therefore, the creators of these applications cannot precisely know which tasks their tool will enable to carry out. Moreover "democratization" of the software tools let occasional users handle concepts and methods developed by and for specialists. Although applications become more and more user friendly, the tasks for which they are used remain complex. These applications are used by users having a heterogeneous degree of expertise. It is important thus that the user interfaces of these applications can adapt, to be able to fit the needs of a particular task for a particular user. As computers "do not forget", it is interesting to keep the suitably modeled traces of use sessions, in order to be able to reuse them to help the realization of new tasks. The reuse of past use episodes is relevant only if the tasks are complex. We propose a way to manage this complexity.

© Springer-Verlag Berlin Heidelberg 2003

Let us imagine the case of a word processing application we want to use to write a CV. It is the first time that we have this task and we don't know very well nor what this kind of document should have as content nor how it should look like physically. We start writing a title, specifying our name, age and begin describing our professional experiences and education degrees. Let us imagine now that our text processor is equipped with an experience gathering system and that it has been already used by several other people (it thus collected their experience). In this case, after having observed us typing several lines, the system can realize that we are using the application in a manner similar to that of another episode collected before (probably one concerning the writing of another resume). According to this information, the system will be able to propose this example, to help us succeed with our CV writing. It could also propose us to specify at the beginning of the document our address, telephone number and email, and it could help us building a convenient layout.

Beyond this example, we developed and applied this approach to provide help for audiovisual document annotation and search. Let us consider the annotation of audiovisual documents. In this application user assigns keywords drawn from a vocabulary to document fragments. We developed this application in our research team and presented it in [2,9,10]. At the beginning, this task is *ad hoc* and the user assigns key words to the document fragments in a personal and intuitive way. If the system is able to capitalize and re-use experience, it will be able to guide the annotation so as to lead to more coherent and structured descriptions among different users. From the first dropped key words, the system can find other documents annotated by these same words or similar words and propose to supplement the current annotation by the missing characteristics or to integrate it in one of the existing description schemas.

These two different applications (text processing and document annotation) illustrate two manners of helping users carrying out their tasks. The assistance in these situations is not done on the use of the application's user interface, but on the realization of the tasks needing creativity, like annotation, document creation, etc. The system aims to reduce the complexity of concrete tasks, when using tools with several degrees of freedom. The assistance relates to "What to do?" type problems rather than to "How to do?" type problems. In the case of the text processor, the question is more, "what to type ?", not "how to type ?". In the case of a document annotation system, the major difficulty does not come from the manner of using the tool, but from the variety of document contents, the size and richness of the vocabulary and the complexity of description schemas.

In this paper we present a use trace model which allows the collection and reuse of user experience, based on a homogeneous and interconnected representation of users, procedures and objects. This model enables assistance in non trivial, creativity requiring situations. Our model uses the Case Based Reasoning (CBR) paradigm in order to reuse experience [11]. Other systems [1,7,16] use similar strategies to provide help, but they don't integrate the three components (users, procedures, objects) in one model. After a formal description of the model we discuss how it can serve to capitalize and re-use experience.

2   The Basic Idea

We consider that in a software application, **users** handle **objects** using **procedures**.

According to our model we memorize the object handling traces by representing the use sessions, the procedures and the objects, in a single directed connected graph. Each one of the three notions (object, procedure, user) is presented in this section in general. They are instaciated in the graph as *abstract nodes* (referring to abstractions, object, procedure and user type definitions) and *concrete nodes* (referring to instances of objects, procedures and users). In order to be used the general Club♣ model has to be applied to a concrete computer program.

2.1   The Objects

Through the use of a computer program, users can manipulate a set of *objects*. The *use model* contains the *objects* and the relations between them we choose to observe. In a text processor, typical *objects* are : the document, a section, a sentence, a word, ... The *objects* can have relations between them, for example : a document is composed by sections, a document has a model. In the general model we will call a relation between two *objects* of the use model : *contextualization* relations. If A and B are *objects,* we could say : A_is_the_context_of_B, B_is_in_the_context_of_A, but we think that other kinds of relations between objects can be included in the use model. In general relation emphasize that two *objects* explain each other.

For a text processor, the *use model* can be composed, as illustrated in Fig. 1, of words, phrases, sections, titles, document models and documents.

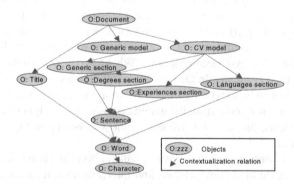

Fig. 1. Example of a *use model* of a text processor application

While observing the use of the application, the objects of the use model are instantiated, instances representing the manipulations carried out on the *concrete objects* through user actions. The use model is to be built for each computer program we want to provide with an intelligent assistant.

2.2   The Procedures

We call *procedure* a manner to use, to manipulate the *objects* of the use model. We call them this way in order to emphasize the difference between these *procedures*, and the task model defined in the knowledge engineering field [3-5,7]. We talk here about a pragmatic point of view on concrete manipulations within a computer program.

Just like it is the case with the relations between *objects* in the use model, the precise semantic of the relations between *procedures* is not predefined in the general Club ♣ model. We will use the term *contextualization relations* to design these relations, expressing the fact that a *procedure* is executed in the context of another *procedure*, or that two *procedures* represent a decomposition of a complex task in two subtasks.

Procedures are typically actions accessible by the menus, buttons and icons of the graphical user interface or simply typing command line instructions. The *procedures* available in a same application are seldom entirely independent.

For example in a text processor the creation of a document passes by the choice of a document model ∥P: Model choice∥ and a suite of section creations ∥P: Create section∥ according to the model. The Fig. 2 presents two arbitrary decompositions in procedures of this task model.

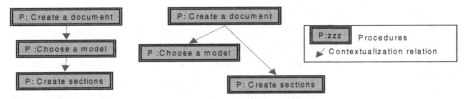

Fig. 2. Two decompositions of a document creation task in a text processor application

We can consider that the *section creation procedure* is executed in the context of a chosen *model*, while a *model* is chosen in the context of a *document creation*. This way we can link the *document creation procedure* to the *model choice procedure* and the *model choice procedure* to the *section creation procedure*. We could also consider that the *document creation procedure* is decomposed in a *model choice* and *section creation procedures*. The set of *procedures* with the relations between them gives us the *procedure model*. A procedure model is a graph the nodes of which represent the *procedures* and the edges the *contextualization relations* between them. These procedure models can be expressed using already existing task modeling tools [6,8,14,15].

2.3   Users

A *user* exploits procedures during a use *session*. Our experience reuse and sharing goal gives the *user* a particular importance. It could be a simple use session attribute but we talk here about tracing a session of <u>one</u> specific user. We thus keep the *concrete user* name to represent the notion of use session.

Procedures are launched by *users*. These users can have different access rights to procedures. In the Club♣ model we include users we want to follow the actions, as nodes of the graph. These user nodes are linked to the nodes representing the procedures they have access to. The model enables tracing the actions of the so defined users.

2.4   Application of the Club♣ Model to a Given Computer Program

In order to apply the Club♣ model to a given application, we have to define first the set of objects (chosen from the *use model*) we want to trace the manipulation. The set of procedures (from the *procedure model*) permitting the manipulation of the chosen objects has to be created next with the contextualization relations attaching them together. The *users* are defined specifying the constraints on the available procedures.

The procedures chosen to be traced together with the nodes representing the users and the edges of the graph linking these nodes compose the *observation model*. Indeed we define here a sort of *point of view* we whish to have while following the use of the computer program. This observation model will provide the *explanation* of the traces gathered during the observation of the use of the program. It creates a filter through which the use of the program is observed.

The observation model for a text processor could be composed of the *document creation procedure*, *model choice procedure* and *section creation procedures*. The creation of the document explains the choice of a model and the creation of sections. In fact in order to create a document, one has to choose a model and create sections. In this case the *use model* is composed by object nodes representing the document, the document model and the section. Defined this way, the application of the Club♣ model enables to trace the use of a text processor.

3   The Club♣ Model Formal Description

We have decided to include in the Club♣ model all the elements we need to trace the use of a computer program: users, procedures and objects. In our previous research [9,10,12] we have developed an audiovisual document annotation system (E-AIS : Extended Annotations-Interconnected Strata) based on a graph structure model. We have also designed several tools, like *potential graphs* [13] for querying this structure.

Formally an instance of the Club♣ model M is composed of:
- a global graph G containing the use model subgraph, the observation model subgraph and the trace subgraph;
- a set of *potential graphs* {PG}, comparison functions and adaptation methods enabling the exploitation of the graph G.

The global graph G is defined as $G=<N,R,L,\nu>$, where N is the set of nodes, R is the set of edges. L is the set of edges labels and ν a function which associates to each edge a label. The set N is composed of three types of nodes N=U∪P∪O. A node can thus be a user u∈U, a procedure p∈P or an object o∈O. The semantic of the edges is given by the type of the nodes they link.

A node can be abstract or concrete. An *abstract node* is defined once for all when applying the Club♣ model to a specified computer program. The *use* and *observation models* are composed by *abstract nodes*. *Concrete nodes* are created when observing the use of the program, they form the trace sub-graph. A *concrete node* is notated [Type : Name, time_code], where Type is either O(object), P(procedure) or U(user), and the time_code is the moment when the *concrete node* was created (Object created, procedure launched, user session started). The *concrete nodes* can be sorted chronologically using this time_code.

3.1   Object Nodes

Objects are nodes representing all observed entities that the user can manipulate and handle in a conscious way. The objects of the Club♣ model are elements of the *use model*, we decided to trace the handling.

An ***abstract object*** is like the class definition. It provides type description for object instances. To each *abstract object* corresponds at least an *abstract procedure* which allows its creation. An *abstract object* can also be in relation with several other *abstract procedures* allowing its handling. Indeed beyond the creation procedures there can be one or more procedures which re-use the object, visualize or modify it. *Abstract objects* can be linked to other *abstract objects* with *contextualization* relations. An *abstract object* is notated «O:object name». On Fig. 3 we have «O:Document», «O:Generic model », «O:CV model », «O:Section», «O:Degrees section », «O:Experiences section », «O:Languages section», «O:Sentence», «O:Word ».

A ***concrete object*** is an instance of an *abstract object*, it has a type, i.e. it is connected to only one *abstract object* by an *instantiation relation*. Every *concrete object* was created by a *concrete procedure*, on the initiative of a *concrete user* at a given time. *Concrete objects* inherit the *contextualization* relations between them from the *abstract objects* they derive from.

3.2   Procedure Nodes

We choose to consider that any use of a computer program can be described through ***procedures***. A procedure is included in the graph because we choose to trace its use. Users have to choose procedures to handle objects. *Procedures* identify specific task signatures, usually connected to the application's graphical interface. A *procedure*, in the Club♣ sense of the word is not necessarily an operation or a task of the application, but a treatment unit chosen to be observed and which enables to handle objects of the use model.

An *abstract procedure* is a *procedure* type. It concerns *abstract objects* (it can be considered as an operator while objects are the operands) and can represent simple or complex user interface functionalities. An *abstract procedure* is notated ‖P :procedure name‖. The contextualization relations between *abstract procedures* do not represent any constraints. They don't indicate any information neither on the order nor on the number of instances when using them. They relate only that something has been done *in the context of* one other thing and will be used in similarity assessments.

A *concrete procedure* is an instance of an *abstract procedure*, situated in time and linked to a *concrete user*. It is linked as well to a *concrete object*. A *concrete procedure* materializes a highly contextual trace of the uses of an *abstract procedure*. Concrete procedures inherit, just like *concrete objects* do, the contextualization relations of their abstract nodes.

3.3   User Nodes

A *user* is the representation of a user session. User nodes are linked to *procedure* nodes by *launched by* relations.

An *abstract user* is notated <U : user name> and materializes a registered user. It does not correspond obligatory to a real person. A registered user can log in the program and his actions will be identified thanks to his sessions. These sessions are materialized by *concrete user* nodes. As a concrete node, the *concrete user* is tagged with it's time code representing the beginning instance of the session.

In the graph of the Club♣ model, relations are labeled. The label is given by the types of the nodes the relations are linking. Table 1 represents these constraints for a relation r∈R. The columns of the table list for a given relation: the type of the origin node (O-object, P-procedure, U-user), the type of the destination node and the label of the relation ($R_{conetxt}$ - contextualization relation, R_{inst} -instantiation relation, R_{creat} - creation relation, R_{launc} - launch relation).

Table 1. Constraints on the label of a relation r∈R, according to the type of the linked nodes. (Oa, Pa, Ua - abstract nodes, Oc, Pc, Uc - concrete nodes)

N°	C1	C2	C3	C4	C5	C6	C7
Start node type	Oa or Oc	Pa or Pc	Oa	Pa	Ua	Pa or Pc	Ua or Uc
End node type	Oa or Oc	Pa or Pc	Oc	Pc	Uc	Oa or Oc	Pa or Pc
v(r)	$R_{context}$	$R_{context}$	R_{inst}	R_{inst}	R_{inst}	R_{creat}	R_{launch}

4   An Example

Fig. 3 represents a concrete example of the global Club♣ graph. For an easier reading we will not represent the direction of the relations, considering that in a figure, an arrow starts always from the upper graph node and goes toward the node below. The observation model allows to trace the document creation according to a particular procedure model. The goal of this example is to illustrate trace construction. The observation model contains only one *user* <U :Jean> and a *procedure* structure which specifies that the document creation procedure (‖P:Create a document‖) is the context of the document model choice procedure (‖P:Choose a model‖), in its turn made up of the section creation procedure (‖P:Create a section‖), the sentence typing procedure (‖P:Type a sentence‖), which is finally the context of the word typing procedure (‖P:Type a word‖). To build the use model we consider the following *objects*: document, generic model, section, sentence and word.

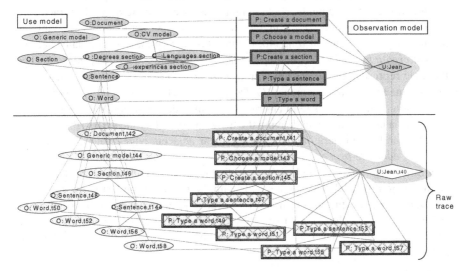

Fig. 3. Global graph representing the Club ♣ model applied to a text processor and the traces of one use session

The example presents only one session when the user created a document according to the generic model, containing a section, contextualizing two sentences, each of them contextualizing two words. Each operation of the user results in the creation of a concrete node in the graph, tagged with a time code. User uses the procedures of the observation model to handle objects, thus leaving traces made of nodes which are instances of these *abstract procedures* and *objects*. We can see that the user Jean started a session at the time t40. He choose the document creation procedure, leaving the trace formed by the nodes [P :Create document, t41] and [O :Document, t42]. After this he selected a document model and created a section. Each action gave birth to nodes in the trace. The user used instances of *abstract procedures* to manipulate *concrete objects*. Each node of the trace derives from an abstract node and is in relation with other concrete nodes.

5   Trace Construction

After having described formally the graph structure formed by the use and the observation model, we present the construction of traces during the use of a computer program. Let us go on with our text processor example. As presented in Fig. 3 the observation model enables the tracing of document creation. The set of concrete nodes on this figure together with their relations form the **raw trace**, while the whole global graph can be considered as the **explained raw trace**. Generally a trace is a connected sub-graph of the global graph G, containing at least one concrete node. The trace contains the *concrete user* node [U :Jean, t40] representing the fact that a user having the *Jean* login began a session at time t40. During this session the user first launched the *document creation procedure*, creating the node [P : create a document, t41] attached to the node representing the session with a *launched relation*, and to the node representing the newly created document [O :Document, t42] with a *creation relation*. All three concrete nodes are linked to abstract nodes they derive from. As a next step the user chooses a document model leaving the trace composed by the nodes [P : Choose a model, t43] and [O :Generic model, t44] and their adjacent edges. The [P : Choose a model, t43] *concrete procedure* is linked to the [P : create a document, t41] by a *contextualization relation*, inherited from their abstract nodes which are connected with a relation having this label. The session ends with the typing of the last word [O :Word, t58]. Every action of the user generates several new nodes and edges in the graph creating this way a highly contextualized trace. These traces are the starting point of our help system. From the trace we can create episodes which will be considered as reusable cases.

6   Potential Graphs and Episodes

Traces can be processed with the help of *potential graphs* in order to obtain *episodes*. In this section we first introduce the *potential graph* and present after the episode construction methods.

   The exploitation of the graph structure is based on a sub-graph-matching algorithm described in [13]. In fact a request is expressed through a so-called *potential graph*. These graphs are made up from several nodes partially filled. For example the request: "Find objects manipulated by <U:Jean> and the procedures used to manipulate them" will give the *potential graph* shown in Fig. 4. A request is solved by searching the matching of this *potential graph* in the global graph. The potential graph elements assigned with a "*" are unspecified nodes, these are in fact what we try to match. The algorithm starts the sub-isomorphism search with the specified nodes and tries to match the rest of the *potential graph* on the global graph following the node types and edge labels. A *potential graph* has to be connected and has to contain at least one specified node. *Potential graphs* have *named nodes*, nodes having a label, the instances of which can be retrieved. In the Club♣ model the named nodes have labels notated Nt$_i$ (trace node n° i). The isomorphism of this *potential graph* will contain *concrete objects* and *concrete procedures* in place of those specified with "*", and these concrete nodes represent the objects and procedures concerning the user <U:Jean>. We have emphasized one instance of an isomorph sub-graph of the global graph on Fig. 3 to the query graph, by the grayed shape, surrounding the nodes: [Odocument,t42], [P:Create a document,t41], [U:Jean,t40] and <U:Jean>. There are 8 other matching sub-graphs in the global graph, containing each *concrete object* and the related *concrete procedures*.

In the Club ♣ model *potential graphs* are used to calculate traces and cut them in episodes. An **episode** is an ordered list of nodes in the global graph G, built by the instanciation of a *potential graph*.

The nodes of the raw trace, sorted by their time-code constitute the **linear raw trace**. This contains every concrete node chronologically ordered. The Fig. 4 presents the *linear raw trace* of the document creation session illustrated on Fig. 3. This trace was obtained by the instanciation of the *potential graph* "linear raw trace" <U :Jean> applied to the global graph G. In order to build linear traces, a *potential graph* has to be instanciated, the matching nodes of the global graph to the named nodes of the *potential graph* retrieved and sorted following a total order (in our case the temporal order). In our example the *potential graph* has two named nodes indicating that every *concrete object* and *procedure* corresponding to them has to be included in the trace.

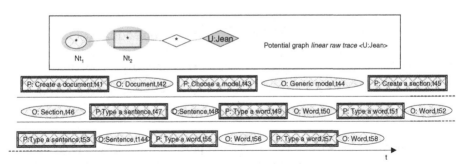

Fig. 4. The *linear raw trace* of the session presented in Fig. 3 and the *potential graph* which served to retrieve it.

The *linear raw trace* can be cut in episodes in different ways. It is possible to retrieve only *procedures* or only *objects*. Another way is to cut it in episodes representing each a different session. Of course, the global graph has to contain in this case more than one session. *Potential graphs* can exploit the structure of the use or observation model of a specific program. Indeed the goal of these models is to provide a rich tracing framework. This way we are considering not only the *linear raw trace* but a larger context of each node as well.

Let us consider the use and observation model of a text processor as presented on Fig. 3. It is possible to exploit the contextualization relations between the *abstract procedures*. Doing this, for this text processor we can create several *potential graphs* in order to retrieve only words, phrases and words, or only phrases, manipulated during one or several sessions. We can consider that a word is a more contextualized object than a sentence which is more contextualized than a section and so on. Fig. 5 represents a set of these *potential graphs*. The first one (**PG_words**) enables to calculate an episode containing the manipulated words only.

If we instantiate this *potential graph* in the global graph of the Fig. 3 it will retrieve the episode episode$_{PG\_Words}$ from the Fig. 6. The second one adds the phrases as well producing the episode episode$_{PG\_sentences\_and\_words}$ from the Fig. 6. We consider that the first episode is *finer* than the second one because it contains only objects coming from the *bottom* of the use model.

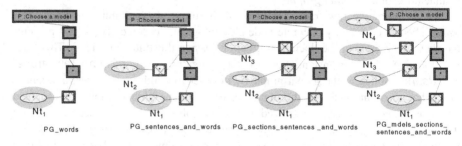

Fig. 5. *Potential graphs* enabling to retrieve traces containing less and less "fine" nodes.

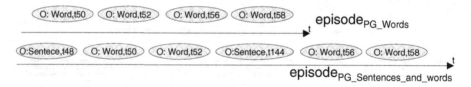

Fig. 6. Episodes calculated with *potential graphs* containing contextualization relations

When applying Club♣ to a concrete computer program it is important to create well structured observation and use models and a convenient set of *potential graphs* in order to get episodes with a high *reusability factor*.

7   Experience Reuse

A computer program equipped with a Club♣ based tracing system can help users in two different manners:

- as an assistant : following user actions continuously and proposing help tips after each action;
- as a counselor : tracing the user actions but only to intercede when help is explicitly asked.

In both cases the help system has to find similar situations in the collected traces, in order to find inspiration in the already found solutions. The fulfilling of tasks is supported by the case based reasoning [11]. The implementation of this technique needs several formalizations.

7.1   The Cases in the Club ♣ Model

In the section 6 we have presented several methods to calculate episodes in the use traces gathered following the Club ♣ model. We consider every episode found this way a *case* in the CBR meaning of the word. These episodes contain as well the problem part of the case as the solution part. The first nodes composing the episode can be considered as the problem and the remaining nodes as the solution. The identification of the target problem and solution is done when help is needed. Generally the target problem is given by the user's last actions and the solution will give his next steps.

The observation and use model applied to the computer program have to enable a tracing that facilitates the identification of problem/solution couples. It is as well necessary to be able to compare and to adapt episodes. To do this we create ordered *potential graph* suites enabling the retrieving of ever finer episodes. With these *potential graphs* the system can calculate episodes representing the current working context with increasing depth explanations, covering a growing period of time. For example while the episode got with first *potential graph* of the Fig. 5 begins at the time t50, the episode created with the second one commences at t48 and if we calculate the episode retrieved with the PG_models_sections_sentences_and_words, its starting time would be t43.

In order to illustrate our approach let us consider the trace left by a novice user writing his CV represented on the Fig. 7. This trace corresponds to the observation model of the Fig. 3. The session begins with the node [U :Jean,t40] and continues with the creation of a document following the generic model. The user types two phrases : one concerning his degrees, the other his experiences. Once he types the word **Assistant**, represented by the node [O :Assistant,t60] he asks himself (and the system) what else can he put on his CV? In this situation the episodes for a case based reasoning cycle are calculated departing from this latter node. Applying the *potential graphs* of the Fig. 5, the episodes of the Fig. 8 are retrieved. These episodes contain only *concrete objects*.

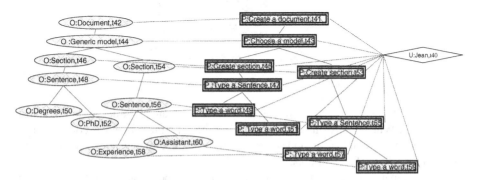

Fig. 7. Traces left by a document creation session

The episode E'1 is retrieved using the *potential graph* : PG_words, the episode E'2 using the PG_sentences_and_words and so on. In this situation the episodes E'1,E'2,E'3,E4 and E5 are potential target cases.

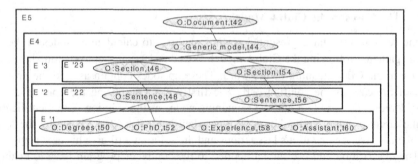

Fig. 8. Overlapping episodes retrieved from a document creation trace

Consider now that another, more expert user had already created a CV. He left the trace represented on Fig. 9. We can notice that this user knew the existence of a CV model and choose it to create the document. He entered his degrees, and the languages he speaks.

When the first user asked for help, both traces were in the global graph G, so the *potential graphs* are instanciated in the trace left during the session identified by the node [U :Pierre, t0] as well. The episodes retrieved from this trace are represented on Fig. 10. We find here the same kind of episodes as on the Fig. 8, this time being potential source cases.

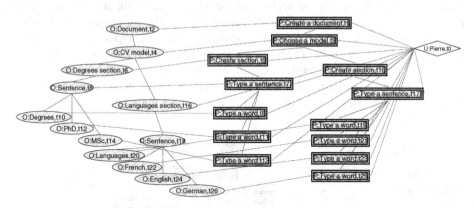

Fig. 9. Traces left by a document creation session

Now that the cases are retrieved, they need to be compared in order to find the most similar ones. When comparing episodes, the number of similar nodes is considered as well as the total number of nodes. We search the longest episode containing the maximum number of similar nodes.

After comparison we find that episodes E'41 and E'1 began with similar nodes, but episodes E'32 and E'2 (Fig. 11) too. As the latter are longer, represent a larger context, we consider the episode E'32 as being a better source case.

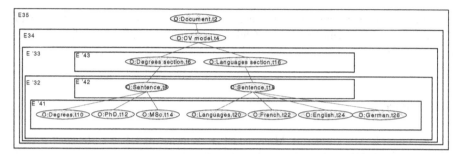

Fig. 10. Overlapping episodes retrieved from a document creation trace

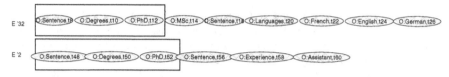

Fig. 11. Two episodes extracted from the traces left by the document creation sessions.

7.2   The Actual Help, Case Adaptation

Once the similar episodes found, several things can be done: the system can simply show the found similar episode to the user in order to give him new ideas. If the applied use and observation model enable it, more advanced adaptation can be done. In our example, we can consider that the generic model is less precise than the CV model, so the system could propose the help asking user to change his document model from generic to CV model and to add a languages section.

8   Conclusion

In this paper we presented an original use trace model, enabling to gather user actions while using a computer program in a homogeneous, highly connected and well formalized structure. The basic idea was to represent as well *users* as *procedures* and *objects* as elements playing a role in the use of a computer program in a same graph. The graph of the Club ♣ model is in fact a very rich log file, with multiple use trace retrieving possibilities. We introduced a robust exploitation tool, the *potential graph*, which enables us to filter in a flexible manner the traces left by users and to create specific episodes aligning nodes of the graph.

We are currently working on a better formalization of adaptation and comparison methods. We plan to consider not only ordered nodes but sub-graphs as cases to compare and to adapt.

The text processor application was used only for simplicity reasons. We are actually working on the adaptation of the Club ♣ model on our audiovisual document annotation system.

References

1. E. Auriol, R. M. Crowder, R. MacKendrick, R. Row and T. Knudsen: Integrating Case-Based Reasoning and Hypermedia Documentation: An Application for the Diagnosis of a Welding Robot at Odense Steel Shipyard. Lecture Notes in Computer Science, Vol. 1650, (1999), 372–384
2. A. Bénel, E. Egyed-Zs., Y. Prié, S. Calabretto, A. Mille, I. Andréa and P. Jean-Marie: Truth in the Digital Library: From Ontological to Hermeneutical Systems. ECDL 2001 European Conference on Research and Advanced Technology for Digital Libraries, Darmstadt (D), Springer-Verlag, Vol. 2163 (2001), 366–377
3. L. Birnbaum, R. Bareiss, T. Hinrichs and C. Johnson: Interface Design Based on Standardized Task Models. Intelligent User Interfaces, San Francisco CA, USA, ACM, ACM, Vol. (1998), 65–72
4. B. Chandrasekaran, J. R. Josephson and V. R. Benjamins: Ontology of tasks and methods. Eleventh Workshop on Knowledge Acquisition, Modeling and Management (KAW '98), Banff, Canada, Vol. (1998), 25
5. J. Charlet, B. Bachimont, J. Bouaud and P. Zweigenbaum: Ontologie et réutilisabilité: expérience et discussion. Acquisition et Ingénierie des Connaissances, Vol. ISBN 2-85428-417-8, (1996), 69–87
6. T. Clarke: Epistemics PC-Pack. http://www.epistemics.co.uk/products/pcpack/tools/ (2001)
7. J. Delgado and N. Ishii: Formal Models for Learning User Preferences, A Preliminary Report. International Joint Conference on Artificial Intelligence (IJCAI-99), Workshop on Learning about Users, Stockholm, Sweden, Vol. (1999), 8p
8. Dukas: Dukas Graphical Task Modeling Tool. http://www.cc.gatech.edu/gvu/user_interfaces/Mastermind/Dukas/ (1998)
9. E. Egyed-Zs., A. Mille, Y. Prié and J.-M. Pinon: Trèfle : un modèle de traces d'utilisation. Ingénierie des Connaissances, Rouen, F, Vol. (2002), 13p.
10. E. Egyed-Zs., Y. Prié, A. Mille and J.-M. Pinon: A graph based audio-visual document annotation and browsing system. RIAO 2000, Paris, France, Vol. 2 (2000), 1381–1389
11. A. Mille: Associer expertise et expérience pour assister les tâches de l'utilisateur. CPE, (1998)
12. Y. Prié: *Modélisation de documents audiovisuels en Strates Interconnectées par les annotations pour l'exploitation contextuelle*. INSA-Lyon, (1999) 270
13. Y. Prié, T. Limane and A. Mille: Isomorphisme de sous-graphe pour la recherche d'information audiovisuelle contextuelle. 12ème congrès Reconnaissance de Formes et Intelligence Artificielle, RFIA2000, Paris, FR, Vol. 1 (2000), 277–286
14. Protégé: Protégé 2000. http://protege.stanford.edu/ (2002)
15. G. Schreiber and J. Wielemaker: ModelDraw. http://www.commonkads.uva.nl/INFO/tools/modeldraw.html (2001)
16. B. Trousse: Evaluation of the Prediction Capability of a User behaviour Mining Approach for Adapative Web Sites. In RIAO 2000, 6th Conference on "Content-Based Multimedia Information Access", Paris, C.I.D. C.A.S.I.S., Vol. (2000), 1752–1761

Case-Based Plan Recognition in Computer Games

Michael Fagan and Pádraig Cunningham

Department of Computer Science
Trinity College Dublin
Ireland
{Michael.Fagan, Padraig.Cunningham}@cs.tcd.ie

Abstract. In this paper we explore the use of case-based plan recognition to predict a player's actions in a computer game. The game we work with is the classic Space Invaders game and we show that case-based plan recognition can produce good prediction accuracy in real-time, working with a fairly simple game representation. Our evaluation suggests that a personalized plan library will produce better prediction accuracy but, for Space Invaders, good accuracy can be produced using a plan library derived from the game play of another player.

1 Introduction

Graphics in computer games have now reached a standard where most users are more than satisfied with the quality available, and it is difficult to differentiate a new game title by the graphics alone. Game designers are turning to Artificial Intelligence (AI) to produce a more interesting and more realistic gaming experience. The main way that AI can help game design is by supporting the development of more realistic non-player characters (NPCs). A first objective in this direction is to support adaptive behaviours where the NPCs do not do the same stupid thing all the time. A fundamental requirement for this is for the NPC to have some model of the player's behaviour that will allow the NPC to anticipate and thus adapt to the player's actions. In AI terms, it would be useful for the NPC to be able to perform plan recognition.

In this paper we present a prototype plan recognition system called COMETS that uses the case-based plan recognition idea [4]. The idea is to have the NPC observe the player's behaviour and identify plans or patterns that recur. Then the NPC can identify future executions of these plans and anticipate what the user will do next. In the case-based plan recognition (CBPR) methodology the observed plans are stored in a case-base (plan library) and the player's behaviour is constantly compared to the case-base to identify the onset of the execution of a recognized plan.

For this initial evaluation we use the classic Space Invaders game. Space Invaders (SI) has been chosen because it is a straightforward example of a game where the player executes plans. While COMETS does produce good predictions for Space Invaders there is no scope within the SI game to react to this information so in future work we need to apply these techniques in other games to exploit the full potential.

In the next section we present a brief overview of research on plan recognition before presenting in sections 3 and 4 the representation of plans used in COMETS.

K.D. Ashley and D.G. Bridge (Eds.): ICCBR 2003, LNAI 2689, pp. 161–170, 2003.
© Springer-Verlag Berlin Heidelberg 2003

Section 5 presents an evaluation of the prediction power of COMETS that considers the impact of case-base size and the provenance of the cases on prediction accuracy. The paper concludes in section 6 with a discussion of some directions for future work.

2 Plan Recognition

Plan Recognition (PR) is the process whereby an agent observes the actions of another agent with the objective of inferring the agent's future actions, intentions or goals. Several methods for plan recognition have been explored. The most notable are deductive [1], abductive [2], probabilistic [3] and case-based [4]. PR approaches may also be classified according to whether the PR process was *intended* [1] or *keyhole* [4]. If the observed agent cooperates to convey his or her intentions to the recognising agent, as in natural language dialogue systems [6], then the PR process is said to be *intended*. Whereas if the relationship between the observing and the observed agents is non-interactive then it is termed *keyhole* PR [7][8].

In some PR systems the plan library is handcrafted by the system designers and often must be complete (see for example the work by Kautz [1]). Building complete plan libraries is a tractable knowledge acquisition task only when the domain complexity is low. In real-world scenarios this is not often the case and constructing complete plan libraries may be out of the question. Furthermore, it is often the case that extraneous plans are included which bloat the plan library with irrelevant information that impacts on the efficiency of the recognition mechanisms.

In recent years efforts has been made to automate the process of building the plan library using Machine Learning (ML) techniques [9][10][4]. Constructing the plan library in this fashion allows the plan library to be personalised, tailoring it to reflect the idiosyncrasies of an individual's behaviour. This is one of the real attractions of the CBPR idea where the plan library can be built from actual data rather than by hand-crafting cases/plans. Since CBPR is in the lazy learning spirit of CBR the plan library can initially be seeded with generic cases with personalised cases being added as more plans are observed.

3 States and Actions

Plans comprise states and actions that enable state transitions. In systems such as STRIPS [12] or PRODIGY [11] a state of the world is represented by a conjunction of first order predicates. An action may only be executed if its preconditions are matched by the state of the world. This idea is simplified in COMETS so that a state is an atomic concept. There are three possible states that make up the *state set*:

{Safe, Unsafe, VeryUnsafe}

The states are an abstraction of what is going on in the game and the player is defined to be in one of these states depending on what conditions are satisfied in the game at that point. These conditions may be likened to the first order predicates that encode the state of the world in PRODIGY [11] or in Kerkez and Cox's CBPR system [4]. The three states are shown in Fig. 1. On the left the player is 'safe' behind a bunker; in the centre the player is 'unsafe' in the open but not under fire; on the right he is in the open under fire and so 'very unsafe'. This state-based representation of SI that is used in COMETS is very simple; while it does capture the progress of the game in general terms, some detail is lost.

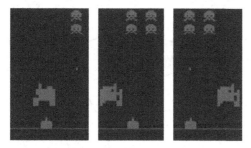

Fig. 1. The three states in the COMETS view of Space Invaders are; *Safe, Unsafe* and *VeryUnSafe*.

Like all planning systems, state transitions are brought about in COMETS by *actions*. In STRIPS-like planning systems [13] an action may only be performed if its *preconditions* are satisfied by the player's/planner's state. If the predictions are met then the action can be performed and the action's *effects* are realised. These preconditions and effects define an action. However, since COMETS is *observing* rather than *managing* the planning process it does not have all the components of a full planning system. For instance, it does not need to check that preconditions are met before an action can take place. Actions are observed to have happened after the fact. All COMETS has to do is record what has happened as a sequence of state-action pairs.

As is the case with the states, there is a predefined set of actions called the *action set*. The action set consists of 5 player actions and one exogenous event. An exogenous event is any event, the system can account for, that occurs in the world that is out of the control of the player. For example, an exogenous event is generated when the player is the target of enemy fire. The action set is as follows and the resulting transitions are shown in Fig. 2:

{fire, hide, emerge, dodge, suicide, exogenous}

So a crucial component of COMETS is the ability to 'watch' the game and abstract what is observed into a plan expressed as a sequence of state-action pairs. This abstraction process involves interpreting the raw game data into a more meaningful format. Sensory inputs include the position of the player, the position of the enemies and the presence of a threatening attack. The player's current state is calculated using this information. This state is stored in the *state register*. Each time the content of the state register changes an action will have occurred; e.g. a transition from *Safe* to *VeryUnsafe* results from an *emerge* action. In this game representation there is only one action that can produce each state transition with the exception of the transition between *Unsafe* and *VeryUnsafe* that can result from *suicide* and *exogenous* actions. In both these states the player is not undercover; the difference is that for *VeryUnsafe* the player is also under fire. The transition from *Unsafe* to *VeryUnsafe* can occur by the player coming under fire (the *exogenous* event) or by the player moving under fire – the *suicide* event.

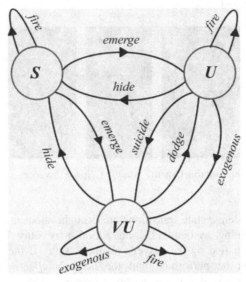

Fig. 2. The state transition diagram for the representation of SI used in COMETS; the arcs represent actions and the nodes represent states.

4 Plans

Plans in COMETS are an ordered sequence of state-action pairs. Plans are assumed to be linear in nature [11][13], i.e. operations in sub-plans are not interleaved. A single SI game is a complete plan. However, the plan recognition process operates on sub-plans that are four steps long (see Fig. 3), the idea being that if game play matches the first three steps in a sub-plan we can guess that the fourth step in this sub-plan will be the player's next action.

4.1 Building the Plan Library

One of the benefits of using CBR for plan recognition is that the plan library can be built automatically by observing actual game play. Kerkez and Cox build their plan library dynamically, as the stacking agent is observed executing new plans in the blocks world or as actions occur in a logistics process. In COMETS, the plan library is built after the player has played the game for three sessions. These sessions yield several plans corresponding to the games played in those sessions. A plan of length n contains $n-(k-1)$ sub-plans of length k. If we view the plan segment of length 6 in

Fig. 3 as a complete plan it consists of 3 sub-plans of length 4. However, all three of these are not of interest. We are only interested in those that turn up systematically. The length 4 as the best length for sub-plans was arrived at after some examination of recorded game play. 3 is too short, and results in too many false matches. While 5 is too long and would not yield enough matches.

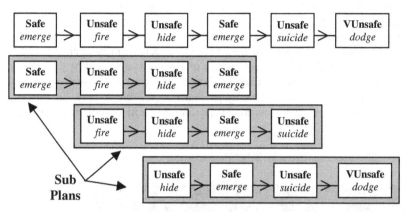

Fig. 3. Sample sub-plans from COMETS.

To build the plan library, the recorded passages of game play are scanned for frequently followed sub-plans. Each sub-plan is assigned a *support* value that is a count of the number of occurrences of that sub-plan in the plans. Sub-plans with support values above a threshold (currently 5) are candidates for inclusion in the plan library. The plan library's quota of sub-plan's is filled with the sub-plans with the highest support values.

4.2 Storing and Retrieving Sub-plans

Since the process of plan retrieval happens continuously while the game is being played, it needs to be computationally efficient. As an example, let us consider a scenario where the player executes the plan segment shown in Fig. 3. After the *Safe/emerge* state-action pair is observed the retrieval mechanism must consider as candidates all sub-plans which start with this state-action pair. This set of sub-plans is called the *conflict pool*. When the next state-action (*Unsafe/fire*) is observed all sub-plans that do not match this are deleted from the conflict pool and all sub-plans that start with this are added to the conflict pool. At this stage the conflict pool will contain all sub-plans with first two steps *Safe/emerge - Unsafe/fire* and also sub-plans with first step *Unsafe/fire*.

COMETS continues like this, adding and deleting sub-plans from the conflict pool until a single sub-plan is found that matches three steps of game play. The player is *recognised* to be executing this sub-plan and the 4th action from that sub-plan is predicted to be the player's next action.

To support this, sub-plans are organised in the plan library using an indexing structure based on an integer encoding of their initial state-action pair. The plan library is in fact a hashtable and sub-plans are stored in bins indexed by a common initial state-action pair. (This is based on the techniques used by Kerkes and Cox [4]).

In summary, COMETS 'recognises' the execution of a sub-plan when it matches three consecutive steps of game play and it is the only candidate to match on three steps. The evaluation in section 5 shows that the policy for managing the plan library has important implications for this uniqueness constraint. We might expect that expanding the plan library to include poorly supported sub-plans will damage retrieval performance and the evaluation shows this to be the case.

Fig. 4 shows a screen shot of the prediction mechanism in operation. The upper text region on the right shows the sequence of actions as observed by COMETS. Below that, the predictions are shown. Each prediction displayed is the final state-action pair from a sub-plan whose first three steps matched the game play. In this example COMETS is doing very well having made three predictions, all three of which are correct.

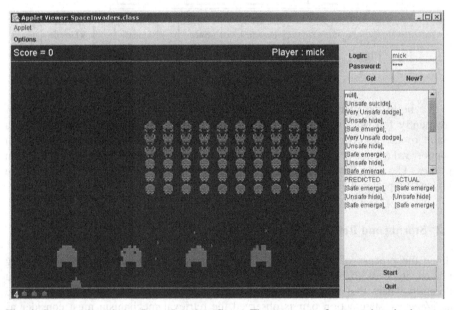

Fig. 4. COMETS observing a Space Invaders Game: The sequence of state-actions is shown on the right with the predictions from COMETS shown below that.

5   Evaluation

In this section we look at the accuracy and frequency of predictions coming from COMETS as the size of the plan library varies. We also look at the impact of personalized plan libraries on accuracy. The measure of the system's accuracy is the proportion of successfully predicted actions in the set of predictions.

5.1 Prediction Accuracy v's Plan Size

The CBPR system was trained over three game sessions as described above. A further three game sessions were used to test the accuracy of the resulting plan library. These accuracy tests were repeated for plan libraries varying in size from 10 to 80. Fig. 5 compares these accuracy figures with the accuracy of randomly generated predictions.

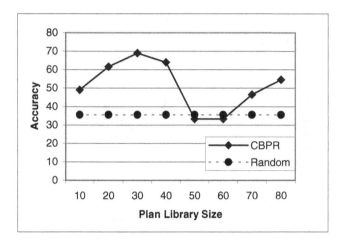

Fig. 5. The accuracy of the CBPR system for different plan library sizes is plotted along side the accuracy of a system performing random prediction.

Fig. 6 shows the change in the prediction rate of the CBPR system as the size of the plan library increases. This is the proportion of user actions for which the system is able to produce predictions. Using a plan library of just 10 sub-plans, the CBPR system will produce predictions in response to 12% of the user's actions. It is important to note that these predictions may be wrong and Fig. 5 shows that a little less than 50% of these are in fact correct. Looking at both graphs, we see that a prediction accuracy of 69% is achievable with a plan library of size 30 with a prediction rate of 7.5%.

The prediction rate drops as the size of the plan library increases. This happens because, with more sub-plans in the library, the chance of matching on three steps of more than one plan increases; i.e. there may be more than one matching plan in the conflict pool. The current implementation has no means of resolving this conflict so no prediction is made.

The other point to notice in the graphs is the drop-off in accuracy as library size goes from 30 to 60 (Fig. 5). This might be viewed as a form of overfitting where the simpler model represented by the library of 30 cases generalizes better to the player's behaviour. The extra cases added to bring the library size up to 60 are poorly supported in the sense that they have occurred less frequently in the observed game play. These cases are noisy examples of the players planning behaviour and damage prediction accuracy. The accuracy rises again above 60 cases but at that stage the prediction rate has fallen to 3%.

This evaluation shows that CBPR can produce predictions with reasonable accuracy in real time. In order to determine the actual 'best' size for the plan library we would need to have some idea of the relative value/cost of good and bad predictions. Clearly, this has no meaning in the context of the SI game as the game does not allow for any adaptive behaviour on the behalf of the NPCs.

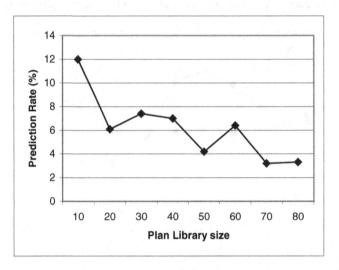

Fig. 6. As the size of the Plan Library grows the frequency of predictions falls.

5.2   Accuracy for Non-personalized Case-Bases

The other question we consider in the evaluation is that of the origin of the plan library (see Table 1). In the evaluation in section 5.1, the training data and test data were produced by the same player, so the library is personalized to that player. It is important to know if the accuracy depends on this, or if reasonable accuracy can be achieved using a plan library produced from someone else's game play (or using a generic plan library). To assess this, three other plan libraries of size 20 were produced from three other players, two intermediate players and a novice. The prediction accuracy for the target player using the plan library from the novice player fell to 39%. But the intermediate players' libraries kept the accuracy up at 56%. This suggests that a personalized library is best but a generic library can be expected to produce fairly good results. This good result with non-personal cases may depend heavily on the constrained nature of the SI game where good players are inclined to be executing the same plans because of the limited potential for variation in game play.

6   Conclusions and Future Work

Our experience with COMETS suggests that CBPR can be used to predict a player's behaviour in a computer game. Not only can CBPR be the basis for adaptive behaviour in computer games, but it also lends itself well to *personalized* adaptive behaviour.

Table 1. This table shows the accuracy of the predictions for a Target Player (Intermediate Standard) using a plan library built from his own play and plan libraries built from the play of others.

Plan Library	Accuracy
Target Player	61.6%
Intermediate A	56.4%
Intermediate B	56.7%
Novice	39%

The performance of the existing system could be improved with a more sophisticated policy for selecting sub-plans for inclusion in the plan library. At present the only criterion is to select the sub-plans with the greatest support in the training data, provided the support is above the threshold of 5 (i.e. the sub-plan was observed 5 times in game play). Our evaluation shows that this allows for plans that contradict one another. There is no benefit in having two sub-plans that match on their first three steps so presumably the one with the weaker support should be deleted. There is scope for considerable research on library maintenance questions such as this.

It is also clear that a lot of useful game information is not captured by the simple plan representation in use in COMETS. We have done some work on a more sophisticated representation based on interval temporal logic [2] and the benefit of this more complex representation needs to be evaluated [13].

Before we can take this research much further, we need to move to a game environment that will allow for adaptive behaviour from the NPCs. Questions about library maintenance policies and library size depend on how the predictions are used and on the utility of predictions and the cost of errors. Are frequent less accurate predictions useful? Or are rarer but more accurate predictions better? There are also interesting questions about the use of generic versus personalised plan libraries that can only be answered in a game environment that allows adaptive behaviour.

We must also recognise that the good coverage we get from a case-base of 30 sup-plans may depend on the constrained nature of the Space Invaders game. A more complex game environment may require a much larger case-base to get reasonable coverage. In a more complex environment a generic case-base may also be much less effective and it may be more important to personalise the case-base to the player to get good performance.

References

1. Kautz., H., A Formal Theory of Plan Recognition and its Implementation, *Reasoning About Plans*, Allen, J., Pelavin, R. and Tenenberg, J. ed., Morgan Kaufmann, San Mateo, C.A., 1991, pp. 69–125.
2. Ferguson, G. and Allen, J.F., Events and Actions in the Interval Temporal Logic, *Journal of Logic and Computation,* Special Issue on Actions and Processes, Vol. 4, No. 5, October, 1994, pp. 531–579.

3. Charniak, E. and Goldman, R., A Bayesian Model of Plan Recognition, *Artificial Intelligence Journal*, Vol. 64, pp. 53–79, 1993.
4. Kerkez, B. and Cox, M., Incremental Case-Based Plan Recognition Using State Indices, *Cased-based Reasoning Research and Development: Proceedings of 4th International Conference on Case-Based Reasoning (ICCBR 2001)*, Aha, D.W., Watson, I., Yang, Q. eds., pp. 291–305, Springer-Verlag, 2001,
5. Cohen, R., Song, F., Spencer, B. and van Beek, P., Exploiting Temporal and Novel Information from the User in Plan Recognition, *User Modelling and User-Adapted Interaction*, Vol. 1, No. 2, 1981, pp. 125–148.
6. Allen, J. F., and Perrault, C. R., Analyzing Intention in Dialogues, *Artificial Intelligence*, Vol. 15, No. 3, 1980, pp. 143–178.
7. Albrecht, D. W., Zukerman, I., Nicholson, A. and Bud, A., Towards a Bayesian Model for Keyhole Plan Recognition in Large Domains, *Proceedings of the 6th International Conference on User Modelling,* 1997, pp. 365–376.
8. Albrecht, D. W., Zukerman, I., and Nicholson, A., Bayesian Models for Keyhole Plan Recognition in an Adventure Game, *User Modelling and User-Adapted Interaction,* Vol. 8, 1998, pp. 5–47.
9. Lesh, N., Rich, C. and Sidner, C., Using Plan Recognition in Human-Computer Collaboration", *Proceedings of the 7th International Conference on User Modelling,* 1999, pp. 23–32.
10. Bauer, M., Acquisition of User Preferences for Plan Recognition, *Proceedings of the 5th International Conference on User Modelling*, 1998, pp.936–941.
11. Veloso, M., Carbonell, J., Perez, A., Borrajo, D., Fink, E., Blythe, J., "Integrating Planning and Learning: The PRODIGY Architecture, *In Journal of Experimental and Theoretical Artificial Intelligence*, Vol. 7, No. 1, 1995.
12. Fikes, R. and Nilsson, N., STRIPS: A New Approach to the Application of Theorem Proving to Problem Solving, *Readings in Planning*, Allen, James, Hendler, James, Tate, Austin, ed., Morgan Kaufmann, San Mateo, C.A., pp. 88–97, 1990 also in *Artificial Intelligence*, Vol. 2, 1971, pp. 198–208.
13. Fagan, M., *Anticipating the Player's Intentions: A Case-based Plan Recognition Framework for Space Invaders*, M.Sc. thesis, University of Dublin, Trinity College, Dublin, Ireland, 2002.

Solution Verification in Software Design: A CBR Approach

Paulo Gomes, Francisco C. Pereira, Paulo Carreiro, Paulo Paiva, Nuno Seco,
José Luís Ferreira, and Carlos Bento

CISUC - Centro de Informática e Sistemas da Universidade de Coimbra.
Departamento de Engenharia Informática, Polo II, Universidade de Coimbra.
3030 Coimbra
pgomes@dei.uc.pt,
http://rebuilder.dei.uc.pt

Abstract. Software design is becoming a demanding task, not only because the complexity of software systems is increasing, but also due to
the pressure that development teams suffer from clients. CASE tools capable of performing more work and of having more intelligent abilities
are needed, so that, they can provide more help to the designer. In this
paper we describe a CASE tool capable of assisting the designer in a
more intelligent way, be it by suggesting new solutions or by learning
user preferences. We detail how the solutions are generated and focus
on the verification process, which enables the new designs to have less
errors. This verification process takes a CBR approach, which has the
advantage of being personalized. We describe experimental results that
show the effect of the verification process in the generated solutions.

1 Introduction

The complexity of software design [2] is increasing at a pace that companies and
development teams have difficulties following. Developing more powerful CASE
(Computer Aided Software Engineering) tools can be a way of increasing the
productivity of software development teams. These tools can help the designer
more effectively in reusing designs and code of previous systems. This task requires knowledge representation formalisms and reasoning mechanisms capable
of providing the software designer useful cognitive functionalities like: retrieving
similar designs, suggesting new designs, learning, verifying diagrams, and more.

One of the main functionalities that the new generation of CASE tools must
have, is to be capable of generating new alternative designs. This is very useful
to the designer, enabling her/him to explore the design space, and possibly saving time and resources. Most of the time, the reuse of software designs implies
adaptation of old designs to the new situation. This adaptation process when
performed by a computational system will generate some inconsistent or incoherent objects in the new design. A verification process is needed to detect and
revise these errors. In this paper we present a CASE tool capable of generating new software designs. We focus on the verification process used to correct

K.D. Ashley and D.G. Bridge (Eds.): ICCBR 2003, LNAI 2689, pp. 171–185, 2003.
© Springer-Verlag Berlin Heidelberg 2003

mistakes made in the generation process. We also describe how this verification process learns new knowledge that will be reused later and that codifies designer preferences.

Case-Based Reasoning [1] is a reasoning mechanism that uses previous experience to solve new problems. This experience is in the form of cases and is stored in a case library for reuse. We think that CBR is suitable for software design verification due to two main reasons: there is no domain model for software design, and users have different preferences. One of the reasons that CBR was developed was to succeed in domains in which there is no model, and consequently rule-based or model-based fail [8]. In software design there is no domain model, which makes CBR the more feasible approach. The second aspect, is that users tend to model systems in different ways, so the verification process has to be user-dependent. In other words, it must convey with the user preferences and not with a general view of the world. Regarding this aspect, CBR is also suitable, providing a way to personalize the verification knowledge for each designer.

There are several approaches to case adaptation in CBR design systems. For instance, CADSYN [9] uses constraint satisfaction algorithms for adaptation. Composer [11] goes further, and combines design composition with constraint resolution. Other approaches to design adaptation involve the application of rules (FABEL [12]), or model-based reasoning (KRITIK [3]). Among these, few revise the generated solutions, and the ones that do it, generally do not learn from this revision process. IM-RECIDE [4] is a CBR design system that uses failure knowledge in the form of failure cases to fix errors in new solutions. It learns failure cases that enable the system to identify design errors, and to correct them.

In this paper we describe our approach to solution verification based on CBR. This approach is implemented in a CASE tool called REBUILDER, and has two main goals: create a corporative memory of software designs, and provide the software designer with a design environment capable of promoting software design reuse in a more intelligent way. The verification process provides the designer a cognitive tool capable of adapting itself to the designer preferences, and at the same time doing verification tasks, which were performed by the designer.

The next section describes the architecture of REBUILDER, it's modules and how they work together. Then section 3 explains how new diagrams are created, describing two generation processes: analogy and case-based design composition. Section 4 focus on the verification process detailing the various parts of this module. It also describes a simple example to illustrate the process. Section 5 describes experimental work that gives an insight on how this mechanism works. Finally section 6 concludes this paper.

2   REBUILDER

This section describes the architecture of REBUILDER, which comprises four different modules: Knowledge Base (KB), UML Editor, KB Manager and CBR engine (see Figure 1).

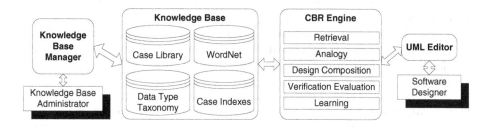

Fig. 1. REBUILDER's Architecture.

The UML editor is the front-end of REBUILDER and the environment where the software designer develops designs. Apart from the usual editor commands to manipulate UML objects, the editor integrates new commands capable of reusing design knowledge. These commands are directly related with the CBR engine capabilities and are divided into two main categories:

- **Knowledge Base actions:** such as connect to KB and disconnect from KB.
- **Cognitive actions:** such as retrieve design, adapt design using analogy or design composition, verify design, evaluate design, and actions related with object classification using WordNet.

The KB Manager module is used by the administrator to manage the KB, keeping it consistent and updated. This module comprises all the functionalities of the UML editor, and it adds case-base management functions to REBUILDER. These are used by the KB administrator to update and modify the KB.

The KB comprises four different parts: case library, which stores the cases of previous software designs; index memory used for efficient case retrieval; data type taxonomy, which is an ontology of the data types used by the system; and WordNet [10], which is a lexical resource that uses a differential theory where concept meanings are represented by symbols enabling a theorist to distinguish among them. Symbols are words, and concept meanings are called synsets. A synset is a concept represented by one or more words. Besides a list of words and the corresponding synsets, WordNet comprises also several types of semantic relations. REBUILDER uses four different type of relations: *is-a*, *part-of*, *substance-of*, and *member-of*. Synsets are used in REBUILDER for categorization of software objects. Each object has a context synset which represents the object meaning. The object's context synset can then be used for computing object similarity (using the WordNet semantic relations), or it can be used as a case index, allowing rapid access to objects with the same classification. Word-Net is used to compute the semantic distance between two context synsets. This distance is used in REBUILDER to assess the type similarity between objects, and to select the correct synset when the object name has more than one synset. This process is called word sense disambiguation [7] and is a crucial task in REBUILDER.

The CBR engine is the responsible module for all the cognitive functionalities of REBUILDER. It comprises five different submodules, each one implementing a different cognitive process that helps the software designer. These submodules are:

Retrieval. The retrieval submodule selects from the case base a set of cases ranked by similarity with the user's query. It enables the software designer to browse through the most similar designs in the case library, exploring different designs alternatives and reusing pieces of cases. This module works like an intelligent search assistance, which first retrieves the relevant cases from the case library and then ranks them by similarity with the query. The cases are presented to the designer only after the cases are ranked. For more details see [5].

Analogy. The analogy submodule generates new solutions using analogical reasoning, which involves selecting case candidates from the case library, then mapping them with the query diagram, and finally transferring knowledge from the source case to the problem diagram, yielding a new diagram. This mechanism generates solutions using only one case, which constraints the type of solutions that it can generate. For more details see [6].

Design Composition. The design composition submodule also generates new solutions from cases in the case library. The main difference to analogy generated solutions is that it can use more than one case to generate a solution. This mechanism can select pieces of cases and then compose them in a new diagram, yielding a solution to the user's query.

Verification and Evaluation. This submodule comprises two functionalities: verification and evaluation. While verification checks the design coherence and correctness. The evaluation mechanism is used to assess the diagram's properties. The verification is manly used in combination with analogy or design composition to look for errors in the generated diagram and to correct them. The evaluation mechanism is at the designer's disposal for listing the design properties, trying to identify shortcomings in a diagram.

Learning. The learning submodule implements several case-based maintenance strategies that can be used by the KB administrator to manage the case library contents. This submodule presents several assessment measures of the case library performance, which provide an important advice to the administrator regarding the addition or deletion of cases.

3 Solution Generation

In REBUILDER solutions are generated using two modules: Analogy and Design Composition. While Analogy creates new diagrams based on one case, Design Composition generates new diagrams based on several cases. The input data used in solution generation is an UML class diagram, in the form of a package. This is the user's query, which usually is a small class diagram in its early stage of development (see Figure 2). This subsection describes in greater detail how these modules generate designs.

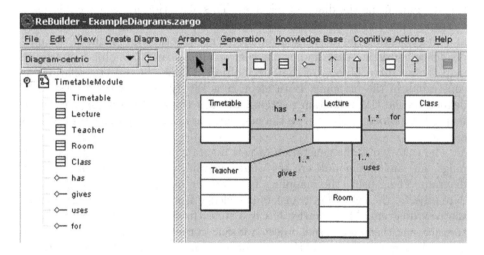

Fig. 2. An example of an class diagram in the early stages of development.

3.1 Analogy

Analogical reasoning is used in REBUILDER to suggest class diagrams to the designer, based on a query diagram. The analogy process has three steps: identify candidate diagrams for analogy; map the candidate diagrams; and create new diagrams by knowledge transfer between the candidate diagram and the query.

Cases are selected from the case library to be used as source diagrams. Most of the analogies that are found in software design are functional analogies, that is, the analogy mapping is performed using the functional similarity between objects. Using the retrieval algorithm in the first phase of analogy enables this kind of analogies, since objects that are functional similar tend to be categorized in the same branch of (or close to) the WordNet *is-a* trees. Thus, the analogy module benefits from a retrieval filtering based on functional similarity (for more details see [6]).

The second step of analogy is the mapping of each candidate to the query diagram, yielding an object list correspondence for each candidate. This phase relies on two alternative algorithms: one based on relation mapping, and the other on object mapping, but both return a list of mappings between objects. The relation-based algorithm uses the UML relations to establish the object mappings. It starts the mapping selecting a query relation based on an UML heuristic (independence measure), which selects the relation that connects the two most important diagram objects. The independence measure is an heuristic used to assign to each diagram object an independence value based on UML knowledge that reflects an object's independence in relation to all the other diagram objects. Then it tries to find a matching relation on the candidate diagram. After it finds a match, it starts the mapping by the neighbor relations, spreading the mapping using the diagram relations. This algorithm maps objects in pairs corresponding to the relation's objects. The object-based algorithm starts the mapping selecting the most independent query object, based on the UML independence heuristic. After finding the corresponding candidate object, it tries to map the neighbor objects of the query object, taking the object's relations as constraints in the mapping. Both algorithms satisfy the structural constraints defined by the UML diagram relations. Most of the resulting mappings do not map all the problem objects, so the mappings are ranked by number of objects mapped.

The last step is the generation of new diagrams using the established mappings. The analogy module creates a new diagram, which is a copy of the query diagram. Then, using the mappings between the query objects and the candidate objects, the algorithm transfers knowledge from the candidate diagram to the new diagram. This transfer has two steps: first there is an internal object transfer, and then an external object transfer. In the internal object transfer, the mapped query object gets all the attributes and methods from the candidate object that were not in the query object. This way, the query object is completed by the internal knowledge of the candidate object. The second step transfers neighbor objects and relations from the mapped candidate objects to the query objects, from the new diagram. This transfers new objects and relations to the new diagram, expanding it.

3.2   Case-Based Design Composition

The Design Composition module generates new diagrams by decomposition and/or composition of case diagrams. The goal of the composition module is to generate new diagrams that have the query objects, thus providing an evolved version of the query diagram. Generation of a new UML design using case-based composition involves two main steps: retrieving cases from the case library to be used as knowledge sources, and using the retrieved cases (or parts of them) to build new UML diagrams. In the first phase, the selection of the cases to be used is performed using the retrieval algorithm described in section 2. The adaptation of the retrieved cases to the target problem is based on two different strategies: best case composition, and best complementary cases composition.

In the best case composition, the adaptation module starts from the most similar case to the problem, mapping the case objects to the problem objects. The case mapped objects are copied to a new case. If this new case maps successfully all the problem objects, then the adaptation process ends. Otherwise it selects the retrieved case, which best complements the new case (in relation to the problem), and uses it to get the missing parts. This process continues while there are unmapped objects in the problem definition. Note that, if there are objects in the used case that are not in the problem, they can be transferred to the new case, generating new objects.

The best complementary cases composition starts by matching each retrieved case to the problem, yielding a mapping between the case objects and the problem objects. This is used to determine the degree of problem coverage of each case, after which several sets of cases are constructed. These sets are based on the combined coverage of the problem, with the goal of finding sets of cases that globally map all the problem objects. The best matching set is then used to generate a new case.

4   Solution Verification

The main idea of verification in REBUILDER is to use the available knowledge sources to verify class diagrams, which are: design cases, WordNet, verification cases, and the designer. Not only REBUILDER generated diagrams can be verified, designer created ones can also be verified. The designer has only to select the diagram to be checked and the verification command to perform it. The designer can also select an option in the settings menu to automatically verify every solution generated by REBUILDER. There are five different types of verification: package, object name, relation, attribute, and method. Verifying an object consists on determining it's validity (true or false), which is to say, if the object is correct or if it is invalid or incoherent with the diagram. In case of being correct it stays in the diagram, otherwise the object can be deleted from the diagram.

One important implementation aspect is that verification cases are stored locally in the designer's client. Thus, each designer has her/his library of verification cases, which makes the system personalized. This is very important since each software designer has her/his way of modelling systems, making verification a personalized task.

4.1   Package Verification

The package verification checks a class diagram starting with the diagram relations, then checking each object's attributes and methods, finally it checks the sub-packages, recursively calling the package verification functionality.

4.2   Name Verification

Name checking applies only to packages, classes and interfaces, and is performed when REBUILDER needs to assign a synset to an object. REBUILDER reasoning mechanisms depend on the correct assignment of synsets to objects, which makes this verification very important. REBUILDER makes a morphological and compositional analysis of the object's name, trying to match it to WordNet words. Once it finds a match it can easily get the list of possible synsets for the given name. Now, two things can happen: the user selects the correct synset, or REBUILDER uses a word sense disambiguation method to do it (it is up to the user to decide).

4.3   Relation Verification

Relation checking is based in WordNet, in the design cases, and in relation verification cases, which are cases describing successful and failure situations in checking a relation validity. These cases are described by: Relation Type {Association, Generalization, Realization, Dependency}, Multiplicity {1-1, 1-N, N-N}, Source Object Name, Source Object Synset, Destination Object Name, Destination Object Synset, and Outcome {Success or Failure}. Two relation verification cases c_1 and c_2 match if:

$$RelationType(c_1) = RelationType(c_2) \land Multiplicity(c_1) = Multiplicity(c_2) \land$$
$$SourceObject(c_1) \equiv SourceObject(c_2) \land DestObject(c_1) \equiv DestObject(c_2) \quad (1)$$

Where $RelationType(c)$, $Multiplicity(c)$, $SourceObject(c)$ and $DestObject(c)$ are respectively: relation type, multiplicity, source object, and destination object of verification case c. Two objects, o_1 and o_2 are said to be equivalent if:

$$o_1 \equiv o_2 \Leftrightarrow (Synset(o_1) \neq \varnothing \land Synset(o_1) \neq \varnothing \land Synset(o_1) = Synset(o_1)) \lor$$
$$((Synset(o_1) = \varnothing \lor Synset(o_2) = \varnothing) \land Name(o_1) = Name(o_2)) \quad (2)$$

Where $Synset(o)$ gives the synset of object o and $Name(o)$ yields the name of object o. All the knowledge sources are used for validating the relation being inspected. The order of search is: relation verification cases, WordNet, design cases and the designer. The verification algorithm for relations is detailed in figure 3.

A WordNet equivalent relation is a relation between two synsets in which one of them is the source object synset and the other is the destination object synset. A design case comprises an equivalent relation if it has two objects connected by a similar relation to the one being investigated, and with equivalent source objects and destination objects. Retrieval of verification cases is based on two steps: first on the relation type, and then by source object name. If there are more than one equivalent cases the outcome with more cases is chosen as the correct outcome. In case of a draw, the system retrieves the newest case.

4.4   Attribute Verification

Attribute checking is based on WordNet, the design cases, and in Attribute Verification Cases, which are cases describing successful and failure situations in checking an attribute validity. These cases have the following description: Object Name, Object Synset, Attribute Name, and Outcome Success or Failure. Two

Search for a equivalent verification case in the library.
    Iffound and outcome is *Success* Then
        Consider the relation valid and exit.
    If found and outcome is *Failure* Then
        Consider the relation invalid and delete it from the diagram, and exit.
    If not found Then
        Continue.
Search for a equivalent relation in WordNet.
    If found Then
        Consider the relation valid, add a new successful verification case and exit.
    Else
        Continue.
Search for a equivalent relation in the design cases.
    If found Then
        Consider the relation valid, add a new successful verification case and exit.
    Else
        Continue.
Ask the user the relation validity.
    If user considers relation valid Then
        Consider the relation valid, add a new successful verification case and exit.
Consider the relation invalid, add a new failure verification case and exit.

Fig. 3. The relation verification algorithm.

attribute verification cases c_1 and c_2 match if: the objects' names and synsets, and attributes' names are the same, or if one of the synsets is null and their names and attributes' names are the same. As in relation verification, all the knowledge sources are used for validating the attribute being inspected. The order of search and the algorithm used is the same as in relation verification (adapted to the attribute situation). A WordNet equivalent attribute is represented by a *substance-of*, *member-of* or *part-of* relation between the synset of the object being inspected and every possible synset of the attribute's name. A design case comprises a similar attribute, if there is an object with the same synset and name comprising an attribute with the same name as the attribute being inspected. Retrieval of verification cases is based on two steps: first on object name and then on object synset.

4.5   Method Verification

Method verification is similar to the attribute verification with the exception that WordNet is not used as a knowledge source, being replaced by an heuristic. The heuristic used is: if the method name has a word that is an attribute name or a neighbor class name then the method is considered valid. Method verification cases describe successful and failure situations in checking a method validity. These cases have the following description: Object Name, Object Synset, Method Name, and Outcome Success or Failure. Two method verification cases c_1 and c_2

match if: the objects' names and synsets, and methods' names are the same, or if one of the synsets is null and their names and methods' names are the same. As in relation verification, all the knowledge sources are used for validating the method being inspected. The order of search and the algorithm used is the same as in relation verification (adapted to the method situation and with WordNet replaced by the heuristic referred before). A design case comprises a similar method, if there is an object with the same synset and name comprising a method with the same name as the method being inspected. Retrieval of method verification cases is performed in the same way as in attribute verification cases.

4.6   Example

This subsection illustrates the verification process described before with an example. Suppose that the designer uses the diagram presented in figure 2 as a problem for the design composition module, resulting in a new diagram. Part of this diagram is presented in figure 4, which shows some inconsistencies, for instance: the generalization between *Teacher* and *Timetable*, or the method *addStudent* in *Timetable*, or the attribute *studentID* in class *Lecture*.

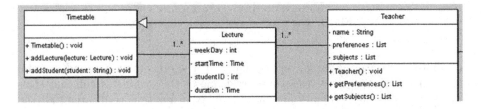

Fig. 4. Part of a class diagram resulting from a design composition operation.

The verification process starts by checking the package containing the new diagram. For illustration purposes we will describe the process checking only the diagram elements considered invalid, the ones mentioned before. When the verification process reaches the generalization between *Timetable* and *Teacher*, the system first searches in the verification cases for an equivalent case, which does not exist. Then it searches for WordNet for an *is-a* relation between the *Timetable* synset and *Teacher* synset, which does not exist. Then searches the design cases that do not have any similar relation, and finally asks the designer for a validation on this relation, which s/he answers that is invalid. Then the system adds a new relation verification case comprising: [Generalization, 1-1, Teacher, 108756476[1], Timetable, 105441050, Failure], and deletes the relation. The next time the system finds an identical relation it will consider it invalid and will delete it from the design. Now suppose it is checking the *studentID* attribute of class *Lecture*, the attribute verification process will search the case library of

---

[1] Synsets are identified by nine digit numbers.

attribute verification cases and it finds an equivalent case: [Lecture, 106035418, studentID, Failure]. The system considers the attribute invalid and deletes it from the diagram. Finally the system checks method *addStudent* from class *Timetable* and the method checking heuristic does not applies, and the design cases have no similar method, then it asks the designer, which considers the method invalid. The method verification algorithm will delete the method and add a new method verification case: [Timetable, 105441050, addStudent, Failure]. We only showed failure situations, but success situations are more frequent than failure ones.

5   Experiments

This section describes the experimental work performed to evaluate the verification mechanism. We have tested the verification with analogy and design composition. Within the design composition we have used both strategies: best case composition and best complementary cases composition (also called best set composition).

5.1   Setup

We have used a Knowledge Base with 60 cases describing software designs. These cases are from four different domains: banking information systems, health information systems, educational institution information systems, and store information systems (grocery stores, video stores, and others). Each design comprises a package, with 5 to 20 objects (total number of objects in the knowledge base is 586). Each object has up to 20 attributes, and up to 20 methods. These designs are defined at a conceptual level, so the design is at an early stage of development having only the fundamental objects.

Twenty five problems were defined, each one having one package with several objects (between 3 and 5), which were related to each other by UML associations or generalizations. These problems are distributed by the four case domains in the following way: banking information systems (6), health information systems (7), educational institution information systems (3), and store information systems (9). For each combination of solution generation method (Analogy, Design Composition - Best Case, and Design Composition - Best Set) by type of object considered (Relation, Attribute or Method) we generated a run with the same 25 test problems and then gathered the data, which was then analyzed by a software engineer.

5.2   Verification in Analogy

Figure 5 presents the cumulative number of objects considered wrong by the user. The X-axis represents the 25 problems used, in this case the presentation order of these problems is considered a progression, since the system learns new

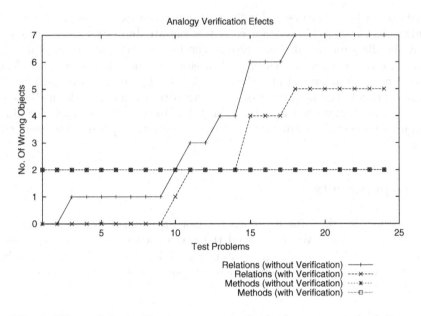

Fig. 5. Effects of the verification process in the Analogy generated solutions.

verification from each problem it solves. We are only considering: relations, attributes and methods. In this case of Analogy solutions, there are no attribute objects considered wrong by the designers. Notice that solutions generated by Analogy generate few wrong objects compared to the ones created by Design Composition. This happens because Design Composition combines parts of different cases, thus generating some inconsistencies. The verification mechanism did not improve the number of wrong methods, but it has improved slightly the number of wrong relations.

5.3   Verification in Design Composition

In the case of verification in Design Composition, figures 6 and 7 show the experimental results. These results show a major improvement in the solution quality, in particular in the methods and relations. The system can effectively drop the number of wrong objects in generated solutions, presenting to the user better solutions.

Table 1 presents the total number of verification cases generated and stored by the verification module, and also the number of questions asked to the user. Notice the difference between the number of verification cases and questions asked to the user. Most of the verification cases come from the design case library (from the design cases) and from WordNet. Since the system learns these new verification cases, the tendency of the number of questions asked to the user is to decline, especially if the designer is working in the same domain.

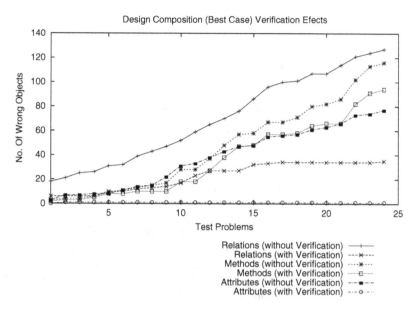

Fig. 6. Effects of the verification process in the Design Composition (Best Case) generated solutions.

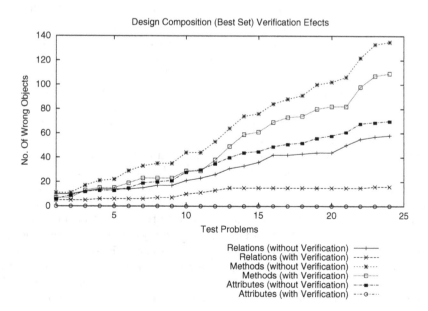

Fig. 7. Effects of the verification process in the Design Composition (Best Set) generated solutions.

Table 1. The total number of verification cases and questions asked to the user.

	Analogy	Best Case	Best Set
No. of Verification Cases (Relations)	244	451	239
No. of Verification Cases (Methods)	511	1210	781
No. of Verification Cases (Attributes)	298	646	430
No. of Questions (Relations)	68	244	145
No. of Questions (Methods)	0	106	104
No. of Questions (Attributes)	3	183	185

6   Conclusions and Future Work

This paper presents an approach to verification of design solutions based on CBR. The main contribution of this work is the use of cases for verification combined with WordNet lexical resource. The experimental work indicates that this approach improves the performance of the adaptation mechanism of RE-BUILDER, making it more robust.

Our approach has the advantage of combining system learning and evolution, with design personalization. As a tool in a CASE environment, the verification module enables an intelligent and personalized assistant, checking possible inconsistencies and errors in diagrams. This tool is especially useful when generated designs are big, escaping from the capabilities of human designers. Another advantage of using CBR, is that the system does not need a domain model to perform verification, at the beginning it might act as a 'dumb' assistant but it has the willing and the ability to learn from it's mistakes.

There are some limitations to our approach, especially when discussing methodological issues. Our approach is intended to be used in an individual level since it is implemented in a CASE tool. Our main argument for this choice, is that each designer has a different way to model the problem being addressed. Starting from this assumption we decided that the case base of verification cases would be local to each client (or designer). When dealing with team development our assumption can have some limitations. Though we defend our point of view by saying that, from our experience, most of the times team development at design level is performed by one or two members, which then discuss their designs with the rest of the team, but only one or two project members are responsible for using the CASE tool for designing the system model. Nevertheless, there are at least two ways of addressing this problem. First, centralizing all the verification cases in one case base accessible by every team member, which would imply the maintenance of such a case base. Or imposing project-wide agreements, which are always difficult to make. Both solutions have problems to be solved.

Future work will go in the direction of checking the classes and interfaces validity, though it is a more difficult goal. Future work will also involve the improvement of word sense disambiguation, which is also crucial to the classification of software objects.

Acknowledgments. This work was supported by POSI - Programa Operacional Sociedade de Informação of Fundação Portuguesa para a Ciência e Tecnologia and European Union FEDER, under contract POSI / 33399 / SRI / 2000, and by program PRAXIS XXI. We would like to thanks the reviewers for their helpful comments on this paper.

References

1. Agnar Aamodt and Enric Plaza, *Case–based reasoning: Foundational issues, methodological variations, and system approaches.*, AI Communications **7** (1994), no. 1, 39–59.
2. Barry Boehm, *A spiral model of software development and enhancement*, IEEE Press, 1988.
3. Ashok Goel, Sambasiva Bhatta, and Eleni Stroulia, *Kritik: An early case-based design system*, Issues and Applications of Case-Based Reasoning in Design (Mahwah, NJ) (Mary Lou Maher and Pearl Pu, eds.), Lawrence Erlbaum Associates, 1997, pp. 87–132.
4. Paulo Gomes, Carlos Bento, and Pedro Gago, *Learning to verify design solutions from failure knowledge*, Artificial Intelligence for Engineering Design, Analysis and Manufacturing **12** (1998), no. 2, 107–115.
5. Paulo Gomes, Francisco C. Pereira, Paulo Paiva, Nuno Seco, Paulo Carreiro, José L. Ferreira, and Carlos Bento, *Case retrieval of software designs using wordnet*, European Conference on Artificial Intelligence (ECAI'02) (Lyon, France) (F. van Harmelen, ed.), IOS Press, Amsterdam, 2002.
6. Paulo Gomes, Francisco C. Pereira, Paulo Paiva, Nuno Seco, Paulo Carreiro, José L. Ferreira, and Carlos Bento, *Combining case-based reasoning and analogical reasoning in software design*, Proceedings of the 13th Irish Conference on Artificial Intelligence and Cognitive Science (AICS'02) (Limerick, Ireland), Springer-Verlag, September 2002.
7. Nancy Ide and Jean Veronis, *Introduction to the special issue on word sense disambiguation: The state of the art*, Computational Linguistics **24** (1998), no. 1, 1–40.
8. Janet Kolodner, *Case-based reasoning*, Morgan Kaufman, 1993.
9. Mary Lou Maher, *Casecad and cadsyn*, Issues and Applications of Case-Based Reasoning in Design (Mahwah, NJ) (Mary Lou Maher and Pearl Pu, eds.), Lawrence Erlbaum Associates, 1997, pp. 161–185.
10. George Miller, Richard Beckwith, Christiane Fellbaum, Derek Gross, and Katherine J. Miller, *Introduction to wordnet: an on-line lexical database.*, International Journal of Lexicography **3** (1990), no. 4, 235 – 244.
11. Pearl Pu and Lisa Purvis, *Formalizing the adaptation process for case-based design*, Issues and Applications of Case-Based Reasoning in Design (Mahwah, NJ) (Mary Lou Maher and Pearl Pu, eds.), Lawrence Erlbaum Associates, 1997, pp. 221–260.
12. Angi Voss, *Case design specialists in fabel*, Issues and Applications of Case-Based Reasoning in Design (Mahwah, NJ) (Mary Lou Maher and Pearl Pu, eds.), Lawrence Erlbaum Associates, 1997, pp. 301–336.

Evaluation of Case-Based Maintenance Strategies in Software Design

Paulo Gomes, Francisco C. Pereira, Paulo Paiva, Nuno Seco, Paulo Carreiro, José Luís Ferreira, and Carlos Bento

CISUC - Centro de Informática e Sistemas da Universidade de Coimbra.
Departamento de Engenharia Informática, Polo II, Universidade de Coimbra.
3030 Coimbra
pgomes@dei.uc.pt,
http://rebuilder.dei.uc.pt

Abstract. CBR applications running in real domains can easily reach thousands of cases, which are stored in the case library. Retrieval times can increase greatly if the retrieval algorithm can not cope with such an amount of cases. Redundancy can also be a problem, focusing retrieval alternatives in a very restricted search space. Basically, the system's performance starts to degrade with the increase of the case-base size. Case-base maintenance allows CBR systems to deal with this problem, mainly through the use of case selection criteria. In this paper we present an experimental study about several case-base maintenance policies developed till now. We adapted and implemented these policies to a CBR system for software reuse and design, testing the applicability of these policies to cases with a complex representation (combination of tree and graph representations).

1 Introduction

The performance of Case-Based Reasoning (CBR, [1,2]) systems depends on several factors. From the similarity measures used for ranking cases, to the adaptation and verification mechanisms, and particularly the content of the case library - the cases used for reasoning. Case-base maintenance (CBM) is an important issue in a CBR system [4]. Several problems can arise if the case-base is not fine tuned, for instance, the system can take too much time to provide a solution to a problem, due to the high number of cases in the case library, or the right cases are not retrieved due to a redundancy problem of the case-base, or more complex issues, like the diversity of a case-base.

CBM has been the focus of several CBR researchers for some time. Smyth and Keane [10] describe a case deletion policy for CBR systems which is based on the idea of preserving the competence of a case-base. They have showed that traditional deletion policies solve the performance problem (when retrieval time performance is poor, due to the high number of cases in the library), but they may fail to preserve the case-base competence. Racine and Yang [8] stress two important issues in CBM, the existence of redundant and inconsistent cases,

K.D. Ashley and D.G. Bridge (Eds.): ICCBR 2003, LNAI 2689, pp. 186–200, 2003.
© Springer-Verlag Berlin Heidelberg 2003

presenting methods to deal with these cases. One important notion in CBM is the competence of a case-base and was introduced by Smyth [11]. This notion is based on the observation that some cases are crucial to the competence of a case-base, while others redundant. Using the notion of case-base competence Zhu and Yang [13] presented a case addition policy rather then deletion. Smyth and McKenna [12] presented a technique for constructing compact competent case-bases, this technique is based on the relative coverage of a case. Leake and Wilson [3] developed a new CBM policy based on the relative performance of a case. Recently McKenna and Smyth [5] have presented a study using several case-base editing techniques.

In our research work, we are developing a CASE tool capable of providing the software designer with several functionalities that we consider intelligent. Some of these capabilities are: retrieving similar designs, suggesting alternative designs, revising designs, learning design knowledge, and others. Our tool, called REBUILDER, basis it's reasoning abilities on cases, which are the main knowledge source and a way of storing the design knowledge of a software development company. REBUILDER is intended to be used at a company level, centralizing the design knowledge and enabling it's reuse. One important issue is the CBM strategy to follow, since the case-base performance is crucial to the system's success. In this paper we explore several CBM policies having in mind REBUILDER as a target application.

The main CBM problem is: what cases should be in the case-base? But for this question to be answered, another question arises: what is the main purpose of the CBR system? and subsequently: what are the main properties that the case-base must have? In order to select an appropriate CBM strategy for RE-BUILDER, we have chosen some of the CBM strategies developed, and we have adapted and implemented them in our system. Most of these strategies are used with a case representation based on vectors of attribute/value pairs. Our approach uses a more complex case representation, where cases are UML (Unified Modelling Language, [9]) diagrams, represented by a tree-like structure, where each node can be a class diagram, which is basically a graph. We are interested on testing the CBM strategies implemented and to study the properties and performance of REBUILDER's case-base.

The next section describes REBUILDER, detailing it's architecture and case representation. Section 3 describes nine different CBM criteria that are implemented in REBUILDER, with the purpose of testing them. Then section 4 presents the performed experiments and the obtained results. Finally, section 5 analyzes the performance of the different CBM criteria, showing the advantages and disadvantages of each criteria. We also draw some conclusions about our case-base properties, and what are the desirable characteristics of REBUILDER case-base.

2   REBUILDER

We developed a CASE tool named REBUILDER whose main goals are: to create a corporation's memory of design knowledge; to provide tools for reusing design knowledge; and to provide the software designer with a design environment capable of promoting software design reuse. This section describes the architecture of REBUILDER and the case representation used.

2.1   Architecture

It comprises four different modules (see figure 1): Knowledge Base (KB), UML Editor, KB Manager and Case-Based Reasoning (CBR) Engine. It runs in a client-server environment, where the KB is on the server side and the CBR Engine, UML Editor and KB Manager are on the client side. There are two types of clients: the design user client, which comprises the CBR Engine and the UML Editor; and the KB administrator client, which comprises the CBR Engine and the KB Manager. Only one KB administrator client can be running, but there can be several design user clients.

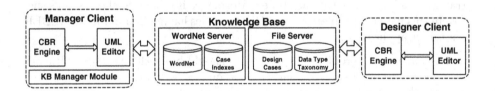

Fig. 1. REBUILDER's Architecture.

The UML editor is the front-end of REBUILDER and the environment dedicated to the software designer. The KB Manager module is used by the administrator to manage the KB, keeping it consistent and updated. The KB comprises four different parts: the case library which stores the cases of previous software designs; an index memory that is used for efficient case retrieval; the data type taxonomy, which is an ontology of the data types used by the system; and Word-Net [6], which is a general ontology that uses a differential theory where concept meanings are represented by symbols enabling a theorist to distinguish among them. Symbols are words, and concept meanings are called synsets. A synset is a concept represented by one or more words. Besides a list of words and the corresponding synsets, WordNet comprises also several types of semantic relations. REBUILDER uses four different type of relations: *is-a, part-of, substance-of*, and *member-of*. Every object in a case has a synset called context synset. This synset categorizes the object in WordNet and enables the use of WordNet as an indexing structure.

The CBR Engine is the reasoning part of REBUILDER. As the name shows, it uses the CBR paradigm to establish a reasoning framework. This module comprises six different parts: Retrieval, Design Composition, Design Patterns, Analogy, Verification, and Learning. The Retrieval sub-module retrieves cases from the case library based on the similarity with the target problem. The Design Composition sub-module modifies old cases to create new solutions. It can take pieces of one or more cases to build a new solution by composition of these pieces. The Design Patterns sub-module, uses software design patterns and CBR for generation of new designs. Analogy establishes a mapping between the problem and the selected cases, which is then used to build a new design by knowledge transfer between the selected case and the target problem. Case Verification checks the coherence and consistency of the cases created or modified by the system. It revises a solution generated by REBUILDER before it is shown to the software designer. The last reasoning sub-module is the retain phase, where the system learns new cases. The cases generated by REBUILDER are stored in the case library and indexed using a memory structure.

2.2   Case Representation

In REBUILDER a case describes a software design, which is represented in UML through the use of Class Diagrams. Figure 2 shows an example of a class diagram representing part of a scheduler system. Nodes are classes, with name, attributes and methods. Links represent relations between classes. Closed-arrow relations represent generalizations, and no-arrow relations represent participative associations. Conceptually a case in REBUILDER comprises: a name used to identify the case within the case library; the main package, which is an object that comprises all the objects that describe the main class diagram; and the file name where the case is stored. UML class diagram objects considered in REBUILDER are: packages, classes, interfaces and relations. A package is an UML object used to group other objects. A class describes an entity in UML and it corresponds to a concept described by attributes at a structural level, and by methods at a behavioral level. Interfaces have only method declarations, since they describe a protocol of communication for a specific class. A relation describes a relationship between two UML objects.

3   Case-Based Maintenance Strategies

Several Case-Based Maintenance (CBM) strategies have been implemented in REBUILDER. Most of these criteria were developed for cases represented as vectors of attribute/value pairs, since we have a complex case representation we had to adapt these strategies to our work. Our main contribution is the adaptation of these strategies to a graph-like case representation,

In REBUILDER the learning mechanism is a tool at the disposal of the KB administrator. When the software designer thinks that a design is worth going into the design repository (the case library) s/he can submit it. This action sends the design to the list of unconfirmed cases in the case library. The KB administrator can then call the *Activate Learning* command to start the CBM

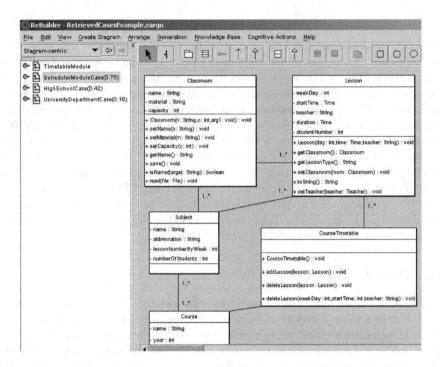

Fig. 2. Example of an UML Class diagram.

process. For each submitted case the learning module runs the CBM strategies selected (by the KB administrator). These strategies give an advice about adding submitted cases to the case library or not, and if there are any cases that should be removed. The final decision is always up to the KB administrator. The next subsections describe the CBM strategies used in REBUILDER and how they were adapted to our case representation.

3.1   Frequency Deletion Criteria

The frequency deletion criteria developed by Minton [7], selects cases for deletion based on the frequency of case access. This implies the existence of an access counter associated with each case. The counter starts with zero and is incremented each time the case is retrieved. A maximum number of cases is established for the case library (called swamping limit). When the learning mechanism is activated, if the number of cases in the library reaches the swamping limit, the less used cases (enough to keep the swamping limit) are selected for deletion. If the swamping limit is not reached, new cases can be added to the case library with their frequency reset. In case there are one or more cases with the same frequency of use, then the one with the oldest access is chosen for deletion. In REBUILDER, if this criteria is not enough, then the smallest case is selected for deletion.

3.2   Subsumption Criteria

The subsumption criteria developed by Racine [8] defines that a case is redundant if:

- Is equal to another case, Or
- Is equivalent to another case, Or
- Is subsumed by another case.

When a new case is to be added to the case library it must be checked for redundancy. If the case is considered redundant, then it is not added to the case library. Cases are redundant when they are subsumed by other cases. In REBUILDER a case C_1 is considered subsumed by case C_2 if the root package of C_1 is subsumed by a package of C_2. A package Pk_1 is subsumed by a package Pk_2 if:

- Pk_1 and Pk_2 have the same synset, And
- All the diagram objects of Pk_1 (except sub-packages) have an equivalent in Pk_2, And
- All sub-packages in Pk_1 are subsumed by a sub-package of Pk_2.

This definition is recursive, which is adequate to the tree-like structure of class diagrams. This process can be time consuming, especially if we are dealing with big design cases.

3.3   Footprint Deletion Criteria

Smyth and Keane [10] developed this criteria, which involves two important notions: coverage and reachability. Coverage of a case is considered to be the neighborhood of the case within a certain adaptation limits, in other words, is the set of problems that a case can solve.

$$CoverageSet(c \in C) = \{c' \in C : Solves(c, c')\} \tag{1}$$

Where C is the case base considered. The reachability set of a case, is the set of cases that can solve this case.

$$ReachabilitySet(c \in C) = \{c' \in C : Solves(c', c)\} \tag{2}$$

Since a target problem in REBUILDER is a class diagram, we say that a case c solves a problem p, when class diagram c subsumes class diagram p, which means:

$$Solves(c, p) = Subsumes(c, p) \tag{3}$$

Using these two concepts, Smyth and Keane divide cases in the case library in four types: pivotal, auxiliary, spanning, and support cases. Pivotal cases represent unique ways to answer a specific query. Auxiliary cases are those which are completely subsumed by other cases in the case base. Spanning cases are cases between Pivotal and Auxiliary cases, which link together areas covered by other cases. Support cases exist in groups to support an idea. The recommended order of deletion is: auxiliary, support, spanning, and pivotal. In REBUILDER Support cases can not be distinguished from Spanning cases, due to the definitions used for coverage and reachability sets. So we decided not to use Support cases. The formal definitions used in REBUILDER for these case types are:

$$Pivotal(c) \Leftarrow \forall c' \in C : \neg Subsumes(c', c)$$

$$Spanning(c) \Leftarrow \exists c' \in C : Subsumes(c', c) \wedge \exists c'' \in C : Subsumes(c, c'')$$

$$Auxiliary(c) \Leftarrow \exists c' \in C : Subsumes(c', c) \wedge \forall c'' \in C : \neg Subsumes(c, c'') \qquad (4)$$

In case of a draw, the similarity between the candidate cases and the new case is used to select the cases to be deleted. The cases most similar to the new case are chosen for deletion.

3.4 Footprint-Utility Deletion Criteria

This criteria, also developed by Smyth and Keane [10], is the same as the Footprint Deletion Criteria, with the exception that when there is a draw the selection is based on the case usage - less used cases are chosen for deletion.

3.5 Coverage Criteria

The coverage criteria as it was first devised by Smyth and McKenna [11], involves three factors: case-base size, case-base density, and case-base distribution. The competence of a case-base is strongly influenced by its size. This is an obvious and easy to understand claim. Another relevant factor is the case-base density, with the local density of a case c within a group of cases G in the case-base C being defined by:

$$CaseDensity(c, G) = \frac{\sum_{c' \in G - \{c\}} Sim(c, c')}{|G| - 1} \qquad (5)$$

Where $Sim(c,c')$ returns the case similarity between c and c'. The third factor that influences a case-base competence is the case distribution. This factor is more complex than other factors because if the CBR system performs adaptation and verification of solutions, this will also influence the case-base distribution (besides retrieval, of course). To assess the competence of a case-base, Smyth and McKenna compute the local case coverage sets and determine how these sets combine and interact to form the case-base competence. They define a competence group as a set of cases which are related to each other, and that make a contribution to the case-base competence, which is independent from other competence groups. The definition of competence groups is based on the shared coverage concept. Two cases exhibit shared coverage if their coverage sets overlap:

$$SharedCoverage(c, c') = true \Leftarrow CoverageSet(c) \cap CoverageSet(c') \neq \varnothing \qquad (6)$$

A competence group can be defined as:

$$CompetenceGroup(G) = \{\forall c_i \in G, \exists c_j \in G - \{c_i\} : SharedCoverage(c_i, c_j) = true\}$$

$$\wedge \{\forall c_k \in C - G, \neg \exists c_l \in G : SharedCoverage(c_k, c_l) = true\} \qquad (7)$$

Smyth and McKenna show that according to this definition a case belongs to only one competence group. Competence group size and number depends on four factors: distribution of cases, density of cases, retrieval mechanism, and adaptation mechanism. Group coverage can be defined by the number and density of cases in the group. The number of cases in the group is easy to measure, group density is given by:

$$GroupDensity(G) = \frac{\sum_{c \in G} CaseDensity(c, G)}{|G|} \qquad (8)$$

Group coverage is based on group size and group density, and is defined as:

$$GroupCoverage(G) = 1 + [|G| \bullet (1 - GroupDensity(G))] \qquad (9)$$

The total coverage of a case-base comprising several competence groups ($G = \{G_1, ..., G_n\}$), is given by the following formula:

$$Coverage(G) = \sum_{G_i \in G} GroupCoverage(G_i) \qquad (10)$$

The learning module of REBUILDER uses these definitions to decide if a case should be added to the case-base and which cases should be remove from the case-base. A new case is added to the case library if: the swamping limit has not been reached or its inclusion increases the ratio case-base coverage/case-base number. We do not use a threshold value for the decision of incorporating a new case into the case-base.

3.6   Case-Addition Criteria

The case-addition criteria [13] involves the notion of case neighborhood, which in REBUILDER is defined as:

$$Neighborhood(c) = \{c' \in C, \tau \in [0, 1] : (RPSynset(c) = RPSynset(c')) \wedge (Sim(c, c') > \tau)\} \quad (11)$$

Where $RPSynset(c)$ is the root package synset of case c, and τ is a threshold value used to define a case neighborhood. This criteria also uses the notion of benefit of a case c in relation to a case set S, which we define as:

$$Benefit(c, S) = \sum_{c' \in Neighborhood(c) - Neighborhood(S)} P(c') \qquad (12)$$

The neighborhood of a set of cases is given by:

$$Neighborhood(S) = \bigcup_{c \in S} Neighborhood(c) \qquad (13)$$

In our implementation of this criteria we defined $P(c)$ as the frequency function of case c, which is computed using an access counter associated with each case in the case library. Then the following algorithm is used to determine a set of cases S defining the optimal case-base coverage.

1. Determine the neighborhood for every case in the case-base.
2. Set S to $\varnothing$.
3. Select a case from $C - S$ with the minimal benefit with respect to the neighborhood of S and add it to S.

4. Repeat step 3 until $Neighborhood(C) - Neighborhood(S)$ is empty or S has k elements.

In the end the cases in S should remain in the case-base, all the others should be removed. To determine if a case, not in the case-base, should be added to the case-base, just add it to the case-base and run the algorithm. In the end, if the case is in S then it should be added to the case-base, otherwise it should not.

3.7   Relative Coverage and Condensed NN

Smyth and McKenna [12] developed this criteria with the goal of maximizing coverage while minimizing case-base size. The proposed technique for building case-bases is to use the Condensed Nearest Neighbor (CNN) on cases that have first been arranged in descending order of their relative coverage contributions. The relative coverage is defined as:

$$RelativeCoverage(c) = \sum_{c' \in CoverageSet(c)} \frac{1}{|ReachabilitySet(c')|} \tag{14}$$

Our implementation of this criteria is detailed in the next algorithm. $CaseBase$ and $NewCase$ are respectively the set of cases in the case-base, and a new case not yet in the case-base.

1. $OrderedSet \leftarrow$ Rank by Relative Coverage $CaseBase$ and $NewCase$.
2. $EvaluatedSet \leftarrow \emptyset$
3. $Changes \leftarrow true$
4. WHILE $Changes$ DO
   a) $Changes \leftarrow false$
   b) FORALL $Case$ IN $OrderedSet$ DO
      i. IF $EvaluatedSet$ can not solve $Case$ THEN
         A. $Changes \leftarrow true$
         B. Add $Case$ to $EvaluatedSet$
         C. Remove $Case$ from $OrderedSet$
5. RETURN $EvaluatedSet$

Using this algorithm if the $NewCase$ makes part of the $EvaluatedSet$ then it should be added to the case-base otherwise it should not. Cases in the case-base that are not in $EvaluatedSet$ should be removed from the case-base.

3.8   Relative Performance Metric

Leake and Wilson [3] developed this criteria based on the notion of relative performance to decide if a case should be added to the case-base or not. The relative performance of a case is defined as follows:

$$RP(c) = \sum_{c' \in CoverageSet(c)} (1 - \frac{AdaptCost(c, c')}{\max_{c'' \in ReachabilitySet(c') - \{c\}} \{AdaptCost(c'', c')\}}) \tag{15}$$

Where $AdaptCost$ is the adaptation cost of transforming c into c', which is defined in REBUILDER as the modulus of the difference between objects in c and objects in c'. A submitted case should be added to the case-base if it's relative performance is higher than a threshold value defined by the KB administrator. In our experiments we have used 0.5 as the threshold value.

3.9   Competence-Guided Criteria

The competence-guided criteria [5] extends previous works of Smyth, and uses the notions of case competence based on case coverage and reachability. This criteria uses three ordering functions:

- Reach for Cover (RFC): uses the size of the reachability set of a case. The RFC evaluation function implements this idea: the usefulness of a case is an inverse function of its reachability set size.
- Maximal Cover (MCOV): is based on the size of the coverage set of a case. Cases with large coverage sets can classify many target cases and as such must make a significant contribution to classification competence.
- Relative Coverage (RC): is defined in a relative coverage criteria.

The algorithm used by this criteria, as implemented in REBUILDER is (*CaseBase* and *NewCase* are defined as previously):

1. *RemainingSet* ← *CaseBase* ∪ *NewCase*.
2. *EditedSet* ← ∅
3. WHILE *RemainingSet* ≠ ∅ DO
   a) *Case* ← Next case in the *RemainingSet* according to the selected ordering function.
   b) Add *Case* to *EditedSet*
   c) Remove all cases in *CoverageSet(Case)* from *RemainingSet*
   d) Update the reachability and coverage sets of the cases in the *RemainingSet*
4. RETURN *EditedSet*

As in the relative coverage criteria, the *NewCase* is only added to the case-base if it is part of *EditedSet*.

4   Experiments

The experimental work has the goal of determining the characteristics of the implemented criteria, mainly in two aspects: computational time and case-base competence. The next subsections explore these two issues.

The case-base used in these experiments comprises 60 cases, each one describing a software design at a conceptual level of abstraction. This implies that cases comprise the basic classes and interfaces, with the main methods and attributes. Each case comprises one package, which encloses 8 to 20 objects (total number of objects in the knowledge base is 586). These cases are from four different domains: banking information systems, health information systems, educational institution information systems, and store information systems. Twenty five problems were defined, each one having one package with several objects (between 3 and 5), which were related to each other by UML associations or generalizations. These problems are distributed by the four domains considered for the cases. It should be noted that despite these defined domains, when solving a problem, the retrieval system can use problems from any domain to solve it. The retrieval algorithm can do this due to the indexing structure (WordNet), which connects every synset.

4.1   Experiment 1 – Computational Time Efficiency

Testing the time performance of all these algorithms is from the research point of view, not so important, we think that for application purposes this is important. Especially when dealing with case-bases that, when in activity, store a huge number of cases, or to study scaling properties of these strategies. In the experiments we have used abbreviations to refer to the strategies: **FDC** - Frequency Deletion Criteria, **SC** - Subsumption Criteria, **FtDC** - Footprint Deletion Criteria, **FtUDC** - Footprint Utility Deletion Criteria, **CC** - Coverage Criteria, **CAC** - Case-Addition Criteria, **RCCNN** - Relative Coverage and Condensed NN, **RPM** - Relative Performance Metric, and **CGC** - Competence-Guided Criteria.

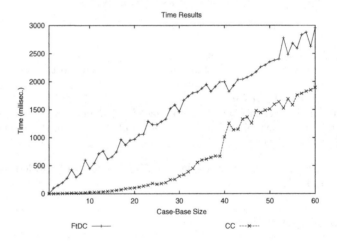

Fig. 3. Computation time results for criteria FtDC and CC.

The results are presented in figures 3 and 4, and show that there are three different groups of criteria, regarding computation time and scalability. The first group comprises FtDC and CC (see figure 3), which have a very different performance from the other criteria. Their computation time grows in a linear way but with a much bigger factor. In particular, FtDC performs worst than CC, at least for the 60 case library used. The second group contains CAC, CGC, FDC, and FtUDC, which in the experiments grow linearly, but with a much lower factor than the first group. FDC and FtUDC are very regular, contrasting with CAC and CGC, which had a slightly exponential growth between iteration 25 and 33. We think that this is due to the sequence of cases used, it possibly was a set of cases that needed more computational time to compute the criteria algorithm. Criteria SC and RPM are the third group, which have very low computational times (bellow one millisecond most of the times). SC is very fast, because among the 60 cases there are no case subsumptions. This results from the subsumption criteria defined (see 3.2), and to the huge search space, from which we have selected 60 'points' close enough to have similarities, but not enough to be subsumed.

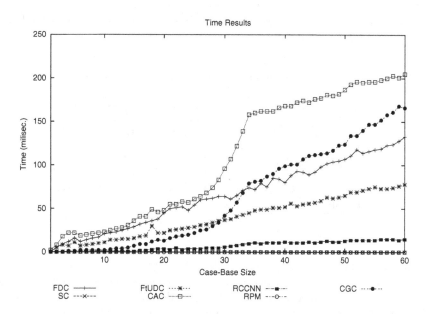

Fig. 4. Computation time results for the other criteria (FDC, SC, FtDUC, CAC, RC-CNN, RPM, and CGC).

4.2   Experiment 2 – Case-Base Competence

The second experiment comprises the variance of the case-base size, using the CBM strategies to define which cases would be part of the case base. We have used six different case-base sizes: 10, 20, 30, 40, 50 and 60. The last one comprises all the possible cases, so there is no need to apply the strategies. The case-base of size 60 is also used as the benchmark for the case base. For each criteria we evaluated the case-base competence using the test problems. For each test problem we ran the retrieval and the adaptation (design composition) algorithms and evaluated the suggested designs, as being relevant or not relevant. For the retrieval, we considered relevant if a retrieved case within the first five was similar to the problem. We defined similar as having the same package synset, and having the same objects (same synset) except one. In the adaptation, only one generated solution was inspected, using the same solution evaluation criteria as in the retrieval.

From the results presented in tables 1 and 2, it can be inferred that the adaptation mechanism makes a big difference in the evaluation of the case-base competence. Even with only ten cases, the case-base has a higher competence than just with retrieval. An explanation for this is that the solution space (UML class diagram space) is huge and the 60 cases are only a very small portion of it. The normal situation is the target problem to be different from the cases in the case-base, which makes the retrieval to find a similar case but not similar enough to solve it. The adaptation mechanism is robust enough to use a retrieved case to solve the target problem.

Table 1. Competence results computed using the CBM strategies, without adaptation.

CB Size	FDC	SC	FtDC	FtUDC	CC	CAC	RCCNN	RPM	CGC
10	24%	24%	4%	24%	24%	4%	24%	24%	24%
20	36%	36%	4%	36%	36%	8%	36%	36%	36%
30	48%	48%	8%	48%	48%	12%	48%	48%	48%
40	48%	48%	16%	48%	48%	36%	48%	48%	48%
50	48%	48%	40%	48%	48%	36%	48%	48%	48%
60	48%	48%	48%	48%	48%	48%	48%	48%	48%

Analyzing the results in respect to the different case-base maintenance policies, and using only these experiments. It is obvious that most of them lost performance when reducing the case-base size, despite that most of the criteria only originate case-bases with lower competence when they lost more than 50% of the cases. This may indicate that there are redundant cases in the case-base, which seems that most of the strategies are enable to identify and remove from the case-base. There is another important aspect regarding the application to this type of case representation. We have the opinion that the subsumption definition influences the applicability of some of the strategies. For instance, we have defined in the implementation of the criteria, that when there are draws between cases, the criteria should choose using the frequency usage of cases (except when the CBM strategy explicitly states what to do). Since most of the cases are not subsumed, there are a lot of draws, which makes this default selection form to be used most of the times. This is why most of the criteria have a similar performance to the FDC one, which is purely frequency based.

5   Discussion

In this paper we have presented a study on the CBM policies applied to a complex case representation. We have come to several conclusions and advices to researchers wanting to develop CBR systems with a complex case representation, and especially in a design domain. First of all, is that the subsumption definition, in which most of the CBM policies are based, is crucial for the good management of the case-base. Due to time constraints, it must be simple to run fast, but on the other hand, it must also be accurate enough to be usable by the CBM

Table 2. Competence results computed using the CBM strategies, with adaptation.

CB Size	FDC	SC	FtDC	FtUDC	CC	CAC	RCCNN	RPM	CGC
10	92%	92%	68%	68%	92%	92%	92%	92%	92%
20	92%	92%	72%	68%	92%	92%	92%	92%	92%
30	96%	96%	92%	92%	96%	92%	96%	96%	96%
40	100%	100%	96%	100%	100%	96%	100%	100%	100%
50	100%	100%	96%	100%	100%	96%	100%	100%	100%
60	100%	100%	100%	100%	100%	100%	100%	100%	100%

policies implemented in the system. In the end it sums up to a trade-off between computation time and accuracy.

Another important issue is the system scalability, because in a real case-base it will probably use thousands of cases with several tens of objects. Though the case-base used is not of that size (it comprises only 586 software objects), it can provide an insight to CBM strategies performance. Several of the implemented strategies in REBUILDER have shown to be scalable, and capable of being used in a real environment.

Last but not least, the adaptation mechanism is also important when selecting a CBM policy for systems with complex case representation, due to the huge dimension of the solution space. Experimental work shows that if the CBR system has a good adaptation mechanism, then the case-base can be smaller and have less similar or redundant cases, since the adaptation mechanisms can overcome the problem of missing cases in the library.

In the specific case of REBUILDER, the more time consuming strategies will have to be dropped, since one crucial aspect of our system is time performance. Our preferred way of using the CBM strategies is as an advice mechanism for the KB administrator, since s/he is the responsible for the case-base coherence. The idea is that a redundant case in the case-base will be pointed out by several CBM strategies, thus making a clear indication to the KB administrator which cases to remove from the case-base.

Future work on this subject will be the study of the influence of several subsumption criteria and what will that imply to the adaptation mechanism. We will also intend to perform these experiments in a bigger case-base. The combination of several policies is also in our future work agenda.

Acknowledgments. This work was supported by POSI - Programa Operacional Sociedade de Informação of Fundação Portuguesa para a Ciência e Tecnologia and European Union FEDER, under contract POSI / 33399 / SRI / 2000, and by program PRAXIS XXI. We would like to thanks the reviewers for their helpful comments on this paper.

References

1. Agnar Aamodt and Enric Plaza, *Case–based reasoning: Foundational issues, methodological variations, and system approaches.*, AI Communications **7** (1994), no. 1, 39–59.
2. Janet Kolodner, *Case-based reasoning*, Morgan Kaufman, 1993.
3. David Leake and David Wilson, *Remembering why to remember: Performance-guided case-base maintenance*, Proceedings of the European Workshop on Case-Based Reasoning (EWCBR-00) (Berlin), LNAI, Springer, 2000, pp. 161–172.
4. David B. Leake, Barry Smyth, Qiang Yang, and David C. Wilson, *Introduction to the special issue on maintaining case-based reasoning systems*, Computational Intelligence **17** (2001), no. 2, 193–195.
5. Elizabeth McKenna and Barry Smyth, *Competence-guided case-base editing techniques*, Proceedings of the European Workshop on Case-Based Reasoning (EWCBR-00) (Berlin), LNAI, Springer, 2000, pp. 186–197.
6. George Miller, Richard Beckwith, Christiane Fellbaum, Derek Gross, and Katherine J. Miller, *Introduction to wordnet: an on-line lexical database.*, International Journal of Lexicography **3** (1990), no. 4, 235–244.
7. Steven Minton, *Quantitative results concerning the utility of explanation-based learning*, Artificial Intelligence **42** (1990), no. 2–3, 363–391.
8. Kirsti Racine and Qiang Yang, *Maintaining unstructured case bases*, Proceedings of the 2nd International Conference on Case-Based Reasoning (ICCBR-97) (Berlin) (David B. Leake and Enric Plaza, eds.), LNAI, vol. 1266, Springer, July 1997, pp. 553–564.
9. J. Rumbaugh, I. Jacobson, and G. Booch, *The unified modeling language reference manual*, Addison-Wesley, Reading, MA, 1998.
10. Barry Smyth and Mark T. Keane, *Remembering to forget: A competence-preserving case deletion policy for case-based reasoning systems*, Proceedings of the Fourteenth International Joint Conference on Artificial Intelligence (IJCAI 95) (San Mateo) (Chris S. Mellish, ed.), Morgan Kaufmann, August 1995, pp. 377–383.
11. Barry Smyth and Elizabeth McKenna, *Modelling the competence of case-bases*, Proceedings of the 4th European Workshop on Advances in Case-Based Reasoning (EWCBR-98) (Berlin) (Barry Smyth and Pádraig Cunningham, eds.), LNAI, vol. 1488, Springer, September 1998, pp. 208–220.
12. Barry Smyth and Elizabeth McKenna, *Building compact competent case-bases*, Proceedings of the 3rd International Conference on Case-Based Reasoning Research and Development (ICCBR-99) (Berlin) (Klaus-Dieter Althoff, Ralph Bergmann, and L. Karl Branting, eds.), LNAI, vol. 1650, Springer, July 1999, pp. 329–342.
13. Jun Zhu and Qiang Yang, *Remembering to add: Competence-preserving case-addition policies for case base maintenance*, Proceedings of the 16th International Joint Conference on Artificial Intelligence (IJCAI-99-Vol1) (S.F.) (Dean Thomas, ed.), Morgan Kaufmann Publishers, July 1999, pp. 234–241.

Optimal Case-Based Refinement of Adaptation Rule Bases for Engineering Design

Hans-Werner Kelbassa

kelbassa@uni-paderborn.de

Abstract. Rule-based systems have been successfully applied for adaptation. But the rule-based adaptation knowledge for engineering design has no static character-istic. Therefore the adaptation problem emerges also as a validation and refinement problem to be solved by global CBR approaches in an optimal way. The optimal refinement of engineering rule bases for adaptation improves the performance of expert systems for engineering design and provides a basis for the revision of the similarity function for the adaptation-guided retrieval. However, selecting op-timal rule refinements is an unsolved problem in CBR; the employed classical SEEK2-like hill-climbing procedures yield local maxima only, not global ones. Hence for the cased-based optimization of rule base refinement a new operations research approach to the optimal selection of normal, conflicting, and alternative rule refinement heuristics is presented here. As the current rule validation and rule refinement systems usually rely on CBR, this is a relevant novel contribution for coping with the maintenance problem of large CBR systems for engineering design. The described global mathematical optimization enables a higher qual-ity in the case-based refinement of complex engineering rule bases and thereby improves the basis for the adaptation-guided retrieval.

1 Introduction

Case-Based Reasoning (CBR) systems have been used for many engineering design applications [23,29,33,8]. Since the CBR systems are being employed with success, the importance of the maintenance of industrial CBR systems is emphasized increasingly [28,13]. This article discusses the adaptation problem of engineering applications with regard to the validation and the refinement of engineering design expertise and presents a novel global case-based approach to the optimal refinement of expert system rule bases.

The automation of engineering design processes has been investigated by many re-searchers. We mention the CBR design assistant ARTDECO which has been developed at the University of Paderborn [33]. While KOLLER believed that engineering design processes could be completely automated [22], FRANKE judged that engineering de-sign would not be completely executable by computer systems [7]. He emphasized that engineering design knowledge does not have a static nature but, due to scientific and technological progress, as well as new administrative regulations (e.g. concerning en-vironmental protection), is subject to change.[1] So it happens that technological limits

---

[1] Franke [7], p. 98ff.

K.D. Ashley and D.G. Bridge (Eds.): ICCBR 2003, LNAI 2689, pp. 201–215, 2003.
© Springer-Verlag Berlin Heidelberg 2003

are becoming obsolete and that prices and costs are not stable. Therefore, in many situations the retrieved historical case solutions have to be adapted, for instance, by using a rule-based adaptation system, and the knowledge used for the design case adaptation step must be validated and refined on a long term basis. Hence the optimal refinement of adaptation rule bases is crucial for the performance of CBR systems [11].

Although there have been considerable automation efforts in the domain of engineering design, the current software systems for the design of mechanical and fluidic systems are not able to win in competition with human engineering expertise a TURING-like test.[2] STEIN ascertained that current engineering design processes for the development of challenging fluidic systems could only be automated partly [33]. As the validation and the refinement of adaptation expertise is crucial for the performance of the engineering knowledge bases, a global optimization approach to the selection of rule refinement heuristics is presented in the following sections [20]. Rule-based systems are widespread and have been succesfully employed in many engineering domains [24,23,27,31]; production rules have also great relevance for future engineering design adaptation systems.

Before the overall refinement optimization approach is presented in the next sections, we distinguish different kinds of adaptation in case-based design as introduced by STEIN AND HOFFMANN [32], and extend this framework with regard to the adaptation-guided retrieval (AGR) in the context of rule-based adaptation systems.

2   Adaptation in Engineering Design

The basic idea of case-based reasoning is to avoid a problem solving start from scratch by using similar case solutions retrievable from a well-maintained case base. Fundamental to CBR is the well-known CBR cycle by AAMONDT AND PLAZA [1] which structures the CBR process in four phases: (1) RETRIEVAL; (2) REUSE; (3) REVISE; (4) RETAIN – the *adaptation phase* belongs to the reuse step. Often the retrieved cases are not identical to the given query case for which at least one (new) solution is to be designed. Hence, in order to meet all technical demands of the given query case, the retrieved *similar* case solution has to be adapted [8]. STEIN AND HOFFMANN (1999) have presented a general description of adaptation levels for engineering design which is extended here with regard to the validation and the refinement of rule-based adaptation systems and similarity functions for the adaptation-guided retrieval. We claim that the refinement of adaptation rule bases should also provide the basis for the refinement of the *similarity function* for the adaptation-guided retrieval (AGR).

In accordance with the CBR cycle, for every query case the most similar case(s) is (are) retrieved. Then for at least one case, which is similar but not identical to the given problem case, an adaptation has to be executed. The basis for the retrieval

---

[2] In computer chess the human world champion KRAMNIK was not able in 2002 to defeat the current best chess program DEEP FRITZ, because it plays on champion level. See SPIEGEL ONLINE: www.spiegel.de and enter keyword "Kramnik"; you will find the article 'Die Lehren aus Kramnik gegen Deep Fritz' dated October 21, 2002; and the article 'Patt zwischen Mensch und Maschine' dated October 19, 2002.

in engineering design is usually a similarity function [23]. Here we have to distinguish two kinds of similarity functions: simple similarity functions, denoted by σ, and similarity functions supporting the adaptation-guided retrieval, denoted by σ_{AGR}.

The similarity measure σ (σ_{AGR}) gets a high value if an available case is very similar to the actual query case (and good adaptable), and a low value otherwise. For a formal description, see STEIN AND HOFFMANN [32] and STEIN [33]. The first CBR systems used a simple similarity measure σ. This measure σ has the drawback that the possibility to adapt the retrieved cases was not taken into account. So it could happen that any non-adaptable case has been retrieved although the case base contained cases which have good adaptation characteristics [31]. Suppose a design adaptation rule base infers for any retrieved design case that any *Feature_23* ensures the case adaptation, but the system validator judges that here *Feature_86* is relevant for the adaptation, and Feature_23 absolutely not. Then it is not sufficient to refine the faulty adaptation rules, rather there should be also a refinement of the similarity function used for the adaptation-guided retrieval. New adaptation possibilities are to be assimilated, and obsolete ones should be discarded in both the rule base and the similarity measure σ_{AGR}.

Now a domain-independent hierarchy of adaptation levels is described which has been introduced by STEIN AND HOFFMANN (1999):

- *Level 0: No Adaptation*
  Engineering design problems can seldom be solved without any modification by a table lookup procedure, i.e. the CBR system retrieved a case which matches completely with the given query. At adaptation level 0 the retrieved case solution has to be accepted only; this is the ideal situation.
- *Level 1: Automatic Adaptation*
  At adaptation level 1, the automatic adaptation is performed without any evaluation based on the scalability and the composability of the developed technical system. Modifications belonging to adaptation level 1 are completely deterministic and therefore the results are sure ones as expected, i.e. the design effects can be completely foreseen, or, at least be estimated sufficiently.
- *Level 2: Automatic Adaptation plus Revise*
  Adaptation on level 2 cannot be executed deterministically, i.e. not without any uncertainty. Therefore, the necessary modifications must be evaluated. The prerequisite for this adaptation level is that an evaluation can be stated. These evaluations are the basis for further modifications until a good design result is reached.
- *Level 3: Adaptation by Human Intelligence and Expertise (Engineers)*
  For the previous adaptation levels there is a feasibility to automate the design adaptation by using appropriate heuristics, technical functions and / or algorithms, so that supervision or evaluation by engineers is not necessary. This is not the situation at adaptation level 3, which requires human intelligence and expertise. At level 3 the adaptation and the evaluation is based on human assessment if the following situations are given: (1) The domain is weakly structured; (2) An automated adaptation is too expensive; (3) The necessary adaptations can easily be executed by humans; (4) Creativity is essential for the solution of the present design problem.

This article deals with adaptation on the level 2 and level 3 which can be carried out by a rule-based adaptation system, at least partly, and considers the rule trace refinement problem which arises if the engineering expert does not agree with the obtained expert system design case solution, i.e., with the adaptation result. Since the rule-based inference system is subject to refinements, the validator enters his critique, for example, concerning wrong intermediate conclusions, by using a validation interface as described by KELBASSA AND KNAUF [20]. So the expert system performance increases as the adaptation rules are being validated in a case by case manner. In general, the optimal refinement of rule bases in reduction-free systems yields an unsolved global refinement selection problem to which a novel solution is presented here. Unfortunately, due to the given space limit the associated σ_{AGR} refinement problem, i.e., the validation and refinement of the similarity measure σ_{AGR}, cannot be discussed in detail in the following.

The state of the art in the area of rule verification is quite advanced, but in the area of rule validation there is no generic validation interface enabling remote validation via the Internet and no overall optimization of rule refinement selection phases for industrial applications [34,6]. At present the available *commercial tools* for the development of rule bases do not provide any *validation system*. There is no satisfying methodical standard for conflict analysis in the selection of the best overall rule refinements [34].

The *rule trace validation phase* can usually be subdivided into (1) the initial rule base evaluation step (case-based validation), (2) the identification of faulty rules, (3) the generation of suitable rule refinements, (4) the selection of the best rule refinements and finally (5) the execution of the selected rule refinements. This article deals with the *selection of the best overall rule refinements for faulty adaptation rules,* which, in current refinement systems, is performed in a heuristic manner [9,3,5] and presents a *mathematical formalization* of the global rule refinement selection problem. The reader who is interested in the creation of suitable rule refinement heuristics is referred to [20, 16,17]. GINSBERG stated that rule base refinement would not be amenable to global mathematical optimization[3]. This pessimistic assertion will be falsified in the following sections whose mathematical outcome is a novel binary maximization problem solvable by linear operations research procedures, i.e. a first global approach to the optimal selection of rule refinements [21].

3   Adaptation Rule Refinement Example

For the elaboration of the global refinement selection problem an higher order refinement example with three refinement classes is discussed now [17,18]. Consider the following adaptation rules contained in an engineering design adaptation rule base RB_0 of any forward-chaining inference system:

$$RB_0 := \{.., R_{18}, ., R_{42}, ., R_{46}, R_{47}, .., R_{54}, ., R_{64}, ., R_{66}, .\}$$
$$R_{18} := \text{IF } (A \wedge B) \text{ THEN } Hypothesis\_1$$
$$R_{42} := \text{IF } (C \vee D) \text{ THEN } Hypothesis\_3$$
$$R_{46} := \text{IF } (Hypothesis\_1 \wedge \neg Hypothesis\_3) \text{ THEN } I_8$$

---

[3] See Ginsberg [9], p. 5 and p. 108f.

$$R_{54} := \text{IF } (Hypothesis\_3 \wedge E) \text{ THEN } I_2$$
$$R_{64} := \text{IF } (A \wedge \neg K) \text{ THEN } Hypothesis\_7$$

Suppose a set of different design cases $c_l \in CB$ ($l \in \{1,..,|CB|\}; l \in I\!N$) retrieved by any CBR system have been processed by the rule-based adaptation system in order to obtain the desired design case adaptation. Every production rule fired generates either a single intermediate design conclusion (design hypothesis) or a single final design conclusion. Here I_2 and I_8 are two different *final* engineering conclusions; the letter I means *interpretation*, i.e. any engineering design proposition. Assume that the production rules in this RB_0 processed the design case base CB and that the engineering expert has entered his evaluation for every case by the validation interface. Validation in this context means that the responsible engineer adopts the proposed expert system adaptation at least partially or not at all. Suppose the rule refinement heuristics listed below have been obtained by the validation system according to the validators rule trace evaluation, i.e. beside (in-)completeness statements every intermediate and every final expert system conclusion got a validation flag: valid or falsified. So the following refinement heuristics RH are to be considered as *rule refinement expertise* – the above adaptation rules became refinement candidates for one or more falsified adaptation cases:

RH1 :=   IF   rule R_{46} is generalized by refinement ϕ_G^2,
            THEN   case set C_1 gets valid reasoning paths (adaptations): $|C_1| = 4$

RH1/2 := IF   rule R_{64} is contextualized by refinement ϕ_C^1,
            THEN   case set C_2 gets valid reasoning paths (adaptations): $|C_{1/2}| = 9$

RH2 :=   IF   rule R_{18} is contextualized by refinement ϕ_C^2,
            and
            rule R_{42} is specialized by refinement ϕ_S^1,
            THEN   case set C_2 gets valid reasoning paths (adaptations): $|C_2| = 1$

RH3 :=   IF   rule R_{46} is generalized by refinement ϕ_G^1,
            and
            rule R_{54} is generalized by refinement ϕ_G^1,
            and
            rule R_{64} is contextualized by refinement ϕ_C^2,
            THEN   case set C_3 gets valid reasoning paths (adaptations): $|C_3| = 8$

RH3/2 := IF   rule R_{46} is specialized by refinement ϕ_S^1,
            and
            rule R_{54} is specialized by refinement ϕ_S^2,
            and
            rule R_{64} is generalized by refinement ϕ_G^3,
            THEN   case set $C_{3/2}$ gets valid reasoning paths (adaptations): $|C_{3/2}| = 15$

In these refinement heuristics the symbols ϕ_C^1, ϕ_C^2, ϕ_G^1, ϕ_G^2, ϕ_G^3, ϕ_S^1, ϕ_S^2 characterize *elementary* rule refinement operations (– see [21,18]). The index C means contextualization ($\phi \in \phi_C$), the index G means generalization ($\phi \in \phi_G$), and the index S means specialization ($\phi \in \phi_S$); the superscript is the class index. The set of all possible rule refinements is $\Phi := \{\phi_C, \phi_G, \phi_S\}$.

It is important to see that the above refinement heuristics are *not alternative ones* because every adaptation case appears once only: $C_1 \cap C_{1/2} \cap C_2 \cap C_3 \cap C_{3/2} = \emptyset$. If refinement heuristics are alternative ones, so, for example, that we should apply either rule refinement heuristic RH4 or RH5 in order to validate a certain case set, then this case set intersection is not empty: $C_4 \cap C_5 \neq \emptyset$. The optimal selection of alternative rule refinement heuristics is formalized below in section 7.

4   First Order Local Case Gain Maximization

This section shows how the rule refinement selection problem is principally solved by the hill-climbing procedure of SEEK2 as described by GINSBERG [9]. The first order greedy heuristics used by SEEK2 select locally between generalizations and specializations only [17]. In the above example we have three rule refinement classes: generalization, specialization, and contextualization. Hence the first order heuristics here have to select between these three rule refinement categories.

Let $Con(R_x)$ be the number of cases in which rule R_x is a context refinement candidate in any refinement heuristic(s) RH, let $Gen(R_x)$ be the number of cases in which rule R_x is a generalization candidate in any refinement heuristic(s) RH, and let $Spec(R_x)$ be the number of cases in which rule R_x is a specialization candidate in any refinement heuristic(s) RH. Then these validation measures enable a SEEK2-like validation module to decide which refinement class is to be executed for any faulty rule R_x [18]. This final target refinement class $Tar(R_x) \in \{\phi_C, \phi_G, \phi_S\}$ for any adaptation rule R_x is selected by the maximum of the functions $Con(R_x) \in IN$, $Gen(R_x) \in IN$, and $Spec(R_x) \in IN$:

$$
Tar(R_x) := \begin{cases}
\phi_C(R_x), & if & Con(R_x) > Gen(R_x) \wedge Con(R_x) > Spec(R_x); \\
\phi_G(R_x), & if & Gen(R_x) > Con(R_x) \wedge Gen(R_x) > Spec(R_x); \\
\phi_S(R_x), & else, i.e., & Spec(R_x) \geq Con(R_x) \wedge Spec(R_x) \geq Gen(R_x).
\end{cases}
$$

As the SEEK2-like calculations maximize the *local* fitness of every refinement candidate $R_x \in RB_0$, for our problem the *first order case gain calculation* results are:

$$Tar(R_{18}) = \phi_C(R_{18}) : \quad Con(R_{18}) = max\{1, 0, 0\}$$
$$Tar(R_{42}) = \phi_S(R_{42}) : \quad Spec(R_{42}) = max\{0, 0, 1\}$$
$$Tar(R_{46}) = \phi_S(R_{46}) : \quad Spec(R_{46}) = max\{0, 4+8, 15\}$$
$$Tar(R_{54}) = \phi_S(R_{54}) : \quad Spec(R_{54}) = max\{0, 8, 15\}$$
$$Tar(R_{64}) = \phi_C(R_{64}) : \quad Con(R_{64}) = max\{9+8, 15, 0\}$$

Accordingly, this hill-climbing result means that only the refinement heuristics RH1/2 and RH2 can be realized, because these are compatible with the locally determined final target refinement classes $Tar(R_x)$. So, for example, the heuristic RH3/2 cannot to be executed, because $Tar(R_{64}) = \phi_C(R_{64})$ is not a generalization. The first order validation gain result G^{1st} is the case gain of RH1/2 and RH2: $G^{1st} = 9 + 1 = 10$ cases.

The methodical selection of optimal rule refinements involving higher order gain calculation leads to a better outcome [17]. It is easy to see that the higher order solution, i.e., firing the higher order rule refinement heuristic RH3/2, yields a better gain result $G = 15 > G^{1st}$ than the first order one.

5   Rule Refinement Conflict Analysis

The elementary refinement operations above are stated with regard to the reference rule R_x, i.e., the refinements all are referring to an unrefined faulty rule $R_x \in RB_0$ of the same rule base. Thus there are difficulties if we try to get a good sequence of elementary refinements for the refinement of any rule R_x which failed in several cases. This *sequence problem* or refinement *reference problem* is not sufficiently solved yet [34].

Let $CS(R_x)$ be the refinement conflict set for any rule $R_x \in RB_0$, which contains all demanded refinements for the rule R_x, i.e., every required refinement operation for this rule appearing in any rule refinement heuristic(s) RH [18]. Accordingly, the conflict sets $CS(\cdot)$ for our concrete refinement selection problem are the following ones:

$$CS(R_{18}) = \{\phi_C^2\} \quad CS(R_{42}) = \{\phi_S^1\} \quad \text{Comment: No conflict with } R_{18} \text{ and}$$
R_{42}.

$$CS(R_{46}) = \{\phi_G^1, \phi_G^2, \phi_S^1\} \quad CS(R_{54}) = \{\phi_G^1, \phi_S^2\} \quad CS(R_{64}) = \{\phi_C^1, \phi_C^2, \phi_G^3\}$$

The conflict sets $CS(R_{18})$ and $CS(R_{42})$ do not reveal any refinement conflict because these sets both have one element only: $|CS(R_{18})| = |CS(R_{42})| = 1$.

The problem specific conflict sets to be investigated are the $CS(R_{46})$, the $CS(R_{54})$, and the $CS(R_{64})$.

Altogether, the conflict analysis regarding the refinement candidates R_{18}, R_{42}, R_{46}, R_{54}, and R_{64}, leads to the recognition that the conflict sets of the latter three rules have to be described by ONE-OF DISJUNCTIONS [21]. These ONE-OF DISJUNCTIONS enable that maximal one of the involved elements can be selected, not more. The ONE-OF relation with two elements can be considered as the exclusive disjunction (XOR). A detailed analysis of this refinement example as well as some definitions are presented in [21]; due to the space limit this refinement conflict analysis cannot be repeated here. The resulting ONE-OF restrictions for CS(R_{46}), CS(R_{54}), and CS(R_{64}) are the following:

$$\text{ONE-OF}(RH1(R_{46}), RH3/2(R_{46}), RH3(R_{46})),$$
$$[\quad \text{ONE-OF}(RH3(R_{54}), RH3/2(R_{54})), \quad]$$
$$\text{ONE-OF}(RH1/2(R_{64}), RH3(R_{64}), RH3/2(R_{64})).$$

The optimization will be on the heuristic level. Therefore, it is not relevant for the following which rules occur in ONE-OF DISJUNCTIONS so that the second ONE-OF above is discarded (stated by [...]), because the third ONE-OF is more restrictive. These constraints can be converted into linear inequalities of an operations research solution.

6   Operations Research Approach

The scientific discipline which is traditionally researching mathematical optimization is termed operations research (acronym: OR) [26,30]. As far as it is known to the author the optimal selection of *conflicting, alternative and normal* rule refinements has not been solved and published by other scientists yet [9].

Usually the various heuristics have different success in the validation of cases, hence the expected total case gain of the best refinement heuristics is maximized. The question whether a certain heuristic is an element of the optimal heuristic set can be answered by a binary decision variable $x \in \{0,1\}$. Accordingly the optimization result $x_j = 1$ $(j \in I\!N)$ means that the j-th heuristic is optimal, whereby the result $x_j = 0$ $(j \in I\!N)$ means that the j-th refinement heuristic is suboptimal and therefore not to be executed. With respect to our special rule refinement selection problem we define the following variables:

$$x_1 \in \{0,1\} := \text{Decision variable for heuristic RH1}$$
$$x_2 \in \{0,1\} := \text{Decision variable for heuristic RH1/2}$$
$$x_3 \in \{0,1\} := \text{Decision variable for heuristic RH2}$$
$$x_4 \in \{0,1\} := \text{Decision variable for heuristic RH3}$$
$$x_5 \in \{0,1\} := \text{Decision variable for heuristic RH3/2}$$

The gain $g_j \in I\!R$ of every refinement heuristic here is the number of falsified cases which are corrected by this heuristic (THEN-part); hence we assign the following gain values: $g_1 = |C_1| = 4$, $g_2 = |C_{1/2}| = 9$, $g_3 = |C_2| = 1$, $g_4 = |C_3| = 8$, $g_5 = |C_{3/2}| = 15$.

Using the gain values g_j (j = 1,...,n) we can also take into account that different design cases have different weights. So, for example, if any gain variable g_{42} is referring to a refinement heuristic which validates three design cases $C_{42} := \{c_4, c_{21}, c_{36}\}$ having the weights $w_4 = 17$, $w_{21} = 25$, and $w_{36} = 44$, then the gain is $g_{42} = 17 + 25 + 44 = 86$. For the sake of clarity different case weights are not used in our specific refinement example. But different case weights are mentioned here, since uniform case weights are a theoretical drawback of several rule base refinement systems [5,9].

The linear *objective function* for the rule refinement selection problem RSP is:

$$Z := \sum_{j=1}^{n} g_j x_j \rightarrow maximum! \qquad (x_j \in \{0,1\}; \; g_j \in I\!R; \; j \in I\!N).$$

Although in our concrete refinement selection sample all gain values are positive, it is stated that $g_j \in I\!R$ (– relevant in the case of undesired side effects). It is also possible to define any *nonlinear* objective function.

Next we come up with the *linear inequalities* for the respective ONE-OF DISJUNC-TIONS. Let $x_1, ..., x_n$ be binary decision variables involved in any ONE-OF conflict, then for a ONE-OF DISJUNCTION the following inequality holds: $x_1 + ... + x_n \leq 1$ $(n \in I\!N)$.

In solving our specific refinement selection problem we process the above two con-crete ONE-OF DISJUNCTIONS:

$$\text{ONE-OF}(RH1, RH3, RH3/2)$$
$$\text{ONE-OF}(RH1/2, RH3, RH3/2)$$

Based on the problem specific definition of the binary decision variables x_j $(j = 1, ..., 5)$ the relevant two ONE-OF inequalities are:

$$x_1 + x_4 + x_5 \leq 1 \tag{I}$$

$$x_2 + x_4 + x_5 \leq 1 \qquad\qquad (II)$$

Thus the special optimization approch to our first refinement selection problem is:

$$4x_1 + 9x_2 + 1x_3 + 8x_4 + 15x_5 \rightarrow maximum!$$

$$
\begin{array}{llll}
\text{subject to} \quad x_1 + & & x_4 + & x_5 \leq 1 \qquad (I) \\
& x_2 + & x_4 + & x_5 \leq 1 \qquad (II) \\
& \multicolumn{3}{l}{x_1, x_2, x_3, x_4, x_5 \in \{0,1\}}
\end{array}
$$

So the general mathematical approach to the conflicting rule refinement selection problem RSP is:

$$
\text{RSP} := \left\{
\begin{array}{l}
\sum_{j=1}^{n} g_j x_j \rightarrow maximum! \\[2ex]
subject\ to \\
\sum_{j=1}^{n} a_{ij} x_j \leq b_i \quad (i = 1, ..., m) \\[2ex]
g_j \in I\!R,\ x_j \in \{0,1\} \quad (j = 1, ..., n) \\[1ex]
a_{ij} \in \{1, 0, -1\},\ b_i \in \{1, 0\} \quad (i = 1, ..., m)
\end{array}
\right.
$$

Due to the restriction $x_j \in \{0,1\}$ this optimization problem is called a *binary integer (maximization) problem*. In our first numeric example m = 2 holds since finally there are only two ONE-OF constraints. As there are no predefined dependencies between the decision variables here $a_{ij} \in \{0,1\}$ holds, else $a_{ij} \in \{1,0,-1\}$ and $b_i \in \{0\}$ can be present.

This refinement selection problem RSP is solvable by several well known OR procedures; in particular a RSP can be solved by using the

- ADDITIVE BALAS' ALGORITHM [2,4,25];
- BRANCH AND BOUND PROCEDURE [26,12];
- GOMORY PROCEDURE [25,26,30];
- BRANCH AND CUT PROCEDURE [12,15].

An important decomposition result has been reported recently by JOSEPH [14]. We expect further scientific progress so that the future relevance of the above procedures cannot be predicted [12].

The optimal solution for our specific RSP is $G^{opt}(0,0,1,0,1) = 16$ cases, and the outcome is that by $x_3 = x_5 = 1$ the heuristics RH2 and RH3/2 are optimal. As $G^{opt} > G^{1st}$ this SEEK2-like maximization result G^{1st} is suboptimal, i.e. no global maximum.

7   Alternative Rule Refinements

Now the selection of additional normal and alternative refinement heuristics is discussed by two further refinement selection examples. The simplest form of alternative refinements is present if there are two rule refinement heuristics validating the same case set.

In this situation we have to ensure that maximal one is realized. Let x_8 and x_9 be the binary decision variables for the alternative refinement heuristics RH4 and RH5, then the ONE-OF constraint for these alternative heuristics is: $x_8 + x_9 \leq 1$.

A powerful refinement optimization should combine the selection of conflicting refinements with the selection of alternative and normal refinements [21]. As not all five refinement heuristics of our first conflict selection example in section 3 are optimal ones, we have to find alternatives for the heuristics RH1, RH1/2, and RH3, after the optimal refinements RH2 and RH3/2 have been executed. Assume that this is done side effect free and that these refinements are listed in a revision protocol which ensures that the rules just refined not become refinement candidates in the following refinement stage(s) again (pendulum problem).

When we start to find out the appropriate alternative refinement heuristics for the remaining falsified case sets, we are going to solve the alternative rule trace problem for a part of the entire refinement problem. In general, it should be possible to find all the alternatives for every refinement heuristic (e.g., by using a refinement generator [5] for exhaustive refinement creation) so that it is possible to compute the optimal refinement heuristic set for known competing, normal and alternative refinement heuristics at the beginning. But this requires more work to be done by the validator and larger financial and time expenditures for the development of engineering adaptation rule bases.

Therefore we prefer to solve a *remainder problem* instead of determining alternatives for all refinement heuristics. The complexity of the refinement problems discussed here is not high. But industrial rule bases can have more than 13 000 rules and therefore it can be difficult and time consuming to develop all refinement alternatives for large scale knowledge bases [27]. However, for small real-world refinement problems it is possible to optimize a set of normal, alternative and conflicting rule refinements at the beginning. This will be elucidated now.

In order to come up with a refinement solution for the remaining falsified case sets associated with heuristics RH1, RH1/2, and RH3, recall that refinement of the rule base $RB_0 \rightarrow RB_1$ yields improved inferences, so that we can suppose that the number of suboptimal elementary rule refinement operations (here: 5) is larger than the number of alternative elementary refinement operations needed still [9]. Facing this situation the following two refinement heuristics are presented which correct rules having the same conclusion as two of the rules just refined:

RH1/3 := IF   rule R_{47} is generalized by refinement ϕ_G^4,
     THEN   case set C_1 gets valid reasoning paths (adaptations): $|C_1| = 4$

RH1/4 := IF   rule R_{66} is generalized by refinement ϕ_G^3,
     THEN   case sets $C_{1/2}$ and C_3 get valid reasoning paths: $|C_{1/2}| + |C_3| = 17$

As there is no conflict between these two refinement heuristics RH1/3 and RH1/4 (different rules), these heuristics can be considered as optimal ones which validate all remaining cases. Although our special refinement problem is completely solved now, we show here how to come up with an OR solution for the selection between *normal, alternative, and conflicting* rule refinement heuristics. Assume we have to solve a selection problem in which the five heuristics of our conflict example are involved, and furthermore also the alternative heuristics RH1/3 and RH1/4 together with the alternative heuristics RH4 and RH5, which both realize the gain $g_8 = g_9 = |C_4| = 18$. All heuristics involved in this second selection example R_{SP}^* are presented in table 1.

Table 1. Selection table for various rule refinement heuristics.

Cases C_1	Cases $C_{1/2}$	Cases C_2	Cases C_3	Cases $C_{3/2}$	Cases C_4
RH1	RH1/2	RH2	RH3	RH3/2	RH4
(x_1)	(x_2)	(x_3)	(x_4)	(x_5)	(x_8)
RH1/3	RH1/4		RH1/4		RH5
(x_6)	(x_7)		(x_7)		(x_9)

Suppose that these alternative heuristics will not cause any new refinement conflict, hence concerning CS analysis it is sufficient to state the above constraints (I, II). The columns in table 1 reveal that for the case sets C_2 and $C_{3/2}$ there are no alternative refinements. So we can make a *preselection*, for example, represented by $x_3 = 1$. As heuristic RH2 is neither a conflicting one nor an alternative one, we classify it as a *normal* heuristic. If one refinement heuristic appears in more than one case set column, as RH1/4 does, every one of these columns can yield a single ONE-OF; here we have two: ONE-OF(RH1/2, RH1/4) and ONE-OF(RH1/4, RH3).

Unfortunately, both ONE-OF restrictions enable redundant results as $x_2 = x_7 = 1$ and $x_4 = x_7 = 1$, although it is sufficient to state $x_7 = 1$ and $x_2 = x_4 = 0$. This minimal refinement outcome can be ensured by the following concrete *either-or constraints* which are mutually exclusive:

$$\text{(either)} \quad x_2 + x_4 < x_7, \text{ i.e., } x_2 = x_4 = 0, x_7 = 1;$$
$$\text{(or)} \quad x_7 = 0.$$

In our first selection example R_{SP} it is not assumed that any decision variable x_i depends on another decision variable x_j ($x_i \neq x_j$; $i, j \in \{1, ..., 5\}$). This situation may arise when the validation of the case(s) associated with decision variable x_j gets a higher priority than the validation of the case(s) associated with decision variable x_i; a priority can be stated by the binary constraint $x_i \leq x_j$. Assume that here for our second specific R_{SP}^* the preference $x_8 \leq x_1$ holds.

The optimal solution for this specific R_{SP}^* is $G^*(0, 0, 1, 0, 1, 1, 1, 0, 1) = 55$ cases. As this optimum is $x_3 = x_5 = x_6 = x_7 = x_9 = 1$, the heuristics RH2, RH3/2, RH1/3, RH1/4, and RH5 are the optimal ones [19]. This means, for example, that again as in the first selection sample the heuristics RH1 and RH1/2 are suboptimal.

SUBSUMPTION. A special alternative is present in the case the IF-part of one refinement heuristic subsumes completely at least one IF-part of another heuristic [21], i.e., if the subset relation $\text{IF}_{x/y} \subset \text{IF}_{x'/y'}$ holds between at least two different IF-parts of the involved refinement heuristics RH. Accordingly, a subsumption example is $\text{IF}_1 \subset \text{IF}_{2/2}$ where

$$RH1 := \{\phi_G^2(R_{46}); |C_1| = 4\} \text{ and}$$
$$RH2/2 := \{\phi_G^2(R_{46}), \phi_C^1(R_{94}); |C_{10}| = 12\}$$

with disjoint case sets: $C_1 \cap C_{10} = \emptyset$. Let x_1 and x_{10} be the decision variables corresponding to the case sets C_1 and C_{10} then we can denote this special kind of alternative by the subsumption relation $\text{SUB} := \{g_1 = g_6 \,|\, x_{10} = 1\}$.

If the refinement heuristic RH2/2 is performed ($x_{10} = 1$), we must neither execute the refinement heuristic RH1 nor RH1/3 in addition (see table 2). This form of *minimal refinement* can be ensured by the ONE-OF inequality: $x_1 + x_6 + x_{10} \leq 1$. Here the ONE-OF inequality has three decision variables, because RH1 and RH1/3 are *alternative* rule refinement heuristics.

In order to come up with the right validation gain outcome we *re-evaluate* the case gain g_{10} for the subsuming refinement heuristic: $g_1 = g_6 = |C_1|$, $g_{10}^* := |C_1| + |C_{10}| = 16$ cases. The subsuming heuristic realizes in addition to its own gain g_{10} the gain of all subsumed (alternative) rule refinement heuristic(s).

SYNERGY. If the combination of several refinement heuristics due to partial subsumption yields a validation case gain which is larger than the cardinality sum of the involved case sets, then we have *synergy*. The technical term synergy is due to H. HAKEN (see [10], p. 352). Synergy means that the combinatorial effect is larger than the sum of all single effects [21]. Let, for instance, the realization of the heuristics associated with decision variables x_{11} and x_{12} have the synergetic effect that the gain $g_8 = g_9$ (associated to variables x_8 and x_9) is *additionally* realized to the gains g_{11} and g_{12}, too:

$$\text{SYN} := \{g_8 = g_9 \,|\, x_{11} = x_{12} = 1\}.$$

The mathematical formalization of this special synergetic effect requires also either-or-constraints, an additional decision variable $x \in \{0, 1\}$ for the objective function ($g_8 x$), an integer variable S for the number of heuristics yielding this synergetic effect: S = 2, and a ONE-OF DISJUNCTION(x_8, x_9, x) which ensures minimal refinement for both alternatives: $x_8 + x_9 + x \leq 1$. The synergetic either-or constraints are:

$$\text{(either)} \qquad x_{11} + x_{12} = S$$
$$\text{(or)} \qquad x_{11} + x_{12} \leq S - 1$$

All rule refinement heuristics of this selection problem $\text{RSP}^\bullet$ are presented in table 2 below. Indeed, this combinatorial rule refinement selection example demonstrates that also synergy can be subject of global optimization.

According to table 2 the concrete OR approach for our extended third $\text{RSP}^\bullet$ is:

Table 2. Selection table for conflicting, normal, and alternative refinement heuristics with subsumption and synergy.   (Legend: $\bullet$:$=$ optimal heuristic $\circ$:= suboptimal heuristic)

Cases $|C_1| = 4$	Cases $|C_{1/2}| = 9$	Cases $|C_2| = 1$	Cases $|C_3| = 8$	Cases $|C_{3/2}| = 15$	Cases $|C_4| = 18$	Cases $|C_{10}| = 12$	Cases $|C_{11}| = 7$	Cases $|C_{12}| = 24$
$\circ$ RH1 $(g_1 x_1)$	$\circ$ RH1/2 $(g_2 x_2)$	$\bullet$ RH2 $(g_3 x_3)$	$\circ$ RH3 $(g_4 x_4)$	$\bullet$ RH3/2 $(g_6 x_5)$	$\circ$ RH4 $(g_8 x_8)$	$\bullet$ RH2/2 $(g_{10}^* x_{10})$	$\bullet$ RH2/3 $(g_{11} x_{11})$	$\bullet$ RH3/3 $(g_{12} x_{12})$
$\circ$ RH1/3 $(g_6 x_6)$	$\bullet$ RH1/4 $(g_7 x_7)$		$\bullet$ RH1/4 $(g_7 x_7)$		$\circ$ RH5 $(g_9 x_9)$			

$$4x_1 + 9x_2 + 1x_3 + 8x_4 + 15x_5 + 4x_6 + 17x_7 + 18x_8 +$$
$$+ 18x_9 + 16x_{10} + 7x_{11} + 24x_{12} + 18x \rightarrow maximum!$$

subject to

$$x_1 + x_4 + x_5 \leq 1 \tag{I}$$
$$x_2 + x_4 + x_5 \leq 1 \tag{II}$$
$$x_1 + x_6 \leq 1 \tag{III}$$
$$x_8 + x_9 \leq 1 \tag{IV}$$
$$x_3 = 1 \tag{V}$$
$$x_7 - My \leq 1 \tag{VI}$$
$$-x_7 - My \leq -1 \tag{VII}$$
$$x_2 + x_4 - My \leq 0 \tag{VIII}$$
$$-x_2 - x_4 - My \leq 0 \tag{IX}$$
$$x_7 + My \leq M \tag{X}$$
$$-x_7 + My \leq M \tag{XI}$$
$$-x_1 + x_8 \leq 0 \tag{XII}$$
$$x_1 + x_6 + x_{10} \leq 1 \tag{XIII}$$
$$x_8 + x_9 + x \leq 1 \tag{XIV}$$
$$x_{11} + x_{12} + Mx \leq M + S \tag{XV}$$
$$-x_{11} - x_{12} + Mx \leq M - S \tag{XVI}$$
$$x_{11} + x_{12} - Mx \leq S - 1 \tag{XVII}$$

$M, S \in I\!N$; M must be a large integer (e.g., $M > n$)

$x_1, x_2, x_3, x_4, x_5, x_6, x_7, x_8, x_9, x_{10}, x_{11}, x_{12}, x, y \in \{0, 1\}$

The optimal solution for this extended heterogeneous selection problem RSP$^\bullet$ is $G^\bullet(0, 0, 1, 0, 1, 0, 1, 0, 0, 1, 1, 1, 1) = 98$ cases. As this optimum is $x_3 = x_5 = x_7 = x_{10} = x_{11} = x_{12} = x = 1$, the rule refinement heuristics RH2, RH3/2, RH1/4, RH2/2, RH2/3, and RH3/3 are the optimal ones.

REVISION. Rule *refinement* means that the cardinality of the refined rule base is kept constant: $|RB_0| = |RB_1|$. If there is no possibility to fix one or more present bugs by rule contextualizations, by rule generalizations or by rule specializations, we should apply rule *revision* operations so that the cardinality of the examined rule base can be changed: $|RB_0| \neq |RB_1|$. This means that new knowledge is integrated by *new* rules and that *obsolete* rules are deleted.

8   Conclusion

The adaptation expertise in engineering design has no static characteristic and is not free of uncertainty. Therefore CBR research for the defined adaptation levels 2 and 3 has to cope with the validation and the refinement of adaptation knowledge bases [32]. It has been claimed that rule base refinement should trigger the revision of the similarity function for the adaptation-guided retrieval σ_{AGR}. The novel global optimization approach described in this article enables a more powerful generation of refinement systems for adaptation rule bases in engineering design. A. GINSBERG's statement concerning the impossibility of optimal rule base refinement has been falsified.[4] The foundation of the mathematical optimization presented above is an analysis of the normal, conflicting and alternative rule refinement relations, and the possibility of assigning validation gain values to the rule refinement heuristics. Discussing three defined examples led to the conclusion that the result of the formal analysis of any rule refinement selection problem is a *binary linear maximization problem* solvable by a binary OR procedure [21]. The application of exact procedures for coping with concrete rule refinement selection problems is innovative since current refinement systems usually employ greedy heuristics and local hill-climbing procedures. It has been shown that the SEEK2-like hill-climbing procedure is suboptimal (local maximum). This article demonstrates that the global selection of rule refinements can be optimized so that large high-performance rule bases in engineering design can be developed more rapidly, and, moreover, suboptimal techniques for rule refinement and rule validation in integrated CBR systems are becoming obsolete [20]. As many rule-based systems have been applied succesfully for adaptation, this is a contribution to the maintenance of future industrial CBR systems.

References

1. Aamondt, A., Plaza, E. 1994. Case-Based Reasoning: Foundational Issues, Methodological Variations, and System Approaches. *AI Communications 7 (1), pp. 39–59*
2. Balas, E. 1965. An Additive Algorithm for Solving Linear Programs with Zero-One Variables. *Operations Research 13, pp. 517–546*
3. Boswell, R. 1999. *Knowledge Refinement for a Formulation System.* Ph.D. Thesis. The Robert Gordon University, Department for Computing and Mathematical Science. Aberdeen, Scotland, U. K.
4. Burkard, R. E. 1972. *Methoden der Ganzzahligen Optimierung.* Vienna: Springer-Verlag
5. Carbonara, L., Sleeman, D. 1999. Effective and Efficient Knowledge Base Refinement. *Machine Learning 37: 143–181*
6. Computer Associates International 2001. *Clever Path AION Business Rules Expert for Windows. Rules Guide 9.1.* New York, USA: Computer Associates International, Inc.
7. Franke, H.-J. 1976. *Untersuchungen zur Algorithmisierbarkeit des Konstruktionsprozesses.* Dissertation. Düsseldorf, Germany: VDI-Verlag
8. Fujita, K., Akagi, S., Sasaki, M. 1995. Adaptive Synthesis of Hydraulic Circuits from Design Cases based on Functional Structure. *Proceedings of the 1995 ACME Design Engineering Technical Conferences – 21st Annual Design Automation Conference, DE-Vol. 82, Vol. 1 (Advances in Design Automation), pp. 875–882.* ISBN 0-7918-1716-4. Boston, Masssachusetts, USA: September 1995
9. Ginsberg, A. 1988. *Automatic Refinement of Expert System Knowledge Bases.* London, U. K.: Pitman Publishing
10. Haken, H. 1983. *Synergetics – An Introduction.* 3rd Edition. Berlin, FRG: Springer-Verlag
11. Hanney, K., Keane, M. T. 1997. The Adaptation Knowledge Bottleneck: How to Ease it by Learning from Cases. In D. B. Leake and E. Plaza (Eds.): *Case-Based Reasoning Research and Development.* LNA 1266, pp. 359–370. Berlin, Germany: Springer-Verlag 1997

---

[4] Ginsberg [9], p. 5: "However since the underlying search space, kb-space, is not a Euclidean vector space, it is impossible to apply the techniques of linear and dynamic programming to this optimization problem."

12. Hillier, F. S., Lieberman, G. J. 2001. *Introduction to Operations Research*. 7th Edition. New York, USA: McGraw Hill, Inc.
13. Iglezakis, I., Roth-Berghofer, T., Anderson, C. E. 2001. The application of case properties in maintaining case-based reasoning systems. In *Schnurr et al. 2001 [29]*, pp. 209–219
14. Joseph, A. 2002. A concurrent processing framework for the set partitioning problem. *Computers and Operations Research 29, pp. 1375–1391*
15. Jünger, M., Naddef, D. (Eds.). *Computational Combinatorial Optimization*. Lecture Notes on Computer Science 2241. Berlin, Germany: Springer-Verlag 2001
16. Kelbassa, H.-W. 1990. Fallbezogene Revision und Validierung von regelbasiertem Expertenwissen für die Altlastenbeurteilung. In W. Pillmann and A. Jaeschke (Eds.): *Informatik für den Umweltschutz*. Informatik-Fachberichte 256, pp. 276–285. Berlin: Springer-Verlag 1990
17. Kelbassa, H.-W. 2002. Higher Order Refinement Heuristics for Rule Validation. *Proceedings of the Fifteenth International Florida Artificial Intelligence Research Society Conference 2002 (FLAIRS 2002), pp. 211–215*. Pensacola, Florida: May 14–16, 2002
18. Kelbassa, H.-W. 2002. Context Refinement – Investigating the Rule Refinement Completeness of SEEK/SEEK2. *Proceedings of the 15th European Conference on Artificial Intelligence 2002 (ECAI 2002), pp. 205–209*. Lyon, France: July 21–26, 2002
19. Kelbassa, H.-W. 2003. Selection of Optimal Rule Refinements. *Proceedings of the 16th International Florida Artificial Intelligence Research Society Conference 2003 (FLAIRS 2003)*. St. Augustine, Florida: May 12–14, 2003
20. Kelbassa, H.-W., Knauf, R. 2003. The Rule Retranslation Problem and the Validation Interface. *Proceedings of the 16th International Florida Artificial Intelligence Research Society Conference 2003 (FLAIRS 2003)*. St. Augustine, Florida: May 12–14, 2003
21. Kelbassa, H.-W. 2003. *Optimal Refinement of Rule Bases*. Forthcoming. Paderborn, Germany
22. Koller, R. 1974. Kann der Konstruktionsprozess in Algorithmen gefasst und dem Rechner übertragen werden? In *VDI-Berichte 219*, pp. 25–33. Düsseldorf, Germany: VDI-Verlag
23. Lenz, M., Bartsch-Spörl, B., Burkhard, H.-D., Wess, S. (Eds.). *Case-Based Reasoning Technology – From Foundations to Applications*. LNAI 1400. Berlin, FRG: Springer-Verlag 1998
24. Marcus, S. (Ed.). *Automating Knowledge Acquisition for Expert Systems*. Boston, USA: Kluwer Academic Publishers 1988
25. Neumann, K. 1975. *Operations Research Verfahren*. Vol. I. Munich, FRG: C. Hanser Verlag
26. Neumann, K., Morlock 2002. *Operations Research*. 2nd Edition. Munich: C. Hanser Verlag
27. Puppe, F., Ziegler, S., Martin, U., Hupp, J. 2001. *Wissensbasierte Diagnose im Service-Support*. Berlin, Germany: Springer-Verlag
28. Roth-Berghofer, T. R. 2003. Knowledge-Maintenance of Case-Based Reasoning Systems: The SIAM methodology. *Künstliche Intelligenz 17 (1)*, pp. 55–57
29. Schnurr, H.-P., Staab, S., Studer, R., Stumme, G., Sure, Y. (Eds.). *Professionelles Wissensmanagement – Erfahrungen und Visionen*. With Proceedings of the 9th German Workshop on Case-Based Reasoning 2001 (GWCBR 2001). Aachen, Germany: Shaker Verlag
30. Schrijver, A. 2000. *Theory of Linear and Integer Programming*. New York: J. Wiley & Sons
31. Smyth, B., Keane, M. T. 1998. Adaptation-guided retrieval: questioning the similarity assumption in reasoning. *Artificial Intelligence 102 (2)*, pp. 249–293
32. Stein, B., Hoffmann, M. 1999. On Adaptation in Case-Based Design. In R. Parenti and F. Masulli (Eds.): *Third International ICSC Symposia on Intelligent Industrial Automation (IIA '99) and Soft Computing (SOCO '99)*. ICSI Academic Press ISBN 3-906454-17-7
33. Stein, B. 2002. *Model Construction in Analysis and Synthesis Tasks*. Habilitation Thesis. University of Paderborn, Department of Computer Science, Paderborn, Germany
34. Vermesan, A., Coenen, F. (Eds.). *Validation and Verification of Knowledge Based Systems – Theory, Tools and Practice. Proceedings of the 5th EUROVAV '99*. Boston, USA: Kluwer Academic Publishers 1999

Detecting Outliers Using Rule-Based Modeling for Improving CBR-Based Software Quality Classification Models

Taghi M. Khoshgoftaar, Lofton A. Bullard, and Kehan Gao

Florida Atlantic University
Boca Raton, Florida, USA
{taghi, lofton, kgao}@cse.fau.edu

Abstract. Deploying a software product that is of high quality is a major concern for the project management team. Significant research has been dedicated toward developing methods for improving the quality of metrics-based software quality classification models. Several studies have shown that the accuracy of such models improves when outliers and data noise are removed from the training data set. This study presents a new approach called *Rule-Based Modeling* (RBM) for detecting and removing training data outliers in an effort to improve the accuracy of a *Case-Based Reasoning* (CBR) classification model. We chose to study CBR models because of their sensitivity to outliers in the training data set. Furthermore, we wanted to affirm the RBM technique as a viable outlier detector. We evaluate our approach by comparing the classification accuracy of CBR models built with and without removing outliers from the training data set. It is demonstrated that applying the RBM technique for eliminating outliers significantly improves the accuracy of CBR-based software quality classification models.

1 Introduction

Over recent years the software engineering community has greatly benefited from the positive effects that software quality models have had on the software development process. In the past, they have been used to improve the fault detection process. Detecting faulty components of a software system prior to deployment can lead to a more reliable operational system, reducing development and maintenance costs. A fault is a defect in the software that causes the executed product to fail [1]. By using an analyst specified threshold of fault-proneness, based on the number of faults, software quality models can be used to classify software modules into one of two classes, fault-prone (*fp*) and not fault-prone (*nfp*). Based on the knowledge of such information, software engineers can take corrective actions which may include, extended reviews, formal proof of correctness, additional testing, and so forth. There are a number of software quality classification models available, such as, logistic regression [2] and case-based reasoning [3,4], that have been used to identify faulty software components.

K.D. Ashley and D.G. Bridge (Eds.): ICCBR 2003, LNAI 2689, pp. 216–230, 2003.
© Springer-Verlag Berlin Heidelberg 2003

Software quality classification models are reliable developmental tools, however, there are important issues that affect their performance and applicability. One such issue is the presence of noise or outliers in the training data set used to calibrate these models. In this paper, an observation (software module) is considered as an outlier when it has correct values for the independent variables (software metrics), but a mislabeled value for its dependent variable (class label). Another type of an outlier, known as an exception [5], is an instance with the correct values for the independent variables, but whose dependent variable is relatively skewed from those of the other instances in the data set. Such an outlier may be observed in quantitative prediction models, e.g., estimating the number of faults. This study focuses on the analysis of the former type of outliers.

Several studies have investigated the effects of outliers on the performance of classification models and have provided some effective detection approach [5, 6,7,8,9]. However, these methods either made an unpractical assumption for the empirical data set [5], or require some hypotheses to classify the modules in the training data set [7,8]. The issue of case deletion from the case library (also known as case-base) has been investigated in some related works, such as [10,11]. However, the case deletion objective of those research works was to construct compact competent case-bases. More specifically, maximizing the range of target problems that can be successfully solved while simultaneously minimizing the case-base size. This study addresses case deletion from a different perspective, i.e., outlier detection and removal.

In this study, we investigate the effects of the removal of outliers from the training data set used to calibrate a Case-Based Reasoning (CBR) software quality classification model. In addition, we explore the effectiveness of using Rule-Based Modeling (RBM) as an outlier detector. The proposed technique follows a simple and logical methodology, lending to its user-acceptance. RBM is composed of a set of Boolean rules [12], where the number of rules depends on the number of significant independent variables in the training data set, as determined by an analyst. We determine outliers using RBM by reviewing the instances assigned to a particular rule. An instance can be assigned to one and only one rule, and each rule is classified as *fp* or *nfp*, based on the probability of the instances associated with that rule being *fp* or not. If an instance is associated with a rule that has a different class label (*fp* or *nfp*) then that instance is a likely candidate to be identified as an outlier.

We opted to investigate the proposed outlier detection technique for classification models built using CBR, because we are interested in determining if they are sensitive to the presence of outliers in the training data set. Our initial assumption is that CBR models are sensitive to the presence of outliers. A CBR model consists of three components, a case library, a similarity function, and a solution algorithm. A case can be thought of as an instance in the training data set, and each case is stored in the case library. When a new case (an instance) is presented to the CBR model, the similarity function is used to calculate the distance between the new case and each of the cases in the case library. The smaller is this distance, the more similar are the two respective modules. Based on these distances, the nearest neighbors are selected and used by the solution algorithm to predict the classification of the target module.

RBM was applied to the training data set, and using a user specified threshold, the fault-proneness of a rule was determined. Using these rules, instances associated with a rule were analyzed to determine if in fact they were outliers. If an instance was identified as an outlier, it was subsequently removed from the training data set.

This case study uses a data set composed of data collected from a very Large Legacy Telecommunications System. The software metrics and fault data were collected from the last four successive system releases. Two CBR models were calibrated based on the training data set; one without detection and removal of outliers, and one after using RBM to detect and remove outliers. The models were compared, and it was observed that the model built without outliers performed significantly better for most of the data sets. No complexity measures were computed, and no assumptions were made about the training data set used to fit the model or the hypotheses that were used to classify the modules. To our knowledge, this is the first study to use RBM to identify outliers.

The rest of this paper is organized as follows. Section 2 contains the methodology and introduces case-based reasoning, the Kolmogorov-Smirnov two-sample test, and rule-based modeling. The system description, the metrics used in this study, the experiment, and the results are discussed in Section 3. Finally, in Section 4 the conclusions are presented.

2   Methodology

2.1   Software Quality Classification with CBR

A CBR classification system consists of three main components: a case library, a similarity function and a solution algorithm. A case library is a set of cases or observations (selected by the analyst) usually obtained from the fit data set. A case consists of all available information about a program module, including its product attributes, its process history, and whether it is fault-prone or not. In a CBR software quality classification model the fault-proneness of a module can be determined by comparing its attributes with those of modules of a previously developed release or similar project. A working hypothesis, i.e., modules with similar attributes belong to the same group, is used to determine the class membership of a target program module.

A similarity function is used to select cases in the case library that are most similar to the current module under investigation. The function determines the distance between the module under investigation and all the cases in the case library. Modules with small distances from the module under investigation are considered similar. There are many similarity functions to choose from, such as City Block distance, Euclidean distance, and Mahalanobis distance [13]. In our study, the Mahalanobis distance is used.

Mahalanobis Distance: This similarity function can be used when the independent variables are *highly correlated*, because it can explicitly account for the correlation among the independent variables [13]. Therefore, when using this distance function the quantitative independent variables do not need to be standardized or normalized. The Mahalanobis distance is given by:

$$d_{ij} = (\mathbf{c}_j - \mathbf{x}_i)' S^{-1} (\mathbf{c}_j - \mathbf{x}_i) \tag{1}$$

where, prime ($'$) represents transpose, $\mathbf{x}_i$ is the vector of independent variables for the target module, $\mathbf{c}_j$ is the vector of independent variable values for case j in the case library, and S is the variance-covariance matrix of the independent variables over the entire case library, S^{-1} is its inverse. The variance-covariance matrix can also be computed for each individual group, i.e., the *fp* and *nfp* groups. However, in this case study such an approach yielded similar results.

Once the distances between the target module $\mathbf{x}_i$ and all cases in the case library have been computed, they are sorted. The set of nearest neighbors $\mathcal{N}$ is defined as the cases with the smallest distances. The number of nearest neighbors, i.e., $n_{\mathcal{N}}$, that will be used for predicting the dependent variable is a model parameter that can be empirically determined.

Data Clustering Classification Rule: In this classification method, the case library is partitioned into two clusters, *fp* and *nfp*, according to the class of each case in the fit data set. For an unclassified case $\mathbf{x}_i$, $d_{nfp}(\mathbf{x}_i)$ is the average distance to the *nfp* nearest neighbor cases, and $d_{fp}(\mathbf{x}_i)$ is the average distance to the *fp* nearest neighbor cases. For a given number of nearest neighbors, $n_{\mathcal{N}}$, our previously proposed *generalized data clustering classification rule* is used to estimate the class of the unclassified case $(\mathbf{x}_i)$, and is given by [4]:

$$Class(\mathbf{x}_i) = \begin{cases} fp, & \text{if } \frac{d_{nfp}(\mathbf{x}_i)}{d_{fp}(\mathbf{x}_i)} \geq c \\ nfp, & \text{otherwise} \end{cases} \tag{2}$$

The right hand side of the inequality, c, is the modeling cost ratio which can be empirically varied as per the needs of a given software system. The classification of the current case would then depend on whether or not the ratio, $\frac{d_{nfp}(\mathbf{x}_i)}{d_{fp}(\mathbf{x}_i)}$, exceeds the chosen value of c.

The accuracy of a software quality classification (two-group) model can be measured in terms of its Type I and Type II misclassification rates. A Type I error occurs when a *nfp* module is classified as *fp*, whereas a Type II error occurs when a *fp* module is classified as *nfp*. In software engineering practices, the penalty for a Type II misclassification is often relatively, more severe than for a Type I misclassification. The cost of a Type I misclassification is the time and effort wasted on additional reviews on a module that does not need it. While the cost of a Type II misclassification is the lost opportunity to review a faulty module, and may involve corrective maintenance efforts during system operations.

An inverse relationship between the Type I and Type II misclassification error rates is observed when varying the parameter c [4]. The desired preferred balance between the two misclassification error rates is dependent on the project requirements. According to our discussions with the development team of the legacy system, the preferred balance for the case study is such that the two error rates are approximately equal, with the Type II error rate being as low as possible.

2.2 Kolmogorov-Smirnov Statistic

Kolmogorov-Smirnov (K-S) two-sample test is a nonparametric statistical test [14]. It is useful in situations where two samples are drawn, one from each of the two possibly different populations, and the analyst wishes to determine whether the Cumulative Distribution Functions (CDFs) of the two samples are from the same or different populations. In the context of this study, we only need to calculate the K-S statistics of the independent variables and their critical values (defined below), which will be used for analysis with RBM.

Suppose that the data consists of two independent random samples, a fp random sample with size n_{fp}, $x_j^{(k)}$ (the jth independent variable for module k), $k = 1, \ldots, n_{fp}$, and a nfp random sample with size n_{nfp}, $x_j^{(l)}$ (the jth independent variable for module l), $l = 1, \ldots, n_{nfp}$. Let $F_{X_j^{fp}}(x_j)$ and $F_{X_j^{nfp}}(x_j)$ represent their respective unknown CDFs. $S_{X_j^{fp}}(x_j)$ is an empirical CDF of fp samples for the jth independent variable, which is defined as the fraction of X_j^{fp} which is less than or equal to $x_j^{(k)}$ for each $x_j^{(k)}$, $k = 1, \ldots, n_{fp}$. Similarly, $S_{X_j^{nfp}}(x_j)$ is defined as the empirical CDF of the nfp sample for the jth independent variable.

To calculate $S_{X_j^{fp}}(x_j)$, $x_j^{(k)}$ must be arranged in an ascending order. For simplicity, assume the ordered sequence is the same as the index k. $S_{X_j^{fp}}(x_j)$ is given by,

$$S_{X_j^{fp}}(x_j) = \frac{N_{fp}(x_j)}{n_{fp}} \tag{3}$$

where $N_{fp}(x_j)$ is the number of elements in the set $\{x_j^{(k)} \mid x_j^{(k)} \leq x_j, k = 1, \ldots, n_{fp}\}$. $S_{X_j^{nfp}}(x_j)$ is given by

$$S_{X_j^{nfp}}(x_j) = \frac{N_{nfp}(x_j)}{n_{nfp}} \tag{4}$$

where $N_{nfp}(x_j)$ is the number of elements in the set $\{x_j^{(l)} \mid x_j^{(l)} \leq x_j, l = 1, \ldots, n_{nfp}\}$. The K-S test statistic is defined as the largest vertical distance between the two empirical CDFs.

$$T_{ks} = \max_{x_j} |S_{X_j^{fp}}(x_j) - S_{X_j^{nfp}}(x_j)| \tag{5}$$

The x_j that corresponds to the maximum K-S distance, T_{ks}, is considered as the critical value, denoted by c_j, of the jth independent variable.

2.3   Rule-Based Modeling

In our study, the RBM classification technique is used to detect outliers in the training data set. Proposed by our research team [12], RBM was developed in order to overcome the limitations of Boolean Discriminant Functions [15].

Table 1. Rules for a model with $m = 3$

Rule #	Binary Code	Rule
0	000	$(x_{i1} \leq c_1) \wedge (x_{i2} \leq c_2) \wedge (x_{i3} \leq c_3)$
1	001	$(x_{i1} \leq c_1) \wedge (x_{i2} \leq c_2) \wedge (x_{i3} > c_3)$
2	010	$(x_{i1} \leq c_1) \wedge (x_{i2} > c_2) \wedge (x_{i3} \leq c_3)$
3	011	$(x_{i1} \leq c_1) \wedge (x_{i2} > c_2) \wedge (x_{i3} > c_3)$
4	100	$(x_{i1} > c_1) \wedge (x_{i2} \leq c_2) \wedge (x_{i3} \leq c_3)$
5	101	$(x_{i1} > c_1) \wedge (x_{i2} \leq c_2) \wedge (x_{i3} > c_3)$
6	110	$(x_{i1} > c_1) \wedge (x_{i2} > c_2) \wedge (x_{i3} \leq c_3)$
7	111	$(x_{i1} > c_1) \wedge (x_{i2} > c_2) \wedge (x_{i3} > c_3)$

In the context of RBM, if m is the number of independent variables then there are 2^m rules. Each rule is a Boolean function consisting of one or more Boolean AND operators, the independent variables' values x_{ij}, and their critical values c_j. Based on its critical value, each independent variable (x_{ij}) can have two possible values, $x_{ij} \leq c_j$ and $x_{ij} > c_j$. Consequently, each rule has a distinct index, representing one of the unique 2^m possible combinations. For convenience, each rule is represented by a binary number of m bits. A binary '0' represents the inequality $x_{ij} \leq c_j$ and a binary '1' represents the inequality $x_{ij} > c_j$. An example of the rules and their representation for $m = 3$ is presented in Table 1.

The Outlier Detection Procedure Using RBM

Let $rule^r$ be the rule with index r, which represents the rule number (**Rule #**) in Table 1.

Step 1: Compute the critical values of the independent variables, based on the fit data set.

Step 2: Choose the m independent variables.

Rank all the independent variables based on their K-S distances. Subsequently, the m most significant independent variables (those with the highest K-S distances) are chosen and used to form the 2^m rules.

Step 3: Compute n^r_{fp} and n^r_{nfp} for $rule^r$, $r = 0, \ldots, 2^m - 1$.

In the context of RBM, each module in the fit data set belongs to (or is associated with) only one rule. The n^r_{fp} is computed as the number of fp modules satisfying $rule^r$, and the n^r_{nfp} as the number of nfp modules satisfying $rule^r$. For some rules, there may be no modules satisfying them, then n^r_{fp} and n^r_{nfp} will be both 0.

Step 4: For each rule, compute its probabilities of being a fault-prone (p_{fp}^r), and not fault-prone (p_{nfp}^r) rule using the following equations:

$$p_{fp}^r = \frac{n_{fp}^r}{n_{nfp}^r + n_{fp}^r} \tag{6}$$

$$p_{nfp}^r = \frac{n_{nfp}^r}{n_{nfp}^r + n_{fp}^r} \tag{7}$$

where n_{fp}^r and n_{nfp}^r are obtained from Step 3. For a given rule, if n_{fp}^r and n_{nfp}^r are both 0, then p_{fp}^r and p_{nfp}^r are assigned a value of -1 to indicate that they are undefined. Such rules are labeled as unknown rules during the modeling process. The rules are arranged in an ascending order of p_{fp}^r, $r = 0, \ldots, 2^m - 1$.

Step 5: Classify each rule, and use them to determine the class membership of each module.

A threshold value (θ) for p_{fp}^r is selected once the rules are ordered according to p_{fp}^r. This threshold determines which rules are to be considered as fp rules and which are to be considered as nfp rules. The rules with $p_{fp} = -1$ are considered as *unknown* rules, and are denoted by unk. Given the selected threshold, the modules are classified as follows:

$$Class(\mathbf{x}_i) = \begin{cases} fp & p_{fp}(rule^r(\mathbf{x}_i)) > \theta \\ nfp & 0 \leq p_{fp}(rule^r(\mathbf{x}_i)) \leq \theta \\ unk & \text{otherwise} \end{cases} \tag{8}$$

where $rule^r(\mathbf{x}_i)$ indicates that module i satisfies rule r.

Step 6: Estimate the preferred threshold value, θ.

Recall that two types of misclassifications can occur in a two-group classification model, Type I and Type II. The preferred balance between the two misclassification error rates can be obtained by selecting the appropriate threshold value, θ. In our study of the high assurance legacy system, the desired balance was such that the two error rates are approximately equal with the Type II error rate being as low as possible.

Step 7: Identify the outliers in each rule and remove them from the fit data set. If for a fp rule, some of the modules that satisfy the rule are labeled as nfp, then those modules can be considered as candidate outliers. Similarly, the fp modules of a nfp rule can be considered as candidate outliers.

3   Empirical Case Study

3.1   System Description

The data sets for this case study were collected from a very Large Legacy Telecommunications System (LLTS), and included software metrics and fault data recorded for approximately 3500 to 4000 updated software modules. The case study consists of four successive releases of new versions of the system, and each release comprised of several million lines of code.

The data collection effort used the Enhanced Measurement for Early Risk Assessment of Latent Defect (EMERALD) tool. A decision support system for software measurements and software quality modeling, EMERALD periodically measured the static attributes of the most recent version of the software code. Table 2 and Table 3 respectively list the software product and execution metrics used for the LLTS case study. Therefore, 28 software metrics were used in our study.

We refer to these four releases as Release 1, Release 2, Release 3, and Release 4. Though a module in all the releases was described by the same number of metrics, each release had a different number of program modules: Releases 1 through 4 had 3649, 3981, 3541, and 3978 modules, respectively. A set of functionally associated source code files was considered as a program module. The independent variables were the 28 software metrics while the dependent variable was the class membership, i.e, *fp* or *nfp*. A module was considered *fp* if it had one or more faults, discovered by customers during system operations.

3.2   Results and Analysis

In this section, we empirically compare and evaluate the performance of the CBR models produced for the experiments. Two models were built, one using the generalized data clustering classification rule on the original fit data set, and one built using the generalized data clustering classification rule on the reduced fit data set yielding from the application of RBM on the original data set to remove outliers.

We used the fit data set to build a RBM model based on the outlier detection procedure presented in Section 2.3. Initially, the K-S statistics and the critical values for the independent variables were computed, and subsequently, the independent variables were ranked in a descending order of their K-S distance. For illustration purposes, in this paper we consider a model based on the seven ($m = 7$) most significant metrics. Other values of m were also considered [12], however, due to space limitations their results are not presented. Therefore, for ($m = 7$) the total number of rules used in the RBM model was $2^7 = 128$. For each rule we computed the probabilities of the rule being a *fp* and a *nfp* rule.

The rules shown in Table 4 are in an ascending order based on the probability of a module being *fp* in each rule. From this table the appropriate value of the threshold, θ, which is used to identify the *fp* and *nfp* rules, is determined. For example (shown in Table 4), any threshold value belonging to {$0.0714 < \theta < 0.0833$} can be selected for designating the last 15 rules as *fp* rules. Table 5 lists the Type I and Type II misclassification rates of the original fit data set for different threshold values. The preferred classification model is illustrated in **bold**. The corresponding threshold, θ, was 0.075. With this threshold, the well-defined (not unknown) rules that were classified as either *fp* or *nfp*, are shown in Table 4.

Theoretically, we could have removed all the modules identified as outliers, i.e., any module with a class label that is different than the class label of the rule the module belongs to. However, in analyzing the RBM results for identifying

Table 2. Software Product Metrics

Symbol	Description
Call Graph Metrics	
$CALUNQ$	Number of distinct procedure calls to others.
$CAL2$	Number of second and following calls to others.
	$CAL2 = CAL - CALUNQ$ where CAL is the total number of calls.
Control Flow Graph Metrics	
$CNDNOT$	Number of arcs that are not conditional arcs.
$IFTH$	Number of non-loop conditional arcs (i.e., if-then constructs).
LOP	Number of loop constructs.
$CNDSPNSM$	Total span of branches of conditional arcs. The unit of measure is arcs.
$CNDSPNMX$	Maximum span of branches of conditional arcs.
$CTRNSTMX$	Maximum control structure nesting.
KNT	Number of knots. A "knot" in a control flow graph is where arcs cross due to a violation of structured programming principles.
$NDSINT$	Number of internal nodes (i.e., not an entry, exit, or pending node).
$NDSENT$	Number of entry nodes.
$NDSEXT$	Number of exit nodes.
$NDSPND$	Number of pending nodes (i.e., dead code segments).
$LGPATH$	Base 2 logarithm of the number of independent paths.
Statement Metrics	
$FILINCUQ$	Number of distinct include files.
LOC	Number of lines of code.
$STMCTL$	Number of control statements.
$STMDEC$	Number of declarative statements.
$STMEXE$	Number of executable statements.
$VARGLBUS$	Number of global variables used.
$VARSPNSM$	Total span of variables.
$VARSPNMX$	Maximum span of variables.
$VARUSDUQ$	Number of distinct variables used.
$VARUSD2$	Number of second and following uses of variables.
	$VARUSD2 = VARUSD - VARUSDUQ$ where $VARUSD$ is the total number of variable uses.

outliers, a conservative attitude was taken in deciding which modules to remove. For $\theta = 0.075$, the *fp* modules that were members of a *nfp* rule with $p_{fp} < 0.02$ were considered as outliers. Similarly, *nfp* modules that were members of a *fp* rule with $p_{fp} > 0.2$ were considered as outliers. Subsequently, we removed 1 *fp* module from $rule^{48}$; 31 *fp* modules from $rule^0$; and, 389 *nfp* modules from $rule^{127}$, all of which are shown in **bold** in Table 4. The 5 modules classified as *nfp* collectively by $rule^{106}$ and $rule^{110}$ were ignored as being outliers because their sample sizes were too small, i.e., 3 and 4, respectively. According to the above discussions, about 11% of the *nfp* modules, and 14% of *fp* modules were removed from the original fit data set. The decisions regarding outlier detection and removal is subjective, and is dependent on the analyst and the system under consideration.

We used the leave-one-out (*n*-fold) cross validation technique to build the CBR models [16]. It is an iterative process in which during each iteration, one

Table 3. Software Execution Metrics

Symbol	Description
USAGE	Deployment percentage of the module.
RESCPU	Execution time (microseconds) of an average transaction on a system serving consumers.
BUSCPU	Execution time (microseconds) of an average transaction on a system serving businesses.
TANCPU	Execution time (microseconds) of an average transaction on a tandem system.

of the n observations in the fit data set is used as the test data and the other $n-1$ are used to train or build the model. Two CBR classification models were built, i.e., one with outliers in the fit data, and one with the reduced fit data set without outliers. For both models, the model parameters: number of the nearest neighbors, $n_{\mathcal{N}}$, and the cost ratio, c, were varied to calibrate a classification model with the preferred balance between the Type I and Type II misclassification rates. As discussed earlier, the preferred balance is such that the two error rates are approximately equal, with the Type II error rate being as low as possible.

In a recent research [17], it was shown that a project specified preferred balance between the Type I and Type II error rates is an effective approach for considering candidate models for high-assurance systems such as LLTS. In the case of high-assurance systems, the proportion of *fp* modules is very small. For a given $n_{\mathcal{N}}$, the cost ratio, c, was varied over a range from 0 to 1 with steps of 0.001. Subsequently, among the respective calibrated models, for the given $n_{\mathcal{N}}$, the model with the preferred balance was selected. A similar process was followed for different values of $n_{\mathcal{N}}$. Table 6 lists the best models for the different values of the modeling parameter, $n_{\mathcal{N}}$. The results of the model fitted with outliers in the fit data set are presented on the left side of Table 6. The preferred balance between the error rates (Type I and Type II) occurred when $n_{\mathcal{N}} = 19$ and $c = 0.629$. The right side of Table 6 presents the results of the model fitted without outliers. The preferred balance between the error rates occurred when $n_{\mathcal{N}} = 15$ and $c = 0.606$. The table also shows the respective Overall error rates for both models.

The classification accuracy was measured with respect to the performance metrics, Type I, Type II, and Overall misclassification rates. Table 7 summarizes the two selected models, and their classification accuracies across the multiple releases of the telecommunication system. It was observed that the Type I and the Overall misclassification rates of the CBR model was significantly improved for all releases when outliers were removed from the training data set. Using cross-validation the Type II misclassification rate was significantly improved for Release 1 (the training data set). This result was also observed for Release 2 when used as a test data set. However, there was no significant change in the

Table 4. Results for RBM rules when $m = 7$

Index	Rule #	n_{fp}	n_{nfp}	P_{fp}	P_{nfp}	Class	Index	Rule #	n_{fp}	n_{nfp}	P_{fp}	P_{nfp}	Class
0-52	others	0	0	-1	-1	unk	90	75	0	1	0	1	nfp
53	1	0	8	0	1	nfp	91	76	0	1	0	1	nfp
54	2	0	54	0	1	nfp	92	78	0	4	0	1	nfp
55	4	0	3	0	1	nfp	93	97	0	8	0	1	nfp
56	5	0	1	0	1	nfp	94	98	0	13	0	1	nfp
57	6	0	3	0	1	nfp	95	114	0	5	0	1	nfp
58	7	0	7	0	1	nfp	96	117	0	1	0	1	nfp
59	8	0	2	0	1	nfp	97	120	0	3	0	1	nfp
60	10	0	2	0	1	nfp	98	122	0	3	0	1	nfp
61	11	0	2	0	1	nfp	99	124	0	1	0	1	nfp
62	12	0	1	0	1	nfp	100	125	0	11	0	1	nfp
63	14	0	3	0	1	nfp	101	**48**	1	75	0.0132	0.9868	nfp
64	15	0	14	0	1	nfp	102	**0**	31	1626	0.0187	0.9813	nfp
65	17	0	1	0	1	nfp	103	99	1	28	0.0345	0.9655	nfp
66	18	0	4	0	1	nfp	104	64	10	231	0.0415	0.9585	nfp
67	19	0	2	0	1	nfp	105	35	1	23	0.0417	0.9583	nfp
68	32	0	43	0	1	nfp	106	49	1	20	0.0476	0.9524	nfp
69	33	0	10	0	1	nfp	107	47	5	85	0.0556	0.9444	nfp
70	39	0	4	0	1	nfp	108	79	1	16	0.0588	0.9412	nfp
71	40	0	2	0	1	nfp	109	16	2	28	0.0667	0.9333	nfp
72	42	0	1	0	1	nfp	110	63	5	70	0.0667	0.9333	nfp
73	43	0	10	0	1	nfp	111	96	2	27	0.069	0.931	nfp
74	44	0	1	0	1	nfp	112	3	1	13	0.0714	0.9286	nfp
75	45	0	2	0	1	nfp	113	123	1	11	0.0833	0.9167	fp
76	46	0	2	0	1	nfp	114	111	19	205	0.0848	0.9152	fp
77	50	0	1	0	1	nfp	115	119	1	10	0.0909	0.9091	fp
78	51	0	26	0	1	nfp	116	80	1	8	0.1111	0.8889	fp
79	53	0	4	0	1	nfp	117	113	5	38	0.1163	0.8837	fp
80	55	0	7	0	1	nfp	118	115	2	15	0.1176	0.8824	fp
81	58	0	1	0	1	nfp	119	103	1	7	0.125	0.875	fp
82	59	0	5	0	1	nfp	120	66	8	54	0.129	0.871	fp
83	60	0	1	0	1	nfp	121	112	15	101	0.1293	0.8707	fp
84	61	0	7	0	1	nfp	122	121	2	13	0.1333	0.8667	fp
85	65	0	1	0	1	nfp	123	34	1	6	0.1429	0.8571	fp
86	67	0	10	0	1	nfp	124	107	2	11	0.1538	0.8462	fp
87	68	0	2	0	1	nfp	125	**127**	108	**389**	0.2173	0.7827	fp
88	70	0	2	0	1	nfp	126	110	1	3	0.25	0.75	fp
89	74	0	5	0	1	nfp	127	106	1	2	0.3333	0.6667	fp

performance for Release 3, and it (model after outlier removal) performed worse for Release 4, with respect to the Type II error rate. We note (based on our discussions with the development team) that the software metric data collection effort for Release 4 was not as complete as the first three releases.

To quantitatively analyze the performances of the two models, a Z-test is performed [18]. The null hypothesis of the Z-test was that the model built with outliers has no worse classification accuracy than the model built without outliers. The alternate hypothesis was that the model built without outliers has a higher

Table 5. RBM: Model Selection ($m = 7$)

Threshold θ	Type I	Type II
0.025	41.35%	13.97%
0.050	32.51%	19.65%
0.075	**25.53%**	**26.64%**
0.085	19.21%	35.37%
0.100	18.92%	35.81%
0.150	11.84%	51.09%

Table 6. Results of CBR (Cross-Validation)

$n_\mathcal{N}$	With Outliers				Without Outliers			
	c	Type I	Type II	Overall	c	Type I	Type II	Overall
1	0.625	0.34327	0.34498	0.34338	0.6	0.23887	0.24365	0.23916
2	0.621	0.34327	0.34498	0.34338	0.603	0.22732	0.22843	0.22739
3	0.626	0.33158	0.33188	0.3316	0.612	0.21973	0.21827	0.21964
4	0.629	0.32807	0.32751	0.32804	0.612	0.21148	0.2132	0.21159
5	0.63	0.32661	0.32751	0.32666	0.609	0.21709	0.2132	0.21685
6	0.635	0.32281	0.32751	0.3231	0.615	0.21181	0.21827	0.21221
7	0.632	0.32749	0.32751	0.32749	0.612	0.21643	0.21827	0.21654
8	0.63	0.32953	0.32751	0.32941	0.608	0.22138	0.21827	0.22119
9	0.631	0.32807	0.32751	0.32804	0.607	0.22336	0.22335	0.22336
10	0.63	0.33158	0.33188	0.3316	0.605	0.22336	0.22335	0.22336
11	0.63	0.32865	0.33624	0.32913	0.601	0.22534	0.22335	0.22522
12	0.625	0.33772	0.33624	0.33763	0.602	0.22204	0.21827	0.22181
13	0.623	0.34064	0.33624	0.34037	0.605	0.21544	0.22335	0.21592
14	0.627	0.33275	0.32751	0.33242	0.603	0.21808	0.21827	0.21809
15	0.628	0.33099	0.32751	0.33078	**0.606**	**0.20983**	**0.20812**	**0.20973**
16	0.628	0.33012	0.32751	0.32995	0.605	0.21016	0.20812	0.21004
17	0.628	0.32749	0.32751	0.32749	0.601	0.2128	0.2132	0.21283
18	0.63	0.32251	0.32751	0.32283	0.598	0.2128	0.2132	0.21283
19	**0.629**	**0.32135**	**0.31878**	**0.32118**	0.597	0.21313	0.2132	0.21314
20	0.63	0.31813	0.32314	0.31844	0.593	0.2161	0.2132	0.21592
21	0.627	0.32105	0.32314	0.32118	0.592	0.2161	0.21827	0.21623
22	0.623	0.32368	0.32314	0.32365	0.59	0.21742	0.21827	0.21747
23	0.619	0.3269	0.32314	0.32666	0.586	0.21874	0.21827	0.21871
24	0.62	0.32281	0.32751	0.3231	0.587	0.2161	0.22335	0.21654
25	0.62	0.32105	0.32751	0.32146	0.585	0.21742	0.22335	0.21778
26	0.62	0.31696	0.32751	0.31762	0.585	0.21445	0.22335	0.21499
27	0.618	0.31901	0.32751	0.31954	0.58	0.21775	0.22335	0.21809
28	0.614	0.32281	0.32751	0.3231	0.58	0.21709	0.22335	0.21747
29	0.614	0.3193	0.32751	0.31981	0.58	0.21379	0.22335	0.21437
30	0.613	0.31871	0.32751	0.31927	0.573	0.2194	0.21827	0.21933

classification accuracy than the model built with outliers. Table 8 presents the
Z-test statistics and the corresponding percentile, p-values. The Z-test results
showed that for Release 1, the classification accuracy was improved at a significance level of less than 1% for the Type I, Type II and Overall misclassification
rates; for Release 2, the classification accuracy was improved at a significance
level of less than 1% for the Type I and Overall misclassification rates, and 33%
for the Type II misclassification rate; for Release 3, the classification accuracy
was improved for the Type I and Overall error rates, and remained the same
($p = 0.5$) for the Type II misclassification rates; for Release 4, the classification
accuracy was improved for the Type I and the Overall misclassification rates, but
decreased to a significance level of less than 24% for the Type II misclassification
rates.

Table 7. Results with and without Outliers

Release #	With Outliers $n_N = 19$ c $= 0.629$			Without Outliers $n_N = 15$ c $= 0.606$		
	Type I	Type II	Overall	Type I	Type II	Overall
Release1	32.14 %	31.88 %	32.12 %	20.98 %	20.81 %	20.97 %
Release2	27.19 %	31.75 %	27.41 %	24.84 %	29.63 %	25.07 %
Release3	32.80 %	23.40 %	32.67 %	29.51 %	23.40 %	29.43 %
Release4	37.01 %	18.48 %	36.58 %	32.48 %	22.83 %	32.25 %

Table 8. Z-test Results

Release #	z-test z-nfp	z-fp	z-total	p-value p-nfp	p-fp	p-total
Release1	10.0811	2.5722	10.4038	0.0000	0.0051	0.0000
Release2	2.3295	0.4461	2.3692	0.0099	0.3278	0.0089
Release3	2.9750	0.0000	2.0534	0.0015	0.5000	0.0200
Release4	4.1928	-0.7285	4.0589	0.0000	0.7668	0.0000

4   Conclusion and Future Work

Software quality classification models have been used to predict the fault-
proneness of software modules. Analysts can use such a prediction to effectively
target software quality improvement activities toward high-risk modules. The
presence of outliers in the training data set can affect the performance of software quality classification models. The goal of this study was to: (1) determine

if the CBR classification model is sensitive to outliers, and (2) investigate RBM as an effective outlier detection technique. In context of CBR-based classification models in our study, a target case/module is classified as *fp* or *nfp* based on its similarity with cases in the case library and the generalized data clustering rule.

An outlier in the training data for our study is defined as a module with correct values for its attributes, but an incorrect value for the class label. The CBR technique is sensitive to these kind of outliers because of its working hypothesis that the quality of a given program module is similar to other program modules with similar attributes. Hence, if a target instance has similar attributes as an instance in a case library, and if the latter instance was mislabeled, then the target instance might be misclassified. To determine the effects of outliers on classification models based on CBR, two models were built: one fitted with a data set that contained outliers, and one fitted with a data set without the outliers that were identified by RBM. Upon comparing the preferred balance between the Type I and Type II error rates of the two models, it was observed that the CBR model built without outliers performed significantly better. More specifically, it had lower Type I and Type II error rates. This confirmed our assumptions about the sensitivity of CBR to noise.

The RBM procedure presented is easy to understand, and can be implemented with ease. It uses a K-S statistic to compute the critical values of the most significant software attributes, and then assigns the membership of each module to one rule. Each rule is classified as a *fp* or a *nfp* rule, based on the probabilities of its associated modules being *fp* and *nfp*. An outlier is detected when a module has a different class label than its associated rule. The results of the study confirmed that RBM was an effective outlier detector. This was clearly indicated by the increase in the classification accuracy (for all four releases of LLTS) of the CBR model calibrated after outlier removal.

Future work will consider extending RBM to allow a correction of the misclassified program modules in the training data set, comparing RBM to different outlier detection techniques; and performing additional empirical studies using RBM as an outlier detector.

References

1. Lyu, M.R., ed.: Handbook of Software Reliability Engineering. McGraw-Hill, New York (1996)
2. Khoshgoftaar, T.M., Allen, E.B.: Logistic regression modeling of software quality. International Journal of Reliability, Quality and Safety Engineering **6** (1999) 303–317
3. Ester, M., Kriegel, H., Sander, J., Xu, X.: A density-based algorithm for discovering clusters in large spatial databases with noise. In: Proceedings of the 2nd International Conference on Knowledge Discovery and Data Mining (KDD-96)., Portland, Oregon, USA (1996) 226–231
4. Khoshgoftaar, T.M., Cukic, B., Seliya, N.: Predicting fault-prone modules in embedded systems using analogy-based classification models. International Journal of Software Engineering and Knowledge Engineering **12** (2002) 201–221 World Scientific Publishing.

230 T.M. Khoshgoftaar, L.A. Bullard, and K. Gao

5. Brodley, C.E., Friedl, M.A.: Identifying and eliminating mislabeled training instances. In: AAAI/IAAI. Volume 1. (1996) 799–805
6. Decatur, S.E., Gennaro, R.: On learning from noisy and incomplete examples. In: Computational Learning Theory. (1995) 353–360
7. Gamberger, D., Lavrac, N.: Noise elimination in inductive concept learning: A case study in medical diagnosis. In: 7th International Workshop on Algorithmic Learning Theory, Sydney, Australia. (1996) 199–212
8. Gamberger, D., Lavrac, N.: Conditions for occam's razor applicability and noise elimination. In: European Conference on Machine Learning. (1997) 108–123
9. Zhao, Q., Nishida, T.: Using qualitative hypotheses to identify inaccurate data. Journal of Artificial Intelligence Research [http://ai-www.aist-nara.ac.jp/doc/people/qi-zhao/JAIR.ps] **3** (1995) 119–145
10. Leake, D.B., Wilson, D.C.: Remembering why to remember: Performance-guided case-base maintenance. In: Proceedings of the 5th European Workshop, EWCBR 2000, Trento, Italy, Springer (2000) 161–172 Lecture Notes in Artificial Intelligence 1898.
11. Smyth, B., McKenna, E.: Building compact competent case-bases. In: Proceedings of the International Conference on Case-Based Reasoning, Monastery Seeon, Munich, Germany, Springer (1999) 329–342 Lecture Notes in Computer Science 1650.
12. Mao, M.: Software quality classification using rule based modeling. Master's thesis, Florida Atlantic University, Boca Raton, Florida USA (2002) Advised by Taghi M. Khoshgoftaar.
13. Bhupathiraju, S.S.: An empirical study of a three-group classification model using case-based reasoning. Master's thesis, Florida Atlantic University, Boca Raton, Florida USA (2002) Advised by Taghi M. Khoshgoftaar.
14. Conover, W.J.: Practical Nonparametric Statistics. John Wiley & Sons, Inc (1971)
15. Schneidewind, N.F.: Software metrics model for integrating quality control and prediction. In: Proceedings of the 8th International Symposium on Software Reliability Engineering, Albuquerque, NM USA, IEEE Computer Society (1997) 402–415
16. Kohavi, R.: A study of cross-validation and bootstrap for accuracy estimation and model selection. In: Proceedings of the 14th International Joint Conference on Artificial Intelligence, IJCAI 95, Montréal, Québec, Canada, Morgan Kaufmann (1995) 1137–1145
17. Khoshgoftaar, T., Yuan, X., Allen, E.: Balancing misclassification rates in classification-tree models of software quality. In: Empirical Software Engineering. Volume 5., Kluwer Academic Publishers (2000) 313–330
18. Zar, J.H.: Biostatisitical Analysis. Second edn. Prentice Hall (1984)

An Empirical Analysis of Linear Adaptation Techniques for Case-Based Prediction

Colin Kirsopp[1], Emilia Mendes[2], Rahul Premraj[1], and Martin Shepperd[1]

[1] Bournemouth University, U.K.
[2] University of Auckland, New Zealand

Abstract. This paper is an empirical investigation into the effectiveness of linear scaling adaptation for case-based software project effort prediction. We compare two variants of a linear size adjustment technique and (as a baseline) a simple k-NN approach. These techniques are applied to the data sets after feature subset optimisation. The three data sets used in the study range from small (less than 20 cases) through medium (approximately 80 cases) to large (approximately 400 cases). These are typical sizes for this problem domain. Our results show that the linear scaling techniques studied, result in statistically significant improvements to predictions. The size of these improvements is typically about 10% which is certainly of value for a problem domain such as project prediction. The results, however, include a number of extreme outliers which might be problematic. Additional analysis of the results suggests that these adaptation algorithms might potentially be refined to cope better with the outlier problem.

1 Introduction

Over the past 15 years case-based reasoning (CBR) has been successfully applied to a wide range of problem domains. Our particular interest is in predicting effort (and related factors such as duration) for software projects. Of course to be useful, such predictions are required at an early stage. This is important because software projects are difficult to justify or manage if it isn't possible to estimate how long they will last and how much effort they will consume. For this reason cost modelling has been an active research topic for more than 30 years. Despite this activity, no one technique has been found to be consistently effective. It has proved to be challenging for a number of reasons. Typically, data sets are small, as projects occur relatively infrequently, perhaps just a few per year. Data is heterogeneous so merging data from different environments is seldom fruitful. Data collection environments are characterised by change, noise and uncertainty. Moreover, software engineering is a predominantly creative activity, consequently we do not have a strong underlying theory.

Various research groups have explored the application of CBR methods to predicting project effort, motivated in part by the obvious similarities between project managers seeking to estimate based on recall of past similar projects, and the formal use of analogies in CBR [17,19,5]. Encouraging results have been

K.D. Ashley and D.G. Bridge (Eds.): ICCBR 2003, LNAI 2689, pp. 231–245, 2003.
© Springer-Verlag Berlin Heidelberg 2003

reported, for example, in an analysis of 9 different data sets and using stepwise regression (SWR) as a baseline, CBR was found to consistently outperform SWR [20]. However, not all results have been this positive [3] and researchers have continued to refine the CBR methods employed. These efforts have included the use of feature and case subset selection [12,13] and the use of adaptation techniques [15,24].

This paper started as an attempt to validate the adaptation scheme previously proposed by Mendes [15]. The reason for wanting an additional validation was to see how well the scheme would work with a set of varied real world data sets, as opposed to the student-based data sets used in the initial validation. However, during the course of the validation it became clear that changes to the original scheme would need to be made both to correct oversights and to allow the scheme to be compatible with a wider range of data sets. These changes were made in collaboration with the original author and are described and justified in section 4.

The work presented is, therefore, both a development of an existing adaptation scheme and a more extensive validation on a variety of industrial data sets.

The remainder of this paper is organised as follows. The next section reviews different case adaptation strategies and then describes a structural adaptation algorithm that has been successfully applied to web projects. The following section provides background on the three case bases used for our analysis. We then describe our method of data collection and analysis. This is followed by the study's results. We conclude with a discussion of the results and make suggestions for follow up work.

2   Related Work on Case Adaptation

One aspect of CBR that is attracting much interest is adaptation. This involves modification of the proposed solution in order to better fit the target case. As well as enabling CBR systems to accommodate novel situations, adaptation may also be useful in counteracting the impact of occasionally retrieving poor cases [18].

The value of adaptation has been investigated by many researchers with varying results. The need for adaptation seems to be largely application dependent. For example, as suggested by Hanney et al. [7], classification tasks might be accomplished with little or no adaptation, while design and prediction applications call for varying degrees of adaptation strategies to achieve acceptable outcomes. Another challenge relates to the difficulties of eliciting the adaptation knowledge [4] although a range of new techniques such as the incremental approach are being investigated [10].

Wilke and Bergmann [25] classify adaptation into three main types:

- null adaptation
- transformational adaptation
- generative adaptation

Null adaptation, the simplest, involves directly applying the solution from the retrieved case(s) to the target case. This is the approach adopted by a simple Nearest Neighbour technique and in a slightly more sophisticated form such as inverse distance weighted mean for kNN when $k > 1$.

With transformational adaptation, the old solution derived from the retrieved case is modified. There are two general approaches to achieving this. First, there is what is often termed *structural* transformation based on some function of the target and retrieved case feature vectors. Examples include Finnie et al. [5] and Hanney and Keane [8]. The other approach — often used when dealing with more complex problem representations — is *rule-based* transformation. Here, rules are either elicited from a domain expert or learnt using an induction algorithm. The use of fuzzy rule induction has also been proposed, see Shiu et al. [21].

Generative adaptation entails deriving the solution to the problem Ôfrom-scratchÕ. In principle, the derivation is handled by the case-based system, largely independent of the case base. Voss [23] describes a number of examples of this approach and more recently Munoz-Avila et al. described a hybrid generative adaptation method that involves user interaction [16].

In the field of software project prediction, cEstor is an early example of an adaptive case-based reasoning system developed by Prietula et al. [17]. The case adaptation knowledge was actually acquired in the raw form from an expert doing the task. This knowledge was translated into procedural rules in the form of if <conditions> then <actions>. The result was good predictions but a lack of generality even to other data sets in the same problem domain.

Finnie et al. [5,6] used structural adaptation for predicting effort using CBR. Their adaptation model was primarily based on the relative size of the source and the target case and involved adaptation by means of a simple linear regression model. Effort was estimated by using a multiplier computed on the basis of the contribution of the selected features to productivity. Overall they found MM-REs[1] for a simple regression model of 62.3%, neural net 35.2% and CBR 36.2% (smaller MMREs are preferred). Structural adaptation has also been applied by Walkerden and Jeffery [24] and Mendes et al. [15]. Both studies employ adaptation rules based on the linear size adjustment to the estimated effort. The linear size adjustment attempts to take into account the difference in size between the target and finished projects. For Walkerden and Jeffery, once the most similar finished project in the case base has been retrieved, its effort value is adjusted to estimate effort for the target project. A linear extrapolation is performed along the dimension of a single 'size' feature that is chosen as being strongly correlated with effort. The linear size adjustment is represented as follows:

$$e_i' = e_i \frac{s_t}{s} \tag{1}$$

where e is the actual effort of a retrieved project, s is the value of a size related feature for that project and e' is the adjusted effort value to be used in

---

[1] Mean magnitude of relative error (MMRE) is a widely used indicator of prediction accuracy and is defined as $\frac{100}{n} \sum_{i=1}^{i=n} \frac{|x_i - \hat{x_i}|}{x_i}$ where n is the number of predictions $\hat{x}$ of x.

calculating the predicted effort for the target case. Note that s_t is the value for the size feature that typically might be a measure of functionality described in the system specification using function points [22]. Mendes et al. [15] apply two types of adaptation rules, both based on linear size adjustment. The first type is called "adaptation without weights", and calculated by generalising the linear size adjustment to an arbitrary number of size related features, and then the estimated efforts generated averaged to obtain an effort estimate (Equation 2). When using this adaptation, all size measures contribute equally towards total estimated effort, indicated by the use of a simple average.

$$\hat{e}_t = \frac{1}{k} \sum_{i=1}^{i=k} \left(\frac{1}{q} \sum_{j=1}^{j=q} e_i \frac{s_{jt}}{s_{ji}} \right) \tag{2}$$

where $\hat{e}_t$ is the predicted effort for the target case, we are basing the prediction on k retrieved cases and there are q size related features. We denote each such feature as $s_{1i} \dots s_{qi}$ for the ith retrieved case.

The second type of adaptation rule they used is called "adaptation with weights". In this type of adaptation, different weights are applied to size metrics to indicate the strength of relationship between a size metric and effort (see Equation 3).

$$\hat{e}_t = \frac{1}{k} \sum_{i=1}^{i=k} \left(\frac{1}{\sum_{j=1}^{j=q} w_j} \left(\frac{1}{q} \sum_{j=1}^{j=q} e_i \frac{s_{jt}}{s_{ji}} \right) \right) \tag{3}$$

where w_j is the weight or relative significance w attributed to the jth size measure s.

As stated in the introduction, to date, our approach has been a null adaptation, and to focus on feature and case subset selection in order to reduce the likelihood of retrieving poor analogies. Given the positive results of other researchers in this problem domain we now examine the impact of using a structural adaptation method i.e. a linear size adjustment similar to that employed by Mendes et al. [15]. This approach is selected because our solution representation is trivial (a single continuous feature) and the case representation is merely a feature vector so the more complex adaptation strategies appear unwarranted at this stage. Moreover, we wish to have a method that generalises to many data sets, unlike say, the method of Prietula et al. [17] where the adaptation rules are couched in terms of the specific features of a particular data set. In addition, we wish to avoid the problems of knowledge elicitation given that we do not possess any deep theory of software project management!

3   Our Data Sets

In this section we provide some background on the three data sets used in our study. These are chosen to represent varying sizes of data set that are commonly encountered in the project prediction domain. The data sets are:

- BT: a small data set ($n = 18$) derived from one division of a large telecommunications company. This is representative of many organisations that embark upon an internal data collection programme to support their effort prediction activities. The data is relatively homogeneous.
- Desharnais: a medium sized data set ($n = 77$) collected by a Canadian software house from projects distributed amongst 11 different organisations.
- Finnish: a large data set ($n = 405$) collected by the benchmarking organisation STTF Ltd. This data is collected over a number of years for a diverse range of software developers thus this is the most heterogeneous of the three data sets. The features are a mixture of continuous, discrete and categorical. However, there are a number of missing data values and also some features that would not be known at prediction time and so are not included in our analysis. Removing features with missing values or after-the-event data, leaves a subset of 42 features that are actually used in the case study. The data set also exhibits significant multi-collinearity, in other words there are strong relationships between features as well as with effort.

Table 1. Example Data Set Classification Scheme

Data set	no. of cases (n)	no. of features (p)	no. of continuous features
BT	18	3	3
Desharnais	77	9	8
Finnish	405	42	37

Table 1 provides some summary information for each of the three data sets. It must be emphasised that the data sets are quite varied not only in terms of size but also in terms of the specific features that have been collected. Building prediction systems from such small case bases as exemplified by the BT data set is a common challenge in this problem domain. The three data sets contrast considerably, from the extreme simplicity of the BT data set to the large number of features and cases contained in the Finnish data set.

4   Method

The techniques to be compared in this study are variants of a linear size adjustment scheme. The techniques used are based on those of Mendes [15], but with some amendments. This study does not assume that all available features are suitable for scaling. Firstly, the data sets used in this paper contain some categorical features and these features are clearly not suitable for linear adjustment. Although differences in categorical features could be used for adaptation we will leave this for further work and concentrate on only the continuous features. Secondly, not all of the continuous features may be suitable for adaptation.

We use robust correlation (e.g., Spearman's rank correlation) as a means of selecting which features will be scaled. The rationale here is that linear scaling would only work if there were a monotonic relationship (at least locally to the target case) between a particular feature and effort. The correlation is intended to be an indication of whether such a relationship exists and so whether linear adaptation is likely to be useful for that feature.

Two variants of linear adaptation are are investigated in this paper. In variant one, only the most highly correlated feature (either positively or negatively) is used for linear size adjustment (single feature adjustment). The second variant applies size adjustment to any feature that is significantly correlated with the dependent variable (multiple feature adjustment).

This study is restricted to the unweighted feature formulation presented in Equation 2. However, there are some issues with this formulation that need to be addressed. Firstly, it is assumed that if $s_{ij} > s_{tj}$ then the effort should be adjusted upward, i.e., that all features are positively correlated to effort. Although this may have been a reasonable assumption in the study from Mendes [15] where all features were size measures, this may not be the case for the data sets in this study where the features represent various attributes of the systems under development or the development environment, e.g. the level of reuse or experience. An alternative formulation for negatively correlated features is presented in Equation 4. Here s_{ij} and s_{tj} have been swapped so that effort will be adjust negatively if s_{ij} increases.

$$\hat{e}_t = \frac{1}{q} \sum_{j=1}^{j=n} e_i \frac{s_{ji}}{s_{jt}} \tag{4}$$

Another issue is that, in Equation 2, $\hat{e}_t$ will become infinite if $s_{ij} = 0$ (as it would if $s_{tj} = 0$ in Equation 4). To avoid this problem, features that would introduce a zero into the denominator (for a particular case) are excluded from the calculation of the adjustment (for that case).

The work of the study will be to build prediction systems based on the variants of linear size adjustment previously described and compare their accuracy. Standard prediction system validation requires a training set and a hold-out set, however, previous studies [9,11] have shown that results vary widely depending on the random allocation of cases in these sets due to the heterogeneity of the data set. Large numbers of such sets may be necessary to provide acceptable confidence limits on the result and to allow statistical testing of apparent differences. The results gained from these adaptation techniques are also compared to case-based prediction without adaptation (simple k-NN prediction) to provide a baseline.

Previous studies have shown that feature subset selection (FSS) prior to building case-based prediction systems can greatly improve their accuracy [1,2, 12,13]. This study investigates whether these strategies can improve a prediction system already tuned using FSS. Although, ideally, FSS should be repeated for each training set, it is computationally prohibitive given the large numbers of prediction systems to be built. Instead we perform one FSS for each treatment of each data set, based on a jack-knife[2] of the entire data set. This means that the same feature subset is used for each training set within a treatment and for some of these training sets it will be sub-optimal. However, since a previous study [13] has shown the optimal feature subset varies little with variations in the randomly sampled cases present in the training set, this should have little impact on the results.

Prediction accuracy is measured using the MMRE and the Sum of absolute residuals $(Sum(|r|))$. MMRE is chosen as it is a standard measure of prediction accuracy in software effort prediction and also because it allows comparison between data sets. The sum of absolute residuals is also used as it is less vulnerable to bias than the asymmetric MMRE [14]. Since the absolute residuals were skewed, we used a non-parametric test to check the significance of our results. The data was naturally paired (the same 100 training and validation sets were used within each data set), so we used the Wilcoxon Signed Rank test to compare the difference in location between two populations. The procedure followed for the data collection is given below:

1. Remove any after-the-event[3] features from the data (other than the dependent variable).
2. No adaptation (simple k-NN)
   a) Do feature subset selection
      Subset search settings:
      - Use mean of the 2 nearest neighbours as the prediction.
      - Jackknife the data set and use the $Sum(|r|)$ as the measure of prediction system accuracy.
      - Search for the feature set that gives the lowest $Sum(|r|)$. Use the most effective search technique for the size of the data set and number of features (by exhaustive search other than for the Finnish data set which uses a forward selection search).
   b) Run 100 validation trials with randomly sampled training sets with a 2:1 split between training and hold-out sets.
   c) Collect MMRE and $Sum(|r|)$ values for each of the 100 sets.
3. Single feature adaptation
   a) Calculate the correlations between the dependent variable and the other (continuous) features. As some of the features are measured on an interval scale and most of the continuous variables are not normally distributed the non-parametric Spearman rank correlation is used.
   b) Do feature subset selection. Subset search settings will be as for 'No adaption' except that linear distance adjustment is used on the feature with the highest correlation (the adjustment is done in the direction of that correlation - positive or negative).

---

[2] Jack-knifing is a form of hold-one-out validation where each case is removed from the training set in turn and the remaining cases used to make a prediction for the holdout case

[3] These are features present in the published data sets that would not be known at prediction time.

     c) Run 100 validation trials based on the same 100 training sets as for 'no adaptation'.

     d) Collect MMRE and $Sum(|r|)$ values.

4. Multiple feature adaptation

     a) Calculate the significant correlations between the dependent variable and the other features at a significance level of α =0.05). Bonferroni adjustment will be used to adjust α based on the number of features to be tested.

     b) Do feature subset selection. Subset search settings are as for 'single feature adaptation' except that all features significantly correlated with effort are used for adjustment.

     c) Run 100 validation trials based on the same 100 training sets as for 'no adaptation'.

     d) Collect MMRE and $Sum(|r|)$ values.

5   Results

5.1   BT Data Set

No Adaptation: Given that the BT data set (following the removal of after-the-event features) contained only 3 independent variables an exhaustive feature selection was straightforward and resulted in only one variable being selected for use. The $Sum(|r|)$ results from running the 100 validation trials using just this feature and no adaptation are given in first boxplot of Figure 1. The median $Sum(|r|)$ is 872 and the median MMRE is 46.6%.

Single Feature Adaptation: In single feature adaptation the feature with the highest Spearman rank correlation is selected. The feature subset selection using single feature adaptation selected two variables. The results for the validation of the single adaptation technique are shown in the second boxplot of Figure 1. The median $Sum(|r|)$ is 877 and the median MMRE is 63.1%.

Multiple feature adaptation: Both (continuous) features must were significantly correlated and so both were adapted.

    The feature subset search using multiple feature adaptation chose the same features as for single feature adaptation. As only one of these FSS selcted features was adapted, the results are identical. These are shown in the third boxplot of Figure 1.

Summary of BT results: Using a two-tailed Wilcoxon signed rank test on the $Sum(|r|)$ values ($\alpha = 0.05$), there are no significant differences between the results from the different treatments indicating we have no grounds for believing that adjustment has either a positive or negative impact upon the accuracy of predictions for this data set.

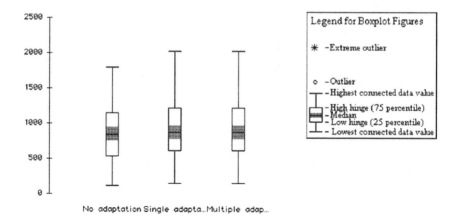

Fig. 1. Boxplot of results for BT data set

5.2   Desharnais Data Set

No adaptation: Following the removal of after-the-event features the Deshar-nais data set contains 9 independent variables, so an exhaustive feature selection was also possible with this data set. The feature subset search resulted in three variables being selected for adaptation. The results from running the 100 validation trials using just this feature set and no adaptation are given in the first boxplot of Figure 2. The median $Sum(|r|)$ is 49377 and the median MMRE is 51.6%.

Single feature adaptation: With single feature adaptation the feature subset selected contained three variables (2 continuous and 1 categorical). The results for the validation of the single adaptation technique are shown in the second boxplot of Figure 2. The median $Sum(|r|)$ is 44754 and the median MMRE is 41.2%.

Multiple feature adaptation: The correlations for four of the features are significant and these were therefore selected for adjustment.

Feature subset selection chose the same three features as for single feature adaptation, and the only feature which is scaled is also the same, the results are identical. These are shown in the third boxplot of Figure 2.

Summary of Desharnais results: Using a two-tailed Wilcoxon signed rank test ($\alpha = 0.05$), there are significant differences between the results from the different treatments. Both adaptation techniques give better results than the simple k-NN treatment ($p \leq 0.0001$).

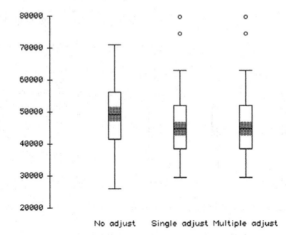

Fig. 2. Boxplot of results for Desharnais data set

5.3   Finnish Data Set

No adaptation: After the removal of features and cases with missing data, the Finnish data set contains 42 independent variables, so an exhaustive feature selection was not possible with this data set. The alternative forward selection search strategy was used instead. The feature subset search resulted in four variables being selected for use. The results from running the 100 validation trials using just this feature set and no adaptation are given in first boxplot of Figure 3. The median $Sum(|r|)$ is 358022 and the median MMRE is 108.8%.

Single feature adaptation: The results for the validation of the single adaptation technique are shown in the second boxplot of Figure 3. The median $Sum(|r|)$ is 320645 and the median MMRE is 71.7%.

Multiple feature adaptation: Since the adaptation must be done in the direction of the correlation, significant positive and negative correlations are handled separately. Of the 37 continuous variables, 16 features were selected for positive adaptation and 10 features for negative adaptation.

The feature subset selected consisted of six features and although this feature set is different from that used for 'single adaptation' (and therefore has different results), there is actually only one scaled variable used.

The results for the validation of the multiple adaptation technique are shown in the third boxplot of Figure 3. The median $Sum(|r|)$ is 310190 and the median MMRE is 71.2%.

Summary of Finnish results: Using a two-tailed Wilcoxon signed rank test ($\alpha = 0.05$), there are significant differences between the results from the different

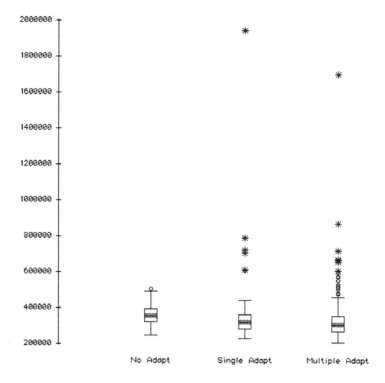

Fig. 3. Boxplot of results for Finnish dataset

treatments. Both single adaptation and multiple adaptation give significantly better results than the simple k-NN treatment ($p \leq 0.0001$ and $p = 0.0069$ respectively). The difference between single adaptation and multiple adaptation is not significant ($p = 0.0555$).

5.4   Analysis of Extreme Outliers

One notable feature of the results where adaptation was applied to the Finnish data set is the large number of extreme outliers produced. Each outlier represents one sampled training set where the $Sum(|r|)$ of the predictions made was particularly high. Further investigation showed that rather than particular training sets producing generally poor results, the poorer $Sum(|r|)$ values were caused by a few extreme predictions. These extreme predictions were in turn caused by extreme adjustment multipliers on these predictions (sometimes as much as several hundred).

What we're particularly interested in is whether linear size adjustment improves prediction as compared to the basic k-NN approach. If there is a relationship between the size of the scaling used when doing adjustment and the likely improvement in prediction, then it may be possible to apply transformation or

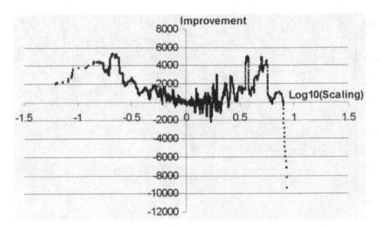

Fig. 4. Scatter plot of scaling against improvement in prediction

capping to the scaling values to reduce the number and size of outliers. In order to investigate this further, the relationship between the size of the scaling and improvement in prediction was examined. Figure 4 shows a smoothed plot of scaling against improvement for single feature adaptation of the Finnish data set. The large amount of random variation in the $Sum(|r|)$ values required smoothing to extract the underlying trend (here a rolling mean of 100 predictions was used). Scaling is shown on a Log_{10} scale to compress the higher scaling values whilst still giving detail for small fractional values present. The points with the most extreme negative improvement values have been omitted to improve the clarity of the diagram.

Figure 4 clearly shows a pattern of improvement against scaling. For scaling values close to zero, improvement is close to zero. This would be expected since at scaling $= 0$ linear size adjustment is equivalent to k-NN and so the results should not differ. As the scaling moves away from zero (in both positive and negative directions) the adjustment improves the accuracy of the predictions. As the scaling continues to move away from zero the level of improvement starts to reduce. For very large adjustment values linear size adjustment produces less accurate predictions. Extrapolating the trend in very small (fractional) scaling suggests that the same would also happen in the negative direction. From figure 4 we can estimate that (for this data set) scaling values above 8 and below 0.05 will (on average) give worse predictions. These values could be used as capping limits on the scaling values.

6   Discussion and Conclusions

This paper is based on an adaptation approach proposed by Mendes [15] that is entirely automatable. This yields the advantage of avoiding explicit knowledge elicitation. It can also be applied without modification or tuning for different data sets containing different features. We have presented a development of the original formulation of this adaptation scheme that is more generally applicable. The proposed method can be now be applied in the presence of features containing values which are zero and where features are negatively correlated to effort. It also adds a mechanism for choosing which features are appropriate for adaptation.

Table 2 gives a summary of the validation results for 2 variants of the proposed adaptation scheme (and a baseline k-NN approach). Two of the three data sets showed statistically significant improvements in prediction accuracy when using linear size adjustment whilst the smallest data set (BT) showed no significant difference in either direction. So it seems that linear scaling adaptation generally improves the accuracy of the predictions. Although the effect size of the improvements might be regarded as modest (improvements in median $Sum(|r|)$ were 9.4% for Desharnais and 13.4% for the Finnish data set) these are cumulative improvements over and above those possible through feature subset selection. Moreover, given the value of many software projects, 10% of total costs may well represent a considerable amount of money. This suggests that this kind of adaptation — despite its naïvety — still has some benefit, particularly for high value predictions where even small improvements in accuracy may be highly beneficial.

Table 2. Summary of results

	BT		Desharnais		Finnish	
	$Sum(|r|)$	MMRE	$Sum(|r|)$	MMRE	$Sum(|r|)$	MMRE
No adaptation (k-NN)	872	46.6%	49377	51.6%	358022	108.8%
Single adaptation	877	63.1%	44754	41.2%	320645	71.7%
Multiple adaptation	877	63.1%	44754	41.2%	310190	71.2%

Although the intention was to see the effect of both single and multiple features being adapted, the suggested method selected a single primary size measure for scaling in each case. This was due to the combination of using feature subset selection to improve accuracy (which also reduces the number of available features) and also the introduced requirement for a feature to be significantly correlated before it could be considered for adjustment.

Applying adaptation to the Finnish data set produced a significant number of extreme outliers. Linear size adjustment assumes that similar cases will have an approximately linear relationship between the adapted features and the target feature. For the Finnish data set, the adapted feature was a size measure (Function Points) and the target feature was effort. The root cause of the outliers was the large variation in productivity (size/effort) for the projects. When apparently similar projects have widely varying productivity, gross errors in estimation can result. However, analysis of the outliers has shown a pattern in the relationship between the level of scaling and the improvement in predictions. This pattern might be exploited to reduce the amount and degree of outliers.

The authors believe the improvements shown are sufficiently encouraging to justify further investigation. However, due to the presence of a few extreme outliers, the authors would advise some caution in using this method in practice.

Further work is necessary to investigate whether transforming or capping the magnitude of the scaling would solve the outlier problem. Work also needs to be done to allow adaptation based on differences in categorical values as well as continuous values.

Acknowledgments. The authors are indebted to STTF Ltd for making the "Finnish" data set available and to Jean-Marc Desharnais and BT for their respective data sets.

References

1. Aha, D. W. and R. L. Bankert, 'Feature selection for case-based classification of cloud types: an empirical comparison'. *AAAI-94 Workshop on Case-based Reasoning*, 1994.

2. Aha, D.W. and R.L. Bankert, 'A comparative evaluation of sequential feature selection algorithms', in *Artificial Intelligence and Statistics V.*, Fisher, D. and Lenz, J.-H., Editors, Springer-Verlag: New York, 1996.

3. Briand, L., T. Langley and I. Wieczorek, 'Using the European Space Agency data set: a replicated assessment and comparison of common software cost modeling techniques'. *22nd IEEE Intl. Conf. on Softw. Eng.*, Limerick, Ireland, Computer Society Press, 2000.

4. Craw, S., J. Jarmulak and R. Rowe, 'Learning and applying case-based adaptation knowledge'. Case-Based Reasoning Research and Development, Proceedings, Lecture Notes in Artificial Intelligence, No. 2080, pp131–145,Springer-Verlag, 2001.

5. Finnie, G.R., G.E. Wittig and J.-M. Desharnais, 'Estimating software development effort with case-based reasoning'. *2nd Intl. Conf. on Case-Based Reasoning*, 1997.

6. Finnie, G.R., G.E. Wittig and J.-M. Desharnais, A comparison of software effort estimation techniques using function points with neural networks, case based reasoning and regression models. *J. of Systems & Software*, 39, pp281–289, 1997.

7. Hanney, K. et al. 'When Do You Need Adaptation?: A Review of Current Practice'. *AAAI-95 Fall Symposium on Adaptation in Knowledge Reuse*, Cambridge, MA, USA, 1995.

8. Hanney, K. and M. T. Keane, 'The adaptation knowledge bottleneck: how to ease it by learning from cases', *2nd Intl. Conf. on Case-Based Reasoning*, 1997.

9. Kadoda, G., M. Cartwright, L. Chen, and M. Shepperd, 'Experiences using case-based reasoning to predict software project effort'. *4th International Conference on Empirical Assessment and Evaluation in Software Engineering*, 17–19 April 2000, Keele University, UK.

10. Khan, A. S. and A. Hoffmann, 'A new approach for the incremental development of adaptation functions for CBR'. Advances in Case-Based Reasoning, Proceedings, Lecture Notes in Artificial Intelligence, No. 1898, pp260–272, Springer-Verlag, 2001.

11. Kirsopp, C. and M. Shepperd, 'Making inferences with small numbers of training sets', *IEE Proceedings – Software* 149(5), 2002.
12. Kirsopp, C., M. Shepperd and J. Hart, 'Search heuristics, case-based reasoning and software project effort prediction', *Genetic and Evolutionary Computation Conference*, New York, USA, July 9–13, 2002.
13. Kirsopp,C. and M. Shepperd, 'Case and Feature Subset Selection in Case-Based Software Project Effort Prediction', Research and Development in Intelligent Systems XIX, Springer-Verlag, 2002.
14. Kitchenham, B.A., S.G. MacDonell, L. Pickard and M.J. Shepperd, 'What accuracy statistics really measure', *IEE Proceedings – Software Engineering* 148(3): pp81–85, 2001.
15. Mendes, E., S. Counsell, and N. Mosley, 'Investigating the use of case-based reasoning adaptation rules for web project cost estimation'. submitted paper, World Wide Web conference 2003.
16. Munoz-Avila, H., D.W. Aha, L.A. Breslow, D.S. Nau and R. Weber, 'Integrating conversational case retrieval with generative planning', in Advances in *Case-Based Reasoning, Proceedings*, Blanzieri, E. and Portinale, L., (Editors), Springer-Verlag. pp210–221, 2001.
17. Prietula, M.J., S.S. Vincinanza and T. Mukhopadhyay 'Software Effort Estimation With a Case-Based Reasoner', *J. of Experimental & Theoretical Artificial Intelligence* 8, pp341–363, 1996.
18. Scott, S., H. Osborne and R. Simpson, 'Assessing Case Value in Case-Based Reasoning with Adaptation'. *World Multiconference on Systemics, Cybernetics and Informatics* (IIIS-99), Orlando, Florida, 1999.
19. Shepperd, M., C. Schofield and B.A. Kitchenham 'Effort estimation using analogy'. *18th Intl. Conf. on Softw. Eng.*, Berlin, IEEE Computer Press, 1996.
20. Shepperd, M. and C. Schofield.'Estimating software project effort using analogies', *IEEE Transactions on Software Engineering* 23(11) pp736–743, 1997.
21. Shiu, S. C. K., D. S. Yeung, C. H. Sun and X. Z. Wang, 'Transferring case knowledge to adaptation knowledge: An approach for case-base maintenance.' *Computational Intelligence* 17(2) pp95–314, 2001.
22. Symons, C.R., 'Function point analysis: difficulties and improvements', *IEEE Transactions on Software Engineering* 14(1): pp2–11, 1988.
23. Voss, A. and R. Oxman. 'A study of case adaptation systems'. *Artificial Intelligence in Design*, pp173–189, Kluwer, 1996.
24. Walkerden, F and R. Jeffery. 'An empirical study of analogy-based software effort estimation'. *Empirical Software Engineering* 4(2),pp135–158, 1999.
25. Wilke, W. and R. Bergmann, 'Techniques and knowledge used for adaptation during case-based problem solving'. *Tasks and Methods in Applied Artificial Intelligence*, LNAI 1416, pp497–505, Springer-Verlag: Berlin, 1998.

A Framework for Historical Case-Based Reasoning

Jixin Ma and Brian Knight

School of Computing and Mathematical Sciences
The University of Greenwich, London, SE10 9LS, U.K.
{j.ma, b.knight}@gre.ac.uk

Abstract. This paper presents a framework for Historical Case-Based Reasoning (HCBR) which allows the expression of both relative and absolute temporal knowledge, representing case histories in the real world. The formalism is founded on a general temporal theory that accommodates both points and intervals as primitive time elements. A case history is formally defined as a collection of (time-independent) elemental cases, together with its corresponding temporal reference. Case history matching is two-fold, i.e., there are two similarity values need to be computed: the non-temporal similarity degree and the temporal similarity degree. On the one hand, based on elemental case matching, the non-temporal similarity degree between case histories is defined by means of computing the unions and intersections of the involved elemental cases. On the other hand, by means of the graphical presentation of temporal references, the temporal similarity degree in case history matching is transformed into conventional graph similarity measurement.

1   Introduction

Case-Based Reasoning (CBR) [1, 2, 3] aims to solve problems and make decisions by retrieving and reusing (possibly revising) solutions from similar, previously solved problems. In conventional CBR systems, the state of the world in the discourse is usually represented by case knowledge in terms of isolated episodes, where the temporal aspect of case knowledge is neglected in most current CBR systems. Generally speaking, CBR is effective in the following situations [4]:

- Where experience, rather than theory, is the primary source of knowledge.
- Where solutions are reusable, rather than being unique to each situation.
- Where the objective is best available solution rather than a guaranteed exact solution.

Over the past two decades, it has been noted that temporal reasoning is essential for many knowledge-based systems where one is interested not only in the representation of distinct snapshots of the state of an enterprise, but also in the history of earlier/future situations [5, 6, 7]. In particular, an appropriate representation and reasoning for temporal knowledge is necessary for many CBR systems, where the history of cases, rather than distinct episodes, plays an important role in solving problems including prediction, explanation, planning, process management and supervision, etc. For instance, in the area of medical information systems, a patient's medical history is obviously very important. In fact, to prescribe the right treatment,

K.D. Ashley and D.G. Bridge (Eds.): ICCBR 2003, LNAI 2689, pp. 246–260, 2003.
© Springer-Verlag Berlin Heidelberg 2003

the doctor needs to know not only the patient's current status, but also his/her previous health situations, including: How long has the patient been ill? Did the patient have the same problem or relevant disease previously? Has the patient had some treatment already before seeing the doctor? Has the patient been allergic to any drugs in the past? And so on. Another example illustrating the need of dealing with the history of cases is given in section 4.3.

Despite the fact that temporal representation and temporal reasoning have been neglected in most conventional CBR systems which only address snapshot episodes, a few interesting approaches have been proposed to incorporate the temporal concepts into isolated elemental cases. Examples of these are that of Nakhaeizadeh [8], of Branting and Hasting [9], of Jaczynski and Trousse [10], of Schmidt, Pollwein and Gierl [11], and of Hansen [12]. It is interesting to note that the underlying time models employed in these systems are all point-based, and therefore, it is required that absolute time points, or absolute point-based intervals, must be associated with the time-dependent objects being addressed. However, for many applications of knowledge-based systems, there may be just some relative temporal knowledge about the time-depended objects, where their precise characters are not available. For example, we may only know that event A happened before event B, without knowing their precise starting-time and finishing-time. Relative temporal knowledge such as this is typically derived from humans, where absolute times are not always remembered, but relative temporal relationships are, and require less data storage than that presented in the complete description.

As the importance of the time domain has become apparent, many other approaches have been proposed, attempting to accommodate the characteristics of relative temporal information. For example, as an early attempt at mechanizing part of the understanding of relative temporal relationships within an artificial intelligence content, Kahn and Gorry's time specialist was developed [13], endowed with the capacity to order temporal facts in three major ways: (1) relating events to dates, (2) relating events to special reference events, and (3) relating events together into before-after chains. However, the most influential work dealing with incomplete relative temporal information in the field of artificial intelligence is probably that of Allen's interval-based theory of time [14, 15]. In [14], Allen introduces his interval-based temporal logic, where intervals are addressed as primitive time elements, and between time intervals there are 13 possible temporal relations; i.e., Equal, Before, Meets, Overlaps, Starts, Started_by, Duration, Contains, Finishes, Finished_by, Overlapped_by, Met_by and After, which may be formally defined in terms of the single primitive relation "Meets" [16].

Recently, Jare, Adamodt and Skalle have introduced an interval-based qualitative approach to temporal reasoning in CBR [17]. Based on Allen's theory of temporal intervals [14], a method for representing temporal cases inside the knowledge-intensive CBR system called Creek has been proposed, focusing on prediction problems for avoiding faulty situations. However, while Allen's theory only addresses intervals as temporal primitives, the approach proposed in [17] actually re-interprets aspects of the theory by considering each interval as delimited by a pair of points.

Usually, in a point-based system where intervals are usually defined as derived objects from points (either as ordered pairs of points, or as set of points), one will be forced to specify if a given proposition holds true at a given point or not. This virtually leads to the annoying *Dividing Instant Problem* (DIP) [18, 19, 20, 21], which is a puzzle encountered when attempting to represent what happens at the boundary instant that divides two successive states.

In addition to the similarity degree for the non-temporal part in Creek, an extra temporal similarity measurement referred as the temporal path strength is introduced [17]. To enable intervals to be related to each other so that a similarity assessment of parameters can be made in order to predict particular states, a dynamic ordering algorithm is developed for matching temporal paths. Such an algorithm requires the corresponding temporal knowledge to be complete for both the input case IC and the current case CC. However, this is not always available in knowledge based systems. For instance, if the temporal knowledge is given in the incomplete form that "I1 Meets I2" and "I3 Meets I4", the *first interval* [17] cannot be decided at all.

It has been claimed in the literature that time intervals are more suited for expression of common sense temporal knowledge, especially in the domain of linguistics and artificial intelligence. In addition, approaches like that of Allen [14] that treat intervals as primitive temporal elements can successfully overcome or bypass the DIP, which, as discussed [21], only arises when one insists on the existence of time points. However, as Galton shows in his critical examination of Allen's interval logic [19], a theory of time based only on intervals is not adequate for reasoning correctly about continuous change. In fact, many common sense situations suggest the need for including time points in the temporal ontology as an entity different from intervals. For instance, it is intuitive and convenient to say that instantaneous events such as "The court was adjourned at 4:00pm", "The light was automatically switched on at 8:00am", and so on, occur at time points rather than intervals (no matter how small they are). Therefore, for general treatments, it is appropriate to include both points and intervals as primitives in the underlying time model, for making temporal reference to instantaneous phenomena with zero duration, and periodic phenomena which last for some positive duration, respectively. On the one hand, approaches that treat both points and intervals as primitive time elements overcomes the limitations of systems based on intervals exclusively. On the other hand, they retain the convenience of expression enjoyed by interval-based approaches [22].

The objective of this paper is to introduce a framework for Historical Case-Based Reasoning (HCBR). In terms of a many-sorted reified logic [23, 24], the formalism is presented in section 2 as follows: In section 2.1, a general time theory that accommodates both points and intervals as primitive time elements is adopted as the underlying temporal basis for the framework. The concepts of fluents and elemental cases are introduced in section 2.2 and section 2.3, respectively. Section 2.4 proposes a formal characterization of case histories; and introduces two similarity values for case history matching, i.e., non-temporal similarity degree and the temporal similarity degree. In section 3, a graphical presentation of temporal references is introduced, which will transform the additional temporal similarity measurement in case history matching into conventional graph similarity measurement. Some examples illustrating the concepts and ideas introduced in the paper are provided in section 4. Finally, section 5 concludes the paper.

2 The Formalism

The formalism will be described in terms of a many-sorted reified logic with equality
[23, 24], consisting of four disjoint sorts of objects T, F, C and H, called *time
elements*, *fluents*, *elemental cases* and *histories*, respectively. We shall denote the
elements of T, F, C and H by (possibly indexed) letters t, f, c and h, and simply adopt
the conventional theory of real numbers.

2.1 The Temporal Basis

For the reason of general treatments, in this paper, we shall take the time theory
proposed previously by Ma and Knight [22] as the temporal basis for making
reference to elemental cases. This time theory addressed both points and intervals as
temporal primitives on an equal footing: neither points have to be defined as limits of
intervals, nor intervals have to be constructed out of points. The distinction between
time intervals and time points is characterized by means of a *duration assignment
function*, Dur, from the set of time elements to non-negative real numbers, i.e., R^{+0}. A time
element t is called an (time) *interval* if Dur(t) > 0; otherwise, t is called a (time) *point*.
Such a temporal theory is indeed an extension to the interval-based axiomitization of
Allen and Hayes [16]. As shown in [22], analogous to the 13 relations introduced by
Allen for intervals [14], there are 30 distinct temporal relations over time elements
including both intervals and points, which can be derived from the single *immediate
predecessor* relation, "Meets". These 30 derived temporal relations can be classified
into the following 4 groups:
- {Equal, Before, After}, which relate points to points;
- {Before, After, Meets, Met_by, Starts, During. Finishes}, which relate points to
  intervals;
- {Before, After, Meets, Met_by, Started_by, Contains, Finished_by}, which relate intervals to
  points;
- {Equal, Before, After, Meets, Met_by, Overlaps, Overlapped_by, Starts,
  Started_by, During, Contains, Finishes, Finished_by}, which relate intervals to
  intervals.

It is important to note that the distinction between the assertion that "point t_1 Meets
interval t_2" and the assertion that "point t_1 Starts interval t_2" is critical: while Starts(t_1, t_2)
states that point t_1 is the starting part of interval t_2, Meets(t_1, t_2) states that point t_1 is one
of the immediate predecessors of interval t_2, but t_1 is not a part of t_2 at all.

2.2 Fluents

In CBR systems, distinct snapshots of the state of the world in the discourse are
usually represented by case knowledge in terms of isolated episodes. Generally
speaking, an episode may be presented by a collection of descriptors that characterize
some certain attributes of the state of the world over the time. From the point of view
of predicate logic, each of these descriptors can be given in terms of a proposition (or

statement) which is either true or false. In this paper, we shall use the term *fluents* [25] to denote propositions whose truth values are dependent on the time, and define the sort of fluents, F, as the minimal set closed under the following rules:

1) If $f_1, f_2 \in F$ then $f_1 \vee f_2 \in F$;

2) If $f \in F$ then $not(f) \in F$.

In order to associate a fluent with a time element, we shall employ a *meta-predicate*, Holds [14, 23, 24], to substitute formula Holds(f, t) for fluent f and time element t, denoting that fluent f holds true over time t.

Remembering that Holds is a meta-predicate, a certain interpretation of its negation is expected. Following Galton's notation [19], we shall use the operator "¬" for both conventional predicate negation and meta-predicate negation, distinct from fluent negation that is symbolised by "not". We impose the following axioms:

(A1) $Holds(f_1 \vee f_2, t) \Leftrightarrow Holds(f_1, t) \vee Holds(f_1, t)$

That is, fluent f_1 or fluent f_2 holds true over time t if and only if one of them holds true over time t.

With respect to points or non-decomposable intervals, i.e., *moments* [16], the relationship between the negation of meta-predicate and the negation of the involved fluent is simply characterized by:

(A2) $\neg \exists t_1, t_2(t = t_1 \oplus t_2) \Rightarrow \neg Holds(f, t) \Leftrightarrow Holds(not(f), t)$

That is, a fluent does not hold true at a non-decomposable time element if and only if its negation holds true at that time element.

However, with respect to decomposable intervals, the interpretation of negation becomes complicated. In fact, by allowing intervals as arguments to meta-predicate Holds, one will face the possibility that a fluent f might holds neither true nor false throughout some interval t. That is, it may be the case that fluent f holds true over some parts of t but also holds false over some other parts. Usually, one might interpret the negative formula ¬Holds(f, t) in two different ways [23, 26]: In the weak interpretation, ¬Holds(f, t) is true if and only if it is not the case that f holds true throughout t, and hence ¬Holds(f, t) is true if f changes its truth-value over time t. In the strong interpretation, ¬Holds(f, t) is true if and only if f holds false throughout t, so neither Holds(f, t) nor ¬Holds(f, t) would be true if fluent f holds true over some parts of t and also holds false some other parts.

Due to the fact that the weak interpretation is appropriate for the standard definition of implication and preserves a simple two-valued logic [26], in this paper, we employ the following axiom to characterise the relation between the truth of a fluent f over a decomposable interval t and its truth over its proper parts:

(A3) $t = t_1 \oplus t_2 \Rightarrow Holds(f, t) \Leftrightarrow \forall t'(In(t', t) \Rightarrow Holds(f, t'))$

Here, $In(t_1,t_2)$ denotes that time t_1 is a proper part of time t_2 [14, 22], that is:

$In(t_1, t_2) \Leftrightarrow Starts(t_1, t_2) \vee During(t_1, t_2) \vee Finishes(t_1, t_2)$

Therefore, (A3) states that, a fluent holds true throughout a decomposable interval if and only if it holds true over/at all the proper parts of the interval.

In addition, we impose:

(A4) $Holds(f, t_1) \wedge Holds(f, t_2) \wedge Meets(t_1, t_2) \Rightarrow Holds(f, t_1 \oplus t_2)$

That is, if a fluent holds true over two adjacent time elements respectively, then it also holds true over their ordered union.

2.3 Elemental Cases

An episode of the world in the discourse, which will be called an (time-independent) *elemental case*, is defined as a collection of fluents. We shall use Belongs(f, c) to denote fluent f belongs to case c. Analogously to Shanahan's approach [27], predicate Belongs is characterised as below:

(A5) $\exists c \forall f(\neg Belongs(f, c))$

That is, there exists a case which is an empty collection of fluents.

(A6) $\forall c \forall f(\neg Belongs(f, c) \vee \neg Belongs(not(f), c))$

That is, any case cannot contain both a fluent and its negation.

(A7) $\forall c_1, f_1(\neg Belongs(not(f_1), c_2)$
$$\Rightarrow \exists c_2 \forall f_2(Belongs(f_2, c_2) \Leftrightarrow (Belongs(f_2, c_1) \vee f_1 = f_2)))$$

That is, any fluent can be added to an existing case to form a new case, as long as the case does not contain the negation of the fluent.

(A8) $c_1 = c_2 \Leftrightarrow \forall f(Belongs(f, c_1) \Leftrightarrow Belongs(f, c_2))$

That is, two cases are equal if and only if they contain exactly the same fluents. In what follows, for the reason of simple representation, if $f_1, ..., f_n$ are all the fluents that belong to case c, we shall represent c as $<f_1, ..., f_n>$; and without confusion, we shall use Holds(c, t) to denote that case c holds over time t, provided that:

(A9) $Holds(c, t) \Leftrightarrow \forall f(Belongs(f, c) \Rightarrow Holds(f, t))$

Also, we shall use Subcase(c_1, c_2) to denote that each fluent belonging to case c_1 also belongs to case c_2:

(A10) $Subcase(c_1, c_2) \Leftrightarrow \forall f(Belongs(f, c_1) \Rightarrow Belongs(f, c_2))$

By (A9) and (A10), it is straightforward to infer that:

$Subcase(c_1, c_2) \wedge Holds(c_2, t) \Rightarrow Holds(c_1, t)$ (Th1)

In addition, we introduce two binary functions, Union and Intersection, over C, so that Union(c_1, c_2) and Intersection(c_1, c_2) denote the *union* of case c_1 and case c_2, and the *intersection* of case c_1 and case c_2, respectively:

(A11) $Belongs(f, Union(c_1, c_2)) \Leftrightarrow Belongs(f, c_1) \vee Belongs(f, c_2)$

(A12) $Belongs(f, Intersection(c_1, c_2)) \Leftrightarrow Belongs(f, c_1) \wedge Belongs(f, c_2)$

2.4 Case Histories

As argued in the introduction, in many CBR applications including prediction, explanation, planning, process management and supervision, solutions depend not only on the snapshots of distinct cases, but also on the temporal history of the cases. In HCBR, and each case history h in H is defined in terms of the follow schema:

CaseHistory(h):

$h = <c_1, ..., c_m>$, where $c_1,...c_m \in C$;

Holds(c_i, t_j), for some c_is and t_js where $1 \leq i \leq m$ and $t_j \in T$;

Meets(t_u, t_v), for some t_us and t_vs which are temporally related to some t_j appearing in Holds(c_i, t_j);

Dur(t_{uORv}) = d_{uORv}, for some t_{uORv}s appearing in Meets(t_u, t_v) where $d_{uORv} \in R^{+0}$.

For the reason of simple expression, in what follows, for a given case history h expressed in the above schema, we shall use a quadruple, ($Holds_h$, T_h, $Meets_h$, Dur_h), to represent the *temporal reference* of h, where $Holds_h$ is the set of all the "Holds" formulae presented in the schema, T_h is the set of all the time elements presented in the schema, $Meets_h$ is the set of all the "Meets" relations presented in the schema, and Dur_h is the set of all the duration assignments presented in the schema.

N.B. Here, the temporal relationships presented in the schema are given in the form of a collection of "Meets" relations between the involved time elements. However, as mentioned in section 2, it can be given in any form of the 30 derived temporal relations, since each of them can be equivalently expressed in terms of the single "Meets" relation between some relevant time elements.

It is straightforward to see that, case history matching is two-fold here, i.e., there are two similarity values need to be computed: the *non-temporal similarity degree* which is based on elemental case matching, and the *temporal similarity degree* which is based on temporal reference matching. In fact, for two case histories h_1 and h_2, where

$$h_1 = <c_{11},...,c_{1m}>$$

and

$$h_1 = <c_{21},...,c_{2n}>$$

we shall define the degree of the history similarity between h_1 and h_2 as:

$$S(h_1, h_2) = w_{nontem}S_{nontem}(h_1, h_2) * w_{tem}S_{tem}(h_1, h_2)$$

where $S_{nontem}(h_1, h_2)$ and $S_{tem}(h_1, h_2)$ stand for the *non-temporal similarity degree* and the *temporal similarity degree*, respectively.

However, in non-temporal matching of case histories h_1 and h_2, due to the fact that elemental cases appearing in case histories are not actually ordered by their index, there is a combinatorial problem in pairing the two case histories in the first place. In general, for $m \geq n$, there are $^mP_n = m!/(m-n)!$ ways of pairing $h_1 = <c_{11},...,c_{1m}>$ and $h_2 = <c_{21},...,c_{2n}>$. Let P denote the set of all possible ordered vectors formed by selecting, in order, n random elemental cases from h_1. It seems reasonable to take the pairing which gives the maximal overall similarity. Hence, in this paper, we shall define the non-temporal similarity degree between h_1 and h_2 as:

$$S_{nontem}(h_1, h_2) = MAX_{p \in P} S_{nontem}(p, h_2)$$
$$\text{where } S_{nontem}(p, h_2) = \sqrt{\Sigma^n_{i=1}w_{ip}s_{ip}(p_i, c_{2i})^2} / \sqrt{\Sigma^n_{i=1}w_{ip}}$$
$$\text{where } p = <p_1, ..., p_n> \text{ and } s_{ip}(p_i, c_{2i}) = |Intersection(p_i, c_{2i})| / |Union(p_i, c_{2i})|$$
$$\text{where } i = 1, ..., n.$$

For $S_{tem}(h_1, h_2)$, the temporal similarity degree between h_1 and h_2, it will be transformed into conventional graph similarity measurement (see next section).

A case history expressed in the schema CaseHistory(h) may be incomplete in various ways. For example, it may substitute formula Holds(c_i, t_i) for only some elemental cases but not for all; in addition, it may only present a partial knowledge of the temporal relationships between the elemental cases, and may contain knowledge of duration for only some of the involved time elements. In this paper, for a given case history h where $h = <c_1,...,c_m>$ with temporal reference ($Holds_h$, T_h, $Meets_h$, Dur_h), we shall define h as (temporally) complete if:

(a) $\forall c_j (1 \le j \le m \Rightarrow \exists t_j \in \boldsymbol{T_h}(\text{Holds}(c_j, t_j))$
(b) $\forall t_u, t_v \in \boldsymbol{T_h}($ $\text{Meets}(t_u, t_v) \in \boldsymbol{Meets_h}$
        $\lor \text{Meets}(t_v, t_u) \in \boldsymbol{Meets_h}$
        $\lor \exists t_1', \ldots, t_n' \in \boldsymbol{T_h}($ $\text{Meets}(t_u, t_1') \in \boldsymbol{Meets_h}$
                    $\land \text{Meets}(t_1', t_2') \in \boldsymbol{Meets_h}$
                    $\cdots$
                    $\land \text{Meets}(t_n', t_v) \in \boldsymbol{Meets_h})$
        $\lor \exists t_1', \ldots, t_n' \in \boldsymbol{T_h}($ $\text{Meets}(t_v, t_1') \in \boldsymbol{Meets_h}$
                    $\land \text{Meets}(t_1', t_2') \in \boldsymbol{Meets_h}$
                    $\cdots$
                    $\land \text{Meets}(t_n', t_u) \in \boldsymbol{Meets_h}))$
(c) $\forall t \in \boldsymbol{T_h} \exists d \in \boldsymbol{R^{+0}}(\text{Dur}(t) = d)$

Otherwise, h is defined as (temporally) incomplete.

In the above, (a) states that, in a complete case history, any elemental case has a reference time over which it holds true; and (b) states that, in a complete case history, any two reference time elements of the corresponding elemental cases are temporal related; finally, (c) states that the relevant duration knowledge is completed.

3   A Graphical Representation

In [28], a graphical representation for expressing temporal knowledge in terms of Meets relations and duration assignments has been introduced by means of a directed and partially weighted graph, where time elements are denoted as arcs of the graph, relation $\text{Meets}(t_i, t_j)$ is represented by t_i being in-arc and t_j being out-arc to a common node, and for time elements with known duration, the corresponding arcs are weighted by their durations respectively.

Such a graphical representation can be directly extended to accommodate the additional "Holds" knowledge in temporal reference ($\boldsymbol{Holds_h}$, $\boldsymbol{T_h}$, $\boldsymbol{Meets_h}$, $\boldsymbol{Dur_h}$) as for case histories. In fact, for each formula $\text{Holds}(c_i, t_j)$, we can simply double name the corresponding arc by both c_i and t_j.

As an example, consider a case history h = $<c_1, c_2, c_3, c_4>$ with temporal reference ($\boldsymbol{Holds_h}$, $\boldsymbol{T_h}$, $\boldsymbol{Meets_h}$, $\boldsymbol{Dur_h}$) where

$\boldsymbol{Holds_h} =$ {$\text{Holds}(c_1, t_1)$, $\text{Holds}(c_2, t_2)$, $\text{Holds}(c_3, t_4)$, $\text{Holds}(c_4, t_8)$}
$\boldsymbol{T_h} =$ {$t_1, t_2, t_3, t_4, t_5, t_6, t_7, t_8, t_9$};
$\boldsymbol{Meets_h} =$ {$\text{Meets}(t_1, t_2)$, $\text{Meets}(t_1, t_3)$, $\text{Meets}(t_2, t_5)$, $\text{Meets}(t_2, t_6)$, $\text{Meets}(t_3, t_4)$,
           $\text{Meets}(t_4, t_7)$, $\text{Meets}(t_5, t_8)$, $\text{Meets}(t_6, t_7)$, $\text{Meets}(t_7, t_8)$}
$\boldsymbol{Dur_h} =$ {$\text{Dur}(t_2) = 1$, $\text{Dur}(t_4) = 0.5$, $\text{Dur}(t_6) = 0$, $\text{Dur}(t_8) = 0.3$}

The corresponding graphical representation of quadruple ($\boldsymbol{Holds_h}$, $\boldsymbol{T_h}$, $\boldsymbol{Meets_h}$, $\boldsymbol{Dur_h}$) can be shown in Fig1. as below:

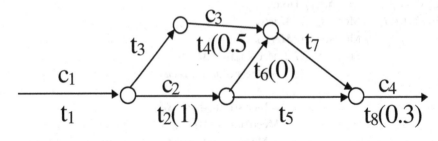

Fig. 1.

In the above graph, there are two simple circuits as shown in Fig2.:

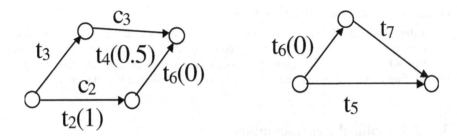

Fig. 2.

It is easy to see that, to ensure the temporal reference itself is temporally consistent, the directed sum of weights in each of these simple circles has to be 0 [28]. This imposes the following two linear constraints:

$$Dur(t_2) + Dur(t_6) = Dur(t_3) + Dur(t_4)$$
$$Dur(t_5) = Dur(t_6) + Dur(t_7)$$

We can easily find a solution to the above linear programming, for instance: $Dur(t_3) = 0.5$, $Dur(t_5) = Dur(t_7) = 1.5$ (In fact, the duration assignment to t_5 and t_7 can be any positive real number, provided that $Dur(t_5) = Dur(t_7)$). Therefore, the temporal reference is consistent. In other words, the corresponding case history is a possible scenario of the modeled world over the time. Otherwise, if there is no solution to the corresponding linear programming of a temporal reference, it will be temporally inconsistent [28], and therefore, the corresponding case history will be an impossible scenario.

As mention in the previous section, in case history matching, in addition to the non-temporal similarity degree which is computed based on elemental case matching, there is an additional similarity value need to be computed, that is the temporal similarity degree which is based on temporal reference matching. However, the graphical presentation of temporal references presented in this paper actually transforms the additional temporal similarity measurement in case history matching into conventional graph similarity measurement. Due to the scope of the paper, we shall not address this issue further.

4   Some Illustrating Examples

The block world is a typical model, especially in artificial intelligence, which has been used to illustrate the application of various formalisms. Consider the following version of the block world in which there are only three blocks, B_1, B_2, and B_3. Each block can be either on the table or immediately on the top of exactly one of the other blocks. Also, each block can have at most one of the other blocks immediately on top of it.

4.1 Examples of Fluents

The state of the 3-block world can be described by the following three kinds of fluents:

Clear(x):   there is no blocks on the top of block x;
OnTable(x):   block x is on the table;
On(x, y):   block x is on the top of block y;

The domain constraints for the 3-block world can be expressed as:

(4.1.1) Clear(x) $\Rightarrow x = B_1 \vee x = B_2 \vee x = B_3$
(4.1.2) OnTable(x) $\Rightarrow x = B_1 \vee x = B_2 \vee x = B_3$
(4.1.3) On(x, y) $\Rightarrow (x = B_1 \vee x = B_2 \vee x = B_3) \wedge (y = B_1 \vee y = B_2 \vee y = B_3)$
(4.1.4) OnTable(x) $\vee \exists y(On(x, y))$
(4.1.5) On(x, y) $\Rightarrow not(x = y) \wedge not(Clear(y))$
(4.1.6) On(x, y) $\wedge On(x, z) \Rightarrow y = z$
(4.1.7) On(x, y) $\wedge On(z, y) \Rightarrow x = z$
     where $\vee$ denotes "exclusive or".

In the above, (4.1.1) – (4.1.3) preserve that there are only three blocks, B_1, B_2, and B_3; (4.1.4) guarantees that each block is either on the table or on the top of one of the blocks, but cannot on both; (4.1.5) states that a block cannot be on itself, and if a block has another block on its top, then its top is not clear; and finally, (4.1.6) and (4.1.7) guarantee that each block can be immediately on the top of at most one of the other blocks and each block can have at most one of the other blocks immediately on top of it, respectively.

4.2 Examples of Elemental Cases, Sub-cases, Unions, and Intersections

It is easy to see that, in the 3-block world, there are in total 13 possible (complete) episodes as shown in Fig3.:

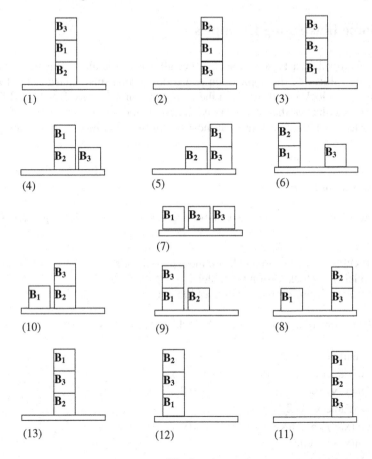

Fig. 3.

These 13 distinct episodes can be presented by the following elemental (time-independent) cases, respectively:

$C_1 = <Clear(B_3), OnTable(B_2), On(B_1, B_2), On(B_3, B_1)>$
$C_2 = <Clear(B_2), OnTable(B_3), On(B_1, B_3), On(B_2, B_1)>$
$C_3 = <Clear(B_3), OnTable(B_1), On(B_2, B_1), On(B_3, B_2)>$
$C_4 = <Clear(B_1), Clear(B_3), OnTable(B_2), OnTable(B_3), On(B_1, B_2)>$
$C_5 = <Clear(B_1), Clear(B_2), OnTable(B_2), OnTable(B_3), On(B_1, B_3)>$
$C_6 = <Clear(B_2), Clear(B_3), OnTable(B_1), OnTable(B_3), On(B_2, B_1)>$
$C_7 = <Clear(B_1), Clear(B_2), Clear(B_3), OnTable(B_1), OnTable(B_2), OnTable(B_3)>$
$C_8 = <Clear(B_1), Clear(B_2), OnTable(B_1), OnTable(B_3), On(B_2, B_3)>$

C_9 = <Clear(B_3), Clear(B_2), OnTable(B_1), OnTable(B_2), On(B_3, B_1)>
C_{10} = <Clear(B_1), Clear(B_3), OnTable(B_1), OnTable(B_2), On(B_3, B_2)>
C_{11} = <Clear(B_1), OnTable(B_3), On(B_2, B_3), On(B_1, B_2)>
C_{12} = <Clear(B_2), OnTable(B_1), On(B_3, B_1), On(B_2, B_3)>
C_{13} = <Clear(B_1), OnTable(B_2), On(B_3, B_2), On(B_1, B_3)>

In addition to the above 13 elemental cases, there are many more. In fact, any proper sub-case of the above 13 cases is an elemental case which stands for some partial configuration of the 3-block world. E.g., C_1' = <Clear(B_3), On(B_3, B_1)> is an elemental case which is a sub-case of both C_1 and C_9, i.e.: Subcase(C_1', C_1) and Subcase(C_1', C_9)

Also, any intersection of two elemental cases is an elemental case. E.g.:

Intersection(C_1, C_{12}) = <On(B_3, B_1)>.

Finally, any union of two elemental cases is an elemental case. E.g.:

Union(C_1, C_{12}) = <Clear(B_3), OnTable(B_2), On(B_1, B_2), On(B_3, B_1), Clear(B_2),
OnTable(B_1), On(B_2, B_3)>

However, it is important to note that, an elemental case does not necessarily stand for a real situation in the modelled world. For instance, Union(C_1, C_{12}) is an impossible case in the 3-block world, since it contracts to the domain constraints (5.1)-(5.7).

From

$$|\text{Intersection}(C_1, C_{12})| / |\text{Union}(C_1, C_{12})| = 1/7$$

we can intuitively see that the similarity degree between elemental cases C_1 and C_{12} is quite low.

4.3 Examples of Case Histories

There are 3 types of actions that may take place to transfer the 3-block world from a certain episode into another:

M(x, y, z): moving block x from the top of y to the top of z.
U(x, y):   removing block x from the top of y and placing it on the table.
S(x, y):   picking up block x from the table and stacking it on the top of block y.

For instance, S(B_3, B_1) transfers C_4 into C_1, and U(B_3, B_1) transfers C_1 into C_4. In fact, the episode-transitions of the 3-block world can be expressed as:

Transfers(S(B_1,B_2),C_7,C_4), Transfers(S(B_1,B_2),C_8,C_{11}), Transfers(S(B_1,B_3),C_7,C_5),
Transfers(S(B_1,B_3),C_{10},C_{13}), Transfers(S(B_2, B_1),C_7,C_6), Transfers(S(B_2,B_1),C_5,C_2),
Transfers(S(B_2,B_3),C_7,C_8), Transfers(S(B_2,B_3),C_9,C_{12}), Transfers(S(B_3,B_1),C_7, C_9),
Transfers(S(B_3,B_1),C_4,C_1), Transfers(S(B_3,B_2),C_7,C_{10}), Transfers(S(B_3,B_2),C_6,C_3),
Transfers(U(B_1,B_2),C_4,C_7), Transfers(U(B_1,B_2),C_{11},C_8), Transfers(U(B_1,B_3),C_5,C_7),
Transfers(U(B_1,B_3),C_{13},C_{10}), Transfers(U(B_2,B_1),C_6,C_7), Transfers(U(B_2,B_1),C_2,C_5),
Transfers(U(B_2,B_3),C_8,C_7), Transfers(U(B_2,B_3),C_{12},C_9), Transfers(U(B_3,B_1),C_9,C_7),
Transfers(U(B_3,B_1),C_1,C_4), Transfers(U(B_3,B_2),C_{10},C_7), Transfers(U(B_3,B_2), C_3, C_6),
Transfers(M(B_1,B_2,B_3),C_4,C_5), Transfers(M(B_1,B_3,B_2),C_5,C_4),
Transfers(M(B_2,B_1,B_3),C_6,C_8), Transfers(M(B_2,B_3,B_1),C_8,C_6),
Transfers(M(B_3,B_1,B_2),C_9,C_{10}), Transfers(M(B_3,B_2,B_1),C_{10},C_9).

Each action takes some certain time to perform, and therefore, if action a transfers case c to case c', where Holds(c, t) and Holds(c', t'), then the temporal relation between t and t' would Before(t, t'), or equivalently, Meets(t, t_a) and Meets(t_a, t') where t_a is the time over which action a takes place. For the reason of simple demonstration, in this example we shall not address the duration assignment to time elements.

Normally, there are some preconditions for the performance of a given action. For instance, to ensure the action of type M(x, y, z) to take place, fluents Clear(x), Clear(z) and On(x, y) must hold. In addition, there may be some other constrains in some specialised applications. For instance, in conventional CBR, C_7 just represents an episode as a snap shot of the 3-block world in time. However, assume the following constraint is imposed additionally:

No further action can take place in case C_7 if fluent On(B_2, B_1) has held previously.

Then, we need to deal with not only the distinct elemental case, but also the case histories. For instance, starting from episode C_1 or episode C_3, the 3-block world can be transferred into episode C_7, e.g.:

Transfers(U(B_3, B_1), C_1, C_4) then Transfers(U(B_1, B_2), C_4, C_7)

and

Transfers(U(B_3, B_2), C_3, C_6) then Transfers(U(B_2, B_1), C_6, C_7)

However, when the 3-block world has been transferred into C_7, the description of episode C_7 itself is not enough for deciding if some further action(s) can take place or not. To make the decision, the corresponding case histories need to be taken into account, i.e.:

H_1 = <C_1, C_4, C_7>;
Holds(C_1, T_1), Holds(C_4, T_4), Holds(C_7, T_7);
Meets(T_1, T_{14}), Meets(T_{14}, T_4), Meets(T_4, T_{47}), Meets(T_{47}, T_7).

and

H_2 = <C_3, C_6, C_7>;
Holds(C_3, T_3), Holds(C_6, T_6), Holds(C_7, T_7);
Meets(T_3, T_{36}), Meets(T_{36}, T_6), Meets(T_6, T_{67}), Meets(T_{67}, T_7).

where T_{14}, T_{47}, T_{36} and T_{67} denote the time elements over which the corresponding actions take place, respectively.

On the one hand, since Belongs(On(B_2, B_1), C_6), and in case history H_2, elemental C_6 "Holds" before case C_7, therefore, no further action can take place from case history H_2, in turn, case history H_2 cannot be extended further into the future. However, on the other hand, On(B_2, B_1) does not belong to any elemental case within case history H_1, thus further actions may take place to change the 3-block world from C_7 into other episodes, and hence extend the case history H_1 itself into the future. For instance, from

Transfers(S(B_2, B_3), C_7, C_8) then Transfers(S(B_1, B_2), C_8, C_{11})

we may get the following case history:

$H_3 = <C_1, C_4, C_7, C_8, C_{11}>$;
$\text{Holds}(C_1, T_1)$, $\text{Holds}(C_4, T_4)$, $\text{Holds}(C_7, T_7)$, $\text{Holds}(C_8, T_8)$, $\text{Holds}(C_{11}, T_{11})$;
$\text{Meets}(T_1, T_{14})$, $\text{Meets}(T_{14}, T_4)$, $\text{Meets}(T_4, T_{47})$, $\text{Meets}(T_{47}, T_7)$,
$\text{Meets}(T_7, T_{78})$, $\text{Meets}(T_{78}, T_8)$, $\text{Meets}(T_8, T_{811})$, $\text{Meets}(T_{811}, T_{11})$.

5   Conclusion

In this paper we have argued that, the history of cases, rather than distinct episodes, plays an important role in many CBR systems, and therefore, an appropriate representation and reasoning for temporal knowledge is needed. Founded on a general temporal theory which accommodates both points and intervals as primitive time elements, we have proposed a framework for Historical Case-Based Reasoning (HCBR), which allows expression of both relative and absolute temporal knowledge. We have introduced the concepts of fluents, elemental cases, and case histories. In case history matching, there are two similarity values need to be computed: the non-temporal similarity degree and the temporal similarity degree. In order to compute the non-temporal similarity degree, based on elemental case matching, the union and intersection of elemental cases is formally defined. In terms of the graphical presentation of temporal references introduced in this paper, the temporal similarity measurement in case history matching is simply transformed into conventional graph similarity measurement.

References

1. Kolodner, J.: *Case-Based Reasoning*. Morgan Kaufmann, San Francisco, California (1993).
2. Leake, D.: *Case-Based Reasoning: Experiences, Lessons, and Future Directions*. AAAI Press, Menlo Park, California (1996).
3. Watson, I.: *Applying Case-Based Reasoning: Techniques for Enterprise Systems*. Morgan Kaufmann, San Mateo, California (1997).
4. Cunningham, P.: CBR: Strengths and Weaknesses. In *Proceedings of 11th International Conference on Industrial and Engineering Applications of Artificial Intelligence and Expert Systems, eds. A Pobil, J. Mira and M. Ali, Lecture Notes in Artificial Intelligence* 1416, Vol.2, (1998) 517–523.
5. Jensen C., Clifford J., Gadia S., Segev A. and Snodgrass R.: A Glossary of Temporal Database Concepts, *SIGMOD RECORD*, 21(3), (1992) 35–43.
6. Keravnou, E.: Modelling medical concepts as time-objects. Eds. M. Stefanelli and J. Watts, eds., *Lecture Notes in artificial Intelligence* 934, Springer (1995) 67–90.
7. Shahar, Y.: Timing is everything: temporal reasoning and temporal data maintenance medicine. Eds. W Horn et al., *AIMDM'99, LNAI* 1620, Springer Verlag (1999) 30–46.
8. Nakhaeizadeh, G.: Learning Prediction of Time Series: A Theoretical and Empirical Comparison of CBR with Some Other Approaches. In *Proceedings of the Workshop on Case-Based Reasoning, AAAI-94*. Seattle, Washington (1994) 67–71.
9. Branting, L. and Hastings, J.: An empirical evaluation of model-based case matching and adaptation. In *Proceedings of the Workshop on Case-Based Reasoning, AAAI-94*. Seattle, Washington (1994) 72–78.

10. Jaczynski, M.: A Framework for the Management of Past Experiences with Time-Extended Situations. In *Proceedings of the 6th International Conference on Information and Knowledge Management (CIKM'97)*, Las Vegas, Nevada, USA, November 10–14, (1997) 32–39.

11. Schmidt, R., Pollwein, B. and Gierl, L.: Medical multi-parametric time course prognoses applied to kidney function assessment. *International Journal of Medical Information* 53, (1999) 253–263.

12. Hansen, B.: Weather reasoning predication using case-based reasoning and Fuzzy Set Theory, *MSc Thesis*, Technical University of Nova Scotia, Halifax, Nova Scotia, Canada (2000).

13. Kahn, M. and Gorry, A.: Mechanizing Temporal Knowledge, *Artificial Intelligence* 9, (1977) 87–108.

14. Allen, J.: Maintaining knowledge about temporal intervals. *Communications of the ACM* 26 (11), (1983) 832–843.

15. Allen, J.: Towards a General Theory of Action and Time. *Artificial Intelligence* 23, (1984) 123–154.

16. Allen, J. and Hayes, P.: Moments and Points in an Interval-based Temporal-based Logic. *Computational Intelligence* 5, (1989) 225–238.

17. Jare, M., Aanodt, A. and Shalle, P.: Representing Temporal Knowledge for Case-Based Reasoning. Proceedings of the 6th Euroupean Conference, ECCBR 2002, Aberdeen, Scotland, UK, September 4–7, (2002) 174–188.

18. van Benthem, J.: *The Logic of Time*, Kluwer Academic, Dordrech (1983).

19. Galton, A.: A Critical Examination of Allen's Theory of Action and Time. *Artificial Intelligence* **42**, (1990) 159–188.

20. Vila, L.: A Survey on Temporal Reasoning in Artificial Intelligence. *AI Communications* **7**, (1994) 4–28.

21. Ma, J. and Knight, B.: Representing the Diving Instant. *The Computer Journal* 46/2, (2003) 213–222.

22. Ma, J. and Knight, B.: A General Temporal Theory. *The Computer Journal* 37/2, (1994) 114–123.

23. Shoham, Y.: Temporal Logics in AI: Semantical and Ontological Considerations, *Artificial Intelligence*, **33**, (1987) 89–104.

24. Ma, J. and Knight, B.: Reified Temporal logic: An Overview, *Artificial Intelligence Review*, 15 (2001) 189–217.

25. McCarthy, J. and Hayes, P.: Some philosophical problems from the standpoint of artificial intelligence, In Meltzer, B. and Michie, D. (eds), *Machine Intelligence* **4** (1969) 463–502.

26. Allen, J. and Ferguson, G.: Actions and Events in Interval Temporal Logic, *the Journal of Logic and Computation*, Vol.4(5), (1994) 531–579.

27. Shanahan, M.: A Circumscriptive Calculus of Events, *Artificial Intelligence*, **77**, (1995) 29–384.

28. Knight, B. and Ma, J.: A General Temporal Model Supporting Duration Reasoning, *Artificial Intelligence Communication*, Vol.5(2), (1992) 75–84.

An Investigation of Generalized Cases

Kerstin Maximini, Rainer Maximini, and Ralph Bergmann

University of Hildesheim
Institute for Mathematics and Applied Computer Science
Data and Knowledge Management Group
31113 Hildesheim, Germany
{k_maximi,r_maximi,bergmann}@dwm.uni-hildesheim.de

Abstract. In the CBR literature from the past 25 years there is a considerable amount of research work that makes use of cases that are subspaces of some representation space rather than points in it. For cases of that kind, different terms have been used such as generalized case, prototype, schema, script, or abstract case. Our analysis of selected publications yields that on the one hand the same term is used for different concepts and on the other hand different terms are used for more or less the same concepts. So our goal is to improve the conceptual clarity by proposing an integrated classification schema for cases. We then use this schema to describe semantically founded ways for similarity definition and computation, depending on the class membership of query and case.

1 Introduction

When looking into the literature describing Case-Based Reasoning, applied to different domains and tasks, one often finds the term *generalized case* or the statement that (some) cases in the case base are *generalized*. Other publications use the concept *prototype* for a very similar application scenario, whereas in publications mostly written in the eighties *schema* and *script* are used. In newer publications the term *abstract case* and *concrete case* is introduced, which shows similarities to generalized cases.

In this paper, we argue that on the one hand the same term is used for different concepts and on the other hand different terms are used for more or less the same concept. So our goal is to improve the conceptual clarity by proposing an integrated classification schema for cases. Such a classification is needed to face the challanges of the current research project *IPQ: IP Qualification for Efficient Design Reuse*[1] funded by the German Ministry of Education and Research (BMBF) and the related European Medea project *ToolIP: Tools and Methods for IP*[2], namely how to handle parameterized cases, whose attributes are not defined independently of each other. The main problems of these generalized cases include their representation formalism, the calculation of similarity, and the implementation of a fast and efficient retrieval. The presented classification

---

[1] IPQ Project (12/2000 - 11/2003). Partners: AMD, Fraunhofer Institute for Integrated Circuits, FZI Karlsruhe, Infineon Technologies, Siemens, Sciworx, Empolis, Thomson Multi Media, TU Chemnitz, University of Hildesheim, University of Kaiserslautern, and University of Paderborn. See www.ip-qualifikation.de

[2] See toolip.fzi.de for partners and further information.

K.D. Ashley and D.G. Bridge (Eds.): ICCBR 2003, LNAI 2689, pp. 261–275, 2003.
© Springer-Verlag Berlin Heidelberg 2003

schema and similarity measures are not specialized to this domain; they are of general nature and can be applied to any CBR application.

The next section of this paper presents selected work from the history of CBR, using generalized cases and related concepts. We derived an integrated classification schema, proposed in section 3. Main focus of this paper lies in the analysis of the similarity measures for the different kinds of case, which is discussed in section 4. We close our paper with a summary and give ideas for future developments in this area.

2   Generalized Cases in the History of CBR

We have reviewed publications describing CBR systems in different application scenarios and different domains, e.g. systems for design, planning, and maintenance in domains like medicine, e-commerce, and architecture. We included also publications about the dynamic memory as a starting point. So the following summary bases upon selected publications of the last 25 years, dealing with the concepts of generalization and abstraction. It is in no way complete, but shows, which terms have been used over the time.

2.1   Dynamic Memory and Cognitive Model

First we want to make clear, that the idea of generalizing cases is not a radically new concept. It was already implicitly present since the very beginning of CBR and instance-based learning research [1,2,3,4,5].

The theory of dynamic memory [6], which is partly implemented in CBR systems [3], proposes a cognitive model and artificial methodology of a memory in which reasoning and learning are inseparable. According to this theory our general knowledge about situations is recorded in *scripts* and the memory is organized by *memory organization packets* (MOPs). MOPs have two functions: They hold general knowledge and they organize specific experiences of that general knowledge in cases. Whereby the cases are the starting point for solving problems and the general knowledge provides guidance in adapting old solutions to fit to new situations. In 1989, Kolodner and Simpson [7] introduced the *generalized episode* which is more or less equivalent to a MOP but describes a general episode instead of a specific one.

2.2   Design

In the early 90s generalization and abstraction of cases have been a topic of research in the design area. For example, every participant involved in the design of a house, like civil engineers, architects, and occupants, has another view to the design. These views are termed *different abstractions* and must be reconciled in the final design. Particularly, all constraints from each abstraction must be regarded for the final design. In the CADRE system [8] the design knowledge for each abstraction is represented in form of so called *design prototypes*, whereby a design prototype is a generalized version of a special design.

Another project in this area was the joint research project FABEL, where amongst other things DOM (domain ontology modelling) in architectural and engineering design has been developed [9,10,11]. The DOM system was designed to assist architects and engineers who are involved in designing the technical installation systems for highly complex buildings by usage of generic concept knowledge and episodic case knowledge. The most interesting knowledge base contains the domain knowledge and is set up with three knowledge containers: *generic knowledge, case knowledge*, and *scheme knowledge*. Design rules like analysis or synthesis rules are represented as *concepts* in the generic knowledge container. *Cases* are snapshots of the designs during the design process (temporally intermediate states of the layout) and therefore can be seen as episodic knowledge. *Schemas* are viewed as generalized cases, because they are created by putting together some similar cases to one more generic pattern. Thereby, equal parts are retained and different parts are replaced with variables. Schemas can be applied to many concrete situations.

2.3 Planning

The PARIS system, extensively described by Bergmann in 1996 [12,13], reuses cases flexibly by application of abstraction and generalization. In the planing domain, the problem part of a case is a representation of the initial and finite state and the solution part is a plan that describes how the finite state can be reached by applying a sequence of operators on the initial state.

Bergmann defines three terms, namely *problem class, solution class*, and *generalized case*. A problem class is a set of problems which is described by a generalized description of the initial and finite state as well as a set of constraints for the initial and finite state. The solution class is a set of solutions (plans) which are described by a sequence of partly instantiated parameterized operators. The generalized case is a problem class together with a solution class. It can be reused directly for a wider range of problems than a specific case and therefors can be seen as a solution schema. The process of transformation of a specific case in a generalized case is called *case generalization*. Beside the concept of generalization also the concept of abstraction has been applied to the cases. Therefore, experience is represented at several different levels of abstraction in an abstraction hierarchy. Based on these levels *concrete cases* and *abstract cases* can be distinguished. The process of transformation of a concrete case into an abstract one is called *case abstraction*. So the PARIS system uses "abstract generalized cases".

Another example of generalized cases in planning systems is the work of Rayner and Harris [14], who compound similar cases to form generalized cases, which are applicable to a wider range of problems.

2.4 Maintenance

In the CBR community the 4Re-cycle [15] is well established as a process description of CBR applications. For maintenance reasons the cycle has been expanded by Reinartz, Iglezakis, and Roth-Berghofer [16,17] with two further steps, namely review and restore. For the restore step they present several operators that modify the case base. Beside others, especially the operators *specialize case, generalize case*, and *abstract cases* are of interest for the scope of this paper. The specialize case operator adds a value to an unset problem attribute, whereas the generalize case operator removes a value from a problem attribute. The abstract cases operator converts two cases with an equal solution into a single case, whereby a relation determines how different attribute values are merged into a single one.

One application that uses these techniques is the ICONS system [18,19]. It is applied in the medical domain to give advise for an appropriate antibiotics therapy for a special patient. It stores patients together with the applied therapies as cases and uses CBR technology for a fast proposal of an antibiotics therapy. Used in every-day's practice, the number of cases would increase continuously and would slow down the retrieval time. To avoid this, the case base is structured by *prototypes*, including the most frequent features of their corresponding cases. Only cases that differ significantly from their prototypes are also stored in the case base.

2.5   Product Design

Increasingly, electronics companies integrate *Intellectual Properties* (IPs) from third parties within their complex electronic systems. An IP is a design object whose major value comes from the skill of its producer [20], and a redesign of it would consume significant time. However, a designer who wants to reuse designs from the past must have a lot of experience and knowledge about existing designs, in order to be able to find candidates that are suitable for reuse in his/her specific new situation. Current CBR systems are not able to handle IPs, because they are descriptions of flexible designs and therefore spawn a design space instead of a point. Their flexibility is based on a number of parameters and dependencies, and valid value combinations for these parameters are constrained by different criteria for each IP.

Bergmann, Vollrath, and Wahlmann [21] characterize the cases that can occur and distinguish between five types: *point case, constant solution generalized case, functional solution generalized case, independent alternative solution generalized case,* and *dependent alternative solution generalized case.* One goal of the IPQ project is to develop case retrieval for case of all these kinds.

3   Proposed Classification Schema

3.1   Case Classification

We now introduce a formal classification schema for cases in attribute-value representation. We consider the *attribute space* $\mathbb{A} = T_1 \times \cdots \times T_n$. T_i are atomic types which are data types with single values like integer, float, boolean, symbol, string, date, or time. Each case has n attributes $A_1, \ldots, A_n$ with an associated type T_i.

We start our definitions with the easiest kind of cases, namely the *point cases*.

Definition 1. *A point case pc is exact one element of the attribute space, $pc \in \mathbb{A}$, i.e., each attribute of pc has a concrete atomic value, unequal to* unknown.

A point case, e.g. c1 in figure 1, can be regarded as a special instance of another concept, namely *generalized cases*.

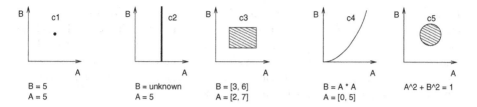

Fig. 1. Examples for the three kind of cases

Definition 2. *A* generalized case *gc is an arbitrary subspace of the attribute space,* $gc \subseteq \mathbb{A}$.

Generalized cases can be interpreted as an (infinite) set of point cases. The main difference in the following two definitions is the kind how this set is defined. The most simple form of a gc is the *attribute independent generalized case* (aigc).

Definition 3. *Assume there exists sets* $\mathbb{A}_1, \ldots, \mathbb{A}_n$ *with* $\mathbb{A}_i \subseteq T_i$. *An attribute independent generalized case* aigc *is defined as* $aigc = \mathbb{A}_1 \times \cdots \times \mathbb{A}_n$. *Consequently, an aigc is a special subspace of the attribute space,* $aigc \subseteq \mathbb{A}$.

Attribute independent generalized cases often occur in applications in which not all attributes of the case are known or where attribute values have been removed, e.g. by maintenance operations. Unknown attribute values are usually interpreted as arbitrary, i.e., they can be considered to spawn the whole attribute dimension in $\mathbb{A}$. Hence, this can be represented by $\mathbb{A}_i = T_i$, e.g. c2 in figure 1. Another common reason for a case to be an aigc is because some attributes hold intervals (range) or sets as values, see c3. Further, a query is usually an aigc, because the solution attributes are not defined.

The second form of gcs are the *attribute dependent generalized cases* (adgc).

Definition 4. *A generalized case* adgc $\subseteq \mathbb{A}$ *that cannot be represented as an aigc is called* attribute dependent generalized case.

Hence, a gc is attribute dependent if the subspace it represents cannot be decomposed into independent subsets for each attribute. Dependencies can be expressed by constraints like demonstrated by c4 and c5 in figure 1. Therefore, these cases are more complex and difficult to handle during retrieval, depending on the form of the spawned subspaces. Roughly speaking, aigcs spawns a subspace which is orthogonal (except aigc with sets) and are therefore manageable in case that similarity measures are also decomposed according to the attributes. For adgcs the subspace is arbitrary and hence it may become computationally very hard to determine the similarity to a pc or another gc [21]. We will explore this issue in detail in section 4.

3.2   Abstraction versus Generalization

In recent CBR literature, the use of multiple representations at different levels of abstraction has been investigated [3,13,22,23,24,25,12,26,27,28,29]. For this kind of approach the term *hierarchical case based reasoning* [22], *stratified case based reasoning* [27] and *reasoning with abstract cases* [12] have been used so far. The basic idea behind all these approaches is to supply experience represented at several different levels of abstraction. To represent different levels of abstraction, the vocabulary is structured into several partially ordered sub-vocabularies, one for each level of abstraction. Based on these levels, two kinds of case can be distinguished:

Definition 5. *A concrete case is a case located at the lowest available level of abstraction, e.g. the leafs of an abstraction tree. An* abstract case *is a case represented at a higher level of abstraction, e.g. the nodes in an abstraction tree.[30]*

Concrete and abstract cases are stored in a case base for reuse when solving new problems. When a new problem must be solved, one (or several) "appropriate" concrete or abstract case is retrieved from the case base and the solution the case contains is reused to derive a solution for the current problem, e.g., by filling in the details that a retrieved case at some higher level of abstraction does not contain.

During the abstraction several cases from a level n are transformed into a single new case c_a on level $n + 1$, see figure 2. The association between c_a and the abstraction

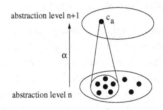

Fig. 2. Abstraction and Generalization

level n is expressed by the equation $g_n(c_a) = \{c | \alpha(c) = c_a\}$ with an abstraction function α. The abstraction function α may be a transformation to another easier to handle representation formalism or just a projection to a subset of the attributes, e.g. by removing less significant ones. Hence, α can be seen as a generalization step, because cases are converted into a gc $g_n(c_a)$ at abstraction level n. But on abstraction level $n + 1$ c_a is usually represented in a more simple way, e.g. as a point case.

Summarizing, abstraction was at all time a generalization together with a simplification of representation formalism and class membership.

4   Consequences for Similarity Measures

In this and the following three chapters we will analyze the similarity computation between a query and a case in the case base, depending on the cases' classes. Therefore, nine combinations have to be distinguished.

	pc (CB)	aigc (CB)	adgc (CB)
pc (Query)	Case 1	Case 2	Case 3
aigc (Query)	Case 4	Case 5	Case 6
adgc (Query)	Case 7	Case 8	Case 9

These nine cases can be grouped in 3 clusters, built up by the retrieval complexity: Similarity computation between non-adgcs (Case 1, Case 2, Case 4, and Case 5) that is decsribed in the following section, similarity computation for scenarios where the case base inludes adgcs (Case 3 and Case 6) that is described in 6, and similarity computation for adgc queries (Case 7, Case 8, and Case 9) that is described in 7.

For the analysis we present typical similarity measures which can of course differ in concrete applications, so they should be understood as examples, but not as the only possible ones.

4.1   Preliminaries

As we have restricted our schema to cases in attribute-value representation, we use the well-known approach to compute the case similarity by combining local similarities with an aggregation function (see [30,31]). A case is described like introduced in section 3.1 by its attribute space $\mathbb{A}$.

Similarity Measure Approach. For every attribute A_i with atomic value type T_i, a local similarity measure is defined in the following way: $sim_{Ai}(x_i, y_i) : T_i \times T_i \to [0,1]$. For every attribute of a gc a local similarity measure of the following way is considered: $sim^*_{Ai}(x_i, y_i) : 2^{T_i} \times 2^{T_i} \to [0,1]$.

A global similarity measure sim can than be calculated for pcs with the help of a monotonous aggregation function $F : [0,1]^n \to [0,1]$ like weighted average, maximum, or minimum, in a way that

$$sim(x,y) = sim((x_1, \ldots x_n), (y_1, \ldots y_n))$$
$$= F(sim_{A1}(x_1, y_1), \ldots, sim_{An}(x_n, y_n))$$

Semantic of Sets. Intervals and sets in the query as well as in the cases may have different semantics. The semantics of an interval or set in the query can be that the user specifies it because the concrete value does not matter to him or her and every value or subset within it would be acceptable (imprecise knowledge) or because he or she searches for a case, covering it (precise knowledge). The semantics of an interval or set in the case can be that either all values are supported (precise knowledge) or one or several are supported but it is not known which ones (imprecise knowledge). The following definition is inspired by Tautz and Althoff [32].

Definition 6. *If the semantics of an interval or a set is that all specified values are addressed and must be true simultaneously we speak of* precise knowledge. *If only a subset is addressed we speak of* imprecise knowledge.

5   Similarity Calculation between Non-adgcs

In this section, the well-understood similarity calculation between non-adgcs is summarized, thus it deals with Case 1, Case 2, Case 4 and Case 5 of the roadmap presented in 4. The most general case is Case 5, namely the calculation of similarity between an aigc query and an aigc case. The other cases are specializations, which are easier to handle.

For the analysis of Case 5 we must consider the reason why the aigcs are generalized cases: is it because some attributes of atomic value type have unknown values or because some attributes have intervals or sets as concrete values, or both. The following subsections follow this discrimination.

5.1   Atomic Unknown

One or more attributes with an atomic value type of query or case have unknown values. In this case, we must distinguish three cases:

1. *Only the attribute value in the case is unknown:* Here we can make use of on an optimistic, pessimistic, or predictand strategy. In an optimistic strategy we assume that unknown values argue for similarity and express that by a local similarity of 1, $sim_{Ai}(x_i, unknown) = 1$. In a pessimistic strategy we assume that unknown values argue against similarity and express that by a local similarity of 0, that means that $sim_{Ai}(x_i, unknown) = 0$. If it is possible to calculate a kind of predictand E for the similarity, we can use the predictand strategy and define the local similarity $sim_{Ai}(x_i, unknown) = E$.

2. *Only the attribute value in the query is unknown:* Here we follow again an optimistic, pessimistic, or predictand strategy, although in the majority of cases the optimistic strategy is the most convenient one. That is because the user does not define values for attributes in the query, whose contents is not important to him or her. So the contents does not care and every values is acceptable. Optimistic strategy means that $sim_{Ai}(unknown, y_i) = 1$. Pessimistic and predictand strategy may be useful in special scenarios and are defined in an analogous way.

3. *The attribute value in case and query is unknown:* Then we can again follow an optimistic, pessimistic, or predictand strategy. Optimistic strategy means that $sim_{Ai}(unknown, unknown) = 1$; pessimistic and predictand strategy are defined in an analogous way.

5.2   Intervals

The attribute value in the query and in the case are intervals. We name the query interval $x_i = [x_{ilb}, x_{iub}]$, the case interval $y_i = [y_{ilb}, y_{iub}]$, and a possible intersection $z_i = [z_{ilb}, z_{iub}]$. We have to distinguish the four combinations of the knowledge types of definition 6.

1. *imprecise query, precise case:*
   With the imprecise query one point is requested from all the possible points of the precise case. Therefore, we just have to distinguish the following two situations:

- $z_i \neq \emptyset$: The local similarity is one, because an arbitrary element of z_i or z_i itself can be returned.
- $z_i = \emptyset$: The local similarity must consider the "distance" from x_{ilb} to y_{iub} and x_{iub} to y_{ilb}, so that

$$sim^*_{Ai}(x_i, y_i) = \max\left(sim_{Ai}(x_{ilb}, y_{iub}), sim_{Ai}(x_{iub}, y_{ilb})\right)$$

Summarizing, a local similarity measure can be defined as:

$$sim^*_{Ai}(x_i, y_i) = \begin{cases} 1 & \text{if } z_i \neq \emptyset \\ \max\begin{pmatrix} sim_{Ai}(x_{ilb}, y_{iub}), \\ sim_{Ai}(x_{iub}, y_{ilb}) \end{pmatrix} & \text{otherwise} \end{cases}$$

2. *imprecise query, imprecise case:*
   The imprecise interval in the case means that a valid value exists in this range, but it is not sure where it is. Unlike the previous case we cannot assume that valid values are in the intersection of query and case interval. Therefore, we must distinguish the three strategies: The optimistic one assumes that valid points are in the intersection, that means this is the same as the previous case. The pessimistic strategy assumes that no valid point is in the intersection which leads to the local similarity

$$sim^*_{Ai}(x_i, y_i) = \min_{\forall x_{is} \in x_i, y_{it} \in y_i} \{sim_{Ai}(x_{is}, y_{it})\}$$

   The predictand strategy calculates the probability that a valid point is in the intersection z_i, e.g. by calculating the relation between the intersection size and the case interval size. Consequently, the similarity measure is defined as:

$$sim^*_{Ai}(x_i, y_i) = \begin{cases} \frac{|y_{iub} - y_{ilb}|}{|z_{iub} - z_{ilb}|} & \text{if } z_i \neq \emptyset \\ 0 & \text{otherwise} \end{cases}$$

3. *precise query, precise case:*
   With the precise query a case is requested whose attribute value covers the complete interval and the precise case specifies an interval with all valid points. Therefore, we have to distinguish the following four situations:
   - $x_i \subseteq y_i$: From the geometrical point of view this means that $y_{ilb} \leq x_{ilb} \leq x_{iub} \leq y_{iub}$. So y_i is a coverage for x_i, and therefore the similarity is one.
   - $x_i \supseteq y_i$: From the geometrical point of view that means that $x_{ilb} \leq y_{ilb} \leq y_{iub} \leq x_{iub}$. The similarity must be lower than one because a coverage was demanded. The similarity can be defined by the percentage of coverage: $sim^*_{Ai}(x_i, y_i) = \frac{|y_{iub} - y_{ilb}|}{|x_{iub} - x_{ilb}|}$.
   - $x_{ilb} \leq y_{ilb} \leq x_{iub} \leq y_{iub}$ or $y_{ilb} \leq x_{ilb} \leq y_{iub} \leq x_{iub}$. This case can be reduced to the preceding case by setting $y_{iub} := x_{iub}$ or $y_{ilb} := x_{ilb}$, respectively.
   - $z_i = \emptyset$: From the geometrical point of view that means that $x_{iub} < y_{ilb}$ or $y_{iub} < x_{ilb}$. The similarity is zero.

   Summarizing, a local similarity measure can be defined with respect to the bound as

$$sim^*_{Ai}(x_i, y_i) = \begin{cases} 1 & \text{if } x_i \subseteq y_i \\ 0 & \text{if } z_i = \emptyset \\ \frac{|y_{iub} - y_{ilb}|}{|x_{iub} - x_{ilb}|} & \text{otherwise} \end{cases}$$

An alternative similarity measure for software engineering experience is defined by Tautz and Althoff [32].

4. *precise query, imprecise case:*
   From the logical point of view the local similarity function can never equal one. Therefore, a concrete definition is very difficult and strongly depends on the application. It can be approximated by usage of the above defined similarity measure for precise query and precise case. Of course, this is not correct, but all cases in the case base have the same problem and therefore are comparable again. Tautz and Althoff [32] defined for this situation an alternative similarity measure.

For the similarity computation in Case 2 (sim between pc query and aigc case), a way to compare a number (from the query) with an interval (from the case) must be found. This is quite simple, because a value x_{i1} can easily be regarded as an interval with coincident lower and upper bounds. The local similarity between the two intervals $x_i = [x_{ilb}, x_{iub}] = [x_{i1}, x_{i1}]$ and $y_i = [y_{ilb}, y_{iub}]$ can than be calculated like described above in the general case.

The same strategy can be applied in Case 4 (sim between aigc query and pc case). Instead of the query point the case point is regarded as an interval and the comparison of two intervals can be performed like described above.

5.3   Sets

The attribute value in the query and in the case are sets. We name the query set $x_i = \{x_{i1}, \ldots, x_{in}\}$, the case set $y_i = \{y_{i1}, \ldots, y_{im}\}$, and a possible intersection $z_i = \{z_{i1}, \ldots, z_{ik}\} = x_i \cap y_i$. We have to distinguish the four combinations of the knowledge types of definition 6.

1. *imprecise query, precise case:*
   With the imprecise query one point is requested from all the possible points of the precise case. Therefore, we have to distinguish the following two situations:
   - $z_i \neq \emptyset$: Analogously to intervals, the local similarity is one.
   - $z_i = \emptyset$: The local similarity must consider the "distances" from the elements of x_i to the ones of y_i. Such a similarity function could be defined as
     $sim^*_{Ai}(x_i, y_i) = \max\{sim_{Ai}(x_{is}, y_{it}) \forall s \in [1, n], t \in [1, m]\}$.
   Summarizing, a local similarity measure can be defined as

$$sim^*_{Ai}(x_i, y_i) = \begin{cases} 1 & \text{if } z_i \neq \emptyset \\ \max_{\forall s \in [1,n], t \in [1,m]} \{sim_{Ai}(x_{is}, y_{it})\} & \text{otherwise} \end{cases}$$

2. *imprecise query, imprecise case:*
   This is analogous to intervals where the three strategies must be distinguished:

$$\text{optimistic: } sim^*_{Ai}(x_i, y_i) = \begin{cases} 1 & \text{if } z_i \neq \emptyset \\ \max_{\forall \left(\substack{s \in [1,n] \\ t \in [1,m]}\right)} \{sim_{Ai}(x_{is}, y_{it})\} & \text{otherwise} \end{cases}$$

$$\text{pessimistic: } sim^*_{Ai}(x_i, y_i) = \min_{\forall x_{is} \in x_i, y_{it} \in y_i} \{sim_{Ai}(x_{is}, y_{it})\}$$

$$\text{predictand: } sim^*_{Ai}(x_i, y_i) = \begin{cases} \frac{|y_i|}{|z_i|} & \text{if } z_i \neq \emptyset \\ 0 & \text{otherwise} \end{cases}$$

3. *precise query, precise case:*
This situation is again analogous to the intervals; several cases can be distinguished. We are summarizing here only the resulting definition of a local similarity measure.

$$
sim^*_{Ai}(x_i, y_i) = \begin{cases} 1 & \text{if } x_i \subseteq y_i \\ \frac{m}{n} & \text{if } x_i \supseteq y_i \\ \frac{k}{n} & \text{if } z_i \neq \emptyset \text{ and } x_i \setminus y_i \neq \emptyset \text{ and } y_i \setminus x_i \neq \emptyset \\ 0 & \text{if } z_i = \emptyset \end{cases}
$$

A more sophisticated similarity measure considers the "distances" between the elements. This method was introduced by Bergmann and Eisenecker [33]:

$$
sim_{Ai}(x_i, y_i) = \frac{1}{n} \sum_{s=1}^{n} \max \{sim_{Ai}(x_{is}, y_{it}) \forall t \in [1, m]\}
$$

By the usage of this similarity measure the similarity for the case $z_i = \emptyset$ must not be zero.

4. *precise query, imprecise case:* With the same argument as for intervals we can again use the similarity function defined in the latter case as approximation.

For the similarity computation in Case 2 (sim between pc query and aigc case), the concrete value of the query must be regarded as a set ($x_i = \{x_{i1}\}$), then the similarity between x_i and $y_i = \{y_{i1}, \ldots, y_{im}\}$ can be calculated like described above in the general case.

The same strategy can be applied in Case 4 (sim between aigc query and pc case). Instead of the query point the case point is regarded as a set and the comparison of two sets can be performed like described above.

5.4 Non Atomic Unknown

Until now we have handled "unknown" only on attributes with atomic value type. Now we will consider the situation how the similarity between unknown and an interval or set can be computed. Therefore, we have analyzed all possible knowledge type combinations and strategies which are presented in Table 1.

Table 1. Unknown in Sets or Intervals

query	case	iq & ic O Pe Pr	iq & pc O Pe Pr	pq & ic O Pe Pr	pq & pc O Pe Pr
unknown	interval or set	1 1 1	1 1 1	0 0 0	0 0 0
interval or set	unknown	1 0 E	1 0 E	1 0 E	1 0 E
unknown	unknown	1 0 E	1 0 E	1 0 E	1 0 E

iq imprecise query
ic imprecise case
pq precise query
pc precise case
O optimistic strategy
Pe pessimistic strategy
Pr predictand strategy

In general, "unknown" for attributes with non atomic types can be handled similarly as for attributes with atomic types. The only difference occurs in the case that the query has the value unknown and the case has a set or interval. In this case the knowledge types have to be distinguished, because an imprecise query always leads to a similarity of one in each strategy and a precise query always leads to zero. Depending on the knowledge types in query and case and the appropriated strategy, the corresponding sim_{Ai}^* for intervals and sets have to be adapted to take the handling of "unknown" into account.

6   Similarity Calculations for Case Bases Including adgcs

This section deals with Case 3 and Case 6 of the roadmap presented in 4, thus the similarity calculation for scenarios where the case base includes adgcs. The more general case is Case 6, namely the calculation of similarity between an aigc query and an adgc case. Case 3 (sim between pc query and adgc case) is a specialization of it.

$$\text{Case 3: } \sup_{\forall y_t \in y} \{sim(x, y_t)\} \qquad \text{Case 6: } \sup_{\forall x_s \in x, y_t \in y} \{sim(x_s, y_t)\}$$

For these cases, the similarity computation is very difficult because the presented problem must be solved. In these equations the association is used that a generalized case is a possibly infinite set of point cases and we are searching the two nearest points. For Case 3, this equation simplifies a little, because the query is a pc instead of an aigc.

Research in this area started a few years ago, but generally accepted assertions or standardized approaches cannot be given for all data types. But the following two methods are very promising and solve the problem for special secnarios.

In 2002 Bergmann and Mougouie [34] presented a solution to calculate the similarity between a pc query and an adgc (Case 3) that is represented through constraints over an n-dimensional real-valued vector space. They have shown that the difficulty of this calculation depends on whether the adgc spawn a convex or nonconvex subspace which is defined by the constraints. For convex constraints and by usage of convex similarity measures, the Topkis-Veinott method can be easily applied to determine exactly the similarity between a pc query and an adgc. If the similarity measure is nonconvex or the adgc contains also nonconvex constraints, the problem is more difficult. For this situation an algorithm is proposed that allows to incrementally compute sequences of upper and lower bounds for the similarity and assures the convergence of the algorithm. It allows to rank the adgc in the case base according to their similarity to the pc query without the exact computation of all similarity measures.

This method is in principal also applicable in Case 6, except that it only works for *unknown* values; intervals and sets are not possible for the query at the current state.

Currently, we investigate [35] another more pragmatic strategy to handle this problem: a converter that samples the subspace spawned by the adgc and creates a number of pcs that are distributed "reasonably" within the subspace. After the conversion of every adgc, the new case base consists obviously of much more cases, but only of pcs. Consequently, standard algorithms for the similarity computation between two point cases can be used. This method is applicable in Case 3 and Case 6.

7 Similarity Calculations for adgc Queries

This section deals with Case 7, Case 8, and Case 9 of the roadmap presented in 4, thus the similarity calculation for scenarios with adgc queries. These cases have not been a topic of research until now. One big problem which has to be solved is to find a possibility to define attribute dependent queries in a user friendly way. Assumed, such a query could be defined – albeit only for simple dependencies – we face the problem to compute the similarity of this query to the cases. This problem may be solved by reducing it to well-known similarity computations, e.g. by changing the cases' model or by converting the query to several point queries, search the most similar cases to all of them, and return a unified set of cases.

Example: Imagine a car-selling domain with an attribute "features", whose type is a set of features like "electronic exterior mirrors", "winter equipment", "rear wing", or "large tires". The user may specify implications like "If the car has electronic exterior mirrors, it should also have winter equipment" and "If the car has a rear wing, it should also have large tires". One solution is to change the representation of the feature attribute from the set to a multiset. The implications can than be converted in the set {{electronic exterior mirrors, winter equipment}, {rear wing, large tires}}, so that we have an aigc query. Another workaround is to request two aigc queries: one with the feature attribute {electronic exterior mirrors, winter equipment} and the second one with {rear wing, large tires}.

8 Summary and Outlook

We have presented an integrated classification schema for cases and have described the similarity computation, depending on the class membership of query and case. We have elaborated that the similarity computation with adgcs is not well researched until now. Hence, the current research should focus on this topic.

The similarity computation may be solved by reducing it to well known similarity computations as touched on in 7. Another idea could be to abstract adgcs with the goal that it becomes an aigc or pc on a higher level of abstraction.

A completely different approach would be the definition of similarity measures on constraints which would enable the comparison of the adgcs' shapes.

This approach is motivated by the different knowledge types (definition 6): imprecise adgc queries can be handled similar to 5, but precise adgc queries can be subdivided in a "coverage request" and a *shape request*. The request of a similar shape leads to the new question how the similarity between constraints, which define the shapes, can be computed. This is not only a theoretical playing, because applications for such scenarios are possible by all means. For example, a designer of furniture searches for a technique to realize a parameterized furniture. In this case the parameterization is the query and the results should be furniture with the same parameterization.

References

1. Schank, R.C., Abelson, R.P.: Scripts, plans, goals and understanding: An inquiry into human knowledge structures. Lawrence Erlbaum Associates, Hillsdale, NJ (1977)

274   K. Maximini, R. Maximini, and R. Bergmann

2. Kolodner, J.L.: Retrieval and Organizational Strategies in Conceptual Memory. PhD thesis, Yale University (1980)
3. Kolodner, J.L.: Case-Based Reasoning. Morgan Kaufmann, San Mateo (1993)
4. Bareiss, R.: Exemplar-Based Knowledge Acquisition: A unified Approach to Concept Representation, Classification and Learning. Academic Press (1989)
5. Salzberg, S.: A nearest hyperrectangle learning method. Machine Learning 6 (1991) 277–309
6. Schank, R.C.: Dynamic Memory: A Theory of Learning in Computers and People. Cambridge University Press, New York (1982)
7. Kolodner, J.L., Simpson, R.L.: The MEDIATOR: Analysis of an Early Case-Based Problem Solver. Cognitive Science 13 (1989) 507–549
8. Hua, K., Smith, I., Faltings, B.: Integrated case-based building design. In Wess, S., Althoff, K.D., Richter, M.M., eds.: Topics in Case-Based Reasoning. Proc. Of the First European Workshop on Case-Based Reasoning (EWCBR-93). Lecture Notes in Artificial Intelligence, 837, Springer Verlag (1993) 436–445
9. Gebhardt, F., Voß, A., Gräther, W., Schmidt-Belz, B.: Reasoning with Complex Cases. Volume 393 of International Series in Engineering and Computer Science. Kluwer Academic Publishers, Boston (1997)
10. Bakhtari, S., Bartsch-Spörl, B., Oertel, W., Eltz, U.: DOM: domain ontology modelling in architectural and engineering design. Fabel-Report 33, GMD, Sankt Augustin (1995)
11. Oertel, W., Bakhtari, S.: Interaction of generic knowledge and cases in DOM. In: Proceedings of the Third Congress on Computing in Civil Engineering, Anaheim, USA (1996)
12. Bergmann, R.: Effizientes Problemlösen durch flexible Wiederverwendung von Fällen auf verschiedenen Abstraktionsebenen. DISKI 138. infix (1996)
13. Bergmann, R., Wilke, W.: On the role of abstraction in case-based reasoning. In Smith, I., Faltings, B., eds.: Advances in Case-Based Reasoning. Lecture Notes in Artificial Intelligence, 1186, Springer Verlag (1996) 28–43
14. Rayner, N., Harris, C.: Mission management for multiple autonomous vehicles (1996)
15. Aamodt, A., Plaza, E.: Case-based reasoning: foundational issues, methodological variations, and system approaches. AI Communications 7 (1994) 39–59
16. Reinartz, T., Iglezakis, I., Roth-Berghofer, T.: On quality measures for case base maintenance. In Blanzieri, E., Portinale, L., eds.: Advances in Case-Based Reasoning (EWCBR'2000). Lecture Notes in Artificial Intelligence, 1898, Springer (2000) 247ff
17. Reinartz, T., Iglezakis, I., Roth-Berghofer, T.: On quality measures for case-base maintenance. Computational Intelligence – Special Issue on Maintaining CBR Systems 17 (2001)
18. Schmidt, R., Gierl, L.: The Roles of Prototypes in Medical Case-Based Reasoning Systems. In Burkhard, H.D., Lenz, M., eds.: 4th German Workshop on CBR — System Development and Evaluation —. Informatik-Berichte, Berlin, Humboldt University (1996) 207–216
19. Schmidt, R., Gierl, L.: Case-based reasoning for antibiotics therapy advice: An investigation of retrieval algortihms and prototypes. Artificial Intelligence in Medicine 23 (2001) 171–186
20. Lewis, J.: Intellectual property (IP) components. Artisan Components, Inc., [web page], http://www.artisan.com/ip.html (1997) [Accessed 28 Oct 1998].
21. Bergmann, R., Vollrath, I., Wahlmann, T.: Generalized cases and their application to electronic designs. In Melis, E., ed.: 7. German Workshop on Case-Based Reasoning (GWCBR'99). (1999) 6–19
22. Smyth, B., Cunningham, P.: Déjà Vu: a hierarchical case-based reasoning system for software design. In Neumann, B., ed.: ECAI 92: 10th European Conference on Artificial Intelligence, August 1992, Vienna. Wiley, Chichester (1992) 587–589
23. Smyth, B.: Case-Based Resign. PhD thesis, Trinity College Dublin (1996)
24. Kambhampati, S., Hendler, J.: A validation-structure-based theory of plan modification and reuse. Artificial Intelligence 55 (1992) 193–258

25. Bergmann, R., Wilke, W.: Building and refining abstract planning cases by change of representation language. Journal of Artificial Intelligence Research **3** (1995) 53–118
26. Bergmann, R.: On the use of taxonomies for representing case features and local similarity measures. In Gierl, L., Lenz, M., eds.: Proceedings of the 6th German Workshop on Case-Based Reasoning. (1998)
27. Branting, K.L., Aha, D.W.: Stratified case based reasoning: Reusing hierarchical; problem solving eposides. Technical Report AIC-95-001, Naval Research Lab (1995)
28. Karchenasse, N., Roger, J.M., Sevila, F.: The hierarchical case-based diagnosis. In Bergmann, R., Wilke, W., eds.: Proceedings of the 5th German Workshop ion Case-Based Reasoning, LSA 97-01E, University of Kaiserslautern, Germany (1997)
29. Cunningham, P., Bonzano, A.: Hierarchical CBR for multiple aircraft conflict resolution. In Prade, H., ed.: Proceedings of the 13th European Conference on Artificial Intelligence, Wiley (1998)
30. Bergmann, R.: Experience Management - Foundations, Development Methodology, and Internet-Based Applications. Lecture Notes in Artificial Intelligence 2432. Springer Berlin, Heidelberg, New York, Hong Kong, London, Milan, paris, Tokyo (2002)
31. Wess, S.: Fallbasiertes Problemlösen in wissensbasierten Systemen zur Entscheidungsunterstützung und Diagnostik. PhD thesis, Universität Kaiserslautern (1995) Available as DISKI 126, infix Verlag.
32. Tautz, C., Althoff, K.D.: Towards engineering similarity functions for software engineering experience. In Göker, M., ed.: 8. German Workshop on Case-Based Reasoning (GWCBR'2000)., DaimerChrysler Research Ulm (2000) 87–97
33. Bergmann, R., Eisenecker, U.: Fallbasiertes schließen zur unterstützung der wiederverwendung objektorientierter software: Eine fallstudie. Technical report, University of Kaiserslautern, Kaiserslautern (1994)
34. Mougouie, B., Bergmann, R.: Similarity assessment for generalizied cases by optimization methods. In: Proceedings of the European Conference on Case-Based Reasoning (ECCBR-02), Springer. (2002)
35. Maximini, R., Tartakovski, A., Bergmann, R.: Investigating different methods for efficient retrieval of generalized cases. In: German Workshop on Experience Management. (2003) accepted.

On the Role of Diversity in Conversational Recommender Systems

Lorraine McGinty[1] and Barry Smyth[1,2]

[1] Smart Media Institute, University College Dublin, Dublin 4, Ireland
Lorraine.McGinty@ucd.ie
[2] ChangingWorlds Ltd., South County Business Park, Dublin 18, Ireland.
Barry.Smyth@ChangingWorlds.com

Abstract. In the past conversational recommender systems have adopted a similarity-based approach to recommendation, preferring cases that are similar to some user query or profile. Recent research, however, has indicated the importance of diversity as an additional selection constraint. In this paper we attempt to clarify the role of diversity in conversational recommender systems, highlighting the pitfalls of naively incorporating current diversity-enhancing techniques into existing recommender systems. Moreover, we describe and fully evaluate a powerful new diversity-enhancing technique that has the ability to significantly improve the performance of conversational recommender systems across the board.

1 Introduction

Conversational recommender systems are forwarded as a potential solution to the information overload problem that are particularly well-adapted to consumer-oriented e-commerce applications [1,2,3,10]. They help users to navigate through complex product spaces in pursuit of suitable products by presenting sets of alternative recommendations (during a series of *recommendation cycles*) and taking advantage of user feedback to guide future cycles [4,5,6,8,7,9,10].

Usually, conversational recommenders adopt a similarity-based recommendation strategy, selecting cases for recommendation because they are are maximally similar to the current user query. However, recently this emphasis on similarity as the primary selection pressure has been brought into question. In particular, the diversity of a set of recommendations has been shown to be important, but largely independent of query similarity [12]. A set of recommendations may be similar to the current query but if they are also very similar to each other - if they lack diversity - then these recommendations provide only limited coverage of the recommendation space. In response a number of researchers have proposed techniques for improving the diversity of a set of recommendations without significantly (if at all) affecting similarity to the user query [2,7,9,10,12]. However, although such techniques make it possible to improve the diversity of a set of recommendations, no attempt has been made to consider how and when such methods should be used properly in conversational recommender systems.

K.D. Ashley and D.G. Bridge (Eds.): ICCBR 2003, LNAI 2689, pp. 276–290, 2003.
© Springer-Verlag Berlin Heidelberg 2003

The assumption that such methods can be used to increase the diversity of each set of recommendations ([12]) is well made. However, the degree to which diversity can be used to improve the efficiency and/or quality of a recommender system has not yet been evaluated. While it has been shown that diversity can be increased within a single recommendation cycle, the degree to which this can help a conversational recommender more efficiently focus in on a good recommendation for the target user, is still unclear. Indeed employing current diversity-enhancing techniques during each recommendation cycle of a conversational recommender is unlikely to deliver optimal results; these techniques are designed to pass-over items that are similar to the target query if they are also similar to concurrent recommendations. Obviously, if the target item is one of these passed-over items, then an opportunity to successfully complete the recommendation task in the current cycle will have been missed.

In this paper we investigate this issue empirically on a range of data-sets, highlighting inefficiencies with current diversity-enhancing techniques. We also present a novel approach to controlling diversity in conversational recommenders called *adaptive selection* and demonstrate that it can lead to significant performance improvements in recommenders that employ preference-based [4,5] and critiquing [3] as their primary forms of feedback.

2   Similarity vs. Diversity in Conversational Recommender Systems

Conversational recommender systems engage the user in an extended dialog to better ascertain a user's specific requirements and needs in order to make relevant recommendations. Shimazu [10] distinguishes between two basic approaches. With *navigation by asking* the user is engaged in a question-answering dialog where they are asked to answer specific questions about the features of their ideal product case. For example, in a PC recommender the user may be asked to provide information about the processor, memory or pricing requirements. In contrast, with *navigation by proposing* the user is instead presented with suggested recommendations and asked to provide feedback regarding the suitability of these suggestions. In particular, the common forms of feedback used in navigation by proposing are preference-based feedback and critiquing. For example, in a PC recommender that uses preference-based feedback a user would simply indicate a preference for PC1 over PC2 or PC3. In a recommender using critiquing the user would indicate such a preference but also provide a critique. For example they might indicate that they are looking for *less expensive* cases than PC1 by critiquing the *price* feature.

Traditionally, conversational recommender systems have followed a similarity-based recommendation policy irrespective of their basic recommendation approach or the type of feedback that they rely on. Accordingly k cases are selected for recommendation because they are maximally similar to the current user query; in the terminology of [9] this set of k cases is called the *standard retrieval set* or *SRS*. However, an important theme in recent CBR research is the extent to which various selection constraints have a role to play during retrieval in addition to similarity (see [2,7,11]). Smyth & McClave [12] highlight how similarity-based approaches have a tendancy to produce recommendations that lack diversity and the problems that this entails. The recommended cases may all be similar to the current query but if they are also very similar to each other then their value, as a set of alternatives for the user to judge, will be compromised. This observation motivates the need for new selection methods capable of delivering a set of recommendations that are diverse as well as being similar to the user query.

The *bounded greedy* technique introduced by [12] was the first attempt to explicitly enhance the diversity of a set of recommendations without significantly compromising their query similarity characteristics; it is worth noting that some loss of similarity is experienced with this approach. The method operates in a similar 2-pass manner. A first pass over the recommendable items (case-base) ranks cases according to their query similarity. The second pass sequentially transfers cases from this ranked list to the final recommendation list such that at each transfer point the case that is selected is the one maximises the product of its similarity to the target query and its diversity relative to the cases that have already been selected; the diversity of a case c relative to a set of cases C is given by Equation 1.

$$RelDiv(c, C) = \frac{\sum_{\forall c_i \epsilon C'} (1 - Sim(c, C_i))}{n} \dots \text{if } C \neq \{\}; 1 \text{ otherwise} \qquad (1)$$

In parallel Shimazu [10] introduced an alternative method for enhancing the similarity of a set of recommendations. In brief, a set of 3 recommendations, c_1, c_2 and c_3, are chosen relative to some query q such that c_1 is maximally similar to q, c_2 is maximally dissimilar to c_1 and then c_3 is maximally dissimilar to c_1 and c_2. In this way, the three cases are chosen to be maximally diverse but unlike the bounded greedy technique above the similarity of c_2 and c_3 to the query is likely to be limited. As such the value of this approach is limited to situations where the set of recommended cases is drawn from a set of cases that are all sufficiently similar to the user query to begin with.

Recently a number of alternative diversity enhancing selection techniques have been proposed. For example, [7] shows that it is sometimes possible to enhance diversity without loss of query similarity. An approach to enhancing diversity based on the idea of *similarity layers* is described. Very briefly, a set of cases, ranked by their similarity to the target query, can be partitioned into similarity layers, such that all cases in a given layer have the same similarity value to the query. To select a set of k diverse cases, the lowest similarity layer that contributes cases to the SRS is identified and a subset of cases from this layer is selected for inclusion in the final recommended set; all cases in higher similarity layers are automatically included. Cases are selected from this lowest similarity layer using an optimal diversity maximizing algorithm. This approach has the ability to improve diversity while at the same time fully preserving the similarity of cases to the user query. However, the diversity improvements obtained are typically less than those achieved by the bounded greedy algorithm. An alternative, and more flexible, diversity enhancing approach is also introduced in [9] based on the analogous notion of *similarity intervals* and the selection of cases from the *rightmost* similarity interval that contributes cases to the SRS; all cases in a given similarity interval are within a specific similarity of the query. The advantage of this approach is that it can achieve greater diversity improvements by relaxing the constraint that query similarity must be preserved. Query similarity is reduced but within a tolerance level defined by α, the width of the similarity intervals.

It is also worth noting that a retrieval technique may not be designed to explicitly enhance diversity but may nonetheless have a beneficial effect by its very nature. *Order-based retrieval* is a good example of such a technique [2]. It is based on the idea that the relative similarities of cases to a query of *ideal* feature values is just one way of ordering a set of cases for recommendation. Order-based retrieval constructs an ordering relation from the query provided by the user and applies this relation to the case-base, returning the k cases at the top of the ordering. The order relation is constructed from the composition of a set of canonical operators for constructing partial orders based on the feature types that make up the user query. The essential point to note is that an empirical evaluation of order-based retrieval demonstrates that it has an inherent ability to enhance the diversity of a set of retrieval results; that is, the cases at the top of the ordering tend to be more diverse than an equivalent set of cases ranked by their pure similarity to the user query (see [2] for further details).

All of the above techniques have been shown to improve the diversity of a single set of recommendations while preserving the similarity of these recommendations to the query to a lesser or greater extent. In other words, using the above techniques it is possible to increase the diversity of a given recommendation set in a single recommendation cycle. However, there has been no attempt to assess the implications of such diversity-enhancing methods across the multiple recommendation cycles that make up the dialog of a conversational recommender system. In particular, most of the above techniques operate by eliminating certain cases from the recommended set: cases that would otherwise have been selected on the basis of their similarity to the user query; cases that are not diverse relative to others that have been selected. If one of these cases happens to be the ideal target case for the user, or a case that may lead more directly to the ideal target, then the efficiency of the conversational recommender may be compromised.

3 Diversity Enhancement in Comparison-Based Recommendation

Comparison-based recommendation is a generic framework for conversational recommender systems that emphasises the roles of case selection, user feedback, and query modification during navigation by proposing. Although initially comparison-based recommendation was proposed as a framework for investigating similarity-based recommenders utilising pure preference-based feedback, it is in fact sufficiently generic to accommodate a range of different recommendation strategies and feedback types. We will describe how it can be adapted to incorporate diversity-enhancing selection techniques such as those described above. Crucially, however, we will also describe an important new technique that introduces diversity into the recommendation process in a more selective way by judging whether it is appropriate or not for a given recommendation cycle.

3.1   Comparison-Based Recommendation

The basic comparison-based recommendation algorithm (Fig. 1) describes an iterative process that starts with an initial user query and terminates when the user is satisfied with one of the recommendations proposed. During each iteration, or recommendation cycle, a set of k cases (or items) are chosen according to some selection mechanism, feedback is provided by the user based on their preference for a given case, and the current query is updated using this feedback.

As it stands the algorithm shown in Fig. 1 utilises simple similarity-based recommendation with preference-based feedback, in which the user indicates a simple preference for one of k recommended cases. Moreover, on the basis of this feedback the user query is replaced with the preferred case for the next recommendation cycle; in previous work we have described and evaluated a range of more sophisticated query revision strategies [4,5]. In addition we have also shown how to adapt comparison-based recommendation to use critiquing as a form of feedback and these modifications are shown in Fig. 2.

3.2   Uniform Diversity Enhancement

It is straightforward to adapt the similarity-based comparison-based recommendation methods to incorporate diversity-enhancing techniques by updating the *ItemRecommend* function. For example, in Fig. 3, we show how the bounded greedy method [12] can be used to update this function when preference-based feedback is used; a similar modification can be made for critiquing. Using this modification we can implement conversational recommender systems that use preference-based or critiquing as a form of user feedback, and that give consideration to query similarity and recommendation diversity during each recommendation cycle. It is vital to note that these adaptations introduce diversity in a uniform manner into each and every recommendation cycle - and in Fig. 3 we set $\alpha = 0.5$ to balance the weight of similarity and diversity during selection.

3.3   Selective Diversity Enhancement

The value of increasing the diversity of the cases in a given recommendation cycle is that it allows for a broader set of alternatives to be presented to the end user. This is likely to be useful at certain stages during the recommendation dialog. For example, if the user's requirements are unclear then presenting a diverse set of cases allows the recommender to cover a number of different points in the

```
1.   define Comparison-Based-Recommend(q, CB, k)
2.   begin
3.     do
4.        R ← ItemRecommend(q, CB, k)
5.        i_p ← UserReview(R, CB)
6.        Q ← QueryRevise(q, i_p, R)
7.     until UserAccepts(i_p)
8.   end


9.   define ItemRecommend(q, CB, k)
10.  begin
11.     CB' ← sort cases in CB in decreasing order of their sim to q
12.     R ← top k items in CB'
13.     return R
14.  end


15.  define UserReview(R, CB)
16.  begin
17.     i_p ← user's preferred case from R
18.     CB ← CB - R
19.     return i_p
20.  end


21.  define QueryRevise(q, i_p, R)
22.  begin
23.     R' ← R - {i_p}
24.     q ← i_p
25.     return q
26.  end
```

Fig. 1. The Comparison-Based Recommendation algorithm using simple similarity-based retrieval with preference-based feedback.

```
1.   define ItemRecommend(q, CB, c, k)
2.   begin
3.      CB' ← {i ∈ CB | Satisfies(i,c)}
4.      CB'' ← sort CB' in by decreasing sim to q
5.      R ← top k items in CB''
6.      return R
7.   end


8.   define UserReview(R, CB)
9.   begin
10.     i_p ← user's preferred case from R
11.     c ← user critique for some f ∈ i_p
12.     CB ← CB - R
13.     return <i_p,c>
14.  end
```

Fig. 2. Modifications to the Comparison-Based Recommendation algorithm for use with critiquing.

```
1.   define ItemRecommend(q, CB, k)
2.   begin
3.     α = 0.5
4.     R ← BoundedGreedySelection (q, CB, k, b, α)
5.     return R
6.   end


7.   define BoundedGreedySelection (q, CB, k, b, α)
8.   begin
9.     CB' := bk items in CB that are most similar to q
10.    R := {}
11.    For j := 1 to k
12.      Sort CB' by Quality(q,i,R) for each case i in CB'
13.      R  := R + First(CB')
14.      CB' := CB' - First(CB')
15.    endFor
16.    return R
17.  end

… where Quality(q,i,R) = α.Sim(q,i)+(1- α)RelDiv(i,R)
```

Fig. 3. Adapting the similarity-based Comparison-Based Recommendation algorithm to incorporate diversity-enhancement techniques.

recommendation space in the hope that one will be a fair match for the user's needs. Indeed similar techniques are used by sales assistants in real-world sales dialogs. When a customer's needs are unclear the sales assistant will present a diverse set of options to try and focus in on a particular type of product. However, as the user's needs become more refined the sales assistant will tend to switch their recommendation strategy, suggesting products that are as similar as possible to the user's known requirements as they home in on the right' region of the product space.

These observations motivate the need for a more sophisticated recommendation strategy, one that adapts its use of similarity and diversity depending on whether the recommender has focused in on the right region of the recommendation space. If the current recommendation focus appears to be correct then a similarity-based strategy is appropriate in order to refine the recommendations in the region of the target item. If the focus appears to be incorrect then recommendation diversity can be increased in order to broaden the search. The trick is how to determine whether or not the recommender is correctly focused.

Adaptive Selection is an attempt to produce a more sophisticated recommendation strategy that is capable of adjusting the balance of similarity and diversity during each recommendation cycle. It takes advantage of the key idea that it is possible to determine whether or not the recommender is correctly focused by determining whether the recent recommendations represent an improvement on those made in the previous cycle. This is achieved by making two modifications to the basic comparison-based recommendation technique. First, instead of making k new recommendations in each new cycle, the current preference case (or the critiqued case) is added to $k-1$ new recommendations; we refer to this as *carrying the preference* (CP). On its own this modification introduces redundancy, in the sense that a previously seen case is repeated in one or more

```
1.    define ItemRecommend(q, CB, k, i_p, i_{p-1})
2.    begin
3.       if(i_p != null) && (i_p == i_{p-1})
4.          R` ← ReFocus(q, CB, k-1)
5.       else
6.          R` ← ReFine(q, CB, k-1)
7.       R ← R`+ i_p
8.       return R
9.    end

10.   define ReFine(q, CB, k)
11.   begin
12.      CB' ← sort CB in decreasing order of their sim to q
13.      R ← top k items in CB'
14.      return R
15.   end

16.   define ReFocus(q, CB, k, i_p, i_{p-1})
17.   begin
18.      α = 0.5
19.      CB' ← sort CB in decreasing order acc to Equation 2
20.      return BoundedGreedySelection(q, CB, k, b, α)
21.   end
```

Fig. 4. Adapting the similarity-based Comparison-Based Recommendation algorithm for the 'adaptive selection' technique with preference-based feedback.

future cycles. However, including the previous preference makes it possible to avoid the problems that ordinarily occur when none of the newly recommended cases are relevant to the user; the user can simply reselect the carried preference case instead of being forced to follow a less relevant recommendation.

More importantly, CP allows us to judge the focus of the recommender. If the user prefers (or critiques) a case other than the carried preference, then it must be because it is closer to the target, and thus positive progress has been made. In this situation diversity is not warranted and the emphasis should be on similarity in the next recommendation cycle. If, however, the user prefers the carried preference case then it suggests that the other $k - 1$ cases are less relevant than the carried case, and thus that the recommender has failed to make positive progress towards the target. In this situation two things happen. First, diversity is introduced into the next recommendation cycle. And secondly, during the selection of the new cases for the next recommendation cycle, the dissimilarity of these candidate cases to the rejected cases is taken into account. The basic idea is to prioritise cases that are not only similar to the query, but also dissimilar from the rejected cases. This is achieved by using the formula given below in Equation 2, where c is a candidate case, c_p is the current preferred case, and C' is the set of $k - 1$ rejected cases.

$$SimDissim(c, c_p, C') = \frac{Sim(c, c_p) + \sum_{\forall c_i \in C'} (1 - Sim(c, c_i))}{k} \qquad (2)$$

The algorithm components in Fig. 4 are the modifications needed to implement adaptive selection in comparison-based recommendation with preference-based feedback. The basic change is that the *ItemRecommend* function must first check whether the carried preference case (i_{p-1}) has been selected by the user as their preference (i.e. $i_{p-1} = i_p$). If it has then the *Refocus* function is called to select a set of $k - 1$ diverse cases for the next cycle; they will be added to the preference case to make up the k cases for the next cycle. If, on the other hand, the carried preference has not been selected (i.e. $i_{p-1} \neq i_p$) then the *Refine* function is called to help the recommender home in on the region of this recent preference in the hope that this region is occupied by the ideal target case. Once again, directly analogous modifications can be made when critiquing is the form of feedback used.

4   Evaluation

So far we have argued for the potential advantages of incorporating diversity enhancing selection techniques into conversational recommender systems. However, we have also argued against the naive use of such techniques - where diversity is enhanced in each and every recommender cycle - pointing out that such strategies are likely to lead to protracted recommendation dialogs in some circumstances. In response we have forwarded the adaptive selection technique as a more selective use of diversity that is likely to improve recommendation efficiency. We test these claims in this section by empirically evaluating the performance of similarity-based and diversity-enhanced recommendation techniques on a number of standard data-sets.

4.1   Setup

Algorithms. We wish to test three basic conversational recommendation strategies: (1) SIM - a pure similarity-based recommender that serves as a benchmark; (2) DIV - a recommender that adopts the uniform diversity enhancing technique described above; and (3) AS - an equivalent recommender that adopts the adaptive selection technique. In addition, we wish to test these recommender systems using two different types of user feedback: preference-based feedback and critiquing. This gives six different recommender systems to test - SIM, DIV, and AS with preference-based feedback and SIM, DIV and AS with critiquing - each implemented using the comparison-based recommendation framework.

Data-Sets. The familiar *Travel* case-base contains 1024 cases, each describing a specific vacation in terms of features such as *location, duration, accommodation, price* etc. The *Whiskey* case-base ([6]) contains a set of 552 cases, each describing a particular Scotch whiskey in terms of features such as *distillery, age, proof, sweetness, flavour, finish* etc.

Methodology. Using a leave-one-out methodology, each case (*base*) in a case-base is temporarily removed and used in two ways. First it serves as the basis for a set of queries constructed by taking random subsets of item features. Here, different numbers's of features are extracted for different queries and, in general, queries with more features are *easier to solve* than queries with few features (see below). Second, we select the case that is most similar to the original base. These cases serve as the recommendation *targets* for the experiments. Thus, the base represents the ideal query for a user, the generated query is the initial query that the user provides to the recommender, and the target is the best available case for the user based on their ideal. Each generated query is a test problem for the recommender, and in each recommendation cycle the users preference is assumed to be the case that is most similar to the known target case. Preference-based or critiquing is applied to this preference case as appropriate; in the case of the latter, a random critique is applied to the preferred case in each cycle. Finally, in our evaluation we set the recommendation window size k to be 3, being the most appropriate number of items to expect a shopper to decide between [10].

Test Queries. For each data set, three different groups of queries are generated of varying degrees of difficulty (*easy, moderate, difficult*); difficulty is based on the number of cycles required by SIM with preference-based feedback.

4.2   Recommendation Efficiency

Perhaps the most basic test of a conversational recommender system concerns its recommendation efficiency [8]; that is, the length of the recommendation dialog for a typical query. Dialog length can be measured in terms of the number of cycles, or the number of unique cases presented, during the dialog. As such, to test recommendation efficiency the leave-one-out method outlined above is used for each query from both data sets across the three recommenders and the average number of cycles and unique items presented to the user are measured.

Results. The results for Travel and Whiskey are summarised in Figs. 5 and 6; in each case graph (a) and (b) relate to preference-based feedback and (c)and (d) relate to critiquing. Graphs (a) and (c) measure efficiency in terms of unique cases - the cycles data has been omitted for space reasons - but graphs (b) and (d) include both unique cases and cycles information in terms of the percentage benefit enjoyed by DIV and AS methods relative to the SIM benchmark.

Analysis. A number of issues are clarified by these results. Firstly, a significant efficiency benefit is enjoyed by DIV and AS, when compared to SIM, in both data-sets, across all query types, and for both types of feedback. For example, using preference-based feedback in Travel, for moderate queries, the SIM method presents the user with an average of about 100 unique cases before the target case is located. By comparison, the DIV method requires only about 53 cases and the AS method requires only 24 cases. Using critiquing in Travel, the equivalent results for SIM, DIV and AS are 40, 35 and 19, respectively. The corresponding relative benefits are shown in Fig. 5(c) for Travel with DIV experiencing a reduction in unique cases of 47% with preference-based feedback but

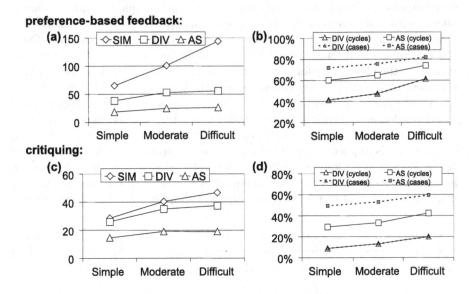

Fig. 5. Efficiency results for the *Travel* dataset using preference-based feedback (a & b) and critiquing (c & d). Graphs (a) and (c) measure efficiency in terms of unique cases. Graphs (b) and (d) include both unique cases and cycles information in terms of the percentage benefit enjoyed by DIV and AS methods relative to the SIM benchmark.

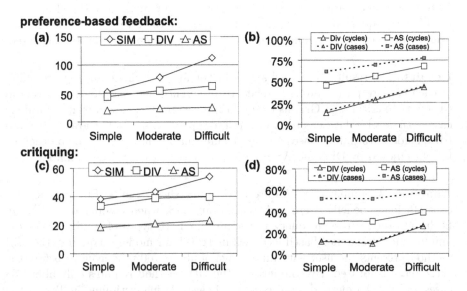

Fig. 6. Efficiency results for the *Whiskey* dataset for preference-based feedback (a & b) and critiquing (c & d).

only 13% for critiquing, relative to SIM. However, AS experiences corresponding reductions of 76% and 53% relative to SIM; similar benefits are presented in terms of the reduction in cycles. Comparable results are also presented in Figs. 5(a-c) for the Whiskey data-set. These results prove that there is a benefit to introducing diversity into conversational recommender systems, but they also show that the straightforward DIV approach is suboptimal compared to AS. Indeed, in both data-sets, the recommenders that employ critiquing enjoy only a limited efficiency improvment (<26%) when using the DIV method, compared to SIM. In contrast, the more sophisticated AS method displays a much greater efficiency advantage, achieving maximum efficiency improvments in excess of 75% (in terms of unique cases) in both data-sets for preference-based feedback, and up to 60% in both data-sets for critiquing. It is also worth highlighting how the efficiency benefits enjoyed by DIV and AS, relative to SIM, are generally increasing with query difficulty in both data-sets and using both types of feedback.

4.3   Preference Tolerance

The above evaluation assumes that the recommendation dialog ends when the pre-determined target case is selected by the user. This is analogous to a user seeking out a very specific case. In reality users are likely to be more flexible in their acceptance criteria, often tolerating cases that are close to, but not an exact match for, their ideal target. To test this we repeat the above experiment but instead of terminating a recommendation dialog when the ideal target has been found, it is terminated once a case is found that is within a specific similarity threshold of the target. We test similarity thresholds from 60% to 100%; 100% corresponds to the previous setup where the dialog terminates with the optimal target case.

Results. The results for Travel and Whiskey are summarised in Figs. 7 and 8; in each figure, graphs (a) and (b) relate to preference-based feedback, while (c) and (d) relate to critiquing. Also the graphs only present the results for queries of moderate difficulty; the results for the simple and advanced queries are broadly similar but omitted, once again, for space-saving reasons.

Analysis. The results are clear. The performance advantages enjoyed by DIV and by AS, relative to SIM, are once again found under less stringent success conditions. For example, in Travel with preference-based feedback, for moderate queries, we find that, on average, SIM expects users to look at about 61 unique cases at the 60% similarity threshold (compared to 100 cases at the 100% threshold). In comparison, under the same conditions, DIV and AS require the user to examine only 31 and 18 cases, respectively (see Fig. 7(a)), representing a reduction of about 49% for DIV and 71% for AS, relative to SIM (see Fig. 7(b)). As the similarity threshold increases, so too does the number of unique cases that the

preference-based feedback:

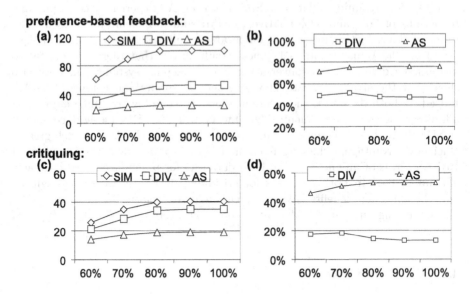

Fig. 7. Preference tolerance results for the *Travel* dataset. Graphs (a) and (b) relate to preference-based feedback, while (c) and (d) relate to critiquing. Graphs (b) and (d) summarise the percentage benefit (in terms of the relative reduction of unique cases) enjoyed by DIV and AS methods relative to the SIM benchmark.

preference-based feedback:

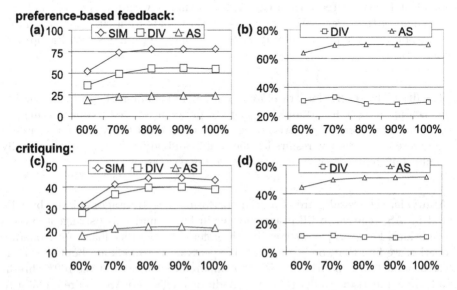

Fig. 8. Preference tolerance results for the *Whiskey* dataset. Graphs (a-d) represent the results described above for this dataset.

user must examine before locating a satisfactory one. Interestingly, while the relative benefit enjoyed by DIV remains relatively constant for changing similarity thresholds, we find that the AS benefit is actually increasing with the similarity threshold. In other words, the ability of AS to improve upon the efficiency of SIM (or indeed DIV) increases as the success criterion becomes more stringent. These results for Travel with preference-based feedback are mirrored by equivalent results for Travel with critiquing (Fig. 7(a-d)). Likewise, the Whiskey results show a similar pattern (Fig. 8(a-d)).

4.4 Conclusions

In this paper we set out to examine the role of diversity as part of the selection mechanism used in various kinds of conversational recommender systems. We highlighted that although some recent research had motivated the use of diversity as part of the recommendation process, so far only very limited evaluation work has been conducted, particularly when it comes to testing the value of diversity across the many cycles of a typical conversational recommender system.

In this paper we have demonstrated that, in general, there is a significant advantage to be gained from introducing diversity into each cycle of the recommendation process. Experiments with a number of complex case-bases show that even a simple uniform approach to introducing diversity has the potential to significantly enhance the efficiency of a conversational recommender system that utilises either preference-based or critiquing forms of feedback. For example, introducing diversity has the potential to reduce the number of unique cases that a user must examine by up to 60% in the case of preference-based feedback and by up to 20% in the case of critiquing.

However, the key contribution of this work is the idea that, powerful and valuable as diversity may be as a key selection constraint, it may not be warranted during every recommendation cycle. Indeed, increasing diversity may result in a loss in recommendation efficiency if the required case is eliminated from the recommended set by the diversity constraint. Accordingly, we have described a novel approach to case selection, called adaptive selection. Our approach takes advantage of similarity and diversity in a more intelligent manner, by determining when best to increase selection diversity and when best to focus on query similarity. Moreover, we have shown that this approach enjoys significant performance improvements over standard similarity-based recommenders and the more traditional (uniform) diversity enhancing techniques mentioned above. For example, adaptive selection can reduce the number of unique cases that a user must examine by up to 80% in the case of preference-based feedback and by up to 60% in the case of critiquing.

To conclude then: we have clarified the role of diversity as a primary selection constraint in conversational recommender systems. Diversity is an important selection constraint. And it can be used to more efficiently guide the recommendation process in many different varieties of conversation recommender systems, especially those that employ preference-based or critiquing as their primary forms of feedback. However, its proper use must be fine-tuned according to the progress being made by the recommender. If the recommender system appears to be close to the target case then diversity should be limited to avoid missing this case. But if the recommender system is not correctly focused then diversity can be used to help refocus the recommender more effectively. The adaptive selection technique is capable of fine-tuning the use of diversity in this way and has the potential to have a major impact on the development of more efficient conversation of recommender systems going forward.

References

1. D.W. Aha, L.A. Breslow, and H. Muñoz-Avila. Conversational case-based reasoning. *Applied Intelligence*, 14:9–32, 2000.
2. D. Bridge. Diverse Product Recommendations using an Expressive Language for Case Retreival. In S. Craw and A. Preece, editors, *Proceedings of the Sixth European Conference on Case-Based Reasoning (ECCBR 2002)*, pages 42–57. Springer, 2002. Aberdeen, Scotland.
3. R. Burke. Knowledge-based Recommender Systems. *Encyclopedia of Library and Information Systems*, 69(32), 2000.
4. L. McGinty and B. Smyth. Comparison-Based Recommendation. In S. Craw and A. Preece, editors, *Proceedings of the Sixth European Conference on Case-Based Reasoning (ECCBR 2002)*, pages 575–589. Springer, 2002. Aberdeen, Scotland.
5. L. McGinty and B. Smyth. Deep Dialogue vs Casual Conversation in Recommender Systems. In F. Ricci and B. Smyth, editors, *Proceedings of the Workshop on Personalization in eCommerce at the Second International Conference on Adaptive Hypermedia and Web-Based Systems (AH 2002)*, pages 80–89. Springer, 2002. Universidad de Malaga, Malaga, Spain.
6. L. McGinty and B. Smyth. The Power of Suggestion. In *Proceedings of the International Joint Conference on Artificial Intelligence (IJCAI 2003)*. Morgan-Kaufmann, 2003. Acapulco, Mexico.
7. D. McSherry. Increasing Recommendation Diversity Without Loss of Similarity. In *Proceedings of the Sixth UK Workshop on Case-Based Reasoning*, pages 23–31, 2001. Cambridge, UK.
8. D. McSherry. Minimizing dialog length in interactive case-based reasoning. In B. Nebel, editor, *Proceedings of the Seventeenth International Joint Conference on Artificial Intelligence (IJCAI 2001)*, pages 993–998. Morgan Kaufmann, 2001. Seattle, Washington.
9. D. McSherry. Diversity-Conscious Retrieval. In S. Craw and A. Preece, editors, *Proceedings of the Sixth European Conference on Case-Based Reasoning (ECCBR 2002)*, pages 219–233. Springer, 2002. Aberdeen, Scotland.
10. H. Shimazu. ExpertClerk : Navigating Shoppers' Buying Process with the Combination of Asking and Proposing. In Bernhard Nebel, editor, *Proceedings of the Seventeenth International Joint Conference on Artificial Intelligence (IJCAI 2001)*, pages 1443–1448. Morgan Kaufmann, 2001. Seattle, Washington, USA.
11. B. Smyth and M. Keane. Adaptation-Guided Retrieval: Questioning the Similarity Assumption in Reasoning. *Artificial Intelligence*, 102:249–293, 1998.
12. B. Smyth and P. McClave. Similarity v's Diversity. In D. Aha and I. Watson, editors, *Proceedings of the International Conference on Case-Based Reasoning (ICBR 2001)*, pages 347–361. Springer, 2001.

Similarity and Compromise

David McSherry

School of Computing and Information Engineering, University
of Ulster, Coleraine BT52 1SA, Northern Ireland
dmg.mcsherry@ulst.ac.uk

Abstract. A common cause of retrieval failure in case-based reasoning (CBR) approaches to product recommendation is that the retrieved cases, usually those that are most similar to the target query, are not sufficiently representative of *compromises* that the user may be prepared to make. We present a new approach to retrieval in which similarity and compromise play complementary roles, thereby increasing the likelihood that one of the retrieved cases will be acceptable to the user. We also show how the approach can be extended to address the requirements of domains in which the user is not just seeking a single item that closely matches her query, but would like to be informed of all items that are likely to be of interest.

1 Introduction

Ideally, the ability of a recommender system to deliver a successful recommendation should be limited only by the available products and the user's willingness to *compromise*. However, a common cause of retrieval failure in CBR approaches to product recommendation is that the retrieved cases, usually those that are most similar to the target query, are not sufficiently representative of compromises that the user may be prepared to make. One reason for this is that the number of cases that can be presented to the user is necessarily restricted in practice [2,5,15]. Another problem is that the most similar cases also tend to be very similar to each other [3,10,15]. For example, it is not unusual in a small retrieval set for all the retrieved products to be made by the same manufacturer. If the user is not prepared to accept this manufacturer, then the system has failed to retrieve an acceptable case. While the user may be prepared to pay more than she intended for the manufacturer she prefers, there is no case in the retrieval set that offers this compromise.

Several authors have questioned the assumption that the most similar case is always the one that is most acceptable or useful [6,14,15]. There is also increasing awareness of the need for recommender systems to offer users a better choice of alternatives than is possible by the k-NN strategy of retrieving the k most similar cases [10,11,15]. In this paper, we present a new approach to retrieval in which the similarity assumption is replaced by a weaker assumption that we refer to as the *compromise* assumption.

The Compromise Assumption. *If a given case C_1 is more similar to the target query than another case C_2, and differs from the target query in a subset of the attributes in which C_2 differs from the target query, then C_1 is more acceptable than C_2.*

K.D. Ashley and D.G. Bridge (Eds.): ICCBR 2003, LNAI 2689, pp. 291–305, 2003.
© Springer-Verlag Berlin Heidelberg 2003

In the personal computer (PC) domain, for example, a case that differs from the user's query only in monitor size is likely to be more acceptable than a less similar case that differs from her query in monitor size and price.

The *compromise-driven* approach to retrieval (CDR) on which we focus in this paper is a special case of a more general approach called *coverage-optimised* retrieval which aims to ensure that for any case that is acceptable to the user, the retrieval set contains a case that is as good or better in some objective sense and so also likely to be acceptable [13]. The compromise assumption is based on one of several *dominance criteria* according to which a given case might be considered as good or better than another case in coverage-optimised retrieval. As we shall see, the CDR retrieval set is constructed in such a way that for any case that is acceptable to the user, the retrieval set contains a case that is more acceptable, or at least equally acceptable, according to the compromise assumption.

A potential problem faced by CDR and other algorithms that aim to offer the user a better choice of alternatives is that in many domains the user is not just seeking a single item that closely matches her query but would like to be informed of all items that are likely to be of interest [10,11]. Typically in such domains, the recommended items (e.g. jobs, rental apartments, bargain holidays) are available for a limited period or sought in competition with other users. A similar problem arises when the recommended items are books, films, or holiday destinations that the user has already read, seen, or visited and would prefer not to repeat.

To offer the user the best possible choice while keeping the size of the retrieval set within reasonable limits, the CDR retrieval set never includes two cases that have identical descriptions or differ from the target query in the same way, a strategy that is clearly at odds with the particular requirements of such domains. For example, another film with the same director, genre, and leading actor as a retrieved case is unlikely to be included in the CDR retrieval set, but may be exactly what the user is looking for.

As we show in the following section, this problem is addressed in CDR by providing the user with immediate access to cases for which a recommended case acts as a *representative* case without having to await the retrieval of additional cases. Other benefits of CDR include the ability to explain why cases are recommended and a new approach to query refinement in which solution quality is held constant during the refinement process.

In Section 2 we describe the complementary roles of similarity and compromise in CDR and how query refinement is supported in the approach. In Section 3, we present an implementation of CDR in a recommender system prototype called *First Case*. In Section 4, we present an empirical evaluation of CDR in comparison with *k*-NN. Related work is discussed in Section 5 and our conclusions are presented in Section 6.

2 Compromise-Driven Retrieval

After giving a brief overview of CDR, we describe the complementary roles of similarity and compromise in the retrieval process, and examine some important properties of the CDR retrieval set.

2.1 Overview of CDR

Although similarity plays an important role in the retrieval process, CDR also assesses each case in terms of the *compromises* it involves; that is, the attributes with respect to which it fails to satisfy the preferences of the user. For example, a PC might satisfy the preferences of the user in terms of price, memory, and processor speed but not in terms of monitor size or manufacturer. In CDR, two cases are deemed to be *alike* if they involve the same compromises. If two or more cases are alike in this way, then only the one that is most similar to the target query is included in the retrieval set. Thus each case in the CDR retrieval set acts as a *representative* for a group of like cases. Cases for which a recommended case acts as a representative case are held in a set of *reference* cases to which the user has immediate access without having to await the retrieval of additional cases.

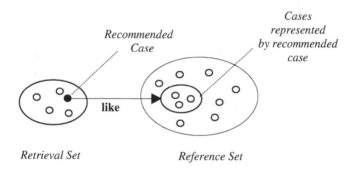

Fig. 1. The retrieval set and reference set in CDR

As Fig. 1 illustrates, cases that involve the same compromises as a recommended case are immediately available in the *reference set* that CDR constructs in addition to the retrieval set. This feature is likely to be of particular benefit in domains (e.g. rental apartments, jobs, films) in which the user would like to be informed of all items that are likely to be of interest. Immediate access to alternatives that involve the same compromises, if any, as a recommended case is also useful when only some of the user's preferences are specified in her initial query. In this way, a user who is prepared to accept the compromises associated with a recommended case may discover cases that offer improvements with respect to *non-query* attributes.

As Fig. 2 illustrates, the user can also ask to see cases that offer *specific* improvements relative to a recommended case. In the PC domain, for example, the user can ask to see cases that are "like this but with more memory". This form of *query refinement* differs from existing approaches [4,5,7,8,9] in that a new query is not initiated in response to a requested improvement or *tweak*. Instead, only cases for which the recommended case acts as a representative case are presented in response to a tweak. As these cases are already available in the CDR reference set, there is again no need for the retrieval of additional cases.

Another distinctive feature of our approach is that solution quality is held constant in that any case presented in response to a tweak must satisfy the user's preferences with respect to the same attributes as the recommended case; that is, it cannot involve additional compromises. In existing approaches, there is no guarantee that a case that satisfies a tweak will not be *less* acceptable to the user in terms of the compromises it involves. However, a trade-off that our approach shares with existing query-refinement techniques is that an improvement in one attribute can often be gained only at the expense of *similarity* with respect to other attributes [5].

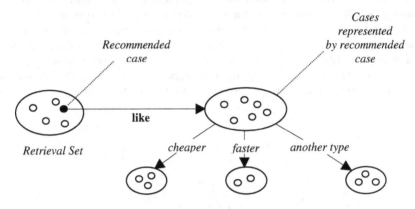

Fig. 2. Query refinement in CDR

2.2 Similarity Measures

Often in recommender systems, retrieval is based on an incomplete query Q in which preferred values are specified for a subset A_Q of the case attributes A. We will refer to $|A_Q|$ as the *length* of the query. The similarity of a given case C to a target query Q is typically defined as:

$$Sim(C, Q) = \frac{\sum_{a \in A_Q} w_a \, sim_a(C, Q)}{\sum_{a \in A_Q} w_a} \tag{1}$$

where for each $a \in A$, w_a is a numeric weight representing the importance of a and $sim_a(C, Q)$ is a local measure of the similarity of $\pi_a(C)$, the value of a in C, to $\pi_a(Q)$, the preferred value of a.

In many e-commerce domains, there are attributes whose values most users would prefer to maximise (e.g. the processor speed of a PC) or minimise (e.g. price). We will refer to these as *more-is-better* (MIB) and *less-is-better* (LIB) attributes respectively and assume that the value specified by the user is a preferred minimum in the case of a MIB attribute, or a preferred maximum in the case of a LIB attribute. Often in practice, the local similarity measure for a MIB attribute assigns the maximum similarity score to any case whose value equals or exceeds the preferred minimum [1,16,17]. However, a potential drawback of this approach is that the system may be unable to distinguish between two cases even when one is clearly superior. In the PC domain, for example, if the user specifies 1.5 GHz as the preferred minimum in terms of processor speed, then the system will be unable to distinguish between two alternatives that are equal in other respects but offer processor speeds of 1.7 GHz and 1.8 GHz.

We have similar reservations about local similarity measures that assign the maximum similarity score to any case whose value for a LIB attribute is less than the preferred maximum. To address this issue, our approach to assessing the similarity of a given case with respect to a MIB or LIB attributes recognises that not all values which exceed a preferred minimum, or fall below a preferred maximum, are likely to be equally preferred. For MIB attributes, the similarity measure used in our experiments is:

$$sim_a(C,Q) = \frac{\pi_a(C) - \min(a)}{\max(a) - \min(a)} \tag{2}$$

where $\min(a)$ and $\max(a)$ are the minimum and maximum values of a in the case library. Our similarity measure for LIB attributes is:

$$sim_a(C,Q) = \frac{\max(a) - \pi_a(C)}{\max(a) - \min(a)} \tag{3}$$

It is worth noting that we measure the similarity or *utility* of a case with respect to a MIB or LIB attribute in a way is that is independent of the target query. As we shall see, however, preferred minimum and maximum values specified by the user play an important role in CDR's ability to support compromise.

Of course, not all numeric attributes can be classified with certainty as MIB or LIB attributes. In the PC domain, for example, the largest available monitor may not be preferred because of the amount of desk space it occupies. Often the user has an ideal value in mind and would prefer a value that is as close as possible to that value. We will refer to such attributes as *nearer-is-better* (NIB) attributes. As usual in practice, we define the similarity of a given case C to a target query Q with respect to a NIB attribute to be:

$$sim_a(C,Q) = 1 - \frac{|\pi_a(C) - \pi_a(Q)|}{\max(a) - \min(a)} \tag{4}$$

As we have argued in previous work, insisting that the user specifies a single preferred value of each nominal attribute in her query may result in failure to retrieve the case that is most acceptable to the user [12]. We have also shown that similarity-based retrieval can be adapted to support more flexible queries in which the user can specify any number of preferred values of a nominal attribute. In the PC domain, for example, the user who is not interested in laptops can select *desktop* and *tower* as her preferred types of computer. Our treatment of nominal attributes in this paper is based on the approach proposed in [12]. That is, we assume that the user can specify any number of preferred values, and define the similarity of a given case C to a target query Q with respect to a nominal attribute to be:

$$sim_a(C,Q) = \max_{x \in \pi_a(Q)} losim_a(C,x) \tag{5}$$

where $\pi_a(Q)$ is the *set* of preferred values of a and for each $x \in \pi_a(Q)$, $losim_a(C, x)$ is a local measure of the similarity of $\pi_a(C)$, the value of a in C, to x.

2.3 The Role of Compromise

In the absence of a product that exactly matches the user's query, what matters is a recommender system's ability to support compromise by offering alternatives that may be acceptable to the user. As Burkhard [6] points out, compromises that the user may be prepared to make are often unrelated to the importance of the attributes in her query and cannot be predicted in advance. For example, even if the user considers price to be very important, she may be prepared to pay a little more for a product that satisfies her preferences with respect to other attributes.

In terms of the attribute types discussed in Section 2.2, a case may fail to satisfy the preferences of the user in one or more of the following ways:

- Its value for a nominal attribute may not be one of the preferred values
- Its value for a MIB attribute may be less than the preferred minimum
- Its value for a LIB attribute may be greater than the preferred maximum
- Its value for a NIB attribute may not be the ideal value

Often the user may be prepared to compromise only on certain attributes, so it is the *combination* of attributes in which a case differs from her query that matters and not just the number of attributes. For any case C and target query Q, we define:

$$compromises(C, Q) = \{a \in A_Q : \pi_a(C) \text{ fails to satisfy the preference of the user}\} \quad (6)$$

If two or more cases involve the same compromises, then only the one that is most similar to the target query is included in the CDR retrieval set. The aim is to ensure that all compromises are represented while keeping the size of the retrieval set within reasonable limits. Instead of being discarded, cases that involve the same compromises as a retrieved case are stored in the CDR reference set.

For any case C_1 in the CDR retrieval set we define:

$$like(C_1, Q) = \{C_2 : C_2 \neq C_1, compromises(C_2, Q) = compromises(C_1, Q)\} \quad (7)$$

That is, $like(C_1, Q)$ is the set of cases that involve the same compromises as C_1 and for which C_1 acts as a representative case. We can now define the CDR reference set for a target query Q as:

$$reference(Q) = \bigcup_{C \in rs(Q)} like(C, Q) \quad (8)$$

where $rs(Q)$ is the CDR retrieval set for Q.

2.4 The Retrieval Process

We are now in a position to describe how the retrieval set and reference set are constructed in CDR. In Fig. 3, *Candidates* is the list of candidates for addition to the retrieval set *RS*. Initially it contains all cases in the case library, in order of non-increasing similarity to the target query Q. We assume that if C_1, C_2 are cases of equal similarity to Q such that $compromises(C_1, Q) \subset compromises(C_2, Q)$ then C_1 is listed before C_2 in *Candidates*, thus ensuring the exclusion of C_2 from the retrieval set.

```
algorithm CDR(Q, Candidates, RS)
begin
  RS ← ϕ
  while |Candidates| > 0 do
  begin
     C₁ ← first(Candidates)
     RS ← {C₁} ∪ RS
     like(C₁, Q) ← {C₁}
     covered(C₁) ← {C₁}
     for all C₂ ∈ rest(Candidates) do
     begin
        if compromises(C₁, Q) ⊆ compromises(C₂, Q)
        then covered (C₁) ← {C₂} ∪ covered(C₁)
        if compromises(C₁, Q) = compromises(C₂, Q)
        then like(C₁, Q) ← {C₂} ∪ like(C₁, Q)
     end
     Candidates ← Candidates - covered(C₁)
  end
end
```

Fig. 3. Algorithm for compromise-driven retrieval

For each case C_1 that it adds to the retrieval set, CDR constructs the set of cases $like(C_1, Q)$ for which C_1 will act as a representative case. It also removes all cases C_2 such that $compromises(C_1, Q) \subseteq compromises(C_2, Q)$ from the list of candidate cases. Thus while cases that involve the same compromises as C_1 are held in the reference set, less similar cases that involve *additional* compromises are discarded.

2.5 The CDR Retrieval Set

An important property that CDR inherits from coverage-optimised retrieval, of which it is a specific instance, is that the retrieval set provides full *coverage* of the case library [13]. That is, for any case that is acceptable to the user, the retrieval set is guaranteed to contain a case that is as good or better in an objective sense and so also likely to be acceptable. The following theorem is a special case of a more general result for coverage-optimised retrieval.

Theorem 1. *For any case C_2 in the case library that is acceptable to the user, the CDR retrieval set contains a case C_1 which is more acceptable than C_2, or at least equally acceptable, according to the compromise assumption.*

Proof. An acceptable case C_2, if any, can fail to be included in the CDR retrieval set only if there is already a case C_1 in the retrieval set such that $Sim(C_1, Q) \geq Sim(C_2, Q)$

and *compromises*(C_1, Q) $\subseteq$ *compromises*(C_2, Q). According to the compromise assumption, C_1 is more acceptable than C_2, or at least equally acceptable.

The significance of this result is that according to the compromise assumption, CDR's ability to deliver a successful recommendation is limited only by the contents of the case library and the user's willingness to compromise. However, the chances of a successful recommendation can be maximised at the expense of cognitive load by presenting all items in the case library to the user. The size of the retrieval sets that a retrieval algorithm produces is thus an important factor in its ability to address the trade-off between satisfaction and cognitive load to which Branting [2] refers.

It follows from our analysis of retrieval-set size in coverage-optimised retrieval [13] that the maximum possible size of the CDR retrieval set for a given query Q is $2^{|A_Q|}$. In practice, the CDR retrieval set is usually much smaller. To illustrate this point, Fig. 4 shows the different ways in which a case can differ from a target query involving the attributes type, monitor, and price in the PC domain. If the most similar case differs from the target query only in monitor, then no case in the CDR retrieval set can differ from the target query in a set of attributes that includes monitor. Thus 4 of the 8 possible ways in which a case retrieved by CDR can differ from the target query are covered by the most similar case.

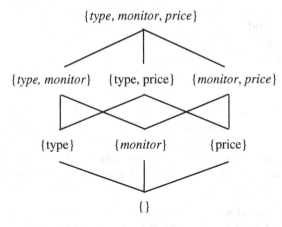

Fig. 4. Possible ways in which a case can differ from a query involving type, monitor, and price in the PC domain

It is worth noting that it is possible with the similarity measures used in our experiments for a case that involves compromise to be more similar to the target query than one that does not, for example if the former has an unusually low price.

The fact that CDR ranks the retrieved cases in order of non-increasing similarity provides a simple solution to the problem that arises when the number of retrieved cases exceeds the maximum permissible size of the retrieval set. In this situation, the cases presented to the user would be the first k cases in the CDR retrieval set. Similarly, when the user asks to see the cases for which a recommended case acts as a representative case, she can be shown the k most similar cases that involve the same compromises.

3 Recommendation in First Case

We now present an implementation of CDR in a recommender system prototype called First Case. The example dialogue in Fig. 5 is based on the PC case library [9], which contains the descriptions of 120 personal computers. Attributes in the case library and weights assigned to them in our experiments are type (8), price (7), manufacturer (6), processor (5), speed (4), monitor size (3), memory (2), and hard-disk size (1). Speed, memory, and hard-disk size are treated as MIB attributes, monitor size as a NIB attribute, and price as a LIB attribute. Minor editing in the interest of clarity includes the format of the user's query. Attributes of the retrieved cases, except manufacturer, are listed in the order: processor, speed, monitor size, type, memory, hard-disk size, and price. The similarity of each case to the user's query is shown in brackets.

First Case: Please enter your query.

User: processor = Intel Pentium, speed ≥ 1900, monitor size = 17, type = desktop or tower, price ≤ 1400

First Case: The following cases are recommended:

Case 38: Intel Pentium, 1700, 15, desktop, 512, 20, 799 (0.93)
Case 50: Intel Pentium, 1700, 17, desktop, 128, 20, 1138 (0.92)
Case 55: Intel Pentium, 1900, 17, desktop, 2000, 40, 1507 (0.90)

User: **why** 50

First Case: Case 50 differs from your query only in speed.

User: **why** 38

First Case: Case 38 differs from your query only in speed and monitor size. It is better than Case 50 in terms of memory and price.

User: **like** 55

First Case: The following cases also differ from your query only in price:

Case 46: Intel Pentium, 1900, 17, tower, 2000, 40, 1507 (0.90)
Case 86: Intel Pentium, 2200, 17, tower, 1024, 120, 2700 (0.82)
Case 75: Intel Pentium, 2200, 17, desktop, 1024, 120, 2700 (0.82)

User: **like** 50 **with more** memory

First Case: The following cases also differ from your query only in speed but have more memory than Case 50:

Case 48: Intel Pentium, 1800, 17, desktop, 256, 40, 1337 (0.91)
Case 39: Intel Pentium, 1800, 17, tower, 256, 40, 1337 (0.91)
Case 102: Intel Pentium, 1500, 17, tower, 256, 80, 1295 (0.89)

Fig. 5. Example recommendation dialogue

As the example dialogue illustrates, First Case can explain why any case is recommended. When the user asks why Case 50 is recommended, First Case explains that it differs from her query only in speed.

First Case can also explain why Case 38, which differs in speed and monitor size, is ranked higher than Case 50, which differs only in speed. Technically, the reason for Case 38 having a higher similarity score is its much lower price. As noted in Section 2.2, our similarity measure for LIB attributes does not assume all values that fall below the preferred maximum to be equally preferred. By way of explanation, First Case highlights the benefits that Case 38 offers in terms of price, one of the attributes in the user's query, and memory, not mentioned in the user's query but known to be a MIB attribute.

The example dialogue also shows how the user can view cases that involve the same compromises as a recommended case. When the user asks to see other cases like Case 55, she is shown three cases that also differ from her query only in price. While two of these alternatives have larger hard disks and faster processor speeds than Case 55, they have less memory and are considerably more expensive.

Finally, the user asks to see cases that are like Case 50 but with more memory. Only three of the five cases presented in response to this request are shown in the example dialogue. Though more expensive than Case 50, which accounts for their lower similarity, two offer faster speeds and larger hard disks as well as more memory. As noted in Section 2.1, solution quality is held constant in that the presented cases, like Case 50, also differ from the user's query only in speed. There may of course be other PCs in the case library that offer more memory than Case 50. However, by stating that the cases presented in response to the user's request also differ from her query only in speed, First Case avoids giving the impression that these are the only available PCs with additional memory.

4   Experimental Results

Following an evaluation of CDR in terms of retrieval-set size for full-length queries on a case library containing over 1,000 cases, we examine the number of cases for which a recommended case typically acts as a representative case in the PC case library [9]. Finally, we present an empirical evaluation of CDR in terms of its ability to support compromise.

4.1   Retrieval-Set Size

Our first experiment examines the size of the retrieval sets produced by CDR for full-length queries on the Travel case library (*www.ai-cbr.org*). This is a standard benchmark containing the descriptions of 1,024 holidays in terms of 8 attributes such as price, region, duration, and season. Our experimental design is based on a *leave-one-out* approach in which we temporarily remove each case from the case library, present its description as a query to a recommender system with retrieval based on CDR, and observe the size of the retrieval set.

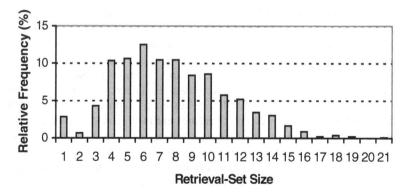

Fig. 6. Size of the CDR retrieval set for full-length queries on the Travel case library

Fig. 6 shows the relative frequency with which each retrieval-set size occurs over all 1,024 queries. Though reaching a maximum of 21 for one query, retrieval-set size is seldom more than 12, the maximum we observed for full-length queries in a similar experiment on the PC case library. The retrieval-set size that occurs with greatest frequency is 6, while the average number of retrieved cases is 7.7. Retrieval-set sizes in the range from 1 to 10 can be seen to account for nearly 80% of queries.

4.2   Cases Represented by a Recommended Case

Our second experiment examines how the number of cases represented by a recommended case in CDR is affected by query length on the PC case library [9]. Again using a leave-one-out approach, we temporarily remove each case from the case library, generate all possible queries of length from 1 to 8 from its description, and present each query to a recommender system with retrieval based on CDR. For each query, we observe the number of cases for which each case in the CDR retrieval set acts as a representative case; that is, the number of cases that involve the same compromises as the recommended case.

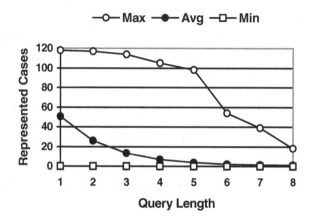

Fig. 7. Numbers of cases for which a recommended case acts as a representative case

For queries ranging in length from 1 to 8, Fig. 7 shows the maximum, average and minimum number of cases represented by a recommended case. It is interesting to note that the minimum number of represented cases is zero for all lengths of query. This means that for a query of any length, there may be no other case in the case library that involves the same compromises, if any, as a recommended case.

Although the average number of represented cases decreases with query length, it remains above 10 until query length reaches 4, a finding which highlights the importance of CDR's support for query refinement as a means of reducing cognitive load. As noted in Section 2.1, the user can ask to see cases that involve the same compromises as a recommended case but offer specific improvements.

For queries involving more than 5 attributes, each recommended case acts as a representative case for only one or two cases on average.

4.3 Supporting Compromise

We have seen that according to the compromise assumption, CDR's ability to deliver a successful recommendation is limited only by the contents of the case library and the user's willingness to compromise. Our final experiment examines how these factors affect CDR's ability to deliver successful recommendations in response to full-length queries on the Travel case library.

Benchmarks in our evaluation are provided by k-NN with $k = 1$, 3, and 30. In view of recent interest in the performance of retrieval algorithms when retrieval-set size is severely restricted [10,15], our evaluation also includes a modified version of CDR called 3-CDR in which the retrieval set is limited to a maximum size of 3. That is, if there are more than 3 cases in the CDR retrieval set, then all but the first 3 cases are discarded.

We assume in this experiment that there is a set of attributes on which the user is prepared to compromise and that she is prepared to accept any case that differs from her query only in these attributes, or in a subset of these attributes. It follows that CDR can fail to deliver a successful recommendation only if there is no such case in the case library. We measure the user's willingness to compromise in terms of the number of attributes on which she is prepared to compromise. Of course, users who are equally willing to compromise in this sense are likely to differ in the combination of attributes on which they are prepared to compromise. For example, there are $^{8}C_3 = 56$ possible combinations of 3 attributes on which the user may be prepared to compromise in a full-length query.

Given a set of 3 attributes on which the user is prepared to compromise, a successful recommendation is one in which the retrieval set contains a case that differs from the target query only in these attributes, or in a subset of these attributes. To obtain an overall success rate for users who are prepared to compromise on 3 attributes, we average the success rates over all combinations of 3 attributes. We similarly determine average success rates for users who are not prepared to compromise on any attribute and for numbers of compromises in the range from 1 to 8.

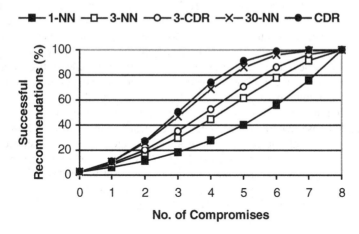

Fig. 8. Successful recommendations in CDR and k-NN for full-length queries on the Travel case library

Again we temporarily remove each case from the case library, now presenting its description as a query to a recommender system running each of the 5 retrieval algorithms in our evaluation. For each query, and each combination of attributes on which the user may be prepared to compromise, we observe which algorithms deliver successful recommendations. Average success rates for each algorithm are shown as percentages in Fig. 8.

In CDR, which we know to be optimal in terms of success rate as measured in this experiment, the user must be prepared to compromise on at least 3 attributes to have more than a 50% chance of a successful recommendation. To equal this chance of success in 1-NN, the user must be prepared to compromise on 6 attributes. It is interesting to note that increasing k from 1 to 3 considerably improves the performance of k-NN. However, with an average retrieval-set size of only 7.7 for full-length queries, CDR continues to outperform k-NN even for $k = 30$.

As might be expected, restricting the size of the CDR retrieval set to a maximum of 3 cases has a considerable effect on the algorithm's performance, reducing average success rates by up to 21%. On the other hand, 3-CDR gives better results than 3-NN for all numbers of compromises in the range from 1 to 7.

5   Related Work

Recently there has been considerable research interest in algorithms that combine measures of similarity and diversity in the retrieval process to achieve a better balance between these often conflicting properties of the retrieved cases [3,10,15]. A basic premise in the approach is that increasing diversity while minimising loss of similarity increases the likelihood that the retrieval set will include an acceptable case. While several authors have provided convincing arguments to support this hypothesis, evaluation of diversification techniques has tended to focus on their ability to address the trade-off between similarity and diversity.

The fact that the size of the retrieval set cannot be predicted in advance is a property that CDR shares with Bridge and Ferguson's *order-based* retrieval [3,4]. Featuring an expressive query language, the latter approach has been shown to be capable of delivering retrieval sets that are inherently diverse. However, there is no ranking of the retrieved cases in order of similarity in order-based retrieval, and so no obvious solution to the problem that arises when the number of retrieved cases exceeds the maximum permissible size of the retrieval set [3].

The techniques used in CDR to provide immediate access to cases for which a recommended case acts as a representative case are adapted from recommendation engineering, in which the user can access cases related to a recommended case by following links in a *retrieval network* [11]. CDR also bears some resemblance to recommendation engineering in the way the retrieval set is constructed, but tends to produce much smaller retrieval sets by excluding any case that is less similar than a retrieved case and involves additional compromises.

6 Conclusions

In terms of its ability to support compromise, a major weakness of similarity-based retrieval is that the retrieved cases are often very similar to each other and not sufficiently representative of compromises that the user may be prepared to make. In compromise-driven retrieval (CDR), similarity and compromise play complementary roles, thereby increasing the likelihood that one of the retrieved cases will be acceptable to the user. The compromise assumption on which CDR is based is weaker than the similarity assumption and therefore less likely to be contradicted by user behaviour. Also a special case of coverage-optimised retrieval [13], CDR ensures that for any case that is acceptable to the user, the retrieval set contains a case that is more acceptable, or at least equally acceptable, according to the compromise assumption.

Our empirical results confirm the superiority of CDR over k-NN in terms of its ability to support compromise. While the size of the CDR retrieval set cannot be predicted in advance, our results suggest that it tends to remain within reasonable limits even for full-length queries on a case library containing over 1,000 cases. In contrast to approaches in which retrieval is based purely on similarity, or on a combination of similarity and diversity measures [10,15], the reasons for including any case in the CDR retrieval set can easily be explained.

We have also shown how the approach can be extended to address the particular requirements of domains (e.g. jobs, rental apartments, films) in which the user is not just seeking a single item that closely matches her query, but would like to be informed of all items that are likely to be of interest. This is an issue that appears to be often neglected in retrieval algorithms [10,11]. Another contribution of the research presented is a new approach to query refinement in which solution quality, in terms of the compromises involved, is held constant during the refinement process. Though motivated primarily by the need to support compromise more effectively in recommender systems, the techniques we have presented in this paper may also be applicable in other areas of CBR that involve compromise such as configuration and design.

References

1. Bergmann, R., Breen, S., Göker, M., Manago, M., Wess, S.: Developing Industrial Case-Based Reasoning Applications: The INRECA Methodology. Springer-Verlag, Berlin Heidelberg New York (1999)

2. Branting, L.K..: Acquiring Customer Preferences from Return-Set Selections. In: Aha, D.W., Watson, I. (eds.) Case-Based Reasoning Research and Development. LNAI, Vol. 2080. Springer-Verlag, Berlin Heidelberg New York (2001) 59–73

3. Bridge, D., Ferguson, A.: Diverse Product Recommendations Using an Expressive Language for Case Retrieval. In: Craw, S., Preece, A. (eds.) Advances in Case-Based Reasoning. LNAI, Vol. 2416. Springer-Verlag, Berlin Heidelberg New York (2002) 43–57

4. Bridge, D., Ferguson, A.: An Expressive Query Language for Product Recommender Systems. Artificial Intelligence Review, 18 (2002) 269–307

5. Burke, R.: Interactive Critiquing for Catalog Navigation in E-Commerce. Artificial Intelligence Review, 18 (2002) 245–267

6. Burkhard, H.-D.: Extending Some Concepts of CBR – Foundations of Case Retrieval Nets. In: Lenz, M., Bartsch-Spörl, B., Burkhard, H.-D., Wess, S. (eds.) Case-Based Reasoning Technology. Springer-Verlag, Berlin Heidelberg New York (1998) 17–50

7. Hammond, K.J., Burke, R., Schmitt, K.: A Case-Based Approach to Knowledge Navigation. In: Leake, D.B. (ed.) Case-Based Reasoning: Experiences, Lessons & Future Directions. AAAI Press/MIT Press, Menlo Park, CA (1996) 125–136

8. Hurley, G., Wilson, D.C.: DubLet: An Online CBR System for Rental Property Recommendation. In: Aha, D.W., Watson, I. (eds.) Case-Based Reasoning Research and Development. LNAI, Vol. 2080. Springer-Verlag, Berlin Heidelberg New York (2001) 660–674

9. McGinty, L., Smyth, B.: Comparison-Based Recommendation. In: Craw, S., Preece, A. (eds.) Advances in Case-Based Reasoning. LNAI, Vol. 2416. Springer-Verlag, Berlin Heidelberg New York (2002) 575–589

10. McSherry, D.: Diversity-Conscious Retrieval. In: Craw, S., Preece, A. (eds.) Advances in Case-Based Reasoning. LNAI, Vol. 2416. Springer-Verlag, Berlin Heidelberg New York (2002) 219–233

11. McSherry, D.: Recommendation Engineering. Proceedings of the Fifteenth European Conference on Artificial Intelligence. IOS Press (2002) 86–90

12. McSherry, D.: A Generalised Approach to Similarity-Based Retrieval in Recommender Systems. Artificial Intelligence Review, 18 (2002) 309–341

13. McSherry, D.: Coverage-Optimized Retrieval. Proceedings of the Eighteenth International Joint Conference on Artificial Intelligence. International Joint Conferences on Artificial Intelligence (2003)

14. Smyth, B., Keane, M.: Adaptation-Guided Retrieval: Questioning the Similarity Assumption in Reasoning. Artificial Intelligence, 102 (1998) 249–293

15. Smyth, B., McClave, P.: Similarity vs. Diversity. In: Aha, D.W., Watson, I. (eds.) Case-Based Reasoning Research and Development. LNAI, Vol. 2080. Springer-Verlag, Berlin Heidelberg New York (2001) 347–361

16. Stahl, A.: Defining Similarity Measures: Top-Down vs. Bottom-Up. In: Craw, S., Preece, A. (eds.) Advances in Case-Based Reasoning. LNAI, Vol. 2416. Springer-Verlag, Berlin Heidelberg New York (2002) 406–420

17. Wilke, W., Lenz, M., Wess, S.: Intelligent Sales Support with CBR. In: Lenz, M., Bartsch-Spörl, B., Burkhard, H.-D., Wess, S. (eds.) Case-Based Reasoning Technology. Springer-Verlag, Berlin Heidelberg New York (1998) 91–113

The General Motors Variation-Reduction Adviser: Evolution of a CBR System

Alexander P. Morgan[1], John A. Cafeo[2], Diane I. Gibbons[1],
Ronald M. Lesperance[1], Gulcin H. Sengir[1], and Andrea M. Simon[3]

[1] General Motors R&D Center, Mail Code 480-106-359, Manufacturing Systems Research
Laboratory, 30500 Mound Rd., Warren, MI 48090-9055,
{alexander.p.morgan, ronald.m.lesperance, diane.gibbons,
gulcin.h.sengir}@gm.com

[2] General Motors R&D Center, Mail Code 480-106-256, Vehicle Development Research
Laboratory, 30500 Mound Rd., Warren, MI 48090-9055,
john.a.cafeo@gm.com

[3] General Motors R&D Center, Mail Code 480-106-390, Electronics and Controls
Integration Laboratory, 30500 Mound Rd., Warren, MI 48090-9055
andrea.m.simon@gm.com

Abstract. The GM Variation-Reduction Adviser (VRA) was originally conceived and prototyped as a CBR system. Feedback from the users led to a variety of changes in the system. It is emerging now as an application destined for all GM assembly plants. This is a fine "success story." However, the VRA has lost so much of its CBR character that it might be best characterized as a "CBR inspired" system rather than a CBR system. In this paper, we describe the original concept and the user feedback that guided its evolution into its current form. Every "real application" has interesting stories about "what worked" and "what didn't." Here, we share some of these stories about our project.

1 Introduction

The Variation-Reduction Adviser (VRA) is a knowledge system for automotive assembly plants, with communication and problem-solving components. It was originally conceived as a case-based reasoning (CBR) system [5] and still retains a number of case-based features. It is being tested in prototype in several plants at this time, and it will be deployed in a production version in the future.

In Section 2, we review the philosophical and application-domain background for the project. Section 3 provides an overview of the VRA. Section 4, which is the core of the paper, describes in some detail the evolution of the system in response to feedback from our assembly plant partners. Section 5 summarizes the main points of Section 4. Section 6 is a Summary and Discussion.

K.D. Ashley and D.G. Bridge (Eds.): ICCBR 2003, LNAI 2689, pp. 306–318, 2003.
© Springer-Verlag Berlin Heidelberg 2003

2 Background

The philosophical background for this work is the grassroots development strategy; the application-domain background is the body shop of an automotive assembly center. These are each discussed below.

2.1 The Grassroots Development Strategy

The grassroots development strategy consists of launching an early prototype in a single location, responding rapidly to feedback, creating a local system that is enthusiastically received, taking the prototype to other locations, and building grassroots acceptance for the evolving prototype. The best location to start with is the one that is clearly a leader, so that "peer pressure" can help build acceptance. At some point, the system is "sold" to top management, when an already enthusiastic user base has been established. This approach is described in detail in [9].

There are disadvantages to beginning without top management support. However, in certain very large and complex organizations even the most eloquent description of unfamiliar tools and methods will tend to be difficult to sell, through unfamiliarity and risk aversion. On the other hand, it is well understood that busy technicians will not voluntarily use anything that is not useful. When a top executive learns that his best workers are enthusiastic about a new tool, the executive will tend to understand the value of the tool and support it.

The VRA was piloted in a leading body shop, that of the Flint (Michigan) Assembly Center. The collaboration of our Flint partners helped us understand what was important and how to make our tool really useful. After a year of feedback and several major revisions, the Flint body shop people were enthusiastic and communicated their enthusiasm to other locations freely. As management at different levels became aware of this success, they offered the VRA strong support. It is currently being tried out at five plants, with more planned. It is our intention to complete the prototype and offer a production version for use in all GM assembly plants.

2.2 The Body Shop of an Automotive Assembly Center

The basic structure of a vehicle is called the body-in-white (BIW). The BIW is measured in meters but must meet its nominal tolerances to within a few millimeters. Otherwise, problems that are difficult to diagnose and cure arise in the final build, such as wind noise, water leaks, and a host of "fit and finish" issues. Typically, stamped sheet metal is welded together into the BIW in the part of the plant known as "the body shop." Parts and paint are then added to the BIW to create the finished vehicle. The BIW, however, is the critical portion of the build for dimensional integrity. Minute deviations in the tooling which holds the metal for welding, or in the thickness of the metal, or in the wear on the weld-gun tips, or in many other process elements, can significantly affect dimensional control. When a problem is detected "downstream" in the process, it can be challenging to discover the source of the problem and find a cure. Working with measurements at various stages of the process, as well as other information, a Dimensional Management (DM) team hypothesizes cause from effect to create a short list of most likely problems, makes visual inspections to refine the list, and makes process adjustments to solve the problem.

The members of the DM Team generally know the process well. This knowledge tends to be very specific, is sometimes documented but often is not, and involves a great deal of three-dimensional intuitive reasoning, as well as experience with the basic materials and machines of the process. Because the DM team members can consider questions such as "If the tooling in a particular station is defective in a particular way, what problems will this cause later in the process?" one might be led to consider a rule-based approach to capturing this knowledge. However, there are several key aspects that suggest "cases" rather than "rules." The most important is coverage; that is, it is difficult to imagine a complete set of rules for such a high-dimensional problem space. A related issue is capturing the three-dimensional and the pictorial nature of the knowledge. In a case-based system, we can evoke the powerful ability of expert humans to interpret and use such knowledge. Finally, in their own problem-solving process, the DM team members work from previous experiences in a way that suggests a case-based approach.

3   Overview of the VRA

3.1   Evolution

The VRA was originally conceived as a classic feature-vector-based diagnostic case-based reasoning (CBR) system. It was quickly realized, however, that a strict feature-based CBR model would not work at all. We then considered a lessons-learned archive indexed by a classic CBR system. However, we wanted something with a more structured knowledge model than this, leading to version 0 of our system, described below. VRA0 quickly became VRA1, which is VRA0 weakly linked to a communication log, provided in response to feedback from users. After VRA1 was further tested, a new version, VRA2, was created, which is very like the classic CBR system indexing a text archive that we resisted at first. Section 4 spends a considerable amount of time describing the evolution from VRA0 to VRA2. Section 4 is the core of our paper, giving considerable insights into the evolutionary system development process demanded by the grassroots philosophy.

3.2 A Case Structure for a Complex Diagnostic Environment

Consider a diagnostic environment in which, for each case, a small subset of a large set of symptoms can arise. Some of these symptoms will be the results of tests. These tests are not performed in any fixed order, but at the discretion of the technician. No particular subset of tests is always performed. A case consists of the presenting symptoms, the results of tests, the results of inspections (a kind of test), the results of actions (*e.g.*, replace a part), and the resolving actions with root causes that complete the case. This formulation fits our domain and also that of the National Semiconductor case described in [10, Chapter 3].

It is clear that a fixed length feature vector cannot capture a case, although it might index a case through simplifications. Here we are interested in a knowledge structure that captures the case more fully than that. For VRA0, we devised the following structure: a case is defined to be a sequence of observations. Observations are classified into a finite number of types. Each type is represented by a templated sentence. These sentences capture symptoms, results of tests, actions, resolutions and a few other types. Each type of observation is represented by a vector of attribute values, the values that go in the slots of the templated sentence. Thus, a case is a sequence of observations of various types, and the types occur in no particular order, although they are taken from a finite set of types. This formal structure seems to be complex enough to capture the diagnostic process, but it is still vastly more structured than free text.

Similarity between cases is built up from similarity between values of attributes and similarity between observations. Here, similarity between individual attribute values is developed from their relative positions in an ontology (see Section 5.2), where each attribute has its own ontology of values. For example, this might be done by counting links in a taxonomy, where more links indicates less similarity. See [3]. Then, observation-to-observation similarity for observations of the same type is defined in strict analogy with classic CBR, since observations of the same type are essentially compatible feature vectors. We favor a domain-specific way of doing this, but a weighted sum of all the attribute-value similarities is also workable. By definition, observations that are not of the same type have similarity zero. Finally, similarity between two cases is computed by matching observations between the two cases and combining similarity scores for the matched pairs. This is done by finding the most similar pair (one from each case), removing these from consideration and matching the second most similar pair, and so on, until one case's observations are entirely matched to a subset of the other case's observations. Then, the pair wise observation-to-observation similarities are combined to get a case-to-case similarity.

We believe that any technical issues around, say, the efficiency of computing similarity this way could have been worked out with the usual clever algorithmics. However, given our user group's preference for free text and their strong need for an emphasis on inter-team communication, we moved on to the approach described in the next section.

3.3 A Knowledge Structure Emphasizing Communication over Problem Solving

After using VRA0, the users asked us to provide them with a log environment, in which a few categorizing attributes are selected via pull-down menus, and then whatever the user wants to say is entered as a block of text. This log system began as a supplement to the CBR system (creating VRA1), but the log flourished while the CBR system languished. Seeing what had to be done, we transferred as many good features from VRA0 as we could to the log system, creating VRA2.

VRA2 has observations, but there is no structure to create cases from them. In fact, many VRA2 observations are just messages from one individual to another. Often, a single observation is a case or a case fragment. Sometimes, two observations are linked to create a case. This is up to the user's discretion, because the core of the VRA2 observation is a free-text block, in which any number of sentences might be written. Attached to this free text are classifying attributes, whose values are chosen by the user from pull-down menus. Here, some structure is restored, but much of the content of the observations is only available in the text. Thus, the clarity of knowledge capture and search of VRA0 are lost in VRA2.

The users like the spontaneity of knowledge entry for VRA2. The drawback is that lessons are mixed indiscriminately with messages, and extracting the essence of the archival knowledge will require further processing.

4 The Evolution of the System Design

4.1 VRA0

The initial version of the VRA was based on a number of assumptions about the work processes of the DM engineer. These assumptions were made based on limited experience: casual observations in the plant, meetings with both plant and non-plant people, and brainstorming with the potential users. A more formal observation period, before starting work on implementation, might have reduced the number of iterations needed to find a satisfactory system design. Here are two assumptions we made, which turned out to be incorrect:

- The problem-solving process is an individual process. In truth, problems are solved by the whole team as a team effort.
- DM engineers are not willing to write very much. The opposite is true.

Our initial assumptions are embodied in the initial design. A case consists of an arbitrary number of observations, classified into types and subtypes (see Section 3.2). The observations are organized into a To Do List and a Completed Observations list. The idea behind the To Do List is to have the DM engineers determine and enter (before actually doing) the steps, processes, and tests they think need to be done. When an item from the To Do List is acted on, it becomes a Completed Observation.

The To Do List Editor is a template-driven form for entering observations. This interface is designed to limit the amount of typing required. The user first classifies what is to be described into one of seven categories, by selecting tabs. This is then further classified by selecting a subtype-classification radio button. At this point, a form can be filled in which captures the relevant information.

Two of the six DM team members tried to work with the program, but it became clear that they would not adopt this interface. While they did understand the value, the system did not fit in well with their workflow. We learned that the problem-solving process at Flint seldom involves a single individual. The norm is to involve multiple people over multiple shifts. The critical need was for team members to be able to informally communicate with each other, requesting tests to be done or shim moves to be made. The results of these tests could then be communicated back to the original requestor, along with suggestions in the form of new requests and analysis.

After some reflection on this, the VRA team met with the DM team to develop a set of improvements. We were told that it was clear, based on experience and our discussions, that there was much value in capturing problems/solutions *for future use*. However, there was a more immediate need: *improving daily communication*.

4.2   VRA1: VRA0 + Daily Log

To address this need, we introduced a bulletin board mechanism, the Daily Log. This log is used to enter any comments or information that a DM team member wants to share. The log is especially useful for transferring information between shifts and for tracking on-going issues that have not yet crystallized into cases.

4.2.1   The Daily Log Module of VRA1

The Daily Log portion of VRA1 turned out to be very useful and was quickly and enthusiastically adopted by the DM team. In the early version of the Daily Log, free text entries were tagged with a minimal amount of information: the **Name** of the person making the entry, the **Shift**, the **Date,** and the factory **Zone**.

This simple version of the Daily Log was used for one month and was soon expanded to include additional tags and functionality at the request of the plant staff; in particular, an **Issue** tag was added. This tag was requested to allow the DM engineer to search on particular types of problems. A *linking mechanism* was also included. It allows the user to link together certain entries either by replying to them or to indicate that an entry is a continuation of a previous problem. The Daily Log was also integrated with the case-based portion of the system: a log entry can be associated with a case and used to start a case. The ability to search, print, and chart Daily Log entries was provided in two additional functions: the Daily Log Report and Daily Log Chart, which provided summaries (textual and visual) over filtered sets of log entries.

The DM team members use the Daily Log Report function to print the past day's entries at the beginning of the shift and carry this printout with them as they perform their duties. They refer to it to remind them of current issues. Also, they will write notes on the printout for later transfer into the Daily Log and/or discussion with colleagues. The Daily Log Chart is often used to give a quick visual summary of the nature of the problems the plant has been encountering over a particular time frame. It is typically used in management reviews and discussions with manufacturing engineers outside of the plant.

4.2.2   Case-Base Module of VRA1

The case-based portion of the VRA also evolved and was tied directly into the Daily Log. Thus, a case can be started in one of two ways: either directly from the case authoring screen (as before) or from the Daily Log screen, where the current entry would be copied into the comment field of a new case. The "to-do" and "completed" classification of observations was abandoned. Observations are merely created, edited, and saved as in any authoring environment. The Body-Location Selector is a main feature of the observation authoring system. It allows the DM engineer to point and click at pictures of sub-assemblies of the BIW and capture a "body location" in both words and as a picture attachment. VRA1 also has the ability to generate case reports as HTML pages or as PowerPoint® slides. The report includes all observations associated with a particular case, as well as all of the associated images.

4.2.3   Issues That Arose Using VRA1

After implementing VRA1, we worked with a variety of people to enter cases into the system. Even though the DM team supervisor told us that the new case-capturing interface was much better, it became clear that it wasn't being used very often. We learned through direct conversions that the DM team believed that they did not have enough time to put the information into the cases. It was obvious that they were thinking about it, because the DM supervisor would often point out log entries and threads that he stated would make a "really good case."

We explained that before he could realize the benefit of searching for similar past cases, there had to be a set of cases in the database upon which to search. The supervisor agreed to assign the responsibility of entering a significant number of cases based on Daily Log entries to a temporary member of his team. We worked with this person and were able to input about 40 cases during his rotation period. However, when he moved into a different department, all case entry stopped. The supervisor then agreed to assign case-authoring responsibility to a co-op college student (freshman). During her month, she was able to document her work with one very extensive case. She found the program easy to use and helpful, as her knowledge of the body shop was limited. After she left, once again all case authoring stopped.

Our conclusion is that this implementation does not fit well into the current workflow for the DM team. There are four main reasons why the DM engineers have used the Daily Log, but not the case-authoring system:

1) The Daily Log improves the way the DM engineers currently work, by improving communication within and between shifts.

2) The case-authoring tool seems redundant to the DM engineer. Having entered a message in the Daily Log, they don't want to have to enter it "again."

3) The case-authoring tool is not in the "workflow" of the DM engineer. The issue is not how easy the tool is to use; a case can be started and a first observation entered in less than two minutes. The issue is that the DM engineer does not perceive that there is a convenient point in the workflow to promote a problem from the Daily Log to a case:

    a) When a problem first presents itself, it is not clear that this will be a "lesson" worth saving.

    b) While solving a problem, the DM engineer is too busy, so a case is not started.

    c) After a problem is solved, there is new problem requiring attention.

4) Even though the DM engineers see the theoretical value of entering a structured case, it does not help them *immediately.*

The one aspect of the case-authoring system that the DM engineers did like was the ability to attach objects to a case. These included both textual and graphic attachments from a variety of sources (statistical charts, digital photos, shim log summaries, etc.).

4.3 VRA2: A New Formulation

We decided to reformulate the VRA to feature what the users would use. The free-text box of the log carries over in VRA2 as the core of an observation, but more attributes are available to annotate this free text, adapted from the case-based part. The **Area** attribute has been expanded to include station information. The **Issue** attribute, along with a new **Issue Detail** attribute, captures the observation-classification categories from the case-based part of VRA1. The observation text continues to serve as the *messaging* mechanism between people and shifts. The observations of VRA2 can have pictures or videos attached to them, by using the standard Microsoft Windows® cut-and-paste mechanism. When a picture is pasted in, the user is asked to caption it, using free text. ("Pull down captioning" was rejected by the users.)

VRA2 currently has two kinds of search, which can be used together:

1. Filtering by attribute value (*e.g.*, Issue = "tooling") or ranges of attribute values (*e.g.*, dates). All records are returned that satisfy the filter specification.

2. Keyword search with exact matching on the free text portions of observations.

This year, we plan to implement a full ontology-guided similarity search (see Section 5.2) on the free text portions of observations. Here, while a new observation is being authored, the concept words and their synonyms in the text will be identified, classified by type, and linked to their proper ontologies. Archived observations will be evaluated in terms of the similarity of their concept words and synonyms to those of the new observation. The "most similar" observations will be offered to the author for viewing during or after the authoring process. Guided by domain-specific evaluations of the importance of certain types of concepts over others, the total observation-to-observation similarity scores will be customized to the application. For example, the "body locations" (e.g., locations on parts and assemblies) should be similar for two observations to be similar, regardless of other matches.

Our plan is for each plant to maintain its own case base, while search from one plant can include case bases at other plants. Case-base maintenance is always an issue in the long term; we trust that the system will be valued enough to motivate minimal maintenance. Also, the various case bases will be searchable by people in the GM engineering and design organizations. If sufficient interest is shown, customized UI's might be created for these other communities.

How will we determine that an observation or set of observations is of archival quality; i.e., a case? The first way of determining this will be to offer the authors an opportunity to say, via a yes-no check box: "useful lesson learned?" These will be reviewed by the data manager and completed or corrected, perhaps in consultation with the original authors. We will consider extending this function of the data manager to include editing observations; for example, completing observations that have no "results" indicated, again perhaps in consultation with the original authors.

5   Knowledge Structure and Ontology for the VRA

The previous section presents a number of details to describe the evolution of the system. Here, we summarize the main features of the different versions, focusing on knowledge structure and ontology. Recall that VRA1 is merely VRA0 with a log.

5.1   Knowledge Structure

Each of VRA1 and VRA2 is organized around *messages* and *cases*. Also, in each version, the cases are linked sequences of *observations*. Further, *attachments* (graphical and other types of objects) form a part of the knowledge structure of each version.

Each case is a *lesson learned*, with descriptions of symptoms, faults, and fixes. The versions differ in a number of details, especially in how observations are structured.

VRA0 has a formally defined case structure, in which a case consists of a title and two sequences: a sequence of observations (which are annotated sentences) and a sequence of attachments (mostly graphical objects). Here, the different elements of a case add up to one lesson learned. The "case as a sequence of observations" structure is described in section 3.2 and in [2, 8]. VRA1 adds a daily log as a separate module, in which messages can be left for individuals, providing a separate *short-term memory*, in contrast to the *long-term memory* of the cases.

The knowledge containers for VRA2 are more flexible and less formally defined than in VRA0, but there are still messages, observations, cases, and attachments. However, in VRA2 an observation is an annotated block of free text; the annotations are strongly structured but the core free text is not. In VRA2, linked sets of observations conceptually frame a case, with symptoms, faults, and actions. The number of observations that link together to make a case varies from one to many. This flexibility results from the fact that observations have a core of free text; typically, VRA0 would require at least two observations to make a case. Further, in VRA2, messages are not formally distinguished from observations. This lack of separation suits the users, although it makes extracting archival cases more difficult. Basically, this is now a separate task that follows knowledge entry. Cases might be identified by an expert reviewer, perhaps assisted by some text-analysis tools. The terms "log entry" and "observation" are used now as synonyms, but in the future we may distinguish between them more formally. As the user interface evolves, we will include an attribute that lets the user identify a record as either a message or as a part of a case. Although a matter of degree and emphasis, "case" is more central to the knowledge containers of VRA0, while "observation" is more central for VRA2.

5.2 Ontology

An ontology is a set of concept terms (standard terms chosen to represent concepts), with relationships defined between them; see [1, 6]. The terms can also be "annotated" with attributes and information about the values the attributes may take on. An ontology must be created, usually by a process of ramping up to full coverage, and it must be maintained, by a process of appending new terms and deleting obsolete ones [4]. Also, synonym lists might be maintained, and (as is common) if the application is global, all these lists may need to be maintained in several foreign languages. The relationships between terms captured in an ontology are especially useful for ontology-guided similarity search. See [7].

The main concept lists for the VRA are grouped by attribute name and organized taxonomically. The free text also has a concept list, consisting of generic names for body locations: ring, dash, box (for a truck), fender, slot, roof, rocker, striker, upper striker hole, back-glass flange, tailgate, "A" pillar, *etc*. This list is used for the current search of the free text portions of observations. Its taxonomic relationships ("part of") will be exploited when the ontology-guided search functionality is implemented (see Section 4.3). These terms are in contrast with the "body location" attribute terms, which are highly specific part names associated with specific models: Rear Seat Belt Shoulder Anchor Plate ASM (L-Zone), Strip (Frame to Outer: H-Zone), Door Frame ASM from E130 (Vision Station), Left Roof Rail REINF ASM from EA020, *etc*. It is typical for a knowledge system to have both kinds of concept terms: generic everyday names for objects typically encountered, and specific parts names and other precise technical terms. Logically, the generic names are generalizations of the technical names; one might imagine a taxonomic tree, with the technical names as leaves of the tree and the generic names as parent links one or two levels above the leaf nodes. This suggests the possibility of automatically modifying text by making terms generic; that is, replacing specific terms with their generic equivalents. This might help us to reuse the knowledge across contexts.

6 Summary and Discussion

6.1 Summary

Working closely with the Flint Assembly Center, we have fielded a prototype of the VRA, which has undergone various modifications. VRA0 is basically the system described in [2, 8]. Recently, this system has been revised, based on feedback and use at Flint, generating the just-completed VRA2. Most of the revisions of the system have to do with fitting in the workflow, rather than with addressing technical problems. The current version has a high degree of user enthusiasm.

Why did the plant people not use the case-authoring environment of VRA0? Basically, there was no immediate value for them, even though they realized it might provide future value. Because the VRA0 case structure was perceived as a formal mechanism by the users, they wanted to "make sure" before promoting something to a case that it was really "worthy." By the time they got around to thinking about it, however, there was no time to actually do it. The creation of cases from daily log entries was viewed as another responsibility to be added to their already long list of responsibilities. Although cases were recognized as good in the long term, the factory environment has a strong "do what's good now" character to it.

Even though we have "gone on" to VRA2, VRA0 is a valuable research prototype. We believe that the formulation of "cases" as a sequence of templated observations might fit certain kinds of diagnostic environments very well; see Section 3.2. When there is a specialized group of case authors and/or when the diagnostic process is already being closely documented (*e.g.*, in police, medical, or biological laboratories), the VRA0 approach might be preferred.

6.2 Practical Lessons Learned from This Project

- The exact form of the user interfaces and their supporting structures cannot be worked out "in advance." Rather, the user community must be given the opportunity to try out prototypes and have them modified based on experience. This is consistent with the grassroots development process noted in Section 2.1.
- The organization of knowledge via a single knowledge unit, an *observation*, can serve as a format for *messages*, for communication between individuals, and for *cases* (= sequences of observations), for archiving of lessons learned, thus providing a unified conceptual structure for short- and long-term communication.
- Improved communication is received with more immediate enthusiasm than providing a problem-solving tool, whose usefulness takes time to establish.

6.3 What's Good and What's Bad about VRA2

Good:
- There is strong user enthusiasm.
- Communicating is facilitated, as well as problem solving.
- Free text allows a total flexibility of expression.
- Filtering using the attributes that annotate the observations provides an easy way to search the observation archive.

Bad:
- The observation database contains a mixture of messages, case fragments, and cases, with no easy way to tell them apart.
- The free text core of observations has all the usual disadvantages for standardizing language, translation into foreign languages, and search.
- The context of the observations is local, with many implicit assumptions and local language eccentricities. The goal of sharing knowledge between plants globally is made more difficult.
- A person to edit observations, separate from the original authors, is now needed: to delete mere messages, to annotate observations with contextual information, to identify cases, and to remove extraneous material, in order to create an archive globally useful for problem solving.

6.4 Final Thoughts

The VRA is a "success story," but qualified by practical considerations, as noted above. It is "case-based inspired," but it has lost much of ist formal structure. Some of this may be recovered, if we successfully implement ontology-guided similarity search. In the tension between knowledge capture and knowledge delivery, we look forward to the day when greater balance can be achieved, perhaps through advances in text understanding and ontology-guided search.

Acknowledgements. We appreciate support from the Flint Assembly Center. In particular, we want to thank Dave Coumes and Dave Holland for allowing us to work with the body shop dimensional control team. We also thank Gene Morrison, Dan Rach, and Nathan Grzymkowski for the information and suggestions they have provided. We acknowledge Glenn Pacer and Gary Telling from the Dimensional Engineering Validation and Variation Reduction Center for their suggestions, comments and support, and Tony Grix and Richard Grimes from Dimensional Engineering for their support. Finally, we would like to thank the reviewers for their positive and helpful suggestions.

References

1. Berners-Lee, T., Hendler, J., and Lassila, O.: The Semantic Web. Scientific American (May, 2001), 35–43
2. Cafeo, J. A., Gibbons, D. I., Lesperance, R. M., Morgan, A. P., Sengir, G. H. Simon, A. M.: Capturing Lessons Learned for Variation Reduction in an Automotive Assembly Plant. Proc. 14th Int. Fla. AI Research Soc. Conf.. AAAI Press, Menlo Park, CA, (2001) 89–92
3. CBR Works, Compendium Document. Empolis Corporation (1998)
4. Das, A., Wu, W., McGuinness, D.: Industrial Strength Ontology Management. In Cruz, Decker, Euzenat, McGuinness, eds. The Emerging Semantic Web. IOS Press (2002)
5. Leake, D. (ed.): Case-Based Reasoning: Experiences, Lessons, and Future Directions. AAAI Press, Menlo Park, California and The MIT Press, Cambridge, Mass. (1996)
6. McGuinness, D.: Ontologies Come of Age. In Fensel, Hendler, Lieberman, Wahlster, eds. Spinning the Semantic Web: Bringing the World Wide Web to its Full Potential. MIT Press (2002)
7. McGuinness, D.: Ontology-enhanced Search for Primary Care Medical Literature. In Proc. Int. Medical Informatics Assoc. Working Group 6 – Medical Concept Representation and Natural Language Processing Conference, Phoenix, Arizona, December 16–19, 1999 (1999)
8. Morgan, A. P., Cafeo, J. A., Gibbons, D. I., Lesperance, R. M., Sengir, G. H. Simon, A. M.: CBR for Dimensional Management in a Manufacturing Plant. Proceedings of the 4th Int. Conf. on Case-Based Reasoning. ICCBR 2001. Vancouver, BC, Canada. (2001) 597–610
9. Morgan, A. P., Cafeo, J. A., Gibbons, D. I., Lesperance, R. M., Sengir, G. H. Simon, A. M.: The General Motors Variation-Reduction Adviser: An Example of Grass Roots Knowledge Management Development. Practical Aspects of Knowledge Management, 4th Int. Conf. PAKM 2002. Vienna, Austria, December 2002. Springer Lecture Notes in Artificial Intelligence. Springer-Verlag, Berlin Heidelberg New York. (2002) 137–143 and 639–645
10. Watson, Ian: Applying Knowledge Management: Techniques for Building Corporate Memories, Morgan Kaufman, New York. (2002)

Diversity-Conscious Retrieval from Generalized Cases: A Branch and Bound Algorithm

Babak Mougouie[1], Michael M. Richter[2], and Ralph Bergmann[3]

[1] Max-Planck Institute for Computer Science,
Stuhlsatzenhausweg 85, 66123 Saarbrücken, Germany
mbabak@mpi-sb.mpg.de
[2] University of Kaiserslautern,
Artificial Intelligence and Knowledge-Based Systems Group
PO-Box 3049, 67653 Kaiserslautern, Germany
richter@informatik.uni-kl.de
[3] University of Hildesheim,
Data- and Knowledge Management Group
PO-Box 101363, 31113 Hildesheim, Germany
bergmann@dwm.uni-hildesheim.de

Abstract. Recommendation systems offer the most similar point cases to a target query. Among those cases similar to the query, some may be similar and others dissimilar to each other. Offering only the most similar cases wrt. the query leads to the well known problem that the customers may have only a few number of choices. To address the problem of offering a *diverse* set of cases, several approaches have been proposed. In a different line of CBR research, the concept of *generalized cases* has been systematically studied, which can be applied to represent parameterizable products. First approaches to retrieving the most similar point cases from a case base of generalized cases have been proposed. However, until now no algorithm is known to retrieve a diverse set of point cases from a case base of generalized cases. This is the topic of this paper. We present a new branch and bound method to build a retrieval set of point cases such that its diversity is sufficient and each case in the retrieval set is a representative for a set of similar point cases.

1 Introduction

In electronic commerce applications, a similarity measure sim is intended to describe the utility of a product p for satisfying a certain query q [3]. The nearest neighbor method then selects the best available product for a given query. In many situations, it is however sufficient to offer products that exceed a given utility (similarity) threshold θ, i.e. $sim(p, q) \geq \theta$. Often there are several different products p that satisfy such a condition and the problem arises which of these products should be offered to the customer. A familiar policy is to present only products that are dissimilar to each other, a concept introduced as *diversity* [13, 6,7]. The reason is that the exact utility function of the customer is not known to the system and dissimilar products may look equally good with respect to the query. In such a situation, the customer can decide on his own which product to choose.

K.D. Ashley and D.G. Bridge (Eds.): ICCBR 2003, LNAI 2689, pp. 319–331, 2003.
© Springer-Verlag Berlin Heidelberg 2003

1.1   Parameterizable Products and Generalized Cases

Nowadays, more complex problems are sold electronically. Typically, such products may be available in many variants. Therefore, the representation of such a product in the product database of the supplier often uses compact notations in the sense that the product has parameters $t_1, \ldots, t_k$. Then a product is described in the form $p(t_1, \ldots, t_k)$ where t_i ranges over some domain $dom(t_i)$. It is also very common that for such a parameterized product not all combinations of parameters are allowed, or certain parameters (e.g. the price or the voltage) may depend on some other parameters. Therefore, the product description must include constraints that describe the parameter dependencies.

When applying CBR for product recommendation, products are represented as cases in the case base. Fixed products are represented using point cases, i.e., point in the representation space of relevant product features. Parameterizable products, however, can be represented in compact form as *generalized cases* [4, 2].[1] A generalized case covers not only a point of the problem-solution space but a whole subspace of it. A single generalized case immediately provides solutions to a set of closely related problems rather than to a single problem only. In general, a single generalized case can be viewed as an implicit representation of a (possibly infinite) set of traditional point cases.

1.2   The Problem: Diversity Conscious Retrieval from Generalized Cases

Mougouie and Bergmann [9] describe the similarity assessment problem for generalized cases as an optimization problem and present several specialized algorithms. However, the problem of retrieving a diverse set of point cases from a set of generalized cases has not yet been addressed. In this paper, we present an algorithm for this problem, which we formulate as follows:

P: *Find a set of point cases from a set of generalized cases that are a) sufficiently similar to the query and b) are sufficiently dissimilar to each other.*

As in our previous work [9], we restrict the applicability of the methods we propose to attribute-value case representations with real-valued attributes only. Discrete attribute values would require a different branch of optimization methods, which we intend to address in our future work.

1.3   Basic Approach

If the generalized cases have the nice property that all their elements are very similar to each other, then the task would be simplified because we could simply replace each generalized case by an arbitrary representative. Unfortunately, generalized cases usually are not of that kind. Therefore, we split our procedure into the following steps:

---

[1] For a discussion of concepts from CBR literature, similar to what we call a generalized case, see [9].

1. Decompose each generalized case into subsets of cases sufficiently similar to each other.
2. Select a representative of each set.
3. For a given query q, find a subset S of representatives which are sufficiently similar to q.
4. Find a set $R \subseteq S$ with sufficiently dissimilar cases.

Different techniques have been proposed in the literature to increase the diversity of retrieved cases from a case base of point cases. Some of them increase diversity while preserving similarity and some decrease similarity in favor of diversity [6,7,13]. Similarity and diversity have been combined into the concept of *quality* of a retrieved set. Our approach differs somewhat from the techniques developed in the literature so far because we start directly with an intuitive problem and make use of the advantages offered by generalized cases.

We start in Section 2, with the elementary definitions behind generalized cases and the formulation of similarity assessment as an optimization problem. Further, we present an application example from micro-electronics design, which we are currently investigating in the German project IPQ. The decomposition of a generalized case is described in Section 3 using a branch and bound algorithm. The construction of a set of representatives S and the construction of the final retrieved set R is described in Section 4. Section 5 summarizes the results and gives an outlook to further research.

2   Generalized Cases, Optimization, and Application Example

To lay the foundation for the remainder of the paper, we now briefly review the basic formal concept of generalized cases and the related similarity assessment described in detail in [4].

2.1   Introduction to Generalized Cases

Let S be the (possibly infinite) representation space for cases. One could assume that this representation space is subdivided into a problem space and a solution space, but we drop this assumption here since it is less appropriate in design domains. There the problem space consists of queries which also describe products; the only difference to the solution space is that query products may not be available. A traditional case c or *point case* is a point in the representation space S, i.e., $c \in S$. A *generalized case* can now be extensionally defined as follows:

Definition 1. (Generalized Case) A *generalized case gc* is a subset of the representation space, i.e., $gc \subseteq S$.

Hence, a generalized case stands for a set of point cases. However, a generalized case should not represent an arbitrary set. In electronic commerce applications, a generalized case stands for a particular product that is available in different variants.

For retrieving generalized cases, the similarity between a query and a generalized case must be determined. As in traditional CBR, we assume that the query is a point in the representation space. We further assume that a "traditional" similarity measure $sim(q, c)$ is given which assesses the similarity between a query q and a point case c. Such a similarity measure can be extended in a canonical way to assess the similarity $sim^*(q, gc)$ between a query q and a generalized case gc as follows: $sim^*(q, gc) := sup\{sim(q, c) \mid c \in gc\}$. Applying sim^* ensures that those generalized cases are retrieved that contain the point cases which are most similar to the query. In electronic commerce applications, we are usually not only interested in the parameterizable product as such, but also in the particular parameter set for which the similarity yields a maximum. In other words, we are interested in the particular point case $c \in gc$ that leads to the best similarity. This is because the customer usually does not buy the parameterizable product, but a fixed product particularly manufactured for him/her given one single specific set of parameters.

For building CBR systems that reason with generalized cases, efficient representations for generalized cases and efficient approaches for similarity assessment must be developed. Obviously, a straight forward approach of computing the similarity for each point case covered by a generalized case and determining the maximum of the similarity values can be quite inefficient if the generalized case covers a large subspace and is impossible if it covers an infinite space.

In the following we restrict ourselves to case representation spaces that are n-dimensional Real valued vector spaces, i.e. $\mathcal{S} = I\!R^n$ and $gc \subseteq I\!R^n$. Further, we assume that the generalized case is intensionally defined by a set of constraints over $I\!R^n$, i.e. a point case is within the generalized cases if for this point all constraints are fulfilled.

2.2   Similarity Assessment as an Optimization Problem

Given the previous definitions for generalized cases, we can now formulate the similarity retrieval problem via the following two optimization problems:
(OP1): get the closest point in a generalized case gc to a query q:

$$\textbf{max } sim(x, q)$$
(OP1)
$$\text{s.t. } h(x) \leq 0,$$

where h is a set of m functions $h_1, h_2, \ldots, h_m$ that represent the gc by $h(x) \leq 0$, i.e., $x \in gc \iff \forall i\ h_i(x) \leq 0$. In this optimization problem, sim is the *objective function* to be maximized and $h(x) \leq 0$ is the *feasible region* for gc, i.e. the set of point cases that fulfill all constraints by which gc is extensionally defined.

(OP2): the closest point in a <u>set</u> of generalized cases to the query.

$$\textbf{max } sim(x, q)$$
(OP2)
$$\text{s.t. } x \in gc_i$$

for some i.

Mougouie and Bergmann [9] introduced the above formulations and presented a cutting plane algorithm to retrieve the nearest neighbor case in the generalized cases to the query. Mougouie [8] and Mougouie and Richter [10] studied branch and bound methods for the same problem. In this paper, we employ the branch and bound method again but this time to construct a diverse retrieval set. This is done by decomposing the generalized cases into some subsets with the property that the cases in each subset are sufficiently similar to each other.

2.3   Marketplace for Electronic Designs

We now present briefly an application example that motivated this theoretical work. Increasingly, companies producing electronic equipments use electronic design objects, called IPs ("Intellectual Properties"), from third parties inside their complex electronic systems. An IP is a design object whose major value comes from the skill of its producer [5], and a redesign of it would consume significant time. However, a designer who wants to reuse designs from the past must have a lot of experience and knowledge about existing designs, in order to be able to find candidates that are suitable for reuse in his/her specific new situation. Currently, electronic marketplaces for IP are coming up that allow the exchange of IP among design companies. The recommendation of reusable IP is an important function of such a market place.

In the current projects IPQ^2 and $ToolIP^3$ we develop such an IP recommendation system [11,12] based on CBR technology. Such an IP is a typical parameterizable product, because it spans a design space. An IP is a flexible design that has to be synthesized to hardware before it can actually be used. The behavior of the final hardware depends on a number of *parameters* of the original design description. The valid value combinations for these parameters are constrained by different criteria for each IP.

The parameters of an example IP (for *discrete cosine transform*) are shown in Table 1 and Fig. 1. These parameters f, a, w, and s heavily depend on each other: increasing the accuracy w of the DCT/IDCT increases the chip area consumption a and decreases the maximum clock frequency f in a particular way, shown in Fig. 1. These relationships define a very specific design space that is spanned by the four mentioned parameters.

Such an IP can easily be represented as a generalized case over the four attributes shown. The constraints shown in Fig. 1 become the constraints of the generalized cases.

---

[2] IPQ (IP Qualification for Efficient Design Reuse) Project funded by the German Ministry of Education and Research, BMBF (12/2000 - 11/2003). Partners: AMD, Fraunhofer Institute for Integrated Circuits, FZI Karlsruhe, Infineon Technologies, Siemens, Sciworx, Empolis, Thomson Multi Media, TU Chemnitz, University of Hildesheim, University of Kaiserslautern, and University of Paderborn. See www.ip-qualifikation.de

[3] ToolIP (Tools and Methods for IP) European Project. See toolip.fzi.de for partners and further information.

Table 1. Selected parameters of the example IP.

parameter	description
frequency f	The clock frequency that can be applied to the IP.
area a	The chip area the synthesized IP will fit on.
width w	Number of bits per input/output word. Determines the accuracy of the DCT. Allowed values are 6, 7, ..., 16.
subword s	Number of bits calculated per clock tick. Changing this design space parameter may have a positive influence on one quality of the design while having a negative impact on another. Allowed values are 1, 2, 4, 8, and no_pipe.

$$f \leq \begin{cases} -0.66w + 115 & \text{if } s = 1 \\ -1.94w + 118 & \text{if } s = 2 \\ -1.74w + 88 & \text{if } s = 4 \\ -0.96w + 54 & \text{if } s = 8 \\ -2.76w + 57 & \text{if } s = \text{no} \end{cases}$$

$$a \geq \begin{cases} 1081w^2 + 2885w + 10064 & \text{if } s = 1 \\ 692w^2 + 2436w + 4367 & \text{if } s = 2 \\ 532w^2 + 1676w + 2794 & \text{if } s = 4 \\ 416w^2 + 1594w + 2413 & \text{if } s = 8 \\ 194w^2 + 2076w + 278 & \text{if } s = \text{no} \end{cases}$$

Fig. 1. Dependencies between the parameters of an example IP

3   General Branch and Bound Algorithm(B&B)

We now describe a branch and bound algorithm for solving the first optimization problem (**OP1**), i.e. finding the most similar point case from a generalized case. Let the objective function be $f(x) = sim(x, q)$ and the generalized case gc be given by $D \equiv h(x) \leq 0$. We put $z = \max \{f(x) : x \in D\}$. The algorithm starts with some set $M_1 \supseteq D$ and decomposes it stepwise into smaller subsets. For each such subset M, we select two points $\underline{z}$ and $\overline{z}$ which are upper and lower bounds for $f(x)$ where $x \in M$. The decomposition process terminates if $\overline{z} - \underline{z}$ is small enough; we get an almost optimal solution for this set M with a controlled error. These optimal solutions for the different sets M are compared and sets with non-optimal solutions are deleted (step 2). This leads finally to an almost optimal solution of the global problem in step 7. Because the set M_1 may contain subsets with no feasible case in it, we need to remove them. This takes place in step 4.

1. Choose $M_1 \supseteq D, x^1 \in D, \overline{z}_1 = q \geq \max f(D)$.
   Set $\underline{M}_1 = \{M_1\}, S_{M_1} = \{x^1\}$,
   $\underline{z}_1 = f(x^1), \overline{z}(M_1) = \overline{z}_1$.
   If $\overline{z}_1 = \underline{z}_1$, stop: x^1 is an optimal solution. Otherwise set $i = 2$.

2. Delete all $M \in \underline{M}_{i-1}$ satisfying $\overline{z}(M) \leq \underline{z}_{i-1}$.
   Let $\underline{R}_i$ be the collection of remaining members of $\underline{M}_{i-1}$.
3. Select a nonempty collection $\underline{P}_i \subset \underline{R}_i$, and construct a partition of every member of $\underline{P}_i$. Let $\underline{P}'_i$ be the collection of all new partition elements.
4. Delete any $M \in \underline{P}'_i$ for which it is known that $M \cap D = \emptyset$. Let $\underline{M}'_i$ be the collection of all remaining members of $\underline{P}'_i$.
5. Assign to each $M \in \underline{M}'_i$ a set S_M and a number $\overline{z}(M)$ such that

$$S_M \subseteq M \cap D, \quad \overline{z}(M) \geq \sup f(M \cap D),$$
$$S_M \supseteq M \cap S_{M'}, \overline{z}(M) \leq \overline{z}(M'),$$

   whenever $M \subset M' \in \underline{M}_{i-1}$. Set $\underline{z}(M) = \max f(S_M)$.
6. Set $\underline{M}_i = (\underline{R}_i \backslash \underline{P}_i) \cup \underline{M}'_i$. Compute
   $\overline{z}_i = \min \{\overline{z}(M) : M \in \underline{M}_i\}$,
   $\underline{z}_i = \max \{\underline{z}(M) : M \in \underline{M}_i\}$.
   Let $x^i \in D$ be such that $f(x^i) = \underline{z}_i$.
7. If $\overline{z}_i - \underline{z}_i \leq \epsilon$(small enough), stop: x^i is a sufficient approximation of the optimal solution.
   Otherwise set $i = i + 1$ and go to step 2.

This branch and bound algorithm describes a solution for **(OP1)**. For solving **(OP2)** we have now two options:

1. Joining the generalized cases into one set and reducing the problem into **(OP1)**.
2. Working on each generalized case individually.

The first method is computationally very involved due to the integrality of the problem; it neglects, in addition, all advantages offered by the generalized cases. Therefore we will use the second method. Here we will obtain a set S_i which is the set of all optimal solutions for each individual generalized case. This is described in the following section. In subsections 4.2 and 4.3, we introduce two methods for building the set $S \subset \bigcup_i S_i$ of representatives which are sufficiently similar to q and finally construct the retrieval set $R \subseteq S$ satisfying the intended dissimilarity conditions.

4   Constructing the Retrieval Sets

Now we slightly modify B&B to build a set S_i of feasible solutions. These feasible solutions are actually point cases located in a generalized case. Let MBB be the modified version of B&B with the following modifications.

1. In step 1 of B&B, add to the algorithm $S_i = S_{M_1}$.
2. In step 6, add to the algorithm

$$S_i = S_i \cup \{x | f(x) = \underline{z}(M), \forall M \in M_i\}. \tag{1}$$

Build S_i such that $S_i = \{x_1, x_2, ...\}$ always has the property that $sim(x_i, q) \geq sim(x_j, q)$ for $i < j$.

Depending on the number of iterations in MBB and our method to divide the feasible region, the set S_i gets bigger and bigger. Since we need only a certain number of cases(k) to construct the retrieval set, therefore we need to choose a subset of $\bigcup_i S_i$ with k elements. This subset will be our retrieval set.

Since the generalized cases are continuous sets, if we choose the subset of $\bigcup_i S_i$ with the most similarity to the target query, this tends to be the subset of just one of S_i's and the diversity of such a retrieval set will be very close to 0. Therefore we have to choose another subset of $\bigcup_i S_i$ with a higher diversity.

In [9], we used a feasible direction algorithm which starting from the points $x \in D$ moves to some closer solutions to the query and finally identifies the optimal solution. In the sequel, we mention the idea of this method again and offer an algorithm based on it. For further material, we refer the reader to [1].

4.1   Feasible Direction Method

Definition 2. *Consider the problem* $\mathbf{max}\, f(x)$ *subject to* $x \in D$*. A nonzero vector* d *is called a* feasible direction *at* $x \in D$ *if there exist a* $\delta > 0$ *such that* $x + \lambda d \in D$ *for all* $\lambda \in (0, \delta)$*. Furthermore,* d *is called an* improving feasible direction *at* $x \in D$ *if there exists a* $\delta > 0$ *such that* $f(x + \lambda d) > f(x)$ *and* $x + \lambda d \in D$ *for all* $\lambda \in (0, \delta)$*.*

Suppose $x \in S_i \subset D_i$. If an improving feasible direction d at x exists, we move along d with a step size λ reaching a new feasible point and we do the same iteration for the new point. If such an improving direction does not exist, we conclude that the current point is a local optimal solution.

Due to the non-linearity of the generalized cases, the existence of local optimal solutions which are not globally optimal is predictable. To locate them, we apply the feasible direction method on each generalized case and use the points in S_i as the starting points. Then we will keep only these local optimal solutions and discard the rest of the points from S_i. S is the set of all local optimal solutions for all i. Finally we will construct $R \subseteq S$ taking the first k nearest points in S to the query.

4.2   The Algorithm to Construct the Retrieval Set(CRS)

Input: The sets $S_i = \{x_1^i, x_2^i, ...\}$ where $sim(x_r^i, q) \geq sim(x_l^i, q)$ for all $r < l$.

for all S_i **do**
{
  $R_i = \{x_1^i\};$ $S_i = S_i \backslash \{x_1^i\};$ $\bar{x}_1 = x_1^i;$ $j = 2;$
  while $(S_i$ not empty$))$ **do**
  {
    Apply the feasible direction method starting at x_j^i to get a local optimal solution $\bar{x}_j$;
    if $(\bar{x}_j \neq x_{j-1}^-)$ **then**
    {

$$R_i = R_i \cup \{\bar{x_j}\};$$
$$\}$$
$$S_i = S_i \backslash \{x_j^i\};$$
$$\text{j++;}$$
$$\}$$
$$\}$$
$$S = \bigcup_i R_i$$
$R = \{x \in S | x$ is among the k nearest neighbors to q from S$\}$.

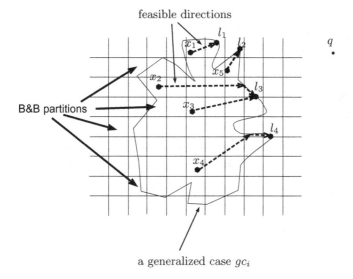

feasible directions

B&B partitions

a generalized case gc_i

Fig. 2. CRS Algorithm

The partition into the squares in Fig. 2 is obtained by our B&B algorithm for a generalized case gc_i. The points $x_1, ..., x_5$ are exactly those from the set S_i but unordered. The arrows starting from the $x_1, ..., x_5$ point in the feasible directions until one reaches a local optimal solution $l_1, ..., l_4$.

The good thing about CRS is that it can be applied during the execution of MBB. Therefore we don't increase the execution time drastically. The disadvantage of CRS is that the retrieval set constructed by CRS consists only of local optimal solutions. Therefore we don't take into account some points which might be good representatives but not necessarily locally optimal. The other problem is that the number of elements in S depends crucially on the behavior of the generalized cases. For example when the generalized cases are convex and the number of them is less than k, then we have less than k local optimal solutions and consequently S will have less than k elements. So we have to revise CRS to add some non-optimal solutions to S. To do so, we introduce some kind of minimum distance requirement between the elements of the retrieval set.

Definition 3. *Let* $R = \{c_1, ..., c_k\}$ *be a retrieval set. We say* R *has the* minimum acceptable diversity *if there exists* $0 < \Delta < 1$ *such that* $sim(c_i, c_j) \leq \Delta$ *for all* $i, j = 1, ..., k$ *and* $i \neq j$. Δ *is called the* minimum border *between the cases in* R.

Now we outline the revised version of CRS.

4.3   RCRS Algorithm

Input: The set $S_i = \{x_1^i, x_2^i, ...\}$ where $sim(x_r^i, q) \geq sim(x_l^i, q)$ for $r < l$.

for all S_i **do**
{
  $R_i = \{x_1^i\}$; $S_i = S_i \backslash \{x_1^i\}$; $j = 2$;
  while (S_i not empty)) **do**
  {
    $\bar{x} = x_j^i$;
    NextPointIsNotFound = True;
    while (NextPointIsNotFound) **do**
    {
        Find an improving feasible direction d starting at $\bar{x}$ such that
        $sim(\bar{x} + \lambda d, x) \leq \Delta; \forall x \in R_i$ and $sim(\bar{x} + \lambda d, q) \leq sim(\bar{x}, q)$
        If d exists **set** $\bar{x} = \bar{x} + \lambda d$;
        else NextPointIsNotFound = False;
    }
    if ($\bar{x} \neq x_j^i$) **then**
    {
        $R_i = R_i \cup \{\bar{x}\}$;
    }
    $S_i = S_i \backslash \{x_j^i\}$;
    j++;
  }
}
$S = \bigcup_i R_i$
$R = \{x \in S | x$ is among the k nearest neighbors to q from S$\}$.

    The idea of the algorithm is to build a set $R_i \subseteq S_i$ such that the similarity between the points in R_i is at most Δ. The points in S_i are picked iteratively, improved by moving along some improving feasible direction, and added to R_i if they have some minimum border to the points already in R_i. In Fig. 3, the circles around the x_j denote the area from which no point can be selected if x_j was chosen before. With the assumption that the points in different generalized cases have a minimum border to each other, the set $S = \bigcup_i R_i$ will have the same property. Therefore the k nearest points in S to q are sufficiently dissimilar to each other. Since these points are chosen in a sorted fashion, they are sufficiently close to q. This guarantees a sufficient diversity and similarity for the retrieval set R.

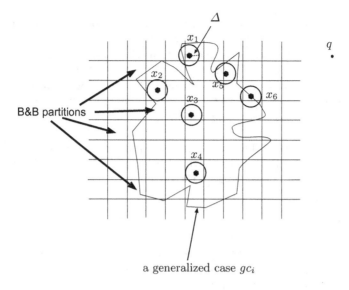

a generalized case gc_i

Fig. 3. RCRS Algorithm

Like CRS, RCRS can be applied during the execution of MBB. This means in (1) we add a point x where $f(x) = \underline{z}(M)$ to S_i if it has a minimum border to the points already in S_i. This reduces the size of S_i and consequently decreases the time complexity of RCRS but deletes some points which might be good choices for the retrieval set.

5   Summary and Conclusion

In this paper, we have analyzed the problem of retrieving the most similar point cases from a set of generalized cases under the additional requirement that the retrieved set should be diverse. We presented a new branch and bound algorithm to solve this problem and thereby significantly extended our previous work on the theory of reasoning with generalized cases [4,9,10,8]. The presented approach makes use of the advantages of generalized cases which put some structure on the set of all cases. We remark also that the retrieval process can be simplified if the customer wants only some minimal similarity to the target query; such situations are not uncommon. Also, this work is again an indication for the fact that optimization theory provides a variety of methods that are useful for similarity assessment in CBR.

Although this paper is a very important step towards solving the diversity-conscious retrieval problem for generalized cases, there are still many open problems to be addressed. Currently, the proposed method is limited to real-valued case representations only. For traditional real-valued optimization problems a huge set of algorithmic methods exist. But as already pointed out in [9,10,8], none of these methods could be used without modification. The problem of similarity assessment for generalized cases must also be analyzed for case-representations including discrete types and constraints and also for mixed representations. In symbolic domains which occur frequently in electronic commerce, optimization methods are far less developed and in our opinion innovative algorithms are necessary. Currently, practical experiences with this algorithm concerning efficiency in real domains, such as the IP reuse domain, is still missing and it is an important part of our future work as well.

Acknowledgements. This work has been partially funded by the BMBF project IPQ. The authors want to thank Alexander Tartakovski for discussions and feedback on earlier versions of the paper.

References

1. Bazaraa, M. S., Sherali, H.D., Shetty, C.M.: *NonLinear Programming, Theory and Algorithms.* Second Edition. 408–474. Wiley, 1993.
2. Bergmann, R.: *Experience Management: Foundations, Development Methodology, and Internet-Based Applications.* Lecture Notes in Artificial Intelligence, Vol. 2432, Springer, 2002.
3. Bergmann, R., Richter, M.M., Schmitt, S., Stahl, A., Vollrath, I.: Utility-Oriented Matching: A New Research Direction for Case-Based Reasoning. *9th German Workshop on Case-Based Reasoning (GWCBR'2001)*, 2001.
4. Bergmann, R., Vollrath, I.: Generalized cases: Representation and steps towards efficient similarity assessment. In W. Burgard, Th. Christaller & A. B. Cremers (Eds.) *KI-99: Advances in Artificial Intelligence* Lecture Notes in Artificial Intelligence, 1701, Springer, 195–206, 1999.
5. Lewis, J.: Intellectual property (IP) components. Artisan Components, Inc., [web page], http://www.artisan.com/ip.html, 1997.
6. McSherry, D.: Diversity-Conscious Retrieval. In: S. Craw & A. Preece (Eds.) *European Conference on Case-Based Reasoning (ECCBR'02).* Lecture Notes in Artificial Intelligence, Springer, 219–233, 2002.
7. McSherry, D.: Increasing Recommendation Diversity Without Loss of Similarity. *Proceedings of the 6th UK Workshop on Case-Based Reasoning*, pp. 23–31, 2001.
8. Mougouie, B.: *Optimization of Distance/Similarity Functions under Linear and Nonlinear Constraints with application in Case-Based Reasoning*, Master thesis, University of Kaiserslautern, Germany, 2001.
9. Mougouie, B., Bergmann, R.: Similarity Assessment for Generalized Cases by Optimization Methods. In: S. Craw & A. Preece (Eds.) *Advances in Case-Based Reasoning, 6th European Conference (ECCBR 2002).* Lecture Notes in Artificial Intelligence, 2416, Springer, 249–263, 2002.
10. Mougouie B., Richter M. M.: Generalized Cases, Similarity and Optimization. In: D. Hutter, W. Stephan (Eds.), *Deduction and beyond*, LNAI 2605, Springer-Verlag, 2003.
11. Schaaf, M., Maximini, R., Bergmann, R., Tautz, C., Traphoener, R.: Supporting Electronic Design Reuse by Integrating Quality-Criteria into CBR-based IP Selection. In: S. Craw & A. Preece (Eds.) *Advances in Case-Based Reasoning, 6th European Conference (ECCBR 2002).* Lecture Notes in Artificial Intelligence, 2416, Springer, 628–641, 2002.

12. Schaaf, M., Visarius, M., Bergmann, R., Maximini, R., Spinelli, M., Lessmann, J., Hardt, W., Ihmor, S., Thronicke, W.: IPCHL – A Description Language for Semantic IP Characterization. *Forum on Specification an Design Languages (FDL'2002)*,2002.
13. Smyth, B., McClave, P.: Similarity vs. Diversity. In: Aha, D.W, Watson, I. (eds.): *Case-Based Reasoning Research and Development*, Springer, pp. 347–361, 2001.

Assessing Elaborated Hypotheses: An Interpretive Case-Based Reasoning Approach

J. William Murdock, David W. Aha, and Leonard A. Breslow

Intelligent Decision Aids Group
Navy Center for Applied Research in Artificial Intelligence
Naval Research Laboratory, Code 5515
Washington, DC 20375
lastname@aic.nrl.navy.mil

Abstract. Identifying potential terrorist threats is a crucial task, especially in our post 9/11 world. This task is performed by intelligence analysts, who search for threats in the context of an overwhelming amount of data. We describe AHEAD (Analogical Hypothesis Elaborator for Activity Detection), a knowledge-rich post-processor that analyzes automatically-generated hypotheses using an interpretive case-based reasoning methodology to help analysts understand and evaluate the hypotheses. AHEAD first attempts to retrieve a functional model of a process, represented in the Task-Method-Knowledge framework (Stroulia & Goel, 1995; Murdock & Goel, 2001), to identify the context of a given hypothesized activity. If retrieval succeeds, AHEAD then determines how the hypothesis instantiates the process. Finally, AHEAD generates arguments that explain how the evidence justifies and/or contradicts the hypothesis according to this instantiated process. Currently, we have implemented AHEAD's case (i.e., model) retrieval step and its user interface for displaying and browsing arguments in a human-readable form. In this paper, we describe AHEAD and detail its first evaluation. We report positive results including improvements in speed, accuracy, and confidence for users analyzing hypotheses about detected threats.

1 Introduction

Terrorist activities are examples of *asymmetric threats*, which occur when a small, secretive group engages in a conflict with a large, powerful (e.g., military, law enforcement) group. Preventing asymmetric threats requires their *detection*. For example, if a law enforcement group detects an attempt by an organized crime group to take over a commercial industry in some region, the law enforcement group can then attempt to stop the takeover or reverse it. Unfortunately, detection is exceedingly difficult for many asymmetric threat domains because their data sets are both large and complex, involving many types of relationships among entities. Thus, detection can require an enormous amount of time.

The DARPA Evidence Extraction and Link Discovery (EELD) program is trying to speed the detection process and increase its reliability by creating software that

K.D. Ashley and D.G. Bridge (Eds.): ICCBR 2003, LNAI 2689, pp. 332–346, 2003.
© Springer-Verlag Berlin Heidelberg 2003

automatically discovers potential asymmetric threats. EELD consists of research and development in three primary areas: evidence extraction, link discovery, and pattern learning. *Evidence extraction* tools convert unstructured data (i.e., raw text) into structured data (e.g., semantic networks or databases). *Link discovery* tools match collections of structured data to known patterns of asymmetric threats. Finally, *pattern learning* discovers new patterns of asymmetric threats. EELD is integrating these three areas to perform fast and accurate detection of threats from organized crime, terrorist groups, etc.

This integrated EELD system runs the risk of generating hypotheses of varying credibility (e.g., false positives). Consequently, an additional challenge arises, namely *elaboration*: providing information to help an intelligence analyst determine whether a hypothesized threat is genuine and decide how to respond to it. To address this, we are developing AHEAD (Analogical Hypothesis Elaborator for Activity Detection), the EELD component that performs hypothesis elaboration. AHEAD takes as input a hypothesis from EELD's link discovery components, along with the evidence used to create that hypothesis, and outputs a structured argument for and/or against that hypothesis. These arguments should help a user (e.g., an intelligence analyst) to quickly and confidently decide whether and how to respond to hypothesized asymmetric threats.

We introduced AHEAD in (Murdock *et al.*, 2003); it uses an interpretive case-based reasoning process consisting of three steps: *case retrieval, solution proposal,* and *solution justification.* These steps are part of the general process for case-based reasoning defined by Kolodner & Leake (1996). Currently, we have implemented only AHEAD's case retrieval step and user interface, which permits an analyst to examine and browse the given hypotheses and the arguments generated by AHEAD. In this paper, we elaborate AHEAD's design and detail its first evaluation. In particular, we test whether its interface can assist the analyst in accurately determining the hypothesized threat's validity, increasing the analyst's confidence in this assessment, and reducing the time required to study the hypothesis before making the assessment. Section 7 describes this experiment, an initial pilot study, and its encouraging results.

2 Motivations and Related Work

In any asymmetric threat domain (e.g., terrorism, organized crime), threats are relatively infrequent and are sufficiently complex that a virtually limitless range of variations exists. Thus, any new threat that arises is unlikely to be an exact or near-exact match to some past instance and is therefore unlikely to be detected or elaborated through using specific concrete cases. Consequently, we are employing *generalized cases* (Bergmann, 2002) to represent asymmetric threats. Specifically, we use functional process models; a single model encodes an abstract representation of a hostile process, such as a takeover of an industry by an organized crime group, and multiple instances of takeovers could match to a single model. Many other systems integrate CBR with other reasoning approaches (e.g., Rissland & Skalak, 1989; Branting, 1991; Goel, Bhatta, & Stroulia, 1997), and some include processes as cases (e.g., Cox 1997; Tautz & Fenstermacher, 2001). AHEAD combines these characteristics in an interpretive process that elaborates hypotheses regarding asymmetric threats.

Sibyl (Eilbert, 2002) is another CBR approach in the EELD program. Sibyl uses CBR for hypothesis generation; it uses generalized cases (to ensure close matches exist for a new input), and its cases closely resemble the evidence in structure and content (to enable fast matching of cases to large bodies of unorganized relational data). AHEAD's cases differ significantly from Sibyl's because they are used for different purposes that impose different demands. Whereas Sibyl searches for threats, AHEAD does not. Instead, it is given a threat hypothesis, which is directly tied to relevant pieces of evidence, and focuses on elaboration of this hypothesis. Thus, AHEAD's cases do not need to be structured for efficient matching to large bodies of evidence. However, they do need to include information not only on *what kinds* of evidence are consistent with a given hypothesized threat, but also on *why* that evidence is consistent with it. Consequently, AHEAD uses *functional* models of processes as cases; such models describe both the actions performed in the process and how those actions contribute to the overall effect.

Although some previous CBR research projects have employed functional process models for explanation, they were not used to generate arguments concerning whether a process is occurring. Instead, functional process models have generally been used to explain a process that the system performed itself (e.g., Goel & Murdock, 1996). AHEAD represents a novel application of model-based CBR to help generate arguments concerning detected activities.

While previous work has studied argumentation in interpretive CBR, that work focused on domains in which detailed models of the processes under examination do not exist (e.g., Aleven & Ashley, 1996) or are best defined in terms of concrete examples (e.g., McLaren & Ashley, 2000). AHEAD employs an innovative structure for the generated arguments, derived from the capabilities provided by functional process models and from the goal of helping an analyst to accept or reject a complex detected hypothesis.

3   Case Representation: TMK Models

Cases in AHEAD are generalizations of concrete event descriptions. For example, instead of describing a single specific industry takeover by a criminal group, a case in AHEAD provides an abstract description of the process by which criminal groups take over industries. AHEAD's representation of processes includes information about how the process is performed and why portions of the process contribute to its overall objective. This representation is known as the TMK (Task-Method-Knowledge) modeling framework (Stroulia & Goel, 1995; Murdock & Goel, 2001). A TMK model is divided into *tasks* (defining what the process is intended to accomplish), *methods* (defining how the process works), and *knowledge* (information that drives the process by providing context).

Figure 1 displays a high-level overview of a sample TMK model that can be used in AHEAD. The rectangles represent tasks, the rounded boxes represent methods, and the oblique parallelograms represent parameters in the knowledge base. Methods include state transition machines that impose ordering constraints on subtasks. Labeled links denote relational information encoded in the tasks and methods. These links connect tasks, methods, parameters, and other links. For example, there is a link labeled *makes* from the *Industry-Takeover* task to the link labeled *controls* from the *Mafiya* parameter to the *Target-Industry* parameter. Those links indicate that an industry takeover produces a state in which the involved mafiya controls the target industry. The bottom of Figure 1 shows ellipses, indicating that those tasks can be further decomposed by additional methods into lower-level tasks.

Because TMK is a functional process modeling language (i.e., it encodes not only the elements of the process but also the purposes that those elements serve in the context of the process as a whole), an argument based on a TMK model can both indicate *which* pieces of evidence are consistent with the given hypothesis and also identify *why* that evidence supports the hypothesis. Consequently, TMK is well suited to addressing AHEAD's knowledge requirements. Models in AHEAD are currently composed manually using domain expertise developed within the EELD program. In future work, we intend to study automatic learning of models from instances and/or interactive support for graphical authoring of models.

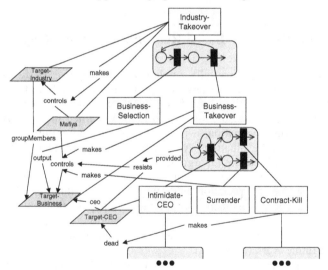

Fig. 1. A partial TMK model of an industry takeover

4 Output: Structured Arguments

AHEAD's argumentation structure is inspired by Toulmin (1958), and specifically concentrates on relating facts from the evidence to specific assertions about the process being performed (Murdock *et al.*, 2003). For example, an argument involving an industry takeover would step through the various events in that takeover (e.g., selecting business, intimidating CEO's). At the root of the argument is the original *hypothesis* that was provided as input to AHEAD. Associated with that hypothesis are individual, atomic *arguments for* the hypothesis and *arguments against* the hypothesis.

Each argument for the hypothesis is an assertion that some portion of the retrieved model is likely to have occurred. Arguments against the hypothesis assert that some portion of the model has not occurred. Some arguments against the hypothesis include links to evidence indicating that the portion of the model did not occur, while others simply indicate a lack of evidence for the event. Each argument for or against includes a statement of what happens in the model and (when applicable) a statement of the purpose of what happens. For example, an industry takeover model states that (under certain circumstances) an organized crime group will kill a CEO of a business because that CEO resists a takeover of that business. In a hypothesis that said (for example) that a particular CEO was killed as part of an industry takeover, there would be an argument for or against involving the assertion that this CEO was killed because he or she resisted an attempt to control the business. That assertion would be included in an argument for the hypothesis if the evidence supported the claim (e.g., if there was a police report saying that a member of that crime group killed that CEO). It would be included in an argument against the hypothesis if there were no supporting evidence or there were evidence contradicting the claim.

5   An Interpretive Case-Based Reasoning Methodology

The AHEAD methodology partially implements *interpretive* CBR (Kolodner & Leake, 1996). Interpretive CBR differs from problem-solving CBR in that it analyzes a given situation (here, a paired hypothesis and its evidence). After case *retrieval*, interpretive CBR *proposes* a solution, which is then *justified* prior to *critiquing* and *evaluation*. Following evaluation, a justified solution may require *adaptation* and then further critique and evaluation. A distinctive element of interpretive CBR is its justification step, which creates an argument for a given interpretation by comparing and contrasting the current situation with the interpretation of the stored situation (to determine whether the interpretation holds for the current situation). The critiquing step tests a justification's argument by applying it to hypothetical situations, prior to evaluation. AHEAD implements retrieval, solution proposal, and solution justification but leaves critiquing, evaluation, and adaptation to the user; we discuss this further in future work (Section 8).

Figure 2 displays AHEAD's functional architecture. Briefly, AHEAD's algorithm consists of three primary steps:

1. *Retrieve*: Given a hypothesis (i.e., a possible terrorist activity) and a library of TMK models representing types of these activities, retrieve the model that best matches that hypothesis.
2. *Propose*: Given the matched model and the evidence leading to the hypothesis, generate the instantiation of that model (i.e., a *trace* in that model) that best matches the evidence. Instantiation is needed because AHEAD's process models are generalizations of concrete cases.
3. *Justify*: Given a model trace and the evidence, analyze the situation described by this evidence and create arguments (both pro and con) explaining why that situation does or does not match that trace.

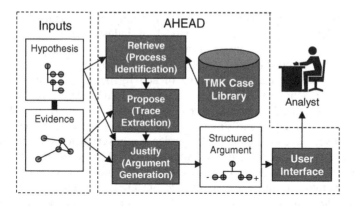

Fig. 2. Functional architecture for AHEAD.

Figure 3 displays procedural pseudocode for these three steps. The three steps are detailed in the following subsections.

---

h: Hypothesis, **e**: Evidence, **L**: Library of process models, **p**: Process model, **t**: Trace (in p), **a**: Argument (both pro and con)

AHEAD(**h**,**e**,**L**) =
        p = identify_process(**h**,**L**)   ; Retrieve
        t = extract_trace(**e**,**p**)   ; Propose
        a = generate_argument(**h**,**e**,**t**) ; Justify
        return(**a**)

Fig. 3. AHEAD's pseudocode.

5.1 Retrieve: Process Identification

The first phase relates the given hypothesis to a TMK process model. It implements a *case retrieval* step by identifying which model in AHEAD's library of TMK models is most relevant to the given hypothesis. AHEAD uses an off-the-shelf analogical mapping tool for retrieval, namely the FIRE Analogy Server (from the Institute for Learning Sciences' Qualitative Reasoning Group at Northwestern University), a general-purpose analogical reasoning tool (Forbus, 2001). Some automated syntactic transformation is required to represent hypotheses and models in the Analogy Server's formalism. The portion of the Analogy Server that AHEAD directly invokes is MAC/FAC (Gentner & Forbus, 1991), which yields for AHEAD (1) the case (i.e., a TMK model) that most closely matches the input hypothesis, and (2) a mapping between elements of the input and the case.

Consider, for example, the following hypothesis: a local organized crime group has taken over the cigarette industry in Kaliningrad and has killed two people during that takeover. AHEAD would invoke MAC/FAC on that hypothesis using the case library of TMK models to retrieve a TMK model of industry takeovers and to map parameters of that model to entities in the hypothesis (e.g., the parameter for target industry would be mapped to the Kaliningrad cigarette industry).

If no model exactly matches the type of activity being performed, MAC/FAC would retrieve an approximate match. For example, if AHEAD receives a hypothesis concerning an organized crime takeover of postal service in some area, MAC/FAC would recognize that the overall structure of the hypothesis resembles the structure of industry takeovers, even though a postal service is a government organization, not an industry. The specific entities in the hypothesis can then be mapped to analogous model elements. This would allow AHEAD to then perform trace extraction and argument generation using this partially relevant model. If there is no model that even comes close to the hypothesis, AHEAD would skip over the trace extraction portion and proceed directly to argument generation (see Section 5.3).

5.2 Propose: Trace Extraction

In the second phase, AHEAD constructs a *trace*: a permissible temporal path through the model with parameter bindings and links to supporting evidence. Because the trace constitutes an elaboration of the hypothesized case, trace extraction is the portion of the general interpretive CBR process (Kolodner & Leake 1996) in which an interpretation is proposed. To illustrate, if an input hypothesis posited an industry takeover, the trace extraction process would start with the mapping between the specific hypothesis and a general model of industry takeovers. It would then determine a temporal path through the model that could produce the observed evidence. Insights from this process would include inferences about what parts of the model have been completed and what parts are underway (e.g., that one company in the industry is being threatened but has not yet been taken over). The trace would include direct links to supporting or contradicting evidence. AHEAD quickly finds relevant evidence because the model is linked to the hypothesis (during analogical retrieval) and the hypothesis is linked to the evidence (in the input).

For example, the model of industry takeovers (Figure 1) involves attempts to take over multiple businesses within the industry, and a business takeover is further decomposed into lower level tasks involving intimidating the CEO of the business and possibly killing the CEO. There are multiple possible paths through the model. For example, if the criminal organization succeeds in taking over a business after intimidating a CEO, then it has no need to kill that CEO. Thus, if the evidence for a particular business takeover suggests that the crime group succeeded through CEO intimidation, then there will be no step in the trace that encodes the killing. However, if the crime group failed to intimidate but did not kill the CEO, then the trace would contain a step that represents the killing (because the model states that it should occur) along with evidence that the step did not occur; this trace step is used during argument generation to create an argument against the hypothesis.

The details of the trace extraction process are illustrated in Figure 4. The inputs to this process are the outputs of the Analogy Server: the model and the mapping between the model and the given hypothesis. The first step in trace extraction is the production of an empty trace (i.e., a trace of the model that asserts that no actions in the model have been performed and that no parameters in the model have been bound). This empty trace is provided to an *atemporal trace-evidence unifier*, which adjusts the trace to be consistent with the evidence at a fixed moment in time. For the empty trace, the unifier adjusts the trace to reflect the world state prior to any actions being taken (i.e., it produces a trace reflecting the initial state). The initial trace is then passed to a *temporal trace iterator*. This subcomponent moves through a single step in the model. It produces a potential updated trace, which indicates that an additional step has been performed, but does not include information about how the evidence supports or contradicts that step. This trace is passed back to the unifier, which does connect the trace at that step to the evidence. The loop between the iterator and the unifier continues until the unifier determines that the final state of the trace corresponds to the current world state. The trace may cover the entire model at this point (suggesting that the process has been completed) or it may only cover part of the model (suggesting that the process is still ongoing).

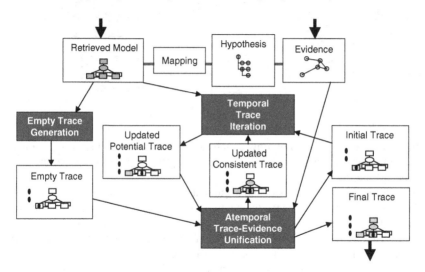

Fig. 4. Details of the trace extraction process.

5.3   Justify: Argument Generation

Finally, AHEAD constructs arguments concerning the hypothesis based on the extracted trace; this constitutes a *justification* step of the general process for interpretive CBR (Kolodner & Leake, 1996). More specifically, the argument generation process steps through the extracted trace and produces arguments for or against the input hypothesis based on the evidence

For example, evidence from a business takeover may suggest that a group intimidated the CEO, did not take over the business, and did not kill the CEO. In this example, one portion of the argument AHEAD produces would support the overall hypothesis of an industry takeover (because intimidating a CEO is part of industry takeovers), while another portion of the argument would contradict the claim (because killing the CEO would be expected under the circumstances but did not occur). A user examining the argument could decide that the latter evidence is strong enough to conclude that an industry takeover has not occurred (i.e., that the intimidation of the CEO was part of some other kind of activity). Alternatively, the user might conclude that the crime group simply acted in an atypical manner or that the activity is still

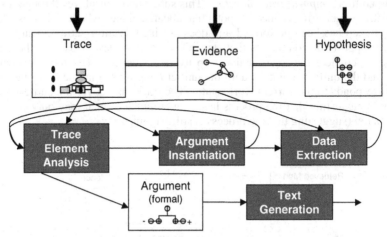

Fig. 5. Details of the argument generation process.

taking place. AHEAD does not draw conclusions of these sorts; it simply presents the relevant information supporting and/or contradicting the hypothesis so that the analyst can make a final judgment.

Figure 5 displays the details of the argument generation process. Each element of the trace is analyzed. Elements of the trace include links to facts that support or contradict them; supporting facts lead to arguments for the hypothesis while opposing facts (or a lack of facts) lead to arguments against the hypothesis. Once the analysis is complete, AHEAD has built a formal structured argument consisting of logical assertions. This formal structured argument (including the original hypothesis, the individual arguments for and against, and the facts supporting those arguments) is translated into semiformal and informal versions via a text generation module. The semiformal version is structured as a nested tree composed of small chunks of English text (e.g., "targeted industry: Kaliningrad cigarette market"). The informal version is structured as full sentences and paragraphs; it is much less concise than the semiformal version but may be helpful for users who are unfamiliar with the exact semantics of the semiformal tree. Users can browse both the informal version and the semiformal version of the arguments (see Section 6); the formal version is intended only for use in automated processing.

There are two extreme circumstances for the execution of the argument generator. In the first, retrieval of the model has failed and thus no trace extraction has been performed. In this situation, the trace element analysis loop runs zero times and no arguments for or against the hypothesis are produced; text generation then operates only on the hypothesis (as the root of the structured argument). Thus AHEAD's user interface is still able to present the hypothesis in an organized, textual format even when it fails to produce any analysis of that hypothesis. The second extreme condition for argument generation is one in which no evidence supporting the hypothesis was found during trace extraction. In this situation, every step in the model will have a corresponding argument against, pointing to a lack of evidence. This result is slightly more informative than the former (i.e., it does give the user a sense of what evidence would be relevant if it were available).

6 Graphical User Interface

AHEAD's user interface allows the user to browse through the semiformal and informal versions of the arguments associated with each hypothesis. Whenever the Argument Generator produces an argument, that argument and the hypothesis that led to it are stored in a library of bindings between hypotheses and arguments. An argument server provides access to this library; it sends the arguments to an argument browser (a web applet). The analyst may then navigate among different hypotheses and related arguments. The browser also has features for switching among semiformal and informal versions of the hypothesis and argument. Furthermore, the browser allows the various elements of the tree representation to be expanded and collapsed, enabling a user to view an abstract overview of the entire argument and then zoom in for details. Finally, the arguments include links to original sources, allowing an analyst to see the arguments' evidential support.

Figure 6 shows a screen shot of AHEAD's argument browser. In this figure, the hypothesis, argument for, and argument against areas are all being presented in semiformal notation. The red and black icons accompanying each argument denote qualitative degrees of certainty (based on source reliability and qualitative heuristics) as indicated by the key at the bottom. For example, complete red squares represent

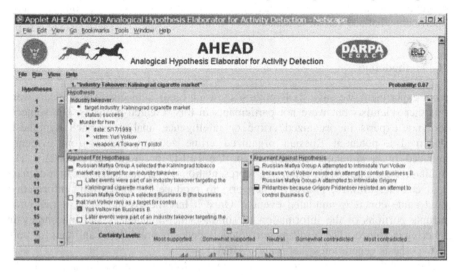

Fig. 6. Screenshot of AHEAD's GUI.

extremely well supported statements while half-filled black squares represent moderately contradicted statements. The example shown in the figure involves an argument in the domain of Russian organized crime, one of the challenge problems in the EELD program. In particular, the hypothesis presented to AHEAD involves an industry takeover decomposed into a set of murder-for-hire events. The argument produced by AHEAD includes concrete steps in this industry takeover and the data that indicates whether those steps occurred in this specific instance. The references to evidence (which appear in blue) are hyperlinks that allow a user to directly access the original source or sources for that evidence. In addition to the view shown in the figure, AHEAD also provides a less compact, informal view in which relationships between elements are written out explicitly (e.g., "An attempt to control a business typically includes an attempt to intimidate the CEO. There is a lack of support for the belief that Russian Mafiya Group A attempted to intimidate Yuri Volkov.").

7 Evaluation

We recently conducted an internal pilot study focusing on AHEAD's user interface and the arguments presented in that interface. In this study users were asked to rank the credibility of presented hypotheses, where only some of the hypotheses were accompanied by their arguments. Because some of AHEAD's automated components (i.e., the Trace Extractor and parts of the Argument Generator) are not yet functional, we constructed outputs for these processes by hand. However, we did follow AHEAD's overall process in producing the arguments for the evaluation, so we expect that when the automated components are complete they will produce outputs comparable to the ones we used in this experiment. Consequently, while this experiment provides an evaluation of AHEAD's GUI and the content of the arguments that AHEAD will produce, it does not investigate the computational costs or accuracy of automatically producing these arguments. We will conduct future experiments that address these issues.

7.1 Methodology

In our experiment, we gave six hypotheses to each of six subjects. The subjects were computer scientists but were not participants in this research project. The subjects were not experts in organized crime or intelligence analysis. Each hypothesis concerned a potential Russian organized crime activity, drawn from evidence produced by a simulator developed for the EELD program (IET, 2002). The simulator steps through a declarative representation of various activities in a domain (e.g., contract killings, industry takeovers) to produce "ground truth" information about some concrete simulated events. Once it has the ground truth, it randomly corrupts portions of the information to simulate incompleteness and inaccuracy in gathering evidence. The resulting corrupted evidence is provided as an input for both the hypothesis generation systems and AHEAD.

Three of the hypotheses concerned a single, isolated contract killing, while the other three involved industry takeovers (i.e., larger, more complex activities that include contract killings as subcomponents).   Two sources were used for the hypotheses: the ground truth answer key provided by the simulator (which is, by definition, absolutely correct) and the SCOPE iGEN module (Eilbert, 2002), an EELD pattern matching system.

In all trials, subjects had access to the *hypothesis* displayed in the top portion of AHEAD's user interface (see Figure 6) and the original *evidence* (in a separate data file). In some trials, subjects also had access to the *arguments* displayed in the bottom portion of the AHEAD user interface. The independent variable studied in this experiment is the presence or absence of the argument. The dependent variables correspond to responses to questionnaires. Each subject was given six hypotheses to evaluate. All subjects received the same six hypotheses, but each one had a different (randomly assigned) subset for which the argument was also presented. For each hypothesis, subjects were asked the following questions:

- How valid is this hypothesis? (1-10)
- How confident are you of your hypothesis validity assessment? (1-10)
- How much time did you spend studying this hypothesis?

At the end of the experiment, subjects were asked to indicate how much they liked the following features of AHEAD, each on a scale of 1-10:

- Presentation of the hypothesis
- Presentation of the arguments for the hypothesis
- Presentation of the arguments against the hypothesis

Finally, participants were asked to provide any additional comments concerning the interface and the displayed content.

7.2   Results

Table 1 displays the mean response values for the questions about the individual hypotheses. On average, users with arguments took 10% less time and indicated a confidence of approximately half a point higher. These are both encouraging results because increasing the speed with which analysts operate and their assessment confidence are primary objectives of this research.

Table 1. Mean results for the two experimental conditions.

Metric	With Argument	Without Argument
Elapsed Time	5:18	5:55
Confidence	7.40	6.86
Error in judgment	**1.83**	**3.01**
Error in confidence	1.70	2.26

Two other values are listed in Table 1. The first is *error in judgment*: a measure of how far the user's estimate of a hypothesis' validity is from the actual validity of that hypothesis. Actual validities were computed by comparing the hypothesis to the original ground truth using the scoring module associated with the EELD simulator;

the scores were scaled to a one to ten range for direct comparison with the users' judged validity. We define error in judgment for a hypothesis as the absolute difference between the judged validity and the scaled (one to ten) actual validity of that hypothesis. The last entry in Table 1 displays the *error in confidence*. Specifically, we define error in confidence for a hypothesis as the absolute difference between how far the user was from being certain (i.e., ten minus the confidence) and how far the user was from being correct (i.e., the error in judgment). On average, users showed lower errors in judgment and lower errors in confidence when they did have arguments than when they did not arguments. These are also important and encouraging results.

All of the results shown in Table 1 were tested for statistical significance using a one-tailed t test assuming unequal variance. The result for error in judgment was found to be statistically significant with $p<.05$ (as indicated by boldface in Table 1); this was very encouraging because correctness is arguably our most important objective. The other results were not statistically significant in this pilot study. Given the observed variances and differences in means, a t test would require about three times as much data to get statistically significant results for confidence and error in confidence and about fifteen times as much data to get statistically significant results for the elapsed time. It may be possible to reduce the amount of data needed in future experiments by having more constrained tasks.

The results for the summary questions were also encouraging. Presentation of the hypothesis and the arguments against the hypothesis received an average rating of 7.5; presentation of the arguments for the hypothesis received an average rating of 8.6. These results suggest a reasonably favorable impression. Some additional comments addressed specific concerns regarding the interface (e.g., layout of the arguments); these comments will help us in designing future versions of the interface.

8 Future Work

We intend to extend the range of capabilities that AHEAD can provide in a purely automated context. The current AHEAD methodology does not include any step in the process in which some conclusion is drawn about whether the hypothesis is valid; the information in the argument is only expected to help a user determine the hypothesis' plausibility. Automated evaluation of structured explanations is a topic that has been addressed in previous CBR research (Leake, 1992). We may build on this work to enable automated evaluation of hypotheses using the arguments that AHEAD constructs. This hypothesis evaluator could be used as a filter (i.e., users would only see those hypotheses that AHEAD assigned a credibility rating above a certain threshold). Furthermore, this ability could be used to identify critical weaknesses in a hypothesis that could then be sent back to the original hypothesis generation system to drive a search for a stronger hypothesis. In our first round of development, we intend to perform automated evaluation using three interrelated Russian organized crime models (contract killing, industry takeovers, and gang wars). In later work we will increase the number of models and address other domains.

Another key element for future work concerns more elaborate evaluation. After completing AHEAD's implementation, we will conduct increasingly informative evaluations and make incremental refinements based on the results. We will pursue three primary improvements in the evaluation process. First, we will increase the number of subjects that perform the experiments to obtain more statistically meaningful results. Second, we will examine a wider variety of experimental conditions; in the current evaluation we compared performance only with and without arguments, but in later evaluations we will compare performance with different parts of the arguments and/or different variations on argument generation and presentation. Third, we will conduct experiments with real-world data and subject matter experts (i.e., analysts). The third improvement is potentially difficult and costly, but it is crucial for realistically evaluating how well AHEAD addresses its motivating problems.

9   Conclusions

Our pilot study provides preliminary support for the following hypotheses concerning the content and presentation of AHEAD's arguments:

- The arguments allow users to make judgments about hypotheses **faster**.
- The arguments enable more **accurate** judgments about hypotheses.
- The arguments give users more **confidence** in their judgments.
- The arguments lead to more **reliable** reports of confidence.

We expect additional development to enable fully automated production of these arguments. Once that work is complete, we will develop new variations on the content and organization of our arguments. We are also in contact with intelligence analysts for their feedback and suggestions on user interface design and argument content. These efforts will enable us to conduct future experiments that contrast different types of arguments and see how each performs along the different metrics we have considered. Such experiments will enable us to produce an increasingly beneficial tool for enabling analysts to understand and react to hypotheses in a wide variety of asymmetric threat domains.

Acknowledgements. Thanks to Dan Fu and Jim Eilbert for providing hypotheses for development and testing of AHEAD, to our subjects, and to Kalyan Moy Gupta and David Leake for discussions. The lead author holds a National Research Council Associateship Award at the Naval Research Laboratory. The work of the other authors is sponsored by the Defense Advanced Research Projects Agency. The views and conclusions contained in this document are those of the authors and should not be interpreted as necessarily representing the official policies, either expressed or implied of DARPA or the United States Government.

References

Aleven, V., & Ashley, K. (1996). How different is different? Arguing about the significance of similarities and differences. *Proceedings of the Third European Workshop on Case-Based Reasoning* (pp. 1–15). Lausanne, Switzerland: Springer.

Bergmann, R. (2002). *Experience management: Foundations, development methodology, and Internet based applications.* New York: Springer.

Branting, K. (1991). Reasoning with portions of precedents. *Proceedings of the Third International Conference on AI and Law* (pp. 145–154). Oxford, UK: ACM Press

Cox, M. (1997). An explicit representation of reasoning failures. *Proceedings of the Second International Conference on Case-Based Reasoning* (pp. 211–222). Providence, RI: Springer.

Eilbert, J. (2002). *Socio-culturally oriented plan discovery environment (SCOPE).* Presentation at the Fall 2002 EELD PI Meeting. San Diego, CA: Unpublished slides.

Forbus, K. (2001). Exploring analogy in the large. In D. Gentner, K. Holyoak, & B. Kokinov (Eds.) *The analogical mind: Perspectives from cognitive science.* Cambridge, MA: MIT Press.

Gentner, D., & Forbus, K. (1991). MAC/FAC: A model of similarity-based retrieval. *Proceedings of the Thirteenth Annual Conference of the Cognitive Science Society* (pp. 504–509). Chicago, IL: Lawrence Erlbaum.

Goel, A., Bhatta, S. & Stroulia, E. (1997). Kritik: An early case-based design system. In M. Maher and P. Pu. (Eds.) *Issues and Applications of Case-Based Reasoning in Design.* Mahwah, NJ: Erlbaum.

Goel, A.K., & Murdock, J.W. (1996). Meta-cases: Explaining case-based reasoning. *Proceedings of the Third European Workshop on Case-Based Reasoning* (pp. 150–163). Lausanne, Switzerland: Springer.

IET [Information Extraction & Transport, Inc.] (2002). *Task-based simulator version 9.1.* Unpublished user's manual. Arlington, VA.

Kolodner, J., & Leake, D. (1996). A tutorial introduction to case-based reasoning. In D. Leake (Ed.) *Case-based reasoning: Experiences, lessons, & future directions.* Cambridge, MA: MIT Press & AAAI Press.

Leake, D. (1992). *Evaluating explanations: A content theory.* Mahwah, NJ: Erlbaum.

McLaren, B.M. & Ashley, K.D. (2000). Assessing relevance with extensionally defined principles and cases. *Proceedings of the Seventeenth National Conference on Artificial Intelligence.* Austin, Texas: AAAI Press

Murdock, J.W., Aha, D.W., & Breslow, L.A. (2003). Case-based argumentation via process models. To appear in *Proceedings of the Fifteenth International Conference of the Florida Artificial Intelligence Research Society.* St. Augustine, FL: AAAI Press.

Murdock, J.W., & Goel, A.K. (2001). Meta-case-based reasoning: Using functional models to adapt case-based systems. *Proceedings of the Fourth International Conference on Case-Based Reasoning* (pp. 407–421). Vancouver, Canada: Springer.

Rissland, E.L & Skalak, D.B. (1989). Combining case-based and rule-based reasoning: A heuristic approach. *Proceedings of the Eleventh International Joint Conference on Artificial Intelligence* (524–530). Detroit, MI: Morgan Kaufmann.

Stroulia, E., & Goel, A.K. (1995). Functional representation and reasoning in reflective systems. *Applied Intelligence,* 9, 101–124.

Tautz, C. & Fenstermacher, K. (Eds.) (2001). Case-base reasoning approaches for process-oriented knowledge management. In R. Weber & C.G. von Wangenheim (Eds.) *Case-Based Reasoning: Papers from the Workshop Program at ICCBR-2001* (Technical Note AIC-01-003, pp. 6–28). Washington, DC: Naval Research Laboratory.

Toulmin, S. (1958). *The uses of argument.* Cambridge, UK: Cambridge University Press.

Soft Interchangeability for Case Adaptation

Nicoleta Neagu and Boi Faltings

Artificial Intelligence Laboratory (LIA),
Computer Science Department, Swiss Federal Institute of Technology (EPFL)
CH-1015 Ecublens, Switzerland
{Nicoleta.Neagu, Boi.Faltings}@epfl.ch http://liawww.epfl.ch/

Abstract. In [1] we propose interchangeability based algorithms as methods for solving the case adaptation for the domain of problems which can be expressed as *Constraint Satisfaction Problems*. In this paper we extend the domain to *Soft Constraint Satisfaction Problems* and give generic adaptation methods based on soft interchangeability concepts.

Many real-life problems require the use of preferences. This need motivates for the use of soft constrains which allows the use of preferences.

We have defined interchangeability for soft CSPs in [2] by introducing two notions: $(^\delta/_\alpha)$substitutability/interchangeability and their algorithms. This paper presents how to build generic adaptation methods based on soft interchangeability. It gives an example of an application of a sales manager system for a car configuration domain and reports test results regarding number of $(^\delta/_\alpha)$interchangeability in random generated problems, thus number of adaptation alternatives.

Keywords: case adaptation, hard/soft constraint satisfaction problems, interchangeability, substitutability.

1 Introduction

In [1], we proposed a generic framework for case adaptation for the domain of problems which can be represented as *Classic Constraint Satisfaction Problems*(CSP). The CSP model can be applied to a wide range of problems [3], well known examples are: diagnosis [4], planning [5], scheduling [6], robot control [7] and configuration [8] but there are still many real life problems which cannot be precisely defined by using classical constraints only. Soft constraints allow for preference levels to be associated to either constraints, or variables, or tuples within the constraints. In this paper we propose adaptation methods for the domains of problems where the knowledge can be represented as a *Soft Constraint Satisfaction Problem*. Certain domains must be represented as hard constraint satisfaction problems in order for the resulting solution to be functional. For example, in the configuration of a product, the components have to match so that the product is functional. However, many other real-life problems are more naturally handled by using soft constraints [9,10]. Classical CSPs consist of a number of choices that need to be made (variables), each of which has an associated number of options (the variable domain) and a set of relationships between choices (constraints). A valid solution to a CSP is an assignment of a value to each variable from its domain with the total set of assignments respecting all the problem constraints. In *soft* CSPs, the significance of the

K.D. Ashley and D.G. Bridge (Eds.): ICCBR 2003, LNAI 2689, pp. 347–361, 2003.
© Springer-Verlag Berlin Heidelberg 2003

constraints is not that a tuple of values for some variables is allowed or not, but rather the *preference* level at which it is allowed. One of the frameworks which formalises *soft* CSPs is the one based on the semiring, see [10]: where each tuple of values in each constraints has an assigned semiring value, to be interpreted as the level of preference of that tuple, or its cost, or any other measurable feature. Further, the constraints are combined according to the semiring operations and the result of the combination is that the assignment for all the variables has a corresponding semiring value too.

In [11], we defined two notions: *threshold* α and *degradation* δ for substitutability and interchangeability, $(({}^{\delta}/_{\alpha})$substitutability/interchangeability). Fortunately, soft constraints also allow weaker forms of interchangeability where exchanging values may result in a degradation of solution quality by some measure δ. By allowing more degradation, it is possible to increase the amount of interchangeability in a problem to the desired level. ${}^{\delta}$substitutability/interchangeability is a concept which ensures this quality. Ideally, one would like to compute values which are interchangeable over global solutions, *full interchangeable*, but this is computational expensive. That is way, the search of this values is computed in local forms, called *neighbourhood interchangeability*. Just as for hard constraints, full interchangeability is hard to compute, but can be approximated by neighbourhood interchangeability which can be computed efficiently and implies full interchangeability. We have defined the same concepts for soft constraints, and prove that neighbourhood implies full $({}^{\delta}/_{\alpha})$substitutability/interchangeability, see [2].

We propose here to apply these techniques in a CBR system where the knowledge domain is represented as a soft CSP. By allowing a certain degradation $delta$ of a case or searching over a certain threshold $alpha$ one can try to realise adaptation. So, in this paper we show how case adaptation can be realised based on these concepts.

The main contribution of this paper is a generic model for the application of soft interchangeability techniques to a large class of CBR adaptation problems (Section 4). We also present an practical product configuration application (Section 2) and examples of our technique within that domain. We conclude the paper with our first experimental results (Section 5) measuring $({}^{\delta}/_{\alpha})$interchangeability occurrence and thus, the number of adaptation alternatives.

Additionally, in Section 3 we recall the main definitions of soft interchangeability/substitutability that are of interest to us, related work is provided in Section 6 while conclusions and further work can be found in Section 7.

2   A Product Configuration CBR System

The CSP model can be applied to a very wide range of problems. We present here how the framework works for a configuration problem example. However, the framework works in the same way for all the problems which can be represented as a CSP.

We have applied and tested constraint satisfaction based methods in a case based reasoning system which function as a sales manager. The case base reasoning system contains cases which represent past sales and consist of a buyer profile and the chosen product. The configuration of the product is modelled as a constraint satisfaction problem. While admissible configurations can be precisely specified as a constraint satisfaction problem, each customer has particular needs that remain largely unformalized. Case-based reasoning maps properties of the customer to these implicit customer needs and product configuration that would fit these needs. Constraint satisfaction techniques can then be used to adapt the proposed solution by the CBR system to the particular customer requirements and preferences.

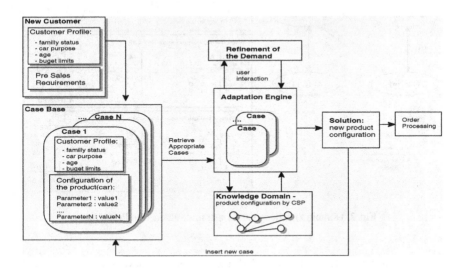

Fig. 1. An electronic sales manager based on a CBR system.

In Figure 1, we represent the general framework of our system. When a new customer makes a new demand, the sales system will search in the case base for similar cases by the use of buyer profile. Each case contains:

- a buyer profile contains:
  - characteristics: like age, family status, using purpose for the car, budget limits in the car investment,
  - particular preferences/requirements for the car.
- the chosen product which contains the configuration of the car as a constraint satisfaction problem solution where each component of the car has assigned a value consistent with all the other components, represented as variables of the CSP, according to the constraints between them.

The retrieved cases are sent to the adaptation engine which communicates with the buyer for further refinement of the demands; and using interchangeability methods adapts the solutions of the product configuration based on the domain knowledge. The domain knowledge is represented as a constraint satisfaction problem. By interacting with these two modules the adaptation engine reaches the new solution which together with the current buyer profile is inserted in the case base. Further, the sale order is send to processing.

In our example we present three models for representing the knowledge, as shown in Figure 2:

- the first example represents the configuration of the product modelled as a classic (hard) CSP where the constraints are either satisfied or not by a tuple of values; in

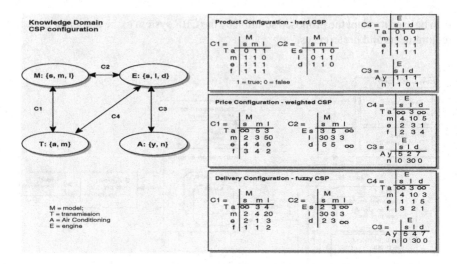

Fig. 2. Domain knowledge as Constraint Satisfaction Problems.

order that the product is functional all the components have to be compatible with one another.

- in the second example we model the price configuration for the cost of the product as a weighted CSP; the weights on the tuples of values represent the cost for each component (by unary constraints) and the costs for combinations of components respectively (by binary constraints).
- the last example represents the delivery of the product modelled as a fuzzy CSP where the preferences on the tuples of values represent the delivery time of the components and the combinations of components according to the constraints between them.

While the configuration of the product has to be expressed with hard constraints in order that the product is feasible, modelling the price and delivery time with soft constraints allows for the use of customer preferences. The found solutions are then ranked according to the optimisation criteria used by the soft constraint system.

3 Background

In the following we give a brief overview of soft CSPs and definitions of different forms of interchangeability.

3.1 Soft CSPs

In many practical applications, constraints can be violated at a cost, and solving a CSP thus means finding a value assignment of minimum cost [1]. Various frameworks for

---

[1] Through the paper we measure the quality of solution by the cost of the CSP, where the quality is good when the cost is low.

solving such soft constraints have been proposed [12,13,14,15,16,17,18]. The soft constraint framework of c-semirings [17] has been shown to express most of the known variants through different instantiations of its operators, and this is the framework we are considering in this paper.

A soft constraint may be seen as a constraint where each instantiation of its variables has an associated value from a partially ordered set which can be interpreted as a set of preference values. Combining constraints will then have to take into account such additional values, and thus the formalism has also to provide suitable operations for combination ($\times$) and comparison ($+$) of tuples of values and constraints. This is why this formalization is based on the concept of c-semiring, which is just a set plus two operations, [17].

A *c-semiring* is a semiring(a tuple) $\langle A, +, \times, \mathbf{0}, \mathbf{1} \rangle$ such that: $+$ is commutative, associative, idempotent, $\mathbf{0}$ is its unit element and $\mathbf{1}$ is its absorbing element; $\times$ is associative, distributes over $+$, commutative, $\mathbf{1}$ is its unit element and $\mathbf{0}$ is its absorbing element.

Soft Constraint Problems. Given a semiring $S = \langle A, +, \times, \mathbf{0}, \mathbf{1} \rangle$ and an ordered set of variables V over a finite domain D, a *constraint* is a function which, given an assignment $\eta : V \to D$ of the variables, returns a value of the semiring.

By using this notation we define $\mathcal{C} = \eta \to A$ as the set of all possible constraints that can be built starting from S, D and V.

Combining and projecting soft constraints. Given the set $\mathcal{C}$, the combination function $\otimes : \mathcal{C} \times \mathcal{C} \to \mathcal{C}$ is defined as $(c_1 \otimes c_2)\eta = c_1\eta \times_S c_2\eta$.

In words, combining two constraints means building a new constraint whose support involves all the variables of the original ones, and which associates with each tuple of domain values for such variables a semiring element which is obtained by multiplying the elements associated by the original constraints to the appropriate subtuples.

Given a constraint $c \in \mathcal{C}$ and a variable $v \in V$, the *projection* of c over $V - \{v\}$, written $c \Downarrow_{(V-\{v\})}$ is the constraint c' s.t. $c'\eta = \sum_{d \in D} c\eta[v := d]$.

Informally, projecting means eliminating some variables from the support. This is done by associating with each tuple over the remaining variables a semiring element which is the sum of the elements associated by the original constraint to all the extensions of this tuple over the eliminated variables. In short, combination is performed via the multiplicative operation of the semiring, and projection via the additive one.

3.2   Degradations and Thresholds in Soft CSPs

Interchangeability in constraint networks proposed by Freuder in [19], captures equivalence among the variables values in a discrete CSP. Two values a and b of a CSP variable v are *interchangeable* if for any solution where $v = a$, there is an identical solution except that $v = b$, and vice versa.

The most straightforward generalization of interchangeability to soft CSP would require that exchanging one value for another does not change the quality of the solution at all. This generalization is likely to suffer from the same weaknesses as interchangeability in hard CSP, namely that it is very rare.

Fortunately, soft constraints also allow weaker forms of interchangeability where exchanging values may result in a degradation of solution quality by some measure δ. By allowing more degradation, it is possible to increase the amount of interchangeability in a problem to the desired level. We define $^\delta$substitutability and $^\delta$interchangeability as a concept which ensures this quality. This is particularly useful when interchangeability is used for solution adaptation.

In a hard CSP, a CSP solution is a value assignment to the variables such that all the constraints are satisfied. In soft CSPs, any value assignment is a solution which have a corresponding semiring value. The semiring values represents the preference value of that solution. This allows broadening the original interchangeability concept to one that also allows degrading the solution quality when values are exchanged. We call this $^\delta$interchangeability, where δ is the *degradation* factor.

When searching for solutions to soft CSP, it is possible to gain efficiency by not distinguishing values that could in any case not be part of a solution of sufficient quality. In $_\alpha$interchangeability, two values are interchangeable if they do not affect the quality of any solution with quality better than α. We call α the *threshold* factor.

Both concepts can be combined, i.e. we can allow both degradation and limit search to solutions better than a certain threshold ($_\alpha^\delta$interchangeability).

By extending the previous definitions we can define thresholds and degradation version of full/neighbourhood substitutability/interchangeability.

As in the classical case, to find full soft interchangeability is computational expensive. However, there are local forms of neighbourhood interchangeability values which can be computed in polynomial time. Here are their definitions:

Definition 1. *Consider two domain values b and a for a variable v, the set of constraints C and a semiring level δ; we say that b is $^\delta$Full Substitutable for a on v ($b \in {}^\delta FS_v(a)$) if and only if for all assignments η,*

$$\bigotimes C\eta[v := a] \times_S \delta \leq_S \bigotimes C\eta[v := b]$$

We define values a and b to be $^\delta$Neighborhood Substitutable if the set of constraints C is limited to the constraints including V, C_v. Further, we define a and b to be $^\delta$Full/Neighborhood Interchangeable if they are $^\delta$Full/Neighborhood Substitutable both ways.

Definition 2. *Consider two domain values b and a, for a variable v, the set of constraints C and a semiring level α; we say that b is $_\alpha$Full substitutable for a on v ($b \in {}_\alpha FS_v(a)$) if and only if for all assignments η,*

$$\bigotimes C\eta[v := a] \geq \alpha \implies \bigotimes C\eta[v := a] \leq_S \bigotimes C\eta[v := b]$$

Similarly to the Definition 1, we define a and b to be $_\alpha$Neighborhood Substitutable if the set of constraints C is limited to the constraints including V, C_v. We define a and b to be $_\alpha$Full/Neighborhood Interchangeable if they are $_\alpha$Full/Neighborhood Substitutable both ways.

As Full Interchangeability needs a big computational effort we use Neighbourhood Interchangeability algorithms to compute interchangeable values, as they can compute in polynomial time and can well approximate Full Interchangeability [2], see algorithms and proofs in [20] .

4 Adaptation Model

In previous work [1], we applied a more restricted interchangeability framework to case adaptation in resource allocation problems. In that approach it was possible to compute NI values which determine choices for a individual variable or a minimal NPI set which finds choices for a subset of variables of the CSP. In this work, we propose adaptation for the problems which are represented as soft constraint satisfaction problems where we use $^\delta_\alpha$interchangeability for updating solutions. In our model the adaptation is realised by interchanging values of one or a subset of variables of CSP by allowing a certain degradation of the solution, while there is no addition or deletion of the constraints of the CSP.

The adaptation model is illustrated here through an example application to a generic product configuration problem. The configuration of the product is defined as a CSP where:

– the components of the product are expressed as the variables of the CSP;
– the domains of the CSP are the sets of values that the components can be;
– the constraints among variables denote the dependency between the components in order that the product to be functional.

In our configuration example, we had used two representative forms of soft CSP : the weighted one to model the price and the fuzzy one to model the delivery time. So, for modelling the price of the product, the modelling of the CSP is the same as for the hard constraint case, only that we have cost for each value assignment of each component (unary constraint) and for each tuple combination over the constraints (binary constraint).

For weighted CSP we use the operations of the semiring $< \Re^+, min, +, +\infty, 0 >$, as in [11]. So, for constraint combination we will have to add the costs in order to obtain the final price.

For delivery time we have used the fuzzy CSP model, where the semiring is defined as $< \Re^+, min, max, +\infty, 0 >$ [3].

4.1 The Architecture of the Adaptation Framework

The architecture of the system is domain-independent; its domain knowledge comes from three external sources: a case library, domain knowledge represented as CSP and user requirements, see Figure 3. Our sales manager system (shown in Figure 1), finds the appropriate product for a new buyer by retrieving cases and adapting their product configurations according to the new requests. The main contribution of this work relates

---

[2] Also Neighbourhood Substitutability can approximate Full Substitutability
[3] Usually the fuzzy CSP is represented by the semiring $< [0,1], max, min, 0, 1 >$, but for modelling this example we had chosen a similar one which uses the opposite order

to the adaptation step of the CBR process. Retrieval is done by using a simple comparison metric over the buyer profile relative to profiles contained in cases and picks out the closest previous cases.

As in Figure 3, the adaptation module receives the retrieved cases from the case base. The module interacts with the user for specific, personalised requirements and with the domain knowledge represented for making consistent adaptations.

The adaptation process proceeds as follows, see Figure 3:

– propose the retrieved cases to the user in order to make a choice;
– ask for the user for
  • specific user requirements on the selected case;
  • a certain price threshold or an allowed degradation of the price (specified as certain limits);
  • a delivery time threshold or an allowed degradation of the delivery time (specified as certain limits);

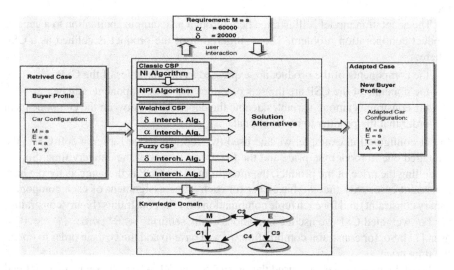

Fig. 3. Domain knowledge as Constraint Satisfaction Problems.

4.2   Example – Degradation and Thresholds

In the following we give an example of how degradation and threshold applies in order to update solutions when the domain knowledge is represented as a soft CSP.

The product catalog can represent the available choices through a soft CSPs, as show in Figure 2. By different representations of the semiring, the CSP represents different problem formulations. Thus, in order to model the cost of the product a weighted CSP might be most appropriate. For a weighted CSP, the semiring preference values model the cost of different components and their integration. The semiring operations and values are: $< \Re^+, min, +, +\infty, 0 >$. This allows one to model optimization problems where the goal is to minimize the total cost of the proposed solution. The cost of the solution is computed by summing up the costs of all constraints, intended as the cost of the chosen tuple for each constraint. Thus the goal is to find the n-tuples (where n is the number of all the variables) which minimize the total sum of the costs of their subtuples (one for each constraint).

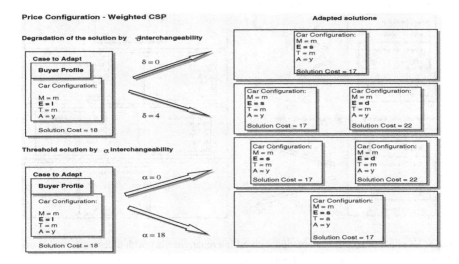

Fig. 4. Example of solution adaptation with NI interchangeability by a degradation δ or over a threshold α knowledge domain is represented as a Weighted CSPs.

In Figure 4, we present an example of solution update where the solution represents price modelling of the product modelled as a weighted CSP. The cost of the current solution is 18 and the user request is to update the value of the engine, here represented by variable E. The cost of the car in the current solution is 18. By allowing a degradation of the solution with $\delta = 0$ the solution updates to E = s and a decrease in the cost to 17. By allowing a degradation of $\delta = 4$ solution can be adapted for variable E either to value s or d where the cost decreases to 17 or increases to 22 respectively. Among all the values of variable E we find that for degradation $\delta = 0$, values s is ^{0}substitutable to values l and d, and l is ^{0}substitutable to d. For a degradation $\delta = 1$, values s and l are ^{1}interchangeable and ^{1}substitutable to d. By allowing a degradation $\delta = 4$, values s and l are ^{4}interchangeable, values l and d ^{4}interchangeable and s is ^{4}substitutable to d. For a degradation δ higher than 5 all the values for component E are $^\delta$interchangeable.

When searching for solutions to a soft CSP, it is possible to gain efficiency by not distinguishing values that could in any case not be part of a solution of sufficient quality. In $_\alpha$interchangeability, two values are interchangeable if they do not affect the quality of any solution with quality better than α, called the threshold factor. In our price modelling example, see Figure 4 we can see that for a threshold $\alpha = 0$, the solution can be updated for variable E with all the other values of its domains as all its values are $_0$interchangeable; this is explained by the fact that since there are no solutions better than $\alpha = 0$, by definition all the elements are interchangeable. For a certain threshold α = 18, values l and d are $_{18}$interchangeable and s can substitute l and d. And for higher α, s can substitute l and d and l can substitute d.

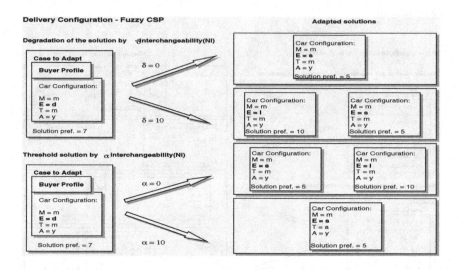

Fig. 5. Example of solution adaptation with NI interchangeability with a degradation δ or over a threshold α when the knowledge domain is represented as a Fuzzy CSPs.

For modelling the delivery time of the car we had used as optimisation criteria a fuzzy CSP. Fuzzy CSP associate a preference level with each tuple of values. Such level is usually between 0 and 1, where 1 represents the best value (that is the tuple is allowed) and 0 the worst, with the semiring $< [0, 1], max, min, 0, 1 >$. In our example we had modelled the delivery time with the semiring $< \Re^+, min, max, +\infty, 0 >$ which is similar to the fuzzy one, but uses an opposite order. Let us called it *opposite fuzzy*. Delay in delivering time is determined by the time to obtain components and to reserve the resources for the assembly process. For the delivery time of the car, only the longest delay would matter. In Figure 5, the solution we have to adapt has a delivery time of 7 days but the user would prefer to change the engine type of the car. For a degradation of the solution $\delta = 0$, we can adapt the solution only by value s for variable E. By allowing a higher degradation of the solution to $\delta = 10$, there are two possible solution adaptation: when variable E takes value s the delivery time stays the same, while when it takes value l the delivery time increases to 10 days. For $\delta = 0$, values s is ^{0}substitutable for values l and d of variable E, while for $\delta = 7$, s and d are becoming ^{7}interchangeable and for $\delta = 10$ all values of variable E are ^{10}interchangeable.

Computing adaptation by $_\alpha$interchangeability for this fuzzy example allows the adaptation of the solution, see Figure 5 to values s and l as well for variable E as all the values are interchangeable for a threshold α. For a threshold $\alpha = 7$, values l and d stay interchangeable, but value s can only substitute l and d, while for higher values of α s can substitute l and d and only d can substitute l.

5   Experimental Results

In order to understand how frequently adaptation based on soft interchangeability would be successful, we have evaluated its occurrence on randomly generated problems. In the following, we give our first results about the occurrence of $(^\delta/_\alpha)$interchangeability in soft CSPs.

We have done our experiments for fuzzy and weighted CSP representing the important class of Soft CSPs dealing with an idempotent and non-idempotent times operation respectively. The motivation for considering both classes comes from the fact that solving Soft CSP when the combination operation is not idempotent is extremely harder [17].

The occurrence of $(^\delta/_\alpha)$interchangeability depends on the soft CSP structure. There are 4 standard parameters which characterize constraint problems:

- problem size, number of variables;
- domain sizes, number of values in the domain;
- problem density, the ratio of the number of constraints relatively to the minimum and maximum number of allowed constraints in the given problem;
- problem tightness, the ratio between the sum of the semiring values associated to all the tuples in all the constraints, and the value obtained by multiplying the 1 element of the semiring (that is the maximum) for the number of all possible tuple (that is the $constraintnumber \times domainsize$).

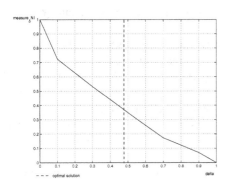

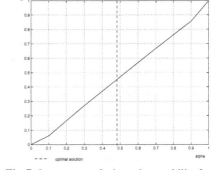

Fig. 6. Occurrence of δ interchangeability for random generated Fuzzy CSPs.

Fig. 7. Occurrence of α interchangeability for random generated Fuzzy CSPs.

During our experiments on fuzzy and weighted CSPs, we had observed that the CSP density and the CSP size do not influence occurrence of interchangeable values. There is a weak dependency on the domain size, thus the number of interchangeabilities increases with the number of resources. There might be a strong dependency on the CSP tightness; it has to be proven in our further research. In Figure 6 and 7 we present our results for fuzzy CSP modelled with the semiring $< [0, 1], max, min, 0, 1 >$ [4]. In Figure 6

---

[4] Note that in our experiments we have used the semiring $< [0, 1], max, min, 0, 1 >$ but in the our example from Section 4 we have the *opposite fuzzy* defined with the semiring $< \Re^+, min, max, +\infty, 0 >$. However, these two models are equivalent and thus the results are relevant for both of them.

and 7, we see how interchangeability occurrence varies with δ and α respectively. The tests are done on sets of random generated problems with 10 variables, with varying density $dens - csp \in \{0.1, 0.2, \ldots, 1\}$ and the maximum domain size $dom - size = \{\frac{n}{10}, \frac{2n}{10}, \ldots, \frac{9n}{10}, n\}$, see model in [21].

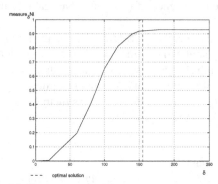

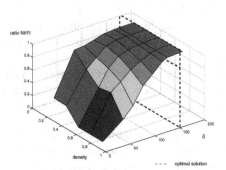

Fig. 8. Occurrence of δ interchangeability for random generated Weighted CSPs.

Fig. 9. Ratio between NI/FI δ interchangeable values for random generated Weighted CSP.

The experiments show that for low semiring values there is a high occurrence of $^\delta NI$ while it decreases till o for higher semiring values, Figure 6.

The number of $_\alpha$interchangeable values is low for low semiring values and increases with the value of the semiring, Figure 7.

In all the graphs we highlight the position of the optimal solution. In fact, when dealing with crisp CSPs there does not exist any notion of optimality, but for soft CSPs each solution has an associated level. It is important to study NI occurrence around optimal solutions because we are often interested in discarding solutions of bad quality.

For $_\alpha$interchangeability we did not find many interchangeabilities around optimal solution where the preference levels over the constraint tuples where uniformly generated. Although there is a high dependence of $^\delta NI$ on the tightness of a soft CSP, it was not proved yet.

For $_\alpha$interchangeability we can see that around the optimal solution the measure of $_\alpha$interchangeable values goes from 0.1 to 0.6.

Similar results hold for $^\delta/_\alpha$interchangeability when dealing with weighted instead of fuzzy CSPs. In Figure 8, we represent $^\delta NI$ occurrence in weighted CSPs. Notice that the shape of the function seems the opposite to that of Figure 6 only because the order in the fuzzy semiring (max-min) is opposite to the weighted semiring (min-sum). Similarly to fuzzy case, in weighted CSPs $^\delta$interchangeability decreases with δ (w.r.t. the semiring order), see Figure 8.

Computing full interchangeable values might be a quite costly operation as it may require computing all the solutions. It has been shown in [20] that full interchangeability ($^\delta/_\alpha FI$) can be approximated by neighbourhood interchangeability ($^\delta/_\alpha NI$).

Since NI computes a subset of FI, it is important to investigate how many interchangeabilities we can find by computing locally neighbourhood interchangeabilities w.r.t. full interchangeabilities. In Figure 9, $ratioNI/FI$ is represented the rate between

Neighbourhood and Full Interchangeability for weighted CSPs. We can see that the ratio stays between 0.7 and 0.9 around optimal solution. In the fuzzy case, from our experiments we reached the conclusion that the $ratio NI/FI$ stays always between 0.7 and 0.95. Thus, NI interchangeability can well approximate FI interchangeability.

6 Related Work

In our previous work [1] we proposed a generic framework to realise case adaptation for the domain of problems which can be represented as crisp CSPs. Here we extend this framework for the domain of soft CSPs as well.

But there are some other approaches to seeing the adaptation problem as a constraint satisfaction problem. One of them was done by Purvis and Pu [22] in a case-based design problem solving domain based on the constraints over discrete CSPs. Their methodology formalises the case adaptation process in the sense of combining multiple cases in order to achieve the solution of the new problem, by applying repair-based CSP algorithm [23]. This method relies only on the knowledge accumulated in the case base where the method proposed by us in [1] considers also information offered by the domain knowledge formulated as CSP. The approaches are different as by method proposed by Purvis and Pu [22] the constraints between specific values of the variables are stored in the case, while adaptation method proposed by us in [1] considers in the case only the solution of the new problem, while the constraints between variables are held in an external module which contains the domain knowledge. We believe that our approach gives more flexibility to the adaptation module but we will study in the future how to combine the two methods for improving the adaptation process.

By extending the framework to the soft CSP domain and thus allowing preferences, the flexibility of the framework is further more improved.

Another approach of adaptation with constraints where the solution of a new problem is built by satisfying the new constraints and by transforming a memorised solution was done by Hua, Faltings and Smith [24] where they proposed a case-based reasoner for architectural design where constraints restrict numerical relationships among dimensions. CADRE introduced the concept of *dimensional reduction*: before attempting to adapt a case, it constructs an explicit representation of the degrees of freedom available for adaptation. However, CADRE defined this approach only for numeric constraints. The adaptation method based on *dimensional reduction* has been tested successfully in the IDIOM project [25].

In the domain of discrete variables, the adaptation space is less obvious. We proposed here a method based on interchangeability for domains of problems which can be expressed as soft CSPs which localise changes in discrete spaces and thus offers a reliable method for determining the closest solution.

7 Conclusions and Future Work

This paper presents methods for case adaptation for the domain of problems which can be represented soft constraint satisfaction problems. By combining with the adaptation methods for crisp CSPs in [1], we can obtain a powerful and generic case adaptation engine.

The adaptation methods for soft CSPs are generic and based on the soft interchangeability concept. We have proved the use of $(^\delta/_\alpha)$substitutability/interchangeability in the adaptation process when the knowledge is represented as soft CSP. The two parameters α and δ allow us to express a wide range of adaptation alternatives. While the threshold α is used to eliminate distinctions that would not interest us anyway, the allowed degradation specifies how precisely we want to optimize the solution.

We presented here as well some preliminary results which measure the occurrence of $(^\delta/_\alpha)$interchangeability thus number of adaptation alternatives. There is a high occurrence of $_\alpha NI$ interchangeability around optimal solution and one can use successfully δ interchangeability for low degradation of the solution, but further study has to be done on that. Moreover, we also show that NI interchangeability, a computable interchangeability method, can well approximate FI interchangeability.

Interesting future directions include:

- algorithms for computing neighbourhood partial interchangeability for soft CSPs;
- further experimental tests to measure dependence of $(^\delta/_\alpha)$interchangeability on soft CSP tightness.
- Classifying case bases of solutions by how re-usable ("adaptable") their solutions are according to allowed δ degradation and/or solution quality relatively to a threshold α.

References

1. Nicoleta Neagu and Boi Faltings. Exploiting Interchangeabilities for Case Adaptation. *In Proc. of the 4th ICCBR01*, 2001.
2. Stefano Bistarelli, Boi Faltings, and Nicoleta Neagu. A Definition of Interchangeability for Soft CSPs. In *ERCIM Workshop(to appear).*, Cork, Ireland, 2002.
3. Van Hentenryck. Generality versus Specificity: An Experience with AI and OR Techniques. *In AAAI-88: Proceedings National Conference on Artificial Intelligence*, pages 660–664, 1988.
4. R Dechter Y. El Fattah. Diagnosing tree-decomposable circuits. *In Proc. of the 14 th IJCAI, pg. 1742–1748*, 1995.
5. H. Krautz and B. Selman. Planning as Satisfiability. *In Proc. of the 10 th Ecai, pages 359–363, Vienna, Austria*, 1992.
6. M. Wallace. Applying constraints for scheduling. *In Constraint Programming, volume 131 of NATO ASI Series Advanced Science Institute Series. Springer Verlag*, 1994.
7. A. Mackworth. Constraint-based Design of Embeded Intelligent Systems. *In Constraints 2(1), pages 83–86, Vienna, Austria*, 1992.
8. R. Weigel and B. Faltings. Interchangeability for Case Adaptation in Configuration Problems. *In Proceedings of the AAAI98 Spring Symposium on Multimodal Reasoning, Stanford, CA, TR SS-98-04.*, 1998.
9. T. Schiex. Probabilistic constraint satisfaction problems, or "how to handle soft constraints?" *In Proc. 8th Conf. of Uncertanty in AI, 269–275*, 1992.
10. Stefano Bistarelli, Ugo Montanari, and Francesca Rossi. Semiring-based Constraint Solving and Optimization. *Journal of ACM.*, 44, n.2:201–236, 1997.
11. Stefano Bistarelli, Boi Faltings, and Nicoleta Neagu. Interchangeability in Soft CSPs. In *Proc. of the 8th CP-2002.*, Ithaca, NY, USA, 2002.

12. E.C. Freuder and R.J. Wallace. Partial constraint satisfaction. *AI Journal*, 58, 1992.
13. D. Dubois, H. Fargier, and H. Prade. The calculus of fuzzy restrictions as a basis for flexible constraint satisfaction. In *Proc. IEEE International Conference on Fuzzy Systems*, pages 1131–1136. IEEE, 1993.
14. Zs. Ruttkay. Fuzzy constraint satisfaction. In *Proc. 3rd IEEE International Conference on Fuzzy Systems*, pages 1263–1268, 1994.
15. H. Fargier and J. Lang. Uncertainty in constraint satisfaction problems: a probabilistic approach. In *Proc. European Conference on Symbolic and Qualitative Approaches to Reasoning and Uncertainty (ECSQARU)*, volume 747 of *LNCS*, pages 97–104. Springer-Verlag, 1993.
16. T. Schiex, H. Fargier, and G. Verfaille. Valued Constraint Satisfaction Problems: Hard and Easy Problems. In *Proc. IJCAI95*, pages 631–637, San Francisco, CA, USA, 1995. Morgan Kaufmann.
17. S. Bistarelli, U. Montanari, and F. Rossi. Semiring-based Constraint Solving and Optimization. *Journal of the ACM*, 44(2):201–236, Mar 1997.
18. S. Bistarelli, U. Montanari, and F. Rossi. Semiring-based Constraint Logic Programming: Syntax and Semantics. *ACM Transactions on Programming Languages and System (TOPLAS)*, 23:1–29, jan 2001.
19. Eugene C. Freuder. Eliminating Interchangeable Values in Constraint Satisfaction Problems. In *In Proc. of AAAI-91*, pages 227–233, Anaheim, CA, 1991.
20. S. Bistarelli, B. Faltings, and N. Neagu. A definition of interchangeability for soft csps. In *Proc. of the Joint Workshop of the ERCIM Working Group on Constraints and the CologNet area on Constraint and Logic Programming on Constraint Solving and Constraint Logic Programming – Selected Papers*, LNAI. Springer-Verlag, 2002.
21. Berthe Choueiry Boi Faltings, Rainer Weigel. Abstraction by Interchangeability in Resource Allocation. In *Proc. of the 14 th IJCAI-95*, pages 1694–1701, Montreal, Canada, 1995.
22. L. Purvis and P. Pu. Adaptation using Constraint Satisfaction Techniques. *In Proc. of the 1st International Conference in CBR, pages 88–97*, 1995.
23. A. Philips S. Minton, M. Johnson and P. Laird. Minimizing Conflicts: A Heuristic Repair Method for Constraint Satisfaction and Scheduling Problems. *In Artificial Intelligence 58, pages 88–97*, 1995.
24. B. Faltings K. Hua and I. Smith. CADRE: case-based geometric design. *In Artificial Intelligence in Engineering 10, pages 171–183*, 1996.
25. C. Lottaz I. Smith and B.Faltings. Spatial composition using cases: IDIOM. *In Proc. of the 1st International Conference in CBR, pages 88–97*, 1995.

Supporting the IT Security of eServices
with CBR-Based Experience Management

Markus Nick, Björn Snoek, and Torsten Willrich

Fraunhofer Institut Experimentelles Software Engineering (IESE)
Sauerwiesen 6, 67661 Kaiserslautern, Germany
{nick, snoek, willrich}@iese.fhg.de

Abstract. Safeguarding security for eGovernment services is an essential in-
gredient for the success of such services. For this purpose, isolated security
efforts are not sufficient. Integrated concepts are required. In the publicly
funded project SKe, we are developing such an integrated approach. One
component of this integrated approach is a CBR-based experience management solution to support the dynamic aspects of IT security. The component
- an intelligent IT security console - supports the daily work of the IT security
personnel and supports them in systematically recording and using experiences in the form of weakly structured cases in their work process. The component is being developed in cooperation with an application partner. The approach is also used in projects with industrial partners.

1   Introduction

eGovernment is becoming a more and more important issue in a number of countries.
For example, in Germany there are initiatives in the federal government and in more
than 130 towns [10]. In the USA, eGovernment is regarded as the next American revolution that is expected by the public [25]. All these initiatives have in common that
"safeguarding security and privacy is the top priority of the public for eGovernment
services". Henceforth, we refer with the term *eService* to such eGovernment services.
An eService is the electronic counterpart of an interactive procedure between governmental organizations and their customers.

To ensure the security of eServices, integrated security concepts are needed that do
not only address the technical issues of IT security but also relevant organizational, cul-
tural, and social aspects as well as legal peculiarities of the implemented administrative
procedure [27]. Furthermore, the security level has to be reasonable, i.e., a good solution has to be found that satisfies the often-conflicting goals of security and usability.
This reasonable security level is one of the bases for user acceptance [18]. Unfortunately, today's IT security concepts are not yet integrated as required for eServices. They
cover only individual aspects and, furthermore, the relationships among these aspects
are not clarified.

In the SKe project[1], we address these issues by iteratively developing and testing a
comprehensive approach to IT security for eServices [20]. This approach consists of

---

[1]   Project SKe - Comprehensives security concepts with dynamic control mechanisms for eService processes; http://www.ske-projekt.de/.

K.D. Ashley and D.G. Bridge (Eds.): ICCBR 2003, LNAI 2689, pp. 362–376, 2003.
© Springer-Verlag Berlin Heidelberg 2003

three major components: First, formal modelling of the eService process and its security aspects is used for identifying and verifying the required security properties of an eService and, second, an electronic security inspector (eSI) supports the continuous monitoring of security measures that can be checked software-technically. The third major component of SKe is the so-called *intelligent IT security console (iSeCo)*, which focuses on systematically collecting and applying IT security experiences about the reaction on security incidents (events, breaches, threats, etc.) in an *experience-based security database (eSDB* or "experience base") [3]. This aims at providing fast and sophisticated support for the daily security-related work of the IT security personnel. For the purpose of the project, it was decided to focus on eService-specific experience [3] and not on general IT security experiences such as the measures from the IT baseline protection manual of the German BSI [9]. Though the results of SKe can be applied to non-governmental eServices as well, the project is especially adapted for eGovernment services. For example, we cooperate with a governmental unit responsible for a financial eService of a major German city as application partner. The partner is involved in the development of the IT security console and will use the system in the context of a case study for the project.

iSeCo and eSDB are typical applications of CBR and of the new field of *experience management (EM)* [7, 24, 6]. The basic idea is rooted in CBR-based diagnosis [12, 14]. However, in contrast to these diagnosis systems, which mainly use structured CBR, we have to deal with weakly-structured cases, which require a Textual CBR approach [13]. Furthermore, the system is designed as a long-lived CBR system with a life-cycle model. As a life-cycle model for the cases, we developed a so-called feedback loop to explain how the cases evolve over time (Section 3) and how the CBR system is integrated in the day-to-day work processes of the users. Furthermore, we have to cope with the diverse environmental requirements ranging from standardization of reactions on security indicents to expert experience exchange about these reactions. For this purpose, the system is designed to be flexibile regarding maintenance strategies and processing on top of one schema. For the maintenance strategies, the required maintenance knowledge is acquired before the system goes into regular use [15].

The remainder of the paper is structured as follows: We applied the goal-oriented EM method DISER [24, 4] to identify the requirements (Section 2) and scenarios that are relevant for managing IT security experience, which are documented an overall process for the required security and knowledge-based activities in [3]. The result was the focus on experience about the reaction on security incidents and -as the core scenario- an experience feedback loop, which integrates the recording and usage of experience into the daily work of IT security personnel. We analysed where CBR can provide "intelligent" support in the feedback loop to enable an effective EM (Section 3). To translate this feedback loop into action, we are developing an intelligent IT security console with CBR support in close cooperation with our application partner (Section 4). Section 5 summarizes status and plans for the evaluation of the IT security console. The paper closes with a summary, conclusion, and overview on ongoing work.

2   Requirements for an EM Solution for IT Security

The experience management (EM) solutions for an intelligent IT security console and eSDB have to be flexible and scalable with respect to the following issues: Different eServices and, therefore, different organisational infrastructures and different experience structures. This leads to different needs regarding "intelligent" support from the EM system. Furthermore, a tight integration into the work process is required to make EM successful, i.e., a proactive, context-sensitive delivery of knowledge within the work process [26]. The experience factory concept serves as organisational principle [6]. By establishing and supporting a feedback cycle with the IT security console, we integrate the recording and usage of experience into the day-to-day work process of the IT security personnel. In an organization, the IT security personnel can be something on a range from a homogeneous group of experts to a group with heterogeneous expertise (i.e., beginners and experts as well). Depending on this variation of expertise of the IT security personnel in an organization, the IT security console ranges from an experience exchange for experts to a standardized "handbook" of reactions to incidents. Our system has to be flexible to support the whole range to support different degrees of standardization.

The system is expected to speed up and improve the reaction to security threats and incidents through the integration of the usage into the daily work with the IT security console. Furthermore, an eSDB is expected to improve the traceability regarding standard cases as well as non-standard cases. In addition, the systematic recording of incidents in the eSDB provides a good basis for preparing security audits. Last but not least, the systematic recording of experience allows maintaining a certain minimal acceptable level of security even when IT security personnel are not available (e.g., on holiday, illness, fluctuation).

Furthermore, we experienced that partners and customers expect scalability with a cheap start for EM initiatives especially when the solution is at the level of functional or organisational units such as departments, where approx. 20-50 users share the same or similar interests with respect to an EM solution.

3   IT Security Experience Feedback Loop and Opportunities for Intelligent Support by CBR

The so-called *experience feedback loop* (Fig. 1) is the core scenario of SKe for the systematic recording and application of IT security experience about the reaction on security incidents from the viewpoint of the IT security personnel. Three additional scenarios refine the feedback loop (see [3] for these scenarios and the initial idead of the feedback loop). This feedback loop is the basis for the intelligent IT security console (Section 4). In the following, we describe the feedback loop and analyse the opportunities for intelligent support -in particular- by CBR.

We differentiate between the roles of an *IT security specialist*, who is an expert in a certain IT security domain, and an *IT security manager (Gr. IT-Sicherheitsbeauftragter)*, who is responsible for assigning tasks to the IT security specialists and monitoring the to-do lists. In small organisations or organizational units, one person can

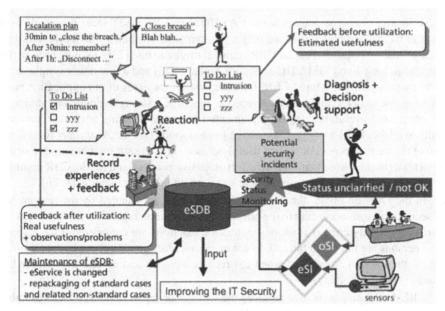

Fig. 1. A feedback loop for IT security experience, which is integrated into the work process.

perform both roles. In contrast, there is a number of IT security specialists in larger organizations.

We distinguish four phases in the loop: security status monitoring, diagnosis & decision support, reaction, and feedback. While the monitoring of the security status is a quasi-continuous task in order to keep the security measures effective, the other three phases are triggered by the recognition of potential security incidents and run sequentially for each of these incidents. The latter three phases resemble the basic CBR cycle [1] at an organizational level [24]. Furthermore, these three phases are similar to CBR-based trouble ticket systems (e.g., [14]) because both deal with the processing of certain incidents by respective personnel. In general, the whole feedback loop shows a tight integration into the work process, which is an enabler for successful knowledge management [26].

In the *security status-monitoring* phase, the electronic security inspector (eSI) monitors software-technically checkable objects using so-called sensors. The organisational security inspector oSI collects respective data on organisational measures or on measures that cannot be monitored by the electronic security inspector eSI for other reasons. All states that cannot be classified as "OK" by eSI or oSI (i.e., people) are compiled in a list of potential security incidents.

In the *diagnosis and decision support* phase, the status is determined for "unclarified" cases. Then respective reactions are proposed based on the experiences and selected by the person(s) responsible for IT security. Depending on severity and potential damage, a priority is assigned to each incident. The incidents to examine are put on a to-do list.

This phase is related to CBR-based diagnosis systems such as helpdesks [12] and trouble ticket systems [14]. In contrast to diagnosis based on structured CBR (e.g., the

CFM-56 aircraft engine diagnosis tool CASSIOPÉE [12]), the IT security console uses cases of weakly structured text and only a few symbolic attributes. Obviously, our type of cases mainly requires Textual CBR retrieval mechanisms ([13] - as, e.g., used in the successful, long-lived SIMATIC system of Siemens [8]) and a few rather simple similarity models from Structured CBR. Because most of the cases of our application partner have one major symptom that selects the reaction, a strong dialogue orientation is not considered useful, but can be implemented in a scale up using advanced commercially available CBR tools such as orenge from empolis GmbH. A stronger formalization of the cases was not considered useful because (a) the users are more used to structured text, (b) the formalization is an effort-intensive process, and (c) the CBR community has success stories for systems with and without this formalization [8, 26].

In the *reaction* phase, the items on the to-do lists are handled by the responsible IT security persons according to the priorities. Furthermore, regarding the escalation hierarchy for highly critical situations, automatic reactions are considered if the responsible persons are not available and do not or cannot react quickly enough (e.g., switching off the internet connection when eSI reports a breach and no-one is available because of a public holiday).

CBR-based diagnosis also includes the therapy or repair actions, which resemble the reaction in the IT security domain. However, for the cases of our application partner and our industrial customers, the typical solution consists of a couple of rather "complex" steps. Most of these steps can be executed only by humans. Furthermore, the human execution of these steps can take some time (e.g., one day for some cases). Therefore, support for logging the execution status of the steps is regarded useful. This logging of the execution status provides also feedback at the step level, i.e., feedback if the step was applied successfully or without success or if the step was left out. This feedback on the utility of the step is useful for repackaging standard cases.

In the *feedback* phase, experience on new or different reactions is recorded and feedback is given, e.g., if there was really a security incident, effect and success of the reaction, actual damage, and prevented damage. This feedback and new experience closes the loop by improving the diagnosis and decision support capabilities.

Because the IT security console is designed as a long-lived CBR system, maintenance issues have to be considered. For our domain, we have to be flexible regarding the degree of standardization of the reactions on security incidents. This requires respective maintenance strategies, processes, techniques, and tools. Furthermore, the feedback should be exploited to base maintenance on facts and experience and not on opinions or ad-hoc actions. Our feedback channels approach [4, 5] describes which feedback indicates which causes and what the respective maintenance is, but the approach does not include something for the required standardization issue. In CBR, [19] describes a maintenance technique for weakly structured cases and [21] provides a collection of maintenance policies for focusing on structured case bases. [11] contains an overview on CBR maintenance as "maintenance policies". However, none of these CBR techniques exploits the knowledge that is represented by the collected feedback. Thus, we choose to use our method EMSIG-KA to derive maintenance policies from the feedback loop as lifecycle model [15]. This includes also the identification of the relevant cases that have to be updated, when an eService is changed.

The systematic recordings on the security incidents can be used for identifying the need for improvements of the IT security and, as a consequence, introduce new measures or upgrade existing measures. Besides simple SQL-based reports, data mining or related techniques can help discover further findings for supporting improvement decisions.

4   A CBR-Based IT Security Console for eServices

The intelligent IT security console implements the core component of the SKe process, i.e., the feedback loop for IT security experience and its related scenarios. These serve as requirements and use cases for the actual system design and development. To ensure intelligent support within the daily work context of the user, we developed a process model and a graphical user interface that completely integrates the intelligent support (*iSupport*) into the work process (Section 4.1). This process model is based on the feedback loop from the previous section. A representation schema is necessary to specify how the knowledge is recorded (Section 4.2). The schema allows distinguishing between standard and non-standard reactions on incidents. Similarity-based retrieval mechanisms realize the iSupports (Section 4.3). The maintenance process particularly supports the repackaging of standard cases and related non-standard cases. The strategy for the maintenance process is adaptable to the needs of the environment (Section 4.4). Finally, the actual implementation is based on a product-line architecture for EM systems (Section 4.5).

4.1   How the System Supports IT Security Personnel

We use a process model to describe how the IT security console supports IT security personnel. The process model is depicted in Fig. 2. Based on the process model, we developed a graphical user interface

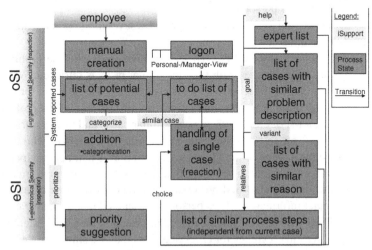

Fig. 2. The process underlying the IT security console

terface (GUI) for the IT security console. In the following, we describe the process and the opportunities for intelligent support in the different steps of the process.

After the login, the system presents the user his personal to-do list and the list of new, open incidents. For an IT security manager the incidents of all IT security specialists can be controlled. New incidents can be reported by eSI (e.g., a port scan) or oSI or entered manually by the IT security personnel.

When a new incident in the list of potential incidents is assigned to a person by himself or by the IT security manager, further situation characteristics are added, which can not be determined automatically. An iSupport proposes a set of categories. Another iSupport proposes the priority level based on similar existing cases. A third iSupport proposes reactions on the incident based on same or similar cases in the past. The user selects the reactions he regards as most useful for dealing with the new incident.

Prioritisation is relevant when there are more than 5-10 tasks in the to-do lists in the typical case for a certain environment. According to our experience from industrial projects, priority decisions are subjective and cannot be made consistently over a longer period neither by a single person nor by several persons. Therefore, iSupport standardizes the priority decisions.

To address the requirements of different environments (i.e., different eServices, organisational structure, and experience structure), we developed different variants for the presentation and modelling of the description of the reaction, which differ in their functionality and degree of formality. Based on example cases from and in discussions with our application partner, we identified structured text (out of a range from plain text to structured decision trees) as the most adequate basis for representing the reaction. A separate representation of steps is necessary to provide support for planning and executing a reaction that takes longer to perform. The variants also differ with respect to their support for parallel execution. A further formalization is required for steps that can be performed automatically. The resulting variant, which was selected by our application partner, supports checklist-style processing and parallel processing of single steps by the IT security personnel.

In the reaction phase, the system provides several iSupports, which are launched by simply pressing a button:

- *"Variant"* aims at identifying alternative causes for the problem. For this purpose, a list of cases with same or similar tasks is retrieved. When an alternative cause is identified, its reaction is also proposed as solution for the current case.
- *"Goal"* aims at finding alternative reactions for solving the problem. For this purpose, a list of cases with same or similar cause and task is retrieved.
- *"Help"* supports persons who have further questions or who do not completely trust the answers of an IT system. As support, a number of experts for the current incident and reaction are identified. This is done by retrieving a list of similar cases from the eSDB and presenting an overview of these cases together with the contact information of the person who handled the respective case in the past.
- *"Relatives"* aims at finding related information for a single step. For this purpose, the systems searches for cases and steps that are similar to the current step (e.g., in the port scan case for the step where the necessity for "open" ports at the firewall is checked, firewall configuration experience would we found). This iSupport requires a representation that supports steps.

The described process refines the feedback loop with respect to the user interaction of the IT security console and shows the integration into the work process as outlined by the feedback loop.

4.2 Modelling the Experience

To support the process model described in the previous section, the cases are structured according to the representation schema as depicted in Fig. 3. For the design of the schema, we had to consider the iSupports, feedback, and maintenance of standard cases (as a dynamic handbook for reactions on security incidents). Furthermore, the structure has to be open for further functionality such as version management.

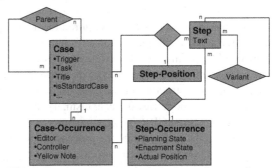

Fig. 3. Excerpt of representation schema for experience on IT security incidents and reaction.

The representation schema distinguishes between *standard cases* ("case", "step-position", and "step") and *concrete cases* ("case occurrence" and "step occurrence"). While standard cases provide a mature description for the reaction in a certain situation, concrete cases describe the application of standard cases for a concrete incident as well as non-standard cases. The application of a standard case can differ regarding the order of the execution of the steps, etc. Such concrete cases are accumulated over time for a standard case [16]. In a maintenance cycle, these concrete cases are used for improving the standard cases. This implements an experience-based improvement cycle for standardized reactions.

The core of a concrete case is the "case occurrence" that includes the attributes of the actual reaction in the concrete case. Besides the "editor" (the responsible IT security person), also "controller" and date & time are stored. The controller is usually the responsible IT security manager. A yellow note allows the editor to store some notes during the processing of the case (e.g., to whom a subtask was assigned). For our application partner, a yellow note is deleted after closing a case. Besides the general situation attributes (trigger, task, title), the steps of the reaction are modelled. The steps themselves are described textually. For the concrete case, the planning and execution is supported at the step level by providing a respective status for each step.

With the concept of separate concrete cases, the representation schema allows to capture knowledge about variations in the application of the standard cases, which is useful for maintenance (see below).

4.3 Case Retrieval

The intelligent support functionality (iSupports) behind the "Help", "Goal", "Variant", and "Relatives" buttons (see Section 4.1) are implemented using similarity based retrieval mechanisms. For example, the "Goal" button aims at finding alternative reactions for solving the respective problem and the "Variant" button aims at identifying alternative causes for the respective problem. Both buttons trigger a search, but the search is performed in different case attributes: "Goals" searches for cases with same or similar cause and task and "Variant" for cases with same or similar task only. Thus, different combinations of the attributes are used for the different iSupports. Most of the attributes are text and only very few attributes are numeric or symbolic (e.g., the eService). The cases are full of domain-specific vocabulary and respective abbreviations.

Because the case structure is required for selecting the fields for the retrieval, information retrieval techniques are insufficient (e.g., the vector space model as basic IR technique [22]). This brings us to Textual CBR, for which domain-specific vocabulary with highest impact on the quality of the retrieval results as demonstrated by [13]. However, besides the structure of the case, all of the mentioned types of attributes have to be supported by the retrieval mechanism. Therefore, we need a combination of Textual CBR and Structured CBR. To generate queries automatically as demanded by the tight integration of the retrieval into the process supported by iSeCo, a text analysis or information extraction from the current case is required. We have implemented a similar solution in the indiGo project [2] using the commercially available tool orenge from empolis GmbH.

As a next step for SKe regarding retrieval, we are investigating how to enhance text similarities (such as [13]) with a feedback-based learning approach in cooperation with our project partner, the knowledge-based systems group at the University of Kaiserslautern. In particular, we want to find out, what feedback is required to make this learning possible, how this can be integrated in the feedback loop -as unobtrusive as possible- and what feedback the user gives "freely" to which extend. To have a maximum flexibility regarding similarity models for this purpose, we use our small Java-based similarity engine RAISIN as an experimentation platform. First results are expected in the summer of 2003.

4.4   Maintenance Strategies, Policies, and Processes

The maintenance processes deal with the question of when to add or update standard cases. For this purpose, there are two classes of concrete cases to be considered: (1) concrete cases that describe the unchanged application of the standard case, where the number of these cases indicates the validity of the standard case; (2) concrete cases that describe an application of a standard case with changes.

Thus, a maintenance strategy has to define (a) the meaning of "changed", i.e., when is a concrete case considered to have been "changed", (b) the handling of "changed" concrete cases, which addresses when, e.g., a "changed" reaction leads to a new standard case that is available for retrieval, and (c) when "cases" and related "case occurrences" are repackaged.

We distinguish between two types of maintenance strategies, which are further parameterised by the implemented meaning of "changed". The open and flexible nature of the described schema supports both maintenance strategies.

For the *meaning of "changed"*, there are a number of different options, which are used for parameterising the basic unmanaged or managed maintenance strategy: A reaction is considered "changed" depending on, e.g., changes in the execution order of the steps, execution of a subset of the steps, or changes in the description of one or several steps. For this purpose, only semantical changes count as changes; e.g., syntactical corrections of text do not count. For our application partner, "changed" reaction means that the semantics of the core "case" or of one or more steps were changed. For this purpose, the user is required to give feedback whether a change is semantic or only syntactical (e.g., correction of typos). Different orders are not considered as "changed" because of the parallel-processing requirement.

The *managed maintenance strategy* is the preferred strategy for handling cases where a certain level of standardization of the reaction is the major goal - for example, when the IT security personnel has a rather diverse level of expertise. Changes to a proposed reaction are only recorded within the "concrete case". The standard case is not changed. In this case, a periodical or evaluation-triggered maintenance by the respective IT security expert is required [17]. This expert decides which histories are integrated in updated standard cases or lead to new variants of standard cases. The editorial work of experts (as eSDB maintainers), i.e., an experience factory in the sense of [6], prevents a decrease in the quality of the experience base. For the revision, the expert can also analyse differences in the order of the execution of the different steps. The different options for the triggering of the maintenance allow a flexible response to the maintenance needs of the different environments.

The strategy of *unmanaged maintenance* is preferred when the IT security personnel are mainly experts and have a high level of expertise. Each time when a proposed reaction is changed, a new standard case is recorded after finishing the handling of the incident. The new standard case is related to the old standard case via the parent relationship.

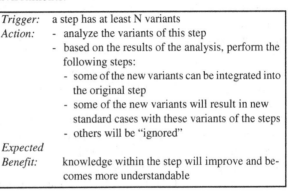

Trigger:	a step has at least N variants
Action:	- analyze the variants of this step
	- based on the results of the analysis, perform the following steps:
	- some of the new variants can be integrated into the original step
	- some of the new variants will result in new standard cases with these variants of the steps
	- others will be "ignored"
Expected Benefit:	knowledge within the step will improve and becomes more understandable

Fig. 4. Maintenance policy for the managed approach focusing on differences in steps to derive new standard cases.

However, this leads to a high number of new standard cases when changes are made frequently. Furthermore, unchecked new standard cases can also lower the quality of the experience base when error-prone cases are added as standard cases. An experience factory is not required, but depending on the meaning of "changed", the system could quickly become full of variants of standard cases. Then, a move to the managed approach would be a solution. Another solution would be to enhance the retrieval technology with diversity to view only one representative case for all variants [23]. A third solution could be the maintenance technique of Racine & Yang [19]. However, the latter two solutions require additional software development and, therefore, conflict with the goal of a cheap start reg. tools (see above). For the mentioned reasons, we chose the managed maintenance strategy.

Using our method EMSIG-KA [15], the maintenance strategies lead to the definition of sets of informal maintenance policies for each type of strategy. For the policies (see Fig. 4 for an example), the above issues and the feedback loop as lifecycle model is considered. These maintenance policies are further refined to operational maintenance guidelines, which can be supported by tools such as the EMSIG framework [17]. This set of maintenance guidelines is application-specific and can be extended with more general maintenance tasks such as the tasks from the SIAM method [21]. Maintenance policies and guidelines together specify a flexible maintenance process for the EM/CBR system.

4.5   Architecture

The system's architecture is an instantiation of IESE's experience base product-line architecture INTERESTS[2] (Fig. 5). For the support of the experience representation schema (Fig. 3) INTERESTS stores its data in a relational data base management system (e.g., PostgreSQL, MS-Access). The applications processes need a stable control flow as much as a complete integration of intelligent technologies (activation happens automatically and invisibly) for realization of the iSupport in the usage process of the IT security console (Fig. 2). For this purpose and to ensure platform independence and scalability, the graphical user interface (GUI) is implemented using JavaServerPages (JSP) and the application logic is modularised as a collection of JavaBeans. Scalability is important right from the start (e.g., when replacing a simple "intelligent" search with a more advanced solution) and is supported by the component-based architecture of INTERESTS. For this purpose, the application uses the INTERESTS API to access different CBR tools. Currently, our in-house solution RAISIN[3] serves as a slim engine and empolis' orenge provides a sophisticated CBR solution. Beneath the application's control flow, the GUI provides access to the experience base (insert, update, change entries) and is one of the interfaces to reports or statistics. Another way to get reports is given by a customized MS-Access GUI. The maintenance policies and respective maintenance guidelines (Section 4.4) are implemented using components of the EMSIG framework [17].

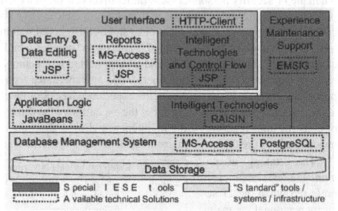

Fig. 5. INTERESTS experience base tools product-line architecture instantiated for iSeCo and eSDB.

5   Evaluation: Status and Next Steps

Based on a design study using real-world cases from the application partner, the concept, user interface, and case representation were reviewed by the application partner. Based on the design study, the most adequate variant for the presentation and represen-

---

[2] INTERESTS = Intelligent Retrieval and Storage System.

[3] RAISIN = RelAtively Intelligent SImilarity eNgine

tation of incidents and reactions as well as relevant opportunities for intelligent support were selected (Section 4.1).

A first version of the IT security console is being implemented and will be "fielded" in the first quarter of 2003. In a first case study in March and April 2003, we will analyse if the system is accepted in practice and is useful, which will demonstrate if the envisioned experience feedback loop works in practice. To analyse the acceptance, we use our standard model for measuring indicators about the acceptance of the system [17, 4]. We combine measuring the usage of the system (i.e., number of queries per iSupport) and feedback on the utility of the retrieved experiences (i.e., the proposed reactions). Combining usage and utility allows obtaining a picture on the acceptance more quickly than just monitoring usage because -in the beginning- usage can also be high because the system is new and everybody plays with it. Additionally, the utility feedback helps to better understand in what the users are really interested. Later, this can be extended with application-specific issues and economic aspects in a more detailed evaluation [4].

Furthermore, for the security department of a telecommunications company, we are coaching the development of a similar system from a simple case processing to a "real" EM solution, which particularly includes an explicit modelling of the reaction steps. This will demonstrate the applicability and usefulness of the experience feedback loop and the concept of the intelligent IT security console in an industrial environment.

6   Conclusion

We identified adequate IT security as an essential for eGovernment applications. In the SKe project, a comprehensive solution for ensuring the IT security of eGovernment applications is being iteratively developed and tested. Managing IT security knowledge is an integral part of the SKe approach. In this context, we are developing a so-called *intelligent IT security console (iSeCo)* with special support for eGovernment web services as a means to use experience management (EM) with CBR for improving the IT security of eGovernment applications.

This intelligent IT security console supports the systematic collection and application of experiences on reactions to security incidents. The general model for the system is provided by an experience feedback loop as lifecycle model that is related to CBR at an organisation level [24] and case-based diagnosis [12, 14] regarding the diagnosis of security incidents. However, the focus is more on the reaction to the incident (i.e., the solution to the diagnosed problem in terms of CBR). In the IT security domain, the reaction is in most cases a longer process and not a single or very few activities as in existing CBR systems for diagnosis [12, 14]. For the modelling of the reactions, we identified for the application partner a rather simple variant that supports planning and enactment of the reaction steps and provides intelligent support during the reaction. However, for industrial partners, we are developing a more complex representation of the reaction, which contains a solution log like a story with positive and negative experiences. Furthermore, cases in the IT security domain are mainly text-based and weakly structured like, e.g., SIMATIC in [8]. Therefore, it requires a combination of Textual CBR and Structured CBR.

The maintenance strategies are chosen depending on the environment, i.e., they depend on the diversity of the expertise of the IT security personnel and the wish/requirement to standardize reactions as well as available resources. Furthermore, the choice regarding the maintenance strategy also has an impact on the environment, i.e., if an experience factory [6] is necessary. Representation schema and architecture are flexible enough to support the different strategies and their variations. Although the maintenance strategies are domain-specific regarding their origin, they are obviously reusable for similar application where the reaction/solution is a "longer process."

We identified a "managed" maintenance strategy as the best solution for a cheap start for our application partner. For this purpose, knowledge about variations in the application of standard cases is collected in the regular usage process. This knowledge is used for repackaging standard cases and related concrete cases during maintenance. Thus, a small experience factory is established, which is one person as case maintainer, who is triggered by operationalized maintenance policies [17] based on the captured knowledge about the relationships among concrete and standard cases. However, this strategy cannot avoid inconsistencies or redundancies when a large amount of cases is important from another system [19]. The case studies will also show how well and how long our approach can avoid inconsistencies in a growing case base as well.

Thus, the iSeCo shows how EM [24, 4, 7, 5] with CBR [12, 14, 13] leads to an intelligent system that is designed as long-lived system with a tight integration of recording and using experience into a process for day-to-day work [26, 16]. Its maintenance strategies are flexible to deal with different environments or changes in its environment. Furthermore, parts of our approaches for acquiring and using maintenance and evaluation knowledge are validated [4, 15, 5, 24, 16].

Regarding the other requirements and expected benefits, we draw the following conclusions: The role model supports the flexibility regarding the organizational structure. The IT security console can be easily adapted to and scaled up regarding the needs of the different environments. The scalable architecture allows an inexpensive start, which is an important requirement of our application partner. The evaluation program for the first version will show if the IT security console is able to establish the experience feedback cycle in practice. So far, representatives of the intended users are expecting a more efficient and effective handling of problems with the financial eService and are looking forward to the first version.

The next steps are the finalization of the first version and a case study with the application partner to show that the intelligent IT security console provides the benefits in the practical application. For the second version, we will focus on (a) the proactive maintenance of the reaction descriptions regarding changes to the eService and (b) learning approaches to improve the textual similarity models based on feedback (cooperation with knowledge-based systems group at the University of Kaiserslautern). Encouraged by the good feedback from the application partner and other projects, we expect that EM with CBR can provide a number of benefits for ensuring the IT security of eServices in eGovernment.

Acknowledgements. We would like to thank the German Ministry of Education and Research (BMBF) for funding the SKe project (contract no. 01AK900B). Furthermore, we would like to thank our colleagues at Fraunhofer IESE, the project members from Fraunhofer SIT, TU Darmstadt, and from the knowledge-based systems group at the University of Kaiserslautern for the fruitful discussions and their support.

References

[1]   A. Aamodt and E. Plaza. Case-based reasoning: Foundational issues, methodological var-iations, and system approaches. *AICom - Artificial Intelligence Communications*, 7(1):39–59, Mar. 1994.

[2]   K.-D. Althoff, U. Becker-Kornstaedt, B. Decker, A. Klotz, E. Leopold, and A. Voss. The indigo project: Enhancement of experience management and process learning with mod-erated discourses. In P. Perner, editor, *Data Mining in Marketing and Medicine*, Lecture Notes in Computer Science. Springer Verlag, Heidelberg, Germany, 2002.

[3]   K.-D. Althoff, S. Beddrich, S. Groß, A. Jedlitschka, H.-O. Klein, D. Möller, M. Nick, P. Ochsenschläger, M. M. Richter, J. Repp, R. Rieke, C. Rudolph, H. Sarbinowski, T. Shafi, M. Schumacher, and A. Stahl. Gesamtprozess IT-Sicherheit. Technical Report Projektbericht SKe - AP3, 2001.

[4]   K.-D. Althoff and M. Nick. *How To Support Experience Management with Evaluation - Foundations, Evaluation Methods, and Examples for Case-Based Reasoning and Experi-ence Factory*. Springer Verlag, 2003. (to appear).

[5]   K.-D. Althoff, M. Nick, and C. Tautz. Improving organizational memories through user feedback. In *Workshop on Learning Software Organisations at SEKE'99*, Kaiserslautern, Germany, June 1999.

[6]   V. R. Basili, G. Caldiera, and H. D. Rombach. Experience Factory. In J. J. Marciniak, ed-itor, *Encyclopedia of Software Engineering*, volume 1, pages 469–476. John Wiley & Sons, 1994.

[7]   R. Bergmann. Experience management - foundations, development methodology, and in-ternet-based applications. Postdoctoral thesis, Department of Computer Science, Univer-sity of Kaiserslautern, 2001.

[8]   R. Bergmann, K.-D. Althoff, S. Breen, M. Göker, M. Manago, R. Traphöner, and S. Wess. *Developing Industrial Case Based Reasoning Applications - The INRECA Methodology*. LNAI. Springer Verlag, 2003. (to appear).

[9]   Bundesamt für Sicherheit in der Informatikstechnik (BSI). *IT Baseline Protection Manual*. Oct. 2002. http://www.bsi.bund.de/.

[10] Bundesministerium des Inneren (BMI). Die eGovernment-Initiative BundOnline 2005. ht-tp://www.bundonline2005.de/, 2000.

[11] D. B. Leake and D. C. Wilson. Categorizing case-base maintenance: Dimensions and di-rections. In B. Smyth and P. Cunningham, editors, *Advances in Case-Based Reason-ing:Proceedings of the Fourth European Workshop on Case-Based Reasoning*, pages 196–207, Berlin, Germany, Sept. 1998. Springer-Verlag.

[12] M. Lenz, H.-D. Burkhard, P. Pirk, E. Auriol, and M. Manago. CBR for diagnosis and de-cision support. *AI Communications*, 9(3):138–146, 1996.

[13] M. Lenz, A. Hübner, and M. Kunze. Textual CBR. In M. Lenz, H.-D. Burkhard, B. Bartsch-Spörl, and S. Weß, editors, *Case-Based Reasoning Technology — From Foun-dations to Applications*, LNAI 1400, Berlin, 1998. Springer Verlag.

[14] L. Lewis and G. Dreo. Extending trouble ticket systems to fault diagnostics. *IEEE Net-work*, Nov. 1993.

[15] M. Nick and K.-D. Althoff. Acquiring and using maintenance knowledge to support authoring for experience bases. In R. Weber and C. G. von Wangenheim, editors, *Proceedings of the Workshop Program at the Fourth International Conference on Case-Based Reasoning (ICCBR'01)*, Washington, DC, 2001. Naval Research Laboratory, Navy Center for Applied Research in Artificial Intelligence.

[16] M. Nick, K.-D. Althoff, T. Avieny, and B. Decker. How experience management can benefit from relationships among different types of knowledge. In M. Minor and S. Staab, editors, *Proceedings of the German Workshop on Experience Management (GWEM2002)*, number P-10 in Lecture Notes in Informatics (LNI), Bonn, Germany, Mar. 2002. Gesellschaft für Informatik.

[17] M. Nick, K.-D. Althoff, and C. Tautz. Systematic maintenance of corporate experience repositories. *Computational Intelligence - Special Issue on Maintaining CBR Systems*, 17(2):364–386, May 2001.

[18] Organization for Economic Development (OECD). Update on official statistics on internet consumer transactions. http://www.oecd.org/pdf/M00027000/M00027669.pdf, 2001.

[19] K. Racine and Q. Yang. Maintaining unstructured case bases. In *Proceedings of the Second International Conference on Case-Based Reasoning*, pages 553–564, 1997.

[20] R. Rieke. Projects CASENET and SKe - a framework for secure eGovernment. In *Telecities 2002 Winter Conference*, Siena, Italy, Dec. 2002. http://www.comune.siena.it/telecities/program.html.

[21] T. Roth-Berghofer. *Knowledge maintenance of case-based reasoning systems. The SIAM methodology*. PhD thesis, University of Kaiserslautern, Kaiserslautern, Germany, 2002.

[22] G. Salton and M. J. McGill. *Introduction to Modern Information Retrieval*. McGraw-Hill Book Co., New York, 1983.

[23] B. Smyth and P. McClave. Similarity vs. diversity. In D. W. Aha and I. Watson, editors, *Case-Based Reasoning Research and Development, 4th International Conference on Case-Based Reasoning, (ICCBR 2001)*, volume 2080 of *Lecture Notes in Computer Science*, pages 347–361. Springer, 2001.

[24] C. Tautz. *Customizing Software Engineering Experience Management Systems to Organizational Needs*. PhD thesis, University of Kaiserslautern, Germany, 2001.

[25] The Council for Excellence in Goverment. Poll "eGoverment - The Next American Revolution". http://www.excelgov.org/, Sept. 2000.

[26] R. Weber, D. W. Aha, and I. Becerra-Fernandez. Intelligent lessons learned systems. *International Journal of Expert Systems - Research & Applications*, 20(1), 2001.

[27] M. A. Wimmer and B. von Bredow. Sicherheitskonzepte für e-Government. Technische versus ganzheitliche Ansätze. *DuD - Datenschutz und Datensicherheit*, (26):536–541, Sept. 2002.

Improving Similarity Assessment with Entropy-Based Local Weighting

Héctor Núñez, Miquel Sànchez-Marrè, and Ulises Cortés

Knowledge Engineering & Machine Learning group, Technical University of Catalonia,
Campus Nord-Edifici C5, Jordi Girona 1-3,
08034 Barcelona, Catalonia, EU
{hnunez, miquel, ia}@lsi.upc.es

Abstract. This paper enhances and analyses the power of local weighted similarity measures. The paper proposes a new entropy-based local weighting algorithm (EBL) to be used in similarity assessment to improve the performance of the CBR retrieval task. We describe a comparative analysis of the performance of unweighted similarity measures, global weighted similarity measures, and local weighting similarity measures. The testing has been done using several similarity measures, and some data sets from the UCI Machine Learning Database Repository and other environmental databases. Main result is that using EBL, and a weight sensitive similarity measure could improve similarity assessment in case retrieval.

1 Introduction

Over the last decade important progress has been made in the Case-based Reasoning (CBR) field. Mainly, because problems are more clearly identified, and research results have led to real applications where CBR performs well. As noticed in [Althoff and Aamodt 1996], in this situation, it has also become clear that a particular strength of CBR over most other methods is its inherent combination of problem solving with sustained learning through problem solving experience. In CBR, similarity is used to decide which instance is closest to a new current case, and similarity measures have attracted the attention of many researchers in the field.

Theoretical frameworks and empirical comparative studies of similarity measures have been described in [Nuñez *et al.* 2003], [Osborne and Bridge 1997], [Osborne and Bridge 1996] and [Sànchez-Marrè *et al.* 1998]. Other research work introduced new measures for a practical use in CBR systems, such as Bayesian distance measures in [Kontkanen *et al.* 2000] and some heterogeneous difference metrics in [Wilson and Martinez 1997]. Also, a review of some used similarity measures was done in [Liao and Zhang 1998]. On the other hand, many researchers have propose discretisation as a methodology to deal with continuous features (i.e. [Kurgan and Cios 2001] and [Wilson and Martinez 1997]).

K.D. Ashley and D.G. Bridge (Eds.): ICCBR 2003, LNAI 2689, pp. 377–391, 2003.
© Springer-Verlag Berlin Heidelberg 2003

In CBR there are a lot of possible frameworks: supervised or unsupervised do-mains, hierarchical or plain case organization, structured or nonstructured case repre-sentation, and so on. This paper focuses on supervised domains, and cases are repre-sented as a vector of feature-value pairs.

This paper aims to analyse and to study the performance of several commonly used measures in addition with a discretisation pre-process, global feature weighting, and local feature weighting, trying to show in an empirical way the utility of a new local feature weighting approach The measures are evaluated in terms of predictive accu-racy on unseen cases, measured by a ten-fold cross-validation process. In this com-parative analysis, we have selected two basic similarity measures (Euclidean and Manhattan), two unweighted similarity measures (Clark and Canberra), two heteroge-neous similarity measures (Heterogeneous Value Difference Metric, and Interpolated Value Difference Metric), two probabilistic similarity measures (SF, MRM) and an exponential weighted similarity measure called *L'Eixample*. Although all these are dissimilarity measures, we can refer to similarity measures by means of the relation:

$$SIM(x, y) = 1 - DISS(x, y)$$

1.1   Related Work

One core task of case retrieval is similarity computation. Many researchers have been trying to improve similarity assessment [Ricci and Avesani 1995]. In recent years, many of them are focusing on feature weighting. Feature weighting is an important issue with a very close relation with similarity assessment. It is intended to give more relevance to those features detected as important, and at the same time, it is intended to give lower importance to irrelevant features. Most general methods for feature weighting use a global scheme. Which associate a weight to all the space of the feature (e.g., [Mohri and Tanaka 1994] and [Kohavi *et al.* 1997]). On the other hand, some local scheme methods have been proposed, such as assigning a different weight to each value of a feature ([Stanfill and Waltz 1986]), or allowing feature relevance to vary across the instances ([Domingos 1997]), or setting weight according to the class value ([Howe and Cardie 1997]), or combining both local and global schemes ([Aha and Goldstone 1992]). In this paper, we argued that a feature may be irrelevant in some subspace of values, but in other subspaces of values it can correctly predict the class of an example. Following this idea, we propose a new local weighting algorithm called EBL. This algorithm is based on entropy of the distribution values of a given attribute. There are some approaches in the literature that use entropy to assign feature weights [Daelemans and Van de Bosch 1992], [Fazil 1999] and [Wettschereck and Dietterich 1995], but these methods are focused on global feature weights instead of local feature weights as EBL is focused on. If a continuous attribute is present, a dis-cretisation pre-process is suggested and a specific weight is associated to each result-ing range or interval. If the attribute is discrete, a specific weight is associated to each possible value. The importance of one specific value (or range) will be determined by the distribution of the class values for that feature value (or range). In other words, if the entropy of the values distribution (or ranges) respect the class values distribution is high, a low weight is set. On the other side, a high weight is associated to a value (or range) showing a low entropy.

In [Wettschereck et al. 1997] a five-dimension framework for feature weighting algorithms is presented: bias, weight space, representation, generality and knowledge. Taking into account that point of view, our approach can be classified as Bias: Preset, Weight Space: Continuous, Representation: Given, Generality: Local and Knowledge: Poor.

The paper is organised in the following way. Section 2 outlines global weighting techniques. In Section 3, background information on local weighting techniques an the new Entropy-Based weighting algorithm is provided. Section 4 presents the results comparing the performance of all distance measures using diverse criteria to handle continuous attributes and feature weights tested on sixteen randomly-selected data-bases from the UCI Machine Learning Repository and other environmental database. Finally, in Section 5 conclusions and future research directions are outlined.

2   Global Weighting Techniques

Global weighting algorithms compute a single weight vector for all cases. A weight is associated to each attribute and this weight is fixed for all the attribute space. Creecy et al. in [Creecy et al. 1992] introduced *cross-category feature importance* (CCF) method. They are trying to assign higher weights to features that occurred in fewer classes. However, this algorithm is not sensitive to the distribution of feature values across classes. Conditional probabilities have been used to assigning feature weights. Mohri and Tanaka [Mohri and Tanaka 1994] reported good performance of their QM2 method that use a set of transformed features based on the originals. The methods selected for the comparison with the new correlation-based methods (global and local) proposed are the Information Gain (IG) method, the Class-Value Distribution approach (CVD) and Class Distribution Weighting (CDW-G). These methods were selected for the comparison because of their good performance and by their different scope based on class value distribution, class projection and feature information gain. For this reason, these methods are described in detail below.

2.1   Information Gain

A feature weighting algorithm should assign low weights to features that provide little information for classification and higher weights to features that provide more reliable information. Following this idea, the *Information gain* from the class membership can be used to assign feature weights. The Information Gain is computed as follows [Fazil 1999]:

$$Info(S) = -\sum_{i=1}^{n} P(C_i, S) * \log(P(C_i, S))$$

where S is the training set, C be the set of n classes. $P(C_i, S)$ is the fraction of examples in S that have class C_i.

If a particular attribute A has v distinct values, the expected information of this attribute is the sum of expected information of the subsets of A according to his distinct values. Let S_i be the set of instances whose value of attribute A is A_i.

$$Info_A(S) = -\sum_{i=1}^{v} \frac{|S_i|}{|S|} * Info(S_i)$$

Then, the difference between $Info(S)$ and $Info_A(S)$ gives the information gained by the attribute A with respect to S.

$$Gain(A) = Info(S) - Info_A(S)$$

The values obtained for each value can be used as a global weight with an appropriate scaling process.

2.2   Class-Value Distribution Approach (CVD)

Although there are some global weighting schemes in the literature [Wettschereck *et al.* 1997], [Mohri and Tanaka 1994], a new approach has been designed. The correlation-based global weighting algorithms developed are based on the idea of assigning higher weights to features showing higher correlation between the value distribution and the class distribution in the sample training set. To that end the correlation matrix, depicted in Table 1, should be used. In our approach [Nuñez *et al.* 2002], the continuous attributes have to be discretized. Afterwards, a specific weight is assigned, both to discretized continuous attributes or discrete attributes.

Table 1.   Correlation Matrix or Contingency Table.

	C_1	C_2	...	C_n	Value Total
V_1	q_{11}	q_{12}	...	q_{1n}	q_{1+}
V_2	q_{21}	q_{22}	...	q_{2n}	q_{2+}
:	:	:	...	:	:
V_m	q_{m1}	q_{m2}	...	q_{mn}	q_{m+}
Class Total	q_{+1}	q_{+2}	...	q_{+n}	q_{++}

Where:

V_i is the *ith* value of the attribute. When the attribute is continuous, V_i represents one interval after the discretisation process.

C_j is the class j.

q_{ij} is the number of instances that have value i and belong to class j.

q_{+j} is the number of instances of class j.

q_{i+} is the number of instances that have value i.

q_{++} is the number of instance in the training set.

To implement the global weighting algorithm a new approach based on estimated probabilities and correlation have been used. The calculated values are in the range [0,1] in ascending order of relevance. In our approach, a correlation matrix is filled for each attribute, representing the correlation between an attribute's values and the class value as show in Table 1.

Two main issues must be taken into account to set appropriates weights: the distribution of the values of the attribute across the classes, and the values associated to a class.

The first one shows how a single attribute's value can determine a class. In the correlation matrix, observing a single row can see this. By observing a column, is it possible to determine the different attribute's values that predict a class. In both cases, it will be ideal to find only one value different to zero in each row and in the column where that value is. This indicates that one attribute's value can predicts a single class, and at the same time, one class is determined only by a single attribute's value. The perfect attribute can be seen like a near-diagonal matrix. To take into account both class and value distribution a third approach has been designed:

$$H_a = \frac{1}{n} \sum_{i=1}^{n} \left(\frac{q_{max,i}}{q_{+,i}} * \frac{q_{max,i}}{q_{max,+}} \right)$$

Where:

n is the number of classes

q_{+i} is the fraction of instances belonging to class i

$q_{max,i}$ is the maximum value of the column i

$q_{max,+}$ is the fraction of instances that have the maximum value $q_{max,i}$

With this addition, the minimum possible value obtained is lower that the obtained in the first approach. So, it is necessary to take it into account in the scaling process. Now the lowest limit will be $1/(|a|*n)$, where $|a|$ is the number of different feature values and n is the number of classes. The weight of the attribute is finally obtained as:

$$W_a = \frac{H_a - \dfrac{1}{|a|*n}}{1 - \dfrac{1}{|a|*n}}$$

In this approach, small addends are necessary to prevent possible zero division in very special conditions.

2.3   Class Distribution Weighting (CDW-G)

Because there is a close relation between the class-distribution global and local methods, both are described in section 3.2.

3   Local Weighting Techniques

Many works have been done concerning assigning weights to features [Wettschereck *et al.* 1997], [Mohri and Tanaka 1994]. But most of them use a *global* weight for the features. *Local* weighting methods assign specific weights to specific values of the attribute. Is it possible that one attribute could be very useful predicting a class according to one of its values, but, when it takes another value, this attribute is not relevant [Ricci and Avesani 1995]. The value difference metric of Stanfill and Waltz [Stanfill and Waltz 1986] assigns a different weight to each value of the feature. Howe and Cardie [Howe and Cardie 1997] propose a class distribution weighting method, which computes a different weight vector for each class in the set of training cases using statistical properties of that subset of data. Creecy et al. [Creecy *et al.* 1992] use per-category feature importance to assign high weights to features that are highly correlated with the class. The Value Difference Metric (VDM) and the Class Distribution Weighting (CDW-L) methods have been selected for a comparison with the new Entropy-Based Local weighting method proposed. These methods were selected for the comparison by their good performance and by their different scope based on probability estimation and weights for each case depending on their class label. For this reason, they are described in detail below.

3.1   Value Difference Metric (VDM)

Stanfill and Waltz proposed the VDM [Stanfill and Waltz 1986]. In VDM the distance between cases is defined as follows:

$$distance(u,v) = \sum_{i=1}^{n} w(i,u_i) * \delta(i,u_i,v_i)$$

where:

$$w(i, p) = \sqrt{\sum_{c=1}^{C} \left(\frac{C_i(p,c)}{C_i(p)} \right)^2}$$

$$\delta(i, p, q) = \sum_{i=1}^{C} \left(\frac{C_i(p,c)}{C_i(p)} - \frac{C_i(q,c)}{C_i(q)} \right)^2$$

where p and q are possible values of an attribute, $C_i(p)$ is the total number of times that value p occurred at an attribute i, and $C_i(p,c)$ is the frequency that p was classified into the class c at an attribute i.

3.2   Class Distribution Weighting (CDW-L)

Howe and Cardie proposed the Class Distribution Weighting method (CDW) in [Howe and Cardie 1997]. CDW starts from the premise that the features that are important to match on are those that tend to have different values associated with different classes. For each class C_j there exist a separate vector $\left\langle W_{f_1 C_j}, ..., W_{f_m C_j} \right\rangle$ of weights for each feature. The weights are assigned to a particular class on a given feature. The weights are calculated as follows:

$$R_{f_i C_j} = \sum_{h=1}^{|a|} \left| a_h(f_i, C_j) - a_h(f_i, T - C_j) \right|$$

where: $a_h(f_i, C_j)$ is the fraction of instances across the training set where f_i takes on the value v_h and belong to class C_j, $a_h(f_i, T - C_j)$ is the fraction of instances across the training set where f_i takes on the value v_h and does not belong to class C_j. This yields a raw weight vector $\left\langle R_{f_1 C_j}, ..., R_{f_m C_j} \right\rangle$ for each class C_j. The final weights $\left\langle W_{f_1 C_j}, ..., W_{f_m C_j} \right\rangle$ are simply the raw weights normalized to sum 1. These local weights are used to obtain global weights (CDW-G) for each feature. The global weights are the average of local weights across all classes to get a single global weight vector. This variant can be expected to perform well in domains where the relevant features are the same for all classes.

3.3   Entropy-Based Local Weigthing (EBL)

Frequently, a single feature may seem irrelevant if you take it in a global way, but perhaps, a range of this feature is a very good selector for a specific class. Our proposal is to assign a high weight to this range, and a low weight to the others. In the tests that have been carried out, entropy values have been used to assign weights to all the ranges. In the following paragraph we present our approach to calculate *local* weights for all values (ranges) and for all attributes. The calculated values are in the range [0,1] in ascending order of relevance. From the correlation matrix, we can obtain the entropy from each value (range):

$$H_{ij} = -\frac{q_{j+}}{q_{++}} \sum_{k=1}^{n} \frac{q_{jk}}{q_{j+}} \log\left(\frac{q_{jk}}{q_{j+}}\right)$$

This entropy H_{ij} belonging to value (range) j from attribute i will be the basis to calculate the weight for the value j following this simple idea. If the value (or range) has a maximum possible entropy ("totally random"), then the weight must be 0. On the other hand, if the value (or range) has a minimum possible entropy ("perfectly classified") then the weight must be 1. The minimum possible entropy is 0 when all the instances with this value (range) belong to the same class. The maximum possible entropy occurs when the instances with this value (range) are equally distributed in all classes and can be calculated as follows:

$$H_{imax} = -\left(\frac{q_{j+}}{q_{++}}\right) \sum_{k=1}^{n} \left(\frac{\frac{q_{j+}}{n}}{q_{j+}}\right) \log\left(\frac{\frac{q_{j+}}{n}}{q_{j+}}\right)$$

This equation is equivalent to:

$$H_{i\,max} = -\frac{q_{j+}}{q_{++}} \log\left(\frac{1}{n}\right)$$

From here, we can interpolate the weight for attribute i value (range) j between 0 and H_{imax} into the range from [0,1]:

$$w_{ij} = 1 - \frac{H_{ij}}{H_{i\,max}}$$

4   Experimental Evaluation

To test the efficiency of the global and local weighting schemas, a nearest neighbour classifier was implemented, using each one of 9 similarity measures: HVDM [Wilson and Martinez 1997], IVDM [Wilson and Martinez 1997], Euclidean, Manhattan, Clark [Lance and Williams 1966], Canberra [Lance and Williams 1966], *L'Eixample* [Sànchez-Marrè *et al.* 1998], SF [Short and Fukunaga 1981] and MRM [Althoff and

Aamodt 1996]. All similarity measures were tested with no weights, with global weights and with local weights including the new entropy-based local-weighting approach. Each similarity measure was tested, with the 6 weighting schemes, in the 16 selected databases from the UCI database repository [Blake and Merz 1998] plus an environmental database. Detailed description of the databases is shown in Table 2 where number of instances in each database (#Inst.), the number of continuous attributes (Cont), ordered discrete attributes (Disc), unordered discrete attributes (NODisc), number of classes (#Class) and missing values percentage (%Mis.).

To verify the accuracy of the retrieval in a CBR system, a test by means of a 10-fold cross-validation process was implemented. The average accuracy over all 10 trials is reported for each data test, for each similarity measure, and for each weighting scheme. The last row named as AV shows the average accuracy for each weighting scheme across all databases The highest accuracy achieved in each data set for the three weighting schemes is shown in boldface in Tables 3a, 3b and 3c.

Table 2. Major properties of databases considered in the experimentation

Database	Short Name	#Inst	Cont	Disc	NODisc	#Class	%Miss
Air Pollution	AP	365	5	0	0	4	0
Auto	AU	205	15	0	8	7	0.004
Breast Cancer	BC	699	0	9	0	2	0
Bridges	BR	108	3	0	8	3	0.06
Cleveland	CL	303	5	2	6	2	0
Flag	FL	194	3	7	18	8	0
Glass	GL	214	9	0	0	7	0
Hepatitis	HE	155	6	0	13	2	5.7
Horse Colic	HC	301	7	0	16	2	30
Ionosphere	IO	351	34	0	0	2	0
Iris	IR	150	4	0	0	3	0
Liver Disorders	LD	345	6	0	0	2	0
Pima Indians Diabetes	PI	768	8	0	0	2	0
Soybean (large)	SL	307	0	6	29	19	21.7
Votes	VO	435	0	0	16	2	7.3
Wine	WI	178	13	0	0	3	0
Zoo	ZO	90	0	0	16	7	0

To get an insight of the level of significance of this value we have done statistical tests of significance using two-tailed paired t-test to verify wether the differences between *L'Eixample*-EBL combination and the other 28 combinations are really significant. At a 95% level of confidence, *L'Eixample*-EBL combination is really significant better than 21 others and only its not significant different from the combinations HVDM-IG, HVDM-EBL, Euclidean-IG, Manhattan-IG, *L'Eixample*-IG, SF and MRM.The later two are very strange results as they have low average values, but due to a high deviation values, the confidence intervals have to be larger, and for that reason the results are these. If you take a look you can see that the more similar combinations are based in the IG method or EBL method. Taking into account that both IG method and EBL method are based in entropy and information gain measures we can conclude that these kind of methods seem to be very promising in feature weighting methods. At an 80% level of confidence, *L'Eixample*-EBL combination is really significant better than 25 others and only its not really significant different from the combinations HVDM-EBL, Manhattan-IG and *L'Eixample*-IG, confirming the above conclusion about entropy-based methods.

Anyway, one have to be in mind that the statistical tests are intended and really significant for large samples, and in our experimentation we have worked "only" with 17 databases. Probably, with more experimentation the statistical results could be confirmed, and perhaps, even better for *L'Eixample*-EBL combination.

Another conclusion is that seems that most methods are not sensitive to the number of classes of the databases.

Table 3a. Generalization accuracy for HVDM and IVDM measures.

| | HVDM | | | | | | | IVDM | | | | | | |
| | | Global Schemas | | | Local Schemes | | | | Global Schemas | | | Local Schemes | | |
	NW	CDW	IG	CVD	CDW	VDM	EBL	NW	CDW	IG	CVD	CDW	VDM	EBL
AP	90.87	93.92	99.44	98.33	96.13	93.36	95.58	82.27	83.93	92.02	87.54	84.76	83.93	84.20
AU	80.05	80.05	81.83	80.05	80.05	80.16	78.66	79.33	80.33	79.32	79.33	78.33	81.76	82.22
BC	97.03	96.81	96.61	96.58	96.81	96.83	96.60	95.09	94.88	94.23	94.45	94.88	95.09	95.51
BR	89.09	89.09	93.09	89.09	88.18	90.09	88.50	85.41	88.00	91.00	89.00	88.00	82.32	87.23
CL	77.29	78.18	76.87	77.61	77.60	78.27	77.59	70.30	73.62	74.99	72.94	75.55	71.62	74.25
FL	59.84	60.27	64.33	59.84	58.79	60.42	61.90	55.53	59.12	66.34	55.48	56.59	57.49	63.80
GL	73.60	73.60	76.64	74.50	73.60	74.97	75.45	72.57	71.14	71.08	71.08	71.58	72.51	70.25
HE	78.50	78.50	81.28	77.35	79.16	79.91	81.83	80.69	80.69	79.32	81.94	82.69	79.39	80.91
HC	79.67	77.71	76.70	80.21	77.71	79.95	**82.24**	79.60	77.17	76.70	79.65	78.77	80.69	79.82
IO	90.87	90.87	90.87	90.30	90.58	90.58	92.86	82.34	82.33	82.33	82.32	82.34	82.92	86.89
IR	92.66	94.66	95.33	95.33	94.66	93.99	95.33	92.66	93.33	93.33	93.33	93.33	92.66	93.33
LD	63.51	64.02	45.61	63.57	64.60	63.50	66.98	65.69	64.51	45.61	67.19	64.54	65.10	65.41
PI	67.86	68.11	64.71	67.21	69.14	68.12	71.99	65.67	66.58	64.45	65.92	67.10	66.06	67.35
SL	89.74	90.76	90.93	89.74	90.03	91.06	91.78	90.91	91.79	91.36	90.91	91.20	91.50	92.08
VO	97.36	96.42	**98.00**	97.47	97.48	96.95	**98.00**	97.47	96.42	**98.00**	96.95	96.95	97.47	**98.00**
WI	97.64	96.47	98.23	94.92	97.05	97.64	99.41	84.31	87.14	89.85	88.79	89.74	88.68	91.28
ZO	**97.00**	**97.00**	**97.00**	**97.00**	**97.00**	**97.00**	96.09	**97.00**	**97.00**	**97.00**	96.00	**97.00**	**97.00**	**97.00**
AV	83.68	83.91	83.97	84.06	84.03	84.28	85.34	80.99	81.65	81.58	81.93	81.96	81.54	82.91

4.1 Discretisation

Some similarity measures have a good performance when the attributes are all continuous or all discrete. Others incorporate mechanisms to deal appropriately all types of attributes. For all the measures and weighting algorithms that need discrete values, we perform a discretisation pre-process over the continuous attributes in such way that the general accuracy can be improved [Dougherty *et al.* 1995]. Discretisation may serve to mark differences that are important in the problem domain. There exist many discretisation algorithms in the literature, and had been compared among them to prove their general accuracy [Dougherty *et al.* 1995], [Ventura and Martinez 1995]. In the experimental test that was carried out, three discretisation methods were used: Equal width intervals, ChiMerge [Kerber 1992] and CAIM [Kurgan and Cios 2001]. Because of the lack of space, we only present the results obtained with the CAIM discretisation method, which recorded the best generalization accuracies. However, all conclusions can be extended to the results obtained with the other discretisation methods used [Nuñez *et al.* 2003].

Table 3b. Generalization accuracy for Euclidean and Manhattan measures.

| | EUCLIDEAN | | | | | | MANHATTAN | | | | | | |
| | Global Schemas | | | Local Schemes | | | | Global Schemas | | | Local Schemes | | |
	NW	CDW	IG	CVD	CDW	VDM	EBL	NW	CDW	IG	CVD	CDW	VDM	EBL
AP	93.36	94.47	99.44	98.05	95.03	93.64	95.02	91.15	94.19	99.44	98.33	95.30	93.63	95.58
AU	74.22	74.22	78.57	75.22	72.70	73.72	75.29	75.52	75.52	**83.85**	76.02	75.52	76.98	81.35
BC	96.16	95.53	97.03	95.53	96.58	96.38	96.81	96.60	96.18	96.40	95.93	96.38	95.96	96.60
BR	81.59	83.59	**93.50**	90.18	84.59	85.59	87.18	82.59	84.59	**93.50**	88.18	82.68	85.59	86.27
CL	78.55	77.53	76.90	75.90	78.85	78.58	79.56	78.86	77.81	76.55	78.51	79.50	79.56	78.55
FL	51.57	58.22	66.01	55.21	51.72	59.42	66.11	51.57	53.73	**66.96**	52.68	51.62	57.26	60.27
GL	68.37	68.39	75.64	70.07	68.29	66.48	70.25	72.63	72.57	78.03	76.20	74.00	74.48	75.81
HE	78.61	78.61	82.61	77.24	77.28	80.42	81.16	76.61	76.61	82.61	79.16	76.61	75.86	81.86
HC	73.99	76.80	76.62	77.58	77.79	77.27	80.71	73.99	76.80	76.62	77.84	76.51	76.74	78.54
IO	86.30	87.16	87.16	88.01	87.44	89.44	92.29	90.87	91.15	91.15	90.30	90.87	90.58	92.57
IR	95.33	**96.00**	95.33	95.33	**96.00**	**96.00**	**96.00**	93.99	95.33	**96.00**	**96.00**	95.33	94.66	**96.00**
LD	62.23	61.13	45.61	64.41	60.86	63.12	64.33	62.89	63.09	45.61	64.11	63.73	62.89	65.51
PI	71.25	70.49	64.71	68.89	70.33	71.64	71.63	69.17	68.38	64.71	67.50	68.51	68.91	71.61
SL	91.36	91.36	91.53	91.36	90.04	92.24	**94.13**	91.36	91.36	91.53	91.36	90.04	91.65	93.40
VO	93.45	96.93	96.51	95.15	95.15	94.93	94.30	93.45	96.40	95.99	95.15	96.10	94.93	94.93
WI	95.40	97.75	98.23	96.69	98.34	97.17	99.41	95.99	96.47	98.23	95.51	95.99	97.64	99.41
ZO	95.18	95.18	**97.00**	95.00	96.09	96.09	96.09	95.18	95.18	**97.00**	**97.00**	96.18	95.18	96.09
AV	81.58	82.55	83.67	82.93	82.18	83.07	84.72	81.91	82.67	84.36	83.52	82.64	83.09	84.96

4.2 Normalisation

A weakness that most of the similarity measures show is that if one of the attributes has a relatively large range of values, it can obscure the meaning of the other attributes when the distance is computed. To avoid this effect, the contribution to the distance of each attribute is normalised, and the common way of doing it is to divide the distance of each attribute by the range (maximum value – minimum value) of the attribute. Thus, the contribution of each attribute to the total distance will be in the rank [0,1]. In the tests carried out in all the databases, the values were normalised for all the continuous attributes in the computation of the Euclidean, Manhattan and *L'Eixample* distance measures. Canberra and Clark distances make a type of normalisation avoiding that attributes influence into others. HVDM and IVDM make a normalisation by means of the standard deviation of the numeric values of the attributes.

Table 3c. Generalization accuracy for Clark, Canberra, SF, MRM and *L'Eixample* measures.

	Unweigthed Metrics				*L'Eixample*						
	Normalised		Probabilistic			Global Schemas			Local Schemes		
	Clark	Canberra	SF	MRM	NW	CDW	IG	CVD	CDW	VDM	EBL
AP	90.61	89.25	99.75	99.75	91.15	**100**	98.88	99.44	96.14	**100**	**100**
AU	68.92	75.59	79.41	72.65	75.52	75.52	82.46	76.52	75.52	76.85	78.35
BC	96.68	96.40	96.62	95.77	96.60	95.96	95.33	94.25	96.38	96.81	**97.23**
BR	80.50	81.41	87.59	86.91	82.59	86.18	92.50	91.18	82.68	87.18	88.27
CL	76.23	77.22	78.82	**80.80**	78.86	77.87	79.53	75.94	78.52	78.58	79.19
FL	51.57	56.05	57.84	58.32	51.57	59.27	60.42	54.21	51.62	63.90	64.43
GL	64.10	65.37	75.81	68.68	72.63	75.89	**79.12**	75.73	74.48	77.75	76.86
HE	83.28	82.39	83.56	**88.23**	76.61	76.61	76.69	76.21	76.61	83.67	84.53
HC	74.13	75.01	75.00	68.06	73.99	78.35	79.65	77.84	75.72	78.52	79.11
IO	90.01	90.59	90.30	88.30	90.87	91.72	91.72	92.57	90.87	94.00	**95.15**
IR	**96.00**	94.66	**96.00**	94.66	93.99	**96.00**	95.33	**96.00**	94.66	95.33	95.33
LD	63.57	60.03	62.66	60.91	62.89	60.21	62.89	64.20	63.72	66.15	**68.16**
PI	63.83	65.04	74.66	**77.38**	69.17	68.64	68.64	67.58	69.03	71.66	72.01
SL	91.22	91.07	51.72	48.05	91.36	91.36	91.81	91.36	90.04	92.38	93.69
VO	93.45	93.45	87.44	91.03	93.45	95.57	96.10	95.15	94.52	95.35	94.30
WI	96.10	97.17	99.52	99.52	95.99	96.58	97.17	96.10	95.99	**100**	98.82
ZO	95.18	95.18	94.09	91.18	95.18	96.09	96.00	96.00	96.18	95.09	96.09
AV	80.90	81.52	81.81	80.60	81.91	83.64	84.96	83.55	82.51	85.48	**85.97**

4.3 Missing Values

In Euclidean, Manhattan, Clark, Canberra, *L'Eixample*, SF and MRM distance measures, a pre-processing task was carried out to substitute the missing input values by the average value obtained of the instances with valid values. This was done for all the attributes. In the case of HVDM, a distance of 1 is given when one of the values compared or both are unknown. IVDM treats the unknown values as any another value. Thus, if the two values compared are both missing, the distance between them is 0.

5   Conclusions and Future Work

Main conclusions after the analyses of the performance among all six weighting schemes and all the similarity measures are that, in general, local weighting approach seems to be better than the global weighting schemes and the unweighted schemes. It can be argued from the whole table examination, and specifically, from the average accuracy of the local weighting schemes. They are generally higher than the other schemes in most databases and in most measures. These results confirm the importance of weighting schemes in case-based similarity assessment. Only IVDM measure seems not to be very sensitive to the weighting schemes.

A new entropy-based local weighting algorithm has been proposed. This local weighting approach (EBL) seems to be better than the other weighting schemes with independence of the similarity measure or database used. Also, it has been confirmed what was found out in a previous study [Nuñez *et al.* 2003]. *L'Eixample* distance similarity measure, which takes into account much information about weights, seems to lightly outperform the other measures, specially when most attributes are continuous, and the inherent potential of the measures is thoroughly used. In previous work [Nuñez *et al.* 2003] it has been showed that *L'Eixample* measure is statistically better than most of the other similarity measures by means of significance tests.

The highest accuracy average over the 17 databases and over all similarity measures corresponds to the combination of *L'Eixample* measure with the EBL weighting method (85.97).

A possible drawback of the EBL method and possible of the IG method is that they are very sensitive to the correlation between feature values and class distribution. If the attributes in a database are not correlated among themselves the methods work very well, but with a great interaction between features, probably the performance of these methods would not be so good.

A first step has been done in the design of suitable weight selection techniques, with the proposed entropy-based local weighting approach.

Future work will be focused on the design, study and analysis of other local weighting algorithms, and also weighting techniques for unsupervised domains will be tackled. The effect of the feature interaction in the EBL method and other methods is being tested with some artificial databases.

Acknowledgements. This work has been partially supported by the Spanish CICyT projects TIC2000-1011 and REN2000-1755, and EU project A-TEAM (IST 1999-10176).

References

1. D.W. Aha, R.L. Goldstone. Concept learning and flexible weighting. *Proceedings of the fourteenth Annual Conference of the Cognitive Science Society.* Bloomington, IN. The Cognitive Science Society, Lawrence Erlbaum Associates. 1992.
2. K. D. Althoff and A. Aamodt. Relating case-based problem solving and learning methods to task and domain characteristics: towards an analytic framework. AI Communications 9(3):109–116, 1996.

3. C.L. Blake, and C.J. Merz. UCI Repository of machine learning databases [http://www.ics.uci.edu/~mlearn/MLRepository.html]. Irvine, CA: University of California, Department of Information and Computer Science. 1998.

4. E. Blanzieri and F. Ricci. Probability Based Metrics for nearest Neighbour classification and Case-Based Reasoning. *Procc. of 3rd International Conference on Case-Based Reasoning,* Munich, 1999.

5. R.H. Creecy, B. M. Masand, S. J. Smith and D. L. Waltz, Trading MIPS and memory for knowledge engineering. *Communications of the ACM* 35:48–64, 1992.

6. P. Domingos. Context-sensitive feature selection for lazy learners. *Artificial Intelligence Review,* 11, 227–253. 1997.

7. W. Daelemans, A. Van Den Bosch. Generalization performance of backpropagation leraning on to syllabification task. *In Proceedings of TWLT3: Connectionism Natural and Language Processing,* pp. 27–37. Enschede, The Netherlands. 1992.

8. J. Dougherty, R. Kohavi and M. Sahami. Supervised and Unsupervised Discretization of continuous Features. *Procc. Of the 12th International Conference on Machine Learning,* pp. 194–202, 1995.

9. N. Fazil. Using Information Gain as Feature Weight. *8th Turkish Symposium on Artificial Intelligence and Neural Networks (TAINN'99),* Istanbul, Turkey. 1999.

10. N. Howe, C. Cardie. Examining locally varying weights for nearest neighbour algorithms. *Proceedings of the Second International Conference on Case-Based Reasoning.* 1997. pp455–466. Berlin: Springer.

11. R. Kerber. Chimerge: Discretisation of Numeric Attributes. *In Proceedings of 9th Int'l Conference Artificial Intelligence,* 1992.

12. R. Kohavi, P. Langley, and Y. Yun. The utility of feature weighting in nearest-neighbour algorithms. *In Proceedings of the European Conference on Machine Learning (ECML97),* 1997.

13. P. Kontkanen, J. Lathinen, P. Myllymäki and H. Tirri.. An unsupervised Bayesian distance measure. Procc. of 5th *Eur. Work.. on Case-based Reasoning (EWCBR'2000).* LNAI-1898, pp. 148–160, 2000.

14. L. Kurgan and K. J. Cios. Discretisation Algorithm that Uses Class-Attribute Interdependence Maximisation, *Proceedings of the 2001 International Conference on Artificial Intelligence (IC-AI 2001),* pp.980–987, Las Vegas, Nevada.

15. G.N. Lance and W.T. Williams. Computer Programs for hierarchical polythetic classification ("similarity analyses") , *Computer Journal, 9,* 60–64, 1966.

16. T.W. Liao, and Z. Zhang. Similarity measures for retrieval in case-based reasoning systems, *Applied Artificial Intelligence,*12,267–288,1998.

17. T. Mohri and H. Tanaka. An Optimal Weighting Criterion of Case Indexing for Both Numeric and Symbolic Attributes, *Aha, D. W., editor, Case-Based Reasoning papers from the 1994 workshop,* AAAI Press, Menlo Park, CA.

18. H. Núñez, M. Sànchez-Marrè and U. Cortés. Similarity Measures in Instance-Based Reasoning. Submitted to *Artificial Intelligence,* 2003.

19. H. Núñez, M. Sànchez-Marrè, U. Cortés, J. Comas, I. R-Roda and M. Poch. Feature Weighting Techniques for Prediction tasks in Environmental Processes. Procc. *of 3rd ECAI'2002 Workshop on Binding Environmental Sciences and Artificial Intelligence (BESAI'2002),* pp. 4:1–4:9. Lyon, France, 2002.

20. H.R. Osborne and D. Bridge. Similarity metrics: a formal unification of cardinal and non-cardinal similarity measures. Procc. of 2nd *Int. Conf. On Case-based Reasoning (ICCBR'97).* LNAI-1266, pp. 235–244, 1997.

21. H.R. Osborne and D. Bridge. A case-based similarity framework. Procc. of 3rd Eur. Work.. on Case-based Reasoning (EWCBR'96). LNAI-1168, pp. 309–323, 1996.
22. F. Ricci and P. Avesani. Learning a local similarity metric for case-based reasoning. *In Proceedings of the 1st International Conference on Case-Based* Reasoning, Berlin, Springer Verlag pages 301–312, 1995.
23. M. Sànchez-Marrè, U. Cortés, I. R-Roda, and M. Poch. L'Eixample distance: a new similarity measure for case retrieval. *Procc. of 1st Catalan Conference on Artificial Intelligence (CCIA'98)*, ACIA bulletin 14–15 pp. 246–253.Tarragona, Catalonia, EU.
24. R.D. Short and K. Fukunaga. The optimal distance measure for nearest neighbour classification. *IEEE transactions on Information Theory.* 27:622–627, 1981.
25. C. Stanfill, D. Waltz. Toward Memory-Based Reasoning, *Communications of the ACM.* 1986.
26. D. Ventura and T.R.Martinez. And Empirical Comparison of Discretization Methods. *Procc. Of the 10th International Symposium on Computer and Information Sciencies*, pp. 443–450, 1995.
27. D. Wettschereck, D. W. Aha, and T. Mohri. A review and empirical evaluation of feature weighting methods for a class of lazy learning algorithms. *Artificial Intelligence Review*, Special Issue on lazy learning Algorithms, 1997.
28. D. Wettschereck and T.G. Dieterich. An experimental comparison of the nearest neighbor and nearest hyperrectangle algorithms. *Machine Learning*, 19:5–28, 1995.[Wilson and Martinez 1997] D.R. Wilson and T.R.Martínez. Improved Heterogeneous Distance Functions, *Journal of Artificial Intelligence Research*, 6, 1–34, 1997.

Collaborative Case Retention Strategies for CBR Agents

Santiago Ontañón and Enric Plaza

IIIA, Artificial Intelligence Research Institute
CSIC, Spanish Council for Scientific Research
Campus UAB, 08193 Bellaterra, Catalonia (Spain).
{santi,enric}@iiia.csic.es
http://www.iiia.csic.es

Abstract. Empirical experiments have shown that storing every case does not automatically improve the accuracy of a CBR system. Therefore, several retain policies have been proposed in order to select which cases to retain. However, all the research done in case retention strategies is done in centralized CBR systems. We focus on multiagent CBR systems, where each agent has a local case base, and where each agent can interact with other agents in the system to solve problems in a collaborative way. We propose several case retention strategies that directly deal with the issue of being in a multiagent CBR system. Those case retention strategies combine ideas from the CBR case retain strategies and from the *active learning* techniques. Empirical results show that strategies that use collaboration with other agents outperform those strategies where the agents work in isolation. We present experiments in two different scenarios, the first one allowing multiple copies of one case and the second one only allowing one copy of each case. Although it may seem counterintuitive, we show and explain why not allowing multiple copies of each case achieves better results.

1   Introduction

Maintaining compact and competent case bases has become a main topic of Case Based Reasoning research. The main goal is to obtain a compact case base (with a reduced number of cases) but without losing problem solving accuracy. Moreover, empirical experiments have shown that storing every case does not automatically improve the accuracy of a CBR system [13]. The last process in the CBR cycle (retrieve, reuse, repair and retain) [1] is in charge of deciding which new cases must be retained. When a case is decided to be retained, it is incorporated into the case base and will be accessible for solving new problems in the future.

Deciding which cases to retain (or to select which cases to learn from) is a concern not only in CBR. A main issue on machine learning is to select which are the examples of the target problem to learn from. Each time a learning system receives a new example, it has two options: use the example to learn

K.D. Ashley and D.G. Bridge (Eds.): ICCBR 2003, LNAI 2689, pp. 392–406, 2003.
© Springer-Verlag Berlin Heidelberg 2003

(retain) or discard it. When a learner retains every example it observes, we are talking of *passive learning*. But when the learner has some strategy to select which are the examples that it is going to learn from, we are talking of *active learning* [4]. The basic idea in active learning is that the learner receives a set of unlabeled examples and decides which of them are interesting to learn from; then the teacher labels the examples that the learner has found interesting and they are used for learning. The main goal of active learning is to minimize the number of examples needed to learn any task without appreciably degrading the performance.

Therefore, we have two different approaches to the problem of selecting which are the most interesting examples (cases) to learn from: the CBR approach and the active learning approach. The basic idea of both is to perform an active selection process through the instance space with the goal of selecting the best examples (cases) to learn from. However, there are also fundamental differences between them. Specifically, active learning strategies try to minimize the number of questions to the teacher, i.e. active learning strategies try to select which are the interesting examples *before* knowing their solution, to avoid the cost associated with labeling them (asking for the right solution from a teacher). CBR case retention strategies do not try to minimize the cost of asking for the solution of the cases, but assumes that this solution is known, since the retain process is performed after the revise process in the CBR cycle. However, we will show that both approaches can be seen under a common framework.

This work extends our previous work on *Ensemble CBR* [11]. Ensemble CBR focuses on *Multiagent CBR Systems* ($\mathcal{M}$AC) where the agents are able to solve problems individually using CBR methods and where only local case bases are accessible to each individual agent. Problems to be solved by an agent can be sent by an external user or by another agent. The main issue is to find good collaboration strategies among self-interested CBR agents that can help improving classification accuracy without compromising case base privacy. In this paper we focus on case retention strategies for Ensemble CBR.

When dealing with a multiagent system both CBR case retention and active learning must be reconsidered. If individual CBR agents apply case retention as if they were in isolation they can be losing relevant information. In a multiagent scenario several learning opportunities arise from the collaboration with other agents. Imagine the following situation: an agent A_i has the opportunity to learn a new example P, but decides that P is not interesting to him. But there is another agent A_j in the system that could obtain a great benefit from learning example P. Both agents would benefit from the fact that the agent A_i does not discard the case but instead gives it or sells it to A_j. Moreover, when an agent retains a new example, the agent can poll the other agents to see if there is anyone else also interested in the new example.

The structure of the paper is as follows. We first present in section 2 a more detailed description of the $\mathcal{M}$AC systems. Then, in section 3 we will present a common framework encompassing both active learning and CBR retention strategies. Within this framework, we will present several strategies exploiting the fact that the agents are inside a multiagent system. Finally, section 4 shows an empirical evaluation of the strategies presented in this paper. The paper closes with related work and conclusions section.

2   Multiagent CBR Systems

Formally, a $\mathcal{MAC}$ system $\mathcal{M} = \{(A_i, C_i)\}_{i=1...n}$ is composed on n agents, where each agent A_i has a case base C_i. In this framework we restrict ourselves to analytical tasks, i.e. tasks (like classification) where the solution is achieved by selecting from an enumerated set of solutions $K = \{S_1 \ldots S_K\}$. A case base $C_i = \{(P_j, S_k)\}_{j=1...N}$ is a collection of problem/solution pairs. Each agent A_i is autonomous and has learning capabilities, i.e. each agent is able to collect autonomously new cases that can be incorporated to its local case base.

Moreover, since we focus on analytical tasks, there is no obvious decomposition of the problem in subtasks. However, collaboration is still interesting because an agent A_i can send a complete problem P to another agent A_j asking for help to solve it. After A_j answers A_i with its own solution for P, A_i can do anything with this solution. A simple way for A_i to use this solution is to compare it with the solution found by itself, if both solutions agree A_i can increase the degree of confidence on the solution found, and if both solutions disagree, maybe it's interesting to send the problem to some other agent to have a third opinion [10].

When an agent A_i asks another agent A_j help to solve a problem the interaction protocol is as follows. First, A_i sends a problem description P to A_j. Second, after A_j has tried to solve P using its case base C_j, it sends back a message that is either :sorry (if it cannot solve P) or a solution endorsement record (SER). A SER has the form $\langle\{(S_k, E_k^j)\}, P, A_j\rangle$, where the collection of *endorsing pairs* (S_k, E_k^j) mean that the agent A_j has found E_k^j cases in case base C_j endorsing solution S_k—i.e. there are a number E_k^j of cases that are relevant (similar) for endorsing S_k as a solution for P. Each agent A_j is free to send one or more endorsing pairs in a SER record.

In our framework, agents use a voting mechanism in order to aggregate the information contained in various SERs coming from other agents. This voting scheme is explained in the next section.

2.1   Voting Scheme

The principle behind the voting scheme is that the agents vote for solution classes depending on the number of cases they found endorsing those classes. However, we want to prevent an agent having an unbounded number of votes. Thus, we will define a normalization function so that each agent has one vote that can be for a unique solution class or fractionally assigned to a number of classes depending on the number of endorsing cases.

Formally, let $\mathcal{A}^t$ the set of agents that have submitted their SERs to the agent A_i for problem P. We will consider that $A_i \in \mathcal{A}^t$ and the result of A_i

trying to solve P is also reified as a SER. The vote of an agent $A_j \in \mathcal{A}^t$ for class S_k is

$$Vote(S_k, A_j) = \frac{E_k^j}{c + \sum_{r=1...K} E_r^j}$$

where c is a constant that on our experiments is set to 1. It is easy to see that an agent can cast a fractional vote that is always less than 1. Aggregating the votes from different agents for a class S_k we have ballot $Ballot^t(S_k, \mathcal{A}^t) = \sum_{A_j \in \mathcal{A}^t} Vote(S_k, A_j)$ and therefore the winning solution class is the class with more votes in total.

This voting scheme can be seen as a variation of *Approval Voting* [3]. In *Approval Voting* each agent vote for all the candidates they consider as possible solutions without giving any weight to its votes. In our scheme, *Approval Voting* can be implemented making $Vote(S_k, A_j) = 1$ if $E_k^j \neq 0$ and 0 otherwise. There are two differences between the standard *Approval Voting* and our voting scheme. The first one is that in our voting scheme agents can give a weight to each one of its votes. The second difference is that the sum of the votes of an agent is bounded by 1. Thus we call it *Bounded-Weighted Approval Voting* (BWAV).

The next section presents the *Committee* collaboration strategy, that uses this voting scheme.

2.2   Committee Collaboration Strategy

In this collaboration strategy the agent members of a $\mathcal{M}AC$ system $\mathcal{M}$ are viewed as a committee. An agent A_i that has to solve a problem P sends it to all the other agents in $\mathcal{M}$. Each agent A_j that has received P sends a solution endorsement record $\langle \{(S_k, E_k^j)\}, P, A_j \rangle$ to A_i. The initiating agent A_i uses the voting scheme above upon all SERs, i.e. its own SER and the SERs of all the other agents in the multiagent system. The problem's solution is the class with maximum number of votes.

Since all the agents in a $\mathcal{M}AC$ system are autonomous CBR agents, they will not have the same problem solving experience (in general, the cases in their case bases will not be the same). This makes it likely that the errors that each agent make in the solution of problems will not be very correlated, i.e. each agent will not err in the same problems. It is well known in machine learning that the combination of the predictions made by several classifiers with uncorrelated errors improves over the individual accuracies of those classifiers [5] ("ensemble effect"). Thus, using the committee collaboration policy an agent can increase its problem solving accuracy because it matches the preconditions of the "ensemble effect".

3   Strategies for Case Retention

In the following sections we will present several strategies that an agent can use to decide which cases to retain. These strategies are used when an agent has the opportunity to learn a new case, and has to decide whether to retain it or not.

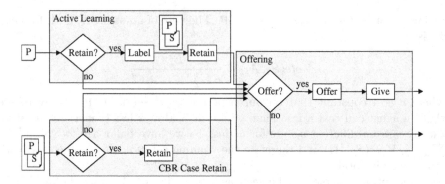

Fig. 1. View of the active learning and CBR case retention decision processes.

As we want to create *case retention strategies* to be used in multiagent scenarios, we divide each full *case retention strategy* in two subprocesses: the individual retention process and the offering process. The individual retention process is responsible of deciding whether a case has to be stored locally or not. The offering process is the responsible of deciding whether to offer a copy of one case or not to some other agents. The way we fulfill each one of these two processes is called a policy. Thus, a retention strategy needs to define an *individual case retention policy* and an *offering policy*. For the *individual case retention policy*, we have seen that there are two different approaches: policies coming from the active learning approach, and policies coming from the CBR case retention approach.

Figure 1 shows the options we have for building a complete case retention strategy. On the left part, we have two different options for the individual case retention policy, and on the right part, we can see the offering policy. Figure 1 also shows the main differences between active learning and CBR case retention: the input to active learning decision policy is a problem with unknown solution, and the input to CBR case retention is a full case (problem plus solution).

In the following sections we will first propose several policies for the individual case retention policy. First we will explain an active learning policy that takes advantage of the fact that the agent is in a multiagent system, and then we will explain several policies from the CBR case retention approach. Finally we will explain with detail the full *case retention strategies* resulting of a combination of all the previous policies with an appropriate offering policy.

3.1   Active Learning Policy

Active learning addresses the problem of deciding if a new example is interesting to be learned or not before knowing its solution. Or alternatively, the question of selecting which are the most interesting examples from a pool of unlabeled examples. But, which criterion can we use to answer these questions?

The answer to the previous question is easier when we restrict to specific learning strategies. For example, if we are learning a concept using the *Version Space* algorithm, we will have three regions in the *Version Space*: a region containing those problems predicted as positive for all currently consistent versions, a region containing those problems predicted as negative for all currently consistent versions, and the so called "region of uncertainty" [4]. In the region of uncertainty, there are problems that some versions predict as positive and that some versions predict as negative. Clearly, only examples pertaining to the uncertainty region will improve our knowledge. Therefore, a good criterion to assess if a new problem is interesting or not in the version space algorithm is whether this new problem falls in the region of uncertainty or not.

For other kinds of learning algorithms, such as neural networks, analogous criteria can be found, Cohn, Atlas and Ladner [4] define strategies to decide whether a new case will be interesting to retain or not for a neural network classifier. However, finding a general criterion applicable to any learning algorithm is difficult. Seung et al. [12], propose the Shannon information measure of the new example as "suitable guide" for the general case. They also propose the *Query by Committee* (QbC) algorithm as an approximation to this measure.

The QbC algorithm suits our framework particularly well, and can be adapted in a straightforward way to work with lazy learning algorithms in a multiagent system. We propose to use an adapted version of the QbC algorithm presented in [12], that uses all the information available in a group of agents to make the decision. Instead of creating a "virtual committee" as in the original Query by Committee algorithm, we will use a real committee composed of several agents. Thus, we propose the following multiagent version of the Query by committee (MAQbC) algorithm:

1. A new problem P arrives to one agent A_i, and A_i has to decide whether to retain P or not.
2. A_i sends problem P to a set $\mathcal{A}$ of other agents in the system (as in the *Committee* collaboration policy).
3. Each agent $A_j \in \mathcal{A}$ solves the problem and each individual classification is sent back to A_i reified as a SER. The agent A_i also solves the problem individually and stores the obtained SER.
4. A_i builds the set $\mathcal{S}$ containing all the SERs sent by the agents in $\mathcal{A}$ and the SER built by itself. Then, A_i measures the degree of disagreement between the SERs contained in $\mathcal{S}$.
5. If the degree of disagreement is high enough, the new problem P is interesting enough to be retained.

As we will use committees with more than 2 members, we need to measure the degree of disagreement. Let us define d, the degree of disagreement, as follows: $d = V_r/((K-1)*V_w)$, where K is the number of possible solutions, V_w are the votes for the most voted solution and V_r are the votes for the rest of solutions. Notice that when there is a clear majority d approaches 0, and that when the disagreement is maximum (each member of the committee votes for a different class) d approaches 1 (the reason for using $K-1$ instead of K is for normalizing the result between 0 and 1).

In order to decide whether a case is interesting or not, we just have to decide a threshold d_0 for the degree of disagreement d. If $d \geq d_0$ the case is considered interesting, and otherwise it is discarded. This policy will be called the *Informative Disagreement* policy:

- *Informative Disagreement (ID) policy*, each time an agent has the opportunity to retain a new case, the case will be evaluated using the MAQbC algorithm, and only if the degree of disagreement is high enough (i.e. $d \geq d_0$), it will be retained.

Notice that the ID policy is not infallible. In fact, in a situation where most agents err in the same way the degree of disagreement will be low enough, and thus the solution will not be asked to the teacher and the case will not be retained. However, this situation is very unlikely because all or most agents have to give the same erroneous class for the current problem.

3.2   CBR Case Retention Policies

The main difference of the CBR case retention policies with the active learning approach is that CBR policies are able to use the solution of the problem to decide whether to retain the case or not.

Deciding which cases to keep in the case base is one of the main issues in case base maintenance, and most of the work done is focused on deleting cases from the case base because the retrieval time has gone beyond the acceptable limits for an application (*swamping problem*). One of the first policies proposed was random deletion proposed by Markovich and Scott [8]. A more complex approach is taken by Smyth and Keane [14], where a competence preserving case deletion policy is proposed. Leake and Wilson [7] propose a policy to delete cases from the cases base using a performance measure. Finally, Zhu and Yang propose in [15] a technique for selecting a subset of cases from a case base using case addition instead of case deletion. This last technique has the advantage of ensuring that the case base coverage will be above a lower bound. However, these strategies are *off-line* strategies, i.e. they store all the cases in the case base, and after doing that, they analyze the content of the case base for selecting which cases to keep and which cases to delete.

We focus on *on-line* case retention strategies, i.e. each time a new problem arrives, the retention strategy is used to decide whether to retain the new case or not. A more similar approach is taken by Aha et al. [2]. They propose two policies for case retention to be applied into instance based learners in order to reduce the number of cases needed to learn. However, they only focus on centralized systems, and we are dealing with multiagent systems. Our approach can be viewed as a generalization of on-line retention policies where the cases that an individual CBR agent decides not to retain can be nonetheless useful for other CBR agents.

For our experiments, we will use three simple retention policies:

- *On Failure Retain (OFR) policy*, each new case received by the agent will be classified individually. Only if this individual classification differs with the real solution class of the problem, it will be retained.
- *Never Retain (NR) policy*, the agent never retains the new cases.
- *Always (AR) Retain policy*, the agent always retains the new cases.

NR policy represents the scenario where no learning is performed by the learning agent, and AR policy represents the scenario of *passive learning* (i.e. when the learning system retains every new example that has the opportunity to retain). The following section will define complete *case retention strategies* using all the previous retention policies (ID, OFR, NR and AR) and several offering policies.

3.3   Case Retention Strategies

In order to build a complete *case retention* strategy, we need to provide both an *individual case retention* policy and an *offering* policy. In this section, for each possible *individual case retention* policy, we will define one or more *offering* policies to form several full *case retention* strategies.

As Figure 1 shows, the *Offering* process has several steps. First, the agent decides whether to offer the case to other agents or not. After the case is offered, the agent has to decide, from the set of agents that answered positively to the offer, to which agent (or agents) the case is to be sent (In our experiments the agents use the *individual case retention policy* to decide whether they are interested in retaining a case offered by another agent.

Before defining the full case retention strategies, we will define two different scenarios. In the first one, we will consider that there are ownership rights over the cases, and therefore, no copies of the cases can be done. In the second scenario, the agents will be free to make copies of the cases, and therefore, multiple agents will be allowed to retain copies of the same case when need be. We will call the first scenario the *non-copy* scenario, and the second one the *copy* scenario. Several strategies for retaining cases can be defined for each scenario. We will now define the *case retention* strategies applicable in each scenario.

***Non-Copy* Scenario Strategies.** In this scenario, we can only allow a single copy of each case in the system. Therefore, only one agent can retain each case. We propose the following strategies for an agent A_i that receives a new problem P to learn:

- *Informative Disagreement - No Offer* strategy (ID-NO): In this strategy, the *MAQbC* algorithm is used to decide whether to retain P locally or not. The case is never offered to other agents.
- *Informative Disagreement - Offer* strategy (ID-O): The *MAQbC* algorithm is used to decide whether to retain locally the case or not. If the case is found interesting, A_i will ask the teacher for the correct solution of P. After that, the agent will know which of the agents (including itself) have failed to solve

the problem correctly. If A_i is one of the agents to fail solving P then the case is retained by A_i. Otherwise, as only one agent can retain P, A_i has to choose one of them (currently this selection is done randomly).

- *Never Retain - No Offer* strategy (NR-NO): No retention nor offering process is done. This represents the case of an agent that has no learning capabilities.
- *Always Retain - No Offer* strategy (AR-NO): The new problem is always retained by A_i, and as only a single copy of the case is allowed, no offering can be made.
- *On Failure Retain - No Offer* strategy (OFR-NO): In this strategy, P is only retained by A_i when A_i was not individually capable of solving P correctly. The case is never offered to other agents.
- *On Failure Retain - Offer* strategy (OFR-O): In this strategy, P is only retained by A_i when A_i was not individually capable of solving P correctly. If the case is not retained, it is offered to the other agents. Then, as we are in the *non-copy* scenario, the agent has to choose just one of the agents that have answered requesting P to send only one copy of it. In our experiments, this selection is done randomly.

Copy Scenario Strategies. All the previous strategies are applicable to this scenario. For this reason, we will only explain here the different strategies that can only be applied to the *copy* scenario:

- *Informative Disagreement - Offer* (ID-O-copy): The difference of this strategy from *ID-O* is that, as we are in the *copy* scenario, no selection process must be done, and all the agents that have failed to solve P can retain it. Therefore, this strategy works as follows: the *MAQbC* algorithm is applied to decide whether to retain P or not. If the case should be retained, after asking the solution of P from a teacher, all the agents that have not correctly solved P receive a copy of it.
- *On Failure Retain - Offer* (OFR-O-copy): A_i retains the case only when A_i was not individually capable of solving P correctly. Then, P is also offered to the other agents. A copy of the case is sent to each agent that answers requesting a copy. Notice that this is possible only because we are now in the *copy* scenario.

There is another combination of policies that generates a new strategy: *Always Retain - Offer* strategy, where the cases are always retained by every agent. However, this is not an interesting strategy because all the agents in the system will have access exactly to the same cases and will retain all of them.

4   Experimental Results

In this section we want to compare the classification accuracy of the *Committee* collaboration policy using all the strategies presented in this chapter. We also present results concerning the resulting size of the case bases.

We use the marine sponge classification problem as our test bed. We have designed an experimental suite with a case base of 280 marine sponges pertaining to three different orders of the *Demospongiae* class (*Astrophorida, Hadromerida* and *Axinellida*). In each experimental run the whole collection of cases is divided in two sets, a training set (containing a 10% of the cases), and a test set (containing a 90% of the cases). The training set is distributed among the agents, and then incremental learning is performed with the test set. Each problem in the test set arrives randomly to one agent in the $\mathcal{MAC}$. The goal of the agent receiving a problem is to identify the correct biological order given the description of a new sponge. Once an agent has received a problem, the *Committee* collaboration policy will be used to obtain the identification. Since our experiments use supervised learning, after the committee has solved the problem, there is a supervisor that tells the agent receiver of the problem which was the correct solution. After that, the retention policy is applied. Each agent applies the nearest neighbor rule to solve the problems. The results presented here are the average of 50 experimental runs.

As these experiments try to evaluate the effectiveness of the collaborative learning policies, it is important that the agents really have an incentive to collaborate. If every agent receives a representative (not biased) sample of the data, they will have a lower incentive to ask for cases to other agents since they already have a good sample. For this reason, for experimentation purposes, the agents do not receive the problems randomly. We force biased case bases in every agent by increasing the probability of each agent to receive cases of some classes and decreasing the probability to receive cases of some other classes. This is done both in the training phase and in the test phase. Therefore, each agent will have a biased view of the data.

4.1 Accuracy Comparison

Figures 2 and 3 show the learning curves for two multiagent systems using all the retain strategies that we have presented. For each multiagent system, 8 strategies have been tested: *NR-NO, AR-NO, OFR-NO, ID-NO, OFR-O, ID-O, OFR-O-copy* and *ID-O-copy*. The figures show the learning curve for each strategy. The horizontal axis of the figures represents the number of problems that the agents have received of the test set. The baseline for comparison is the *NR-NO* strategy, where the agents do not retain any cases, and therefore (as we can see in the figures) they do not learn, resulting in an horizontal learning curve around an accuracy of about 50% in all the settings. This is because the training set is extremely small, containing just 28 cases to be distributed between the agents (The *Committee* collaboration policy has proven to obtain results above 88% in this dataset when the agents have a reasonable number of cases [9]). For the experiments that use the *ID* policy, we have set the parameter $d_0 = 0.3$ for the 5 agent scenario and $d_0 = 0.25$ for the 8 agent scenario.

Considering the other seven strategies we can see that they fall in two groups. The first one containing all the non-offering strategies (*AR-NO, OFR-NO* and *ID-NO*) and the second one containing all the offering policies (*OFR-O, ID-O,*

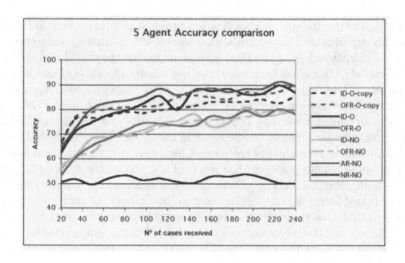

Fig. 2. Accuracy comparison for a $\mathcal{M}$AC system composed of 5 agents.

OFR-O-copy and *ID-O-copy*). Notice also that all the strategies in the offering group have higher accuracies than the strategies in the non-offering group. Let us now analyze them in turn.

Concerning the non-offering strategies, in the 5 agent scenario (Figure 2), they are practically indistinguishable in terms of classification accuracy. They all start with an accuracy of about 55% and reach (after receiving all the cases of the test set) an accuracy of about 80%. If we look at the 8 agent scenario on Figure 3, we can see that we have nearly the same situation. All the non-offering policies start with an accuracy of about 53% and end with an accuracy of about 82%. In this scenario the *ID-NO* strategy seems to work a little better than *AR-NO* and *OFR-NO*. Summarizing, we can say that they all are significantly better than the *NR-NO* strategy but to distinguish between them we have to take in consideration more factors than only accuracy (see section 4.2).

Concerning the group of offering strategies, both Figures 2 and 3 show that the *non-copy* strategies obtain higher accuracies than their respective *copy* scenario versions (i.e. *OFR-O* obtains higher accuracies than *OFR-O-copy* and *ID-O* obtains higher accuracies than *ID-O-copy*). Concerning the *copy* strategies, *OFR-O-copy* obtains higher accuracies than *ID-O-copy*. This difference is not so clear with the *non-copy* strategies, because in the 5 agent scenario *OFR-copy* obtains higher accuracies than *ID-O*, but they both reach accuracies of about 89% in the 8 agent scenario. Summarizing, we can say that *OFR-O* is slightly better than *ID-O* and that both are clearly better than their *copy* scenario versions. The explanation is that if we allow multiple copies of a case in the system, we are increasing the error correlation between the agents. Moreover, the "ensemble effect" [6] states that the combination of uncorrelated classifiers has better results that the combination of correlated ones; increased correlation is the cause of *OFR-O-copy* and *ID-O-copy* achieving lower accuracies than *OFR-O* and *ID-O*.

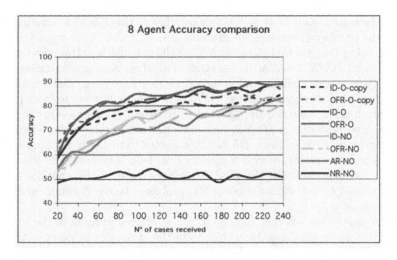

Fig. 3. Accuracy comparison for a $\mathcal{MAC}$ system composed of 8 agents.

Table 1. Average case base size of each agent at the end of the learning process.

	5 Agents	8 Agents
ID-O-copy	35.93	30.81
OFR-O-copy	56.81	56.18
ID-O	23.96	17.65
OFR-O	34.26	25.70
ID-NO	39.21	28.24
OFR-NO	16.09	11.00
AR-NO	56.00	35.00
NR-NO	5.60	3.50

Comparing both groups of strategies, all the offering strategies obtain always higher accuracies than all the non-offering strategies. Therefore, we can conclude that it is always better for the *Committee* collaboration policy that the agents offer cases to the other agents; the reason is that cases not interesting for some agents can be found interesting by some other agents. In other words, collaboration is better than non collaboration for the retention policies.

4.2   Case Base Size Comparison

Table 1 shows the average size of each individual case base at the end of the learning process (i.e. when all the 252 cases of the test set have been sent to the agents). In all the experiments the size of the initial case base (distributed among the agents) is just 28 cases (the training set). When the agents use the *NR-NO* strategy, since they do not retain any new cases, they just keep the initial cases. For instance, we can see in the 5 agents scenario (where the agents have in average a case base of 5.60 cases) that 5 times 5.60 is exactly 28 — exactly the number of cases in the training set.

Comparing the case base sizes reached by the non offering strategies (*AR-NO*, *OFR-NO* and *ID-NO*) that achieved nearly indistinguishable accuracies, we can see that there is a great difference among their case base sizes. The strategy that obtained smaller case base sizes was *OFR-NO*, with 16.09 average cases per case base in the 5 agent scenario, and 11.00 average cases per case base in the 8 agent scenario. The next one is *ID-NO*, and the one that obtained the biggest case base sizes was *AR-NO*. Thus, *OFR-NO* is better than the other two, because has the same accuracy but with a smaller case base size. However, we have to take into consideration that the *ID-NO* strategy uses less information, because it doesn't need to ask the solution of the problems before deciding whether to retain them or not.

In the case of the offering strategies, the strategies working in the *non-copy* scenario obtain smaller case base sizes than the strategies working in the *copy* scenario. This is not surprising, because in the *copy* scenario we allow multiple copies of each case to be retained, thus increasing the amount of cases retained by the agents. Since they also obtain better accuracies this result still reinforces the fact that the strategies working in the *non-copy* scenario obtain better results than the strategies working in the *copy* scenario. These strategies obtain higher accuracies because the error correlation is lower and then the ensemble effect is stronger.

Comparing the strategies based in active learning (*ID-O* and *ID-O-copy*) with the strategies based in CBR case retention (*OFR-O* and *OFR-O-copy*), we see that active learning strategies obtain smaller case base sizes. However, we are unable to say that *ID-O-copy* is better than *OFR-O-copy* because *OFR-O-copy* obtained higher classification accuracies. Comparing *ID-O* with *OFR-O*, we can see that *ID-O* obtains smaller case base sizes, but *OFR-O* obtained slightly higher accuracies.

5   Conclusions

As we have seen, some retention strategies for Ensemble CBR are clearly better than others. For instance, offering strategies always obtain greater case base sizes than non-offering strategies. But this increase in case base size is highly justified by a large increase in classification accuracy. Therefore, we can conclude that for $\mathcal{M}$AC systems using the *committee* policy it is better for an agent to offer cases to other agents.

Strategies working in the *copy* scenario have an increased case base size with a lower accuracy. Therefore they are clearly worse than the *non-copy* strategies. This may seem not intuitive, but it's an expected issue of the "ensemble effect" since copied cases increase the error correlation between agents.

Comparing strategies coming from active learning and strategies coming from CBR case retention, there is no clear winner. Strategies based on CBR case retain (*OFR-NO*, *OFR-O* and *OFR-O-copy*) usually obtain higher accuracies, but strategies based on active learning (*ID-NO*, *ID-O* and *ID-O-copy*) obtain smaller case bases (except for *ID-NO*, that obtains relatively large case bases).

Moreover, while comparing active learning strategies with CBR case retention strategies we have to take into consideration more factors. The first one is that active learning strategies do not need to ask for the right solution for every problem before deciding whether to retain it or not. Thus, they can avoid a lot of questions to the teacher. Moreover, we also have to take into consideration that the Informative Disagreement (*ID*) policy has to be tuned to each system with the adequate threshold d_0. In our experiments we have found that this is very easy when the committee has a not too small number of members. However, when the committee is very small (for instance we have experimented with a committee of 3 agents), it's not possible to find a d_0 that obtains good results, because there are very few possible values for the degree of disagreement d.

At the beginning of the experiments section we have said that, in order to give the agents an incentive to collaborate, we have forced biased case bases in every agent by increasing the probability of each agent to receive cases of some classes and decreasing the probability to receive cases of some other classes. To see the effect of retention policies under unbiased conditions, we have performed all the experiments presented in this section but randomly distributing the cases in the agents rather than forcing biased case bases. We found that the difference between offering and non-offering strategies is smaller than in the scenario of biased case bases, but that offering strategies still improve the performance. This result was expected, since when the agents receive the problems randomly, each agent receives a representative sample of examples, reducing the need of obtaining cases from other agents. In the unbiased scenario both non-offering strategies (*OFR-NO* and *AR-NO*) obtain slightly (but significantly) lower accuracies than *OFR-O*, and the same happens with *ID-NO* respect to *ID-O*. The reason for the small increment in accuracy of the offering policies (*OFR-O* and *ID-O*) is that when agents use offering policies, all the agents in the system have access to a greater amount of cases, and thus they retain more cases on average, leading to a slightly higher individual accuracy. This increment in individual accuracy is the cause of the small increment in accuracy of the offering policies in the unbiased scenario.

Summarizing, there are two main conclusions. The first one is that for case retention cooperating with other agents is always beneficial, since the offering policies always perform better than non-offering policies and *committee* collaboration policy works better than individual problem solving. The second conclusion is that working in the *non-copy* scenario to avoid error correlation between the agents' case bases is preferable, since we can obtain more benefits from the *committee* collaboration policy. This second result is quite interesting, because it could seem intuitive to think that the more cases each agent is allowed to retain, the greater classification accuracy the committee will obtain. Moreover, the restriction introduced by the *non-copy* scenario (only one copy of each case allowed in the system) could seem arbitrary, but the reduction of the error correlation between the agents obtained has a strong enough effect to prefer it to the *copy* scenario. It remains as future work to explore intermediate scenarios between the *copy* and *non-copy*, to see if a better tradeoff between individual accuracy and error correlation can be found.

Finally, notice that the ID policy (used in active learning) takes into account information obtained from other agents. As a future work, we plan to develop new CBR case retention policies that also take advantage of information obtained from other agents.

Acknowledgements. The authors thank Josep-Lluís Arcos of the IIIA-CSIC for his support and for the development of the Noos agent platform. Support for this work came from CIRIT FI/FAP 2001 grant and projects TIC2000-1414 "eInstitutor" and SAMAP (MCYT-FEDER) TIC2002-04146-C05-01.

References

[1] Agnar Aamodt and Enric Plaza. Case-based reasoning: Foundational issues, methodological variations, and system approaches. *Artificial Intelligence Communications*, 7(1):39–59, 1994.

[2] David W. Aha, Dennis Kibler, and Marc K. Albert. Instance-based learning algorithms. *Machine Learning*, 6(1):37–66, 1991.

[3] Steven J. Brams and Peter C. Fishburn. *Approval Voting*. Birkhauser, 1983.

[4] David A. Cohn, Les Atlas, and Richard E. Ladner. Improving generalization with active learning. *Machine Learning*, 15(2):201–221, 1994.

[5] L. K. Hansen and P. Salamon. Neural networks ensembles. *IEEE Transactions on Pattern Analysis and Machine Intelligence*, 12:993–1001, 1990.

[6] Anders Krogh and Jesper Vedelsby. Neural network ensembles, cross validation, and active learning. In G. Tesauro, D. Touretzky, and T. Leen, editors, *Advances in Neural Information Processing Systems*, volume 7, pages 231–238. The MIT Press, 1995.

[7] David B. Leake and David C. Wilson. Remembering why to remember: Performance-guided case-base maintenance. In *EWCBR-2000*, LNAI, pages 161–172. Springer Verlag, 2000.

[8] S. Markovich and P. Scott. The role of forgetting in learning. In *ICML-88*, pages 459–465. Morgan Kaufman, 1988.

[9] S. Ontañón and E. Plaza. Learning when to collaborate among learning agents. In *ECML-2001*, LNAI, pages 394–405. Springer-Verlag, 2001.

[10] Santiago Ontañón and Enric Plaza. Learning to form dynamic committees. In *Int. Conf. Autonomous Agents and Multiagent Systems AAMAS'03*, 2003.

[11] Enric Plaza and Santiago Ontañón. Ensemble case-based reasoning: Collaboration policies for multiagent cooperative cbr. In I. Watson and Q. Yang, editors, *In Case-Based Reasoning Research and Development: ICCBR-2001*, number 2080 in LNAI, pages 437–451. Springer-Verlag, 2001.

[12] H. S. Seung, Manfred Opper, and Haim Sompolinsky. Query by committee. In *Computational Learing Theory*, pages 287–294, 1992.

[13] B. Smyth. The utility problem analysed: A case-based reasoning persepctive. In *EWCBR-96*, LNAI, pages 234–248. Springer Verlag, 1996.

[14] Barry Smyth and Mark T. Keane. Remembering to forget: A competence-preserving case deletion policy for case-based reasoning systems. In *IJCAI-95*, pages 377–382, 1995.

[15] Jun Zhu and Qiang Yang. Remembering to add: Competence-preserving case-addition policies for case base maintenance. In *IJCAI-99*, pages 234–241, 1999.

Efficient Real Time Maintenance of Retrieval Knowledge in Case-Based Reasoning

David W. Patterson, Mykola Galushka, and Niall Rooney

Northern Ireland Knowledge Engineering Laboratory
School of Information and Software Engineering
University of Ulster at Jordanstown,
Newtownabbey, County Antrim,
Northern Ireland
{ wd.patterson, mg.galushka, nf.rooney }@ulster.ac.uk

Abstract. In this paper, we investigate two novel indexing schemes called D-HS and D-HS+PSR(II) designed for use in case-based reasoning systems. D-HS is based on a matrix of cases indexed by their discretised attribute values. D-HS+PSR(II) extends D-HS by combining the matrix with an additional tree-like indexing structure to facilitate solution reuse. DHS+PSR(II)'s novelty lies in its ability to improve retrieval efficiency over time by reusing previously encountered solution patterns. Its benefits include its accuracy, speed and ability to facilitate *efficient real time* maintenance of retrieval knowledge as the size of the case-base grows. We present empirical results from an analyses of 20 case-bases and demonstrate the technique to be of similar competency to C4.5 yet much more efficient. Its performance advantages over C4.5 are shown to be especially apparent when tested on case-bases which grow in size over time.

1 Introduction

The nearest neighbour (NN) algorithm is a commonly used similarity metric in Case-based reasoning (CBR). Its appeal includes its simplicity, its transparency, its robustness in the presence of noise and the fact that it does not require training. Over the years researchers have studied the nearest neighbour algorithm in detail to try and improve upon its competency. For example its noise tolerance has been improved by retrieving k nearest cases and introducing a 'voting' scheme to combine the various predictions [15]. Attribute values have been weighted according to their significance to help deal with the curse of dimensionality [14], cases themselves have been weighted to increase the retrieval probability of more competent cases [3,2,10] and approaches developed to improve the manner in which symbolic attributes are dealt with [14,2,3]. All of these improvements have focused on improving the competency of the NN algorithm. A major drawback of the algorithm, due to its exhaustive search through the case-base for the most similar case, remains its efficiency. This is especially poor for large case-bases. A serious consequence of this poor efficiency in CBR is an exacerbation of the effects of the utility problem [13].

K.D. Ashley and D.G. Bridge (Eds.): ICCBR 2003, LNAI 2689, pp. 407–421, 2003.
© Springer-Verlag Berlin Heidelberg 2003

Case indexing has been widely applied in CBR as a method of improving search efficiency to combat the effects of the utility problem. As only a selective portion of the case-base is made available during retrieval, search time is reduced and the efficiency of identifying a possible solution is increased dramatically. Unfortunately building and maintaining a competent index is not an easy task as it is highly dependent on the retrieval circumstances [4], which are constantly changing in real world applications. Therefore the indexing structure (retrieval knowledge) of the case-base must be maintained to reflect this. This maintenance of retrieval knowledge can be a major burden on CBR systems. If the indexing scheme is poor or maintenance is ignored, cases with good solutions to the target problem may be overlooked as they reside in a different part of the case-base inaccessible under the current indexing scheme. This can lead to the complex adaptation of less suited cases, a reduction in competency and in severe situations, problem-solving failures. Therefore, due to poor retrieval knowledge or insufficient maintenance, in an attempt to improve efficiency, competency is often sacrificed [11].

Researchers have applied generic indexing strategies borrowed from the machine learning community for this purpose. ID3, C4.5 and k-d trees have all been used reasonably successfully in both commercial and research based CBR applications. ID3 and C4.5 make a recursive, greedy, heuristic choice of possible partitions within the case-base. Typically the heuristic choice is based on the values of a single attribute and an impurity measure (such as information gain or Gini index) to choose the best attribute to split upon. The basic approach to kd-trees is to recursively build a tree which splits the search space into areas which contain a number of similar cases according to a given similarity measure. Both the decision tree and k-d tree approaches are widely known to have problems when it comes to maintenance. For example adding or removing cases from a decision tree can lead to a degradation in accuracy unless the tree is totally re-built. Similarly adding or deleting cases from a kd-tree, without rebuilding, can have an unpredictable outcome on its search performance.

Additionally a number of researchers have developed *CBR specific* indexing strategies designed for particular CBR applications as opposed to using the more generic machine learning approaches. Although these have been successful in their own right they have limitations. For example some indexing strategies have proven difficult to maintain over time or have tended not to be very generic as they are too specific to the domain for which they were developed. This means it is difficult to apply them to other domains. Others still have proven to be too labour intensive to be of practical use in real world domains. For example, Deangdej [4] devised a dynamic indexing structure to retrieve cases at run time from a case-base of over two million cases in an insurance domain. This is an interesting approach in that indexes are generated dynamically in real time in response to target problems. Unfortunately it requires specific domain knowledge from an expert (which may not always be available in every domain) to guide the process and cannot cope with the addition of new cases to the case library, thus it cannot be maintained easily. Fox [5] developed an introspective reasoning technique for dynamically refining case indexes based on previous retrievals in a case-based planning domain. Unfortunately, although it was successful at maintaining retrieval knowledge, it required quality domain knowledge initially to build a model based component which is then used to drive the introspective indexing technique. The luxury of having this type of knowledge readily available cannot be assumed in all domains. Zhang & Yang [16] take an indexing like approach to reducing redundancy in case-bases, based on a neural network model. Unfortunately this approach is very labour intensive as it relies on feedback from the user as to the quality of the retrieval in order to maintain and optimize the index. Aha [1] presented a methodology of continually refining a case library in the domain of conversational CBR to improve both competency and efficiency. This, effective as it is, is designed for the very specialised domain of conversational CBR and cannot be converted into a generic indexing approach usable by conventional CBR application domains. Smyth has devised an indexing scheme based on a case competence model [19], which improves retrieval competency and efficiency. This is domain knowledge free, is not labour intensive and is generic but it does have large processing overheads associated with it, for example to determine competence groups. Patterson et al. [11] demonstrated the use of k-Means clustering to indexing in CBR. This is a generic approach requiring no domain knowledge, nor input from the user that also has a very low maintenance overhead. It was demonstrated how the index could be generated and maintained in real time whilst still remaining just as competent and more efficient than k-NN.

The retrieval techniques proposed in these experiments are called Discretised Highest Similarity (D-HS) [12] and Discretised Highest Similarity with Pattern Solution Reuse II (D-HS+PSR(II)) which is an updated version of the algorithm first presented in [12], which showed the efficiency benefits of the technique compared to nearest neighbours. Both can be viewed as *generic* indexing schemes for CBR systems, developed in a similar spirit to Patterson et al. [11]. They are generic in that they require no domain specific knowledge and can be applied to any CBR task using attribute-value vectors as the case representation. They are designed to have low maintenance overheads and need no input from the user. DHS+PSR(II) extends D-HS and uses the principal of pattern reuse to improve retrieval efficiency and also facilitates the *real time* maintenance of the indexing structure (retrieval knowledge), which is a major limitation of the generic machine learning indexing strategies and many of the specific application driven CBR approaches outlined previously. This approach is a hybrid technique consisting of D-HS combined with a tree like structure for pattern reuse. The tree structure can be viewed as a reduced form of the case-base from where initially retrievals are attempted, if retrieval fails then a solution is formed from the D-HS (unreduced case-base) and the tree is updated so that the next time a similar solution is required it can be solved from the tree. Additionally anther benefit of D-HS is that it also be used as a source of similarity or adaptation knowledge by the system.

The main aims of this research were 2-fold. It had been shown in [12], that D-HS+PSR was much faster than NN whilst providing at least the same competency.

Firstly we wanted to determine its efficiency and accuracy compared to C4.5. Secondly we wanted to examine the maintainability of the retrieval technique in real time. Thus we investigated the incremental nature of the approach (emulating the growth of a real world case-base over time) with a view to assessing the maintainability of the retrieval knowledge and efficiency of the technique in comparison to C4.5. In the experiments we analyse the performance of both D-HS and D-HS+PSR(II) in comparison to C4.5.

Section 2 outlines the methodology employed to construct the retrieval technique. Section 3 describes the experimental techniques for the incremental and non incremental experiments. Section 4 provides the results and discussion for the experiments outlined in Section 3. Finally conclusions are drawn and future work outlined in Section 5.

2   Methodology

2.1   D-HS

The training cases were processed to create a matrix M where each cell $M(i,j)$ contains a list of cases whose normalised attribute value x for attribute i lies in an interval $1/d_i * (j-1) <= x < 1/d_i * |j, j=1.d_i$. For nominal attributes the value of d_i is simply the number of possible attribute values. For continuous numeric attributes, we chose d_i to have the value of 10 (as this was found to give competent results in [12]) so in essence numeric attributes are discretised into 10 intervals. A target case was said to match a case from the case-base on a particular attribute value if both of their attribute values fell into the same discretised interval as defined in equation 1.

$$similarity(C_1,C_2) = \sum_{j=1}^{d} match(C_1(j),C_2(j))$$

where   (1)

d is the number of attributes and

$match(C_1(j),C_2(j)) == 1$ or 0

At least N (N = 5 in our experiments) cases from the matrix, with highest matching count were considered for retrieval as part of a *retrieval set* for a Target. This retrieval set was then used to predict a majority class for target problems. Figure 1 shows an example of how the D-HS was constructed using the example case-base where cases consist of 3 attributes (A1-A3) and a solution field S. It also describes the retrieval process for a target T. For simplicity it shows how each case attribute value was discretised into one of 5 intervals. A count was kept of the number of times the attributes of each case in the case-base case fell into the same discretised intervals as the corresponding attribute of the target, T. All cases, which overlap with T, are shown in bold in Figure 1. This means that the similarity function has maximal value if two cases agree on all their attribute values and 0 if they agree on none of their attribute values.

Example Dataset

Case	A1	A2	A3	S
C1	0.1	0.3	0.9	0.6
C2	0.2	0.9	0.4	0.3
C3	0.4	0.3	0.1	0.2
C4	0.5	0.3	0.1	0.8
C5	0.3	0.1	0.6	0.4
C6	0.9	0.5	0.3	0.3
C7	0.3	0.3	0.2	0.3
C8	0.3	0.3	0.1	0.2
C9	0.2	0.5	0.5	0.3
C10	0.3	0.5	0.5	0.3
T	0.3	0.5	0.5	?

Matrix

Interval:	1	2	3	4	5
A1	C1	C2,C5,C7, C8,C9, C10, T	C3,C4		C6
A2	C5	C1,C3, C4 C7,C8,	C6,C9, C10, T		C2
A3	C3, C4, C8	C6,C7	C2,C9, C10, T	C5	C1
Interval range:	0.0-0.2	0.2-0.4	0.4-0.6	0.6-0.8	0.8-1.0

Matching Count Table

Cases	Count
C2	2
C5	1
C6	1
C7	1
C8	1
C9	3
C10	3

C2,C5,C6 C7,C8,C9 ,C10

Retrieval Set

Cases	S
C2	0.3
C5	0.4
C6	0.3
C7	0.3
C8	0.2
C9	0.3
C10	0.3

Solution 0.3

Fig. 1. Retrieval using D-HS

2.2 D-HS+PSR(II)

This D-HS approach could be speeded up further by creating a tree like representation of the cases in the case-base. It was seen that, especially for larger case-bases, there was a high probability that a number of different target cases shared the same matrix retrieval pattern (as a result of the attribute value discretisation process) as cases in the case-base.

An auxiliary retrieval tree structure was therefore built, which mirrored the exact matrix intervals each particular case fell into for each of its attributes. Figure 2 shows a partial tree for cases 1, 5, 9 & 10. Attribute decision nodes, A1,A2,A3, discriminate among the matrix intervals a case's attribute falls into. At each leaf node of the tree is stored the actual cases which are indexed via the particular retrieval pattern of its attributes. Utilizing the tree, to exactly match a target case's interval pattern, could negate the need for a matrix lookup when the pattern is recognized by the tree. If the target interval pattern is not recognized, then the matrix can still be used to solve the problem. From Figure 2 it can be seen that each level of the tree corresponds to a specific attribute and each node in the tree can potentially be split into the number of discretised intervals for that attribute. Each node has child pointers to the next attribute. The tree structure shown in Figure 2 corresponds to the same cases in the case-base as shown in the previous example. The 1st attribute of case 1 falls into interval 1, its 2nd attribute falls into interval 2 and the 3rd attribute falls into interval 5, so the tree is traversed as shown and case 1 stored at the leaf node and can be indexed by a retrieval pattern of {1,2,5}. The diagram demonstrates how the target case T with retrieval pattern {2,3,3} is solved using the tree. The retrieval patterns within the tree can be viewed as new 'case structures', which can be used to solve target problems. They can be seen as a generalization of the case knowledge contained within the D-HS.

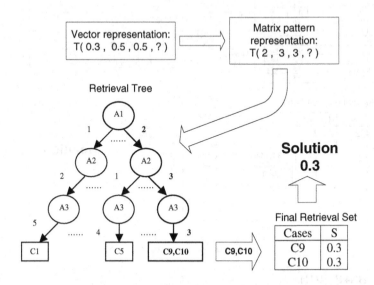

Fig. 2. Retrieval using the tree in D-HS+PSR(II)

It should be noted that the solutions produced by the tree will be identical to D-HS as it simply reuses solutions determined previously by the D-HS. Obviously it is faster to form a solution from the tree than the D-HS, as the tree look-up of the initial retrieval set can be done in a time factor proportional to the number of attributes, whereas with D-HS, formation of the initial retrieval step is dependent on how many cases have some overlap with the target case. The D-HS+PSR(II) technique has an initial overhead in setting up the tree structure but for large data sets with good solution reuse this should be compensated for by the improved speed by which problems can be solved by as opposed to using the matrix alone. A major advantage of D-HS+PSR(II) is that updating the system with new cases can be achieved in real-time. An in depth analysis of the incremental nature of both the D-HS retrieval and D-HS+PSR(II) compared to C4.5 is provided in Section 4.

3   Experimental Technique

3.1   Experiment 1 – D-HS, D-HS+PSR(II) and C4.5 Performance

In this experiment the accuracy and efficiency of D-HS and D-HS+PSR(II) were analysed in comparison to that of C4.5, one of the most widely used indexing algorithms. Twenty case-bases were taken from the UCI machine learning repository all of which had classification type solution fields. These case-bases contain a range of numeric, ordinal and unordered nominal values. Missing attributes were replaced using a means or modal technique. Although the technique works equally well with regression type problems, classification case-bases were used here because C4.5, used to benchmark the performance of D-HS+PSR(II), cannot operate with regression problems. The case-bases were partitioned into a training and a test case-base and analysed using 10-fold cross validation. The auxiliary tree structure was built and used only during the test phase. Classification accuracies were recorded for each technique after 10 fold cross validation based on the percentage of correct classifications. Two tailed paired t-tests (with a 95% confidence interval) were carried out to see if the difference between the accuracies produced by the different indexing approaches were statistically significant. The time taken to carry out the 10 fold cross validation was recorded as an indication of retrieval efficiency for each technique.

3.2   Experiment 2 – Incremental Learning Experiments

In these experiments the case-bases were split into training (composed of 90% of the cases) and test case-bases as before. The training case-base was then split further into 10 equal sized partitions. The first partition was used to build the matrix in D-HS and D-HS+PSR(II) and the test set used to build the tree during retrieval in DHS+PSR(II), as described in Section 3. Each partition of data was then added to the index structure(s) in 9 increments.   Accuracies and efficiencies were noted after each increment. However unlike in the cross validation process of 3.1 , the tree structure was maintained in real-time after each increment, as now described. After each incremental addition of the next training partition, each child node of the tree was marked as being valid or invalid with a given probability p. Those marked as valid *could* be used directly to form solutions during the next test phase and were *not* updated to reflect the new case knowledge contained in any newly added partition of cases. Nodes marked as invalid could *not* be used directly to form a solution for target cases whose retrieval pattern preexisted in the tree, but instead a solution was sought from the matrix and the relevant branch of the tree updated. These nodes *were* updated to reflect the new case knowledge contained in the newly added partition of cases (i.e. those recently appended to the matrix in the most recently added partition). The motivation behind this maintenance approach was to maximise the amount of solution re-use from the tree while at the same time facilitating an update process on the tree structure. Evaluation was again carried out as before. This process was repeated until all 9 partitions had been added to the index structure(s). By varying the value of the reuse parameter p the amount of tree maintenance can be adjusted. Larger values of p will result in more efficient retrievals times but will probably affect the overall accuracy of the technique for the worse. Conversely by lowering p the efficiency of the technique will suffer somewhat but accuracy should benefit from a more charitable maintenance policy. In these experiments the value of p was set to 0.5. To enable the performance of the technique to be assessed, C4.5 was analysed using the same incremental approach (using 10 partitions) and its respective accuracies and efficiencies noted at each stage for each case-base. As the C4.5 indexing structure can not be updated in real time, the structure was built from scratch after each addition of a partition.

4   Experimental Results and Discussion

4.1 Experiment 1 – D-HS, D-HS+PSR(II) and C4.5 Performance

Experiments were carried out as described in Section 3.1. The results can be seen in Table 1.

Table 1. Accuracies for D-HS, D-HS+PSR(II) and C4.5 retrieval techniques.

Case-base	Accuracy		
	D-HS	D-HS+PSR(II)	C4.5
ADULT	83.38	83.38	**86.07**
BALANCE	**83.06**	**83.06**	75.84
BREAST CANCER	95.45	95.45	95.45
COLIC	80.41	80.41	**85.03**
CREDIT	84.78	84.78	85.80
DIABETES	68.88	68.88	72.38
DERMATOLOGY	94.80	94.80	93.18
ECHOCARDIOGRAM	86.32	86.32	88.68
GLASS	61.39	61.39	68.27
HEART	**83.16**	**83.16**	73.90
HEPATITIS	84.62	84.62	78.83
IONOSPHERE	89.15	89.15	87.46
LETTER	86.98	86.98	86.84
MUSHROOMS	100	100	100
SEGMENT	90.43	90.43	**96.83**
SONAR	75.93	75.93	73.10
VEHICLE	69.73	69.73	69.15
VOTE	93.10	93.10	**96.32**
VOWEL	**79.90**	**79.90**	79.09
WAVEFORM	73.76	73.76	**75.46**

From this it can be seen that accuracies are indeed identical between the D-HS and D-HS+PSR(II) for all case-bases tested (this is expected as D-HS+PSR(II) reuses solutions previously determined by the D-HS). D-HS/D-HS+PSR(II) outperform C4.5 with 9 case-bases, 3 of which were statistically significant (bold font –Balance Heart and Vowel), and C4.5 outperforms D-HS+PSR(II) with 9 case-bases, five of which were statistically significant (bold font- Adult, Colic, Segment, Vote and Waveform). For 2 case-bases (Mushrooms & Breast Cancer) the two techniques were equally accurate. From these results it can be concluded that all techniques are equally accurate for the case-bases studied. It is interesting to note that where C4.5 was statistically significantly more accurate it was by a small percentage (3.72% on average) whereas where the D-HS was statistically significantly more accurate it was by more than double this amount (5.8 % on average). Table 2 shows the efficiencies of the relevant retrieval techniques, given as a ratio compared to C4.5. A ratio less than 1 indicates C4.5 is more efficient and a ratio more than 1 indicates C4.5 is less efficient.

Table 2. Efficiency ratios of retrieval for D-HS and D-HS+PSR(II) compared to C4.5

Case-base	Efficiency	
	D-HS	D-HS+PSR(II)
ADULT	0.21	0.24
BALANCE	0.92	0.85
BREAST CANCER	**1.49**	**1.60**
COLIC	**1.50**	**1.37**
CREDIT	**1.25**	**1.17**
DBT	**3.05**	**2.85**
DERMATOLOGY	0.66	0.60
ECHOCAR	**2.62**	**1.87**
GLASS	**2.92**	**3.17**
HEART	**2.57**	**2.27**
HEPATITIS	**2.27**	**2.13**
IONOSPHERE	**6.56**	**5.58**
LETTER	**1.06**	**1.07**
MUSHROOMS	0.02	0.02
SEGMENT	**1.28**	**1.26**
SONAR	**7.65**	**6.09**
VEHICLE	**5.55**	**4.70**
VOTE	0.44	0.41
VOWEL	**8.78**	**7.86**
WAVEFORM	**2.35**	**2.21**

From this it can be seen that for 5 case-bases C4.5 is more efficient (Adult, Balance, Dermatology, Mushrooms, and Vote) whereas for the other 15 case-bases both the D-HS and D-HS+PSR(II) are more efficient (shown in bold). Therefore both the D-HS and D-HS+PSR(II) are much more efficient indexing approaches than C4.5. It should also be noted that once the D-HS and D-HS+PSR(II) gave equivalent efficiencies (Mushrooms) and for 4 case-bases (Adult, Breast Cancer, Glass and Letter) D-HS+PSR(II) was more efficient than the D-HS. This is because here the time taken to construct the tree is compensated for by the time saved reusing previously encountered solutions using the tree, as opposed to constructing them from scratch each time from the D-HS. It is known that C4.5 tends to be less efficient when dealing with numeric as opposed to nominal attributes. In addition D-HS will tend to suffer in efficiency if a number of nominal values have a high number of possible values. This was reflected in the results where the best improvement in efficiency using D-HS+PSR(II) was for Sonar, a dataset composed of 60 numeric attributes and the worst improvement was for MUSHROOMS a dataset consisting of only nominal attributes some of which had more than 10 values.

To summarise these findings, C4.5 may be slightly more accurate on the case-bases investigated but the D-HS and D-HS+PSR(II) are much more efficient. Additionally the D-HS and D-HS+PSR(II) always provide the same accuracies but overall the D-HS is the more efficient of the two techniques.

Where D-HS+PSR(II) has a real advantage with respect to conventional indexing approaches such as C4.5, is in its ability to work incrementally in real time. To prevent a loss in accuracy, C4.5 must be reconstructed from scratch whenever new cases are added to the case-base, which is a drain on system resources and reduces the usability of the approach with respect to its use in CBR. To demonstrate the incremental nature of D-HS+PSR(II) the experiments in the next section were carried out.

4.2   Experiment 2 – Incremental Learning Experiments

Table 3 shows the accuracy results for the incremental building of D-HS for 20 case-bases with the probability of reuse set to 0.5. Accuracies shown are an average for the 10 fold cross validation process on the complete case-bases (after all partitions have been added). Values in bold were significantly different.

The first point of note is that for these incremental experiments D-HS and D-HS+PSR(II) may not necessarily demonstrate the same accuracies as they did in the original non incremental experiments. This is because as cases are added incrementally to the D-HS, it is not until after retrieval that the tree structure is fully updated to reflect these additions. We do not believe this to be a significant factor – a position that is vindicated by analyzing the results between these two techniques. If we examine the results for the D-HS and D-HS+PSR(II) alone it can be seen that 14 case-bases show no significant differences in accuracies between the 2 techniques. Of the 6 case-bases that show significant differences 3 (Balance, Letter and Vowel) are more accurate with the D-HS whereas the other 3 (Diabetes, Glass and Ionosphere) are more accurate with D-HS+PSR(II). Therefore we can conclude that there is no real preference for one approach compared to the other with respect to accuracy, when building a case-base incrementally.

Comparing D-HS+PSR(II) to C4.5 it can be seen that there was a significant difference in accuracies with 8 case-bases with the other 12 giving no significant difference in accuracy. On 6 occasions C4.5 was more accurate (Adult, Colic, Letter, Segment, Vote and Waveform) and on the other 2 occasions D-HS+PSR(II) was more accurate (Heart and Balance).

Table 3. Comparison of the average accuracies for the incrementally built case-bases

Case-base	Comparison Between			Comparison Between	
	D-HS	D-HS+PSR(II)		D-HS+PSR(II)	C4.5
ADULT	83.38	83.06		83.06	**86.07**
BALANCE	**83.06**	82.75		**82.75**	75.84
BREAST CANCER	95.45	95.45		95.45	95.46
COLIC	80.41	81.76		81.76	**85.03**
CREDIT	84.78	85.36		85.36	85.80
DIABETES	68.88	**71.49**		71.49	72.38
DERMATOLOGY	94.80	94.80		94.80	93.18
ECHOCARDIOGRAM	86.32	86.37		86.37	88.68
GLASS	61.39	**67.40**		67.40	68.27
HEART	83.16	80.85		**80.85**	73.90
HEPATITIS	84.62	85.17		85.17	78.83
IONOSPHERE	89.15	**90.60**		90.60	87.46
LETTER	**86.98**	86.11		86.11	**86.84**
MUSHROOMS	100	99.94		99.94	100
SEGMENT	90.43	90.13		90.13	**96.83**
SONAR	75.93	77.79		77.79	73.10
VEHICLE	69.73	69.61		69.61	69.15
VOTE	93.10	92.86		92.86	**96.32**
VOWEL	**79.90**	73.43		73.43	79.09
WAVEFORM	73.76	73.88		73.88	**75.46**

It was observed that 5 of the 6 case-bases where C4.5 was significantly more accurate than D-HS+PSR(II), were the same as those where C4.5 was more accurate with the non incremental experiments, namely Adult, Colic, Segment, Vote and Waveform (Table 1). This re-emphasises the competency of the incremental, real time approach to retrieval knowledge maintenance of D-HS+PSR(II). The 6th case-base, which didn't originally show a significant difference in accuracy in Table 1, was Letter, and it was hypothesized that the reason for a significant difference with the incremental experiments was due to not enough maintenance within the incremental D-HS+PSR(II) approach. Therefore these experiments were repeated for this case-base and the reuse parameter p reduced from 0.5 to 0.25. This improved the accuracies for Letter to 0.87, which was now seen to be equivalent to C4.5. It can be concluded that the drop in accuracy observed with Letter compared to that obtained using the D-HS, is due to the value of p being set too high and not enough maintenance being carried out as a result. Setting p originally to 0.5 was done as an initial investigation into the approach for incremental building of the index and proved an appropriate setting for the case-bases on average.

These results were very encouraging because for more than two thirds of case-bases (14 in total), D-HS+PSR(II) either gave the same accuracies to C4.5 or statistically different and better. Additionally where C4.5 provided significantly different results which were better, the improvement in accuracy displayed over D-HS+PSR(II) was small (3.1%) whereas where D-HS+PSR(II) provided significantly different results which were better the improvement was larger (6.93%). From this it can be concluded that when building case-bases incrementally D-HS+PSR(II) is an appealing approach to adopt.

Next we examined the incremental efficiencies of the three approaches. The results for this are shown in Figure 3. Two lines are displayed, one shows how the retrieval efficiency for the D-HS approach varied, compared to the efficiency of C4.5, as the number of partitions added to the case-base was increased (i.e. the size of the case-base was incrementally increased). The other shows how the retrieval efficiency for the D-HS+PSR(II) approach varied, compared to C4.5, as the number of partitions added to the case-base was increased. Due to space restrictions it was not possible to show individually how the efficiency of each of the 20 case-bases varied as the number of partitions increased. Therefore we have shown the *average* incremental efficiency ratio compared to C4.5 for the D-HS and D-HS+PSR(II) for each of the 20 case-bases.

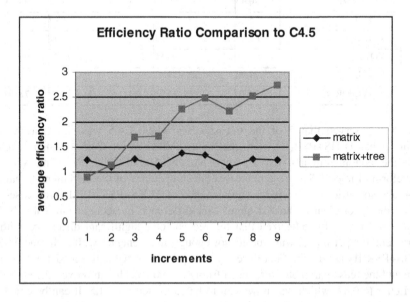

Fig. 3. Comparison of average incremental efficiencies for the D-HS and D-HS+PSR(II) compared to C4.5

From Figure 3 it can be seen that as the number of partitions added to the training case-base increases the D-HS technique remains fairly constant at a ratio around 1.25 times faster than C4.5. Therefore, as the accuracies of the D-HS were comparable to C4.5 for the case-bases examined, it can be concluded that as the D-HS is more efficient, it is a more desirable approach with respect to these two parameters. More significantly, from Figure 3, it can be seen that D-HS+PSR(II) improves in a linear fashion compared to C4.5 as the size of the case-base grows. Therefore the larger the case-base becomes over time, the more significant the efficiency of the technique will be. With only one partition added to the case-base (and no tree structure formed) its efficiency was much poorer than the D-HS and on average 0.95 that of C4.5 (it is less efficient because no tree structure is in place and must be built from scratch, which not only takes time but prohibits any reuse of previous solutions). With the addition of the second partition the efficiency ratio immediately rises to 1.2 times that of C4.5 and is comparable to D-HS. This is because D-HS+PSR(II) is reusing the knowledge stored in its tree structure formed after the addition of the first partition. As the third and fourth partitions are added the efficiency ratio rises to 1.7 and as the fifth partition is added to it now 2.35 times more efficient than C4.5. Finally when the last partition is added its efficiency is 2.7 that of C4.5. It should be noted that as the partitions are added, the tree structure is maintained in *real time* (as determined by the reuse parameter p) to ensure that accuracy is not compromised to achieve this improvement in efficiency. The results in Table 3 demonstrate that accuracy is not sacrificed. As with the D-HS approach accuracies for D-HS+PSR(II) were comparable to C4.5 during the incremental building of the case-bases, therefore it can be concluded that when efficiencies are taken into consideration, D-HS+PSR(II) is the most desirable of the three indexing approaches investigated with respect to the incremental building of case-bases.

5   Conclusions and Future Work

In this work we provide an analysis of 2 novel (related) indexing techniques, namely the D-HS and D-HS+PSR(II), in comparison to C4.5. In a study of 20 case-bases they are shown to have similar competency to C4.5 but to have better efficiency. Additionally an investigation into the incremental nature of the algorithms was performed. When the indexes are constructed in an incremental manner, the efficiency of D-HS+PSR(II) is shown to be superior to both the D-HS and C4.5. Its efficiency gain over C4.5 is especially noteworthy proving to be almost 3 times more efficient based on the case-bases used in the study. The significance of this is that it is an ideal indexing approach to use in CBR, as most other approaches do not facilitate such efficient maintenance of retrieval knowledge in real time. Furthermore, it is simple, generic, has low processing overheads, it is not labour intensive, and does not require domain knowledge. Additionally, although classification problems have been the focus in this study, the indexing approaches presented are versatile enough to work equally well on regression problems.

Future work will include utilising D-HS to highlight the areas of the problems space, where the system presently lacks knowledge to solve problems, thus drawing attention to these areas for future case knowledge acquisition. Theoretically if all cells in the D-HS have values present then there would be complete problem space coverage in that a solution could be found for all target problems. One approach to discovering any missing D-HS knowledge would be to rely on the expert to actively acquire it but a more appealing and elegant approach would be to use machine-learning techniques to automatically discover the missing case knowledge. The D-HS would be used in this instance as a knowledge acquisition tool. Other issues for further study include, investigating how the approaches deal with missing attribute values (we have carried out experiments concerning this and found the techniques to be robust but for purposes of brevity have not been able to present them in this paper), the relationship between case knowledge and adaptation knowledge and an improvement to the D-HS+PSR(II) technique so it can more efficiently deal with nominal attributes. In addition, a study of variable sized D-HS intervals and the weighting of attributes and retrieval cases will be carried out.

References

[1]   Aha, D. W. and Breslow, L. Refining conversational case libraries. In Proceedings of the 2nd International Conference on Case-based Reasoning,-ICCBR-97, pp 267–276, Providence RI, USA, 1997.

[2]   Anand, SS; Patterson, DW and Hughes, JG. Knowledge Intensive Exception Spaces, AAAI-98, pp 574–579, 1998.

[3]   Cost, S.; and Salzberg, S. 1993. A Weighted Nearest Neighbour Algorithm for Learning with Symbolic Features. *Machine Learning* 10: 57–78.

[4]   Deangdej, J., Lukose, D., Tsui, E., Beinat, P. and Prophet, L. Dynamically creating indices for two million cases: A real world problem. In Smith, I. And Faltings, B. eds., *Advances in Case-Based Reasoning, Lecture Notes in AI*, .Springer-Verlag. 105–119. Berlin: Springer Verlag 1996.

[5]   Fox, S. and Leake, D.B. Using Introspective reasoning to refine indexing. In roceedings of the 14th International Joint Conference on Artificial Intelligence. Montreal, Canada, August, pp 391–387. 1995.

[6]   Hanney, K. and Keane M. Learning Adaptation Rules from a Case-Base, Proc. Advances in Case-Based Reasoning, 3rd European Workshop, EWCBR-96, pp179–192, Lausanne, Switzerland, November 1996.

[7]   Hunt, J.E., Cooke, D.E. and Holstein, H. Case-memory and retrieval based on the immune system. 1st International Conference on Case-Based reasoning (ICCBR-95), pp 205–216, 1995.

[8]   McSherry, D. Automating case selection in the construction of a case library. Proceedings of ES99, the19th SGES International Conference on Knowledge-Based Systems and Applied Artificial Intelligence, Cambridge, pp 163–177, December 1999.

[9]   Patterson, D., Anand, S.S., Dubitzky, D. and Hughes, J.G. Towards Automated Case Knowledge Discovery in the M^2 Case-Based Reasoning System, *Knowledge and Information Systems*:An International Journal, (1), pp 61–82, Springer Verlag, 1999.

[10] Patterson, D; Anand, SS; Dubitzky, D and Hughes, JG. A Knowledge Light Approach to Similarity Maintenance for Improving Case-Based Competence. Workshop on Flexible Strategies for Maintaining Knowledge Containers 14th European Conference on Artificial Intelligence, ECAI 2000, pp 65–77, 2000.

[11] Patterson, D., Rooney, N. & Galushka, M. Towards Dynamic Maintenance of Retrieval Knowledge in CBR. Proceedings of the 15th International FLAIRS Conference. AAAI Press, 2002

[12] Patterson, D., Rooney, N. & Galushka, M. Efficient Similarity Determination and Case Construction Techniques For Case-Based Reasoning. 4th European Conference on CBR, pp 292–305, 2002.

[13] Smyth, B. and Keane, M. Remembering to Forget.: A Competence-Preserving case Deletion Policy for Case-Based Reasoning Systems. Proceedings of 14th IJCAI, pp377–382. 1995.

[13] Stanfill, C. and Waltz, D. ,Towards Memory-based Reasoning. *Communications of the ACM.* 29(12): 1213–1228, 1986.

[14] Wettschereck, D.; Aha, D.; and Mohri, T. A Review of Empirical Evaluation of Feature Weighting Methods for a Class of Lazy Learning Algorithms, *Artificial Intelligence Review Journal*, 1997.

[15] Zhang, Z. and Yang, Q. Towards lifetime maintenance of case-based indexes for continual case-based reasoning. In Proceedings of the 8th International Conference on Artificial Intelligence: Methodology, Systems, Applications, Sozopol, Bulgaria, 1998.

Incremental Learning of Retrieval Knowledge in a Case-Based Reasoning System

Petra Perner

Institute of Computer Vision and Applied Computer Sciences
August-Bebel-Str. 16-20
04275 Leipzig
ibaiperner@aol.com

Abstract. Case-base maintenance typically involves the addition, removal or revision of cases, but can also include changes to the retrieval knowledge. In this paper, we consider the learning of the retrieval knowledge (organization) as well as the prototypes and the cases as case-based maintenance. We address this problem based on cases that have a structural case representation. Two approaches for organizing the case base are proposed. Both are based on approximate graph subsumption.

1 Introduction

Case-based reasoning is used when general knowledge is lacking, but a set of cases is available which can be made available for reasoning immediately. Such a system contains different knowledge containers which may change during the life-time of a CBR system and by doing so the performance of the CBR system will improve. These knowledge containers [1] are: the vocabulary knowledge (used to describe the cases and the problem domain), the retrieval knowledge (including indexing and similarity knowledge), and the adaptation knowledge. The process of changing the knowledge containers is called case-base maintenance.

Case-base maintenance typically involves the addition, removal or revision of cases, but can also include changes to the retrieval knowledge [2][3]. In this paper, we consider the learning of the retrieval knowledge (organization) as well as the prototypes and the cases as case-based maintenance. We address this problem based on cases that have a structural case representation. Such representations are common in computer vision and image interpretation [4], building design [5], timetabling [6] or gene-nets.

In this paper we propose a similarity measure for an attributed structural representation. We describe two approaches for organizing the case base. Both are based on approximate graph subsumption. The first approach is based on a divide-and-conquer strategy whereas the second is based on a split-and-merge strategy which better allows to fit the hierarchy to the actual structure of the application, but requires more complex operations. The first approach uses a fixed threshold for the similarity values. The second approach uses for the grouping of the cases an evaluation function.

K.D. Ashley and D.G. Bridge (Eds.): ICCBR 2003, LNAI 2689, pp. 422–436, 2003.
© Springer-Verlag Berlin Heidelberg 2003

The paper is organized as follow: In Section 2 we will describe the concepts for CBR indexing and learning. The definition of a structural case, the similarity measure are presented in Section 3. Our two approaches for case-base organization and learning are described in Section 4. We compare our methods to related work in Section 5. Finally, conclusions are given in Section 6.

2   Concepts for CBR Indexing and Learning

2.1   Case Base Organization and Retrieval

Cases can be organized into a flat case base or in a hierarchical fashion. In a flat organization, we have to calculate similarity between the problem case and each case in memory. It is clear that this will take a considerable amount of time even when the case base is very large.

To speed up the retrieval process, a more sophisticated organization of the case base is necessary. This organization should allow separating the set of similar cases from those cases not similar to the recent problem at the earliest stage of the retrieval process. Therefore, we need to find a relation t that allows us to order our case base:

Definition 1: A relation t on a set CB is called a partial order on CB if it is reflexive, antisymmetric, and transitive. In this case, the pair $\langle CB, t \rangle$ is called a partial ordered set or poset.

The relation can be chosen depending on the application. One common approach is to order the case base based on the similarity value. The set of cases can be reduced by the similarity measure to a set of similarity values. The relation $\leq$ over these similarity values gives us a partial order over these cases. The derived hierarchy consists of nodes and edges. Each node in this hierarchy contains a set of cases that do not exceed a specified similarity value. The edges show the similarity relation between the nodes. The relation between two successor nodes can be expressed as follows: Let z be a node and x and y are two successor nodes of z, then x subsumes z and y subsumes z. By tracing down the hierarchy, the space gets smaller and smaller until finally a node will not have any successor. This node will contain a set of similar cases. Among these cases has to be found the most similar case to the query case. Although we still have to carry out matching, the number of matches will have decreased through the hierarchical ordering. The nodes can be represented by the prototypes of the set of cases assigned to the node. When the hierarchy is used to process a query, the query is only matched with the prototype. Depending on the outcome of the matching process, the query branches right or left of the node. Such hierarchy can be created by hierarchical or conceptual clustering [7], k-d trees [8] or decision trees [9]. There are also set membership-based organizations known, such as semantic nets [10] and object-oriented representations [11].

The problem is to determine the right relation t that allows to organize the case base, a procedure for learning prototypes and case classes, and a similarity measure.

3 Structural Representation and Structural Similarity Measure

Before we can describe our approach to maintaining the retrieval knowledge in detail we introduce the basic definitions and notation that will be used in this paper.

3.1 Definition of a Case

The structural representation of a case can be described as a graph. If we assign attributes to the nodes and the edges, then we have an attributed graph defined as follow:

Definition 2

W ... set of attribute values, A ... set of all attributes, $b: A \rightarrow W$ partial mapping, called attribute assignments, B ... set of all attribute assignments over A and W.

A graph $G = (N, p, q)$ consists of

$\quad N$ ... finite set of nodes

$\quad p: N \rightarrow B$ mapping of nodes to attribute assignment

$\quad q: E \rightarrow B$ mapping of edges to attribute assignment, where

$\quad\quad E = (N \cdot N) - I_N$ and I_N is the Identity relation in N.

For generality we will not consider specific attribute assignments to the nodes and the edges. To give the reader an idea what these attributes could be we will consider the cases to be images such as the ultrasonic image. The images show defects such as cracks in a metal component taken by an ultra sonic image acquisition system called SAFT. A defect comprises of several reflection points which are in a certain spatial relation to each other. Here the nodes could be the objects (reflection points) in the image and the edges are the spatial relation between these objects (e.g. right-of, behind, ...). Each object has attributes (e.g. size, mean gray level value,..) which are associated to the corresponding node within the graph. We will not describe the application in this paper, nor will we describe how these objects are extracted from the images, combined into a graph and labeled by symbolic terms. For these details we refer to [4]. For demonstration purpose we will use the four graphs shown in Figure 1a-1d.

3.2 Similarity Measure, Mean of a Graph, and Graph Subsumption

We may define our problem of similarity as to find structural identity between two structures. However, structural identity is a very strong requirement. An alternative approach is to require only part isomorphism.

Definition 3

Two graphs $G_1 = (N_1, p_1, q_1)$ and $G_2 = (N_2, p_2, q_2)$ are in the relation $G_1 \leq G_2$ iff there exists a one-to-one mapping $f: N_1 \rightarrow N_2$ with (1) $p_1(x) = p_2(f(x))$ for all $x \in N_1$ and (2) $q_1(x, y) = q_2(f(x), f(y))$ for all $x, y \in N_1, x \neq y$.

Definition 3 requires identity in the attribute assignments of the nodes and the edges. To allow proximity in the attributes labels, we introduce the following way to handle similarity. In Definitions 3 we may relax the required correspondence of attribute assignment of nodes and edges to that we introduce ranges of tolerance:

If $a \in A$ is an attribute and $W_a \subseteq W$ is the set of all attribute values which can be assigned to a, then we can determine for each attribute a a mapping: $dist_a : W_a \rightarrow [0,1]$.

The normalization to a real interval is not absolutely necessary but advantageous for the comparison of attribute assignments.

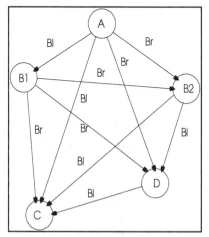

Fig. 1a. Graph_1

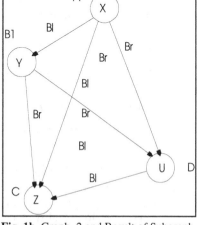

Fig. 1b. Graph_2 and Result of Subgraph Isomorphism to Graph_1

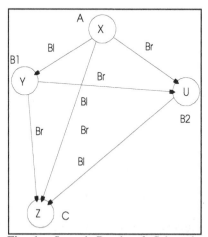

Fig. 1c. Second Result of Subgraph Isomorphism of Graph_1 and Graph_2

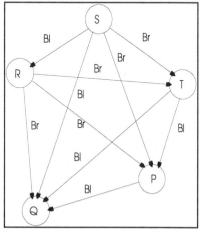

Fig. 1d. Graph_3 and Results for Subgraph Isomorphism to Graph_2

For example, let a be the attribute spatial_relation as it is in e.g. in the ultra sonic image the relation between the nodes and $W_a = \{behind, \quad right, \quad behind\_left, \quad in\_front\_right, \ldots \}$ then we could define:

$dist_a(behind\_right, behind\_right) = 0$
$dist_a(behind\_right, infront\_right) = 0.25$
$dist_a(behind\_right, behind\_left) = 0.75$.

Based on such a distance measure for attributes, we can define different variants of distance measure as mapping:

$dist : B^2 \rightarrow R^+$ (R^+ is the set of positive real numbers) in the following way:

$$dist(x, y) = \frac{1}{D}\sum_{a \in D} dist_a(x(a), y(a)) \text{ with } D = domain(x) \cap domain(y).$$

Usually, in the comparison of graphs not all attributes have the same priority. Thus it is good to determine a weight factor w_a and then define the distance as follows:

$$dist(x, y) = \frac{1}{D}\sum_{a \in D} w_a \cdot dist_a(x(a), y(a))$$

For definition of part isomorphism, we get the following variant:

Definition 4

Two graphs $G_1 = (N_1, p_1, q_1)$ and $G_2 = (N_2, p_2, q_2)$ are in the relation $G_1 \leq G_2$ iff there exists a one-to-one mapping $f : N_1 \rightarrow N_2$ and thresholds C_1, C_2 with

(1) $dist(p_1(x), p_2(f(x))) \leq C_1$ for all $x \in N_1$

(2) $dist(q_1(x, y), q_2(f(x), f(y))) \leq C_2$ for all $x, y \in N_1$ $x \neq y$.

Obviously it is possible to introduce a separate constant for each attribute. Depending on the application, the similarity may be sharpened by a global threshold:

If it is possible to establish a correspondence g according to the requirements mentioned above, then an additional condition should be fulfilled: $\sum_{(x,y) \in g} dist(x, y) \leq C_3$, where C_3 is the global threshold.

The mean graph can be computed as follows:

Definition 5

A Graph $G_p = (N_p, p_p, q_p)$ is a prototype of a Class of Cases $C_i = \{G_1, G_2, ..., G_t(N_t, p_t, q_t)\}$ iff $G_p \in C_i$ and if there is a one-to-one mapping $f : N_p \rightarrow N_i$ with

(1) $p_p(x_i) = \frac{1}{n}\sum_{n=1}^{t} p_n(f(x_i))$ for all $x_i \in N$ and

(2) (2) $q_p(x_i, y_i) = \frac{1}{n}\sum_{n=1}^{t} q_n(f(x_i), f(y_i))$ for all $x_i, y_i \in N$.

On the basis of the part isomorphism, we can introduce a partial order over the set of graphs. If a graph G_1 is included in another graph G_2 than the two graphs are in the relation $G_1 \leq G_2$ and the number of nodes of G_1 is not higher than the number of nodes of G_2. We can also say G_1 subsumes G_2 and we can write $G_1 \succ G_2$. We can use these relations to organize our case base and on the other hand it allows us to discover the underlying concept of the domain.

4 Case Base Organization and Learning

We propose an hierarchical organization schema of the case base that can be up-dated incrementally. Two approaches are described in the following section. Both are based on approximate graph subsumption. The first one is based on a divide-and conquer strategy whereas the second is based on an evaluation function and a split-and-merge strategy.

4.1 Approach I

4.1.1 Index Structure
The initial case base may be built up by existing cases. Therefore, a non-incremental learning procedure is required in order to build the index structure. When using the system, new cases may be stored into the case base. They should be integrated into the already existing case base. Therefore, we need an incremental learning procedure.

Cases in the case base are representations between graphs. As an important relation between structural cases we have considered similarity based on part isomorphism. Because of this characteristic it is possible to organize the case base as a directed graph.

In the following, we will define the index structure of the case base as a graph that contains the graphs described above in the nodes:

Definition 7

H is given, the set of all graphs.
A index graph is a tupel $IB = (N, E, p)$, with

(1) $N \subseteq H$ set of nodes and

(2) $E \subseteq N^2$ set of edges. This set should show the partial isomorphism in
the set of nodes, meaning it should be valid $x \le y \Rightarrow (x, y) \in E$ for all $x, y \in N$.

(3) $p : N \to B$ mapping of case names to the index graph (also the attribute
values for the case class).

Because of the transitivity of part isomorphism, certain edges can be directly derived from other edges and do not need to be separately stored. A relaxation of point 2 in definition 5 can be reduced storage capacity.

In the nodes of the index graph are stored the names of the case and not the case itself. Note that case identifiers are stored into the nodes of the directed graph, not the actual cases. The root note is the dummy node.

It may happen that by matching two graphs we will find two solutions, as it is shown in Figures 1a-1d. This will result in an index structure as shown in Figure 2. The hypergraph will branch into two paths for one solution. That means at $n=4$ we have to match twice, once for the structure $\{A, B1, C, D, B2\}$ and the other time for the structure $\{A, B1, C, B2, D\}$. Both will result in the same solution, but by doing so the matching time will double. The solution to this problem could be that in the index structure a link to point p will advise the matcher to follow this path. But this will only be the right solution if the increase in the number of nodes from one step to another is one and not more. Otherwise more than one solution will still be possible and should be considered during the construction and up-date of the index structure.

4.1.2 Incremental Learning of the Index Structure

Now the task is to build up the graphs of IB into a supergraph by a learning environment.

Input:

Supergraph $IB = (N, E, p)$ and graph $x \in H$.

Output:

modified Supergraph $IB' = (N', E', p')$ with $N' \subseteq N \cup \{x\}, E \subseteq E', p \subseteq p'$.

At the beginning of the learning process or the process of construction of index graph N can be an empty set.

The attribute assignment function p' gives the values $(p'(x), (dd))$ as an output. This is an answer to the question: What is the name of the image name that is mirrored in the image graph x?

The inclusion $N' \subseteq N \cup \{x\}$ says that the graph x may be isomorphic to one graph y contained in the case base, so $x \leq y$ and also $y \leq x$ hold. Then no new node is created, which means the case base is not increased.

The algorithm for the construction of the modified index structure IB' can also use the circumstance that no graph is part isomorphic to another graph if it has more nodes than the second one.

As a technical aid for the algorithm we introduced a set N_i. N_i contains all graphs of the case base IB with exactly i nodes. If the maximal number of nodes of the graph contained in the case base is k, then: $N = \bigcup\limits_{i=k}^{k} N_i$.

The graph which has to be included in the case base has l nodes $(l > 0)$. By comparison of the current graph with all graphs contained in the case base, we can make use of transitivity of part isomorphism for the reduction of the nodes that have to be compared. The full algorithm for the construction of the hierarchy is shown in Figure 3.

If we use the approach described in Section 3.2 for uncertainty handling, then we can use the algorithm presented in Section 3.5 without any changes. But we should notice that for each group of graphs that is approximate isomorphic, the image graph that occurred first is stored in the case base. Therefore, it is better to calculate for every instance and each new instance of a group a prototype and store it in the index structure of the case base.

Figure 4 illustrates this index hierarchy. Suppose we have given a set of structural cases, where the supergraph is the empty graph. Then we open the first node in the supergraph for this case at level n which refers to the number of nodes this structural case has, and make a link to the root node which is the dummy node. Then a new case is given to the supergraph. It is first classified by traversal of the tentative supergraph. If it does not match with a case stored in case base then a new node is opened at the level which refers to the number of nodes this structural case has and a link to the root node is made. If the node matches with the case in the supergraph and if the case is in the relation $G_1 < G_2$, then a new node is opened at the level k, the link between the root node and the recent node is removed and a link between the new node and the old node is inserted and another link from the new node to the root is installed. This procedure is repeated until all cases are inserted into the supergraph.

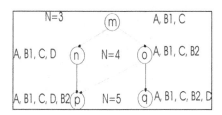

Fig. 2. Hypergraph and the Problem of two solutions

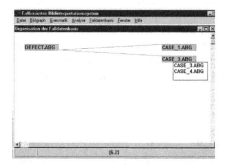

Fig. 4. Example of Case Base Organization

Algorithm

E' := E;
Z := N;
for all y∈ N₁
if x ≤ y then [IB' := IB; return];
N' := N ∪ {x};
for all i with 0 < i < l;
for all y ∈ N₁ \ Z;
for all y ≤ x then [Z := Z \ {u | u ≤ y, u ∈ Z};
E' := E' ∪ { (y,x)}];
for all i with l < i ≤ k
for all y ∈ N₁ \ Z
if x ≤ y then [Z := Z \ {u _ y ≤ u, u ∈ Z };
E' := E' ∪ { (x,y)}];
p' := p ∪ { (x, (dd : unknown))};

Fig. 3. Algorithm of Approach I

4.1.3 Retrieval and Result

Retrieval is done by classifying the current case through the index hierarchy until a node represented by a prototype having the same number of nodes as the query is reached. Then the most similar case in this case class is determined. The output of the system are all graphs y in the image database which are in relation to the query x as follows: $(x ≤ y ∨ x ≥ y) ≤ C$ where C is a constant which can be chosen by the user of the system.

Cases that are grouped together in one case class can be viewed by the user by clicking at the node which opens a new window showing all cases that belong to the case class. The node itself is labeled with the name of the graphs in this example but can be also labeled with a user given name.

The visualization component allows the user to view the organization of his case base. It shows him the similarity relation between the cases and case classes and by doing this gives him a good understanding of his domain.

4.2 Approach II

Whereas in Section 4.1 the index structure is built based on a divide-and-conquer technique, in this approach we use a strategy which is more flexible to fit the hierarchy dynamically to the cases. It does not only allow to incorporate new cases into the hierarchy and open new nodes by splitting the leaf nodes into two child nodes. It also allows to merge existing nodes and to split existing nodes at every position in the hierarchy.

4.2.1 Index Structure

A concept hierarchy is a directed graph in which the root node represents the set of all input instances and the terminal nodes represent individual instances. Internal nodes stand for sets of instances attached to those nodes and represent a super concept. The super concept can be represented by a generalized representation of this set of instances such as the prototype, the median or a user-selected instance. Therefore a concept C, called a class, in the concept hierarchy is represented by an abstract concept description and a list of pointers to each child concept $M(C) = \{C_1, C_2, ..., C_i, ..., C_n\}$, where C_i is the child concept, called a subclass of concept C.

4.2.2 Learning

When several distinct partitions are incrementally generated over the case base, a heuristic is used to evaluate the partitions. This function evaluates the global quality of a single partition and favors partitions that maximize potential for inferring information. In doing this, it attempts to minimize intra-case class variances and to maximize inter-case class variances. The employment of an evaluation function avoids the problem of defining a threshold for class similarity and inter class similarity. The threshold is to determine domain-dependent and it is not easy to define them a priori properly. However, the resulting hierarchy depends on a properly chosen threshold. We will see later on by example what influence it has on the hierarchy.

Given a partition $\{C_1, C_2, ..., C_m\}$, the partition which maximizes the difference between the case class variance s_B and the within case class variance s_W is chosen as the right partition:

$$ SCORE = \frac{1}{m} \left| s_B^{*2} - s_W^{*2} \right| \Rightarrow MAX \; ! \tag{1} $$

The normalization to m (m-the number of partitions) is necessary to compare different partitions.

If G_{pj} is the prototype of the j-th case class in the hierarchy at level k, $\overline{G}$ the mean graph of all cases in level k, and G^2_{vj} is the variance of the graphs in the partition j, then:

$$SCORE = \frac{1}{m} \left| \sum_{j=1}^{m} p_j \left(G_{pj} - \overline{G} \right)^2 - \sum_{j=1}^{m} p_j G^2{}_{vj} \right| \tag{2}$$

where p_j is the relative frequency of cases in the partition j.

It might happen that the reasoning process results in the answer: "There is no similar case in the case base". This indicates that such a case has not been seen before. The case needs to be incorporated into the case base in order to close the gap in the case base. This is done by classifying the case according to the case base and a new node is opened in the hierarchy of the case base at that position where the similarity relation holds. The new node represents a new case class and the present case is taken as case representative.

The evidence of new case classes increases when new cases, where the evaluation measure holds, are incorporated into the node. This is considered as learning of case classes.

When learning a class of cases, cases where the evaluation measure holds are grouped together. The case that appeared first would be the representative of the class of these cases and each new case is compared to this case. Obviously, the first case to appear might not always be a good case. Therefore it is better to compute a prototype for the class of cases as described in Section 3.3.

In the same manner we can calculate the variance of the graphs in one case class. The resulting prototype is not a case that exists in reality. Another strategy for calculating a prototype is to calculate the median of the case in a case class.

The constructed case classes and the hierarchy are sensitive to the order of case presentation, creating different hierarchies from different orders of the same cases. We have already included one operation to avoid this problem by learning of prototypes. Two additional operations [12] should help it recover from such non-optimal hierarchies. At each level of the classification process, the system considers merging the two nodes that best classify the new instance. If the resulting case class is better according to the evaluation function described in Section 4.2.2.1 than the original, the operation combines the two nodes into a single, more abstract case class. This transforms a hierarchy of N nodes into one having N+1 nodes.

The inverse operation is splitting of one node into two nodes. This is also known as refinement. At each level, the learning algorithm decides to classify an instance as a member of an existing case class, it also considers removing this case class and elevating its children.

If this leads to an improved hierarchy, the algorithm changes the structure of the case base hierarchy accordingly.

4.2.3 Algorithm

Now, that we have defined our evaluation function and the different learning levels, we can describe our learning algorithm. If a new case has to be entered into the case base the case is tentatively placed into the hierarchy by applying all the different learning operators described before. The operation which gives us the highest evaluation score is chosen. The new case is entered into the case base and the case base hierarchy is reorganized according to the selected learning operation. Figure 6 shows the CBR learning algorithm in detail.

4.3 Discussion of the Two Approaches

The results in Approach I shown in Figure 4 are two nodes containing a set of cases each. The second node is highlighted in Figure 4 and shows that the two cases (Case 3 and Case 4) are belonging to the same case class. The first node shows only the name of Case 1 but also contains Case 2. The partition {1,2} and {3,4} is reached by a threshold of 0.0025 for the similarity. Matching has to be performed three times for this structure. First, matching the prototypes is performed and afterwards is determined the closest case in the case class of the prototype with the highest similarity. If we increase the threshold to 0.02 than we obtain the partition {1,2,4}{3}. This hierarchy still has two nodes but the time for matching is increased since now in one node there are three cases that should be matched.

The four cases are placed into four separate nodes each when using a threshold less than 0.001. Thus, for this hierarchy matching has to be performed four times.

This example shows how the threshold effects the resulting hierarchy.

Algorithm II automatically selects the best partition {1,2} and {3,4}. The predetermination of a threshold is not necessary. This algorithm protects the user from a try-and-test procedure in order to figure out the best threshold for the similarity of his application and besides that it guarantees that the hierarchy will not grow too deep or too broad. The evaluation measure as well as the allowed operations over the hierarchy keep the hierarchy in balance according the observed cases.

5 Related Work

Bunke and Messmer [13] used a network of model graphs for matching graphs which is created based on the subgraph isomorphism relation. They calculated off-line each possible permutation from each model graph and used them to construct the network. This network was then used for matching the graphs. In their approach they did not consider approximate graph matching, nor can their approach be used in an incremental fashion. The resulting structure is a network of model graphs not a directed graph. It also requires that the network is complete. In contrast, our approach can tolerate incompleteness. The approach of Bunke et al. is also used by Burke [6].

An approach for tree structured cases has recently been described by Ricci and Senter [15]. It assumes that cases are in a tree-structured representation or can be transformed into this structure which is not always possible.

The two approaches described in this paper are based on approximate graph subsumption and can be used in an incrementally fashion. The first approach is based on a divide and conquer strategy and requires a fixed threshold for the similarity value. A similar approach has been used by Börner et al. [14] for an application in building design. Their approach is not incremental and groups cases together which have different numbers of nodes. The importance of a concept is described by its probabilities and they assume a large enough case base.

An approach which uses such a flexible strategy as our approach II is to our knowledge not used by anyone for building the index structure of a CBR system.

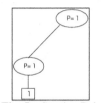

Fig. 5a. Starting Point

Insert Case 2		
Insert to existing node	Create a New Node	Node Merging
P= 1,2 → P= 1,2 → 1 2	P= 1,2 → P= 1 → 1 ; P= 2 → 2	P= 1,2 → P= 1,2 → P= 1 → 1 ; P= 2 → 2
SB = 0	SB = 0,00018172	SB = 0,00018172
SW = 0,00018172	SW = 0	SW = 0
SCORE= 0,00018172	SCORE = 0,00018172	SCORE = 0,00018172
Resulting Case Base		

Fig. 5b. Insert Case 2 into the case base

Insert Case 3		
Insert to existing node	Create a New Node	Node Merging
P= 1,2,3 → P= 1,2,3 → 1 2 3	P= 1,2,3 → P= 1,2 → 1 2 ; P= 3 → 3	P= 1,2,3 → P= 1,2,3 → P= 1,2 → 1 2 ; P= 3 → 3
SB = 0	SB = 0,0255671	SB = 0,0255671
SW = 0,0156513	SW = 0,0001211	SW = 0,0001212
SCORE = 0,0156513	SCORE = 0,0254459	SCORE = 0,0254459
	** Resulting Case Base **	

Fig. 5c. Insert Case 3 into Case Base

Insert Case 4			
Insert to existing node_1	Insert to existing node_2	Create a New Node	Node Merging
P= 1,2,3,4 → P= 1,2,4 → 1 2 4 ; P= 3 → 3	P= 1,2,3,4 → P= 1,2 → 1 2 ; P= 3,4 → 3 4	P= 1,2,3,4 → P= 1,2 → 1 2 ; P= 3 → 3 ; P= 4 → 4	P= 1,2,3,4 → P= 1,2,4 → P= 1,2 → 1 2 ; P= 4 → 4 ; P= 3 → 3
SB = 0,0159367	SB = 0,0250232	SB = 0,0218856	SB = 0,0204
SW = 0,0120498	SW = 0,0008960	SW = 0,0000795	SW = 0,00009086
SCORE = 0,0038869	SCORE = 0,024127 *Result	SCORE= 0,021805	SCORE = 0,0203091

Fig. 5d. Insert Case 4 into Case and Final Case Base

Input:	Case Base Supergraph CB
	An unclassified case G
Output:	Modified Case Base CB´

Top-level call:	Case base (top-node, G)
Variables:	A, B, C, and D are nodes in the hierarchy
	K, L, M, and T are partition scores

Case base (N, G)

IF N is a terminal node,
        THEN Create-new-terminals (N, G)
            Incorporate (N, G)
      ELSE   For each child A of node N,
                Compute the score for placing G in A.
                Compute the scores for all other action with G
                Let B be the node with the highest score K.
                Let D be the node with the second highest score.
                Let L be the score for placing I in a new node C.
                Let M be the score for merging B and D into one node.
                Let T be the score for splitting D into its children.

                IF K is the best score
                        THEN Case base (P, G) (place G in case class B).
                        ELSE IF L is the best score,
                              THEN Input a new node C
                                      Case base (N, G)
                            Else IF M is the best score,
                                Then let O be merged (B, D, N)
                              Case base (N, G)
                                    Else IF T is the best score,
                                        Then Split (B, N)
                                        Case base (N, G)

Operations over Case base

Variables: X, O, B, and D are nodes in the hierarchy.
                 G is the new case

Incorporate (N, G)
     Update the prototype and the variance of case class N

Create new terminals (N, G)
     Create a new child W of node N.
     Initialize prototype and variance

Merge (B, D, N)
     Make O a new child of N
     Remove B and D as children of N
     Add the instances of P and R and all children of B and D to the node O
     Compute prototype and variance from the instances of B and D

Fig. 6. Algorithm II

6 Conclusions

We consider a case to be a structural representation such as an attributed graph. Such representations are useful to describe multimedia objects such as images, text documents, log-files or even in building design, software engineering, and timetabling. The similarity between these objects must be determined based on their structural relations as well as on the similarity of their attributes.

The retrieval and matching of structural representation are time-consuming processes and often NP complex. To reduce the time complexity, efficient organization of the case base is essential. We propose two approaches which enables cases to be organized the cases in a hierarchical fashion so that we can discover the underlying concepts of the domain over time. Our two approaches for maintaining and incremental learning the index hierarchy are based on approximate graph subsumption. The first approach requires an off-line defined threshold for the similarity value and can only construct new case classes. Once a case class has been established the structure cannot be reversed. This is only possible in the second approach since it can merge and split nodes at any position in the hierarchy. This approach does not rely on a fixed threshold for similarity. Instead, an evaluation function is used to select the right partition. This gives the flexibility needed when incrementally building the index.

References

1. M.M. Richter, Introduction, In: M. Lenz, B. Bartsch-Spörl, H.-D. Burkhardt, and S. Wess (Eds.), Case Based Reasoning Technology: From Foundations to Applications, Springer Verlag 1998. LNAI 1400.
2. D.B. Leake and D.C. Wilson, Categorizing Case-Based Maintenance: Dimensions and Directions, In: B. Smyth and P. Cunningham (Eds.), Advances in Case-Based Reasoning, Springer Verlag 1998, LNAI 1488, pp. 196–207.
3. S. Craw, J. Jarmulak, and R. Rowe. Maintaining Retrieval Knowledge in a Case-Based Reasoning System, Computational Intelligence, vol. 17, No. 2, 2001, pp. 346–363.
4. P. Perner, Case-Based Reasoning For Image Interpretation in Non-destructive Testing, 1st European Workshop on Case-Based Reasoning, Otzenhausen Nov. 1993, Proc. SFB 314 Univ. Kaiserslautern, Hrsg. M. Richter, vol. II, pp. 403–410
5. F. Gebhardt, A. Voss, W. Gräther, and B. Schmidt-Belz. Reasoning with complex cases. Kluwer 1997
6. E.K. Burke, B. MacCarthy, S. Petrovic, and R. Qu, Case-Based Reasoning in Course Timetabling: An Attributed Graph Approach, In: D.W. Aha and I. Watson (Eds.), Case-Based Reasoning Research and Development, Springer Verlag 2001, LNAI 2080, pp.90–103.
7. P. Perner, Different Learning Strategies in a Case-Based Reasoning System for Image Interpretation, Advances in Case-Based Reasoning, B. Smith and P. Cunningham (Eds.), LNAI 1488, Springer Verlag 1998, pp. 251–261.
8. S. Wess, K.-D. Althoff, and G. Derwand, Using k-d Trees to Improve the Retrieval Step in Case-Based Reasoning, In: S. Wess, K.-D. Althoff, and M.M. Richter (Eds.) Topics in Case-based Reasoning, Springer Verlag 1993, pp. 167–182.
9. D. McSherry, Precision and Recall in Interactive Case-Based Reasoning, In: D. W. Aha and I. Watson, Case-Based Reasoning Research and Development, Springer Verlag 2001, LNAI 2080, pp. 392–406.
10. M. Grimnes and A. Aamodt, A Two Layer Case-Based Reasoning Architecture for Medical Image Understanding, In: I. Smith and B. Faltings (Eds.), Advances in Case-Based Reasoning, LNAI 1168, Springer Verlag 1996, pp 164–178.
11. R. Bergmann and A. Stahl, Similarity Measures for Object-Oriented Case Representations, In Proc.: Advances in Case-Based Reasoning, B. Smith and P. Cunningham (Eds.), LNAI 1488, Springer Verlag 1998, pp. 25–36.

12. J.H. Gennari, P. Langley, and D. Fisher, "Models of Incremental Concept Formation," Artificial Intelligence 40 (1989) 11–61.
13. H. Bunke and B. Messmer. Similarity measures for structured representations. In S. Wess, K.-D. Althoff, and M.M. Richter (eds.), Topics in Case-Based Reasoning, Springer Verlag 1994, pp. 106–118
14. K. Börner, E. Pippig, E.-Ch. Tammer, and C.H. Coulon, Structural Similarity and Adaptation, in: I. Smith and B. Faltings, Advances in Case-Based Reasoning, Spinger Verlag 1996, pp.58–75
15. F. Ricci and L. Senter, Structured Cases, Trees and Efficient Retrieval, In Proc.: B. Smyth and P. Cunningham, Advances in Case-Based Reasoning, Springer Verlag 98, pp. 88–99.

Case Base Management for Analog Circuits Diagnosis Improvement

Carles Pous, Joan Colomer, Joaquim Melendez, and Josep Lluís de la Rosa

Institut d'Informàtica i Aplicacions. Universitat de Girona
Avda. Lluís Santaló s/n E-17071 Girona, (Catalonia)
carles@eia.udg.es

Abstract. There have been some Artificial Intelligence applications developed for electronic circuits diagnosis, but much remains to be done in this field, above all in the analog domain. The purpose of this paper is not to give a general solution, but to contribute with a new methodology. Our aim is to develop a methodology for analog circuit diagnosis based on improving the well-known fault dictionary techniques by means of new cases addition or adaptation towards a Case Based Reasoning system. As an example, a fault dictionary method have been studied in detail. It has been used as starting point for case base construction to be applied to a real electronic circuit. The faults considered are parametric, permanent, independent and simple.

1 Introduction

Diagnosis of circuits is based on the analysis of the circuit response to a certain input stimuli. Therefore, it is necessary to generate stimuli signals and to acquire measures in particular circuit nodes. There are plenty of methods proposed for diagnosing analog electronic circuits as cited in [1]. But for these last decades automating fault diagnosis using Artificial Intelligence techniques are becoming an important research field on this topic.

A classification and review of AI techniques for electronic circuits diagnosis is given in [2]. *Artificial Intelligence techniques* could be applied either as a reinforcement of other techniques or as themselves. *Fuzzy techniques*, *Neural networks*, *Expert systems* and *Case Based Reasoning (CBR)* can be cited among all of them. According to Fenton et al. the approaches to intelligent diagnosis can be classified, as shown in Figure 1, in:

Traditional approaches are based on IF-THEN rules, and they are intuitive. On the other hand the difficulty of acquiring knowledge from the experts and its lack of dealing with novel faults are its main shortcoming. Besides, once the system is built it has a fixed performance. There is no possibility to learn.

Model-Based approaches make use of models to predict faults from the real circuit. Its main disadvantage is its inability to deal with unsimulated faults and difficulties in expert knowledge acquisition to build the causal model. They have also a fixed level performance.

K.D. Ashley and D.G. Bridge (Eds.): ICCBR 2003, LNAI 2689, pp. 437–451, 2003.
© Springer-Verlag Berlin Heidelberg 2003

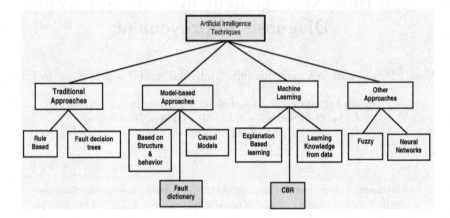

Fig. 1. AI methods classification

Machine Learning approaches take advantage of previous successful or failed diagnoses, and they use this knowledge in order to improve the system performance. But, in general, big data bases with suitable data are necessary if good results are desired.

Other approaches. Fuzzy and Neural Network techniques can be cited in this group. The former provides a very intuitive way of representing knowledge, and they are typically combined with other techniques. The latter have the power of modelling unknown predicted faults when they are trained.

The future trends are hybrid solutions of the above classification. This is one of the research fields that has major interest; in particular the combined use of models and cases as particular situations.

The main goal of this paper is to propose a new methodology for analog electronic circuits diagnosis based on CBR cycle. In our case fault dictionary techniques are used as starting point for Case Based Reasoning System construction in order to avoid the limitations that fault dictionaries have.

The paper is organized as follows. Next section gives a brief overview of the fault dictionaries and their lacks. Section 3 introduces the proposed methodology to built the CBR system. Afterwards, in Section 4 the methodology is applied to a real electronic circuit and the results are shown. Conclusions and future work are given in last section.

2   Fault Dictionaries and Their Limitations

Fault dictionaries are techniques based on quantitative calculations. Selected measures are obtained from the faulty system, and stored in a table. These values will be then compared with the measures obtained from the system under test. The comparison is typically performed by the neighborhood criterion, obtaining distances or minimizing certain indexes. The class of the nearest extracted case is taken as diagnosis. The main difficulties the fault dictionary system have to deal with are the tolerances and the existence of non previously considered faults. As a consequence, the measures acquired from the real system could not match with the stored ones. The goal is to obtain a dictionary as reduced as possible, but robust to tolerances at the same time. A classification of the main fault dictionaries methods can be found in [1].

It often happens that certain faults produce the same circuit measures. So, it is impossible to distinguish between them. They form what is called an *ambiguity group*. Ambiguity groups depend on the test points selected (number and place where they are taken) and the measurement accuracy. Once the basic dictionary is built, these groups have to be detected. There are several methods to do this, like the ones proposed in [3] or in [4].

3   The Proposed Case-Based Reasoning System

Fault dictionaries can be seen as a simplified approach to Case-Based Reasoning for classification. Thus, our proposal is based on extending the fault dictionary towards a Case Based Reasoning system. This CBR system is detailed in the following subsections.

3.1   Case Memory and Case Base Construction

The case structure is chosen to be the same used in the fault dictionary, including a field with an associated diagnosis corresponding to the case (Table 1).

Table 1. Case Structure

Case Num	Measure. 1	Measure. 2	...	Measure. n	Class
Case i	M1i	M2i	...	Mni	Fault i

Then, a fault dictionary with one case representing each fault considered is built and the detection of ambiguity groups is done. As in faults dictionaries a good start is to select ±20% and ±50% from the nominal values of the components. These faults seem to be distributed well enough in order to cover a possible set of typical faults.

CBR systems need a good case base with significant cases. Since in present days there are powerful circuit simulation tools such us PCAD, Protel, etc., and there are good models of the different devices, it is not difficult to simulate hundreds of circuit failures in a reasonable time. According to [5], resistors and capacitors have a gaussian distribution of their values. When simulating, the values of the components are randomly changed inside their tolerance margin. In order to find possible cases produced by the tolerances for a particular measure, several simulation have to be carried out. In our approach, Monte-Carlo method

has been selected. After several tests, the authors stated that more than 2000
runs wides the measure interval unnecessarily, while the gaussian 3σ deviation
doesn't change. Therefore, 2000 runs for each considered fault, with Monte-Carlo
method using gaussian randomly distributed values of the components are used
to generate the dictionary cases.

As the cases with tolerance have been generated randomly, there are redundant data stored. Since the dictionary is huge, related to the number of
components to test, instance prune techniques are applied in order to reduce the
dictionary size, while keeping or even improving its accuracy. The IB3 (Instance-
Based learning algorithm) and DROP4 methods proposed in [9] are applied to
the spread obtained dictionaries generated by Monte-Carlo. These techniques
are based on the improvements of the nearest neighbor algorithm.

Similar to the hierarchy proposed in [6], case base hierarchy is defined considering several levels depending on circuit complexity. Figure 2 shows the idea.

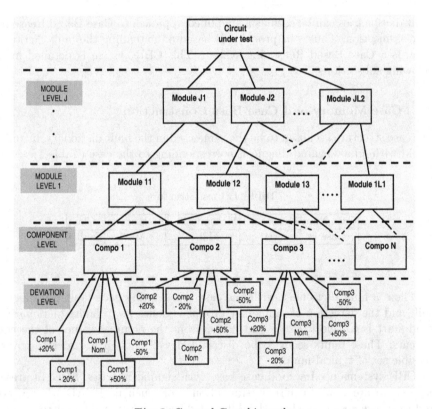

Fig. 2. General Case hierarchy

The last level corresponds to the faulty component deviation ($\pm 20\%$ or
$\pm 50\%$). Since sometimes it will not be possible to diagnose with such a pre-

cision, the upper level is defined as the component level (*compo1*, *compo2*, ...,
compoN). At this point, the system will be only able to diagnose what component is wrong, but not the fault deviation. Also, it is possible that certain faults
can only be located just at a certain module, but not deep inside it. So, going
to upper levels, the circuit is divided in modules. The number of module levels
J depends on the circuit complexity. From this level to the superior ones, it is
necessary to have certain knowledge on the circuit topology in order to built the
case base hierarchy. A possible algorithm to decompose the circuit in hierarchical
blocks is proposed in [7] or in [8].

At the same time, it has been decided to split the case base in two bases: the
Main Case Base (MCB) and the Specific Case Base (SCB). The former contains
the reminder cases after reduction algorithm is applied. Dropped cases are those
that are classified correctly by the reminder cases or cases that are incorrectly
classifed, but their introduction to the MCB is going to spoil previous cases
classification. These last ones will be introduced in the SCB. The decision about
if the new case is going to spoil the classification is done using the *neighbor*
and *associate* concepts implemented in the DROP4 (Decremental Reduction
Optimization Procedure) algorithm. This algorithm is described in detail in [9].

Hence, each base will provide us with a possible diagnosis when considering
a new case. It will be necessary to give a certainty coefficient C_{MCB} or C_{SCB} to
each proposed diagnosis, or combine them, if it is necessary. Figure 3 illustrates
this idea. An interpretation of the certainty coefficients and how to deal with
them is explained later on this paper.

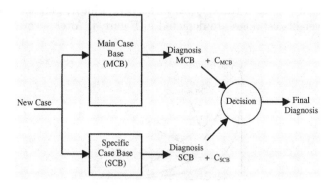

Fig. 3. Two case bases composition

3.2   Case Retrieval

It is necessary to define a metric and the number of cases to retrieve from the case
base. Among all possible distance functions, the normalized Euclidean distance
has been chosen. Attributes Normalization is necessary because of their different

order of magnitude. So, the distance between two instances is calculated as shown in equation 1

$$E(\vec{x}, \vec{y}) = \sqrt{\sum_{i=1}^{m} \left(\frac{x_i - y_i}{range_i} \right)^2} \tag{1}$$

Where $\vec{x}$ and $\vec{y}$ are the vector instances to be compared, x_i and y_i are the corresponding attribute value i, and m is the number of attributes; $range_i$ is the difference between the maximum and minimum value of the attribute i.

The number of cases k to retrieve from the MCB will be according to the value of k that produces the best diagnosis results. Normally is an small odd number. For the SCB the number of extracted cases is one, since retrieving more specific cases will probably bring a wrong proposal from the SCB.

3.3   Case Reusing

Once the k nearest neighbors are extracted from the MCB, an examination of the extracted cases class has to be done. The simplest way is to count the cases corresponding to each class. The final classification is the result of this voting procedure. But this simple method does not take into account any information about the distance. Then, as proposed in [9] a weight can be given to the extracted cases according to its distance to the new case (distance-weighted voting). Wilson proposes three types of kernels: Linear, gaussian or exponential. These weight-distances are depicted in Figure 4. After several tests, in our

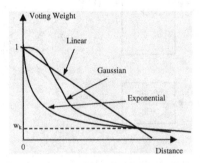

Fig. 4. Distance-Weighted kernels

case, the distance-weighted method that performs better is the exponential one. Exponential kernel is given by the following formula:

$$w_j = w_k^{\frac{D_j}{D_k}} \tag{2}$$

where w_k is the weight given to the kth neighbor, and D_k and D_j are the distances to the kth neighbor and the jth neighbor respectively. As it can be seen, the bigger the distance from the new case to the jth neighbor, the lower the weight given to the jth neighbor. The diagnosis provided by the MCB will be the class voted with the biggest weight, and the certainty coefficient is the same associated weight.

For the SCB only the nearest case will be extracted with its corresponding weight. The weight is calculated using the following equation:

$$w = w_k^{\frac{D}{D_{MCB_1}} \bullet n} \tag{3}$$

where D is the distance to the extracted SCB case, D_{MCB_1} the distance to the first extracted MCB case, and n an index to control the exponential decay. The diagnose proposed by the SCB will be the class of the closest extracted SCB case, and the certainty coefficient $C_{SCB} = w$.

The class corresponding to the diagnosis given by each case base can be different. At this point, several possibilities have to be studied. Lets consider the situation in which MCB produces a diagnosis with a higher weight $C_{MCB} > C_{SCB}$. This situation can be interpreted as a new case clearly closer to the MCB provided class. On the other hand, if $C_{MCB} < C_{SCB}$ the case will be clearly closer to the SCB class. And finally, if $|C_{MCB} - C_{SCB}| \leq \epsilon$ the solution provided by the MCB and SCB are both possible. Then, the diagnosis will be given by the higher common hierarchy level. Table 2 resumes this decision process.

Table 2. Diagnosis decision

$C_{MCB} > C_{SCB}$	Decision is what MCB says
$|C_{MCB} - C_{SCB}| \leq \epsilon$	Decision is passed to superior common hierarchy level
$C_{MCB} < C_{SCB}$	Decision is what SCB says

The threshold ϵ selected is decisive and it has a great influence on the final results. At this moment, there is no a methodology proposed to find the optimal value of ϵ. So it has been obtained by trial and error.

3.4   Case Revising and Retaining

When a new situation is produced, retrieved cases from the case base will provide us with a possible diagnosis. If the diagnosis is correct, it means that there is enough information on the case base. Hence, it is no necessary to retain the new case. On the other hand, if the retrieved cases produce a misclassification of the new case, some learning has to be incorporated in the base. In our case, the system will learn by adding new cases, without adapting them. When a new case retention is necessary, there are two possibilities: 1- New case retention does not influence previous cases classification and 2- Its retention will produce other previous cases misclassification. On the first situation, the new case can be introduced in the MCB base without any problem. But in the second one, the introduction of the new case in them MCB could be worst. Therefore it is introduced in the SCB.

The influence that a new case retention will have on the diagnosis of the present MCB case base is evaluated using the associates concept described in [9]. Once neighbor and associates of the new case are calculated, two situations can be given. It could be that new case does not have associates. This implies that the new case is not one of the k nearest neighbors of the existing cases in the case base. Hence, its introduction will not affect on the previous classification of the cases already contained in the case base. On the other hand, if the new case has associates, it is necessary to evaluate how these associates are affected by the new case. If there is no change on the classification of the associates due to the introduction of the new case, it can be added to the case base. Nevertheless, if at least one of its associates is misclassificated , the case can not be introduced directly in the case base, since it will solve its own classification but it will spoil some associates diagnosis. The Revising and Retaining algorithm is summarized in Figure 5

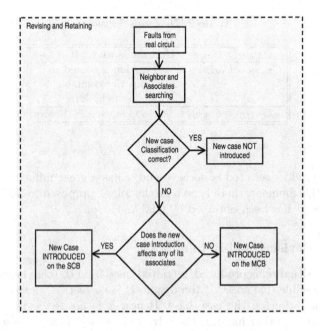

Fig. 5. Revising and Retaining Process detailed

In order to test the methodology and to make it more comprehensive, it has been applied to a real circuit. This example is given in the following section.

4   Example on a Real Circuit

4.1   Circuit under Test

The selected system is a biquadratic filter shown in Figure 6. This circuit is used as a benchmark in the bibliography [10] [11] [12].

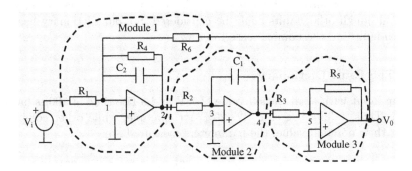

Fig. 6. Circuit under test

The nominal values of the components in the example are: R1=2.7K, R2=1K, R3=10K, R4=1.5K, R5=12K, R6=2.7K and C1=C2=10nF. A component is considered faulty when its value differs more than 10% from nominal. Component real values are affected by 10% tolerance.

4.2   Measures Selection

In order to select a diagnosis method or methods, it is necessary to fix the type of fault to be detected. This paper is focused on the detection and location of *parametric, permanent, independent* and *simple* faults. These characteristics are described in detail in [13]. The dictionary based on a temporal method described in [10] is taken as example. In this case, the stored data in the dictionary are certain characteristics of the circuit response to a saturated ramp input.

The parameters used to characterize the faults are:

− *Steady state (V_{est})*: Final value at which the output tends to.
− *Overshoot (SP)*: Defined as

$$SP = \frac{V_{\max} - V_{est}}{V_{est}} 100 \tag{4}$$

where V_{max} is the amplitude maximum value reached at the output.

- *Rising time (tr)*: Time used by the output to rise from the 10% to 90% of the steady state value.
- *Delay time (td)*: Interval of time between the moment that the input and the output get to the 50% steady state value.

In [10] it is highlighted that choosing a smaller ramp rise time, doesn't imply better diagnostic results. A method to help in the selection of an appropriate ramp rise time is not provided.

The initial proposed faults to detect are deviations of $\pm 20\%$ and $\pm 50\%$ from the nominal values of the passive components (a set of 32 faults). These faults seem to be distributed well enough in order to cover a possible set of typical faults, although other faults could be considered. So, our dictionary has a row for each fault and the nominal case (33 rows).

4.3   The Fault Dictionary

A ramp input with a saturation value of 1 V and a rise time of $100\mu s$ has been chosen. Thus, taking the case R2+20%, for example, while other components stay at their nominal value, the parameters measured are:

$$SP = 4.51\%,\ td = 19\mu s,\ tr = 76\mu s\ \text{and}\ V_{est} = -0.99V.$$

For all the initially considered faults, the temporal dictionary has 33 rows and 4 columns and is shown in Table 3

Table 3. Classic dictionary for the ramp input

Fault	SP%	$T_d(\mu S)$	$t_r(\mu S)$	V_{est} (V)	Fault	SP%	$T_d(\mu S)$	$t_r(\mu S)$	V_{est} (V)
R1+20	4.4029	15	76	-0.8332	R5+20	4.6189	12	75	-0.9999
R1-20	4.4029	15	76	-1.2498	R5-20	3.9447	20	77	-1.0002
R1+50	4.4029	15	76	-0.6665	R5+50	4.8682	9	76	-1.0002
R1-50	4.4029	15	76	-1.9996	R5-50	2.1315	31	86	-0.9996
R2+20	4.0473	19	77	-1.0001	R6+20	4.0473	19	77	-1.2001
R2-20	4.6614	11	75	-1.0000	R6-20	4.6614	11	75	-0.8000
R2+50	3.3711	24	80	-1.0003	R6+50	3.3711	24	80	-1.5004
R2-50	5.2359	5	75	-0.9999	R6-50	5.2359	5	75	-0.4999
R3+20	4.0473	19	77	-1.0001	C1+20	4.0473	19	77	-1.0001
R3-20	4.6614	11	75	-1.0000	C1-20	4.6614	11	75	-1.0000
R3+50	3.3711	24	80	-1.0003	C1+50	3.3711	24	80	-1.0003
R3-50	5.2359	5	75	-0.9999	C1-50	5.2359	5	75	-0.9999
R4+20	5.7311	12	73	-0.9994	C2+20	5.7085	16	73	-0.9997
R4-20	2.4917	19	80	-1.0000	C2-20	3.0781	15	77	-1.0000
R4+50	6.9145	10	71	-0.9990	C2+50	7.6834	17	72	-1.0005
R4-50	0	29	92	-1.0000	C2+50	1.0031	15	80	-1.0000
					Nom	4.4029	15	76	-0.9998

Giving a look to the Table 3, faults R2+20, R3+20 and C1+20 have identical attributes. The same could be said for the same components and faults -20% and $\pm 50\%$. It will be impossible to distinguish between them taking the cited measures at the output circuit V_0. Then the dictionary could be reduced to 25 rows table, where [R2+20 R3+20 C1+20] forms an ambiguity group. The same happens for [R2-20 R3-20 C1-20], [R2+50 R3+50 C1+50] and [R2-50 R3-50 C1-50].

4.4   Case-Based Reasoning System Proposed

In order to include tolerance effect a Monte-Carlo simulation has been done. 501 randomly chosen runs gaussian distributed have been produced for each considered fault. Hence the new dictionary will have 33x501 = 16533 cases. If the ambiguity sets grouping is applied, then the dictionary size is reduced to 25x501 = 12525 cases. $Matlab^{TM}$ has been used as simulation tool.

The hierarchy proposed in Figure 2, can be particularized for the given circuit as shown in Figure 7. The modules are depicted in the circuit of Figure 6. The division in three modules has been made by simple inspection because the circuit is very simple. For more complex circuits the algorithms proposed in [3] or in [4] can be applied.

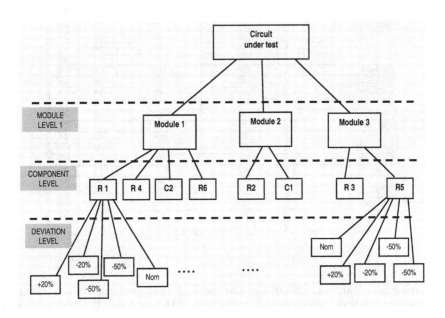

Fig. 7. Circuit Case hierarchy

For dictionary size reduction, three neighbors (k=3) have been used to decide the output class of an input case. In the reduction dictionary step each of them is taken with the same weight when voting.

According to [9], the incremental algorithms are less computational consuming than decremental ones, but the latter usually produce shortest case bases.

For the IB3 method the 12525 cases of the spread dictionary are reduced
to 2457 (19.61% of the spread dictionary cases retained), while using DROP4
to 1112 (8.8% of the spread dictionary cases retained). These new reduced case
bases are tested using a randomly generated case set with 100 simulations for
each considered fault (a total of 2500 test cases). Again, the Euclidean distance
is used and the class of the closest extracted case is taken as a classification of
the input case. Table 4 resume the percentage of correct classifications and gives
a comparison of the diagnosis capability provided by the classic dictionary, the
spread one, and the reduced ones.

Table 4. Reduction Methods comparison. Ramp input

Fault	Classic dictionary	Spread dictionary	DROP4	IB3
R1+20	84	83	85	77
R1-20	87	94	90	90
R1+50	99	98	99	97
R1-50	100	100	100	100
R2+20,R3+20,C1+20	41	30	41	35
R2-20,R3-20,C1-20	36	35	35	31
R2+50,R3+50,C1+50	79	78	83	72
R2-50,R3-50,C1-50	94	99	96	98
R4+20	85	89	87	78
R4-20	88	84	88	80
R4+50	98	98	98	98
R4-50	100	100	100	100
R5+20	47	33	46	36
R5-20	38	40	38	43
R5+50	82	78	83	75
R5-50	91	93	94	93
R6+20	79	78	79	78
R6-20	86	83	82	74
R6+50	98	99	100	100
R6-50	100	100	100	100
C2+20	82	75	74	76
C2-20	89	90	90	83
C2+50	99	99	99	95
C2-50	100	100	100	100
NOM	69	61	72	57
Average	**82.04**	**80.68**	**82.36**	**78.64**

Analyzing Table 4, DROP4 is the method that performs better diagnosis
percentage with the most reduced dictionary. Hence, even DROP4 is computationally more expensive than IB3 reduction, it results in a greater storage
reduction and, it will produce computational savings during execution there-
after. As it has been explained before, the voting procedure is carried out using
a distance-weighted exponential kernel.

The reduced case base obtained by DROP4 method is used as MCB. During
the reduction process, the dropped cases that are going to be misclassified by
MCB are introduced in the SCB if its addition in the MCB is going to spoil the
MCB diagnosis. As a result, MCB is composed originally by 1112 cases and SCB
by 967.

For testing proposes, the same test case set used to compare reduction algorithms efficacy is applied to our CBR system. At the present moment, the exponent n used to calculate the weight w associated to the extracted SCB cases is taken as $n = 1$. The threshold ϵ is chosen to be $\epsilon = 0.1$. This value has been obtained by inspection of the solutions and their associated weights provided by MCB and SCB. Table 5 shows some possible results for several test cases.

Table 5. Results obtained by MCB & SCB

Case Number	Fault Simulated	C_{MCB}	MCB Decision	C_{SCB}	SCB Decision	Final Diagnosis
34	R1+20	0.7338	R1+20	0.7341	R6-20	Module 1
107	R1-20	0.3018	R1-20	0.3945	R5+20	R1-20,R5+20
113	R1-20	0.4671	R6+20	0.6382	R1-20	R1-20
431	R2+20	0.2378	R1+20	0.4494	R2+20	R2+20
689	R2+50	0.2261	R5-20	0.4661	R5+20	R5+20
1762	R6-20	0.6057	R1+20	0.3074	R6-20	R1+20
2032	C2+20	0.6913	C2+20	0.6993	R2+20	C2+20,R2+20
2043	C2+20	0.4054	C2+20	0.6178	R5-20	R5-20
2166	C2-20	0.7284	C2-20	0.8099	R4-20	Module 1
2428	Nom	0.2445	R1+20	0.4408	Nom	Nom
2524	Nom	0.4129	R5+20	0.4816	R2-20	R5+20,R2-20

Results like test case 1762 are very common. Although the isolated fault proposed by SCB is wrong, the decision is clearly taken by MCB as $C_{MCB} = 0.6057 > C_{SCB} = 0.3074$, and it is correct. But some times, there are test cases like 113, 431 and 2428 that produces $C_{MCB} < C_{SCB}$. Hence the decision is given by SCB and the correction performed over the MCB initial decision is clearly improved. On the other hand cases like test case 2043, the MCB correct decision is spoiled by SCB conclusion. The particularity of test case 34 and 2166 is that $|C_{MCB} - C_{SCB}| \leq \epsilon = 0.1$. Then the decision is taken by the upper common hierarchy level. Giving a look to Figure 7, it corresponds to $Module1$ in both situations. It is clear that sometimes hierarchy consideration produces a precision loss. Finally, there are test cases like 689 that both, MCB and SCB, provide a wrong decision. The solution in a situation like this one is to retain the case. If applying DROP4 algorithm the final decision is that this new case is not suitable for MCB, it will be introduced in the SCB. The results obtained by our CBR system are displayed and compared in Table 6.

There is a slight improvement over the other proposed systems. The advantage is that CBR system can learn from new situations. A new fault can make the fault dictionary to give a wrong diagnosis. On the other hand, the designed CBR system can learn from this new situation. The same can happen when measures are taken from the real circuit. Furthermore, simulations do not take into account noise on the measures. Hence real measures can cause the fault dictionary diagnosis to fail. It is expected that CBR system will be more robust to noise.

Table 6. Improvement Using MCB & SCB

Fault	Classic dictionary	DROP4	With MCB & SCB
R1+20	84	85	84
R1-20	87	90	90
R1+50	99	99	98
R1-50	100	100	100
R2+20,R3+20,C1+20	41	41	42
R2-20,R3-20,C1-20	36	35	44
R2+50,R3+50,C1+50	79	83	82
R2-50,R3-50,C1-50	94	96	94
R4+20	85	87	87
R4-20	88	88	89
R4+50	98	98	98
R4-50	100	100	100
R5+20	47	46	49
R5-20	38	38	43
R5+50	82	83	82
R5-50	91	94	95
R6+20	79	79	76
R6-20	86	82	82
R6+50	98	100	100
R6-50	100	100	100
C2+20	82	74	74
C2-20	89	90	89
C2+50	99	99	100
C2-50	100	100	100
NOM	69	72	69
Average	**82.04**	**82.36**	**82.68**

5   Conclusions and Future Work

This work shows how reduction techniques produces an improvement in Analog circuit diagnosis. The decision of introducing special cases in a separate base SCB gives a better diagnosis, but a deeper study about how to choose ϵ, w_k, and n for the SCB weight calculation should be done. Also, further research is necessary to study how to organize SCB. The hierarchy solves the problem of ambiguous decision between MCB and SCB at the expense of precision loss.

The Euclidean distance function can be improved by the use of attribute weights. Some studies have been done based on the sensitivity analysis, but it is still in progress.

Reduction algorithms DROP4 and IB3 are proved to be more effective compared with the spread dictionary. The number of instances is drastically reduced and the diagnosis results are even improved with the DROP4. Hence, using this reduced dictionary as initial MCB is a good start. Distance-weighted voting using the exponential kernel is proved to give the best results.

Although DROP4 gives us good results as a learning method for new cases, there will be an implementation using IB3 in order to test how an incremental method can cope with new cases. The main problem is that IB3 is highly affected by the order that instances are removed. Therefore, special care should be taken when applying this method.

The learning method produces just a small improvement on the final test. It can be interpreted that after reduction, the case base has reached its maximum learning, hence, when new situations of the considered faults are produced due to tolerances, there will be almost no learning.

A low isolation success percentage for faults like R2+20 is obtained. This occurs because there is a great overlapping with other set of considered faults. This can be improved introducing other node measures, although this improvement will take place for all the presented methods.

References

1. Bandler, J., Salama, A.: Fault diagnosis of analog circuits. Proceedings of the IEEE **73** (1985) 1279–1325
2. Fenton, W.G., McGinnity, T.M., Maguire, L.P.: Fault diagnosis of electronic systems using intelligent techniques: A review. IEEE Transactions on Systems, Man and Cybernetics. Part C: Applications and Reviews **31** (2001) 269–281
3. Starzik, J., Pang, J., Manetti, S., Piccirilli, M., Fedi, G.: Finding ambiguity groups in low testability analog circuits. IEEE Transactions on Circuits and Systems. Fundamental Theory and Applications **47** (2000) 1125–1137
4. Stenbakken, G., Souders, T., Stewart, G.: Ambiguity groups and testability. IEEE Transactions on Instrumentation and Measurement **38** (1989) 941–947
5. Boyd, R.: Tolerance Analysis of Electronic Circuits Using Matlab. Electronics Engineering. CRC Press (1999) ISBN: 0-8493-2276-6.
6. Voorakaranam, R., Chakrabarti, S., Hou, J., Gomes, A., Cherubal, S., Chatterjee, A.: Hierarchical specification-driven analog fault modeling for efficient fault simulation and diagnosis. International Test Conference (1997) 903–912
7. Sangiovanni-Vicentelli, A., Chen, L., Chua, L.: An efficient heuristic cluster algorithm for tearing large-scale networks. IEEE Transactions on Circuits and Systems **cas-24** (1977) 709–717
8. Chen, Y.: Experiment on fault location in large-scale analog circuits. IEEE Transactions on Instrumentation and Measurement **42** (1993) 30–34
9. Wilson, D., Martinez, T.: Reduction techniques for instance-based learning algorithms. Machine Learning **38** (2000) 257–286
10. Balivada, A., Chen, J., Abraham, J.: Analog testing with time response parameters. IEEE Design and Test of computers (1996) 18–25
11. Kaminska, B., Arabi, K., Goteti, P., Huertas, J., Kim, B., Rueda, A., Soma, M.: Analog and mixed-signal benchmark circuits. first release. (IEEE Mixed-Signal Testing Technical Activity Committee)
12. Soma, M.: A desing for test methodology for active analog filters, IEEE (1990) 183–192
13. Duhamel, P., Rault, J.: Automatic test generation techniques for analog circuits and systems: A review. IEEE Transactions on Circuits and Systems **Cas-26** (1979) 411–440

Empirical Analysis of Case-Based Reasoning and Other Prediction Methods in a Social Science Domain: Repeat Criminal Victimization

Michael A. Redmond[1] and Cynthia Blackburn Line[2]

[1] Mathematics & Computer Science, La Salle University, 1900 W. Olney Ave, Philadelphia, PA, 19141, (215) 951-1096,
redmond@lasalle.edu

[2] Department of Law & Justice Studies, Rowan University, 201 Mullica Hill Road, Glassboro, NJ 08028, (856) 256-4500
line@rowan.edu

Abstract. Case-Based Reasoning (CBR) has been used successfully in many practical applications. In this paper, we present the value of Case-Based Reasoning for researchers in a novel task domain, criminology. In particular, some criminologists are interested in studying crime victims who are victims of multiple crime incidents. However, research progress has been slow, in part due to limitations in the statistical methods generally used in the field. We show that CBR provides a useful alternative, allowing better prediction than via other methods, and generating hypotheses as to what features are important predictors of repeat victimization. This paper details a systematic sequence of experiments with variations on CBR and comparisons to other related, competing methods. The research uses data from the United States' National Crime Victimization Survey. CBR, with advance filtering of variables, was the best predictor in comparison to other machine learning methods. This approach may provide a fruitful new direction of research, particularly for criminology, but also for other academic research areas.

1 Introduction

Case-Based Reasoning (CBR) has been an active research area and has been used successfully in many practical applications. While it has also aided researchers in other academic fields, with some exceptions [1], the tendency has been to explore technical fields. In this paper, we present the value of Case-Based reasoning for researchers in the social science field of criminology. Some social science research questions are difficult to study using traditional methodologies due to limitations in statistical methods. For example, in criminology, the interesting issue as to why some crime victims are repeatedly victimized has been infrequently studied. The ability to predict who might be at-risk for being a "multiple victim" would be of value in public

K.D. Ashley and D.G. Bridge (Eds.): ICCBR 2003, LNAI 2689, pp. 452–464, 2003.
© Springer-Verlag Berlin Heidelberg 2003

education and crime prevention. Sociologists and criminologists have explored this issue to some extent, but are limited by statistical assumptions and data requirements associated with commonly used statistical methods. In this paper, we show that CBR provides a useful alternative for the study of victimization data. A fairly simple CBR approach has been used to make predictions successfully, and generate interesting hypotheses as to what features, or *variables* (in social science usage) are important predictors of multiple victimization. We believe that this approach could be useful for aiding other social science research. For CBR, this paper presents a test-bench in which CBR achieves better prediction accuracy than related methods, providing a successful application of CBR research.

1.1 Background

Research on multiple victimization demonstrates that not only are crime victims rare in the general population, but that multiple victimizations are very rare and are possibly unique [2]; [3]; [4]; [5]; [6]; [7]; [8]. Victimization tends to follow a very skewed distribution with most people being victimized zero times, a few people being victimized once, and very few people being victimized more than once. There have been attempts at model fitting and other statistical modeling designed to explain the skewed distribution of multiple victimization [5], [8]. However, limitations in statistical methods prevent true prediction. Some problems include:

1. Many models are of limited use when using a large number of variables (e.g. multiple regression)
2. Many models rest on assumptions about the data or the relationships among the data – assumptions the data are random, assumptions of independence, assumptions of linear or curvilinear relationships
3. Nominal variables are common in real data, but are not handled well by basic statistics
4. Some models may require the elimination of "outlier" cases in order to achieve a better fit

In contrast, CBR presents several advantages to victimization prediction. First, CBR has no inherent limit to the number of variables that can be used without being negatively affected. CBR does not rely on assumptions in order to predict values for cases – there is no need to assume random data, independence (multicollinearity is not a problem), or linear or curvilinear relationships. Further, CBR easily accommodates all variables (versus some other models which have limited use when it comes to binary, nominal, ordinal, or interval variables).

1.2 Case Based Reasoning

A discussion of basic CBR methodology is not included here, as it is assumed that the audience is familiar with these methods. Interested readers desiring extended introduction can review basic CBR methodology in Kolodner [9], Leake [10], and Watson [11]. While CBR has been applied to many different tasks in many different problem-domains, its application for social science has been rare. While it has been quite popular for legal reasoning [12]; [13];[14], it has received less use involving crimes, victims, arrests and other criminal justice concerns.

Perhaps related, but a closer relative to CBR for legal reasoning, Shiu [15] presented a system for determining of sanctions for government employee negligence. Toland and Lees [16] argued that CBR is potentially useful for solving crimes and suggested in particular the domain of suspect generation. However, this work is still in the development process. Redmond and Baveja [17] developed a system, Crime Similarity System (CSS), that uses case-based retrieval to match communities on three dimensions (crime, socioeconomic environment, and law enforcement) in order to find communities from which a given community can learn better or more efficient law enforcement strategies, practices, or techniques. Line and Redmond [18] investigated the use of CBR for predicting community crime rates. The above appears to represent the only use of CBR in related domains.

In the rest of this paper, the empirical experiments performed using data related to criminal victimization are presented; first the methodology is discussed, then the results. Finally, conclusions and future work are discussed.

2   Experimental Methodology

The researchers utilized the 1995 National Crime Victimization Survey (NCVS) [19] and utilized the person level records. In the full dataset this includes N=32,539 cases. The researchers chose any potentially relevant variables for inclusion as independent variables (features) (N=78) guided by criminological research. Criminology studies of victimization have focused on lifestyle [20] and routine activities [21] of the potential victims. These perspectives have influenced what features (variables) are included in the NCVS. There are clearly limitations in this data. The variables included in the survey involve the potential victim and his/her household, and include only limited data about the community, and the community is not identified, so these additional variables cannot be added.

Given the available variables, the number of variables was intentionally chosen to be large in order to present a feature selection or weighting challenge to the system, rather than having a knowledgeable human filter the variables tightly. Any variable that could be even loosely related was included, to be filtered by the program. Pre-processing included coding each individual as to his/her victimization status, "multi-victim" or not. All possible victimizations – both against the person and against property – were included. The task is to correctly predict to which category a person belongs based on available features.

A stratified random sample of 1000 subjects was pulled from the full dataset for experimentation. The subset data was created so that it included 500 multi-victimized and 500 non-multi-victimized people. This stratification allowed us to focus on the multi-victimized people who are of most interest and who are relatively rare in the full dataset. If a pure random sample was used, a program could get a high percentage of predictions correct merely by predicting that nobody was victimized multiple times.

All experiments followed a 10-fold cross validation methodology. Thus, in each experiment, for each fold being tested, there are 900 training cases and 100 test cases. The results are averaged across the results from each of the 10 folds to get a mean percent correct. Further, in our experiments, we did 10 such 10-fold cross validations for each method being evaluated, as suggested by Witten and Frank [22, p127]. This controlled for any variability in whether similar cases were separated or in the same fold and allowed the application of statistical tests, such as t-tests, on the results without violating independence assumptions. All tests were done on the same randomly generated folds, so paired sample statistics can be used.

3   CBR Experiments

In order to predict victimization (multiple victimizations or not multiple victimizations), the researchers tested a variety of methods ranging from the simple to moderately complex.   In terms of the common CBR terminology, none of the experiments involved use of "Adaptation," or complex "Retrieval," such as using "Indexing." The K-nearest neighbor approach to CBR retrieval ([23], [24]), sometimes referred to as instance-based learning, was used for all CBR experiments.

The simplest possible CBR method is 1-Nearest Neighbor, without adaptation, where the prediction is made by predicting the same value for the dependent variable in the test case as the value in the most similar training case. Better performance can be obtained, to a point, by using more neighbors. One similar neighbor could be unusual (essentially an outlier) and could lead to an incorrect prediction. Adding more neighbors (increasing K) essentially brings more information to bear on the prediction. However, as more neighbors are added, the neighbors being used are getting less similar to the case being predicted. At some point it is expected that increasing K will lead to worse performance instead of better.

Table 1. Results for Simple K Nearest Neighbor, Stratified NCVS Subset

Method	Pct Correct	Significance Compared to Previous
Chance	50.00	
1NN	56.57	< .0001 (single sample test)
5NN	59.05	< .001
10NN	60.95	< .001
15NN	61.80	< .05
20NN	62.70	< .05
25NN	62.88	
30NN	63.28	< .05
35NN	63.04	
40NN	63.40	
50NN	63.94	
60NN	64.43	< .05
70NN	64.09	< .05 worse
75NN	63.88	< .05 worse
80NN	63.81	
90NN	63.58	
100NN	63.32	< .05 worse

Table 1 shows results of simple K-nearest neighbor with different values for K, as applied to the stratified subset of the NCVS data. Accurate prediction steadily climbs with greater K, peaks at 60NN, and then gradually declines. Statistical p values are shown for differences that are statistically significant in comparison to the preceding level for K. It may be disturbing to some that a prediction based on 60 previous cases is being considered case-based, but it is still a far cry from generalization based on all 900 cases in the training set. Prediction is still "lazy," done as needed, based on a selection of exemplars.

As discussed above, doing this sort of prediction on the NCVS data using statistical methods would violate statistical assumptions and requirements for types of data. For comparison to other relevant methods of doing the same kinds of predictions, it is valuable to compare the instance-based, K-Nearest Neighbor, approach to other data mining methods. The same data was used with the WEKA data mining software [22], a leading suite of publicly available, open source, data mining tools (http://www.cs.waikato.ac.nz/ml/weka). Table 2 shows results with learning methods that are compatible with the current data (binary dependent variable, a mix of binary, nominal, ordinal, and ratio independent variables), with results sorted by percent correct in the experiment. None of these methods beat the simple 60NN.

Table 2. Results for Alternative Machine Learning Approaches, Stratified NCVS Subset

Method	Percent Correct	Significance Comparison With 60NN (all worse than 60NN)
Hyperpipes	51.47	< .001
Kernel Density[1]	54.35	< .001
K Star [26]	54.80	< .001
One R [27]	58.20	< .001
Voted Perceptron [28]	59.42	< .001
Artificial Neural Net[2]	60.05	< .001
J48 Decision Tree[3]	61.55	< .001
Decision Table [30]	62.18	< .001
Decision Stump [31]	62.40	< .001
Logistic [32]	63.63	<. 005
Sequential Minimal Optimization [33]	64.29	

The next step was to try to improve upon simple K-Nearest Neighbor. The simple KNN uses all features and treats each feature as equally important. No criminologist would believe that all 78 independent variables are equally important. Likewise, CBR and machine learning researchers know that some features are more important than others in many task domains. As in many machine learning tasks there is a feature selection/ weighting problem to address [34]; [35]; [36]. Prediction performance should be able to be improved via removing unneeded variables and/or weighting the importance of variables.

---

[1] A Weka version of common Kernel Density approach [25]
[2] A Weka version of common neural net that learns via backpropagation
[3] Part of Weka data mining tool. Based on Quinlan's C 4.5 [29]

"Feature Selection" or "Feature Weighting" approaches commonly are divided in "filter" and "wrapper" methods [37]. Filter methods process the data before the learning method is used, in order to make the task easier for the learning method. Wrapper methods essentially use the learning method itself as a test of the feature selection or weighting. During training, the performance is tested on a "validation set" of data, separate from the training and test sets. Then training continues though making adjustments in response to validation performance, and then performance is re-tested on the validation set, etc. Actual testing is then done on the test set, which has not been involved at all in the training. The researchers tried several filter approaches. The results of using each of these filter approaches, then using 60NN, are shown in Table 3 (sorted by percent correct).

The filter approaches all look for differences between cases that are multiple victims and those that are not. These will each be briefly discussed in turn. The information gain approach uses the foundational entrophy metric [38]. This filter method, implemented in the WEKA data mining tools, looks for the variables that produce the most information gain if cases are divided into groups based on each of the variables. Rounded information gain ("IG round") adjusts the results of information gain, based on Kohavi, Langley, and Yun's [39] finding that it can be better to have weights on features be taken from a small set of possibilities, rather than the infinite possibilities offered by continuous weights. The intent is to reduce overfitting. Therefore, in this approach, weights generated based on Information Gain were rounded to the nearest 0.5 (0, 0.5, 1, 1.5 etc). Correlated Feature Subsets (CFS) [40] selects features based roughly on correlations between independent variables and dependent variables – with adjustment methods invented for dealing with binary, nominal, and ordinal variables. This research directly used an implementation of Hall's algorithm that is provided with the WEKA data mining software. Variable Distribution by Category (VDC) sets weights using a less formally proven technique using the same intuition as Information Gain and Correlated Feature Subsets – variables whose distribution of values differ significantly between the categories for the dependent variable are more heavily weighted. Variables whose distribution of values does not differ between categories have a zero weight and are essentially discarded.

While the difference between VDC and CFS is not statistically significant, nor likely practically significant, based on the (slightly) better performance and the more formal justification for it, further refinements were pursued based on improving upon the filtering done by CFS.

Table 3. Results for 60NN After Various Filter Approaches

Filter Method	Percent Correct	Significance in Comparison with Simple 60 NN
IG round	63.89	< .05 worse
Info Gain	64.35	
VDC	64.86	< .05
CFS	64.97	< .05

The CFS method selects features; it does not assign weights (importances) to those selected. The next research step was to determine if a wrapper approach to learning weights could improve upon the selection of variables using the CFS filter. As predictions of validation set data are being marked correct or incorrect, variables that lead to correct validation set cases to be matched are rewarded and variables that lead to incorrect training cases to be matched are punished. The amount of reward depends on degree of similarity of the correct case to the current case, and for a given variable the amount the variable favors the correct case. The amount of punishment for a variable's weight based on an incorrect prediction is almost the reverse – it depends on the degree of similarity of the incorrect case to the current case, and for each given variable, the amount the variable favors the incorrect case. This process is then repeated until a stopping condition is met. Only after the learning for a fold is stopped is the resulting weighted similarity function used for doing the real tests.

Following this learning regimen, 60NN with variables first filtered by CFS then weights learned, the program was able to get 65.36% correct. This is not significantly better than the 64.97% correct for CFS only, statistically or otherwise. Various adjustments to the learning algorithm did not further increase performance. Further research in this area will be tried, but at this point, it appears that the most significant benefit is in selecting variables using CFS. Also, it is important to note that the number of neighbors used is very important in the accuracy of predictions. By using 60NN, the program is, in a way, forming a bunch of "on-the-fly," or ad hoc, generalizations. This is more flexible than generating one generalization that works for all cases, as many of the other data mining methods, such as One R, Decision Tree, Decision Table, do.

One of the interesting aspects of the last two sets of experiments in this research for social scientists is that the feature selection/weighting methods learn which features are most important for successfully predicting whether somebody will be a "multi-victim" of crime. A large number of variables considered potentially relevant, involving the individual's lifestyle and routine activities, were included. Some were judged to be more valuable in predictions than others by learning and filtering approaches, and as a result of that heuristic judgment predictions were improved. For the CBR researcher, the key question is "did the method improve performance?" But once it is shown that it did, to the social science researcher, the question is "Which features (variables) were determined to be important?" Instance-based learning with feature selection/weighting provides the social science researcher a fruitful alternative to using statistical approaches. The Appendix shows a list of all features used in the study, whether each variable was selected for use by CFS used as a filter, and the average weight given to those remaining variables by the best wrapper weight learning method. Interestingly, some of the variables included in the most successful prediction model are surprising to criminologists. For instance, some that might be considered surprising include:

- # of household members age 11 and under
- 1 Adult with children
- Victim got married
- Age of victim

These are interesting as they are not something that a criminologist might overlook because they may counter-indicate multiple victimization. Specifically, research on crime victims tends to show (rather regularly) that significant changes in the life course, such as aging, getting married, and having children, tend to remove potential victims from lifestyle experiences that leave them open to the potential of victimization. In other words, older, married adults with children are less likely to go out to clubs and to live what are often referred to as "riskier" lifestyles. However, to a computer algorithm, a variable that aids prediction by counter-indication is just as visible as a variable that aids prediction by being an indicator of risk.

The researchers had a few criminologists try to identify important variables. None of these human-generated variable lists (or weighted lists) was able to obtain predictive performance equal to that obtained via computer algorithms' processing of the data. One possible explanation is that the criminologists were thrown off by their biases – biases that were not reflected in the data. Another is that the basic assumption behind data mining is true - that the scale of data and ability of computer processing and algorithms enables discovery of new information unknown to humans. The selection and weighting of variables by filter and wrapper methods represent hypotheses of what variables are important, and can be a productive source of future social science research.

Interestingly, as another control, two computer science students using IT tools (Microsoft Excel and Access) tried to identify important features as well. None of these variable lists was able to obtain predictive performance equal to that obtained via the best CBR results either. It might well be argued that K-nearest neighbor and feature selection/weighting are better tools for such search. Part of the reason for use of databases and spreadsheets in business is to help identify what is important. Yet, it may be that CBR methods are better at identifying important features than even human-assisted analysis using IT tools.

4 Discussion and Conclusion

The results indicate that predicting victimization using the K-Nearest Neighbor technique and CBR holds promise. While the results are not particularly overwhelming, it appears that this may be because the prediction task is rather challenging. The results obtained using the CBR approach are better than that obtained through using other machine learning data mining approaches. In fairness, some of the other methods can be tuned; it is possible that experts in those approaches could obtain better performance through tuning. Beyond providing the best predictions, the CBR with advance filtering provides hypotheses that can generate future research in the task domain. Further, the model is not bound by assumptions or other statistical limitations that limit many methods currently in use in criminology. Thus, there are compelling reasons to pursue the K-Nearest Neighbor and CBR techniques in researching victimization. Further, we believe that this domain is merely an example, and that other social science research topics may be amenable to similar application of nearest neighbor techniques.

The use of Case Based Reasoning and the K-Nearest Neighbor approach are unique in the study of victimization, and largely within the criminal justice field and much of social science research. This use may provide a fruitful opening of a new research methodology to some areas that have been previously limited to statistical approaches.

From a CBR perspective, this work provides yet another validation of the usefulness of CBR in another task domain. It also shows a successful use of Hall's [40] Correlated Feature Subsets algorithm as a filter approach in preparation for K-nearest neighbor prediction. In future work, we are interested in further exploring more different feature selection and weighting methods (as in [34], [35]). We also are interested in extending the work of Line and Redmond [18] to explored filter and wrapper approaches to feature selection and weighting. Further, as noted above, this work is not a particularly sophisticated application of CBR. It does not employ all of the stages in the CBR cycle. We are interested in exploring whether adaptation can be used in such a data-rich, but perhaps knowledge-poor area.

References

1. McLaren, B. M. and Ashley, K. D., Assessing Relevance with Extensionally Defined Principles and Cases; In the Proceedings of AAAI-2000, Austin, Texas, August 2000.
2. Collins, J. J., B. G. Cox, and P. Langan: Job Activities and Personal Crime Victimization: Implications for Theory. Social Science Research 16 (1987) 345–360.
3. Johnson, S. D., K. Bowers, and A. Hirschfield. New Insights into the Spatial and Temporal Distribution of Repeat Victimization. British Journal of Criminology 37 (1997) 224–241.
4. Lasley, J. R. and J. Rosenbaum: Routine Activities and Multiple Personal Victimization. Social Science Research 73 (1988) 47–50.
5. Osborn, D. R. and A. Tseloni: The Distribution of Household Property Crimes. Journal of Quantitative Criminology 14 (1998) 307–330.
6. Sampson, R. J. and J. D. Wooldredge: Linking the Micro- and Macro-Level Dimensions of Lifestyle-Routine Activity and Opportunity Models of Predatory Victimization. Journal of Quantitative Criminology 3 (1987) 371–393.
7. Robinson, M. B. Burglary Revictimization: The Time Period of Heightened Risk. British Journal of Criminology 38 (1998) 78–87.
8. Sparks, R. F. Multiple Victimization: Evidence, Theory, and Future Research. The Journal of Criminal Law & Criminology 72 (1981) 762–778.
9. Kolodner, J. Case-Based Reasoning. Los Altos, CA: Morgan Kaufmann. (1993)
10. Leake, D. Case Based Reasoning: Experiences, Lessons, and Future Directions. Menlo Park, California: AAAI Press/MIT Press. (1996)
11. Watson, I.D. Applying Case-Based Reasoning: Techniques for Enterprise Systems. Los Altos, California: Morgan Kaufmann,. (1997)
12. L. Karl Branting: *Reasoning with Rules and Precedents: A Computational Model of Legal Analysis*, Kluwer Academic Publishers, Dordrecht, December 1999.
13. Ashley, K.D., 1991. Reasoning with cases and hypotheticals in HYPO, *International Journal of Man-Machine Studies* 34 (6) 753–796.
14. Kevin D. Ashley, Edwina L. Rissland: Compare and Contrast: A Test of Expertise. *AAAI 1987*: 273–278
15. Shiu, S.C.K: An Object-Oriented Expert System for Awarding Punishment for Serious Discipline Cases. In Workshop Proceedings on Practical Case-Based Reasoning Strategies for Building and Maintaining Corporate Memories, Munich, Germany (1999) II.3-II.8.
16. Toland, J. and B. Lees Applying Case-Based Reasoning to Law Enforcement. International Association of Law Enforcement Intelligence Analysts Journal 15(2003)

17. Redmond, M. A. and A. Baveja: A Data-Driven Software Tool for Enabling Cooperative Information Sharing Among Police Departments. European Journal of Operational Research 141 (2002) 660–678.
18. Line, C. Blackburn and M. Redmond: Predicting Community Crime Rates Using Artificial Intelligence Case-Based Reasoning Techniques. Paper presented at the annual meetings of the American Society of Criminology, Washington, D. C. (1998)
19. U. S. Department of Justice, Bureau of Justice Statistics National Crime Victimization Survey. Washington, D. C. (1995)
20. Hindelang, M.J., M. R. Gottfredson, and J. Garofalo: Victims of Personal Crime: An Empirical Foundation for a Theory of Personal Victimization. Cambridge, MA: Ballinger Publishing Company. (1978)
21. Cohen, L. E. and M. Felson: Social Change and Crime Rate Trends: A Routine Activity Approach. American Sociological Review 44 (1979) 588–608.
22. Witten, I. H., and E. Frank. Data Mining, Practical Machine Learning Tools and Techniques with Java Implementations. San Francisco, CA: Morgan Kaufmann Publishers. (2000)
23. Cost S., and S. Salzberg: A weighted nearest neighbor algorithm for learning with symbolic features. Machine Learning 10 (1993) 57–58.
24. Aha, D. W.: Lazy Learning. Artificial Intelligence Review 1:1–5 (1997).
25. Silverman, B. W. Density Estimation for Statistics and Data Analysis. Chapman and Hall: London. (1986)
26. Cleary, J.G. and L. E. Trigg: K*: An Instance- based Learner Using an Entropic Distance Measure. In Armand Prieditis, Stuart J. Russell (Eds.), Proceedings of the Twelfth International Conference on Machine Learning. Stanford University, CA, Morgan Kaufmann Publishers. (1995)
27. Holte, R.C. Very Simple Classification Rules Perform Well on Most Commonly Used Datasets. Machine Learning 11 (1993) 63–91.
28. Freund, Y. and R. E. Schapire: Large Margin Classification Using the Perceptron Algorithm. Proceedings of the 11th Annual Conference on Computational Learning Theory. New York, New York: ACM Press. (1998)
29. Quinlan, Ross C4.5: Programs for Machine Learning. San Mateo, CA.: Morgan Kaufmann Publishers. (1993)
30. Kohavi, R. The Power of Decision Tables. In N. Lavrac and S. Wrobel, (Eds), Proceedings of European Conference on Machine Learning, Lecture Notes in Artificial Intelligence 914, Springer Verlag, Berlin, (1995) 174–189.
31. Iba, W., and P. Langley Induction of One-Level Decision Trees. Proceedings of the Ninth International Conference on Machine Learning. Aberdeen, Scotland: Morgan Kaufmann. (1992)
32. Le Cessie, S. and J. C. Van Houwelingen Ridge Estimators in Logistic Regression. Applied Statistics 41 (1997) 191–201.
33. Platt, J. Fast Training of Support Vector Machines using Sequential Minimal Optimization. In B. Schölkopf, C. Burges, and A. Smola (eds.), Advances in Kernel Methods – Support Vector Learning. Boston, MA: MIT Press. (1998)
34. Wettschereck, D., D. W. Aha, and T. Mohri: A Review and Comparative Evaluation of Feature Weighting Methods for Lazy Learning Algorithms. Artificial Intelligence Review 11 (1997) 273–314.
35. Bonzano, A., P. Cunningham, and B. Smyth: Using Introspective Learning to Improve Retrieval in CBR: A Case Study in Air Traffic Control. ICCBR 1997: 291–302
36. Blum, A. L. and P. Langley: Selection of relevant features and examples in machine learning. Artificial Intelligence 97 (1997) 245–271

37. John, G., R. Kohavi, and K. Pflger: Irrelevant Features and the Subset Selection Problem. In W. W. Cohen and H. Hirsh, (eds.), Machine Learning: Proceedings of the Eleventh International Conference. San Francisco, CA: Morgan Kaufmann Publishers, (1994)
38. Shannon, C. E. A Mathematical Theory of Communication. Bell System Tech. Journal., 27 (1948) 379–423, 623–656.
39. Kohavi, R., P. Langley, P., and Y. Yun: The Utility of Feature Weighting in Nearest-Neighbor Algorithms. In L. C. Aiello (Ed), Proceedings of the Ninth European Conference on Machine Learning. Prague: Springer-Verlag. (1997)
40. Hall, M. A. Correlation-Based Feature Selection for Discrete and Numeric Class Machine Learning. Proceedings of the Seventeenth International Conference on Machine Learning. Stanford University, CA, Morgan Kaufmann Publishers. (2000)

Appendix A – Independent Variables, CFS Filtering, and Wrapper Weight Learning

Independent Variable	Type	Selected by CFS?	Ave Weight (across folds)
Tenure Own/Rent	Nominal	Yes	3.10
Land Use Urban/Rural	Nominal		
Farm Sales	Nominal		
Regular Home (House, Apt, Flat)	Binary		
Dorm - Student Qtrs.	Binary		
Other Living Qtrs.	Binary		
Number of Housing Units in Structure	Ordinal		
Outside Access to Household	Nominal		
Household Income Range	Ordinal		
Principal Person Relationship to Reference Person	Nominal		
Age of Reference Person	Ratio	Yes	6.27
Reference Person Marital Status	Nominal		
Reference Person Got Married	Binary		
Reference Person Got Widowed	Binary		
Reference Person Got Divorced	Binary	Yes	9.33
Reference Person Got Separated	Binary		
Reference Person Gender	Binary		
Reference Person Armed Forces Member	Binary		
Reference Person Education Completed	Ordinal		
Reference Person Enough Education	Binary		
Reference Person Race	Nominal		
Reference Person Hispanic Origin	Binary		
# Household Members – age 12 and up	Ratio		
# Household Members – age 11 and under	Ratio	Yes	9.23
Business Operated from Address	Binary		

Business with Sign Operated from Address	Binary		
Number of Vehicles Owned by Household	Ratio		
Take Household Security Measures	Binary		
Town Watch in Area	Nominal		
Participate on Town Watch in Area	Nominal		
College / University	Binary		
Public Housing	Nominal		
2 Adults with Children	Binary		
1 Adult with Children	Binary	Yes	1.94
2 Adults without Children	Binary	Yes	4.09
Extended Family – has Other Relatives	Binary		
Household with Nonrelatives	Binary		
Household with Singles	Binary		
Female Headed Household	Binary		
Female Only Adult	Binary		
Place Size of Residence	Ordinal	Yes	1.70
Place Region	Nominal		
Place MSA Status	Nominal	Yes	3.64
Reference Person Attending Post-Secondary Education	Nominal		
Person Relationship to Reference Person	Nominal		
Age of (Possible) Victim	Ratio	Yes	4.92
(Possible) Victim Marital Status	Nominal	Yes	0.51
(Possible) Victim Got Married	Binary	Yes	9.97
(Possible) Victim Got Widowed	Binary		
(Possible) Victim Got Divorced	Binary		
(Possible) Victim Got Separated	Binary		
(Possible) Victim Gender	Binary		
(Possible) Victim Armed Forces Member	Binary		
(Possible) Victim Education Completed	Ordinal		
(Possible) Victim Enough Education	Binary		
(Possible) Victim Race	Nominal		
(Possible) Victim Hispanic Origin	Binary		
How often possible victim went shopping	Ordinal		
How often possible victim went out in evening	Ordinal	Yes	5.12
How often possible victim used public transportation	Ordinal	Yes	6.07
Number of Months Living at Current Address (Possible) Victim	Ratio	Yes	5.52
Number of Times Moved Last 5 Years (Possible) Victim	Ratio	Yes	5.64
(Possible) Victim Had Job Last Week	Binary		
(Possible) Victim Had Job Within Last 6 Months	Binary		
(Possible) Victim Had Job in Medical Profession	Binary		
(Possible) Victim Had Job in Mental Health Profession	Binary		

(Possible) Victim Had Job in Teaching Profession	Binary		
(Possible) Victim Had Job in Law Enforcement Profession	Binary		
(Possible) Victim Had Job in Jail Guard Profession	Binary		
(Possible) Victim Had Job in Security Profession	Binary		
(Possible) Victim Had Job in Salesclerk Profession	Binary		
(Possible) Victim Had Job in Bartending Profession	Binary		
(Possible) Victim Had Job in Bus Driving Profession	Binary		
(Possible) Victim Had Job in Taxicab Profession	Binary		
(Possible) Victim Kind of Employer	Nominal		
(Possible) Victim Kind of Area Where Work	Nominal		
(Possible) Victim Works for College / University	Binary		
(Possible) Victim Attending Post-Secondary Education	Nominal	Yes	1.14

A Hybrid System with Multivariate Data Validation and Case Base Reasoning for an Efficient and Realistic Product Formulation

Sina Rezvani and Girijesh Prasad

Intelligent Systems Engineering Laboratory, School of Computing and Intelligent Systems,
University of Ulster, Londonderry BT48 7JL, N. Ireland, UK
Tel: +44 28 71375489, Fax: +44 28 70327004
s.rezvani@ulst.ac.uk

Abstract. This applied research paper presents a novel hybrid system, which provides a systematic approach for an efficient and realistic case retrieval, retention and testing of product formulations. The underlying idea is to build a case library of practical and viable product formulations with consistent quality patterns, flexible process attributes and constituent proportions. To avoid the storage of non-representative and unrealistic cases within the case library, a strict multivariate validation method has been imposed on the system. The input formulation, whether it be a single suggestion on product formulation as a query, an optimized case or a collection of tests, is validated against the most similar formulation cluster in the case library determined through the Principal Component Similarity factor and Mahalanobis distance. T^2 and Q-statistics as multivariate data validation methods are employed to determine whether the input formulations match the most similar cluster of datasets in the case library. The synergistic use of univariate control charts and the graphical plot of variable relations between the input formulation and the most similar case provide information on variables, which cause a mismatch. If the value of the culprit variable cannot be rectified to match the dataset in the case library, the new input formulation can only be retained after an empirical validation in the main manufacturing area.

1 Introduction

Within the polymeric industry, we are looking for ways to identify new product formulations, which improve product performance attributes in connection with classified applications and minimize manufacturing cost. The validated and realistic formulations, such as day-to-day manufacturing data during the normal manufacturing operations, are stored in a case library according to their application area for future use. Further formulations such as collections of batch tests, mathematically optimized or hypothetically forwarded product formulations can either be retained in the system after a multivariate validation against the stored dataset in the case library or as a new product formulation. Currently, accessible literatures do not have any provision for multivariate data validation, which is necessary for obtaining representative product formulation in the case library.

K.D. Ashley and D.G. Bridge (Eds.): ICCBR 2003, LNAI 2689, pp. 465–478, 2003.
© Springer-Verlag Berlin Heidelberg 2003

Input formulations take the form of a simple suggestion on improved product formulation, optimized cases or a collection of batch tests. After determining the most similar formulation cluster within the case library using Principal Component similarity factor and Mahalanobis distance, these can be validated with the help of T^2 and Q-statistics using Principal Component models. Validated input formulations can be directly fed to the case library if they are not duplicates. Those input formulations, which do not pass the multivariate validation, are examined for problematic parameters. Variables, which exceed the univariate control limit, can be detected using control charts. If however parameters are within the control range, the relationship between them can be studied by employing the most similar cases as a template. If input formulations do not pass the test, the following action plan is implemented: firstly, the problematic or culprit variables will be adjusted to fit the historical dataset; secondly, the product formulation cluster can be extended by changing the control limits of those variables, which do not affect the overall performance of product formulations while improving economical factors. Finally, if product formulations, which promise an improvement of performance attributes, cannot be adjusted to match the available datasets in the case library, new product formulations have to be devised and extensively tested before integration within the case library.   The proposed system thus offers the integration of consistent properties within the case library, the maintenance of multivariate specification and a feature to identify problem variables with the help of validated product formulations. Furthermore, the case library only contains good data points, which can be utilized to optimize formulations, predict missing information and identify key parameters. In connection with the retrieval of desirable product formulations, the system allows maximum flexibility within the manufacturing operation and restricts quality deviation. Nonetheless, a wide range of performance attributes can be generated by having a broad diversity in product formulations.

The next section gives an overview of the hybrid system and highlights its advantages and limitations. The synergistic use of Multivariate and univariate data validation modules will be explained and the role of CBR for identifying problem variables will be described. In Section four, a case study within a polymeric manufacturing company will demonstrate the benefit of this system for the industry.

2   System Overview

Figure 1 shows an overview of the hybrid system. The individual blocks are numbered for clarity. Input formulations (1) such as collections of batch tests, mathematically optimized (3) or hypothetically forwarded product formulations enter the system for validation. Furthermore, queries can be directly passed on to the case library (2) for a similarity analysis. A relational database with connectivity to a CBR engine capable of performing different similarity analyses builds up the CBR system. After removing any obvious outliers (4), the most similar data cluster (8) to the input formulations will be calculated (6) to validate the data. Using the principal component models derived from the selected data cluster in the case library (5), the principal component scores and from it the estimated parameters (7) can be utilized to validate the data in a multivariate way. T-square analysis (9) represents the deviation of the input formulation from the data population in the case library [1] whereas Q-statistics

(10) monitors the goodness-of-fit between the input formulation and the model [2]. Input formulations, which pass the two-mentioned tests are considered as validated and can be retained in the case library (11). Residual charts are utilized to identify problem variables associated with invalid input formulations (12).

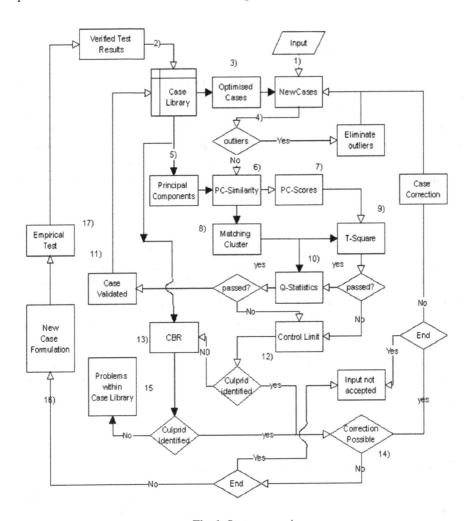

Fig. 1. System overview

In special cases, where the test is multivariate invalid and the residuals are within control limit, the problem could arise on the ground of incorrect interrelations between parameters, low variability or exceptionally asymmetric distribution of the data. At this stage, a CBR system (13) is employed, which finds the most similar cases as a template. This can be analyzed against the pattern of the input formulation using charts illustrating the course of standardized variables with the most similar cases. If parameters are adjustable, the corrected input formulation has to re-enter the system for re-validation (14). Otherwise, either a new product formulation has to be established or the parameter control limits have to be redefined (16). In such a case, the formulation has to be empirically tested before it enters the case library (17). In an extreme situation, where the culprit-parameters are not identifiable, the problem lies within the data cluster selected from the case library (15). Here, the data cluster has to be re-examined to ensure enough parameter variability.

2.1 Case Base Reasoning System

As part of this product formulation and recommendation system, a conventional CBR system has been established with a specially designed relational database, which serves as the case library. With the system, three different similarity functions (*SIM*) are used. Nearest neighbor relation [3] between the query $(x \in X)$ and the case library $(c \in C)$ $NN(x,c) :\Leftrightarrow \forall c_i \in C : SIM(x,c) \geq SIM(x,c_i)$ perfectly works for general queries on product recommendations, whereas simple Euclidean scores with unified weight allocation $SIM(x,c) = 1/n(\sum 1/(1+|x_i - c_i|)$ provides the ideal template for examining invalid input formulation patterns against most similar cases in the case library. For more specific queries, Fuzzy Logic scores $SIM(x,c) :\Leftrightarrow \forall c^* \in C : \mu_x(c) \geq \mu_x(c^*)$ can be generated [4]. To carry out effective reasoning, Fuzzy Logic rules as a powerful decision support accept imprecise and vague formulations and translate multiple antecedents (if Y is A) into a possibility measure for the consequent (then Z=B) $P_{C|A} = \sup \min[\mu_A(x), \mu_C(x)]$ from the case library C. To make some antecedents more important than others, weighting factors (*f*) enter into the model $\mu_A(x)^f = \max[(1-f), \mu_A(x)], \forall x \in X, f \in [0,1]$ changing the possibility of the consequent to $P_{C|A} = \min[P_{C_1|A_1}^{f_1}, P_{C_2|A_2}^{f_2}, ..., P_{C_n|A_n}^{f_n}]$.

Compared to the conventional system, stricter rules are imposed on the retention of input formulations in the case library. The formulations can be integrated within the case library either after a multivariate validation or through empirically tested formulations. Cases are grouped into different product formulation clusters. New input formulations are validated against that cluster which is most similar to it.

2.2 PCA Similarity Factor and Mahalanobis Distance

It is not useful to analyze input formulations containing a collection of experimental results with the entire case library, since this approach affects the efficiency of the analysis and increases the computational load. For this reason, we select a data cluster, so-called candidate pool, which is most similar to our input formulation [5]. The candidate pools can either be a set of predefined product formulations or dynamically moving data windows, which screen the case library to identify an area most similar to the input formulation. The latter is more appropriate for chronologically recorded datasets and allows comparing process behavior between the input formulation and previously recorded information in the case library. Thus, such a method is predestined for identifying abnormal situations and fault diagnosis within process monitoring. Predefined candidate pools, however, hold time independent information about data cluster such as variability, relationships among parameters and tendencies and serve as a template for supervised pattern matching.

The principal component model ($Z_{n \times k}$) of input formulation ($X_{i \times n}$) contains k number of eigenvectors corresponding to n variables. The same type of model ($Y_{n \times k}$) has to be built for the candidate pool ($C_{j \times n}$). The k number of models can be determined using stopping rules such as cross validation, Scree-plot or individual residual variances, where $k \leq n$. Consequently the dimension of PC-scores for the input formulation decreases to $i \times k$ and the PC-scores for the candidate pool will decline to $j \times k$. The PCA similarity factor [6] can be calculated accordingly using the equation 1. PCA- similarity can also be expressed in a geometrical form considering the angles (θ) between the eigenvectors of $Z_{n \times k}$ and $Y_{n \times k}$.

$$S = \frac{trace(Z'YY'Z)}{k} = \frac{1}{k} \sum_{m=1}^{k} \sum_{n=1}^{k} \cos^2 \theta_{mn} \tag{1}$$

The PCA similarity factor compares the similarity in term of spatial orientation. Datasets with similar spatial orientation however can be located far from each other. In this case, the distance similarity factor[5] based on the Mahalanobis distance defined in equation 2 can be employed, where Σ_X^+ is the pseudo inverse of input formulation covariance, $\overline{C}_{1 \times n}$ is the row matrix of the average values of n variables in each cluster within the case library and $\overline{X}_{1 \times n}$ is the average value matrix of the input formulations.

$$Dist_{Mahalanobis} = \sqrt{(\overline{C}_{1 \times n} - \overline{X}_{1 \times n}) \Sigma_X^+ (\overline{C}_{1 \times n} - \overline{X}_{1 \times n})'} \tag{2}$$

2.3 Multivariate Validation

Based on the selected candidate pool, a Principal Component Analysis is performed, which is a multivariate projection method. In recent years, multivariate analyses are often utilized to analyze databases accumulated in industry in order to improve process performance and product quality. Improving the operations of existing processes involves developing better methods for the analysis of historical operating policies, process trouble-shooting, process monitoring, abnormal situation detection, fault isolation and process and product optimization [7].

To generate PCA models, the eigenvectors ($z_i \in Z$) associated with the covariance matrix (Σ) of the original dataset and the corresponding eigenvalues ($l_i \in L$) of those Principal Components, which account for the most variation within the dataset, are used to transform n correlated variables $[x_1, x_2,...,x_n]$ into k new uncorrelated variables $[p_1, p_2,...,p_k]$ where $k \leq n$ [8]. Accordingly, a high dimensional and complex dataset can be reduced to a simpler and less complex data image reflecting most of the coherent information in the data multitude [9]. To find out k, we use Individual Residual Variances as a stopping rule, considering over 85% of explained variability within the dataset [10].

To compute PCA, batch method and neuro-PCA have been suggested in the literature [11]. For relatively small case dimensions, the batch method is often the preferred method. The computational requirement can increase to an unmanageable degree if the number of parameters grows excessively. The generalized Hebbian algorithm, Oja Rules, and the Rubnner Model as well as the Adaptive Principal Component Extraction (APEX) and the Földiák's model are the main Principal Component Analysis methods based on Neural Network.

Principal Component Scores of the suggested formulations can be calculated using the Principal Component model derived from the candidate pool C. Here, the data is standardized by subtracting the row matrix of the mean values $\overline{C}_{1\times n}$ and by dividing it by the row matrix of the standard deviation $\sigma_{1\times n}$. The Principal Component scores ($P_{j\times k}$) of the selected cluster in the case library, which are defined in equation 3, are calculated using the eigenvectors Z retained in the model. To generate the scores for the input-formulation, $C_{j\times n}$ is replaced by the values in the input formulation $X_{r\times n}$ with r number of inputs.

$$P_{j\times k} = [(C_{j\times n} - (\overline{C}'_{1\times n} \cdot 1_{1\times j})') . / (\sigma'_{1\times n} \cdot 1_{1\times j})'] Z_{n\times k} \tag{3}$$

T-Square test as a multivariate validation can be performed using either the batch or model based approach. To reduce computational load and test-sensitivity, which can be caused by random variation and noise within the input data, the latter is the preferred approach. Here, the test data are validated against the estimated product features from Principal Component models. The use of a principal component model has the following advantages:

    a.   The case is validated in a multivariate way accounting for interrelationships among parameters.

    b.   A model is used instead of the whole data group in the case library. This improves computational load.

    c.   Cases are often subjected to noises. Using a principal Component Model we ignore those parts of the dataset, which contribute to a small variation within the case library.

    d.   Instead of monitoring each parameter, a single value will give us the information about the validity of a case.

Since we need to estimate the value of parameters using the model prior to the T-square test, different algorithms have been suggested in the literature to perform this task. General PCA defined in equation 4 and Parallel Factor analysis for batch examination in equation 5 are often used for static systems [12],

$$X_{r\times n} = \hat{X}_{r\times n} + E_{r\times n} = P_{r\times k} . Z'_{n\times k} + E_{r\times n} \tag{4}$$

where $\hat{X}_{j\times n}$ is defined as the predicted values of an input formulation $X_{j\times n}$, Z as the Eigenvectors (Loading vector) and E as the prediction Error for r number of inputs, n number of variables and k number of Principle Components retained in the model.

$$X_{r \times i \times n} = \hat{X}_{r \times i \times n} + E_{r \times i \times n} = P_{r \times k} \cdot (W_{n \times k} \circ Z_{n \times k})' + E_{r \times i \times n} \quad (5)$$

Instead of loading vectors alone, we use scaled vectors partitioned into 2 Parts W (weight) and Z (eigenvector) using Khatri-Rao product within PARAFAC. For dynamic Systems, Multiscale PCA, DISSIM based on Karhunen-Love algorithm and moving PCA [13] have been employed successfully.

Having generated the PC-models and the estimated dataset, T^2 can be calculated using equation 6 where Σ is the covariance matrix and x_i is the value of the input formulation. A T^2 value below the control limit based on the F-distribution demonstrates a sound input formulation, which matches the candidate pool in a multivariate manner. Here, equation 7 shows the calculation of the control limit. $F_{n,j-n,\alpha}$ symbolizes an F-value in respect of n variables, j observations and a confidence level of α. It is also possible to calculate T^2 using the Principal Component scores P defined in equation 8 with respect to diagonal matrix L (equivalent to eigenvalue) [14].

$$T^2_{calc} = (x_i - \hat{x}_i)' \Sigma^{-1} (x_i - \hat{x}_i) \quad (6)$$

$$T^2_{n,j,\alpha} = \frac{n(j-1)}{j-n} F_{n,j-n,\alpha} \quad (7)$$

$$T^2_{calc} = P' L^{-1} P \quad (8)$$

In contrast to T^2 test, Q-statistics is based on unexplained residuals and shows the variation, which cannot be explained by the Principal Component based model. It is complementary to T-square. Growing T-square and moderate Q-statistics shows a drift of the query with regard to the variation within the historical case library. High Q-statistics and moderate T-square however are signs for an external cause, which affects the suggested input formulation. The equation 9 shows the calculation of residuals Q, where e is defined as individual elements of the error matrix E and p_i is the Principal Component scores, which are not retained in the model². Clearly, it can be seen that this model tries to explain those parts of the model, which are not described by Principal Components. It is in fact the sum of the Principal Component scores, which are not retained in the model. Using the input formulation $x \in X$ and the retained eigenvectors in the model $z \in Z$, the error matrix is defined as shown in equation 10.

$$Q = (x - \hat{x})'(x - \hat{x}) = e'e = \sum_{l=k+1}^{n} p_l^2 \quad (9)$$

$$E_{r \times n} = X_{r \times n} (I - Z_{n \times k} Z'_{n \times k}) \quad (10)$$

With regard to the control limit of Q-statistics, some literatures suggest the use of χ^2. This approach is not correct and should be replaced by Q_a defined in equations 11 and 12 where l_i is the Eigenvalues, K the number of Principal Components retained in the model and p the number of variables. The upper and lower tail of distribution is represented by C_a [15]. Input formulations, which pass the T^2 test and Q-test, are seen as validated and can be saved as a new case in the case library.

$$h_0 = 1 - \frac{2 \sum\limits_{i=k+1}^{p} li \sum\limits_{i=k+1}^{p} li^3}{3 \sum\limits_{i=k+1}^{p} li^2} \tag{11}$$

$$Q_a = \sum\limits_{i=k+1}^{p} li \left[\frac{C_a \sqrt{2 \left(\sum\limits_{i=k+1}^{p} li^2 \right) h_0^2}}{\sum\limits_{i=k+1}^{p} li} + \frac{\left(\sum\limits_{i=k+1}^{p} li^2 \right) h_0 (h_0 - 1)}{\left(\sum\limits_{i=k+1}^{p} li^2 \right)} + 1 \right]^{1/h_0} \tag{12}$$

2.4 Identification of Culprits

Cases, which pass T^2 and Q-test are considered as validated and can be retained in the case library as a new case. Cases, which do not pass the test, have to be examined using univariate techniques to identify parameters, which cause the problem. In equation 13, each parameter is measured against an upper and lower confidence level, where σ represents the standard deviation, κ the upper and lower control limits and $t_{df,\alpha}$ the t-distribution with df degree of freedom and α level of confidence. The nth average value of each variable is symbolized by $\bar{x}_n$.

$$\kappa = \bar{x}_n \pm t_{df,\alpha} \cdot \sigma_i \tag{13}$$

If the multivariate tests show an invalid case query despite the case values being within the allowed boundary, then the interrelationship between variables can cause the invalidity. To compare these interrelations, graphs of all parameters are compared with the most similar cases to identify interrelational problems. With regard to a single case query and a unified historical case formulation cluster, the similarity calculation is based on the Euclidean distance. Using the entire historical case library, the similarity of a series of input tests, which has been performed under the same condition, can be assessed by using the candidate pool.

If the case query cannot be amended in the way that it fits the multivariate nature of the historical case library then it might be possible that there is a distribution problem within the historical case library, which has to be changed. All case queries, which can be amended, are fed back to the system after the correction. In a new run the input formulations will be retested. If it is not possible to match an input formulation to the dataset in the case library, this formulation can be integrated in the case library after empirical evaluations.

2.5 Case Retention

Here, the process of case retention in the case library falls into four groups. During optimal manufacturing processes, cases can be collected for the entry into the case library. Here, it is vital to record realistic and well-monitored parameters. Secondly, further input formulations resulting from tests in laboratories or experiences can be added to the case library if they match the pattern of a candidate pool in the case library. Additionally, they have to contribute to the variability of the dataset in the case library. If there is a mismatch between the input formulation and the candidate pool, it is possible to redefine the parameter limits within the case library, provided that the parameter change does not affect the overall performance of the product. The decision about this can be made by regression models, empirical tests or by analyzing the historical dataset. The latter presupposes a good knowledge about the interaction between variables. Within the scope of this project, general linear models and multivariate data projection methods such as self-organizing maps were utilized to outline the interactions between parameters. Finally, a new product formulation can be established as a new candidate pool if the parameters cannot be adjusted to match the historical dataset. In the last two cases, it is essential to validate the formulations empirically before they enter the case library.

The variability in the case library in connection with each candidate pool provides the necessary scope for improved economical process attributes, efficient manufacturing route and optimized raw material usage while performance attributes remain desirably limited to a specific application score allowing consistent product formulation. An improved flexibility in connection with product performance qualities can be achieved by an increasing diversity of candidate pools.

3 Case Study

The research work reported in this paper is part of an undertaking, which is a collaborative work between the University of Ulster and the medical packaging company Perfecseal Ltd. in the United Kingdom. Perfecseal Ltd. supplies the medical packaging industry with proprietary formulated adhesive coated substrates. Fiber free opening, controlled bond strength and porosity as well as stability of physical properties during and after sterilization characterize the nature of the products. Data on normal manufacturing operations such as raw material inputs and process conditions have been recorded systematically with regard to optimal product performance attributes. To extend the assortment of potential formulation for more flexibility in the market place and to select a manageable number of commercially viable products with a wide range of applications, laboratory based trials provide alternative formulations. Systematic validation and integration of these results within the case library is vital for the selection of quality products with improved cost factors, optimized manufacturing routes and efficient use of raw materials.

Within the scope of this project, empirically validated laboratory based formulations enter into the case library along with information on normal manufacturing operations. These can be a newly designed product or the extension of a previously established formulation. To avoid a profuse growth of cases, only representative ones are transferred from the database to the case library while duplicates are removed. Eighteen different product formulations have been established here. Laboratory based formulations were used solely to improve the variability of raw material proportion and process values. Before entering any input formulations such as simple queries, suggestions for a new product and optimized or extrapolated cases into the case library, these were validated against available candidate pools. Cases marked as invalid have to pass laboratory tests or be implemented successfully in the main manufacturing area before they enter the case library.

To find the appropriate candidate pool for a multivariate analysis, Matlab was utilized to perform Similarity PCA and to calculate the distance similarity factor. The T^2 analysis based on original values of the dataset may result in the type I error due to the random variation and noise within the dataset. In contrast, T^2 based on PCA improves the results. To minimize type I error, a comparative analysis of alternative methods is accessible in the literature [16]. A series of Matlab programs were established to calculate the above-mentioned calculations (see figure 2). Control limits are adjustable to different confidence levels. As an alternative approach, the *Chi*-square based control limit can be activated as an alternative to the T^2 control limit based on F-distribution [1]. For non-Gaussian distributions, it was proved that the *Chi*-square converges the T^2 control limit with a growing number of samples [17]. The Q-statistics in figure 3 show the observations 1, 13 and 25 as well as 26, which cannot be modeled well with the PCA and need to be examined more closely. The use of original values instead of Principal Component model offers the advantage of avoiding Q-statistics but it increases the chance of occurrence of type I error. The synergistic use of Q-statistics, T^2 based on PCA and original values minimizes the number of observations, which have to be examined more closely in respect of contributing culprits. The three plots in figure 2 and 3 illustrate the fact that observation 23 is the only invalid case in this example.

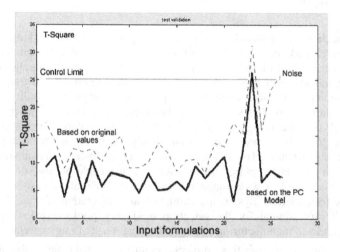

Fig. 2. T^2 analysis

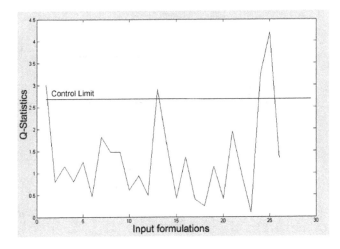

Fig. 3. Q-statistics

To identify the culprit parameters, univariate control charts were employed in connection with those observations, which did not pass the multivariate validation. As shown in figure two, the observation number 23 is over the T^2-limit and needs to be examined more closely. The standardized values of important parameters ($\bar{x}_i = 0, \sigma_i = 1$) are plotted within figure 4. As can be seen from the graph, variables one and two are over the control limit.   Additionally, similar cases can be interactively selected or estimated from the PCA model and activated within the univariate control chart as in figures four and five. This approach allows examining the behavioral patterns of the input formulations or in this instance the test in contrast to the most similar cases. The tendency of the three initial variables within figure four shows that the invalidity of the test is not just due to the residuals but it moreover illustrates the relational dependencies between the variables. Figure 5 demonstrates the behavioral pattern of a valid input formulation in contrast to the most similar case. Although here the patterns are slightly different, the interdependencies between variables remain relatively similar. Interactively, any number of cases with different similarity degrees here can be selected using a program written in the Matlab environment.

3.1 Generation of New Product Formulations

To generate desirable product formulations from the case library, different similarity analyses (mentioned in section 2.1) have been established. As a CBR engine, we use Induce-it and a Matlab based program. The case library is a relational database with tables on raw material proportion and process parameters. Furthermore individual raw material and operation expenses are recorded here along with the costs for alternative constituents and process routes. Each entry is assigned to a specific product formulation and is indexed accordingly. The optimal manufacturing route in most

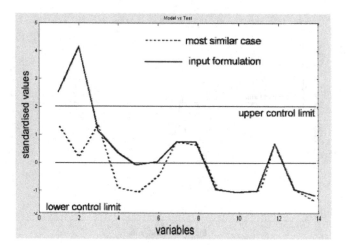

Fig. 4. Univariate Control Chart

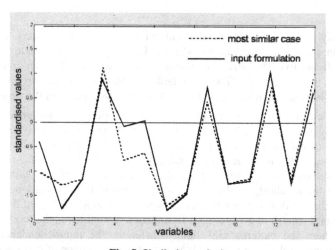

Fig. 5. Similarity analysis

cases is the most economical setting. For this reason the total cost for each formulation generated from the available raw materials and process expenses is forwarded to the CBR system along with the product performance attributes for the formulation of appropriate products. Highest weight is given to the total product formulation cost and the most crucial quality parameters. To give high weights to those parameters with high variability causes the system to get stuck in a specified span of observations and consequently it is the cause for inefficient results. As a rule of thumb, we allocate high weight to variables with low variability and vice versa. In connection with best formulations, the process parameters and raw material proportions can be selected and examined more closely using the database. Selected cases can be used for optimization and extrapolation. Within this project we used the Simplex method for linear optimization and Genetic Algorithm or the Quasi-Newton method for non-linear optimization. The latter was used for optimizations with a relatively large number of constraints. Mathematically modified formulations were validated and empirically tested.

4 Conclusion

The forwarded work offers a systematic approach to maintain and retain product formulations in a case library. As with standard CBR systems, comparable cases can be retrieved, adapted and optimized for diagnostic, decision-making and problem-solving reasons. As an extension to the conventional method, any input formulations are validated against a candidate pool, a defined cluster of recorded datasets in the case library, which is most similar to the input formulations, prior to any retention. Problem variables are identified with the help of sound and realistic datasets in the case library. As part of the data validation, interrelational dependencies between variables are taken into account using multivariate analyses and their behavioral pattern can be examined using the CBR system.

The synergistic effect of CBR and multivariate data validation provided an opportunity to have an increased variability in process parameters and raw material proportion while a relatively consistent quality could be balanced within each candidate pool. This feature was helpful to establish flexibility within the manufacturing area without affecting the quality. However, this alone does not provide a comprehensive variability in the performance attributes in terms of a relatively broader range of process parameters and constituent proportions. For this, a diversity of clusters was stipulated within the case library to counteract this effect. With these twin approaches, the most appropriate formulation having the desired quality with minimum cost could easily be determined.

Acknowledgement. The authors wish to express their sincere thanks to Invest Northern Ireland (INI) Ltd. and Perfecseal Ltd., for supporting this project through a START grant No. ST202.

References

1. N. Ye, S.M. Emran, et al., Multivariate Statistical Analysis of Audit trails for Host-based Intrusion Detection, IEEE Transaction on Computers, July 2002, 51, 7
2. Computer-Based Monitoring and Fault-Diagnosis: A Chemical Process Case Study, ISA Transactions, 2001, 40, 85–98,
3. K.P. Sankar, S.D. Tharam, S.Y. Daniel (eds), On the Notation of Similarity in Case Based Reasoning and Fuzzy Theory, in Soft Computing in Case Based Reasoning, 2001, Springer Verlag,
4 K.P. Sankar, S.D. Tharam, S.Y. Daniel (eds), Fuzzy Logic Based Neural Network for Case Based Reasoning, in Soft Computing in Case Based Reasoning, 2001, Springer Verlag,

5. A. Singhal D.E. Seborg, Matching Patterns from Historical Data Using PCA and Distance Similarity Factors, Proceedings of the American Control Conference, VA June 2001, Arlington, 25–27

6. W. J. Krzanowski, The combination of PCA Between-Groups Comparison of Principal Components. *J. Amer. Stat. Assoc.*, 1979, **74**, 367, 703–707,

7. T. Kourti, Process Analysis and Abnormal Situation Detection, IEEE Control Systems Magazine, October 2002

8. J.E. Jackson, A User Guide to Principal Components, John Wiley & Sons Inc, 1991, pp. 4–25,

9. P. Ralston, G. DePuy, J.H. Graham, Computer-based Monitoring and Fault Diagnosis: Chemical Process Case Study, ISA Transactions, 2001, 40, 85–98

10. J.E. Jackson, A User Guide to Principal Components, John Wiley & Sons Inc, pp. 41–50, (1991)

11. K.I Diamantaras, S.Y. Kung, Principal Component Neural Networks Theory and Applications, A Wiley-Interscience Publication, 1996, 74–121,

12. D. J. Louwerse, A. K. Smilde, Multivariate statistical process control of batch processes based on three-way models, Chemical Engineering Science, 2000, 55, 1225–1235

13. M. Kano, K. Nagao, et al., Comparison of statistical process monitoring methods: application to the Eastman challenge problem, Computers and Chemical Engineering, 2000, 24, 175–181,

14. J.E. Jackson, A User Guide to Principal Components, John Wiley & Sons Inc, 1991, 21–24

15. J.E. Jackson, G. Mudholkar, Control Procedures for residuals associated with Principal Component Analysis, Technometrics, 1979, 21, 341–349

16. R.T. Fouladi, R.Ronald, D. Yockey, Type I Error Control of Two-Group Multivariate Tests on Means under conditions of Heterogenous Correlation structure and varied Multivariate Distributions, Commun. Statist.-Simula, 2002, 31, 3, 375–400

17. A. Dembo, Q.M. Shao, Large and Moderate Deviation for Hotteling's T2-Statistics, Stanford University and University of Oregon, 1991

Product Recommendation with Interactive Query Management and Twofold Similarity

Francesco Ricci, Adriano Venturini, Dario Cavada, Nader Mirzadeh,
Dennis Blaas, and Marisa Nones

eCommerce and Tourism Research Laboratory
ITC-irst
via Sommarive 18
38050 Povo, Italy
{ricci,venturi,dacavada,mirzadeh,blaas,nones}@itc.it

Abstract. This paper describes an approach to product recommendation that combines in a novel way content- and collaborative-based filtering techniques. The system helps the user to specify a query that filters out unwanted products in electronic catalogues (content-based). Moreover, if the query produces too many or no results, the system suggests useful query changes that save the gist of the original request. This process goes on iteratively till a reasonable number of products is selected. Then, the selected products are ranked exploiting a case base of recommendation sessions (collaborative-based). Among the user selected items the system ranks higher items that are similar to those selected by other users in similar sessions (twofold similarity). The approach has been applied to a web travel application and it has been evaluated with real users. The proposed approach: a) reduces dramatically the number of user queries, b) reduces the number of browsed products and c) the selected items are found first on the ranked list.

1 Introduction

Recommender systems are applications exploited in e-commerce sites to suggest interesting and useful products and provide consumers information to facilitate the decision-making process [12]. Recommender systems research is motivated primary by the need to cope with: information overload, lack of user knowledge in a specific domain, cost-benefit tradeoff optimization, interaction cost minimization.

Building real operational recommender systems that tackle all the above problems is extremely complex and requires: long user requirements elicitation, task modelling, tuning of recommendation algorithms, development and test of the graphical user interface. This holistic approach has been stressed in our previous paper [10] where we described an application to trip planning, aimed at recommending to a leisure traveller a good bundling of trip products (locations, accommodation, attractions, activities, events). In this paper we want to focus on the basic recommendation technology that we have developed, stressing the

K.D. Ashley and D.G. Bridge (Eds.): ICCBR 2003, LNAI 2689, pp. 479–493, 2003.
© Springer-Verlag Berlin Heidelberg 2003

general aspects, its wider applicability, and presenting the empirical evaluation results conducted with real users. The ultimate goal of the proposed recommendation technology is to help its users through a ranked list of products (from electronic catalogues) taking into account a wide variety of needs and wants (explicit vs. implicit, must vs. optional, long term vs. short term, personal vs. group) in an efficient and effective way.

Recommender systems implicitly assume that user's needs and constraints can be converted/mapped, by means of appropriate recommendation algorithms, into product selections using "knowledge" managed by the system. Burke distinguishes three types of recommendation approaches: collaborative- or social-filtering; content-based and knowledge-based [4]. Here we distinguish only between collaborative- and content-based assuming a more comprehensive definition of knowledge. Hence, for instance, even a simple archive of sequences containing the items bought by users, is a source of knowledge for a collaborative-based approach[1].

In content-based filtering approaches, the user expresses needs, benefits and constraints and the system matches this description with items contained in a catalogue of products. Products are typically ranked according to the degree of matching with the user query. Content-based approaches may possibly exploit the history of past user queries to build a user profile, ultimately stressing the importance of matching the needs collected during a specific recommendation session. Case-Based Reasoning recommendations have often been viewed as a derivation of content-based approaches, where the problem description comprises the user needs and constraints and the solution(s) is (are) the items retrieved. Content-based approaches appear to have as a major drawback to be unable to produce a sufficient degree of diversity, as they stick to the explicit needs expressed in the user query [15]. Moreover, designing dialog support techniques aimed at helping the user to express explicitly his needs has always been considered as a major issue in the CBR community. This has motivated a lot of research on conversational case-based reasoning [8,9], non-standard retrieval approaches (order-based [3], query tweaking [5]), attribute selection methods [13], structured case retrieval [6].

Collaborative-based approaches [2] collect user ratings on offered products and/or user previously bought product information to identify similarities between users and cross recommend to a user those products, not yet considered, and highly ranked or bought by similar users. Collaborative approaches are strong in suggesting new items that the user may not know. Conversely, collaborative-based approaches require a vast amount of user feedback before producing satisfactory recommendations and are not able to take into account session-dependent (contextual) user needs. Moreover collaborative filtering is applicable only when products to be recommended are standardized, i.e. sold in the same form to several users, and a user is likely to buy many items of the same

---

[1] Actually there are other recommendation methodologies, see for instance [5], but because of lack of space we limit the discussion to collaborative- and content-based approaches that are by far the most popular.

type through the same web site. Product types that do have these characteristics include CDs, books and movies. But there are other products (e.g. travels, cameras, cars, computers) that are not amenable to collaborative-based recommendation. It is not likely that information about the cars previously owned by a user could predict the next car a user may buy. Or, the fact that a user once travelled to New York does not mean that the user will never go there again (a collaborative-based recommender does not suggest twice the same product).

The above mentioned shortcomings of both content- and collaborative-based filtering has motivated us to design a more powerful methodology, which is described in Section 2. The formal definition of case base and query model is given in Section 3. Section 4 describes the whole recommendation process and its sub-components: the query evaluation and product rankings algorithms. The empirical evaluation of the proposed methodology is given in Section 5. Finally, Section 6 gives the conclusion and outlines some future work.

2   A New Methodology for Recommender Systems

We have designed a novel hybrid collaborative/content based recommendation methodology that is further motivated by the following requirements:

- Products may have a complex structure, where the final recommended item is an aggregation of more elementary components. For instance a trip may bundle a flight, an accommodation and a rental car, or a desktop computer may be sold together with a printer, a monitor and a scanner.
- Both short term (goal oriented) preferences and long term (stable) preferences must influence the recommendation. Short term preferences are highly situation dependent, tend to be hard constraints, and should dominate long term preferences. For instance, if the user searches for a business flight the system must shade the influence of a previous history of 'no frills' flights bought by the user for a leisure travel.
- The recommendation methodology must fit into the ubiquitous form-based information search interfaces that the majority of e-Commerce web systems provide. This would make the methodology seamlessly pluggable into existing systems.
- The lack of an initial memory of any user interactions with the system or buying should not prevent completely the applicability of the methodology. Thus, unregistered users should be allowed to get recommendations.

In the proposed methodology a case models a unique human-machine interaction session and collects: all the information provided by the user during the session, the products selected, and some stable user related preferences and demographic data if he is registered. A recommender system based on this methodology stores these cases in a repository (case base) in addition to the catalogues of products (databases). This is in contrast with standard CBR recommender systems that view the catalogue of products as a case base.

All input features provided by the user during an interaction session fall into two (not mutually exclusive) categories: content and collaborative features. Content features are those features that can be constrained in the users' queries, and they are used as descriptors of the products in the catalogues. For instance, in a hotel description the hotel category and the presence of a garage are content features. Conversely, the nationality of the user or the travel purpose could be used to describe a trip, and naturally is not part of the any description of the products found in the catalogue. In this setting these are collaborative features since they can be used to measure user/session similarity.

When the recommender searches for similar recommendation sessions, it uses the collaborative features acquired from the user. We have applied various strategies to obtain these features. In our first recommender system (ITR [10]), they are collected in the first stage of the interaction, whereas a second application (Dietorecs [7]) even the products selected at a given point play the role of collaborative features. After a small set of similar recommendation sessions is computed, the items in the result set of the user query are ranked using a double similarity computation. A score for each item in the result set is computed by maximizing the product of the case similarity (between the current case and the retrieved cases) and the item similarity (between a selected item and the item of the same type contained in the retrieved case). The selected items are finally presented to the user in decreasing score order. The overall effect is that content features dominates the selection process and determine what is in the result set. Then the collaborative features are exploited to order the result set, popping up items that are recommendable because they are similar to those selected by other users in similar recommendation sessions.

We have empirically evaluated the proposed methodology in a between subjects test. A first users group planned a vacation with a system built with the proposed recommendation methodology. A second group solved the same task with a system variant in which we discarded the interactive query management and ranking functions. We have proved that the proposed methodology drastically reduces the number of queries issued, the number of items that the user browsed, and sorts the result list in such a way that selected items are displayed earlier.

3   Case Model

In our approach, a case represents a user interaction with the system, and therefore is built incrementally during the recommendation session. A case comprises the following main components:

- **Collaborative Features (clf)** are features that describe general user's characteristics, wishes, constraints or goals (e.g. desire to relax or to practise sports). They capture preferences relevant to the user's decision-making process, which cannot generally be mapped into the features of products in the electronic catalogues. These features are used to measure case (session) similarity. A knowledge of the domain and the decision process is essential to select the right collaborative features [10].

- **Content Queries (cnq)** are queries posed over the catalogues of products. Content queries are built by constraining (content) features that describe products listed in the catalogues. Products may belong to different types (e.g. an accommodation or an event).

- **Cart** contains the set of products chosen by the user during the recommendation session represented by the case. A cart represents a meaningful (from the user's point of view) bundling of different products. For instance, a travel cart may contain some destinations, some accommodations, and some additional attractions.

- **Vote** is a collection of votes given by the user to the products contained in the cart.

Figure 1 shows an example in the tourism domain. It represents a user, who is single, has a medium budget, and is looking for a vacation (destinations and accommodation) where he can practice some sports and relax (collaborative features). Then there are the queries (over the product catalogues) constructed by constraining content features of the products: for instance, he wants to stay in a three star hotel, which has a private parking lot and has a cost per night less then 50 Euro. The destination should be a resort suitable for rock climbing and hiking activities. Given these preferences, the user is supposed to have selected and added to his cart the Azalea Hotel, and the Cavalese and Canazei resorts. In this example, the user has selected two destinations by querying the destination catalogue. Note that, the user has not yet specified any vote over the selected products (vote=null).

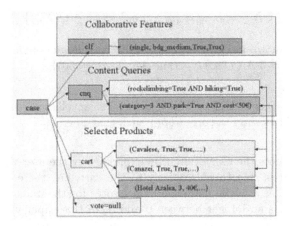

Fig. 1. An example of case. The collaborative features are TravelParty, Budget, Sports, and Relax.

More formally, the Case Base (CB) is defined as following:

$$CB \subseteq CLF \times CNQ \times CART \times V$$

Collaborative Features Space (CLF) is a vector space $CLF = \prod_{i=1}^{l} CLF_i$, where CLF_i is set of symbols, a finite subset of the integers or a real interval. In our example, $CLF = TravelParty \times Budget \times Sports \times Relax$. Where $TravelParty = \{single, family\}$, $Budget = \{low, medium, high\}$ and $Sports = Relax = \{True, False\}$. In the example shown, the features specified by the users are $clf = (single, medium, True, True)$.

Content Queries (CNQ) is the space of all the queries that the user can specify over products in the catalogues. We assume that each product p can be represented as a vector of features $X = \prod_{i=1}^{n} F_i$. F_i can be, as above, a set of symbols, a finite subset of the integers or a real interval. A catalogue $CX \subset X$ is said to be of type X. A query q over a catalogue CX is the conjunction of simple constraints, where each constraint involves only one feature. More formally, $q = (c_1, \cdots, c_m)$, where $m \leq n$, and:

$$c_k = \begin{cases} f_{i_k} = v_k & \text{if } F_{i_k} \text{ is symbolic} \\ l_k \leq f_{i_k} \leq u_k & \text{if } F_{i_k} \text{ is finite integer or real} \end{cases} \quad (1)$$

where f_{i_k} is a variable of type (with domain) F_{i_k}, $v_k \in F_{i_k}$, and $l_k, u_k \in F_{i_k}$ are the boundaries for the range constraint on a real valued feature. Let $Q(X)$ be the space of all the queries over X. Furthermore, let us assume that there are N product types $X_1, \ldots, X_N$. Then we denote by $Q = \bigcup_{i=1}^{N} Q(X_i)$ the space of all the queries on the catalogues. We finally denote with $CNQ = \mathcal{P}(Q)$, the set of all subsets of queries over $X_i, \cdots, X_N$, i.e.

$$CNQ = \{cnq = \{q_1, \cdots q_k\} \ s.t. \ q_i \in Q(X_{j_i})\}$$

In the example shown in Figure 1, $cnq = \{(rockclimbing = true \ AND \ hiking = true), (category = 3 \ AND \ park = true \ AND \ cost \leq 50)\}$.

CART is defined as $CART = \mathcal{P}(\bigcup_{i=1}^{N} X_i)$, i.e. an element $cart \in CART$ is subsets of products: $cart = \{p_1, \cdots, p_k\}$ such that $p_i \in X_{j_i}$.

Vote (V) represents the case evaluation expressed by the user who has built it. The vote in fact is structured similarly to the cart, i.e., there is a elementary vote for the cart as a whole and elementary votes for the items in the cart. An elementary vote is an integer between 0 and 5. In this paper we shall not deal with this component since collaborative-filtering in our approach is not based on user votes (see [1] for a description of its usage in a more general case similarity metric).

4   Product Recommendation

This section describes the proposed approach to support the user in the selection and recommendation of products. The overall process is shown in Figure 2. The user interacts with the recommender system by querying recommendations about a product type (e.g., a destination). To simplify the notation, we will consider just one product space X, and $q \in cnq$ will denote the user's query. The system either recommends some products, or, in case the query fails, suggests some query refinements. The RecEngine module manages the request. First, it invokes the EvaluateQuery function (1) of the Intelligent Query Manager module (IQM), by passing the query. This function searches the catalogue for products matching the query. If too many[2] or no product matches the input query q, then EvaluateQuery analyzes q and determines a set of query refinements to suggest. These refinements are presented to the user as a set of features. If there are too many results then three features are selected and the user is asked to provide a value for one of them to narrow down the search result (attribute selection). Conversely if no result can be found the system explains to the user the cause of the failure, i.e., it lists those constraints that if relaxed would allow the query to return some results. The EvaluateQuery function is described in Section 4.1.

When the number of items retrieved is satisfactory then the products are ranked by invoking the Rank method (2). Rank receives the collaborative features clf of the current case and the set of products selected by the EvaluateQuery function. The clf features are used to retrieve the 10 most similar cases, and the products contained in these retrieved cases are then used to rank the user selected products. Finally, the ranked products are returned to the user. The Rank algorithm is described in Section 4.2.

4.1   EvaluateQuery Algorithm

The goal of the EvaluateQuery algorithm is to find out the products matching the content query expressed by the user. EvaluateQuery and the Intelligent Query Management module are aimed at helping the user to reformulate the query when failures occur. Because of lack of space we only sketch the description of that module. The reader is referred to [11] for further details.

The EvaluateQuery algorithm is described in Figure 3. It receives as input a query q, over a product catalog CX. It returns the products P matching the query q, and a set of query refinement suggestions R. R is a set of triples, each containing a feature f_{i_k}, a constraint c_k over the feature f_{i_k}, and the suggested operation op_k (add, modify, or remove from q). In line 1, the SearchCatalog function is invoked, passing the q query as parameter. The function searches through the catalogue for products matching q, and returns the set of matching products. Line 2 evaluates the size of the result set. If the number of selected products is above a certain threshold, the TightenQuery function is invoked (line 3). This function, using information related to the product catalogue data

---

[2] in our experiments this threshold was set to 10.

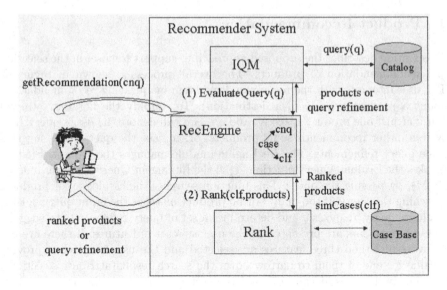

Fig. 2. Recommendation process.

distribution (entropy and mutual information), returns a set of features (three) suggested to the user to further constrain the search. The user can chose one (or more) and provide a value (symbolic feature) or a range of values (numeric feature).

Actually, TightenQuery returns a set of triples $(f_i, null, add)$, where f_i is a feature and $c_i = null$, since the TightenQuery function cannot guess the exact value (or range of values) the user may want to specify for a suggested feature. Line 5 tests the empty result set condition. If the result set is empty, the RelaxQuery function is called (line 6). This function searches for those q modifications (constraint relaxation) that will allow q to retrieve some results. The suggested modifications are again returned as set of triples (f_i, c_i, op_i), where $op_i = remove$ for symbolic features and $op_i = modify$ for finite integer or real features, and c_i represents the new (larger) range to be set. If neither relaxation nor tightening is invoked, the result set P is returned (line 9).

4.2   RankProducts Algorithm

The RankProducts algorithm ranks the products retrieved by EvaluateQuery. Ranking is computed exploiting two similarity metrics: first, the case base is accessed to retrieve the (10) most similar cases (reference cases) to the current one. This similarity-based retrieval uses the collaborative features. Then, the products contained in the carts of the retrieved reference cases (reference products) are used to sort the products selected by the user's query. The basic idea is that among the products in the result set of the query one will get a better score if it is similar/equal to a product (of the same type) bought by a user with similar needs and wants. The Figure 4 describes the algorithm in detail.

CX is the product catalog
q is the user's query
$P = \{p_1, \cdots, p_k\}$ the products selected by the user query q.
$R = \{(f_{i_1}, c_1, op_1), \cdots, (f_{i_m}, c_m, op_m)\}$, $op_j \in \{add, modify, remove\}$, c_j is a
       constraint on feature f_{i_j} to be: added, modified or removed (op_j)

$EvaluateQuery(q, CX)$
1   $P \leftarrow SearchCatalog(q, CX)$
2   **if** $Size(P) > threshold$
3       $R \leftarrow TightenQuery(q, CX)$
4   **return** R
5   **else if** $Size(P) = 0$
6       $R \leftarrow RelaxQuery(q, CX)$
7   **return** R
8   **else**
9   **return** P

Fig. 3. The EvaluateQuery algorithm.

The Rank function receives the current case c, the set of products P retrieved by the function EvaluateQuery, and the case base CB. It returns the products P ranked. First it retrieves from CB the reference cases RC (line 1). Here, the similarity query uses the collaborative features clf. In line 3, RP is defined as the products contained in the reference cases RC[3]. Note that products in RP and P are of the same type. In line 4, the Score of each product p_i is computed as the maximum of $Sim(c, rc_j) * Sim(p_i, rp_j)$ over all the reference products rp_j (the similarity functions are described in Section 4.3).

Computing the final product score as the multiplication of cases and products similarity mimics the collaborative-filtering (CF) approach, but there are some notable differences. First, differently from a standard CF approach, only the first nearest neighbor case is considered, i.e., the case that yields the maximum value for $Sim(c, rc_j) * Sim(p_i, rp_j)$. The rationale for this choice is that we can use the retrieved case to explain the score value to the user. Secondly, we do not consider the votes given by other users to the product to be scored, as is common in CF. Conversely, we use the similarity of the product to be scored to products selected in a similar case (user session) as a sort of implicit vote: if another user in a similar session has chosen that product or a similar one, this is an indication that this product fits the needs that are shared by the current user and the previous user.

Let us consider the following simple example. Let us assume that the collaborative features in CLF are TravelParty (symbolic), Budget (numeric), Sports

---

[3] For sake of simplicity we assume that each reference case rc_i contains just one product rp_i of the same type of the products to be ranked, but the same approach applies also when more products are contained in a case.

$RC = \{rc_1, \cdots, rc_{10}\}$ retrieved cases
$RP = \{rp_1, \cdots, rp_{10}\}$ products inside the reference cases
c is the current case
CB is the case base
$P = \{p_1, \cdots, p_k\}$ the products selected by the user query

---

$Rank(c, p, CB)$
1 $RC \leftarrow FindSimilarCases(c, CB)$
2 $RP \leftarrow ExtractReferenceProducts(RC)$
3 **for each** $p_i \in \{p_1, \cdots, p_k\} = P$
4      $Score(p_i) \leftarrow \max_{j=1 \cdots 10}\{Sim(c, rc_j) * Sim(p_i, rp_j)\}$
5 $P \leftarrow Sort\{p_1, \cdots, p_k\}$ according to $Score(p_i)$
6 **return** P

Fig. 4. The Rank algorithm.

(boolean), Relax (boolean), that the product features in X are DestName (symbolic), RockClimbing (boolean), Hiking (boolean), and that the collaborative features of the current case c are: $clf = (single, medium, true, true)$. Assume that a user query q has retrieved the products: $p_1 = (Predazzo, true, true)$ and $p_2 = (Cavalese, true, true)$. Then FindSimilarCases retrieves two cases rc_1, rc_2, whose similarities with the current case cc are $Sim(cc, rc_1) = 0.75$ and $Sim(cc, rc_2) = 1$. Let further assume that rc_1 and rc_2 contain the product $rp_1 = (Campiglio, true, true)$ and $rp_2 = (Cavalese, true, true)$ respectively. Moreover, the products similarities are (see Section 4.3 for the similarity definition): $Sim(p_1, rp_1) = 0.66$, $Sim(p_1, rp_2) = 0.66$, $Sim(p_2, rp_1) = 0.66$, $Sim(p_2, rp_2) = 1$. The score of each p_i is computed as the maximum of $Sim(cc, c_j) * Sim(p_i, rp_j)$, thus: $Score(p_1) = max\{0.75 * 0.66, 1 * 0.66\} = 0.66$, and $Score(p_2) = max\{0.75 * 0.66, 1 * 1\} = 1$. Then finally p_2 is scored better than p_1.

4.3 Similarity Measure

For both case and product similarity we use a modified version of the Euclidean Overlap Metric (HEOM) [16]. If $x, y \in \prod_{i=1}^{n} F_i$ are two generic feature vectors, then:

$$d(x, y) = \frac{1}{\sqrt{\sum_{i=1}^{n} w_i}} \sqrt{\sum_{i=1}^{n} w_i d_i(x_i, y_i)^2} \qquad (2)$$

where:

$$d_i(x_i, y_i) = \begin{cases} 1 & \text{if } x_i \text{ or } y_i \text{ are unknown} \\ overlap(x_i, y_i) & \text{if the } i\text{-th feature is symbolic} \\ \frac{|x_i - y_i|}{range_i} & \text{if the } i\text{-th feature is finite integer or real} \end{cases}$$

where $range_i$ is the difference between the maximum and minimum value of a numeric feature F_i, and $overlap(x_i, y_i) = 1$ if $x_i \neq y_i$ and 0 otherwise. In addition we have integrated this metric with a cut-off concept. For each feature there is a cutoff value $0 \leq \lambda_i \leq 1$. If one feature distance $d_i(x_i, y_i)$ is greater than λ_i then the overall distance $d(x, y)$ becomes 1. So, for instance, if the cut-off value for the feature "cost" is 0.2 then two items having a normalized cost difference greater than 0.2 are considered as maximally distant (or minimally similar). Using cut-offs, features can be made maximally important in a non-linear way, and this cannot achieved with a weighting schema.

If $c = (clf, cnq, cart, v)$ and $c' = (clf', cnq', cart', v')$ are two cases and $p, p' \in X = \prod_{i=1}^{n} F_i$ are two products then:

$$Sim(c, c') = 1 - d(clf, clf') \text{ and } Sim(p, p') = 1 - d(p, p').$$

By the above definition any similarity value is in a range between 0 and 1, since the distance functions have their image values in the same range.

5   Evaluation Results

We have empirically evaluated the methodology introduced in section 2. We built two variants of the same showcase called ITR+ and ITR-[4]. ITR+ fully implements the proposed methodology and ITR- is obtained by discarding from ITR+ the interactive query management and ranking functions. In other words, the second system has almost the same GUI but is not able to recommend changes to a content-based query when a failure occurs and does not provide any sorting of the selected products (the visualization order reflects the position in the catalogue). ITR- does not use the case base of recommendation sessions, it only searches in the electronic catalogues. The two systems, as query result, present three recommendations per page. A sample recommendation page is shown in Figure 5. We randomly assigned users to ITR- and ITR+ without mentioning the fact that we were testing two variants. In fact, the tests for two user groups were performed on two different days. First, ITR- was used by 19 users and then ITR+ by 16. The ranked recommendations computed by ITR+ were based on 35 cases. Among these cases, 20 were inserted by ourselves and 15 were obtained by the ITR- trial. The users were students of the University of Trento, coming from different Italian regions and European countries, and some administrative personnel of the University. The assigned task was the same, i.e., to select a set of travel products to arrange a vacation in Trentino. Before solving the task, users took their time to learn the system without any direction from those that administered the test, they used only the instructions on the web site. A number of objective measures, which were taken by logging the user activity, are shown in Table 1. It includes the average values (in a user group) and standard deviations of the measures taken for each recommendation session. Values marked with * (**) means a significant difference at the 0.1 (0.05) probability level, according to an unpaired t-test.

---

[4] ITR+ is accessible at http://itr.itc.it.

Fig. 5. Recommended events (example).

The input information provided by the two groups were essentially equal. The user provided (on average) 12.3 (ITR-) and 11.5 (ITR+) collaborative features, and in each query they constrained 4.7 (ITR-) 4.4 (ITR+) content features on average. Therefore apparently the proposed recommendation functions did not influence the users eagerness to provide information about their preferences.

The situation changes when we observe the number of queries executed and the output of the system. Users of ITR- issued a larger number of queries than those using ITR+, i.e., 20.1 vs. 13.4. Moreover, it is interesting to note that the maximum number of submitted queries for ITR- is 81 vs. 29 for ITR+. The reduction in the number of queries is due to the interactive query management support. Moreover, ITR- outputs on average a significantly larger number of results for each user query (42.0) than ITR+ 9.8. We believe that this caused the difference in the number of pages displayed by the two systems. In fact ITR- displayed 93.3 pages per session and ITR+ 71.3. In both cases the number of pages displayed is linearly correlated with the number of issued queries, with correlation coefficients: 0.67 (ITR-) and 0.78 (ITR+). It is interesting to note that the session duration is actually a bit longer for ITR+ and this fact shows that ITR+ users have devoted much more time than ITR- users to browse the information content rather than navigating through the system.

Table 1. ITR+ vs. ITR-, objective measures per user session.

	ITR-	ITR+
Queries issued by the user	20.1±19.2	13.4±9.3*
Content features in a query (average)	4.7±1.2	4.4±1.1
Collaborative features provided	12.3±1.4	11.5±2.0
Results per query (average)	42.0±61.2	9.8±14.3**
Page displayed	93.3±44.3	71.3±35.4**
Items in the case	5.8±3.9	4.1±3.4
Session duration (minutes)	28.5±9.5	31.0±12.3
System suggested query relaxations	n.a.	6.3±3.6
User accepted query relaxations	n.a	2.8±2.1
System suggested query tightenings	n.a.	2.1±2.5
User accepted query tightenings	n.a.	0.6±0.9
Selected item position in the result list	3.2±4.8	2.2±2.9**

Regarding the usage of the query tightening (system suggests new features to add) and relaxation (system suggests constraints to discard or change), we note that users seem more inclined to use the relaxation rather than the tightening. The first was suggested by the system 6.3 times per session, and this means that approximately 50% of the queries had a "no result" failure. The user accepted one of the proposed relaxation 2.8 times, i.e. almost 45% of the time. We consider this a good result, taking into account the user behavior that is often erratic and not always focussed in solving the task. The corresponding results for query tightening are less convincing. A tightening suggestion was proposed by the system 2.1 times per session, which accounts for 16% of the user queries and was accepted by the user 0.6 times, i.e., 28% of the times it was suggested. We must observe that tightening was suggested by ITR+ when more than 10 items satisfied the user query. This could be a too small value, and we do not have comparisons with other tightening methods (e.g. those based on pure entropy or information gain maximization). But this result suggests that query tightening (also called attribute selection methods [13]) could have been overemphasized in the CBR literature. The impression we got from the users and from the result of a questionnaire, is that users seem to be able to refine a query when there are too many results, but it is more difficult for them to understand why a query fails to return any item.

Finally, we comment on the last measure in Table 1, namely the position of the item selected by the user in the recommended list. We recall that ITR- shows the query results in the same order as they are found in the catalogues, whereas ITR+ sorts the product using the proposed twofold similarity computation. The difference for the two systems is significant at the 0.05 level (t-test, unpaired, one-tail) and shows that ITR+ ranks the items selected by the user higher in the result list than ITR-. The average position of a selected item is 2.2 in ITR+ compared with 3.2 in ITR-. The last two numbers are computed on all the user queries that ended up with selection of an item (i.e. saved in the cart).

6   Conclusions and Future Work

In this paper we have presented a novel approach to products recommendation that exploits both content-based and collaborative-based filtering.[5] The proposed methodology helps the user to specify a query that filters out unwanted products in electronic catalogues (content-based). A human/computer interactive dialogue is managed till a reasonable amount of products is selected. Then, the selected products are ranked exploiting a case base of recommendation sessions (collaborative-based). Among the user selected items the system ranks higher items similar to those selected by other users in similar sessions (twofold similarity).

The approach has been applied to a web travel application and it has been empirically evaluated with real users. We have shown that the proposed approach: a) reduces the number of user queries, b) reduces the number of browsed products and c) the selected items are found first on the ranked list.

The future work will be devoted to the exploitation of the whole case in the collaborative stage, i.e., in using the complete case structure to match similar recommendation sessions [1]. Moreover we are investigating other recommendation methodologies that are driven by the presentation of selected examples more than by question answering [14]. The goal is to provide a range of recommendation functions for an large set of users free to adopt multiple decision styles [7].

References

1. B. Arslan and F. Ricci. Case based session modeling and personalization in a travel advisory system. In F. Ricci and B. Smyth, editors, *Proceedings of the AH'20002 Workshop on Recommendation and Personalization in eCommerce*, pages 60–69, Malaga, Spain, May, 28th 2002.
2. J. Breese, D. Heckerman, and C. Kadie. Empirical analysis of predictive algorithms for collaborative filtering. In *Proceedings of the Fourteenth Conference on Uncertainty in Artificial Intelligence*, Madison, WI, July 1998. Morgan Kaufmann Publisher.
3. D. Bridge and A. Ferguson. Diverse product recommendations using an expressive language for case retrieval. In S. Craw and A. Preece, editors, *Advances in Case-Based Reasoning, Proceedings of the 6th European Conference on Case Based Reasoning, ECCBR 2002*, pages 43–57, Aberdeen, Scotland, 4 - 7 September 2002. Springer Verlag.
4. R. Burke. Knowledge-based recommender systems. In J. E. Daily, A. Kent, and H. Lancour, editors, *Encyclopedia of Library and Information Science*, volume 69. Marcel Dekker, 2000.
5. R. Burke. Hybrid recommender systems: Survey and experiments. *User Modeling and User-Adapted Interaction*, 12(4):331–370, 2002.

[5] This work has been partially funded by CARITRO foundation (under contract "eCommerce e Turismo") and by the European Union's Fifth RTD Framework Programme (under contract DIETORECS IST-2000-29474).

6. P. Cunningham, R. Bergmann, S. Schmitt, R. Traphöner, S. Breen, and B. Smyth. Websell: Intelligent sales assistants for the world wide web. In R. Weber and C. Wangenheim, editors, *Procs. of the Workshop Programme at the Fourth International Conference on Case-Based Reasoning*, 2001.

7. D. R. Fesenmaier, F. Ricci, E. Schaumlechner, K. Wöber, and C. Zanella. DIETORECS: Travel advisory for multiple decision styles. In A. J. Frew, M. Hitz, and P. O'Connors, editors, *Information and Communication Technologies in Tourism 2003*, pages 232–241. Springer, 2003.

8. M. H. Göker and C. A. Thomson. Personalized conversational case-based recommendation. In *Advances in case-based reasoning: 5th European workshop, EWCBR-2000, Trento, Italy, September 6-9, 2000: proceedings*, pages 99–111. Springer, 2000.

9. K. M. Gupta, D. W. Aha, and N. Sandhu. Exploiting taxonomic and causal relations in conversational case retrieval. In S. Craw and A. Preece, editors, *Advances in Case-Based Reasoning, Proceedings of the 6th European Conference on Case Based Reasoning, ECCBR 2002*, pages 133–147, Aberdeen, Scotland, 4 - 7 September 2002. Springer Verlag.

10. F. Ricci, B. Arslan, N. Mirzadeh, and A. Venturini. ITR: a case-based travel advisory system. In S. Craw and A. Preece, editors, *6th European Conference on Case Based Reasoning, ECCBR 2002*, pages 613–627, Aberdeen, Scotland, 4 - 7 September 2002. Springer Verlag.

11. F. Ricci, N. Mirzadeh, and A. Venturini. Intelligent query managment in a mediator architecture. In *2002 First International IEEE Symposium "Intelligent Systems'*, pages 221–226, Varna, Bulgaria, September 10-12 2002.

12. J. B. Schafer, J. A. Konstan, and J. Riedl. E-commerce recommendation applications. *Data Mining and Knowledge Discovery*, 5(1/2):115–153, 2001.

13. S. Schmitt, P. Dopichaj, and P. Domínguez-Marín. Entropy-based vs. similarity-influenced: attribute selection methods for dialogs tested on different electronic commerce domains. In S. Craw and A. Preece, editors, *Advances in Case-Based Reasoning, Proceedings of the 6th European Conference on Case Based Reasoning, ECCBR 2002*, pages 380–394, Aberdeen, Scotland, 4 - 7 September 2002. Springer Verlag.

14. H. Shimazu. ExpertClerk: Navigating shoppers buying process with the combination of asking and proposing. In B. Nebel, editor, *Proceedings of the Seventeenth International Joint Conference on Artificial Intelligence, IJCAI 2001*, pages 1443–1448, Seattle, Washington, USA, August 4-10 2001. Morgan Kaufmann.

15. D. O. Sullivan, D. Wilson, and B. Smyth. Improving case-based recommendation, a collaborative filtering approach. In S. Craw and A. Preece, editors, *Advances in Case-Based Reasoning, Proceedings of the 6th European Conference on Case Based Reasoning, ECCBR 2002*, pages 278–291, Aberdeen, Scotland, 4 - 7 September 2002. Springer Verlag.

16. D. R. Wilson and T. R. Martinez. Improved heterogeneous distance functions. *Journal of Artificial Intelligence Research*, 11:1–34, 1997.

Unifying Weighting and Case Reduction Methods Based on Rough Sets to Improve Retrieval

Maria Salamó and Elisabet Golobardes

Enginyeria i Arquitectura La Salle, Universitat Ramon Llull,
Psg. Bonanova 8, 08022 Barcelona, Catalonia, Spain
{mariasal,elisabet}@salleurl.edu

Abstract. Case-Based Reasoning systems usually retrieve cases using a similarity function based on K-NN or some derivatives. These functions are sensitive to irrelevant or noisy features. Weighting methods are used to extract the most important information present in the knowledge and determine the importance of each feature. However, this knowledge, can also be incorrect, redundant and inconsistent. In order to solve this problem there exist a great number of case reduction techniques in the literature. This paper analyses and justifies the relationship between weighting and case reduction methods, and also analyses their behaviour using different similarity metrics. We have focused this relation on Rough Sets approaches. Several experiments, using different domains from the UCI and our own repository, show that this integration maintain and even improve the performance over a simple CBR system and over case reduction techniques. However, the combined approach produces CBR system decrease if the weighting method declines its performance.

1 Introduction

The success of any Case-Based Reasoning (CBR) system depends on its ability to select the right case for the right target problem [Aamodt and Plaza, 1994]. The quality of the information in the case memory is one of the key issues. When the information is redundant, irrelevant, or noisy and/or unreliable, the success of the CBR system when classifying is more difficult. The case memory is a key piece in a CBR cycle because it is present in the whole process. Although we concentrate on CBR systems, the need for information with high quality is also present in other machine learning techniques (e.g. decision trees). Many researchers have addressed the improvement of this quality, most of them using two major approximations to it: (1) weighting or feature selection methods and (2) prototype selection or reduction techniques (identified as case reduction methods in the CBR community). Both approaches are focused on the information but they concentrate on different dimensions: the first one focuses on the features (attributes) while the second one focuses on the cases (instances).

K.D. Ashley and D.G. Bridge (Eds.): ICCBR 2003, LNAI 2689, pp. 494–508, 2003.
© Springer-Verlag Berlin Heidelberg 2003

The motivation of this paper is addressed after a previous analysis of three majors factors on the retrieval phase, see figure 1. The first factor is that weighting methods are influenced by the case memory size. At the same time, as a second continuous factor is the positive influence of weighting methods when using the similarity function to retrieve the most similar cases. Finally, the case memory itself is influenced by the similarity due to the policy applied when retaining which is dependant on the correct classification of the new case.

In this paper, we concentrate on an analysis of a combined approach between weighting and case reduction techniques, as a consequence of previous analysis. The combined approach include two of the main parts of the retrieval phase. In this case, we use Proportional Rough Sets method (PRS) as a weighting method and the Accuracy Classification Case Memory (ACCM) algorithm as a case reduction technique. Finally, we tested this combination using several similarity functions in order to test if there is some clear positive or negative interaction between the methods in the combination.

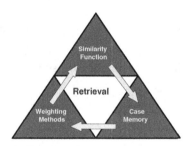

Fig. 1. Dependencies schema in the retrieval phase.

The paper is organized as follows. Section 2 describes the motivation for the paper. Next, Section 3 details the proposed unification between weighting methods and case reduction methods. Section 4 describes the experiments and analyses the results obtained. Then, Section 5 introduces some related work. Finally, Section 6 presents some conclusions and further work.

2   Motivation

The motivation of this paper originates in a previous analysis on the behaviour of weighting methods. This previous analysis [Salamó and Golobardes, 2002] demonstrated the positive influence of weighting methods and the relationship between weighting methods and case memory growth. Although the paper concentrated on weighting methods, the results can be extrapolated to feature selection methods.

In the previous paper, we tested the weighting methods using several datasets, each one with 9 proportions of the case memory. Proportions are in the range $X \in \{10\%, 20\%, \ldots, 90\%\}$ of the initial case memory for training where the remaining cases are used for testing. Each proportion was generated 10 times and the accuracy results of each test are averaged. Here we present the most significant results obtained in our previous paper for the *echocardiogram* (see figure 2(a)), *iris* (see table 1) and *mammogram* (see figure 2(b)) datasets. Details of datasets can be seen in section 4.1.

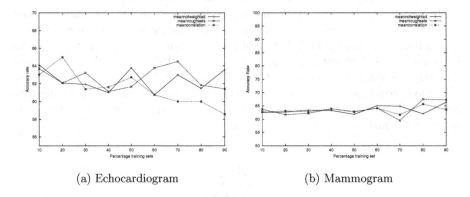

(a) Echocardiogram   (b) Mammogram

Fig. 2. Figures describing the accuracy of the CBR system when increasing the training case memory size.

Table 1. Mean average accuracies results for the *Iris* dataset. The columns show the results for a non weighting approach (¬W), Proportional Rough Sets (PRS) and Sample Correlation (Corr) weighting methods.

Prop. Train	Mean ¬W	Mean PRS	Mean Corr
40%	96.22	96.00	96.22
60%	95.33	95.50	96.16
70%	95.11	95.33	95.77
80%	97.00	97.00	97.33
90%	96.66	96.66	97.33

As a summary of previous results, we can notice that the system performs better when using weighting methods. The most important point is that the CBR improves with enough case memory. However, it is noticeable that the case memory increase also produces a declination on performance when the case memory increases too much. Thus showing also that the number of cases included in the case memory influences the performance of the weighting methods. This influence can be seen in figures 2(a) and 2(b). These figures show the evolution of performance when the case memory increases. In conclusion, it is important to remark that the performance of the weighting seems to depend on the case memory size and also depend on the quality of the cases present in it, as reported in all datasets analysed.

Although the results are not conclusive in the previous paper, previous observations motivated us to perform the experiments and analysis described in this paper.

3 Unifying Weighting and Case Reduction Methods Based on Rough Sets

After demonstrating the influence of the case memory over weighting methods, we present in this section a combined approach between weighting methods and case reduction methods. The proposed solution is based on Rough Sets. Here we present a unification of two kinds of algorithms that work well separately.

The most important point is that they have the same foundations, even though they use different policies: in one case to weight features and on the other hand to maintain or delete cases.

First of all, we present a summary of Rough Sets foundations of all algorithms. Next, we describe our weighting method and case base maintenance method tested and how they are unified in the CBR system.

3.1 Rough Sets Foundations

The rough sets theory defined by Zdisław Pawlak, which is well detailed in [Pawlak, 1982,Pawlak, 1991], is one of the techniques for the identification and recognition of common patterns in data, especially in the case of uncertain and incomplete data. The mathematical foundations of this method are based on the set approximation of the classification space.

Within the framework of rough sets the term *classification* describes the subdivision of the universal set of all possible categories into a number of distinguishable categories called elementary sets. Each elementary set can be regarded as a rule describing the object of the classification. Each object is then classified using the elementary set of features which can not be split up any further, although other elementary sets of features may exist. In the rough set model the classification knowledge (the model of the data) is represented by an equivalence relation IND defined on a certain universe of objects (cases) U and relations (attributes) R. IND defines a partition on U. The pair of the universe objects U and the associated equivalence relation IND forms an approximation space. The approximation space gives an approximate description of any subset $X \subseteq U$.

Two approximations are generated by the available data about the elements of the set X, called the lower and upper approximations (see figure 3). The lower approximation $\underline{R}X$ is the set of all elements of U which can *certainly* be classified as elements of X in knowledge R. The upper approximation $\overline{R}X$ is the set of elements of U which can *possibly* be classified as elements of X, employing knowledge R.

In order to discover patterns of data we should look for similarities and differences of values of the relation R. So we have to search for combinations of attributes with which we can discern objects and object classes from each other. The minimal set of attributes that forms such a combination is called a **reduct**.

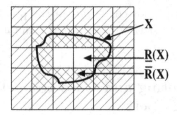

Fig. 3. The lower and upper approximations of a set X.

Reducts are the most concise way in which we can discern objects classes and which suffices to define all the concepts occurring in the knowledge.

3.2 Proportional Rough Sets Weighting Method (PRS)

The relevance of each feature in the system is computed using the proportional appearance at the reducts of information.

$$For\ each\ feature\ f\ computes: \mu(f) = \frac{card(appearance\ f\ in\ RED(R))}{card(\ all\ RED(R))} \quad (1)$$

An attribute f that does not appear in the reducts has a feature weight value $\mu(f) = 0.0$, whereas a feature that appears in the core has a feature value $\mu(f) = 1.0$. The remaining attributes have a feature weight value depending on the proportional appearance in the reducts. This weighting method has been selected because it has a good behaviour on different application areas. The comparison of this weighting method and well known weighting methods is detailed in [Salamó and Golobardes, 2002].

3.3 Accuracy-Classification Case Memory Maintenance Method (ACCM)

ACCM algorithm has been selected, from different Rough Sets case reduction techniques [Salamó and Golobardes, 2003], because in previous experiments it presents a good balance between reduction and accuracy. This algorithm uses a categorisation model of the case memory. Next, we briefly introduce the main definitions.

Categorisation model of case memory. The distribution of the case memory is done using a categorisation in terms of their *coverage* and *reachability*, which are adapted to our needs. In the case of coverage it is measured using Rough Sets theory, equally it does the weighting method. The reachability is modified in order to be employed in classification tasks.

Definition 1 (Coverage)
Let $T = \{t_1, t_2, ..., t_n\}$ be a training set of instances, $\forall\, t_i \in T$:
$Coverage(t_i) = AccurCoef(t_i) \oplus ClassCoef(t_i)$

The $\oplus$ operation is the logical sum of both values. When $AccurCoef$ value is 1.0, the $Coverage$ is 1.0 but when it is 0.0 value, the $Coverage$ is $ClassCoef$ value.

Definition 2 (AccurCoef)
This measure computes the *Accuracy* coefficient (**AccurCoef**) of each case t in the knowledge base (case memory) T as:

$$For\ each\ instance\ t \in T\ it\ computes : AccurCoef(t) = \frac{card\ (\ \underline{P}(t))}{card\ (\ \overline{P}\ (t))} \quad (2)$$

Where $AccurCoef(t)$ is the relevance of the instance t; T is the training set; $card$ is the cardinality of one set; P is the set that contains the *reducts* obtained from the original data; and finally $\underline{P}(t)$ and $\overline{P}(t)$ are the presence of t in the lower and upper approximations, respectively.

The accuracy measure expresses the degree of completeness of our knowledge about the set P. It is the percentage of possible correct decisions when classifying cases employing t. We use the accuracy coefficient to explain if an instance t is on an internal region or on a outlier region. The values of the measure when there exists only one case t as input is limited to $\{0,1\}$. When the value is 0.0 it means an internal case, and a value of 1.0 means an outlier case. Inexactness of a set of cases is due to the existence of a borderline region. The greater a borderline region of a set (greater $\overline{P}$), the lower the accuracy of the set.

Definition 3 (ClassCoef)
In this measure we use the *quality of classification* coefficient (**ClassCoef**). It is computed as:

$$For\ each\ instance\ t \in T\ it\ computes :$$
$$\mu(t) = \frac{card\ (\ \underline{P}(t))\ \cup\ card\ (\ \underline{P}(-t))}{card\ (\ all\ instances)} \quad (3)$$

Where $ClassCoef(t)$ is the relevance of the instance t; T is the training set; $-t$ is $T - \{t\}$ set; $card$ is the cardinality of a set; P is a set that contains the reducts; and finally $\underline{P}(t)$ is the presence of t in the lower approximation.

The $ClassCoef$ coefficient expresses the percentage of cases which can be correctly classified employing the knowledge t. This coefficient has a range of real values in the interval $[0.0, 1.0]$. Where 0.0 and 1.0 mean that the instance classifies incorrectly and correctly respectively, the range of cases that belong to its class. The higher the quality, the nearer to the outlier region.

Definition 4 (Reachability)
Let $T = \{t_1, t_2, ..., t_n\}$ be a training set of instances, $\forall t_i \in T$:

$$Reachability(t_i) = \left\{ \begin{array}{ll} Class \ (t_i) & if \ it \ is \ a \ classification \ task \\ Adaptable(t', t_i) & if \ it \ is \ not \ a \ classification \ task \end{array} \right. \quad (4)$$

Where $class(t_i)$ is the class that classifies case t_i and t'$\in$ T.

Accuracy-Classification Case Memory (ACCM) algorithm. Once we have computed the AccurCoef and ClassCoef, we apply for the original case memory algorithm 1 to select the cases that have to be deleted from the case memory. The cases not selected are maintained in the case memory. An extended explanation of this can be found in [Salamó and Golobardes, 2003].

The main idea of this reduction technique is to benefit from the advantages of both measures separately. Firstly, it maintains all the cases that are outliers, so cases with an AccurCoef = 1.0 value are not removed. This assumption is made because if a case is isolated, there is no other case that can solve it. Secondly, the cases selected are those that are nearest to the outliers and other cases nearby can be used to solve it because their coverage is higher.

Algorithm 1 ACCM

```
1. SelectCasesACCM (CaseMemory T)
2. confidenceLevel = 1.0 and freeLevel = ConstantTuned (set at 0.01)
3. select all instances t ∈ T as SelectCase(t) if it satisfies:
   coverage(t) ≥ confidenceLevel
4. while not ∃ at least a t in SelectCase for each class c that reachability(t) = c
5.    confidenceLevel = confidenceLevel - freeLevel
6.    select all instances t ∈ T as SelectCase(t) if it satisfies:
      coverage(t) ≥ confidenceLevel
7. end while
8. delete from CaseMemory the set of cases selected as SelectCase
9. return CaseMemory T
```

3.4   Unification of Weighting and Case Reduction Methods

The meta-level process of the unification can be described in three steps, as shown in figure 4. This process is performed in an initial phase prior to the CBR cycle. The first step discretises the initial training set of instances, using Fayyad and Irani's algorithm [Fayyad and Irani, 1993], in order to use Rough Sets theory. The second step searches for the reducts of knowledge using the Rough Sets theory. Finally, the third step uses the reducts of knowledge to extract the proportional appearance of each attribute and AccurCoef and ClassCoef measures. The last measures are used to compute the cases that have to be maintained and removed from the case memory using the algorithm 1 ACCM, thus reducing the initial training case memory. Weights are used when computing the similarity function.

Our approach based on the combination of PRS and ACCM has been done from the point of view of Rough Sets theory. The selection of this approach is done for two main reasons: (1) both methods share a common basis, what make it possible to obtain a higher speed because the central point of computations are the same; (2) both methods have demonstrated in previous papers their good behaviour in front of a great number of problems, PRS analysis versus well known weighting methods (e.g. ReliefF [Kononenko, 1994], CFS [Hall, 2000]) can be seen in [Salamó and Golobardes, 2002] and ACCM details can be found in [Salamó and Golobardes, 2003] where an analysis versus known case reduction techniques (e.g Instance Based learning (IB1-IB4) algorithms [Aha, 1992] and instance prunning techniques (DROP1-DROP5) [Wilson and Martinez, 2000b]) is performed.

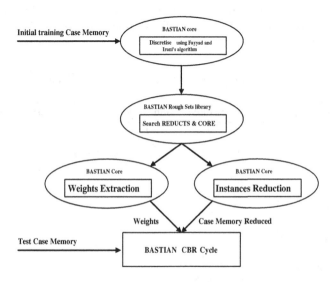

Fig. 4. Unification process in BASTIAN platform.

A sequential alternative, first case reduction and in second place weighting based on the reduced case memory, will be part of our future work. However, this sequential alternative have two main drawbacks at first sight: (1) it is not possible to improve execution time; (2) if the basis are the same, the reduced case memory will contain the same characteristics as the initial one to extract weights. Thus computing twice the same parameters. Last drawback will be true if the case memory reduction works well.

4   Experimental Analysis

This section is structured as follows: first of all, we describe the testbed used in the experimental analysis; then we analyse the results obtained from the weighting methods, the case reduction technique and the the combined approach of both techniques in our CBR system.

4.1   Testbed

The evaluation of the performance rate is done using sixteen datasets which are detailed in table 2. Datasets can be grouped in two ways: *public* and *private*. **Public datasets** are obtained from the UCI repository [Merz and Murphy, 1998]. **Private datasets** [Golobardes et al., 2002] come from our own repository. They deal with *diagnosis* of breast cancer (*Biopsy* and *Mammogram*) and a *synthetic* dataset (TAO-*grid* which is obtained from sampling the TAO figure using a grid). These datasets were chosen in order to provide a wide variety of application areas, sizes, combinations of feature types, and difficulty as measured by the accuracy achieved on them by current algorithms. The choice was also made with the goal of having enough data points to extract conclusions.

Table 2. Details of the datasets used in the analysis.

	Dataset	Ref.	Samples	Num. feat.	Sym. feat.	Classes	Inconsistent
1	*Audiology*	*AD*	226	61	2	24	Yes
2	*Biopsy (private)*	*BI*	1027	24	-	2	Yes
3	*Breast-w*	*BC*	699	9	-	2	Yes
4	*Credit-A*	*CA*	690	5	9	2	Yes
5	*Glass*	*GL*	214	9	-	6	No
6	*Heart-C*	*HC*	303	6	7	5	Yes
7	*Heart-H*	*HH*	294	6	7	5	Yes
8	*Heart-Statlog*	*HS*	270	13	-	2	No
9	*Ionosphere*	*IO*	351	34	-	2	No
10	*Iris*	*IR*	150	4	-	3	No
11	*Mammogram (private)*	*MA*	216	23	-	2	Yes
12	*Segment*	*SG*	2310	19	-	7	No
13	*Sonar*	*SO*	208	60	-	2	No
14	*TAO-Grid (private)*	*TG*	1888	2	-	2	No
15	*Vehicle*	*VE*	846	18	-	4	No
16	*Vote*	*VT*	435	-	16	2	Yes

The study described in this paper was carried out in the context of BAS-TIAN, a *case-***BA***sed* **S**ys**T**em *for class***I***fic***A***tio***N**. All techniques were run using the same set of parameters for all datasets: a **1-Nearest Neighbour Algorithm** that uses a list of cases to represent the case memory. Each case contains the set of attributes, the class, the AccurCoef and ClassCoef coefficients. Our goal in this paper is to test the combination of weighting and case reduction methods. For this reason, we have not focused on the representation used by the system. The retain phase uses the following policy: *DifSim*, which only stores the new case if it has a different similarity from the retrieved case. Thus, the learning process is limited to this simple policy. Future work will be focused on improving the retain policy.

The configuration of BASTIAN system is different from previous papers, producing some changes on previous results. The percentage of correct classifications has been *averaged* over *stratified ten-fold cross-validation* runs. To study the performance we use paired *t-test* on these runs.

4.2   Experiment 1. Analysis of Separated Components and the Unified Approach for the Retrieval Phase

This section analyses each component studied (similarity function, weighting and case reduction method) in this paper versus the combined approach. The results are shown in table 3, where the similarity function analysed is an overlap metric for nominal attributes and normalised Euclidean distance function for linear attributes, the weighting approach is Proportional Rough Sets (PRS) method, the case reduction method is Accuracy Classification Case Memory (ACCM), and the combined approach is named ACCM+PRS.

Table 3. Results for all datasets showing the percentage of correct classifications. Last column shows the case memory size obtained when using ACCM in two previous columns. We use paired t-test at the 1% significance level, where a • and a ○ stand for a significant improvement o degradation of PRS, ACCM and ACCM+PRS related to Euclidean. We also show paired t-test at the 5%, where a † or ‡ stand for a significant improvement or degradation.

Ref.	Euclidean	PRS	ACCM	ACCM+PRS	size
AD	75,36	77,93	71,84	72,58	70,00
BI	83,17	82,37	83,07	80,79	88,01
BC	95,86	96,14	94,99	95,00	77,36
CA	81,76	81,19	82,20	81,77	84,30
GL	66,30	76,56†	67,29	73,42	74,95
HC	74,20	76,19	73,58	73,91	82,02
HH	72,82	76,96•†	73,82	76,58•†	85,63
HS	74,07	81,11	76,29	78,89	79,67
IO	86,33	87,75	87,20	86,60	83,77
IR	95,33	96,00	96,66	96,66	89,03
MA	62,95	65,79	63,56	65,84	89,19
SG	97,35	97,31	97,40	97,10	57,59
SO	86,83	83,25	86,90	83,71	71,71
TG	96,13	96,66	96,29	96,29	95,87
VE	69,43	70,44	68,48	67,55	72,35
VT	86,65	88,23	90,78	91,49†	79,23
Mean	81,53	83,37	81,90	82,39	80,04

The results show that the combination, between PRS weighting method and ACCM case reduction method, obtains an average behaviour on performance for the majority of datasets. The behaviour of the combination depends initially on the behaviour of the weighting method. When PRS and ACCM increases the accuracy, in comparison with Euclidean, the combined approach also increases the prediction accuracy, as can be seen in *heart-h* and *tao-grid* datasets. The results also show that an increase combined with a decrease on performance in PRS or ACCM produces an increase on performance if one of the methods achieve a great difference on the initial performance (e.g. *glass* and *vote*). Another interesting observation is that when PRS or ACCM declines its performance, the combination performance loss is not as great as the first one.

All the results show that the combination of the case reduction and weighting methods is on average positive on the CBR system. The ACCM maintains some negative results obtained when weighting (e.g. *vote*), and at the same time, PRS maintains or improves some negative results obtained by ACCM (e.g. *mammogram*). Maybe the results are not so high as expected, but it is also important to note that the reduction of the case memory is performed while achieving a robust CBR system.

4.3 Experiment 2 – Comparison of the Combined Approach versus Similarity Function

After considering the previous results, we want to analyse the influence of the similarity function in our combined approach. We want to observe if the similarity function produces an increment or decrement in the performance of the system. In this case, we test Camberra, Clark, Manhattan, Euclidean and Minkowski -set up r=3- (Cubic) similarity functions combined with ACCM+PRS approach.

Table 4. Results for all datasets showing the percentage of correct classifications.

Ref.	Camberra	Clark	Manhattan	Euclidean	Cubic
AD	75,58	**76,98**	72,58	72,58	72,53
BI	78,19	78,60	**80,80**	80,79	79,86
BC	94,29	93,32	**95,55**	95,00	93,99
CA	82,58	**82,87**	82,20	81,77	81,04
GL	70,63	67,12	**76,34**	73,42	72,00
HC	**76,86**	75,47	74,22	73,91	72,89
HH	78,59	**78,93**	77,24	76,58	76,58
HC	**79,63**	77,78	78,15	78,89	79,26
IO	**91,76**	91,47	90,62	86,60	82,91
IR	95,33	96,00	96,00	**96,66**	**96,66**
MA	60,28	60,14	61,21	**65,84**	64,46
SG	93,85	91,13	**97,45**	97,10	96,62
SO	76,66	70,11	82,35	83,71	**84,26**
TG	95,76	95,76	**96,29**	**96,29**	**96,29**
VE	68,31	67,48	**69,02**	67,55	65,79
VT	**91,49**	**91,49**	**91,49**	**91,49**	**91,49**
Mean	81,86	80,91	**82,59**	82,39	81,66

The results on table 4 show some great differences between different similarity functions. One of the major points to notice is that no one is able to achieve a maximum values in all datasets. Camberra function can deal well with datasets that contain a great number of missing values and at the same time a reduced set of cases, whereas Manhattan function is better than the usual Euclidean or Cubic distance functions.

4.4 Experiment 3 – Comparison of the Combined Approach versus IDIBL

Finally, we test a similar approach to our combined approach. However, in this case, the comparison has been performed using the information present in the paper that describes IDIBL method [Wilson and Martinez, 2000a]. So t-test can not be performed, and only a briefly comparison using nine datasets can be showed in table 5.

Table 5. Results for nine datasets showing the percentage of correct classifications.

Ref.	IDIBL	Manhattan K=1	Manhattan K=3
BC	97,00	95,55	95,12
GL	70,56	76,24	76,24
HC	83,83	74,22	74,22
HO	73,80	71,79	75,29
IO	87,76	90,62	90,62
IR	96,00	96,00	96,00
SO	84,12	82,35	83,70
VE	72,62	69,02	69,02
VO	95,62	91,49	90,08
Mean	84,59	83,03	83,37

The results are slightly lower in our combined approach. IDIBL approach has its own weighting method, its own case reduction method as our combined approach, but uses a different number of neighbours (K=3) and uses a different similarity function. Table 5 show the results for IDIBL in second column, our Manhattan similarity distance function using K=1 neighbours in third column and K=3 neighbours in the last column. The differences between IDIBL approach and our combined approach, in our opinion, is mainly produced by the similarity function used. Wilson and Martinez have reported that distance functions are not suitable for some kind of problems and the IVDM similarity function perform better than these kind of functions. For future work we will test their function in our combined approach. Another important difference between both approaches is that IDIBL tunes up parameters twice, while our approach does it only once. As explained in the unification process, this is part of our further work. Although the comparison is not fair in all parameters tested, we think that our results are promising and the IDIBL results address us to further investigate some improvements on the combined approach.

5   Related Work

There is little related work focused closely on the approach presented in this paper. One of the few closely ones to our proposal is the refinement of retrieval knowledge by optimising the feature/weights after case base maintenance [Craw and Jarmulak, 2001]. The difference of this approach compared to our proposal is that the refinement of retrieval is performed all at the same time. Some work focused on similarity is also related to our proposal. The most similar approach is IDIBL algorithm [Wilson and Martinez, 2000a]. However, it uses a different similarity metric, uses K=3 neighbours and find parameters twice. Many researchers have point out that it is important to obtain diversity in order to improve similarity, particularly in so-called *recommender systems* [Smyth and McClave, 2001]. McSherry in [McSherry, 2002] shows that it is possible to increase diversity without loss of similarity. Our present analysis argues that diversity maintained using CBM technique can help similarity and weighting during the retrieval phase.

Related work on weighting methods can be placed in two main categories: *Wrappers* and *Filters*. We concentrate on *filters* due to the fact that our PRS approach is a filter method. *Filters* use general characteristics of the data to evaluate features and operate independently of any learning algorithm. Many filter methods for feature selection have been proposed recently, and a review of them can be found in [Blum and Langley, 1997]. The simplest filtering scheme is to evaluate each feature individually measuring its correlation to the target function (e.g. using a mutual information measure) and then select K features with the highest value. The *Relief* algorithm, proposed by Kira and Rendell [Kira and Rendell, 1992], follows this general paradigm. Kononenko proposed an extension of it [Kononenko, 1994], called *ReliefF*, that can handle noisy and multiclass problems. Unlike *Relief*, *CFS* [Hall, 2000] evaluates and hence ranks feature subsets rather than individual features. The *CFS* algorithm is a subset evaluation heuristic that takes into account the usefulness of individual features for predicting the class along with the level of intercorrelation among them. In our weighting method, the relevant features are extracted using the reduction of feature space computed by the Rough Sets theory.

On the other hand, many researchers have addressed the problem of case memory reduction [Wilson and Martinez, 2000b] and different approaches have been proposed. The most similar methods to our approach are those focused on increasing the overall competence, *the range of target problems that can be successfully solved* [Smyth and Keane, 1995], of the case memory through case deletion. Strategies have been developed for controlling case memory growth. Several methods such as competence-preserving deletion [Smyth and Keane, 1995] and failure-driven deletion [Portinale et al., 1999], as well as for generating compact case memories [Smyth and McKenna, 2001] through competence-based case addition. Leake and Wilson [Leake and Wilson, 2000] examine the benefits of using fine-grained performance metrics to directly guide case addition or deletion. These methods are specially important for task domains with non-uniform problem distributions. ACCM approach uses a global policy to delete cases using a Rough Sets competence model [Salamó and Golobardes, 2003]. Reinartz and

Iglezakis [Reinartz and Iglezakis, 2001] presented the maintenance integrated with the overall case-based reasoning process.

6   Conclusions

The aim of this paper has been to analyse and demonstrate the combination of weighting and case reduction techniques based on Rough Sets in the retrieval phase. First of all, this paper has presented the influence of case memory growth on weighting methods in a CBR system. Secondly, it has also presented a Rough Sets proposal that combines weighting and case reduction methods. The most important fact of the unification is that they share common foundations. Different experiments have shown the unification of both approaches produces maintenance or even an improvement on performance. The maintenance or improvement of the prediction accuracy is highly related to the initial behaviour of the weighting method, as denoted in the experiments, and not mainly to the case reduction method. The results also show that unification produces a robust system, because the system performance does not decrease too much if the weighting method does not perform good weights. Our further work will be focused on testing different Rough Sets case reduction methods and to combine different measures of feature relevance to improve the CBR system when the weighting method does not work efficiently. Also, to test different similarity functions not based on distance.

Acknowledgements. This work is supported by the *Ministerio de Ciencia y Tecnologia*, Grant No. TIC2002-04160-C02-02. We wish to thank *Enginyeria i Arquitectura La Salle - Ramon Llull University* for their support to our Research Group in Intelligent Systems. Finally, we wish to thank the anonymous reviewers for their useful comments.

References

Aamodt and Plaza, 1994. Aamodt, A. and Plaza, E. (1994). Case-Based Reasoning: Foundations Issues, Methodological Variations, and System Approaches. In *AI Communications*, volume 7, pages 39–59.

Aha, 1992. Aha, D. (1992). Tolerating noisy, irrelevant and novel attributes in instance-based learning algorithms. *International Journal of Man-Machine Studies*, (36):267–287.

Blum and Langley, 1997. Blum, A. and Langley, P. (1997). Selection of Relevant features and Examples in Machine Learning. In *Artificial Intelligence*, volume 97, pages 245–271.

Craw and Jarmulak, 2001. Craw, S. and Jarmulak, J. (2001). Maintaining Retrieval knowledge in a case-based reasoning system. *Computational Intelligence*, 17(2):346–363.

Fayyad and Irani, 1993. Fayyad, U. and Irani, K. (1993). Multi-interval discretization of continuous-valued attributes for classification learning. In *19th International Joint Conference on Artificial Intelligence*, pages 1022–1027.

Golobardes et al., 2002. Golobardes, E., Llorà, X., Salamó, M., and Martí, J. (2002). Computer Aided Diagnosis with Case-Based Reasoning and Genetic Algorithms. *Knowledge-Based Systems*, (15):45–52.

Hall, 2000. Hall, M. (2000). Correlation-based feature selection of discrete and numeric class machine learning. In *Proc. International Conference on Machine Learning*, pages 359–366. Morgan Kaufmann.

Kira and Rendell, 1992. Kira, K. and Rendell, L. (1992). A practical approach to feature selection. In *Proceedings of the 9th International Conference on Machine Learning*, pages 249–256.

Kononenko, 1994. Kononenko, I. (1994). Estimating attributes: Analysis and extensions of RELIEF. In *Proceedings of the Seventh European Conference on Machine Learning*, pages 171–182.

Leake and Wilson, 2000. Leake, D. and Wilson, D. (2000). Remembering Why to Remember: Performance-Guided Case-Base Maintenance. In *Proceedings of the Fifth European Workshop on Case-Based Reasoning*, pages 161–172.

McSherry, 2002. McSherry, D. (2002). Diversity-Conscious Retrieval. In *Proceedings of the 6th. European Conference on Case-Based Reasoning*, pages 219–233.

Merz and Murphy, 1998. Merz, C. J. and Murphy, P. M. (1998). UCI Repository for Machine Learning Data-Bases [http://www.ics.uci.edu/~mlearn/MLRepository.html]. *Irvine, CA: University of California, Department of Information and Computer Science.*

Pawlak, 1982. Pawlak, Z. (1982). Rough Sets. In *International Journal of Information and Computer Science*, volume 11.

Pawlak, 1991. Pawlak, Z. (1991). *Rough Sets: Theoretical Aspects of Reasoning about Data.* Kluwer Academic Publishers.

Portinale et al., 1999. Portinale, L., Torasso, P., and Tavano, P. (1999). Speed-up, quality and competence in multi-modal reasoning. In *Proceedings of the Third International Conference on Case-Based Reasoning*, pages 303–317.

Reinartz and Iglezakis, 2001. Reinartz, T. and Iglezakis, I. (2001). Review and Restore for Case-Base Maintenance. *Computational Intelligence*, 17(2):214–234.

Salamó and Golobardes, 2002. Salamó, M. and Golobardes, E. (2002). Analysing rough sets weighting methods for case-based reasoning systems. *Inteligencia Artificial. Revista Iberoamericana de Inteligencia Artificial*, (15):34–43.

Salamó and Golobardes, 2003. Salamó, M. and Golobardes, E. (2003). Hybrid deletion policies for case base maintenance. In *FLAIRS-2003*, page To appear.

Smyth and Keane, 1995. Smyth, B. and Keane, M. (1995). Remembering to forget: A competence-preserving case deletion policy for case-based reasoning systems. In *Proceedings of the Thirteen International Joint Conference on Artificial Intelligence*, pages 377–382.

Smyth and McClave, 2001. Smyth, B. and McClave, P. (2001). Similarity vs. Diversity. In *Proceedings of the 4th. International Conference on Case-Based Reasoning*, pages 347–361.

Smyth and McKenna, 2001. Smyth, B. and McKenna, E. (2001). Competence Models and the maintenance problem. *Computational Intelligence*, 17(2):235–249.

Wilson and Martinez, 2000a. Wilson, D. and Martinez, T. (2000a). An integrated instance-based learning algorithm. *Computational Intelligence*, 16(1):1–28.

Wilson and Martinez, 2000b. Wilson, D. and Martinez, T. (2000b). Reduction techniques for Instance-Based Learning Algorithms. *Machine Learning, 38*, pages 257–286.

A Knowledge Representation Format for Virtual IP Marketplaces

Martin Schaaf, Andrea Freßmann, Marco Spinelli, Rainer Maximini, and
Ralph Bergmann

University of Hildesheim, Data- and Knowledge Management Group
PO Box 101363, 31113 Hildesheim, Germany
{schaaf, fressmann, spinelli, r_maximi,
bergmann}@dwm.uni-hildesheim.de
www.dwm.uni-hildesheim.de

Abstract. For the design of *Systems on Chip* (SoC) it is essential to reuse previously developed and verified *virtual components* in order to meet nowadays requirements in reliability, correctness, and time-to-market. On the downside, deciding about reusing a third-party component in a design situation can consume substantial time and resources. This is especially true in situations where many potential candidates exist due to the large amount of functional, non-functional, and quality related aspects of each component. In order to facilitate the search for components in an internet-based market scenario, we have developed a retrieval system that utilizes structural CBR. The approach relies on XML descriptions of each component that constitute the case base. In this paper we present IPCHL, which was originally intended to be a simple schema for such descriptions. As a consequence of the growing demands for structured documentation, IPCHL has become a representation format for virtual component descriptions incorporating many of the CBR knowledge containers.

1   Introduction

The term of *Electronic Design Automation* (EDA) has been assigned to the current academic and industrial research activities that tackle the development of new methodologies, standardized description techniques, and tools for the design of microelectronic circuits. An important area that depends on efficient EDA is the design of so-called *Systems on Chip* (**SoC**). SoCs combine multiple functionalities on one chip and are the building blocks for a wide range of consumer electronic devices such as mobile phones or DVD players. Nowadays, SoCs are designed by reusing already existing modules, which are called *Virtual Components* or *Intellectual Properties* (IPs). SoC designers do no longer rely only on their own developed components but also on IPs offered by external vendors. Companies like sci-worx are even specialized in providing IPs for functionalities of general interest like audio decoding or error correction. The amount of IPs offered in the World Wide Web grows daily and the task of searching for potential IPs suitable for a given design situation can be very time consuming. This is especially true due to the huge amount

K.D. Ashley and D.G. Bridge (Eds.): ICCBR 2003, LNAI 2689, pp. 509–521, 2003.
© Springer-Verlag Berlin Heidelberg 2003

of functional and non-functional aspects that have to be taken into account. In order to allow virtual marketplaces to emerge, a standardized IP documentation is required, which can be read by humans and processed by computers. Furthermore, there must be a tight integration of computer support into the development methodology of designers. This is the aim of the project *IP Qualification* (IPQ), an EDA project founded by the German Ministry of Education and Research (BMBF) and initiated with several industrial partners. Within IPQ, we have developed an intelligent retrieval approach that supports designers in their search for IPs. The approach utilizes structural CBR by comparing the designer's situation with the characterization of IPs. The basic retrieval strategy combining functional, non-functional, and quality related aspects of IPs has been described in [13]. In the following paper we present the IPQ market scenario based on web services that build the environment of the retrieval application. The focus lies on the concepts of the **IP Characterization Language** (IPCHL) that was designed for representing IP characterizations and motivated by CBR-specific requirements. Because of the growing demand from the industrial partners for standardization of all IP related information, newer releases of IPCHL incorporate many of the CBR knowledge containers providing the necessary semantic for communication and cooperation between the different services within the virtual marketplace for IP.

2   The Virtual Marketplace Scenario of IPQ

A System on Chip typically combines several functionalities on one integrated circuit, for instance a SoC may contain a Java execution engine together with an audio decoding unit. In contrast to traditional integrated circuits, which are individually designed and highly optimized, the focus of SoCs lies on high integration and cost reduction. Such aspects are prevalent for consumer electronics like mobile phones. Nowadays, technology allows SoCs to become very complex and, due to the immense functionality aggregated on one chip, verification is time consuming.

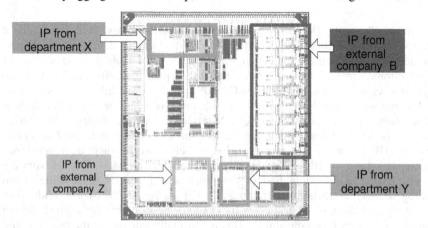

Fig. 1. IPs Integrated on a *System on Chip*

Very similar to newer advancements in software engineering, a possible solution for SoCs is to reuse already existing and fully verified components so called *Virtual Components* or *Intellectual Properties (IPs)*. IPs are specifications in a hardware description language like VHDL or Verilog and one distinguishes between *Soft IP, Firm IP*, and *Hard IP*. The difference between Soft IPs and Hard IPs lies in the degree of flexibility and, therefore, reusability. While a Soft IP is a high-level specification of the intended functionality independent from the technology (e.g. CMOS) of the resulting SoC, a Hard IP is specifically designed for one target technology. Everything between Hard and Soft IP is called Firm IP. Fig. 1 shows an example of a SoC that has been produced from a specification incorporating IPs from multiple vendors.

2.1   Architecture of the IPQ Virtual Marketplace

In order to support designers for selecting and integrating IPs into their actual design, the IPQ Virtual Marketplace for IPs offers a variety of web services for purchasing IPs as well as transferring between different IP repositories (see Fig. 2). A so-called *IP Basar* currently under development brokers requests from the design gate, which is the interface between the marketplace and the designers, to registered services.

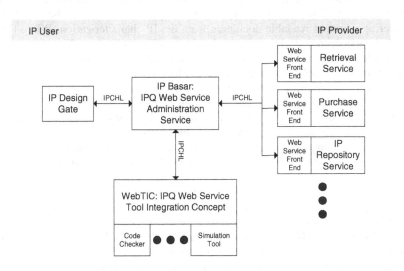

Fig. 2. IPQ Web Service Architecture

The *WebTIC* interface connects also web service unaware applications, e.g. code checkers or a simulation tool.

All services depicted in Fig. 2 utilize XML formats for the IP itself (content) and its description or characterization. The XML application for the IP Characterization is named IPCHL and it has been derived from requirements of CBR-based retrieval services. It is a structured representation format for the various CBR specific knowledge containers.

3   Representing Knowledge for CBR-Based IP Retrieval

When applying the structural CBR approach, knowledge items are described by a *characterization* constructed from a previously developed domain vocabulary. State-of-the-art CBR systems utilize an object-oriented vocabulary representation [8; 1; 2]. Such representations can be seen as an extension of the attribute-value representation. They make use of the data modeling approach of the object-oriented paradigm including *is-a* and other arbitrary binary relations as well as the inheritance principle. In the domain of IP retrieval, each IP is represented by an XML characterization that acts as a semantic index or semantic markup. The set of all characterizations constitutes the case base and, because that is in fact a set of XML files, it is possible to transfer each characterization across the Internet by utilizing standard web communication facilities like *web services*. That was an important requirement from the market scenario described above.

When using a modern CBR retrieval engine like the Open Retrieval Engine orenge from empolis Knowledge Management GmbH [6], cases can be accessed from various data sources, e.g. relational databases, but the domain vocabulary itself is represented in a proprietary format, typically, only of interest for the engine itself. For the aim of IPQ it was a basic requirement to have an explicitly specified vocabulary because it contains much important knowledge about the domain that is of interest for other services as well. For example, a *catalog builder* can use the vocabulary for rendering a human readable document from the IP characterization. While the aspect of documentation based on an explicitly specified conceptualization is a typical application scenario for ontology-based systems like OntoBroker [4] or Protégé [7], it was clear that a CBR-based retrieval should be retained.

Another requirement from our application scenario was a certain degree of flexibility. With respect to the current state of EDA research, it is not simply possible to develop a single problem oriented domain vocabulary sufficient for all IP vendors. The situation very much resembles the problems currently tackled by Ontology-based Knowledge Management approaches where a proper and explicit description of all kinds of knowledge is nearly as important as the problem solution itself [3]. Hence, our objective was to develop an explicit XML-based representation of a CBR domain vocabulary tailored for IP retrieval specific needs that is a conceptualization of each particular IP characterization. From a slightly different perspective, such a vocabulary defines the primitives and the structure of each IP characterization. In the following we will present the **IP** Characterization Language (IPCHL) that has been developed as a knowledge representation language specific for CBR applications within the EDA domain. We start with the first release of IPCHL that was basically for domain vocabularies. We will then show further enhancements of IPCHL that capture other knowledge types of the CBR knowledge container model as well.

4   The Initial Version of IPCHL

As mentioned before, the initial release of IPCHL has been developed with the aim of being an explicit CBR vocabulary representation tailored for IP retrieval and is extensively described in [12]. For readers convenience, we will give a brief overview of the language and the rationales behind here.

On a very high level, two different attribute types constitute the set of potential properties for the characterization of IPs:

- *Application attributes* that refer to properties important to decide about the applicability of an IP in a given design situation
- *Quality criteria* that characterize the IP and its deliverables according to its quality.

Both types are subject to current standardization efforts of the VSIA (Virtual Socket Alliance). For the application attributes, the document „Virtual Component Attributes (VCA) With Formats for Profiling, Selection and Transfer Standard Version 2 (VCT 2 2.x)" [16] presents a variety of attributes together with proposals for their syntactical representation. For the quality criteria, the decision about several standardization proposals donated by the VSIA members is still pending. A candidate, for example, is the OpenMORE Assessment Program from Synopsis [14]. VSIA and OpenMORE approaches only identify necessary attributes and criteria. Their integration into a representation format is not tackled there and left to future work.

For the characterization of IPs by elementary properties it is essential to be compliant with the standards of the VSIA. It will ensure a wider acceptance because it is expected that tools like design checkers will commit to these standards, too. However, because of the fact that the standardization is still in progress, it is necessary to rely only on the stable parts and allow enhancements as required. Hence, a major part of IPCHL is an XML Schema definition of both catalogues as depicted in Fig. 3.

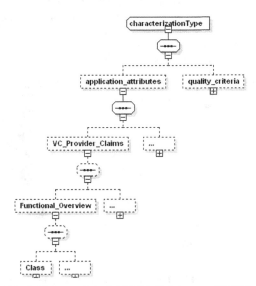

Fig. 3. Excerpt of the initial XML Schema of IPCHL

For unique identification, each attribute is referenced by a complex name that is a path of the XML document tree. The complex name is built from the name of the attribute itself and a sequence of categories, which are counterparts of the corresponding sections of the VSIA respective OpenMORE catalogues [14; 16]. For example, the fully qualified name of the attribute *class* in Fig. 3 is *Characteri-zationType/Application_Attributes/VC_Provider_Claims/Functional_Overview/Class*. Note that these categories structure the various attributes but do not classify the particular IPs. They are much like packages in UML that serve the purpose to organize the different elements of the model (e.g. diagrams, classes etc.) but should not be confused with the hierarchical structure of the model itself.

Following the CASUEL approach [8], a CBR domain vocabulary is a hierarchy of classes that is built from a taxonomical property elicited from the domain of discourse. Such a property becomes a classifier. In our application scenario, it is a property from the IP characterization. For example, a potential candidate for this is the functional class taxonomy defined in [16] by the VSIA and shown in Fig. 3. Similar to typical object-oriented modeling approaches, the classifier determines the set of remaining properties relevant for a corresponding instance. E.g. an attribute like *sampling frequency* does only apply to IPs of the class *audio converter* respective its subclasses. In fact, an attribute for itself has no meaning without the context given by the class for which they apply. This was the crucial point when developing the domain vocabulary. Because each industrial partner had his own directives for structuring his IP asset, it was simply not possible to fix a particular taxonomy within IPCHL as a standard. Hence, we specified only XML constructs for defining taxonomies and building associations between individual taxonomy nodes of and subsets of the other properties. Consequently, the checking for compliance of particular cases (IP Characterization and IP Content) as instances of the vocabulary could no longer be delegated to standard XML Schema parsers. The combination of the XML Schema specification of IPCHL and a concrete taxonomy makes the CBR domain vocabulary, which is also named an *IPCHL Profile* or, for emphasizing that it is a format for the IP characterization, *IP Characterization Schema*.

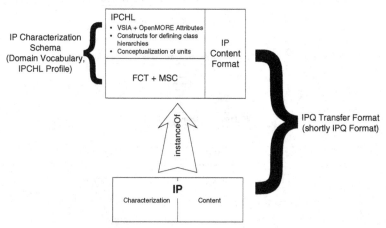

Fig. 4. IPCHL Container Overview

Fig. 4 provides an overview of the different types of knowledge involved in the IPQ market scenario. It furthermore shows the role of IPCHL within the scope of the *IPQ Transfer Format* that is the set of all formats for information potentially transferred across organizational boundaries. Because the taxonomical properties *functional class taxonomy* (FCT) and *market segment classification* (MSC) are explicitly mentioned in the standardization catalogue of the VSIA [16] they are provided as default IPCHL profiles. The IP Provider deploying the IP retrieval application can define other taxonomies acting as classifiers. In addition, IPCHL provides a conceptualisation for units used within the IP context e.g. *mV* for power consumption or *Hz* for frequencies. The IP is an instance and consists of the characterization and the content. From the perspective of traditional CBR systems, the IP is the case with the characterization as problem description and the content as solution.

5   Extending IPCHL toward a Flexible IP Knowledge Representation Language

With the initial release of IPCHL only the domain vocabulary and the IP characterization are explicitly represented. Although the remaining knowledge types of the CBR container model, e.g. similarity measures, provide highly valuable knowledge [10] as well, they were only internally available in the retrieval engine we used for the CBR application (orenge, see [6]). Beside a growing demand from the industrial partners to have at least the similarity measure explicitly represented, it also became clear that the set of properties for IP characterization identified by the VSIA [16] was not sufficient for specialized application domains e.g. error correction. Hence, it was required that properties can be defined on behalf of the IP Provider.

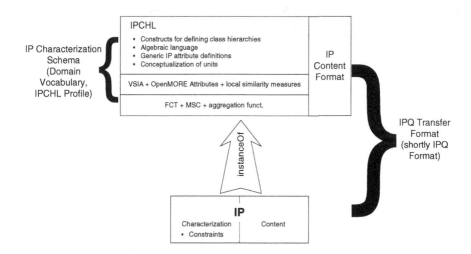

Fig. 5. Extended IPCHL V2 Knowledge Containers

Therefore, we have extended IPCHL according to Fig. 5, the new release of IPCHL now only contains a set of generic attribute type definitions, constructs for defining class hierarchies, a conceptualisation for units, and an algebraic language specification for defining similarity measures, and constraints used in generalized cases (see below). The VSIA and OpenMORE attributes, which were first-class citizens of the initial IPCHL release, are now refinements of these attribute types provided as a default IPCHL profile that can be enhanced by IP Provider specific profiles. Attribute Types refined in an IPCHL profile must define a local similarity function by making use of the algebraic language specified in IPCHL. Depending on the particular set of attributes, profiles contain the taxonomies that provide the hierarchy of the domain model. Again, the functional class taxonomy and the market segment classification are provided by default. In addition, each taxonomy node specifies an aggregation function for the attributes associated to the particular concept. At the time of writing, only simple aggregation function utilizing weighted can be defined and IPCHL provides the following attribute types:

- ValueType: ValueType is a basic attribute type.
- SingleValueType: A ValueType that is restricted to a single value.
- IntervalType: An attribute of this type defines an interval with boundaries "Maximum" and "Minimum".
- IntervalWithTypicalValueType: This type is composed of an IntervalType and a SingleValueType that acts as a standard value.
- TaxonomyType: When referencing a taxonomy this type is used. It contains one or more elements called "Node" by which taxonomy paths can be selected.
- TaxonomyDependendType: This type is composed of one or more SingleValueTypes and optionally makes it possible to define additional taxonomies that are not standardized before.
- PickListType: Picklists are a set of multiple alternative values that can be defined by using this type.
- CategoryNodeType: This type specializes category types.

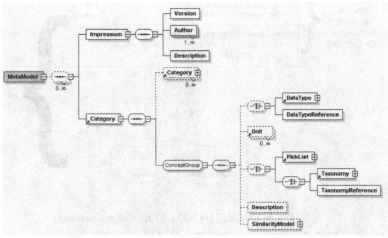

Fig. 6. Excerpt of the new XML Schema of IPCHL

Another challenge was to represent so-called *parametrizable IPs* (PIPs), which refer to a kind of IP that has a certain degree of flexibility for improved reusability. Parametrizable IPs can be seen as generalized cases because they do not cover only a point of the case space but a whole subspace of it [9]. Following the approach given in [9], generalized cases are specified by a set of constraints that span the subspace of a generalized case by defining the functional dependencies between parameters. Although generalized cases are still subject to current research, we had to take precautions for defining constraints on the IP characterization instance level.

Fig. 6 gives a brief impression of the XML Schema defined behind IPCHL. As shown, each IPCHL profile already contains information about the author and comes with a version number assigned. This is useful for tracing the history of a profile. Furthermore, this information is necessary for distinguishing different profiles in a distributed setting.

6   Perspectives of IPCHL

As mentioned before, the purpose of IPCHL is not only restricted to knowledge representation. In addition, it is a part of the contract (or protocol) between different web services of the IPQ market scenario affecting other project partners as well. From the beginning, we have been in a strong cooperation with our industrial IPQ project partners and they contributed to the following tasks:

- Elicitation of retrieval relevant attributes and their weights as feedback from daily practice.
- Visualization of the retrieved IPs
- Feedback for attributes and taxonomies

A first result from the cooperation was the integration of proprietary attributes or taxonomies beside ones identified by the VSIA und OpenMORE. Both standards are simple catalogues not sufficient for automatic reasoning about IPs. Consequently, they contain only an enumeration of attributes and lack the necessary structure. Typically, IP providers have a large amount of information about IPs, which depends on the functionality, not covered by the standard attributes. The demand for proprietary attributes resulted in the new release of IPCHL. Because it no longer relies on already existing standards, knowledge acquisition from the industrial partner became even more important. Therefore, a Java-based IPCHL editor has been developed that facilitates the development of IPCHL profiles as well as the editing particular IP Characterizations. The editor, IPCHL etc. are currently evaluated by the industrial partners. Consequently, overall market scenarios can be evaluated as soon as the necessary infrastructure that has been adopted by the other partners.

Future extensions of CBR-based IP retrieval should cover some kind of explanations because designer typically want to double-check retrieval results. It has been shown that under certain circumstances retrieval results are totally unexpected when the intended relevance of designers does not match the pre-defined weights of the IP vendor. For that reason, an explanation component will be integrated that can give very useful information if slight changes to the weight model would result in a totally different retrieval sets. A first prototype of an explanation module utilizes a sensitivity analysis interpreting the similarity model. By achieving this, users can interactively play with the retrieval system and test the influences of similarity modifications to the result set. Very related to this, is the general requirement for user specific weight models. The representation of user specific models as well as their integration in IPCHL will be an issue for the next release.

7 Related Approaches

In the following we present three related approaches to SoC development support. These approaches have not been chosen arbitrarily. They represent the different directions of SoC design support currently researched. While the VSIA (Virtual Socket Interface Alliance) aims to provide a technical foundation for IP transfer based on characterizations of virtual components (VC) or IPs [16] by identifying and cataloguing so-called Virtual Component Attributes (VCA), the company Design & Reuse [5] hosts an Internet portal with IP retrieval functionality for the IP community. The third approach from Synchronicity [15] focuses on solutions for design collaboration and design management in order to speed the development of SoCs. In contrast to the activities of the VSIA, both companies rely on own developed proprietary formats for representing IP specific knowledge. However, the intended target applications (IP marketplaces respective Tools for SoC collaboration) are very similar to those of the IPQ project and, for that reason, they have to be considered, here.

8 VSI Alliance – Virtual Component Attributes

The Virtual Socket Interface (VSI) Alliance is an industrial consortium of well-known international companies. The main goal of the VSIA is the improvement of the SoC development and the integration of software and hardware VCs from multiple sources [17]. The VSIA comprises several working groups, which have different IP standardization tasks assigned. Examples are the development of technical foundations for the IP transfer between design tools as well as the standardization of attributes that enable a quality-based assessment of IPs. As one of the leading industrial consortia, the standards of the VSIA are widely accepted. The document VCT 2 *(VSI Alliance Virtual Component Attributes With Formats for Profiling, Selection, and Transfer Standard)* proposes a set of specific attributes, their structure, and syntax for IP exchange. For example, VCT 2 contains the definition of a market segment classification (MSC), the functional class taxonomy (FCT). Although the VCT 2 currently lacks the necessary formality required for a unique representation format, it is a good starting point for distributed IP marketplaces. However, experience has shown that a proper IP description also comprises a lot of attributes specific for the intended target application of the IP. These attributes cannot be specified in advance but are essential for intelligent support like the CBR retrieval service proposed in this paper. Therefore, it is important to maintain a certain degree of flexibility for the set of IP attributes, which, of course, cannot be accomplished by the VSIA standardization approach.

9 Design and Reuse

Design And Reuse (D&R) hosts an Internet portal and offers several services related to IP reuse. D&R claims to be the world's largest directory of silicon IP and SoC design platforms. The D&R approach is a web-based solution with access to registered users. As described in [11], an "entry portal" is provided for companies in order to collect information about external IPs. The aim of D&R is to facilitate the search for IPs by distinguishing different catalogues:

- Silicon IP/SoC: Search for silicon IPs
- Verification IP: essential companions to virtual component or IPs in order to verify IPs
- Software IP: IPs ranging from embedded OS to communication stacks and application software.
- IP Search/Find Club: The worldwide place to trigger most strategic IP business deals.

The first three of these different IP catalogues allow a keyword search with or without an additional guidance by a functional taxonomy.

Under certain conditions, the search process is facilitated by some optional attributes like IP type (soft, firm, hard, model), technology (ASIC, FPGA), and verified technology. Unfortunately, these attributes are not represented later in the result set that only contains the block name and provider.

The IP Search/Find Club is different. This kind of search facilitates strategic IP business deals. Large system houses and customers are allowed to post their IP demands.

For composing an IP request, users have to fill out a form with item, functionality, integration requirements etc. D&R forwards incoming requests to qualified IP providers who can contact the customer directly while being tracked by D&R. Without any pre-selection, this can cause a lot of work for providers processing the requests. Unfortunately, no information is available if the pre-selection is done manually or automatically. Finally, D&R supports IP users in finding experts like providers, appropriate tools or other general information about IPs.

The internal representation of IPs stored in a catalogue comprises meta-data about the IP itself [11]. Depending on the classification of the IP, several data formats are defined by using XML DTD's. In contrast to services based on IPCHL, handling the D&R representation format library requires a significant number of different parsing methods.

Compared to the CBR-based IP retrieval approach of IPQ, the D&R search mechanisms neither utilize intelligent retrieval techniques nor do they provide the ability to specify additional search information that makes use of the XML-based IP representation. The combination of text-based search combined with the functional taxonomy used as decision-tree leaves much of the work to the searching users. However, as long as the amount of functional similar IPs does not grow too large, the search facilities seem to be sufficient. However, the D&R approach does not support the precision of IPCHL-based searches.

10 Synchronicity

Synchronicity provides solutions for deploying IP design methodologies including multi-site engineering. Hence, the focus is on products enabling team communication, data sharing, and third-party tool integration. Team communication comprises sharing of ideas, bug reports, and engineering change information in distributed environments. Synchronicity's solution for IP searching is IP Gear that incorporates an IP catalog and a helpdesk application. IP Gear splits into two suites. The Publisher Suite for moving design related information within and between companies. This suite provides a comprehensive infrastructure for minimizing design chain latency across the enterprise. The Catalog is a server that manages IP information by representing web pages. The helpdesk works with past solutions for answering requests. The Consumer Suite provides IP retrieval by connecting suppliers using the Publisher Suite. Furthermore, this suite has the same access to the helpdesk as the Publisher Suite. Consumers are assured to retrieve the latest and correct IP versions that include updates, notifications and incremental releases. Consumers can search for IPs by browsing through a component hierarchy or by using a key word search. Results are presented as links to their web pages. Similar IPs are indicated and their differences are visually highlighted. Although Synchronicity provides solutions for every step of a design flow, IP search facilities are restricted to text-based search or navigation in taxonomies. A structured representation of the IP documentation, which is typically created during IP design, is not considered. For the Synchronicity approach, standardization issues and interoperability aspects are the crucial points because of the proprietary representation format that is non-disclosed.

11 Conclusion

In this paper we presented IPCHL, a flexible and extensible representation format for IP-specific knowledge. Originated from a CBR application that enables efficient and intelligent support for IP selection in an internet-based market scenario, IPCHL meets the requirements to become a standard committed by a variety of services. This is typically not easy to achieve because the different CBR knowledge containers do not distinguish between ontological and problem-specific knowledge. Beside the domain vocabulary underlying a structural CBR application, other knowledge types like similarity models can be either problem or domain specific. In our approach we reflected the different scopes by distinguishing between local similarity measures for generic types defined by IPCHL itself and local similarity measures defined within an IPCHL profile.

IPCHL may become a language that supports distributed CBR approaches in the near future. As a declarative representation language enables interesting new approaches like CBR applications tightly integrated into the IP design workflow.

References

1. Arcos J., Plaza E.: Reflection in NOOS: An object-oriented representation language for knowledge modelling. In: IJCAI-95 Workshop on reflection and meta-level architecture and their applications in AI, (1995).
2. Bergmann, R., Wilke, W., Vollrath, I. & Wess, S.: Integrating general knowledge with object-oriented case representation and reasoning. In: H.-D. Burkhard & M. Lenz (eds.) 4th German Workshop: Case-Based Reasoning - System Development and Evaluation, Informatik-Berichte Nr. 55, Humboldt-Universität Berlin, (1996) 120–127.

3. Bergmann, R., Schaaf, M.: On the Relations between Structural Case-Based Reasoning and Ontology-based Knowledge Management, Proceedings German Workshop on Experience Management, April (2003).
4. Decker S., Erdmann M., Fensel D., Studer R.: Ontobroker: Ontology based access to distributed and semi-structured information. In R. Meersman et al. (eds.), DS-8: Semantic Issues in Multimedia Systems. Kluwer Academic Publisher (1999).
5. Design & Reuse Homepage. http://www.us.design-reuse.com/, last visited 01/27/2003.
6. empolis knowledge management GmbH: The orenge Framework - A Platform for Intelligent Industry Solutions Based on XML and Java. Whitepaper, empolis knowledge management GmbH, Kaiserslautern (2001).
7. Grosso E., Eriksson H., Fergerson R.W., Tu S.W., Musen M.M.: Knowledge Modeling at the Millenium – The Design and Evolution of Protégé-2000. In: Proc. the 12th International Workshop on Knowledge Acquisition, Modeling and Management (KAW'99), Banff, Canada, October (1999).
8. Manago, M., Bergmann, R., Wess, S., Traphöner, R.: CASUEL: A common case representation language. ESPRIT Project INRECA. Deliverable D1, University of Kaiserslautern (1994).
9. Mougouie, B., Bergmann, R.: Similarity Assessment for Generalized Cases by Optimization Methods. In: S. Craw & A. Preece (eds.) European Conference on Case-Based Reasoning (ECCBR'02). Lecture Notes in Artificial Intelligence, Springer (2002).
10. Richter, M. M.: The Knowledge Contained in Similarity Measures. Invited talk at the First International Conference on CBR, ICCBR (1995).
11. Saucier, G., Brüning, A., Radetzki, M., Pfirsh, T.: IP XML GATEWAY. Medea Workshop (2002). http://www.us.design-reuse.com/encapsulation/paper002.pdf/, last visited 20/03/2003.
12. Schaaf, M., Visarius, M., Bergmann, R., Maximini, R., Spinelli, M., Lessmann, J., Hardt, W., Ihmor, S., Thronicke, W., Franz, J., Tautz, C., Traphöner, R.: IPCHL - A Description Language for Semantic IP Characterization, Forum on Specification & Design Languages, September (2002).
13. Schaaf, M., Maximini, R., Bergmann, R., Tautz, C., Traphöner, R.: Supporting Electronic Design Reuse by Integrating Quality-Criteria into CBR-Based IP Selection, Proceedings 6th European Conference on Case Based Reasoning, September (2002).
14. Synopsis Inc., Mentor Graphics Corporation: OpenMORE Assessment Program for Hard/Soft IP Version 1.0, http://www.openmore.com (2001).
15. Synchronicity Homepage. http://www.synchronicity.com/, last visited 01/27/2003.
16. VSI AllianceTM, Virtual Component Transfer Development Working Group: Virtual Component Attributes (VCA) With Formats for Profiling, Selection, and Transfer. Standard Version 2.2 (VCT 2 2.2) (2001).
17. VSI Alliance. http://www.vsi.org/, last visited 03/30/2003.

Managing Experience for Process Improvement in Manufacturing

Radhika B. Selvamani and Deepak Khemani

A.I. & D.B. Lab, Dept. of Computer Science & Engineering I.I.T.Madras, India
khemani@iitm.ac.in
bradhika@peacock.iitm.ernet.in

Abstract. Process changes in manufacturing are often done by trial and error, even when experienced domain personnel are involved. This is mainly due to the fact that in many domains the number of parameters involved is large and there exists only a partial understanding of interrelationships between them. This paper describes a framework for keeping track of process change experiments, before they qualify as full cases. Process changes happen as a result of diagnosis done by the expert, following which some therapy is decided. The paper also presents an algorithm for diagnosis and therapy based on induction on discrimination trees constructed on specific views on the set of problem parameters.

1 Introduction

Case Based Reasoning (CBR) has effectively been used in many domains to store and retrieve past cases to solve new problems. By storing and retrieving problem solving instances CBR is instrumental in exploiting experience in the simplest way. It is because of this simplicity that this cycle of CBR makes it a natural tool for knowledge management in various domains [1]. It has the ability to accrue a vast amount of experience in the form of problem solution pairs when it is embedded in any activity in which human solvers operate. But, by its nature, as a problem solving aid it is limited to reusing solutions from the past to similar problems. In such a scenario CBR system learn when human experts solve more problems. In this paper we explore ways in which the data available in case bases can be utilized to help the experts arrive at new solutions.

Storing and retrieving individual experiences is only the first stage of knowledge-based activity. There are many problems where the collective experience available with a problem solver plays a role in arriving at a solution. Traditionally the AI community has attempted to model abstract knowledge as rules directly. Such knowledge is acquired if a domain expert with a knowledge engineer can articulate the rules. Machine learning approaches investigate the automatic acquisition of knowledge in compact forms, or target functions [2]. Meanwhile, the data mining community has occupied itself with discovery of rules and associations from raw data.

K.D. Ashley and D.G. Bridge (Eds.): ICCBR 2003, LNAI 2689, pp. 522–536, 2003.
© Springer-Verlag Berlin Heidelberg 2003

But often the goals of this exercise are loosely stated, since the objective is discovery of some interesting associations [3].

In this paper we describe a methodology of exploiting a repository of stored experiences, for specific goals. The objective of our induction algorithm is to identify a cause of a frequently occurring undesirable event, for example a particular kind of defect in manufacturing. Further, while adding this functionality to a CBR system in an industrial setting, we observe that different stakeholders in an organization make different kinds of knowledge demands. At one end a trainee is keen to learn what is routine, while at the other end the expert seeks to understand and classify what is out of place. This understanding often happens in stages, with the aid of repeated experiments with different ways of doing things. A knowledge management system should allow for such tentative knowledge to exist, even to be exploited, while it is being tested in the crucible of performance. In this paper we look at how experts explore the space of solutions, and how a case repository can maintain such tentative knowledge, and also the kind of support it can provide in arriving at informed solutions.

Section 2 describes the diagnosis problem in a manufacturing domain, and section 3 looks at experienced knowledge and its use in such a setting. Section 4 considers process improvement and section 5 describes an appropriate architecture to handle changing knowledge. Section 6 looks at how knowledge is used in the organization. Section 7 looks at an approach to diagnosis and repair followed by some results and concluding remarks.

2 Manufacturing Domain

We seek to extend an existing CBR implementation [4] in a refractory blocks manufacturing setting. Refractory blocks are manufactured by melting a mix of materials at high temperatures in an electrocast furnace, and pouring the melt into a mould. The blocks then need to be annealed to room temperature, and if everything has gone right, go through a finishing process before being inspected. The entire process may take a few months, and since the material and energy inputs are substantial too, there is a high premium on success. In the implementation described above, the CBR system acquires cases by data acquisition embedded in the shop floor. The process shops capture the information needed for a case as part of their routine [1], which becomes the case acquisition process of CBR systems. The quality control department detects problems in the final products and uses the retrieval cycle of CBR to get a solution from the case base. The CBR system retrieves a single case or a set of cases which matches the problem and process parameters of the final product.

2.1 Beyond Instance Based Solutions

There are situations when traditional CBR systems retrieving a single case for a given problem may not be able to provide a solution. Instance based CBR requires a successful case in its repository. In any manufacturing scenario process improvement exercises are periodically done to improve the quality of the products. New cases are created after some informed trial and error by domain experts. A knowledge management system could support this activity in two ways. One, by guiding the trial and error process with analysis of the past data. Particularly when the system may have large amount of knowledge captured and stored. Two, by allowing tentative process knowledge to exist while it is being tested, until a decisive case is at hand.

2.2 Defects in Manufacturing

Manufacturing processes are usually distributed among different shops and comprehensive expertise is not easy to acquire. Also the processes are prolonged involving many parameters. With a large number of parameters contributing to the product it is often difficult to pinpoint causes for defects [4]. In many ill understood domains, for instance foundries, manual analysis in the domain may be difficult and error prone. In such situations experts take recourse to trial and error methods to identify the cause of the problem. This brings in a need to integrate this problem solving activity into the CBR system. Also better diagnosis methods that aid experts would increase the usability and acceptability of the knowledge systems in the manufacturing domain.

3   CBR in Experience Management

CBR methodology originated from the cognitive field of human understanding and has been widely applied since late eighties. The Experience Factory approach gained importance during early nineties [5,6]. Experience management involves apart from knowledge storage and retrieval, sophisticated knowledge acquisition techniques, role identification exercise (of the stake holders), and dispersion of the knowledge widely referred to as "saying the right thing at the right time" [7]. Since the mid nineties CBR has been used both on the organizational experience factory process level as well as the technical experience base implementation level. Much of the work was focused on the software industries. [8, 9]. Knowledge management including experience management using CBR tools gained importance in different domains [10, 11]. Experience knowledge acquisition and usage in a manufacturing domain is different from other domains. A manufacturing domain requires any experience management solution to be embedded into the manufacturing process, rather than be developed as a stand-alone system for storage and dissemination of knowledge [12].   The CBR structures itself into the three main issues of knowledge management namely knowledge creation, knowledge integration and knowledge dissemination.

3.1   Knowledge Retrieval for Different Stake Holders

An instance-based implementation of CBR employs retrieval of past cases and adaptation of slightly different retrieved cases to solve the current problem. This makes the CBR attractive for training of novices and making day-to-day simple process decisions for the other employees. But it is of little or of no practical use for experts seeking to solve more complex problems. Since experts are involved in critical decisions regarding process improvement they tend to use CBR for just validation of their thoughts. At the same time if the experts were to ignore the CBR system the system in turn would be deprived of their experience. This concern for the issue of making CBR more useful to domain experts leads to the exploration of certain real problems faced by stakeholders in an organization. The following are the demands that different stakeholders may make on the system.

Requirements of the Trainees
- Browsing through the case base helps the trainees to learn about the domain
- Knowledge of how specific processes have evolved over time and the methods employed for design alterations would help understand why a particular process is being used.
- Knowledge of allowable process modifications *and* modifications that led to failure would facilitate informed modification / adaptation.

Requirements of the Case Author
- Knowledge about strength of cases. The more the case finds a match with a real problem, the greater its utility.
- Visualization of case matching. This would allow the author to validate the notion of similarity used by the retrieval system.
- Ease of maintenance of the system.

Requirements of the Domain Experts
- When there exist unsolved problems: For example focusing on a particular kind of defect an expert may look for some means of analysis of the past data to relate a set of process parameters to the defect.
- Experts need to be satisfied by the reasoning process involved in the analysis.

Requirements of the Design Department
- The process knowledge in the domain is not static. Changing environment and requirements often demand changes in the design process. In the absence of a precise domain theory, a CBR system could support a new process development.
- Statistical data stored with a case base could initiate changes in the design handbook.

In the next section we describe the process improvement scenario.

4 Process Improvement Cycle

Manufacturing poses problems continuously. In many domains it is more of an art rather than a science. There is a process cycle in the domain (Fig. 1). Applying the specified parameters for a particular process results in an outcome, which may be the defect in the manufactured product. The solution provided by the experts when the output is undesirable is usually a change in some of the process parameters. The changed process is applied in the domain to observe the outcome.

The process is revised until the desired outcome is obtained, a point at which the process is presumably flawless. Then, the process and the outcome form a complete case. In the intervening period, when the new problem is being experimented with, the experience instances remain as tentative cases.

4.1 Suitability of the Domain

The process cycle described above suits most domains where a trial and error change in the system is adopted to find remedies. The manufacturing domain has been chosen for our discussion. In this domain, parameters include the design specification of the product, but the diagnosis and alterations, which are discussed later in the paper, are applied only for the features involved in the production process, which can be modified affecting the outcome of the product. The defect description forms the outcome of the case. The alterations suggested for the production parameters in the trial case form the solution of the case. Since the complete case needs no further trial to be done, it does not require a solution part.

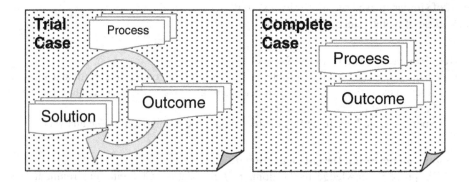

Fig. 1. Trial Case and a complete case in the process improvement cycle

5   Architecture for CBR in Process Improvement

5.1   CBR Module

The CBR module has two functionalities, case retrieval and diagnosis (Fig. 2). While retrieval takes place on flat structure of cases, diagnosis is done on hierarchical organization of a set of case instances [13, 14].

Case Retrieval. Conceptually CBR systems have a single case base used by the retrieval engine. But in the approach described here we have two different types of cases, trial cases and complete cases, stored respectively in a Trail Case Base (TCB) and a Complete Case Base (CCB). Any new case in the domain first enters the trial case base. When a process that consistently avoids the defects is found, the case graduates to the complete case base. A complete case is a case that has passed through the trials in the domain and has been finalized by the domain experts. Case history consists of all the instances belonging to the same trial in the TCB and the completed case in the CCB. It may be observed that retaining the instances, many of which have been classified under one case, is important for knowledge discovery tasks. A completed trail history will have cases both in the TCB as well as the CCB. A partial trial history may not have a case in the CCB. During retrieval for any new instance all the best matching cases are retrieved from both the TCB and the CCB.

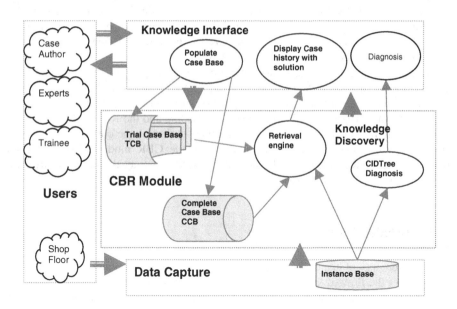

Fig. 2. Architecture for CBR in Process Improvement

Diagnosis. When a trial case has a bad outcome with sufficient number of instances, it needs improvement. Diagnosis process relates the outcome with the process parameters and therapy suggests alternative values for the parameters causing the defects. Our approach to diagnosis is described in section 7. Following diagnosis a new trial case is formed with the altered parameter values which is stored in the trial case base and the process is modified by the design department accordingly, for the products manufactured with the specified design in the case.

5.2 Knowledge Interface

The interface serves the purpose of capturing the knowledge from the experts as well as displaying the knowledge stored in the case base. It also lets users visualize the diagnosis process, so that they are convinced with the results. This is an extension over the information retrieval subsystem in the previous work [4]. A knowledge interface should cater to the different kinds of users for effective distribution of knowledge among stake holders. The various functionalities of the CBR module discussed above are useful for stakeholders at various levels in the domain. The shop floor personnel use the system for capturing and storing the data prevailing in the domain. The trainees, the domain experts and the technical staff involved in maintaining the system (case author) use the knowledge interface according to their needs. Access to the case history benefits the trainees who are new to the domain, enabling them to acquire the expertise of the manufacturing process. The domain experts on the other hand may use the system for analysis into the domain and solving new problems. Finally the maintenance of the cases within the case base is done by the case authors using the match values and the utility measures provided along with the cases during the retrieval. It is the case authors who define the case base, populating it with records from the instance base.

The data capture module taps into capture the data that prevails in the domain as a routine process, maps the data to required ontology and stores the formatted data in the instance base. Details about case acquisition and storage may be obtained from [4]. The instance base is used both by the CBR module and the Knowledge Interface. Provisions are provided in the knowledge interface to display the collected data which can be used to carry out further analysis using the CBR module. The diagnosis module in the CBR system uses the instance base to construct the memory structure needed for the investigation process.

6   Knowledge Flow

The requirements of the various stakeholders have been mentioned in section 3.1. Fig. 3 shows the flow of knowledge among various stakeholders. The instances of the newly manufactured products are provided to the users initially so that they can select the one, which is of their interest. The CBR module retrieves a set of case history matching the product instances, which may be of interest for new employees to know about the domain. The case author using the match value obtained during retrieval decides the case where the new data fits. If it does not fit anywhere, it is added as a new trial case. When they feel that the utility of a particular trial case is large and the outcome is not desirable, they can analyze the domain using the diagnosis and therapy module to get suggestions for process improvement.

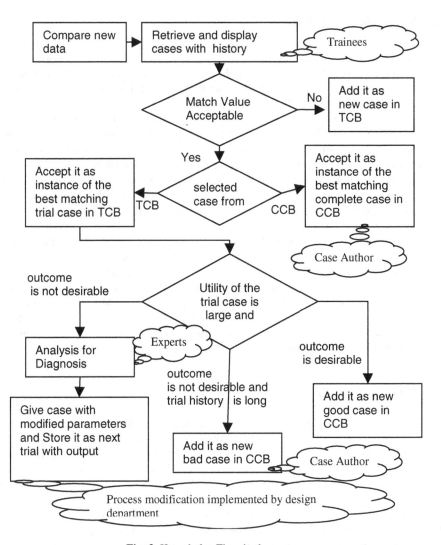

Fig. 3. Knowledge Flow in the system

The design department, which takes care of process modifications, needs to validates the suggestions using the cases in the case base and perhaps modify the design handbook. After looking at the trial history the design department can finalize the trials to form a complete case to populate the CCB. The CCB has both cases arrived at by a successful trial experiment and bad cases that mark the manufacturing processes that lead to undesirable outcome.

7 Diagnosis and Repair

We assume that defects can be traced to some parameter value setting. Looking at a case instance there would be no way of determining the parameter that is responsible for the defect. This is because a CBR system does not bring out any correlation or causal connections amongst the various attributes. However, looking at a significantly large set of defect cases it may be possible to isolate the culprit. We describe below a methodology that first builds a discrimination tree over a suspect set of parameters, and then uses a statistical measure to pick out the most likely fault choices. These parameters for example pertain to a particular sub process on the shop floor. We describe below an algorithm to do induction on discrimination trees constructed on specific views on the database.   The system discovers plausible faulty choice of process parameters, and also suggests a therapy derived from successful past instances.

The previous work in the domain of aluminium casting discusses process improvement by trouble shooting and closing the loop of the manufacturing process [11]. It emphasizes the need for tracking the outcome of applying a case in the domain. Our work progressed with a goal to capture the outcome of a case and hence facilitating experiments in the existing domain processes. Data Mining techniques are often used to extract the required organization knowledge from the Experience base. [15]. We use classification trees for fault diagnosis using interestingness measures specially designed to focus the task.

7.1 CIDTree Methodology

The analysis for diagnosis is done over hierarchically organized cases. A methodology called CIDTree, cause induction in discrimination tree has been developed for diagnosis of the defect. Preliminary results based on the algorithm are described in [16]. The goal of building a CID Tree is to isolate those process parameters that could have led to the defect under consideration. Not only would one want to know the identity of the parameter, one would also like to determine the values of that parameter, which lead to the defect. The CID Tree is built as follows. First the user needs to identify the candidate set of attributes that are suspected. In our system this is done by selecting a view of the manufacturing process that focuses on a particular shop floor. Then the instances in the instance base are clustered to form two classes, good and bad, depending on the defect that needs to be analyzed. Next, the system uses c4.5 algorithm [17] to build a decision tree to segregate the defective cases from the non-defective ones. Ideally the algorithm would come up with a tree as shown in Fig.4(a). This tree has two leaf nodes, marked "Flawed" and "Suggestion" with zero entropy [17]. In practice however such a clean segregation may not occur and a larger tree with nodes containing a mix of defective and non-defective cases will be generated as in Fig.4(b). Here some parameter choices may be seen in the context of other parameter choices when the flawed node is deeper in the tree. The task now is to identify the most likely "flawed " node. We use a measure described below to determine the most likely set of flawed nodes, that identify the process

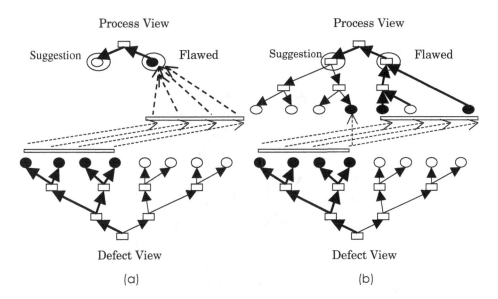

Fig. 4. Overlapping Clusters of the Process View with those of the Defect View Identifying the Flawed Node

parameter values that are likely to be the' cause of the defect. The sibling of the flaw node that is most successful becomes the suggested change in the parameter value.

Interestingness measure. Although specification of the task-relevant data and the kind of knowledge to be mined may substantially reduce the number of patterns to be generated, a data mining process may still generate a large number of patterns. Typically only a small fraction of these patterns will actually be of interest to the given user. A smaller set can be extracted by specifying interestingness measures or objective measures that estimate the simplicity, certainty, utility and novelty of patterns. The objective measures are based on the structure of patterns and the statistics underlying them [18]. Usually the interesting measure for a decision tree is its number of nodes or leaves. But we use this tree for functionality other than classification. Our interestingness measure calculation and the results are consequently different. After building the tree we classify all the instances under each decision node and determine the number and nature of the instances classified. We apply the objective measures to this tree structure to get the relevance score of the attributes with respect to defects. The relevance support is a measure of the attribute choice being related to the defect. Support and confidence are two widely used measures to determine the usefulness of an association rule mined from the database [18]. The interestingness measure for the association pattern (Current Node => Defect) in Fig. 5 is calculated as shown below.

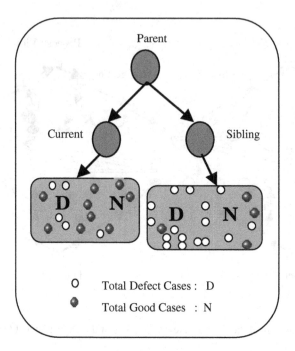

Fig. 5. Distribution of cases at the nodes and leaves

Support of an association pattern refers to the fraction of the total data tuples for which the pattern is true.

Support of (A=>B) = # (tuples with both A and B) / # (tuples in the data base) .
Where #(x) refers to number (x) .

Support (Current Node = > Defect)
= Fraction of defects under current node over all cases in the instance base
= $D_1/(N+D)$.

Confidence is the validity or trustworthiness of the pattern (ie) Fraction of defect cases out of all cases classified under current node.

Confidence of (A=>B) = # (tuples with both A & B) / # (tuples with A) .

Confidence (Current Node => Defect)
= Fraction of defect cases under current node over all cases classified under the current node
= $D_1/(N_1+D_1)$.

Maximize support and confidence (Current Node => Defective):

$$D_1{}^2 / (N+D) * (N_1+D_1 \quad . \tag{1}$$

Minimize support and confidence (Current Node => Non-Defective):

$$N_1{}^2 / (N+D) * (N_1+D_1) \quad . \tag{2}$$

Minimize support and confidence (Sibling Node => Defective):

$$D_2{}^2 / (N+D) * (N_2+D_2) \quad . \tag{3}$$

Maximize support and confidence (Sibling Node => Non-Defective):

$$N_2{}^2 / (N+D) * (N_2+D_2) \quad . \tag{4}$$

Relevance of Current Node in causing the defect

$$D_1{}^2 N_2{}^2 / D_2{}^2 N_1{}^2 \quad . \tag{1 x 4 / 2 x 3}$$

Example. The diagnosis process has been tested in a domain manufacturing carborundum blocks [5]. There are two shops providing process parameters, the foundry and the furnace. The products manufactured have defects like cracks, spalls and hottear due to wrong parameter specifications. Process parameters for about 206 blocks manufactured in the domain was available in the instance base. There were 45 blocks. The instance base was manually clustered to defective and non-defective cases. Defective cluster had 38 instances and non-defective cluster had 168 instances. The induction tree was built for this training set of 206 instances. The number of defective and non-defective cases classified under each node is calculated as shown in Fig. 6. D denotes number of defective cases and N denotes number of non-defective cases. The relevance score is calculated for the nodes as shown in Table 1. The nodes 3 and 6 have high relevance with the defect and the nodes 4 and 5 are suggested respectively as the therapy. This can be seen visually in the Fig. 6. The arrow points towards the best alternative below each node. The relevance score is given below the arcs.

8 Conclusions and Future Work

The prime objective of the work described here is better process management. The Experience/Knowledge management tool is an application with a CBR system. We identify different needs of the different stakeholders. Two important requirements are to manage tentative process change experiments, and to provide decision-making support to experts to experiment with process changes. Cause identification for defects is done by induction over past experience and remedial actions are produced as a corollary. The cause is a flawed choice node, and the therapy is a (successful) sibling of the flawed node. The results of tests done in a few cases have been encouraging. In the new EM framework, the suggested therapy may be experimented with and stored as cases. Validation over a period of time will lead to its acceptance as a standard operating procedure. Future work is towards exploration of the diagnosis process using different induction algorithms

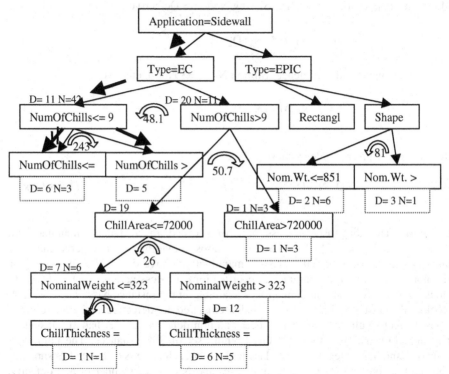

Diagnosis: If Type = EC and NumOfChills <= 9 then NumOfChills <=6 causes cracks. **Therapy** : Allow numofchills > 6

Fig. 6. The discrimination tree and the induction process for diagnosis of cracks over the foundry parameters. D = Number of Defect cases. N = Number of good cases. The tail of the arc points towards the node relevant in causing defect and the head towards the alternative good node. The relevance scores are given below the arcs. The highest score is 243 and that gives the diagnosis and therapy. For score calculation refer Table 1

Table 1. Results tabulated on diagnosis of cracks over Foundry parameters. Possible Diagnosis (Node 3, 6) and suggested therapies (Node 4, 5) . The table was formed on the information derived at the nodes of a discrimination tree built over foundry parameters. D = defect cases classifieds under the node. N = Good cases classified under the node. Score 243 is the highest

Node No	Nodes	D Defect	N None	Score = $(D2^2*N1^2)/(N2^2*D1^2)$	1/Score	
1	NumOfChills<= 9	11	42			
2	NumOfChills > 9	20	11	48.19		
3	NumOfChills<= 6	6	3			Diagnosis
4	NumOfChills > 6	5	39		243	Therapy
5	Nom. Wt. <= 851	2	6			Therapy
6	Nom. Wt. > 851	3	1	81		Diagnosis
7	ChillArea<=720000	19	8			
8	ChillArea >720000	1	3	50.76		
9	NominalWeight <=323	7	6			
10	NominalWeight >323	12	2	26		
11	ChillThickness = 1	1	1			
12	ChillThickness = 25	6	5	1		

References

1. Watson, I.: Applying Case-Based Reasoning: Techniques for Enterprise Systems. Morgan Kauffman Publishers, Inc. San Francisco, CA , (1997) 61–77
2. Mitchell, Tom M.: Machine Learning. McGraw-Hill Companies, Inc., Singapore (1997)
3. Pazzani, Michael J.: Knowledge discovery from data ?, IEEE Intelligent Systems and their applications, Special issue on Data Mining II, Vol. 15, No. 2, March/April 2000, pp. 10–13
4. Khemani, D., Selvamani, Radhika B., Dhar, Anando R., Michael, S.M.: InfoFrax : CBR in Fused Cast Refractory Manufacture. in S. Craw, A. Preece (Eds.): Advances in Case-Based Reasoning, 6th European Conference, ECCBR 2002, Aberdeen, Scotland, UK,. Proceedings, LNAI 2416, (2002) 560–574
5. Althoff, K.-D., Decker, B., Hartkopf, S., Jedlitschka, A., Nick, M., Rech, J.: Experience Management: The Fraunhofer IESE Experience Factory, P. Perner (eds).: In Proc. Industrial Conference Data Mining. July (2001) Leipzig 24.–25
6. Birk, A., Surmann, D., Althoff, K.-D.: Applications of Knowledge Acquisition in Experimental Software Engineering. Fensel, D., Studer, R.: (Eds.): Knowledge Acquisition, Modeling, and Management (EKAW'99), Springer Verlag, (1999) 67–84.
7. Fisher, G.,Ostwald J.: Knowledge Management: Problems, Promises, Realities, and Challenges. In: Special issue on Knowledge Management. IEEE Intelligent Systems, Vol. 16, no. 1, Jan./Feb. (2001) 60–72
8. Bergmann, R., Breen, S., Göker, M., Manago, M., Schumacher, J., Stahl, A., Tartarin, E., Wess, S., Wilke, W.: The INRECA-II Methodology for Building and Maintaining CBR Applications. (1998)

9. Althoff, K.-D., Becker-Kornstaedt, U., Decker, B., Klotz, A., Leopold, E., Rech, J., Voss, A.: The indiGo Project: Enhancement of Experience Management and Process Learning with Moderated Discourses. In P. Perner (Ed.): Data Mining in E-Commerce, Medicine and Knowledge Management, Springer Verlag, Lecture Notes in Computer Science. (2002).
10. Althoff, K.-D., Bomarius, F., Müller, W. & Nick, M.: Using a Case-Based Reasoning for Supporting Continuous Improvement Processes. In: P. Perner (ed.): Proc. German Workshop on Machine Learning, Technical Report. Institute for Image Processing and Applied Informatics, Leipzig, (1999).
11. Price, C ., Pegler, I S., Ratcliffe, M B., McManus, A.: From troubleshooting to process design: closing the manufacturing loop. In proc. 2nd International Conference, ICCBR-97, Providence, Rhode Island, USA, July 25–27, Lecture Notes in Computer Science 1266 Springer (1997)
12. Michael, S. M., Khemani, D.: Knowledge Management in Manufacturing Technology, In Proceedings of the International Conference on Enterprise Information System 2002, Ciudad Real,, Spain, Vol. I. (2002) 506–512
13. Schank, Roger C.: Dynamic Memory Revisited. Cambridge University Press, Cambridge, London, NewYork (1999)
14. Kolodner, J.: Case-Based Reasoning. Morgan Kaufmann Publishers,Inc., SanMateo, California (1993).
15. Patterson, D., Anand, S S., Dubitzky, W., Hughes, J G.: Towards Automated Case Knowledge Discovery in the M2 Case-Based Reasoning System. In Knowledge and Information Systems: An International Journal. Springer Verlag, Vol. 1 (1999) 61–82.
16. Selvamani, Radhika B., Khemani D.: Investigating Cause for Failures in Discrimination Tree from Multiple Views. In the proceedings of the International Conference of Knowledge Based Computer Systems, Mumbai (2002)
17. Quinlan, J.R., C4.5: Programs for Machine Learning. Morgan Kaufmann Publishers,Inc., SanMateo, California (1993)
18. Han,. J., Nishio, S., Kawano, H., Wang, W.: Generalization based data mining in object oriented database using an object cube model. Data and Knowledge Engineering, Vol. 25 (1998) 55–97

Using Evolution Programs to Learn Local Similarity Measures

Armin Stahl and Thomas Gabel

Kaiserslautern University of Technology, Computer Science Department
Artificial Intelligence - Knowledge-Based Systems Group
67653 Kaiserslautern, Germany
stahl@informatik.uni-kl.de, tgabel@rhrk.uni-kl.de

Abstract. The definition of similarity measures is one of the most crucial aspects when developing case-based applications. In particular, when employing similarity measures that contain a lot of specific knowledge about the addressed application domain, modelling similarity measures is a complex and time-consuming task. One common element of the similarity representation are *local similarity measures* used to compute similarities between the values of single attributes. In this paper an approach to learn local similarity measures by employing an evolution program — a special form of a genetic algorithm — is presented. The goal of the approach is to learn similarity measures that sufficiently approximate the *utility of cases* for given problem situations in order to obtain reasonable retrieval results.

1 Introduction

When developing case-based applications, the definition of accurate similarity measures is one of the most important tasks. Even if a reasonable amount of high-quality case knowledge is available, the overall problem-solving capability of a CBR system strongly depends on the similarity measure employed. Only if it is possible to retrieve cases that are really useful for the current problem-solving situation, the full potential of the available case knowledge can be exploited.

According to the traditional CBR paradigm, namely *"similar problems have similar solutions"*, the concept of *similarity* can be characterised as a heuristic used to estimate the *utility* of cases for particular problem-solving situations. However, the specific semantic of the term "similarity" generally depends on the employed similarity measures. In traditional CBR applications similarity often was interpreted as a kind of *similar look*. Similarity measures that are defined according to this semantic only consider the syntactical differences between the entities to be compared. Popular examples are the Hamming distance, the simple matching coefficient, the Euclidean distance and other simple distance metrics. In what follows, we call such measures *knowledge-poor similarity measures (kpSM)*. While such measures can easily be defined, the drawback of them is that they do not consider the particular coherences of the addressed application domain.

K.D. Ashley and D.G. Bridge (Eds.): ICCBR 2003, LNAI 2689, pp. 537–551, 2003.
© Springer-Verlag Berlin Heidelberg 2003

This often leads to bad retrieval results due to an insufficient approximation of the cases' utility.

Hence, in many recent CBR applications the term similarity is interpreted differently. Instead of only measuring syntactical differences, here, the *utility* of cases is approximated by considering the specific semantic of the case knowledge. This means, particular knowledge about the domain has to be encoded into similarity measures in order to obtain a well-founded utility approximation [1]. A very simple form of such *knowledge-intensive similarity measures (kiSM)* are specific feature weights that are used to express the different importance of the single case features.

Unfortunately, the use of kiSM is generally coupled with a significant drawback. To be able to define such measures, at least a partial understanding of the underlying application domain is required. However, CBR is often applied in domains where this understanding is nearly missing completely. And even if the domain is partially understood, the acquisition and formal representation of the required domain knowledge usually leads to additional development effort. This additional effort may prevent the use of kiSM, although they might significantly increase the efficiency and/or competence of the CBR system to be developed.

One possibility to avoid the mentioned drawback is the application of machine learning techniques to simplify the acquisition of similarity knowledge. Unfortunately, existing approaches to learn similarity measures are mostly restricted to classification domains only and cannot be employed directly in other application domains like e-commerce or general knowledge management scenarios. Further, existing approaches focus mainly on learning feature weights. However, when employing more sophisticated kiSM, major portions of the domain knowledge are usually encoded in complex *local similarity measures* used to compute similarities between single attribute values.

In this paper an approach to learn local similarity measures by using an evolution program — a special form of a genetic algorithm — is presented. The described approach bases on our general framework for learning similarity measures that has already been presented in [11,12]. First we will discuss the basic difficulties that arise when defining kiSM manually and we review our general learning framework. After that we describe a new learning algorithm used to extend the framework on learning local similarity measures. To show the general applicability of the algorithm the results of a first experimental evaluation are presented. Finally, we close with a discussion of related work and an outlook on future research issues.

2   Defining Knowledge-Intensive Similarity Measures

In contrast to simple syntactical measures, the definition of accurate kiSM requires a difficult knowledge acquisition and engineering process. To guarantee reasonable retrieval results, knowledge about the utility of cases for particular problem situations has to be acquired and formalised. Basically, this knowledge strongly depends on the underlying application domain and the concrete application scenario of the CBR system to be developed. For example, the following aspects might influence how to estimate the utility of cases:

- Consider a traditional CBR scenario, like a classification or diagnosis task. Even if the domain is not completely understood, domain experts often possess *partial knowledge about the relationship between problems and solutions*. So, they know, for example, upper bounds for tolerable differences between the query and the cases' attribute values to ensure that a case is still relevant for a given problem situation.
- A different situation occurs in e-commerce or general knowledge management scenarios. Here, the utility of cases is not only determined by the domain, but also by the *individual preferences of the customers/users*. To be able to provide personalised recommendation functionality, the CBR system has to employ similarity measures that consider the preferences of individual customers/users or at least the preferences of certain customer/user classes.
- When providing case adaptation functionality, the semantic of the similarity measure is different to that in a retrieval-only system. Here, it is not appropriate to estimate the utility of a case for the given query directly. Instead, the similarity measure must approximate the utility of a case with respect to the available adaptation possibilities, i.e. it has to *guarantee the retrieval of easily adaptable cases* [10,7].

When defining kiSM, one is often confronted with major problems that complicate or even avoid a good approximation of cases' utility. The kind of problems arising depends on the particular application scenario, for example:

- In traditional classification/diagnosis scenarios, *insufficient explicit domain knowledge* might be available. Possible reasons are, for example, a poorly understood domain, or the fact that an experienced domain expert is not available or too expensive.
- Even if an experienced domain expert is available, s/he is *usually not familiar with the similarity representation formalisms* of the CBR system. So, the formalisation of the provided knowledge might be very expensive because it might only be available in natural language.
- The knowledge about the real utility of cases might be not available at all during the development phase of the CBR system. When applying personalised similarity measures in an e-commerce or knowledge management scenario, the *knowledge can only be provided by the users themselves* during the use of the system.
- The *knowledge might only be available in another representation form*. For example, to estimate the adaptability of cases, one has to transfer adaptation knowledge into the similarity measure.

2.1   Representing Similarity Measures

In the following we assume an attribute-value based case representation and a commonly used structure to represent similarity measures consisting of

1. *local similarity measures* used to compute similarities between values of individual attributes,
2. *attribute weights* used to express the importance of individual attributes with respect to the utility approximation,
3. an *amalgamation function* used to compute the final similarity value for a given query and a case, based on local similarities and attribute weights.

Because this paper deals with local similarity measures we focus now on this part of the entire similarity representation. Generally, the representation of local measures strongly depends on the data type of the corresponding attribute. The two mostly used kind of types are numeric types, like Integer or Real, and different symbolic types, like unordered symbols, ordered symbols, and taxonomies. In this paper, we focus on two common representation formalisms that can be used to represent local similarity measures for numeric and symbolic data types. To reduce the dimensionality of similarity measures, commonly used commercial CBR tools derive similarity for numeric attributes from the difference of the values to be compared, leading to following definition:

Definition 1 (Similarity Function). *Let a be a numeric attribute with a defined value range of $D_a = [d_{min}, d_{max}]$. Under a **similarity function** for D_a, we understand a function $sim_a : [(d_{min} - d_{max}), (d_{max} - d_{min})] \longrightarrow [0, 1]$ that computes a similarity value out of the interval $[0, 1]$ based on the difference between a case value $c = d_x$ and a query value $q = d_y$ with $d_x, d_y \in D_a$.*

Definition 2 (Similarity Table). *Let a be a symbolic attribute with a defined list of allowed values $D_a = (d_1, d_2, \ldots, d_n)$. A $n \times n$-matrix with entries $x_{i,j} \in [0, 1]$ representing the similarity between the query value $q = d_i$ and the case value $c = d_j$ is called **similarity table** for D_a.*

Figure 1 shows two examples of local similarity measures that might be used in a product recommendation system used to recommend personal computers. The first measure is a similarity table for a symbolic attribute RAM-Type and the second measure represents a similarity function for a numeric attribute CPU-Clock. The semantic of these measures is an estimation of the utility of the technical properties of a given PC with respect to the given customer requirements. For example, if the customer wants to buy a PC with DDR-RAM and gets a PC with SD-RAM this leads to a significantly decreased similarity (0.5) because the performance of SD-RAM is poor compared with the performance of DDR-RAM. On the other hand, the similarity with respect to the CPU-Clock is only decreased if the case value is smaller than the query value. A higher value always leads to a similarity of 1.0 because the customer will probably be satisfied if he gets an even faster PC, provided that other properties still match his demands (e.g. the price).

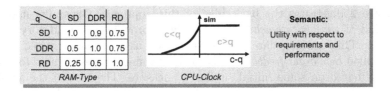

Fig. 1. Examples of Local Similarity Measures

2.2 Bottom-Up Procedure

To allow a comfortable definition of local similarity measures, common CBR tools[1] provide powerful graphical modelling tools. Nevertheless, manually defining accurate local similarity measures is still a complicated and time-consuming task. It requires an analysis of each attribute to identify its influence on the utility of cases. Further, the estimated influence has to be encoded into an appropriate similarity measure by using the modelling facilities of the employed CBR tool. However, this bottom-up procedure has some general drawbacks:

- The procedure is very time-consuming. For example, consider a symbolic attribute with 10 allowed values. This requires the definition of a similarity table with 100 entries!
- Sometimes its not possible to estimate the influence of each attribute sufficiently due to the lack of reasonable domain knowledge. However, domain experts are often able to estimate the utility of whole cases for particular problem situations.
- Due to the complexity of the representation, users often make definition failures by mistake. Unfortunately, the identification of such failures is very difficult.
- Usually the quality of the completely defined similarity measure is not validated in a systematic way. Existing approaches (e.g. leave-one-out tests and measuring classification accuracy) only measure the overall performance of the CBR system, that is, of course, also influenced by other aspects, for example, the quality of the case data.

2.3 Alternative Strategy: Learning

In [12] we proposed an alternative strategy for defining kiSM that can be characterised as a top-down approach compared with the bottom-up procedure described in the previous section. The basic idea of this approach is to acquire only high-level knowledge about the utility of cases for some set of given problem situations. The necessary low-level knowledge required to compute the utility of cases for new problem situations is then extracted from the acquired high-level knowledge by employing machine learning techniques.

---

[1] For example, the commercial CBR shells CBR-WORKS and ORENGE of empolis knowledge management GmbH, formerly tecinno GmbH.

Figure 2 illustrates the basic idea of this approach. Generally, it requires some kind of *similarity teacher* that is able to provide the mandatory training data [12]. This training data can be described as a set of corrected retrieval results called *case order feedback*. This means training queries are used to perform retrievals based on some initial similarity measure. The task of the similarity teacher is then the analysis of the obtained retrieval results with respect to the actual utility of the retrieved cases for the given queries. Obvious deficiencies have to be corrected by reordering the cases. Note, that the approach does not require feedback for all retrieved cases. Even information about the utility of a single case might be useful, for example, in an e-commerce scenario where the customer does not buy the most similar product but another one contained in the retrieval result. Of course, then a greater number of training queries is required to obtain a reasonable training data set. To be able to compare the obtained retrieval results with the case order feedback provided by the similarity teacher, a special error function has to be defined that measures the "distance" between the two given partial orders. Finally, the task of the learning algorithm is to minimise this error function by modifying the initial similarity measure.

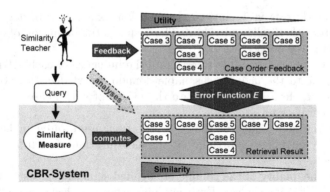

Fig. 2. Learning through Utility Feedback

Generally, the actual learning task, i.e. the minimisation of the error function, can be performed by any accurate learning algorithm. For example, in [11,12] we used a gradient descent algorithm to learn attribute weights. Below we present an approach that employs an evolution program to learn local similarity measures.

3   Learning Local Similarity Measures

3.1   Evolution Programs

Evolution programs and genetic algorithms, respectively, are search algorithms based on the mechanics of natural selection, natural genetics, and the principle of the "survival of the fittest". In every generation a new set of artificial creatures (individuals) is created using pieces (genes) of the genome of individuals of the previous generation (crossover). Occasionally, mutations are introduced, sometimes leading to improved fitness. For the foundations of and more details on EPs and GAs the reader is referred to [8,5].

For the following reasons we decided to employ an evolutionary program for the purpose of optimising local similarity measures:

- Evolutionary strategies have proved to provide powerful and robust mechanisms for the search for an optimum in complex search spaces.
- Optimisation techniques that try to minimise an error function's value with the help of its derivation, such as gradient descent methods, are difficult to apply here. Since local similarity measures depict complex entities that are characterised by several parameters, it is not feasible to find an adequate error function that can be derived with respect to these parameters.
- Local similarity measures can adequately be represented as individuals within an evolutionary process.

In standard genetic algorithms individuals are commonly represented as bit strings – lists of 0s and 1s – to which evolutionary operators, such as crossover or mutation, are applied. One drawback of that representation is the difficulty in incorporating constraints on the solution that a single individual stands for. Moreover, the calculation of the similarity between a query and a case (as depicted in Section 2.1) is mainly based on real-valued numbers, which can only be extracted from bit strings in a round about way. For these reasons we developed an evolutionary algorithm that makes use of "richer" data structures and applies appropriate genetic operators, while still being similar to a standard genetic algorithm.

3.2   Representation of Individuals

In order to be able to learn local similarity measures as defined in Definition 1 and 2, i.e. similarity functions and tables, we have to settle on how to represent the respective individual. Further, we need a formalism that maps those individuals, as used in the evolutionary algorithm, to a local similarity measure.

Assume an arbitrary similarity function sim_a according to Definition 1. Since sim_a is continuous in its value range D_a it is generally not possible to describe it with a finite number of parameters (in certain cases that may be possible, but in general it is not). Thus, we employ an approximation based on a number of sampling points:

Definition 3 (Similarity Function Individual, Similarity Vector). *An individual I representing a similarity function sim_a for the numeric attribute a is coded as a vector V_a^I of fixed size s. The elements of that **similarity vector** are interpreted as **sampling points** of sim_a, between which the similarity function is linearly interpolated. Hence, it holds for all $i \in \{1, \ldots, s\}$: $v_i^I = (V_a^I)_i \in [0, 1]$.*

The sampling points are distributed equidistantly over the value range D_a of attribute a. Figure 3 illustrates how a local similarity measure for a numeric attribute is modelled. The length s of the similarity vector may be chosen due

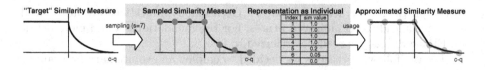

Fig. 3. Representation of Similarity Vectors as Individuals

to the demands of the application domain: The more elements V_a^I contains, the more accurate the approximation of the corresponding similarity function, but on the other hand the higher the computational effort.

Similarity tables, as the second type of local similarity measures of concern, are represented as matrices of floating point numbers within the interval $[0,1]$. The definition following is in the main no different to Definition 2, however, we need it due to the notation it introduces:

Definition 4 (Similarity Table Individual, Similarity Matrix). *An individual I representing a similarity table for a symbolic attribute a with a list of allowed values $D_a = (d_1, d_2, \ldots, d_n)$ is a $n \times n$-matrix M_a^I with entries $m_{ij}^I = (M_a^I)_{ij} \in [0,1]$ for all $i, j \in \{1, \ldots, n\}$.*

3.3   Specialised Genetic Operators

Genetic operators are responsible for the creation of new individuals and have a major influence on the way a population develops. The operators we use are quite different from classical ones since they operate in a different domain (real-valued instead of binary representation). However, because of underlying similarities, we divide them into the two standard groups: mutation and crossover operators.

Mutation Operators. Operators of this class are the same for both kinds of local similarity measures we are dealing with. They change one or more values of a similarity vector V_a^I or matrix M_a^I according to the respective mutation rule. Doing so, the constraint that every new value has to lie within the interval $[0,1]$ is met. The second constraint that needs to be attended concerns the reflexivity of local similarity measures. The similarity between a query q and a case c should always be 1.0, if it holds $q = c$. As a consequence, the medial sampling point of a similarity vector should be 1.0 as well as the elements m_{ii}^I of a similarity matrix for all $i \in \{1, \ldots, n\}$. Since any matrix can be understood as a vector, we describe the functionality of our mutation operators for similarity vectors only:

- *Simple mutation*: If $V_a^I = (v_1^I, \ldots, v_s^I)$ is a similarity vector individual, then each element v_i^I has the same chance of undergoing a mutation. The result of a single application of this operator is a changed similarity vector $(v_1^I, \ldots, \hat{v}_j^I, \ldots, v_s)$, with $1 \leq j \leq s$ and $\hat{v}_j^I$ chosen randomly from $[0,1]$.
- *Multivariate non-uniform mutation* applies the simple mutation to several elements of V_a^I. Moreover, the alterations become smaller as the age of the population is increasing. The new value for v_j^I is computed after

$\hat{v}_j^I = v_j^I \pm (1 - r^{(1-\frac{t}{T})^2})$, where t is the current age of the population at hand, T its maximal age, and r a random number from $[0, 1]$. Hence, this property makes the operator search the space more uniformly at early stages of the evolutional process (when t is small) and rather locally at later times.

- *In-/decreasing mutation* represents a specialisation of the previous operator. Sometimes it is helpful to modify a number of neighbouring sampling points uniformly. The operator for in-/decreasing mutation randomly picks two sampling points v_j^I and v_k^I and increases or decreases the values for all v_i^I with $j \leq i \leq k$ by a fixed increment. Assume, the local similarity measure for the attribute CPU-Clock (see Section 2.1) as the optimisation goal and an individual I for whose similarity vector it holds: $v_i^I < 0.9$ for all $i < \frac{s}{2}$. Here, a mutation, that increases the similarity value for several neighbouring sampling points left of the y-axis, will bring I nearer to its optimisation goal.

Crossover Operators. Applying crossover operators, a new individual in the form of a similarity vector or matrix is created using elements of its parents. Though there are variations of crossover operators described that exploit an arbitrary number of parents, we rely on the traditional approach using exactly two parental individuals, I_A and I_B.

- *Simple crossover* is defined in the usual way: A "split point" for the particular similarity vector or matrix is chosen. The new individual is assembled by using the first part of the parent I_A's similarity vector or matrix and the second part of parent I_B's.
- *Arbitrary crossover* represents a kind of multi-split-point crossover with a random number of split points. Here, we decide by random chance for each component of the offspring individual whether to use the corresponding vector or matrix element from parent I_A or I_B.
- *Arithmetical crossover* is defined as the linear combination of both parent similarity vectors or matrices. In the case of similarity matrices the offspring is generated according to: $(M_a^{I_{new}})_{ij} = m_{ij}^{I_{new}}$ with $m_{ij}^{I_{new}} = \frac{1}{2}m_{ij}^{I_A} + \frac{1}{2}m_{ij}^{I_B}$ for all $i, j \in \{1, \ldots, d\}$.
- *Row/column crossover* is employed for similarity tables, i.e. for symbolic attributes, only. Rows and columns in a similarity matrix contain coherent information, since their similarity entries refer to the same query or case value, respectively. Therefore, cutting a row/column by simple or arbitrary crossover may lead to less valuable rows/columns for the offspring individual. We define row crossover as follows: For each row $i \in \{1, \ldots, n\}$ we randomly determine individual I_A or I_B to be the individual for that row. Then it holds $m_{ij}^{I_{new}} = m_{ij}^{I_P}$ for all $j \in \{1, \ldots, n\}$. Column crossover is defined accordingly.

3.4   Controlling the Learning Procedure

Given a particular attribute a and the mandatory training data (case order feedback, see 2.2), our algorithm settles how to represent local similarity measures for that type of individuals. It then proceeds through evolutionary techniques (each of the genetic operators described above is employed with a specified probability), creates new similarity measures while abolishing old ones, in order to search for the *fittest individual*, whose corresponding local similarity measure yields the minimal value of the error function for the training data. The control structure of our implementation is similar to a standard genetic algorithm [5] and proceeds at a high level as follows:

1. Generate an initial population P_a of random local similarity measures for the respective attribute.
2. Evaluate each $I \in P_a$ by assigning a fitness value and a lifetime value. For the computation of a local similarity measure's fitness we use a slight modification of the index error (see [11]), a distance measure that regards the number of realignments that are necessary to make the retrieval results (for a specific set of queries), to which that measure leads, match with the case order feedback given by the similarity teacher. Of course individuals with smaller fitness values are considered to be fitter, since the mentioned error function has to be minimised. Moreover, we assign a lifetime value to each individual that corresponds to its fitness value, telling for how many generations the individual is maximally allowed to remain in the population.
3. Randomly select mating partner from P.
4. Create a set P_o of new individuals by applying crossover operators and reproducing mutation to the selected mating partners.
5. Mutate the individuals in P_o (adaptive mutation).
6. Increase age for each $I \in P_a$, evaluate each $I \in P_o$, and form $P_a := P_a \cup P_o$.
7. Remove dead (lifetime below 0) and the most unfit individuals from P_a.
8. Repeat step 3 and following.

The algorithm is also capable of learning several local similarity measures simultaneously. Given a set of attributes $\{a_1, \ldots, a_m\}$, for which local similarity measures are to be learnt, a population P_{a_i} is generated for each attribute a_i. Thus, it is possible to optimise the local similarity measures for all attributes of the case representation simultaneously.

4   Experimental Evaluation

To evaluate the presented learning algorithm we have chosen a similar experiment as already described in [11]. The idea of this experiment is to learn a similarity measure that considers the provided adaptation possibilities during the retrieval of useful cases. When providing adaptation functionality, it is generally insufficient to determine how well a case matches the current problem situation in order to obtain an accurate approximation of the utility of cases. Instead, the similarity measure has also to pay attention to the *adaptability of cases* [10,7]. For example, consider again a product recommendation system for the PC domain. In Figure 1 we have already shown local similarity measures that might be used to estimate the utility of PCs with respect to the customers' requirements. However, these measures have to be modified if the used CBR system also provides possibilities to adapt retrieved PCs. Then, the measures shown in Figure 4 might be more accurate. Here, the similarity between SD-RAM and DDR-RAM (bold) is always considered to be 1.0 due the compatibility of these RAM types. The similarities concerning the RD-RAM (grey shadowed) are not changed because this RAM type is incompatible with the other types and therefore adaptation is impossible. Further, the similarity function for the CPU-Clock is also modified. The assumption here is that it is possible to replace slow CPUs against faster ones as long as the difference between the clock rates does not exceed a critical value[2] x.

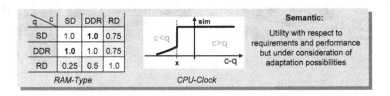

Fig. 4. Considering Adaptability in Local Similarity Measures

4.1   The Experiment

The case model of our PC domain consists of 11 attributes $a_1, \ldots, a_{11}$ (5 numeric and 6 symbolic attributes) that describe the technical properties of a PC. For each attribute we defined a local similarity measure used to estimate the utility of particular PCs for a given query. However, these similarity measures do not consider the customisation possibilities provided by a set of adaptation rules.

To obtain the required training data S we have generated case order feedback by creating 600 queries randomly, performing adaptation of all retrieved cases (in our experiment 20) and reordering the (adapted) cases by measuring their utility with help of the initially defined similarity measure. For our experiments (see Figure 5) we divided S at the ratio of 1 : 2 into a subset S_{train} of training examples and S_{test} of test examples used for evaluation. Prior to the utilisation of our evolutionary algorithm we learnt the 11 attributes' feature weights w_i with the help of the approach introduced in [11]. When learning the involved local measures sim_{a_i}, we make use of these optimised feature weights and do not modify them any further. Our learning algorithm creates and manages a population of appropriate individuals for each attribute (5 populations of similarity vectors and 6 of similarity matrices). In a kind of round-robin optimisation the delineated evolutionary techniques are applied to these 11 populations and thus the PC domain's local similarity measures are optimised simultaneously.

Evaluating the learning results, we determine a new retrieval result (based on the learnt similarity measure) for each query contained in the training examples of S_{test}. Regarding the quality of these case orders we revert to the quality measure $CR1_i$ and $CR3_i$ as defined in [12]. These measures express the percentage

---

[2] Motherboards usually only support a limited CPU clock range.

(in relation to $|S_{test}|$) of those retrievals that return the optimal case as most similar one and, respectively, among the 3 most similar ones. The optimal case for a specific query q is determined by S_{test} and denotes that case which yields the highest utility for q after having been adapted.

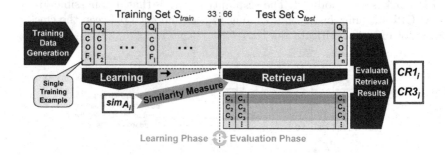

Fig. 5. The Experiment

To achieve an understanding of the amount of training data needed we have repeated the procedure of similarity measure optimisation for incrementally increasing subsets of S_{train}. Further, we have focused on our learning algorithm's convergence behaviour and analysed the quality measures' development by time (by number of evolutionary generations). In order to obtain statistically significant results we have repeated the described learning process 10 times, using newly generated training and test data, and calculated the worst, average, and best values for the mentioned quality measures.

4.2 Results

Figure 6a) shows the gradual optimisation of the global similarity calculation due to the number of evolutionary generations, making use of all 200 training examples from S_{train} (evaluated on S_{test}). Here, in the left part of the chart the initial improvement resulting from feature weight learning is to be seen. The right part illustrates the further improvement of the quality measures as yielded by the optimisation of local similarity measures. After about 300 generations the evolutionary algorithm converges to an optimum, on average enhancing the value of quality measure $CR1_{200}$ from 36.3% to 45.6%, and $CR3_{200}$ from 66.3% to 75.3%[3]. Figure 6b) illustrates the influence of the size of the training set S_{train} on the quality of the learning results. Here, at each case the worst, average, and best value (reached after 300 generations of the evolutionary algorithm) of $CR1_i$ and $CR3_i$ are shown.

The results presented here indicate the fundamental capabilities of our approach to learn local similarity measures with the help of an evolutionary al-

---

[3] Note, that a single run of the optimisation process in the presented application domain for $|S_{train}| = 200$ and for 200 evolutionary generations takes about 7 hours on a P-IV machine with 1.8 GHz.

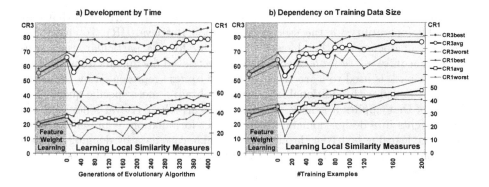

Fig. 6. Evaluation Results

gorithm. In a domain where case adaptation is applied, our algorithm clearly improves the quality of a similarity measure so that it takes the possibilities of case adaptation into consideration. With respect to the required amount of training data, we expected to need more training examples compared with the learning of attribute weights to achieve reasonable results due to the much more complex search space. And indeed, in our experiment about 100 training examples are required to ensure stable learning results. Using smaller training data sets, the algorithm sometimes tends to over-fit the presented data leading to poor results on the independent test data. Nevertheless, assumed that enough training data is available, the experimental results show that our approach is able to improve the retrieval quality clearly. At least in the presented application scenario the amount of training data is not a crucial problem because it is generated automatically and so the risk of over-fitting is marginally low.

When omitting prior feature weight optimisation and starting the local optimisation for the fixed weights of the given utility measure, the learnt local similarity measures result in an even more noticeable improvement of $CR1$ and $CR3$. The reason is that it is obviously possible to simulate the effect of feature weights partially with accurate local similarity measures.

5 Related Work

When talking about learning in CBR, traditionally the focus lays on the acquisition of new case knowledge. Concerning the learning of similarity measures, existing approaches are restricted to learning attribute weights. Several techniques have been developed to improve the accuracy of case-based classification systems [13,2,14,9,15]. However, these techniques are difficult to apply in domains without classified case data, like e-commerce and general knowledge management domains. An alternative approach to learn customer preferences in e-commerce is presented in [3]. The training data used here, called *return-set selections*, is comparable with the case order feedback presumed by our approach. However, it also focuses only on attribute weights to represent preferences of customers.

Another research field that deals with the retrieval of information that may have different utility for the user is Information Retrieval (IR). To ensure the retrieval of documents that have a high utility for the particular user, some systems acquire *relevance feedback* about the retrieved documents from the user. This feedback is used to learn the *actual user context* represented by the user's query extended with additional key terms to obtain a more specific query [4].

Work that applies a genetic algorithm to learn the retrieval index and feature weights in a design domain, namely tablet formulation, is presented in [6]. Here, the learning is driven through the available case data by defining a fitness function that measures the retrieval quality of a special leave-n-out test.

6   Conclusion and Outlook

In this paper we have presented an approach that can be seen as a first step towards the learning of knowledge-intensive local similarity measures. Such measures are commonly used in many current application domains, in particular when employing powerful commercial CBR shells that provide graphical modelling tools. The advantage of our learning approach is that it avoids some major problems that arise when defining similarity measures manually. On the one hand, it may simplify the definition process clearly, on the other hand, it may also help to define similarity measures that represent a better approximation of the underlying utility function. In our point of view, the major strength of the learning approach is its more goal directed fashion compared with the manual procedure. Instead of tuning numerous single representation elements of the entire similarity measure, like weights and local similarity measures, the similarity definition is directly based on the expected outcome of the similarity computation, namely the utility of cases for particular problem situations. However, like other machine learning techniques, the success of the approach strongly depends on the available training data. Only if acquiring the required training data requires less effort than a manual definition of the similarity measure, the learning approach might be useful. A typical example are domains that require case adaptation. Here, the training data might be generated automatically like described in Section 4. However, in [11] we have already discussed other domains and application scenarios where our learning framework might be applied successfully.

An interesting issue for future research is the consideration of additional, easy to acquire background knowledge during the learning process (see also [11]). This might decrease the risk of over-fitting small training data sets and therefore could also decrease the amount of training data required to obtain accurate learning results. Further, additional experiments with real-world application domains are necessary to show the general applicability of our approach.

References

1. R. Bergmann, M. M. Richter, S. Schmitt, A. Stahl, and I. Vollrath. Utility-oriented matching: A new research direction for Case-Based Reasoning. In *Professionelles Wissensmanagement: Erfahrungen und Visionen. Proceedings of the 1st Conference on Professional Knowledge Management*. Shaker, 2001.
2. A. Bonzano, P. Cunningham, and B. Smyth. Using introspective learning to improve retrieval in CBR: A case study in air traffic control. In *Proceedings of the 2nd International Conference on Case-Based Reasoning*. Springer, 1997.
3. K. Branting. Acquiring customer preferences from return-set selections. In *Proceedings of the 4th International Conference on Case-Based Reasoning*. Springer, 2001.
4. A. Göker. Capturing information need by learning user context. In *Working Notes of the Workshop on Learning about Users, 16th International Joint Conference in Artificial Intelligence*, 1999.
5. J.H. Holland. *Adaptation in Natural and Artificial Systems*. The University of Michigan Press, 1975.
6. J. Jarmulak, S. Craw, and R. Rowe. Genetic algorithms to optimise CBR retrieval. In *Proceedings of the 5th European Workshop on Case-Based Reasoning*. Springer, 2000.
7. D. Leake, A. Kinley, and D. Wilson. Linking adaptation and similarity learning. In *Proceedings of the 18th Annual Conference of the Cognitive Science Society*. Hillsdale, NJ: Lawrence Erlbaum, 1996.
8. Z. Michalewicz. *Genetic Algorithms + Data Structures = Evolution Programs*. Springer, 1996.
9. F. Ricci and P. Avesani. Learning a local similarity metric for case-based reasoning. In *Proceeding of the 1st International Conference on Case-Based Reasoning*, pages 301–312. Springer, 1995.
10. B. Smyth and M. T. Keane. Retrieving adaptable cases: The role of adaptation knowledge in case retrieval. In *Proceedings of the 1st European Workshop on Case-Based Reasoning*. Springer, 1993.
11. A. Stahl. Learning feature weights from case order feedback. In *Proceedings of the 4th International Conference on Case-Based Reasoning*. Springer, 2001.
12. A. Stahl. Defining similarity measures: Top-down vs. bottom-up. In *Proceedings of the 6th European Conference on Case-Based Reasoning*. Springer, 2002.
13. D. Wettschereck and D. W. Aha. Weighting features. In *Proceeding of the 1st International Conference on Case-Based Reasoning*. Springer, 1995.
14. W. Wilke and R. Bergmann. Considering decision cost during learning of feature weights. In *Proceedings of the 3rd European Workshop on Case-Based Reasoning*. Springer, 1996.
15. Z. Zhang and Q. Yang. Dynamic refiniement of feature weights using quantitative introspective learning. In *Proceedings of the 16th International Joint Conference on Artificial Intelligence*, 1999.

Playing Mozart Phrase by Phrase

Asmir Tobudic[1] and Gerhard Widmer[1,2]

[1] Austrian Research Institute for Artificial Intelligence, Vienna,
[2] Department of Medical Cybernetics and Artificial Intelligence,
University of Vienna, Austria

Abstract. The article presents an application of instance-based learning to the problem of expressive music performance. A system is described that tries to learn to shape tempo and dynamics of a musical performance by analogy to timing and dynamics patterns found in performances by a concert pianist. The learning algorithm itself is a straightforward *k*-nearest-neighbour algorithm. The interesting aspects of this work are application-specific: we show how a complex, multi-level artifact like the tempo/dynamics variations applied by a musician can be decomposed into well-defined training examples for a learner, and that case-based learning is indeed a sensible strategy in an artistic domain like music performance. While the results of a first quantitative experiment turn out to be rather disappointing, we will show various ways in which the results can be improved, finally resulting in a system that won a prize in a recent 'computer music performance' contest.

1   Introduction

The work described in this paper is another step in a long-term research endeavour that aims at building quantitative models of expressive music performance via AI and, in particular, machine learning methods [9,10]. This is basic research. We do not intend to engineer computer programs that generate music performances that sound as human-like as possible. Rather, the goal is to investigate to what extent a machine can automatically build, via inductive learning from 'real-world' data (i.e., real performances by highly skilled musicians), operational models of certain aspects of performance, for instance, predictive models of tempo, timing, or dynamics. In this way we hope to get new insights into fundamental principles underlying this complex artistic activity, and thus contribute to the growing body of knowledge in the area of empirical musicology (see [4] for an excellent overview).

In previous work, we managed to show that a computer can indeed find interesting regularities of musical performance. A new rule learning algorithm [12] succeeded in discovering a small set of simple, robust, and highly general rules that predict a substantial part of the note-level expressive choices of a performer (e.g., whether she will shorten or lengthen a particular note) with surprisingly high precision [11]. But these rules described only very local, low-level aspects (things a performer does to a particular note), and indeed, the

K.D. Ashley and D.G. Bridge (Eds.): ICCBR 2003, LNAI 2689, pp. 552–566, 2003.
© Springer-Verlag Berlin Heidelberg 2003

'expressive' performances produced by the computer on the basis of the learned rules were far from sounding musical.

Music performance is a highly complex activity, with performers tending to shape the music at many different levels simultaneously (see below). The goal of our current work is to complement the note-level rule model with a predictive model of musical expression at higher levels of the musical structure, e.g., the level of *phrases*. This paper presents our first steps in this direction. An instance-based learning system is described that recognizes performance patterns at various abstraction levels and learns to apply them to new pieces (phrases) by analogy to known performances. The learning algorithm itself is a straightforward k-nearest neighbour algorithm. The interesting aspects of this work are thus not so much machine-learning-specific but application-specific: we show how a complex artistic artifact like the tempo/dynamics variations applied by a musician can be decomposed into well-defined training examples for a learner, and that case-based prediction is indeed a sensible strategy in an artistic domain like music performance. While the results of a first quantitative experiment turn out to be rather disappointing, we will show various ways in which the results can be improved, finally resulting in a system that — while still far from being able to attain the musical quality of human musicians — won a prize in a recent 'computer music performance' contest.

The paper is organized as follows: Section 2 briefly introduces the reader to the notion of expressive music performance and its representation via performance curves. Section 3 then describes how the training examples for the learner are derived (by decomposing complex performance curves into elementary 'expressive shapes' that can be associated with musical phrases at different levels), and specifies our learning algorithm. Section 4 presents first results of systematic experiments. Various ways of improving these are shown in Section 5, and Section 6 briefly talks about the qualititative, musical side of the results, including the above-mentioned computer music performance contest. Current and future research plans are then discussed in the final Section 7.

2   Expressive Music Performance and Performance Curves

Expressive music performance is the art of shaping a musical piece by continuously varying important parameters like tempo, dynamics, etc. Human musicians do not play a piece of music mechanically, with constant tempo or loudness, exactly as written in the printed music score. Rather, they speed up at some places, slow down at others, stress certain notes or passages by various means, and so on. The most important parameter dimensions available to a performer (a pianist, in particular) are tempo and continuous tempo changes, dynamics (loudness variations), and articulation (the way successive notes are connected). Most of this is not specified in the written score, but at the same time it is absolutely essential for the music to be effective and engaging. As such, expressive

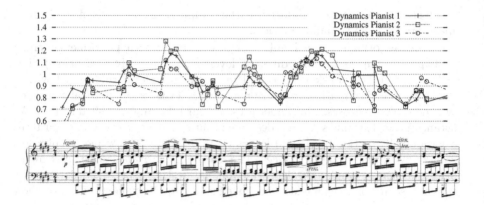

Fig. 1. Dynamics curves (relating to melody notes) of performances of the same piece (Frédéric Chopin, Etude op.10 no.3, E major) by three different Viennese pianists (computed from recordings on a Bösendorfer 290SE computer-monitored grand piano).

performance is a phenomenon of central interest in contemporary (cognitively oriented) musicology.

In the following, we will restrict ourselves to two of the most important parametric dimensions: *timing* (tempo variations) and *dynamics* (loudness variations). The tempo and loudness variations applied by a musician over the course of a piece (if we can measure them, which is a problem in its own right) can be represented as *tempo* and *loudness curves*, respectively. For instance, Figure 1 shows *dynamics curves* — the dynamics patterns produced by three different pianists in performing the same piece. Each point represents the relative loudness with which a particular melody note was played (relative to an averaged 'standard' loudness); a purely mechanical, unexpressive rendition of the piece would correspond to a perfectly flat horizontal line at $y = 1.0$. Variations in tempo can be represented in an analogous way.

Musically trained readers will notice certain high-level patterns or trends in the curves in Figure 1 that seem to correlate with lower- and higher-level phrases of the piece (e.g., a global up-down, *crescendo-decrescendo* tendency over the large phrase that covers the first four bars, and a consistent patterning of the one-bar subphrases contained in it). Extracting and learning to apply such high-level expressive patterns is the goal of the work presented here.

3   Learning Task and Algorithm

3.1   Deriving the Training Instances: Multilevel Decomposition of Performance Curves

Our starting material is the scores of musical pieces plus measurements of the tempo and dynamics variations applied by a pianist in actual performances of these pieces, represented as *tempo* and *dynamics curves*. Both tempo and loudness are represented as multiplicative factors, relative to the average tempo and dynamics of the piece. For instance, a tempo value of 1.5 for a note means that the note was played 1.5 times as fast as the average tempo of the piece, and a loudness of 1.5 means that the note was played 50% louder than the average loudness of all melody notes. In addition, the system is given information about the *hierarchical phrase structure* of the pieces, currently at four levels of phrasing. Phrase structure analysis is currently done by hand, as no reliable algorithms are available for this task.

Given a performance (dynamics or tempo) curve, the first problem is to define and extract the *training examples* for phrase-level learning. Remember that we want to learn how a performer 'shapes' phrases at different structural levels by tempo and dynamics 'gestures'. To that end, the complex curve must be decomposed into basic expressive 'gestures' or 'shapes' that represent the most likely contribution of each phrase to the overall observed performance curve.

As approximation functions to represent these shapes we decided to use the class of second-degree polynomials (functions of the form $y = ax^2 + bx + c$), because there is quite a consensus in musicology that high-level tempo and dynamics are well characterized by quadratic or parabolic functions [5,7,8] (but see section 5.4 below). Decomposing a given performance curve is an iterative process, where each step deals with a specific level of the phrase structure: for each phrase at a given level, we compute the polynomial that best fits the part of the curve that corresponds to this phrase, and 'subtract' the tempo or dynamics deviations 'explained' by the approximation. The curve that remains after this 'subtraction' is then used in the next level of the process. We start with the highest given level of phrasing and move to the lowest.

As by our definitions, tempo and dynamics curves are lists of multiplicative factors, 'subtracting' the effects predicted by a fitted curve from an existing curve simply means dividing the y values on the curve by the respective values of the approximation curve.

More formally, let $N_p = \{n_1, ..., n_k\}$ be the sequence of melody notes spanned by a phrase p, $O_p = \{onset_p(n_i) : n_i \in N_p\}$ the set (sequence) of relative note positions of these notes within phrase p (on a normalized scale from 0 to 1), and $E_p = \{expr(n_i) : n_i \in N_p\}$ the part of the performance curve (i.e., tempo or dynamics values) associated with these notes. Fitting a second-order polynomial onto E_p then means finding a function $f_p(x) = a^2x + bx + c$ that minimizes

$$D(f_p(x), N_p) = \sum_{n_i \in N_p} [f_p(onset_p(n_i)) - expr(n_i)]^2$$

Given an performance curve $E_p = \{expr(n_1), ..., expr(n_k)\}$ over a phrase p, and an approximation polynomial $f_p(x)$, 'subtracting' the shape predicted by $f_p(x)$ from E_p then means computing the new curve

$$E'_p = \{expr(n_i)/f_p(onset_p(n_i)) : i = 1...k\}.$$

The final curve we obtain after the fitted polynomials at all phrase levels have been 'subtracted' is called the *residual* of the performance curve [13].

To illustrate, Figure 2 shows the dynamics curve of the last part (mm.31–38) of the Mozart Piano Sonata K.279 (C major), first movement, first section. The four-level phrase structure our music analyst assigned to the piece is indicated by the four levels of brackets at the bottom of each plot. The figure shows the stepwise approximation of the performance curve by polynomials at three of the four phrase levels, as well as how much of the original curve is accounted for by the four levels of approximations, and what is left unexplained (the *residuals*).

3.2   Learning and Prediction

Given performance curves decomposed into levels of phrasal shapes, the learning task is to predict appropriate tempo or dynamics shapes for new musical phrases (at any level) on the basis of examples of known phrases with associated shapes. More precisely, what is to be predicted for each example are three coefficients a, b, c that define an approximation polynomial $y = ax^2 + bx + c$. The learning algorithm is a simple nearest-neighbour algorithm [2]; we first decided to use only the one nearest neighbour for prediction, because it is not entirely clear how several predictions (triples of coefficients) should be combined in a sensible way.

The similarity between phrases is computed as the inverse of the standard Euclidean distance. For the moment, phrases are represented simply as fixed-length vectors of attribute values, where the attributes describe very basic phrase properties like the length of a phrase, melodic intervals between the starting and ending notes of the melody, information about where the highest melodic point (the 'apex') of the phrase is, the harmonic progression between start, apex, and end, whether the phrase ends with a cadential chord sequence, etc. Given such a fixed-length representation, the definition of the Euclidean distance is trivial.

At prediction time, the shapes predicted by the learner for nested phrases at different levels must be combined into a final compositive performance curve that is then evaluated (and can be used to produce a computer-generated 'expressive' performance). This is simply the inverse of the curve decomposition problem. Given a new piece to produce a performance for, the system starts with an initial 'flat' performance curve (a list of 1.0 values) and then successively multiplies the current value by the phrase-level predictions.

Formally, for a given note n_i that is contained in m hierarchically nested phrases $p_j, j = 1...m$, the expression (tempo or dynamics) value $expr(n_i)$ to be applied to it is computed as

$$expr(n_i) = \prod_{j=1}^{m} f_{p_j}(onset_{p_j}(n_i)),$$

where f_{p_j} is the approximation polynomial predicted as being best suited for the jth-level phrase p_j by the nearest-neighbour learning algorithm.

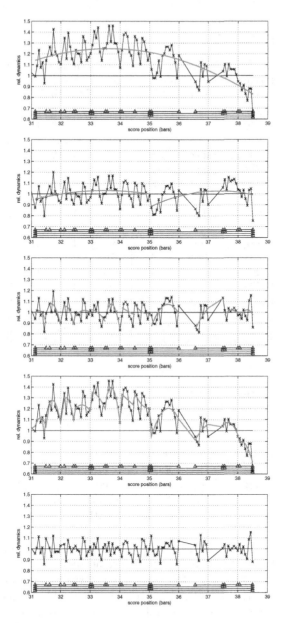

Fig. 2. Multilevel decomposition of dynamics curve of performance of Mozart Sonata K.279:1:1, mm.31–38. From top to bottom: (1) original dynamics curve (black) plus the second-order polynomial giving the best fit at the top phrase level (grey); (2+3) each show, for two lower phrase levels, the dynamics curve after 'subtraction' of the previous approximation, and the best-fitting approximations at this phrase level; (4): 'reconstruction' (grey) of the original curve by the polynomial approximations; (5): *residuals* after all higher-level shapes have been subtracted.

Table 1. Mozart sonata sections used in experiments (to be read as <sonataName>:<movement>:<section>); *notes* refers to 'melody' notes.

Piece	tempo	time sig.	notes	phrases at level 1	2	3	4
K.279:1:1	fast	4/4	391	50	19	9	5
K.279:1:2	fast	4/4	638	79	36	14	5
K.280:1:1	fast	3/4	406	42	19	12	4
K.280:1:2	fast	3/4	590	65	34	17	6
K.280:2:1	slow	6/8	94	23	12	6	3
K.280:2:2	slow	6/8	154	37	18	8	4
K.280:3:1	fast	3/8	277	28	19	8	4
K.280:3:2	fast	3/8	379	40	29	13	5
K.282:1:1	slow	4/4	165	24	10	5	2
K.282:1:2	slow	4/4	213	29	12	6	3
K.282:1:3	slow	4/4	31	4	2	1	1
K.283:1:1	fast	3/4	379	53	23	10	5
K.283:1:2	fast	3/4	428	59	32	13	6
K.283:3:1	fast	3/8	326	53	30	12	3
K.283:3:2	fast	3/8	558	79	47	19	6
K.332:2	slow	4/4	477	49	23	12	4
Total:			5506	714	365	165	66

4   A First Experiment

4.1   The Data

The data used in the following experiments were derived from performances of Mozart piano sonatas on a Bösendorfer SE 290 computer-controlled piano by a Viennese concert pianist. The SE 290 is a full concert grand piano with a special mechanism that measures every key and pedal movement with high precision and stores this information in a format similar to MIDI. From these measurements, and from a comparison with the notes in the written score, the tempo and dynamics curves corresponding to the performances can be computed.

A manual phrase structure analysis of some sections of these sonatas was carried out by a musicologist. Phrase structure was marked at four hierarchical levels. The resulting set of annotated pieces available for our experiment is summarized in Table 1. The pieces and performances are quite complex and different in character; automatically learning expressive strategies from them is a challenging task.

4.2   Quantitative Results

A systematic *leave-one-piece-out* cross-validation experiment was carried out on these data. Each of the 16 sonata sections was once set aside as a test piece, while the remaining 15 pieces were used for learning. The learned

Table 2. Results of piece-wise cross-validation experiment. Measures subscripted with D refer to the 'default' (inexpressive) performance, those with L to the performance produced by the learner. *Mean* is the simple mean, *WMean* the weighted mean (individual results weighted by the relative length (number of notes) of the pieces).

	dynamics					tempo				
	MSE_D	MSE_L	MAE_D	MAE_L	$Corr_L$	MSE_D	MSE_L	MAE_D	MAE_L	$Corr_L$
kv279:1:1	.0383	.0409	.1643	.1543	.6170	.0348	.0420	.1220	.1496	.3095
kv279:1:2	.0318	.0736	.1479	.1978	.4157	.0244	.0335	.1004	.1317	.2536
kv280:1:1	.0313	.0275	.1432	.1238	.6809	.0254	.0222	.1053	.1071	.4845
kv280:1:2	.0281	.0480	.1365	.1637	.4517	.0250	.0323	.1074	.1255	.3124
kv280:2:1	.1558	.0831	.3498	.2002	.7168	.0343	.0207	.1189	.1111	.7235
kv280:2:2	.1424	.0879	.3178	.2235	.6980	.0406	.0460	.1349	.1463	.4838
kv280:3:1	.0334	.0139	.1539	.0936	.7656	.0343	.0262	.1218	.1175	.5276
kv280:3:2	.0226	.0711	.1231	.2055	.4492	.0454	.0455	.1365	.1412	.3006
kv282:1:1	.1126	.0476	.2792	.1737	.7609	.0295	.0320	.1212	.1216	.3689
kv282:1:2	.0920	.0538	.2537	.1829	.6909	.0227	.0443	.1096	.1555	.2863
kv282:1:3	.1230	.0757	.2595	.2364	.6698	.1011	.0529	.2354	.1741	.8104
kv283:1:1	.0283	.0236	.1423	.1206	.5907	.0183	.0276	.0918	.1196	.2409
kv283:1:2	.0371	.0515	.1611	.1625	.4469	.0178	.0274	.0932	.1197	.1972
kv283:3:1	.0404	.0319	.1633	.1324	.5993	.0225	.0216	.1024	.1083	.4300
kv283:3:2	.0417	.0399	.1676	.1457	.5305	.0238	.0244	.1069	.1116	.3060
kv332:2	.0919	.0824	.2554	.2328	.5599	.0286	.0436	.1110	.1529	.1684
Mean:	.0657	.0533	.2012	.1718	.6027	.0330	.0339	.1199	.1308	.3877
WMean:	.0486	.0506	.1757	.1662	.5584	.0282	.0332	.1108	.1285	.3192

phrase-level predictions were then applied to the test piece, and the following measures were computed: the *mean squared error* of the learner's predicted curve relative to the actual performance curve produced by the pianist ($MSE = \sum_{i=1}^{n}(pred(n_i) - expr(n_i))^2/n$), the *mean absolute error* ($MAE = \sum_{i=1}^{n}|pred(n_i) - expr(n_i)|/n$), and the *correlation* between predicted and 'true' curve. MSE and MAE were also computed for a *default* curve that would correspond to a purely mechanical, unexpressive performance, i.e., a performance curve consisting of all 1's. That allows us to judge if learning is really better than just doing nothing. The results of the experiment are summarized in Table 2, where each line gives the results obtained on the respective test piece when all others were used for training.

At a first glance, the results look rather disappointing. We are interested in cases where the *relative errors* (i.e., MSE_L/MSE_D and MAE_L/MAE_D) are less than 1.0, that is, where the curves predicted by the learner are closer to the pianist's actual performance than a purely mechanical rendition. In the dynamics dimension, this is the case in 11 out of 16 cases for MSE, and in 12 out of 16 for MAE. Tempo seems basically unpredictable: only in 5 (MSE) and 3 (MAE) cases, respectively, did learning produce an improvement over no learning, at least in terms of these purely quantitative, unmusical measures Also, the correlations vary between 0.77 (kv280:3:1, dynamics) and only 0.17 (kv332:2, tempo).

Averaging over all 16 experiments, it seems that dynamics seems learnable under this scheme to some extent — the relative errors being $RMSE = 0.811$, $RMAE = 0.854$ (unweighted), $RMSE = 1.041$, $RMAE = 0.945$ (weighted) respectively — while tempo seems hard to predict in this way — all relative errors are above 1.0.

5   Improving the Results

The above result were rather disappointing. Even keeping in mind that artistic performance of difficult music like Mozart sonatas is a complex and certainly not entirely predictable phenomenon, we had hoped that there would be something predictable about phrase-level tempo and dynamics that a learner could pick up. But the above results are not the end of the story, and in the following sections we explore ways in which they can be improved — at the end we will end up with a system that at least partly makes surprisingly good predictions and even won a prize in a performance contest (see Section 6).

5.1   More Homogeneous Training Sets

One way of improving the results is by noting that Mozart piano sonatas are highly complex music, with a lot of diversity in character. Splitting this set of rather different pieces into more homogeneous subsets and performing learning within these subsets should make the task easier for the learner. For instance, it is known in musicology that absolute tempo has quite an impact on what performance patterns sound acceptable. And indeed, it turns out that simply separating the pieces into fast and slow ones and learning in each of these sets separately considerably increases the number of cases where learning produces an improvement over no learning, both in the dynamics and the tempo domain. Table 3 summarizes the results in terms of wins/losses between learning and no learning for both learning settings. The improvement is obvious. However, the tempo domain is still a problem, with only 7 wins out of 16 cases.

Table 3. Summary of wins vs. losses between learning and no learning; + means curves predicted by the learner better fit the pianist than a flat curve (i.e., relative error < 1), − means the opposite. First line: piece-level cross-validation over all pieces; second line: learning and testing on fast and slow pieces separately.

Training set	MSE/dynamics	MAE/dynamics	MSE/tempo	MAE/tempo
all pieces	11+/5-	12+/4-	5+/11-	3+/13-
slow / fast	14+/2-	14+/2-	7+/9-	7+/9-

5.2   Varying Numbers of Neighbours and Phrase Levels

All the results so far were produced by a k-NN learner with $k = 1$. We initially chose $k = 1$ because we could not think of a meaningful way to combine the predictions of several neighbours — simple averaging of polynomial coefficients or curves seemed not very sensible from a musical point of view. But in experiments it turned out that in the absence of a more informed combination strategy, even simple averaging of several neighbours' predictions can substantially improve the quality of the predicted curves. Table 4 shows the results obtained by increasing the number k of neighbours used in the prediction. The dynamics results in particular show substantial improvement — the RMSE (MSE_L/MSE_D) drops from 1.041 for $k = 1$ to 0.654 for $k = 10$, the RMAE from 0.946 to 0.787, and the correlation improves. There is also some improvement in the tempo dimension, with at least the RMSE dropping below 1.0. The attendant slight drop in correlation indicates that with increasing k, the learner tends to reproduce fewer of the local tempo changes of the pianist, while improving the overall fit at higher levels.

In further experiments, it turned out that the highest level of phrasing that was marked by our musicologist — extended phrases that span several, sometimes many, bars — was not well mirrored in the performances by our pianist. Ignoring the highest phrase level and learning and predicting only at the lower three phrase levels leads to even better result, as shown in the last rows in Table 4. Finally, learning beats no learning even in the tempo dimension.

Table 4. Varying the numbers of neighbours and phrase levels. Top: errors (weighted means over all test pieces). Bottom: wins/losses relative to default.

Variant	dynamics					tempo				
	MSE_D	MSE_L	MAE_D	MAE_L	$Corr_L$	MSE_D	MSE_L	MAE_D	MAE_L	$Corr_L$
4 levels, 1NN	.0486	.0506	.1757	.1662	.5584	.0282	.0332	.1108	.1285	.3192
4 levels, 2NN	.0486	.0395	.1757	.1520	.5637	.0282	.0299	.1108	.1239	.3105
4 levels, 3NN	.0486	.0354	.1757	.1466	.5918	.0282	.0297	.1108	.1231	.2871
4 levels, 5NN	.0486	.0336	.1757	.1424	.6114	.0282	.0292	.1108	.1208	.2786
4 levels, 10NN	.0486	.0318	.1757	.1382	.6166	.0282	.0276	.1108	.1157	.2960
3 levels, 10NN	.0486	.0312	.1757	.1380	.6096	.0282	.0271	.1108	.1136	.2937

Variant	MSE/dynamics	MAE/dynamics	MSE/tempo	MAE/tempo
4 levels, 1NN	11+/5-	12+/4-	5+/11-	3+/13-
4 levels, 2NN	12+/4-	13+/3-	7+/9-	4+/12-
4 levels, 3NN	12+/4-	14+/2-	6+/10-	2+/1=/13-
4 levels, 5NN	14+/2-	14+/2-	8+/8-	5+/11-
4 levels, 10NN	14+/2-	15+/1-	10+/6-	6+/10-
3 levels, 10NN	15+/1-	15+/1-	11+/1=/4-	9+/7-

5.3   Improving the Musical Quality by Learning Local Rules

As Figure 2 above shows quite clearly, hierarchically nested quadratic functions tend to reconstruct the larger trends in a performance curve quite well, but they cannot describe all the detailed local nuances added by a pianist, e.g., the emphasis on particular notes. Local nuances will be left over in what we call the *residuals* — the tempo and dynamics fluctuations left unexplained by the phrase-level polynomials. These can be expected to represent a mixture of noise and meaningful or intended local deviations.

In order to also learn a model of these intended deviations, we applied a rule learning algorithm to the residuals. The goal was to induce note-level rules that predict when the pianist will significantly lengthen or shorten a particular note relative to its context, or play it significantly louder or softer. The learning algorithm used was PLCG, which has been shown to be quite effective in distinguishing between signal and noise and discovering reliable rules when only a part of the data can be explained [12]. Combining the learned rules with a simple numeric prediction scheme again based on a k-NN algorithm produces a partial model of note-level nuances that predicts local timing and dynamics changes to be applied to some individual notes.

Combining these note-level predictions with the phrase-level predictions yields an additional slight reduction in MSE and MAE both for tempo and dynamics, but the difference is almost negligible (though consistently in favour of the combined learner). The interesting fact is that the correlation values improve significantly. For instance, combining the note-level model with the *3 levels, 10NN* learner yields (weighted mean) correlations of 0.6182 for dynamics and 0.3588 for tempo — for tempo in particular, this is significantly higher than any of the values in Table 4. Obviously, the note-level model captures some important local choices of the pianist (which also strongly contribute to the musical quality of the performance).

5.4   A Fairer Comparison

A final way of 'improving' the results is to note that the error measures we used so far in this paper may not be quite appropriate. What was compared was the performance (tempo or dynamics) curve produced by composing the polynomials predicted by the learner, with the curve corresponding to the pianist's actual performance. However, what the k-NN learner learned from was not the actual performance curves, but an *approximation*, namely, the polynomials fitted to the curve at various phrase levels. And maybe this approximation is not very good to begin with. This is partly confirmed by a look at Table 5, which summarizes how well the four-level decompositions (without the residuals) reconstruct the respective training curves.[1] The dynamics curves are generally better approximated by the four levels of polynomials than the tempo curves, and the difference is dramatic. That may explain in particular why our tempo results were so poor.

---

[1] That is, we look not at the performance of the learning system, but only at the effectiveness of approximating a given curve by four levels of quadratic functions.

Table 5. Summary of fit of four-level polynomial decomposition on the training data. Measures subscripted with D refer to the 'default' (mechanical, inexpressive) performances (repeated from table 2), those with P to the fit of the curves reconstructed by the polynomial decompositions.

	MSE_D	MSE_P	$RMSE$	MAE_D	MAE_P	$RMAE$	$Corr_P$
dynamics	.0486	.0049	.1008	.1757	.0501	.2851	.9397
tempo	.0282	.0144	.5106	.1108	.0755	.6814	.6954

Table 6. Summary of errors resulting from comparing the learner's predictions to the 'reconstructed' training curve rather than the actual performance curve produced by the pianist. Shown are weighted means over all training examples.

	dynamics					tempo				
Variant	MSE_D	MSE_L	MAE_D	MAE_L	$Corr_L$	MSE_D	MSE_L	MAE_D	MAE_L	$Corr_L$
4 levels, 1NN	.0437	.0457	.1665	.1543	.5936	.0141	.0190	.0811	.0959	.4517
4 levels, 2NN	.0437	.0345	.1665	.1394	.5995	.0141	.0158	.0811	.0919	.4361
4 levels, 3NN	.0437	.0304	.1665	.1339	.6296	.0141	.0156	.0811	.0922	.4020
4 levels, 5NN	.0437	.0286	.1665	.1292	.6522	.0141	.0151	.0811	.0894	.3829
4 levels, 10NN	.0437	.0268	.1665	.1249	.6571	.0141	.0135	.0811	.0831	.4137
3 levels, 10NN	.0437	.0262	.1664	.1246	.6489	.0141	.0130	.0811	.0806	.4155

The finding implied by Table 5 has implications for musicology, where it has hitherto been believed (but never systematically tested with large numbers of real performances) that quadratic functions are a reasonable model class for expressive timing (e.g., [7,13]). But it also suggests that the above way of computing prediction error was not entirely fair. It would seem more appropriate to compare the predicted curves not to the actual performance curve, but to the approximation curve that is implied by the four levels of quadratic functions that were used as training examples.[2] Correctly predicting these is the best the learner could hope to achieve. Table 6 shows the error figures we obtain in this way, for all the k-NN learners described above.

As can be seen, the situation indeed now looks better for our learner (compare this to Table 4 above). Note the substantially higher correlations in the tempo domain — it is obviously easier to predict approximated curves than real curves. There is also some improvement in terms of the numbers of wins vs. losses against the default. For example, with 3 levels of phrasing and 10 nearest neighbours (last line in Table 6) we get win/loss ratios of 15+/1- for dynamics (both for MSE and MAE) and 11+/1=/4- (MSE) and 10+/6- (MAE) for tempo. That is the best we managed to obtain so far.

---

[2] Actually, the most direct comparison would be between the predicted and 'true' polynomial coefficients; but numeric errors and correlations at this level would be hard to interpret intuitively or musically.

Of course, this 'trick' of changing the definition of error does not change the musical quality of the results, but it gives a more realistic picture of the capabilities of nearest-neighbour learning in this domain.

6   Musical Results

The musical quality of the results is hard to describe in a paper. Generally, the quality varies strongly between pieces, and even within pieces — passages that are musically sensible are sometimes followed by rather extreme errors, at least in musical terms. One incorrect shape can seriously compromise the quality of a composite performance curve that would otherwise be perfectly musical. The quantitative measures MSE, MAE, and correlation are not necessarily indicative of the quality of the listening experience.

Figure 3 tries to give the reader an impression of how well the learning system (phrase-level + note-level) can predict how a pianist is going to play a given passage. This is a case where prediction worked quite well, especially concerning the higher-level aspects. Some of the local patterns were also predicted quite well, while others were obviously missed.

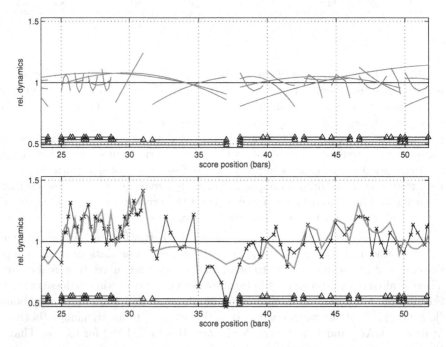

Fig. 3. Learner's predictions for the dynamics curve of Mozart Sonata K.280, 3rd movement, mm. 25–50. Top: quadratic performance shapes predicted for phrases at four levels; bottom: composite predicted dynamics curve resulting from phrase-level shapes and note-level predictions (grey, without markers) vs. pianist's actual dynamics (black, with markers).

The curve shown in Figure 3 is from a computer-generated performance of the Mozart piano sonata K.280 in F major that was produced by the 1-NN learning algorithm + rules learned from the residuals, after training on other sonatas. A recording of this performance was submitted to an International Computer Piano Performance Rendering Contest[3] (RENCON'02) in Tokyo in September 2002, where it won Second Prize behind a rule-based rendering system that had been carefully tuned by hand. The rating was done by a jury of human listeners. While this result does in no way imply that a machine will ever be able to learn to play music like a human artist, we do consider it a nice success for a machine learning system. This was an early result, and we expect further improvement by increasing the number of neighbours k, refining the strategy for combining predictions, and introducing contextual knowledge (see below). We hope to demonstrate some interesting sound examples at the conference.

7   Conclusions

To summarize, this paper has presented a system that combines case-based with rule-based learning in the difficult domain of expressive music performance. First experimental results are at least encouraging. Case-based learning for expressive performance has been proposed before in the domain of expressive phrasing in jazz [1,6], where the promise of CBR was shown, but the evaluation was mostly qualitative and based on relatively small numbers of phrases. The work presented here thus constitutes the first large-scale quantitative evaluation of case-based learning for expressive performance (against a high-class concert pianist). On the other hand, the CBR approach taken in [1] was richer than our simple instance-based prediction method in that it also involved adaptation operators. That is something we might also try, in order to optimise the way phrase shapes are fitted into their respective musical context.

There are numerous other possibilities for improvement that are currently being investigated. One obvious limitation is the propositional attribute-value representation used to characterize phrases, which does not permit the learner to refer to details of the internal structure and content of phrases. Here, we now investigate the use of first-order logic representations and ILP methods [3].

A related problem is that phrasal shapes are predicted individually and independently of the shapes associated with (or predicted for) other, related phrases, i.e., phrases that contain the current phrase, or are contained by it. Obviously, this is too simplistic. Shapes applied at different levels are highly dependent. We are now trying to introduce dependency information via the notion of *context*; very preliminary experiments with a new relational instance-based learner with a context-sensitive similarity measure indicate that this may be fruitful.

A general problem with nearest neigbour learning is that it does not produce interpretable models. As the ultimate goal of our project is to contribute new insights to musical performance research, this is a serious drawback. Along

---

[3] yes, there is such a thing ...

these lines, we will investigate both feature selection/weighting and alternative learning algorithms.

Acknowledgments. This research is made possible by a START Research Prize by the Austrian Federal Government, administered by the Austrian *Fonds zur Förderung der Wissenschaftlichen Forschung (FWF)* (project no. Y99-INF). Additional support for our research on machine learning and music is provided by the European project HPRN-CT-2000-00115 (MOSART). The Austrian Research Institute for Artificial Intelligence acknowledges basic financial support from the Austrian Federal Ministry for Education, Science, and Culture. Thanks to Werner Goebl for performing the harmonic and phrase structure analysis of the Mozart sonatas.

References

1. Arcos, J.L. and López de Mántaras (2001). An Interactive CBR Approach for Generating Expressive Music. *Journal of Applied Intelligence* 14(1), 115–129.
2. Duda, R. and Hart, P. (1967). *Pattern Classification and Scene Analysis.* New York, NY: John Wiley & Sons.
3. Dzeroski, S. and Lavrac, N. (eds.) (2001). *Relational Data Mining: Inductive Logic Programming for Knowledge Discovery in Databases.* Berlin: Springer Verlag.
4. Gabrielsson, A. (1999). The Performance of Music. In D. Deutsch (ed.), *The Psychology of Music (2nd ed.)*, 501–602. San Diego, CA: Academic Press.
5. Kronman, U. and Sundberg, J. (1987). Is the Musical Ritard an Allusion to Physical Motion? In A. Gabrielsson (ed.), *Action and Perception in Rhythm and Music*, 57–68. Stockholm, Sweden: Royal Swedish Academy of Music No.55.
6. López de Mántaras, R. and Arcos, J.L. (2002). AI and Music: From Composition to Expressive Performances. *AI Magazine* 23(3), 43–57.
7. Todd, N. (1989). Towards a Cognitive Theory of Expression: The Performance and Perception of Rubato. *Contemporary Music Review, vol. 4*, pp. 405–416.
8. Todd, N. McA. (1992). The Dynamics of Dynamics: A Model of Musical Expression. *Journal of the Acoustical Society of America* 91, 3540–3550.
9. Widmer, G. (2001). Using AI and Machine Learning to Study Expressive Music Performance: Project Survey and First Report. *AI Communications* 14(3), 149-162.
10. Widmer, G. (2002). In Search of the Horowitz Factor: Interim Report on a Musical Discovery Project. In *Proceedings of the 5th International Conference on Discovery Science (DS'02)*, Lübeck, Germany. Berlin: Springer Verlag.
11. Widmer, G. (2002). Machine Discoveries: A Few Simple, Robust Local Expression Principles. *Journal of New Music Research* 31(1).
12. Widmer, G. (2003). Discovering Simple Rule in Complex Data: A Meta-learning Algorithm and Some Surprising Musical Discoveries. *Artificial Intelligence* (in press).
13. Windsor, W.L. and Clarke, E.F. (1997). Expressive Timing and Dynamics in Real and Artificial Musical Performances: Using an Algorithm as an Analytical Tool. *Music Perception* 15(2), 127–152.

Using Genetic Algorithms to Discover Selection Criteria for Contradictory Solutions Retrieved by CBR

Costas Tsatsoulis and Brent Stephens

Information and Telecommunication Technology Center
Department of Electrical Engineering and Computer Science
The University of Kansas
tsatsoul@ittc.ku.edu

Abstract. In certain domains a case base may contain contradictory but correct cases. The contradictory solutions are due to known domain and problem characteristics which are not part of the case description, and which cannot be formally or explicitly described. In such situations it is important to develop methods that will use these criteria to select among the competing solutions of the matching cases Our domain of application was the assignment of billing numbers to the shipment of goods, and the case base contained numerous cases of similar or even identical problems that had different solutions (billing numbers). Such contradictory solutions were correct and an outcome of domain constraints and characteristics that were not part of the cases and were also not formally known and defined. It was assumed that the frequency with which a solution appeared among the retrieved cases and the recency of the time the solution had been applied were important for selecting among competing solutions, but there was no explicit way for doing so. In this paper we show how we used genetic algorithms to discover methods to combine and operationalize vague selection criteria such as "recency" and "frequency." GAs helped us discover selection criteria for the contradictory solutions retrieved by CBR retrieval and significantly improved the accuracy and performance of the CBR system.

1 Introduction

When selecting case-based reasoning (CBR) for use in a particular domain, it is assumed that similar problems lead to similar solutions, so previous experience can be reused in the formulation of a new solution. Additionally, CBR systems assume that the case base used to describe the previous experiences is consistent and correct and that knowledge represented by it remains accurate. The ability of CBR systems to reason accurately is lost if these assumptions do not hold.

Recent work in CBR is looking into developing techniques to resolve some of the problems associated with incorrect, conflicting and noisy cases by performing maintenance on a case base (among many: [8], [17], and [20]). The motivation for doing maintenance is to reduce the size of the database, maintain consistency,

K.D. Ashley and D.G. Bridge (Eds.): ICCBR 2003, LNAI 2689, pp. 567–580, 2003.
© Springer-Verlag Berlin Heidelberg 2003

and maximize domain coverage. This is done by strategically eliminating or combining cases to get rid of redundancy or inconsistency.

There are domains, though, where traditional case base maintenance techniques are not appropriate, and may lead to loss of important knowledge and information. Our work focuses on domains where the case base is large (hundreds of thousands of cases), very redundant, and contains contradictory cases. The redundancy needs to be preserved since it is a proxy of "best practices." In other words, the frequency by which an action was taken in a certain situation is an important indicator of whether this action should be chosen in future situations. The contradictory cases can be due to data input errors, but, often, they represent cycles in best practices. If the actions taken in a certain situation depend on business or other cycles, then two contradicting cases may each be correct at appropriate times. If the attribute that distinguishes between the cases is inaccessible, then both cases will be retrieved, but there is no way to select between them.

In such domains, a CBR system would retrieve a large number of cases proposing different solutions or actions, and a simple pruning based on similarity is not an appropriate selector of the best case. One possible solution to this problem is to let a user decide between the cases retrieved. This has several limitations: first, since too many cases are retrieved, the user has to analyze all of them; second, the accuracy of the case selection process is limited by the ability of the user, so an expert user may be needed; lastly, the overall workload on a user may actually increase when using the system, because of the need to perform manual case selection.

In the work presented in this paper we used the characteristics of the case base (redundancy and cyclic nature of actions) to develop an automated way to select the best case. We experimentally examined a variety of equations that combine the frequency, recency, and similarity of a case to identify the best possible way to combine these characteristics to improve retrieval. We used genetic algorithms (GAs) to find the parameters of these equations, and experimented with two different fitness metrics for the GA.

GAs have been used in previous CBR systems either as loosely coupled preprocessors (e.g. to find the weights of similarity functions) or as tightly coupled CBR components (e.g. to perform case adaptation). Conversely, CBR has been used to seed GAs to reduce the amount of search and the number of generations. Much of this work is discussed in Section 6, "Previous Research."

We applied our system to a large case base of billing records for shipments to clients. The shipment characteristics were used by the CBR system to identify similar cases and to assign the appropriate billing code. In situations where simple CBR retrieval resulted in conflicting billing codes, the application of the GA-derived selection equations resulted in selecting the correct solution out of the competing cases in 80–90% of the time. In the best case, simple CBR retrieval found a unique billing code in approximately 45% of the problems and the GA-derived selection criteria found the correct code in approximately 30% of the problems, resulting in a combined 75% accuracy; the remaining 25% of the problems remained unsolved. Our experiments showed that the integration of standard CBR retrieval with retrieval using the GA-generated case selection criteria consistently and dramatically increased the accuracy of the selected billing codes (e.g., from 45% to 75%). This, in turn, indicated that: first, in case bases which contain redundant and contradictory information that is due to case characteristics that are not part of the case (in other words, the contradictory information is not incorrect), the frequency, recency and similarity of a case can be combined to improve retrieval; and, second, GAs are an appropriate method to identify the parameters used in combining these values in an efficient manner.

2 Domain of Application

The actual problem our research addressed was to use CBR to identify the billing code for shipments by the Burlington Northern and Santa Fe Railway Company (BNSF) [1]. The billing code in turn identifies the exact division of a particular company that should be billed for a shipment. The billing is done by BNSF employees except in cases where, for a variety of reasons, they are not sure which billing code to apply. Also, in some cases, the employees enter the incorrect code, the bill is rejected by the client, and returns to the BNSF accounting system for correction. Our system would assign the correct billing code to shipments that either had no code or were returned because they had the wrong code. According to BNSF there are approximately 5000 such billing statements per month.

Each shipping record consists of a very large number of attributes describing originating location, destination, transit points, type of cargo, type of car used, and other domain-specific information totaling over 700 attributes. BNSF maintains a multi-terabyte database of paid bills that keeps growing at approximately 600,000 billing records per month.

The database of paid bills is mostly correct, but there are records in it that contain incorrectly entered information and billing codes. Since the database is maintained over a long period of time, certain billing codes have changed, and these changes lead to billing codes that are no longer accurate and should not be used. Finally, during certain periods of the year it is possible that the billing codes will change, so that billing numbers may no longer be correct.

The high-level goal of our CBR system was fairly simple: given a new shipment, select the appropriate billing code by matching it against the database of previous billing cases (i.e. paid bills). The difficulty was that in so doing our system would retrieve many billing codes from cases that were either old, incorrect, or not valid for the current cycle of operations. When discussing the problem with the BNSF billing experts they indicated that there were two major selection criteria they would use to resolve any conflicts: the *volume* or *frequency* and the *recency* of a billing number. In other words, how many times a billing number had been used in the past coupled with how recently the number had been used.

---

[1] BNSF operates a railroad network with 33,000 route miles in North America

The combination of these two parameters is not straightforward, though. Cyclic billing means that some recent billing records would be correct, but have much less frequency than older ones that were generated over a long period of time. On the opposite end, a recent record may be simply incorrectly entered by BNSF personnel and should not necessarily override voluminous but older records.

Traditional case base maintenance techniques were of no help, since the conflicting cases were, in most situations, correct for different billing cycles and conditions, and such cycles and conditions were not consistent across all customers, nor were they always dependent on available information (for example, a customer moved temporarily to a new address, requiring a new number, and then moved back to their original offices, requiring the old number, but this happened in no predictable fashion). The case base did not have obsolete information that could be simply pruned; it contained current, sometimes conflicting, billing cases. To capture all rules and information regarding the definition of billing cycles and changes would be a very expensive and error-prone exercise.

3   CBR System

The basic CBR system for retrieval of the most similar cases used a simple, weighted nearest-neighbor matching of 20 features of the shipping record that required a billing number and the cases in the billing record case base. Weights were determined by BNSF experts of the domain, who also determined the attributes that were used in the matching process. The threshold over which a case was considered similar was varied experimentally between 1 and 0.9 in increments of 0.02 to identify any trends in retrieval. In this particular application varying the similarity threshold led to trivial and expected results: a lower threshold retrieved a larger set of similar cases and had fewer inputs that retrieved no similar cases.

Once the initial matching is complete, a billing code is assigned only if all retrieved cases above the cut-off threshold have the same billing code (something that happens in approximately 45% of the problems submitted to the CBR system). Otherwise the cases are analyzed by additional processing which uses the GA-created selection criteria, as described next. Billing problems that retrieve no similar cases are left for users to determine the appropriate billing code.

4   Generating Weighted Solution Selection Criteria

When CBR retrieved different billing codes, leading to conflicts as to the solution the system should select, our system needs to decide which of the billing codes to pick. As mentioned, the selection of the most appropriate case should be based on a combination of the recency of the billing case, its frequency (how often it has been used), and its similarity to the current billing problem. At issue was how to combine these parameters in a way that led to the selection of the correct billing case. We experimented with different equations and weighted parameters using genetic algorithms (GAs).

Before we describe the equations we used, we need to define two parameters: *frequency* and *recency*. Frequency is simply the relative frequency of a billing number in the cases retrieved. So, for example, if we retrieve 100 cases that are over the matching threshold, and 60 of them have the same billing number 12345, then the frequency of 12345 is 0.6. To compute the recency of a billing number we first need to define the cut-off distance, in other words the number of days after which a billing number is considered outdated. Each day between the current date and cutoff date is assigned a number between 0 and 1, computed linearly over the time interval. So, for example, if the cutoff date is 5 days in the past, the current date has value 1.0, yesterday has value 0.8, two days ago is 0.6, etc. The recency of a billing number is the normalized sum of the recency value of each case retrieved that has this number.

We defined six different weighted solution selection metrics:

1. A linearly weighted frequency: $\alpha \times frequency - \beta$
2. An exponentially weighted frequency: $\alpha \times e^{-(\beta(1-frequency))} + \gamma$
3. A step function for frequency: $\left\lceil \frac{frequency}{1/\alpha} \right\rceil \times \beta$
4. A linearly weighted recency: $\alpha \times recency - \beta$
5. An exponentially weighted recency: $\alpha \times e^{-(\beta(1-recency))} + \gamma$
6. A step function for recency: $\left\lceil \frac{recency}{1/\alpha} \right\rceil \times \beta$

We also defined two simple retrieval methods to be used as comparisons:

1. Most recent: Select the billing number that is in the most recent case
2. Most frequent: Select the billing number that appears most often in the whole set of retrieved cases

Next we used GAs to find the parameters of the six equations described above. We ran nine different experiments, one each for a different maximum similarity threshold (1, 0.98, 0.96, 0.94, 0.92, and 0.90). We repeated our experiments using two different fitness functions, to investigate the effect of the fitness function on the selection of the appropriate solution. The first fitness function was based only on the percentage of the problems that were solved correctly (i.e. were assigned the correct billing number). The second fitness function combined the percentage of the problems solved correctly with the difference between the matching value of the highest-ranked case that had the correct solution and the matching value of the highest-ranked case that had an incorrect solution; the goal was to have high accuracy but also to punish incorrect solutions that matched highly. Figure 1 shows the overall solution accuracy for the two fitness functions; since the fitness function that takes only percent correctness into account performed significantly worse, we will only discuss our results using the second fitness function.

The genetic algorithm was run for 1000 generations per experiment. Each generation population consisted of 200 individuals. The likelihood for crossover

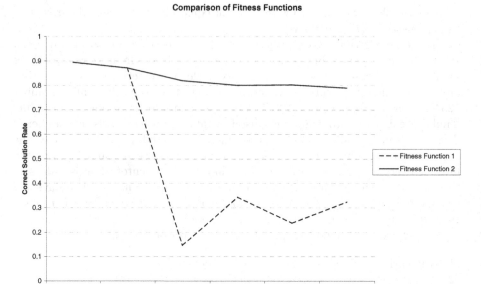

Fig. 1. Comparison of the overall results of the two fitness functions. "Fitness Function 1" uses only the percentage of correct solutions and performs significantly worse as the matching threshold for case selection is lowered.

was 99 percent, and the likelihood for mutation was 1 percent. The parameters we wanted to determine where encoded as bit strings. For example, for the exponentially weighted frequency equation, the GA tried to find the parameters α, β, an γ; for the linearly weighted recency equation, the GA tried to find the parameters α, β, and the cutoff date distance; etc. We used a case base of 500 cases for training and another one of 500 cases for testing. The training cases were again divided into five sub-sets of 100 cases each. The GA switched between training sub-sets for each generation, in an effort to avoid overfitting the solution.

The numbers generated were floating point with resolution of 0.001. For the exponential formulas we used 19 bits to encode the α parameter, 17 bits to encode the β parameter, and 20 bits to encode the γ parameter. For the linear formulas we used 17 bits to encode the α parameter and 10 bits to encode the β parameter. There are integer parameters, too, for example the date length is encoded in 9 bits (the date length is the number of days in the past when recency is set to zero), and the step number and step height each are encoded in 10 bits. The parameters for each equation are stored in a single chromosome of maximum length 90 bits. As already mentioned, the fitness function combined the percentage of the problems solved correctly with the difference between the matching value of the highest-ranked case that had the correct solution and the matching value of the highest-ranked case that had an incorrect solution.

For example, the GA found the following parameter values for the exponentially weighted recency equation when the similarity threshold was set to 0.90: cutoff date distance= 17 days; equation: $0.089 \times e^{-(0.053(1-recency))} + 0.085$

Next, we used the same GA process to discover the parameters of a *combination formula*, $\sum_{i}^{8} w_i \times f_i$ where w_i are the parameters and f_i are the outputs of the six formulas and the two simple solution selection methods ("most recent" and "most frequent"). The weight for each formula was encoded as a 10-bit string in the GA.

5 Results

After running the GAs, for each similarity threshold we had three formulas that weighted recency, three that weighted frequency, and one formula that combined the previous six and the two simple selection criteria of "most recent" and "most frequent." These nine selection criteria were tested on the 500 problems of our test set, and the results are shown on Figures 2 and 3 (note that three criteria, most frequent solution, and step and exponential weighted frequency, had identical results). We ran three different experiments with the same test set and all resulted in similar equations and the results were within one percentage point. While more experiments may be needed, our initial results indicate that the formulas generated by the GAs are stable and produce almost identical results. The results we are showing in the following graphs are from a single experiment.

Figure 2 shows the percentage of correct solutions (billing codes) that were identified by the nine different selection criteria as a function of the similarity threshold used. The combination formula does the best, and is the most consistent across changing threshold values. Note that the ratio of correct solutions is computed as a percentage of the solutions that the system found, and does not include situations where no solution could be found. Because of this, the graphs of Figure 2 are slightly misleading, since they could lead to the naive conclusion that the best performance can be achieved using a similarity threshold of 1.0, or, in other words, by demanding a perfect match. Figure 3 shows a better comparison of the nine selection criteria.

Figure 3 uses as an evaluation criterion the "contribution to the overall solution." This metric indicates how many correct solutions were found, versus (1) incorrect solutions, plus (2) cases where there were no competing solutions (i.e. all retrieved cases had the same billing number[2]), plus (3) problems where no solution was identified since no case matched at or above the matching threshold. So, this rate is the percentage of problems for which competing cases where retrieved times the percentage of them that were solved correctly. We believe that this is a better criterion of the overall performance of the selection metrics, since it indicates the contribution that the selection metrics make to the overall

---

[2] As mentioned, when cases are found and retrieved, in approximately 45% of the problems there are no competing solutions. So, the solution selection criteria are used in the remaining 55% or of the problems

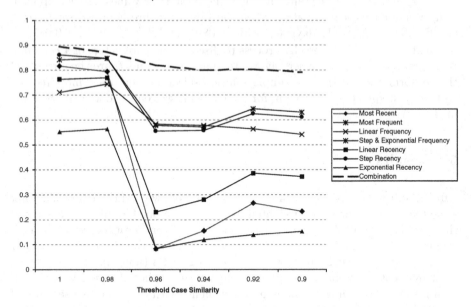

Fig. 2. Comparison of the nine solution selection criteria as a function of the percent of problems they solve correctly versus the similarity threshold used for case selection.

quality of the solution. Figure 2, on the other hand, shows the accuracy of the selected solution in cases where the system *can find a solution*.

For example, for a matching threshold of 1.0, CBR retrieval returned 24 cases without conflicting billing numbers, and 25 cases with conflicting billing numbers. Of the latter, we used the GA-generated combination formula to select the correct number and did so successfully in 22 instances (approximately 88%). So, at matching threshold of 1.0, the success of the simple CBR retrieval is 24 out of 500 (5%), while the combined system is 46 out of 500, or approximately 9%. The success of the GA-generated combination formula for the same threshold was 22 out of 476 (that is, 500 test cases minus the 24 that had no conflicting billing numbers), or approximately 4.6%. This 4.6% is the *contribution* of the GA-based selection criteria to the overall solution quality.

The combination method gave the best overall results, contributing 31% points to the overall solution quality. There seem to be no obvious trends for the other criteria. Interestingly, the "simple" solutions of selecting either the most frequent or the most recent solution do diametrically different, with frequency giving much better results than recency. On the other hand, the recency of a solution is important, as shown by the success of the "step recency" formula. Currently we have no insights as to the reasons the graphs look as they do, and, as discussed in Section 7, "Conclusions," we are performing more experiments to help gain a better understanding of the behavior of the GA-generated selection criteria. Since the current experiment dealt only with small variations in the matching threshold, it is possible that the behaviors shown by the individual plots are small permutations that will not seem important as we extend our experiments to smaller matching threshold, say down to 0.6.

Despite the performance of the individual selection criteria, though, it is clear that the combination method performs substantially better than the others, and especially against the simple selection methods of "most recent" and "more frequent."

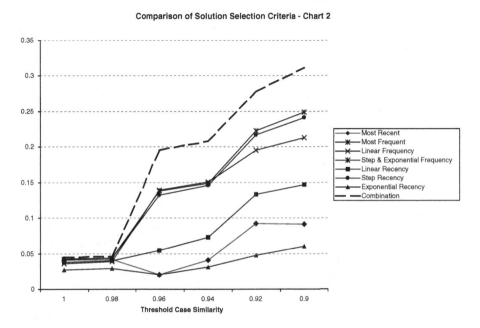

Fig. 3. Comparison of the nine solution selection criteria as a function of the contribution they make to the overall solution quality (expressed as percentage added to the combined CBR+GA system's accuracy) versus the similarity threshold used for case selection.

6   Previous Research

There has been a substantial volume of research that integrated CBR with genetic algorithms (GAs). Some of the previous work used CBR to seed GAs, so that they would not start from a random configuration of chromosomes, but, instead, start from a generation that —based on experience— was "close" to the required solution. For example, Ramsey and Grefenstette [14] presented a GA that was initialized by cases that contained descriptions of past GA runs (e.g. task environment and parameter values), and where CBR aimed to focus the GA to the current environment and situation. Liu [9] injected 5–15% of cases into a GA system for the design of gate-level circuits. Similarly, Perez et al.[12] used a case base of designs to seed a GA that also evolved circuits at the gate level. The work by Job et al. [4] is also very similar, in that it uses cases to seed an FPGA design program that uses GAs.

Other research used GAs to adapt solutions retrieved by CBR. This work is very similar to the one where CBR is used to seed GAs (the retrieved solutions can be seen as the GA seeds), but the focus is more on CBR than GAs. For example, structural design cases were adapted using GAs in the work described in [3]: CBR was used to retrieve up to four cases from a case base, that were then used as the initial population for a GA that evolved them to generate the most appropriate solution. A GA was also used to adapt designs that conform to feng shui rules and that were retrieved by CBR [1]. As in previous such work, the cases were used as "seeds" for the GA that then adapted them using standard GA techniques. The authors concluded that the combined CBR and GA system solved the same percentage of problems as a GA system alone, but that it generated designs of better quality and in faster times. A slightly different approach was taken in the work by Purvis and Athalye [13], where the generation of a solution from multiple retrieved cases was seen as a CSP problem that was solved by a CA.

The work in the CIGAR system [10] integrates GA seeding by a case base with the adaptation by a GA of the solutions generated by CBR. CIGAR uses a case base to inject part (10–15%) of a population at every GA step when attempting to solve a new problem in an evolutionary manner; as the GA proceeds, the solutions offered by the original cases are evolved by crossover and mutation to adapt to the new problem; new solutions are then learned by getting stored in the case base.

A large body of research has focused on determining the weights of features used in case matching using a GA. Early work [5] used GAs to find feature weights for a k nearest neighbor algorithm. Skalak [16] demonstrated how GAs can be used to perform feature selection and showed how this can be of great help in reducing computational costs without sacrificing accuracy in pattern recognition problems. Oatley et al. [11] used a GA to optimize the values of the weights of features used to compute similarity. Similar work is described in Shin and Han [15], where GAs are used to decide on the best indexing features for a CBR system for stock market prediction. In Kool et al. [7], the weight, selection, and ordering of features is performed using a GA and a case-based approach, and the two techniques are compared in the domain of memory-based language processing.

A very preliminary study of using GAs for CBR maintenance was discussed in [2]. In this work a set of representative cases were selected, and then their feature weights were modified by a GA to allow the cases to "move" in the problem space. Communication between case-controlling agents would eventually guide the GA to position all cases in a way that would provide the minimal representative case base.

Soh et al. [18] and Soh and Tsatsoulis [19] have examined using GAs to create a case base. In their work they define a set of domain-specific evaluation criteria for the quality of cases, but no actual case base exists initially. GAs are then used to generate populations of cases that fit the evaluation criteria and that are then used by a standard CBR system for problem solving.

Our work is not really similar to most previous work that combined CBR and GAs. Closest to our approach is the research that learns feature weights, since it attempts to improve retrieval, which is what our system also tries to do. Our work, though, applies GAs to cases where traditional CBR matching and retrieval has failed, and assumes that information that is *not* part of the feature set of the case (and, consequently, not known or not knowable) is what would improve retrieval.

Finally, early work on the CBR system PARADYME [6] used the recency with which a particular source case was last used as preference heuristic between retrieved cases that had the same similarity value. PARADYME's main goal was to show how different goals should lead to weighting case features differently, and the psychologically inspired factor of recency was just a simple post-retrieval criterion. While the goals of our system are similar to PARADYME's use of recency (select between competing cases), as mentioned in our discussion of the domain, cyclic billing means that some recent billing records would be correct, but have much less frequency than older ones; on the other, a recent record may be simply incorrectly entered by personnel and should not necessarily override voluminous but older records. Because of these complexities, it was necessary to learn/evolve the formulas that combine similarity, frequency and recency for case selection. Note also that in our work "recency" does not reflect when a case was used last (i.e. by the CBR system), but when the action described by a case was last performed.

7   Conclusions

In certain domains a case base may contain contradictory but correct cases. The contradictory solutions are due to known domain and problem characteristics which are not part of the case description, and which cannot be formally or explicitly described. In such cases, it is important to develop methods that will use these criteria to select among the competing solutions of the matching cases. We showed how one can use genetic algorithms to discover methods to combine and operationalize vague selection criteria such as "recency" and "frequency." In our domain it was assumed that these criteria were important for selecting among competing solutions, but there was no explicit way for doing so. GAs helped us develop simple equations that combined the solution selection criteria, and significantly improve the correctness of the system. In the best case experiment, the GA-developed selection criteria added approximately 31% correct solutions to the CBR system as compared to using simple weighted matching and retrieval. For our application this translates to over 1500 bills per month that would be send to the correct payee and would not be contested, resulting in substantial savings and in uninterrupted payments for shipments.

We observed that formulas combining all selection criteria performed better than ones considering a single criterion. We also discovered that the selection of the fitness function for genetic learning had a significant impact on the solution, and different fitness functions should be experimented with before committing to one. In our, albeit only three, experiments we noticed that the selection criteria generated by the GAs were very similar and led to almost identical results.

We intend to continue our experiments with decreasing similarity thresholds in an effort to see if contributions to the overall solution quality offered by the GA-generated selection criteria can be improved beyond the current 31%, and to find the point where —as we expect— performance will start declining.

More generally, CBR retrieval has —in most cases— resulted in the selection of the best matching case (or a small number of top matching cases), from which a solution is then adapted. Most work has concentrated on finding the best features, or the best weights, or has used the user to guide the ultimate selection, as done in Conversational CBR. The assumption has been in most cases that the similarity assessment process was sufficient to guide the problem solver to the best case from which to start adaptation. Our work in an, admittedly, uncommon domain of application, has led us to believe that in cases where there is no guarantee that the feature set describing a case adequately represents the problem instance, or that it would lead to correct case retrieval, the use of case selection criteria used after the similarity assessment phase can greatly improve performance.

Many case bases start as company data bases or textual documents, and their contents were never designed to be cases or be useful in establishing similarity between them. In such environments, the developers of the CBR system must try to elicit from experts further selection criteria and rules. Another possibility, as we have shown, is to have the experts identify which characteristics that are not part of the case description they use in selecting between cases, and then use these characteristics to learn the actual selection equations. In our work, the expert-defined characteristics were frequency and recency; in other domains they may be different. Our experiments showed that GAs are a good way of generating these selection criteria equations, and significantly improved the performance of the CBR system. While more experimentation will be necessary, it seems that the selection functions are stable and might be modeling inherent properties of the domain and of the expert case selection process. It would be interesting to attempt a similar experiment in a more "traditional" CBR application, and to study whether GA-generated selection criteria would do a better job selecting the best case from a subset of matching cases as compared to selecting the best matching case.

Acknowledgments. This work was supported in part by the Burlington Northern and Santa Fe Railway Company. The comments by the anonymous reviewers helped us improve the exposition of our work.

References

1. de Silva Garza, A.G. and M.L. Maher: "An Evolutionary Approach to Case Adaptation," in Proceedings of 3rd Int. Conf. on CBR (ICCBR-99),K.-D. Althoff, R. Bergmann and L.K. Branting (Eds.), Berling: Springer-Verlag, (1999) 162–172.
2. Huang, Y.: "An Evolutionary Agent Model of Case-Based Classification," in Proceedings of 3rd European CBR Workshop (EWCBR-96), I. Smith and B. Faltings (Eds.), Berling: Springer-Verlag, (1996) 193–203.
3. Hunt, J.: "Evolutionary Case Based Design," in Progress in Case-Based Reasoning: 1st UK Workshop, I.D. Watson (Ed.), Berlin: Springer-Verlag, (1995) 17–31.
4. Job, D., Miller, J. and Shankararaman, V.: "Combining CBR abd GA for Designing FPGAs," in Proceedings of 3rd Int. Cnf. on Computational Intelligence and Multimedia Applications, (1999) 133–137.
5. Kelly, J.D. and Davis, L.: "A Hybrid Genetic Algorithm for Classification," in Proceedings of 12th Int. Conf. on AI (IJCAI-91), (1991) 645–650.
6. Kolodner, J: "Selecting the Best Case for a Case-Based Reasoner," in Proceedings of 11th Ann. Conf. of the Cognitive Science Society, Hillsdale, NJ: Larence Erlbaum Associates, (1989) 155–162.
7. Kool, K., Daelemans, W. and Zavrel, J.: "Genetic Algorithms for Feature Relevance Assignment in Memory-Based Language Processing," in Proceedings of 4th Conf. on Computational Natural Language Learning and of the 2nd Learning Language in Logic Workshop, Lisbon, Somerset, NJ: Association for Computational Linguistics, (2000) 103–106.
8. Leake, D. B. and Wilson, D. C: "Case-Base Maintenance: Dimensions and Directions," in Proceedings of European Workshop on Case-Based Reasoning. Springer-Verlag, Berlin Heidelberg New York (1998) 196–207.
9. Liu, X.: "Combining Genetic Algorithms and Case-based Reasoning for Structure Design," M.S. Computer Science Thesis, University of Nevada at Reno (1996).
10. Louis, S.J. and Johnson, J.: "Robustness of Case-Initialized Genetic Algorithms," in Proceedings of 12th Int. Florida AI Research Society (FLAIRS-99), (1999) 129–133.
11. Oatley, G., Tait, J. and McIntyre, J.: "A Case-based Reasoning Tool for Vibration Analysis," in Applications and Innovations in Expert Systems VI: Proceedings of the BCS Expert Systems Conference, R. Milne, A. Macintosh and M. Bramer (eds.), Berlin: Springer-Verlag (1998).
12. Perez E.I., Coello, C.A. and Aguirre, A.H.: "Extracting and Re-Using Design Patterns from Genetic Algorithms using Case-Based Reasoning," in Proceedings of the Genetic and Evolutionary Computation Conference, GECCO-2002, Langdon, W.B. et al. (Eds.), San Francisco, CA: Morgan Kaufmann Publishers, (2002).
13. Purvis, L. and Athalye, S.: "Towards Improving Case Adaptability with a Genetic Algorithm," in 2nd Int. Conf. on CBR (ICCBR-97), Leake, D.B. and E. Plaza (Eds.), Berlin: Springer-Verlag, (1997) 403–412.
14. Ramsey, C.L. and Grefenstette, J.J.: "Case-Based Initialization of Genetic Algorithms," in Proceedings of 5th Int. Conf. on Genetic Algorithms, (1993) 84–91.
15. Shin, K. and Han, I: "Case-based Reasoning Supported by Genetic Algorithms for Corporate Bond Rating," J. of Expert Systems with Applications 16(2), (1999) 85–95.
16. Skalak, D.B: "Prototype and Feature Selection by Sampling and Random Mutation Hill Climbing Algorithms," in Proceedings of 11th Int. Conf. on Machine Learning, (1994) 293–301.

17. Smyth, B. and McKenna, E.: "Modeling the Competence of Case-Bases," in Proceedings of 4th European Workshop on Case-Based Reasoning, EWCBR-98, Lecture Notes in Artificial Intelligence 1488, Smyth, B. and Cunningham, P. (Eds.), Berlin: Springer Verlag, (1998) 208–220.
18. Soh, L-K., Tsatsoulis, C., Jones, M. and Agah, A: "Evolving Cases for Case-Based Reasoning Multiagent Negotiations," in Proceedings of the Genetic and Evolutionary Computation Conference, GECCO-2001, Spector, L. et al (Eds.), San Francisco, CA: Morgan Kaufmann Publishers, 909 (2001).
19. Soh, L-K. and Tsatsoulis, C.: "Combining Genetic Algorithms and Case-Based Reasoning for Genetic Learning of a Casebase: A Conceptual Framework," in Proceedings of the Genetic and Evolutionary Computation Conference, GECCO-2001, Spector, L. et al (Eds.), San Francisco, CA: Morgan Kaufmann Publishers, (2001) 376–383.
20. Zhu, J and Yang, Q.: "Remembering to Add: Competence-Preserving Case-Addition Policies for Case Base Maintenance," in Proceedings of the Fifteenth Int. J. Conf. on Artificial Intelligence. Morgan Kaufman (1999) 234–239.

Using Case-Based Reasoning to Overcome High Computing Cost Interactive Simulations

Javier Vázquez-Salceda, Miquel Sànchez-Marrè, and Ulises Cortés

Knowledge Engineering & Machine Learning Group,
Technical University of Catalonia, Campus Nord-Edifici C5, Jordi Girona 1-3,
08034 Barcelona, Catalonia, EU
{jvazquez, miquel, ia}@lsi.upc.es

Abstract. This paper describes an innovative usage of Case-Based Reasoning to reduce the high computing cost derived from running large interactive simulation scenarios within the framework of advanced training systems. The paper discusses the ideas, implementation and a preliminary evaluation within the framework of the European IST research project A-TEAM.

1 Introduction

Over the last decade an important progress has been made in the Case-based Reasoning (CBR) field. Specially, because problems are more clearly identified, and research results have led to real applications where CBR performs well.

Case-Based Reasoning paradigm provides advanced intelligent training systems with a great learning flexibility. In advanced environmental training systems, the use of simulation exercises is a common feature. Providing the trainees with realistic skills in emergency management is an important learning feature of the advanced environmental training systems. Simulation exercises are good tools to practice environmental emergency management in a real scenario without causing damage to the environment, and complement other static learning issues of the pedagogical components of a training system. Commonly, simulation exercises have a major disadvantage: the computer time consumption is very high, as the simulation exercises usually involve complex mathematical models that are implemented with very time-expensive computer algorithms, and complex picture images, generated by highly time-consuming computer algorithms.

At this point, the role of the Case-Based Reasoning and its derived technologies appears as a possible solution. The CBR module can retrieve the appropriate previously computed simulation exercise/s according to the pedagogical issues of the learning units of an advanced intelligent training system, and/or according to the degree of trainees' expertise. The CBR module can pre-compute and store in a Case Library the most representative simulation exercises in off-line computation. Afterwards, in an

K.D. Ashley and D.G. Bridge (Eds.): ICCBR 2003, LNAI 2689, pp. 581–594, 2003.
© Springer-Verlag Berlin Heidelberg 2003

interactive on-line learning session with a trainee, the CBR module can retrieve the most appropriate set of simulation exercises avoiding huge computation time delays. Not only the CBR module can retrieve appropriate cases, but also it can adapt some retrieved cases to fit a new required simulation exercise foreseeing the simulation results, by means of some domain knowledge. Therefore advanced intelligent training systems will become a more interactive, pedagogically flexible and user-friendly training systems.

In Environmental sciences, CBR has been applied in different areas with different goals, because of its general applicability. It has been used in information retrieval from large historical meteorological databases (Jones and Roydhouse, 1995), in optimisation of sequence operations for the design of wastewater treatment systems (Krovvidy and Wee, 1993), in supervisory systems for diagnosing and controlling WWTP systems (Sànchez-Marrè et al, 1997a), in decision support systems for planning forest fire fighting (Avesani et al, 1995), in case-based prediction for rangeland pest management advisories by (Branting et al, 1997), or in case-based design for process engineering (Surma and Brauschweig, 1996).

In the environmental emergency management there have been some works, especially within the CBR planning field, such as the works of (Avesani et al., 2000; Ricci et al., 1999). But the merging of interactive simulation and CBR have not been exploited too much. There is a project (Sadek 2001; Sadek et al., 1999) about the development of a Prototype Case-Based Reasoning for Real-time Freeway Traffic Routing. This project developed a prototype Case-Based Reasoning Decision Support System for the on-line management of freeway traffic in the presence of incidents. The system uses input data from loops and closed-circuit TV cameras to develop optimal routing strategies that are to be relayed to travellers via variable message signs (VMS) and highway advisory radio (HAR). Also there some work in the training and education within the medical domain using CBR techniques such as the work of (Bichindaritz and Sullivan, 2002).

The paper is organised in the following way. Section 2 describes the framework of the A-TEAM project. In Section 3, the case structure within the system is detailed. Section 4 presents the case library interactions. Section 5 is devoted to the design and development of the CBR server. An application of the system in a particular domain is detailed in section 6. Finally, in Section 7 conclusions and future research directions are outlined.

2 The A-TEAM Project

The CBR Module is one of the components of the A-TEAM System that provides information to the RTXPS module, as depicted in fig.1:

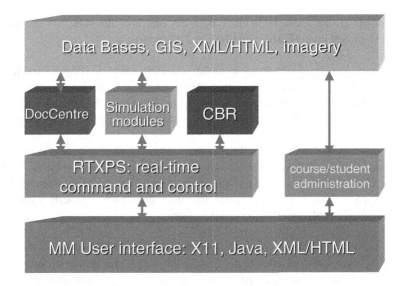

Fig. 1. Overview of the A-TEAM modular architecture

The A-TEAM system provides to the trainee a multimedia course structured in lessons with text, images and short videos, where the evolution of the student is tracked by means of some tests. Most of contents of the courses (the lesson's text, images, videos and the multiple-choice tests) are provided to the RTXPS module by DocCentre. But there are other kind of tests that make A-TEAM system innovative: the interactive emergency situations.

Interactive simulated emergency situations are a special kind of tests where the trainee, alone or with other trainees in a shared scenario, has to solve an environmental emergency that is shown in their display. The trainee has to take the proper decisions to manage the emergency. These kinds of tests evaluate the trainee skills in emergency management, and are one of the key features of the A-TEAM system. Some of these emergency situations are completely set by the content provider, that is, the one who builds the course material. But there are times that the trainee is allowed to change some of the parameters involved in the emergency (such as wind speed, wind direction, wind temperature and so on) in order to see the influence each change in one of them has in the emergency.

Some of the emergency situations can be computed on-line by the Simulation Modules and delivered directly to the RTXPS system, but some others are so complex that it takes several minutes to compute them, so they shouldn't be generated on-line. In order to keep the student focused in the lesson, it has been decided to avoid delays in computation of complex scenarios by means of having them pre-computed and stored in a way that lets a fast recovery of the information when RTXPS makes a request of one of those pre-computed situations.

One option to store the information of situations could be a Relational Database. It is a widely used technology to store and recover information in several information systems. However, the recovery is made by exact match of the values of the query. So using a Database in A-TEAM could lead to 2 alternatives:

- Pre-compute any possible scenario that a student could need for his training. This first option is unfeasible when there are emergency scenarios partially driven by the student's choice in the parameters, as the set of possible situations to store and retrieve would grow to million or even more combinations of those parameter values.
- To let only the content provider or the student to choose emergencies that currently are stored in the database. That is, that the queries made by the RTXPS to the CBR Module should match the exact values of the situations stored. This option makes that if there's a query that does not matches exactly with any pre-computed simulation, then no result is given.

As we saw in section 1, one of the main capabilities of a CBR system is the recovery of the best results, the ones that better fit with the values provided in the query. Instead of the "exact match" criteria, CBR systems use a "*similarity*" criterion (Núñez et al., 2003) that can be defined for each domain. Similarities allow to recover not only the exact result for the query (if exists) but also recover the most similar ones. In our CBR system *L'Eixample* similarity measure has been used (Sànchez-Marrè et al., 1998).

So the role of the CBR system is as storage facility for the pre-computed simulations so complex that they cannot be made on-line. In this new approach the pre-computed simulations are stored as cases in the Case Library. The queries that came from the RTXPS system are attended by the CBR module, which seeks for the most similar, pre-computed simulations to the one the RTXPS requests.

2.1 Integration of the CBR Module with the Other A-TEAM Modules

The CBR Module is integrated in the A-TEAM system as an independent module interacting with other modules in the system. These interactions of the CBR Module with the other modules can be divided in two steps (see figure 2):

- off-line: the Simulation Modules can provide the CBR with all the pre-computed data about complex emergencies (accidental spills, transportation accidents, fire, explosion, atmospheric dispersion) that could be useful to be recovered on-line.
- on-line: for each request from the RTXPS module, the CBR gives the best simulation according to a previously established similarity criteria.

Off-line interactions among the simulation modules and the CBR module are made by e-mail by means of a predefined format. On the other hand, the way on-line interactions are done is based on the work done in the WP06 (Integration and Implementation), that defines the A-TEAM system as a network-distributed service composed by:

- The Main Server, including the RTXPS system, the DocCentre System and the Data-bases
- The on-line UDM Simulation Server
- The CBR Server

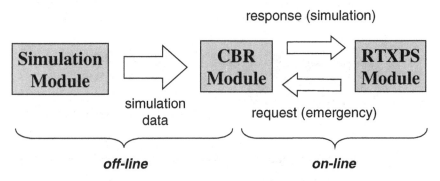

Fig. 2. Interactions of the CBR Module with the RTXPS module and the off-line Simulation Modules

The communication among all the distributed parts is made through the World Wide Web by means of an HTTP protocol. This distribution of computation allows that hard computational issues such as the emergency simulation or the CBR can be placed in powerful machines, speeding-up the response and decreasing the hardware needs for the end-users' platforms.

In the whole architecture (shown in figure 1), the CBR Server is the part of the A-TEAM system that does the CBR functionalities explained above. It is hosted in a powerful machine to a) store all the pre-computed simulation for all the test cases, and b) attend the on-line requests it receives in parallel, computing lots of similarities among the query and the stored cases to retrieve the better stored simulation.

3   Filling the Case Library: A Case in the A-TEAM System

As mentioned before, the case library stores the simulation exercises too complex to be built on-line. So *"feeding"* the case library with all those simulations is an off-line process where the content developers and the Simulation Modules managers are involved in order to create the information the CBR's Case Library will store.

While designing a course, the content developers should decide which examples will be shown, which images, the tests to be performed by the trainee and so on. Some of the examples or the tests could be emergency simulations that also have to be designed with the managers of the Simulation Modules, in order to find the proper simulation model to the simulation proposed and thus, the format of the inputs and outputs for that model.

While designing a complex emergency simulation (that is, a simulation that should be pre-computed off-line and stored by the CBR), the information that should be collected and built is composed by the parts depicted in figure 3:

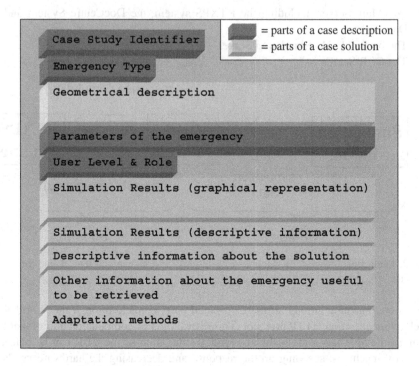

Fig. 3. Information associated to an emergency simulation.

Case Study Identifier and Emergency Type

The Case Study Identifiers are useful to distinguish among the different case studies (Austria, Italy, Switzerland, Portugal and United Kingdom), while the Emergency Types are useful to identify the kind of emergency (such as Road Tunnel, Chemical Plant, etc.). These identifiers are set for the whole A-TEAM system.

Geometrical Description

It is all the useful geometrical information about the topology (mountains, roads, buildings, etc.) of the place where the emergency will be simulated. This piece of information is not used as part of the case in the Case Library, as it's only useful for the Simulation Modules in order to run their simulation. More details about the format of these data are provided in deliverables of A-TEAM project (A-TEAM, 2003).

Parameters of the emergency

These are the parameters that set the initial state of the emergency. They are established for each type of emergency. For instance, in emergencies that involve gas dispersion, some of the parameters are Wind speed, Wind direction, Air Temperature, Exit velocity (of the dangerous substance that is spilled), etc.

These parameters are not only useful to the Simulation Modules as input of their runs, but also to the CBR as part of the case description.

User Level and Role

This piece of information is placed if needed. Useful to tag emergency exercises designed specifically for a given trainee profile (a team coordinator, a fireman, etc.) or a certain level of expertise (beginner, intermediate, expert). This is needed when the content developer decides that different user profiles (roles) or levels of expertise need different simulations to be shown.

Simulation Results

They are the result of the runs of the Simulation Modules to be stored for a later delivery to RTXPS when requested, as part of the case solution.

They consist on two kinds of data:

- The graphical information is useful to run the simulation on the trainee's display. Examples of this kind of data are 2D map representations of the emergency, gas concentration isolines, bar graphs, etc.
- The descriptive information is useful to provide the trainee with some numerical features or to be used in the RTXPS as part of the course management. Examples of this kind of information are the final values of temperature in the affected area, the concentration values of toxic substances in that area.

Descriptive information about the solution

Along with the simulation results, it could be useful to include some information (maybe only some hints) about the proper solution to solve the emergency, or the proper measures to make the area to return to a normal state (for instance, the procedures to be taken to clean the area from the toxic substances).

Other information about the emergency

This is another piece of information placed only if needed. Is up to the content developers to figure if they need more information associated with each simulation, so it should be stored with the rest of data.

Adaptation Methods

As stated before, it is unfeasible to pre-compute all the possible emergency simulations the user will need. The similarity-based retrieval of CBR systems partially addresses this issue, by retrieving not the exact simulation requested but the most similar one. But there is another step that can fit the solution given by the case retrieved to the actual simulation requested: the adaptation step.

Adaptation can be made from the best case's solution or from the joint of some of the best cases. It allows creating new solutions from the case solutions stored in the Case Library. In the A-TEAM context that means that it is not needed to have pre-computed all the possible simulations with all the possible combinations in the input parameters if there's a method to adapt the results of the most similar emergency situations to the current one requested by the RTXPS.

The adaptation step is a domain-dependent process, so that means it has to be designed for each emergency type. Depending on the kind of information to adapt it can be expressed as a mathematical functions (to compute some sort of interpolation), a piece of computer code or a list of rules to be applied.

4   Introduction of Cases in the Case Library

In order to build a case library for a given case study and a given type of emergency, there are needed two kinds of information:

- The parameter descriptions: it is a metadata file used by the RTXPS system to describe each of the parameters that it uses in its reasoning process. These metadata files, which we will refer as the RTXPS parameter descriptors, are used as a standard notation in the rest of the A-TEAM system, so they are also an useful input for the CBR system.

- The Simulated Emergencies: the Simulation Modules following the specifications of the content providers provide these data. Each of the simulated emergencies would become a case in the Case Library.

In figure 4 the inputs of the CBR are depicted:

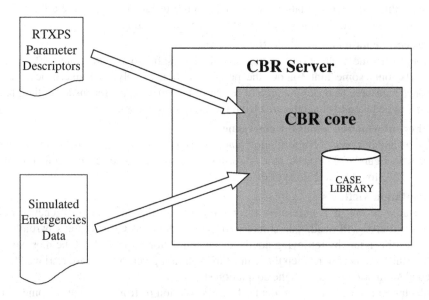

Fig. 4. The off-line inputs of the CBR server

Both inputs are files sent by e-mail or placed in a restricted ftp site to be downloaded. The format of the RTXPS parameter descriptors are describe in the A-TEAm project documentation (A-TEAM, 2003). The format of the Simulated Emergencies file depends on whether the content developer decided that different user profiles (roles) or levels of expertise need different simulations to be shown. As explained before, when there were emergency exercises designed specifically for a given kind of trainee a piece of information, named User Level & Role in figure 5, is added.

```
CASELIB

HEAD
CI <ATEAM_case_study_id>
ET <A_TEAM_emergency_type_id>
INPUTP_ORDER
P <RTXPS_param_descriptor>
P <RTXPS_param_descriptor>
...
P <RTXPS_param_descriptor>
ENDINPUTP_ORDER
TRAINEE CASE_SPECIFIED
OUTPUTP_ORDER
P <RTXPS_param_descriptor>
P <RTXPS_param_descriptor>
...
P <RTXPS_param_descriptor>
ENDOUTPUTP_ORDER
ENDHEAD

BODY
CASE
N <num_case>
INPUTP
<val1> <val2> ..... <valn>
ENDINPUTP
TRAINEE
T <ATEAM_trainee_role_id>
...
T <ATEAM_trainee_role_id>
T <ATEAM_trainee_expertise_level>
...
T <ATEAM_trainee_expertise_level>
ENDTRAINEE
OUTPUTP
<val1> <val2> ..... <valn>
ENDOUTPUTP
OUTPUTG
<Graphic_Output_Data>
ENDOUTPUTG
SOLUTION
<Solution_Data>
ENDSOLUTION
MOREINFO
<More_information_data>
ENDMOREINFO
ENDCASE

CASE
...
ENDCASE

...

ENDBODY
ENDCASELIB
```

Fig. 5. Example of format of the Simulated Emergencies File

As shown, the input is a tagged text file composed by a) some headers, with information regarding the whole simulations, and b) a body, where each case block holds the data of a single simulation. In order to decrease the size of the file, the relation among parameter names and values is set by defining an order in the head section. So, the order of the parameter names (which should follow the standard names set by the RTXPS descriptor file) is the order of their respective values for each simulation.

5 Design and Implementation of the CBR Server

As part of the distributed A-TEAM system, the CBR Server should attend all the requests for pre-computed simulation that the main RTXPS server makes remotely. To do this, a new component should be added to the CBR server shown previously in figure 6: the HTTP server.

So, with this addition, the CBR Server is composed by:
- The HTTP server: this component deals with the communication issues of the CBR server. It is a front-end that can manage multiple HTTP connections from one or several RTXPS servers, decoding the HTTP request to get the query and sending it to the CBR core. Then it encodes the result provided by the CBR core and sends it back to the RTXPS server.
- The CBR core: this component receives several on-line queries through the HTTP server, and it returns the best pre-computed solution for each query. The current implementation lets the core to run all the searches in parallel.

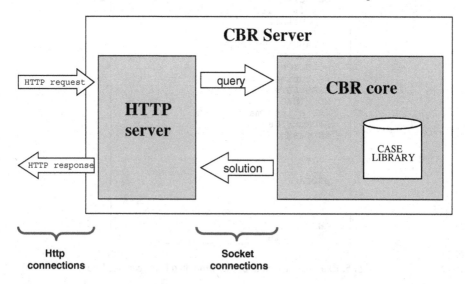

Fig. 6. The on-line inputs of the CBR Server

Java technologies have been chosen for both the HTTP server and the CBR core, not only because of its portability but also because of the multi-threading and secure networking mechanisms it provides. Therefore, the HTTP server can be any commercial server that manages Java servlets, while the CBR core is a multi-threaded application.

The sequence diagram in figure 2.9 describes in detail all the fluxes of information created in an on-line query. It shows how an HTTP request is processed: the Web Server creates a new thread of execution and calls the method doPost of the Java Servlet (class CBRServlet), which, in turn, calls its doGet method (HTTP Get and HTTP Post requests are processed the same way by the servlet).

The doGet method obtains the query information, and opens a Socket connection to the CBR server (class CBReasoner), that is waiting for connections from the *HTTP server*. When receiving such a connection, it creates a new thread of execution (class ServerThread) to manage the request of information. The ServerThread class uses the method importFromData of class ATeamCase to create a new case from the raw data it receives through the socket, and then starts a reasoning cycle to obtain the result. The result is sent back through the socket connection to the *Java Servlet*, where the result is translated into an HTTP response format and then sent back by the *Web Server*. It is important to note that, as either the Java Servlets and the server threads use Java threads to run, the CBR server can manage more than one request concurrently.

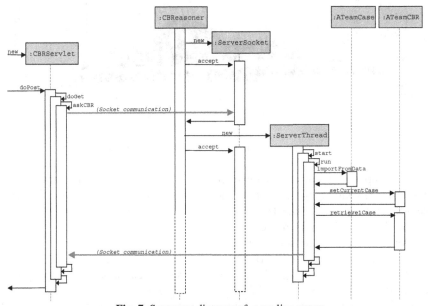

Fig. 7. Sequence diagram of a on-line query.

6 An Application: A Railway Tunnel Scenario

As an example of application, now one of the test cases of the CBR server within the A-TEAM project will be presented. The test case consists of a simulation exercise placed in a 6.3 km. Long tunnel: the Grauholz tunnel, north of Bern, Switzerland, which is a link for east to west traffic between Zurich and Geneva, and for north to south traffic through the Alps (see figure 8).

The simulation exercise aims to present different scenarios to the student to be solved, from a train that develops a small fire in a container without dangerous goods involved to a bigger incident where a train derails inside the tunnel and releases relevant amounts of fuel oil and starts burning, heating up the tanker(s) and possibly, creating a chain reaction (rupture of the containment, thermal decomposition and formation of toxic gas) that scales up the incident. Part of the simulation exercise includes the assumption that there are passengers in the tunnel to be saved, either from the same train that started the fire or a passenger train approaching from the other direction into the tunnel which could not be stopped in time and entered the tunnel.

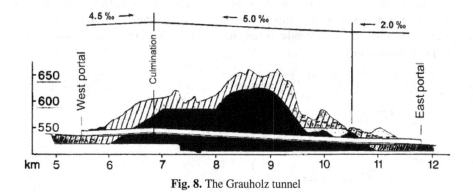

Fig. 8. The Grauholz tunnel

For each emergency case, a number of physical parameters describing the scenario characteristics were computed. For the emergency intervention and self rescue actions of people in the tunnel, the development of the following parameters during the emergency situation (fire) are crucial and constitute the output of the simulations for the whole volume of the tunnels:

- Air Temperature in the tunnel (K)
- Air pressure in the tunnel (kg/(m s2))
- Air flow speed in the tunnel (m/s)
- Tracer in the tunnel (kg/m3), is meaning the concentration of an inert pollutant (i.e. smoke).

An example of the output provided by the CBR server is depicted in figure 9. The output shows the parameters of the case plus the temperature distribution inside the tunnel (the image shows the snapshot of the tunnel 25 min after the fire started). At the bottom of the window there is a navigation tool that allows going forward/backward in the simulation time, and up/down in the tunnel (to see the temperature distribution from the ground to the ceiling of the tunnel).

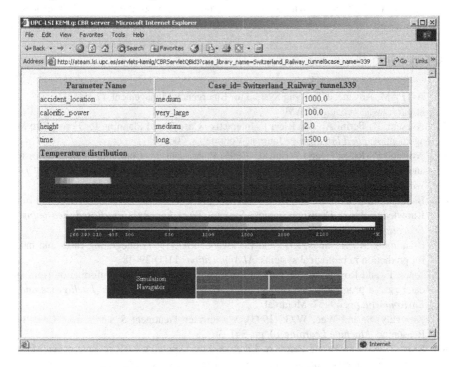

Fig. 9. Output of the CBR server for the railway scenario.

7 Conclusions and Future Work

The CBR server described within this paper has been experimentally evaluated from a qualitative point of view. The environmental manager experts who are in charge of training courses have assessed some test cases, such as the railway tunnel scenario and a road tunnel scenario.

Preliminary evaluation has shown a very good performance and accuracy in the CBR system. Only some adjustments for graphical outputs are being updated to satisfy the requirements of the users.

In the near future a more statistical and numerical evaluation will be made as the other modules and components of the A-TEAM project will be successfully integrated, and a deeper evaluation will be possible.

Also, as the design of the core of the CBR server is a very general tool it can be applied to other environmental and advanced intelligent training systems. Other domains of applications will be studied.

Acknowledgements. This work has been partially supported by the Spanish CICyT project TIC2000-1011, REC2000-1755, and EU project A-TEAM (IST 1999-10176). The authors wish the acknowledge the work and effort of all the A-TEAM partners.

References

1. A-TEAM. Advanced Training System for Emergency Management. (2003). http://www.ess.co.at/ATEAM/.
2. Avesani, P., Perini A., and Ricci F. Interactive Case-Based Planning for Forest Fire Management. *Applied Intelligence* Journal, Volume 13, 2000.
3. Avesani, P., Ricci, F and Perini, A. (1995) P. Avesani, F.. Combining human assessment and reasoning aids for decision making in planning forest fire fighting. Procc. *of IJCAI Workshop on Artificial Intelligence and the Environment*, pp. 71–74, Montréal.
4. Bichindaritz I. and Sullivan, K.M. Generating Practice Cases for Medical Training from a Knowledge-Based Decision-Support System. *Workshop on Case-Based Reasoning for Education and Training*, Abeerdeen, Scotland. September 4th, 2002.
5. Branting. L.K., Hastings, J.D., and Lockwood, J.A. (1997) Integrating cases and models for prediction in biological systems. *AI Applications* 11(1):29–48.
6. Jones, E. and Roydhouse, A. (1995). Retrieving structured spatial information from large databases: a progress report .Procc. of *IJCAI Workshop on Artificial Intelligence and the Environment*, pp. 49–57, Montréal.
7. Krovvidy, S. and Wee, W.G. (1993). Wastewater Treatment Systems from Case-Based Reasoning. *Machine Learning* 10, pp. 341–363.
8. Ricci F., Avesani P. and Perini A. Cases on Fire: Applying CBR to Emergency Management. *New Review of Applied Expert Systems Journal*, Vol. 5, 1999.
9. Núñez H., Sànchez-Marrè M. and Cortés U. Similarity Measures in Instance-Based Reasoning. Submitted to *Artificial Intelligence*, 2003.
10. Sadek A.W., Smith B.L. and Demetsky M.J. (2001). A Prototype Case-Based Reasoning Decision Support System for Real-time Freeway Traffic Routing. *Transportation Research*, Part C, Vol. 9(5).
11. Sadek A.W., Smith B.L. and Demetsky M.J. (1999). Case-Based Reasoning for Real-time Traffic Flow Management. *Computer-Aided Civil and Infrastructure Engineering*, Vol. 14(5).
12. Sànchez-Marrè, M., Cortés, U. R-Roda, I., Poch, M., and Lafuente, J. (1997a) Learning and Adaptation in WWTP through Case-Based Reasoning. *Microcomputers in Civil Engineering* 12(4):251–266.
13. Surma, J. and Brauschweig, B. (1996) Case-Based Retrieval in Process Engineering: Supporting Design by Reusing Flowsheets. *Engineering Applications of Artificial Intelligence*. 9(4): 385–391.

Predicting Software Development Project Outcomes

Rosina Weber, Michael Waller, June Verner, and William Evanco

College of Information Science & Technology, Drexel University
3141 Chestnut Street Philadelphia, PA 19104
{rosina.weber,mwaller}@drexel.edu;
{june.verner,william.evanco}@cis.drexel.edu

Abstract. Case-based reasoning is a flexible methodology to manage software development related tasks. However, when the reasoner's task is prediction, there are a number of different CBR techniques that could be chosen to address the characteristics of a dataset. We examine several of these techniques to assess their accuracy in predicting software development project outcomes (i.e., whether the project is a success or failure) and identify critical success factors within our data. We collected the data from software developers who answered a questionnaire targeting a software development project they had recently worked on. The questionnaire addresses both technical and managerial features of software development projects. The results of these evaluations are compared with results from logistic regression analysis, which serves as a comparative baseline. The research in this paper can guide design decisions in future CBR implementations to predict the outcome of projects described with managerial factors.

1 Introduction and Background

Software development project failure can be very costly. Risk factors that can determine project failure tend to become evident only in the later stages of software development life cycle; often too late to steer a project safely back on course. As a result, software project managers can be aided greatly by tools that can identify likely success or failure at an early stage, as well as those factors that may contribute to development problems. Our goal is to develop a tool that can make a good prediction of a project's outcome early in the development life cycle and indicate success or risk factors. This tool has to be flexible enough to accommodate managerial features and be able to manage a variety of knowledge tasks (e.g., capture, reuse) comprising a knowledge management (KM) system.

We chose case-based reasoning (CBR) for this tool because CBR is a methodology [1] that can support the flexible automation of the entire process. Additionally, CBR is appropriate for software development related tasks because the methodology resembles human judgment [2]. CBR also offers advantages to support KM efforts [4, 5, 6, 7]. CBR is characterized as a lazy learner that predicts the outcome of new cases by using a k-nearest neighbor classifier, thus presenting some potential benefits to predict project success (e.g., a relatively small training cost and effort conjugated with an explanation for the classification [3]).

K.D. Ashley and D.G. Bridge (Eds.): ICCBR 2003, LNAI 2689, pp. 595–609, 2003.
© Springer-Verlag Berlin Heidelberg 2003

There are a number of different techniques that can be used to implement CBR; the current view is that certain design choices can bias the system's quality [8, 9]. Therefore, we need to test different techniques and select the one that performs best with the problem data. Our data was collected from 122 software developers who responded to a questionnaire about a software project they had recently worked on. The questions addressed both technical and managerial features of the chosen software development projects.

Past work using CBR for prediction of software development projects has focused on the technical, quantifiable aspects of software development, predicting, for example, development effort [2, 8, 9] rather than addressing qualitative managerial factors. In [9], Watson et al. compared three CBR techniques and found that the weighted Euclidean distance was the most accurate method for predicting development effort for web hypermedia software. In [2] Finnie et al. compared CBR techniques with linear regression analysis. They predicted effort represented by a continuous dependent variable, which is better suited for linear regression models. Kadoda et al. [8] also predicted software development effort with CBR and compared its performance with stepwise regression. They concluded that there is strong association between features of the dataset (e.g., training set size, nature of the cost function) and the success of a technique, and that the best technique can be determined on the basis of each dataset [8].

The use of CBR to help manage software engineering projects is commonly associated with the experience factory (EF) [10, 11] - a framework that structures the reuse of experience and products obtained during the software development life cycle. For example, Althoff et al. [7] have adopted the EF model to create an experience base to reuse experiences and products obtained in the development of CBR systems. Our approach differs because our core goal is to predict success and provide advice to software project managers. Our strategy is not intended to explicitly record methods employed in one development and enable detailed reuse, but simply to gather general experience in software development projects in order to identify success factors. In our approach, it is the user's responsibility to search for mitigants when a given factor seems to suggest potential failure. Our approach is more superficial and designed for easier implementation and acquisition.

When using CBR to manage or predict success of managerial projects, sometimes the number of features describing these projects may outnumber the number of cases. The way Cain et al. [11] dealt with this problem was by incorporating domain knowledge to choose the features to explain success or failure. They combined the notion of explanation-based learning (EBL), which uses domain knowledge to generalize a concept from a training example [13]. Their parameterized combination of CBR plus EBL is detailed in Subsection 3.3.

We tested different techniques to assess how well they performed with our data. After testing unweighted measures we used a hill-climbing feedback method to learn weights and prevent imperfect features from participating equally in predicting project outcome. We then introduced and investigated a weighted version of the CBR plus EBL approach. As we identify the best similarity measure to provide accurate outcome predictions, we will introduce a method to use this technique to identify success factors with CBR. Because failure factors may have multiple mitigants, managers will have the information necessary to avoid project pitfalls.

We also used a non-CBR technique, logistic regression (LR) [14], to predict the outcomes for the same dataset. LR is generally considered the most accurate statistical technique for modeling dichotomous dependent variables, particularly in datasets with fewer than 100 examples, but it is also a method that tends to be expensive [14]. Cleary et al., explain that LR is a highly desirable statistical model and should be used for model fitting and hypothesis testing [14]. Hence, we use LR as a point of comparison for testing various CBR techniques.

This paper is organized as follows. Section 2 discusses the questionnaire used for data collection. Section 3 describes the prediction techniques we used. In Section 4 we evaluate the techniques used and describe our results. Section 5 extends the use of the most accurate CBR technique to identify software project success factors. In Concluding Remarks, we present our conclusions and future work.

2   Collecting Software Development Project Data

The collection method is crucial in obtaining reliable data. Once data is collected and understood by a KM system it can be managed to systematically benefit other projects. Verner [15, 16] is a software engineer who collected the data we used in this research to investigate software project critical success factors. The data was collected for the sole purpose of analyzing software development projects and identifying the factors that determine project success or failure.

Table 1. Examples of questions in the questionnaire

ID	Question
q2_1	What was the level of involvement of the customers/users?
q2_4	Were the customers/users involved in making schedule estimates?
q3_3	Was the scope of the project well defined?
q3_5	Did the customers/users make adequate time available for requirements gathering?
q3_7	Did the requirements result in well-defined software deliverables?
q4_2	Was the delivery date decision made with appropriate requirements information?
q4_8	Did the project have adequate staff to meet the schedule?
q4_11	Did the schedule take into account staff leave, training, etc.?

Removing all variables that describe features unknown early in a project resulted in a total of 23 variables. The questionnaire incorporates both objective and subjective human judgments about these projects. Table 1 provides some example questions, which will be further discussed in this paper, referenced by their ID. The format of these answers are *yes/no* and multiple-choice.

This questionnaire addresses the areas of *management support, customer/user interaction, requirements, estimation* and *scheduling*, in relation to project outcome. The outcome section originally included questions that allowed for conflicting answers. The questionnaire asked for project success or failure from the perspective of the organization and from the perspective of the developer answering the question. We merged these variables into a single variable and removed all projects where outcome variables were in conflict. After eliminating the conflicting answers, the initial group of 122 project records was reduced to 88 – 67 describing successful projects and 21 describing failed projects.

3   Techniques to Predict Project Outcomes

Our goal is to design a system to systematically acquire software development project data and understand it within a KM framework. A case-based reasoner predicts the outcome of new projects in this system. In this section, we discuss the CBR system we implemented to evaluate different similarity measures to predict project's outcome, describe CBR techniques and LR.

3.1   CBR Implementation

Our CBR implementation uses the data gathered with the questionnaire discussed in Section 2, from which we created a case base with 88 cases described by 23 features and a binary variable for project outcome. This implementation entails the use of four subtasks of the retrieve CBR process, namely, *identify features*, *initial match*, *search*, and *select* [17]. These are standard implementations except for the *select* subtask. In order to accommodate situations in which multiple cases have the same similarity but different outcomes, we broke all ties by selecting the class of the case with the next highest similarity. We treat all features as symbolic; if they have the same value the similarity equals one, otherwise it equals zero; there are no intermediary degrees for similarity.

Currently, our implementation does not identify factors that contribute to success or failure. The results discussed later in this paper will lay the foundation for the development of a method to provide identification of these factors along with an outcome prediction. Suggesting countermeasures based upon these factors is an additional step to incorporate.

3.2   Unweighted k-NN

We first implemented CBR with a traditional unweighted k-NN classifier to serve as a baseline to compare with predictions developed with other techniques. This measure simply considers the number of similar features between a candidate case and a target case.

3.3   Explanation-Based Learning

Explanation-based learning (EBL) uses domain-specific knowledge to generalize a concept [13]. Cain et al. [11] used the EBL notion to explore feature relevance -in a combined approach with CBR - to classify a dichotomous dependent variable because the features in their dataset outnumbered the cases. We investigate their CBR+EBL approach because we are designing a tool with an evolving collection process, and thus having more features than cases is a future possibility. The work described in [11] has successfully classified foreign trade negotiation cases (50 cases, 76 features) by applying the CBR+EBL approach. The approach entails a parameterized similarity measure that incorporates both elements of traditional CBR (exploring the similarity of features between projects) and elements of EBL (exploring features' relevance supported by domain knowledge). The parameterized Equation (1) of CBR+EBL introduced in [11] is given by similarity measure S:

$$S = \frac{\sum_{i=1}^{n} \alpha * sim\ (case_{\ i}, cue_{\ i}) + \beta \sum_{i=1}^{n} relevance\ (case_{\ i}) * sim\ (case_{\ i}, cue_{\ i})}{n + \left(\beta \sum_{i=1}^{n} relevance\ (case_{\ i}) \right)} . \quad (1)$$

To implement the CBR+EBL approach, we need to acquire domain-specific knowledge and choose appropriate values for α and β.

Knowledge acquisition for EBL. This knowledge elicitation process is aimed at determining a relevance factor *1* or *0* for each possible question answered in the questionnaire. These factors represent, respectively, whether or not the answers influence the project's outcome. Thus, a factor *1* is given when the answer for a question is such that it supports the outcome of that specific project. For example, software engineering knowledge mandates that, to be successful, projects should have a schedule (consequently the lack of a schedule could explain failure). Therefore, there are two possible answers for the question asking whether the project had a schedule: yes or no. The final factor *1* or *0* can only be obtained when we also consider the given project's outcome. Thus, in a project with outcome of success, if the answer to the question about the existence of the schedule is also yes, then the relevance factor is *1*; because, based on domain knowledge, we can state that this answer supports the outcome of success. The relevance factors vary as shown in Table 2.

We interviewed two software engineers for consistency and represented the knowledge with simple rules. For example, Figure 1 shows a multiple-choice question from the *customer/user* section of the questionnaire, and its associated rule obtained through knowledge acquisition from experts.

Table 2. Relevance factors for question about existence of schedule

Does the project have a schedule?	Project outcome is	Relevance Factor is
Yes	Success	1
Yes	Failure	0
No	Success	0
No	Failure	1

By implementing rules for all features where an association occurs based on domain-specific knowledge, we were able to determine the relevance factor of a particular feature for a case. Some features can be left without rules because no association was evident. For example, the Yes/No question q1_7, "Did senior management impact the project in any other way?" does not directly assess the type of impact and thus was the only feature in our dataset left without a rule. This question exemplifies how we use EBL to help evolve the collection method; by confirming the importance of a given question through its impact on project outcomes (question q1_7 will be removed or reworded in the next version of the questionnaire).

Question:
"2.1 What was the level of involvement of the customers/users?
1. none   2. little   3.some   4. reasonable level   5. high involvement"
Rule:
IF ((outcome is success) AND (answer is either (4) OR (5))) OR
IF ((outcome is failure) AND (answer is either (1) OR (2)))
THEN relevance factor equals 1, otherwise relevance factor equals 0.

Fig. 1. Example question and its associated rule

Experts were able to provide associations for nearly all questions because the entire questionnaire was conceived and designed with the sole purpose of analyzing software development projects. Considerable research has been published in this area [e.g., 16, 18].

An aspect that we did not implement concerns combinations of features. It is possible, and very likely, that experts using domain knowledge could find associations between two or more features. One association could explain a given outcome, while another may neutralize the effect of individual features. We did not extend our investigation to address this, although we will consider this aspect in future research.

Determining α and β. Equation (1) expresses similarity S as the weighted distance between two cases that incorporates β as a weight measurement for the relevance factor. In the EBL component, features are considered relevant when their values support the outcome of each case, and thus they are assigned a relevance factor. Therefore, different cases have different sets of relevant features. The CBR component of the equation, represented by α, explores the similarity of features between cases. The final step in applying the parameterized equation from [11] is to define values for α and β. The authors [11] who conceived the equation do not explicitly recommend values for α and β; they used $\alpha = 1$ and $\beta = 15$. They stated that the equation is not very sensitive to β and that β values greater than one will produce similar results.

The baseline for these parameters occurs when $\alpha = 0$, in which case only the EBL component is evaluated and different values for β do not impact the accuracy. When $\beta = 0$, however, the equation evaluates simple feature counting (unweighted k-NN). We also evaluated the sensitivity of variations of these two parameters with respect to our data. Initially we set $\alpha = 1$, and then 5, 10 and 20 and varied β in search of the greatest accuracy. We found the maximum accuracy to occur in multiple pairs of points for α and β. To account for the sensitivity of these parameters in different datasets, to ensure consistency of the results, and given that the authors in [11] claim that values above one for β do not impact the results, we chose to use four different pairs for α and β: (1,1), (5,7), (10, 11.5), and (20, 32). Though we perform all the tests using all the pairs, we will present only the results obtained with the first pair (1,1).

Given the bias imposed by applying the same effect to all features (some may be irrelevant) [19] on the case-based component of the formula, we next investigate variable feature weights. Our goal is to extend the CBR+EBL approach (Equation (1)) by adding a representation of relative feature relevance to that awarded by domain knowledge. Hence, once we have the feature weights for all the variables, we implement the combined version of the parameterized equation:

$$S' = \frac{\sum_{i=1}^{n} w_i * sim\,(case_i, cue_i) + \beta \sum_{i=1}^{n} relevance\,(case_i) * sim\,(case_i, cue_i)}{\sum_{i=1}^{n} w_i + \left(\beta \sum_{i=1}^{n} relevance\,(case_i) \right)} \; ; (2)$$

where we use individual weights instead of α. To ensure the consistency of the results, we compute S' (Equation (2)) for $\beta = 1$ and $= 15$. The results are discussed in Section 4.

3.4   Feature Weight Learning

The framework for feature weighting methods described in [19] suggests the use of incremental hill-climbing methods when the dataset contains interacting features. We selected gradient descent (GD), which is a hill-climber that uses feedback from the similarity measure when examining each case.

GD can be implemented and modified by adjusting its geometric parameters. We used starting step size 0.5, ending step 0.02, step size update 0.9, and the number of cases tested was 10. These parameters resulted most effective in our preliminary tests. Having obtained weights to account for the relative importance of each feature, we used these weights to predict project outcomes using the weighted k-NN and weighted CBR+EBL.

3.5   Logistic Regression

LR is generally considered the most accurate and theoretically appropriate statistical technique for modeling dichotomous dependent variables, particularly in datasets with fewer than 100 examples, though it is also a method that tends to be expensive [14]. Cleary et al., explain that LR is a highly desirable statistical model and should be used for model fitting and hypothesis testing [14]. It is appropriate for our data because outcome is a dichotomous variable. LR produces a formula that predicts the probability of an occurrence as a function of the independent variables. LR overcomes the problem with linear models producing values for the probability outside the range of (0,1) desired for a dichotomous dependent variable [19]. Unlike ordinary least squares (OLS) regression, LR does not assume linearity of relationship between the independent variables and the dependent, does not require normally distributed variables, and in general has less stringent requirements with respect to the data.

4   Evaluation

First we want our evaluation to determine which of the CBR techniques performs best across three accuracy metrics when predicting project outcomes with our dataset. Second we want to compare the performance of the CBR techniques to LR for each metric. Third, we want to determine whether the weighted version of CBR+EBL (S') is more accurate than its unweighted version.

4.1   Methodology

We represent the performance of these techniques by using three metrics. *Accuracy* represents the number of correct predictions in relation to the total predictions. *True positives* represent the number of correct predictions of projects with outcomes of success. *True negatives* give the number of correct predictions of projects with outcomes of failure. In this paper, values of accuracy, true positives and true negatives are expressed as percentages.

The origin of the data is explained in Section 2. We used the data generated by the questionnaire and also prepared for LR. It has 23 symbolic features describing 88 training examples; 67 successes and 21 failures.

For the evaluation we used stratified sampling by randomly choosing six pairs of training sets (test sets were the complements), with 44 cases each, maintaining the overall proportion of positive and negative examples across all sets. Training sets 1, 3 and 5 have 33 positive and 11 negative examples; training sets 2, 4 and 6 have 34 positive and 10 negative examples. We will present our results in terms of the average and standard deviation across these six test sets.[1]

LR and the weighted forms of CBR require the use of training sets. Training sets were used to either generate equations for LR or learn feature weights. Once completed, the training parameters were then tested on the testing sets, i.e. on data not included in training.

4.2   Results

A summary of our results is presented in Table 3. These results were obtained by applying unweighted k-NN, (unweighted) CBR+EBL, weighted k-NN, weighted

---

[1] Though we believe LOOCV is preferable, applying LR would require that we developed 88 sets of equations, therefore we relied on stratified sampling.

CBR+EBL with β=1, and logistic regression (LR). The results are given with the average and standard deviations across the six test sets.

Table 3. Average and standard deviation for accuracy, true positives, and true negatives

Technique	Accuracy		True Positives		True Negatives	
	Ave.	St.Dev	Ave.	St.Dev	Ave.	St.Dev
Unweighted k-NN	76.9	1.7	85.6	2.1	49.6	9.2
CBR+EBL	**80.7**	3.4	85.6	6.2	**65.4**	10.0
Weighted k-NN	78.4	4.9	84.6	5.0	58.8	11.4
Weighted CBR+EBL	74.6	7.8	77.7	12.1	65.3	10.5
LR	80.5	5.3	**88.9**	12.3	29.1	34.3

On the *first hypothesis* evaluated, we found CBR+EBL to be the most accurate among the CBR techniques for all three metrics. It performed just as well as the baseline (unweighted k-NN) in predicting successful projects, and was superior in the other two metrics, though one should note that the standard deviation resulted from the CBR+EBL performance is higher than the baseline. The results also confirm the conclusions presented in [11] that CBR+EBL outperforms unweighted k-NN. These results support the conclusion to adopt CBR+EBL, particularly because we can expect to have case bases in which the number of features is greater than the number of cases, which seems to be no obstacle for CBR+EBL.

With respect to the *second hypothesis* evaluated, CBR+EBL slightly outperformed LR in the average accuracy, but LR presented a higher standard deviation. In the average of true positives, LR was superior. LR predicted successful projects well, but was not able to predict failed cases as accurately (less than 30% for true negatives). This was likely due to the sparsity of data among the group of failed software projects (i.e., 21 out of 88). Inclusion of additional failed project cases would very likely improve these results.

Given that the data for successful projects is sufficiently dense, the metric true positives in Table 3 emphasizes the loss in accuracy caused by using a combination of feature weights and the EBL measure (weighted CBR+EBL). This is the only technique not able to predict at least 80% of successful projects. Even the unweighted k-NN performs well, easily finding similar cases among positive examples. LR is the most accurate in this metric.

The relative lack of negative examples (or failed projects) makes the accuracy of CBR+EBL stand out. This is probably the reason why CBR+EBL tends to be more accurate in general. Even with fewer negative examples, it provides better predictions. Our results suggest that there is an advantage in using CBR especially CBR+EBL-with this type of data, which may often be sparse in real world problems. Therefore, we recommend CBR+EBL to predict the (binary) outcome of software development projects.

For the *third hypothesis* evaluated, we wanted to compare the performance of the weighted version of CBR+EBL (*S'*) with respect to the unweighted *S*. *S'* provided the lowest accuracy with the highest standard deviation. It actually performed more poorly in predicting successful projects from dense data than it did predicting failed cases from sparse data.

These results suggest investigating further why the weighted version of CBR+EBL did not perform well in accuracy and true positives but performed much better (with respect to other techniques) in true negatives. The variation in performance of LR suggests an association with the number of negative examples; hence we want to investigate if a similar association could be made.

Possible causes for performance of *S'*. Table 3 shows that the weighted version of CBR+EBL outperforms all techniques that do not use domain knowledge for the metric true negatives. This may suggest that the combination of both the CBR and EBL components would be appropriate to learn from sparse data (and predict failed projects). When we compare the performance of the unweighted versions alone, CBR+EBL performs (a little) better than k-NN for accuracy, exactly the same as k-NN for true positives, and (much) better than k-NN for true negatives. This comparison suggests that when we add the EBL component, the performance improves with respect to true negatives. Additionally, if we analyze the weighted versions, the weighted CBR+EBL performs worse than the weighted k-NN. It performs just as poorly for true positives and better only for true negatives. These facts, combined with the high standard deviations, found for the weighted CBR+EBL measure, instigate further examination. Given this preliminary analysis, our hypothesis is that when we combine feature weights with the EBL component, it overestimates the relative importance of some features. This is detrimental to predictive accuracy with dense data, but when applied to sparse data, the method seems to work fairly well. In future work, we will perform a second experiment to evaluate this hypothesis; in this paper, we simply examine further our results.

In order to fully gauge the effect of combining feature weights with EBL, we examine the weights and the EBL component in different test sets. The weights were determined by gradient descent (see Section 3.4), while the EBL component is provided by the assignment of relevance factors (see Section 3.3). Table 4 ranks the six variables that received the largest number of relevance factors overall. The final row shows the performance of the weighted CBR+EBL for true positives for these sets. The two columns in Table 4 dedicated to the two test sets show each variable's overall ranking within each test set based upon their feature weights (the higher the number, the smaller the weight). For example, variable q3_7[2] was fourth among the variables overall in terms of the number of relevance factors assigned, ranked fourth in test set 2 and 16th in test set 6.

Table 4. Relevance factors and weights in test sets 2 and 6

Rank	Variable ID	Test Set 2	Test Set 6
1	q3_5	1	4
2	q3_3	5	19
3	q4_8	15	3
4	q3_7	4	16
5	q4_2	3	17
6	q3_8	7	10
True Positives	-	58.8	85.3

---

[2] See meaning of feature in Table 1.

The analysis of Table 4 shows that five of the six variables were heavily weighted in test set 2 (rankings 1, 3, 4, 5, 7) and lightly weighted in test set 6 (rankings 10, 16, 17, 19). When comparing these rankings to the performance for true positives, it is clear that where the majority of these variables were heavily weighted, weighted CBR+EBL performed the most poorly and where these variables were most lightly weighted, CBR+EBL performed the most accurately. This supports our interpretation that prediction accuracy decreases when the same features receive high weights and are assigned relevance factors in the majority of the cases (overestimating the relative importance of some features). We will evaluate this hypothesis in future work, because if the combination of the two techniques increases prediction accuracy when the dataset is sparsely populated, this measure can be used in these cases.

5   Associating Outcomes to Project Management

This paper's final challenge is to make use of the most accurate technique to perform an additional task. We would like to determine which factors have the strongest associations with particular project outcomes. These could then be highlighted as critical risk factors in projects heading for failure, allowing a project manager to identify key strengths and weaknesses early enough to establish corrective measures when needed.

Given the suitability of LR, we again use it as a benchmark. The LR process includes the identification of the variables that most strongly predict the dependent variable; thus, predictor variables are a byproduct of LR. Based on LR, the variables that have the most influence on project outcome are q3_3, q3_5, q4_2, and q4_8.

We use the parameterized equation S (CBR+EBL) to suggest predictor variables by predicting the outcome of each of the four questionnaire sections separately. We compare these prediction results with the prediction generated using the entire dataset. Isolated problem areas and features that predict outcome nearly as well as the entire dataset are assumed to be those most responsible for project outcome.

Table 5. Average accuracy (in %) for the four sections across the six test sets

Problem Area	Ave.	Std dev.
Management Support	70.08	7.39
Customer/User	77.65	1.71
Requirements	75.38	6.17
Estimation/Schedule	76.51	5.12

Table 5 shows the average accuracy in each of the four sections for the six test sets. Given the similarity of average accuracy of the three problem areas *customer/user*, *requirements*, and *estimation-schedule*, our strategy is to further examine these three areas for potentially useful predictors. We will exclude the *management support* section because of its lower accuracy when compared to the other sections.

In order to further investigate the three problem areas, we assess the frequencies of the relevance factors in each test set. Our assumption is that features that have scored a higher number of relevance factors are those most responsible for the project outcome. We note that these tests were performed on test sets with 44 cases, so that a feature that has, for example, been assigned a relevance factor 29 times, has influenced 65.9% of the cases. Table 6 summarizes the averages across the six test sets for the four most relevant variables in each of the three sections. These variables are the ones with the best potential to be predictors. Among these variables, q3_3 and q3_5 in the *requirements* section, and q4_8 and q4_2 in *estimation-schedule* are also the variables identified by LR.

Table 6. Average assignments of relevance factors

Customer-user		Requirements		Estimation and Schedule	
Variable ID	Ave	Variable ID	Ave	Variable ID	Ave
q2_1	29.5	q3_3	33.3	q4_2	30.0
q2_3	26.7	q3_5	33.5	q4_1list	22.5
q2_4	22.2	q3_7	30.3	q4_8	31.7
q2_6	25.7	q3_8	30.0	q4_11	22.0

We now examine the variable with the highest relevance factor frequencies (q3_5) to determine whether it has been valued because it is relevant to successful or failed projects. For this last analysis, we do not want to use averages, so we select test sets five and six because they are the sets that present relevance frequencies that are the most similar to the averages for the *requirements* section.

In test set 5, feature q3_5 supported successful outcomes in 87.9% of the cases, that is, 29 out of 33. It supported failure outcomes in 45.5% of the cases, 5 out of 11. In test set 6, q3_5 supported success in only 26 of 34 cases, which represented 76.5% of the cases. The number of failed projects supported by q3_5 in this set was 7, representing 70% of the cases (7 out of 10).

Looking exclusively at these two test sets, q3_5 supported success in over 80% of the cases; and supported failure in almost 60% of the cases. It would be premature to state whether this feature can be considered as a critical success factor in successful or failed projects. Further study is necessary to identify a method to validate such conditions for a variable. Because this variable deals with the time dedicated for requirements gathering by the *customer/users*, it is easy to accept it conceptually as a critical factor for both success and failure in this instance.

These tests are not conclusive but show promising results for further research into automatically determining success and risk factors. Further research will delve more deeply into methods for identifying critical factors for success and failure; this will help project managers to better understand failure and how to increase chances of success by taking action early in software project development.

6   Concluding Remarks

This paper extends our understanding of the amenability of using CBR to support KM tasks for managing knowledge from projects described by managerial factors. We conclude that the parameterized CBR+EBL similarity measure [11] is the most accurate technique for this application. The second most accurate CBR technique, weighted k-NN, performed nearly as accurately as CBR+EBL overall, but it did not perform as well for predicting project failures because it appears to be less tolerant of sparse data sets. When the dataset was sufficiently dense, CBR+EBL performed at or above the level of all other methods and it stood out when the data was sparse. For this reason, the CBR+EBL measure is the best choice for this type of prediction.

With respect to the CBR techniques we used, one intriguing result was that the weighted k-NN performed similarly to CBR+EBL (S) in some instances but combining the two methods (S') generally decreased prediction accuracy. We believe that this is because the two methods provide similar relative levels of importance to the same data and a combination of these methods ultimately overstates the relative strength of these variables. In general, this may lead to less accurate prediction results. As discussed in Subsection 4.2, however, when we analyzed prediction for sparse data sets, it is possible that the combination of these methods will allow for a strong association between key factors and outcomes. It is also important to note, however, that even with sparse data, the combination of these methods did not outperform the CBR+EBL method alone. Probing this question more deeply will be a focus of future research.

The accuracy provided by logistic regression suggests its use as a benchmark for the prediction accuracy of a case base, when the dependent variable is dichotomous. These techniques cannot be considered as competitive alternatives for supporting a KM framework because LR poses higher engineering requirements, as it requires statistical expertise and a complex process of analysis. These tasks may be more easily performed using a CBR technique, which has less stringent engineering requirements. The primary cost benefit of CBR is manifested through automation – knowledge acquisition and system reuse may be fully automated so that staff members may use the tool without needing in-depth knowledge about the techniques used by the tool.

We have shown how to detect potential predictor variables for project success. Our work identifies q3_3, a well defined project scope; q3_5, customers/users making adequate time for requirements gathering; q4_2, a delivery decision (schedule) made with adequate requirements information; and q4_8, assignment of adequate staff to meet the project schedule, as the success factors in our dataset. It is noteworthy that CBR has found q3_5 to be the most important factor for both project success and failure. As project managers well know, estimation of a reasonable schedule is impossible without good requirements; good requirements and a well-defined project scope go hand-in-hand; and good requirements are essential for assigning adequate staff to a project schedule.

There are a few areas of future work that we wish to explore: evaluate the causes of the performance of S', validate predictor variable identification, investigate the use of predictor variables to derive mitigants for project management, and analyze combinations of features to assign relevance factors in EBL. In the CBR implementation, we will incorporate the step that indicates the success or failure factors.

Acknowledgements. Rosina Weber's research is supported in part by the National Institute for Systems Test and Productivity at USF under the USA Space and Naval Warfare Systems Command grant no. N00039-02-C-3244, for 2130 032 L0, 2002.

References

1. Watson, I.: CBR is a methodology not a technology. Knowledge Based Systems, 12 (5–6) (1999) 303–308
2. Finnie, G.R., Wittig, G.E., Desharnais, J.M.: A Comparison of Software Effort Estimation Techniques: Using Function Points with Neural Networks, Case-Based Reasoning and Regression Models. Journal of Systems Software 39 (1997) 281–289
3. Aha, D. W.: Feature weighting for lazy learning algorithms. In H. Liu & H. Motoda (eds.): Feature Extraction, Construction and Selection: A Data Mining Perspective. Norwell, MA, Kluwer (1998) 13–32
4. Aha, D.W., Becerra-Fernandez, I., Maurer, F., & Muñoz-Avila, H.: (eds.) Exploring Synergies of Knowledge Management and Case-Based Reasoning: Papers from the AAAI Workshop (Technical Report WS-99-10). Menlo Park, CA, AAAI Press (1999)
5. Watson, I.: Knowledge Management and Case-Based Reasoning: a perfect match? In Proc. of the Fourteenth Annual Conference of the International Florida Artificial Intelligence Research Society Menlo Park, CA, AAAI Press (2001) 118–122
6. Weber, R., Aha, D.W., Becerra-Fernandez, I.: Intelligent lessons learned systems. International Journal of Expert Systems Research & Applications 20 1 (2001) 17–34
7. Althoff, K.D., Nick, M., Tautz, C.: CBR-PEB: An Application Implementing Reuse Concepts of the Experience Factory for the Transfer of CBR System Know-How. In Proc. of 7th German Workshop on Case-Based Reasoning, Würzburg (1999) 39–48
8. Kadoda, G, Cartwright, M., Shepperd, M.: Issues on the Effective use of CBR Technology for Software Project Prediction. In Aha, D., Watson, I., (eds.): Case-Based Reasoning Research and Development, LNAI, 2080, Springer (2001) 276–290
9. Watson, I., Mendes, E., Mosley, N., Counsell, S.: Using CBR to Estimate Development Effort for Web Hypermedia Applications. In Proc. of the Fifteenth Annual Conference of the International Florida Artificial Intelligence Research Society. Menlo Park, CA, AAAI Press (2002) 132–136
10. Basili, V.R., Caldiera, G., Rombach, H.D.: Experience Factory. In J. J. Marciniak, (ed), Encyclopedia of Software Engineering 1 (1994) 469–476
11. Jedlitschka, A., Althoff, K.-D., Decker, B., Hartkopf, S., Nick, M.: Corporate Information Network (COIN): The Fraunhofer IESE Experience Factory, IESE-Report No. 034.01/E. Version 1.0, May (2001)
12. Cain, T., Pazzani, M. J., Silverstein, G. Using domain knowledge to influence similarity judgment. In Proc. of the Case-Based Reasoning Workshop. Washington, DC, Morgan Kaufmann (1991) 191–202
13. Mitchell, T., Keller, R., Kedar-Cabelli, S.: Explanation-based generalization: A Unifying View. Machine learning 2 (1986) 47–80
14. Cleary, P.D., Angel, R.: The Analysis of Relationships Involving Dichotomous Dependent Variables, Journal of Health and Social Behavior 25 (1984) 334–348
15. Verner, J. M, Overmyer, S. P. and McCain, K. W.: In the 25 Years Since the Mythical Man-Month What Have we Learned About Project Management? Information and Software Technology 41 (1999) 1021–1026
16. Procaccino, J.D., Verner, J.M., Overmyer, S. P., Darter, M.: Case Study: Factors for Early Prediction of Software Development Success, Information and Software Technology 44 (2001) 53–62
17. Aamodt, A., Plaza, E.: Case-Based Reasoning: Foundational Issues, Methodological Variations, and System Approaches. Artificial Intelligence Communications 7(1) (1994) 39–59.
18. Reel, J.S.: Critical Success Factors in Software Projects, IEEE Software 16(3) (1999) 18–23

19. Wettschereck, D., Aha, D.W.: Weighting features. Veloso, M., Aamodt, A. (eds). Case-Based Reasoning Research and Development, LNAI 1010, Springer-Verlag (1995) 347–358

20. Whitehead, J.: Willingness to Pay for Bass Fishing Trips in the Carolinas. In An Introduction to Logistic Regression, Writing up results. (1998) Available online (last visited 03/31/2003): http://personal.ecu.edu/whiteheadj/data/logit/

An SQL-Based Approach to Similarity Assessment within a Relational Database

Graeme M. West and James R. McDonald

Institute for Energy and Environment, University of Strathclyde, 204 George St,
Glasgow, G1 1XW
graeme.west@strath.ac.uk, j.macdonald@eee.strath.ac.uk
http://www.isap.eee.strath.ac.uk

A common issue with case-based reasoning (CBR) systems, particularly those
that are distributed over a network, is the time required to determine the closest
match to the current case. Research has been carried out in this area to try to
improve the situation by distributing some of the calculation to the client side
thereby reducing the burden on the server. In CBR applications, the case library is stored in some format such as a relational database or flat files that the
software interprets in order to perform similarity assessment between the current case and each case in the database. In this paper a novel approach is proposed where the retrieval of the case information and the calculation of the
similarity values are performed in one action. This does not incur the same
burden upon the server in terms of calculation, as all that is required is a larger
database lookup via SQL. As the case base needs to be queried regardless of
the CBR technique used to obtain the case information, it is proposed that a
combined similarity assessment and case retrieval would provide a fast method
of case retrieval.

1 Introduction

There are a number of existing perspectives of integrating CBR systems with databases, such as the three-tier architecture described in [1]. Different design variants
are discussed but in general, databases do not support CBR technology and therefore
the CBR technology needs to be placed in either the client or the server application.
If similarity assessment is to be carried out on the client machine, and thus decrease
the burden on the server machine, then there is the issue of selecting the most appropriate cases to return to the client for analysis. Generally, it is not advisable to send
the entire case library across the network due to bandwidth constraints, particularly if
the case library is large. Relaxation algorithms reported in [2], and adapted in [3] and
incremental approaches to identifying the most discriminatory parameters [4] can reduce the number of cases to be examined. Additionally, [5] describes some of the issues associated with effective retrieval and states that the ideal approach to integrating
CBR and databases from a technical point of view is to perform the similarity calculation within the database. It cites the lack of a standardised language as a barrier to
realising case-based retrieval within a database. An approach to similarity-base retrieval is then presented which uses relaxation techniques to progressively query the

K.D. Ashley and D.G. Bridge (Eds.): ICCBR 2003, LNAI 2689, pp. 610–621, 2003.
© Springer-Verlag Berlin Heidelberg 2003

case-base until the k most similar cases are returned to main memory. This approach removes the need to hold the entire case-base in case memory before calculating all the similarities and selecting the best k matches. It provides a comparison of both methods and shows that the proposed approach offers significant advantages in time. There are reported issues with large values of k, such as a degree of incompleteness, resulting in poor performance as additional relaxation steps were undertaken to compensate.

This paper describes an alternative approach to implementing the CBR similarity assessment within a database using standard table designs and SQL only. It removes the need to move any of the cases into main memory to perform the similarity calculations and so ensures that up-to-date values are always used. This is achieved by representing similarity assessment as a set of pre-calculated partial similarities. As all the similarities already exist within the database, a set of table joins between the case table and these similarity tables and a filter using the current case parameter values can be performed. As a result, an ordered case library can be returned, from most to least similar. This is particularly useful if there is bandwidth constraints caused by a network as the user can control the number of solutions that are returned. A process of discretization is used, which may make this approach unsuitable for some CBR applications. A series of tests that show discretization is unsuitable for CBR applications is described in [6], where the similarities are derived from lazy learning algorithms. However, for applications where the similarity values are derived from a domain expert it is shown later that the loss in accuracy from discretization is acceptable.

A sample set of retrieval tests are reported on, using a test case-library of varying size. These preliminary results indicate a rapid retrieval time with little loss in accuracy.

As CBR can be applied differently to solve different types of problems such as design and classification, there are a few caveats and assumptions about the situations where this proposed approach should be used. These are:

◆ This approach applies to CBR systems that use relational databases for storing the case information. It is also assumed that all the cases follow a homogeneous case structure (i.e. all the cases are described by a common set of features). No provision for case-bases stored in other formats, such as object oriented or flat files, is made (although this may still be applicable if they can be interpreted in the same manner).

◆ The reasoning approach adopted should be a nearest neighbour type approach as opposed to a rule induction-based approach. That is to say that the case base is queried in a single operation rather than as a series of questions and answers as in an induction-based approach.

◆ The CBR system is distributed (the case base held centrally with user(s) making requests from separate, client machine(s)) with a reasonable size of case base as there will be little or no gain in performance on smaller case bases.

♦ The indexing parameters used to describe the case can be either symbolic or numeric (i.e. part of a set range). For ranges of values, the bounds of the range should be known as is required by the standard nearest neighbour algorithm. There is currently no consideration for case-bases that use textual features.

♦ Case adaptation is not considered here. It is assumed that the CBR system is used to identify the most similar cases from its library. What to do with the most similar case is left to the user.

♦ A process of discretization is used in this approach, which can affect the final percentage similarity obtained. However, it will be shown that the impact on accuracy is of little overall consequence as the assignment of similarity values for symbolic representations is subjective and, if appropriately designed, can outweigh the loss of accuracy in the numeric values.

The next section describes the architecture required to implement similarity assessment within a database. This is followed by an example of the approach applied to protection scheme design.

2   Database Architecture

In order to perform the similarity assessment within the database, three main types of table are required:

• A table that stores all the case information including a column for each indexing parameter value and its associated look-up value. The actual case information may be stored as a link or location to the actual case.

• A table for each indexing parameter, detailing the possible values that it can take for symbolic indexing parameters or the bands of possible values for numeric parameters.

• A table describing similarity for each indexing parameter. For symbolic parameters, these can be derived from an expert or through an instance-based learning approach. For numeric values, this will consist of a pre-calculated set of similarities derived from a standard distance function.

2.1 Symbolic Features

Similarity values for symbolic features can be represented within CBR through a similarity matrix. This matrix is often populated with the aid of a domain expert to assign values to the relationships between different values for the given feature. However, this often occurs on an ad-hoc basis [7] and is an area that requires further investigation. Figure 1 shows an example of a typical similarity matrix. This matrix is represented within a database table by three columns, the current value, the case value and the similarity. A further consideration is to include an additional column that details any rationale associated with the similarity value for each attribute-value pair. This does not affect the retrieval function directly but could be useful for explaining the final overall match for any given case. Additionally, this rationale can be useful should modifications to the similarities be required. There are, however, issues concerned with capturing this rationale such as the knowledge elicitation effort required, the availability of the experts and the expert's ability to quantify similarity. These issues are currently under investigation.

	Red	Orange	Green
Red	1.0	0.8	0.1
Orange	0.8	1.0	0.1
Green	0.1	0.1	1.0

→

Current Value	Case Value	Similarity
Red	Red	1.0
Red	Orange	0.8
Red	Green	0.1
Orange	Red	0.8
Orange	Orange	1.0
Orange	Green	0.1
Green	Red	0.1
Green	Orange	0.1
Green	Green	0.8

Fig. 1. Similarity Matrix

2.2 Numeric Features

Similarity calculation for features which have numeric values are usually carried out using a nearest neighbour algorithm. Complex calculations such as this cannot readily be performed within a database using SQL. However, simple addition, subtraction, multiplication and division is permissible. Therefore, the similarity values need to be pre-calculated based on the nearest neighbour algorithm then a look up performed based on the current and case values. The minimum and maximum values of the parameter must be known in order to normalise the results. From this range a number of equally spaced bands of values can be established. Similarity values for each band can then be calculated based on the mid-point value of each band. The numeric parameter can now be treated as a symbolic one, as described above. Therefore, a set of similarity values for each possible value (or range of values) needs to be pre-calculated and stored within the appropriate database table. Each parameter value for the current case and the case from the case library under consideration are used to look-up the pre-calculated similarity value from the appropriate similarity table. Each of these partial similarities is combined to provide an overall similarity value. This process is repeated for each case in the case library and an ordering function can be used to highlight the most similar case(s).

2.3 Sample Calculation

Presented next is a sample look-up calculation is presented based upon a numeric parameter with values within the range 0-999. Firstly, the range is divided into a number of equal sized bands, in this case 20.

(0-49), (50-99), (100-149), (150-199), ... , (950-999)

Using a Euclidean distance measure, the similarity value between a current value of 87 and a case value of 105 would be calculated as follows:

87 appears in the band (50-99). Mid-range value of this band is 74.5
105 appears in the band (100-149). Mid-range value of this band is 124.5

Assuming a weighting value of 1,

$$Similarity = 1 - \frac{|CaseValue - CurrentValue|}{OverallRange} = 1 - \frac{|124.5 - 74.5|}{999} = 95\%$$

This type of calculation would be performed for all possible combinations of values, so using 20 bands would require 400 calculations. However, with this particular case, it can be seen that the similarity reduces by 5% for each band difference between the current and case values. It should be noted that there is no restriction on the formula used to calculate the similarity and it need not follow a one-to-one cardinality. For example, if a case value of A and a current value of B are 70% similar does a case value of B and current value of A also have a similarity of 70%? Due to the number of calculations involved, a small program or stored procedure should be used to generate these similarity tables.

2.4 Similarity Assessment

When a similarity assessment is performed in the case table, each parameter value is effectively replaced by its equivalent partial similarity value taken from the appropriate row of that parameter's similarity table. The layout of the tables is shown in figure 2, which illustrates a simple example of a case base containing 2 indexing parameters, P1 and P2. P1 has possible values A, B and C while P2 has possible values red, orange and green. P1 and P2 both have their own similarity table.

Case Base Table

Case Name	P1 Value	P2 Value
Case X	A	red
Case Y	A	green
Case Z	C	orange

P1 Similarities

Current Value	Case Value	Similarity
A	A	1.0
A	B	0.7
A	C	0.2
B	A	0.7
B	B	1.0
B	C	0.4
C	A	0.2
C	B	0.4
C	C	1.0

P2 Similarities

Current Value	Case Value	Similarity
red	red	1.0
red	orange	0.8
red	green	0.1
orange	red	0.8
orange	orange	1.0
orange	green	0.1
green	red	0.1
green	orange	0.1
green	green	1.0

Fig. 2. Table Layout

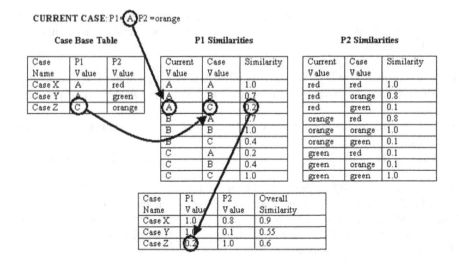

Fig. 3. Calculating similarity for one parameter value

Figure 3 illustrates one partial match where the current case value for P1, A, is compared with the value from Case Z for P1, C, from the P1 Similarity table. This process is repeated comparing the values for each parameter for the current case with each one within the case base. The overall similarity is calculated from the average of each of the partial similarities. At this stage, weighting values could also be included. The equivalent SQL statement, which would be used to return an ordered list of the cases from the case base, along with their overall similarities is:

```
SELECT [Case Name], ((([P1 Similarities].[Similarity]+ [P2
Similarities].[Similarity])/2) AS Overall Similarity FROM
[Case Base Table], [P1 Similarities], [P2 Similarities]
WHERE [P1 Similarities].[Current Value]="A" AND [P2 Simi-
larities].[Current  Value]="orange"  AND  [P1  Similari-
ties].[Case Value]=[Case Base].[P1 Value] AND [P2 Simi-
larities].[Case  Value]=[Case  Base].[P2  Value]  ORDER  BY
Overall Similarity
```

The output from this statement is shown in table 1.

Table 1. Ordered set of results from SQL statement

Case Name	Overall Similarity
Case X	0.9
Case Z	0.6
Case Y	0.55

As the number of parameters increases, then the length of the SQL statement increases proportionally. For each additional parameter, four elements are required in the SQL statement:

♦ The contribution to overall similarity in the SELECT part of the SQL statement
♦ The call to the parameter's similarity table within the FROM part of the statement
♦ Filtering the similarity table based on the current parameter value in the WHERE clause
♦ Filtering the similarity table for each case in the case table in the WHERE clause

There are additional SQL commands that could further optimise the results, such as the SELECT TOP or LIMIT statement, which restricts the number of results that are returned and subsequently sent across the network. At this stage, exact matching of certain parameters could also be introduced where appropriate to reduce the number of cases requiring consideration.

2.5 Weightings

In the above example, the weighting values were all assumed to be equal. However, it is straightforward to introduce an additional table that holds the relative weighting value for each parameter. These weighting values would be introduced to the SQL statement at the point where the overall similarity is calculated. In addition, a number of sets of weighting values representing different situations, such as different stages within a design task or different views such as cost-based or technical, could also be included. Depending upon the application, a different set of weighting values could be selected and used.

2.6 Accuracy Issues

Using a look-up table for indexing features that have symbolic representations is a standard approach for CBR systems. The similarity values are usually derived from experts and though this tends to be carried out on an ad-hoc manner, this paper assumes these values have already been successfully captured. For numeric features, a nearest neighbour algorithm is usually used to calculate similarity based on Euclidean distance, which results in a precise value for similarity. When using a look-up table for the similarity values, the range of possible values must be separated into a number of equal "bands". The more bands, then the more "accurate" the result. In general, the worst-case error will be the inverse of the number of bands. For example, if a parameter can have any possible value between 0 and 999 and there are 20 bands (0-49, 50-99, 100-149,......, 950-999) then the accuracy will be 5%. Although this seems quite a significant inaccuracy, when compared to those obtained for symbolic values where the expert is asked to assign values then these tend to be very subjective and often will not be accurate any better than 10%. As the similarity is based on a combination of all the partial similarities from all the parameters, the accuracy depends upon the average of these values and also on any associated weightings. For domains where the majority of the indexing parameters have a numeric value, this approach may be unsuitable. However, in situations where there are a large number of symbolic parameters whose similarity values have been derived from a human expert then this degree of inaccuracy is acceptable. It should be noted that in the main case base table, the band value for a numeric parameter should be stored for the similarity assessment but the original (actual) value could also be stored. This permits an accurate assessment of the similarity value to be carried out on the best matches using a nearest neighbour calculation if required.

3   Performance Tests

The approach of using the SQL statement to perform the calculation was tested to ensure that the modified SQL similarity assessment would not adversely affect the overall performance of the system. The increased time required to execute this more complex statement was compared with the standard look-up time and the difference could be used to compare with other methods, which require an external calculation of similarity (plus any additional relaxation algorithms, etc). A series of tests were carried out to gauge the performance of using pre-calculated similarity values. Three sizes of test case library were used: 800 cases, 3,200 cases and 12,800 cases. Each case is described by five symbolic parameters and five numeric parameters. Each symbolic parameter contained five possible values and the numeric values were examined using two levels of discretization, 10 and 100 value bands. A mySQL database, version 3.23.42, was used. It should also be noted that a number of database indexes were used to increase the efficiency of the database look-up. The cases were generated using random values for each parameter. The tests were performed using SQLyog [8], a free mySQL front end. The times noted in the results are approximate values only, and the speed of look-up is also dependant on the specification on the machine running the database (in this case a 1.7GHz processor with 128MB RAM) and if any other applications are also being run concurrently.

The results are shown in table 2. The column "Look-up time including similarity assessment" represents the total time required by the database to execute the SQL query and display the case base, from most to least similar, on the screen. No indication of the time required to send this returned information across a network is indicated here, although this can be controlled by limiting the results sets to the top few cases as described above. This time should be compared to the time to retrieve the case values, perform all the similarity calculations and order the results. As can be seen by the "Look-up time for retrieving the case library" column, the time for retrieval of the information from the database is negligible. As the final row indicates, the time taken to perform the similarity assessment on 12,800 cases, for any given input case, is around 2 seconds with an accuracy of $\pm 1\%$ on the numeric parameters (compared with a calculation). Additionally, the look-up time does not seem to increase significantly with an increased level of discretization. This may be due to the way that databases organise their indexes in order to improve retrieval times. However, a larger level of discretization will require a larger table to store all the permissible values, which will in turn lead to a larger database file and associated database index file.

Table 2. Test Results

Size of Case Library	Level of Discretization	Look-up time including similarity assessment	Look-up time for retrieving case library
800	10	141ms	31ms
800	100	157ms	31ms
3200	10	500ms	31ms
3200	100	547ms	31ms
12800	10	2016ms	31ms
12800	100	2078ms	31ms

As all the processing is performed on the server, issues could arise when multiple users are querying the database simultaneously. This situation will arise regardless of the approach used to calculate similarity, as the database will still need to be queried in order to obtain the case information. If the approach described in this paper were to be used in conjunction with a large database with many users requiring simultaneous access, then this issue would require further investigation. A solution may be to use powerful databases such as Oracle or Microsoft SQL Server that are designed for handling large quantities of data and simultaneous users.

The processing power of a machine required to undertake this type of calculation has only been widely available within the past few years. Further developments in processor speed and with decreasing memory costs should make the discretization inaccuracies obsolete within the next few years.

4   Application

The techniques described have been applied to provide CBR support to the design of protection schemes for transmission networks [9]. During protection scheme design it is often desirable to examine documents from previous, similar design projects. A web-based design decision support system called DEKAS (Design Engineering Knowledge Application System) was developed, which utilises CBR to provide support to the various activities within protection scheme design. The case-base consists of about 200 core protection designs described by 18 parameters. Of these 18 parameters, 5 are numeric parameters and 13 are symbolic parameters. The similarity table for one of the simpler parameters, substation type, is shown in figure 4. It shows the similarity value for each combination of substation type value, as well as a record of the rationale behind the value, which may be useful for updating the similarity values at a future date.

The entire protection scheme design process has been modelled within DEKAS. This consists of a number of models, some of which detail the activities required to be undertaken in order to complete a task and others which provide the user with links to all the relevant documents required to complete a given activity. Some of the documents, such as policies and standards, are required regardless of the project undertaken. Other documents are specific to the current project and are linked to through a supporting electronic design file, where a variable of the current project name is used to identify the relevant documents to return to the user. Finally, the user is provided with relevant documents from similar, completed designs. The CBR system identifies the most similar cases whose case names are used to retrieve the relevant documents from the supporting electronic design files. This process is shown in figure 5.

ID	SubType CurrentValue	SubType CaseValue	Similarity Value	Rationale
1	Unknown	Unknown	1	Exact Match
2	Unknown	GIS	0	Not enough information about the current case
3	Unknown	AISin	0	Not enough information about the current case
4	Unknown	AISout	0	Not enough information about the current case
5	GIS	Unknown	0	Not enough information about the target case
6	GIS	GIS	1	Exact Match
7	GIS	AISin	0	No Match
8	GIS	AISout	0	No Match
9	AISin	Unknown	0	Not enough information about the target case
10	AISin	GIS	0	No Match
11	AISin	AISin	1	Exact Match
12	AISin	AISout	0.7	Both are air insulated substations which can exhibit similar properties
13	AISout	Unknown	0	Not enough information about the target case
14	AISout	GIS	0	No Match
15	AISout	AISin	0.7	Both are air insulated substations which can exhibit similar properties
16	AISout	AISout	1	Exact Match

Fig. 4. Similarity table for symbolic parameter "Substation Type"

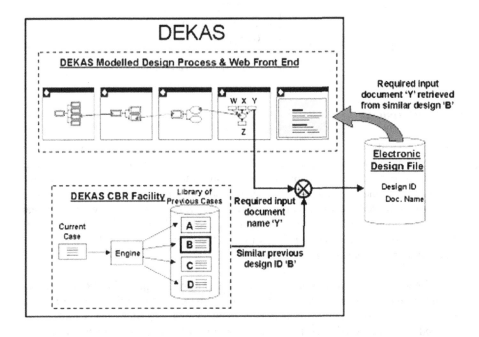

Fig. 5. Support offered by DEKAS

Figure 6 illustrates a sample model from a protection design activity: production of thermal rating schedules. This shows links to relevant documentation required to undertake the activity and, in addition, links to documentation from a similar previous design are provided. The CBR system performs the similarity assessment and highlights the most similar case(s), in this case "Project 1754 Refurbishment". This information is used to identify the relevant documents from a supporting file structure, which are then returned to the user through the web-interface as requested.

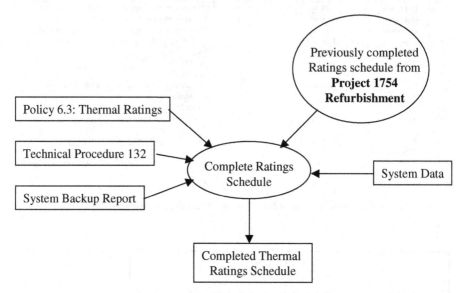

Fig. 6. Support of thermal rating calculation

5   Conclusions

This paper has illustrated a new approach to implementing CBR similarity assessment contained entirely within a database using standard table design and SQL statements. The results produced are promising but require further comparison to alternative similarity assessment techniques. The new approach offers advantages in quicker retrieval times by reducing the number of cases delivered across a network, and platform independence, by using standard database tools and techniques. The biggest issue with developing a successful system using the new approach is the identification and capture of appropriate similarity values.

As outlined earlier, this approach is not suitable for all types of CBR, particularly where automatic adaptation is required. Where this method is probably most applicable is in internet-type applications, where many people are accessing a single casebase and all that is required is to identify (not adapt) an ordered list of the most similar items. This has obvious applications in e-commerce where large online catalogues are available but hard to navigate through. However, there is the requirement for structure to be in place within these catalogues to allow similar indexing parameters to be compared and these may prove to be prohibitive in implementing such as system. Additionally, due to the discretization process that is undertaken, a loss of overall accuracy in terms of final calculated value may occur. As discussed, the discretization error can be improved by increasing the number of value bands, at the cost of increasing the size of the database and database index file.

As the result returned via the SQL statement is a list of the most similar cases to the current case, it can be readily implemented within any computing environment that allows databases to be queried through SQL. Additionally, as the user can control the number of cases that are returned, there are potential applications where bandwidth is a major limitation, such as mobile WAP applications.

References

1. Donner, M. and Roth-Berghofer, T.,: "Architectures for Integrating CBR-systems with Databases for E-commerce", Proceedings of the 7th German Workshop on Case-Based Reasoning, GWCBR '99
2. Kitano, H. and Shimazu, H.,: "The Experience Sharing Architecture: A Case Study in Corporate-Wide Case-Based Software Quality Control", Case-Based Reasoning: Experiences, Lessons and Future Directions, Leake, D.B. (Ed), AAAI Press
3. Watson, I. and Gardingen, D.,: A Distributed Case-Based Reasoning Application for Engineering Sales Support, Proceedings 16th International Conference on Artificial Intelligence (IJCAI-99), Vol. 1: pp. 600–605.
4. Hayes, C., Doyle, M., Cunningham, P.,: Distributed CBR Using XML, Internal Report Trinity College Dublin, (1998), TCD--CS-1998-06.
5. Schumacher, J. and Bergmann, R.,: "An Efficient Approach to Similarity-Based Retrieval on Top of Relational Databases", 5th European Workshop on Case-Based Reasoning, 2000
6. Ventura, D and Martinez, T. R.,: "An Empirical Comparison of Discretization Methods", Proceedings of the Tenth International Symposium on Computer and Information Science, 1995
7. Watson, I.,: Applying Case-Based Reasoning: Techniques for Enterprise Systems, Morgan Kaufmann, (1997) p182
8. SQLyog v2.51, MySQL front end, downloaded from http://www.webyog.com/
9. West, G. M, Strachan, S. M., Moyes, A., McDonald, J. R., Gwyn, B., Farrell, J.,: Knowledge management and decision support for electrical power utilities, Knowledge and Process Management, Volume 8, Issue 4, (2001)

Knowledge Capture and Reuse for Geo-spatial Imagery Tasks*

David C. Wilson, Michela Bertolotto, Eoin McLoughlin, and
Dympna O'Sullivan

Smart Media Institute, Department of Computer Science, University College Dublin,
Belfield, Dublin 4, Ireland
{david.wilson,michela.bertolotto,eoin.A.mcloughlin,
dymphna.osullivan}@ucd.ie

Abstract. The continuously increasing amount and availability of geo-spatial image data is giving rise to problems of information overload in organisations that rely on digital geo-spatial imagery. Intelligent support for relevant image retrieval is needed in order to help manage large geo-spatial image libraries. Moreover, managing the knowledge implicit in using geo-spatial imagery to address particular tasks is crucial for capturing and making the most effective use of organisational knowledge assets. We are developing case-based knowledge-management support for large geo-spatial image repositories, which incorporates sketch-based querying for image retrieval; image manipulation and annotation tools for highlighting and composing relevant aspects of task-relevant imagery; and automatic context-based querying for retrieving relevant previous task experiences. This paper describes our approach to knowledge capture and reuse through task-based image annotation, and it introduces the environment we are developing for capture and reuse of task knowledge involving geo-spatial imagery.

1 Introduction

With advances in technology for digital image capture and storage, the geosciences and spatial information engineering have experienced an explosion of available image data. Collections of geo-spatial imagery, such as digital satellite and aerial photographs, are also becoming more complex with improvements in remote sensing (e.g., infrared) and scanning techniques. Intelligent Geo-spatial information systems have thus become crucial for addressing the problem of imagery information overload by retrieving the most relevant geographic image data and associated information. Such systems play a central role in the larger picture of supporting organisational tasks that require the retrieval and analysis of geo-spatial imagery. Moreover, as geo-spatial information systems are employed to address specific tasks, the expert interactions, analyses, and conclusions—based

---

* The support of the Research Innovation Fund initiative of Enterprise Ireland is gratefully acknowledged.

K.D. Ashley and D.G. Bridge (Eds.): ICCBR 2003, LNAI 2689, pp. 622–636, 2003.
© Springer-Verlag Berlin Heidelberg 2003

on relevant imagery—come to represent a substantial organisational knowledge asset.

For example, a company that uses geo-spatial data for civil development projects may employ such a system to assist in selecting the location for a new airport. From a task-based standpoint, the most relevant work product lies not merely in the applicable visual data, but in descriptions of why and how the information has been collected and to what ends it has been successfully (or unsuccessfully) employed. A clear advantage is provided by capturing and leveraging not only essential underlying information but also a measure of the human expertise involved in seeking out, distilling, and applying the information required for organisational tasks. This serves both to facilitate workflow by providing access to best-practice examples, as well as to grow a repository of task-based experience as a resource for support, training, and minimizing organisational knowledge-loss as a result of workforce fluctuations.

As part of an overall effort in intelligent geo-spatial information systems, we are developing case-based knowledge management support for libraries of geo-spatial imagery. The research draws on a substantial body of work in case-based knowledge management (e.g., [Minor & Staab 2002; Fenstermacher & Tautz 2001; GWCBR-01 2001; Aha *et al.* 1999]. The goals of our geo-spatial knowledge management approach are to provide:

- digital image libraries for effective data organisation and efficient transmission to distributed clients
- sketch-based user interaction enabling a more natural mode of interaction in describing the context for retrieval
- a flexible task environment to support analysis and elucidation of relevant geo-spatial image information that can easily be integrated as part of existing workflow
- case-based tools to support intelligent capture and re-use of encapsulated task-based interactions and context

This paper focuses on the last two goals in providing a "knowledge-light" [Wilke *et al.* 1997] interactive approach to the fundamental issues of case acquisition and context-sensitive retrieval. A more general overview of the project can be found in [Bertolotto, Carswell, & Wilson]. The research challenge here is to enable capture and reuse of task-based knowledge as users interact with image libraries, in an unobtrusive manner. To this end, we are developing a task-based environment that facilitates users in work that already involves selecting, composing, and summarizing the aspects of digital imagery in support of their current task. From the user's perspective the image interaction tools provide them with a convenient way to organize and store a set of insights about relevant imagery that form a coherent basis for them to draw on in reporting their findings as part of a normal workflow process. By providing our reasoning system access to behaviours and results as users highlight relevant image aspects and make notes (for themselves), we can capture those insights in a form that the system can use.

Our approach to knowledge capture is very much in the spirit of work for capturing rationale in aerospace design [Leake & Wilson 2001] and automotive design feasibility analysis [Leake *et al.* 1999]; however, the emphasis here is on making use of self-directed annotations provided by users as a means of task analysis support, rather than on prompting users for particular kinds of choices. The method of annotating multimedia is related to annotating for the semantic web (e.g., [Champin, Prié, & Mille 2001]) and multimedia indexing (e.g., [Worring *et al.* 2002]), which focus on developing and leveraging annotated descriptions of the media content. Here, we focus rather on a task-centric view of annotation, providing for and employing annotations about how an image relates to the task at hand, though this will necessarily involve some reference to image content which may later be used to refine indexing. Multimedia database approaches such as QBIC [Flickner *et al.* 1995] provide for image segmentation and annotation, but also focus on contextualizing individual images, rather than task experiences. Previous work in CBR has made use of multimedia cases (e.g., [Burke & Kass 1996; Barber *et al.* 1992]), but the case media is not employed directly for retrieval; rather, the case indices are crafted semantic representations of the media content, an overhead we seek to avoid. While we make use of the information as part of task similarity rather than task structure, the system is instrumented to collect information about user interactions in terms of browsing and usage in a manner similar to the usage model in [Egyed-Zsigmond, Prié, & Mille 2003].

This paper presents our initial task environment implementation for annotating imagery, capturing experiences and rationale, and reusing previous experiences based on textual annotations. We begin by describing the image library interaction that provides a baseline for knowledge capture. Section 3 goes on to describe the user tools available for image annotation that enable capture of domain knowledge by monitoring user behaviour. Section 4 introduces our methods for annotation-based retrieval. We conclude with a discussion of initial test results and a description of future work.

2   Image Retrieval

Geo-spatial information represents the location, shape of, and relationships among geographic features and associated artifacts, including map and remotely sensed data. In this research, we focus on managing the large quantities of geo-spatial information available in raster format (digital images, with spatial position implicit in pixel ordering), primarily digital aerial photos, satellite images, and raster cartography. Geo-spatial imagery is employed in a wide range of applications, such as intelligence operations, recreational and professional mapping, urban and industrial planning, and touristic systems. Typically, geo-spatial imagery will also include *metadata* information, such as: date and time of image acquisition; date and time of introduction to system; scale/resolution; location of the image, expressed in hierarchically arranged geographic entities (e.g., state, country, city); sensor information; and imagery type (e.g., black & white, colour, infrared).

Based on these image characteristics, our system provides a baseline functionality of image querying. A typical task-based query to our image repository is a straightforward request to a geo-spatial image database, and it could consist of specified metadata, semantic information, and a sketched configuration of image-objects [Carswell, Wilson, & Bertolotto 2002; Agouris, Carswell, & Stefanidis 1999a; Agouris, Carswell, & Stefanidis 1999b]. The metadata criterion would include such information on image scale or location, while the semantic criterion would match against any specially tagged information (if any) about the type (purpose, etc.) of objects within images of interest. Note that this semantic information is image-centric (e.g., contains hospital), rather than task-centric as with our annotations. The sketch would include information on desired image-objects and their configuration. For example, if the user were interested in retrieving images that would aid construction of a new airport in Boston, the query would:

- Process the metadata to retrieve all images that match to the specified criteria (e.g., images from Boston).
- From this subset of images, use any available semantic information (e.g., airplanes, terminal) to further constrain the result set.
- From this subset of images, select imagery indexed by object-features that best match the user sketch.
- Process the spatial relations of the sketch scene on the last image subset and return a prioritized list of imagery as the query result.

The user can formulate an image library query using any combination of these elements. Our work on integrating the various similarity measures present in the system is ongoing, and in this paper we focus on image retrieval using metadata alone. A description of our image content similarity measure can be found in [Carswell, Wilson, & Bertolotto 2002; Carswell 2000].

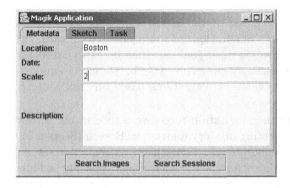

Fig. 1. Metadata Entry

When a user logs in to the application, they are directed to an interface that enables them to search directly for images that correspond to their current task needs. Queries can be constructed using a combination of metadata, semantic information, and pen-based sketch input. The metadata screen allows a user to formulate a query based on the image location, scale, creation date, and semantic keys. For example, a user might be interested in building an airport near Boston and wish to view recent images of possible building sites and related areas. As shown in Figure 1, the user could enter the location as Boston and a small scale value, as they wish to view large areas of land. Once the user has formulated their query using any combination of the search screens, they can initiate the search.

The resulting matching images are returned to the search screen in a new tab. Matching images are displayed as a list of thumbnails with their associated matching percentage score (out of 100), as shown in Figure 2. A subset of the metadata for each image is available as tooltip text when mousing over the image. The user can browse the images retrieved in the results screen and select any images that are relevant to the task at hand. The selected images are collected in the current user context and made available for manipulation and annotation, as described in Section 3.

3   Annotation Tools for Knowledge Capture

In order to assist the user in organising information about relevant imagery and to facilitate knowledge capture, we have developed tools for direct image ma-nipulation, including filters, transformations, highlighting, sketching, and post-it type annotations. These allow the user to identify regions of interest that can be linked to clarifications, rationale, and other types of annotations (e.g., multime-dia). The manipulations and annotations do not alter the underlying images or geo-spatial information, rather they are layered to provide a task-specific view. This enables the capture and refinement of more general task-based ideas and rationale. A typical interaction with the system, then, can capture sketches and geo-spatial queries posed by the user, the results that were found to be useful, as well as the user's annotations of the results. All of the contextual knowledge required to address the task goal can thus be captured as an experience case, enabling an increasingly powerful cycle of proactive support, as described in Section 4, with case-based suggestions based on task context. These cases are referred to as *sessions*.

To illustrate the annotation tools, we return to our airport example. After retrieving and selecting imagery relevant to Boston (Section 2), the user can ma-nipulate and/or annotate each image using a substantial set of tools, as shown in Figure 3. The tools are a subset of what might typically be found in a full-fledged image processing suite. We have selected the kinds of image manipulations that would be most useful in helping to analyse and focus on image features (e.g., high-pass filtering). All of the sketching manipulations can be performed in a variety of colors and brush styles. The architecture has also been designed to facilitate the addition of new types of image tools as the need arises.

The user can then go on to add personal media annotations to the image as a whole or to particular highlighted image aspects. Currently, the system supports annotation by text and audio, though retrieval is focused on text. In Figure 3, our example user has highlighted some aircraft and airport buildings and has added a textual annotation and uploaded an audio file, which are represented by icons painted on the image. The user can click on either of these icons to display a pop-up description. The system also supports annotation by cut, copy and paste between a given image and other images in the dataset, as well as images in any application that supports clipboard functionality for the given operating system. A user's entire process of image interaction in the system is stored as an encapsulated session case. Note that a session can be saved and re-opened to continue processing later.

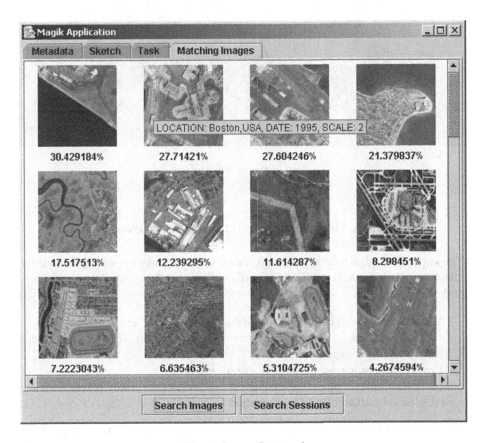

Fig. 2. Image Retrieval

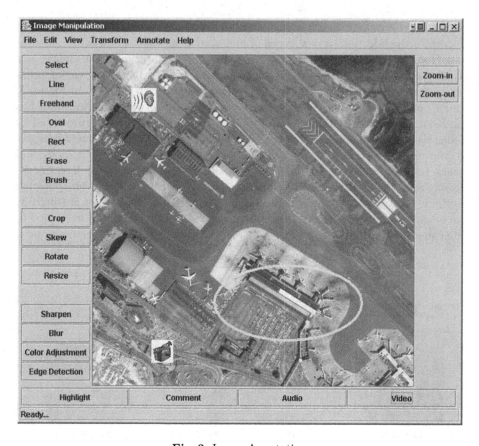

Fig. 3. Image Annotation

4   Annotation Based Similarity and Retrieval

The capture of task-based experience cases is the foundation of the knowledge management process. It enables an increasingly powerful cycle of proactive support that can:

- Make available relevant task knowledge from a user's own previous work,
- Facilitate knowledge sharing by retrieving potentially relevant knowledge from other user experiences,
- Provide a training support for novice users, and
- Enable automatic proactive support by retrieving potentially relevant knowledge based on the partial task context.

In the first phase of the work, we are focusing our annotation-based retrieval on textual annotations, using Information Retrieval metrics (e.g., [Salton & McGill 1983]) as a basis for similarity.

We presume that image retrieval is taking place toward some goal in the context of an overall workflow. Given a textual representation of the task context, we can match previously annotated session images to the current context. This allows both querying by task context alone, as well as providing an additional factor that can be taken into account in conjunction with the original image query components. Moreover, the task descriptions and image query elements can be used to retrieve entire sessions as relevant to supporting the current task.

Task descriptions could be provided by the user directly. Since we expect our system to be used in the context of an overall workflow, we have designed the system to link directly with upstream task descriptions, as they are provided to the user. This could also allow multiple users to share the same context for cooperative tasks. We also take relevant parts of any metadata provided as part of the task description context. In the case of our Boston airport development example, a task description could be given as shown in Figure 4.

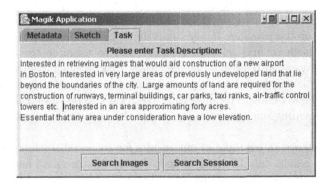

Fig. 4. Task Description

The system task-based retrieval employs indexes in three separate spaces.

1. Annotation Index - IR vector space across all textual annotations, where each annotation represents a "document"
2. Image Index - IR vector space across all images, where the text for each image is composed of the combined text from all annotations and metadata
3. Session Index - IR vector space across all sessions, where the text for each session is composed of the task description and user metadata query information

These indices are used in two different types of retrieval: image retrieval and session retrieval.

4.1   Image Retrieval

Task-based image retrieval serves two purposes. First, task-based similarity can be used directly to access annotated images in the image library. Second, it can be integrated with similarities from the other types of query information, such as by image content, to provide a more refined overall metric for retrieval. In either case, the resulting images are presented through the same type of interface, as shown in Figure 2, for consistent interaction. In searching for relevant images, similarity is computed as follows:

- if image passes metadata filter
  - compute similarity in the image index
  - compute and average similarities for each attached annotation in the annotation index
  - compute the final image score as the average of overall image and individual annotation similarities

4.2   Session Retrieval

As the system builds up encapsulated user interactions, another type of retrieval is enabled, retrieving entire previous task-based sessions. This enables a current user to look for the previous image analysis tasks that are most similar to the current task both to find relevant imagery and to examine the decisions and rationale that went into addressing the earlier task. One challenge in retrieving previous sessions has been how to present an entire session to the user in a manner that is compact enough to allow multiple results to be viewed simultaneously while still providing enough information for the user to discriminate potential relevancy.

Figure 5 shows an example of our results for retrieved sessions, displayed in an additional results tab. In order to keep session listings small and still provide enough discriminatory information, each session result is summarized to include the following:

- Basic session information on author and creation date
- Percent similarity score (out of 100)
- The most discriminating query information (if more than one) for the session (since we have captured which results were actually used, we know which queries were most fruitful)
- The most important annotation text (annotations, words, and phrases from the session that have the highest similarity to the current user's context)
- Thumbnail versions of the most important images (those from the session with the highest similarity to the current user's context)

By providing relative ranking for session elements, we can tailor the session view to a reasonable amount of available space for displaying results.

In searching for relevant sessions, similarity is computed as follows:

- compute similarity in the session index
- for each previous session above a threshold similarity
  - compute the number of images annotated in that session as a fraction of the total number of images returned

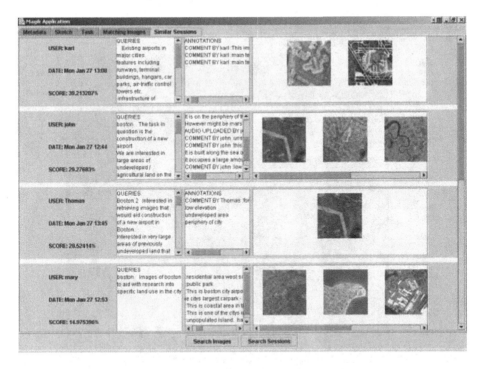

Fig. 5. Session Retrieval

- compute the number of images browsed in that session as a fraction of the total number of images returned
- compute the final session score as the weighted sum of session similarity, proportion of annotated images, and proportion of browsed images

The proportions of annotated and browsed images provide a measure of the relative usefulness of a given session, and they are are given a parameterized weighting relative (currently lower) to the session index similarity component.

If the user wishes to view the annotations made to an image returned in a similar session, they may do so by clicking on the thumbnail, which brings up the image and all its annotations in the image manipulation screen, as shown in Figure 6. The user may further annotate this image if they wish and/or retain the previous users annotations by adding it to their current session image context. Once the user saves the desired previous/new annotations, all of these annotations are transferred to the current user's view of the image. The user may perform many different queries and annotate or manipulate many images during the course of a session, and these are all saved as part of the users profile when they exit the application.

Because the knowledge management system is tightly coupled with the tasks that the user is performing, the system also has the capacity to make proactive recommendations in a natural and unobtrusive manner by monitoring the user's

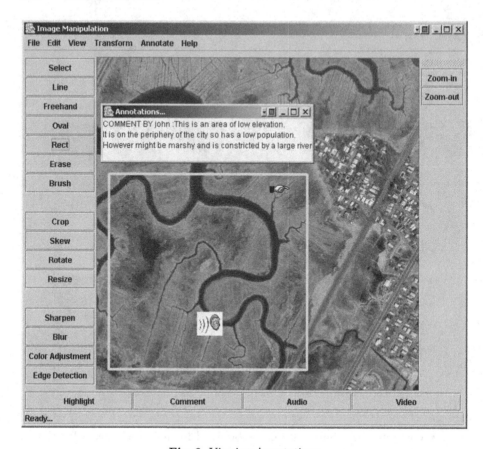

Fig. 6. Viewing Annotations

current task context. This is the next step for this work in augmenting the retrieval capabilities. Based on increments in the geo-spatial image information accessed and annotations provided, the system can correspondingly anticipate and update what previous experiential knowledge would be relevant at that stage, making it available to the user. The knowledge is provided unobtrusively, so that it need only be accessed when required. Thus the process of knowledge retrieval does not distract from the task at hand, yet makes relevant knowledge available just-in-time.

5   Evaluation

For the initial phase of the implementation, we have conducted testing with a library of 50 images used in 17 different task scenarios for novice task-domain users. The current experiments are designed more to test whether the system is performing as expected rather than to provide an absolute measure of utility.

Sessions were completed each in one pass, without engaging in feedback and refinement. The ideal way to test the system, of course, would be to conduct human trials with task-domain experts.

5.1 Image Retrieval

In order to test how the image retrieval improves over time with the addition of annotations, an empty library of sessions and annotations was created and a series of new task sessions were built via system interaction. Within each session annotations were added to images selected by the users as relevant to the task. We outlined six categories of task description, corresponding to the civil development in the following areas: airports, hotels, bridges, hospitals, stadiums and shopping centers. An example task description might be: "build a shopping center near the outskirts or suburbs of the city where infrastructure is good and land is inexpensive."

Different task descriptions were entered, corresponding to each of the six different categories, and ranked images were returned to the user. The matching scores were recorded for each image, and the user selected images for annotation that seemed relevant to the task description. The annotations were stored, but not indexed, in order to provide a baseline retrieval performance for the system with annotations. After 17 sessions were added, the experiment was repeated using the same task descriptions to measure how the image scores change after the textual annotations were indexed and included.

Table 7 shows the results for the most relevant 5 images (as judged by the user) for each session. The left/right columns give the similarity respectively without and with indexed annotations. As expected, there was an overall increase in the image matching scores, demonstrating the usefulness of including textual annotations for retrieval.

5.2 Testing Similar Sessions

In order to evaluate the retrieval of similar sessions, three new task descriptions (to the 17) were then constructed in three of the predefined categories. The top three similar sessions returned by the application were analyzed and their results deemed to be relevant or irrelevant.

The first task description corresponded to the "Airport" category. The task description outlined a scenario in which a user was interested in viewing images of existing airports in order to aid them with the development of a new airport facility. They sought general information concerning airport locations and orientations with regard to the urban areas which they service, land elevation, and the average land space occupied.

The top three similar sessions returned for the airport category had similar session scores of 40.68%, 15.14% and 14.82% respectively. The session user of the first similar session had entered a task description describing how they wanted to construct a new airport. It differed from the task description of the current session, however, in that the user was not interested in retrieving images

Query	Image 1		Image 2		Image 3		Image 4		Image 5	
1	0	12.32	7.8	12.1	0	9.7	3.8	7.16	4.6	6.08
2	35.68	51.95	31.54	53.11	26.33	44.03	23.8	40.5	36.07	38.13
3	27.35	36.71	20.62	29.99	12.49	5.86	9.5	0	18.73	0
4	40.63	52.34	31.18	48.16	29.65	45.93	7.55	38.35	23.44	37.32
5	22.64	33.32	17.68	27.07	18.39	26.82	16.64	26.32	24.56	24.85
6	0.09	13.06	0.05	11.44	1.49	11.2	4.1	11.01	0.5	9.8
7	0	10.96	1.69	10.68	0	6.67	0	5.78	0	5.2
8	10.2	15.56	3.5	14.68	0.06	12.81	6.9	10.96	5.7	8.8
9	13.2	0	7.9	5.2	7.51	2.1	6.4	3	4.45	3.9
10	12.58	18.57	10.28	15.51	9.32	14	8.04	11.73	7.19	10.81
11	6.1	11.62	2.3	10.85	0.08	8.07	2.1	5.69	0.06	4.06
12	27.3	20.84	12.2	20.43	16.7	19.01	0	17.2	11.8	9.7
13	0	5.1	0	4.99	0	4.5	0	4.13	0	2.6
14	0	16.56	16.5	16.09	10.31	10.07	0.7	9.98	0	9.31
15	9.8	14.79	3.6	13.56	10.8	13.65	5.8	11.11	3.54	6.75
16	7.21	10.97	2.7	10.02	8	9.95	4.29	8.24	2.6	5.01
17	6.43	15.2	2.4	11.09	6.4	9.7	10.2	13.29	8	10.7

Fig. 7. Image Retrieval Results

of existing airports. Rather, they wished to view areas of land that would be suitable for new development. Both task descriptions contained text associated with the airport domain such as elevation and land-space, as did some of the annotations uploaded by the user of the similar session to the images returned in their session. This session was deemed to be useful in fulfilling our current task description.

The task description associated with the second retrieved session was a request for images related to land usage in the selected cities. Some of the images returned by the similar session depicted the city airport, and the user had made annotations in this regard. The session score was higher because some more general use terminology, such as land and urban appear in both queries. The session was deemed to be moderately related to our current task.

The third most similar result session was interested in finding appropriate urban areas in which to construct a stadium. The tasks are similar in terms of the construction context, and this is reflected in the session score. For example, the land sites required for both developments are relatively large when compared to many other development domains. In both cases it is preferable for the development sites to be located away from the center of urban areas, given cost and the scale of previous development. This session also seems to see gains in similarity from more general use terminology that parallels the domains. We expect that there would be more marked differences allowing for finer distinctions with task-domain experts and more substantial task descriptions. This session was deemed to be quite similar to ours, but not very relevant.

Similar evaluations were carried out in the development categories of "Bridge"—top 3 sessions: 35.59% (relevant), 14.65% (very relevant), and 13.79%

(not relevant)—and "Hotel"—top 2 sessions: 52.19% (relevant) and 20.14% (relevant). Only 2 sessions were retrieved in total for the "Hotel" task. While these results are only indicative, they do show that the system performing as expected. Retrievals presented sessions deemed relevant to the user within the top results returned. There are many factors that need to be accounted for in larger scale testing, including a larger range of categories, scaling the number of annotations, and refining vocabulary toward more domain-specific usage.

6   Conclusion

We have introduced a case-based reasoning approach to knowledge capture and reuse in the context of a knowledge management system for task-based geo-spatial imagery retrieval. Experiments show the initial system implementation performing as expected, and we hope to scale testing as the implementation progresses. As the system matures, we expect to provide knowledge support in a flexible manner that can be easily integrated with existing infrastructure, and we intend to make use of existing standards for communication between system modules and for external communication. For example, we will incorporate Geography Markup Language (GML)[1] support for geo-spatial information, as the standard develops. We will also investigate the possibility of adding other resources, such as chaining the supporting experience cases, as well as other media such as video. We plan to investigate the possibility as well for structuring the knowledge internally in such a way that we can access additional upstream workflow information for further retrieval context, as well as providing a flexible output format (e.g., Docbook) that could automatically be used to generate workflow output, such as linking to standard reporting tools. We also note that our system has much wider potential applications beyond geo-spatial imagery, such as medical imagery, and we expect that such techniques will prove valuable in many fields that rely on image analysis.

References

Agouris, P.; Carswell, J.; and Stefanidis, A. 1999a. An environment for content-based image retrieval from large spatial databases. *ISPRS Journal of Photogrammetry & Remote Sensing* 54(4):263–272.

Agouris, P.; Carswell, J.; and Stefanidis, A. 1999b. Sketch-based image queries in topographic databases. *Journal of Visual Communication and Image Representation* 10(2):113–129.

Aha, D.; Becerra-Fernandez, I.; Maurer, F.; and Muñoz-Avila, H., eds. 1999. *Proceedings of the AAAI-99 Workshop on Exploring Synergies of Knowledge Management and Case-Based Reasoning.* AAAI Press.

Barber, J.; Bhatta, S.; Goel, A.; Jacobsen, M.; and Pearce, M. 1992. AskJeff: Integrating case-based reasoning and multimedia technologies for interface design support. In Gero, J., ed., *Artificial Intelligence in Design*, 457–476. Boston: Kluwer.

---

[1] www.opengis.org

Bertolotto, M.; Carswell, J. D.; and Wilson, D. Managing geo-spatial imagery and knowledge. In *Proceedings of the 10th Geographical Information Systems Research—UK Conference (GISRUK)*, 28–31.

Burke, R., and Kass, A. 1996. Retrieving stories for case-based teaching. In Leake, D., ed., *Case-Based Reasoning: Experiences, Lessons, and Future Directions*. Menlo Park, CA: AAAI Press. 93–109.

Carswell, J. D.; Wilson, D. C.; and Bertolotto, M. 2002. Digital image similarity for geo-spatial knowledge management. 58–72. Berlin: Springer-Verlag.

Carswell, J. 2000. *Using Raster Sketches for Digital Image Retrieval*. Ph.D. Dissertation, University of Maine, Orono, Maine, USA.

Champin, P.-A.; Prié, Y.; and Mille, A. 2001. Annotating with uses: a promising way to the semantic web. In *K-CAP 2001 Workshop on Knowledge Markup and Semantic Annotation*, 79–86.

Egyed-Zsigmond, E.; Prié, Y.; and Mille, A. 2003. Club (trèfle): a use trace model. In *Proceedings of the Fifth International Conference on Case-Based Reasoning*.

Fenstermacher, K., and Tautz, C., eds. 2001. *Proceedings of the ICCBR-01 Workshop on Case-Based Reasoning Approaches for Process-Oriented Knowledge Management*.

Flickner, M.; Sawhney, H.; Ashley, J.; Huang, Q.; Dom, B.; Gorkani, M.; Hafner, J.; Lee, D.; Petkovic, D.; Steele, D.; and Yanker, P. 1995. Query by image and video content: The QBIC system. *IEEE Computer* 28(9):23–32.

2001. *Proceedings of GWCBR-01: Knowledge Management by Case-Based Reasoning: Experience Management as Reuse of Knowledge*.

Leake, D. B., and Wilson, D. C. 2001. A case-based framework for interactive capture and reuse of design knowledge. *Applied Intelligence* 14(1).

Leake, D.; Birnbaum, L.; Hammond, K.; Marlow, C.; and Yang, H. 1999. Integrating information resources: A case study of engineering design support. In *Proceedings of the Third International Conference on Case-Based Reasoning*, 482–496. Berlin: Springer Verlag.

Minor, M., and Staab, S., eds. 2002. *Proceedings of the German Workshop on Experience Management*.

Salton, G., and McGill, M. 1983. *Introduction to modern information retrieval*. New York: McGraw-Hill.

Wilke, W.; Vollrath, I.; Althoff, K.-D.; and Bergmann, R. 1997. A framework for learning adaptation knowedge based on knowledge light approaches. In *Proceedings of the Fifth German Workshop on Case-Based Reasoning*, 235–242.

Worring, M.; Bagdanov, A.; v. Gemerr, J.; Geusebroek, J.-M.; Hoang, M.; Schreiber, A. T.; Snoek, C.; Vendrig, J.; Wielemaker, J.; and Smeulders, A. 2002. Interactive indexing and retrieval of multimedia content.

Index Driven Selective Sampling for CBR

Nirmalie Wiratunga, Susan Craw, and Stewart Massie

School of Computing
The Robert Gordon University
Aberdeen AB25 1HG, Scotland, UK
{nw,smc,sm}@comp.rgu.ac.uk
http://www.comp.rgu.ac.uk

Abstract. In real environments it is often difficult to obtain a collection of cases for the case base that would cover all the problem solving situations. Although it is often somewhat easier to generate potential problem cases that cover the domain tasks, acquiring the solutions for the problems captured by the cases may demand valuable time of a busy expert. This paper investigates how a Case-Based Reasoning system can be empowered to actively select a small number of useful cases from a pool of problem cases, for which the expert can then provide the solution. Past cases that are complete, containing both the problem and solution, together with partial cases containing just the problem, are clustered by exploiting a decision tree index built over the complete cases. We introduce a Cluster Utility Score *ClUS* and Case Utility Score *CaUS*, which then guide case selection from these clusters. Experimental results for six public domain datasets show that selective sampling techniques employing *ClUS* and *CaUS* are able to select cases that significantly improve the accuracy of the case base. There is further evidence to show that the influence of complete and partial cases utilised by these scores needs also to consider the number of partitions created by the case base index.

1 Introduction

The main knowledge source in a Case-Based Reasoning (CBR) system is the case base. Typically a case consists of a problem description and the solution, or case label. When a new problem is encountered, a case with a similar problem part is retrieved from the case base, and its solution is reused. The availability of suitable cases is one of the arguments that supports the use of CBR for many problem-solving tasks. However, for some tasks the knowledge engineering effort can be significant [5].

There may be knowledge acquisition problems associated with other knowledge containers; e.g. specialised retrieval knowledge is required, or the problem solving relies on the availability of effective adaptation knowledge. However, it may also be caused by a lack of suitable cases. There may be few problem-solving experiences to record as cases, as in our tablet domain where the complex formulation task has been captured in relatively few manufactured tablets [4]. It could even be that the case base is biased with some areas of the problem space

K.D. Ashley and D.G. Bridge (Eds.): ICCBR 2003, LNAI 2689, pp. 637–651, 2003.
© Springer-Verlag Berlin Heidelberg 2003

being very poorly represented. Although this is often a consequence of a sparse case base, it can also occur in a plentiful case base, where there are holes in the coverage. Finally, a plentiful source of problems might be easily available but acquiring solutions for these problems might be harder: e.g. easy access to patient information related to a disease but acquiring laboratory results might be costly; or easy access to documents on the web but acquiring relevance feedback is time consuming.

The approach we investigate here is selective sampling, where although a source of new problems is readily available, the choice of cases for the case base is crucial because constraints limit the availability of case labels. This is a relatively common problem in a real environment, where labelling many problems with the expert's solution may require significant interaction with a busy expert. Unlabelled cases are often generated by analysing all labelled cases that are available with the aim of identifying holes in the domain [9], or random case generation might be adopted when there are no labelled cases initially. Unlike the labelling task, generating unlabelled cases does not typically require the assistance of an expert.

The work described in this paper performs an informed selection from a set of unlabelled cases. The expert must subsequently label only this subset, thereby reducing the demand on the expert. However, we must ensure that the informed selection of relevant cases does not hamper the competence of the case base by omitting cases that uniquely solve problems. Although we do not directly deal with the case discovery problem, we believe that useful insight in this direction can also be gained from the selective sampling approach presented in this paper.

The remainder of this paper describes our approach and evaluates it on several public domain case bases. Existing work in case selection and discovery are discussed in Section 2. A generic selective sampling process is presented in Section 3. It exploits a domain model created by labelled cases to sample unlabelled cases. Section 4 outlines how we use a case base index as our domain model to cluster all cases (labelled and unlabelled) in order to select unlabelled cases that are potentially useful, using heuristics described in Section 5. The approach is evaluated on several public domain datasets in Section 6, before we draw some conclusions in Section 7.

2   Related Work in Case Selection

The problem of unavailability of labelled cases and sample selection of relevant cases from a set of unlabeled cases falls under the paradigm of active learning and more specifically, selective sampling. Much work has been done in selective sampling of examples mainly related to training classifiers: using information about the statistical distribution of case feature values for nearest neighbour algorithms [8]; using a committee-based approach combined with expectation maximization for text classification [10]; and using a probabilistic classifier that selects cases based on class uncertainty for C4.5 [7]. Increasingly, estimation and prediction techniques with roots in statistics are being applied to classifiers with resulting improved accuracy [3].

Partitioning all labelled and unlabelled cases is a common approach that is employed by many active sampling techniques. Clustering cases in this manner helps identify interesting cases; i.e. those that have the potential to refine the domain model learned thus far. But the use of cases for training classifiers differs from their use for a CBR system. In CBR, case retrieval is typically aided by a case base index, and retrieved cases may be directly reused to solve the new problem, or revised before being presented as a solution. The case base index which partitions cases into distinct problem solving areas in a CBR system will be exploited in this paper as a means to cluster labelled and unlabelled cases. Importantly by using the case base index we ensure that both the retrieval and adaptation stages influence the case selection process as opposed to simply exploiting the statistical distribution of cases.

Other CBR researchers utilise the CBR process when partitioning the cases. Smyth & Keane's coverage and reachability [13] are used to form competence groups of cases which can be used to solve each other [15]. These competence groups define the coverage of the case base, and allow narrow gaps to be identified where new cases can be proposed [11]. Competence groups are identified by applying the CBR retrieval and adaptation to cases in the case base. Boundary cases are pairs of cases, one from each of a pair of similar competence groups, chosen because they are most similar to each other. New cases are proposed that are midway between the boundary cases of the pairs of most similar competence groups. Their motivation is that close competence groups are more likely to merge with the addition of a new case that spans the narrow gap between them. This approach applies the model of the CBR reasoning to identify clusters of cases and hence small gaps between clusters.

CaseMaker [12] is an interactive knowledge acquisition tool that suggests potentially useful new cases for the case base by evaluating the coverage of possible new cases. It also applies the retrieval and adaptation knowledge to identify new cases.

This paper explores the same problem of identifying potentially useful cases to add to the case base. The case base index is used as a means to cluster the existing cases, to analyse the spread of existing cases and to suggest new cases that fill gaps identified by the clustering. Although retrieval and adaptation knowledge is not explicitly applied, the use of the index implicitly captures this knowledge. In contrast to competence-based case discovery [11], we select new cases that are dissimilar to existing ones, rather than discovering cases between close boundary cases. Although narrow gaps between large groups are interesting it is also vital to identify gaps within existing groups or even isolated gaps outwith existing groups.

3   Selective Sampling Process

The approach we investigate here is informed selection, where a source of new problems is available, and selective sampling identifies the most useful problems for which the expert should provide solutions, so that new cases can be added. This approach can also be used for case discovery where possible new problems are generated, and those that are selected for inclusion can be validated for consistency by the expert when he provides the solution.

Figure 1 outlines the selective sampling process for a set of unlabelled cases U by incorporating knowledge from labelled cases L. It would not be unusual to expect L to comprise a very small number of cases, while U would ideally contain a large set of cases. An initial model is created using the cases in the labelled set L. Using this model, cases in both L and U are partitioned to form clusters. The aim is that each cluster contains cases that reflect the common problem solving behaviour abstracted by the model. In this paper we use a C4.5 decision tree as the model. Each cluster may contain zero or more cases from L, U, or both. The next step selects K clusters. This selection should ideally be guided by the labelled and unlabelled cases grouped together in a cluster. Once the K clusters are chosen, unlabelled cases are selected from these clusters. Max-Batch-Size is simply a constant that restricts the number of cases selected per sampling iteration.

```
L = set of labelled cases
U = set of unlabelled cases
LOOP
      model ← create-domain-model(L)
      clusters ← create-clusters(model, L, U)
      K-clusters ← select-clusters(K, clusters, L, U)
      FOR 1 to Max-Batch-Size
            case ← select-case(K-clusters, L, U)
            L ← L ∪ get-label(case, oracle)
            U ← L \ case
UNTIL stopping-criterion
```

Fig. 1. Selective sampling process

Case selection is incremental, and once labelled, by obtaining the solution from a domain expert or oracle, the new cases are appended to L, and U is updated accordingly, before a new domain model is created. So the aim then is to select cases that are most likely to trigger refinements (or improvements) to the domain model. This selection process iterates until a desirable level of accuracy is achieved on L, a sufficient number of new cases are added, or until the participation limit of the oracle is reached.

4   Case Base Index: A Domain Model for Sampling

Several commercial CBR tools (e.g. RECALL, REMIND and KATE) use decision trees to index the case base in order to improve the efficiency of case retrieval [1]. Additionally these trees provide a useful means to explain the underlying reasoning for the retrieval. In previous work, we have shown that optimising the case base index improves the reuse stage [6] and that the partitions created by the case base index can further be exploited to acquire adaptation knowledge [16]. Therefore a CBR case base index forms a useful domain model since it identifies the areas of different problem solving behaviours in a case base. Here we look at how a case base index is created and how it can be used to form clusters.

4.1   Decision Tree Indexing

Figure 2 illustrates how a case base index can be created by inducing a C4.5 decision tree. The case base contains 20 (labelled) cases for a classification task with three classes X, Y and Z. The 3 decision nodes are tests associated with 3 of the features that describe the problem scenario captured by a case. Now let us see how the decision tree index is used within CBR retrieval. Assuming that a new problem is described as $f_1 = a$ and $f_2 = d$, then the tree would be traversed reaching the leftmost leaf node containing 5 labelled cases. These 5 cases form the relevant cases for the new problem, and by applying k-Nearest Neighbour (k-NN), we obtain the k nearest neighbours for the new case that lie within the leaf partition. Notice that here retrieval knowledge encompasses the nodes traversed and the feature weights that might be employed by k-NN. The new solution is obtained by reusing the majority solution suggested by the retrieved k cases, possibly with an adaptation stage added.

4.2   Index-Based Clustering

For sampling purposes we wish to partition all our cases so that cases in a given cluster share common retrieval and/or adaptation knowledge. The obvious candidates for a cluster are cases that are grouped together in a leaf node of the decision tree. Although leaf nodes of a case base index contain only labelled cases, the decision tree can be applied to unlabelled cases to allocate them to a leaf node, and hence a cluster. The problem description part of an unlabelled case alone is sufficient for tree traversal. Therefore, once an index is created using labelled cases, it is trivial to identify also the leaf nodes to which the unlabelled cases belong. Figure 3 shows the same index after 18 unlabelled cases are introduced. Here we have 5 clusters: three containing either unlabelled or labelled cases and the other two containing a mixture of labelled and unlabelled cases.

Since the initial index was created with a small number of labelled cases, it is likely that the decision nodes, and hence the traversal paths, need to be refined. Therefore the clusters which are created according to the index are also bound to capture this incorrect traversal behaviour. The aim then is to

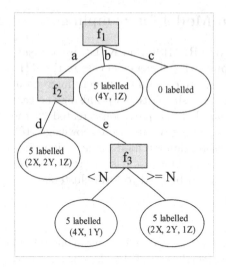

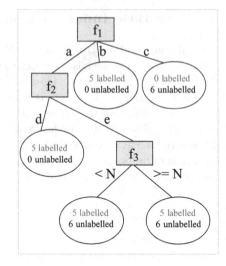

Fig. 2. Decision tree index   **Fig. 3.** Index for clustering

identify clusters that contain useful cases in that they solve diverse problems whose solutions would provide useful new cases for the case base. Moreover the addition of these cases will bring about changes to the case base index, thereby refining the retrieval and adaptation stages.

5   Cluster and Case Selection

In this section we look at the sort of evidence that will aid the identification of interesting clusters that are likely to contain useful new cases. Figure 4 illustrates a detailed view of the 5 clusters formed in Figure 3. The small rectangles denote cases, and labelled cases are distinguished by shading and labels.

Since clusters (i) and (iii) do not contain any unlabelled cases there is no need to concentrate on them, because they are not a source of new cases. In contrast cluster (ii) contains 6 unlabelled cases and, since there are no labelled cases representing this area of problem solving, it would be useful to select this cluster. If however we had to select between clusters (iv) and (v), each containing some labelled and unlabelled cases, we would wish to pick the one that contains atypical cases; i.e. the cluster with low intra-cluster similarity. Additionally, the fact that there is a greater mixture of labelled cases with cluster (v) indicates more uncertainty, and so it should be considered most fruitful.

Once an interesting cluster is identified what criteria should we employ to ascertain the usefulness of a new case? Certainly a case that is representative of other unlabelled cases is useful because by selecting such a case we cover a greater number of problem solving situations. In contrast selected cases also need to be different from labelled cases that are already in the cluster. With cluster (ii) the bold rectangle indicates a candidate case that is sufficiently representative

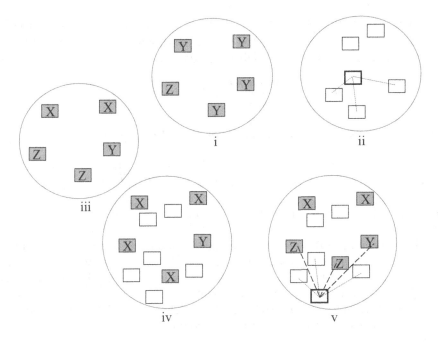

Fig. 4. Selecting a cluster

of (ii), in that it has the least distance to its unlabelled 3 nearest neighbours. With cluster (v) the bottom-most case is sufficiently similar to its unlabelled 3 nearest neighbours but also farthest away from its labelled 3 nearest neighbours, and so would be a good candidate case for selection.

5.1   Cluster Utility Score

We first consider the problem of choosing the most interesting cluster. We look at how distances between cases and information gleaned from both labelled and unlabelled cases can be exploited when formulating a Cluster Utility Score $ClUS$.

For a given case c in a cluster C, our first metric estimates the average distance $distance_N$ between c and its neighbourhood of k nearest neighbours in C.

$$distance_N(c, C, k) = \frac{1}{k} \sum_{n \in N_k(c,C)} distance(c, n)$$

where $N_k(c, C)$ returns the k nearest neighbours of c in C, and $distance(i, j)$ is the normalised distance between cases i and j.

The simplest utility score for cluster C is the average $distance_N$ for the cases in the cluster. However, we further wish to influence this by the error associated with the incorrectly classified labelled cases in the leaf node of the decision tree corresponding to the cluster C. The intuition behind this is that if two clusters have the same score then the cluster containing cases with different class labels should be chosen over a cluster containing cases with similar class labels. Therefore *ClUS* combines the average neighbourhood distance $distance_N$ and the entropy of C's subset of labelled cases L_C.

$$ClUS(C) = \frac{entropy(L_C)}{|C|} \sum_{c \in C} distance_N(c, C, k)$$

where *entropy* is the standard information theoretic measure

$$entropy(L_C) = - \sum_{i=1}^{m} \left(\frac{l_i}{|L_C|} \right) log_2 \left(\frac{l_i}{|L_C|} \right)$$

m is the number of classes, and l_i is the number of cases in L_C belonging to class i .

However in a decision tree with nominal attributes, a leaf node may contain no labelled cases (e.g. cluster (ii) in Figure 4). Entropy is meaningless because L_C is empty, but yet this is an interesting cluster for case selection. To overcome this problem we increment the class counts for each cluster by one. Thus l_j becomes $l_j + 1$, and $|L_C|$ becomes $|L_C| + m$. The revised definition for *entropy* follows and is used in the definition of *ClUS* above.

$$entropy'(L_C) = - \sum_{i=1}^{m} \left(\frac{l_i + 1}{|L_C| + m} \right) log_2 \left(\frac{l_i + 1}{|L_C| + m} \right)$$

Let us demonstrate the effect in a binary classification domain. If a leaf contains only unlabelled cases then the revised entropy for this cluster is 1 ($log_2 2$). However if there are labelled cases for each class, say 6 positives and 1 negative, then the class counts will be updated to 7 positives and 2 negatives, and the cluster entropy will be reduced from 1 to 0.76.

5.2   Case Utility Score

While *ClUS* captures the uncertainty within a cluster, the case-utility-score *CaUS* captures a case's impact on refining the case base index. The decision nodes that are traversed in order to reach a leaf node are chosen because of their ability to identify labelled cases with similar retrieval behaviour, by discriminating them from the rest of the labelled cases. Essentially the cases in a cluster share a common traversal path, and those that are likely to cause a change are unlabelled cases that are least similar to labelled cases in the cluster. However we would also like to ensure that selected cases are representative of any remaining unlabelled cases in the cluster.

CaUS is calculated for a case c in a selected cluster C by calculating the distances to remaining labelled cases in L_C and the unlabelled cases in the cluster U_C. Since we are only interested in selecting unlabelled cases labelled cases will have a *CaUS* score of zero. The diversity measure (adapted from [14]) assigns higher scores to cases that are farthest away from labelled cases, but also favours cases that are part of a tightly knit neighbourhood of unlabelled cases. Essentially it attempts to address the trade-off between selecting labelled cases that are not too similar to already labelled cases in the cluster, yet ensuring that they are sufficiently similar to unlabelled cases, thereby representing a higher proportion of unlabelled cases in C.

$$CaUS(c, C) = \begin{cases} 0 & \text{if } c \in L_C \\ diversity(c, C) & \text{otherwise} \end{cases}$$

$$diversity(c, C) = distance_N(c, L_C, k) * (1 - distance_N(c, U_C, k))$$

5.3   Sampling Heuristics

Let us revisit Figure 1 and see how the different steps fit together. create-domain-model uses available labelled cases to derive a model; here the case base index. This model is used to partition all the labelled and unlabelled cases to form clusters. *ClUS* is calculated for each cluster. These scores identify K-clusters from which we select cases based on their *CaUS*s. Case selection is incremental, in that once a selected case is labelled, the L_C and U_C are updated, before another unlabelled case is selected.

Several incremental sampling techniques have been implemented with the more informed sampling techniques employing *ClUS* and/or *CaUS* for cluster and case selection.

- RND selects a cluster randomly and selects cases randomly (without replacement) ;
- RND-CLUSTER selects one cluster randomly and incrementally selects the cases with highest *CaUS* from this cluster;
- RND-CASE selects the one cluster with highest *ClUS* but selects cases randomly;
- INFORMED-S selects a single cluster with highest *ClUS* and incrementally selects highest *CaUS* cases from this cluster;
- INFORMED-M selects K (multiple) clusters (K=3) with highest *ClUS* and selects the case with highest *CaUS* from each cluster. Notice here case selection need not be incremental, hence the L_Cs and U_Cs are updated once in a single sampling iteration.

With all techniques in each iteration of the sampling loop unlabelled cases are incrementally selected until a sample of Max-Batch-Size is formed. We use RND as the technique with which to compare the more informed selection techniques. RND-CASE and RND-CLUSTER demonstrate the impact of *ClUS* and *CaUS* independently. INFORMED-S and INFORMED-M both use *ClUS* and *CaUS*, and should be better able to pick useful cases compared to RND-CLUSTER and RND-CASE. However it is harder to postulate the impact of selecting from a single cluster versus multiple clusters; it is likely that this is domain dependent.

6   Evaluation

We evaluated the different case selection techniques to determine whether informed case selection leads to case bases with increased accuracy. We selected six datasets from the UCI ML repository [2]. They have varied number of features, number of classes, proportion of nominal to numeric features, and some have missing values. In order to simulate similar problem-solving experiences in the case base the size of each dataset was doubled by randomly duplicating cases. The intuition behind this is that an informed sampling technique would avoid selecting similar problem-solving experiences that are already covered by the labelled cases in the case base. Two of the domains have in excess of 400 cases (House votes and Breast cancer). For these, a training set of 350 is randomly selected while the remaining cases form the test set. For the smaller domains (Zoo, Iris, Lymphography and Hepatitis), we formed a training set size of 150 and a disjoint, similarly sized, test set. Experiments with five increasing training set sizes were carried out starting at:

- 150 with an increment of 50 for the larger training sets; and
- 50 with an increment of 25 for the smaller training sets.

Although all cases in the training set are labelled for experimentation purposes, these labels are ignored until cases are selected from the training set. The labelled cases (L) forming the case base is initialised by selecting 35 cases from the training set (we use 15 for the smaller domains), the rest of the cases form the set of unlabelled cases (U). The sampling process terminates once 3 sampling iterations are completed, simulating a sampling process constrained by expert availability. The `Max-Batch-Size` is set at 3 which generally gives a selection technique the opportunity to select not more than 9 new cases for the case base.

The experiments aim to evaluate the effectiveness of informed case selection on case base accuracy and the efficiency on sampling time. We note the time taken to complete the sampling iterations. The accuracy of the case base, now with the newly sampled cases, is evaluated on the test set by a straightforward k-NN. The graphs plot the average accuracy over 25 trials for increasing training set size.

6.1   Accuracy Results

Figures 5 (a) and (b) show average accuracy results for the Zoo and Iris domains. Both have no missing values, while Zoo has 7 classes and 18 features (all nominal), Iris has 3 classes and 4 features (nominal + numeric). As expected we see a significant difference between informed selection techniques INFORMED-S and INFORMED-M compared to RND (Zoo p=0.001 and Iris p=0.001). Although with Zoo we see that the difference between informed techniques and RND increase with increasing training set size this is not obvious with Iris. This might be explained by the contrasting difference in average index complexity (or number of nodes): 3 for iris and 8 for Zoo. When comparing INFORMED-M and INFORMED-S we see that the increase achieved by the former is significantly higher for Zoo

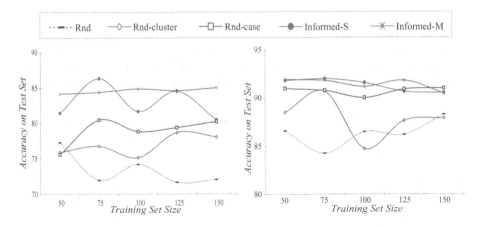

Fig. 5. Results for: (a) Zoo (b) Iris

(p=0.016), but that there is no difference for Iris (p=0.371). Again this is related to the relative difference in concept complexity, hence the difference in
the number of partitions or clusters. It also suggests the need to consider more
than one cluster and possibly the inter relationship of clusters when selecting
cases for domains with flatter and broader indices such as Zoo. The performance
of RND-CLUSTER is less consistent compared to RND-CASE. This is interesting
because it confirms that working hard at selecting a cluster is important.

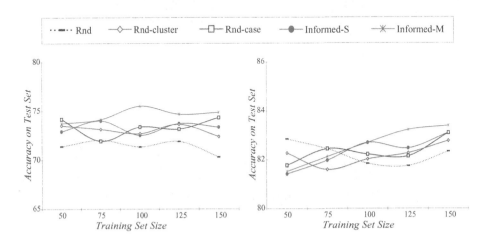

Fig. 6. Results for: (a) Lymphography (b) Hepatitis

Evaluation results for Lymphography and Hepatitis domains appear in Figures 6 (a) and (b). These domains have similar number of features (19 and 20),
but Lymphography has nominal and numeric with 4 classes, while Hepatitis is

binary classification with nominal features. Additionally the Hepatitis dataset contained missing values and when building the index a fraction of a case with missing values passes down each branch of an unknown decision node. For clustering, this means that a case with missing values can end up in two or more clusters. Here, we assigned cases with missing values to a single leaf; i.e. the leaf associated with the highest case fraction.

Again we find a significant difference between the informed techniques and RND (Lymphography p=0.001 and Hepatitis p=0.001). With Lymphography the average concept complexity is 9 and, as with Zoo, INFORMED-M's performance is significantly better than INFORMED-S (p=0.005). With certain test runs RND-CASE has out performed INFORMED-S suggesting that random case selection is better than selection based on $CaUS$. We believe that there can be a danger of exploiting information from already labelled cases where selection can be too biased by labelled cases in the cluster; here with $CaUS$ the distances to labelled cases $distance_N$, may become an undesirable influence when the distribution of labelled cases is skewed, possibly explaining the improved performance of random case selection. With Hepatitis the increase in accuracy by the informed techniques over RND though significant is small (2%) compared with other domains. It seems that the initial selection of labelled cases forming the case base already achieved high accuracy, therefore the impact of the newly sampled 9 cases seems to be less obvious.

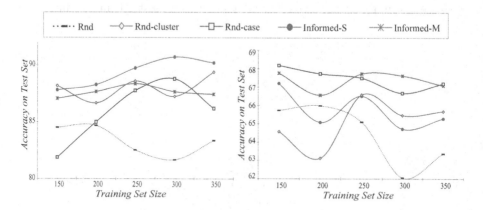

Fig. 7. Results for: (a) House votes (b) Breast cancer

The results from the larger datasets; House votes and Breast cancer appear in Figures 7 (a) and (b). These are both binary classed domains containing missing data. House votes has 16 binary valued features while Breast cancer has 9 multi-valued features. With House votes we have a significant improvement with INFORMED-M and INFORMED-S over RND (p= 0.001). The concept complexity with House votes on average is 3 which suggests fewer partitions of the case base explaining INFORMED-S's significant improvement over INFORMED-M's performance (p = 0.023).

Unlike the House votes domain, Breast cancer is more complex because the features are not just binary valued. Still the results are very encouraging, in that we have significant improvements with all informed techniques. We also see that RND-CASE has significantly better performance over INFORMED-S and RND-CLUSTER. This is most likely due to the increased concept complexity (here an average of 7, with a depth bound of 5 on the index tree) and so increased number of partitions to the case base. With fewer labelled cases in a cluster, $CaUS$ would have been overly influenced by the labelled cases particularly in $distance_N$. This then suggests that for $CaUS$ we need to consider the distribution of labelled cases and use this information to regulate the influence of labelled cases on $CaUS$.

6.2   Efficiency Results

So does the increase in accuracy justify the increase in training time? For domains with many features, and in particular those with many classes (e.g. Zoo), there is almost a 3-fold increase in training time with INFORMED-M compared to RND (see Table 1). This increase can amount to as much as a 40-60 seconds difference and for the larger datasets with 350 cases a 5-fold increase can mean up to a 150 second difference. For real applications this is an obvious drawback. However since the main processing cost is associated with the pairwise case distance calculation associated with $ClUS$, an efficient feature subset selection technique will help improve efficiency.

Table 1. Increased training time ratio of INFORMED-M compared to RND

Training set size	50	75	100	125	150
Zoo	1.1	1.6	2.3	2.6	2.9
Iris	1.5	1.7	1.9	2.1	2.3
Lymphography	1.5	1.9	2.1	2.4	2.6
Hepatitis	1.9	1.9	2.1	2.1	2.3

Training set size	150	200	250	300	350
House Votes	2.3	2.8	3.4	3.9	4.5
Breast Cancer	2.6	3.3	4.1	4.4	4.7

Generally when operating with a fixed expert availability time constraint the trade-off here depends on whether during this time we wish to present an expert with: fewer yet different problems selected using informed techniques; or many problems selected randomly with the hope that a sufficient spread of problems is covered.

7   Conclusions

The idea of exploiting the partitions formed by the case base index as the basis
for selective sampling for CBR is a novel contribution of this paper. It is also
a sensible thing to do because the index invariably captures the CBR system's
problem solving behaviour. The sampling approach is iterative and attempts to
identify new cases that when added into the case base are most likely to trigger
refinements to the index. The paper introduces a cluster utility score *ClUS*,
which reflects the uncertainty within a cluster by deriving information from
both labelled and unlabelled cases. High scores denote interesting clusters that
are a source of useful unlabelled cases. A further case utility score *CaUS* then
helps rank these cases by maximising distances to labelled cases yet minimising
distances to unlabelled cases.

The effectiveness of informed sampling techniques using *ClUS* and *CaUS* was
demonstrated on 6 public domain datasets. In general, a significant improvement
in test accuracy was observed with these techniques compared to random sampling. Case selection from multiple clusters outperformed selection from a single
cluster on several domains. However there seems to be an obvious relationship
between index depth and breadth, and hence the partitions, and the sampling
techniques. Generally for an index with fewer leaf nodes, selection from a single
cluster works better but the opposite is true for a flatter index.

In this paper we have primarily concentrated on a case base index created by
a decision tree structure formed using C4.5's information gain ratio. However,
we are keen to see how the sampling approach presented in this paper might be
more generally applied with other case base indexing schemes, such as k-means
and bottom-up clustering. Another area of interest is to explore how incomplete
case base indices might be manipulated as evidence of holes in the case base and
then to exploit this as a means to discover new cases.

Selective sampling tools are useful for CBR systems whether labelled cases are
plentiful or not. If there is a constraint on availability of labels then certainly a
CBR system with sampling capability will be very attractive. Conversely if there
are many labelled cases then sampling techniques can be adapted as a means
to identify few yet useful cases thereby ensuring that CBR retrieval efficiency is
maintained.

References

1. Aha, D.W., Breslow, L.A.: Comparing simplification procedures for decision trees
   on an economics classification task. Technical Report AIC-98-009, Navy Center
   for Applied Research in AI, Washington DC, 1998
2. Blake, C., Keogh, E., Merz, C.: UCI repository of machine learning databases,
   1998. http://www.ics.uci.edu/~mlearn/MLRepository.html
3. Cohn, D., Ghahramani, Z., Jordan, M.I.: Active learning with statistical models.
   Journal of Artificial Intelligence Research, 4:129–145, 1996
4. Craw, S., Wiratunga, N., Rowe, R.: Case-based design for tablet formulation. In
   Proceedings of the 4th European Workshop on Case-Based Reasoning, pages 358–
   369, Dublin, Eire, 1998. Springer

5. Cunningham, P., Bonzano, A.: Knowledge engineering issues in developing a case-based reasoning application. *Knowledge-Based Systems*, 12:371–379, 1999
6. Jarmulak, J., Craw, S., Rowe, R.: Genetic algorithms to optimise CBR retrieval. In *Proceedings of the 5th European Workshop on Case-Based Reasoning*, pages 136–147, Trento, Italy, 2000. Springer
7. Lewis, D.D., Catlett, J.: Heterogeneous uncertainty sampling for supervised learning. In *Machine Learning: Proceedings of the 11th International Conference*, pages 148–156, New Brunswick, NJ, 1994. Morgan Kauffman
8. Lindenbaum, M., Markovich, S., Rusakov, D.: Selective sampling for nearest neighbour classifiers. In *Proceedings of the 16th National Conference on Artificial Intelligence (AAAI 99)*, pages 366–371, Orlando, FL, 1999. AAAI Press
9. Liu, B., Wang, K., Mun, L.F., Qi, X.Z.: Using decision tree induction for discovering holes in data. In *Proceedings of the 5th Pacific Rim International Conference on Artificial Intelligence (PRICAI-98)*, pages 182–193, 1998
10. McCallum, A., Nigam, K.: Employing em in pool-based active learning for text classification. In *Proceedings of the 15th International Conference on Machine Learning*, pages 359–367, 1998
11. McKenna, E., Smyth, B.: Competence-guided case discovery. In *Proceedings of the 21st BCS SGES International Conference on Knowledge Based Systems and Applied Artificial Intelligence (ES 01)*, pages 97–108, Cambridge, UK, 2001. Springer
12. McSherry, D.: Automating case selection in the construction of a case library. In *Proceedings of the 19th BCS SGES International Conference on Knowledge Based Systems and Applied Artificial Intelligence (ES 99)*, pages 163–177, Cambridge, UK, 1999. Springer
13. Smyth, B., Keane, M.T.: Remembering to forget. In *Proceedings of the 14th International Joint Conference on Artificial Intelligence (IJCAI 95)*, pages 377–382, Montreal, Quebec. 1995. Morgan-Kaufmann
14. Smyth, B., McClave, P.: Similarity vs. diversity. In *Proceedings of the 4th International Conference on CBR*, pages 347–361, Vancouver, BC, Canada, 2001. Springer
15. Smyth, B., McKenna, E.: Competence models and the maintenance problem. *Computational Intelligence*, 17(2):235–249, 2001
16. Wiratunga, N., Craw, S., Rowe, R.: Learning to adapt for case-based design. In *Proceedings of the 6th European Conference on Case-Based Reasoning*, pages 421–435, Aberdeen, Scotland, 2002. Springer

Case Base Reduction Using Solution-Space Metrics

Fei Ling Woon[1], Brian Knight[2], and Miltos Petridis[2]

[1] Tunku Abdul Rahman College, School of Arts and Science, Kuala Lumpur, Malaysia
f.woon@gre.ac.uk
[2] University of Greenwich, School of Computing and Mathematical Sciences,
London SE10 9LS, UK
{b.knight, m.petridis}@gre.ac.uk

Abstract. In this paper we propose a case base reduction technique which uses a metric defined on the solution space. The technique utilises the Generalised Shepard Nearest Neighbour (GSNN) algorithm to estimate nominal or real valued solutions in case bases with solution space metrics. An overview of GSNN and a generalised reduction technique, which subsumes some existing decremental methods, such as the Shrink algorithm, are presented. The reduction technique is given for case bases in terms of a measure of the importance of each case to the predictive power of the case base. A trial test is performed on two case bases of different kinds, with several metrics proposed in the solution space. The tests show that GSNN can out-perform standard nearest neighbour methods on this set. Further test results show that a case-removal order proposed based on a GSNN error function can produce a sparse case base with good predictive power.

1 Introduction

Case-Based Reasoning (CBR) is a methodology for reasoning from experiential information. The classical cycle for CBR (see e.g. [20,12]) is that of retrieval of similar cases, adaptation of the cases to produce a solution, revision of the case base where the solution is not satisfactory and retention of the revised case base. The efficiency of the process in the first two stages of this cycle, retrieval and adaptation, has been studied by several authors recently.

Yang [23] addressed the problem by proposing a method that selects an optimal case base from a given set of cases, based on nearest neighbour retrieval. In his paper, no adaptation is considered, hence the nearest neighbour solution is applied to the target problem. Smyth *et al.* [17, 18, 19] have also addressed similar problems by means of an algorithm based on a calculation of 'relative competence' of cases. Relative competence is used to measure the importance of cases, and consequently provides a means to optimize case base performance. Smyth and Keane point out that competence depends upon both retrieval and adaptation.

Lately, Salamo and Golobardes [15] invented a competence model that uses deletion and building techniques based on rough set theory in classification tasks. In their work, a set of equivalence relations are used to determine the core and reduct of knowledge (i.e. a set of cases) which can then be used for filtering unwanted cases. They proposed a set of frameworks that work on different domains to examine

K.D. Ashley and D.G. Bridge (Eds.): ICCBR 2003, LNAI 2689, pp. 652–664, 2003.
© Springer-Verlag Berlin Heidelberg 2003

whether to keep the boundary cases or create new cases in order to produce an optimum case base. Many results have been published in their paper in comparison with other reduction methods such as the IBL2-4 algorithms [1, 2], CNN [8], DROP1-5[21], and etc. on some data sets.

In fact case selection techniques have been investigated in the guise of both case-base maintenance and instance-based learning (IBL). According to Mitchell [13], IBL and CBR share some common properties: (1) they implement "lazy" learning, (2) they classify new instances by nearest neighbour methods. IBL has historically focused on learning algorithms for case-based prediction.

Among case-base maintenance models in CBR and reduction methods for IBL, k-Nearest Neighbour (k-NN) [4, 13] and the Distance Weighted Nearest Neighbours (DWNN) [13] are common retrieval methods used in prediction. k-NN predicts the solution for a given target query based on the output classification of its k-nearest neighbours assuming that the output class of the target query is the most similar to the output class of its nearby instances in Euclidean distance. However, the DWNN weights the contribution of each of the k-nearest neighbours according to its distance to the target query. In the discrete-valued domain, both the k-NN and DWNN work on a voting basis. For continuous-valued target functions, mean value and weighted average of its k-nearest neighbours are applied to k-NN and DWNN correspondingly.

In this paper, we propose a generalised reduction technique of the Shrink [10] algorithm, and examine its use to find an optimum sparse case base. This reduction technique plugs the GSNN algorithm [11] into the Shrink algorithm. GSNN is used to estimate the output classification of a given target query, and thence to estimate the contribution of each case to the predictive power of the case base. Reduction in the Shrink algorithm is based on the contribution of cases to the predictive power. The experimental results in Section 4 show that such a reduction technique which uses a solution space metric can be implemented. A ten-fold cross validation test [22] is performed on the Iris data set and on a pneumatic conveying particles problem to examine the predictive power of case bases at different stages in a decremental fashion. The former is a classification problem. The latter is a practical problem that exists in pneumatic conveying industry [9]. One of the major industry concerns is to investigate how parameters such as the air velocity, loading ratio, the collision angle of the bend and etc. affect particle attrition. The aims of the test are to investigate the feasibility of using such a reduction technique to extract an optimum case base from data provided by the user, and to use the simulation result as a bench mark to evaluate the predictive power of the reduced case base. The test results confirm that GSNN can out-perform k-NN and DWNN on these problems with several measures, depending upon metrics defined in the solution space.

Furthermore, due to the inherent nature of GSNN, a case-removal order can be defined in terms of the GSNN error function. When implementing the case-removal order, good predictive power can still be achieved even with very sparse case bases.

2   The Generalised Shepard Nearest Neighbour Algorithm

The Generalised Shepard Nearest Neighbour algorithm [11] is a retrieval method which has two features of interest in case base reduction. It is an interpolative method operating over nominal values, which shows good predictive power for sparse case bases. Also, it allows us to exploit knowledge of any distance metric defined over the solution space. We show in Section 3 that this feature is of use in case base reduction, in that the solution space similarity can be used effectively in ordering case removal. The GSNN algorithm forms a basis for a reduction technique incorporating solution space metrics. The use of solution space metric can achieve a sparse case base with good predictive power.

The algorithm assumes that there exists a distance metric $d_x(x,x_i)$ in the X (problem) space and also a metric $d_y(y,y_i)$ in the Y (solution) space. There are no other restrictions on these spaces, which may be continuous (real valued) or discrete (nominal valued) or, indeed, mixed. In real-valued domains, the method reduces to a localised version of Shepard's method [16], which is a global method. GSNN uses k nearest neighbours to produce a solution

$$\hat{y} = arg \ \underset{y \in Y}{Min} \ I(y) \ . \tag{1}$$

where $I(y)$ is a measure of the deviation of the value y from its prediction based on its k nearest neighbour. $I(y)$ is defined entirely in terms of distance metrics $d_x(x, x_i)$ and $d_y(y, y_i)$, taking the form:

$$I(y) = \sum_1^k d_y(y, y_i)^2 d_x(x, x_i)^{-p} / \sum_1^k d_x(x, x_i)^{-p} \ . \tag{2}$$

$I(y)$ may be seen as the distance weighted mean square deviation of y from the neighbouring solutions y_i. The deviation of y is measured by the solution space metric $d_y(y,y_i)$, and distance weighting w_i is measured by $w_i = \dfrac{1}{d_x(x_q, x_i)^p}$, normalised so that $\sum_1^k w_i = 1$. Here k is a positive integer that specifies the number of nearest neighbours retrieved and p is a positive integer which controls the distance weighting effect. In what follows we have taken p = 1.

The GSNN algorithm has more general applicability than k-NN and DWNN, allowing general solution space similarity metrics. We can in fact show that a special case of GSNN is in fact DWNN. Take the case that the solution space Y is the real number domain R, and take $d_y(y, y_i) = |y - y_i|$. In this case, we can calculate the minimum value of I(y) from the condition $\partial I / \partial y = 0$. This gives:

$$y \sum_1^n \| x - x_i \|^{-p} \ = \ \sum_1^n \| x - x_i \|^{-p} y_i \ .$$

and we see that y is given by a distance weighted average value, identical with DWNN.

However, GSNN differs markedly from DWNN when the solution space is discrete, whereupon DWNN resorts to a voting mechanism. GSNN will also allow more general solution domains, such as vector domains with continuous or mixed elements, as long as a metric is defined on Y.

In summary, the GSNN algorithm works equally well with real and nominal domains for both x and y. Its novelty lies in: (i) the inclusion of a problem space distance metric, $d_y(y,y_i)$, and (ii) its ability to implement interpolation over nominal domains. In [11], it has been shown to work well on sparse databases with nominal valued solutions.

3   Use of the GSNN Algorithm in Reduction Methods

In order to use GSNN in case base reduction methods, and to compare it against other methods, we first need to re-cast such a technique, to be cognizant of the special feature of GSNN, viz. that it can exploit the existence of a solution based metric. In this section, we show how one such method, the decremental method can be generalised so that GSNN can be used.

Many reduction techniques use the k-NN algorithm [13] for a target query approximation in classification tasks. In fact, much fruitful research work has been done over past decades on reduction algorithms. A wide range of such algorithms have been developed for Instance-Based Learning: for example, CNN [8], RNN [6], Shrink[10], IBL[1,2], DROP[21], Explore[3] and etc. Generally, these reduction algorithms can be divided into three main categories: Incremental, Decremental and Batch [21]; and other growing and reducing reduction methods such as Explore, ELGROW [3] and etc.. In this paper, we concentrate on decremental methods, to investigate the feasibility of using GSNN in substitution for other nearest neighbour methods in case base reduction.

First we review the general reduction method. If we take D be the domain of cases, and $c \in D, C \subseteq D, R \subseteq C, S \subseteq C$, we can formulate the general reduction algorithms as :

```
Function R(C):
Begin
          R=C
          While CandidateSet(R) ≠  Null
           R ← R - Select(CandidateSet(R))
          loop
End
```

Here, C is the initial set of cases, R is the Reduced set. The function CandidateSet (R) returns a set of cases. The function Select (S) returns a case: Select (S) ∈ S, where S represents a candidate set $S \subseteq R$.

Reduction techniques such as Shrink reduce the case base according to this general algorithm, so that each iteration of the algorithm produces a case base with one less case. The case to be removed is decided upon by first obtaining a candidate set from the current R. In all the reduction methods listed here, this is done by using a nearest neighbour algorithm to obtain an estimated solution $\hat{y}$ for each case c ∈ R. Inclusion in the candidate set is then based on the difference between $\hat{y}$ and the true solution y_t. The candidate set is usually taken to be the set of cases such that

$$\left| y_t - \hat{y} \right| = 0 \quad . \tag{3}$$

The argument here being that for these cases satisfying (3) y_t is perfectly predicted by its nearest neighbours, and therefore adds little new information to the case base.

The second phase of the removal strategy is represented by the Select() function. Usually this is a random selection of a single case from the candidate set. If the candidate set is empty, the algorithm will halt. This can happen using condition (3) to define the candidate set whilst the case base is still quite large. However, we may replace (3) by the condition:

$$\left| y_t - \hat{y} \right| = Min_R \left| y_t - \hat{y} \right| \quad . \tag{4}$$

On the right of this equation is the minimum value of the difference between $\hat{y}$ and the true solution y_t for cases in R. This difference could be 0 or positive. Equation (4) will be satisfied by all cases with a difference equal to this minimum. This set is therefore the candidate set, which must always contain at least one member while R itself is not empty. We can therefore continue the reduction to produce case bases of any size, as long as $|R| > k$. When $|R| > k$ there are not enough interpolation points to produce estimates $\hat{y}$ for any case in R.

In order to use GSNN, we need to generalise (4), to allow solution space metrics other than simple differences to be used. In fact, the obvious generalisation is represented by the condition:

$$d(y_t, \hat{y}) = Min_R d(y_t, \hat{y}) \quad . \tag{5}$$

We see that (5) is obtained from (4) by taking $d(y_t, \hat{y}) = \left| y_t - \hat{y} \right|$, i.e. the simple linear difference.

4   Experimental Results

To examine how the GSNN algorithm might work on real case bases, and to measure its performance when embedded in a reduction method, we performed a trial test on the Iris dataset [5] and on a pneumatic conveying particles degradation dataset [9, 7]. The reduction method is then used to find a minimum case base.

We have chosen the Shrink algorithm from among reduction methods available due to its decremental fashion of eliminating cases. The Shrink algorithm begins by placing all training instances into a case base and then prunes the case base by removing instances that are correctly classified by the remaining subset. It is somewhat similar to RNN [6] except that RNN considers whether the classification of other instances would be affected by the instance's removal. Like other some other reduction methods, the Shrink algorithm retains boundary cases but it is sensitive to ordering effects.

The fact that GSNN takes advantage of interpolative mechanism and use of solution-space metric, has indeed shown itself to be a complement to the Shrink algorithm. With GSNN, a removal order can be implemented using formula (5) in the Shrink algorithm to further remove the cases to find a minimum case base.

The benefits of the algorithms proposed here, in comparison with the many existing case reduction algorithms are: (i) the algorithm can exploit the existence of a similarity metric in the solution space. This applies particularly for nominal values, for instance, with the Iris classification problem shown in Section 4.1, (ii) this algorithm can achieve sparse case bases with good predictive power.

To verify the above argument, the standard 10-fold cross validation test has been performed for analysis with different k values where k is the number of nearest neighbours retrieved.

In the 10-fold cross validation test, cases in the dataset are randomized and then partitioned into 10 sets. Each set is in turn used a test set while the other sets are used as training set. We repeat this 10 times since there are 10 partitions. The test results obtained is the average result of the 10 test sets. Also we used the same partitions in all tests. This test examines two aspects of the method: (i) Case base storage size, and (ii) Prediction Accuracy. We compare the performance of GSNN using two different solution space metrics (GSNN-1 and GSNN-2) with both the standard k-NN and DWNN method.

4.1   Experiment 1: The Iris Classification Problem

The Iris data set contains 3 classes of 50 instances each, where each class refers to a type of Iris plant.   We take the problem space X to be R^4 , so that $x = (x_1, x_2, x_3, x_4)$ is a point in problem space, where $x_1 = $ sepal width, $x_2 = $ sepal length, $x_3 = $ petal width, $x_4 = $ petal length. The solution space Y = { setosa, versicolour , virginica }. For this problem, we need to define distance metric in both problem space X, and solution space Y. For the problem space we define distance according to a weighted sum of attributes. For convenience, we assign equal weight = ¼ for each attribute, so that:

$$d_x(x, x') = \tfrac{1}{4}\left(\left| x_1 - x_1' \right| + ... \right) .$$

For the Y space, we need to construct $d_y(y, y')$. In GSNN-1, we use a distance metric $d_y(y, y')=0$ if y = y', $d_y(y, y')=1$ otherwise. This metric corresponds to the view that the three Iris classes are each totally dissimilar to each other. It is interesting to notice that

GSNN-1 behaves like DWNN in all tests. This suggests that DWNN (and k-NN) also implicitly treat solution classes as mutually dissimilar.

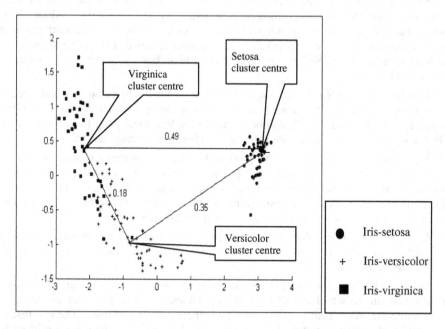

Fig. 1. Principal component plot of The Iris dataset. This shows a figure consisting of three different classifications of Iris plants, together with the associated cluster centres. The distances between the cluster centres represents the distance between the Iris classes in GSNN-2

In GSNN-2 we take the Iris classes to bear some similarity to each other. Fig. 1 shows a principal components plot of the dataset. Although this is only a 2-dimensional representation, it indicates that class versicolour lies somewhat "between" classes setosa and virginica (although not *linearly* between). To reflect this view of the classes bearing some similarity to each other, we use the distances between cluster centres to represent the distance between the classes.

These distances are shown in the following matrix:

	setosa	versicolour	virginica
setosa	0	.35	.49
versicolour	.35	0	.18
virginica	.49	.18	0

Table 1 shows the results of these tests. The Shrink algorithm was used to find reduced case bases with 19 cases and with 3 cases. The table shows how effective these reduced case bases were in classifying a target query, using 10-fold cross validation, in comparison with the complete case base and various retrieval methods. These results confirm that the GSNN which uses solution-space metric can outperform the two other nearest neighbour methods for case bases using the Shrink algorithm. In particular, the GSNN-2 sparse case bases with only 3 cases demonstrate better classifying power than either k-NN or DWNN.

Table 1. Average Correct Predictions in estimating Iris dataset using 10-fold cross validation

Embedded methods in the Shrink algorithm	Case base size	k-NN (%)	DWNN (%)	GSNN-1 (%)	GSNN-2 (%)
k=1	135	92.67	92.67	92.67	92.67
	19	87.33	87.33	84.67	87.33
	3	52.67	52.67	64.67	83.33
k=2	135	92.67	92.67	92.67	92.67
	19	84.0	87.33	87.33	87.33
	3	34.0	52.67	60.67	84.0
k=3	135	94.67	94.0	94.67	94.67
	19	92.0	88.0	89.33	90.67
	4	50	42.0	61.33	66.0
k=4	135	94.67	94.67	94.67	94.67
	19	92.0	89.33	89.33	89.33
	5	52	56.0	70.67	67.33
k=5	135	94.0	94.67	94	94
	19	91.3	90.0	94	92.67
	6	36.37	40.67	59.33	58.67

4.2   Experiment 2: Pneumatic Conveying Particles Degradation

Pneumatic conveying is an important transportation technology in conveying solid bulks in industry. Attrition of powders and granules during pneumatic conveying is a problem that has existed for a long time. One of the major industry concerns is to investigate how parameters such as air velocity, loading ratio, the angle of the bend and etc. affect particle attrition. Such knowledge is of great use in the design of conveyors. CBR models are currently under investigation for estimation of conveyor design quality, which may affect particle degradation and erosion of pipe bend. However, experimental cases are expensive to produce, and suitable sparse case-bases are desirable.

In the second trial test, we have collected 50 cases in the form of <problem, solution> pairs from a pneumatic conveyor simulation model, which simulate pneumatic conveying of sugar. The simulation model is used to measure particle degradation and the velocities of the air and particles at the outlet. These cases are generated at random by a user to construct a case base with a total of 50 cases, each with a unique solution.

k-NN and DWNN both work on the basis of a voting function [13]. The present condition of the case base, with only one unique solution corresponding to each problem presented in the case base, would affect the predictive power of the case base when using 10-fold cross validation. Both the k-NN and the DWNN methods will never give the exact solution because the test set is separated from the training set. Because CBR is an approximation technique [14], there is no guarantee for a correct solution, and adaptation become necessary for unseen problems.

In the particle degradation problem, the problem domain consists of the attributes: velocity of air and velocity of particles at the outlet, distribution of class size. The solution domain consists of attributes: velocity of air and suspension density at the inlet and the angle of bend. This problem is formulated based on the user's interest in finding appropriate parameters for a desired distribution of particles in different size class. The distance metric in both the problem domain and solution domain are computed by using the weighted sum of attributes with equal weight on all attributes as Iris problem distance metric.

However, the solution domain is a mixed domain with a vector of y = (angle, air velocity, suspension density), where the angle of the bend can only be 45 degree and 90 degree according to the user. A simple mean value for k-NN and the weighted mean for DWNN in prediction of the target query would not be appropriate use on this set. Therefore, we use a classifier with a given tolerance which can be used in prediction on this set. We classify a case with error outside the tolerance as incorrect, and otherwise it is classified as correct.

Table 2. Average Correct Predictions obtained from several different retrieval methods using a classifier based on the average error with a tolerance, $\varepsilon = 0.163$

Embedded methods in the Shrink algorithm	Case base size	k-NN (%)	DWNN (%)	GSNN-1 (%)	GSNN-2 (%)
k=1	45	60	60	60	60
	30	58	58	58	58
	5	32	32	32	32
k=2	45	50	60	60	66
	30	44	58	58	64
	5	24	32	32	36

As mentioned in Section 4.1, GSNN-1 behaves like DWNN in all tests. This is due to the inherent nature of the data set collected from the user. The data set consists of 50 unique <problem, solution> pairs in which we would expect both DWNN and GSNN-1 give the same result regardless of the value of k since they both weighted the contribution of each of the k nearest neighbour by problem distance and that the solution distance is a {0,1}. Thus, we would expect the one nearest case to the target query will always be the estimated value of the target solution.

Notice also that for k > 1, GSNN-2 seems to out-perform k-NN on this set by approximately 50%.

5   The Candidate Set Condition

In this section we examine the effect of the candidate set condition on the reduction algorithm. The candidate set conditions (4), (5) have the general form:

$$M(\, y_t, \hat{y}\,) = Min_R M(\, y_t, \hat{y}\,)\quad . \tag{6}$$

where $M(y_t, \hat{y})$ is a measure of how important y_t is to the case base's predictive power. In Section 4, it appears that in both test examples $M = d(y_t, \hat{y})$ is better than $M = \left| y_t - \hat{y} \right|$. However a better gauge of how important y_t is to the case base is a measure of how close y_t is to being selected. We show that the measure

$$M = \left| I(y_t) - I(\hat{y}) \right|\quad . \tag{7}$$

is such a measure. We know from (1) that:

$$\hat{y} = arg\ \underset{y \in Y}{Min}\ I(y)\quad .$$

Hence, $I(\hat{y}) = Min\ (I(y))$ is a measure of the deviation between the estimated value and its k- neighbours prediction. Similarly $I(y_t)$ is a measure of the deviation between the true value and its k-neighbour prediction. Hence the expression: $I(y_t) - I(\hat{y})$ is a measure of how near y_t is to being selected as the estimated value. If $I(y_t) - I(\hat{y}) = 0$, then y_t will definitely be selected . If $I(y_t) - I(\hat{y}) \gg 0$, then y_t is a long way from being selected.

5.1   Experiment 1 with Alternative Candidate Set Conditions

Taking $M = \left| I(y_t) - I(\hat{y}) \right|$ in the candidate set criterion, we re-ran the Shrink test of the previous section. The results are given in Table 3. They show that a very sparse case base can be found, giving good predictive power using $M = \left| I(y_t) - I(\hat{y}) \right|$.

Note that the results shown in Table 3 implementing the candidate set condition (7) in the removal of cases are not only better than using (5), but also far better than the prediction of using k-NN and DWNN retrieval. As in Table 4, when k=1, $M = \left| I(y_t) - I(\hat{y}) \right|$ is 1.8 times better than k-NN and DWNN and 2.7 times better than k-NN and 1.8 times better than DWNN when k=2.

Table 3. Average Correct Predictions in estimating the Iris dataset for GSNN-2 –Shrink algorithm with different removal strategies using 10-fold cross validation

$M(y_t, \hat{y})$	Case base size	k=1	k=2
$d(y_t, \hat{y})$	3	83.33%	84%
$\left\| I(y_t) - I(\hat{y}) \right\|$	3	96%	93.33%

Table 4. Average Correct Predictions in estimating the Iris dataset for GSNN-2 –Shrink algorithm with removal strategy: $\left\| I(y_t) - I(\hat{y}) \right\|$ and different retrieval methods using 10-fold cross validation

Retrieval methods	Case base size	k=1	k=2
GSNN-2 with removal strategy: $\left\| I(y_t) - I(\hat{y}) \right\|$	3	96.0 %	93.33%
k-NN	3	52.67%	34.0 %
DWNN	3	52.67%	52.67%

5.2   Experiment 2 with Alternative Candidate Set Conditions

As in 5.1, we repeat the same test on the pneumatic conveying particles problem:

Table 5. Average Correct Predictions in estimating the Pneumatic conveying particles dataset for GSNN-2 –Shrink algorithm with different removal strategies using 10-fold cross validation

$M(y_t, \hat{y})$	Case base size	k=1	k=2
$d(y_t, \hat{y})$	5	32.0 %	36.0 %
$\left\| I(y_t) - I(\hat{y}) \right\|$	5	42.0 %	42.0 %

Note that again the results shown in Table 5 by implementing the candidate set condition (7) in the removal of cases are better than using (5), and gives better prediction than using k-NN and DWNN retrieval on this set as shown in Table 6.

Table 6. Average Correct Predictions in estimating the Pneumatic conveying particles dataset for GSNN-2 –Shrink algorithm with removal strategy: $\left|I(y_t) - I(\hat{y})\right|$ and different retrieval methods using 10-fold cross validation

Retrieval methods	Case base size	k=1	k=2
GSNN-2 with removal strategy: $\left|I(y_t) - I(\hat{y})\right|$	5	42.0 %	42.0 %
k-NN	5	32.0 %	24.0 %
DWNN	5	32.0 %	32.0 %

6   Conclusion

In this paper we have set out a case base reduction technique which uses a metric defined on the solution space. The reduction technique utilises the GSNN algorithm to estimate nominal or real valued solutions in case bases with solution space metrics. A generalised reduction technique is given for such case bases in terms of a measure $M(y_t, \hat{y})$.

Experimental results are given for the classification of the Iris case base and pneumatic conveying particles dataset. The tests show that the reduction technique can out-perform standard nearest neighbour techniques on these sets. A version of the technique, where M is defined in terms of the GSNN error function, $I(y)$, gave the best results.

References

1.   Aha, D. W., *"Tolerating noisy, irrelevant and novel attributes in instance-based learning algorithms"*, International Journal of Man-Machine Studies, 36, (1992) 267–287.
2.   Aha, D. W., Kibler, D., & Albert, M. K., *"Instance-Based Learning   Algorithms"*, Machine Learning, 6, (1991) 37–66.
3.   Cameron-Jones, R. M., *"Instance Selection by Encoding Length Heuristic with Random Mutation Hill Climbing"* Proceedings of the Eighth Australian Joint Conference on Artificial Intelligence (1995) 99–106.
4.   Cover, T. M., Hart, P., *"Nearest Neighbour Pattern Classification"*, IEEE Transactions on Information Theory, 13, (1967) 21–27.
5.   Fisher, R. A., *"The use of Multiple Measurements in Taxonomic Problems"*   Annual Eugenics, 7, Part II, (1936), pp.179–188; also in *"Contributions to Mathematical Statistics"* (John Wiley, NY, 1950).
6.   Gates, G. W., *"The Reduced Nearest Neighbour Rule"*, IEEE Transactions on Information Theory, 18(3), (1972) 431–433.

7.   Hanson, R., Allsopp, D., Deng, T., Smith, D., Bradley, M. S. A., Hutchings, I. M., Patel, M. K., *"A Model to Predict the Life of Pneumatic Conveyor Bends"*, Proc Instn Mech Engrs Vol 216 Part E: J Process Mechanical Engineering, IMechE, (2002) 143–149.

8.   Hart, P.E., *"The Condensed Nearest Neighbour Rule"*, IEEE Transactions on Information Theory, 14, (1968) 515–516.

9.   Kalman, H., *"Attrition of Powders and Granules at Various Bends during Pneumatic Conveying"*, Powder Technology 112, Elsevier Science S.A. (2000) 244–250.

10. Kibler, D. & Aha, D. W., *"Learning Representative Exemplars Of Concepts: an Initial Case Study"*, Proceedings of the Fourth International Workshop on Machine Learning, Irvine, CA: Morgan Kaufmann (1987) 24–30.

11. Knight, B., Woon, F., *"Case Base Adaptation Using Solution-Space Metrics"*, to be appear in: Proceedings of the 18th International Joint Conference on Artificial Intelligence, IJCAI-03, Acapulco, Mexico (2003).

12. Kolodner, J., *"Case Based Reasoning"* Morgan Kaufmann Publishers; ISBN: 1558602372; (November 1993).

13. Mitchell T, *"Machine Learning"*, McGraw-Hill Series in Computer Science, WCB/McGraw-Hill, USA, (1997) 230 – 247.

14. Richter, M., *"Case-Based Reasoning: Past, Present, Future"*, ICCBR 2001, Vancouver, Canada.

15. Salamo, M., Golobardes, E., *"Deleting and Building Sort Out Techniques for Case Base Maintenance"*, LNAI 2416: published by Springer, Germany.6th European Conference, ECCBR-02, September, Aberdeen, Scotland, UK (2002) 365–379.

16. Shepard, D., *"A Two-dimensional Interpolation Function for Irregularly- Spaced Data"*, Proceeding of the 23rd National Conference, ACM, (1968) 517–523.

17. Smyth, B., Keane, M. T., *"Remembering to Forget: a Competence-Preserving Deletion Policy for Case-Based Reasoning Systems"* In: Proceedings of the 14th International Joint Conference on Artificial Intelligence. Morgan-Kaufmann. (1995) 377–382.

18. Smyth, B., McKenna, E., *"Modeling the Competence of Case-Bases"* In: Smyth, B. & Cunningham, P. (eds.): Advances in Case-Based Reasoning. Lecture Notes in Artificial Intelligence, Vol.1488. published by Springer-Verlag, Berlin Heidelberg New York (1998) 208–220.

19. Smyth, B., McKenna, E., *"Building Compact Competent Case-Bases"* Lecture Notes in Artificial Intelligence, Vol.1650: published by Springer-Verlag. 3rd International Conference on Case-Based Reasoning, ICCBR-99, Seeon Monastery, Germany, (July 1999) 329–342.

20. Watson, I. D., *"Applying Case-Based Reasoning: Techniques for Enterprise Systems"*, Morgan Kaufmann Publishers; ISBN: 1558604626; (July 1997).

21. Wilson, D. R., Martinez, T. R., *"Reduction Techniques for Instance-Based Learning Algorithms"*, Machine Learning, 38: Published by Kluwer Academic Publishers, Netherlands, (2000) 257–286.

22. Witten, I. H., Frank, E., *"Data Mining"*, Practical Machine Learning Tools and Techniques with Java Implementations, Morgan Kaufmann Publishers; (2000) 125–127.

23. Yang, Q., Zhu, J., *"A Case-Addition Policy for Case-Base Maintenance"* Computational Intelligence, Vol. 17, No.2, published by Blackwell Publishers, (2001) 250–262.

CBM-Gen+: An Algorithm for Reducing Case Base Inconsistencies in Hierarchical and Incomplete Domains

Ke Xu and Héctor Muñoz-Avila

Department of Computer Science and Engineering
19 Memorial Drive West
Lehigh University
Bethlehem, PA 18015, USA
{kex2,hem4}@lehigh.edu

Abstract. We propose an algorithm, CBM-Gen+, to refine case bases for hierarchical and incomplete domains. In these domains, the case bases are the main source of domain information because of the absence of a complete domain theory. CBM-Gen+ revises the existing cases when a new solution is captured. The main purpose of this revision is to reduce inconsistencies in the cases. We will prove that CBM-Gen+ is sound relative to the captured solutions. We also perform experiments showing that CBM-Gen+ is on average at least as efficient as a previous approach for constructing case bases for hierarchical domains.

1 Introduction

One of the main current research topics in CBR is case base maintenance (Leake & Wilson, 1998; Watson, 1997, Chapter 8). In recent years researchers have formulated case base maintenance (CBM) policies for reducing the size of the case base without losing coverage (Racine & Yang, 1997; Kitano & Shimazu, 1996; Smyth & Keane, 1998), for constructing compact case bases (Smyth & McKenna, 1999), for refining case libraries (Aha & Breslow, 1998), and for adding new cases (Ihrig & Kambhampati, 1996; Muñoz-Avila, 2001).

In this paper we present an approach for case base maintenance in hierarchical and incomplete domains. In hierarchical domains high-level tasks are decomposed into simpler tasks. Incomplete domains are those for which no complete domain theory exists explaining how to solve problems in that domain. An example of such a domain is project planning. Project Planning is a business process for successfully delivering one-of-a kind products and services under real-world time and resource constraints. Project plans are hierarchical in nature being expressed in so-called work-breakdown structures. Work-breakdown structures closely resemble a hierarchical (HTN) plan representation (Muñoz-Avila et al, 2002). There is no complete domain theory for generating project plans. Knowledge about how to formulate project plans is mostly episodic, even though general guidelines have been formulated to help with the project plan elicitation (PMI, 1999).

In previous work we proposed an algorithm, Gen+, for acquiring cases automatically by capturing user sessions with project planning tools (Mukammalla & Muñoz-Avila, 2002). The main motivation for our case acquisition procedure was to make case capture transparent to the user. Cases captured with Gen+ are

K.D. Ashley and D.G. Bridge (Eds.): ICCBR 2003, LNAI 2689, pp. 665–678, 2003.
© Springer-Verlag Berlin Heidelberg 2003

generalizations of project planning episodes. The main advantage of this generalization is that it increases the opportunities for reusing the cases. In addition, cases contain pieces of project plans rather than complete project plans. Again, this results in greater flexibility since pieces of different projects can be combined to create new projects. However, Gen+ can over-generalize project planning episodes. That is, potential instantiations of the cases may not be valid in the target domain.

Because of the generalization procedure in Gen+, multiple cases may be applicable for a given problem. Thus, any of these cases can be reused. If a problem and a solution were captured to acquire a case, there is no guarantee that the case will be reused when the problem is given once again. Depending on the domain, reusing a different case may yield an incorrect solution. In such situations, we say that Gen+ is not sound relative to the captured solutions. This may be a surprising result but it is a trade-off issue between soundness and coverage. As pointed out in (Mukammalla & Muñoz-Avila, 2002), if cases are not generalized, a very large case base will be required to obtain an adequate coverage.

We will present a new procedure, CBM-Gen+, for refining cases having a hierarchical representation. Cases still are generalized solutions as in Gen+. However, CBM-Gen+ revises previously acquired cases when a new case is captured. This revision process is performed when potential conflicts between the new and the existing cases are identified. Thus, it is possible that the order in which the solutions are captured will determine which cases will be reused. We will show that CBM-Gen+ is sound relative to the captured solutions. That is, if S is a solution for a problem P and (P, S) is used to learn generalized cases in a case base, then S will be generated as a solution whenever P is given as a problem.

This property is a weak version of soundness for planning procedures. We cannot ensure that every solution generated is correct in the target domain unless we make some stronger assumptions (e.g., (Muñoz-Avila et al, 2001)). Still, this property guarantees soundness for those problems whose solutions have been previously captured.

As we will see, existing cases may be split into two separate cases during the revision process in CBM-Gen+. As a result, the case bases generated with CBM-Gen+ are generally larger than the case bases with Gen+ even if they received the same input cases. Despite this, we will describe experiments showing that, in average, problem solving with CBM-Gen+ case bases is not less efficient than with Gen+ case bases. Furthermore, our experiments suggest that problem solving with CBM-Gen+ is much faster if the input problems are solvable.

2   The Gen+ Procedure

In (Mukkamalla & Muñoz-Avila, 2002), a procedure, Gen+, is presented to acquire cases representing pieces of a project plan. The main motivation of Gen+ is to assist users in the development project plans by using hierarchical case decomposition techniques (Muñoz-Avila et al, 2002). Starting point for this approach is the recognition that the representations commonly used for project plans are very similar to the hierarchical task network (HTN) representations. Thus, HTN planning techniques can generate project plans.

2.1   Cases Contents

In HTN planning, high-level tasks are decomposed into simpler tasks. This decomposition process continues until so-called primitive tasks are obtained. Primitive tasks indicate concrete actions to be undertaken. HTN planning techniques requires the availability of a domain theory capturing all possible decompositions in the target domain.   Such a requirement is unfeasible in project planning where users follow general guidelines and their own experience rather than a well-determined collection of rules. For this reason, our KBPP approach advocates capturing episodic project planning episodes as cases that have an HTN-like representation.

Cases have the form *(:case h cond ST)*, where *h* is the task being decomposed, *cond* is a collection of conditions, *ST* is a collection of subtasks. Given a task *h'*, if *h* matches *h'* with a substitution β (i.e., $h\beta = h'$) and the instantiated conditions *cond*β are satisfied in the current situation with a substitution α, then the case can be used to decomposed *h'* into *ST*$\beta\alpha$.

2.2   Case Capture

Given a case *C = (:case h cond ST)*, the generalization of *C*, denoted by Gen+(*C*) is obtained by considering each parameter, ψ, occurring in the arguments of the head, conditions, or subtasks of *C* (Mukkamalla & Muñoz-Avila, 2002). Two situations may occur: first, if the type of ψ is known, then all occurrences of ψ in *h*, *cond*, and *ST* are replaced with a unique variable, ?ψ. If tName denote the type of ψ, then the condition (tName ?ψ) is added to *cond*. This condition indicates that any instantiation of ?ψ must be of type tName. Second, parameters for which the type is not known are not generalized. In addition the following constraints are added as conditions of the case:

- For each two different variables, ?x and ?y, of the same type, the constraint (:different ?x ?y) is added
- For each constant, c, and each variable, ?x, the constraint (:different ?x c) is added

The condition (tName ?ψ) is added to reduce the chances of over-generalization. Although over-generalization may still occur, the alternative (e.g., not generalizing the cases) will require too many cases to get adequate coverage. If there is a maximum of n task names, with an average number of m arguments and each argument can take an average number of v values, there are nm^v different tasks. We require at least one case for each task. Thus, we would require at least nm^v cases. Notice that this is the minimum number of cases required. But we may need more cases to obtain a better coverage because similarity is computed not only based on the tasks but also on the current situation (e.g., available resources).

As an example, suppose that the equipment equip103 must be delivered between two specific locations. Table 1 shows a concrete solution for this task, namely, contracting the delivering company Deliver Incorporated (first column). Gen+ stores this solution by adding variables with their corresponding types (second column).

Table 1. A concrete solution and the corresponding Gen+ case

Concrete Solution	Gen+ Case 1
Task:	Task:
(deliver equip103 dept107 office309)	(deliver ?e ?d ?o)
Condition (resources):	Condition:
Deliver_inc	(deliverCompany ?fd)
equip103	(equipment ?e)
dept107	(depot ?d)
office309	(office ?o)
Subtask:	Subtask:
(contract Deliver_inc equip103 dept107 office309)	(contract ?fd ?e ?d ?o)

3 Soundness Relative to the Captured Solutions

One of the most challenging aspects of working with domains such as project planning is the lack of a domain theory. The Gen+ procedure fills this gap by proposing generalizations of the solutions it receives as inputs. Depending on the domain, these generalizations may be correct. However, it is easy to construct examples where instantiations of the case do not model the target domain correctly. Furthermore, as more cases are added to the case base, problem-solution pairs used as input to generate cases may not be necessarily reconstructed. This motivates the following definition:

Definition: Suppose that a collection of pairs (P_i, S_i) is given, where P_i is a problem and S_i is a solution for P_i in a target domain. Suppose that this collection is used as input for a procedure to construct a case base CB. The procedure is said to be **sound relative to the captured solutions** if for every problem P_i, the solutions generated using CB are correct in the target domain.

This definition presupposes a correct case reuse algorithm. In our work, we use the SiN reuse algorithm which is provable correct (Muñoz-Avila et al, 2001).

We can now show that Gen+ is not sound under this definition: continuing with the example shown in Table 1, suppose now that a new solution and the corresponding generalized case shown in Table 2 are added to the case base. The main difference between the solution in Table 1 and the new solution is that the equipment is delivered in two stages. First, Deliver Incorporated is once again contracted to deliver the equipment to depot55. Second, one of the company's own truck is used to make the final delivery to office700. The generalized case is also shown in Table 2. Suppose that the reason why this delivery must be performed in two stages is because there is no company that delivers goods from dept107 to office700. Lets assume that the case base consists of both Gen+ cases and that the task and the conditions in the first column of Table 2 are given once again as a new problem. With this assumption, it is obvious that Gen+ Case 2 is applicable because it is the generalization of the concrete solution. Gen+ Case 1 is also applicable because its conditions are a subset of the conditions of Gen+ Case 2. However, under our assumption selecting Gen+ Case 1 is incorrect. Thus, Gen+ is not sound relative to the captured solutions.

Table 2. Second concrete solution and the corresponding Gen+ case

Concrete Solution	Gen+ Case 2
Task:	Task:
(deliver equip103 dept107 office700)	(deliver ?e ?d ?o)
Condition (resources):	Condition:
Deliver_inc	(deliverCompany ?fd)
Unlimited_Deliver	(deliverCompany ?ud)
equip33	(equipment ?e)
dept107	(depot ?d)
office70	(office ?o)
depot55	(depot ?d1)
truck654	(truck ?t)
Subtask:	(:different ?d ?d1)
(contract Deliver_inc equip33 dept107 Depot55)	Subtask:
(internalDeliver truck654 equip33 depot55 office70)	(contract ?fd ?e ?d1 ?o)
	(internalDeliver ?t ?e ?d1 ?o)

4 The CBM-Gen+ Procedure

CBM-Gen+ and Gen+ both capture problem-solution pairs and generalize them to construct case bases. The difference is that Gen+ simply adds generalized cases into the case base without making any revisions. On the other hand, CBM-Gen+ may refine existing cases and the new case before adding it into the case base. *Unless stated otherwise, in the remaining of this paper, we assume that the all the cases have been generalized.* As before, a case *(:case h cond ST)* consists of three parts: the task h, the conditions cond, and the subtasks ST.

4.1 Preliminaries

We introduce some definitions before detailing the CBM-Gen+ algorithm:

- *Notation:* Given a case C = *(:case h cond ST)*, T(C) denotes the task *h*, P(C) represents the conditions *cond* and ST(C) represents the subtasks *ST*.

- *Task-Match*: two cases C and C' task-match, if there is a substitution θ such that: $T(C)\theta = T(C')$.

- *Condition Intersection Set*: If two cases C and C' task-match with a substitution θ. $P(C)\theta$ denotes the instantiated conditions in C. The intersection set of $P(C)\theta$ and $P(C')$ is called the condition intersection set of C and C', which contains every condition appearing in both $P(C)\theta$ and $P(C')$. The condition intersection set of cases C and C' is denoted as $P(C \cap C')$.

- *Condition Difference Set:* Given two sets of conditions P(C) and P(C'), $P(C) - P(C')$ denotes the set difference of P(C) and P(C').

- *Parent case* and *Child Case*: For two cases C and C', if ST(C) contains only one subtask, i.e., ST(C) = {st}, and T(C') = st, then C is called the parent case of C'. C' is called a child case of C.

- *Leaf Case*: A case C is called a leaf case if C has a parent case but no child cases in the case base.

- *Root Case*: A case C is called a root case if C has no parent case.

As with Gen+, the cases in CBM-Gen+ are stored in a plain list. However, in CBM-Gen+, there is a logical connection as illustrated in Figure 1. If the only subtask of C is equal to the head of C1 and C2 (i.e., ST(C) = {T(C1)} = {T(C2)}), C can be seen as the parent case of C1 and C2 (C1 and C2 can be seen as the child cases of C).

The case base may contain several root cases. In addition, CBM-Gen+ will guarantee that no child case will have more than one parent case, and each parent case has exactly two child cases.

Root Case / Parent Case

Leaf Case / Child Case

Fig. 1. Example illustrating the relations between cases

4.2   The Main Algorithm

The CBM-Gen+ algorithm receives as input a new case N. The algorithm first finds a root case C that tasks-matches with N and calls the auxiliary procedure Insert(N,C). If the case base is empty or N does not task-match a root case then N is inserted as a new root case in the case base and the procedure ends. The procedure CBM-Gen+ is shown below:

```
Procedure CBM-Gen+(N)  {
        IF CB is empty or N does not task-match with any root case THEN
                Add N into CB as a root case;
        IF CB is not empty, THEN {
                IF N task-match a root case C in CB THEN {
                        Insert(N, C)   }}}
```

We are going to define now the auxiliary procedure Insert(N, C). The parameter N represents the new generalized case to be added into the case base, and C represents an existing case. When Insert(N, C) is called from the CBM-Gen+ procedure, C is a root case. But the procedure may be called recursively with child cases. We identify three main situations. The first situation occurs when P(N∩C) is a strict subset of P(N) and P(C). The pseudo-code for this situation is shown below:

IF P(N∩C) is a strict subset of P(N) and P(C) THEN {
      Add the following cases in CB:
          N∩C   = (:case T(C) P(N∩C) {vT})
          C-(N∩C) = (:case vT P(C)-P(N∩C) ST(C))
          N-(N∩C) = (:case vT P(N)- P(N∩C) ST(N))
      Remove C from CB   }

The task vT is a new task not mentioned anywhere in the case base. This situation is illustrated in Figure 2. The new root case will have as preconditions the intersection P(N∩C). The left child case of the new root case will have as preconditions: P(C)-P(N∩C). The right child case will have as conditions P(N)- P(N∩C). Notice that the original case C can be reconstructed by taking the task of the new root case, collecting the conditions of the left child case and of the new root case, and taking the subtasks of the left case. The new case N can be reconstructed in a similar fashion.

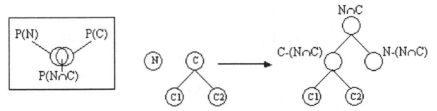

Fig. 2. P(N∩C) is a strict subset of P(N) and P(C)

The second situation occurs when P(N) is a strict subset of P(C). The pseudo-code for this situation is shown below:

IF P(N) is a strict subset of P(C) THEN {
      Add the following cases in CB:
          N∩C   = (:case T(C) P(N) (vT))
          C-N∩C = (:case vT P(C)-P(N), ST(C))
          N- N∩C = (:case vT, ¬(P(C)-P(N)) ST(N))
      Remove C from CB   }

As before vT is a new task name. If *cond* is a collection of conditions, ¬*cond* is the disjunction of the negation of each condition in *cond*. This situation is illustrated in Figure 3. The new root case has P(N) as conditions. The left child case has P(C)-P(N) as conditions and the right child case has ¬(P(C)-P(N)) as conditions. As before, the case C can be reconstructed by taking the task of the new root case, collecting the conditions of the left child case and of the new root case, and taking the subtasks of the left case.

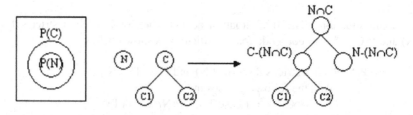

Fig. 3. P(N) is a strict subset of P(C)

The third situation occurs when P(C) is a strict subset of P(N). The pseudo-code for this situation is shown below:

```
IF P(C) is a strict subset of P(N) THEN {
        IF C is a leaf case THEN {
                Add the following cases in CB:
                        N∩C = (:case T(C)  P(C)  {vT})
                        C-(N∩C) = (:case vT ¬(P(N)-P(C))  ST(C))
                        N-(N∩C) = (:case vT  P(N)-P(C)  ST(N))
                Remove C from CB
        }ELSE {
                Let C1 and C2 be the child cases of C and ST(C) = {vT}
                Let  N' = (:case vT  P(N)-P(N∩C)  ST(N))
                IF |P(N') ∩ P(C1))| ≥ |P(N') ∩ P(C2))| THEN
                        Insert(N', C1)
                ELSE Insert(N', C2)   }}
```

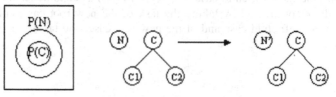

Fig. 4. P(C) is a strict subset of P(N)

As before, vT is a new task name. There are two possibilities. If C is a leaf case then we add N∩C as the new root, and C-(N∩C) and N-(N∩C) as the child cases (see Figure 4). The negation in C-(N∩C) ensures that either N or C are selected. The situation in which C is not a leaf is illustrated in Figure 5. The algorithm will call recursively insert with the case C1 or C2 that has more common conditions with N'.

Fig. 5. P(C) is a strict subset of P(N)

Table 3. Refinement of Case 1 with CBM-Gen+

CBM-Gen+ Root Case	CBM-Gen+ Child Case 1	CBM-Gen+ Child Case 2
Task: (deliver ?e ?d ?o) Condition: (deliverCompany ?fd) (equipment ?e) (depot ?d) (office ?o) Subtask: (vT ?fd ?e ?d ?o)	Task: (vT ?fd ?e ?d ?o) Condition: (¬(:different ?d ?d1) ∨ ¬(deliverCompany ?ud) ∨ ¬(depot ?d1) ∨ ¬(truck ?t)) Subtask: (contract ?fd ?e ?d ?o)	Task: (vT ?fd ?e ?d ?o) Condition: (deliverCompany ?ud) (depot ?d1) (truck ?t) (:different ?d ?d1) Subtask: (contract ?fd ?e ?d1 ?o) (internalDeliver ?t ?e ?d1 ?o)

4.3 Example

We will illustrate the CBM-Gen+ procedure with the generalized cases, Case 1 and Case 2, of Tables 1 and 2. Suppose that initially Case1 is added as a new root in the case base. Suppose next that Case2 is added. Under these circumstances, we will be in the second situation of the insert algorithm. The reason for this is that the Case1 task-matches Case 2 and the conditions of Case 1 are a subset of the conditions of Case 2. The resulting case base is illustrated in Table 3. The task and the conditions of the root case, CBM-Gen+ Root Case, are the same as those in the original Case 1. The subtask of the root case is a new task named vT. The child cases of the root case, CBM-Gen+ Child Case 1 and CBM-Gen+ Child Case 2, contain the conditions P(Case 2)-P(1Case 1) and ¬(P(Case 2)-P(Case 1)) respectively. Their subtasks contain the original subtasks from Case1 and Case2 respectively.

5 Soundness of CBM-Gen+

In Table 3, notice that whenever Child Case 2 is applicable then Child Case 1 is not applicable. Thus, if we give the same task and conditions as in the first column of Table 2, Child Case 2 will be applicable but Child Case 1 will not. This illustrates that CBM-Gen+ is sound relative to the captured solutions. In this section we are going to sketch proof demonstrating that this is always the case.

Theorem: Let $\{(:case_1\ h_1\ cond_1\ ST_1), (:case_2\ h_2\ cond_2\ ST_2), ..., (:case_n\ h_n\ cond_n\ ST_n)\}$ be a collection of concrete cases. If this collection is used to learn generalized cases using CBM-Gen+, then ST_i and only ST_i will be generated as a solution whenever $(h_i, cond_i)$ is given as a problem.

Proof: (sketch) Without loss of generality, we will assume that if we generalize the input cases, they task-match. If this is not the situation we can simply split the input cases into separate collections such that generalized cases in the same collection task-match. Suppose that, for some i and j, the conditions $cond_i$ is a subset of $cond_j$. That is, $cond_i = \{p_1, p_2, ...p_m\}$, $cond_j = \{p_1, p_2, ...p_m, p_{m+1}, ... p_{m+k}\}$. If $(h_j, cond_j)$ is given as a problem, then ST_j must be returned because the task and the conditions of the generalized case of $case_j$ match h_j and $cond_j$ respectively. The decomposition ST_i will not be returned because the conditions of the generalized case of $case_j$ do not match $cond_j$. The reason is that the generalization of $case_j$ with CBM-Gen+ will contain not only the generaliation of the conditions $cond_i$ but also the disjunction of the negation of the condtions in the Condition Difference Set of $case_j$ and $case_i$ (i.e., $(\neg p_{m+1} \vee \ldots \vee \neg p_{m+k})$), which cannot be satisfied in $cond_j$.

This proof is a sketch. As mentioned during the insertion algorithm, each generalized case may be split into several cases. Typically, for rebuilding the case, the path from a root case to a leaf case must be followed collecting all preconditions along the way. The details of this proof are too cumbersome and we omit these details for the sake of simplicity.

6   Empirical Evaluation

We performed an experimental evaluation of CBM-Gen+. The goal of these experiments was to see the impact of the overhead in CBM-Gen+ as a result of adding new cases when compared to Gen+.

6.1   Domains

We used the same domains that were created originally for demonstrating Gen+ (Mukkamalla & Muñoz-Avila, 2002). These domains are an HTN version of the Logistics domain (Veloso and Carbonell, 1993). In the Logistics domain, packages need to be moved between different places. Trucks and planes are used to transport objects. These experiments also used a subset of the UMTranslog (Erol et al, 1994). The subset of UMTranslog extends the logistics domain by defining objects that can be a combination of the various types such as *liquids* and *perishables*. For example, milk can be defined as a liquid and perishable object. The transportation means in the extension can be a combination of various types such as *tanker* and *refrigerated*. Each type is specially suited to transport one object type. For example a refrigerated tanker truck is suitable to transport milk.

6.2   Experimental Setup

A random problem generator feeds problems to the HTN planner SHOP that uses our subset of the UMTranslog domain to generate solution plans (Nau et al, 1991). In the previous work, Gen+ was integrated with SHOP to generate solutions that were acquired as cases automatically. In this experiment, we used CBM-Gen+ to generate a case base for SHOP, a correct case reuse HTN algorithm (Mukkamalla & Muñoz-Avila, 2002). SHOP was run with Gen+ and CBM-Gen+, and the same test set.

The UMTranslog knowledge domain used in the experiment contains 85 cases. A problem generator was used to generate the test set. The generator can randomly generate a problem with a certain number of packages. The more packages in a problem, the more complicated the problem will be, and the more time will be needed by SHOP to solve the problem. In our test set, the number of packages was incremented from 1 to 6. Five problems were randomly generated for each number of packages. Thus the test set contained a total of 30 problems.

The generator can formulate randomly a group of problems with the same number of packages once a time. But since SHOP will try to solve these problems separately, there is no difference whether we input a group of problems to SHOP or input the same problems one after another. That is the reason we generated the problems in the test set one by one.

6. 3   Results and Discussion

Figure 6 shows the results when the input problems are solvable. It plots the number of packages in the problems (x-axis) versus the average required time (y-axis). We observe that when there is a solution for a problem, SHOP with CBM-Gen+ will find the solution using less time than the one with Gen+ by a factor of at least 20%.

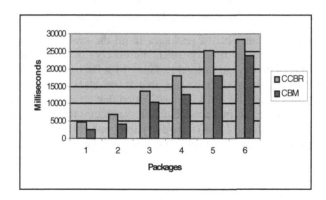

Fig. 6. Average Time for Solvable Problems

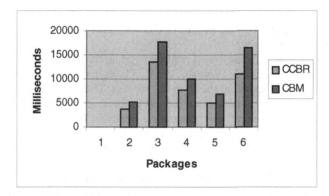

Fig. 7. Average Time for Unsolvable Problems

Figure 7 shows the results for the unsolvable problems. This figure plots the number of packages in the problems (x-axis) versus the average required time (y-axis). In this situation, SHOP with CBM-Gen+ needs at least 20% more time than with Gen+ to determine that there is no solution for the given problem.

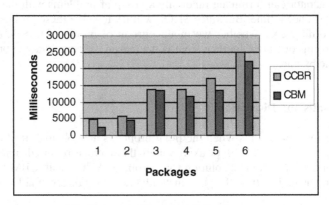

Fig. 8. Average Time for All Problems

Figure 8 shows the number of packages in all the problems of the whole test set versus the average required time (y-axis). We observe that the problem-solving time with CBM-Gen+ is in average faster then Gen+ by a factor of at least 10%.

This experiments shows that despite that more cases are generated with CBM-Gen+, still it runs faster than with Gen+. Notice that case bases generated with both procedures are represented in a plain list. We conjecture that if we add physical links for the corresponding logical links between parent and child cases that result from the CBM-Gen+ procedure, time for problem solving will be reduced even further.

7 Related Work

In the system CaMeL (Elgami et al, 2002), a process is shown that allows automatic elicitation compiled knowledge forms from cases. A similar kind of process developed in (Hanney, K., & Keane, 1996) for eliciting rules from cases. In our work, we propose to modify existing generalized cases rather than extracting rules/compiled knowledge from the cases.

Prodigy/Analogy is a case-based planning system that uses a similar criterion to the one discussed in Figure 2 (Veloso, 1994). Cases having common conditions are grouped together for speeding the retrieval process. There is a fundamental difference with our approach: the domains in Prodigy/Analogy are complete. That is, there is a complete domain theory for generating plans. The role of the cases in Prodigy/Analogy is to provide meta-level knowledge by indicating how to use the domain theory for solving problems efficiently. In contrast, cases in our approach contain knowledge about the domain otherwise unavailable. As a result, plans in Prodigy/Analogy are always correct and thus case revision, the main motivation for the CBM-Gen+ algorithm, is unnecessary. As a result, situations such as the ones illustrated in Figures 3 and 4 are not considered in Prodigy/Analogy.

In the PARIS (Bergmann & Wilke, 1995), a method to abstract and generalize concrete cases is also introduced. Then difference between the PARIS and GGS is that the first one requires a compelte domain theory and abstract operators, while the latter one captures cases without requiring any domain theory or operators.

8 Discussion and Final Remarks

CBM-Gen+ will find fewer solutions than Gen+ when conflicting cases are captured. In our examples, we constructed two case bases, one for Gen+ and the other one for CBM-Gen+, using the same problem-solution pairs as input (see Tables 1-3). We observed that in the CBM-Gen+ case base, Case 1 is not applicable in situations in which Case 2 is applicable. In contrast, Case 1 is always applicable when Case 2 is applicable in the Gen+ case base. The lost coverage in CBM-Gen+ relative to Gen+ corresponds to those solutions generated with conflicting cases. As we discussed, these are the solutions that may cause Gen+ not to be sound relative to the captured solutions. With the CBM-Gen+ algorithm, in the worst situation, if the number of cases in the original case base is N, then the newly generated case base will have 2N-1 cases. Thus, the case base generated by CBM-Gen+ will run into the utility problem only if the original case base runs into this problem.

Whether to use CBM-Gen+ or Gen+ is a trade-off issue. For those domains in which conflicting cases cause no loss of soundness, using Gen+ is adequate since more coverage will be gained. On the other hand, CBM-Gen+ is a better alternative for domains in which the soundness is lost as a result of conflicting cases. For example, in knowledge-based planning, user confidence, which is a crucial requirement, can be improved as a result of the gains in soundness.

As discussed in the section 2.2, not generalizing the cases will demand very large case bases. This is the reason why we use case generalization. One could argue that we may not need many concrete cases if a more powerful similarity procedure and/or adaptation procedure is used. However, trying to obtain such procedures will just shift the generalization problem that we are addressing in this paper from the case representation container to the similarity knowledge and/or the adaptation knowledge container.

We also show experiments demonstrating that CBM-Gen+ runs faster than Gen+ on the same domain and input cases with which Gen+ was originally evaluated. We conjecture that if we add physical links for the corresponding logical links between parent and child cases that result from the CBM-Gen+ procedure, the time for problem solving will be reduced even further.

References

Aha, D.W., and Breslow, L. Refining conversational case libraries. In: *Proceedings of the Fourth European Workshop on Case-Based Reasoning (EWCBR-98).* Providence, RI: Springer. 1998.

Bergmann, R. & Wilke, W. (1995). Building and refining abstract planning cases by change of representation language. *Journal of AI Research.* Volume 3, (pp. 53–118).

Erol, K., Nau, D., & Hendler, J. HTN planning: Complexity and expressivity. In: *Proceedings of the Twelfth National Conference on Artificial Intelligence* (pp. 123–1128). Seattle, WA: AAAI Press, 1994.

Ihrig, L. & Kambhampati, S. Design and implementation of a replay framework based on a partial order planner. In Weld, D., editor, In: Proceedings of AAAI-96. IOS Press, 1996.

Ilghami, O., Nau, D.S., Muñoz-Avila, H., & Aha, D.W. (2002) CaMeL: Learning Methods for HTN Planning. To appear in *Proccedings of the The Sixth International Conference on AI Planning & Scheduling (AIPS'02)*, 2002.

Hanney, K., & Keane, M. T. *Learning Adaptation Rules From a Case-base.* August. In I. Smyth & B. Faltings (Eds.), Advances in Case-Based Reasoning. Amsterdam: Springer Verlag, 1996.

Kitano, H. and Shimazu, H., The Experience-Saring Architecture: A Case Study in Corporate-Wide Case-Based Software Quality Control *Case-Based Reasoning,* AAAI/MIT Press, 1996

Leake, D.B, & Wilson, D. Categorizing Case-Base Maintenance: Dimensions and Directions. In: *Advances in Case-Based Reasoning: Proceedings of EWCBR-98,* Springer-Verlag, Berlin. 13 pages.

Mukammalla, S. & Muñoz-Avila, H. Case Acquisition in a Project Planning Environment. In proceedings of the Sixth European Conference on Case-Based Reasoning (ECCBR-02). Springer, 2002.

Muñoz-Avila, H., Aha, D.W., Nau D. S., Breslow, L.A., Weber, R., & Yamal, F. SiN: Integrating Case-based Reasoning with Task Decomposition. To appear in *Proceedings of the Seventeenth International Joint Conference on Artificial Intelligence (IJCAI-2001).* Seattle, WA: AAAI Press, 2001.

Muñoz-Avila, H., Gupta, K., Aha, D.W., Nau, D.S. Knowledge Based Project Planning. To appear in *Knowledge Management and Organizational Memories.* 2002.

Nau, D., Cao, Y., Lotem, A., & Muñoz-Avila, H. SHOP: Simple hierarchical ordered planner. *Proceedings of the Sixteenth International Joint Conference on Artificial Intelligence (IJCAI-99).* Stockholm: AAAI Press, 1999.

Racine, K., & Yang, Q. Maintaining Unstructured Case Bases, inCase-Based Reasoning Research and Development, In Leake D., B., and Plaza E., (Eds). Proceedings of the International Conference on Case Based Reasoning, Springer, 1997.

Smyth, B., and Keane, M.T., Remembering to forget: A competence-preserving case deletion policy for case-based reasoning systems. *In: Proceedings of the Fourthteen International Joint Conference on Artificial Intelligence (IJCAI-95).* AAAI Press, 1995.

Veloso, M. *Planning and learning by analogical reasoning.* Berlin: Springer-Verlag, 1994.

Watson, I., Applying Case-Based Reasoning: Techniques for Enterprise Systems. Morgan Kaufmann Publishers, 1997.

Maintaining Consistency in Project Planning Reuse

Ke Xu and Héctor Muñoz-Avila

Department of Computer Science and Engineering
19 Memorial Drive West
Lehigh University
Bethlehem, PA 18015, USA
{kex2,hem4}@lehigh.edu

Abstract. In this paper we describe an application of JTMS technology for maintaining consistency of pieces of a project plan obtained by case reuse. In our approach project plans are constructed interactively with the support of a CBR module. The user can either make edits to a project plan, or call a case reuse module for completing parts of it. As the user is making modifications on the project plan, conditions about applicability of the cases may change. We present an implementation of JTMS technology on a commercial tool for project planning to detect possible inconsistencies in reusing cases as a result of these changes.

1 Introduction

Project planning is a business process for successfully delivering one-of-a kind products and services under real-world time and resource constraints. One-of-a kind means that the product or service differs in some distinguishing way from similar products or services (Anderson *et al.*, 2000). Several software packages for project management are commercially available. These include *MS Project*™ (Microsoft) and *SureTrak*™ (Primavera Systems Inc). These interactive systems help users elicit a work-breakdown structure (WBS), which indicates how high-level tasks can be decomposed into simple work units. These packages also contain a suite of tools to control the scheduling of the tasks and the management of resources.

In previous work (Muñoz-Avila et al, 2002), a knowledge-layer for existing tools supporting project planning was proposed. This approach, called knowledge-based project planning (KBPP) advocates the use of CBR technology to reduce the time required to generate WBSs. The main motivation for using CBR in this context is that knowledge about how to formulate project plans is mostly episodic, even though general guidelines have been formulated to help with the project plan elicitation process (PMI, 1999; Liebowitz, 1999).

We implemented KBPP on top of *MS Project*™ (Mukkamalla & Muñoz-Avila, 2002). During trials with this implementation we identified a problem that is due to the interactive nature of the KBPP process. When the user requests the KBPP system to complete parts of a project plan, the system responds by determining applicable cases and reusing them. Case applicability is determined based on two factors: the task being completed and the available resources. The problem may arise if the user later changes the available resources and/or the task being solved. An inconsistency occurs when cases previously reused are no longer applicable. We refer to these

K.D. Ashley and D.G. Bridge (Eds.): ICCBR 2003, LNAI 2689, pp. 679–690, 2003.
© Springer-Verlag Berlin Heidelberg 2003

inconsistencies as *case reuse inconsistencies*. These can be seen as semantic inconsistencies and are complementary to the syntactical inconsistencies that most commercial project planning tools can detect. A typical syntactical inconsistency is the over allocation of resources.

To deal with case reuse inconsistencies, we implemented a new component, the Goal Graph System (GGS), in our KBPP system. GGS is based on the Redux architecture, which is a justification truth-maintenance system (JTMS) for dealing with planning contingencies (Petrie, 1992). GGS keeps track of all modifications being performed to the current project plan in a data structure called the Goal Graph (GG). These modifications include user edits and case reuse episodes. Edits that may result in case reuse inconsistencies will trigger a JTMS propagation process in GG. Any inconsistencies detected are displayed to the user in a non-intrusive manner, allowing him to decide at what point he wants to deal with them. GGS has two crucial properties: first, GGS can propagate the effects of user edits rapidly. Second, GGS has a sound JTMS propagation mechanism that ensures the detection of all inconsistent pieces of the project plan.

In this paper we are going to explain in detail the different kinds of case reuse inconsistencies that may occur in project planning, how these are detected by GGS and discuss details of the Goal Graph.

2   Related Work

Our studies are closely related to replanning. In replanning, a plan is modified when some changes occur in the problem situation making pieces of the original plan invalid (Petrie, 1991). In the CAPlan/CbC system, replanning techniques are used to implement an adaptation procedure (Muñoz-Avila et al, 1996). CAPlan/CbC also uses a variation of the Redux architecture. The main difference with our KBPP system is that CAPlan/CbC assumes that a complete domain theory is available indicating all possible planning steps. In KBPP such an assumption is not possible since most of the domain knowledge is episodic and no complete domain theory exists. A second major difference is that the KBPP must be as non-intrusive as possible. When inconsistencies are detected, they are pointed out in the interface but there is no automatic replanning process. A third difference is that our KBPP system uses a hierarchical task network (HTN) representation compared to the STRIPS plan representation in CAPlan. HTNs have been shown to be more expressive than STRIPS (Erol et al, 1994). As a result, our use of the Redux architecture had to be adjusted accordingly.

A complementary problem to WBS elicitation is the problem of resource allocation. Initial research has been done to address resource allocation in the context of project management (Srivastava, Kambhampati & Minh, 2000).

3   Knowledge-Based Project Planning

In (Muñoz-Avila et al, 2002), KBPP is proposed to assist planners in the development of WBS by using a hierarchical case decomposition algorithm. This approach is based on the observation that so-called Work-breakdown structures (WBS), as the main project planning representation paradigm is called, have a one-to-one correspondence with the hierarchical task networks (HTNs).

Figure 1 shows a snapshot of a work-breakdown structure in Microsoft Project. The task *Distribute-packages* is decomposed into four subtasks (first column): *Distribute package100 from Allentown to NYC, Distribute package200 from Bethlehem to Beijing, Distribute package300 from Easton to Newark*, and *Distribute package400 from LU to UIC*. Some tasks are called activities and represent concrete actions to be performed. For example, *drive truck47 to Allentown* is considered an activity. Tasks have assigned resources (second column). For example, the task *Drive truck47 to Allentown* has two assigned resources: truck47 and Allentown. Finally, tasks have ordering relations among them (third column). For example, the task *Drive truck47 to Allentown* is ordered before the task *Load truck47 with package100*. More generally, there are 3 kinds of relations in a WBS:

- Task - subtask relations
- Task-resource assignments
- Task- task ordering relations

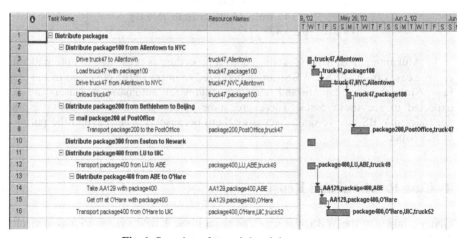

Fig. 1. Snapshot of a work-breakdown structure

Cases contain 1-level decompositions in the WBS and consist of the following elements:

- Task h to be decomposed.
- Subtasks ST decomposing h if the case is applicable
- Conditions C indicating when the case is applicable
- Ordering relations between the subtasks

Cases represent generalizations of WBSs. That is, cases contain variables instead of the original elements mentioned in the WBS. For example, in place of the element package100, cases use the variable ?package100 (variables are denoted with a question mark). Table 1 shows the case for the decomposition of the task *Distribute package100 from Allentown to NYC* from Figure 1. This task is represented as (distribute ?package100 from ?Allentown to ?NYC). The four subtasks are represented using the same convention. For example, the subtask *Drive truck47 to Allentown* in Figure 1 is represented in the case as (drive ?truck47 to ?Allentown). The four resources associated with the subtasks are used to define the conditions of the case. The conditions indicate the type of the resource. For example, the resource Allentown is used to define the condition (city ?Allentown).

Table 1. A generalized case for a WBS decomposition

Case 1
Task:
(distribute ?package100 from ?Allentown to ?NYC)
Condition:
(city ?Allentown)
(package ?package100)
(city ?NYC)
(truck ?truck47)
Subtask:
(Drive ?truck47 to ?Allentown)
(Load ?truck47 with ?package100)
(Drive ?truck47 from ?Allentown to ?NYC)
(Unload ?truck47)

In (Mukammalla & Muñoz-Avila, 2002) a procedure is presented to automatically capture cases from WBSs. WBSs are generalized to improve the coverage of the case base. Since the case capture and reuse procedures are automatic, end-users are not expected to see these cases. There are some issues regarding soundness of the generalized WBS but we omit discussing them because they are beyond the purpose of this paper.

4 Case Retrieval and Reuse

Given a task *t* in the WBS, the user can request the KBPP system to automatically decompose *t* into subtasks. The KBPP system selects applicable cases by performing the following two tests:

1. The task of the case matches t.
2. The conditions of the case match the existing resources.

For Example, the case in Table 1 is applicable to decompose the task *Distribute package300 from Easton to Newark* from Figure 1. First, the task of the case matches this task with the substitution {?package100 → package300, ?Allentown → Easton, ?NYC → Newark}. Second, the conditions match existing resources. A truck, truck33, is available. The list of available resources in MS Project can be viewed under the so-called Resources Sheet. For determining the applicability of a case, the KBPP system collects all available resources that are not used by any task whose scheduled times overlaps with the task being decomposed. In this way, the KBPP system ensures that only free resources will be assigned.

Once an applicable case is selected, its subtasks are used to decompose the target task. Figure 2 shows the resulting decomposition when the case in Table 1 is used to decompose the task *Distribute package300 from Easton to Newark*. Notice that in addition to the decomposition, the resources used to match the conditions of the case have been assigned. This assignment is necessary to maintain consistency in the usage of resources.

	ⓘ	Task Name	Resource Names	y 19, '02	May 26, '02	Jun 2, '02	Jun
				M T W T F S S	M T W T F S S	M T W T F S S	
1		⊟ Distribute packages					
2		⊟ Distribute package100 from Allentown to NYC					
3		Drive truck47 to Allentown	truck47,Allentown	truck47,Allentown			
4		Load truck47 with package100	truck47,package100	truck47,package100			
5		Drive truck47 from Allentown to NYC	truck47,NYC,Allentown		truck47,NYC,Allentown		
6		Unload truck47	truck47,package100		truck47,package100		
7		⊟ Distribute package200 from Bethlehem to Beijing					
8		⊟ mail package200 at PostOffice					
9		Transport package200 to the PostOffice	package200,PostOffice,truck47			package200,PostOffice,truck47	
10		⊟ Distribute package300 from Easton to Newark					
11		Drive truck33 to Easton	truck33,Easton	truck33,Easton			
12		Load truck33 with package300	truck33,package300	truck33,package300			
13		Drive truck33 from Easton to Newark	truck33,Newark,Easton	truck33,Newark,Easton			
14		Unload truck33	truck33,package300		truck33,package300		
15		⊟ Distribute package400 from LU to UIC					
16		Transport package400 from LU to ABE	package400,LU,ABE,truck49	package400,LU,ABE,truck49			
17		⊟ Distribute package400 from ABE to O'Hare					
18		Take AA129 with package400	AA129,package400,ABE	AA129,package400,ABE			
19		Get off at O'Hare with package400	AA129,package400,O'Hare	AA129,package400,O'Hare			
20		Transport package400 from O'Hare to UIC	package400,O'Hare,UIC,truck52		package400,O'Hare,UIC,truck52		

Fig. 2. Snapshot of the refined WBS after case reuse

5   Case Reuse Inconsistencies

A case reuse inconsistency occurs if a case C that was used to decompose a task t into subtasks in the WBS is no longer applicable as a result of edits made by the user in the project plan. This kind of semantic inconsistency is reflected by the fact that if t had been decomposed after the edits were made, C would not have been selected. Instead, either a different case would have been selected or no applicable case would have been found. We will now discuss the kinds of edits in a project plan that may result in case reuse inconsistencies.

5.1   Inconsistency by Change in a Resource

These inconsistencies occur when the user removes a resource or replaces a resource with another one of different type. Since the resources are used to determine the applicability of a case, these kind of changes will usually make the case non applicable with the current instantiation of the variables. An example of such an inconsistency occurs if the user removes truck33 from the subtasks of the task

Distribute package300 from Easton to Newark from Figure 2. In this situation, the condition (truck ?truck47) of the case in Table 1 is no longer valid. Thus, the decomposition of the tasks into the subtasks is invalid. Another example of an inconsistency occurs if the user replaces the recourse truck33 with truck10 in the activity *Load truck33 with package300*. The inconsistency occurs because all dependent tasks using truck33 need to be changed as well.

5.2   Inconsistency by Change in a Task

These inconsistencies occur when the user removes or renames a task. Since the task is used to determine the applicability of the cases, the case will be no longer applicable. For example, if the task *Distribute package300 from Easton to Newark* from Figure 2 is renamed as *Distribute package300 from Easton to Reading*, then the decomposition is no longer valid.

5.3   Inconsistency by Change in an Ordering Link

These inconsistencies occur when the ordering between tasks is removed. Since the applicability of a case is made based on the free resources that are available at a certain point of time, removing an ordering link may cause some conditions not to be satisfied. In Figure 2, assume that the decomposition of the task *mail package200 at post office* into the task *Transport package200 to the PostOffice* was performed by case reuse. If the ordering link from the task *Unload truck47* to the task *Transport package200 to the PostOffice* is removed, the case may not be applicable. The reason for this is that truck47 is used by both tasks and eliminating the ordering link will make both tasks be performed at the same time, while the resource can only be assigned to one of them.

The reader who is familiar with tools such as MS Project may recognize that MS Project will detect this kind of conflict. This syntactic inconsistency takes place because the resource can only be used at most once during any period of time. Thus, we have a situation in which a syntactic and a semantic inconsistency take place at the same time and for the same reason. The user has several alternatives to solve these inconsistencies. Solving the semantic inconsistency will ensure that the syntactic inconsistency is also solved. However, the opposite is not necessarily true. If the user decides to remove the resource truck47 from the task *Unload truck47*, the syntactic inconsistency will be solved but the semantic inconsistency still remains since the case is inapplicable.

6 The Goal Graph System

We have seen how edits in a project plan may result in case reuse inconsistencies. The simple examples of case reuse inconsistencies discussed previously show only one task decomposition being affected. However, edits may have a domino effect in which several pieces of the plan will become inconsistent. The Goal Graph System was created for two reasons: first, we wanted a mechanism to propagate the effects of user edits rapidly. Second, we wanted a sound mechanism to ensure detection of all inconsistent pieces.

At the core of the Goal Graph System is the Goal Graph (GG), which is based on the Redux architecture. Redux combines the theory of justification-based truth maintenance system (JTMS) and constrained decision revision (CDR) (Petrie, 1992). In a truth maintenance system (TMS), assertions (called nodes) are connected via a tree-like network of dependencies. The combination of JTMS and CDR provides the ability to performed dependency-directed backtracking, which is adopted in GG to propagate changes.

6.1   Justification Truth Maintenance Systems

In JTMS, each assertion is associated with a justification (Doyle, 1986). A justification consists of two parts: an IN-list and an OUT-list. Both IN-list and OUT-list of a justification are sets of assertions. The assertions in the IN-list are connected to the justification by "+" links, while those in OUT-list are linked by "-" links. The validation of an assertion is supported by the justification that it is associated with, i.e., an assertion is believed when it has a valid justification. A justification is valid if every assertion in its IN-list is labeled "IN" and every assertion in its OUT-list is labeled "OUT". If the IN- and OUT-lists of a justification are empty, it is called a *premise justification*, which is always valid. A believable assertion in JTMS is labeled "IN", and an assertion that cannot be believed is labeled "OUT". To label each assertion, 2 criteria about the dependency network structure need to be met: *consistency* and *well-foundness*. Consistency means that every node labeled IN is supported by at least one valid justification and all other nodes are labeled OUT. Well-foundness means that if the support for an assertion only depends on an unbroken chain of positive links ("+" links) linking back to itself, then the assertion must be labeled OUT.

In a consistent JTMS, each node is labeled either IN or OUT. A node is labeled IN when it has a valid justification, i.e., the assertions in the IN-list of the justification are all labeled IN, and the assertions in the OUT-list of the justification are all labeled OUT. A node is labeled OUT if either it has an invalid justification (which means that either some assertions in the IN-list are labeled OUT, or some in the OUT-list are labeled IN, or both situations occur), or it has no associated justification that supports it.

6.2   The Goal Graph

The goal graph represents relations between goals, operators and decisions. A goal is decomposed into subgoals by applying an operator. The applied operator is called a decision. The assignments represent conditions for applying the operator. Figure 3 shows the relationship between a decomposed goal, its subgoals, the operator list, the decision, and the assignments.

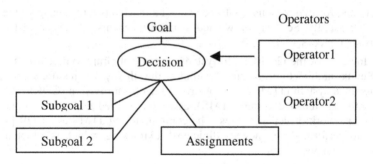

Fig. 3. A decision in the goal graph

Figure 4 shows a sketch of the goal graph. The first goal list from the top represents the main goals. A goal may have several decisions, one for each possible operator that can be chosen to achieve the goal. In GG, decisions decompose goals into the subgoals. A decision contains a goal list, storing all the subgoals of the goal. Assignments needed for applying the decision to the goal are collected in an assignment list, which is also contained in the decision.

A JTMS mechanism is built on GG. A decision is valid if all the assignments in its assignment list are valid, and all the subgoals in its goal list are valid. Valid decisions are labeled "IN". For a goal, all the decisions in its decision list labeled "IN" are applicable, which means the goal can be decomposed by those valid decisions.

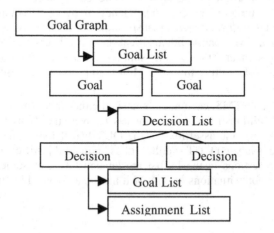

Fig. 4. Sketch of a goal graph

If for some reason, the validity of some assignments of a valid decision changes, then the decision may become invalid. GG incorporates a JTMS mechanism, so that the changes can be automatically propagated.

6.3   The Goal Graph in KBPP

For applying the Goal Graph System into KBPP, we mapped the elements of our KBPP approach into Goal Graphs. Since tasks are decomposed into subtasks, tasks were mapped into goals. A task may be associated with some resources. These resources are mapped as assignments in GG. Ordering relationships between tasks are also mapped into assignments.

Table 2. Map of KBPP elements into GG

KBPP	Goal Graph
Task	Goal
Subtask	Subgoal
Task-Resource assignment	Assignment
Ordering link	Assignment
System-made decompositions	Operator
User-made decompositions	Operator

One of the most challenging aspects of our work was to cope with the interleaving of user-made task decompositions and system-made decompositions (i.e., case reuse). We decided to map both kinds of decompositions as operators since they decomposed goals into subgoals. Decisions are labeled as user-made or system-made depending on the situation. The reason for this is that only system-made decompositions can be determined to be semantically inconsistent. Thus, GGS needs to know whether a decision is user-made or system-made during the JTMS propagation procedure.

In summary, the mapping of KBPP into GG results in the following dependencies:

- Subtasks depend on their parent tasks
- Subtasks depend on the decision (user-made, system-made) introducing them
- Decisions depend on the task they accomplish
- Task-resource assignments and ordering links depend on the decision that added them

These dependencies determine the next elements that are accessed in the JTMS propagation process.

6.4   Implementation and Example

We implemented the Goal Graph System in java and established a communication module between GGS and Microsoft Project (called MSP from now on). When the user or the system makes some changes to the project plan, such as adding or deleting a task or reusing a case, GG is updated. Figure 5 shows the decision representing the decomposition of the task *Distribute package300 from Easton to Newark* depicted in Figure 2. Notice that the decision has been labeled system-made because the case in Table 1 was reused to obtain this decomposition.

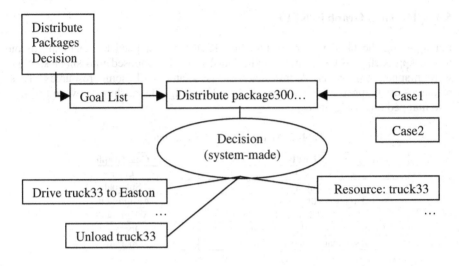

Fig. 5. Representation of a task decomposition in GG

	ⓘ	Task Name	Resource Names	y 19, '02	May 26, '02	Jun 2, '02	Jur
				M T W T F S S	M T W T F S S	M T W T F S S	S
1		⊟ **Distribute packages**					
2		⊟ **Distribute package100 from Allentown to NYC**					
3		Drive truck47 to Allentown	truck47,Allentown	▓truck47,Allentown			
4		Load truck47 with package100	truck47,package100	▓truck47,package100			
5		Drive truck47 from Allentown to NYC	truck47,NYC,Allentown	▓truck47,NYC,Allentown			
6		Unload truck47	truck47,package100	▓truck47,package100			
7		⊟ **Distribute package200 from Bethlehem to Beijing**					
8		⊟ **mail package200 at PostOffice**					
9		Transport package200 to the PostOffice	package200,PostOffice,truck47			▓package200,PostOffice,truck47	
10	⟡	⊟ **Distribute package300 from Easton to Newark**					
11	⟡	Drive truck33 to Easton	Easton	▓Easton			
12	⟡	⟡ Notes: 'OUT' ·······0	package300	▓package300			
13	⟡	Newark	Newark,Easton	▓Newark,Easton			
14	⟡	Unload truck33	package300	▓package300			
15		⊟ **Distribute package400 from LU to UIC**					
16		Transport package400 from LU to ABE	package400,LU,ABE,truck49	▓package400,LU,ABE,truck49			
17		⊟ **Distribute package400 from ABE to O'Hare**					
18		Take AA129 with package400	AA129,package400,ABE	▓AA129,package400,ABE			
19		Get off at O'Hare with package400	AA129,package400,O'Hare	▓AA129,package400,O'Hare			
20		Transport package400 from O'Hare to UIC	package400,O'Hare,UIC,truck52		▓package400,O'Hare,UIC,truck52		

Fig. 6. Snapshot of a case reuse inconsistency. The icons denote affected tasks

Coming back to the example about inconsistencies by changing resource, if the resource truck33 is no longer available (e.g., the user deletes it), this will cause the decision to become invalid. In turn the subtasks (e.g., Unload truck33) will become invalid. Any subtasks of these subtasks will become invalid as well. In addition, the goal *Distribute package300 from Easton to Newark* will become invalid (However its parent task, *distribute-packages*, will not become invalid since the other 3 children are still valid). GG allows a systematic propagation of these changes by following the dependencies between the plan elements.

Once inconsistencies are detected by GG, a special icon is displayed in front of the affected tasks (Figure 6). This icon notifies the user about the inconsistency in an unobtrusive manner. Since the JTMS propagation is done after each edit, inconsistencies will be marked immediately after the infringing edit is made.

7 Conclusions and Future Work

Knowledge-based project planning is a promising application field of CBR technology. The knowledge in KBPP is mostly episodic and represented in a formalism that facilitates its automatic case capture and reuse. Early trials with an implementation of KBPP on top of a commercial tool made evident a consistency problem that is due to the interactive nature of the KBPP process. The problem arises when pieces of a project plan obtained with case reuse become invalid because of user edits. We presented a complete catalog of edits that may result in case reuse inconsistencies. These kinds of semantic inconsistencies are complementary to syntactical inconsistencies that most commercial project planning tools can detect. In this paper we presented GGS, the component of our KBPP system that was developed to addresses this problem. GGS maintains a Goal Graph representing dependencies between the pieces of a project plan. The Goal Graph offers a natural representation for project plans and facilitates the detection of case reuse inconsistencies. When edits are made to the project plan, a JTMS propagation procedure detects inconsistencies. These inconsistencies are then displayed to the user in a non intrusive manner.

In future work we plan to extend GGS to be able to automatically suggest repairs to the case reuse inconsistencies. In addition we are planning to deploy our KBPP system in an adequate environment to evaluate its impact in an organization (Davenport & Prusak, 1997).

References

1. Anderson, V.; Bradshaw, D.; Brandon, M.; Coleman, E.; Cowan, J.; Edwards, K.; Henderson, B.; Hodge, L.; & Rundles, S. (2000). Standards and Methodology of IT Project Managment. *Technical Report.* Office of Information Technology. Georgia Institute of Technology.
2. Davenport, T; & Prusak, L. (1997). *Working Knowledge, How Organizations Manage What They Know.* Harvard Business School Publishing.
3. Erol, K; Hendler, J; & Nau D.S. (1994). HTN Planning: Complexity and Expressivity. In *Proceedings of the National Conference on Artificial Intelligence (AAAI-94).* AAAI Press.
4. Liebowitz, J. (1999). *Knowledge Management Handbook,* CRC Press, Boca Raton, FL.
5. Mukammalla, S. & Muñoz-Avila, H. Case Acquisition in a Project Planning Environment. In *Proceedings of the Sixth European Conference on Case-Based Reasoning* (ECCBR-02). Springer, 2002.
6. Muñoz-Avila, H. & Weberskirch F.: Planning for Manufacturing Workpieces by Storing, Indexing and Replaying Planning Decisions. In *Proceedings 3rd International Conference on AI Planning Systems* (AIPS-96), AAAI-Press, 1996.
7. Muñoz-Avila, H., Gupta, K., Aha, D.W., Nau, D.S. Knowledge Based Project Planning. In *Knowledge Management and Organizational Memories.* 2002.

8. Petrie, C. (1991). *Planning and Replanning with Reason Maintenance*. PhD thesis, University of Texas at Austin, Computer Science Dept.
9. Petrie, C. (1992). Constrained decision revision. In *Proceedings of AAAI-92*. AAAI Press.
10. Project Management Institute (PMI). (1999). PMI's A Guide to the Project Management Body of Knowledge (PMBOK® Guide). *Technical Report*. Release No.: PMI 70-029-99. Project Management Institute.
11. Srivastava, S.; Kambhampati, R.; Minh, B. (2001). Planning the Project Management Way: Efficient Planning by Effective Integration of Causal and Resource Reasoning in RealPlan. ASU CSE *Technical Report*.

Case Mining from Large Databases

Qiang Yang and Hong Cheng

Department of Computer Science, Hong Kong University of Science and Technology,
Clearwater Bay, Kowloon Hong Kong
{qyang, csch}@cs.ust.hk
http://www.cs.ust.hk/~qyang

Abstract. This paper presents an approach of case mining to automatically discover case bases from large datasets in order to improve both the speed and the quality of case based reasoning. Case mining constructs a case base from a large raw dataset with an objective to improve the case-base reasoning systems' efficiency and quality. Our approach starts from a raw database of objects with class attributes together with a historical database of past action sequences on these objects. The object databases can be customer records and the historical action logs can be the technical advises given to the customers to solve their problems. Our goal is to discover effective and highly representative problem descriptions associated with solution plans that accomplish their tasks. To maintain efficiency of computation, data mining methods are employed in the process of composing the case base. We motivate the application of the case mining model using a financial application example, and demonstrate the effectiveness of the model using both real and simulated datasets.

1 Introduction

To motivate the case mining problem, consider a financial application example. Suppose that a certain ABC Bank is interested in initiating a marketing campaign to encourage its customers to sign up for a new loan program. Suppose that we are given two datasets on (1) customer information and (2) past marketing action logs on customers in (1) and the final outcomes in loan-signup results. Tables 1 and 2 show an example of a customer database table together with some examples of past marketing actions on customers. Suppose that we are interested in building a campaign plan for a new customer Steve. Based on the past campaign actions for people like Steve, there are many candidate actions that one can suggestion. For example, we can use two of the past cases for John and Mary. If we follow the plan for John, we can first give him a personal phone call and then send him a gift. Alternatively, we can decrease the mortgage rate for Steve, followed by offering a new Credit card. The latter plan follows that of Mary's success. In either situation, the ABC bank might have a relatively high chance of converting Steve from a reluctant customer to a willing one.

K.D. Ashley and D.G. Bridge (Eds.): ICCBR 2003, LNAI 2689, pp. 691–702, 2003.
© Springer-Verlag Berlin Heidelberg 2003

The above problem can be formulated as a case-based reasoning problem, where the key issue is to find a good role model for customers such as Steve, and apply case retrieval and adaptation techniques [9,10] to find low-cost plans for these customers on a case-by-case basis. Our approach is to first identify typical problem descriptions as potential role models from the customer database (Table 1). Then for each typical problem, a cost-effective plan is found to be associated with each negative-class role model (Table 2); they are stored in a case-base as a plan. Then, for each new problem, we find a similar problem description and adapt its plan in the case base.

Table 1. An example of customer database. The last attribute is the class attribute.

Customer	Salary	Cars	Mortgage	Loan
John	80K	3	None	Y
Mary	40K	1	300K	N
...	...	...	...	...
Steve	40K	1	None	N

Table 2. Action-log database example containing marketing actions and outcomes

Advisee	Action1	State1	Action2	State2
John	Phone call	Feature-values for John	Send gift	Feature-values for John
Mary	Lower mortgage	Feature-values for Mary	Credit card	Feature-values for Mary

In this paper, we focus on how to find the case base from a given database efficiently. A challenging issue facing the construction of the case base is the large size of the database and large amount of data. To solve the scale-up problem, we exploit data mining techniques, including clustering and association rule mining algorithms [2, 5, 8, 14]. Cluster center objects, also known as the medoids, are obtained from the customer database to produce the basis for cases from customers belonging to both the negative class (problem descriptions for new problems) and the positive class (where Class=Yes in the final results table). Association-rule mining is applied to the action-log database to produce typical plans to be associated with the problem-objective pairs. The resultant case base is then used for problem solving for new customers. Because we extract high-quality cases from large databases using data mining techniques, we call this method *case mining*. Empirical results are obtained to demonstrate that the case-mining algorithms are scalable and achieve a balance between quality and efficiency.

2 Related Work

Case mining is closely related to case-base maintenance, whereby the case base structure, index and knowledge representation are updated to improve problem-solving performance. The most recent special issue of *Computational Intelligence Journal* on case-based maintenance [6] highlighted this interest and progress. Smyth and Keane [15], who defined case-base competences based on how cases in an existing case base are related to each other, addressed the maintenance issue by proposing a deletion-based algorithm. Their maintenance policy is aimed at removing as much redundancy form a case base as possible by reducing the overlap between cases or groups of cases. Subsequently, Smyth and McKenna [22] and Yang and Zhu [16] explored how other policies can be applied to case-based maintenance. Leake, Kingly and Wilson [10, 11, 17] analyzed the case-base maintenance problems and cast them into a general framework of *revising* the content and structure of an existing case base.

Aamodt et. al [1] presented learning algorithms for similarity functions used in case retrieval. In our formulation, case mining is targeted for large, un-indexed raw databases rather than an existing case base. The indexing problems have been an issue of intensive study in the past, including work in [4, 19, 20]. The indexing literature assumes that there is already a case base in existence, whereas in this paper we explore how to find the case base from historical databases. Patterson et. Al [21] discussed how to apply the K-means algorithm for case-base maintenance.

The work is also related to case-based planning [9, 18], which derives a new plan based on plans stored in case bases. However, case-base planning has mainly focused on case adaptation; instead, we focus on how to exploit the distribution of massive data to obtain statistically well-balanced case bases.

3 Mining Problem Descriptions

Our algorithm is divided into two phases. In phase one, we take the customer database and find a set of typical cases by applying clustering algorithm to it. The result is a set of positive-class and negative-class objects. In order to find the typical cases, we apply two different algorithms including a clustering algorithm and an SVM-based algorithm. In phase two, we find a plan for each negative-class role model to form a potential case. Care is taken in the search process to find only high-utility plans.

We wish to find K typical cases to populate the case base, where the parameter K is user defined; later we discuss another method (SVM) which does not require K to be specified. These cases should be highly representative of the distribution of the customer information in the original customer database. They will serve as the initial states for our planner to work on in the next phase.

We consider all *negative* instances in the database as the training data for mining the problem descriptions of the case base. Our first method applies the clustering algorithms to the negative instances, as described in more detail in Table 3. The training database consists of the negative instances of the original database.

Table 3. Algorithm *Centroids-CBMine* (database DB, int K)

Steps	Begin
	casebase= emptyset;
1	
2	DB = *RemoveIrrelevantAttributes*(DB);
3	Separate the DB into DB+ and DB−;
4	Clusters+ = *ApplyKMeans*(*DB−, K*);
5	**for each** *cluster* in Clusters+, **do**
6	C = *findCentroid*(cluster);
7	*Insert*(C, *casebase*);
8	**end for;**
9	Return *casebase*;
	End

In the algorithm *Centroids-CBMine* in Table 3, the input database DB is a raw database. There are two classes in this database, where the negative class corresponds to population of initial states for a marketing plan. Step 2 of the algorithm performs feature extraction by applying a feature filter to the database to remove all attributes that are considered low in information content. For example, if two attributes $A1$ and $A2$ in the database are highly correlated, then one of them can be removed. Similarly, if an attribute A has very low classification power for the data as can be computed using information theory, then it can be removed as well. In our implementation, we apply a C4.5 decision-tree learning algorithm to the database DB. After a decision tree is constructed, the attributes that are not contained in the tree are removed from the database; these are the irrelevant attributes.

Step 3 of the algorithm separates the training database into two partitions, a positive-class subset and a negative-class subset. Step 4 of the algorithm performs the K-means clustering on the negative-class sub-database [5]. K-means finds K locally optimal center objects by repeatedly applying the *EM* algorithm on a set of data. Other good clustering algorithms can also be used here in place of K-means. Step 6 of the algorithm finds centroids of the K clusters found in the previous step. These centroids are the bases of the case base constructed thus far, and are returned to the user. Finally, Step 9 returns the case base as the output.

The centroid-based case-mining method extracts cases from the negative-class cluster center objects and takes into account only the negative class distribution. By considering the distribution of both the positive and negative class clusters, we can sometimes do better. In general, it may be better to find the boundary between the two distributions, and to select cases from the dense areas on that boundary. This is the intuition behind the SVM-based case mining algorithm.

The key issue then is to identify the cases on the *boundary* between the positive and negative cases, and select those cases as the final ones for the problem descriptions. This has two advantages. First, by using the boundary objects as cases, from the past plans, we may determine that some objects are in fact not convertible to the positive class; these are the objects that are not similar to any of the problem descriptions in the case base. The case-based reasoning algorithm cannot solve these cases. Second, because the cases are the support vectors themselves, there is no need to specify the input parameter K as in the Centroids-CBMine algorithm; the parameter K is used to determine the number of clusters to be generated in K-means. This corresponds to parameter-less case mining, which is superior because in reality, the number of cases to be generated is typically unknown ahead of time. We observe that the cases along the boundary hyper-plane correspond to the support vectors found by an SVM classifier [7, 13]. These cases are the instances that are closest to the maximum margin hyper-plane in a hyperspace after an SVM system has discovered the classifier [7, 13].

By exploiting the above idea, we have a second problem-description mining algorithm called SVM-*CBMine( )*. In the first step, we perform SVM learning on the database to locate the support vectors. Then we find the support vectors and insert them into the case base. This algorithm is illustrated in Table 4.

Table 4. **Algorithm** *SVM-CBMine* (database *DB*, int *K*)

Steps	**Begin**
1	*casebase* = empty set;
2	*Vectors = SVM(DB)*;
3	**for each** *negative* support vector C- in *Vectors* **do**
4	Insert(C-, *casebase*);
5	**end for**
6	Return *casebase*;
	End

4 Mining the Plans

Having obtained the problem descriptions as "seeds" for the cases in the case base, we now consider the problem of finding solution plans to be associated with these descriptions with an aim to convert all negative-class cases to positive. Our algorithm is a state-space search algorithm that search an AND-OR tree. AND-OR trees are used to deal with the problem of uncertainty in planning. The plans produced are probabilistic in nature; they are aimed at succeeding in converting the customers to positive class with low cost and high success probability.

Given the *customer* table and the *action log* database, our first task is to formulate the problem as a planning problem. In particular, we wish to find a method to map the customer records in the customer table into states using a statistical classifier. This task in itself is not trivial because it maps a large attribute space into a more concise space. When there are missing values in the database, techniques of data cleaning [14] can be applied to fill in these values.

Next, the state-action sequences in the *action log* database will be used for obtaining action definitions in a state space, such that each action is represented as a probabilistic mapping from a state to a set of states. To make the representation more realistic, we will also consider the cost of executing each action.

To summarize, from the two tables we can obtain the following information:

• $f_s(r_i) = s_j$ maps a customer record r_i to a state s_j. This function is known as the customer-state mapping function;

• $p_c(s)$ is a probability function that returns the probability that state s is in a desirable class. We call this classifier the state-classification function;

• $p(s_k \mid s_i, a_j)$ returns the transition probability that, after executing an action a_j in state s_i, one ends up in state s_k.

Our planning algorithm divides the resulting plan in stages, where each stage consists of one action and a set of possible outcome states resulting from the action. In each stage the states can be different possible states as a result of the previous action, and the action in the stage must be a same, single action. In our formulation, we define a utility function of a plan to be $u(s)$ for a state s, where the function is defined as

$$u(s) = \max_a((\sum_{s \in S} P(s' \mid s,a) * u(s')) - cost(a))$$

where, at a leaf node t, the function u is defined as the utility of the node which is $P(+|t)$, and $cost(a)$ is the cost of the action a.

A major difficulty in solving the planning problem stems from the fact that there are potentially many states and many connections between states. This potentially large space can be reduced significantly by observing that the states and their connections are not all equal; some states and action sequences in this state-space are more significant than others because they are more frequently "traveled" by traces in the *action-log table*. This observation allows us to use an approach in which we exploit planning by abstraction.

In particular, significant state-action sequences in the state space can be discovered through a frequent string-mining algorithm [2]. We start by defining a minimum-support threshold for finding the frequent state-action sequences. Support represents the number of occurrences of a state-action sequence from the *action log database*. More formally, let *count(seq)* be the number of times sequence "seq" appears in the database for all customers. Then the support for sequence "seq" is defined as the frequency of the sequence. Then, a string-mining algorithm based on moving windows will mine the *action log database* to produce state-action subsequences whose support is no less than a user-defined minimum-support value. For connection purpose, we only retain substrings both beginning and ending with states, in the form of $< s_i, a_i, s_{i+1}, a_{i+1}, ..., s_n >$.

Once the frequent sequences are found, we piece together the segments of paths corresponding to the sequences to build an abstract AND-OR graph in which we will search for plans. If $< s_0, a_1, s_2 >$ and $< s_2, a_3, s_4 >$ are two segments found by the string-mining algorithm, then $< s_0, a_1, s_2, a_3, s_4 >$ is a new path in the AND-OR graph. Since each component of the AND-OR graph is guaranteed to be frequent, the AND-OR graph is a highly concise and representative state space.

Based on the above heuristic estimation methods, we can perform a best-first search in the space of plans until the termination condition is met. The termination conditions are determined by the probability or the length constraints in the problem domain. For the initial state s, if the expected value $E(+|s)$ exceeds a predefined threshold *Success_Threshold*, i.e. the probability constraint, we consider the plan to be good enough and the search process terminates. Otherwise, one more action is attached to this plan and the new plans are inserted into the priority queue. $E(+|s_i)$ is the expected state-classification probability estimating how "effective" a plan is at transferring customers from state s_i. Its calculation can be defined in the following recursive way:

$$E(+|s_i) = \sum p(s_k|s_i, a_j) * E(+|s_k) ; \text{ if } s_i \text{ is a non-terminal state; or}$$

$$E(+|s_i) = P(+|s_i) \text{ if } s_i \text{ is a terminal state.}$$

We also define a parameter *Max_Step* that defines the maximum length of a plan, i.e. the length constraint. We will discard a candidate plan, which is longer than the *Max_Step* but its $E(+|s_i)$ value is less than the *Success_Threshold*. We now consider optimality of the algorithm.

5   Efficiency Experiments

We run tests on both artificial data sets and realistic data sets to obtain the performance of the case mining algorithm. In this paper, we are primarily interested in the speed in which to obtain the case bases, especially when the database reaches a large size. Our other ongoing work is aimed at showing the quality of the mined case bases. Thus, our interest in these tests is how the CPU time changes with different experimental parameters. In the sequel, we separately test the problem description and the planning algorithms. The experiments are performed on an Intel PC with one Gigahertz CPU.

5.1   Testing Problem Description Mining

Our first test is aimed at establishing the efficiency of the problem-description mining algorithm, which determines whether the case mining framework can be scaled up or not. It uses an artificial dataset generated on a two-dimensional space (x, y), using a Gaussian distribution with different means and co-variance matrix for the positive (+) and the negative (–) classes (Figure 1). Our purpose is to demonstrate the effect of data distribution and model size on the switching-plan quality and efficiency. When the means of the two distributions are separated, we expect the class boundaries are easy to identify by the SVM-based method. As can be seen, the time it takes to build and execute the model increases with K, the number of cases in the case base (Figure 2). As the two distributions move close to each other such that there are no clear boundaries, the SVM-based method selects nearly all the negative examples as cases in the case base, resulting in a bloated case-base. Thus, its time expense is also very high (Figure 2). In this case, the *CenroidCaseMine* method is preferred.

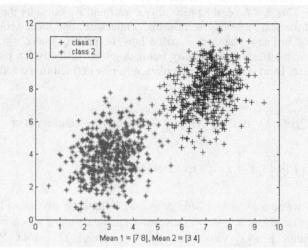

Fig. 1. Distribution of the class 1=positive (+) and class 2=negative (*) data.

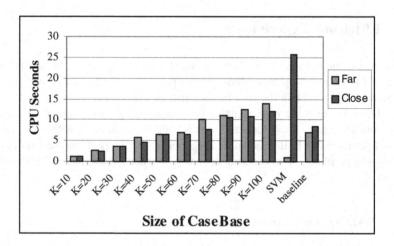

Fig. 2. Comparison of CPU time for different distributions between two distributions that are either "Far" apart or Closely mixed.

For large-scale tests, we performed an experiment using the IBM QUEST synthetic data generator (http://www.almaden.ibm.com/cs/quest/syndata.html). We generated the training dataset with 9 attributes, 50% positive class and 50% negative class. An excerpt of the database is shown in Table 5.

In the dataset, the Salary attribute is uniformly distributed from 20000 to 150000, the commission values are set so that if Salary >= 75000, Commission = 0; otherwise it is uniformly distributed from 10000 to 75000. The Age attribute is uniformly distributed from 20 to 80, the Education attribute is uniformly chosen from 0 to 4, and the Car attribute includes the make of the car, and is uniformly chosen from 1 to 20. The ZipCode attribute is uniformly chosen from 9 available zip codes, and the House Value attribute is uniformly distributed from $0.5*k*100000$ to $1.5*k*100000$, where $0 <= k <= 9$ and the House Value depends on the ZipCode. The YearsOwned attribute is uniformly distributed from 1 to 30, and the Loan attribute is uniformly distributed from 0 to 500000. Then we compared the running time to train a 50-case case base for the centroid-based method and CPU time for the SVM based method. Our results are shown in Table 6. It is clear from the table that with large data, the centroid-based method is able to scale up much better than the SVM based method.

Table 5. An excerpt from the synthetic dataset.

Salary	Commission	Age	Education	Car	...
65498	49400	61	1	2	...
24523	0	70	2	3	...
78848	0	20	2	6	...
74340	29463	45	0	3	...
42724	0	32	1	4	...

Table 6. CPU-time comparison of Centroid-based Method and SVM-based method.

$Log_{10}(N)$, N=Database size	CPU Time (Seconds)	
	Centroid-based	**SVM**
2	0.7	0.7
2.5	1.6	1.9
3	6.5	14.3
3.5	23.1	319.2
4	95.8	3,834.9
4.5	312.9	No result in 5 hrs
5	1,938.4	No result in 7 hrs

5.2 Testing Problem Description Mining

In this second test, we assume that we have obtained a case base of typical problem descriptions from the negative examples in the training set. Our task now is to find a plan for each negative description. These plans will serve as the cases that can be

adapted for new problems in the future. In this experiment, we test the efficiency of
the algorithm for a single problem description in a case.

We again used the IBM Synthetic Generator to generate a *Customer* dataset with
two classes and nine attributes. The positive class has 30,000 records representing
successful customers and negative has 70,000 representing unsuccessful ones. Those
70,000 negative records are treated as starting points for *Marketing-log* data generation. We evaluated the quality of the plans via simulation. From this input, we set out
to find a case base of marketing plans to convert customers to a successful class. This
testing process corresponds to the testing phase for a trained model in machine learning. In this simulation, if there is a plan suitable for converting a customer record, a
sequence of actions is carried out on that record. The plan will then change the customer record probabilistically. At the end, the classifier is used to decide whether the
changed record has turned into a successful one.

When *Success_Threshold* is low, many states are considered positive, and thus plans
can be easily and quickly found for most of the initial states in the graph. We can
observe this from Figure 3: planning time is low with low *Success_Threshold*. As the
Success_Threshold increases, so does the planning time. When *Success_Threshold* is
too high, no plan can be found for some initial states. The *Time* is much higher because the searching process doesn't terminate until all the plans expanded longer than
Max_Step. The search efficiency also depends on other parameters. *MinSupport* is
another important factor. When *MinSupport* is low, more plans in the action log qualify to be in the abstract state space, and thus search takes a longer time. We can also
see from Figure 4 that the CPU time drop is greater when the MinSupport increases
from one to 100. However, the planning time drop slows down between MinSupport
value of 100 and 1000. This suggest to us that we should use a support value of
around 100, since at this value we can achieve the balance of a relatively large number
of plans to be included in the search space and a low planning time.

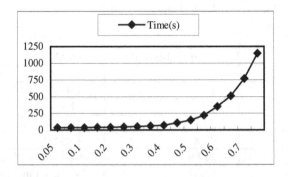

Fig. 3. CPU Time vs. Success_Threshold. MinSupport = 100

6   Conclusions and Future Work

In this paper, we presented a case mining algorithm for discovering a case base from a
large database. The central issue of the problem lies in the discovery of high-quality

case bases that balances the efficiency for extracting the case base, the cost of the adaptation plans and the probability of success. This is what we call the case-mining problem. For the data distribution where the two classes are clearly separated, the SVM-CBMine algorithm, which is an SVM-based method, should be used. When the data distributions are not separated well by a boundary, the cluster-centroids based method is recommended. Furthermore, we designed a planning system for finding probabilistic plans where the probability of success is taken into account. The efficiency of the case mining algorithm is validated against large databases. In the future, we will continue to explore quality of case mining results and the related problem of case adaptation in this framework.

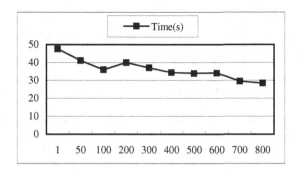

Fig. 4. CPU Time vs. *MinSupport*.   Success_Threshold=0.05.

References

[1] A. Aamodt, H. A. Sandtorv, O. M. Winnem: Combining Case Based Reasoning and Data Mining – A way of revealing and reusing RAMS experience. In Lydersen, Hansen, Sandtorv (eds.), *Safety and Reliability; Proceedings of ESREL '98*, Trondheim, June 16–19, 1998. Balkena, Rotterdam, 1998.

[2] R. Agrawal and R. Srikant. 1994. *Fast algorithm for mining association rules*. Proceedings of the Twentieth International Conference on Very Large Databases. pp 487–499

[3] C. L. Blake, C.J. Merz (1998). *UCI Repository of machine learning databases* Irvine, CA: University of California, Department of Information and Computer Science. http://www.ics.uci.edu/~mlearn/MLRepository.html

[4] A. Bonzano, P. Cunningham and B. Smyth *Using Introspective Learning to Improve Retrieval in CBR: A Case Study in Air Traffic Contol*, in Leake D., Plaza E. (eds.) `Case-Based Reasoning Research and Development, Second International Conference on Case-Based Reasoning ICCBR 1997, Springer Verlag, Berlin 1997.

[5] P. S. Bradley and U. M. Fayyad. *Refining initial points for **k-means** clustering*. In Proceedings of the Fifteenth International Conference on Machine Learning (ICML '98), pages 91–99, San Francisco, CA, 1998. Morgan Kaufmann.

[6] *Computational Intelligence Journal, Special Issue on Case-base Maintenance*. Blackwell Publishers, Boston MA UK. Vol. 17, No. 2, May 2001. Editors: D. Leake, B. Smyth, D. Wilson and Q. Yang.

[7] G. C. Cowley. *MATLAB Support Vector Machine Toolbox. v0.54B* University of East Anglia, School of Information Systems, Norwich, Norfolk, U.K. NR4 7TJ, 2000. http://theoval.sys.uea.ac.uk/~gcc/svm/toolbox

[8] P. Domingos and M. Richardson. Mining the Network Value of Customers. Proceedings of the Seventh ACM SIGKDD International Conference on Knowledge Discovery and Data Mining. August 2001. ACM. N.Y. N.Y. USA

[9] K. Hammond. Explaining and Repairing Plans that Fail. *Artificial Intelligence*, 45(1–2):173–228, 1990.

[10] D. Leake. *Case-based Reasoning -- Experiences*, Lessons and Future Directions. AAAI Press/ The MIT Press, 1996.

[11] D. Leake, Kinley, A., & Wilson, D. (1995). Learning to improve case adaptation by introspective reasoning and CBR. In Proceedings of First International Conference on Case-Based Reasoning. Sesimbra, Portugal.

[12] C. X. Ling and C. Li. *Data mining for direct marketing: Problems and solutions*. In Proceedings 4th International Conference on Knowledge Discovery in Databases (KDD-98), New York, 1998.

[13] J.C. Platt, *Fast training of support vector machines using sequential minimal optimization*, in Advances in Kernel Methods – Support Vector Learning, (Eds) B. Scholkopf, C. Burges, and A. J. Smola, MIT Press, Cambridge, Massachusetts, chapter 12, pp 185–208, 1999.

[14] J. Quinlan C4.5: *Programs for Machine Learning*. Morgan Kaufmann Publishers, Inc., San Mateo, CA.

[15] B. Smyth and M. T. Keane. *Remembering to forget: A competence--preserving deletion policy for case--based reasoning systems*. In Proceedings of the 14th International Joint Conference on Artificial Intelligence, pp 377–382, 1995

[16] Q. Yang and J. Zhu. A Case-addition Policy for Case-based Reasoning. *Computational Intelligence Journal*, Special Issue on Case-based Maintenance. Blackwell Publishers, Boston MA UK. Vol. 17, No. 2, May 2001. Pages 250–262.

[17] D. C. Wilson and D. B. Leake *Maintaining Case-based Reasoners: Dimensions and Directions*. Computational Intelligence Journal. Vol. 17, No. 2. May 2001

[18] M. Veloso. (1994). *Planning and learning by analogical reasoning*. Number 886 in Lecture Notes in Artificial Intelligence. Springer Verlag.

[19] D. Wettschereck and D.V. Aha. Weighting features. In Proceedings of the First International Conference on Case-Based Reasoning, ICCBR-95, pages 347–358, Lisbon, Portugal, 1995. Springer-Verlag.

[20] Zhong Zhang and Qiang Yang. Feature Weight Maintenance in Case Bases Using Introspective Learning. *Journal of Intelligent Information Systems*, Kluwer Academic Publishers, 16, Pages 95–116, 2001. The Netherlands.

[21] D. Patterson, N. Rooney, M. Galushka, S. S. Anand: Towards Dynamic Maintenance of Retrieval Knowledge in CBR. In Proceedings of the Fifteenth International Florida Artificial Intelligence Research Society Conference, 2002, Florida, USA. AAAI Press 2002, pages 126–131.

[22] B. Smyth, and E. McKenna, Building Compact Competent Case-Bases. In *Proceedings of the third International Conference on Case-based Reasoning*, Springer-Verlag, Munich, Germany, 1999, pp 329–342.

Case Base Maintenance for Improving Prediction Quality*

Farida Zehraoui, Rushed Kanawati, and Sylvie Salotti

LIPN-CNRS, UMR 7030, Université Paris 13, 99, Av Jean Baptiste Clément 93430
Villetaneuse, France.
{rushed.kanawati,sylvie.salotti,farida.zehraoui}@lipn.univ-paris13.fr

Abstract. We propose a new case base maintenance strategy which allows the improvement of the prediction quality of CBR system.
This strategy combines the learning of new selected cases, the reduction of the use of noise cases, and the removal of not useful cases. We describe in this paper the case based reasoning system, in which we have associated new measurements for the source cases. These measurements vary with the use of the cases to get target cases solutions.

Keywords. Case base maintenance, Large data bases, Case based reasoning, Prediction.

1 Introduction

Maintenance of case based reasoning (CBR) system is one of the central topics of research in case based reasoning area today. CBR system maintenance aims to implement policies in order to revise the various knowledge containers in the system for improving the future reasoning [4]. Maintenance becomes necessary for systems, which are conceived to be used over long periods and/or which will treat great volumes of data and cases. Among the various knowledge containers that can be aimed by maintenance, most of the current works is concentrated on case base maintenance (MBC), e.g., How to reduce the case base size, in order to increase the efficiency (concerning the time required for solving target case), without reducing system competence (concerning the problems which can be solved by the system)? Various strategies are proposed in the literature.
This paper reports the problem of predicting user behaviour in an e-commerce site. We are interested, particularly, in the prediction of the final goal { buy, not buy } of the site's user. To make this, we use a case based reasoning methodology, which is based on the experiences of users who have navigated in similar ways. The site users' web log file provides these experiences. We propose an approach where a case represents a precise experience in navigation (sub- navigation). For that, we distinguish the *case base*, which contains these sub-navigations, from the *navigation base*, which contains complete navigations [2]. The navigation base is very large. As several cases can be extracted from navigation, the case base is

---

* This research is supported by Numsight Consulting.

K.D. Ashley and D.G. Bridge (Eds.): ICCBR 2003, LNAI 2689, pp. 703–717, 2003.
© Springer-Verlag Berlin Heidelberg 2003

also likely to be very large. The search time for source cases can be expensive. In addition some cases extracted from the log files data can present noise for our system, decreasing the prediction quality.

Most of the case based maintenance approaches focuses on increasing the system efficiency, our strategy aims to improve the prediction quality and the system efficiency. It gives the priority to retrieve the source cases from the case base, instead of extracting them from the navigation base, which increases the system performance. The navigation base in our system allows increasing the case base coverage by adding selected cases. We have add to each case in the case base new measurements, which contribute to:

- *Prediction quality improvement:* this is done by filtering the cases in the retrieval phase and choosing the best solution in the adaptation phase. The case filtering is not time consuming, it consists in associating a variable similarity threshold for each case. This threshold depends on its use in the system. In the adaptation phase, a confidence is associated to each solution provided by source cases. This confidence is a function of the measurements.
- *Increasing performance:* this is done by reducing the case base.

To summarize, our strategy allows the learning of selected new cases, while reducing the use of noise cases and removing those, which are not useful.

The paper is organized as follows: Section 2 describes case base maintenance problem and presents some recent works. Section 3 details our prediction system and the case base maintenance strategy. In Section 4, we compare our case base maintenance approach to related work introduced in Section 2. Section 5 comments our experimental results. Finally, section 6 presents the current state of our research and future work.

2   Case Base Maintenance

The growing use of Case-Based Reasoning applications has brought with an increased awareness on the importance of the maintenance of CBR systems. In recent years, most of the works were focused on case base maintenance. A good definition of the case base maintenance can be found in [4]:

A case base maintenance implements policies for revising the organization or/and contents of the case base in order to facilitate future reasoning for a particular set of performance objectives.

This definition shows that case base maintenance is concerned with performance improvement, and is significantly affected by two factors: the competence and the efficiency.

The competence represents the number and the type of problems that the system can solve.

The efficiency concerns the time required for solving the target case.

However, increasing the competence does not mean increasing the number of cases, otherwise the system efficiency can be degraded rather than improved. Therefore, most of the works on case base maintenance are focused on reducing the case-base size, while preserving competence. Two different strategies have been developed in order to reduce the case base size:

The first one is the *selective deletion*. It deletes cases according to a case deletion policy. It can be made with techniques involving the utility [7] for each case or involving the overall competence of a case-base. Smyth and McKenna [10,11] have proposed several approaches for case deletion based on the coverage and reachability properties.

The coverage set of a case c is the set of cases that can be solved by c.

The reachability set of a case c is the set of cases that can be used to solve c.

One of these approaches uses the relative coverage of a case. This concept represents the contribution of a case in the case base coverage. Deleted cases are those which have the smallest relative coverage [11].

In [12] a new case deletion policy is proposed. It deals with the problem of limited memory space. Even if a CBR system admits only a limited number of stored cases in the memory, there will still exist a storage-space problem if some of these cases that vary in size. This policy aims at releasing the space in the case memory, which can help to preserve competence and establish a theoretical lower bound for competence.

The second strategy is the selective addition. It consists in constructing a new reduced case base from the current one.

Smyth and McKenna [11] have also proposed a hybrid solution for case base reducing which uses the condensed nearest neighbours (CNN) algorithm. It takes as entries the cases ordered following the relative coverage.

Similarly, Leake and Wilson [6] have proposed relative performance. Their strategy is based on selecting cases following this notion. Yang and Zhu [15] have constructed a reduced case base using the coverage notion. They define the case coverage as the neighbours of the case with some adaptation limits.

An other strategy, different from the previous ones, consists in keeping all the cases in the case base and improving the system efficiency by partitioning the case base. This reduce the search space in the retrieval phase.

Yang and Wu [13] have proposed an approach based on two ideas:

- The first one is clustering, where a large case base is decomposed into groups of closely related cases, which form, distributed case bases.
- The second idea is to allow a user to retrieve the distributed case bases by incrementally selecting the attributes that are information-rich.

All these works, aim to improve the system efficiency. We are interested in maintaining prediction system in complex domain where data contains noise. In our approach, the maintenance strategy increases the prediction quality and the efficiency. We will describe our strategy and compare it with existing ones in Section 4.

3   System Specification

In the CBR cycle, we want to use the case base as much as possible. The cases retrieve is done first in the case base. If the system does not provide any prediction, then cases are extracted from the sequence base. Several cases are retrieved and used to get the target case solution. If the cases used for resolution are extracted from the navigation base, then some of them are added to the case base.

3.1   General Description

For more clarity, we start by introducing some notations that are used later in the paper. A navigation q of a site user represents an ordered set of states.

A state $E_q^j = (v_i)$, $1 \leq i \leq n$ of the navigation q is characterized by values v_i $(1 \leq i \leq n)$ of n characteristics $c_i (1 \leq i \leq n)$ and by its position j in the navigation q. In our application, a state represents successive similar pages [1], and the characteristics represent the number of the pages in the state, the time, ...etc.

The presented problem, consists in predicting the value s_i of a property S of the states succeeding the current state of the navigation (this property can represent, for example, a characteristic of the following or the final state of the navigation. In our application it represents the final goal { buy, not buy } of the site's user). A target case represents the p last states (p is a system parameter) of the current navigation (figure 1).

Cases, called *source cases*, that are similar to the target case, are retrieved from the case base or extracted from the navigation base. A source case represents a part of navigation. It is composed of:

- *The problem part* which represents a part of the navigation with a fixed length p: it is a succession of p states.
- *The solution part* which represents the property value $s_i \in S$.

3.2   Case Base Maintenance Approach

Similarly to [2], a case extracted from the navigation base is called *a potential case* and a case contained in the case base is called *a concrete case*. Additional measurements are associated to concrete cases like in [2,8]. These measurements are used to improve the prediction quality and to reduce the case base size. We propose the new measurements that are presented below:

- *Positive contribution CP* represents the number of successful retrievals. It takes into account the number of cases, which provide the target, case solution.
- *Negative contribution CN* represents the number of unsuccessful retrievals. It also takes into account the number of cases, which provide the target case solution.
- *Case quality* represents the rate of the case success in solving target cases: $QC = \frac{CP}{CN+CP}$.

---

[1] This is done in order to reduce navigations length

Current navigation

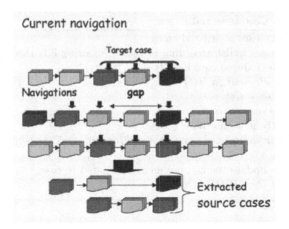

Fig. 1. Source case retrieve from the navigation base. The last 3 states of the current navigation represent the target case. Similar cases are extracted from the navigation base allowing the presence of gaps between two successive states.

- *Extent ET* determines a neighbourhood of the case, which contains the cases covered by this case. This neighbourhood can contain cases with different solutions. *ET* defines a variable similarity threshold for each source case $case_i$: $\alpha(case_i) = 1 - ET(case_i)$.

Initialisation and update of these measurements are made in the CBR cycle and are described in section 3.3.

Our maintenance strategy consists in:

- Learning some selected cases extracted from the navigation base (see Retain phase in §3.3).
- Reducing the use of noise cases, which deteriorate the system competence by decreasing their extent (ET). This leads to increase their similarity threshold.
- Reducing the case base size, off line [4]. The notion of coverage is used to construct a reduced case base. The coverage set of a case c is the set of cases which are similar to c and have the same solution as c.

A concrete case $case_i$ is considered as noise if its quality is bad ($QC(case_i) < d'$ where d' is a threshold defined in the system).

The case base size reduction consists in constructing, from the case base, a reduced case base (initially empty) by gradually adding cases (selective addition strategy). First, these cases are ordered by their decreasing extent. If two cases have the same extent, they are ordered by their decreasing quality, and then put in the reduced case base. A case c is not added to the reduced case base (not useful case) if c is covered by an other case c' in this base and if the neighbourhood of c is include in the neighbourhood of c'. Case base reduction is done following algorithm 3.1.

Algorithm 3.1 Case base reduction.

$list \leftarrow ()$//list is a set of ordered cases
Order the BC cases in list according to their decreasing ET, then QC
// Construct the reduced case base RBC
$RBC \leftarrow \{first\_element\_in\_list\}$
For all case $case_i \in list$
   For all case $case_j \in RBC$
   //NBC is the new case base
   If $[(1 - Similarity(case_i, case_j) + ET(case_i) < ET(case_j)) \wedge (sol(case_i) = sol(case_j))]$
        then update the measurement associated to $case_i$
     Else $NBC \leftarrow RBC \cup \{case_i\}$
     endIf
   endFor
endFor

3.3   CBR System Architecture and CBR Cycle Description

The system consists mainly of two modules (figure 2): the *naive engine* and *the intelligent engine*. A module called *controller* manages these two modules. When a new problem is presented to the system, the intelligent engine triggers the CBR cycle. In this cycle, the source cases are retrieved from the case base. If this module does not provide prediction, the naive engine is activated. This one triggers the CBR cycle. In this cycle, the source cases are extracted from the navigation base. Some extracted cases are added to the case base in the learning phase. The case base reduction is done regularly by the system.
CBR cycle phases are described bellow.

Retrieve phase: The system memory contains two principal parts:

– The navigation base that contains complete navigations.
– The case base that contains the extracted cases from navigations (concrete cases).

The search of source cases similar with the target case is done by retrieving the k first cases, for which the similarity with the target case exceeds a threshold, from the case base or by extracting them from the navigation base. The similarity measure is an aggregation of states similarities (the states' order in a case is taken into consideration). The case search is done first in the case base. The similarity threshold, in this case, is a function of the extent of each source case (algorithm 3.2). This threshold filters the retrieved cases.
If no prediction is provided using this base, then the search is done in the navigation base using a constant similarity threshold (α_0).

Reuse phase: After every retrieve phase, several source cases are retrieved. For each value s_i of S contained in retrieved source cases solutions, we associate

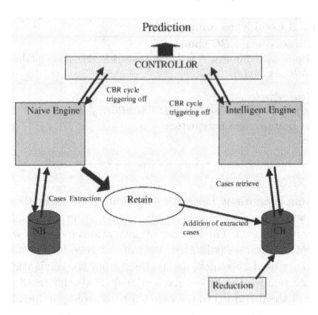

Fig. 2. CBR system architecture.

Algorithm 3.2 Cases retrieval from the case base.

For all $case_i \in BC$ //BC is the case base
//case base retrieve
    IF $Similarity(case_i, case_{target}) > 1 - ET(case_i)$ **then** $case_i$ is retrieved
    endIf
endFor

---

a confidence measurement. The confidence of a value s_i is a weighted average of the average similarity of all extracted cases with solution s_i and the proportion of these cases among all extracted cases. The average similarity $Similarity\_Av(s_i)$ associated to a value s_i of S is computed in a different way when retrieved cases are concrete (retrieved from the case base) or potential (extracted from the navigation base). In the average similarity computed from concrete cases, the quality of these cases is taken into consideration (algorithm 3.3). The value s_i with the greatest confidence is predicted. If several values of S have confidences close[2] to that of s_i, then the system can not perform the prediction.

Retain phase: In this phase, we perform two operations:

- Adding navigations to the navigation base.
- Adding cases to the case base.

---

[2] We have defined a threshold β. If the difference between two confidences don't exceed β, we say that they are close.

Algorithm 3.3 Confidence computation.

If retrieved cases $case_j \in BC$ **then**

    For all proposed value $s_i \in S$ // $QC(case_j)$ is the $case_j$ quality

$$Similarity\_Av(s_i) \quad = \quad \frac{1}{\sum_j QC(case_j)} \quad * \quad \sum_j (QC(case_j) \quad *$$

$Similarity(case_j, case_{target}))$

      $Conf(s_i) = A * percentage(s_i) + B * Similarity\_Av(s_i)$

      // A and B are system parameters.

    endFor

endIf

Using a simple heuristic performs the addition of navigations to the navigation base, which consists in adding every navigation for which the length is greater than or equal to p. The number of navigations increases with time. Since the memory of our system is limited, we can not keep all the navigations. Another heuristic is used to remove navigations from the navigation base (in our application, we remove the oldest navigations). Potential cases extracted from the navigation base are added to the case base. To avoid putting all the extracted cases at each prediction (this will produce a large case base), we have used an heuristic to select representative cases. It consists in:

- Clustering the extracted cases that have the same solution as the ones of the target case. We have used the similarity matrices algorithm [1], which uses only the similarity information between cases. This algorithm first transforms the similarity matrix to an equivalent matrix and then determines several clusters based on the rule "case c and case c' belong to the same cluster if and only if $similarity(c, c') \geq \alpha_0$", where α_0 is the similarity threshold defined previously.
- Selecting from each group a representative case: the case that minimizes the sum of the *distances* to the other cases of the same group.

These representative cases are added to the case base. This addition takes into account the similarities of selected cases to the target case and the diversity of these cases to each other [9].

Measurements initialisation: When a case is added to the case base, its measurements are initialised as follows:

$CN = 0$, $CP = \frac{1}{m}$, $QC = 1$ and $ET = 1 - \alpha_0$

where m is the number of selected representative cases and α_0 is the similarity threshold.

Measurements update: When the prediction is made by the case base, updates are performed for the retrieved concrete cases (algorithm 3.4).

- If the prediction is correct, then the CP of cases which have contributed to make the prediction increases.
- If the prediction is not correct, then the CN of cases which have contributed to make the prediction increases. If the QC of these cases is smaller than a certain threshold d', their ET decreases.

Algorithm 3.4 Case measurements update.

For all target case $case_i$
    If $sol(case_i)$ is made by BC **then**   //BC is the case base
    For all case $case_j$ extracted from BC
      If $valPredict = sol(case_j)$ **then**
      // $valPredict$ is the predicted value in S
          If $sol(case_j) = sol(case_i)$ **then**
            $CP(case_j) = CP(case_j) + \frac{1}{nb}$
            // nb is the number of extracted cases which have contributed
            to make prediction
         Else
            $CN(case_j) = CN(case_j) + \frac{1}{nb}$
            If $QC(case_i) < d'$ **then** $ET(case_i) \leftarrow ET(case_i) - pr(ET)$
            //d' is a system parameter and $pr(ET)$ is a function of ET
            endIf
          endIf
        endIf
      endFor
    endIf
endFor

Reduction phase: The case base reduction previously described (in algorithm 3.1) is applied to the system. This phase is triggered off-line. It is done periodically, after a certain number of predictions.

4 Discussion and Related Work

We have proposed a new case base maintenance strategy for CBR prediction system in an e-commerce site. The system memory consists of two bases:

- Navigation base that contains complete navigations.
- Case base that contains parts of navigations.

We have added measurements for performing the maintenance to the concrete cases. Conversely to the traditional CBR systems, the cases added to the case base are not target cases but potential cases extracted from the navigation base like in [2]. Moreover, several cases can be added to the case base during every CBR cycle.

First, we select cases added to the case base by constructing clusters in the set of extracted cases from the navigation base and by choosing a case from each cluster. The algorithm we use is the similarity matrix algorithm [1].

The notions of similarity and diversity of cases introduced in [9] are used in the retrieve phase. In our approach, we have used these notions in the retain phase in order to increase the case base coverage.

The maintenance measurements are updated at every CBR cycle. These measurements determine the relevance of a case according to its use for solving target cases:

- *The extent of a case* determines a neighbourhood of the case, which contains cases covered by this case. But this neighbourhood can contain cases with different solutions. The coverage set of a case is the set of the cases, which are in its neighbourhood and which have the same solution as this case.

- *The quality of a case* represents the rate of the case success to solve the target cases, which are presented to the system.

- *The positive and negative contributions* measure the frequency of the successful and unsuccessful use of the cases to solve target cases. This frequency takes into consideration the number of cases what take part in the resolution of each case.

The coverage defined by Smyth and Mckenna [10,11] consists in considering the coverage set of a case C as being the set of the neighbours of C (according to the defined similarity measurements) such as the solution of C can be adapted to solve these cases. In [15], the case coverage represents the neighbourhood of a case following the adaptation cost (set of cases for which the solution is closer to that of this case).

The case coverage, in our approach, is defined as in [10,11] except that the concept of adaptation is different. The cases, which really cover the target case, are those which have the same solution as the target case (we are interested in a classification problem).

Generally, in CBR systems, the problem-solution regularity is assumed. This regularity represents the relation between similarity measurements of problems and those of solutions [5]. In our approach, we suppose that the assumption of problem-solution regularity is satisfied on average i.e., that it is satisfied by the majority of the cases, which justifies the use of CBR, but this does not exclude the presence of noise cases. Consequently, any case similar to the target case is a potential candidate to belong to it reachability set (paragraph 2). For this, the adaptation phase consists in giving a solution to the new target case from a set of cases (not only one) by taking into consideration the similarities of these cases with the target case and their proportion. Moreover, the concepts of case extent and case quality allow to treat the problem of the noise. The concepts of positive and negative contributions can also enable us to remove the obsolete cases (that was not taken into account in our approach). The concepts related to the cost of adaptation cannot be used in our approach since we are interested in a classification problem.

The idea of tracking success and failures to determine which case to retain is proposed in [8]. But in their approach, the potentially dangerous cases (which fail in the adaptation) or useless cases (which are not retrieved for a long time) are directly deleted, while in our approach, noise cases' use is progressively reduced and not useful cases are deleted. The notions of success and failures defined in our approach are different from those defined in [8], where the success and failures concern the case adaptation (in a failure situation, the CBR system don't provide solution), while in our approach, the success and failures are related to the quality of the solution provided by the system. In a failure situation, the system predicts false solution (this is due to the presence of some noise cases). The representation of a case like parts of a navigation was proposed in the BROADWAY recommendation approach [2] which was applied to support users during their navigation on the web (the BROADWAY-V1 system [3]).

In our system, the ET measure is used to reduce the utilisation of noise cases without deleting them by increasing their similarity threshold. In BROADWAY-V1 system, the similarity threshold is constant for all cases, while in our approach, it is variable .

In the BROADWAY-V1 system, a maintenance strategy was proposed, the measurements, cited above, are associated to a concrete case:

- The number of successful retrievals of case
- The quality of case $= \frac{number\_successful\_retrievals}{number\_retrievals}$

These measurements, used in BROADWAY-V1, allow to improve prediction (use of case quality in reuse phase) and to reduce the case base.

In our approach, the positive contribution (CP) is close to the number of successful retrievals but in our measure, we take into account the number of cases which provide the target case solution (when several cases are used to get the target case solution, the CP of these cases are increased differently from when only one case provides the solution). The definition of the quality is similar but also takes into account the case contribution to target cases resolution. We have also proposed new measurements which are the negative contribution (CN) and the extent (ET).

In BROADWAY-V1 system, the case base reduction is limited to the removal of cases which are not used for a long time (obsolete cases). In our approach, we study the state of the case base and similarities existing between cases which are in this case base (coverage) and we use the QC and the ET of cases to do it.

Q. Yang and Al. [14] present an approach to apply case-based reasoning to Web navigation for next-page prediction. They have combined the data mining and the case based reasoning in order to mine the cases efficiently. They have developed techniques allowing different case bases to be combined in order to yield a overall case base with higher quality than each individual ones. They have use some case quality measures used in data mining:

- Support of case is defined as the percentage of strings in the web log in which the case successfully applies.
- Confidence of case is defined as the conditional probability that the solution part of the case falls in the target case solution part.

The support measure uses the notion of prediction success but it is different from our "CP" measure (the number of cases, which provide the target case solution is taken into consideration in CP). The confidence, in our work is provided by several cases and not associated to individual cases. QC and ET measures provide the case quality.

One important difference between the Yang et Al.work and this one is that this paper focuses on the effect of an innovative method for case-base maintenance in improving prediction quality end performance.

5   Experimental Results

We have performed several experiments on a log files of an e-commerce web site, where approximately 3000 navigations are registered every day. We have designed and implemented a CBR system in order to predict, as soon as possible, the final goal { buy, not buy } of a site's user. Using experiences of users, which have navigated in a similar way, does this. The navigations of the site's users are registered and stored in the navigation base. A source case describes a part of past navigation. A target case represents the succession of the p last states of ongoing navigation ($p = 3$). A state represents successive pages having certain common characteristics. The property S is the user goal. It takes two values: S = { buy, not buy }.

For space limitation, we show only the results related to the prediction quality improvement. The experiments consist in comparing the results of a prototype of the system using only the navigation base (labelled by "without CBM" in the figures showed below) with a prototypes for which we have applied our maintenance strategy (labelled by "with CBM" in the figures showed below). To compare the prediction quality of these two approaches, we have used the following metrics:

- *Recall:* represents the ratio of the number of correct predictions to the number of queries.
- *Precision:* represents the ratio of the number of correct predictions to the number of all predictions.
- *Prediction rate:* represents the ratio of the number of predictions to the number of queries.

In the experiments, the test base contains 10000 navigations where there is approximately 10% of buyers (navigations in which the users buy).

In figures {3, 4, 5}, we have computed the comparison metrics at each users' click in their navigations.

These figures show the results {recall, precision and prediction rate} improvement provided by the addition of the case base and the maintenance strategy in the CBR system. We note that the CBR system can't predict before 3 clicks of the user because $p = 3$.

Table1 shows the frequency of the use of the case base and the navigation base by the system in order to perform the prediction.

It shows the use frequency (use rate) of the case base for each user goal ("buy", "not buy"). We note that the case base is used more frequently than the navigation base.

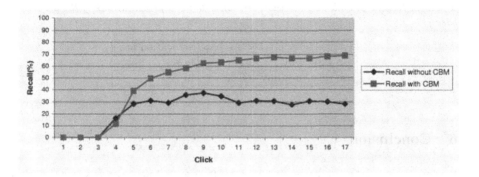

Fig. 3. Recall comparison.

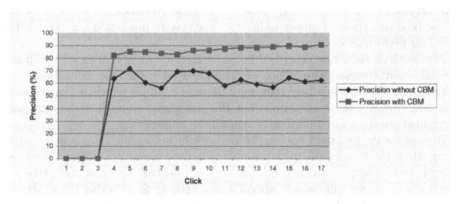

Fig. 4. Precision comparison.

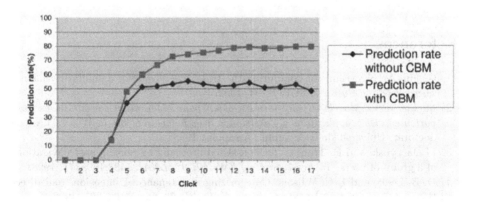

Fig. 5. Prediction rate comparison.

Table 1. *Results provided by the case base after the two presentations of the same test base*

	Case base	Navigation base
Use rate "buy"	62 %	38 %
Use rate "not buy"	60 %	40 %

6   Conclusion

We have proposed a maintenance strategy for a case based reasoning prediction system. This strategy allows to manage the system memory that contains the case base and the navigation base. The case based maintenance strategy is based on the selection of the cases to retain, the idea of tracking success and failures to determine which cases to retrieve and the selective addition strategy for the case base reduction. It allows to improve the system prediction quality and the system performance.

The case base reduction described in the system, does not guaranty a significant reduction of the case base. Thus, we are interested in the case indexation.

To reduce the sequence base size, we have used a simple heuristic that consists in removing the oldest sequences, but this don't guarantees that the sequences retained are the most representative of all the sequences.

To improve the proposed system, future work includes conceiving a new system , in which the case length (p) is variable (p is fixed in our system) and the cases are indexed using neural networks. Since the case base contains cases that are sub-sequences, we will use a temporal neural network for indexing them. We will propose also a heuristic in order to reduce the sequence base.

Acknowledgement. We would to thank S. Fabre, E. Janvier and M. Malek for their help in the realization of this work.

References

1. G. Fu. An algorithm for computing the transitive closure of a similarity matrix. *Fuzzy Sets and Systems*, 51:189–194, 1992.
2. M. Jaczynski. *Modèle et plate-forme à objets pour l'indexation par situations comportementales : application à l'assistance à la navigation sur le Web*. Thèse de doctorat, Universit de Nice-Sophia Antipolis, 1998.
3. M. Jaczynski and B. Trousse. *www* assisted browsing by reusing past navigations of a group of users. *In Proceedings of EWCBR'98, LNAI*, 1488:160–171, 1998.
4. D. B. Leake and D.C. Wilson. Categorizing maintenance: Dimensions and directions advances in case-based reasoning. *EWCBR-98*, pages 196–207, 1998.
5. D. B. Leake and D.C. Wilson. When experience is wrong: Examining cbr for changing tasks and environments. *Proceedings of the third International Conference on Case-Based Reasoning, ICCBR-99, Springer-Verlag*, 1999.

6. D. B. Leake and D.C. Wilson. Remembering why to remember: Performance-guided case-base maintenance. *Advances in Case-Based Reasoning: Proceeding of EWCBR-2K, Springer-Verlag*, 2000.

7. S. Minton. Qualitative results concerning the utility of explanation-based learning. *Artificial Intelligence*, 42:363–399, 1990.

8. L. Portinale, P. Torasso, and P. Tavano. Speed-up, quality and competence in multi-modal case-based reasoning. *ICCBR-99*, pages 303–317, 1999.

9. B. Smyth and P. McClave. Similarity vs. diversity. *In 3rd International Conference on Case-based Resoning ICCBR'01.*, pages 347–361, 2001.

10. B. Smyth and E. McKenna. Modelling the competence of case-bases. *Advances in Case-Based Reasoning, 4th European Workshop, EWCBR-98*, pages 208–220, 1998.

11. B. Smyth and E. McKenna. Building compact competent case-bases. *In Proceeding of the third International Conference on Case-Based Reasoning*, pages 329–342, 1999.

12. F. Tonidandel and M. Rillo. Releasing memory space through a case-deletion policy with a lower bound for residual competence. *ICCBR 2001, LNAI 2080*, pages 546–560, 2001.

13. Q. Yang and J. Wu. Keep it simple: A case-base maintenance policy based on clustering and information theory. *In Proceeding of Canadian AI Conference. Montreal, Canada*, 2000.

14. Q. Yang, H. H. Zhang, and I. T. Li. Mining high-quality cases for hypertext prediction and prefetching. In 4th *International Conference on Case Based Reasoning (ICCBR-2001)*, pages 744–755, Vancouver BC, Canada, July 2001.

15. Q. Yang and J. Zhu. A case addition policy for case-base maintenance. *Computational Intelligence Journal, A Special Issue on Case-Base Maintenance. Blackwell Publishers, Boston MA UK*, 17(2):250–262, 2001.

Context-Awareness in User Modelling: Requirements Analysis for a Case-Based Reasoning Application

Andreas Zimmermann

Fraunhofer Institut for Applied Information Technology
Schloß Birlinghoven
53754 Sankt Augustin, Germany
Andreas.Zimmermann@fit.fraunhofer.de

Abstract. The paper describes an approach of using the case-based reasoning methodology in context-aware systems. It elaborates how this technique can be applied to generate recommendations based on the contexts of users respectively objects especially in a mobile scenario. By combining case-based reasoning methodology and context awareness a new and powerful way of modelling and reasoning from contexts emerges. Using cases to enclose contexts will enhance the possibilities to compare contexts, determine certain values of context-similarities, and reflect this information in the process of generating recommendations. Furthermore, this contribution tries to show how the users' behaviour can be learnt in a case-based fashion and how the users' way of thinking can be simulated.

Keywords: User Modelling, Personalization, Context Modelling, Context-Awareness, Generalised Cases, Time-Extended Cases

1   Introduction

Since the 1980's software architects design systems for the adaptation of information to the user for a variety of reasons. There are lots of works on adaptive systems ranging from the aspect of

- how to analyze the user's behaviour and draw inferences about the user's knowledge, interests, goals, etc.
- how to represent and store information about users
- how to use this information about users to adapt a lot of information system parameters to the individual user or groups of users
- why to support and plan for adaptations and what is the real gain of such adaptive methods.

E-Commerce and marketing systems have extensively exploited user tracking data in existing systems, and the idea of personalization is currently taking corporate portals and public applications to the next stage. As Alfred Kobsa pointed out in [11]:

K.D. Ashley and D.G. Bridge (Eds.): ICCBR 2003, LNAI 2689, pp. 718–732, 2003.
© Springer-Verlag Berlin Heidelberg 2003

"Since personalization has already been demonstrated to benefit both the users and the providers of personalized services and since personalization is therefore going to stay, it is practically certain that generic tool systems will be needed in the future as well."

In the last years a new dimension was added to user tracking. By the usage of location tracking systems users cannot only be tracked in the information space but also in the physical space. This allows for a variety of new applications and is also an important new step in user modelling and adaptive systems. Basically speaking the growing number of resources of data about a user enables more valid inferences and much more contextualized interactions of users and adaptive systems. The adaptation of information selection and presentation based on a changing context has been described in a variety of approaches [6, 9, 15]. The ideas presented in this paper are the outcome of the LISTEN project, which is an ongoing project conducted by the Fraunhofer Institut Sankt Augustin and described now in more detail.

1.1 The LISTEN Project

The LISTEN project deals with the audio augmentation of real and virtual environments [8]. The users of this system move in physical space wearing wireless motion tracked headphones and listen to audio sequences emitted by virtual sound sources placed in the environment. The audio pieces vary according to the user's spatial position and orientation of his/her head. A first LISTEN prototype is intended to be applied to an art exhibition at the Kunstmuseum in Bonn [17]. The visitors of the museum experience personalized audio information about paintings by August Macke.

Combining high definition spatial audio rendering technology with advanced user modeling methods enables context-sensitive audio-augmented environments. The physical environment is augmented through a dynamic soundscape, which users experience over their headphones for. Fine-grain motion tracking is essential for the LISTEN approach because full auditory immersion can only be reached when the binaural rendering process takes into account the rotation of the user's head. A sophisticated 3-dimensional spatial reproduction of the virtual auditory scene takes into account the current position and orientation of the user's head in order to seamlessly integrate the virtual scene with the real one. Speech, music and sound effects are dynamically arranged to form a personalized and situated soundscape, offering information related to visual objects placed in the scenery as well as creating context-specific atmospheres.

Next to the automatic adaptation of soundscapes to the position and orientation of the user's head, the audio stream is controlled in two ways: 1) events (mediated interaction), that are used to start and stop the playback of information items in form of audio recordings, and 2) continuous control (immediate interaction) changing parameters in the audio-generation of the presentation (e.g. a sound that gets continuously louder as you approach a certain position within the space). The several models of the system are described now:

The *world model* describes the physical environment the user moves through interacting with the system. In the LISTEN environment, the space model contains the geometric information of the environment and its visual objects. The LISTEN world model is a detailed virtual reality based geometric model.

The *augmentation layer,* on top of the world model, defines areas (Zones, Segments, Triggers) within the world model; these areas contain active information or sound objects the users of the system interact with. The augmentation layer filters the position and motion of the user by dividing the dimensions the user moves through (location and orientation) into meaningful constraints and deriving continuous parameters from them. By defining zones and segments, the user's focus obtains a valuable meaning.

The *domain model* holds information about sound objects and other hypermedia objects connected to the physical space via the augmentation layer by using meta data. The domain model builds up a virtual acoustic space, in which the location of virtual sound sources and spaces are defined. Stopping in front of a visual object generates aural information about the art piece. Moving the head and body activates a further audio source, where music deepens the user's impressions, or the voice of a commentator talks about the artist or describes the period the painting originates from.

The *user model* contains knowledge and profile information about the system's users. While the user moves in physical space, events are sent to the user model and by these events the model is refined. This model is the most sophisticated and relevant one in the definition of the LISTEN project.

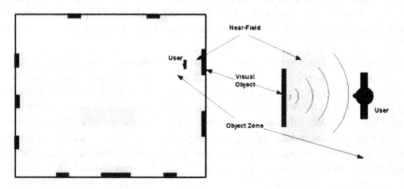

Fig. 1. Space Model of the LISTEN Application in a Museums Environment

In Figure 1 we show the scenery of the application of LISTEN in a museum environment. The zones, which are connected to the visual objects placed within the environment, are divided into *object zones* and *near fields*. The object zones are associated with specific sound information about their connected visual object from a general perspective. The near fields are connected to smaller parts of the visual objects and contain a more detailed sound information. Within the near field, the orientation of the user's head plays a more important role than in the more general object zone. The right hand picture shows an example of a sound emerging directly from the painting. The LISTEN system also allows the sound sources to be placed to certain parts of the painting or to be moving around.

This contribution describes how case-based reasoning techniques have been applied to achieve the context-awareness of the system. It is illustrated how context descriptions are represented as cases and how the case-based reasoning methodology was employed in order to find similar contexts of visitors and exhibits in a mobile scenario and to submit recommendations based on this similarity. In addition, this context-aware system benefits from some basic properties of case-based reasoning like extensibility and dynamic, transparency through explainablility and insusceptibility to fuzziness and uncertainty.

In the course of the LISTEN project, we further try to employ case-based reasoning as a simulation of the users' way of thinking and elaborate its role as a context-aware system in the field of user modelling. For this reason Section 2 comes up with a brief description of a general framework for a context-adaptive systems architecture. By means of this framework necessary extensions to the case-based reasoning methodology may be identified in order to achieve context-awareness.

Section 3 illustrates the application of case-based reasoning in the LISTEN project. It shows an approach of how contexts are modelled as cases and how simple recommendations can be generated.

In Section 4 three ideas are presented for a further extension of this approach, in order to achieve the goal of simulating the users' way of thinking with the help of the case-based reasoning methodology.

2   Framework for Context-Adaptive Systems

Recently, many projects make use of user modelling components and personalization engines in order to make systems adaptable and adaptive to the users' behaviour. Many of these components are specialized applications, tailored to one special domain or environment and rarely reusable in other or subsequent applications. Common problems that emerge during the development and the reusability of components are

- a strong dependency on the domain
- lack of open standards and interfaces
- no uniform representations of user profiles and models
- different views on user profiles
- the use of different information sources
- huge amount of interaction data
- causality of events
- highly dynamic domains, where variable properties change their values in short time intervals

Several approaches from the background of user modelling define different functionalities for the acquisition of information about users, for the information representation and the production of personalized content and adapted navigation structures. This chapter describes our approach to organize the functionality provided by user modelling and personalization servers from the literature and cluster them into layers. From this a model is developed that abstracts from specialized and specific solutions that work in situ of personalized applications. Based on this model for context-adaptive systems possible benefits and roles of the case-based reasoning methodology can be analysed.

Figure 1 illustrates this layered approach in a transparent way. The four main layers, sensor, semantic, control and indicator/actuator layer, are described in more detail now.

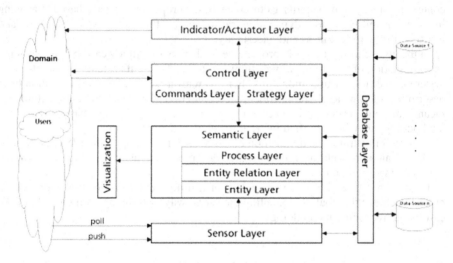

Fig. 2. General framework for context-adaptive systems

2.1   Sensor Layer

The very first functional layer serves as an information collector. A network of *sensors* is placed within in the environment and connected to variable parameters of the domain. These sensors recognize every change within the environment and are used especially for the perception of the users' interaction with this environment. Note that these sensors are to be configured domain dependent, but the corresponding software objects are implemented in a generalised and abstract way.

The sensors receive their information bits from the domain via *push* or *poll*. They work synchronously triggered by time intervals, asynchronously by events or on demand and hence deliver a temporal diffuse stream of data to the sensor layer. Depending on the characteristics of the domain, the sensors have to deal with highly dynamic alterations and their values or states may change in short time intervals. The content of the evolving data vectors is mapped to appropriate software objects on the semantic layer.

2.2 Semantic Layer

The semantic layer semantically enriches the data vectors delivered by the sensor layer by assigning values to software objects that are further processed. This layer defines the context model of an adaptive system. The context model captures the current situation the users act in, their preferences, interests, their social dependencies, and so forth. In addition, the context model contains information about the users environment (cf. Section 3.1). The following subsections describe the context modelling procedure in more detail. On its way through these sub-layers of the semantic layer the sensor information successively gains a meaning.

Entity Layer. The entity layer accommodates predefined context-frames that represent classes of objects or object templates. In a first step, information bits received from the sensor layer are assigned to attributes of the contexts frames and from this, corresponding objects are instantiated.

Entity Relationship Layer. The objects on the entity layer relate to each other in certain ways (e.g. visitor *looking at* a painting). On the entity relationship layer relations are modelled in an UML-like terminology, in order to express associations, aggregations, compositions and additional dependencies.

Process Layer. This layer observes the evolution or process of contexts or parts of contexts over time. The application of time series and history modules, statistic models and intelligent algorithms support this observation procedure. Since several inference mechanisms may derive different assumptions about the context, a system for breaking up contradictory evidences or inconsistencies should be employed if necessary. On this level, plans of users are recognized and learnt. The components located on the process layer are modules, that are put together and on top of each other. For this purpose each of these modules is implemented by using well defined interfaces and following common component concepts. Thus, this concept opens the ability to easily implement new, or reuse and replace old components as required.

The semantic layer completely covers the profiling task of personalization engines. In addition this layer prepares mechanisms for the succeeding matching task and provides different views on the data captured about context for the control layer. Algorithms that perform tasks like matching customers to products can then be utilized for feature- [5] or content based filtering [3, 14], collaborative filtering [7] or similar approaches.

2.3 Control Layer

Based on the intelligent models and the data provided by the semantic layer the control layer generates sequences of commands in order to control the behaviour of the components located on the indicator/actuator. It is composed of the two component types *commands* and *strategic*, that are plugged together via well-defined interfaces.

Commands Layer. On the commands layer the system answers simple requests from external systems or applications by formulating appropriate queries to the semantic layer. Basically speaking this layer knows how to handle all information about the current context of a user and basic adaptive methods are realized. Additionally, aimed feedback loops are triggered (e.g. by the initiation of a questionnaire) in order to obtain direct user input at the sensor layer.

Strategic Components. On the strategic layer the system decides on the highest level whether to behave active or reactive in the interaction. The basic underlying principles, which the user will experience as the essential distinction made on this layer, are pacing and leading. The decision is drawn by a variety of intelligent methods based on the interaction history and certain thresholds that trigger the change of the strategic behaviour of the context adaptation process.

2.4   Indicator/Actuator Layer

The indicator/actuator layer handles the connection back to the domain. For the control layer this engine represents an API of the domain and implements domain-dependent methods that directly change variable parameters of the environment. Adaptive methods like prompting are compiled into a set of domain specific functions.

This general framework has been developed during the implementation of the LISTEN project and serves as a basis for realizing context awareness. Within this framework the case-based reasoning methodology has been applied for modelling user behaviour and providing recommendations to the user. Therefore a case-based reasoning module has been placed on the process layer (cf. Section 2.2). The data for generating case instances is provided by sensors that are connected to attributes of the case description. A scheduler component located on the controlling layer triggers queries to the case-based reasoning system. The main task to apply the case-based reasoning technology to the framework is to find an appropriate representation of contexts as cases. A representation approach is illustrated in the next chapter.

3   Contexts and Cases

Context as a means for adaptation of information selection and presentation has been described in a variety of ways and approaches [6, 9, 15]. Nevertheless the underlying problem of identifying similarities and differences between different constellations of context parameters has not been discussed intensively in the literature. Identifying important context parameters to describe a user interaction is an essential issue when designing context aware information services.

3.1   Context Modelling

A user has a context and a context encloses a user. Overall a context captures the current situation the users act in. Several approaches have defined context models and described different aspects of context taken into account for context-aware systems. For example, Schilit et al. have mentioned [15]: where you are, who you are, and what resources are nearby. Dey and Abowd [6] discuss several approaches for taking into account the computing environment, the user environment, and the physical environment and distinguish primary and secondary context types. Primary context types describe the situation of an entity and are used as indices for retrieving second level types of contextual information.

In this work the context modelling approach is based on the four dimensions of a context which Gross and Specht have considered in [9]. They form the basis for identifying important features of situations individually for each user:

Identity: The identity of a person gives access to the second level of contextual information. In some context-aware applications highly sophisticated user models hold and infer information about the user's interests, preferences, knowledge and detailed activity logs of physical space movements and electronic artefact manipulations. The group of people that share a context can also define the identity of a context.

Location: The location can be considered as a parameter that can be specified in electronic *and* physical space. An artefact can have a physical position or an electronic location described by an URL. Location-based services as one type of context aware applications can be based on a mapping between the physical presence of an artefact and the presentation of the corresponding electronic artefact [9].

Time: Time is an important dimension for describing a context. Beside the specification of time in CET format categorical scales as an overlay for the time dimension are mostly used in context-aware applications (e.g., working hours vs. weekend). For nomadic information systems a process-oriented approach can be time dependent (similar to a workflow).

Environment or Activity: The environment describes the objects and the physical location of the current situation. In several projects approaches for object modelling and building taxonomies or ontology about their interrelations are used for selecting and presenting information to a user.

The basic idea now is to model the different contexts of all domain objects as cases in a way that a similarity value can be determined by a case-based reasoning system in order to retrieve similar (i.e. shared) contexts in a mobile scenario for recommendation purposes.

3.2   Case Modelling

The important question to answer is now: What are the common aspects between user contexts in user modelling and cases in case-based reasoning as we want to express the users way of thinking? First, a context and a case seem to be similar in their definition as a description of aspects of a situation. Of course, contexts obtain a more punctual sense concerning time and cases on the other hand may also represent entire processes. But an object-oriented hierarchy of attribute-value pairs, which is the most common modelling technique for cases used in case-based reasoning, is also a powerful "language" for expressing both contexts and user models.

Second, the differentiated relevancy of single concepts of a situation description is a common property of contexts and cases, as well. In case-based reasoning aspects of the case description can be weighed differently dependent on the similarity measure, the user's adjustments or cases of the case base. People being in the same situation and thus sharing their contexts may assess this situation differently and certain aspects of the context description may be of different relevance.

Three major properties of user models are: The model should always be up-to-date, should cope with changing and highly dynamic user focuses (no deadlock) and should support different views on the user data. A straight forward approach of memorizing every interaction between the user and the domain, which is captured in a context, addresses these properties. In contrast to [10] context snapshots of the users are encapsulating in one case-base for each user and thus, an intelligent implicit user profile is represented. In the following the advantages and difficulties that emerge with this approach will be elaborated.

Figure 1 illustrates our approach of representing a case by mapping the problem-solution pairs of a case description to context-recommendation pairs. The problem description complies with the description of the context. As this context description covers the four dimensions mentioned in Section 3.1, the case's problem description is a four dimensional vector of complex attributes. The solution description of the case is an object identifier which points to an object representing the solution (cf. Section 3.3).

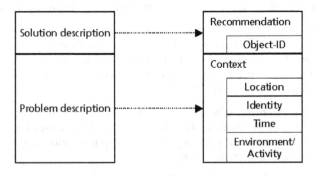

Fig. 3. Case Representation of a Context Description

Every sensor scanning the environment is connected to one attribute of an object's context description. One sensor may deliver an update value for its associated attribute on a time slice or event basis. Some objects like exhibits in a museum hold a *static context*, which does not change very often. Other objects like people moving around own a highly *dynamic context*, which changes frequently.(e.g. a position tracking system may deliver an update value every 10 ms). Both dynamic and static parts of a contexts are to be transformed into a case of a case-based reasoning system. Dynamic attributes raise a problem, because case-based reasoning systems cannot handle continuous domains appropriately and mainly work on discreet point-cases in a n-dimensional space.

Hence, a technique that performs a discretization of a continuous domain is needed. For this purposes we propose taking snapshots of the domain in discrete time intervals. Like a camera freezes the current environment and captures it on a picture, a snapshot freezes the current values of all sensors and assigns them to their corresponding attributes of the context description. Obviously, the granularity of the delivered information depends on the frame rate of the snapshots. All static attribute values of a context can then be transferred into one single case and stored in the case base of a case-based reasoning system for further processing.

This snapshot is enriched by some static information like a user's name, age and interest in artworks, derived information (e.g. rule-based, neuronal networks, etc.) and the point in time indicating when the snapshot was taken. If the snapshots were taken every five seconds, the moving person would leave a trace of cases in the case base.

3.3   Generating Simple Recommendations

The preceding section has described a mobile context modelling approach using the case-based reasoning system. This section now briefly introduces how this system generates simple recommendations. The context is represented as a four dimensional vector stored as a case in the case base and referring to a certain point in a four dimensional space. In our similarity assessment we put a high weight onto the location, the time and the interests of a user. Thus, around each point case a sphere emerges, whose appearance depends on the weights assigned to the several attributes.

If the context of a certain object changes, for example because its position has changed, the case-based reasoning system is able to detect the similarity value exceeding a certain threshold value and thus, to notice two or more overlapping spheres. If two contexts are similar, we define a recommendation to one domain object as a link to the other object that is associated with its specific context. The context of one object is interpreted and presented as a recommendation to the other object.

Mostly, the target for a recommendation are users, because they are somehow able to understand und interpret a recommendation. But also exhibits of a museum, restaurant or gas station may process a recommendation. For example, a recommendation to a restaurant could be a message like this: "Promote your Italian food; some tourists are approaching!"

Example: A visitor is walking through an exhibition wearing wireless headphones. After some time the system detects a high similarity between the visitor and a certain painting, because the visitor's interest in impressionism matches with the painting's creation date and he also is walking by this painting. After this detection, the system looks up valuable information about this specific painting in its database and provides any available audio information to the visitor through the headphones. Later the visitor shares his context with another visitor because they both showed the same behavior in moving through the museum. The system plays a certain attractor sound ("Pssst") in order to focus both visitors' attention on each other.

Depending on the particular task or view on the data the context descriptions of the similar objects can be interpreted and formulated as a recommendation appropriately. In order to realize a future collaborative task the system may send an email to all users sharing similar contexts. This email would contain information on why a contact should be established at each case. A recommendation task would implement the transmission of a message to the mobile device of the user explaining why the restaurant a few steps ahead is so special for him/her. In addition, the experiences the system stored about the user may also be exploited for refining the explanation of a recommendation.

4   Adapting the Case-Based Reasoning Methodology

The preceding sections describe the current state of a ongoing project, in which case-based reasoning was employed, in order to make a museums guide context-aware. An method was introduced that shows how context modelling and case-based reasoning can come together. This approach has to be further extended and improved. This section is about benefits and problems of this approach, and presents ideas to overcome some of these problems.

4.1   Generalising Sets of Cases

Tracking the interaction processes between a user and objects of a specific domain (e.g. location based services) means dealing with a huge amount of data. If a single context snapshot is mapped to a case of a case-based reasoning system, the case base of this system would explode and retrieval algorithms would suffer from complexity. Much research effort has been taken for reducing the size of case bases. Many of them simply forget cases that are very similar to old cases and thus, do not contribute to the system's knowledge. But simply deleting cases from the case base always means a loss of information.

A few years ago generalised cases were introduced in [2] as a mean for reducing the size of the case base by summarizing several similar cases in one single case. Many retrieval and reuse problems of generalised cases have been addressed so far. An automated creation of generalised cases from a set of cases has not been researched, yet. The subdivision of the problem into three sub problems of ascending complexity is proposed:

- Clustering: The first step of the generalisation process is the identification of similar cases, that may be grouped together. This clustering procedure should be implemented with regard to the similarity measure. Many clustering algorithms already exist, that may suitable for this task, but neuronal networks like self-organizing maps should also be considered.

- Generalisation: The succeeding step after clustering is the transformation of these clusters into one single case. The generalisation algorithm can be performed on an attribute basis. From this hyper-rectangles [2, 18] can be derived representing a new case in the case base.

- Specification: Depending on the quality of the generalisation process, the newly created generalised case may cover more point cases than necessary. Therefore, a set of constraints among the attributes are to be formed and specified.

It has to be investigated how an automated generalisation process has side-effects on maintaining different views and the retrieval process (automatic indexing). In addition, if several distributed case-bases are used (i.e. one for each user), a consolidation of sets of case-bases may have different generalisation results.

4.2   Different Views and Shared Contexts

Today many methods exist that show with success how to support users in using information technology by seeking similar objects within a domain (e.g. recommend similar objects to similar users or find similar users for collaboration). Different views on the data covered by the user profiles are possible: The view may be directed inwards or outwards dependent on whether the own profile is adequate for a recommendation or other user profiles are to be consulted.

In a case-based reasoning terminology realizing different views on cases means the usage of different attribute weights, that can be adjusted personally and learnt from user feedback. These weights can be taken into account differently for finding similar situations in the history of a user (or a group of users) and to give appropriate context-aware recommendations to mobile users and compute a user interest model. Important features of a rapidly changing user interest model can be represented adequately with a weighting of context parameters of the current user situation.

This view of seeking similar objects or users may be widened and formulates a shared context approach: Users and objects of the domain share similar contexts. Examples for shared context situations are a couple driving in the same car looking for a restaurant or two museum visitors looking at the same statue from opposite sides. Should their contexts be merged into one context of a new single object and how could this be achieved? How do recommendations to this newly emerged object look like?

It has to be investigated if there is benefit to gain from recognizing that people or even objects share the same contexts and in particular which aspects of their contexts they share with each other. The extended view leads to an implementation of flexible similarity measures that can be instantiated in a personalized way. In addition, if a shared context is detected, an amalgamation of case bases and similarity measures has to be considered. An overlay model of domain concepts can be used in order to determine similarities on different levels of abstraction.

4.3   Modelling Episodes of Cases

A user who is tracked in an environment leaves a trace of context snapshots in this environment. From an automated concentration of context accumulations a graph of points of interest can be derived and by superposition of different user graphs users with similar behaviour can be identified. In addition, if we analyzed the evolution of the user's contexts over time, we would recognize several patters in the user's behaviour.

Each context snapshot builds up on an antecessor and results in a successor, because several causal implications exist between contexts (e.g. causality of time). If the corresponding cases of a case-based reasoning system are extended by a time information, a set of time-extended cases composes one episode with a start and an end point in time. Thus, every case obtains a history and a future and predicting the future of a case could be made possible by the following proposition: Two cases with a similar history have a similar future. Continuing this approach leads to the problem of finding an appropriate representation of time-extended cases and episodes as well as to a definition of a similarity measure for episodes, time and time periods.

The representation of facts and relations concerning time and space are investigated with special effort in the similarity assessment (common sense logic). In [10] the representation of temporal knowledge in a case is based on Allen's thirteen temporal relations [1]. In order to maintain an up-to-date user profile, this Ph.D. uses a set of cases capturing previous interactions rather than a single composite case for one user profile. Thus, a more feasible solution has to be investigated that complies with the generalisation algorithms as well. In addition, the mentioned approaches do not take into account the length or any other qualifier of the time intervals to be compared, since a time interval may shrink to a point in time in comparison with another time interval.

If context modelling is performed using the case-based reasoning methodology and its strong capability of representing cases, an additional problem occurs: Different parts of a case description may possess different time stamps, as well. The context of a user has to cover several properties of the user and the user's environment, which are taken from a set of sensors placed in the environment and may be delivered asynchronously. Thus, the case description is split up into parts with different time stamps and distributed among different sources. There is a decision to be taken about whether or not a specific part really belongs to a specific case description. In addition, a mechanism is to be developed, in order to reunite distributed case descriptions.

5   Conclusion and Future Work

By means of the exemplary environment of the LISTEN project (i.e. visitors walking through a exhibition hall wearing wireless headphones) this paper has shown, that concepts of case-based reasoning are proper for their application as a context-aware system in user modelling.

As a guideline for the development of such context-aware systems a general framework for a context-adaptive systems architecture was presented. Different layers for the contextualization framework for different target applications are identified. These layers describe functional clusters of sensor input, semantic enrichment, control for adaptive methods and a rendering layer for different target applications.

In this paper a method for reasoning from user (respectively object) contexts in a mobile scenario has been introduced. The underlying case-based reasoning engine determines similarities between contexts and generates recommendations, if the similarity value exceeds a certain threshold value. Based on this approach, a multifaceted field of possibilities for future work emerges. First, the way recommendations are generated or formulated should be improved. The information represented by the context description should be exploited by a subsequent application and used to build meaningful recommendations. In addition, the history of origin of this recommendation may also be taken into account, as well as user profiles of similar users, who share the same contexts. In this connection privacy issues have to be addressed, also.

Second, the realisation of different views requires attribute weights of a situation description, that can be learnt by some learning mechanism based on user feedback. Thus, different vectors of weights can be used in the current situation to model different user views on the domain objects. Indeed, we expect that one of the drawbacks of the LISTEN system will be *the lack of explicit user feedback*. Computer users are known for providing little feedback if they are expected to rate the quality of items recommended to them. The lack of explicit feedback causes difficulties in clearly distinguishing between interesting and non-interesting objects. We can assume that in case of the LISTEN system, users will provide no (or at most very little) explicit feedback. In these situations, some systems use heuristics to determine positive and negative evidence of the user's information interest (i.e. unselected objects are negative examples [16]). Another approach developed in [12] uses significant analysis aiming at selecting those features that are extraordinarily important to the user for identifying relevant objects.

Third, the comprehension of time and space in the case-based reasoning methodology entails benefits and problems at the same time, that have to be addressed in future. The three major concepts, shared contexts, generalisation of case sets and modelling of episodes, were presented in this connection, that demand extensions to the case-based reasoning methodology.

References

1. Allen, J.F. (1983), Maintaining Knowledge about Temporal Intervals. In: Communications of the ACM 26, 11, University of Rochester, pp. 832–843.
2. Bergmann, R. (1996), Effizientes Problemlösen durch flexible Wiederverwendung von Fällen auf verschiedenen Abstraktionsebenen. Ph.D., University of Kaiserslautern.
3. Balabanovic, M. and Shoham, Y. F., (1997), Content-Based, Collaborative Recommendation. In: Communications of the ACM, March 1997, Vol.40, No. 3, pp. 77–87.
4. Basu, C., Hirsh, H. and Cohen, W. (1998), Recommendation as Classification: Using Social and Content-Based Information in Recommendation. In: Proceedings of the Fifteenth National Conference on Artificial Intelligence, Madison, WI, pp. 714–720.
5. Billsus, D., and Pazzani, M. J. (1999), A Hybrid User Model for News Classification. In: Kay J. (ed.), UM99 – User Modeling Proceedings of the Seventh International Conference, Springer-Verlag, Wien, New York 1999, pp. 99–108.
6. Dey, A.K. , Abowd, G.D. (1999): Towards a Better Understanding of Context and Context-Awareness. GIT-GVU-99-22, College of Computing, Georgia Institute of Technology.
7. Delgado J., Ishii N., Ura T. (1998), Content-based Collaborative Information Filtering: Actively Learning to Classify and Recommend Documents. In: Proceedings of the CIA'98, Paris, France, July 1998, LNCS 1435. Springer Verlag, Wien, New York 1998.
8. Eckel, G. (2001), LISTEN – Augmenting Everyday Environments with Interactive Soundscapes. In: Proceedings of the I3 Spring Days Workshop "Moving between the physical and the digital: exploring and developing new forms of mixed reality user experience", Porto, Portugal 2001.

9. Gross, T., Specht, M. (2001), Awareness in Context-Aware Information Systems. In: Mensch&Computer – 1. Fachübergreifende Konferenz, Bad Honnef, Germany, Oberquelle, Oppermann and Krause (Eds.) Teubner, pp. 173–182.
10. Jære M., Aamodt, A., Skalle, P. (2002), Representing Temporal Knowledge for Case-Based Prediction. In: Proceedings of the 6th European Conference on Case-Based Reasoning (ECCBR2002), Aberdeen, Scotland, UK, pp. 174–188.
11. Kobsa, A. (2001), Generic User Modeling Systems. In: User Modeling and User-Adaptive Interaction, 11 (1–2), pp. 49–63.
12. Mladenic, D. (1996), Personal WebWatcher – Implementation and Design. Technical Report IJS-DP-7472, Department of Intelligent Systems, J. Stefan Institute, Slovenia, 1996.
13. Pazzani M. J. and Billsus D. (1997), Learning and Revising User Profiles: The Identification of Interesting Web Sites. In: Machine Learning 27, pp. 313–331.
14. Pazzani, M. (1999), A Framework for Collaborative, Content-Based and Demographic Filtering. In: Artificial Intelligence.
15. Shilit, B.N., Adams, N.I., Want, R.(1994), Context-Aware Computing Applications. In Proceedings of the Workshop on Mobile Computing Systems and Applications (IEEE Computer Society, Santa Cruz, CA, pp. 85–90.
16. Schwab, I., Pohl, W. and Koychev, I. (2000), Learning to Recommend from Positive Evidence, In: Proceedings of Intelligent User Interfaces, ACM Press 2000, pp.241–247.
17. Unnützer, P. (2001), LISTEN im Kunstmuseum Bonn, KUNSTFORUM International, Vol. 155, June/July 2001, pp. 469/70.
18. Zimmermann, A. (2000): Generalised Cases: Representation and Application-Oriented Adaptation of Electronic Designs. In: Proceedings of the 8th German Workshop on Case-Based Reasoning (GWCBR2000), Lämmerbuckel, Germany.
19. Zimmermann, A., Lorenz, A., Specht, M. (2002), Reasoning From Contexts. In: Proceedings of the 10th GI-Workshop "Adaptivität und Benutzermodellierung in interaktiven Softwaresystemen", Hannover, Germany

Author Index

Aggour, Kareem S. 5
Aha, David W. 332
Aiken, Jim 107
Arcos, Josep Lluís 20
Ashley, Kevin D. 65
Avesani, Paolo 35

Bento, Carlos 171, 186
Bergmann, Ralph 261, 319, 509
Bertolotto, Michela 622
Bjørnestad, Solveig 50
Blaas, Dennis 479
Blackburn Line, Cynthia 452
Bonissone, Piero P. 5
Breslow, Leonard A. 332
Brüninghaus, Stefanie 65
Bullard, Lofton A. 216

Cafeo, John A. 306
Carreiro, Paulo 171, 186
Cavada, Dario 479
Champin, Pierre-Antoine 80
Cheetham, William E. 5, 96
Cheng, Hong 691
Colomer, Joan 437
Corchado, Emilio S. 107
Corchado, Juan M. 107
Cortés, Ulises 377, 581
Craw, Susan 637
Cunningham, Pádraig 122, 161

Díaz-Agudo, Belén 131
Doyle, Dónal 122

Egyed-Zsigmond, Elöd 146
Evanco, William 595

Fagan, Michael 161
Faltings, Boi 347
Fernandez, Florentino 107
Ferrari, Sara 35
Ferreira, José Luís 171, 186
Freßmann, Andrea 509
Fyfe, Colin 107

Gabel, Thomas 537

Galushka, Mykola 407
Gao, Kehan 216
Gervás, Pablo 131
Gibbons, Diane I. 306
Golobardes, Elisabet 494
Gomes, Paulo 171, 186
Gonzalez, Manuel 107
González-Calero, Pedro A. 131
Grachten, Maarten 20

Kanawati, Rushed 703
Kelbassa, Hans-Werner 201
Khemani, Deepak 522
Khoshgoftaar, Taghi M. 216
Kirsopp, Colin 231
Knight, Brian 246, 652

Leake, David B. 1
Lesperance, Ronald M. 306
López de Mántaras, Ramon 20
Loughrey, John 122

Ma, Jixin 246
Massie, Stewart 637
Maximini, Kerstin 261
Maximini, Rainer 261, 509
McDonald, James R. 610
McGinty, Lorraine 276
McLoughlin, Eoin 622
McSherry, David 291
Melendez, Joaquim 437
Mendes, Emilia 231
Mille, Alain 146
Mirzadeh, Nader 479
Morgan, Alexander P. 306
Mougouie, Babak 319
Muñoz-Avila, Héctor 2, 665, 679
Murdock, J. William 332

Neagu, Nicoleta 347
Nick, Markus 362
Nones, Marisa 479
Núñez, Héctor 377

O'Sullivan, Dympna 622
Ontañón, Santiago 392

Paiva, Paulo   171, 186
Patterson, David W.   407
Pavese, Marc   5
Pereira, Francisco C.   171, 186
Perner, Petra   422
Petridis, Miltos   652
Plaza, Enric   392
Pous, Carles   437
Prasad, Girijesh   465
Premraj, Rahul   231
Prié, Yannick   146

Redmond, Michael A.   452
Rezvani, Sina   465
Ricci, Francesco   479
Richter, Michael M.   319
Riloff, Ellen   4
Rooney, Niall   407
Rosa, Josep Lluís de la   437

Salamó, Maria   494
Salotti, Sylvie   703
Sànchez-Marrè, Miquel   377, 581
Schaaf, Martin   509
Seco, Nuno   171, 186
Selvamani, Radhika B.   522
Sengir, Gulcin H.   306
Shepperd, Martin   231
Simon, Andrea M.   306

Smyth, Barry   276
Snoek, Björn   362
Solnon, Christine   80
Spinelli, Marco   509
Stahl, Armin   537
Stephens, Brent   567
Susi, Angelo   35

Tobudic, Asmir   552
Tsatsoulis, Costas   567

Vázquez-Salceda, Javier   581
Venturini, Adriano   479
Verner, June   595

Waller, Michael   595
Weber, Rosina   595
West, Graeme M.   610
Widmer, Gerhard   552
Willrich, Torsten   362
Wilson, David C.   622
Wiratunga, Nirmalie   637
Woon, Fei Ling   652

Xu, Ke   665, 679

Yang, Qiang   691

Zehraoui, Farida   703
Zimmermann, Andreas   718